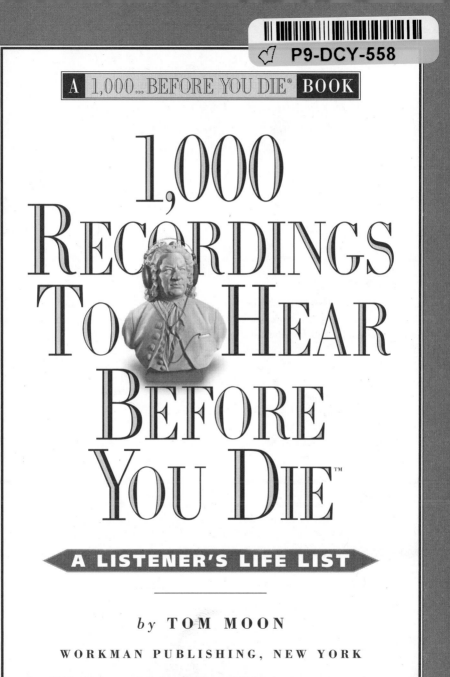

A **1,000...** BEFORE YOU DIE® **BOOK**

1,000 RECORDINGS TO HEAR BEFORE YOU DIE™

A LISTENER'S LIFE LIST

by **TOM MOON**

WORKMAN PUBLISHING, NEW YORK

*"When I hear music, I fear no danger.
I am invulnerable. I see no foe. I am related
to the earliest times, and to the latest."*

—HENRY DAVID THOREAU

Library of Congress Cataloging-in-Publication Data is available.

ISBN 978-0-7611-3963-8 (pb); 978-0-7611-4941-5 (hc)

Layout and interior design by Katherine Tomkinson
Icon design by Alan Kikuchi

Workman books are available at special discount when purchased in bulk for
premiums and sales promotions as well as for fund-raising or educational use.
Special editions or book excerpts also can be created to specification.
For details, contact the Special Sales Director at the address below.

Workman Publishing Company, Inc.
225 Varick Street
New York, NY 10014-4381
www.workman.com

Printed in the United States of America
First printing August 2008

10 9 8 7 6 5 4 3 2 1

For Kim and Savannah

✦ ✦ ✦

In memory of George Horan,
who opened the door . . .

Acknowledgments

This book was born with the help of a constellation of passionate, energetic, and extremely generous people. It could not have happened any other way. My debts are many, and they begin with my mom, Margaret Moon Koryda, who's supported me in every way imaginable and been an inspiration besides.

My family put up with constant schedule upheavals, crazy hours, and on long car trips, a listening diet that might be best described as "challenging." My wife, Kim, and my daughter, Savannah, never complained—they were right with me for the whole journey. Their love, patience, and positivity literally kept me going. Every day.

My friends got used to not seeing me much, and yet still managed to support me—sometimes just by answering my "daily poll" e-mails (which Art Blakey? *Moanin'* or *A Night at Birdland* Vol. 1?). Among those who provided key lifelines and dispatches from the world beyond my office: Stephen Fried, Bob Broockman, Sharon Cloud, Aaron Levinson, Brad Rubens, and the members of MusicMusicMusic, the informal gathering of record producers and deep musical thinkers in Philadelphia. The evenings I spent with them provided me with countless gems.

One attraction of this project was that it forced me to explore types of music I knew only casually. My most acute need was in classical music and opera. Though I'd read scores and listened to the great masterworks in music school, I lacked a sense of the context. I needed a guru, and found an amazing one in a cubicle not far from mine at the *Philadelphia Inquirer*. The critic David Patrick Stearns instantly grasped the scope of the mission. He opened his library to me, and walked me through a lifetime's worth of musical astonishments in all shades and hues. Our discussions helped refine my thinking, and sharpened my responses to all sorts of music. Many of his preferred recordings became mine. This book would not exist without him.

Every writer should have an editor who listens as intently as Margot Herrera does. Margot believed in my ability to actually *execute* the big idea of this book years before I did. She was curious about the music I discovered, and able to translate my runaway enthusiasm into understandable English. More significantly, she maintained, throughout, a clear sense of the book's mission and its "tone"—when she wasn't buying an idea, it wasn't to be bought. Lots of times I had doubts; Margot never wavered. Her relentless energy and high spirit propelled this project every step of the way. I fear I am spoiled forever.

Anthony DeCurtis came on board as a line editor and right away the project hit another level; his input snapped my sometimes flabby prose into shape, and his insights made every entry better. Recently we did a bit of mental math and realized he'd been editing me at *Rolling Stone* and other places for twenty years. For enduring that with such grace and sensitivity, he deserves either an award or a mental health exam. Probably both.

Another saint was assistant editor Cassie Murdoch. Throughout, Cassie handled a blinding array of details without blinking—she organized my ragtag lists into spreadsheets that are works of art, caught glitches in the text, and kept the endless volleys of editing on track, all while offering great insights.

The first day I walked into Workman, I was struck by the spirit of teamwork that seemed to define the place. The folks who worked on this book brought not only skill and professionalism, but also heart and soul. Publisher Peter Workman was generous with his time and insights, and along the way proved open to ideas both conventional and not so. The same is true of editor-in-chief Suzie Bolotin, designer Katherine Tomkinson, creative director David Matt, and Doug Wolff in the production department. Production editor Carol White guided the book

> **While working as a critic, I was fortunate to converse with—and learn from—hundreds of recording artists.**

down the long and winding road from manuscript into galleys into pages, with the able help of her assistant Adrianna Borgia. Barbara Peragine spent countless hours typesetting it. Photo editor Aaron Clendening searched high and low for appropriate images. The copy editor, Tim DeWerff, caught factual errors, while two hardworking interns, Mike Miller and Alicia Matusheski, provided valuable input. The incredible Rob Sternitzky flagged down still more errors and, just as importantly, challenged my facile assumptions—his catches made an enormous difference in the final product. Cathy Dorsey organized this mass of information into a thoughtful index.

Many thanks are due the folks who are dedicated to spreading the word about this book—COO Walter Weintz, Brianna Yamashita and Amy Corley in publicity, Katie Ford in marketing, Pat Upton in licensing, copy/web/advertising guru David Schiller, and Justin Nisbet of workman.com.

At key moments, additional help was cheerfully provided by Steve Hochman, Dominic Umile, and Glenn Chapman. I'm deeply grateful to all.

A special thanks goes to Patricia Schultz, the author of the *1,000 Places* books, for sharing this incredible concept. Patricia set a high bar: Her vivid descriptions and crisp writing inspired me to communicate more clearly.

While working as a critic, I was fortunate to converse with—and learn from—hundreds of recording artists. It's impossible to list all of them, but here are some whose enthusiasm still rings in my ears, and as a result lives in these pages: Keith Richards, Al Green, Bono and U2, Rickie Lee Jones, Jeff Tweedy, Beck, Jimmy Page, Paul Simon, Leonard Cohen, Dave Matthews, Pat Metheny, Ahmir "?uestlove" Thompson, the Red Hot Chili Peppers, Radiohead, Pearl Jam, Elliott Smith, Branford Marsalis, Wynton Marsalis, Pat Martino, Joe Lovano, Ryan Adams, Walter Becker and Donald Fagan, Patti Smith, Joe Boyd, the Roots, Jill Scott, David Gilmour, Shirley Horn, Paul Westerberg, Coldplay, Norah Jones, Sting, Trey Anastasio, Neko Case, Tom Waits, Sonny Rollins, Prince, Keith Jarrett, Caetano Veloso, Frank Zappa, Peter Gabriel, Fiona Apple, Ibrahim Ferrer, Chuck D, Ry Cooder, Herbie Hancock, Miles Davis.

Countless people in the media were part of this journey too. Over the years, I've been fortunate to work with amazing editors—including Bob Boilen and Brendan Banaszak at National Public Radio, Jason Fine at *Rolling Stone*, Bruce Warren and David Dye at WXPN, and Linda Hasert at the *Philadelphia Inquirer*. Among those in the music business who suggested and

helped track down music for this project, a very partial list would include Ambrosia Healy, Melissa Cusick, David Bither, Carla Sacks, Tina Pelikan, Liz Rosenberg, Ken Weinstein, Jim Merlis, Mark Satloff, Marilyn Laverty, Allison Elbl, Regina Joskow, Tracy Mann, Felice Ecker, Steve Martin, Harry Weinger, Dennis Dennehy, Don Lucoff, Bob Merlis, Bill Bentley, Steve Berkowitz, Michael Cuscuna, Matt Hanks, JR Rich, Tom Cording, Lori Earle, Larry Jenkins, Deb Bernadini, Amy Lombardi, Kris Chen, Tracy Zumott.

There is no way to properly account for all those who have shaped my awareness as a musician, writer, critic, and listener. One starting point would be the critics who inspired so many shopping trips—Jon Pareles, Richard Harrington, Robert Christgau, Ben Ratliff, David Fricke, Greg Kot, Will Hermes, Alan Light, Tim Page, Alex Ross, and the late Robert Palmer and Whitney Balliett. I've been lucky to encounter teachers who enlightened me about not just the inner workings of music, but also its infinite nuances—including my composition professor, Ron Miller, and my high school band director, George Horan.

I've learned, though, that everyone can be a teacher—I owe a great deal to strangers, record store clerks, and DJs who said "check this out!" and shared something of their hearts. Thanks for that. A thousand zillion times over.   ✦

Contents

Special Indexes, *continued*

Chasing the Essential

When I began work on this book in the fall of 2004, the big number in the title didn't rattle me much. Music critics love to make lists. Given a few minutes, we can crank out a roundup of All-Time Best Singles, or Greatest Beethoven Symphony Performances, or the Most Mind-Bending Guitar Solos. I'd generated scores of such lists over the twenty years I spent covering music at the *Philadelphia Inquirer*, *Rolling Stone*, NPR's *All Things Considered*, and elsewhere. Along the way, I'd encountered more than my share of spine-tingling records. I figured I'd be able to pull together at least a thousand worthy candidates, no sweat.

It was the "Before You Die" part that tripped me up.

Now there's nothing wrong with a gentle reminder that the clock's ticking, that it could be "party over" for any of us at any time. The awareness of mortality tends to bring clarity—as in, time is running out so consider what you listen to carefully. But even with that idea foremost in my mind, it seemed impossible to get to the essence of something as vast and elusive as music. Can any one list hope to represent the full range of riches? Is there such a thing as a single universally beloved classic recording? Are there ten? A hundred? A thousand?

Eventually, after wrestling with these irresolvable questions for a while, I came to see the title as a mandate: Everything here had to have some incandescent life-changing energy inside it. To be true to the book's mission, each choice had to be a peak experience, music so vibrant it could lift curious listeners out of the mundane and send them hurtling at warp speed in a new direction—toward ecstasy, perhaps, or coolsville. Obviously those encounters couldn't come secondhand—I had to dive in and dig, as though on a vision quest. I couldn't hold each piece to some abstract criterion, either; pure pleasure was the only meaningful metric. I had to trust my ears. And heart.

Every day for more than three years, I went off searching. This book is the product of my journey. It's been an odyssey powered by the thrill of discovery and governed by a simple notion: That the more you love music, the more music you love. As I chased down recordings from all over the world, just about every day brought unexpected revelations—sometimes a life lesson would arrive wrapped inside the weary groan of a bluesman; sometimes a single devastating chord change said all there is to say about heartache. My hope is that these jumping-off points will inspire more searches, lifetimes of exploration.

✦ ✦ ✦

There is no standard map to follow in search of great music. You have to go your own way. Likewise, there's no foolproof strategy for creating a list like this. Inevitably, I was drawn to works of lasting significance—they're prime examples of just how all-consuming and intense music can be. At the start, I assembled a preliminary list of World Culture Greatest Hits—Mozart's late symphonies, Bob Dylan's *Blonde on Blonde,* John Coltrane's *A Love Supreme,* Jessye Norman singing Strauss's *Four Last Songs.* I listened with minimal distractions.

It would be a shame to perish before spending an hour inside the tangle of taut, perfect images spun by Joni Mitchell.

Often, I thought about that ticking clock—how it would be a shame to perish before spending an hour inside the tangle of taut, perfect images spun by Joni Mitchell. Before hearing the consummate technical mastery of classical pianist Vladimir Horowitz. Before being immersed in the mesmerizing soundscapes created by Radiohead.

I thought also about Duke Ellington's notion that there are only two kinds of music—good music, and "the other kind." I wanted the good kind, music that feels vital and alive whether the listener happens to know the backstory or not. I investigated plenty of titles that are regarded as key to the evolution of music as an art form, but I didn't blindly follow the endorsements of experts—the music still had to connect on a visceral level.

With those timeless classics thundering inside my head, I went scavenging for lesser-known works that might hit me with the same force. The hunting-and-gathering became an obsession, but when I think back, it really was just an extension of the kind of searching I did as a kid. In a sense, preliminary research for this project began in the band room at Langley High School in Northern Virginia, in the presence of an irascible white-haired trumpet player named George Horan. More Miles Davis than Mr. Holland, Horan considered himself a musician first and a teacher second. He viewed music as a calling and was deeply offended by any lackluster performance—if you weren't cutting it, he'd bellow, "You think time is a magazine!" I can still remember him corralling the jazz band to listen to Steely Dan's *Aja* shortly after it came out. With little conductor-like gestures and exhortations to "check this out," Horan revealed the mysteries embedded in the music's architecture. He taught us to dig deeper, that if you listen closely, there's always more to hear.

As he did with so many others, Horan set my course—I've spent my adult life studying, playing, composing, and writing about music, and all of those experiences are woven into the pages of this book. I worked for several years as a professional musician, which some days meant playing the circus and some days meant backing great singers like the suave Cheo Feliciano. I toiled in cruise ship orchestras and in rock bands, and for a year toured with jazz trumpeter Maynard Ferguson. On just about every gig, I encountered gifted musicians who were as excited about records as I was. We'd spend hours scrutinizing the circuit-breaking genius of Miles Davis's '60s quintet, or the dense forests of sound conjured by Frank Zappa. The titles my coworkers recommended often zoomed onto my list of personal favorites; I carried them with me from place to place and shared them as often as possible. I'm sharing them again in this book.

I cast a wide net, in the hope of making the book as diverse as possible. I'd ask people at parties what records I absolutely should not miss; I took note of what was playing on the jukebox. I read liner notes, pored over books, scrutinized those All-Time Best lists the British music magazines seem to generate every other month. And I read reviews from customers at online retailers. If somebody wrote passionately about how a piece of music inspired them, I needed to hear it. Not every rave panned out, but a surprising number did—scores of the entries in this book were completely unknown to me when I began working on it.

And I went back through the hundreds of interviews I'd done with musicians and recording artists in my two decades as a journalist—among them, Keith Richards, Miles Davis, Caetano Veloso, Beck, and Keith Jarrett. In almost every conversation, I'd ask what music had profound impact on their lives. Perhaps because they know how hard it is to document an elusive inspiration, artists speak with open awe about records that affected them. Their insights became part of my understanding of music, and their recommendations are an important part of this book.

At one point the list of possible titles ballooned to more than three thousand. Then what I remember as the "pain and misery" phase began. It was possible to make a solid case for each of the choices, but I still had to winnow the list. Often it came down to which piece hit me the hardest. I agonized over which Talking Heads record to include. I found myself embroiled in loud arguments about which jazz organist was the hippest—my favorite, Richard "Groove" Holmes, didn't make the final round, because his blazing intensity wasn't consistently evident on record. This happened over and over again, in every genre—the book's metaphoric cutting-room floor is cluttered with genius.

✦ ✦ ✦

Along the way more fundamental issues arose. Should this project focus on single songs, individual movements, or larger pieces—that is, old-fashioned long-playing albums? No question, these days the single-track download is king. I spotlighted some singles here, but eventually concluded that the lone track doesn't reveal enough about an artist. Spend a while inside an album, and a deeper impression emerges—of the artist, and the time of the work's creation.

Whether or not the tracks are conceptually linked, there are usually "threads" of ideas and images running through great albums: It's one thing to hear the magnificently ruminative second movement from Schubert's B-Flat Piano Sonata; it's quite another to follow the piece from its initial phrase. The only way to "get" the composer's intent is to take the full ride.

> **This journey taught me that there's great treasure waiting on the other side of wherever you draw your territorial lines.**

Likewise, by grabbing just "Money," the single from Pink Floyd's *Dark Side of the Moon,* you miss the sweep and grandeur of the album.

Listening this way requires patience, curiosity, and that most precious commodity, time. I'd argue it's worth it. No matter how fast the download speed, music still unfolds in real time, one stanza after another. It's a journey. Not every recording will come jumping out to leave a strong first impression. Sometimes great music takes a while to get under your skin. But when it does, it stays there.

Then there was the question of how to organize the book. Categorizing the music by genre was an obvious route, but on reflection it seemed the only way to honor the spirit of the project was to present the entries dictionary-style, alphabetically by artist. Finding renegade jazz pianist Cecil Taylor next to sensitive singer-songwriter James Taylor, who abuts the Russian composer Tchaikovsky underscores the astounding range of musical expression available, while subtly discouraging people from hanging out in the genre neighborhoods (ghettos?) they know best. This journey taught me that there's great treasure waiting on the other side of wherever you draw your territorial lines. Those wishing to drill deeply into specific areas will find genre indexes in the back, starting on page 894. But my hope is that adventurous readers will flip through the pages, land on something at random, seek out the music, and have an unexpected eureka! moment.

✦ ✦ ✦

There's a scene in *Almost Famous,* Cameron Crowe's semiautobiographical film about his unlikely rise as a teenage rock critic, that illustrates the kinetic thrill of discovering music. The Cameron character's big sister has just left home, and he's checking out her record collection—gazing meaningfully at Cream's *Wheels of Fire* and *Led Zeppelin II* as though trying to decipher sacred texts. When he opens the gatefold of the Who's rock opera *Tommy*, he finds a note: "Listen to *Tommy* with a candle burning and you will see your entire future."

He follows the instructions, drops the needle on the hi-fi, and hears those galvanizing guitar chords, a call-to-arms across generations. Even though he's maybe ten years old, he promptly gets that glassy look in his eyes that says, "Please don't disturb this cosmic moment." With this one scene, which has no dialogue, Crowe makes manifest something music lovers know in their bones: That if you listen intently, you will encounter more than just constellations of cool sounds—that lurking within them is information worth having, perhaps even a signpost pointing you toward the next key step on your journey.

That's how music works. It can take your blues, dust them in a wicked mojo, sneak them to that crossroads where the Devil hangs out, and swap them for a veggie burrito made by a blissed-out Deadhead in a parking lot. This might not be exactly what you ordered, but it might inspire you all the same. Music can shred your illusions, show you ways of getting along in the world, expose vices and vanities, bring calm to moments of turbulence. It can shine a light on the traps that await you on your path, and offer a sneak preview of what life feels like when you fall into them. It can send your fantasies into overdrive and magnify the reality of your surroundings. As Leonard Bernstein once said, music can "name the unnameable and communicate the unknowable." But don't take his word. Or mine. Put one of these thousand records on, light a candle, and see what happens.   ✦

Navigating This Book

The recordings in this book are arranged alphabetically by artist. This is true regardless of musical style, except in the case of classical music. Most classical titles appear under the composer's name, but some are found under the performer's. This occurs where the performance is of primary interest—for its superlative quality or historical significance. Because this could be potentially confusing, there are two special indexes devoted to classical music and opera, one for composers and one for performers. Thus, to find every recording of compositions by Beethoven mentioned in the book, consult the Classical and Opera Composers index on page 921. To track down a particular soloist or orchestra, consult the Classical and Opera Performers index on page 926.

When there are multiple artists included on the same title, the work appears under V, for Various Artists. In the case of a collaboration between two equally billed artists, the entry appears under the last name of the first artist listed on the work. (For example, the entry about the Bill Evans–Jim Hall title *Undercurrent* appears in E, for Evans.)

Following each entry is a short listener's guide that includes basic information—the year of release, genre, issuing label, and suggestions of KEY TRACKS that are representative of the work as a whole. The GENRE designation is intended as a general reference point; descriptions of music by style or category are notoriously imprecise (so much so that in some cases multiple genres are listed). There are also recommendations for further listening: CATALOG CHOICE identifies one or more other works by the same performer or composer. NEXT STOP offers a recording by a different artist whose work is somehow related (or similar to) the work discussed in the entry. AFTER THAT suggests a recording that is less directly related, and may represent a slightly larger leap.

Starting on page 909, you will find a series of themed "occasion" indexes—Music to Inspire Reflection, Get the Party Started, Roadtrip Soundtrack, to name a few—with recommendations drawn from the entries.

Every effort has been made to spotlight recordings that are commercially available. However, due to the vagaries of the music business, some titles mentioned here may have already fallen out of print. To obtain these, a bit of detective work may be necessary. The list of sources, on page 893, includes websites and retail stores that specialize in obscure or hard-to-find music.

My blog, links to buy the music, and a forum for sharing your favorites can be found at www.1000recordings.com.   ✦

ABBA ✦ Dimi Mint Abba and Khalifa Ould Eide ✦ The Muhal Richard Abrams Orchestra ✦ The Abyssinian Baptist Choir ✦ AC/DC ✦ John Adams ✦ Johnny Adams ✦ Ryan Adams ✦ The Cannonball Adderley Quintet ✦ King Sunny Ade ✦ Aerosmith ✦ Mahmoud Ahmed ✦ Air ✦ Arthur Alexander ✦ Alice in Chains ✦ Mose Allison **A** ✦ The Allman Brothers Band ✦ The Almanac Singers ✦ Herb Alpert and the Tijuana Brass ✦ Los Amigos Invisibles ✦ Albert Ammons and Meade "Lux" Lewis ✦ Marian Anderson ✦ The Animals ✦ Aphex Twin ✦ Fiona Apple ✦ The Arcade Fire ✦ Martha Argerich ✦ Louis Armstrong ✦ Arrested Development ✦ Art Ensemble of Chicago ✦ Fred Astaire ✦ Chet Atkins and Les Paul ✦ Albert Ayler

The Craft of the Hit Song

Gold

ABBA

An entire industry has grown up around the worship of ABBA, the two former couples from Sweden who became one of the pop powerhouses of the 1970s. There's the long-running Broadway revue *Mamma Mia!*, books, anthologies, and even a museum in Stockholm, all dedicated to the glory of pop songs that can seem, to unbelievers, like lightweight, airbrushed nothingness.

Love or hate ABBA, this much is difficult to dispute: The singles this quartet released between 1974 and 1979 are models of impeccable craft, ranking with the most carefully sculpted radio fare of all time. Principal songwriters Björn Ulvaeus and Benny Andersson started out like many in Europe circa 1970—they learned to sing in English, and tried to imitate the radiant refrains and gilded vocal harmonies of the Beatles. They got good at it right away (see "Waterloo," the first worldwide hit from 1974) and grafted that stuff onto the beats of the 1970s, notably disco and Euro-style funk. Then ABBA polished everything to a blinding sheen.

Gold is one of the Top 40 bestselling albums of all time worldwide.

That gloss explains some of the success, especially considering that in terms of nuts and bolts, songs like "Mamma Mia" are fairly inconsequential. But some of the group's other massive singles—"SOS," "Knowing Me, Knowing You," and the unstoppably buoyant, often overlooked "Fernando"—contain refrains so damn giddy they can't be easily purged from the brain. These tightly scripted songs are an excellent starter kit for those wanting to investigate the DNA of post-Beatles pop.

GENRE: ☆ Pop. **RELEASED:** 1992, Polar/Polydor. **KEY TRACKS:** "SOS," "Dancing Queen," "Waterloo," "Take a Chance on Me," "Fernando." **CATALOG CHOICE:** *Arrival.* **NEXT STOP:** The Cardigans: *Life.* **AFTER THAT:** Duran Duran: *Rio.*

Severe, Stirring, Beguiling: Another Side of Africa

Moorish Music from Mauritania

Dimi Mint Abba and Khalifa Ould Eide

The traditional music of Mauritania exists between worlds. It encompasses both the devotional aspect of Islamic life in North Africa, and the rhythmic energy and group interplay of sub-Saharan "black" Africa. For centuries the desert republic has functioned as a crossroads, a place where various African and Arabic cultures, from Berber to Wolof and Tuareg, have met. That's reflected in the sounds: The indigenous music combines the calm authority of the ancients—some texts are based on centuries-old Islamic poetry—with the urgent cries of modern life. When a singer of Dimi Mint Abba's persuasive power is involved, the contrasts and irreconcilable differences fade into music of fierce, transcendent passion—songs of devotion that need no translation.

Abba and her husband, Khalifa Ould Eide, were both born into the *iggawin*, or griot, tradition. In Mauritania, griots are a caste apart, regarded simultaneously as truth-telling folksingers, keepers of the poetry and heritage, and wizards in possession of paranormal powers. Abba's family is a particularly influential one: In 1960, after the Islamic African nation won independence from France, her father wrote what became the Mauritanian national anthem. He's also credited with helping to "modernize" traditional music, by replacing the four-stringed instrument known as the *tidinit* with the six-string guitar.

On this recording, made in London in 1990, Abba's husband provides the accompaniment (on *tidinit* and/or guitar), and their two daughters add percussion and chanted vocals. Abba sings and handles the percussion instruments traditionally played by women, including the *ardin*, which is akin to the West African *cora* or calabash harp. These simple settings provide Abba with a sturdy framework for her vocals, which are largely improvised. Like other Islamic singers, Abba doesn't always stay within a given tonality—when she's really riled up, her ad-libs veer into wild quarter-tones and semitones that are manifestations of pure spirit. While everything on this set sparkles, of particular note is "Sawt Elfan" (Art's Plume), which brought Abba the top prize at a 1977 competition in Tunis. Through a series of riveting verses, Abba asserts that artists make more consequential contributions to society than warriors. The fervent, resolute singing she does here pretty much ends that argument.

GENRE: 🌐 World/Mauritania. **RELEASED:** 1990, World Circuit. **KEY TRACKS:** "Waidalal Waidalal," "Yar Allahoo," "Sawt Elfan." **CATALOG CHOICE:** *Music and Songs of Mauritania.* **NEXT STOP:** Tinariwen: *Amassakoul.* **AFTER THAT:** Andy Palacio and the Garifuna Collective: *Wátina.*

Effortless, Unpredictable Free Jazz

Blu Blu Blu

The Muhal Richard Abrams Orchestra

Outbursts of childlike joy and growling blues catcalls animate the music of Muhal Richard Abrams, the pianist and composer who is one of the stealth legends of modern jazz. A founding member of the Chicago-based Association for the Advancement of Creative Musicians (AACM), one of the most influential outfits dedicated to progressive jazz, Abrams was on the scene when free jazz was coalescing in the 1960s. With his debut recording as a leader in 1967 and many of the titles that followed, he expanded the toolkit of the typical jazz radical with ideas from blues and New Orleans music.

This 1990 session is one of several thrilling Abrams works for large ensemble (another is the hard-to-find *Rejoicing with the Light*) in which angular, inventive written material is offset by slightly unhinged solo passages. The band includes trumpeter Jack Walrath, vibraphonist Warren Smith, and a whistler named Joel Brandon, whose feature, "One for the Whistler," is a suite that includes a desultory ballad and an agitated Afro-Cuban polyrhythm. (Those curious to hear what a jazz whistler sounds like when he's got the spotlight should cue up "Stretch Time," which features a spry, if short, Brandon excursion.) The spirited title track is a tribute to Muddy Waters; Abrams got his start playing blues

Abrams taught himself how to play on a small spinet piano.

and R&B, and this is one of a long line of originals that celebrates (and strengthens) the link between gut-level blues and the visceral expressions of the jazz avant-garde.

Other musicians have had trouble getting those styles to mesh. Abrams, a free-jazz subversive, does it effortlessly, creating unpredictable music distinguished by a bustling big-city exuberance.

GENRE: 🎵 Jazz. **RELEASED:** 1991, Black Saint. **KEY TRACKS:** "Blu Blu Blu," "One for the Whistler," "Stretch Time." **CATALOG CHOICES:** *Rejoicing with the Light; Sightsong; View from Within.* **NEXT STOP:** Art Ensemble of Chicago: *Urban Bushmen* (see p. 28). **AFTER THAT:** Henry Threadgill: *Too Much Sugar for a Dime.*

What 120 Zealous Souls Can Do

Shakin' the Rafters

The Abyssinian Baptist Choir

The rhythm sections that toil behind gospel choirs can usually be found way in the back of the mix, providing unobtrusive backbeats designed to send the singing higher with as little fanfare as possible. Professor Alex Bradford, a stage personality, pianist, and singer who was the music minister at Newark's Abyssinian Baptist Church in the 1960s, alters that approach on this live recording, to thrilling effect. The musicians serve as catalysts, not accompanists—their crisp, unified attack sets the tone for the soloists. It galvanizes the choir. Runs the show.

The three mortals who make up this screaming locomotive of a rhythm section jolt the 120 Abyssinian voices out of the Sunday-services routine into near-ecstatic communication they sustain from the beginning of this disc to the end. The songs are mostly Bradford originals, expressions of faith and praise that emulate the works of legendary gospel composer Thomas A. Dorsey (see p. 233). Several of them belong alongside Dorsey's best, including "Said I Wasn't Gonna Tell Nobody," which is resolute from the opening line, and the 6/8 blues "He Is Such an Understanding God." Loaded with crackling call-and-response exchanges and outbreaks of intricately contrapuntal soul-clapping jubilation, these feature hot solo singing from Calvin White and Margaret Simpson, but they're never really solo vehicles. The choir is right there, contributing asides and shouts, blasting past doubt and despair with a contagious energy most often associated with the early days of rock and roll.

GENRE: 🎵 Gospel. **RELEASED:** 1960, Columbia. (Reissued 1991, Sony Legacy.) **KEY TRACKS:** "Said I Wasn't Gonna Tell Nobody," "He Is Such an Understanding God." **NEXT STOP:** Gospel Soul Children: *Gospel Soul Children of New Orleans.* **AFTER THAT:** Various Artists: *Jubilation! Great Gospel Performances,* Vols. 1 and 2.

Lean Mean Arena Rock

Back in Black

AC/DC

Before he began producing his ex-wife Shania Twain's enormously lucrative high-gloss country-pop, Robert John "Mutt" Lange largely defined the sound of bad-boy arena rock. His productions—particularly this career effort for Aussie rockers AC/DC, which has sold over sixteen million copies in the U.S. alone, and its Def Leppard counterpart *Pyromania*, which kick-started a pop-metal revolution—defined an entire strain of '80s suburban rebellion. Even when the music itself wasn't terribly threatening, Lange gave it a distinct whiff of badass menace.

Back in Black was AC/DC's most popular album, selling more than 42 million copies worldwide.

Back in Black is one of Lange's crowning achievements, a delicate balance of power and finesse that defined the commercial side of heavy music for years after its release. Recorded in 1980, just two months after AC/DC's lead singer Bon Scott died (according to the coroner's report, he'd "drunk himself to death"), it is a ten-song feast of tightly wound, enormously disciplined stomp rock. New singer Brian Johnson was as willing to shred the upper end of his voice as Scott had been, and Lange made sure that every walloping rhythm guitar supporting Johnson's tales of lasciviousness (check out "What Do You Do for Money Honey") weighed in at industrial strength—and was executed with surgical precision.

The album's tightly wound radio songs—"Shoot to Thrill," the proud peacock strut "Back in Black," and the explosive "You Shook Me All Night Long"—share a mean streak. The rhythm section gets right near the boiling point and then hangs there, waiting for the schoolboy-uniform–wearing Angus Young to deliver demonically twisted lead guitar that pushes things over the edge. He always comes through: Every last solo here is a thrill ride.

GENRE: 🎸 Rock. **RELEASED:** 1980, Atlantic. (Reissued 2003, Epic.) **KEY TRACKS:** "Shoot to Thrill," "What Do You Do for Money Honey," "Back in Black," "You Shook Me All Night Long." **NEXT STOP:** Def Leppard: *Pyromania.* **AFTER THAT:** Thin Lizzy: *Jailbreak.*

Big Chord Changes

Harmonium

John Adams
San Francisco Symphony Orchestra and Chorus (Edo de Waart, cond.)

When the noted minimalist John Adams began writing this piece for chorus and large orchestra using poems by Emily Dickinson and John Donne, he confronted a paradox of poetry: Though the lines might hold hints of rhythms and reveries, or carry the forlorn tone of a cello playing alone in the distance, they can lose resonance when yoked too tightly to music. The poet's discipline is about proportion and order; the moment a melody swells too aggressively into the forefront, the spell is broken.

John Adams started composing at the age of 10.

Adams overcomes this by treating the text as just another element, not the center-ring attraction. Often the words take a back seat to his elaborate schemes of tension and release; *Harmonium* is really a study of magical chords and the many ways a resourceful composer might resolve them. Sometimes, on the setting of Donne's "Negative Love," the harmony seems static, with Adams moving massive blocks of consonant harmony around slowly, shifting tones one at a time in the manner of a "dissolving" shot in a film. At other times, notably on the transcendental "Wild Nights," Adams creates extended passages of gathering-storm portent, building tension over several minutes until there's an eruption. This sends orchestra and chorus lunging into an unexpected new key center, a wild frontier where new phantoms lurk.

"Because I Could Not Stop for Death" is even more visual. Adams follows Dickinson's character on a journey, perhaps in a slow-moving carriage, through the things she knew in life. The "fields of gazing grain" and other images come outfitted with shimmering and distinct textures; by the end, as the speaker in the poem heads toward eternity, the music acquires the faint bluish luster some near-death survivors have described as the "channel" between life and death.

This is one of two Adams pieces from roughly the same period with "Harmony" in the title. *Harmonielehre*, the caustic commentary on twelve-tone music, is more beloved by critics. It's a big work, with brainy transitions that utilize the same types of tension/release schemes found in *Harmonium*, only in more animated, gee-whiz ways. Though *Harmonium* is less immediately gratifying and murkier, it resonates more profoundly. When Adams engineers one of his epic chord changes, you don't merely appreciate the craft and the way the words figure in, you feel it in your gut.

GENRE: 🎷 Classical. **RELEASED:** 1984, ECM New Series. **KEY TRACKS:** Part 1: "Negative Love"; Part 2: "Because I Could Not Stop for Death," "Wild Nights." **CATALOG CHOICES:** *Harmonielehre,* City of Birmingham Symphony (Simon Rattle, cond.); *Grand Pianola Music,* Solisti New York (Ransom Wilson, cond.). **NEXT STOP:** Steve Reich: *Reich Remixed.* **AFTER THAT:** Miles Davis: *The Complete In a Silent Way Sessions* (see p. 210).

An Astounding Opera, as Fresh as the News

The Death of Klinghoffer

John Adams
Christopher Maltman, Sanford Sylvan, Yvonne Howard,
London Symphony Orchestra (John Adams, cond.)

I n the liner notes of *Earbox*, a ten-CD retrospective of his work, John Adams recalls that this operatic account of the 1985 hijacking of the *Achille Lauro* cruise ship was a magnet for controversy: *"The Death of Klinghoffer* started eliciting opinions even before a note of it had been heard outside my studio."

The second of Adams's "docu-operas" (after *Nixon in China*), *Klinghoffer* had a difficult birth, in part because its subject reflected ongoing tensions between Israel and Palestine. Leon Klinghoffer was a wheelchair-bound Jew killed during the hijacking. His murderers were Palestinians. The opera begins with two "prologues" contrasting the plight of impoverished Palestinians ("Chorus of the Exiled Palestinians") with the middle-class comfort of American Jews ("Chorus of the Exiled Jews"). From there, Adams and librettist Alice Goodman use the hijacking and the graphic murder as the springboard for extended choral meditations on war, human cruelty, and the ephemerality of life. Adams said that his models were the Passions of Bach—"grave, symbolic narrative poems supported by large chordal pillars"—and the connection is easy to hear. Though Adams's music pulsates with distinctly modern rhythms, he gives the choir deep, pondering melodies. Bach's choirs express awe over spiritual mysteries; Adams's group sings as though trying to make sense of the incomprehensible.

Many critics initially considered *Klinghoffer* a step backward from the brighter *Nixon in China*. Adams made changes, but still the opera wasn't performed much during the 1990s; some critics dismissed it as more a "hot topic" curio than a serious musical work. Although there are several notable audio recordings, this innova- tive film adaptation, shot on a cruise ship in the Mediterranean, deserves credit for engendering a reappraisal of *Klinghoffer*. Unlike most filmed opera productions, there is no lip-synching; the characters are captured singing live, on camera. During the chorales, the screen fills with archival footage from the aftermath of World War II, and faux-archival footage that chronicles the backstories of various characters. These effects are stupendous; they simultaneously sharpen the specifics of the plot and connect this incident to the sorry cavalcade of human tragedy.

Adams was perhaps the most significant composer of the late twentieth century, and *Klinghoffer* helps explain why. The subject matter is volatile, but Adams completely avoids sensationalism. His music is as taut as the soundtrack of an adventure film, with moments of uneasy calm that gradually balloon into towering declarations. At times his overlapping themes achieve a powerful symbiosis: the beautiful, the terrifying, and the sorrowful, all swirled together.

GENRE: 🌐 Opera. **RELEASED:** 2004, Philips. **KEY TRACKS:** Prologue: "Chorus of the Exiled Palestinians"; Act 1: "We Are Very Sorry for You"; Act 2: "I've Never Been a Violent Man." **ANOTHER INTERPRETATION:** London Opera Chorus, Orchestra of the Opéra de Lyon, (Kent Nagano, cond.). **CATALOG CHOICE:** *Shaker Loops, The Wound-Dresser,* Bournemouth Symphony Orchestra. **NEXT STOP:** Philip Glass: *Koyaanisqatsi.*

A Perfect Combination of Singer and Song

The Real Me:
Johnny Adams Sings Doc Pomus

Johnny Adams

D oc Pomus brought knowing maturity and a strong sense of the blues to the often blithe Brill Building pop of the early '60s. First along with his writing partner Mort Shuman, and later with any number of musicians

(including, on this album, pianist Mac Rebennack, better known as Dr. John; see p. 237), the polio-plagued lyricist wrote about being swept up in—or strung out on—romance. His songbook includes "Lonely Avenue," the monster Ray Charles hit; "Teenager in Love," made famous by Dion and the Belmonts; and the Drifters classics "This Magic Moment" and "Save the Last Dance for Me."

"Mr. Adams can invest life and death into every song he sings, moving from shouts to quivering phrases that seem to be dripping tears."
—*The New York Times*

Not everyone has the chops to sing Pomus persuasively, and the songs he wrote when he returned to music in the late 1970s, after spending a decade as a professional gambler, are a particular challenge. These address universal emotions without glossing over life's complexities; they're simple odes that require a singer to provide some vulnerability, some trace of humanity, to complete them.

The largely unknown singer Johnny Adams (1932–1998) understood this. A dynamo from New Orleans whose forte was blues and R&B, Adams attacked Pomus's songs like a boxer, mixing direct blows with evasive maneuvers. He'd been interpreting Pomus for years when, in 1990, he asked the legend to write some new songs for an album he was planning. Pomus put together several

songs and then fell ill, dying of lung cancer early the next year. Adams continued the project, combining the newly penned Pomus pieces (including the positively stunning "Blinded by Love" and "She's Everything to Me") with songs written earlier. The result is music of unexpected subtlety: Singing of heartbreak like he's been there too many times, Adams spins Pomus's simple themes into potent, disarmingly casual blues confessions. His vocals are spectacular throughout, partly because he never looks for pity, and partly because he's so completely at home in front of this hard-swinging New Orleans band, which features Dr. John and guitarist Duke Robillard. A dream pairing of singer and songwriter, this probably should have happened a decade or two sooner.

GENRE: 🎵 Blues. **RELEASED:** 1991, Rounder. **KEY TRACKS:** "Blinded by Love," "She's Everything to Me," "Imitation of Love," "There Is Always One More Time." **CATALOG CHOICE:** *Room with a View of the Blues.* **NEXT STOP:** Irma Thomas: *True Believer.* **AFTER THAT:** Little Milton: *If Walls Could Talk.*

Young, Sad, High = Songwriting Genius

Heartbreaker

Ryan Adams

In the years after this album established him as a solo performer on the rock and roll radar, Ryan Adams wrote hundreds of songs, and recorded them at a frenzied pace. In 2005 alone he issued three CDs, one of them a two-disc set. The overdrive hasn't helped Adams much commercially or critically—a recurring theme in reviews of his work is how much he could use an editor.

This set was recorded before the deluge. Its fourteen wry, introspective tunes stand in stark contrast to everything else in Adams's discography: It was made in a moment when every song wasn't just an exercise, but actually held significance for him. Part of that could be attributed to the circumstances of its creation. In the six months prior to the sessions, Adams broke up with a longtime girlfriend and dissolved his much-acclaimed band, Whiskeytown, after a series of notably erratic live performances. He immediately took to the road solo, and after several tours sought the help of singer-songwriter Gillian Welch and guitarist and singer David Rawlings. The three set up in a Nashville studio and knocked out the intimate *Heartbreaker* in two weeks.

Starting with the wise-beyond-years, medium-tempo ramble "To Be Young (Is to Be Sad, Is to Be High)," *Heartbreaker* shows Adams getting comfortable in an impressive range of styles. There are country ballads that express a restless

drifter's longing for home ("Oh My Sweet Carolina," a lustrous duet with Emmylou Harris), and slow rockers that express a more caustic view ("Come Pick Me Up," which is anchored by an unperturbed, almost jolly banjo). There's one brisk country fantasia ("My Winding Wheel") and songs of yearning ("Call Me on Your Way Back Home") that are made poignant by Adams's blown-apart-and-not-hiding-it delivery. The intimacy of the surroundings, and the lingering, long-distance ache Welch and Rawlings bring to the tracks, help make *Heartbreaker*'s songs sound like unearthed classics. Though he later mastered the technical aspects of recording, Adams here communicates with a raw "you-are-there" urgency—he catches the essence of being young and high, sure of everything and nothing, enthralled with life's possibilities and at the same time drowning in an ocean of conflicting feelings. In other words, his heart's in here.

GENRE: 🎸 Rock. **RELEASED:** 2000, Bloodshot. **KEY TRACKS:** "My Winding Wheel," "Oh My Sweet Carolina," "To Be Young (Is to Be Sad, Is to Be High)." **CATALOG CHOICES:** *Rock N Roll; Gold.* **NEXT STOP:** The Jayhawks: *Hollywood Town Hall.* **AFTER THAT:** Grant Lee Buffalo: *Fuzzy.*

An Overdose of Smiling Riffs

At the Lighthouse

The Cannonball Adderley Quintet

Some jazz musicians feed on torment. Julian "Cannonball" Adderley (1928–1975) specialized in its opposite—a bubbly, endlessly effusive, happy jazz. Throughout his career, from an early stint in Miles Davis's band to his own hard-grooving "soul-jazz" combos of the '60s, the alto saxophonist spread sunshine wherever he went. The tune could be demanding bebop, or a sorrowful blues, but when Cannonball rolled in, the storm clouds dissolved. His collaboration with singer Nancy Wilson stands as one of the breeziest jazz vocal documents of all time. His take on bossa nova, in collaboration with Sergio Mendes on *Cannonball's Bossa Nova,* is equally upbeat.

Then there's this consistently great live album, which overflows with zesty, smiling riffs. Listen for just a few minutes, and you can't miss the secret of the Adderley group: These guys know how much fun jazz can be, and they charge through a series of up-tempo toe-tappers as though determined to spread that joy around.

At least part of the exuberance originates with Adderley's tone, which many regard as the "quintessential" sound of the alto saxophone. It's bright and lively, tart, and at the same time thoroughly warm. There's puppy-dog playfulness in it; at times gregarious laughter comes tumbling between the lines. When, on the opening jump "Sack o' Woe," Adderley dishes out a blue moan, he slips and slides around, creating unbroken curves of deliciously slurred pitches.

The nickname "Cannonball" was a childhood corruption of "cannibal," describing the saxophonist's enormous appetite.

Later, on a blazing fast "Our Delight," he sounds like he's bursting at the seams, alive with energy he can barely handle.

Recorded in 1960, *At the Lighthouse* catches Adderley's group—featuring his brother Nat on cornet, Victor Feldman on piano, and the perpetually underesteemed rhythm team of Sam Jones (bass) and Louis Hayes (drums)—looking back at the spangly side of hard bop, and forward to the grittier rhythms that would become the group's signature later in the decade. Several pieces fall somewhere between those extremes, and of them, Feldman's surging "Azule Serape" is the best. It moves through several different grooves, and, like all of Adderley's greatest work, masks its formidable structural challenges beneath a vivacious, perpetually untroubled good-time veneer.

GENRE: 🎵 Jazz. **RELEASED:** 1960, Riverside. (Reissued 2001, Blue Note.) **KEY TRACKS:** "Sack o' Woe," "Azule Serape," "Our Delight," "What Is This Thing Called Love?," "Big P." **CATALOG CHOICES:** *Mercy, Mercy, Mercy!; Cannonball Adderley and Nancy Wilson; Cannonball's Bossa Nova.* **NEXT STOP:** Grant Green: *Solid.* **AFTER THAT:** Elvin Jones: *Live at the Lighthouse.*

Juju Mojo, at Full Strength

The Best of the Classic Years

King Sunny Ade

A frica is the motherland of rhythm, and the place where music that speaks of great hardship often winds up sounding blissfully angelic. It's also the world capital for music that unlocks the pelvis. This compilation of material the Nigerian guitarist King Sunny Ade (born Sunday Adeniyi) recorded in his homeland in the early '70s is a shining example of all that. Juju is music of extraordinary liquidity, propelled by precisely pitched talking drums and intertwined electric guitar conversations, sometimes four at once. There are vocals, and Ade's band, which during this period contained up to sixteen instrumentalists and singers, often gathers itself into a church choir. The prayerful themes float over isolated, sometimes hyperactive strands of guitar counterpoint, with rhythmic repetitions that lead, slowly but surely, to illumination.

These songs established Ade and his band, first known as the Green Spot Band and later the African Beats, as preeminent masters of what musicologists consider "classic" juju.

Ade is also known as the Minister of Enjoyment.

They're also the recordings that inspired Island Records founder Chris Blackwell to sign Ade and, using techniques that made Bob Marley a star, launch him as another global icon. Ade never reached that kind of acclaim, but that's hardly his fault: Those later recordings are marred by goopy rock-style production. To experience the careful synchronization that makes juju go, start here. Inside these interlocking rhythms and restless conversations between guitars and drums is music of mesmerizing power.

GENRE: 🌐 World/Nigeria. **RELEASED:** 2003, Shanachie. **KEY TRACKS:** "Synchro System," "Ibanuje mon iwon," "Sunny ti de." **CATALOG CHOICE:** *Juju Music.* **NEXT STOP:** Commander Ebenezer Obey: *Juju Jubilee.* **AFTER THAT:** I. K. Dairo: *Ashiko.*

Teenage Boy Bliss

Toys in the Attic

Aerosmith

A erosmith didn't invent blues-rock, wasn't the first band to dish bawdy lyrics, and really brought nothing innovative to the game—unless you count the scarves vocalist Steven Tyler tied around his microphone stand. Yet with its third album, *Toys in the Attic*, the Boston quintet took the basic three-chord guitar scheme, added some old-fashioned showbiz razzle-dazzle, and gave "rawk" a new attitude.

Toys is thirty-seven minutes of teenage-boy air-guitar bliss—all double-time peel-outs and leering talk of fast girls, with a hit of rebellion on the side. Its pulverizing backbeats and tightly wound riff boogie ooze horniness ("Walk This Way," still the prototype rock strut). Its songs about drugs ("Uncle Salty" and "Sweet Emotion," the cleverest deployment of bass marimba in rock history) are disciplined verse-chorus odes disguised as spacey meandering.

An instant hit that sold millions and established the band as arena headliners, *Toys* solidified the trick that the "Toxic Twins" songwriting team, vocalist Tyler and guitarist Joe Perry, would turn for decades: slightly sleazy bad-boy stuff made irresistible by fireworks-on-cue hookcraft.

GENRE: 🎸 Rock. **RELEASED:** 1975, Columbia. **KEY TRACKS:** "Walk This Way," "Uncle Salty." **CATALOG CHOICES:** *Rocks; Pump.* **NEXT STOP:** Van Halen: *Van Halen.* **AFTER THAT:** Mötley Crüe: *Dr. Feelgood.*

Girl Trouble, on a Lofty Plane

Éthiopiques, Vol. 7: Erè Mèla Mèla

Mahmoud Ahmed

E*rè Mèla Mèla* opens with questions, sung in the Amharic language of Ethiopia: "When? Today or tomorrow? When will we gaze into one another's eyes?" Even if you don't know that the song is about a faraway lover,

Mahmoud Ahmed's voice gives it away: He sounds frustrated, unwilling to accept that a long separation might be in store.

He's like lovesick souls everywhere, with one big exception: He has a band pumping out wonderfully liquid beats behind him. The rhythms on this record are unlike anything else you're likely to hear from Africa—or anywhere else. Moving with a snakelike grace, the Ibex band layers tightly fitted guitar parts over tumbling ritual-ceremony drum pulses. Ahmed gets inside the bubbly flow of the music and dispenses wriggling, athletic, off-the-cuff-sounding vocals. Like other vocalists from his homeland, he seeks a speaking-in-tongues type of ecstatic state. His voice often trembles, kept

Erè Mèla Mèlà was originally released in Ethiopia in 1975.

aloft by the gentle but steady propulsion. Drawing on the psychedelic side of Jamaican dub, the traditional Amharic five-note scale, and traces of jazz and R&B phrasing, Ahmed describes love as a deep and unending devotion. He's one of those singers whose every chant seems to come from a spiritual place. Listen long enough, and that's where you'll end up too.

GENRE: 🌐 World/Ethiopia. **RELEASED:** 2002, Buda Musique. **KEY TRACKS:** "Erè Mèla Mèla," "Fetsum Deng Ledj Nesh." **CATALOG CHOICE:** *Almaz.* **NEXT STOP:** Tlahoun Gèssèssè: *Éthiopiques, Vol. 17.* **AFTER THAT:** Mulatu Astatke: *Éthiopiques, Vol. 4.*

The Last Whoopee Cushion Squawk Before Orthodoxy Set In

Air Lore

Air

This head-swiveling assault on jazz history was recorded in May 1979, not exactly a high time for jazz. Yet it documents a creative peak: Here are three wise and accomplished members of the free-jazz community discovering the tremendous symmetry at work inside Scott Joplin's ragtime follies and the early blues of Jelly Roll Morton. Then, having observed and celebrated those qualities, the three—saxophonist Henry Threadgill, bassist Fred Hopkins, and drummer Steve McCall—go toddling around like cartoon characters in a chase scene. They bash the tunes with billowing gales and squawks, short detours into thundering funk, sudden stop-time breaks, and expansive solos.

What happens two minutes into "Buddy Bolden's Blues" is characteristic: As Threadgill begins his alto solo, the ambling parade rhythm evaporates, replaced by triple-fast bebop. Nobody misses a beat as Bolden is propelled a few decades into the future.

Air Lore is jazz as living breathing music, in which old ideas from sixty or more years back help to fertilize radical new approaches. Shortly after this album's release, that recycling—which is crucial to jazz and present throughout its evolution—got twisted around by the "new traditionalists." These young musicians scorned free jazz, ridiculed its practitioners, and championed a narrow definition of the music. It's likely they never really listened to this timeline-trampling, back-to-the-future experiment, which reminds that before it became a cultural preservation project, jazz was fun.

GENRE: 🎵 Jazz. **RELEASED:** 1979, Arista/Novus. **KEY TRACKS:** "The Ragtime Dance," "Buddy Bolden's Blues," "Weeping Willow Rag." **CATALOG CHOICE:** *Live Air.* **NEXT STOP:** Charles Mingus: *Blues and Roots.* **AFTER THAT:** Henry Threadgill: *Too Much Sugar for a Dime.*

Call Him Lonesome

The Ultimate Arthur Alexander

Arthur Alexander

Most people who rode on the social-services bus that Arthur Alexander drove around Cleveland for much of the '80s didn't really know who he was. They weren't aware of his "other" career—as a singer and songwriter who blended country and soul in ways no one had done before. Being a soft-spoken fellow, he didn't talk much about why, after years on the edges of the music business, he ended up driving a bus. Some accounts say he left the music business to overcome substance abuse problems, others attribute his disappearance to a debilitating illness.

Alexander's cover was blown in 1993, when a "comeback" album, *Lonely Just Like Me*, appeared. The album reawakened interest in his sly, genre-blurring singing, and drew new attention to his unusual track record as a songwriter. An early original, "Anna (Go to Him)," was covered by the Beatles, and one of his biggest hits, "You Better Move On," reached number 24 on the pop charts. (It was later done by the Rolling Stones.) Alexander's 1962 version of the latter, which is part of this collection, was the very first recording made at the legendary Muscle Shoals studio in Alabama—Alexander and songwriter Rick Hall converted an old tobacco warehouse themselves—and it began a career that, despite hot flashes, never fully took off.

That lack of success is a great mystery, because there's passion and grit inside everything Alexander recorded. His nimble, unassuming voice had a touch of George Jones in it; like Jones, he could make generic odes of lost love instantly riveting. At the same time,

Arthur Alexander started his singing career with Spar Music in 1960.

Alexander was a Southern soul man with Otis Redding's ability to work a groove; one head-swiveling moment on this collection comes on the up-tempo "Shot of R&B," an ebullient party song that should have been massive. Though it's not a full-career retrospective, this compilation gathers most of Alexander's most heart-wrenching work from the 1960s. Those enchanted by it should seek out *Lonely Just like Me*, the album that rescued him from the footnotes. Though he'd been gone from active performance for more than a decade, Alexander hadn't lost a step: His plaintive vocals are nothing less than astounding. Alexander, just fifty-three, was promoting *Lonely* when he fell ill and died.

GENRE: 🎙 R&B. **RELEASED:** 1993, Razor & Tie. **KEY TRACKS:** "Anna (Go to Him)," "You Better Move On," "Shot of R&B," "Call Me Lonesome." **CATALOG CHOICES:** *Lonely Just like Me; Rainbow Road: The Warner Bros. Recordings.* **NEXT STOP:** James Carr: *You Got My Mind Messed Up* (see p. 143). **AFTER THAT:** O. V. Wright: *The Soul of O. V. Wright.*

Pure Junkie Menace

Dirt

Alice in Chains

Seattle's Alice in Chains has a reputation as a drug-plagued heavy band, purveyors of dark and stormy sludge-rock thickened by abrasive guitar dissonance. That's only part of the story. This quartet, built around the extraordinary guitarist Jerry Cantrell and singer Layne Staley (1967–2002), was interested—during the making of *Dirt*, anyway—in sharp musical contrasts: Its most bludgeoning songs contain outbreaks of utterly lovely harmony singing. Its rhythm guitar attack is studded with jerky, odd-meter prog-rock riffs.

Those juxtapositions are the soul of *Dirt*, the second full-length Alice in Chains effort, a sweet counterpoint to the band's relentlessly bleak imagery. You follow Staley and his crew into the dankest dungeon of junkie-existentialist despair, because there's always at least a glimmer of light waiting at the end of the tunnel.

Alice in Chains (clockwise from left): Sean Kinney, Jerry Cantrell, Mike Inez, and Layne Staley.

Dirt arrived in the fall of 1992, after the music scene in Seattle began to explode. Though much more of a hard rock band than a grunge or "alternative" band, Alice in Chains benefited from the media frenzy surrounding Nirvana; *Dirt* sold three million copies, a success that some believe hastened the band's demise. Staley's drug problems deepened, preventing the band from touring regularly, and hindered recording efforts as well. Subsequent records lack the extensive palette of *Dirt*—the lone notable effort that follows this is *Jar of Flies*, the first EP ever to enter at the top of *Billboard*'s album chart.

GENRE: 🄜 Rock.
RELEASED: 1992, Columbia.
KEY TRACKS: "Angry Chair," "Down in a Hole," "Would?," "Rooster." **CATALOG CHOICE:** *Jar of Flies*. **NEXT STOP:** Temple of the Dog: *Temple of the Dog*. **AFTER THAT:** Days of the New: *Days of the New*.

The Musings of a Hipster Cynic

Allison Wonderland

Mose Allison

66 I don't worry about a thing 'cause I know nothin's gonna be alright." "Stop this world, let me off, there's too many pigs in the same trough." "Your mind is on vacation and your mouth is working overtime."

These and other withering assessments of the human condition are the hallmark of the Tippo, Mississippi–born pianist and singer Mose Allison, whose recordings in the 1960s found a vital middle ground between jazz and blues, hipster jive and social commentary. One part Mark Twain and one part Willie Dixon, Allison began by interpreting the blues "straight"—his early records,

At age 5, Mose Allison realized he could play the piano by ear.

including the "Back Country Suite" and "Parchman Farm," featured here, reveal a student of boogie and New Orleans barrelhouse who's also familiar with more modern bebop blues derivations.

By the mid-'60s, when he signed on with Atlantic Records, Allison was in the grip of a misanthropic muse. He began writing original songs, many built on traditional outlines—anyone who's heard a few twelve-bar blues tunes will recognize the basic formulations of his backing tracks on this career-highlights anthology. What sets him apart are the lyrics, which include eccentric rants on the evils of city life, musings on the corrupting influence of women, and fanciful mock-academic riffs on the alchemy of love ("Your Molecular Structure"). They're a hipster's wry take on what's wrong with the world, served with a glib bounce in the step and a twinkle in the eye, and a laconic style that's well suited to the task of lampooning assorted vanities.

GENRE: 🎵 Vocals. **RELEASED:** 1994, Rhino/Atlantic. **KEY TRACKS:** "Your Mind Is on Vacation," "Stop This World," "Everybody Cryin' Mercy," "Ever Since I Stole the Blues." **CATALOG CHOICE:** *Down Home Piano.* **NEXT STOP:** Jamie Cullum: *Twentysomething.* **AFTER THAT:** Oscar Brown Jr.: *Sin and Soul* (see p. 122).

An Essential Live Rock Document

At Fillmore East

The Allman Brothers Band

T he Allman Brothers Band was just beginning to generate national attention when it pulled into Manhattan's Fillmore East auditorium for its first headlining stand in March 1971. All four shows from the run, including a final one that was delayed for hours because of a bomb scare (and didn't end until around 6 A.M.), were recorded. Producer Tom Dowd took the tapes, trimmed down some solos and completely edited others, and delivered *At Fillmore East*, the album that transformed this fast-rising curiosity from Macon, Georgia, into one of the truly great American rock bands of all time.

The Rock and Roll Hall of Fame called the Allman Brothers Band "the principal architects of Southern Rock."

There were lots of wonderful live acts in rock circa 1971. But the thrashing first choruses of "Statesboro Blues" and "Trouble No More" suggest that this one is different. It's a rock band built on a jazz notion: that the journey can be more interesting than the simple attention-grabbing refrain. Loose and free-floating solos involve the entire band, including the drum tandem of Butch Trucks and Jaimoe (Jai Johanny Johanson). Everything develops organically and everyone's united in search of the kind of collective musical ecstasy that's usually found on John Coltrane records.

The long-haul truckers of rock, the Allmans establish a groove and keep it cranking. They're happy as long as the boogie is scooting along and nobody's stopping them from doing eighty-five miles an hour down the freeway. Dowd once described the Allmans' twin-lead-guitar attack—Duane Allman playing slide and Dicky Betts on six-string—as "frightening," and this album shows you why. When one finishes his climb to the mountaintop, the other begins, taking "Whipping Post" and "In Memory of Elizabeth Reed" to new frenzied plateaus. Just when *that* settles down, along comes organist (and vocalist) Gregg Allman, working out on a hot-sounding Hammond B3 to extend the marathon a bit further. (Check out his romp through the eight-minute "Stormy Monday.")

Fillmore East, now expanded with additional performances, established the Allmans among the rock elite, but, almost immediately, the band hit hard times: In October 1971, fourteen days after the album went gold, Duane was killed on his motorcycle. The band picked up again, and its next release, *Eat a Peach* (so named because it was a peach truck that killed Duane), included an entire album of live music from the Fillmore date as well as sedate, beautifully contemplative studio material.

Since then, the group, led by Gregg Allman, has shown remarkable resilience: No matter who's on stage, the band seems to recapture at will the greasy-boogie locomotion of the Fillmore recordings. That's no small feat, given that *At Fillmore East* remains one of the best live albums in rock history. Ornery and loud, it's perfect driving music for the road that goes on forever.

GENRE: 🎸 Rock. **RELEASED:** 1971, Mercury. **KEY TRACKS:** "Midnight Rider," "Whipping Post," "Statesboro Blues." **CATALOG CHOICES:** *Eat a Peach*. Gregg Allman: *Laid Back*. **NEXT STOP:** Lynyrd Skynyrd: *One More from the Road*.

Folk Activism Begins Here

Complete General Recordings

The Almanac Singers

Modern folk music might have started before this—musicologist Alan Lomax once fixed the date at March 3, 1940, when Pete Seeger and Woody Guthrie met at a migrant worker benefit concert. But these 1941 recordings, which feature Seeger (initially identified as "Pete Bowers") and Guthrie, mark a beginning in terms of temperament: Here, typical folk fare (songs of the sea) is offset by early activist screeds on the rights of workers and American involvement in World War II.

The Almanac Singers, an avowedly leftist group that included Sonny Terry, Brownie McGhee, Lee Hays, and Millard Lampell, flip-flopped on the war. Its first album, *Songs for John Doe*, which collected singles issued in 1941, was loudly against it,

Refusing to fit the mold of pop singers, the Almanac Singers often performed in their street clothes.

but within a year, the group, recognizing that pacifism was no longer a plausible platform after Germany's invasion of the Soviet Union, was writing pro-war tales of bravery. One of its most celebrated later songs was "Round and Round Hitler's Grave."

The group was branded for its leftist leanings; although the Almanac Singers were responsible for the term "hootenanny" (which it defined as an informal gathering of folk singers and listeners), when ABC-TV put together a folk show of that name in the early '60s, Seeger was banned. But the Almanac approach—simple declarations answered by hardscrabble vocal harmonies—spread widely. The group's sound was seized by many folk performers, and became the basic blueprint for the folk boom of the 1950s. Among the borrowers were the Weavers, the subsequent group formed by Seeger and Hays, which rerecorded "Hard, Ain't It Hard" and other Almanac songs, and carried the group's spirit into the next iteration of folk, which began in the late '50s.

GENRE: 🌐 Folk. **RELEASED:** 1941, General. (Reissued MCA.) **KEY TRACKS:** "Hard, Ain't It Hard," "The Dodger Song." **CATALOG CHOICE:** Pete Seeger: *If I Had a Hammer (Songs of Hope and Struggle)*. **NEXT STOP:** The Weavers: *At Carnegie Hall*. **AFTER THAT:** The Kingston Trio: *College Concert*.

More Songs About Food . . .

Whipped Cream and Other Delights

Herb Alpert and the Tijuana Brass

America wasn't exactly clamoring for instrumental pop in the winter of 1965. And it's safe to say there was little demand for an album that contained foods in all the song titles. And yet several months after its release,

a Herb Alpert and the Tijuana Brass single called "A Taste of Honey" ballooned into a monster hit, and this album landed in the *Billboard* Top 10, where it stayed for an astounding sixty-one weeks (eight of them at number one). TV's *The Dating Game* pounced on the craze, using "Whipped Cream" to introduce the bachelorettes, and the later hit "Spanish Flea" to bring on the bachelors.

The model here was actually covered in shaving cream.

What explains the left-field success of the Tijuana Brass? Certainly some credit goes to the album's cover, which features a sultry model swathed in whipped cream. (Alpert, who co-owned the creative, independent A&M Records with Jerry Moss, recalled, years later, that this was the album where he "realized how important it is to be visual with instrumental music.") And the band's general sound was decidedly unique in those early British Invasion days—no other recording act was fusing traditional Mexican music (the mariachi fanfares that herald bullfights) with jazz, Brazilian samba, and R&B, a curious but utterly workable combination that has enshrined Alpert as a patron saint of lounge exotica ever since.

While so much subsequent instrumental pop (Kenny G et al.) is just noodling indulgence, *Whipped Cream* works because the Brass (which, until this album erupted, was really just a bunch of L.A. studio musicians) focuses so singlemindedly on rhythm, even on such calmer selections as "Tangerine." They all play as though it's their responsibility to sustain the sense of motion—of particular note are the athletic bass lines of Pat Senatore, which respect mariachi tradition while grooving like it's already 1969. Then, on top, the famed Brass approaches each theme as a percussive endeavor, punching out staccato phrases with militaristic precision. Hearing these tunes now, divorced from their moment, is instructive: What's often dismissed as pure period froth turns out to have some juicy meat on the bone.

GENRE: ✪ Pop. **RELEASED**: 1965, A&M. **KEY TRACKS**: "A Taste of Honey," "Tangerine," "Whipped Cream." **CATALOG CHOICES:** *Whipped Cream and Other Delights, Rewhipped; Going Places!* **NEXT STOP**: Chuck Mangione: *Feels So Good.* **AFTER THAT**: Jim Hall: *Concierto.*

The Now Sound of the Latin Diaspora

Arepa 3000: A Venezuelan Journey into Space

Los Amigos Invisibles

Despite the subtitle, there's no space exploration on the second U.S. release from the super-inventive Venezuelan dance band Los Amigos Invisibles. There is, however, a fair bit of time travel: One minute the six-piece ensemble is chasing (and nattily embellishing) a retro '60s mod vibe, complete with shimmering organ. Then along comes a snappy drum loop, and suddenly the pulse quickens, and we're three hours into some Ibiza rave circa 2000, with the DJ spinning a weird mix of samba and stutter-stepping rhythm at 180 beats per minute.

Lead singer Julio Briceno at the Coachella Music Festival in 2006.

Those transitions happen fast and reveal much about the intentions of this unusual outfit: Los Amigos approach music the way a globetrotting DJ would, segueing between eras and styles without ever compromising the essential Latinness of the pulse. In these grand, campy songs, hints of old-school cha-cha bump into Brazilian *batucada*, and grooves that echo rumbling '70s funk magically transform into gaudy disco fantasies (one of which is titled "Masturbation Session"). Often music drawn from such far-flung sources feels like gim- mickry. Not this stuff. Following the example of Funkadelic, an obvious inspiration, Los Amigos Invisibles start with authentic grooves, and add the nuttiness on top. The lyrics of "El baile del Sobón" amount to a derisive parody of the rituals of merengue; the music, meanwhile, is a totally locked-up and utterly reverent celebration of the dance style. That cheeky commingling offers a hint of what the next utopia might sound like if Los Amigos have anything to do with it: One globe under a giddy pan-Latin groove.

GENRE: 🌐 World/Venezuela. **RELEASED:** 2000, Luaka Bop. **KEY TRACKS:** "Mujer policía," "La vecina," "Masturbation Session," "No le matas mano." **CATALOG CHOICE:** *Superpop Venezuela.* **NEXT STOP:** Funkadelic: *One Nation Under a Groove.* **AFTER THAT:** Bloque: *Bloque* (see p. 100).

Talk About an Auspicious Start

The First Day

Albert Ammons and Meade "Lux" Lewis

John Hammond's Spirituals to Swing concert at Carnegie Hall in December 1938 (see p. 811) did more than expose groundbreaking jazz and blues musicians to New York audiences for the first time: It created demand for their services among record labels. Producer Alfred Lion was so wowed by the boogie-woogie pianists Meade "Lux" Lewis (1905–1964) and Albert Ammons (1907–1949) that he set up a label of his own to record them. Just two weeks later, the intrepid Lion captured eight tunes by Lewis (including a five-part original suite called "The Blues"), nine by Ammons, and two jovial, fast-moving duets. In a single day. The results became the very first recordings pressed by the Blue Note label.

They're also some of the least ostentatious piano-boogie recordings of all time. The feeling throughout is loose and relaxed, as both pianists are inclined to paw through ambling themes rather than do the high-octane show-off thing. Lewis is the nuts-and-bolts guy; his pieces move at an easygoing clip, and drift out of tempo every once in a while. Ammons is the barn burner: His "Boogie Woogie Stomp" swings with a giddy ferociousness, like he's dancing with the piano. His aptly titled "Bass Goin' Crazy" is a series of scale-like runs with a serious wow factor.

Lots of boogie had that impact. What sets Ammons and Lewis apart is their shared insistence that there's more going on than just dazzling look-how-fast-the-left-hand-moves demonstrations. *The First Day* has the expected bells and whistles—the wildcatting lines, irreverent shout choruses, and slipping and sliding mayhem that spans the length of the keyboard. But it's also got some blues reflection in it, and moments of poignancy that are precious now, considering how showbiz-sensational boogie-woogie soon became.

GENRE: 🎵 Jazz. **RELEASED:** 1939, Blue Note. **KEY TRACKS:** "Bass Goin' Crazy," "The Blues (Pts. 1–5)," "Boogie Woogie Stomp," "Nagasaki" (duet). **CATALOG CHOICES:** Ammons: *Eight to the Bar.* Lewis: *The Blues Piano Artistry of Meade "Lux" Lewis.* **NEXT STOP:** Pete Johnson: *King of Boogie.* **AFTER THAT:** Willie "The Lion" Smith: *Relaxin' After Hours.*

A Voice That Challenged America

Spirituals

Marian Anderson

After hearing Marian Anderson (1897–1993) sing in Salzburg in 1935, conductor Arturo Toscanini remarked that "a voice like hers is heard only once in a hundred years." Alas, it took a while for listeners in her homeland to appreciate the smooth contralto with a superb range. Like many African American artists, Anderson faced ongoing and entrenched racial discrimination. Ironically, she rose to prominence after one such incident: In 1939, the Daughters of the American Revolution canceled an Easter Sunday recital in Washington, D.C., because of Anderson's color. This caused an uproar: First Lady Eleanor Roosevelt renounced her DAR membership, and a free concert at the Lincoln Memorial was scheduled. Seventy-five thousand people came to hear her sing. The performance made her a star and a symbol of equal rights.

Anderson received numerous honors and prizes during her lifetime, including Kennedy Center Honors and a Grammy for Lifetime Acheivement.

On the program that day were several spirituals, songs of faith, many of which originated during slavery. Anderson learned these songs as a child—beginning at age six, she sang in church choirs in Philadelphia, often teaching herself the soprano, alto, tenor, and bass parts. She later went through rigorous operatic training, but managed to retain her feeling for the austere and often haunting melodies of spirituals.

Recorded between 1936 and 1952, this collection offers an excellent introduction to spirituals, and contains some of the greatest recordings Anderson ever made. There are definitive piano-and-voice versions of well-known pieces ("Go Down, Moses," "Nobody Knows the Trouble I've Seen"), as well as lesser-known compositions ("Soon-ah Will Be Done," "Ride On, King Jesus") that Anderson helped to rehabilitate. Recognizing that typical opera-singer discipline won't help bring these songs to life, Anderson sings with great resolve and an evangelist's firmness, taking church singing just one step toward art song. Anderson had other career milestones after this—in 1955, she became the first African American to sing a principal role at the Metropolitan Opera—but her singing here towers above even those significant accomplishments. As she interprets these simple songs, Anderson brings listeners face-to-face with the stoic dignity and stirring melody that rose up in response to an ignoble chapter of American history.

GENRES: 🎻 Classical ✝ Gospel.
RELEASED: 1953, RCA. (Reissued 1999.)
KEY TRACKS: "Go Down, Moses," "Let Us Break Bread Together," "My Lord, What a Morning," "De Gospel Train." **CATALOG CHOICE:** *Brahms Alto Rhapsody and Lieder.*
NEXT STOP: Jessye Norman: *The Essential Jessye Norman.* **AFTER THAT:** Archie Shepp and Horace Parlan: *Goin' Home* (see p. 694).

The Ruin of Many . . .

"The House of the Rising Sun"

The Animals

O f the many brothels in the folklore of New Orleans, none is more legendary than the one run by Madame Marianne LeSoleil Levant from 1862 to 1874. The so-called House of the Rising Sun (from a translation of her name) inspired one of the most enduring songs in American music, a cautionary tale about what happens to a poor girl who follows a drunkard to New Orleans. (Hint: He disappears, and she becomes miserable working in the sex trade.)

Based on the tune of a traditional English ballad, the original—with lyrics folklorist Alan Lomax traced to the Kentucky duo of Georgia Turner and Bert Martin, though exact authorship is impossible to verify—is sung from the woman's perspective. It was first recorded in 1934 by the Smoky Mountain singers Clarence Ashley and Gwen Foster, and since then has been modified endlessly—Nina Simone renders it as a disconsolate moan, Bob Dylan sings it in a severe tone on his debut album. The most famous iteration of the song, the Animals' 1964 chart-topping hit, is also one of the more radically altered: Fearing that a song about prostitution wouldn't get on the radio, the British band changed the lyrics into a sermon about the more generic evils of drinking and

The group was dubbed "The Animals" because of their raucous stage antics.

gambling, sung from a male perspective.

Amazingly, this doesn't diminish the song. Surrounded by a halo of haunting reverb and the hovering chords from Alan Price's organ, Eric Burdon winds his way through the arpeggiated guitar line as though counseling a little brother about the traps that await out in the big world. He knows he's made a mess of things, and though there's the hint of shame in his delivery, he won't play the typical helpless wayward drunk. Singing sorrowfully but not in defeat, he asks for compassion the way all the great soul singers do, by making clear that what happened to him could happen to anybody.

GENRE: 🎸 Rock. **RELEASED:** 1964, MGM. **APPEARS ON:** *The Animals.* **OTHER INTERPRETATIONS:** Nina Simone: *Four Women;* Joan Baez: *Joan Baez* (see p. 39). **CATALOG CHOICE:** *Animalism.* **NEXT STOP:** Blind Willie Johnson: *The Complete Blind Willie Johnson* (see p. 400).

The Home Brew of a Genius

Selected Ambient Works 85–92

Aphex Twin

Like lots of people involved in electronic dance music, Richard D. James—operating under the nom de pop Aphex Twin—learned how to use synthesizers and beat boxes (and even sandpaper on a turntable instead of a vinyl record) to make powerful, transformative music. He created some notable stuff in the early '90s, earning a reputation (and significant cash) as a remixer with a knack for scrumptious, detailed tracks. Meanwhile his heart was elsewhere. For his own amusement, he began exploring less frenetic pulses that pull apart the building blocks of electronica. With this measured, understated music—collected on the homemade *Selected Ambient Works 85–92*—James became the patriarch of ambient techno.

To most of humanity, "ambient techno" will seem another meaningless genre classification, and a contradiction besides—techno connotes pulse and motion, while ambient music suggests sounds that could hover in the air for hours. James reconciles these ideas brilliantly. He surrounds simple, steady beats with synthesized "auras" that seem to envelop the sound field, radiating calm. His settings are uncluttered. At times the sharp edges of electronica are blunted by the recording, which was allegedly made on a primitive four-track cassette machine. This turns out to be a positive: While much club music is so pristine as to be off-putting, the soundscapes on *Selected Ambient Works*—particularly the eerily pastoral "Ageispolis" and "Pulsewidth"—are mysterious, inviting in a fuzzy analog way.

This album is one of a small cluster of electronica records designed for listening and reflection. Incredibly, it's also got a bit of the Ecstasy generation's joy in it. Taking just a step away from clubland, James finds himself in a detached, desolate netherworld, yet with the energy and the lust of the club still ringing in his ears. This inspires music that aims for the scope of a symphony orchestra, and the sudden subtle emotional ripples of great piano-trio jazz. Listen on headphones to fully appreciate the bubbling and bright possibilities James found while puttering in the lab.

GENRE: 🅦 Electronica. **RELEASED:** 1993, Apollo. (Reissued 2002, PIAS America.) **KEY TRACKS:** "Ageispolis," "We Are the Music Makers," "Pulsewidth," "Delphium." **BUYER BEWARE:** Volume 2 of *Selected Ambient Works*, issued the following year, is nothing like this—mostly oceanic washes of texture with very little rhythm. **NEXT STOP:** Jon Hassell/Brian Eno: *Fourth World*, Vol. 1: *Possible Musics*. **AFTER THAT:** David Torn: *Cloud About Mercury*.

A Ninety-Word Title, and It Doesn't Begin to Sum This Up . . .

When the Pawn . . .

Fiona Apple

Something profound happened to Fiona Apple between her debut and the making of this, her second record. When she first appeared, on the smoldering 1996 million-seller entitled *Tidal*, the New York singer, songwriter, and pianist seemed a competent if undistinguished student of Nina Simone and less original torch singers. Three years later, at the age of twenty-two, Apple delivered one of the great rococo leaps of the rock era, this series of dialogs with diffident, recalcitrant, or otherwise insensitive lovers set to flamboyant, tightly wound music.

Theories abound about the possible causes of the transformation. Apple herself explained at the time that she was just curious about songs and structures. "I didn't want to be trapped by a style. . . . The whole idea about music is to develop your own instincts, which is hard when the culture is telling you to sound a certain way and think a certain way." At least partial credit goes to Jon Brion, who produced *When the Pawn . . . .* He surrounds Apple's impetuous poutage with oompah beats and carnival horns, stomping-feet Broadway bluster, and bits of funk. Brion created some funhouse orchestrations that are the musical equivalent of the sad clown's painted smile. They cast Apple's personal torments in upbeat, surprisingly accessible settings.

Brion's schemes also offer Apple a wide

range. She mewls over one verse and belts the next, and on several tracks, including the galumphing "On the Bound," her eruptions come out of nowhere, as though triggered by a stray bitter memory. These outbursts fit the profile Apple creates with her lyrics: She's unstable, difficult, maybe even damaged goods. On "To Your Love," she apologizes, "Please forgive me for my distance, pain is evident in my existence." A few songs later, she tells some poor man to run away "Fast as You Can," before he gets himself in deeper. There's something irresistible about that, a woman with the quintessential come-

Fiona Apple is an evocative live performer.

hither voice warning potential suitors to run, lest they fall.

GENRE: 🎸 Rock.
RELEASED: 1999, Epic.
KEY TRACKS: "Fast as You Can," "On the Bound," "To Your Love." **F.Y.I.:** *When the Pawn* is the shorthand name of this album; the ninety-word title begins: *When the Pawn Hits the Conflicts He Thinks like a King What He Knows Throws the Blows* and goes on from there. **CATALOG CHOICE:** *Tidal.* **NEXT STOP:** Alanis Morissette: *Jagged Little Pill* (see p. 522).
AFTER THAT: Nellie McKay: *Get Away from Me.*

The First Rock Masterpiece of the New Millennium

Neon Bible

The Arcade Fire

Those who saw the Arcade Fire perform around the time of *Funeral*, its 2004 debut, walked away with that "I've seen the future of rock and roll" look in their eyes. The Montreal band tends to overwhelm people. Just the array of instruments it employs can be daunting: The songs depend on strings and xylophone, gongs and hurdy-gurdy, odd vintage keyboards, as well as guitar, bass, and drums. Ten musicians scurry around the stage in perpetual motion, switching instruments and changing textures to provide the proper cushioning for the grim and often fatalistic pronouncements of songwriter Win Butler.

Lots of rock bands confuse sheer mass of sound with grandeur. Not the Arcade Fire. It concentrated on live performance before it ever hit the studio, and as a result developed unusual ways to underscore and sharpen whatever Butler is obsessing over in the lyrics.

Funeral catches this in a nascent, homemade phase; with *Neon Bible*, the Arcade Fire is in full control of its massive forces. The music billows and swells into a rich orchestral splendor; just as quickly it can become haunting and spare. Every shade serves some purpose—though its songs contain choreographed peaks, the drama of the Arcade Fire feels organic. It's the sound of ten multi-instrumentalists, acolytes in the church of rock, putting every shred of convention (and savage guitars and arcane percussion instruments) into vividly pulsating true-believer music.

Neon Bible took most of a year to make. It was recorded in a church, because the band found studios too constricting. Its songs are about faith, and what happens to ordinary people when their faith has been shattered and disillusionment sets in. That's pretty standard subject matter, but in most rock anthems, the music strides solemnly while the lyrics supply the hope. *Neon Bible* turns that upside down: The lyrics are borderline despondent, and whatever sunshine there is resides in the cresting, bursting-with-possibility music. On the New Wave–ish suite "Black Wave/Bad Vibrations," for example, Butler radiates ambivalence while the band

barrels along like conquering heroes, determined to use all available colors and tones to rouse him from his torpor. These contrasts make *Neon Bible* the first rock masterpiece of the new millennium.

GENRE: 🎸 Rock. **RELEASED:** 2007, Merge. **KEY TRACKS:** "Black Mirror," "Keep the Car Running," "Intervention," "Black Wave/Bad Vibrations." **CATALOG CHOICE:** *Funeral.* **NEXT STOP:** The Cure: *The Head on the Door* (see p. 198). **AFTER THAT:** Jeff Buckley: *Grace* (see p. 126).

Subtle Power at the Piano

Prokofiev: Piano Concerto No. 3
Ravel: Piano Concerto in G

Martha Argerich
Berlin Philharmonic (Claudio Abbado, cond.)

Concert soloists are usually revered for their command of difficult material, or capacity for dazzling technical displays. Near the end of the first movement of Maurice Ravel's Piano Concerto in G, pianist Martha Argerich displays a distinctly different kind of power: The ability to freeze the entire Berlin Philharmonic in its tracks.

The Ravel is a clattering pastiche, with echoes of Gershwin's *Rhapsody in Blue.* Argerich skips through a short solo passage, and when the strings re-enter, Ravel's score asks the pianist to provide crisp upper-register frosting for a series of pretty string-ensemble chords. But Argerich doesn't oblige immediately. She hangs back, forcing the ensemble to listen long enough to fall in sync with her rhythm, which is anything but obvious. Coyly, deliberately, she places each chord just a whisker behind where it should metrically go. Inside that split-second hesitation is a drama that cannot be notated, and Argerich makes the most of the "stolen" space: When the pulse returns, she has snapped all

involved to a higher level of attention.

Such moments are an Argerich trademark; one joy of her recordings is hearing her seize upon the tiny gems other soloists trample over. Particularly when she's accompanied by an alert orchestra—as the Berlin, here conducted by Claudio Abbado, certainly is—her pauses and accents form an alternate reading of a piece, teasing out lyricism at every legitimate moment.

An enigmatic presence who retired from solo recording in 1984, Argerich didn't rely on sensitivity alone: The Prokofiev work, which is on the same disc, reveals her as a percussive, endlessly agile instrumentalist capable of summoning fury when necessary. She dispatches the demanding runs with lightness and ease, gathering clusters of notes into elegant larger shapes. This approach can make Argerich seem capricious, if not glib. Listen again, because it's not blustery technique, but a meta-mastery that defines her iconoclastic readings.

GENRE: 🎵 Classical. **RELEASED:** 1996, Deutsche Grammophon. (Recorded 1967.) **CATALOG CHOICES:** *Chopin, The Legendary 1965 Recording; Ravel: Piano Concertos.* **NEXT STOP:** Leif Ove Andsnes: *Grieg, Schumann Piano Concertos* (see p. 327). **AFTER THAT:** Van Cliburn: *My Favorite Rachmaninoff.*

The Spark That Set the Fire of Jazz

The Complete Hot Fives and Hot Sevens

Louis Armstrong

Louis Armstrong was perhaps the most complete human embodiment of American exuberance. A daredevil musician and singer, he channeled all sorts of dazzling emotions into sound. He made the trumpet squeal with delight and roar with mock fury. His solos molded the rapid-fire exchanges of Dixieland and the big-town strut of the blues into the ad hoc, constantly mutating vocabulary that became jazz. The recordings he made in Chicago between 1925 and 1928 amount to the first significant documents of the genre, and a template for virtually everything that came later. They're peppery, chattery works of up-tempo fire punctuated by Armstrong's whimsical trumpet playing—improvisational outbursts in which the melodies were ad-libbed and the ad-libs were invariably melodic.

Louis Armstrong was nicknamed "Satchmo," short for "satchel mouth."

This four-disc set represents the moment when Armstrong (1901–1971) transformed jazz into a soloist's art. The trumpeter had been moving in that direction before these sessions, as early as 1922, when he accompanied the legendary New Orleans trumpeter Joe "King" Oliver to Chicago. Armstrong left Oliver in 1924, and the next year he and his wife—the pianist Lil Hardin Armstrong, whose assertive barrelhouse style complemented his own playing—began recording for the Okeh label, with a quintet. The gems from those sessions—"Cornet Chop Suey," "Potato Head Blues," and others—cast the cross-talking exuberance of Dixieland in more sophisticated musical trappings. Subsequent sessions, especially those featuring Lil Hardin's replacement, Earl Hines, are even more inventive, and far more harmonically adventurous.

The *Hot* recordings reverberated well beyond Armstrong's immediate circle. Instrumentalists everywhere copied his approach to interpretation, and arrangers in bands large and small began incorporating "solo" passages into their charts. Armstrong became a music star, then an entertainer. But the *Hot Fives and Hot Sevens* endure: the spark that started the fire known as jazz.

GENRE: 🅙 Jazz. **RELEASED:** 2001, Sony Legacy. **KEY TRACKS:** "Weather Bird,"

"St. James Infirmary," "Potato Head Blues." **CATALOG CHOICE:** *The Complete RCA Victor Recordings, 1930–1956.* **NEXT STOP:** Wynton Marsalis: *The Marciac Suite.* **AFTER THAT:** Lester Bowie: *The Great Pretender.*

Life-Affirming Alternative Rap

Three Years, Five Months, and Two Days in the Life of . . .

Arrested Development

The title refers to the amount of time it took the idealistic Atlanta hip-hop group Arrested Development to find a record label willing to issue this, its first effort. That there were few executives who believed in the group's life-affirming, socially aware messages is dismaying, especially considering this hit their desks before gangsta rap broke big. Even more incredible is the way rapper Speech and his counterparts handled the rejection: They pressed on, taking in feedback but retaining the basic ideology. Before anybody else did, they believed in this music.

The group accepting the award for Best Rap Video at the MTV Video Music Awards in 1992.

The group's persistence was rewarded: On the strength of its searching single "Tennessee" and several follow-ups, Arrested Development became a sensation. The album sold over four million copies and brought the group two Grammys including, in a first for hip-hop, Best New Artist.

It's easy to hear why Arrested Development clicked —*Three Years* is the giddy utopianism of early Sly and the Family Stone grafted onto a hip-hop rhythmic frame. Many of the tracks aim to galvanize through messages of self-reliance and responsibility, with grabby chanted choruses reinforcing the slogans.

Some talk of empowerment ("Give a Man a Fish"), while several of the medium-tempo tracks directly discuss race and faith, invoking Sly's positivity more directly—"People Everyday" is a flip update of the 1969 hit "Everyday People." Other alternative-minded rappers before and after Arrested Development (especially A Tribe Called Quest) offer more intricate musical foundations, and weightier messages. But these stirring and exuberant tracks endure: Cue this up whenever you need to be reminded that in hip-hop, inner strength can matter just as much as blustery street bravado.

GENRE: 🅗 Hip-Hop. **RELEASED:** 1992, Chrysalis. **KEY TRACKS:** "Mama's Always on Stage," "Tennessee," "Fishin' 4 Religion." **CATALOG CHOICE:** Speech: *Spiritual People.* **NEXT STOP:** A Tribe Called Quest: *The Low End Theory* (see p. 786). **AFTER THAT:** P.M. Dawn: *Jesus Wept.*

A New Kind of Jazz Storytelling

Urban Bushmen

Art Ensemble of Chicago

L eft. Right. Left. When the marching starts, it feels like it's only gonna be a momentary diversion. Or at least you hope so. It keeps going. LeftRightLeft. And then along comes Lester Bowie, the impish magician of the trumpet, playing a military reveille, more or less straight. Commands are shouted in the distance, and pretty soon the whole Art Ensemble of Chicago is in step. The woodwind players Joseph Jarman and Roscoe Mitchell swap clarinet lines like they're on the streets of the French Quarter.

This surreal but not quite grand processional, part of a tune called "Sun Precondition Two/Theme for Sco," reflects the special genius of the Art Ensemble of Chicago, the five-piece group responsible for some of the most vividly imagined free jazz of the 1970s and '80s. Rather than attempt linear narratives, the members of the Ensemble go after sprawling scenes—that march is one of several wide-angle, highly visual portrayals on this two-disc live set, which was recorded in Munich in 1980. Others include a percussion exchange with tuned woodblocks, "Bush Magic," that sounds like it's happening in an African village square. Then comes an opposite extreme, "Urban Magic," during which solo passages are punctuated by (what else?) whistles and sirens.

The soloists handle themselves well, but the Art Ensemble's music sinks or swims on the strength of the constantly shifting structures going on behind them. Everyone plays several instruments—Jarman alone is credited with twenty-two, including the full range of saxophones, bass pan drums, and bassoon—and because they're actively involved in creating the atmospheres, the asides they drop in are often as interesting as whatever's in the spotlight. That's the beauty of free jazz as practiced by the Art Ensemble: It thrives not on one big idea but a thousand little ones.

GENRE: 🎷 Jazz. **RELEASED:** 1982, ECM. **KEY TRACKS:** "Bush Magic," "Sun Precondition Two/Theme for Sco," "New York Is Full of Lonely People," "Ancestral Meditation." **CATALOG CHOICES:** *Nice Guys; People in Sorrow.* **NEXT STOP:** Lester Bowie: *The Great Pretender.*

The Standard Starting Point for Singing Standards

Steppin' Out: Astaire Sings

Fred Astaire

T o discover why Fred Astaire never got tangled up on his feet, listen to him sing. The most superlative dancer in film history, Astaire (1899–1987) had an exacting sense of phrasing and the ability to traipse through tricky vocal lines with an unflappable serenity. The composers of the Great American Songbook—George and Ira Gershwin, Irving Berlin, Cole Porter, Jerome Kern—depended on Astaire to introduce their songs to the world, and though he didn't have the most sterling voice or the sexiest persona, his innate musicality made him very well suited to that task.

Virtually every jazz and saloon singer who reinterpreted these songs was familiar with his precise, unassuming treatments, which became the standard starting point for the singing of standards.

In 1952, during a rocky stretch at the box office (*The Belle of New York* had just tanked), Astaire and a top-shelf jazz combo gathered in Los Angeles to rerecord songs he'd done in musicals and films. The pianist Oscar Peterson was at the helm, and among the supporting cast was the virtuosic guitarist Barney Kessel and tenor saxophonist Flip

Fred Astaire could dance *and* sing.

Phillips. First collected on the four-LP *The Astaire Story* and now available as this single-disc "highlight" reel, these performances call from an era when poise mattered. Though the music around him gets "hot," there's nothing even remotely torrid about Astaire's singing—he catches the essential shape of such durable themes as "Dancing in the Dark," and then gets out of the way, leaving the instrumentalists plenty of breathing room. The atmosphere throughout is buoyant and assured, as Astaire, whose voice sounds warmer here than on the original soundtrack recordings, serves as an eager tour guide to these great songs, pointing out exactly what he finds so wonderful about each one.

GENRE: 🎵 Vocals. **RELEASED:** 1953, Verve. (Reissued 1994.) **KEY TRACKS:** "Dancing in the Dark," "The Way You Look Tonight," "I Won't Dance," "The Continental." **CATALOG CHOICE:** *The Essential Fred Astaire.* **NEXT STOP:** Tony Bennett: *Steppin' Out.* **AFTER THAT:** Chet Baker: *Let's Get Lost* (see p. 40).

An Honest-to-Goodness Picking Party

Chester and Lester

Chet Atkins and Les Paul

If the effusive volleys of the opening track, "It's Been a Long, Long Time," don't tell all about these sessions, which feature two of the world's most expressive electric guitarists, what comes next will. As country guitarist Chet Atkins (1924–2001) and jazz pioneer Les Paul (born 1915) begin a medley of "Moonglow" and the theme from "Picnic," the two are heard discussing possible introductions. Atkins offers one idea and before anything seems set, Paul starts playing, and the song takes off.

This whole affair is governed by that sense of spontaneity. It isn't a country record, though Atkins's twangy guitar defines the canvas. It's not a jazz record either, despite Paul's liquid tone. Rather, the album is thirty-six minutes of utterly relaxed carousing, a consistently surprising dialogue between masters who enjoy each other's company. They harmonize and fly in formation on "Out of Nowhere." They trade six-string tricks on a spry version of "Caravan" that has both men wrestling with the ghost of Django Reinhardt.

Atkins, who'd done a series of successful instrumental records before this, explains in the liner notes why he was anxious to work with Paul, who invented the solid-body electric guitar and other music-making devices. "He really does know everybody who's playing and what they're doing on the instrument," Atkins said. "Of course, a lot of stuff they're doing now, Les was doing in 1937." And the low-key stuff these two did together here? Guitarists are *still* trying to figure all of it out.

GENRES: 🌐 Country 🎷 Jazz. **RELEASED:** 1977, RCA. **KEY TRACKS:** "Caravan," "Out of Nowhere," "It Had to Be You." **CATALOG CHOICES:** Atkins: *Mister Guitar*. Paul: *The Hit Makers!* **NEXT STOP:** Speedy West and Jimmy Bryant: *Stratosphere Boogie* (see p. 854).

The Full Ayler Assault

Spiritual Unity

Albert Ayler

A striking feature of Albert Ayler's best live album, *Live in Greenwich Village*, is the applause between songs. Here he is, tearing out the drummer's guts with his saxophone, really reaching for a visceral communication that is truly new. And at the end of each piece, the audience responds in a cordial and completely noncommittal way. Nobody sounds revved to be hearing one of the masters of free-jazz anarchy—this is subscription-series applause.

Even the jazz faithful struggle with Ayler (1936–1970), one of the genre's most polarizing talents. On this wild ride of a record, his best studio work, the multi-instrumentalist scatters bleats and whinnies and lashing gales of sound in all directions. He might start with something familiar: "Ghosts," his impression of a gospel prayer meeting, is built on steady call-and-response. But as Ayler gets going, his R&B honking and discordant leaps from the top of the horn to the bottom push the music into unfriendly, destabilized territory. Pretty soon bassist Gary Peacock and drummer Sonny Murray find themselves in a three-way musical fistfight, dodging Ayler's jabs and hooks while dishing out their own.

"It's not about notes anymore," Ayler told an interviewer in the early 1960s, drawing a distinction between his work and that of more traditional jazz musicians. "It's about feelings." And while those feelings can come across as harsh, Ayler's commitment is unassailable. Listen to *Spiritual Unity* for just a few minutes, and you can tell he's into the music with every ounce of breath. Chasing ideas that were just beyond the common musical vocabulary of the time, he played what he felt in the moment, and didn't stop to worry about how it might be going over. Which perhaps explains why his audiences were sometimes rendered speechless.

GENRE: 🎷 Jazz. **RELEASED:** 1965, ESP. **KEY TRACKS:** "Ghosts, First Version," "Spirits." **CATALOG CHOICES:** *The Complete Live in Greenwich Village*; *Bells*. **NEXT STOP:** Pharoah Sanders: *Karma*. **AFTER THAT:** Don Cherry: *Eternal Rhythm*.

Baby Huey and the Babysitters ✦ J. S. Bach ✦ Bad Brains ✦
Erykah Badu ✦ Joan Baez ✦ Anita Baker ✦ Chet Baker ✦ The
Balfa Brothers ✦ Hank Ballard and the Midnighters ✦ Afrika
Bambaataa and the Soul Sonic Force ✦ The Band ✦ Samuel
Barber ✦ Ray Barretto ✦ Béla Bartók ✦ Cecilia Bartoli ✦ Count
Basie and His Orchestra ✦ Waldemar Bastos ✦ Batacumbele
✦ Bauhaus ✦ The Beach Boys ✦ Billy Bean ✦ The Beastie
Boys ✦ The Beatles ✦ The Beau Brummels ✦ Sidney Bechet
✦ Beck ✦ Ludwig van Beethoven ✦ Bix Beiderbecke ✦ Harry
Belafonte ✦ Peter Bellamy ✦ Belle and Sebastian ✦ Vincenzo
Bellini ✦ Bembeya Jazz National ✦ Jorge Ben ✦ Benedictine
Monks of the Abbey of St. Maurice and St. Maur, Clervaux
✦ Tony Bennett and Bill Evans ✦ Alban Berg ✦ Luciano
Berio ✦ Hector **B** Berlioz ✦ Leonard
Bernstein and Stephen Sondheim
✦ Chuck Berry ✦ Vishwa Mohan Bhatt
and Ry Cooder ✦ Asha Bhosle ✦ Big Daddy Kane ✦ Big
Star ✦ Georges Bizet ✦ Björk ✦ Black Flag ✦ Black Sabbath
✦ Rubén Blades and Willie Colón ✦ Blind Blake ✦ Art
Blakey and the Jazz Messengers ✦ Bobby "Blue" Bland
✦ Paul Bley ✦ The Blind Boys of Alabama ✦ Blind Faith
✦ Blondie ✦ Bloque ✦ Jerry Bock and Sheldon Harnick ✦
Dock Boggs ✦ Bonnie "Prince" Billy ✦ Boogie Down
Productions ✦ James Booker ✦ Booker T. and the MGs ✦ Lô
Borges ✦ Boston ✦ The Bothy Band ✦ Boukman Eksperyans
✦ David Bowie ✦ The Boys of the Lough ✦ Johannes Brahms
✦ Anthony Braxton ✦ Bright Eyes ✦ Benjamin Britten ✦
Big Bill Broonzy ✦ Chuck Brown and the Soul Searchers
✦ Clifford Brown–Max Roach Quintet ✦ James Brown ✦
Oscar Brown Jr. ✦ Ruth Brown ✦ Jackson Browne ✦ Anton
Bruckner ✦ Jeff Buckley ✦ Lord Buckley ✦ Tim Buckley ✦
Buckwheat Zydeco ✦ Buffalo Springfield ✦ The Bulgarian
Women's National Radio and Television Chorus ✦ Solomon
Burke ✦ Burning Spear ✦ R. L. Burnside ✦ Kate Bush ✦
William Byrd ✦ The Byrds ✦ David Byrne and Brian Eno

Bigger Than a Footnote

The Baby Huey Story: The Living Legend

Baby Huey and the Babysitters

Even those who typically resist the impulse to glorify the "good old days" have to admit that conditions for live music in the U.S. were generally better in the 1960s and '70s than at any time since. Virtually every decent-sized city had a variety of nightspots—neighborhood jazz rooms, coffeehouses, and scruffy venues where local rock and R&B bands could hone skills and make mistakes while developing a sound. (Without such fertile soil in the Bay Area, for example, there might never have been a Sly Stone, Grateful Dead, or Santana.)

"Baby Huey" got his nickname from the 1950s cartoon duck.

If you happened to pass through Chicago in the late '60s, you might have encountered one shining light of the local club scene, the formidable Baby Huey and his explosive band, the Babysitters. A classic well-known unknown, towering within the music community there but a footnote beyond, the massive four-hundred-plus-pound singer had a voice built for shouting and a gift for crooning intimate soul confessions as well as belting hard rock. In fact, his militaristically tight, incredibly energetic band was fluent in everything happening in pop music at the start of the '70s—guitar flourishes in the style of Jimi Hendrix (Huey counted Hendrix among his friends), passionately shouted Memphis-soul vocals, and elaborate horn arrangements.

Huey (whose given name was James Thomas Ramey) was the initial attraction, but the ten-piece band's intense live perfor-mances and fresh take on the union of jazz and rock eventually drew the attention of soul legend Curtis Mayfield, who signed the band to his Curtom label. Mayfield was producing the Baby Huey debut when its star dropped dead in a hotel room. He was twenty-six years old. The record was unfinished—there are more instrumentals than would have probably appeared on the completed album had Huey lived. But what survives is essential listening—a spine-chilling version of Sam Cooke's "A Change Is Gonna Come" and an original called "Listen to Me" that has been routinely sampled (the most famous appropriation comes on Eric B. and Rakim's 1988 "Follow the Leader"). Track this down for the pure pleasure of discovering a could-have-been-massive voice, and to be reminded that not all the great talent in the world makes it onto the radio.

GENRE: 🎙 R&B. **RELEASED:** 1971, Curtom. (Reissued 2004, Water.) **KEY TRACKS:** "Listen to Me," "Hard Times," "A Change Is Gonna Come." **NEXT STOP:** Charles Wright and the Watts 103rd Street Rhythm Band: *Express Yourself.* **AFTER THAT:** Eric B. and Rakim: *Follow the Leader.*

A Starting Point for Bach

The Brandenburg Concertos

J. S. Bach

Concerto Italiano (Rinaldo Alessandrini, cond.)

These six lively pieces for small orchestra are regarded as key to the puzzle that is baroque superstar Johann Sebastian Bach (1685–1750). In his day, however, these and other instrumental works were almost afterthoughts, less significant than the cantatas (see p. 372) and other religious-themed music he wrote. What has changed over the past 250 years is the appreciation for Bach's range and imagination. While indisputably beautiful, the religious works are accompaniments to ceremony, and so usually follow prescribed paths. When he's free of those liturgical obligations, Bach's renegade streak emerges. He cuts loose a bit, makes up his own rules, experiments with structure and texture.

This recording from Concerto Italiano won three Gramophone awards.

The Brandenburgs were written over two years, from 1719 to 1720, to fulfill a commission from an aristocrat in the German principality Brandenburg-Schwedt, and no two utilize the same instrumentation—the orchestra shrinks and expands to fit the requirements of each piece. The transfixingly logical Concerto No. 4 is built around solo recorder (don't laugh, it's a magical sound!), while several others feature clusters of three or four soloists interacting with each other in what came to be called "concerto grosso" form.

One thrill of the Brandenburgs is following Bach as he scurries around trying to resolve chords in perfect (and often stupendously elaborate) ways. Never content to go straight from point A to point B when there's a chance to take a fifteen-city detour, Bach loads up the Brandenburgs with harmonic deviousness, and drawn-out chordal inventions that take forever to unravel. (To hear one typically elongated chord sequence, check out the opening movement of the fifth concerto.)

There are hundreds of Brandenburg recordings. This one, by one of Europe's premier chamber orchestras, is notable for its warm acoustics (it was recorded live in Rome's Salone d'Ercole at the Palazzo Farnese) and for the ensemble's adherence to Bach's indications of tempo and mood. Some modern conductors slow things down in interpreting the cycle, transforming sprightly minuets into more ponderous music. Here, the dances move the way Bach intended them to—vividly. It's Bach having fun on a rare day off from church.

GENRE: 🎵 Classical. **RELEASED:** 2005, Opus 111. **KEY TRACKS:** No. 3: second movement. No. 4. No. 5: cadenza. **ANOTHER INTERPRETATION:** *Brandenburg Concertos 4, 5, 6*, Musica Antiqua Köln (Reinhard Goebel, cond.). **CATALOG CHOICES:** *Bach Cantatas*, Lorraine Hunt Lieberson (see p. 372); *The Art of the Fugue*, Glenn Gould. **NEXT STOP:** Georg P. Telemann: *Water Music*, Musica Antiqua Köln (Reinhard Goebel, cond.). **AFTER THAT:** Wolfgang A. Mozart: *Eine kleine nachtmusik*, Berlin Philharmonic (Herbert von Karajan, cond.).

Solo Masterworks for an Unlikely Instrument

Complete Sonatas and Partitas for Solo Violin

J. S. Bach
Arthur Grumiaux

The violin is an unlikely candidate for unaccompanied solo works. It's a linear instrument, geared toward melody and designed to glide atop harmony outlined by others. This didn't stop Bach from writing a daunting series of pieces for it. In these lively caprices, the baroque composer—who was, according to some biographers, a decent violinist himself—sets up elaborate schemes that utilize the violin's full range of sounds.

On some passages in the Sonatas and less-formal Partitas, Bach expects the violinist to play chords by voicing two or three strings (the so-called double stop or triple stop). He uses those fleeting chords to anchor extended forays through intricate sequences that sometimes wander a while before arriving at a calming resolution. Along the way, Bach sets all sorts of traps—in Partita No. 2 in D Minor, he uses extended arpeggios to define each new tonality, and ornate curlicues to embellish them. The Partitas have a loose, suitelike structure, with no set number of movements. They're often derived from dances: The triple-meter Giga section of Partita No. 2 zooms along, lively and fearless. That piece's final Chaconne movement, the longest single section in the set, is similarly animated, spiraling through a series of themes and astoundingly smart inventions. Its abundant melodic riches make the Chaconne one of Bach's towering achievements.

Bach composed over 1,000 known pieces of music.

As he wanders through Bach's towering structures, French violinist Arthur Grumiaux focuses on graceful details, like an enthusiastic guide conducting an architectural tour. He has the technical command to dispatch Bach's hairpin turns, but doesn't use it in a showy way—he drills down to the center of the music, finding the compositional logic at every step. This, coupled with Grumiaux's delicate yet firm tone, makes his reading of the Partitas and Sonatas less about athleticism and more about pure music. Throughout, you sense that he could skate through the piece, playing up the surface flash, but chooses not to. He'd rather illuminate Bach's fantastical inner workings instead.

GENRE: 🎸 Classical. **RELEASED:** 1961, Philips. (Reissued 2007.) **KEY TRACKS:** Partita No. 2 in D Minor. Sonata No. 3 in C. **ANOTHER INTERPRETATION:** Julia Fischer. **CATALOG CHOICE:** *Inventions and Sinfonias,* Glenn Gould. **NEXT STOP:** W. A. Mozart: *Violin Sonatas,* Itzhak Perlman, Daniel Barenboim. **AFTER THAT:** W. A. Mozart: *Piano Sonatas,* Christoph Eschenbach.

The Old Testament of Keyboard Music, Reborn

The Well-Tempered Clavier, Book 1

J. S. Bach
Till Fellner

C lassical music lovers consider this set of forty-eight preludes and fugues as the "Old Testament" of piano literature, and Beethoven's Piano Sonatas as the New. Just as the biblical document marks the beginning of a civilization, Bach began work on these during the codification of equal temperament, which standardized intervals between pitches to make a uniform scale. This was one of those upgrades that had to happen: It enabled music written in one key to be transposed to another, while retaining the same basic harmonic relationships.

Bach wrote the two books of *Well-Tempered Clavier* over two decades, from 1722 to 1744, as material for his students to play. Both books encompass polar-opposite characteristics of his work: The preludes, which have no set form, situate gregarious themes over interesting harmonic progressions. If they're the "art," the fugues represent the "craft": They're exercises in counterpoint in which two distinct musical "cells," or ideas, go running off in different directions and then reflect back on each other in parroted echoes and staggered rejoinders. Fugues have fixed rules, and Bach both upholds and bends them as he goes, exhausting possibilities with characteristic German thoroughness.

Bach understood that different keys projected different tones and colors, and he wrote to exploit those. His C Major Prelude, for example, is a totally open book, with a recurring figure that occasionally dips, via chromatic lines, into the relative minor. Later, working in "stormier" keys like E-flat or D-flat, his fugue subjects become more reflective, at times almost lyrical. That one set of pieces designed for utilitarian purposes could accommodate so many majestic, musically substantial ideas is a testament to the peerless Bach.

Pianist Till Fellner, who was born in Vienna in 1972 and studied with concert pianist Alfred Brendel, uses featherweight touches to bring this incredibly rich, detailed music to life. There's a great openness to his approach, and a sense that each note is getting special attention—the muted passage in the C-Sharp Minor fugue is extreme in this regard, a slight, yet stunning recasting of Bach's gesture that gives the music a modern timbre. Fellner gets help from the ambience of the recording: Like many ECM discs, it has a generous amount of sonic "warmth." Recommended for those who are seeking to broaden their classical music horizons, this contemplative reading of a masterwork has the power to inspire.

GENRE: 🎹 Classical. RELEASED: 2004, ECM. KEY TRACKS: C-Sharp Minor; E Major; G Minor. ANOTHER INTERPRETATION: The Glenn Gould Edition. CATALOG CHOICE: *Violin Concertos*, Andrew Manze, Academy of Ancient Music (Rachel Podger, cond.). NEXT STOP: Ludwig van Beethoven: *Piano Sonatas, Opp. 109, 110, 111*, Mitsuko Uchida. AFTER THAT: Glenn Gould: *The Art of the Fugue*.

The World, in Music

Mass in B Minor

J. S. Bach

Chorus and Orchestra of the Collegium Vocale (Philippe Herreweghe, cond.)

The Bohemian-Austrian composer Gustav Mahler once argued that a symphony should incorporate and reflect the whole world. Good examples abound in his Second and Eighth Symphonies, which combine towering orchestral themes, extended passages for solo vocal, and other sections written for a large choir. However, Mahler was not the first to aspire to such comprehensiveness: Some 150 years earlier, J. S. Bach wrote the luminous and expansive Mass in B Minor, which is as close to a comprehensive inventory of human emotion—from grief to exaltation to doubt to wonder—as music gets.

Bach completed this mass in 1749, shortly before his death in 1750.

Here the baroque master gathers everything he'd used in the more modest, contained cantatas that were his bread and butter—elaborate counterpoint, active running melodies, chorales of voices moving in contrasting waves—and sprawls them over an extra-large canvas. Then he takes the whole shebang to church. The Mass stands with the St. Matthew Passion and the St. John Passion among the key pillars of Bach's religious output.

The Christe of the opening section celebrates God incarnated as man, and establishes the tone of mystery and awe that prevails throughout. As the Mass unfolds, its traditional sections and cadences find Bach exploring various aspects of religious devotion—there are passages that suggest trembling fear of a vengeful God, or the serenity of a true believer. The piece ends with the churchgoing equivalent of fireworks—a fantastical expression of what the "heavenly reward" might actually sound like.

This version of the Mass is notable for its exquisite detail. The piece is considered among the most challenging in the choral repertoire, and often it's performed with a huge assemblage of voices. The Collegium Vocale is much smaller—just twenty-three singers. Recent scholarship suggests that Bach, a practical composer, wrote for a handpicked group, with one voice to a part. That makes this configuration closer to his design. Each voice plays a critical role in bringing the rousing melodic inventions to life: Compare this with one of many cast-of-thousands renditions, and you may find that the gargantuan approach is overkill—the smaller forces render Bach's agile lines, particularly those written for interior voices, with breathtaking clarity.

GENRE: 🎼 Classical. **RELEASED:** 1998, Harmonia Mundi. **KEY TRACKS:** Kyrie Eleison; Domine Deus. **ANOTHER INTERPRETATION:** Bach Choir of Bethlehem. **CATALOG CHOICE:** *St. Matthew Passion,* Choir of King's College, Cambridge (Stephen Cleobury, cond.). **NEXT STOP:** George Frideric Handel: *Messiah* (see p. 341). **AFTER THAT:** Johannes Brahms: *A German Requiem,* Philharmonia Orchestra and Chorus (Otto Klemperer, cond.).

The Refinement of an Unlikely Sound

I Against I

Bad Brains

Adam Yauch of the Beastie Boys once described the Bad Brains' self-titled 1982 debut as "the best punk/hardcore album of all time." That may be an overstatement, but this Washington, D.C., foursome did have seismic and overnight impact—its thrashy, superfast speed-punk attack, paired with melodies (and philosophy) drawn from reggae and dub, was unlike anything else in hardcore. While most punks were lucky to lurch to the end of a song together, this rhythm section, which got its start playing jazz, turned out keyed-up music loaded with jolting and abrupt switchbacks.

On stage H.R. is "like James Brown gone berserk, with a hyperkinetic repertoire of spins, dives, back-flips, splits, and skanks." —*Village Voice*

Bad Brains is thirty-six minutes of full-tilt mayhem, with a few thoughtful downtempo dub tracks for respite. This follow-up is more refined. It was made four years later, after the band had broken up and re-formed, and was thinking about music in considerably more expansive terms. Steady road work taught the Brains the importance of pacing; the biggest change on *I Against I* is the variety of tempos and grooves, and vocalist H.R.'s contortions— he sings some songs in an aggravated whine, others like a bellowing drill sergeant.

Several of these tunes, notably "Secret 77," are almost featherweight pop. The reggae element, which was dear to H.R. ("Human Rights," born Paul D. Hudson), flourishes on the antiviolence title track and the chilling spiritual "House of Suffering." Yet this is still a hardcore band: Even when the melodies exude hopeful rasta positivity (see "Re-Ignition"), the anchoring rhythms, which include ripping funk backbeats or fitful heavy rock, are anything but idyllic.

And in truth, the fine points associated with different musical styles don't matter much when this daredevil rhythm section is at work. Sounding almost supernaturally cohesive, like they're all breathing with the same lungs, the Bad Brains go headfirst at everything safe and staid about rock. Guitarist Dr. Know (Gary Miller) stomps on the canvas with severe blockhead chords, then turns around and serves up crying single-note leads that are as gentle as droplets of rain.

Bridging the abrasive energy of punk and the blissed-out tones of reggae in ways much more aggressive than such British acts as the Specials, the Bad Brains put forth an idea that was radical in punk then, and remains that way now: that a sound of relentless harshness could carry expressions of great sensitivity.

GENRE: 🎸 Rock. RELEASED: 1986, SST. KEY TRACKS: "House of Suffering," "I Against I," "She's Calling You." F.Y.I.: According to Bad Brains lore, H.R. recorded the vocals of "Sacred Love" over the phone from prison, while serving time on a marijuana charge. CATALOG CHOICE: *Bad Brains.* NEXT STOP: Minor Threat: *Complete Works.* AFTER THAT: 24-7 Spyz: *Harder than You.*

This Gun Is Loaded . . .

Mama's Gun

Erykah Badu

An alternative to the perfectly coiffed line-dancing machine-music of Janet Jackson, Destiny's Child, and others, Erykah Badu makes booty calls to consciousness. First on her acclaimed 1997 debut, *Baduizm,* and more sharply on this rousing and resolute follow-up, Badu recasts the party-animal hip-hop/R&B "flygirl" as a confident woman who's wide awake, defiant in the face of the "penitentiary philosophy" that limits her potential. Through songs she calls "think jams," she defines herself in the positive, particularly where body image is concerned, yet never forgets the message she got over and over again growing up: "Remember there in school one day I learned I was inferior—water in my cereal" goes one couplet.

Badu had her share of life turmoil in the three years between her debut, which established her as a powerful voice in the burgeoning "neo-soul" subgenre, and this follow-up. A romance with Outkast's André 3000 (né Benjamin) led to the baby-mama drama immortalized on the Outkast hit "Ms. Jackson" and a breakup. Badu toured extensively around her debut, and through those performances discovered the virtues of on-the-fly interaction between live musicians. When it came time to record *Mama's Gun,* the singer and songwriter, who grew up in Dallas (and attended the same high school as Norah Jones), carried those lessons into the studio. She put together a top-shelf band around Roots drummer Ahmir "?uestlove" Thompson, and let the ideas fly. "Just about everything on the album was a jam," she explained in an interview shortly before the album's release, "just something we were trying, to get the flow going."

The looseness liberates the word-centered Badu. Before, she was a decent hip-hop MC with a coy sense of rhythm; at different times on *Mama's Gun,* she sounds like she's fronting the classic James Brown band, or a torchy jazz group, or a futuristic electronic crew whose stutter-step beats defy drum-programming logic. Each setting inspires wildly different harangues, spirited extemporaneous riffing that was once the lifeblood of rhythm and blues. Before that militaristic line-dancing took over.

GENRE: 🎙 R&B. **RELEASED:** 2000, Motown. **KEY TRACKS:** "Cleva," "Booty," "Kiss Me on My Neck," "In Love with You." **CATALOG CHOICE:** *Worldwide Underground.* **NEXT STOP:** Macy Gray: *On How Life Is.* **AFTER THAT:** Mary J. Blige: *Mary.*

Grammy award–winning Erykah Badu in one of her signature headwraps.

The Arrival of a Subtle Folk Voice

Joan Baez

Joan Baez

Near the end of "East Virginia," one of fifteen traditional songs Joan Baez interprets on her debut album, there's an unexpected display of musicianship. Baez has been singing in full, almost loud, voice when suddenly she drops into pianissimo and modulates her guitar accompaniment accordingly. She handles most of the transfixing final verses this way, not in a stage whisper exactly, but a muted, death-pondering voice.

Such dynamic contrasts, common in classical music, happen much less frequently in folk. Baez uses the hush to heighten the already dramatic narrative. Her framing of the tale—another in the long line of bitter odes about unrequited love—becomes as riveting as the story itself.

That attention to detail turns up throughout this influential debut. At the dawn of the 1960s, the singers associated with the "folk revival" were thinking big thoughts and concerning themselves with rattling the populace awake. They weren't always thinking about fine points like dynamics. That's one reason Baez was so important: Leaving the hectoring to others, she brought texture and contrast and subtlety to the coffeehouse.

Recorded in the summer of 1960, when she was nineteen, *Joan Baez* presents the singer's calm, crystalline soprano on a program of tragic ballads and lullabies. A dedicated student of American music, Baez developed highly personal treatments of traditional songs—her arrangement of "I Know You Rider" is said to have inspired the Grateful Dead to explore the tune. And those who know the Stanley Brothers' "Man of Constant Sorrow" from *O Brother, Where Art Thou?* will be enchanted by Baez's rendering. "Girl of Constant Sorrow"—which was left off the original album and appears as a bonus track on the 2001 reissue—gives that eternal melody a slightly different, but no less woeful, spin.

GENRE: 🎵 Folk. **RELEASED:** 1960, Vanguard. (Reissued 2001.) **KEY TRACKS:** "East Virginia," "House of the Rising Sun," "Mary Hamilton," "John Riley," "I Know You Rider." **CATALOG CHOICE:** *Blessed Are . . . .* **NEXT STOP:** Richie Havens: *Mixed Bag.* **AFTER THAT:** Buffy Sainte-Marie: *It's My Way!*

Sultry Upscale Soul

Rapture

Anita Baker

Named after a Smokey Robinson song, the "Quiet Storm" radio format originated at Howard University's WHUR in the mid-1970s, and within several years became a staple of the nighttime airwaves coast to coast. The concept was simple: Quiet Storm was aimed expressly at lovers. It focused on low-key urban music, often ballads. Tune in, and you could count on hours of delicate aural seductions, sometimes undifferentiated vaguely jazzy sounds that flickered easily, like candlelight.

Plenty of artists (Luther Vandross, Lionel Richie) targeted the Quiet Storm format, but few nailed its tone and temperament the way Anita Baker did on her major-label debut, *Rapture*. The album quickly sold over a million copies, spawned several songs that remain Quiet Storm classics ("Caught Up in the Rapture," "Sweet Love"), and established Baker as a singer of uncommon poise and sophistication.

Rapture endures primarily because of the way Baker, a Detroit-based singer who grew up listening to Sarah Vaughan, Dinah Washington, and others, approaches the task of singing sweet nothings. While the reigning pop divas (Whitney Houston et al.) load every phrase with heaping helpings of pain, Baker hangs way back, letting her voice ooze over the subtle, at times sedate accompaniment. She sounds, throughout, as if she is caught up in a kind of deep bliss, a zone of feeling from which she can be candid about the wonders of the love she shares.

Even when she's talking about ecstasy, Baker is restrained—she takes her leisurely time with every note. Singing in this deliberate and unhurried way, she fulfills the romance requirement of Quiet Storm while aligning herself with João Gilberto, Billie Holiday, Roberta Flack, Miles Davis, and other masters of musical quietude.

GENRE: 🎙 R&B. **RELEASED:** 1986, Elektra. **KEY TRACKS:** "Sweet Love," "Caught Up in the Rapture." **CATALOG CHOICE:** *My Everything.* **NEXT STOP:** Cassandra Wilson: *Blue Light 'til Dawn* (see p. 869). **AFTER THAT:** Alice Russell: *Under the Munka Moon.*

Getting Lost, in a Mist, with the Master

Let's Get Lost: The Best of Chet Baker Sings

Chet Baker

C het Baker was the polar opposite of those jazz singers who approach the microphone intending to wow their audiences. He sang haltingly, as though deep in doubt. He didn't demand attention. Instead, his confiding tones made romance seem infinitely beguiling, something almost beyond comprehension. This disc was culled from recordings made in the 1950s before heroin ravaged his body and blunted the little-boy-blue purity of his voice. It is among the most beautiful respites in all of jazz.

Baker (1929–1988) was a longtime heroin addict. This made him notoriously unreliable; at times he'd take recording dates just to score enough money to feed his habit. The upheavals in his life didn't always seep into his art, however. When he was on, he displayed a control of nuance that made him the music world's Monet, a master of mists and gentle inflections. Here, Baker is in the company of sympathetic West Coast jazz players. He's obviously comfortable, unafraid to appear vulnerable. These all-time-great performances of "I Remember You," "My Funny Valentine," and "You Don't Know What Love Is" have a gliding, unperturbed aura; they're jazz singing as a private internal discussion. Baker defines not just the melodic outlines of a song, but a way of feeling within it. He melts the music without ever raising his voice, and when he's finished doing that, he picks up the trumpet and blows sweet, lyrical solos that take things to a slightly different place. Baker once observed that his singing and playing were intertwined: "If I hadn't been a trumpet player, I don't know if I would have arrived at singing that way. I probably wouldn't have."

Chet Baker helped pioneer cool jazz in the 1950s.

GENRE: Jazz.
RELEASED: 1989, Pacific Jazz/Capitol. **KEY TRACKS:** "My Funny Valentine," "My Ideal," "But Not for Me," "I Remember You," "You Don't Know What Love Is."
CATALOG CHOICE: Gerry Mulligan: *The Best of the Gerry Mulligan Quartet with Chet Baker.* **NEXT STOP:** Paul Desmond: *Take Ten* (see p. 220). **AFTER THAT:** Nick Drake: *Five Leaves Left* (see p. 235).

A Landmark of Cajun Music

The Balfa Brothers Play Traditional Cajun Music

The Balfa Brothers

When the Balfa Brothers of Mamou, Louisiana, light into a zippy Cajun two-step, what transpires is stately and unflappable dance music made with the polite manners of old ladies sitting around a sewing circle.

That's not a knock: In great Cajun music, everyone sticks to his or her knitting. The fiddles handle their woeful, seesawing melodies, the guitars are strummed in straightforward, unremarkable fashion, and the percussion—which comes from the triangle and the washboard—defines the tempo in efficient, nothing-fancy strokes.

The Balfas are masters of this clockwork interdependence, which gives the simple odes of traditional Cajun music a juiced-up exuberance. Listen to this family band keep time, and what you hear is more than care-

"A culture is preserved one generation at a time."
—Dewey Balfa

ful execution. You hear great spaces between the notes, moments where it seems everyone breathes at the same instant and then leans back into the groove with the same amount of elbow grease. Building on this unity, the brothers Dewey, Will, Rodney, and Harry bring extraordinary lightheartedness to nimble waltzes and songs of devotion.

The Balfas grew up hearing traditional Cajun music—their father, a sharecropper, sang the songs of his French ancestors almost daily, at a time when many French-speaking settlers in southern

Louisiana spoke English in order to assimilate. Dewey and his brothers played small dances and local affairs until 1964, when they were invited as a last-minute replacement at the Newport Folk Festival. They caused a sensation, but it wasn't enough to land the group a record deal.

Dewey Balfa knocked on the doors of small record companies throughout the region, and was twice turned down by Swallow Records owner Floyd Soileau, before Soileau agreed to record a tryout single. That led to *Play Traditional Cajun Music*, which was released in 1965. Amazingly, despite the album's success and the group's stature as key preservers of Cajun culture, it took nine years for Swallow

to record a follow-up, *The Balfa Brothers Play More Traditional Cajun Music*. Both volumes are included on this disc, which is the text from which all the Cajun artists that surfaced during the Cajun revival of the 1970s and '80s—from Wayne Toups to Michael Doucet and BeauSoleil—learned the craft.

GENRE: 🌐 Folk. **RELEASED:** 1965, Swallow. (Reissued 2005.) **KEY TRACKS:** "'Tit galop pour Mamou," "Chère joues roses," "Family Waltz," "Madeleine," "Enterre-moi pas." **CATALOG CHOICE:** *Legends of Cajun Music.* **NEXT STOP:** Michael Doucet and BeauSoleil: *Bayou Deluxe* (see p. 233). **AFTER THAT:** Various Artists: *J'ai été au bal* (DVD and/or CD).

The Original Twist and So Much More

Singin' and Swingin' with . . .

Hank Ballard and the Midnighters

Hank Ballard's first step into pop culture consciousness came with a trio of bawdy 1954 singles that immortalized a girl named Annie. "Work with Me Annie" and its two sequels ("Annie Had a Baby," "Annie's Aunt Fanny")

were banned by many radio stations as too explicit, but each sold over a million copies and established Ballard, who grew up in Alabama, as an original voice. His basic trick: pairing music that had the fervent vocal appeal of rhythm and blues with caterwauling dance rhythms—and lyrics filled with risqué double entendres.

As his career progressed, Ballard sought more than to merely titillate. This hot 1957 date reveals him as a songwriter of significant range, capable of sorrowful, blues-inflected ballads and pieces that feel as giddy as doo-wop but without the dewy-eyed

". . . Rock 'n' roll is good for the soul, for the psyche, for your everything."   —Hank Ballard

naïveté. *Singin' and Swingin'*'s big hit, "Teardrops on Your Letter," is a timeless early-rock song that somehow never became a standard; just about everything else shows that Ballard was not only willing to experiment (see the moody atmosphere of "I'll Be Home Someday," which sounds like it could have been recorded a decade later, during the height of psychedelia), but capable of crafting new hybrids of gospel, R&B, and rock and roll. This album's commercial claim to fame, though, is the B side to "Teardrops," "The Twist," which was rerecorded by Chubby Checker and became one of the biggest singles in rock history as well as a dance craze. Checker's version follows the outline of the Ballard recording, adding a touch of teenage enthusiasm and little else. Check out the original to hear Ballard's group ride a significantly tighter roadhouse-rocking rhythm. Sure it's coarse, but it has that heedless devil-may-care quality that animates all great party music.

GENRE: 🄮 Rock. **RELEASED:** 1959, King. **KEY TRACKS:** "Teardrops on Your Letter," "Last Goodbye," "I'll Be Home Someday," "Sweet Mama, Do Right." **CATALOG CHOICE:** *Sexy Ways: The Best of . . .* **NEXT STOP:** Various Artists: *Cameo-Parkway 1957–1967* (see p. 806). **AFTER THAT:** Wynonie Harris: *Bloodshot Eyes.*

Hot Enough to Rock the Planet!

"Planet Rock"

Afrika Bambaataa and the Soul Sonic Force

I f there ever was a machine-based rhythm so funky its very DNA demands note-by-note dissection, this hyperkinetic robot dance is it. The snare drum that sits at the front of "Planet Rock" isn't like any recognizable acoustic instrument—it's a phenomenon of fizzy attack, with a long tail of bubbles trailing behind. The high-hat cymbals snap with a satisfying hiss. The kick drum is a whomp to the gut. These drums—pounded out on the now-legendary Roland 808 electronic beatbox, which became standard in hip-hop recording studios after this single—outline a pattern common to lots of early hip-hop. But there's a difference: The beat syncs up with elements of Kraftwerk's "Numbers," and the melody comes directly from the title track of the German group's *Trans-Europe Express* (see p. 433).

This integration of ideas is, of course, the core craft of the hip-hop DJ. Afrika Bambaataa, a pioneer from the South Bronx who took his name from a nineteenth-century Zulu chief, kicked the game up a few levels with this track, which has become an essential part of every club DJ's toolkit. The demonically inventive

Bambaataa was a pioneer of the hip-hop awareness group Universal Zulu Nation.

drum programming of "Planet Rock" spread beyond hip-hop, shaping such subsequent dance styles as Miami bass and Detroit techno. With conceptual help from Arthur Baker and keyboardist John Robie, Bambaataa blended the 808 riff and the Kraftwerk bits into a single groove, then added syncopated orchestra stabs and catcalling team vocals from the Soul Sonic Force crew. The basic "Planet Rock" pattern (as well as its exact drum sounds) has turned up on countless hip-hop records, and still the original stands apart—riveting from that first slammed downbeat, it's a hit of instant audio euphoria.

GENRE: 🄮 Hip-Hop. **RELEASED:** 1986, Tommy Boy. **APPEARS ON:** *Planet Rock: The Album.* **NEXT STOP:** EPMD: *Strictly Business.* **AFTER THAT:** Cut Chemist: *Live at Future Primitive Sound Session.*

Come Hear the Band

The Band

The Band

It's as if an itinerant old-time medicine show somehow skipped a few generations, pulled off a two-lane Arkansas highway in 1910, and woke up in 1968, with its remaining potions turned to hallucinogens. Of course the time travelers had stories to tell—about the wily old South, where men with names like Virgil and Eustace tended the land, and there was pride just in surviving.

Four Canadians and one Southern "ringer" (drummer Levon Helm, who grew up in Arkansas), the Band caught what was wild and romantic about America, and framed it in ramshackle grandeur with a touch of a hippie-era batik. The musicians first played together backing rockabilly singer Ronnie Hawkins, but became cohesive backing Bob Dylan during his shift from acoustic folk to rock. When the Band moved out of the Big Pink house in Woodstock, New York, the group of talented multi-instrumentalists discovered they had something different, but no less profound, to say on their own. That's instantly evident in the story-songs on their first album, *Music from Big Pink,* and this masterpiece—a one-two punch the likes of which rock and roll hasn't seen since.

Just the titles from this record suggest Southern Gothic stories: "Up on Cripple Creek." "The Night They Drove Old Dixie Down" (Joan Baez's biggest hit). "Across the Great Divide." "King Harvest (Has Surely Come)," a hymn about trade unionism. When Robbie Robertson's considered guitar quips and the "barrelhouse" piano of Richard Manuel are added to the swampy yarns, the result is a glimpse into a mythic rural America that may or may not have existed. It's a place where accordions wheeze soft and low and honest voices gather into a ragged choir of the devoted, singing just for the communal joy of it.

GENRE: 🎸 Rock. **RELEASED:** 1969, Capitol. (Reissued 2000.) **KEY TRACKS:** All of them. **CATALOG CHOICE:** *Music from Big Pink.* **NEXT STOP:** Tom Waits: *Foreign Affairs.* **AFTER THAT:** The Grateful Dead: *Workingman's Dead.*

Symphonic Music for Meditation

Adagio for Strings

Samuel Barber
St. Louis Symphony Orchestra (Leonard Slatkin, cond.)

The brooding surges and keening tones of Samuel Barber's *Adagio for Strings* suggest the work of a troubled soul in the late autumn of life, reflecting on things past. In fact, Barber wrote the piece at the ripe old age of twenty-six, initially conceiving it as the slow movement of his 1936 String Quartet. He provided a full symphonic orchestration two years later, and virtually rocketed to fame soon after, when the piece was championed by celebrated conductor Arturo Toscanini. It became one of the few works by an American composer performed regularly by Russian orchestras during the cold war.

Over his musical career Samuel Barber earned two Pulitzers.

And it wasn't long before the Adagio reached those who didn't pay much attention to classical music: Its stately pace suited it to ceremonies of public mourning (it was played during funeral observances for Franklin D. Roosevelt and John F. Kennedy) and any number of poignant films, including *The Elephant Man* and the Vietnam drama *Platoon.*

Perhaps because of its somber air and long questioning tones, the Adagio is often included on those classical anthologies devoted to "relaxing" music. It's that and more, a singularly moving eight-minute journey suited to any introspective occasion. Alternately stormy and tranquil, with brooding counterlines that rise from the cellos and basses answered by hovering sustained notes

from the violins, the piece creates its own atmosphere. Some recorded versions lean toward an almost florid excess, utilizing glacially slow tempos to manufacture drama. This 1981 version by the St. Louis Symphony, conducted by Leonard Slatkin, is haunting precisely because it's so spare. Slatkin fixates on the solemnity of Barber's score, and renders it cleanly, luring listeners into a transfixing zone of reflection that Barber built out of chords that hang, perpetually unresolved, in the air.

GENRE: 🎵 Classical. **RELEASED:** 1981, Telarc. **COLLECTOR'S NOTE:** This themed collection of nocturnal pieces includes Ralph Vaughan Williams's magnificent (and underappreciated) "Fantasia on a Theme by Thomas Tallis," a string-orchestra recontextualization of a Tallis religious work from the 16th century. **ANOTHER INTERPRETATION:** New York Philharmonic (Leonard Bernstein, cond.). **CATALOG CHOICE:** *Piano Concerto No. 1,* John Browning, St. Louis Symphony Orchestra (Leonard Slatkin, cond.). **NEXT STOP:** Maurice Ravel: *Pavane for a Dead Princess,* Berlin Philharmonic (Herbert von Karajan, cond.).

Salsa Caliente

Barretto Power

Ray Barretto

Cue this up to experience the fire that starts with calloused hands striking skins, those perfectly timed wallops and thundering slaps that send musicians and dancers into the stratosphere. They're all over this album,

one of four the conga player and bandleader Ray Barretto recorded in 1972. The music will

be simmering pleasantly along, and suddenly Barretto drops in one galvanizing phrase, maybe just a single resounding "thwack" on the conga, and like magic, everything gets hotter.

Barretto (1929–2006) had a vast repertoire of these devices. As the musical director of the Fania All Stars, he used them to inspire the players in his invariably well-rehearsed bands to go deeper into the groove. That leadership is audible on the opening track, "Oye la noticia." It begins as a medium-tempo dance tune, but right around the three-minute mark, Barretto breaks into a marathon conga roll that sends an unmistakable signal: Change is coming. The percussionists heed his call. Within seconds, they begin smacking the rhythm around, adding inspired jabs. These don't simply outline the beat but pummel it into submission with phrases that require both brute strength and tremendous dexterity.

This album is aptly titled. Though slightly less exploratory than some of Barretto's jazz-leaning works of the '70s (notably the electri-

The album art was designed by Izzy Sanabria, creator of some of Fania Records' best-known covers.

fied *Acid*), it presents his band, the cream of the Fania crew, at an absolute rip-roaring peak. Every tune, from the suave "Quitate la mascara" to the boogalooing "Right On," alternates between lively vocal exchanges and swaggering instrumental solos that percolate, thrillingly, for minutes on end. These, too, are "sculpted" by Barretto. Leading with the drums, he pushes his band right to the brink of a riot, encouraging upheaval. And then, when chaos seems imminent, he restores order, using those same slaps and pops to remind the musicians that no matter how far "out" they get, they're still in the dance music business.

GENRE: 🌐 World/Latin. **RELEASED:** 1972, Fania. **KEY TRACKS:** "Oye la noticia," "Right On," "Quitate la mascara," "Power." **CATALOG CHOICES:** *Acid; Rican/Struction; Que vive la musica.* **NEXT STOP:** Mongo Santamaria: *Mongo Introduces La Lupe.* **AFTER THAT:** Jerry Gonzalez: *Rumba para Monk.*

The Shape-Shifting Genius of Bartók

Six String Quartets

Béla Bartók
Takac Quartet

Like a film director working without a script, Hungarian composer Béla Bartók (1881–1945) follows an impulsive, nonlinear path through these six astounding pieces for string quartet, which represent a peak of twentieth-century music. He rarely stays in any one key center for long. His themes tumble out, sometimes getting discarded immediately and sometimes coalescing into purposeful ensemble bursts, occasionally piling on top of each other like a multicar crash on the freeway.

Written between 1908 (when the composer was twenty-seven) and 1939, the String Quartets outline the arc of Bartók's progression from dutiful post-romanticist to folklorist to one of the most original composers of all time. He was hardly the only composer to investigate folk forms, but unlike most, he did not settle for the quaint and pretty endearments that had already been anthologized. Bartók strapped a gramophone onto the back of a donkey and headed for the most remote Transylvanian villages to get the tunes down exactly, and what he came back with was gritty, cranky, idiosyncratic stuff, which he used as the springboard for his later musical investigations. Today, such an investigation seems smart and in some ways inevitable; when Bartók began, many considered it a folly.

Bartók integrates the folk material stealthily, often picking up the swirl of a dance or emulating, in the picky string pizzicato passages he marked "barbaro," the rhythmic cadence of a century-old vocal tune. He's never gratuitous, and he never slums. He sometimes replicates the emotions underpinning the folk themes in total, but is more often inclined to fracture them, creating music that

is supremely beautiful one minute (the nighttime mist that envelops the third movement of No. 4) and jarringly disruptive (the torrid first movement of No. 6) the next.

The Hungarian Takac Quartet relishes Bartók's extremes. While it catches and celebrates the idiosyncracies in the score, it manages to give the composer's knotty, imposing structures a good airing out—rendering this heavy music with an animated brightness that's more typically associated with children's songs.

GENRE: & Classical. **RELEASED:** 1998, Decca. **KEY TRACK:** No. 4. **ANOTHER INTERPRETATION:** Emerson String Quartet. **CATALOG CHOICE:** *Music for Strings, Percussion, and Celesta* (see below). **NEXT STOP:** Kronos Quartet: *Night Prayers* (Music by Joan Jeanrenaud). **AFTER THAT:** Osvaldo Golijov: *Oceana*.

Group Togetherness, on a Grand Scale

Concerto for Orchestra; Music for Strings, Percussion, and Celesta

Béla Bartók
Chicago Symphony Orchestra (Fritz Reiner, cond.)

Everyone should experience the thrill of hearing a hundred or more musicians racing toward and then landing on the same downbeat at the same millisecond, with nary a whisker out of place. When a great orchestra is in sync, there's nothing quite like it in all of music—the mass of sound registers as something more than precision, a no-room-for-doubt chop that splits the air cleanly into "before" and "after." The notes become secondary to the slashing exactitude of placement.

You don't encounter this kind of precision every day. James Brown's bands had it. The Count Basie Orchestra, too. Prince has it. Many orchestras don't have it anymore—a mushy,

behind-the-beat approach has taken root in the wind sections of some major symphonic groups. In the 1950s (and for a while after), the Chicago Symphony Orchestra was among the most detail-oriented; its recordings under Fritz Reiner, including this pair of unconventional Bartók works, are shining examples of group togetherness on a grand scale.

With its angular lines and abrupt changes of direction, *Music for Strings, Percussion, and Celesta* is a showpiece for those dramatic downbeats, offering a series of challenges that can vex even the most precision-minded ensemble. The Chicago Symphony rises to the task, putting serious oomph into those attacks—particularly during the frenzied and thrilling final movement, when the piano becomes the knife edge of the percussion section.

The longer and somewhat more substantial *Concerto for Orchestra* is an odd beast. It doesn't adhere to concerto form or the template for a symphony. Bartók envisioned it as a series of dialogs between various soloists and the larger group, and also between various sections. That's how it starts, with a foreboding low-strings murmur and an answering theme played by winds and harp. Similar exchanges crop up throughout—the second movement, subtitled "The Game of Pairs," is a capricious exercise in which the long and winding theme is carried by pairs of instruments that trade off at unexpected intervals. The third movement "Elegia," which is organized around a flowing melody, contains some of the most beautiful hallucinations ever played by a symphony orchestra.

There, and, really, throughout the piece, Bartók expects his interpreters to animate the material with crisp execution, but not overshadow its intricate web of themes and variations with too many interpretive flourishes. Reiner, who was Hungarian and knew Bartók personally, does this instinctively. He brings each crescendo to a satisfying brink, and then leaves space so that the individual attacks register as distinct events. Approaching the score not as notes but a series of textural challenges, Reiner brings Bartók to life with the balance of force and finesse that only happens when a hundred musicians play as one.

GENRE: 🎷 Classical. **RELEASED:** 1958, RCA. **KEY TRACKS:** *Music for Strings: Adagio. Concerto for Orchestra:* "Elegia," Finale. **ANOTHER INTERPRETATION:** Chicago Symphony Orchestra (James Levine, cond.). **CATALOG CHOICE:** *Violin Concerto No. 2, Rhapsodies Nos. 1 and 2,* Chicago Symphony Orchestra (Pierre Boulez, cond.). **NEXT STOP:** Igor Stravinsky: *The Rite of Spring* (see p. 750). **AFTER THAT:** Frank Zappa: *Boulez Conducts Zappa: The Perfect Stranger,* Ensemble InterContemporain.

The Alchemy of an Evening

Bartók: Concerto No. 3 for Piano and Orchestra; Tchaikovsky: Symphony No. 6

Béla Bartók and Pyotr Ilyich Tchaikovsky
Annie Fischer, Bavarian Radio Symphony Orchestra (Ferenc Fricsay, cond.)

The arm-waving is the easy part. For most conductors and music directors, the real challenge happens offstage, when assembling pieces with vastly different sonorities and textures into an exhilarating evening of music.

This live concert, by the Bavarian Radio Symphony on November 24, 1960, illustrates the mixmaster's art. It features Hungarian conductor Ferenc Fricsay interpreting two deeply emotional pieces, the last major works by their respective composers.

Fricsay's programming tactic here might be described as "high contrast." Bartók's Piano Concerto No. 3, written in 1945, is characteristically percussive, defined by modern angular chords and splashes of unexpected color. Tchaikovsky, the classicist who finished this symphony, nicknamed the "Pathétique," just before he died in 1893, explores dark emotions while upending convention (unlike most symphonies, the first and last movements here are slow, with the middle two more animated). Bartók demands a fiery attitude and significant agility from the soloist. Tchaikovsky expects the orchestra to melt into his melancholy.

Despite these differences, the pieces work marvelously in juxtaposition. This reading of the Bartók showcases the fiery and unsentimental Hungarian pianist Annie Fischer, who makes her first entrances with the steely efficiency of a school administrator. Bartók's tone softens in the second movement, a "night music" essay that drifts from one haunting abstraction to the next, and Fischer concentrates on the placement of every note. Pretty soon Fricsay—an underappreciated master of shading—gets the whole orchestra inside that deliberative mood. Together they create a kind of witching spell,

Béla Bartók was a pioneer of ethnomusicology—the study of music in its cultural context.

a thick atmosphere that carries through the Bartók and, incredibly, extends into the slow opening movement of the Tchaikovsky.

With Bartók still ringing in the hall, the *Pathétique*'s initial themes—a gathering storm of disconsolate tones and swelling surges—become even more breathtaking. The pieces come from different eras and contain wildly contrasting sonorities, yet under Fricsay's baton they coalesce into a single impression, an evening of music that is even more stirring than the sum of its powerfully affecting parts.

GENRE: 🎧 Classical. **RELEASED:** 1989, Orfeo. **KEY TRACKS:** Bartók: second movement. Tchaikovsky: first and fourth movements. **ANOTHER INTERPRETATION:** Tchaikovsky: Leningrad Philharmonic (Evgeny Mravinsky, cond.; see p. 768). **CATALOG CHOICE:** Bartók: *Six String Quartets* (see p. 46). Tchaikovsky: *Symphonies Nos. 4, 5, 6,* Berlin Philharmonic (Herbert von Karajan, cond.). **F.Y.I.:** Fricsay recorded Tchaikovsky's Sixth several times; this version is almost eight minutes longer than his 1953 rendering, an indication of how a conductor's approach to a piece can change over time. **NEXT STOP:** *Beethoven Piano Sonatas,* Annie Fischer. **AFTER THAT:** Gustav Mahler: *Symphony No. 4* (see p. 468).

The Pleasures of Italy, in Sound

The Vivaldi Album

Cecilia Bartoli

Cecilia Bartoli was on a two-pronged rescue mission when she undertook her own research into the baroque-era operas of Antonio Vivaldi (1678–1741) in the late 1990s. She was primarily interested in resurrecting the works, which are more "mannered" than modern operas, and thus not often programmed. At the same time, she was searching for palatable material to sing: Bartoli has a down-to-earth voice and jaw-dropping agility that earned her comparisons with the great Beverly Sills (see p. 518). But she's a mezzo-soprano, and the opera repertoire offers few leading roles for mezzo-sopranos. Far fewer of those are in Italian, her native language. So Vivaldi was a logical move both musically and professionally; it offers her the chance to shine on underappreciated material.

Bartoli makes the most of it. Rather than tackle large excerpts or full works, she culls arias from the composer's numerous operas—in some ways this is a highlight reel, curated by a singer who's interested in the most musically (and theatrically) compelling platforms.

Recognizing that the plot lines are fairly "stock," Bartoli emphasizes the moments when Vivaldi breaks away from the tottering niceties of baroque to offer up divine melodic morsels. These are the passages that make the hearts of musicians race, and Bartoli brings them to life with a touch of Italian pride and

Cecilia Bartoli has won four Grammys for her contributions to classical music.

pronounced sensuality. She sweeps technically demanding lines into tossed-off showers of pixie dust, and though these sometimes feel showy, they're hardly just blurs of notes. She's one of those rare singers who can tear around and never land even a smidgen away from the intended pitch.

While Bartoli understands (and is capable of brilliantly executing) the theatrical element in Vivaldi, her handling of the arias tends toward gentler and more entrancing interpretations. On the aria "Zeffiretti, che sussurrate" from an unknown opera, she rolls right through the echoing effects, holding the melody with pride; she's even more resolute on "Sventurata navicella" (from *Il Giustino*), which has a mystical aura and a voluptuous melody. Bartoli sings it like she knows exactly how precious it is.

GENRE: 🎼 Classical. **RELEASED:** 1999, Decca. **KEY TRACKS:** "Zeffiretti, che sussurrate." *Il Giustino:* "Sventurata navicella." *La fida ninfa:* "Alma oppressa." **CATALOG CHOICE:** *An Italian Songbook.* **NEXT STOP:** Douglas Moore and John Latouche: *The Ballad of Baby Doe.* (see p. 518). **AFTER THAT:** Jessye Norman: *The Jessye Norman Collection.*

The Definition of Swing

Complete Decca Recordings

Count Basie and His Orchestra

T he first great minimalist of jazz, Count Basie said more with three carefully placed notes than most musicians do with three thousand. The pianist, organist, and bandleader had a distinctive touch and the rare ability to get a whole band swinging just through offbeat plinks and chordal jabs. Basie (1904–1984) was born in Red Bank, New Jersey, and after studying briefly with Fats Waller (see p. 843), was hired as an accompanist on the vaudeville circuit of the 1920s. He wound up in Kansas City, Missouri, and in 1929 became the pianist for the Bennie Moten band. His experience playing for dancers during that town's party boom of the 1930s taught him that sometimes the simplest ideas are the most effective ones. After Moten died in 1935, Basie built his own big band around this concept, and stuck to it for almost fifty years. His legacy isn't a single tune, but the singular swing feel, which reverberated from the piano through his tight band and into the culture at large.

Basie shows that teamwork counts. Because in isolation, the individual ingredients that go into Basie's music seem unspectacular—the steady chop of acoustic guitar chords (from Freddie Green, the band's unwavering secret weapon), the plink-plink dance of a few stray chords from Basie's piano, or the brass chirping its riffs with staccato certainty. Assembled just so, these ordinary elements become a screaming locomotive of rhythm, boogying down the tracks and levitating just above them, sweeping up everything in its path.

This three-disc anthology documents the

Count Basie led the Count Basie Orchestra for nearly 50 years.

first great Basie band, circa 1937, just after it arrived in New York. The starring role goes to the torrid rhythm section—guitarist Green, drummer Jo Jones, bassist Walter Page, and Basie—a combination talent scout John Hammond found "overwhelming" when he first heard the band live in K.C. But also on hand are some of the most exciting soloists ever to grace the bandstand, among them trumpeter Buck Clayton and saxophonists Lester Young and Chu Berry (heard here in an epic battle on "Cherokee"); several tracks also feature the authoritative singer Jimmy Rushing. The material is basic blues shouts (the first recording of the Basie anthem "One O'Clock Jump" is here) and juiced-up ragtime ("Pennies from Heaven"), plus novel pop songs like "Honeysuckle Rose," which Basie interprets as a breezy stride. As the emphasis switches from soloist to shout chorus and back, nobody showboats for long, because all Basie hands know that the groove is the holy grail. Get this to discover the feel-good essence of swing.

GENRE: 🎵 Jazz. RELEASED: 2000, Decca/MCA. KEY TRACKS: "Listen My Children and You Shall Hear," "Roseland Shuffle," "One O'Clock Jump." CATALOG CHOICE: *Atomic Swing*. NEXT STOP: Bennie Moten: *1923–1927*. AFTER THAT: Jimmie Lunceford: *Rhythm Is Our Business*.

Laments from a Native Son of Angola

Pretaluz

Waldemar Bastos

hen Waldemar Bastos defected to Portugal from his native Angola during its civil war in the 1970s, he encountered music that was to change his life—fado, the heart-heavy "blues" of Portugal, in which love affairs end messily and fate is usually cursed. Incorporating bits of the fado sound with African folk-song, Bastos then looked at what he'd left behind. His music, he once said, offers a "response to the fratricide in Angola, a simple message emphasizing the value of all life." His music became popular in his homeland, and though both warring factions embraced his songs, he didn't feel safe enough to return there to perform.

Pretaluz, released internationally in 1998, tells of Bastos's journey through a series of prayerlike meditations. These draw the agile guitar patterns of African pop and the sentimental melodies of fado into a boundaryless sound—music that connects continents without being

Pretaluz was Waldemar Bastos's first full-length American release.

ostentatiously "multi-culti." Singing wise aphorisms about envy ("Kuribota") or lamenting, in a trembling voice, the cruelty of war ("Sofrimento"), Bastos goes about the work of soul healing with a quiet humility. He's less a social commentator than a poet with gaze fixed on the long view, and throughout this mesmerizing cycle his objective isn't to force change, but to remind anyone embroiled in conflict about beauty, goodness, and the always underestimated power of love.

GENRE: 🌐 World/Angola. RELEASED: 1998, Luaka Bop. KEY TRACKS: "Kuribota," "Morro do Kussava," "Menina." NEXT STOP: Boukman Eksperyans: *Kalfou Danjere* (see p. 108).

The Spirit of the Drum

Con un poco de songo

Batacumbele

At the center of Cuba's Santeria religion are the *bata* drums. Congalike and hourglass-shaped, these instruments, of African origin, give a deep and stirring sound, and are used to play specific patterns calling

to individual deities in ritual ceremonies. So when, in the early '80s, a group of experimental Puerto Rican musicians in a band known as Batacumbele began playing *bata* and conga alongside drums used for traditional Puerto Rican rhythms like *bomba* and *plena*, eyebrows raised all over the Caribbean. Some veteran Cuban musicians worried that this revered instrument was being debased for secular ends.

Con un poco de songo started a cult following for Batacumbele.

In fact, Cuban popular groups—among them the esteemed Los Van Van, originators of the then-hot style called *songo*—had been using the *bata* in dance music for years. All Batacumbele was doing was broadening the rhythmic palette by incorporating bits of its own tradition. When Cubans heard it they went wild: "After we played several pieces, the audience rose to their feet shouting '¡Viva Puerto Rico! ¡Batacumbele con bata!' and waving their handkerchiefs in the air," percussionist Giovanni Hidalgo recalled of tours in 1981 and 1984.

Batacumbele's debut recording, *Con un poco de songo*, explains the ebullient reaction. It's a sleek, sophisticated sound, with tricky piano and bass figures darting around a percussion section that's deep into its own conversation. The vocal chants often seem borrowed from a religious ceremony, but even in the jazzy moments, the presence of the *bata* drums guarantees that there's some ancient spirits in the mix.

GENRE: 🌐 World/Cuba. **RELEASED:** 1989, Disco Hit. **KEY TRACKS:** "Se le ve," "La jibarito," "A la i ole." **CATALOG CHOICE:** *En aquellos tiempos.* **NEXT STOP:** Irakere: *Misa negra.* **AFTER THAT:** Truco y Zaperoko: *Música universal.*

The Dawning of a New Gloomy Day

In the Flat Field

Bauhaus

B auhaus is often credited with "inventing" goth rock, the style known for foreboding lyrics enveloped by shades of gray and black bleakness. Whether the credit is deserved or not (goth is one of those subgenres

that oozed from several directions at once), the goth-culture association has overshadowed something essential about the four-piece: In the beginning, it could raise serious hard rock hell.

Consider "Double Dare" from this electrifying debut, which was reissued with surprisingly sharp bonus tracks in 1988. It begins with Daniel Ash's almost primitive two-measure guitar riff, a metallic cattle-prod that's so saturated with fuzz-tone it hardly sounds like a guitar at all. Vocalist Peter Murphy sings the opening lines ("I dare you to be real") like he's positioning himself as the next Jim Morrison, but soon drops the air of mystery to belt more forcefully. By the end, his voice is as abrasive as the guitar, ravaged in its attempt to keep up with the heaving intensity around him.

Bauhaus are (from left) bassist David J, singer Peter Murphy, drummer Kevin Haskins, and guitarist Daniel Ash.

Named for the German art movement of the early twentieth century (in fact, the band's original name was Bauhaus 1919), the group formed in Northampton, England, in 1978, when punk was popping out all over. There's some of the franticness of that era in the songs of *Flat Field*—the tightly wound and infectiously hooky "God in an Alcove" could be early R.E.M.—but more often Bauhaus replaces punk jitters with a taut, restrained sense of rhythm. The band's measured and at times dispassionate attack intrigued British hipsters—one early champion was influential BBC Radio 1 personality John Peel—and after a series of singles, Bauhaus released *In the Flat Field*. The album has that goth sense of grandeur, but not, thankfully, the haughty, self-important pomposity that later made goth the preferred affectation of spoiled suburban brats. Instead, Murphy and the others treat dissatisfaction and frustration as learning opportunities. They move *through* the emotional states they describe, rather than wallowing endlessly in them. And that, needless to say, makes all the difference.

GENRE: 🎸 Rock. **RELEASED**: 1980, 4 AD. **KEY TRACKS**: "Double Dare," "God in an Alcove," "Stigmata Martyr," "Nerves." **CATALOG CHOICE:** *Mask.* **NEXT STOP:** Nine Inch Nails: *The Downward Spiral* (see p. 552). **AFTER THAT:** Killing Joke: *Killing Joke.*

Forever Picking Up . . .

"Good Vibrations"

The Beach Boys

66 **G**ood Vibrations" sits alone between the two artistic skyscrapers of Brian Wilson's career—the 1966 *Pet Sounds*, for which this single was originally intended, and the even more experimental *Smile*,

the "concept" work that he shelved after more than a year of work and god-only-knows-what inner turmoil. The episodic suite is an embarrassment of melodic riches. It's all singable, yet really hard to sing. It's catchy, but not in the same way "Surfin' USA" is catchy. Each new section scales a totally different mountain range. One minute we're doot-doot-doodling along a happy hokey surfer dude landscape, the next we're in the fjords, with cascading vocal lines raining down a Beethovenian homage to the glory of nature.

The Beach Boys have more Top 40 hits than any other U.S. rock band.

utes and thirty-five seconds. It's the most idiosyncratic of pop experiences, an almost disconnected bag of tricks held together by, of all things, the high-pitched theremin, an otherworldly-sounding electronic instrument that responds to hand motions. The single, which Wilson once described as a "pocket symphony," uses the squiggling trajectory of the theremin to represent positive vibrations in motion. Though it ventures all over the place, "Good Vibrations" somehow remains locked on that Total

The legend: Beach Boys songwriter Wilson removed the song from *Pet Sounds* because he didn't think it was finished. When the album didn't immediately become a hit, he went back to "Good Vibrations" and spent several months (and over $50,000, a then-unheard-of sum for a single) shuttling between studios trying to catch all the fragmented magic he heard in his head. In all, Wilson used over 70 hours of tape to create the single, which lasts three min-

Joy frequency, the one that Wilson, and Wilson alone, owns.

GENRE: ⭐ Pop. **RELEASED:** 1966, Capitol. **APPEARS ON:** *Smiley Smile.* (It was rerecorded for *Brian Wilson Presents Smile,* released by Nonesuch in 2004.) **CATALOG CHOICE:** *Pet Sounds* (see next page). **NEXT STOP:** There is none. This is the highest expression of the art of the pop single.

God Only Knows Where We'd Be Without This

Pet Sounds

The Beach Boys

S ooner or later Brian Wilson had to grow up. Summer might last forever, but at some point slinging surf music was gonna get old. To grow as an artist, it seemed, he needed to get around "I Get Around." This carefully

sculpted and lavishly arranged set of songs is Wilson's most "mature" music-making—and represents a high-water mark of pop craft in general. *Pet Sounds* is the California sunshine of the early Beach Boys as seen through darker lenses by people just old enough to remember when life really was carefree. Its characters have adult knowledge of the world's cruelties—they've been burned in love and are contending with what it means to be responsible. Bittersweetness creeps around the edges of the gliding harmonies and featherweight lead vocals. The Beach Boys' once purely exuberant melodies are now etched with poignant brushstrokes.

"*Pet Sounds* encompasses everything that's ever knocked me out and rolled it all into one."
—Eric Clapton

From the opening track, a vision of romantic bliss so idealized it has to be fantasy ("Wouldn't It Be Nice"), *Pet Sounds* travels the road between youthful hope and nostalgia—with brief detours for cautionary tales about drugs (the bonus track "Hang On to Your Ego") and meditations on the mysteries of life ("God Only Knows"). Though it's somewhat unified in terms of text, *Pet Sounds* is remarkably diverse in the orchestration department—virtually every track comes with its own set of instrumental touches, from the chiming bells of "Wouldn't It Be Nice" to the kettle drums that frame "Sloop John B."

Though *Pet Sounds* did have several

charting singles ("Caroline No," "Wouldn't It Be Nice," "Sloop John B"), the record didn't get massive promotion from Capitol; incredibly, it took until 2000 for the album to reach the million-copies-sold plateau. Despite those figures, *Pet Sounds* (and the later single "Good Vibrations," which Wilson initially intended as part of this album) has influenced just about everyone who makes pop music.

It's also an illustration of the reciprocal nature of pop inspiration: Wilson cited the Beatles' *Rubber Soul*, released in December 1965, as a primary catalyst for *Pet Sounds*. In turn, Paul McCartney has said that he was deeply affected by *Pet Sounds* during the making of the Beatles' *Sgt. Pepper's Lonely Hearts Club Band*. McCartney was once quoted as saying, "I figure no one is educated musically 'til they've heard *Pet Sounds*."

GENRE: 🅡 Rock. **RELEASED:** 1966, Capitol. (Reissued 1999.) **KEY TRACKS:** "Wouldn't It Be Nice," "Sloop John B." **COLLECTOR'S NOTE:** The reissue contains both the original monophonic mixes Wilson preferred and the subsequent stereo ones. **CATALOG CHOICE:** *Brian Wilson Presents Smile.* **NEXT STOP:** The Beatles: *Sgt. Pepper's Lonely Hearts Club Band* (see p. 60).

The Trio: Rediscovered

Billy Bean

T his one goes out to the near greats and the should-have-beens. All styles of music have them—the sidemen who could throw down in a big way but never got a break, the players who made others tremble but somehow got lost on the way to the spotlight. They are the utility infielders of music, existing in the half-light of liner notes and the memories of those who happened to be on the scene when once they roared. Their obscurity can be attributed to a zillion different twists of fate—they missed the gig where the talent scout showed up, they were the "wrong" color or gender, they fell victim to substance abuse, they just didn't look the part.

Among these is the jazz guitarist Billy Bean, whose crisp and hyper-articulate style set him apart from many of his peers. Active during the 1950s and '60s, the Philadelphia native cut his teeth supporting Red Callender, Bud Shank, Herbie Mann, and Charlie Ventura, among others. In between the journeyman work, Bean led a trio featuring pianist Walter Norris and bassist Hal Gaylor that worked the Manhattan jazz circuit in 1960. This group caught the ear of legendary pianist Bill Evans, who arranged for a record contract. The three made exactly one record, entitled *The Trio* (1961), which disappeared without attracting much attention.

Bean himself completely disappeared a year or so after that release, leaving behind a handful of small recordings (notably two with guitarist John Pisano, *Take Your Pick* and *Makin' It*). His output barely rated a short

While little-known jazz guitarist Billy Bean was highly respected and worked with many jazz greats, he only made one album as a frontman.

mention in Leonard Feather's *Biographical Encyclopedia of Jazz*, yet there was just enough to fuel a tiny myth. Decades later, some prominent guitarists—among them Pat Metheny and John Scofield—began to talk about Bean in glowing terms, as the rare technician whose lines are dauntingly complex, yet at the same time filled with sneaky, disarmingly beautiful melodies. Virtually everything on this drummer-less set bolsters that assessment: Cue up the snapping "Have You Met Miss Jones?" or the intricate "Porgy and Bess Medley" to hear a man with a unique, highly developed voice on his instrument, swinging delightfully, making wild leaps and rarely missing a beat. The audience wasn't there to pick up on it, but the tape survives all the same—a reminder that greatness can sometimes slip through the cracks, and go unnoticed for decades. Or, sometimes, forever.

GENRE: 🎵 Jazz. **RELEASED:** 1999, String Jazz. (Originally released 1961, Riverside.)
KEY TRACKS: "Porgy and Bess Medley," "Motivation," "Lush Life," "Have You Met Miss Jones?" **CATALOG CHOICE:** *Makin' It Again* (with John Pisano, Dennis Budimir). **NEXT STOP:** Hazel Scott: *Relaxed Piano Moods.* **AFTER THAT:** Ira Sullivan and Joe Diorio: *Breeze and I.*

Great Beats, Astute Rhymes from Hip-Hop's Heyday

Paul's Boutique

The Beastie Boys

C huck D of Public Enemy once said that after this album appeared in 1989, the unspoken consensus among the hip-hop elite was that the Beastie Boys, a trio of white rappers from Brooklyn, "had better beats" than just about anyone in the game.

To be sure, the rhythm beds of this record are astounding. Rather than punching out a simple beatbox rhythm or rejiggering sampled phrases, Beasties Adam "Ad-Rock" Horovitz, Michael "Mike D" Diamond, and Adam "MCA" Yauch, along with the production team known as the Dust Brothers, break things down to an almost cellular level. On some tunes, each individual drum tone is drawn from a different source. Then, the group crams tons of information where the beats would ordinarily

Paul's Boutique is "the *Pet Sounds/Dark Side of the Moon* of hip-hop."
—*Rolling Stone* magazine

go, and drops in more sampled exclamations to punctuate the lyrics or provide ironic running commentary. Consider "Shake Your Rump": A sizzling bit of high-energy funk, its drum tones are derived from recordings by the Sugar Hill Gang, Bob Marley ("Could You Be Loved"), jazz drummer Paul Humphrey, and a disco track by Harvey Scales called "Dancing Room Only," not to forget one of the memorable drum fills, which comes from Led Zeppelin's "Good Times Bad Times." The vocal interjections are culled from a similarly lengthy list that includes hip-hop's favorite patron saint, James Brown.

These painstakingly assembled samples set *Paul's Boutique* apart from just about everything else in popular music. They also hail from the very end of what might be called the "free" era

of hip-hop: The Beasties used most of the material without permission from the original creators. Less than two years after this release, a landmark lawsuit changed common hip-hop practice about samples, making it prohibitively expensive to reference other recordings in the collage style heard here.

Paul's Boutique is notable for other reasons. It documents the Beastie Boys' substantial evolution as lyricists: Once known for chuckleheaded enthusiasms—their first hit was "(You Gotta) Fight for Your Right (to Party!)," and their debut, *Licensed to Ill*, was dismissed in some quarters as "frat-rap"—the trio became a machine-gunning quip dispenser, flattening rivals with wisecracks while shouting down all sorts of biases and double standards. A vivid diatribe, "Egg Man" encapsulates a bit of stereotype-busting Beastie ideology: "You made the mistake, you judged a man by his race, you go through life with egg on your face."

GENRE: 🎤 Hip-Hop. **RELEASED:** 1989, Capitol. **KEY TRACKS:** "Shake Your Rump," "Hey Ladies," "Egg Man," "Looking Down the Barrel of a Gun." **CATALOG CHOICES:** *Licensed to Ill; To the Five Boroughs.* **NEXT STOP:** Beck: *Odelay.* **AFTER THAT:** Luscious Jackson: *Fever In Fever Out.*

A Hard Day's Night

The Beatles

I f you haven't listened closely to "A Hard Day's Night" since the transistor radio era, prepare for a shock. The eponymous song that kick-starts the Beatles' third full-length album is so familiar, it's like the furniture in the living room—there but unnoticed. Pay attention, and you may find yourself astounded all over again by this tuneful ode of complaint, which finds John Lennon double-tracking his voice to give the effect of a duet. He's groaning—cheerfully of course—about the trials of being an on-the-go pop idol.

It's a giddy adrenaline rush, and like everything that follows, it's the very essence of pop. Released at the height of Beatlemania in 1964, *A Hard Day's Night* is the first Beatles album designed to accompany a film (some consider it the best of that bunch), and the first to feature nothing but Lennon/McCartney originals, all of them about the gooeyest of songwriter subjects, love. Among its well-known singles are "Can't Buy Me Love" and "Tell Me Why," but virtually everything could be a single, including the enraged "You Can't Do That," the type of acidic breakup song Lennon later made a specialty.

And then there are the disarmingly lovely ballads—"Things We Said Today," "If I Fell," "And I Love Her." Utilizing a variety of guitar sounds (George Harrison's twelve-string figures prominently) and vocal approaches (powerful unison singing for "And I Love Her," sliding barbershop-style inner-voice harmonies on "If I Fell"), these offer hints of the more sophisticated Beatles music that was around the corner. Compact marvels of feeling, these never come off as fancy or pretentious—the melodies float along, lighter than air, blessed with pop innocence and at the same time suggesting a knowing beyond years.

GENRE: 🎸 Rock. **RELEASED:** 1964, Capitol. **KEY TRACKS:** "And I Love Her," "Things We Said Today," "If I Fell," "You Can't Do That," "I Should Have Known Better," "Tell Me Why." **CATALOG CHOICES:** *Please Please Me; Rubber Soul* (see below). **NEXT STOP:** Badfinger: *Straight Up.* **AFTER THAT:** ABBA: *Gold* (see p. 2).

Rubber Soul

The Beatles

I n the discography of any other pop band, a collection that offers "Nowhere Man," "Drive My Car," and "In My Life" would rank as a never-to-be-surpassed career peak. Not so for the Beatles: What follows *Rubber Soul* (that would be *Revolver, Sgt. Pepper's Lonely Hearts Club Band,* etc.) gives off such a zillion-watt glare it tends to render these last great bursts of Beatles earnestness somewhat slight by comparison.

That's unfortunate, because *Rubber Soul*—which is the home of "Michelle," "Norwegian Wood," and the utterly perfect three minutes known as "You Won't See Me"—is among the most historically significant of the group's long-players. It's the aftermath of the movie *Help!,* and the band slyly sidesteps Fab Four frenzy by bringing a more poignant swoon into the songs. Things don't always work out, and there's a touch of grown-up bittersweetness running through even the joyful refrain of "In My Life." It's also the beginning of the serious studio adventuring, which brings with it more nuanced arrangements, trickier narrative entanglements, and trippier vocal harmonies (the serpentine slides of "The Word" foreshadow some of this). In addition, some Beatles scholars iden-

tify "In My Life" as the last true collaboration between principal writers John Lennon and Paul McCartney; though they continued to refine each other's ideas, they didn't cowrite many songs after this.

Above all, *Rubber Soul* is straight-up craft from a group of people who are at peak power but aren't interested in reinventing the wheel, stars who've yet to feel the need to drop a protective veil. (See *The White Album,* p. 61, for that.) Its fourteen songs come drenched in an inescapable form of pop love—for the pure song as it takes flight, and the possibilities waiting. When this is playing, you can't help feel some of that.

GENRE: 🎸 Rock. **RELEASED:** 1965, Capitol. **KEY TRACKS:** "Norwegian Wood," "In My Life," "Michelle." **CATALOG CHOICES:** *Revolver* (see below); *White Album* (see p. 61); *Abbey Road* (see p. 62). **NEXT STOP:** Badfinger: *No Dice.* **AFTER THAT:** Big Star: *Third/Sister Lovers.*

The Modern (Not Mod) Beatles

Revolver

The Beatles

Revolver is the big hinge in the discography of the Beatles. Their previous album, *Rubber Soul,* offers a program of wistful love songs. The next one, *Sgt. Pepper's Lonely Hearts Club Band,* begins the band's headfirst charge into experimentation. *Revolver* connects the two. It has the plaintive earnestness of the early band, and the radical curiosity—about sound, subject matter, composition—that defined everything after.

Although the band had already been exploring, this time they're brazen and much more thorough about it: "Tomorrow Never Knows," which finds Lennon reading excerpts from the Tibetan Book of the Dead, plays like a test to see how far into terrifying dissonance pop can go. Similarly, "Taxman," the bitterest song George Harrison ever wrote, voices a cynicism then unusual in pop. "Good Day Sunshine" is its opposite—a grand attempt at the flamboyantly rococo, pure pop joy for its own sake. But wait, there's more. *Revolver* contains another foray into classical Indian music ("Love You To"), and the band's first acid-trip cartoon ("Yellow Submarine"). It's the home of a feather-pillow McCartney ode, "Here, There, and Everywhere," that schooled Burt

Bacharach and a generation of tunesmiths, and also "Eleanor Rigby," the odd still-life that is richer in character development than many three-hour movies.

Every track lives in its own sonic wonderland—here's where the Beatles expand the toolbox, with clever implementation of sitar, brass band, harpsichord, and string quartet. And yet, characteristically, none of the exotica seems ostentatious: The Beatles and producer George Martin seek what the songs demand and not a note more. This sense of honoring the material

Revolver's cover art was created by German-born bassist and artist Klaus Voormann.

is what makes *Revolver* utter perfection, at once the wildest and most cohesive listening experience the Beatles ever created.

GENRE: 🎸 Rock.
RELEASED: 1966, Capitol.
KEY TRACKS: "Love You To," "Taxman," "For No One," "Got to Get You into My Life."
CATALOG CHOICES: *Rubber Soul* (see p. 58); *Sgt. Pepper's Lonely Hearts Club Band* (see below). **NEXT STOP:** The Zombies: *Odessey and Oracle* (see p. 889). **AFTER THAT:** XTC: *Skylarking* (see p. 878).

Lend Me Your Ears . . .

Sgt. Pepper's
Lonely Hearts Club Band

The Beatles

T he tracks of magnetic tape the Beatles and producer George Martin loaded up so lavishly at Abbey Road in 1966 and '67 are quite possibly the most scrutinized pop-culture documents in history. Every last speck of

Sgt. Pepper's Lonely Hearts Club Band has been transcribed and dissected, chopped into bits and reassembled, fed into computers, and run through Bible Code–style cryptographic software. Academics have spent years poring over "A Day in the Life," drawing parallels to James Joyce, doing psychological workups of the dream-sequence segments. Heck, whole books have been written about the photo montage on the cover.

So everything, even those Ringo lead

This album was on the U.S. *Billboard* 200 chart for 175 weeks.

vocals, has been under the microscope. Now what? What's the end result of all this scholarship? Is our understanding substantially enriched?

Don't let anyone feed you any theories about this music. The ideal way to approach it, of course, would be with totally fresh ears, shed the "All Time Best" estimations and the endless accolades that have attached, like barnacles, to it and encounter it on your own terms. Play it backward if you have to. See if it can lead you into other states of consciousness. Consider whether it's grown lame and corny. Glean what truth, if any, it holds for you. Of course anyone who ever took Art Appreciation knows that's the way to encounter all creative works. But it's especially true with something like *Sgt. Pepper*, which arrives loaded with "important masterwork" baggage. Get caught up in the endless tireless analysis, and you can miss the very meaning of music, so beautifully expressed by John Lennon in that dreamy voice

from across the universe: "I'd love to turn you on . . . ."

GENRE: 🎸 Rock. RELEASED: 1967, Capitol. KEY TRACKS: "Lucy in the Sky with Diamonds," "A Day in the Life," "With a Little Help from My Friends." CATALOG CHOICES: *Abbey Road; Let It Be . . . Naked* (the 2003 reissue that strips producer Phil Spector's orchestral embellishments, leaving the original Beatles recordings). NEXT STOP: There is none.

"The Tension Album"

The Beatles (The White Album)

The Beatles

In *Here, There, and Everywhere*, his account of his years spent as the Beatles' recording engineer, Geoff Emerick contends that not until the sessions for this double album did the four members of the Beatles bring problems (or girlfriends, notably John Lennon's future wife, Yoko Ono) into the recording studio. And when they did, disaster followed. The sessions to record *The Beatles* (now better known as *The White Album*) began in the spring of 1968, after the Beatles returned from India, and Emerick describes the climate as "poisonous." He writes: "If John had made a nasty crack about the Maharishi that George resented, they would have a go at each other while gathered around a microphone to do backing vocals. . . . If George dared question any of Paul's suggestions, Paul would get in a snit."

Having shared the creative fruits of so much togetherness, it was probably inevitable that the Beatles would also show the world what happens when the flame dims, when daily interaction is defined by cold war–style flare-ups. *The White Album*, which McCartney later described as "The Tension Album," documents the painful fraying of the Fab Four, the moment when the musicians retreat into their own zones to do their own

things—with or without help from the others.

It's a wonder anything of lasting value emerged from the sessions. Certainly the double album is a different creature from anything else by the Beatles. Wildly erratic where previous albums are unified, it contains faux-rustic folk tales ("Rocky Raccoon"), noisy one-offs ("Helter Skelter"), unmitigated schmaltz ("Good Night," sung by Ringo Starr), and two of John Lennon's most plaintive ballads ("Julia," "Dear Prudence"). While there's a great degree of brazen experimentation, there's also plenty of striking quintessential Beatles music—this is the album that contains Harrison's masterpiece "While My Guitar Gently Weeps," after all.

Much has been made about the diffuse nature of *The White Album*, and even without knowing the gory details of its tumultuous birth, it's clear that something's amiss. The wheels are falling off. Profound dissolution is in progress. And these guys, God bless them, are still singing. Sometimes even together.

GENRE: 🅑 Rock. RELEASED: 1968, Apple/EMI. KEY TRACKS: "Dear Prudence," "Wild Honey Pie," "Back in the U.S.S.R.," "Blackbird," "While My Guitar Gently Weeps,"

"Julia." CATALOG CHOICES: Abbey Road (see below); George Harrison: All Things Must Pass (see p. 345). NEXT STOP: Elliott Smith: XO (see p. 716). AFTER THAT: Magnetic Fields: Sixty-nine Love Songs (see p. 465).

". . . In the End, the Love You Take Is Equal to the Love You Make"

Abbey Road

The Beatles

The sixteen-minute medley that closes *Abbey Road* is arguably the most resourceful act of scrap-scavenging in pop music history. A parade of discards and song fragments waiting to be finished, it presents the Beatles cleaning out the cupboards, and tossing anything once deemed workable—a neglected bit of Lennon psychedelia ("Sun King"), an unfinished music-hall production number by McCartney ("Carry That Weight")—into one last meal.

The group had just endured two fractious recording projects (*The White Album,* see previous page, and *Let It Be,* which was mostly recorded before *Abbey Road* but released

The Beatles have had more number one albums (19!) than any other group.

after). The breakup was a foregone conclusion, but somehow they were still "together" enough to do justice to these short, cannily sequenced vignettes. The tunes of the medley wander all over the musical map, as do the many songs on the two-disc *White Album.* But unlike that sprawling set, each theme here is a perfect miniature that lasts just long enough to convey a single crystalline thought. Some episodes unfold in seconds. "The End," the final punctuation mark, consists of a single Zen-koan couplet: "And in the end, the love you take is equal to the love you make." Could there be a better epitaph for the band that taught the world all you need is love?

Recorded in a month during the summer of 1969, *Abbey Road* offers plenty more than just the medley. Two of George Harrison's most illuminated melodies are here—the idyllic ballad "Something" and "Here Comes the Sun." Also here is the most convincing exploration of blues and progressive rock the Beatles ever attempted, "I Want You (She's So Heavy)." And then there's "Because." Another of the band's hazy acid-dream moments, its nine swooning vocal parts (three each for McCartney, Lennon, and Harrison) align into a spine-tingling, lighter-than-air sound. Like much of *Abbey Road,* it's a stupendous display of pop imagination that evaporates immediately, leaving you at once immensely satisfied and yearning for more. Sort of like the Beatles themselves.

GENRE: 🅑 Rock. RELEASED: 1969, Apple/EMI. KEY TRACKS: "Come Together," "Something," "Because," side two medley. CATALOG CHOICE: The Beatles (The White Album) (see previous page). NEXT STOP: There is none.

A Psych-Mod Blast from the Bay

Triangle

The Beau Brummels

The Beau Brummels started out as an artistically credible American response to the British Invasion, and with this album became something else—purveyors of delicately scored mystical rock that captured the crisscrossing currents of 1967.

Named after a nineteenth-century British dandy, the Bay Area group began by openly emulating aspects of mod culture—they copped the haircuts, the twee lyrics, and the vocal harmonies so successfully, some who heard the early singles "Laugh Laugh" and "Just a Little" (both produced by Sylvester Stewart, aka Sly Stone) thought the group *was* British.

"Laugh Laugh" is named one of the 500 greatest songs by the Rock and Roll Hall of Fame.

written by guitarist Ron Elliott are infused with the directness and discipline of British pop. They're tart, lively, and disarmingly beautiful compositions that showcase Sal Valentino's magnetic voice—which, on "Only Dreaming Now" (one of several dream-inspired odes), dwells in a languid, almost gloomy atmosphere. *Triangle* was not a commercial success, but it remains an unusual artistic one—the rare bridge between the sunshiny straightforwardness of mid-'60s pop and the fuzzy opaqueness of psychedelia.

That impression changed with *Triangle*, which replaces the youthful earnestness of the early Brummels singles with hazy, occasionally obtuse lyrics about Middle Earth, wild psychedelic orchestrations (from the great Van Dyke Parks, who plays harpsichord on "Magic Hollow"), and touches of the chiming guitars and daring vocal harmonies of the Byrds. The sound is rich, but at a core level, the songs

GENRE: 🅱 Rock. **RELEASED:** 1967, Warner Brothers. (Reissued 2003, Collectors Choice.) **KEY TRACKS:** "Magic Hollow," "Are You Happy?" **CATALOG CHOICES:** *Introducing the Beau Brummels; Magic Hollow.* **NEXT STOP:** The Grateful Dead: *Workingman's Dead.*

The First Great Saxophone Soloist

Sidney Bechet: Ken Burns Jazz

Sidney Bechet

The legend of Sidney Bechet goes like this: One of seven kids from a Creole family in New Orleans, he started on the clarinet, and quickly developed a reputation for a shrill, piercing sound that could be as brash as a trumpet.

Musicians had trouble working with him because he constantly wanted to be the lead voice. This only got worse when, on the first of many European tours, he stumbled on a soprano sax in a store and switched instruments on the spot. Suddenly Bechet was like a human siren—his wide vibrato careening atop whatever else was going on, the wild pitch-bends of the soprano offering him more expressive range than the clarinet ever could. (On many of his best recordings, however, Bechet plays both clarinet and soprano.)

Sidney Bechet began playing the clarinet when he was 8 years old.

The first international jazz musician, Bechet (1897–1959) was largely unknown in America. But through his early touring with vaudeville troops, he became a fixture in Europe. Many of the recordings here were made during Bechet's regular returns to the U.S.—the racing "Shag" was recorded in 1932 by a small group he co-led called the New Orleans Feetwarmers, while his "Polka Dot Stomp," from 1934, is one of several recordings masterminded by bandleader and vocalist Noble Sissle. Bechet eventually settled in France, and died there a beloved figure.

Bechet continued to grow as a musician, incorporating tunes from the Great American Songbook into his repertoire of rags and hot blues—his creepin'-around 1939 hit version of George Gershwin's "Summertime" is one highlight of this career-spanning single-disc compilation, which was issued in conjunction with the Ken Burns documentary series *Jazz*, and is the best Bechet primer available. Everyone needs some Bechet in their lives, if only to be reminded about the exuberant razzle-dazzle that was a crucial part of early jazz.

GENRE: 🎵 Jazz. **RELEASED:** 2000, Columbia/Legacy. **KEY TRACKS:** "Wild Cat Blues," "Shag," "Summertime," "Blue Horizon." **NEXT STOP:** Bix Beiderbecke: *Singin' the Blues,* Vol. 1 (see p. 71). **AFTER THAT:** Jimmie Noone: *Apex Blues.*

When There's No More Confetti to Throw . . .

Mutations

Beck

Two years after his critically drooled-over smash *Odelay,* cagey post-modernist Beck Hanson offered this set, which was produced by Radiohead Svengali Nigel Godrich. Beck and his record label insisted at the time that it wasn't the "official" follow-up, and in artistic terms, it's a galaxy away: If *Odelay* is bright primary colors and flashing dance floor lights, *Mutations* is rustic earth tones and pastel shades blurred artfully together. The most concise introduction to Beck's zany record making, it's one of the most creative pop music statements of the 1990s.

Beck's interest in croaky country tunes and strange blues offshoots was well documented before *Mutations*—he'd followed his breakthrough single "Loser" with the lo-fi *One Foot in the Grave* (1994). A few songs on *Mutations* echo the general bent of that release, notably "Cancelled Check," which is appointed with pedal-steel guitar beamed straight from some lonely jukebox on the outskirts of Nashville. More often, though, Beck fits elements of roots music into an ancient-meets-modern patchwork. The lyrics of "Nobody's Fault but My Own" borrow from Blind Willie Johnson's holy blues "Nobody's Fault but Mine" to tell a fairly conventional bluesman's tale of regret, but the melody is a study in questioning, upturned half steps, and the surrounding music contains everything from random splashes of synthesizer to spacey psychedelic guitars.

The common perception of Beck is that of a reckless mixmaster, a crazed Iron Chef chucking odd sounds and radioactive images into a busy soup. There's some of that on *Mutations*, but it's held in check—with this

Beck won the Grammy for Best Alternative Music Performance for *Mutations*.

album, Beck's lyric non sequiturs no longer dictate the whole game. Rather, they're part of tightly structured songs, with sly chord sequences and bracingly beautiful melodies that hang in the air, unresolved. These transform conventional genre studies—the samba evocation "Tropicalia," the Delta postcard "Bottle of Blues"—into highly personal creations. If you're new to Beck, start here: This diverse, deliriously inspired collection will make you curious to hear everything he's done.

GENRE: 🎸 Rock. RELEASED: 1998, DGC/Bong Load. KEY TRACKS: "Cold Brains," "Nobody's Fault but My Own," "We Live Again," "Tropicalia," "Bottle of Blues." CATALOG CHOICES: *Odelay; Sea Change.* NEXT STOP: Caetano Veloso: *Cê.* AFTER THAT: Ween: *Black Pepper.*

A Chamber Music All-Star Session

"Archduke" Trio, Kreutzer Sonata

Ludwig van Beethoven
Jacques Thibaud, Pablo Casals, Alfred Cortot

This is the chamber-music equivalent of the Three Tenors—a summit of megastars tackling key pieces in the repertoire. Just one difference: When this was recorded, between 1927 and 1929, these three were actually in their prime, and profoundly attuned to each other, having played together (initially for their own pleasure) for more than twenty years.

As a result, these versions of Beethoven's endlessly singing "Archduke" Trio, dedicated in 1811 to the composer's pupil Archduke Rudolph, is surprisingly elastic, with subtle lurches forward and passages where the three gently slow the tempo, as though guided by a single hand, to accentuate a particular phrase. This unity approaches almost paranormal levels in the second Scherzo movement of the "Archduke," when the three, in tandem, execute an extended crescendo not in one tempo, as it's written, but with several glancing millisecond pauses added for drama along the way.

For all the group cohesion, the mighty "Archduke" (more formally known as Piano

Trio in B-flat Major, Op. 97), the gem of Beethoven's middle period, also highlights the contrasting personalities: Pianist Cortot brings a languid romanticism to everything he plays, and an elegance shared by his countryman Thibaud, who plays violin. The Catalan cellist Casals, meanwhile, infuses the music with a fiery animation; it's his gorgeously emphasized long tones that give the Andante third movement its anchor.

There are other treasures on this disc—including the only known Thibaud/Cortot recording of Beethoven's Violin Sonata No. 9 (the "Kreutzer") and a transfixing run through the cello/piano *Magic*

Beethoven dedicated 11 major works and four canons to his patron Archduke Rudolph.

Flute Variations, which finds Cortot surrounding the beefy cello lines with dainty, almost transparent rejoinders from the piano.

GENRE: 🎻 Classical. **RELEASED:** 2002, Naxos. **KEY TRACKS:** All of them. **ANOTHER INTERPRETATION:** *Beethoven Piano Trios*, Vol. 2, Itzhak Perlman, Vladimir Ashkenazy, Lynn Harrell. **NEXT STOP:** Felix Mendelssohn: *Trio in D Minor*, Thibaud, Cortot, Casals. **AFTER THAT:** Robert Schumann: Cello Concerto, Pablo Casals, Prades Festival Orchestra (Eugene Ormandy, cond.).

Intimate String Quartets, Played by an Orchestra

String Quartets, Opp. 131, 135

Ludwig van Beethoven
Vienna Philharmonic Orchestra (Leonard Bernstein, cond.)

The great conductor and composer Leonard Bernstein once said that his best performances seemed to happen "while I'm away." The implication: That his well-documented ability to drive a symphony orchestra to volcanic (some detractors said "oversized") climaxes came not from any willful direction on his part, but from the cosmos. Maybe he was being modest. More likely he was talking about losing himself, disappearing into the music and making his creative decisions from a deeply intuitive place.

Bernstein must have been really gone when he led the Vienna Philharmonic through this recording of two late string quartets by Ludwig van Beethoven. The idea to transpose works written for four players to an orchestra's string section wasn't his—while a sophomore at Harvard, he attended a performance of the Boston Symphony, conductor Dimitri Mitropoulos's American debut, which included Beethoven's Opus 131 quartet played this way.

The performance made an impression on him and, years later, when he found himself in front of the august Vienna Philharmonic, he asked the group to try the piece, one of Beethoven's late masterworks, in rehearsal. Apparently there were objections—many in the classical music world oppose this type of meddling, arguing that the quartet is an intimate forum, and its themes don't resonate the same way when pumped up. According to legend, however, before the end of the first movement, a rhapsodic adagio, the ensemble was won over.

It's easy to hear why. Bernstein makes sure that the four "voices" remain distinct, and gets the group to move with the intuitive grace of a quartet that's played together for years. He honors the unusual logic of Beethoven's lines, which veer far from traditional classical form. (Opus 131 has seven movements, and Opus 135 opens with a lightweight first movement, saving the meat for the final two.) Part of the strange symmetry can be attributed to Beethoven's health. Most pieces Beethoven wrote after his hearing loss are "about" something—his Seventh Symphony, for instance, is about dance. These two string works, both written in 1826, are not about anything. They're pure music, journeys through unusual chord progressions that are kept on track by slight (and usually unsingable) melodic threads, and development sections that sometimes feel like detours.

The most vivid illustration of Bernstein's performance genius comes in the slow movements. Though he was known to pursue musi-cal extremes, the Adagio of Opus 131 and the Lento of Opus 135 find the conductor demanding balance and subtlety, and getting that plus a mountain-stream liquidity from the Vienna. The result is one of the most sublime recordings in all of music. If, indeed, it was made while Bernstein was "away," we should all find out where he went and make plans to go there immediately.

GENRE: 🎷 Classical. **RELEASED:** 1979, Deutsche Grammophon. (Reissued 1992.) **KEY TRACKS:** Opus 135: Lento (third movement), Allegro (fourth movement). Opus 131: Adagio (first movement), Andante (fourth movement). **ANOTHER INTERPRETATION:** *Late String Quartets,* Emerson String Quartet. **CATALOG CHOICE:** *Symphonies Nos. 4 and 6,* Columbia Symphony Orchestra (Bruno Walter, cond.). **NEXT STOP:** Ottorino Respighi: *Pines of Rome,* Chicago Symphony Orchestra (Fritz Reiner, cond.).

A Massive Mass

Missa Solemnis

Ludwig van Beethoven
New Philharmonia Chorus and Orchestra (Otto Klemperer, cond.)

Beethoven gave future interpreters a set of massive challenges with the *Missa solemnis.* It's been called the greatest unperformable masterpiece, and with good reason. Just in terms of manpower, the piece calls for four solo singers, a large chorus, and an orchestra. To do it justice, a conductor must operate like an air traffic controller at rush hour, guiding large forces through a crowded soundscape so that they work in tandem, and, ideally, interact with each other.

Then there's the not-small matter of what Beethoven (1770–1827) expects the human voice to do. This was written during the composer's late period, when he was cut off from the world by his deafness. Though his previous writing shows he understood the particulars of vocal range, the *Missa* and Ninth Symphony both push the limits, with one key difference: The difficult vocal passages happen only in the last movement of the symphony, and they're pretty much nonstop in this mass. As he ponders the meaning of earthly and divine existence, Beethoven sends his singers to the highest heights, and gives them demanding intervallic exercises to puzzle over along the way. He divides the words between full chorus and the soloists, and at times asks that they bat lines back and forth in torrid exchanges that can be hard singing work. His idea of a respite are the prayers of forgiveness and gratitude the four principals (here, soprano Elisabeth Söderström, contralto Marga Hoffen, tenor Waldemar Kmentt, bass Martti Talvela) usually sing alone. Each of these is spectacular.

This recording shows how powerful the *Missa solemnis* can be when the army of performers involved seek clarity above all. Conductor Otto Klemperer, a sure hand with Beethoven, thinks strategically throughout, insisting on a deliberate rhythmic foundation that comes in handy as the Gloria section gathers momentum. The orchestra barrels into a dizzying, bigger-than-big fugue that has "climax" written all over it; but where some

groups race ahead to exploit the excitement, Klemperer keeps things earthbound. The score moves through a series of increasingly dramatic false endings (a favorite Beethoven tactic), and eventually, as the end draws near, Klemperer lightens up. The extra-large group, suddenly turned loose, blows lustily through to the finale, bringing new animation to some of Beethoven's most exalted themes.

GENRE: 🎸 Classical. RELEASED: 1966, EMI. (Reissued 2001.) KEY TRACKS: Kyrie; Gloria; Credo. CATALOG CHOICE: *Mass in C, Elegaic Song,* Atlanta Symphony Orchestra and Chorus (Robert Shaw, cond.). NEXT STOP: Giuseppe Verdi: *Requiem* (see p. 832). AFTER THAT: Richard Strauss: *Four Last Songs* (see p. 750).

A Tour of the Great One's Pianistic Thinking

Piano Concertos Nos. 1–5

Ludwig van Beethoven
Rudolf Serkin, Chorus and Symphony of the Bavarian Radio (Rafael Kubelík, cond.)

Beethoven's piano concertos are in-between works—they're not quite as personal or intimate as his thirty-two piano sonatas, and at the same time not loaded with the grand gestures of his symphonies. They demand a spirit at the keyboard who's both technically assured and more than a little bit contemplative; as a pianist, Beethoven had control of both extremes, and wrote for the instrument as though everyone who'd play his music was similarly equipped.

Rudolf Serkin (1903–1991) actually was. These live recordings come from a series of 1977 performances, when the pianist was in his mid-seventies, and they hit a high gallop and sustain it for jaw-dropping stretches of pure greatness that will make you say, "We should all be this alert at his age." The Munich critic Wolfgang Schreiber, who reviewed the

performances, wrote that Serkin had "retained the ability to interpret . . . even seemingly hackneyed works as though he is experiencing and expressing them for the first time. He can still bring to Beethoven's piano concertos a sense of spontaneous freshness."

Not that these works are hackneyed at all—just uneven. The first two are display pieces intended to dazzle; the flashes of great thematic development are bonuses. Number 3, written between 1800 and 1803, is among the earliest indications of Beethoven's mastery of the dark and imposing minor-key music that would dominate his later output; its second movement is one gloriously pensive tone poem. The fourth opens with an extended meditation that some hear as an instrumental counterpart to Hamlet's "To Be or Not to Be" speech. It evolves into a series of reflections and reveries, episodes that move at various speeds, from stately processional to scampering stride and everything in between.

Then there's the Fifth, nicknamed the "Emperor" by the composer's friend Johann Baptist Cramer (Beethoven rarely appended such sobriquets). Written just before deafness ended the composer's performing career, its first movement contains some of the more exuberant piano-plus-orchestra passages Beethoven wrote—lunging runs that set the brilliant solo lines into a complex latticework of orchestration. The second movement, built around a

Rudolf Serkin was awarded the Presidential Medal of Freedom in 1964.

sleeper cell of just a few notes, has a hymn-like quality. This set also includes the Choral Fantasy, Op. 80, composed in 1808, which is considered by many to be a minor Beethoven work, even though it contains a prototype of the "Ode to Joy" theme that he developed in great detail in the Ninth Symphony.

GENRE: 🎵 Classical.
RELEASED: 2005, Orfeo.
KEY TRACKS: Concerto No. 3: second movement. Concerto No. 4: first movement. Concerto No. 5. **ANOTHER INTERPRETATION:** Walter Gieseking: *Gieseking Plays Beethoven.* Recorded in Berlin in January 1945, this version of the "Emperor" has the sound of antiaircraft fire in the distance during the first-movement cadenzas. **CATALOG CHOICE:** *Favorite Piano Sonatas,* Vladimir Ashkenazy.

Works for Piano and Orchestra, as Beethoven Intended

Piano Concertos Nos. 4 and 5

Ludwig van Beethoven
Arthur Schoonderwoerd, Ensemble Cristofori

When our modern orchestras gather to play Beethoven, are we hearing what the composer intended? According to those involved in the period-instruments movement, in many cases the answer is no— modern instruments, while more practical and easier to play in tune, are also louder and at times less subtle. The steel strings that replaced catgut strings for violin and cello are more brittle. And the ensembles are considerably larger: Beethoven wrote these works for piano and orchestra in 1807 and 1809 intending them to be played by twenty musicians (in a ballroom no less!), not an army of eighty or a hundred. What a composer intended as a fleeting coloristic dab can, in modern rendering, translate into a massive thunderclap.

This recording offers an excellent encounter with the early-music philosophy, which shares a kinship with heirloom vegetable farming and other back-to-basics movements. From the very first notes of the Fourth Concerto, the Cristofori ensemble lures listeners away from the big, the towering, and the modern, and into a place where each attack is a discreet and precious event. This changes the entire dynamic of the music making: In many performances of the Fourth, the orchestra bullies the piano, and by the end there's a kind of chilly standoff. Here, it's as though we're embroiled in a deep discussion between the two different fields of sound. If there's a psychological winner, it's not the orchestra, as is usually the case, but the keyboard, with its nimble and fantastic flourishes glancing off the big string chords.

Soloist Arthur Schoonderwoerd keeps the dialogue going through both of these majestic pieces. He plays the fortepiano—that tinkly, super-precise missing link between the harpsichord and the modern piano—with an almost exaggerated militaristic articulation, and a keen sense of when to duck behind the curtain of the ensemble. He offers a buoyant perspective on Concerto No. 5, the mighty "Emperor," savoring the long arching melodies of the Adagio second movement without making them overwrought. His performance affirms all the glory and heroism of Beethoven's great melodies, while drawing attention to the delicate balances of light, and shade, and the colors Beethoven put there—qualities that have been overwhelmed by modern orchestral interpretation.

GENRE: 🎼 Classical. RELEASED: 2005, Alpha Productions. KEY TRACKS: Concerto No. 4: first movement. Concerto No. 5: second and third movements. ANOTHER INTERPRETATION: Piano Concerto No. 5: Rudolf Serkin, New York Philharmonic (Leonard Bernstein, cond.). CATALOG CHOICE: Late Piano Sonatas, Solomon Cutner. NEXT STOP: Martha Argerich: Chopin, The Legendary 1965 Recording.

The Mother Lode of Symphonic Music

Symphonies Nos. 1–9

Ludwig van Beethoven
Tonhalle Orchestra of Zurich (David Zinman, cond.)

Here, Beethoven flies. Literally. Conductor David Zinman approaches this mighty cycle of nine symphonies by following a newly researched edition of the scores (the so-called Bärenreiter version), and adhering to the tempo markings the composer intended. This turns out to be a touch radical: Over many decades of Beethoven interpretation, a consensus has taken hold that insists on slow tempos, which can impose a heft and a solemnity that isn't always in the score. Zinman says booyah to all that, and goes the other way: Passages known for their relative stability (the opening movement of the Sixth Symphony, the Turkish march in the fourth movement of the Ninth) move more freely and reach more dizzying heights. What once could seem plodding now moves at a freer, and often more fanciful, gait.

It's not Beethoven remixed, but it's close, and whether you own a more traditional reading of the cycle or are just beginning to explore this trove of symphonic amazingness, this version merits attention. Zinman and the members of the (smallish) Tonhalle Orchestra of Zurich sound like they're rediscovering these pieces every step of the way. There's a real involvement in the rendering, a commitment to framing Beethoven so that his enormous riches reveal themselves in new ways. This renegade spirit prevails throughout the cycle, from the spry early works that showcase the orchestra's uncommon agility, through the later ones that gently but unmistakably magnify the glory of Beethoven's motifs. These performances benefit from Zinman's uniformly light approach: By the last few symphonies, which positively glow, it's hard to believe that these works were dismissed as inferior during Beethoven's life.

The pieces themselves are, of course, awesome, endlessly wondrous achievements. The first two show Beethoven's mastery of the rules governing orchestral composition, while the third, the stirring "Eroica," finds him exploding that convention; the piece is twice as long as most orchestral works of its time, and contains an outpouring of valiant, heights-scaling melodies. Number 4, written for a small-ish orchestra, is all summery lightness. The Fifth is famous for that inescapable four-note opening hook, but is equally significant for its brilliant development passages. The "Pastorale" Sixth Symphony is a series of nature scenes (the final movement, portraying a vigorous storm, is rendered torridly here), and is often cited as a precursor to impressionism. The Seventh was once described by Richard Wagner as "the apotheosis of dance itself." The Eighth is regarded as Beethoven's "difficult" symphony, and is the least performed of the cycle, and yet contains dazzling passages. The Ninth marks the first time a composer integrated a full chorus into an orchestra; its final "Ode to Joy" offers glorious, utopia-seeking sound as the path to peace and brotherhood.

Heard in chronological order, they document an artistic and emotional arc that encompasses nearly a quarter century (1800–1824) from the composer's early days as a virtuoso to his final inward years as a hearing-impaired eccentric. To recklessly oversimplify this progression: Along the way lies political jubilation (No. 3), the torment and disillusionment brought by the onset of deafness (No. 5), love of nature (No. 6), love of dance (No. 7), and love of mankind (No. 9). The recordings in this book are not ranked—competition has no place in music. Still, some works are more important than others. The Beethoven symphonies are to music what the American Revolution was to world history, a necessary seismic shift from which there was no turning back.

GENRE: 🎼 Classical. **RELEASED:** 1999, Arte Nova. **KEY MOMENTS:** Symphony No. 3: fourth movement. Symphony No. 5: first movement. Symphony No. 9. **OTHER INTERPRETATIONS:** Berlin Philharmonic (Herbert von Karajan, cond., 1963); NBC Symphony (Arturo Toscanini, cond.; circa 1950). **CATALOG CHOICE:** *Violin Concerto* (see p. 496). **NEXT STOP:** Gustav Mahler: Symphony No. 9 (see p. 470). **AFTER THAT:** Miles Davis: *Kind of Blue* (see p. 208).

The Sweet Side of Early Jazz

Singin' the Blues, Vol. 1

Bix Beiderbecke

O f all the hotshots who made important music between early jazz and the rise of swing in the 1930s, the cornetist Bix Beiderbecke (1903–1931) is among the least appreciated. That's partly because he wasn't a typical hotshot: The self-taught musician gravitated toward the downcast and the contemplative, using his pure, piercing tone to make a potent first impression. Like every jazz aspirant of the 1920s, Beiderbecke toiled in the shadow of Louis Armstrong. But the lean, pomade-wearing kid born to second-generation German parents from Davenport, Iowa, wisely didn't try to imitate Satchmo. Instead, Beiderbecke pursued a sound that emphasized finesse over raw power. He understood the stop-time tricks and other conventions of early jazz, and filled each break with disarmingly wistful phrases that could not be easily copied.

"Lots of cats tried to play like Bix; ain't none of them play like him yet." —Louis Armstrong

All of *Singin' the Blues*, Vol. 1, was recorded in 1927, the year in which Beiderbecke went from Midwestern jazz curiosity to the star soloist of the Paul Whiteman Orchestra. (According to legend, the latter position did him in: Beiderbecke, an alcoholic, died longing to return to the freedom of a small group.) During that year, Beiderbecke and his longtime foil, the saxophonist Frankie Trumbauer, played in New York and cut these sprightly small-group sides, little gems of early jazz notable for their spiffed-up arrangements and restrained, at times almost "cool," solos. Beiderbecke was exploring harmony outside of standard jazz—his famed piano composition included here, "In a Mist," reveals the influence of Claude Debussy. On some of Beiderbecke's most engaging solos, such as "Singin' the Blues" and "I'm Coming Virginia," he darts around the accompaniment, which includes Eddie Lang on single-string guitar, hinting at a modernity that was years (maybe even decades) away.

GENRE: 🎷 Jazz. **RELEASED:** 1990, Columbia/Legacy. **KEY TRACKS:** "Singin' the Blues," "I'm Coming Virginia," "In a Mist," "Humpty Dumpty." **NEXT STOP:** Louis Armstrong: *The Complete Hot Fives and Hot Sevens* (see p. 26). **AFTER THAT:** Benny Moten: *Benny Moten's Great Band of 1930*.

"Day-O" Done Dramatically

At Carnegie Hall

Harry Belafonte

A decade into his recording career, the singer Harry Belafonte had mastered what was then common practice for live performers: Rather than merely sing hits, artists would cluster songs into thematic groups, creating miniature music-theater tableaux. Belafonte's shows opened with a set entitled "Moods of the American Negro" and contained a segment called "In the Caribbean" that featured his hits "The Banana Boat Song (Day-O)" and "Jamaica Farewell," and another spotlighting folk songs from "'Round the World."

The evening was tightly scripted and cleverly connected, and yet on this landmark live set drawn from two benefit concerts in April 1959, the dapper Belafonte manages to make it sound impromptu. He's electric even when he whispers, and when he puts his full lung power behind a song like the a cappella opener "Darlin' Cora," he's downright devastating. He obviously enjoys hearing the way this famous hall cradles his instrument. (Indeed, this is a gem of a recording, with more warmth and dimension than was common at the time; details like the crack of Danny Barrajanos's conga drum are gloriously free of distortion, and the forty-seven-piece orchestra is there when needed, but never intrusive.)

Belafonte was riding a string of hits, notably the island idyll "The Banana Boat Song (Day-O)," at the time of this appearance; that song and another bit of island wisdom, "Man Smart (Woman Smarter)," helped keep this album on the charts for three full years. As both a singer and actor, he'd developed a reputation as a maverick (a few albums later his *The Midnight*

Special would be the first recording of a young harmonica player named Bob Dylan), primarily for confronting racial issues often glossed over at the time. Whether this singer's singer is delivering African American spirituals, the keening Irish ballad "Danny Boy," or his singalong debut hit "Matilda," it is his ability to communicate the soul of a people that gives Belafonte's interpretations such stirring power. Still.

GENRE: 🎵 Vocals. **RELEASED:** 1959, RCA. **KEY TRACKS:** "Darlin' Cora," "Matilda," "Man Smart (Woman Smarter)," "The Banana Boat Song (Day-O)." **CATALOG CHOICES:** *Calypso; Belafonte Returns to Carnegie Hall.* **NEXT STOP:** Jill Scott: *Beautifully Human/Words and Sounds,* Vol. 2.

Harry Belafonte is considered the "King of Calypso."

An Opera of Folk Songs

The Transports

Peter Bellamy

This 1977 "opera" aligns with the topical and historical songwriting that became fashionable during the folk revival of the early 1960s. At that time, Scottish poet Ewan MacColl and others developed extended story-songs that often held a novel's worth of detail—one, MacColl's 1965 *The Ballad of John Axon,* told about a railroad man who dies trying to stop his runaway train. British singer and songwriter Peter Bellamy (1944–1991) was deeply influenced by this style; his discography includes five albums devoted to the poetry of Rudyard Kipling as well as *The Transports,* one of the hidden beauties of traditional folk.

The Transports uses period instruments and British ballad forms to tell the sad but true tale of Henry Cabell and Susannah Holmes. Convicted under British law of larceny, they were part of the "First Fleet" of criminals transported by boat to Australia in the eighteenth century. Bellamy starts by setting the scene in England, with songs that describe the socioeconomic forces that vex lower-class citizens ("Us Poor Fellows"). In the manner of opera, the songs are all sung "in character," with each of the principals played by a well-known folk singer (June Tabor, A. L. Lloyd, Martin Carthy,

Mike and Norma Waterson, among others). Bellamy often wrote new lyrics for traditional songs, transforming sea chanteys into sprawling songs about the hardship of the voyage and human misery in general. These are sung with a hearty pub-going zest, by people who obviously enjoy playing a role (the work has been presented theatrically several different times in London). The participants also seem to enjoy Bellamy's wry lyrics, which are studded with fascinating historical perspective and a strong empathy for those being transported. Though it's purely pleasurable from start to finish, *The*

Transports is so loaded with detail it's hard to avoid learning something as it unfolds.

GENRE: 🎵 Folk. **RELEASED:** 1977, Topic. (Reissued 1997, Free Reed.) **KEY TRACKS:** "Us Poor Fellows," "The Black and Bitter Night," "The Robber's Song," "The Green Fields of England." **BUYER BEWARE:** The "Silver Edition" box offers the original recording plus a 1997 "re-creation" by contemporary artists, which is not nearly as engrossing. **NEXT STOP:** Ewan MacColl: *The Ballad of John Axon.* **AFTER THAT:** Oysterband: *Holy Bandits.*

Pop Splendor with a Pinch of Bittersweet

If You're Feeling Sinister

Belle and Sebastian

Stuart Murdoch, the fragile-sounding lead voice of Belle and Sebastian, began writing songs during a seven-year bout with chronic fatigue syndrome. The long recuperation gave the former DJ and record-store clerk time to work out exactly how his music should sound, and when he recovered his health, he began to assemble a band that could realize his particular vision. "I wanted the trumpet to be as important as the guitar," Murdoch told National Public Radio in 2006. "And the cello as important as the drums."

On this, the second Belle and Sebastian album, the expanded instrumental palette reflects the splendor of '60s pop cut with Murdoch's sometimes acidic view of the world. "Seeing Other People" is typical: After several verses and a devastatingly clever refrain, the trumpet charges in, on loan from the Burt Bacharach archives, to sketch a beautiful theme. Elsewhere the cello (played by Isobel Campbell, who sings some leads and backing vocals in a willowy half-whisper) or harmonica provide the uplifting counterpoint, offsetting the distressed tone of the lyrics with lively music seemingly designed to help the downhearted keep the faith.

Belle and Sebastian was a seven-piece for this album (personnel has changed with each project); its instrumental passages last just long enough for the lyrics, which tell of nasty breakups, unrealized aspirations, and other disillusionments, to sink in. Among those lyrics is this Murdoch gem: "All I wanted was to sing the saddest songs, if somebody sings along I'll be happy now." His songs, wry and mordant, suggest that true happiness is a much more complicated proposition.

GENRE: 🎸 Rock. **RELEASED:** 1997, Matador. **KEY TRACKS:** "Seeing Other People," "Me and the Major," "The Boy Done Wrong Again." **CATALOG CHOICES:** *Dear Catastrophe Waitress; The Life Pursuit.* **NEXT STOP:** The Smiths: *Hatful of Hollow.* **AFTER THAT:** Olivia Tremor Control: *Dusk at Cubist Castle.*

A Diva at Peak

Norma

Vincenzo Bellini

Maria Callas, Ebe Stignani, Chorus and Orchestra of La Scala (Tullio Serafin, cond.)

Those who don't know *Norma* may be surprised to recognize the hymn-like "Casta diva," Norma's first entrance in Act 1. It's the music Susan Sarandon is listening to while bathing her arms and breasts in lemon juice in an early scene of the film *Atlantic City.* The piece, one of the most famous tunes in all of opera, is Norma's rhapsodic description of the moon, a pagan hymn of worship. Sung here by the much-worshiped opera goddess Maria Callas, it's suffused with a particular kind of awe that sets up the story to follow, a retelling of the Medea legend casting Norma as a Druid princess in love with a Roman general. The plot, in a nutshell: Love sours, Norma threatens to kill the general's two children, tense confrontations ensue.

Maria Callas is often hailed as La Divina.

The achingly beautiful "Casta diva," an aria in two parts, signals what composer Vincenzo Bellini (1801–1835) has in store for his heroine: long, lavish melody lines that tremble and blossom into showcases, yet are not unduly ostentatious. The role covers tremendous dramatic territory—it's considered the Mount Everest of Italian "bel canto" opera, the style that emphasizes the beauty of the vocal line over dramatic expression. And Callas, under the direction of the conductor who was her Svengali, Tullio Serafin, takes great advantage of it, intoning her lines the way she imagines the troubled Norma would. In the liner notes, Callas explains that "Norma resembles me in a certain way. She seems very strong, very ferocious at times. Actually, she is not, even though she roars like a lion." This performance has the roar, but is more notable for Callas's depth, her ability to convey details of the character in highly personal ways.

This recording is the first of two versions featuring Callas, the jet-setting beauty who was married to Aristotle Onassis (before being dumped for Jacqueline Kennedy). It's also the best. It contains all the qualities that made Callas one of the most revered figures of twentieth-century music—her gilded and complex voice, in peak form here; her disciplined phrasing and pinpoint control of trills and grace notes; her nervous energy, which is particularly well suited to Norma's unhinged moments. Spend some time with "Casta diva" and "Ah! bello a me ritorna" to experience the kind of effortless singing that can stop you in your tracks.

GENRE: 🎵 Opera. **RELEASED:** 1954, EMI. **KEY TRACKS:** "Casta diva," "Ah! bello a me ritorna," "Si, fino all'ore estreme." **CATALOG CHOICE:** *I Puritani*, Maria Callas, Chorus and Orchestra of La Scala (Tullio Serafin, cond.). **NEXT STOP:** Gaetano Donizetti: *Lucia de Lammermoor,* Maria Callas, Chorus and Orchestra of La Scala (Tullio Serafin, cond.).

Massive African Mambo

The Syliphone Years

Bembeya Jazz National

S everal years after Guinea won its independence from France in 1958, the new government began a program intended to promote cultural heritage. In music, that meant that the established dance bands and orchestras that specialized in rhythms not native to Guinea were disbanded, and new ensembles were encouraged to make music based on indigenous traditions. Government officials had a hand in assembling the new groups, and when they reached the town of Beyla, near the border with Liberia, they put together a horn ensemble first called Orchestre de Beyla and later renamed for the nearby Bembeya River.

Like most musicians, the assembled players shared a curiosity about music from all over the world. But they were canny enough to recognize that survival depended on what the government considered "authenticity"; so the tracks on the group's first album, from 1961, included a calypso, a mambo cha-cha, and four folkloric pulses identified as "rhythme Africaine."

But as the group evolved, it strayed from that initial directive. Its specialty became the polyrhythmic music of Cuba, which, of course, descended from the polyrhythmic music of West Africa. To this intercontinental cauldron Bembeya added multiple electric guitars playing spiderwebbed African-style riffs, and spirited call-and-answer exchanges between singer Demba Camara and the active horn section. It's possible to identify the various regional traits, but after a while it all blends into a sound of pure joy that spreads generously in all directions. Resistance to this buoyant pulse is futile—before you're even aware of it, you may find yourself dancing.

GENRE: 🌐 World/Guinea. **RELEASED:** 2004, Sterns Africa. **KEY TRACKS:** "Camara mousso," "Montuno de la sierra," "Beyla," "Sabor de guajira." **CATALOG CHOICE:** *Bembeya Jazz.* **NEXT STOP:** Orchestra Baobab: *Specialist in All Styles.*

Music from Utopia's Dance Floor

Africa/Brazil

Jorge Ben

F urther proof that the ideology of funk spread well beyond America's "chocolate cities," *Africa/Brazil* represents a rare trifecta: It links the propulsion of African music to fluid Brazilian samba to the party-time outlandishness of mid-'70s Parliament-style funk. And because the tunes are by Jorge Ben, there's pure idealistic sweetness running throughout. Ben is one of Brazil's underappreciated treasures, a prolific composer who came along after the upheavels of *tropicálismo,* offering gentle and serene melodies that were recorded, with great success, by many of the country's big singing stars.

Africa/Brazil was inspired, at least in part, by touring: When Ben visited Africa in 1975, he met Afrobeat legend Fela Kuti (see p. 436) and jammed with African rhythm masters. Upon returning home, Ben assembled an amazing (and amazingly large) ensemble that included African percussion and a chorus of voices, and built his songs around easygoing open-ended jams or, in the case of the slithering "Ponta de lanca africano," parade beats. The result was a rare melding of polyrhythms and heritage music that was downright radical. Describing it in words reduces what was a profound vision to a chemistry experiment. As music, it instantly makes sense, a union of the ancient and the urbane that could only happen on utopia's dance floor.

Jorge Ben's career took off when a record producer heard him at a nightclub.

GENRE: 🌐 World/Brazil. **RELEASED:** 1976, Universal. **KEY TRACKS:** "Ponta de lanca africano," "Xica da silva." **CATALOG CHOICE:** *A tabua de esmeralda.* **NEXT STOP:** Banda Black Rio: *Maria Fumaca.* **AFTER THAT:** Tom Zé: *Fabrication Defect* (see p. 887).

Soul-Stirring, Enchanting Chant

Salve Regina: Gregorian Chant

Benedictine Monks of the Abbey of St. Maurice and St. Maur, Clervaux

The incantations known as plainchant have punctuated the Roman Catholic service for centuries, but it's safe to say that not until the blockbuster *Chant* appeared, in 1994, did most modern ears get hip to the sound.

A live document of the Benedictine Monks of Santo Domingo de Silos praying, *Chant* was hyped as a rare peek into the monastic life, which makes it either really cool or slightly voyeuristic. Serene cover art (monks in the clouds!) and electronica remixes (!) helped *Chant* to become the most unexpected smash hit of 1994.

It's not, however, the most striking available rendition of Gregorian chant. That distinction belongs to *Salve Regina,* which was also recorded live (at the Clervaux monastery in France in 1957). It features the monks of the Abbey of St. Maurice and St. Maur praying in tones so strong, the vast and austere beauty of Gregorian chant becomes inescapable.

Many of these pieces begin with the anchoring drone of an organ sustaining a single tone. Then come the voices, methodically working through the unmoored and affectless melodies, which rarely resolve on a regular schedule. The drone magnifies the detached, hollow-vessel character of the singing: As they pare back the outside world and focus on the chants as pathways to illumination, the monks sound like they're deeply immersed in prayer, and cannot be disturbed. There's no ambition in the voices, and certainly no ornamentation.

But there is seeking going on here—if nothing else, the monks chant knowing that their tones can never fully resolve, at least not in a way satisfying to Western ears. This does not stop them. They press on, following the labyrinthine lines until they find something that sounds suspiciously like peace.

GENRE: 🎼 Classical. **RELEASED:** 1958, Philips. **KEY TRACKS:** "Te Deum," "Adoro te," "Salve Regina," "Regina Caeli," "O Salutaris Hostia." **NEXT STOP:** John Adams: *Harmonium* (see p. 6). **AFTER THAT:** The Hilliard Ensemble: *Pérotin*.

Jazz Vocals Unplugged, Without a Net

The Tony Bennett–Bill Evans Album

Tony Bennett and Bill Evans

Even the most accomplished saloon singer can sound corny in the recording studio, where no glasses clink, no lovers swoon, and it's up to the voice to manufacture the magic that flows like whiskey in a nightclub.

Among those with an appreciation for the studio's special demands is Tony Bennett. Forever associated with the enduring city song "I Left My Heart in San Francisco," the buoyant, big-voiced belter got past contrivance better than just about anyone. On a series of surprisingly consistent recordings for Columbia in the 1960s, Bennett melted the artifice of the studio by finding the drama within little

After this album, the duo recorded *Together Again* in 1976.

gestures. His best recordings overflow not just with musical sophistication, but an enthusiasm for life, and a real understanding of all sorts of heartache. Bennett hugs the microphone in an up-close embrace, and his proximity draws listeners right next to him. He treats the singer's platform less like a confessional than a nice spot at the bar where you go to tell stories and nurse wounds.

This recording, the first of two meetings between Bennett and jazz pianist Bill Evans,

offers the most intimate glimpse of that skill in action. It's just piano and voice, and from the opening stanza of "Young and Foolish," Bennett signals that he's not interested in the responsible American Songbook interpretation. Instead he sounds like he's wallowing in regret, an adult looking back with sadness at long-gone moments of foolishness. Evans is right there with him; as happens throughout, he elaborates on the emotional territory Bennett has described, carrying the singer's particular shade of blue into a realm of parallel heartbreak. The tempoless ballads are sometimes heroic and always sublime—this may be the all-time best reading of "But Beautiful." More unexpected are swingers like "When in Rome," which finds Bennett telling of rascally joys with a devil-may-care irreverence. The song's a little corny, no denying that. And the jiving and jousting these two do is anything but.

GENRE: 🎵 Vocals. **RELEASED**: 1975, Fantasy. **KEY TRACKS**: "Young and Foolish," "Some Other Time," "But Beautiful," "My Foolish Heart." **CATALOG CHOICES**: Tony Bennett:

The Ultimate Tony Bennett; Basie/Bennett. Bill Evans: *Alone*. **NEXT STOP**: Frank Sinatra: *September of My Years*. **AFTER THAT**: Sammy Davis Jr.: *Sammy Davis Jr. Sings and Laurindo Almeida Plays*.

Atonality Can Tell a Story

Wozzeck

Alban Berg
Hamburg State Philharmonic (Ingo Metzmacher, cond.)

Soldier Wozzeck has it rough. He's harassed by his military superior, poked and prodded in the name of medicine by a quack, and cuckolded by his common-law wife. None of these self-absorbed characters notices when he begins to slowly fall apart. For all the overt brutality he endures, it's this blithe indifference that ultimately sends him into madness.

Or maybe it's the music playing around him. A student of Arnold Schoenberg, whose dissonant twelve-tone approach to composition ignited firestorms of controversy in classical music, Alban Berg (1885–1935) packs this opera

Alban Berg composed *Wozzeck* between 1914 and 1922.

with every ear-stretching device at his disposal. His prickly porcupine score relies on the atonality's jarring quality—its sudden changes of direction, its flashes of rage—to trace the progress of a fast-advancing inner delirium.

In adapting Georg Büchner's unfinished play (and lifting its text directly in many cases), Berg doesn't just do torment for torment's sake. He conjures different colors for each character and plot twist, and his intricately shaded confrontations bring listeners close to an emotional rawness. The exchanges exhibit a humanity missing from his teacher's compositions. Indeed, with this work and his similar orchestral efforts, Berg proved to the music world's many skeptics that Schoenberg's tactics can be more than number-crunching hoodoo.

Premiered in 1925 at the Berlin State Opera, *Wozzeck* instantly provoked outrage; only later was it embraced as one of the towering achievements of twentieth-century music. It is innovative not just for the drama embedded in its sounds, but also for its structure—a series of short, disconnected scenes that don't always track in linear sequence. This 1999 live performance, guided by Ingo Metzmacher, catches all the harrowing turbulence of the score, without adding any extra angst. Wozzeck doesn't need *that*.

GENRE: 🎵 Opera. **RELEASED**: 1999, EMI. **KEY TRACKS**: Act 1, Scene 4: "Doctor"; Act 3, Scene 3: "Wozzeck and Marie." **ANOTHER INTERPRETATION**: New York Philharmonic (Dimitri Mitropoulos, cond.). **CATALOG CHOICE**: *Chamber Concerto*, BBC Symphony Orchestra (Pierre Boulez, cond.). **NEXT STOP**: John Adams: *Nixon in China*, Orchestra of St. Luke's (Edo de Waart, cond.).

Two Key Works of the Twentieth-Century Violin Repertoire

Alban Berg: Violin Concerto
Igor Stravinsky: Violin Concerto

Alban Berg, Igor Stravinsky
Mark Kaplan, Budapest Festival Orchestra (Lawrence Foster, cond.)

A lban Berg learned about the capabilities of the violin by listening to Louis Krasner, the musician who commissioned this piece for $1,500, practice. In the summer of 1935, Krasner visited the composer. While working or talking with his wife, Berg would listen as his guest improvised several rooms away. According to a biography, whenever the violinist would begin to work on a passage from the repertoire, Berg would loudly tell him to stop—insisting, "No concertos, just play!"

Berg, the most accessible of the Second Viennese school of composers, was evidently seeking the instrument's tones and colorations, how it "speaks" in different registers and settings. Berg's preparation resulted in one of the towering achievements of concerto form, a burst of inspiration that, unlike most of his compositions, was written quickly. (He died, after complications from a bee sting, before the piece was premiered.)

The two-movement work begins with tones that suggest a violin being casually tuned up, and then travels through a series of "visions" that each lean on different aspects of the violin's character. These include frenetic passages that transpire on rickety haunted-house stairs, lamentations filled with quietly weeping long tones, and odd atonal echoes of a Viennese waltz.

On this recording, violinist Mark Kaplan plays up the swelling emotion of Berg's melodies. At times the violin seems to streak across the sound spectrum, a ribbon of silver dancing over the challenging chords and fractured themes Berg has placed in its path. The piece is knotty, and at times off-putting; Kaplan makes it sing. And wail.

The Stravinsky Violin Concerto is more straightforward, and requires a completely different aesthetic approach from Kaplan. Where Berg changes moods in jarring ways, Stravinsky sets up his soloist (and his listener) for whatever tumult lies ahead. The great ballet composer uses chord clusters and small inventions to steadily increase the tension, and by the time the score arrives at a crashing downbeat or other climactic moment, the violinist has laid the groundwork. Kaplan navigates the piece with little evident effort—managing the contours of what many consider a "lesser" Stravinsky work, and by doing so, making it seem plenty great.

GENRE: 🎼 Classical. **RELEASED:** 2002, Koch International Classics. **KEY TRACKS:** Berg: first movement. Stravinsky: third movement. **ANOTHER INTERPRETATION:** Berg: Daniel Hope, BBC Symphony Orchestra (Paul Watkins, cond.). Stravinsky: Hilary Hahn, Academy of St. Martin in the Fields (Sir Neville Marriner, cond.). **CATALOG CHOICE:** Berg: *Wozzeck* (see previous page). Stravinsky: *The Rite of Spring* (see p. 750). **NEXT STOP:** Witold Lutosławski: *Concerto for Piano and Orchestra,* Krystian Zimerman, BBC Symphony Orchestra (Lutosławski, cond.). **AFTER THAT:** Einojuhani Rautavaara: *On the Last Frontier,* Helsinki Philharmonic Orchestra (Leif Segerstam, cond.).

Sinfonia for Eight Voices and Orchestra

Luciano Berio

London Voices, Göteborgs Symfoniker (Peter Eötvös, cond.)

This piece can seem an inventory of worries on the minds of ordinary Americans in 1968, the year it premiered. In the first movement, there's a tumultuous explosion that has been described as the musical equivalent of the atomic bomb—which was, at the time, the elephant in the cold war living room. Then comes a prayer of sorts spelling out the name "Martin Luther King," the civil rights leader who'd recently been murdered. The third movement features voices babbling in several languages and extravagant collisions of themes, several echoing Wagner, a cacophony that has been interpreted as a comment on rapid population growth. In the fourth, Luciano Berio (1925–2003) attempts to draw order out of the preceding Tower of Babel soundscape. In the fifth section, which wasn't finished when the New York Philharmonic premiered it, the Italian composer uses huge, zooming lunges as his finale; some heard these as an admiring, if veiled, response to the U.S. space program.

The Sinfonia can be appreciated both for its topicality and as an extension of the experimental spirit running through the culture at the time. That spirit didn't penetrate the fortresslike confines of the concert hall very often: The thriving avant-garde was alienated from traditional presenters, and its composers rejected history-steeped sounds as ferociously as orchestra audiences rejected new works. The Sinfonia is one of the few firebrand pieces of the era to be embraced by the classical establishment.

It deserves to be heard now for the way Berio integrates the voices into the overall fabric—sometimes the chattering crowd is the main element demanding attention, and sometimes the scattered voices haunt the periphery. The London Voices heard in this recording approach Berio with gusto—when they recite the scraps of text in the third movement, they do so with a great sense of purpose. It can be tricky to discern exactly what's under discussion, and at times that feels deliberate: Like other twentieth-century composers, Berio doesn't necessarily want to make things too easy on his listeners.

Berio fought with anti-Nazi groups during World War II.

GENRE: 🎧 Classical. **RELEASED:** 2005, Deutsche Grammophon. **KEY TRACKS:** "O King" (second movement); fifth movement. **ANOTHER INTERPRETATION:** New York Philharmonic (Leonard Bernstein, cond.). **NEXT STOP:** Béla Bartók: *Concerto for Orchestra* (see p. 47). **AFTER THAT:** Steve Reich: *Different Train*, Kronos Quartet.

One Composer's Pursuit of the Romantic Ideal

Symphonie fantastique

Hector Berlioz

Orchestre Révolutionnaire et Romantique (Sir John Eliot Gardiner, cond.)

Hector Berlioz was inspired to write this unusual symphonic tone poem in 1827, when an English Shakespeare troupe visited Paris. Smitten with its leading lady, Harriet Smithson, Berlioz sought her affection. He had little success at first, but his efforts led him to the work's guiding theme—a man pursuing his romantic ideal to the gates of Hell. Eventually he got the girl and they married, at which point he discovered that the onstage illusion was better than the reality. By then his piece was in circulation, hailed for its unusual orchestrations and vividly realized theme. It became his signature work.

Symphonie fantastique details the journey of a lovesick artist who, having glimpsed the feminine ideal, is involved in an all-consuming chase. Berlioz seized that "idée fixe" and exploited all its possibilities, using his command of color and shading—and unorthodox chordal resolutions (after examining the score, Rossini was heard to say "Thank God it's not music!")—to tell his story. Berlioz expanded the idea set forth in Beethoven's "Pastorale" Symphony No. 6, that an orchestra could echo and emulate natural phenomena. In Berlioz's conception the male lead smokes copious amounts of opium, and finds himself beset by visions.

Berlioz intended the five-movement piece to be a work of drama, an opera without words. He furnished his audience with a "programme" that summarizes the overall intent and the motivations of its characters within the

Hector Berlioz was a pioneer of musical Romanticism.

individual scenes—this text, reprinted in the liner notes, serves as a helpful guide to the temperaments each section explores. The opening movement is entitled "Daydreams-Passions," and here Berlioz lays out the basic motifs that will recur, in altered form, in the subsequent movements. The revisitations are fantastical all right—the second movement is an endlessly whirling waltz, while the fourth, the "March to the Scaffold," is drenched in a lugubrious, murderous dread. The fifth section includes a burlesque parody of the "Dies Irae" theme used in Catholic funeral services.

To replicate the sound opening-night patrons would have heard, this recording utilizes the composer's original orchestrations, as well as the seating plan used at the piece's Paris Conservatory premiere. The string section's instruments have gut strings, which provide a less aggressive attack, and they forgo the constant vibrato that became fashionable later. This gives the strings a warm and enveloping sound; it also clears space for other colors, including a contraption known as the ophicleide that has the bell of a bugle and the double reed of a bassoon. Not all the instruments are that exotic, but many of the sonorities Berlioz assigns them are, as advertised, fantastic.

GENRE: ♪ Classical. RELEASED: 1993, Philips. KEY TRACKS: "Daydreams-Passions" (first movement); "In the Meadows" (third movement); "March to the Scaffold" (fourth movement). ANOTHER INTERPRETATION: Boston Symphony Orchestra (Charles Munch, cond.). NEXT STOP: Modest Mussorgsky: *A Night on Bald Mountain,* Chicago Symphony Orchestra (Fritz Reiner, cond.). AFTER THAT: Ottorino Respighi: *Pines of Rome,* Chicago Symphony Orchestra (Fritz Reiner, cond.).

Trojan Horse and All

Les Troyens

Hector Berlioz

Monteverdi Choir and Chorus of the Théâtre du Chatelet; Orchestre Révolutionnaire et Romantique (Sir John Eliot Gardiner, cond.)

This operatic retelling of Virgil's *Aeneid* begins just before the fall of Troy, with Cassandra (sung here by Anna Caterina Antonacci) sharing visions of impending disaster that no one seems to heed. The fall itself takes up Part One of this two-part, five-act work, and its broad story outline turns out to be perfect for opera: There's lots of violence and retribution set to the chaotic swirls that were a specialty of Hector Berlioz's instrumental music, notably his best-known *Symphonie fantastique* (see previous page). The singing is fierce and impassioned. And in the end, nearly everybody dies.

Part Two has the love story. Aeneas arrives in Carthage to protect Queen Dido's peaceful kingdom. She falls in love, but he's summoned to Italy (the gods have decreed he must resettle his band of surviving Trojans there). Dido, devastated, falls apart. Her kingdom crumbles.

A literary obsessive, Berlioz (1803–1869) wrote the libretto for *Les Troyens* himself. He began work on it at age fifty-three, without a commission, and finished the massive piece two years later. He didn't expect it to be produced—opera companies regarded its staging as challenging, its long numbers devoted to mundane matters (one celebrates a bountiful crop) as indulgent, and the melodies for the central tenor role of Aeneas to be daunting in the upper register. The piece was largely neglected until after World War II, when several full productions, including a British one helmed by conductor Sir Thomas Beecham, prompted a rethinking.

Les Troyens sits in chronological proximity to Wagner's epic works, and is often dismissed as inferior to them. That's unfair: Though the piece has large tidal-wave washes of sound that resemble Wagner, Berlioz's construction is very different. He builds his crescendos from small events, not massive Wagnerian planks—if you listen closely to this crisp rendering of the piece, what emerges is less blunt bigness than a mosaic of sound, enriched by countless details.

This production, captured live as part of a celebration marking the two hundredth anniversary of Berlioz's birth and available on DVD, is another period recording—the small string contingent uses gut strings, and the wind sections include strange instruments no longer common in orchestras. Conductor Sir John Eliot Gardiner avoided loud Wagnerian voices for the main roles, casting a singer who specializes in French art song, Susan Graham, as Dido (Didon in French). Because the instrumental forces are small, the vocalists don't have to scream but can play their roles with great freedom. This turns out to be pure genius, as it brings Berlioz's sensational towers of sound to a human, and very accessible, scale.

GENRE: 🌐 Opera. **RELEASED:** 2004,

BBC/Opus Arte. **KEY TRACKS:** Act 1: "Récit du"; Act 2: "Complices de sa gloire." **CATALOG CHOICE:** *Symphonie fantastique* (see p. 82). **NEXT STOP:** Richard Wagner: *Lohengrin,* Plácido Domingo, Jessye Norman, Vienna Philharmonic (Georg Solti, cond.).

To Live and Die on the Mean Streets

West Side Story

Leonard Bernstein and Stephen Sondheim
Original Broadway Cast

In all of Western music, the most extreme interval is the tritone. Spanning six half-steps, it instantly engenders a feeling of tension—it's unsettled, transitory, restless. Music students sometimes have trouble hearing it, or at least they did until this smart retelling of Shakespeare's *Romeo and Juliet* opened in 1957. The melody of "Maria," one of its most enduring songs, begins with a striving tritone that resolves upward. The phrase so neatly captures the power of this interval, it's been used in theory classes to help students remember its unique sonority.

After assimilating those first few notes of the "Maria" theme, don't be surprised if you start hearing tritone inventions throughout this magnificent score. Composer Leonard Bernstein (1918–1990) splashes the interval across the incidental music, gives it to the brass as an upturned unanswered question, buries it inside the orchestrations for other tunes. A simple melodic kernel, it's perfect for the rapid transitions of this boisterous tale of a turf battle among youth gangs in 1950s New York City.

In retelling Shakespeare, lyricist Stephen

Tony (Larry Kert) serenading Maria (Carol Lawrence) on her balcony.

Sondheim doesn't get bogged down in the details of the conflict. The white and Puerto Rican gangs do what gangs do: They fight over a piece of street. (Ironically, the location is the neighborhood that was torn down to make room for Lincoln Center.) Sondheim concentrates on the emotional undercurrents, and his tunes coalesce into a deeply moving portrait of kids who find romance and rivalry intertwined.

Tony (a reluctant member of the "American" gang known as the "Jets") and Maria (whose brother is the leader of the Puerto Rican gang the Sharks) meet at a dance, and are thoroughly smitten with each other. For obvious reasons they have to be secretive about the affair, and in one deviation from the Shakespeare plot, Maria doesn't die at the end but threatens to kill herself in front of everybody, so aggrieved is she over the gang warfare death of Tony. (Bernstein cited that scene, which is spoken and not sung, to refute the common notion that *West Side Story* is an opera.)

This original cast album, which features sparkly performances from Larry Kert (Tony) and Carol Lawrence (Maria), deserves some credit for making *West Side Story* into a cultural icon. The musical wasn't a massive hit right away—it closed after a respectable 732 performances, and then immediately hit the road. After that, the album took off, creating demand for a return Broadway engagement and, eventually, the 1961 film. The version that is currently available features the original Broadway cast, crisp remastering, and a selection of bonus tracks. They're interesting, but hardly necessary after the likes of "Tonight, Tonight," "Maria," and "Something's Coming," some of the most expansive, powerful tunes ever heard on Broadway.

GENRE: 😊 Musicals. **RELEASED:** 1957, Columbia. (Reissued 1998.) **KEY TRACKS:** "Maria," "Tonight, Tonight," "Something's Coming," "Gee Officer Krupke." **ANOTHER INTERPRETATION:** Operatic version with Kiri Te Kanawa, José Carreras. **CATALOG CHOICE:** Bernstein: *Candide,* London Symphony Orchestra (Bernstein, cond.). Sondheim: *Company,* Original Broadway Cast. **NEXT STOP:** Alan Jay Lerner and Frederick Loewe: *Camelot,* Original Broadway Cast. **AFTER THAT:** Jonathan Larsen: *Rent,* Original Broadway Cast.

Duckwalking into History

The Anthology

Chuck Berry

❝**D**on't give me any sophisticated crap," John Lennon once told an interviewer. "Give me Chuck Berry." Rock's first great guitarist and the originator of so many of its archetypal anthems, Berry appeared as a change agent, blasting away at postwar cultural stagnation with a heedless, joyriding roar. He was the first rock figure to skewer the elite (see "Roll Over Beethoven"), and the best at backing up his taunting words with diabolical guitar. Everything he did, and certainly everything contained on this set, was a jolt of illicit pleasure, or generational rebellion, or both. Berry's cocktail of jump blues, hillbilly giddyap, and pure hormonal energy was so potent that everyone who followed (including Elvis Presley,

"If you tried to give rock and roll another name, you might call it 'Chuck Berry.'" —John Lennon

who was a year away from Sun Studios when Berry's first single, "Maybelline," hit) had to have at least a sip. Lennon considered Berry his teacher; Brian Wilson of the Beach Boys once described his group as "Chuck Berry guitar with Four Freshmen harmonizing."

For all of his abandon, Berry *was* sophisticated—in his deliriously inventive lyrics and sly musicianship. He understood the nuances of blues (his early B sides were downcast, last-set club blues in the style of Charles Brown) and the shuffling propulsion of swing. Many of his signature riffs, including "Johnny B. Goode," are essentially big-band horn catcalls translated for the electric guitar. His solos are feats of firewalking wonder, made more impressive when you consider that in concert, he was often doing an elaborate dance step (the duckwalk, the buggy ride) while performing. Unlike virtually all who copied him, Berry cranked out solo breaks that weren't just a smidgen hotter than the vocals, but exponentially more intense. The notion of rock as catharsis starts (and some would say ends) right here.

There have been many Berry anthologies, none of them perfect. The single-disc *The Great 28* is the most succinct barrage of hits, but it skips key B sides and at least one gem, "You Never Can Tell." This two-disc set, issued in 2000, is more comprehensive and features the sharpest sound of any Berry reissues.

GENRE: 🎸 Rock. **RELEASED:** 2000, Chess/MCA. **KEY TRACKS:** "Roll Over Beethoven," "Reelin' & Rockin'," "Little Queenie." **CATALOG CHOICE:** DVD: *London Rock and Roll Show* (1972). **NEXT STOP:** Bo Diddley: *Bo Diddley* (see p. 223). **AFTER THAT:** John Lennon: *Rock 'n' Roll*.

An Auspicious Encounter

A Meeting by the River

Vishwa Mohan Bhatt and Ry Cooder

This 1992 disc is one of the most animated of the many cross-cultural conversations that sprouted in the wake of "world beat" awareness in the 1980s. Representing the Americas is Ry Cooder, the canny California master of blues-style bottleneck slide guitar. Hailing from Jaipur, India, is Vishwa Mohan Bhatt, a specialist in Hindustani North Indian classical music who uses a steel rod to play an elaborate eight-stringed instrument of his own design. Supported by tabla player Sukhwinder Singh Namdhari and Cooder's son Joachim on *dumbek* (drum), the two find commonality on four rapt, contemplative duets that incorporate Indian drones and flatted "blue" notes.

Meeting was recorded shortly after the two men met. Nothing was planned. Bhatt and Cooder simply sat down to play, and took turns leading. One piece, "Longing," suggests the extended structure of Indian raga, but never quite circles around the way ragas do. Cooder plays the hymn "Isa Lei," and Bhatt follows at a respectful distance, contributing elaborate squiggling asides and, in several places, swooping nosedives that

sound almost impossible to do on a stringed instrument. Amazingly, the conversation has no one-upmanship in it. Both men are seeking aptness, not dazzle. As a result, when they "slide" between pitches and blend microtones together, their improvisations are totally sweet. They come from different traditions, and here by this river they wind up in the same musical zone, communicating in the universal language of carefully tugged and twanged strings.

GENRE: 🌐 World/India. **RELEASED:** 1992, Water Lily Acoustics. **KEY TRACKS:** "Longing," "Ganges Delta Blues." **CATALOG CHOICE:** Vishwa Mohan Bhatt and Jerry Douglas: *Bourbon & Rosewater.* **NEXT STOP:** Ry Cooder and Ali Farka Touré: *Talking Timbuktu.* **AFTER THAT:** Ali Farka Touré and Toumani Diabaté: *In the Heart of the Moon.*

A Few of Her Thousands of Songs . . .

The Rough Guide to Asha Bhosle

Asha Bhosle

The Indian singer and film star Asha Bhosle has, over decades of recordings, developed as a kind of singing deity with supernatural powers. (She's immortalized that way in Cornershop's winning 1997 single "Brimful of Asha.") Spend a few minutes listening to Bhosle, who got her start by singing the "bad girl" songs in Bollywood B movies of the 1950s, and this reverence becomes understandable: Her voice is easygoing and endlessly captivating, playful in a flirty, girlish way and at the same time radiating a grown woman's confidence. Since her early films, she's amassed a

Bhosle did playback singing for over 950 Bollywood movies.

discography containing over twenty thousand entries, which those who keep track of such things say puts her at or near the top of the "Most Prolific" list. She's sung in more than a dozen languages, done everything from light films to folk songs, classical music to pop and jazz (on the least compelling song here, "Ika Mina Dika," she attempts a campy American swing the liner notes describe as "rock and roll") to the musical settings of love poetry known as *ghazals*.

Such an impressive list wouldn't mean much if Bhosle was just another sweet voice. But on many of the recordings featured here, which were culled with her assistance to represent the many facets of her career, she appears as something of a divine presence, whose wondrously textured voice exudes grace, magic, possibility.

You don't have to know what she's saying,

or have even a basic appreciation of Indian music, to be moved by her extraordinary performances: She is one of those singers whose great technical facility makes every languid, seemingly tossed-off phrase riveting.

Because of her hyperproductivity, surveying Bhosle's career can be difficult. This single-disc volume offers a telescopic overview. It includes two pieces from her albums and many selections from film soundtracks—the down-tempo "Mera kuchh saaman," from the film *Ijaazat* (1987), has a Dusty Springfield sultriness, while the gliding "Jaame kya haal ho kai," from *Maa Ka Aanchal* (1970), showcases her command of so-called light classical Hindustani music. Incredibly, it doesn't matter that these tracks visit different styles or were recorded during different eras: All are unified by Bhosle's incandescence.

GENRE: 🌐 World/India. **RELEASED:** 2003, World Music Network. **KEY TRACKS:** "Mera kuchh saaman," "Jaame kya haal ho kai," "Sapna mera toot gaya," "Neeyat-e-shauq." **NEXT STOP:** Sheila Chandra: *Weaving My Ancestors' Voices.* **AFTER THAT:** Cornershop: *When I Was Born for the Seventh Time.*

Long Live the Kane

Big Daddy Kane

Recorded in 1988 during what many consider old-school hip-hop's artistic zenith, *Long Live the Kane* offers a glimpse of the moves, motivations, and morals of the typical hip-hop don. The mighty Kane (Antonio Hardy) was a part of the New York scene from its early days, and through a brain-scrambling assortment of devastating putdowns, battle taunts, and boasts about his own cleverness, he breaks down exactly what's involved in rocking the house. It's Old-School Hip-Hop 101.

Unlike the latter-day rap stars who still cop from his playbook, Kane never just leans on one kind of narrative. He's an operator around the ladies. But he's also a formidable wordsmith who can spin an extended story out of thin air—a skill he touts on the blistering "Set It Off." And on "I'll Take You There" (which is built on the Staple Singers' hit) and "Word to the (Mother) Land," he appears as a socially aware black man, voicing dismay over conditions in urban neighborhoods. Kane wasn't the first to deliver socially aware raps, but he's among the most influential: Common and other truth-telling rappers of the 1990s cite this record as early inspiration.

It's interesting to hear a statement of purpose like "Ain't No Half Steppin'" after even cursory exposure to 1990s gangsta rap, with its endless cartoonish confrontations and routine degradation of women. Like the gangstas, Kane doesn't suffer fools. But he's not exactly prone to whipping out the Glock and shooting to settle a disagreement—he'd rather use humor to silence an adversary. And where the gangstas rely on an almost generic horror-film menace in the backing tracks, Kane and producer Marley Marl foster a feeling of bright, freestyling spontaneity, with spongy, danceable beats, squiggly synth sounds, and needle-to-the-eardrum noises. The bubbling stew keeps everything copacetic like it was back in the day, when rappers weren't afraid to show vulnerability. And a deep respect (love, really) for the rhyming art defined the discourse.

GENRE: 🎙 Hip-Hop. **RELEASED:** 1988, Cold Chillin'/Warner Bros. **KEY TRACKS:** "Ain't No Half Steppin'," "I'll Take You There," "Raw," "Just Rhymin' with Biz." **CATALOG CHOICE:** *It's a Big Daddy Thing.* **NEXT STOP:** LL Cool J: *Mama Said Knock You Out.*

Key Secret Texts of Power-Pop

#1 Record/Radio City

Big Star

In its September 9, 1972, report on *#1 Record*, the debut release of the Memphis rock four-piece Big Star, the music industry trade magazine *Billboard* enthused: "Each and every cut on this album has the inherent potential to become a blockbuster single. The ramifications are positively awesome."

Needless to say, the predictions of imminent stardom were greatly exaggerated. Despite across-the-board raves from critics, no blockbuster single was forthcoming. In fact, Big Star fell victim to utterly typical business problems: Its label, Ardent Records, had trouble with distribution from Stax and later Columbia Records. As a result, there were no records in stores for people to buy. The positive notices were squandered.

Disillusioned, principal writers Chris Bell and Alex Chilton, who in Lennon/McCartney fashion wrote strikingly different types of songs but shared writing credit, had a falling out. Bell left the band in December, during work on the follow-up *Radio City*. As a result, the second album (and a third, the more psychedelic *Sister Lovers*) is mostly a showcase for Chilton, though the liner notes indicate that Bell did contribute ideas to a few of the revved-up rockers.

The first two Big Star records, now reissued on a single CD, are great treasures, if for somewhat different reasons. *#1 Record* offers Bell's fierce, unapologetically grabby pop ("Feel") as well as Chilton's more philosophical songs ("The Ballad of El Goodo").

Big Star's singer and guitarist Alex Chilton.

The *Billboard* scribe might have been a tad too generous—several tracks, like the rollicking Stones-influenced shout "Don't Lie to Me," are sparkling album tracks, not singles. Still, the basic Big Star equation—an appreciation for Memphis R&B backbeats, elaborate vocal harmonies, and other British Invasion finery—is hard to deny.

Bell's departure took away that vocal-group dimension, but it unleashed a torrent of staggeringly creative songs from Chilton. *Radio City* spans quite a range—there are contemplative ballads that make the most of Chilton's bewildered voice; shadowy, sinister rockers; and even a slowly unfolding space trance in the style of Pink Floyd, "Daisy Glaze." The album didn't fare any better than its predecessor in the marketplace, but to those who love power-pop, its exultant melodies are essential texts.

GENRE: 🎵 Rock. **RELEASED:** *#1 Record:* 1972, Ardent; *Radio City:* 1974, Ardent. (Reissued 1992, Fantasy.) **KEY TRACKS:** "Feel," "The Ballad of El Goodo," "In the Street," "Thirteen," "You Get What You Deserve," "Back of a Car." **CATALOG CHOICE:** *Sister Lovers.* **NEXT STOP:** Badfinger: *Straight Up.* **AFTER THAT:** The Raspberries: *Raspberries.*

Tobacco Girl Takes On the World

Carmen

Georges Bizet

Victoria de los Angeles, Nicolai Gedda, French Radio Orchestra and Chorus (Sir Thomas Beecham, cond.)

C*armen* opens in a Seville public square on a hot day. The local police sing an idle, workaday tune while keeping watch over the bustle; they're really waiting to glimpse the women who work in the tobacco factory as they take lunch. The officials have a few favorites, among them the tempestuous heroine, who displays, from her very first entrance, a talent for drawing male attention Madonna might envy.

An exotic Gypsy beauty who tells fortunes and projects a regal air that's above her station, Carmen turns out to be a magnet for love troubles: In the course of this colorful essay on free-spiritedness and jealousy, she snares a young corporal, Don José, then a dashing toreador, Escamillo; she disrupts work and gets into brawls with women, all the while smoking copiously. Georges Bizet establishes each character with distinct hues he returns to, fleetingly, as the tale unfolds. His bawdy large-ensemble moments are organized around hummable tunes—not least of them the magisterial "Toreador" march and the orphan girl's lament "Je dis, que rien ne m'épouvante."

Although Bizet plotted out other operas and comic operas late in his life, Carmen was his last multi-act work: He died at age thirty-six, just three months after its premiere, not knowing that the piece would become an operatic standard. He conceived Carmen using spoken dialog, but the presenting company requested that the narrative exposition be set to music,

Georges Bizet composed his first symphony at age 16.

in traditional recitative style. That task was unfinished at his death, and was handled by the far less adventurous composer Ernest Guiraud, whose labored connective music moves the story along in fitful lurches.

Carmen is now often presented the way Bizet intended, but one of the most enduring recordings—this 1959 version, conducted by Sir Thomas Beecham and featuring Victoria de los Angeles as Carmen and a forceful Nicolai Gedda as Don José—utilizes Guiraud's recitatives. That's its only flaw: Beecham keeps the Castilian flourishes restrained and helps everyone involved seize, then celebrate, Bizet's coy lyricism. Those seeking music bubbling with passion but containing little of the pomposity associated with opera will find this delightful.

GENRE: 🎵 Opera. **RELEASED:** 1960, EMI/Angel. **KEY TRACKS:** Act 1: "L'Amour est un oiseau rebelle"; Act 3: "Je dis, que rien ne m'épouvante." **CATALOG CHOICE:** L'Arlésiennes Suites Nos. 1 and 2, London Symphony Orchestra (Claudio Abbado, cond.). **NEXT STOP:** Maria Callas: *Highlights from Carmen.*

A Sound World Like None Other

Homogenic

Björk

Björk is an island. While most artists of the mix-and-match 1990s can seem imprisoned by their sources, the Icelandic auteur exists apart from hers, defying all attempts at rock-critic math. She is perhaps her generation's most successful avant-garde thinker, yet creates sounds that are grandly ear-catching even when they're not conventionally accessible. She borrows beats from clubland but doesn't make dance music. While her work carries distant, yet discernable traces of inspiration—*Low*-era David Bowie, for example—it's impossible to draw a direct line between her and literally anything that came before.

That's downright unbelievable considering Björk arrived in an age when everyone in pop music was a recycler of some sort. Her first two albums showed she had a pretty good idea of how to balance radical sonics against the comforting regularly scheduled undulations of pop songs. This one finds her junking most of that script: Rather than sampling drum loops the way most electronic beatmakers do, Björk starts with skronky guitars and "found" sounds, then processes them until they become unlikely percussion instruments. This gives the rhythmic backdrops an exotic texture, which she enhances by programming strange halting pauses and odd hiccups, and

Björk described *Homogenic* as "emotionally confrontational."

surrounding those with the dense, sometimes foreboding sounds of the Icelandic String Octet.

The textures inspire wild and sprawling songs that express frustration (and, just as often, resignation) over failed romance, or dismay and self-recrimination over perceived shortcomings. *Homogenic*'s lyrics can be tortured, and at times impenetrable, but the deeper you get into Björk's cavernous sound-schemes, the more the words seem irrelevant. She's found a way to have these fantastically mangled sounds tell the stories.

GENRE: 🎸 Rock. **RELEASED:** 1997, Elektra. **KEY TRACKS:** "Hunter," "Bachelorette," "All Neon Like," "Immature." **CATALOG CHOICES:** *Debut; Post.* **NEXT STOP:** Juana Molina: *Segundo* (see p. 511). **AFTER THAT:** St. Etienne: *So Tough.*

The First Great Blast of L.A. Punk

Damaged

Black Flag

The L.A. punk band Black Flag had been recording for several years when, at a New York show in 1981, a fan named Henry Rollins jumped up on stage and began singing. In a gesture that resonated throughout the punk world, the band invited Rollins to join. (The singer at the time, Dez Cadena, was more interested in playing guitar anyway.) Suddenly what had been a good band became a trailblazing one.

Rollins, who grew up in Washington, D.C., matched guitarist and leader Greg Ginn's hell-bent energy, firing off bellicose screams that maximized the impact of the guitar sparks. He brought East Coast attitude to the one-time surf-

punk band from Huntington Beach, California. Rollins taunted and challenged listeners. He chortled in ways that made Ginn's surprisingly cogent lyrics—about vapid consumerism and the soul-sucking offerings of network TV as well as such standby punk subjects as alienation and despair—sound like his own thoughts.

To be sure, Rollins, who after Black Flag went on to develop a separate career as a surly political commentator and spoken word artist, is plenty intense here—so much so that the band's major-label distributor, MCA Records, initially refused to release the album, terming it "anti-parent." Just as crucial, though, is Ginn, whose rhythm guitar rings with the purpose and energy of a crusade in progress. Ginn mixes dissonant serrated chords and spearing single lines (and very

Henry Rollins sang his heart out for Black Flag from 1981 until 1986.

brief solo explosions) into a veritable index of punk guitar pulverization.

GENRE: 🎸 Rock.
RELEASED: 1981, SST. **KEY TRACKS:** "Depression," "TV Party," "Gimme Gimme Gimme."
CATALOG CHOICE: *My War.*
NEXT STOP: X: *Wild Gift* (see p. 878). **AFTER THAT:** Helmet: *Size Matters.*

I . . . Am . . . Iron Man!

Paranoid

Black Sabbath

Before British rock singer Ozzy Osbourne was a one-joke reality TV star, before he allegedly bit the head off a live bat in concert, before he became a caricature of stoned celebrity excess, he was the first master of rock and roll psychodrama. And this, the second Black Sabbath album, is his Inventory of Primal Fears and Thrilling Nightmares of Great Portent. This stuff is not for the faint of heart: Meet the boy who's shunned by others, trapped in his own paranoid delusions (the title track). Step into the dark hall where the "Iron Man" dwells; he's a machine devoid of soul who knows "nobody wants him." (He'd be something to shun were he not powered by one of the most devastating two-measure riffs in all of gui-

Ozzy Osbourne during one of his tamer moments on stage.

tardom.) Shudder at the craven scheming of the "War Pigs." Beware the "Hand of Doom," with its foreboding fuzztone fingers.

Recorded live in the studio in just three days, *Paranoid* neatly defines the sound and

the philosophical disposition of heavy metal. Its obsessions (hate, the supernatural, war, alienation) became the obsessions of every other band aspiring to hardness. Its basic premise—that we must atone for the inherent evil of mankind—became the cornerstone upon which an overwhelming preponderance of heavy metal texts are built.

Running through these eight tunes is a feeling of malevolence waiting just out of sight. The vibe's so thick that Osborne doesn't have to do much; he bellows a little something about fairies wearing boots, and suddenly it's the witching hour. Black Sabbath's original lineup—Osborne, guitarist Tony Iommi, bassist Terry "Geezer" Butler, and drummer Bill

Ward—watched what the fast-ascending Led Zeppelin (see p. 442) was doing, and realized that blues rock, then huge in England, could travel down different roads. Zeppelin made it mystical. And Sabbath cranked it up, creating battle music of brute Wagnerian force and *Ben Hur* scope. This album, the first full realization of Sabbath's power, was a hit almost instantly, but is equally significant for its influence on the hard rock that followed.

GENRE: 🎸 Rock. **RELEASED:** 1971, Warner Bros. (U.K. release, 1970.) **KEY TRACKS:** "War Pigs," "Paranoid," "Iron Man." **F.Y.I.:** Kurt Cobain once described his band Nirvana as "a cross between Black Sabbath and the Beatles." **CATALOG CHOICE:** *Master of Reality.* **NEXT STOP:** Metallica: . . . *And Justice for All.* **AFTER THAT:** Pantera: *Vulgar Display of Power* (see p. 575).

Subversive Salsa

Siembra

Rubén Blades and Willie Colón

From a distance, *Siembra* sounds like much of the high-intensity Latin dance music that came out of New York in the late '60s and '70s: a chattering, trombone-heavy horn section, rhythms so persuasive they practically force your feet to move, and strings swirling in disco-fantasia flourishes (it was, after all, 1978).

But unlike most salsa of the period, there's a riot going on inside the celebration. The percussive and progressive Panamanian singer Rubén Blades sends sharp commentary shooting through several of these original songs, transforming what is typically considered party music into a platform for consciousness raising. Naturally he's coy about it, operating under the cover of often enchanting melodies, and the crazy quilt accompaniments generated by his collaborator, Bronx-born trombonist and arranger Willie Colón. Some songs are utterly straightforward harangues—"Plastico" lampoons the runaway consumerism of American (and Latin American) culture. It begins with garish disco strings, then slams them into an ultracomplex salsa rhythm, as though he's presenting his music as an outright challenge to the Disco Duck. Other tunes make their points more stealthily. "Pedro Navaja" borrows the struc-ture of the Bobby Darin hit "Mack the Knife," spinning the timeless Peter Gay/Kurt Weill tale of a small-time neighborhood operator into a parable of barrio life. (The piece ends with sirens blaring and an ironic "I like to live in America," sung in heavily accented *West Side Story*–ish English.)

Siembra proved incendiary. It quickly took up residence on Latin radio, and within a year became the top-selling tropical album of all time. Blades and Colón were credited with giving voice to an overlooked sector of American society and bringing topicality to a form often dismissed as exclusively for dancing. The album triggered a wave of similarly spirited (if less trenchant) salsa commentary. The duo split after an unsuccessful follow-up, and both continued to thrive, Colón as a bandleader capable of wrapping dance music in sumptuous orchestrations, Blades in the company of the rock-leaning band Seis del Solar, whose second album, *Escenas*, is the closest he's come to *Siembra*'s rare alchemy of music and message. That's not to say the subsequent work isn't magical: It's just that *Siembra* set a seriously high bar.

GENRE: 🌐 World/Latin. **RELEASED:** 1978, Fania. **KEY TRACKS:** "Buscando guyaba,"

"Pedro Navaja," "Plastico." **CATALOG CHOICE:** Willie Colón: *The Good, the Bad and the Ugly*. **NEXT STOP:** Larry Harlow Orchestra: *Hommy*. **AFTER THAT:** Roberto Roena y Su Apollo Sound: *5*.

The First Shredder

Ragtime Guitar's Foremost Fingerpicker

Blind Blake

Everyone who cares about the art of the guitar needs to know about Blind Blake, one of the men of mystery and intrigue roaming the blues highway in the 1920s and '30s. Arguably the first guitar shredder, Blake specialized in what's known as "ragtime guitar," which requires guitarists to mimic the lockstep boom-chink ragtime rhythms more commonly played on piano. For some practitioners, just keeping the beat going was challenge enough. Blake had no trouble there—his rhythm rocks like a freight train, steady and strong. He then added a level of difficulty, lacing deft ad-libbed ideas into every available break.

Blind Blake, circa 1927, in one of the only photographs of him known to exist.

These are bursts of pure genius, and a primary attraction of this twenty-three-track career overview. On most pieces, Blake starts out singing, in the unremarkable manner of countless early bluesmen. Accompanying himself, he sometimes generates enough rhythm to sound like a full band; as tunes like "Diddie Wa Diddie" and "Too Tight Blues #2" progress, Blake drops in conceptually forward-looking phrases that sparkle with a spirit of impromptu composition, a just-makin'-it-up-as-we-go-along invention. At times these lively creations suggest a strange dichotomy:

Blake's singing aligns with the conventions of the 1920s, while the guitar playing suggests the more daring approaches associated with the late '40s.

Little is known about Blake, who recorded approximately eighty tracks for Paramount between 1926 and his death in 1933. He was revered by musicians yet not a star in any sense. He died in obscurity, even though his high-stepping up-tempo rambles and chilling tales of death ("Rope Stretching Blues") have really no equal in his time. To amaze and astound the guitar hero in your life, cue up "Blind Arthur's Breakdown." Some great guitar minds of today are still baffled by that one.

GENRE: 🔵 Blues. **RELEASED:** 1990, Yazoo. **KEY TRACKS:** "Blind Arthur's Breakdown," "Diddie Wa Diddie," "One Time Blues," "Southern Rag," "Rope Stretching Blues." **NEXT STOP:** Blind Boy Fuller: *Truckin' My Blues Away*. **AFTER THAT:** Blind Lemon Jefferson: *The Best of Blind Lemon Jefferson*.

Hard-Swinging Hard Bop

Moanin'

Art Blakey and the Jazz Messengers

The horn players who spent time as part of the Jazz Messengers—the finishing school run by drummer Art Blakey whose alums include Wayne Shorter, Lee Morgan (heard in sparkling form here), and Curtis Fuller—revered the drummer as the great fire starter of small-group jazz. With just a carefully placed rim shot or a surging press roll, Blakey would nudge soloists along. The tenor saxophonist Johnny Griffin, another Messengers vet, once explained that these devices were Blakey's way of gently pushing his soloists: "He'd make one of those rolls and say 'No, you can't stop yourself now.'"

In 2005, Blakey received the Grammy Lifetime Achievement Award.

title track, which inspires a lip-slurring love letter from Morgan, and two pieces from saxophonist Benny Golson—the adventurous "Blues March" and the breezy stroll "Along Came Betty." Far from typical hard-bop blowing session quickies, these intricate tunes thrive on the Blakey zen, that ability to guide the music with strokes that are firm, definite, and vibrating with the feeling of swing.

Close listening to the lively *Moanin'* reveals that side of Blakey, his ability to stir sparks out of thin air. It also shows how important the compositions were to his hard-bop laboratory. This set features some of the most engaging Messengers tunes ever recorded, among them pianist Bobby Timmons's prayer-meeting

GENRE: 🎵 Jazz. **RELEASED:** 1958, Blue Note. **KEY TRACKS:** "Moanin'," "Along Came Betty," "Blues March." **CATALOG CHOICE:** *A Night in Tunisia.* **NEXT STOP:** Horace Silver Quintet: *Song for My Father* (see p. 702). **AFTER THAT:** Lee Morgan: *The Sidewinder.*

A Scintillating Voice Stands . . .

Two Steps from the Blues

Bobby "Blue" Bland

Bobby "Blue" Bland wasn't an elder statesman of anything when he recorded these astounding soul-blues singles in the late '50s. He just sounds that way. On songs that celebrate commitment and cry about the heartaches that inevitably follow, Bland, who was in his late twenties, brought the blues to new levels of intimacy. He found an emotionally expressive terrain the volatile kingpins of Delta blues ignored and, before he'd even been recording for very long, developed it into a sound that influenced an entire generation of singers—Otis Redding, Wilson Pickett, and all the rest.

A founding member, along with B.B. King, of the Memphis aggregate known as the Beale Streeters, Bland was first recorded in 1951, on a single produced for Chess by Sam Phillips that went nowhere. The singer entered the military in 1952, and when he returned to civilian life in 1955, he found himself in demand right away, performing with harmonica ace Junior Parker and recording singles for Duke Records.

Bobby Bland was inducted into the Rock and Roll Hall of Fame in 1992.

Soon after, Duke was bought by notorious record-biz hustler Don Robey (another in a line of businessmen to claim songwriting credit to skim publishing royalties from artists). In what became a blessing for Bland, Robey paired him with the smart musician and arranger, Joe Scott, who discovered and exploited Bland's innate smoothness.

Many of the singles here, including "Cry, Cry, Cry" and "Lead Me On," were written by Deadric Malone and arranged (often cannily underarranged) by Scott. Bland delivers each with a predator's patience and clearly enjoys having his vocals reinforced by the equally distraught guitar ad-libs of Clarence Holliman. Bland's laments about the love that's gone proceed at a slow and steady pace, and by the time he utters the raw vocal appeal he calls a "squall" (see "Little Boy Blue," his zenith, for a few memorable ones), he's thoroughly set a scene. All he has to do is whimper a little bit, and he whisks his listeners to his specific spot on the misery index, a place that isn't two steps away, as Bland claims, but deeply immersed in the blues.

GENRE: 🎵 Blues. RELEASED: 1961, Duke. KEY TRACKS: "I Pity the Fool," "Little Boy Blue," "Cry, Cry, Cry," "I'll Take Care of You." CATALOG CHOICE: *Call on Me.* NEXT STOP: Albert King: *Born Under a Bad Sign* (see p. 425). AFTER THAT: Little Milton: *If Walls Could Talk.*

Music for Brooding

Fragments

Paul Bley

Free jazz is an acquired taste, and unless you happened to have a hipster older brother who passed along his Ornette Coleman and Archie Shepp obsessions, chances are good you didn't acquire it. Even those who click intellectually with the basic notion of free jazz—that structure can be derived minute-by-minute, via the tussles of group interaction, rather than via a predetermined form—can find its caterwauling shrieks to be rough sledding.

Some veterans empathize with this, and in the years since the avant-garde heyday of the late '60s, have sought to create music that tempers the defiant skronk with more melodic expressions. The visionary pianist Paul Bley, who has played with Charlie Parker, Sonny Rollins, and members of Coleman's most important quartet, has been among the most effective "translators" of the free impulse. His massive discography includes straight-ahead bop and extemporaneous forays into harsh solo piano dissonance and stops at virtually every point in between. *Fragments*, a 1986 date featuring guitarist Bill Frisell, woodwind master John Surman (whose brooding low tones on the baritone saxophone and bass clarinet are particularly captivating), and drummer Paul Motian, is among his most lyrical endeavors, and one of the underappreciated gems of the '80s.

The elegies and laments each musician wrote for *Fragments* share a sound like they might have been inspired by the same vast desert landscape. There's none of the clutter that usually accompanies free playing; also absent are the ego-driven "look-at-me" marathons. The pieces exist in a space of overriding calm. Bley considers every chord and cluster carefully, and his musing temperament spreads to his accomplices, particularly Frisell, whose echoey sustained notes hover over the relaxed music like storm clouds. Inside this deliberative atmosphere, the group catches something that eluded many others: music that has an anything-goes openness while referring, however obliquely and intermittently, to a governing form.

GENRE: Jazz. **RELEASED:** 1986, ECM. **KEY TRACKS:** "Monica Jane," "Line Down," "Once Around the Park." **CATALOG CHOICES:** *Open, to Love; Tears* (solo piano). **NEXT STOP:** Keith Jarrett: *My Song* (see p. 394). **AFTER THAT:** Bill Frisell: *Lookout for Hope.*

Here's Gospel 2.0

Spirit of the Century

The Blind Boys of Alabama

When most music obsessives think about gospel, it's usually in the past tense, something that happened a long time ago. Of course some know about the reverent recordings Marion Williams (see p. 865) made in the 1980s and '90s, and about groups like the Fairfield Four and the Dixie Hummingbirds (see p. 226), whose legends have evolved over decades of gracious harmonizing. But in recent decades not much of interest has appeared under gospel—unless you count Kirk Franklin's dim R&B bait-and-switch routines.

Recorded in 2000, *Spirit of the Century* suggests that all

The Blind Boys formed over 70 years ago. They won a Grammy for this album.

gospel needed was a little bit of old-fashioned jukejoint energy. Here are freshly hopped-up versions of revival-tent standbys, including a version of "Amazing Grace" set to the chords of "The House of the Rising Sun." Also included are rock-era pieces cut from the same message-music cloth—notably the Rolling Stones' "I Just Wanna See His Face," treated as an up-tempo jubilee, and Tom Waits's yowling better-get-ready parade song "Jesus Gonna Be Here." They're sung by one of the most storied groups ever to travel the gospel highway: The Blind Boys of Alabama first formed in 1937 at a state school for the blind, and under the direction of Clarence Fountain became one of the powerhouse harmony acts, contributing important works in the '50s, '60s, and '70s.

Spirit, which features cameos from Ben Harper, harmonica virtuoso Charlie Musselwhite, and British bassist Danny Thompson, may not be the single best Blind Boys title available. But it's the one that set the group's comeback in motion. It's also the best illustration of the group's adaptability—its

knack for savoring the riches of the epoch just past while hurtling, at fearless speed, into the new one. The spotlight throughout is on the singers, reverent voices who know exactly what to do when the man upstairs sends down a double dose of great-gosh-almighty.

GENRE: ✝ Gospel. **RELEASED:** 2001, Real World. **KEY TRACKS:** "Jesus Gonna Be Here," "Run On for a Long Time," "Amazing Grace," "Nobody's Fault but Mine," "Motherless Child." **CATALOG CHOICES:** *Collectors Edition; The Gospel at Colonus.* **NEXT STOP:** Ben Harper and the Blind Boys of Alabama: *There Will Be a Light.* **AFTER THAT:** Mavis Staples: *Have a Little Faith.*

The First (Best) Rock Supergroup

Blind Faith

Blind Faith

Nobody in rock ever petitioned the heavens quite the way Steve Winwood did during the brief flicker that was Blind Faith. An agile singer as a teenager, Winwood had demonstrated deep appreciation of soul and

R&B on several hits with the Spencer Davis Group ("I'm a Man," "Gimme Some Lovin'") and his own Traffic. But in this setting, surrounded by Eric Clapton's questioning lead guitar, the herculean drumming of Ginger Baker, and oceans of reverb, his voice became almost celestial.

Winwood sings like he's got one last chance to redeem himself. His performance on "Sea of Joy," one of several originals he wrote for *Blind Faith*, is a marvel of optimism—at once perfectly formed and utterly spontaneous. His ecstatic vocals connect the rhythm section's gallop-

Steve Winwood began performing when he was only 8 years old.

ing roar to moments of placid, lakeside-at-sunset calm. .

Blind Faith began after Cream—Clapton's massively popular blues-rock power trio—soured in the fall of 1968. Looking for a different sound and less discord, Clapton sought out Winwood for some informal jamming in early spring 1969. The two hit it off immediately, and when former Cream drummer Baker turned up uninvited, the nucleus of rock's first supergroup was in place.

Refined through jamming, Blind Faith's music was less dense and more transparent than that of Cream; its open spaces showcased

Clapton's sonic discoveries (often here he's playing through the rotating Leslie speaker used for organ) as well as surging, gloriously apt guitar counterlines.

News of the collaboration sparked outsized anticipation, and as *Blind Faith* was released in July 1969, extensive tours of Europe and the U.S. were booked. The supergroup's first gig was in front of 100,000 people in London's Hyde Park, and the first U.S. show, at Madison Square Garden in New York, was marred by rioting. The band never lived up to expectations in live performance and called it quits in October 1969. The 2001 Deluxe Edition's added material (which includes four intermittently diabolical extended jams) suggests that had it somehow managed to survive the hype, Blind Faith might have taken rock down even more radical roads.

GENRE: 🎸 Rock. **RELEASED:** 1969, Polydor/Universal. (Deluxe Edition issued 2001.) **KEY TRACKS:** "Sea of Joy," "Can't Find My Way Home," "Presence of the Lord." **NEXT STOP:** Derek and the Dominos: *Layla and Other Assorted Love Songs* (see p. 219). **AFTER THAT:** Traffic: *The Low Spark of High-Heeled Boys.*

New York Punk Pop for the Ages

Parallel Lines

Blondie

L ooking at the publicity shots and listening to the first two Blondie albums, it's tempting to dismiss the band as a trend-chasing marketing creation. Singer Debbie Harry and her musicians are accessorized to the nines, trying to at least look like denizens of the New York punk scene that birthed the Talking Heads and the Ramones. Musically, though, they're not nearly as assertive; Blondie sounds like it's a little bit afraid of punk, not sure whether to charge fully into its confrontations.

Those first two albums are warm-ups for *Parallel Lines.* This time, Blondie blows past the punk trappings in pursuit of a postmodern amalgam of the Dixie Cups and the Ronettes and David Bowie glam. And, oh yes, a crucial visionary pinch of disco (check out the huge single "Heart of Glass"). The singles and the songs that could have been singles filter girl-boy relationship woes into thrilling pop

Six *Parallel Lines* songs were issued as singles.

constructs that depended not just on Harry's attitude, but her ability to channel the exuberance of the Phil Spector girl groups (especially on "Picture This"). Though they hit common themes (love as a drag is one), the songs of *Parallel Lines* each claim their own spots on the spectrum that starts at punk desperation and ends at bubblegum bliss.

GENRE: 🎸 Rock. **RELEASED:** 1978, Chrysalis. **KEY TRACKS:** "Heart of Glass," "Hanging on the Telephone," "Picture This." **CATALOG CHOICE:** *Blondie.* **NEXT STOP:** The Runaways: *The Runaways.* **AFTER THAT:** Eurythmics: *Sweet Dreams (Are Made of This).*

Thoroughly Mixed Mezcla

Bloque

Bloque

L atin music changed radically in the 1990s. After decades of tame attempts at pop assimilation—see the Miami Sound Machine et al.—there came a generation of artists raised intent on *mezcla*, the ad hoc mixing sounds and styles inspired by American hip-hop. These musicians had deep traditional roots (Bloque's core members backed Colombian pop *vallenato* star Carlos Vives) and wide musical curiosities, and, while proud of their heritages, they were selective about showing it. Many felt let down by previous generations: Bloque leader Ivan Benavides once explained that Bloque grew out of "the immense black hole that was created by the media revolution in the '60s, when Colombian people forgot to create their own modern music while they were busy trying to learn how to dance to the sound of the . . . Beach Boys."

The eight-piece Bloque was among the most ambitious of this rogue wave, which included bands like Colombia's Aterciopelados and Mexico's Los de Abajo and others grouped under the classification "rock en español." On this high-octane international debut, Bloque definitely rocks, in a rainbow of ways—sometimes its pulse has a heavily Brazilian feel, and some-times the beat is looser and more psychedelic, like Santana on a mushroom high. The songs are real songs, not repetitive vamps, and many reach a peak when guitarist Ernesto Ocampo, a student of heavy metal, steps up to solo. Moods change radically from song to song: The album offers jolly limbo-line dances, sultry *son montuno* rhythms, and solemn chants that suggest a super-secret midnight tribal ritual. Crucially, this approach to *mezcla* is totally organic. While the commercial rock en español bands parade their crudely pasted-together influences, Bloque blows right past gratuitous grabbing, with a global pastiche that's celebratory, and visionary.

GENRE: 🌐 World/Colombia. **RELEASED:** 1998, Luaka Bop. **KEY TRACKS:** "Nena," "Sin lagrimas," "Ay donde andara." **NEXT STOP:** Aterciopelados: *La pipa de la paz.* **AFTER THAT:** Los Amigos Invisibles: *Arepa 3000* (see p. 19).

All the Riches, Baby, Don't Mean Anything

Fiddler on the Roof

Jerry Bock and Sheldon Harnick
Original Broadway Cast

W hen Gwen Stefani, the lead singer of the rock band No Doubt, took a solo turn in 2005, she launched it with a role-reversing remake of "If I Were a Rich Man," this musical's most familiar tune.

The update was set to a vaguely Middle Eastern beat, and added a refrain ("All the riches, baby, don't mean anything") as well as a gold-digging rap manifesto from Stefani's frequent collaborator, Eve.

It was a stroke of genius, the rare instance of a song from ancient history (well, 1964) commenting trenchantly on the modern world: As Tevye, the wise milkman played by Zero Mostel (1915–1977) in this original Broadway cast version, knew, everybody everywhere spends at least some time chasing the bling. Stefani's peers might want to investigate more of the songs Jerry Bock and Sheldon Harnick wrote for this Broadway evergreen: They're sharp appraisals of human nature propelled by spry, memorable melodies. There are breathless expressions of hope ("Matchmaker, Matchmaker") and near-frantic dances ("Wedding Celebration/The Bottle Dance"), and meditations on the cycle of life ("Sunrise, Sunset") that feel sullen and rhapsodic at once.

These and other tunes help to tell the story of Tevye and his three daughters, who marry for love and not riches—that oldest of story-telling devices. Set in a closely knit Jewish community, the musical tells of life in the

Zero Mostel (above) won a Grammy Award for his role in *Fiddler on the Roof.*

days before the formation of Israel, when Jews weren't surprised when they had to leave their villages on short notice. One recurring insight has to do with the way traditions hold a culture together, particularly when that culture is as precarious as a fiddler on the roof.

As handled by the original Broadway cast, this *Fiddler* is a spry creation, informed by a zest for life and a parallel understanding of its cruelties. Mostel is the main draw. His crisp diction and casual yet idiomatic phrasing light up Tevye's every line; by the time he finishes his vivid "If I Were a Rich Man," you know his character intimately. According to legend, Mostel was a terror on stage, sometimes improvising different lines or stopping entirely to provide the audience with sports scores. This performance, with its quaint wisdom and winking lightness, suggests he was more than worth the trouble.

GENRE: 😊 Musicals. **RELEASED:** 1964, RCA. **KEY TRACKS:** "If I Were a Rich Man," "Sunrise, Sunset." **CATALOG CHOICE:** *She Loves Me.* **NEXT STOP:** Gwen Stefani: *Love. Angel. Music. Baby.* **AFTER THAT:** Mitch Leigh and Joe Darion: *Man of La Mancha,* Original Broadway Cast.

The Wise Man of Wise County

Dock Boggs:
His Folkways Years, 1963–68

Dock Boggs

ise County is in the extreme southwestern portion of Virginia, near the state's borders with Kentucky and Tennessee. It's craggy Appalachian country, where for generations coal mining was the primary employment.

It's also a cradle of much traditional American music. Bristol, the town that straddles the Virginia-Tennessee line, is where the Carter Family made the first commercially available country recordings. Bluegrass pioneer Ralph Stanley was born in nearby Stratton. Not far from there, in Norton, Moran Lee "Dock" Boggs (1898–1971) grew up. The youngest of ten children, Boggs was working in a coal mine by age twelve.

Though he's the least famous of the Virginia pioneers, Boggs ranks among the most inventive. He was one of the first to explore the connection between Appalachian mountain music and the blues; his early recordings "Sugar Baby" and "Country Blues" from the 1920s opened up a conversation between the Virginia hills and the Mississippi Delta that continues today.

Boggs's chosen instrument was the banjo. But he didn't play it in the brusque "clawhammer" style of Charlie Poole and others. Instead, using an "up-picking" technique borrowed from finger-style guitarists, he plucked single notes and chords using three fingers, an approach that gave his accompaniments a marked sophistication. These rarely, however, overshadow the man's plaintive, forever besieged vocals. As he applies this contrivance-free voice to common mountain songs, Boggs transforms the death-haunted echoes of rural blues, murder ballads, and cautionary tales of bleak prison life into time-stopping miniatures. His songs are the

tragic soundtracks playing in the background of worried lives—be they obsessed and cruel lovers ("Pretty Polly") or unrepentant alcoholics ("Drunkard's Lone Child").

These chilling pieces were decades ahead of the musical sensibilities of the late '20s, and Boggs knew it: Frustrated by his lack of success, he sold his banjo in 1933 and abandoned music, making his living for a while as a bootlegger. He was rediscovered in the early 1960s by Mike Seeger of the New Lost City Ramblers, and persuaded to record for Folkways.

This two-disc set, from 1963–1968, finds Boggs revisiting his core repertoire some forty years after the initial recordings. He doesn't make any radical changes. His voice is more weathered, almost harrowingly so, but he sings with the same fierce spirit, trusting that the truths of these sturdy, old-as-the-hills tunes will endure.

GENRE: 🄲 Folk. RELEASED: 1997, Revenant. KEY TRACKS: "Sugar Baby," "Danville Girl," "Pretty Polly." CATALOG CHOICE: *Country Blues: Complete Early Recordings: (1927–29)*. COLLECTOR'S NOTE: Boggs obsessives should prepare to hunt for *Country Blues,* which is out of print. NEXT STOP: The Stanley Brothers: *The Complete Columbia Recordings* (see p. 735). AFTER THAT: Robert Johnson: *The Complete Recordings* (see p. 404).

Another Doleful Singer-Songwriter at His Brooding Peak

I See a Darkness

Bonnie "Prince" Billy

66 "If I am gone and with no trace," Will Oldham advises in the first stanza of this earthy and creakily sung record, "I will be in a minor place." This, it turns out, is his musical comfort zone. All eleven odes in this set are brooders—loaded with images that suggest hidden internal turmoil and lachry- mose melodies he might have overheard while walking on winding mountain roads.

"Minor" though it may be, this place is not slight: Like Nick Drake and a few others, Oldham, working here as Bonnie "Prince" Billy, explores conflicted emotional states with great clarity and, when necessary, a withering self-awareness. Hearing his idle, stargazing songs, it's easy to imagine the Louisville, Kentucky, singer and guitarist scrawling in a journal in some remote locale, methodically sorting out his troubled relationships. On the title track, which is addressed to a longtime friend and drinking companion, he wonders whether this person detects the darkness that "comes blacking in my mind." The song moves at a glacial, inevitable pace, an audio representation of encroaching darkness.

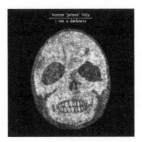

I See a Darkness is the first album on which Oldham used the name Bonnie "Prince" Billy.

Oldham is one of the most prolific songwriters to emerge in the 1990s. He's also among the most gifted. Working in a variety of contexts and guises—first he recorded as Palace Songs, then Palace Brothers, then under his own name

or Bonnie "Prince" Billy—he's written credible alt-country as well as enduring modern folk songs that have a timeless feel.

In some ways, *I See a Darkness,* which is his most consistently engrossing work, can be seen as a precursor to the "new folk" movement that spawned Sufjan Stevens (see p. 742) and many others. Yet Oldham follows his own quirky path. The roots elements keep him grounded and give his often mystical images surprising resonance. Get close enough, and you may see and, even more important, *feel* that darkness.

GENRE: 🎸 Rock. **RELEASED:** 1999, Palace. **KEY TRACKS:** "Minor Place," "Another Day Full of Dread," "Knockturne." **CATALOG CHOICE:** *The Letting Go.* **F.Y.I.:** Before his singing career took off, Oldham starred in several films, including John Sayles's *Matewan.* **NEXT STOP:** Sufjan Stevens: *Illinoise* (see p. 742). **AFTER THAT:** Jim O'Rourke: *Eureka.*

Murder Triggers a Hip-Hop Transformation

By All Means Necessary

Boogie Down Productions

Until his longtime collaborator and DJ, Scott La Rock (real name Scott Sterling), was murdered in 1987, the MC known as KRS-One (Kris Parker) specialized in terse confrontational rap. The tunes on the

duo's then-current release *Criminal Minded* are blow-by-blow descriptions of drug deals gone sour, humorous taunts, and mercilessly clever, if often foulmouthed, wordplay. Parker might have followed that direction for years, but when Sterling was shot trying to break up an argument at a Bronx party, Parker's outlook changed.

He began calling himself "the Teacher," and as he explains on this album's opening track "My Philosophy," became interested in raising consciousness about drugs and violence, advocating education as a way out of poverty for young African Americans. This album, the first Parker released after the murder, contains tracks developed by Sterling. It's among the most galvanizing calls to responsibility in hip-hop history.

A high school dropout who lived in homeless shelters as a teenager and schooled himself, on his own, in public libraries, Parker might not have found his way to hip-hop were it not for Sterling, a social worker by day and DJ by night. The two met at a Bronx shelter when Parker, then nineteen, arrived after a short stint in jail (for selling marijuana). They formed a group, Boogie Down Productions, and within months were being scouted by labels looking for the next great hip-hop sound.

Where he'd previously glorified thug life, Parker argues, sometimes stridently, for hip-hop as an agent of social change on *By All Means Necessary* (which adapts a phrase commonly used by Nation of Islam activist Malcolm X). The most overt statement along those lines comes on the chanted "Stop the

Both the album's title and cover refer to Malcolm X.

Violence," but throughout, Parker the street intellectual uses his commanding voice to rattle listeners awake and his castigating rhyme style to galvanize them to create change. The proof of his persuasive abilities can be heard throughout much of the hip-hop made subsequently: Just about every rapper intent on sending positive messages has borrowed something from KRS-One, whose name is an acronym for "Knowledge Reigns Supreme Over Nearly Everyone."

GENRE: 🎤 Hip-Hop. **RELEASED:** 1988, Jive/RCA. **KEY TRACKS:** "Stop the Violence," "Illegal Business," "Jimmy." **CATALOG CHOICES:** *Criminal Minded.* KRS-One: *The Return of the Boom Bap.* **NEXT STOP:** Public Enemy: *It Takes a Nation of Millions to Hold Us Back* (see p. 618). **AFTER THAT:** Eric B. and Rakim: *Paid in Full* (see p. 260).

A Gumbo from the Piano Prince

New Orleans Piano Wizard Live!

James Booker

James Booker (1939–1983) took a rogue's delight in messing with established texts. On stage, the New Orleans pianist and singer would interrupt a tune, any tune, to add zany detours. Booker had classical training until he was twelve; he'd sometimes lunge into flamboyant arpeggios and other faux-baroque show-off moves. Irreverence dominated his performances: Almost nightly, he'd take some corny old song—like the easy-listening standard "Something Stupid" heard on this 1977 performance at a Zurich boogie-woogie summit—and pump it into a hip-shaking tour de force.

The pirate-patch-wearing Booker was, however, an erratic human being. He spent much of his career under the influence of various intoxicants. He was frequently in debt, and though a regular on the New Orleans club circuit, he recorded sporadically—only three albums of his work were released in his lifetime, and none of them features him on the organ, where, as private tapes demonstrate, he seemed to grow extra hands.

Although this date doesn't show the full range of his repertoire, it's carefully recorded and finds Booker playing on a well-maintained grand piano—a big step up from the rickety upright at one of his main New Orleans haunts, the Maple Leaf Bar. Between the eighty-eight-key heroics are several sparkling vocal pieces, including the torchy "Come Rain or Come Shine" and "Please Send Me Someone to Love," both of which reveal him to be a deeply moving ballad singer. Listen just once, and you will wonder why James Booker, manic wizard of the piano, remains such a well-kept secret.

GENRES: 🔵 R&B 🟡 Jazz ⚫ Blues.
RELEASED: 1987, Rounder. **KEY TRACKS:** "On the Sunny Side of the Street," "Something Stupid," "Let Them Talk." **CATALOG CHOICES:** *Junco Partner; Spiders on the Keys; A Taste of Honey.* **NEXT STOP:** Professor Longhair: *New Orleans Piano* (see p. 616).
AFTER THAT: Eddie Bo: *The Hook and Sling.*

Groovy Instrumentals from a Cradle of Soul

Melting Pot

Booker T. and the MGs

During its tenure as the rhythm section for Otis Redding and virtually everyone else who sang for Memphis-based Stax Records, the team of keyboardist Booker T. Jones, guitarist Steve Cropper, bassist Donald "Duck" Dunn, and drummer Al Jackson Jr. set an impossibly high standard for backbeat music. Cue up virtually any Stax side and check out the sublime force sizzling away unobtrusively in the background. They make it easy for the singers to hit that sweet spot.

Melting Pot was Booker T. and the MGs' last album for Stax Records.

The task of supporting singers gave the musicians serious cohesion, and because singers are notoriously unpredictable, Jones and his crew enjoyed plenty of studio downtime for unstructured playing. The rhythm section's biggest hit, "Green Onions," happened during a spontaneous jam while they waited for singer Billy Lee Riley, who never showed.

A top ten hit in 1962, "Green Onions" is a loping boogie in the John Lee Hooker tradition that's been endlessly repurposed by dance-music DJs and hip-hop mavens. Alas, "Green Onions" was also endlessly repurposed by Booker T. and the MGs: The group's next album featured a carbon copy called "Mo Onions," and even years later, on this last great studio effort, the group returned to the same terrain—see the aptly titled "Kinda Easy Like," which adds tightly harmonized wordless vocals (à la a '40s girl group) from the Pepper Sisters.

Melting Pot was recorded in New York instead of the group's home studio in Memphis. The spotlight's on steady surging grooves—the title track rides an effortless, butter-churning polyrhythm for eight minutes, and includes a sneaky solo from the magnificent Cropper, whose succinct, searing lines virtually define the crossroads of blues and rock. Booker T. and the MGs were among the most potent of the hard-grooving instrumental-soul bands of the '60s, and arguably had more impact than outfits led by saxophonists King Curtis and Junior Walker. The group disbanded shortly after this album's release, and was at work on a comeback album in 1975 when Jackson, the drummer, was murdered in a robbery attempt. The crime has never been solved.

GENRE: 🎵 R&B. **RELEASED:** 1971, Stax. **KEY TRACKS:** "Melting Pot," "Back Home," "Fuquawi," "Kinda Easy Like." **CATALOG CHOICES:** *Green Onions; Hip Hug-Her.* **NEXT STOP:** Jr. Walker and the All Stars: *Shotgun.* **AFTER THAT:** King Curtis: *Live.*

Fifteen Stunning Miniatures in Thirty Minutes

Lô Borges

Lô Borges

Imagine being a young musician in Brazil in the late 1960s, a time when horizons in music were changing by the day. All around you possibilities were opening: At home, the leading lights were reinventing indigenous forms as *tropicália*, a radical movement that would become enormously influential. From far away came the impossibly pretty, world-changing harmonies of the Beach Boys and the ambitious songwriting of the Beatles.

Of those inspired by these developments (Caetano Veloso, Gilberto Gil, Milton Nascimento), the most criminally overlooked is Lô Borges, a singer and guitarist from Belo Horizonte whose debut is one of the lost gems of world pop. Borges grew up around Milton Nascimento and Wagner Tiso among others, and was involved in Nascimento's powerful song-cycle about childhood, 1972's *Clube da esquina* (see p. 540). While writing and recording that album, Borges compiled a set of more idiosyncratic songs for his own project, pieces built on slurpy rock/funk rhythm patterns and languid, almost mystical vocal melodies, with lyrics about unrequited and rediscovered love.

These pieces don't simply paste California sunshine onto generic bossa nova: Rather they're slyly intricate études, coy in their use of rock rhythm but suffused with the elegant melodic slopes central to all Brazilian music. Borges borrowed both musical ideas and recording techniques from rock. There's lots of vocal and instrumental layering, and several pieces feature guitarist Toninho Horta unleashing swervy and dramatic solos in the background, a counterpoint to the vocal refrains. Borges came up with a deft assimilation—music that's elaborate (in a *Pet Sounds* way; see p. 55) but never fussy, built with reverence for detail (see the carefully webbed guitar arpeggios that define "Homem da rua") and a surplus of soul. From a distance, these fifteen short works breeze by, generically pretty and not terribly demanding. Up close, they're exquisite, elusive miniatures that reveal new dimensions each time you hear them.

GENRE: 🌐 World/Brazil. **RELEASED:** 1973, EMI. **KEY TRACKS:** "Nao foi nada," "Calibre," "Toda essa agua." **CATALOG CHOICE:** Milton Nascimento: *Clube da esquina* (see p. 540). **NEXT STOP:** Caetano Veloso: *Estrangerio.* **AFTER THAT:** Juana Molina: *Segundo* (see p. 511).

A Feeling, Amplified

Boston

Boston

"More than a Feeling" is more than the prototypical three-chord guilty pleasure sing-along of the '70s. Beneath its screaming-bullet guitars and correspondingly shrill vocals is a tale of obsession: One man's pursuit of a particular guitar sound he hadn't heard anywhere else.

The backstory: Guitarist Tom Scholz, a mechanical engineering graduate of MIT with a day job at Polaroid, literally spent years in his basement exploring novel ways to amplify and record the guitar. His research yielded an array of different techniques—among them a way to capture the sound of fingers striking the strings of an acoustic guitar (heavily processed acoustic guitar is a secret weapon of this album) along with special effects that give ordinary chords an almost palpable texture. He also went a bit nutty with a homemade multitracking rig, painstakingly stacking individual riffs and counterlines into massive guitar symphonies.

Though the album is a showcase for Scholz's unorthodox sonics, there is, amazingly, almost no guitar wanking here: On every track, this semi-mad scientist uses a different set of textures and tricks to support Brad Delp's multitracked vocals. The epic stomp "Long Time" features howling whammy-bar sustained notes as a near-constant backdrop, while "Peace of Mind" has a grittier, less airbrushed attack. With its rare balance of gee-whiz sounds and reliable hookcraft, *Boston* remained the top-selling debut album of the rock era until Whitney Houston's self-titled release in 1985. Its high-gloss guitars were copied by scores of bands, and so were its riffs: Nirvana's "Smells Like Teen Spirit" is a natty confluence of "More than a Feeling" and "Louie, Louie." Scholz took more than two years to follow up the hit (the uneven *Don't Look Back*, 1978), then eight years to release album number three, which came out in 1986. Vexed by lawsuits, personnel changes, and Scholz's perfectionism, Boston never reached anywhere near this level of inspiration again.

GENRE: 🅑 Rock. **RELEASED:** 1976, Epic. **KEY TRACKS:** "More than a Feeling," "Foreplay/Long Time." **NEXT STOP:** The Who: *Who's Next* (see p. 859). **AFTER THAT:** Free: *Fire and Water.*

Worth It for the Title Alone

Old Hag You Have Killed Me

The Bothy Band

The songs on *Old Hag You Have Killed Me* are old. Really old. They've been handed down from generation to generation by musicians who regard them as sacred texts, inviolate works of Celtic heritage that are never to be tampered with. The Bothy Band somehow missed the memo about that: The six-piece band shoots jigs, reels, and ballads full of adrenaline and a touch of progressive-rock drama, not to mention traces of the funky clavinet—that spikey-sounding keyboard instrument Stevie Wonder plays on "Superstition."

The Bothy Band played together from 1974 to 1979.

Though it only existed in its best lineup for three years, and made just three studio albums, the Bothy Band rattled the Celtic world with its revitalizations. Listening to "Music in the Glen," it's possible to get a sense of this: It begins as a showcase for the happy fiddling of Kevin Burke, but after a minute or so the band comes thundering in, with heavy power chords from multi-instrumentalist Donal Lunny on the stringed instrument known as the *bouzouki*. Right away they hijack the grassy-hillside vibe, with jolting phrases that have more in common with Gentle Giant–style progressive rock than anything ancient.

Determined to avoid the obvious, these six don't let too many of the beautiful melodies settle into placidness. They've rejiggered the music to show off the group's magical teamwork and technical command, so some tunes are played at blindingly fast tempos, while others contain flashy speed changes sure to give dancers fits. Often these fantastic passages seem to evaporate too quickly, and that's a key to understanding the Bothy Band: It makes traditional Irish music for the short-attention-span set, working overtime to avoid the cycles of verse-chorus repetition. For this reason—if not the utterly perfect title that recalls an age when Old Hags were known to terrorize their men—this is an excellent way to begin an exploration of Celtic music.

GENRE: 🌐 World/Celtic. **RELEASED:** 1976, Green Linnet. **KEY TRACKS:** "Music in the Glen," "The Kid on the Mountain," "Farewell to Erin," "The Maid of Coolmore." **CATALOG CHOICES:** *The Bothy Band; After Hours.* **NEXT STOP:** Genesis: *The Lamb Lies Down on Broadway* (see p. 305). **AFTER THAT:** Nightnoise: *The Parting Tide.*

Songs of Subversion

Kalfou Danjere

Boukman Eksperyans

The credits on *Kalfou Danjere/Dangerous Crossroads* begin: "Recorded in May 1992 in the midst of political mayhem at Audiotek Studios, Port-au-Prince, Haiti." Mayhem, indeed. The year before, in a cultural crackdown by Haiti's military government, the family band Boukman Eksperyans was harassed and banned from the country's annual February carnival. The reason: Its enormously popular song "Kalfou Danjere," a fable about how those who lie and cheat will be judged at the metaphysical cross-

roads, was interpreted by the government as a subversive commentary. Soldiers began turning up at the group's (infrequent) live performances and, members said later, intimidating them.

Like many Haitian acts, Boukman Eksperyans (named for a voodoo priest who worked to unify slaves during a successful revolt against France in 1804) slips thinly disguised outrage about current events into its songs, often via double entendre and coded slang. But those messages come under the cover of pure sweetness, carried by music that, in the tradition of Bob Marley, aims to uplift as much as to agitate. The rhythms, many built on drum machines and complementary hand-drumming, exude a festive feeling, while the singers, both as soloists and members of the chorale, share an uncommon sense of mission: Whether they're tossing around a voodoo chant or supplying somber hummed responses to a dancing lead, they bring the quality of prayer and reflection to every track on this remarkable disc. Rarely has music born in—and concerned with—conflict sounded so centered, hopeful, serene.

GENRE: ⊕ World/Haiti. **RELEASED:** 1992, Island/Mango. **KEY TRACKS:** "Tande m tande," "Jou nou revolte." **NEXT STOP:** Bob Marley and the Wailers: *Survival.* **AFTER THAT:** Boukan Ginen: *Rev au nou.*

Rock Stardom as a Phantasmagoria

The Rise and Fall of Ziggy Stardust and the Spiders from Mars

David Bowie

Before virtually anyone else, David Bowie understood that rock and roll of the 1970s needed an element of fantasy. He made this a personal mission, and fashioned a repertory company of alter-egos in theatrical guises—among them sleazy streetwalkers, space-dwelling dope fiends, and cross-dressers tottering precariously on platform heels. These constructs are, in some ways, more memorable than the spotty albums on which they appear. Until *Ziggy.*

Though its "story" dissolves early on, and its sexual brazenness is long past outré, *Ziggy* is British rocker Bowie's urtext.

It's also one of the great glam statements of the '70s, a clever distillation of T. Rex, Mott the Hoople, and Andy Warhol, in which the sublime and the sordid sit next to each other. Bowie had already grabbed attention a few times by

As Ziggy Stardust, Bowie sported bright red hair and fierce outfits.

this point, with *Space Oddity, Hunky Dory,* and the enduring title track from *The Man Who Sold the World.* Having tasted stardom, sharp social critic Bowie (né David Jones) was evidently both attracted and horrified by it; these songs are a frightened and frightening account of a space alien rock star sent to free the youth of the world from inhibition. Sometimes the places he and his entourage, the Spiders, go are a real trip ("Suffragette City," an all-time classic rocker), and sometimes they're all too real ("Rock and Roll Suicide," "Moonage Daydream"). No matter where he lands,

Bowie fully immerses listeners in the freaky feel and smell of the place. He also gets the horniness and holiness of rock ritual—one more recently released bonus track, "Sweet Head," proclaims: "Before there was rock, you only had God." He also understands the yearning for meaning, and depicts the Spiders, and the freaks who pay to see them, with compassion. Like him, they're both skeptics and true believers, participants in a sordid traveling tableau. Their exploits form

an allegory about stardom as phantasmagoria that seems downright prescient in our celebrity-obsessed age.

GENRE: 🎸 Rock. **RELEASED:** 1972, Virgin. **KEY TRACKS:** "Suffragette City," "Moonage Daydream," "Five Years," "It Ain't Easy." **CATALOG CHOICES:** *Young Americans; Heroes.* **NEXT STOP:** T. Rex: *Electric Warrior* (see p. 785). **AFTER THAT:** Mott the Hoople: *All the Young Dudes.*

Intimate Setting Yields Incredible Interplay

Live at Passim

The Boys of the Lough

Recorded at the famed Harvard Square folk club Passim over three nights in 1974, this lively disc serves as an introduction to the traditional songs of Ireland, Scotland, and Shetland, at least the ones heard in pubs and at dances. As was the fashion at the time among Celtic ensembles, the Boys of the Lough lean on the old ways of doing things, often assembling several brief pieces together into "sets": Track four, for example, knits together three Irish reels, "The Boys of Twenty-Five," a boisterous country dance called "The Boyne Hunt," and "Chase Her Through the Garden." There are no seams between these fast-moving pieces. Instead, the band tumbles from one to the next, using brief instrumental caprices to link disparate tunes.

In performance, the Boys of the Lough display the kind of steady-handed agility often associated with jazz musicians—their straightforward songs are enlivened by conversational asides (many from mandolin virtuoso Dave Richardson) and moments of almost giddy, unexpected joy. The quartet became one of the more celebrated ensembles during the Chieftains-led explosion of interest in Celtic music in the early '70s, and this disc shows why. Few other groups kick up as

lively a ruckus as this one does on the early selections, and just when you get accustomed to the whimsical stuff, along comes an ode like "The Flower of Magherally" to remind you how heavy-hearted—and disarmingly lovely—Celtic music can be.

The disc's accompanying booklet contains brief descriptions of the pieces, often tracing their lineage and offering insight into the band's intentions. This comes in handy when listening to "The New Set," which finds the Boys knitting together several jigs and a reel before ending with an altered mazurka. On paper, that suggests something of a train wreck. In performance, it's delightful.

GENRE: 🌐 World/Celtic. **RELEASED:** 1975, Philo. **KEY TRACKS:** "General Guinness," "The Boys of Twenty-Five," "The Hound and the Hare," "The New Set." **CATALOG CHOICE:** *The Boys of the Lough.* **NEXT STOP:** The Chieftains: *4* (see p. 165). **AFTER THAT:** Dick Gaughan: *Handful of Earth.*

A Low-Key Way to Begin Exploring the Classics

Sonatas for Cello and Piano, Opp. 38, 99, 108

Johannes Brahms
Yo-Yo Ma, Emanuel Ax

It's not easy to undertake an exploration of classical music. Most critics seem to be talking some encrypted decoder-ring language, underscoring the perception that classical music is a rarefied world apart. It seems as if there

are about thirty recordings of the same piece available but no *Wine Spectator*–style rating system to help differentiate one from another. So where to go when you want to add to a collection that starts and ends with Beethoven's Fifth?

One possible approach: Avoid the symphonic repertoire and investigate something "smaller," like these entrancing sonatas that come from opposite ends of Brahms's creative output. Here is lively, approachable music that is heroic in spots and contemplative in others, a range that mirrors that of many great symphonies. But

American cellist Yo-Yo Ma has won 15 Grammy Awards.

there's less throat-clearing ceremony—the focus throughout is on the shining beauty of Brahms's melodies. The first work, Opus 38 in E Minor, from 1865, is a youthful rush of harmonic gamesmanship; Opus 99 in F Major moves with the more measured gait of an older person. The final one, Opus 108 in D Minor, is a transcription of a violin sonata (see p. 113); it's the most lyrical and introspective of the three.

And when played with the empathy that Yo-Yo Ma and Emanuel Ax bring, they can suggest the kind of rambling conversation that follows a holiday feast. Parts of Opus 99 are devoted

to extravagantly showy volleys: The cello suggests a notion, the piano provides an elaborate response, and pretty soon the two instruments are swatting big ideas back and forth. The themes, particularly the one that drives the Adagio second movement of Opus 99, spring from a zone of deep yearning. A particular delight of this recording is the blend Ma and Ax, frequent collaborators, achieve: At times it sounds as though the cello is lodged deep in the midsection of the keyboard, and Ax uses a soft, bell-like tone to coax Ma a bit more into the forefront. As they weave ideas together and joust playfully, you can hear just how enchanted these two musicians are by these rich scores.

GENRE: 🎧 Classical. **RELEASED:** 1992, Sony Classical. **KEY TRACKS:** Opus 38: first movement (Allegro non troppo). Opus 99: second movement (Adagio affettuoso). **ANOTHER INTERPRETATION:** Jacqueline du Pré and Daniel Barenboim. **CATALOG CHOICE:** *Violin Sonatas* (see p. 113). **NEXT STOP:** Edward Elgar: *Cello Concerto, Sea Pictures,* Jacqueline du Pré, London Symphony Orchestra (Sir John Barbirolli, cond.).

Craft, on an Orchestral Scale

The Four Symphonies

Johannes Brahms
NDR Symphony (Gunther Wand, cond.)

The symphonies of Johannes Brahms are built on granite foundations—solid musical ideas that can initially seem less than sexy. Where Beethoven seeks to push limits of harmony, phrase length, and rhythm, Brahms (1833–1897) establishes a comfortable basic perimeter, and never lets the heavy machinery venture outside of it. His four pieces for orchestra represent a scholarly consolidation of everything he knew; he didn't begin writing symphonies until after he turned forty, telling students he believed it was not a form to be tackled by the young. So, not surprisingly, there's little youthful impulsiveness in them: Sometimes Brahms's themes seem to lumber along. Just when you're about to give up, he tosses out a soaring melody, a blossom of pure grace that not merely redeems, but greatly expands, what came before it.

"Brahms has . . . the reputation for being a grump, even though few could also be as lovable as he."
—Gustav Jenner

Each of the symphonies—which are often packaged together because they share strategies and temperaments—shows off a different facet of Brahms's melodic genius. The tight cell that defines Symphony No. 2, for example, is just three ordinary notes. From this simple beginning, the composer leads his listeners through a watch-what-I-can-do romp—he inverts the line, turns it sideways, and then, when he gets to the triumphant final movement, augments the core phrase with a few additional notes. These spark a new game of variations.

Brahms lived much of his adult life in sexual frustration. While boarding at the home of Robert and Clara Schumann, he fell in love with Clara.

Their relationship never went anywhere, not even after Robert died, and Brahms pined away, lamenting the lost love of his life. As a result, he put his anguish on display in his compositions—it's audible in the slow opening to Symphony No. 1, and the second and fourth movements of Symphony No. 4. As played by the NDR Symphony, with Gunther Wand at the helm, the finale of the Fourth Symphony is like a dying man's flashback dream, with scenes of tragedy and joy bursting forth and then receding over a recurring pattern of eight chords. Brahms treats each event as a discrete scene, supporting them with slight changes of color, piling world upon world in a way that makes the mood swings consistently surprising.

GENRE: 🎵 Classical. **RELEASED:** 1983, RCA. **KEY TRACKS:** Symphony No. 2: first movement. Symphony No. 4. **ANOTHER INTERPRETATION:** Vienna Philharmonic (Leonard Bernstein, cond.). **CATALOG CHOICE:** *Double Concerto,* Isaac Stern, Yo-Yo Ma, Chicago Symphony Orchestra (Claudio Abbado, cond.). **NEXT STOP:** Ludwig van Beethoven: *Symphonies Nos. 3 & 8,* Cleveland Orchestra (George Szell, cond.). **AFTER THAT:** Franz Schubert: *Eight Symphonies,* Berlin Philharmonic (Karl Böhm, cond.).

Brahms, with No Excess Charisma

Violin Sonatas, Opp. 78, 100, 108

Johannes Brahms
Josef Suk, Julius Katchen

Sometimes composers "front-load" the beginning of a piece to capture the audience's attention. And sometimes instrumentalists, even great ones, do the same, starting a piece with exaggerated flourishes. Then, once attention is sufficiently grabbed, "real" music making can begin. The Czech violinist Josef Suk and American pianist Julius Katchen take an opposite approach on Brahms's Violin Sonata, Op. 100: They start unassumingly, following the momentum of Brahms's line, letting the theme unfold at its own pace. Pretty soon, pure music flows out of the wondrous calm. The fragmentary ideas gather into the first great "theme"—an outpouring of ecstatic lyricism from the violin. By movement's end, what started as a matter-of-fact discussion between two musicians has blossomed into a complete, and demanding, idea.

That sensitivity prevails throughout this performance of three peak-period Brahms sonatas, written in 1879, 1886, and 1888. It's audible in the gentleness of the piano phrasing of Opus 78, which is nicknamed the "Rain" Sonata for its steady, consoling rhythms. And it's there in the final movement of Opus 108, when the interplay

Brahms devised swells into symphonic gales that foretell a tragedy. Here, Brahms's painstaking exactness becomes clear: The parts are independent and largely equal—a sharing that leads to high-spirited passages.

Suk and Katchen performed together regularly for decades (until Katchen died in 1969), and developed a devoted, if small, following. Their taciturn readings have grown in stature as classical music has gotten charisma-happy: Here is clear, clean, old-school interpretation, with no outsized gestures, just beautiful, logical Brahms.

GENRE: 🎧 Classical. **RELEASED:** 1967, Decca. **KEY TRACKS:** Opus 78: first movement. Opus 108: third movement. **CATALOG CHOICE:** *Piano Trios,* Josef Suk, Julius Katchen, János Starker. **NEXT STOP:** Raphael Ensemble: *Brahms String Sextets, Nos. 1 and 2.*

The Piano Glows Here

Piano Concerto No. 2

Johannes Brahms
Sviatoslav Richter, Chicago Symphony Orchestra (Erich Leinsdorf, cond.)

This is like John Barrymore playing Hamlet—an auspicious pairing of genius performer and masterpiece. Written between 1878 and 1881, the Piano Concerto No. 2 is Brahms's most formidable offering for piano and orchestra, a dense work in which elements of symphonic form are utilized to fulfill the virtuoso-showcase imperatives of the concerto. It's a full meal of a piece, and Russian pianist Sviatoslav Richter (1915–1997), one of the most agile, electrifying pianists of his day, devours it. This recording, which was made during his first tour of the U.S. in 1960, takes Brahms to deeply emotional places.

Richter is one of "the most powerful musical communicators of our time." —Glenn Gould

Brahms gives each of the four movements the character of a Romantic-era symphony—the second is a tense scherzo (marked "allegro appassionato"), the third a doleful andante. There are fleet-fingered, technically demanding passages for the soloist—at times in the first two movements, Richter sounds like he's shoving the strings to the sidelines, insisting on center stage. When he gets there, he earns the attention by rattling out low-register chords, or dashing off commanding technical passages, including several rollicking descending lines that feel like a tumble down a long flight of stairs.

Richter's playing traverses extremes of sound. He's able to bring a superhuman force to the crescendos and executes jarring peaks that bring the first movement to a torrid close. But these heated flashes are followed almost immediately by calmer atmospheres, and whenever Brahms calls for a light touch, Richter provides it, insinuating himself into the fabric of the ensemble. The quieter moments (particularly those in the astoundingly serene third movement) showcase another Richter signature—the pearly, glowing "resonance" he coaxes from the piano. Even on this vintage live recording, that rare quality shines through.

GENRE: 🎧 Classical. **RELEASED:** 1961, RCA. **KEY TRACKS:** First movement (Allegro Non Troppo); third movement (Andante). **CATALOG CHOICE:** *The Four Symphonies* (see p. 112). **NEXT STOP:** Franz Liszt: *Two Piano Concertos, Piano Sonata* (see p. 449). **AFTER THAT:** Ludwig van Beethoven: *The Late Sonatas*, Richard Goode.

Extreme Saxophonistics

For Alto

Anthony Braxton

For his second recording under his own name, Anthony Braxton devised solo pieces he said were inspired by and dedicated to musicians and friends who'd influenced him. The nine-minute piece for composer John Cage finds Braxton, one of the visionaries of avant-garde jazz, rifling through a blur of intervallic caprices, then stopping abruptly (in Cage-like fashion) as if to change a setting on the horn, before launching a series of shrieks that ascend up to frequencies only canines can hear. In the context of these squiggles and clusters, structure is elusive at best.

For Alto is dizzying and maddening, dense and challenging, inventive and off-putting. It's also among a handful of great solo saxophone recordings in jazz, alongside the unaccompanied tunes on Eric Dolphy's *Far Cry*. Like Dolphy's frenetic solo endeavors, Braxton's *For Alto* can be appreciated as a work of great gale-force invention—to hear the altoist at peak, check out the segment inspired by pianist Cecil Taylor, during which his alto chases echoes of the blues. And yet, some sections do have governing compositional ideas, and as is true of Braxton's later compositions for ensembles of various sizes, they're represented by geometric diagrams in the accompanying booklet. (One clue about Braxton's enterprise comes in liner notes he wrote for this but didn't use, in which the saxophonist and composer expresses great regard for the avant-garde musical strategies concepts of Karlheinz Stockhausen.)

The sheer amount of music here is

Over the course of his career, Anthony Braxton has released over 100 albums.

overwhelming. Even though Braxton uses contrasting tones and techniques to make each piece a distinct experience, it can be too much to appreciate in one sitting. Taken in small doses, however, *For Alto* is a riveting blast of fresh air, radically adventurous early gems from one of the most important thinkers in jazz.

GENRE: 🅙 Jazz.
RELEASED: 1969, Delmark.
KEY TRACKS: "To Composer John Cage," "To Pianist Cecil Taylor."
CATALOG CHOICES: *Five Pieces; News from the '70s.* **F.Y.I.:** An avid chess player, Braxton supported himself for a while in the 1960s as a chess "hustler" in New York City's Washington Square Park. **NEXT STOP:** Eric Dolphy: *Far Cry.* **AFTER THAT:** Dave Holland: *Conference of the Birds* (see p. 362).

An Auteur Paints His First Masterpiece

I'm Wide Awake, It's Morning

Bright Eyes

The new millennium's first New Dylan, Conor Oberst has a whiny voice and a penchant for piling up run-on sentences. (The title of his 2002 breakthrough, *Lifted, or The Story Is in the Soil, Keep Your Ear to the Ground,* is indicative.) A proud antisinger, he sometimes shouts when he's run out of more artful moves. He can sound royally pissed off whether provoked or not. Like others of his generation, he throws spectacular me-so-wounded tantrums that at times seem overly dramatic.

Amazingly, on this staggering set of songs, these traits aren't as grating as you'd think—they snap Oberst's accounts of betrayal and duplicity into a kind of emo high drama. The Nebraska native, who goes by the nom de rock

Bright Eyes, started recording at age fourteen. With this record, made when he was twenty-two, he surrounds the guitar-and-voice screeds that populated earlier albums with strikingly varied accompaniments. These defy genre classification—tunes that tell of existential crisis, like "We Are Nowhere and It's Now," are cradled by gentle meditating mandolin and piano, the love child of upbeat country and slouchy slacker rock.

The set suggests that Oberst has come

to recognize the limits of ranting and raving. Always attentive to (some would say "obsessed" with) his words, Oberst for the first time here seems just as interested in finding musical ways to enhance and expand his meanings. The stark, lovely melodies (check "At the Bottom of Everything") are augmented with swelling strings, carnival horns, and other funhouse trappings. But perhaps the best evidence of Oberst's evolution is the presence of Emmylou Harris (see p. 344) on

Conor Oberst (right) lists the Cure, Neil Young, and Emmylou Harris among his influences.

several selections. One of the great harmony vocalists of all time, Harris smooths the edge of Oberst's voice, blunts the bitterness of his tone. Their intertwined voices send a paranoid meditation on freedom, "Landlocked Blues," into a floating, deliciously ethereal airspace. A place that *sounds* free.

GENRE: 🎸 Rock. **RELEASED:** 2005, Saddle Creek. **KEY TRACKS:** "At the Bottom of Everything," "We Are Nowhere and It's Now," "Landlocked Blues," "Road to Joy." **CATALOG CHOICE:** *Lifted, or The Story Is in the Soil, Keep Your Ear to the Ground.* **NEXT STOP:** Calexico: *The Black Light.* **AFTER THAT:** Ed Harcourt: *Here Be Monsters.*

A British Seafaring Saga, Set to Music

Peter Grimes

Benjamin Britten
Jon Vickers, Heather Harper, Royal Opera House Orchestra and Chorus (Sir Colin Davis, cond.)

An outsider with rage-a-holic tendencies, the fisherman Peter Grimes is mistrusted by the people of his small town. He has a habit of hiring boy apprentices and losing them at sea. The opera opens at a court hearing (there's no overture), where Grimes, sung here by Jon Vickers, convinces the authorities that the latest situation was accidental. The people remain suspicious—much of the dialog consists of gossip: In one telling scene, Grimes enters a tavern during a storm only to find that he's the main topic of conversation, and of course he's shunned. Later Grimes returns from an expedition having lost another apprentice. This turns the town into an angry mob. The final scene is a heartbreaker: Grimes arrives onstage alone, barely outrunning the crowd. His only friend tells him his best option is to take the fishing boat out to sea, and commit suicide by sinking it. He's last seen heading away from the shore. End of opera.

Peter Grimes is British composer Benjamin Britten's second opera, and his most famous. It was premiered in 1945, and it represents something unusual for twentieth-century music: Its language is thoroughly modern, built from sharp angles and juxtapositions, yet avoids atonality.

The motifs hold plenty of challenges—some of the leading roles walked out before the premiere, claiming their parts were unsingable—but are also, in their own way, rhapsodic.

Usually, the sexual orientation of composers doesn't impact our understanding of a piece—Handel was probably gay and who cares? Britten (1913–1976) is a different story. He was gay, and wrote with sympathy about outsiders like Grimes; it's highly unlikely that Grimes would be as resonant a character had its composer not been acquainted with social stigma, disapproving neighbors, and all the rest.

The role of Peter Grimes was introduced by Britten's longtime partner, Peter Pears, who became one of the great English tenors of his time. When this austere production appeared in the 1970s, Vickers drew significant criticism—according to legend, Britten walked out on the performance. There are pronounced differences: Pears played Grimes as a sensitive soul caught in brutal circumstances; Vickers approaches the character as more of a blue-collar brute.

One additional reason to seek out the Vickers version is the Royal Opera House Orchestra, which wrings every ounce of drama from Britten's sea scenes. These aren't the peaceful lapping waves of Debussy's *La mer*. In conductor Sir Colin Davis's rendering, Britten's ocean is a vast, heaving, relentlessly uncontrollable force, cruel, random, and unforgiving. In other words, perfect for the subject.

GENRE: 🎵 Opera. **RELEASED:** 1978, Philips. **KEY TRACKS:** Act 1: "The Truth . . . the Pity . . . and the Truth"; Act 2: "Fool to Let It Come to This." **OTHER INTERPRETATIONS:** Peter Pears, Covent Garden Royal Opera House Chorus and Orchestra (Britten, cond.). *Four Sea Interludes from Peter Grimes,* London Symphony Orchestra (Andre Previn, cond.). **CATALOG CHOICE:** *Death in Venice,* Peter Pears. **NEXT STOP:** Igor Stravinsky: *Rite of Spring* (see p. 750).

The Best of Early Broonzy

The Young Big Bill Broonzy, 1928–1935

Big Bill Broonzy

During the 1940s, Big Bill Broonzy was one of the kingmakers of Chicago blues—he recommended that several labels record a young unknown named Muddy Waters, and was revered as a wise elder by the city's guitarists, mainly for his steady-rolling ragtime guitar rhythm and the nimble "flatpicking" technique also used by Charley Patton and Blind Lemon Jefferson.

Before that, though, Broonzy (1898–1958) recorded some hugely entertaining early sides—rollicking pieces that combine the urgency of rural blues from the Mississippi Delta region (he was born in Scott, Mississippi) with a smooth, winkingly urbane singing style that was rare in country blues.

This collection spotlights some of Broonzy's best early work, including the piano-guitar duet "Good Liquor Gonna Carry Me Down" and a lusty vocal on "I Can't Be Satisfied" that became a touchstone for subsequent generations. (Waters's version of the song, his first big hit, hews close to this one.)

Beyond their appeal as straight-up entertainment, several tracks are of historical interest: They're collaborations between Broonzy and the pianist "Georgia Tom," aka Thomas Dorsey (see p. 233), who went on to become a major force in gospel music as the author of countless hymns.

Dorsey is anything but pious here, as he dispenses tavern-tested piano-isms and contributes to the bawdy banter between Broonzy and singer Jane Lucas. These energetic performances present Broonzy as one of the first blues artists to amalgamate

Big Bill Broonzy's style was influenced by spirituals, ragtime, and country blues.

elements of different styles into a seamless and highly personal sound. Even at this early stage, his approach to the blues was seriously contagious: Dorsey, for one, never sounded happier than he does on these sides.

GENRE: 🎵 Blues.
RELEASED: 1992, Yazoo.
KEY TRACKS: "Good Liquor Gonna Carry Me Down," "Hokum Stomp." **CATALOG CHOICE:** *Big Bill Broonzy Sings Folk Songs.* **NEXT STOP:** Muddy Waters: *Sings Big Bill Broonzy.* **AFTER THAT:** Lonnie Johnson: *Blues and Ballads.*

Go-Go Gets Real Gone

Any Other Way to Go?

Chuck Brown and the Soul Searchers

To hear why the Washington, D.C.–based guitarist and bandleader Chuck Brown calls his music go-go, check out this live performance, which catches Brown and his band the Soul Searchers at a zinging peak. Honed

in sweaty and inhospitably crowded D.C. nightclubs, this hybrid style is all about forward motion. Its simple bass-and-drums backbeat has hypnotic power—often the same groove cruises for hours, serving as the foundation for a high-speed chase through unlikely musical worlds. On an average night, Brown weaves bits of *Star Wars* music or TV cartoon themes (check out the version of "Woody Woodpecker" here) between jazz, torch songs, and funk chants.

Chuck Brown, the creator of go-go, is a local legend in Washington, D.C.

This set begins with an update of Duke Ellington's "It Don't Mean a Thing If It Ain't Got That Swing," which serves as a clue about what follows: This rubbery, high-intensity groove swings like the proverbial barnyard gate. The tunes flow together as a medley; they're often connected only by Brown's chicken-scratching rhythm guitar, which resembles Ike Turner's wickedly terse approach. Soloists from the horn section claim the spotlight briefly and then disappear, and every now and then the groove stops abruptly, only to roar back with greater force. It's impossible to remain still when the Soul Searchers are playing: If you're not dancing, you're at least nodding your head.

The so-called "Godfather of Go-Go," Brown taught his groove to several generations of musicians—among his disciples were E.U. (which had a hit with "Da'Butt" from the *School Daze* soundtrack), and the more progressive Trouble Funk. When those bands began to attract national attention in the late 1980s, Brown seemed destined to break big. Things didn't quite work out—his studio sides could be erratic—but Brown, undaunted, never stopped performing. As the live *Any Other Way To Go?* makes clear, he continued to expand the go-go horizons—check out the way he and the Soul Searchers twist a jazz standard like "Moody's Mood for Love" into a risqué booty call.

GENRE: 🅡 R&B. **RELEASED:** 1988, Verve. **KEY TRACKS:** "Moody's Mood for Love," "Family Affair," "Harlem Nocturne." **CATALOG CHOICE:** *This Is a Journey . . . Into Time.* **NEXT STOP:** Trouble Funk: *Live.* **AFTER THAT:** The Soul Rebels: *Rebelution.*

The Sound of Jazz Precision

Clifford Brown and Max Roach

Clifford Brown–Max Roach Quintet

Some jazz trumpet players paint pretty landscapes, others smear notes like they're spreading butter on a biscuit. Clifford Brown—the pied piper of post bop who was killed in 1956 at age twenty-five in an accident on the Pennsylvania Turnpike—played like he was lighting firecrackers. His attack was dizzyingly precise. He placed notes exactly on the part of the beats he intended to hit. He had the spark of great bebop and the lazy warmth of cool jazz. And whether the music moved at a technically demanding clip or was to be caressed at ballad tempo, the soft-spoken musician his friends called "Brownie" had a way of nudging things toward greatness. "He could change from a meek lamb, musically, into a fierce tiger," saxophonist Benny Golson once said of Brown, whose recording career spanned just four years. "He could play the bottom, top, loud, soft. He was playing the whole instrument."

This album, the first of several featuring a group Brown co-led with drummer Max Roach (1924–2007), offers endless examples—the exquisite bebop of "Daahoud," the fanciful clip of "Parisian Thoroughfare," the slalom-like chord sequence of Brown's original "Joy Spring," which catches him doing one of the neatest bob-and-weave maneuvers in all of jazz.

Also notable is Golson's "Blues Walk," which Brown treats more like a blues chase—he keeps the trumpet in constant motion, tossing out genius lines left and right, and when he finally finishes, it feels like he's just run a marathon. And somehow carved a masterpiece of sculpture along the way.

GENRE: 🅙 Jazz. **RELEASED:** 1955, EmArcy. **KEY TRACKS:** "Joy Spring," "Jordu," "These Foolish Things," "The Blues Walk." **CATALOG CHOICES:** Brown: *The Beginning and the End.* Roach: *We Insist!: Freedom Now Suite* (see p. 647). **NEXT STOP:** Booker Little: *Out Front* (see p. 450).

Hardest-Working Man Lives Up to His Billing

Live at the Apollo (1962)

James Brown

"**A**re you ready for Star Time?" emcee Lucas "Fats" Gonder asks the fifteen hundred fans assembled for the Apollo Theater's late show on October 24, 1962, the week of the Cuban missile crisis. The question is, of course, utterly academic: By the time Gonder, who also plays organ, finishes his list of James Brown's hits and begins introducing "Mr. Dynamite," "The Amazing Mr. Please Please Please Himself," Star Time is well under way. Brown enters during the third chorus of the scampering blues called "The Search" and, while the faithful are still screaming, launches a forty-minute assault that would go on to become one of the most thrilling live albums in pop history.

Brown was ready—in the liner notes to the deluxe edition he recalls weeks spent practicing every detail of his act for this engagement, his fifth at the Apollo as a headliner. (Like many R&B artists, he knew it as a place where even seasoned performers are tested, and knew, also, that positive word of mouth from the show would travel everywhere.) Starting with "I'll Go Crazy," Brown doesn't merely tame the notoriously fickle Apollo crowd, he blows them clear to the red-velvet back wall of the theater. In the two minutes of "Think," Brown and his agile Famous Flames create a rippling wave of raw emotion; whirling together love ballads including "I Found Someone" and "Please, Please, Please," he offers a pleading epic on the vicissitudes of romance.

Brown subsidized the Apollo recording himself, after King Records honcho Syd Nathan refused, arguing that no live record could sell without an accompanying single. After hearing the tapes, the executive relented and agreed to release *Live at the Apollo,* which has endured ever since as an indispensable primer on the fine points of live performance. Unexpectedly, the album became a monster hit, Brown's first million-seller. And it did get played on the radio—individual songs during the day, and longer stretches of it at night. Rocky G, the program director of New York's WWRL radio station, once said that "People were always calling in, asking us to play 'JamesBrown-LiveattheApollo'—one word, like it was the name of one of his songs."

Brown returned to the storied Harlem theater to record another live album in 1968, at a time when the band was hotter, and more tuned to the funk. He reprises several of the songs from the 1962 version ("Think" among them) and, listening back-to-back, you can hear how a few years of intense roadwork toughened up the tune. The highlight of this set is a medley of "Let Yourself Go," "There Was a Time," "I Feel All Right," and "Cold Sweat" that lasts twenty riveting minutes and could easily have gone twenty more.

GENRE: 🎙 R&B. **RELEASED:** 1962, King. **KEY TRACKS:** "Please, Please, Please," "Think." **CATALOG CHOICE:** *Revolution of the Mind.* **NEXT STOP:** Funkadelic: *One Nation Under a Groove.* **AFTER THAT:** D'Angelo: *Voodoo.*

Ain't It Funky Now?

Soul Pride:
The Instrumentals, 1960–1969

James Brown

A secret history of the 1960s lurks inside this two-disc survey. It concerns the "other" James Brown (1933–2006), the bandleader and sometime organist who carried the grooves that made him famous into after-hours gigs and late-night recording sessions. Brown recorded more than eleven full-length instrumental albums during the '60s; he and the band played down-and-dirty slow blues, roaring boogaloo, and an intense agitated jazz-funk. These records didn't sell a lot, but they were influential: Rhythm section players from all corners of popular music study them still.

Drop in anywhere, and you'll encounter a band accustomed to the demanding work of backing the Godfather of Soul. Except here, everybody's laying back just a smidgen. Solos stretch on expansively—hear Maceo Parker, the master of horn funk, at full steam, cue up "The Popcorn," a serving of hotly tongued saxophone explosiveness. Brown himself is more than a name on the marquee: Check the big-band blues "Sumpin' Else" and the live up-tempo "Devil's Den" to hear him play smart, scooting organ solos. Also here is the original mix of "Funky Drummer," the showcase for the mighty Clyde Stubblefield.

These recordings show exactly what goes into the wound-tight James Brown groove. Every musician understands how his contribution, even if it's a simple two-note horn riff, fits into the big picture. The rhythm section snaps out backbeats that are loose yet taut, agitated yet restrained—on this bandstand, the biggest sin is to overplay. When everybody's locked together, the result is a backbeat that deserves to be regarded as a national treasure.

GENRE: 🎵 R&B. **RELEASED:** 1992, Polydor. **KEY TRACKS:** "Hold It," "Sumpin' Else," "Devil's Den," "Gittin' a Little Hipper," "The Popcorn," "Sudsy." **CATALOG CHOICE:** *In the Jungle Groove.* **NEXT STOP:** Sly and the Family Stone: *There's a Riot Goin' On.* **AFTER THAT:** Idris Muhammad: *Power of Soul.*

The Band Lasted a Year, Impacted Generations

"Sex Machine"

James Brown and the JB's

An unstoppable force through most of the 1960s, James Brown hit a rough patch in 1969, when his longtime band, known as the Famous Flames, walked out on him. For most fussy and demanding singers, this might be a catastrophe; for Brown, it proved to be a new lease on life. A few months later, in early 1970, Brown hired a Cincinnati group known as the Pacemakers, who'd been pestering people at the James Brown Productions office. Among the teenage musicians were bassist William Collins and his brother, guitarist Phelps Collins—better known as "Bootsy" and "Catfish," respectively.

Here's how good the group was: Among the fruits of its first day in the recording studio was "Get Up (I Feel Like Being a) Sex Machine."

That was not beginner's luck. It's pure rhythm euphoria built from the simplest of tools, just a two-note recurring guitar phrase and a tightly wound bass figure. A minimalist in the studio, Brown was constantly seeking these kinds of all-day vamps; inside his extemporaneous vocals is the sound of a man who knows he's hit paydirt, and is determined to enjoy every funky minute. Nobody has to work hard to keep things going—already masters of the controlled burn, the Collins brothers might be playing the same phrase over and over, but by leaning into certain notes, and adding slight emphasis in key places, they keep the vamp at the very edge of percolation. Whatever happens on top of it—at

The original version of "Sex Machine" opens with a short dialogue between Brown and the JB's.

one point Brown asks tenorman Robert MacCollough to "blow me some 'Trane, brother"—is, in a real sense, totally secondary.

"Sex Machine" became a hit, and its architecture served as the template for much of Brown's '70s work, even though this band would only record with Brown for a year. The best way to encounter the tune is on the compilation *Funk Power 1970: A Brand New Thang*, which includes the ten-minute studio jam of "Sex Machine" and the single mix, as well as "Super Bad" and "Talking Loud and Saying Nothing." Its nine tracks (there's also an antidrug public service message) amount to the last bursts of true greatness from the Godfather—incendiary 1000-watt groove vamps that defined a whole new phase of funk.

GENRE: 🎤 R&B. **RELEASED:** 1970, Polydor. **APPEARS ON:** *Funk Power 1970: A Brand New Thang* (1996, Polydor). **CATALOG CHOICE:** *Love Power Peace, Live at L'Olympia, Paris, 1971,* which, despite its too-fast tempos, is the best document of the JB's band in performance. **NEXT STOP:** Sly and the Family Stone: *Stand!* (see p. 713). **AFTER THAT:** Bootsy Collins and Bootsy's Rubber Band: *Ahhh . . . The Name Is Bootsy, Baby!*

The Best from the Thinking Person's Hipster

Sin and Soul

Oscar Brown Jr.

The gavel falls, and Oscar Brown Jr., playing the role of slave auctioneer, begins "selling" a fifteen-year-old girl from the Dahomey region of Africa. In brisk and businesslike patter, the Chicago-born singer, songwriter, and playwright reels off her attributes like a car salesman touting the latest features.

The a cappella "Bid 'Em In" is coarse and crass, and impossible to forget. Certainly

Brown, an African American, is repulsed by this chapter in history—yet throughout the "auction," which lasts a minute and twenty-eight seconds, he never breaks character. He comports himself the way slave owners did, not bothering to examine his actions. Or their implications.

The Chicago-based Brown (1926–2005) was a master of this kind of theatrical role play—elsewhere on his instant classic debut *Sin and Soul* he imagines himself toiling on a chain gang ("Work Song," the Nat Adderley composition for which Brown wrote lyrics), and plays a loser trying to remain suave while the world crumbles around him ("But I Was Cool"). Too much of an entertainer to dwell forever on the tragic, Brown leavens his commentary with more playful songs, including the amazing "Dat Dere," which celebrates the endless questioning curiosity of children.

Sin and Soul was one of two albums involving Brown released in 1960. The other was Max Roach's *We Insist! Freedom Now Suite* (see p. 647). These works established Brown as a visionary, one of a handful of African American artists whose bold work set the tone for the Afrocentrism that erupted later in the decade. What makes Brown so effective is that his message is strong but never merely confrontational: When he sings his original "Brown Baby" (which was famously covered by Mahalia Jackson), it's a lullaby, driven by a father's resolute hope for the child he holds, and really all children: "When out of men's hearts all the hate is hurled," he sings, "you're gonna live in a better world."

GENRES: 🅐 Jazz 🅥 Vocals. **RELEASED:** 1960, Columbia. (Reissued 1996 as *Sin and Soul . . . and Then Some*.) **KEY TRACKS:** "Work Song," "Bid 'Em In," "Signifyin' Monkey," "Dat Dere." **COLLECTOR'S NOTE:** The reissue includes five tracks Brown wrote for his short-lived Broadway musical *Kicks and Co.* **CATALOG CHOICE:** *Mr. Oscar Brown Jr. Goes to Washington.* **NEXT STOP:** Nina Simone: *Anthology* (see p. 705). **AFTER THAT:** Public Enemy: *Fear of a Black Planet.*

She Put the R&B in R&B

Miss Rhythm

Ruth Brown

Ruth Brown's brash, bright, brilliantly sung early hits helped set the table for the rhythm and blues explosion of the 1950s. Initially influenced by Dinah Washington (see p. 847), Brown learned early how to turn out a sorrowful torch song—check out her blue inflections on the big band warhorse "Sentimental Journey" here. Then, aided by rhythmically adventurous backing musicians versed in jazz and blues, she transported that wise way of singing to the lively rhythms of jump blues and its offshoots. The result was something mesmerizing—music suffused with the rashness of young love and informed by a veteran crooner's knowledge about the perils of romance.

Miss Rhythm gathers Brown's key early singles for Atlantic Records, many of which were not released on albums at the time. It's a showcase for tremendously disciplined singing, defined by Brown's attention to the subtleties of the beat, and her judicious ad-libbing. Among its delights are "Teardrops from My Eyes," which topped the R&B charts for eleven weeks in 1950, and "Mama, He Treats Your Daughter Mean." This being the

'50s, there are dance-craze songs ("Mambo Baby") and several rockin' gems by Leiber and Stoller, the hit-making team behind the Coasters ("I Can't Hear a Word You Say").

These singles and others put Atlantic Records on the map—before Ray Charles came along, Atlantic was known as "the house that Ruth built." Brown wasn't able to maintain that success, however, and by the mid-'60s she'd dropped out of sight. After working as a maid, she returned in the 1980s to mount a sustained comeback. At that time, Brown was also among a handful of R&B pioneers who successfully campaigned to collect unpaid royalties; her work helped change the way labels compensated often-neglected heritage artists.

GENRE: 🎖 R&B. **RELEASED:** 1989, Atlantic. (Singles recorded 1949–1960.) (Reissued 1999, Collectables.) **KEY TRACKS:** "Teardrops from My Eyes," "Lucky Lips," "Sentimental Journey," "Mama, He Treats Your Daughter Mean." **CATALOG CHOICE:** *Have a Good Time.* **NEXT STOP:** Esther Phillips: *Burnin'.* **AFTER THAT:** LaVern Baker: *LaVern Baker.*

Self-Inquiry as Art

Late for the Sky

Jackson Browne

Jackson Browne has the ability to sing about fantastic tangles of emotions and make it seem as if he's been there—or, more impressively, is there still. His songs examine messes in progress, and relationships that unravel unexpectedly. The action might be limited, but Browne keeps close watch on the emotional temperature: By the end of one of his epics (like, say, "Before the Deluge" here) you may feel wrung out, like you've just lived through a two-hanky feature film.

And at the same time you're enriched, because Browne, the most introspective of the California singer-songwriters, has a way of drawing illumination (if not consolation) out of painful circumstances. On the classic *Late for the Sky*, his third effort, the songs are the surprisingly unself-conscious thoughts of a lost seeker—someone who's out there by himself, running down the big questions. This inquiry leads him into the minefields of memory ("Fountain of Sorrow,"

Jackson Brown was inducted into the Rock and Roll Hall of Fame by his friend Bruce Springsteen in 2004.

in which a photograph opens the floodgates) and extended, voyeuristic character studies ("For a Dancer," perhaps the most beautiful song in Browne's book).

If you only get to hear one Browne song in your life, make it "The Late Show," which suggests that Browne, known primarily as a word guy, has a knack for the cinematic. The mood is all pent-up restlessness. Browne's protagonist is waiting in the car ("let's just say an early model Chevrolet"), trying to convince his lover that it's time to escape.

"You go and pack your sorrows," he tells her. "The trash man comes tomorrow./Leave it by the curb, and we'll just pull away." At that culminating moment, where you'd expect a massive swell, the music becomes eerily placid. A piano plinks calmly. The next sound is a perfectly timed car door slamming, which kicks things into overdrive. Skies part. Motor revs. And guitarist David Lindley, Browne's secret weapon, serves up poignant weeping leads that send the couple riding off into the L.A. sunset, destination unknown.

GENRE: 🎸 Rock. **RELEASED:** 1974, Asylum. **KEY TRACKS:** "The Late Show," "For a Dancer," "Fountain of Sorrow." **CATALOG CHOICES:** *Running on Empty; Jackson Browne.* **NEXT STOP:** Neil Young: *After the Gold Rush* (see p. 885). **AFTER THAT:** David Baerwald: *Triage.*

A Massive Symphonic Homage to Wagner

Symphony No. 7 in E

Anton Bruckner

Royal Scottish National Orchestra (Georg Tintner, cond.)

The knock against the Austro-German symphonist Anton Bruckner (1824–1896) goes like this: He was obsessed with the sweeping gestures of Richard Wagner and quick to echo Wagner's devices in pieces that wandered and swelled portentously but wound up lacking melodic substance. Bruckner's symphonies are long (No. 8 lasts eighty minutes). The conductor Arturo Toscanini once complained that the devout Catholic "never gets off his knees," loading even his symphonic music with a suffocating piousness.

This work, Bruckner's biggest hit, turns those negatives into virtues—it's a grandiose, majestic statement in which each theme feels like a thoughtful offering to the glory of God. It was written in 1883, and at least partly inspired by the death of Wagner: Bruckner told a conductor friend that the second movement, the Adagio in C-Sharp, came to him just after a premonition of Wagner's demise. Although the tone is set by trembling strings in the opening movement, the piece takes off in the ominous, enveloping second movement, which lasts twenty-five minutes. If he's stingy with memorable melodies

"Bruckner: half simpleton, half God."   —Gustav Mahler

elsewhere, Bruckner lays out a feast here, and his serpentine strung-together lines, written on church organ, grapple with big unanswered questions that don't resolve in conventional amen-cadence ways.

The Adagio helps clarify Bruckner's historical place: He's the evolutionary link between Wagner and Mahler, transforming some of Wagner's dramatic impulses to orchestral music. The young Mahler attended the Vienna premiere of Bruckner's Third Symphony and recalled it as a key moment.

This version of Bruckner's seventh symphony, recorded in 1999, is conducted by Georg Tintner, who was educated in Austria but, like many other artists, fled the Nazis. It catches him late in his career—learning he had terminal cancer, he committed suicide not long after making this recording—and is the jewel in a sparkling, deeply restrained set of recordings of all nine Bruckner symphonies.

GENRE:  Classical. **RELEASED:**
1999, Naxos. **KEY TRACK:** Adagio
(second movement). **CATALOG CHOICES:**

Masses Nos. 2 and 3, English Chamber
Orchestra (Daniel Barenboim, cond.).
NEXT STOP: Gustav Mahler: *Symphony
No. 4* (see p. 468).

A Voice Prematurely Lost

Grace

Jeff Buckley

Reading the eulogies and appreciations of Jeff Buckley—the singer and songwriter who drowned in Memphis in 1997 at age thirty—it was easy to feel that a major voice, if not the last best hope of rock, had been
stilled. In fact, Buckley, the son of cult songwriter Tim Buckley (see next page), was then at work on just his second full album. The rhapsodic praise for him was based on this one set of songs—and transcendent live shows during which he'd practically levitate off the ground, singing airborne melodies in a voice kissed with equal helpings of angelic purity and demon lust. Buckley struck some admirers as a rock god à la those of the

David Bowie listed *Grace* as "one of the 10 albums he'd bring with him to a desert island."

mystical late 1960s, a singer forever in search of unattainable ecstasy. At the same time he could sound like a tortured Sylvia Plath type, desperate to convey a particular depth of feeling. He could wail like an opera singer nearing the big final scene, and create extemporaneous themes like a jazz player. Among his favorite singers was the *qawwali* master Nusrat Fateh Ali Khan (see p. 422), whose reeling, stemwinding improvisations have no parallel in Western music.

Grace stands alone in '90s rock. It's a showcase for an unforgettably poised singing voice in an era of leather-lung shouters, and it locates fertile ground somewhere between classic rock and the scruffier music happening in the wake of grunge. Buckley took the episodic outbursts

of Nirvana and surrounded them with elegant, yearning melodies that echo the late Beatles. He wrote more than a few epics: "Mojo Pin" volleys between pensive moments and thundering Led Zeppelin tumult.

At each step he knows exactly which musical textures should surround his voice. At times he sings over a chorus of forceful rhythm guitars and at other moments Buckley's voice stands alone in an ethereal mist. These contrasts make *Grace* so riveting. At a time when many rockers rejected anything that smacked of "classic rock," Buckley bathed in its long shadow, delighted in its mysticism, reveled in possibilities his peers scoffed at. In the process he showed several generations that profoundly new rock and roll doesn't necessarily involve the wholesale rejection of what came before.

GENRE:  Rock. **RELEASED:** 1994,
Columbia. **KEY TRACKS:** "Mojo Pin," "Last
Goodbye," "So Real," "Hallelujah." **CATALOG
CHOICES:** *Live at Sin-e; The Grace EPs;
Sketches (for My Sweetheart the Drunk).* **NEXT
STOP:** Elliott Smith: *XO* (see p. 716). **AFTER
THAT:** Jeremy Enigk: *Return of the Frog Queen.*

Dig This Crazy Jive . . .

His Royal Hipness

Lord Buckley

A jazz-scene rule-breaker who defined hipster culture at least a decade before the Beat poets, Richard Meryle "Lord" Buckley (1906–1960) was probably the only performer who could claim this trifecta: He jammed with Charlie Parker, was championed by Frank Zappa, and was enshrined in pop culture history by Bob Dylan. (There's a picture of Buckley on the mantel behind Dylan on the cover of *Bringing It All Back Home.*)

Beloved by underground types and virtually ignored by everyone else, Buckley's best trick was translating history into highly caffeinated jive. When, for example, he tells the story of "Marc Antony's Funeral Oration," the line "Friends, Romans, countrymen, lend me your ears" becomes "Hipsters, flipsters, and finger-poppin' daddies, knock me your lobes." Buckley put a metaphysical spin on Jesus ("The Nazz," who was, in his parlance, "a carpenter kitty") and Gandhi ("The Hip Gan"). All of Buckley's subjects got the same treatment: Approaching historical figures as mythic jazz cats, he spun their legends in torrents of words that blur the

Lord Buckley also gave his friends and family noble titles.

patois of African Americans of the Deep South and the reverential airs of British aristocracy.

On this, the best existing anthology, Buckley uses instrumental accompaniment (organ, drums) sparingly. But he displays a serious sense of rhythm—anybody who's going to riff at such breakneck intensity better know where the downbeat is. He also has an uncanny ability to mimic various singing styles. His loving evocation of Louis Armstrong doing "When the Saints Go Marching In" at the end of "The Nazz" is an imitation so good it's double happiness—a loving celebration of the original that, like so much Lord Buckley, goes slyly beyond.

GENRE: 🎵 Vocals. **RELEASED:** 1992, Discovery. **KEY TRACKS:** "The Nazz," "The Hip Gan," "Gettysburg Address." **NEXT STOP:** Ken Nordine: *Word Jazz.*

A Masterpiece of Mystic Folk-Rock

Dream Letter: Live in London, 1968

Tim Buckley

R estless soul Tim Buckley (1947–1975) never stayed in one artistic place for long. At the time of his London Records debut in 1968, the singer, songwriter, and guitarist had two somewhat twee, rococo psychedelic folk-rock albums under his belt. Though both were acclaimed by critics, Buckley began moving in a different direction almost immediately—subsequent albums (particularly *Happy Sad*, from 1969) contain tunes with much looser structures, platforms for Buckley's wordless vocal flights and jazz-like group interplay.

This tour document, which features guitarist Lee Underwood and vibraphonist David Friedman, captures a potentially awkward transitional moment for Buckley—he is thinking in expansive, free-form terms, while his audience is expecting the saturnalia dreamscapes and wordy confessions of *Goodbye and Hello*. He manages to satisfy all here, looking both forward and backward in a way that makes *Dream Letter* a concise and ideal introduction to his work. Buckley serves up gorgeously pliant, questioning treatments of his familiar material as well as new songs in which his bliss-seeking voice is enhanced by Underwood, who sprinkles guitar serenity in the margins.

The group sounds like it's been play-

Like father, like son: Tim is the father of Jeff Buckley (see p. 126).

ing together for years (in fact, British bassist Danny Thompson was recruited just for these gigs); they bring a spirit of purposeful seeking to Buckley's sometimes cryptic meditations and story songs. The notoriously flinty Buckley expands (but never tramples) his writing, by occasionally changing around the DNA of his melodies à la Bob Dylan. Several times he juxtaposes verses from different originals together: After a strong verse of his literary "Pleasant Street," he launches into a passionate rendition of the Motown hit "You Keep Me Hangin' On." It's a stroke of genius, the linking of crazy abstraction with a hook so urgent and universal it lights up everything around it.

GENRES: 🎵 Folk 🎸 Rock. **RELEASED:** 1991, Manifesto/Bizarre-Straight. **KEY TRACKS:** "Buzzin' Fly," "Dolphins," "Morning Glory," "Pleasant Street/You Keep Me Hangin' On." **CATALOG CHOICES:** *Goodbye and Hello; Happy Sad.* **NEXT STOP:** Van Morrison: *Too Late to Stop Now.*

Believe the Title

Buckwheat's Zydeco Party

Buckwheat Zydeco

Stanley Dural Jr. spent much of the 1960s playing soul and R&B on the club circuit in the South. An adroit organist and gruff singer, he followed James Brown's example as a bandleader: He expected the music to be tight, played by musicians who showed up ready to entertain people. Sometime in the 1970s, just as interest in rural forms of Cajun music was awakening among young people, Dural began experimenting with his father's accordion and the music known as "zydeco" that the legend-ary Clifton Chenier (see p. 160) spearheaded in the 1950s. It wasn't long before Dural and his southern Louisiana musicians fluent in soul and Cajun styles came up with dance floor dynamite—a tastefully modernized version of the zydeco rhythm, buttressed with horns, a stomping rhythm section, and soul-revue panache. This idea spread quickly: Several generations of zydeco bands, most notably Beau Jocque and the Zydeco Hi-Rollers, followed Dural's example, covering rock songs and spicing up the tradition.

Zydeco Party contains material from the two albums Dural (stage name Buckwheat Zydeco) made for Rounder in the early '80s, just before signing a major-label contract. The timing is crucial: Though Dural crafted intermittently strong records after this, he fell victim to the excesses of "star time," cluttering his titles with pointless special guests and funk vamps that last way too long. Even his zydeco started to feel very Los Angeles.

Here, though, Dural and his quintet are still scrapping. Their rhythmic refinements aren't yet etched in stone, and as far as material's concerned, it's anything goes—

Buckwheat Zydeco (far left) jamming with Robert Plant (center) and Neil Young (right).

there's even a version of the Little Richard standby "Tutti Frutti." They're striving for common ground between New Orleans boogie and the stately Clifton Chenier waltzes and the greasier side of Stax-Volt R&B. When they hit the sweet spot—see "Hot Tamale Baby" and "Zydeco Boogaloo"—it's the musical equivalent of a high-revving big rig that's just discovered a previously untapped cruising gear. And intends to roll that way all night.

GENRE: 🌐 Blues. **RELEASED:** 1987, Rounder. **KEY TRACKS:** "Hot Tamale Baby," "Ya-Ya," "Someone Else Is Steppin' In," "Tutti Frutti," "Zydeco Boogaloo." **CATALOG CHOICE:** *On a Night Like This.* **NEXT STOP:** Beau Jocque and the Zydeco Hi-Rollers: *Pick Up On This!* **AFTER THAT:** Boozoo Chavis: *Johnnie Billy Goat.*

A Short-Lived but Influential Supergroup

Retrospective

Buffalo Springfield

I f the Rock Gods gave awards, Buffalo Springfield would deserve consideration for "Most Accomplished in the Least Amount of Time." The pioneering band, whose members included folk troubadours Stephen Stills, Neil Young,

Richie Furay, Dewey Martin, Bruce Palmer, and (later) Jim Messina, came together in 1966 and lasted less than two years. They made two albums as a cohesive group and another in a more splintered every-man-for-himself fashion, and in that time developed an earthy melding of folk, country, and rock that, along with the early albums of the Byrds, hugely influenced California pop rock of the '70s.

Buffalo Springfield's eponymous debut finds the group casting about for its sound—attempting its own approximation of tightly scripted British Invasion pop (Stephen Stills's beautiful "Sit Down I Think I Love You") as well as exploring barroom odes (Neil Young's "Nowadays Clancy Can't Even Sing") and percussion-spiced rockers ("Pay the Price"). The follow-up is erratic for different reasons. There are great tunes from Stills and Young, and three less interesting ones from Furay.

Both albums are consequential; neither captures the group's full story. As a result, *Retrospective* is the most satisfying way to encounter Buffalo Springfield. This carefully assembled collection begins with Stills's "For What It's Worth," one of the sage check-your-head anthems of the 1960s. Then it moves in a musically logical, nonchronological sequence that argues for the group's standing among the most adventurous outfits in an adventurous time. All the tunes now enshrined in Classic Rock history are here—Young's harrowingly psychedelic "Mr. Soul" and Stills's Laurel Canyon meditation "Bluebird" and surprisingly powerful "Rock and Roll Woman"—and many of them offer moments

The band chose its name from the side of a steamroller made by the Buffalo-Springfield Roller Company.

of gut-wrenching paradigm-shifting guitar from Stills.

That's one surprise waiting for those who haven't thought much about Buffalo Springfield recently: While Young has received the lion's share of the love from rock pundits, Stills—whose music is trenchant and graceful in equal measure—is overdue for reappraisal. Just one pass through the work of Buffalo Springfield, and you'll hear why.

GENRE: 🎸 Rock. **RELEASED:** 1969, Atco. **KEY TRACKS:** "For What It's Worth," "Mr. Soul," "Bluebird," "Broken Arrow." **CATALOG CHOICE:** *Buffalo Springfield.* **NEXT STOP:** Stephen Stills: *Stephen Stills.* **AFTER THAT:** The Stills-Young Band: *Long May You Run.*

Folk Singing Made Chilling

Le mystère des voix bulgares

The Bulgarian Women's National Radio and Television Chorus

L ined up in a large chorus or gathered into groups of two and three, the female singers of Bulgaria transport traditional harvest songs to a realm of celestial beauty. They coo quietly in far-off murmuring tones, then break

into strident ear-stretching harmonies and cascading three-part chorales that beg for, and rarely receive, conventional resolutions. They whoop like bellicose drill sergeants or offer lithe, vibratoless melodies, and at peak moments of agitation their massed voices can emulate the frenzy of crows scattering.

They've been singing this way for centuries in Bulgaria, using tricks handed down over generations from master to apprentice. But only beginning in the 1970s, through the work of Bulgarian composer Philip Koutev and the musicologist Marcel Cellier, did the

world begin to appreciate this rich, haunting sound. Koutev composed works based on traditional songs from Thrace and other regions, often rescuing dormant performance practices that, despite the neglect, sound surprisingly modern. The recordings of the Radio and Television choir, made in Bulgaria in the early '80s and issued internationally in 1987, show just how intricate this ensemble singing can be: Avoiding the "sweet" harmonies of Western music (thirds and sixths) in favor of strident ninths and whole steps, the women cast everything, even the simple expression of gratitude for a good crop, in delicate shades of otherworldly yearning.

This album became a cult classic in the U.S. and Europe, and led to several tours featuring the principal vocalists. Unfortunately, demand for Bulgarian singing was so great that assorted entrepreneurs took advantage of it, flooding the market with less than thrilling records from less accomplished ensembles—

including, of all things, "dance remix" records. These pure, beautiful voices didn't need *that* kind of help.

GENRE: 🌐 World/Bulgaria. **RELEASED:** 1987, Nonesuch. **KEY TRACKS:** "Svatba," "Mir stanke le." **NEXT STOP:** Trio Bulgarka: *The Forest Is Crying.* **AFTER THAT:** *Márta Sebestyén and Muzsikás* (see p. 686).

An Old Soul's Welcome Return

Don't Give Up on Me

Solomon Burke

O ne of the unexpected positive trends in the music business of the late 1990s was the return of long-neglected soul, gospel, and R&B singers. A talent who'd been completely off the radar for twenty years or more would

generate a bit of buzz via the re-release of classic records. This sometimes became the prelude to a full comeback, complete with duets with current stars, ardent hosannas from critics, and tours. After a decade of recording for smallish labels, veteran gospel harmony specialists the Blind Boys of Alabama (see p. 97) experienced a full-scale career revitalization, as did Howard Tate (see p. 763) and others.

Solomon Burke was originally a preacher in his hometown of Philadelphia.

Just one hitch: In many cases the new recordings turned out to be pale echoes of what came before. Solomon Burke is one of the very few members of the old-timers' club whose late-innings work is as strong as the hits of his heyday. That's saying something, because Burke was part of the mighty soul roster at Atlantic Records in the 1960s. A dynamo of lived-through-it-all groans and subtle inflections, his delivery was authoritative, his vocals a study in beseeching urgency, whether he was making a

plea ("Send Me Some Loving") or offering to comfort ("Cry to Me"). When the hits dried up for Burke in the 1970s, he didn't jump onto the oldies circuit. He returned to his ministry, opened a chain of mortuaries, and was very selective about his music work. This preserved his voice, as he noted in an interview during the launch of *Don't Give Up on Me*: "I was very fortunate. . . . I didn't have to do my 20 minutes on a revue every night, all that grueling travel. When it's time to sing, I feel like I can sound the way people expect me to sound."

Sure enough, Burke's voice is remarkably well preserved on *Don't Give Up*—the bass end is full, and his throaty high notes positively wail. It helps that he's not trying to re-create the whiplashing Atlantic sound: The songs here, written by such noted rockers and Burke disciples as Tom Waits, Bob Dylan, Nick Lowe, and others, are reflective, truth-seeking processionals. The crown jewel is "Diamond in Your Mind," a lazy two-step written by Tom Waits and sung by Burke in his best Louis Armstrong style. As he looks back at the high time when "money was something that you throw from the back of trains," Burke urges his flock to remain focused on the positive, and sings in a way that makes that diamond seem like it's right there, within reach.

GENRE: 🌑 R&B. **RELEASED:** 2002, Fat Possum/Anti. **KEY TRACKS:** "Diamond in Your Mind," "Stepchild," "Don't Give Up on Me," "Fast Train." **CATALOG CHOICE:** *Home in Your Heart: The Best of Solomon Burke* (which covers his great Atlantic output). **NEXT STOP:** Otis Redding: *Otis Blue* (see p. 636). **AFTER THAT:** James Carr: *Anthology*.

A Reggae Call to Consciousness

Marcus Garvey

Burning Spear

With his forlorn observation "No one remembers . . . old Marcus Garvey," reggae artist Winston Rodney (aka Burning Spear) embarked on a campaign to resurrect a key figure of black nationalism, the Jamaican journalist and entrepreneur who engineered the "Back to Africa" movement of the early twentieth century.

At the time of this release, Garvey was known to schoolchildren in Jamaica as little more than an important historical figure. Rodney's passionate, articulate songs draw connections between Garvey's ideas and modern social problems, and argue that for people of African descent all over the world, understanding and embracing African heritage is a crucial part of moving forward. His songs are a key early example of consciousness reggae; whenever some upstart singer invokes Garvey today, and many do, Rodney and the all-star band that created this album are at least partially responsible.

Rodney isn't a stellar singer—most of the vocals on *Marcus Garvey* are repetitive chants that utilize a range of about four notes. But they have a hypnotic quality: As he asks, again and

Burning Spear, Bob Marley, and Marcus Garvey were all born in Saint Ann's Bay, Jamaica.

again, "Do you remember the days of slavery?" Rodney's repetitions somehow communicate the whole dismaying legacy of that era. He doesn't itemize the injustices. Doesn't have to.

Rodney can take things easy because the band, which includes guitarists Tony Chin and Earl "Chinna" Smith, bassist Robbie Shakespeare, and the adroit backing singers Rupert Willington and Delroy Hinds, achieves an effortless percolation. Their echoey laid-back atmospheres help make *Marcus Garvey* a rare strain of message music, with the ideals and the uplift radiating through every element of the groove.

GENRE: 🌐 World/Jamaica. **RELEASED:** 1975, Island/Mango. **KEY TRACKS:** "Slavery Days," "Old Marcus Garvey," "Jordon River," "Resting Place." **CATALOG CHOICE:** *Live.* **NEXT STOP:** Hugh Mundell: *Africa Must Be Free by 1983* (see p. 532).

Better Be Sitting Down for This One . . .

Wish I Was in Heaven Sitting Down

R. L. Burnside

Until he was in his sixties, R. L. Burnside (1926–2005) made his living as a farm laborer in the Mississippi hill country. The gravel-voiced singer had been taught guitar by his neighbor, the legendary Mississippi Fred McDowell, and played juke joints from time to time—he was first recorded in 1967, by musicologist George Mitchell. In 1992, Burnside and another nearby guitarist Junior Kimbrough (see p. 423), were featured in the film *Deep Blues,* triggering record deals, tours, and eventually a wide revival of interest in what had been a fast-vanishing rural blues style.

After several relatively traditional efforts, Burnside shocked the blues world in 1996 by collaborating with the high-energy Jon Spencer Blues Explosion on *A Ass Pocket Full of Whiskey,* which featured hip-hop scratching, odd "found" sounds, and other urban accoutrements. That record hasn't aged well; its nonidiomatic touches seem gratuitous now. The subsequent *Wish I Was in Heaven Sitting Down* gently integrates those devices into a throaty impressionistic wail that is still, at bottom, the blues.

Throughout this set, Burnside brings an echo-chamber spookiness to the most ordinary blues clichés—when, on "Nothing Man," he talks about neglect, his words "I wish my mother would have loved me" are chillingly wooden. The album opens in a downcast mood, with the syrup-slow "Hard Time Killing Floor," and though the pace quickens (for the chugging "Miss Maybelle" and a stuttering cover of "Chain of Fools"), Burnside is most effective when he lingers over his thoughts, muttering like an old man who's lost in the sonic scrapheap around him. If your blues vocabulary stops at the highly polished guitar pronouncements and effusive vocals of latter-day B.B. King, seek out Burnside, whose coarseness recalls a time before the blues was show business.

GENRE: 🅰 Blues. **RELEASED:** 2000, Fat Possum. **KEY TRACKS:** "Chain of Fools," "Hard Time Killing Floor," "Wish I Was in Heaven Sitting Down." **CATALOG CHOICE:** *Too Bad Jim.* **NEXT STOP:** Junior Kimbrough: *All Night Long* (see p. 423). **AFTER THAT:** The Black Keys: *Thickfreakness.*

The Debut of a Pop Iconoclast

The Kick Inside

Kate Bush

Under normal circumstances, any song called "Wuthering Heights" that begins with the line "Out on the wiley, windy moors, we'd roll and fall in green," would be something to avoid, another pretentious grab at literature from yet another pop lyricist desperate for material. But these are not normal circumstances. The singer and songwriter Kate Bush was eighteen when she recorded this. A piano prodigy from Bexleyheath, England, with a taste for cinematic art-rock and a penchant for bracing (if slightly eccentric) imagery, she was clearly precocious. Few eighteen-year-olds would dare transpose the Gothic manners of Emily Brontë's novel onto a song of steamy yearning.

By sixteen, Bush had developed a reputation for her silvery voice, four-octave-range, and original songs that invoked paranormal phenomena. Pink Floyd guitarist David Gilmour became an advocate; he financed the demo tape that got her signed and, along with Pink Floyd producer Andrew Powell, spent two years developing the young artist. "Wuthering Heights" was the first fruit of this collaboration: Released in early 1978, it was a massive U.K. hit (actually boosting sales of the Brontë book), and the album established Bush internationally—no small feat considering that its off-kilter music stood apart from everything on the charts at the time. Although Bush released more commercial music subsequently, the weeping-willow melodies and majestic refrains of *The Kick Inside* remain her boldest statement, a tour of a mystic netherworld of Heathcliffs and healers led by a girl who's just beginning to puzzle out the meaning of it all.

GENRE: ⭐ Pop. RELEASED: 1978, EMI. KEY TRACKS: "The Saxophone Song," "Moving," "Them Heavy People." CATALOG CHOICE: *Hounds of Love*. NEXT STOP: Tori Amos: *Little Earthquakes*. AFTER THAT: Cocteau Twins: *Treasure*.

Keyboard Music Starts Here

Harpsichord Music

William Byrd
Gustav Leonhardt

A student of Renaissance composer Thomas Tallis, who was a contemporary of William Shakespeare and Giovanni Palestrina, William Byrd (1543–1623) is sometimes called the "Father of Music." This was because of his unique position as a composer: He was one of the very first musicians of the late Renaissance period to use keyboard instruments (rather than just human voices) to explore ideas about counterpoint and harmony. Talk about radical: By pursuing pleasing sounds, and not just using music to accompany text, Byrd changed the world.

Imagine the vastness of the frontier he faced doing so. There were few rules in place about the form an instrumental piece might take (many of his works for harpsichord resemble vocal songs, with verse after verse). Ideas about symmetry and harmony were not fixed—not even in the vocals of sacred music, which Byrd wrote and understood. Some pieces are clearly intended to reflect dances—these are notated as "Galliards" and "Pavans"—and others have an almost funereal quality, deliberating at painfully slow tempos. Sometimes Byrd's phrases end in a questioning tone, as though he's imitating an interrupted conversation with large ideas left unresolved.

And though he concentrated on the chords, Byrd did slip in little curlicues and other ornamentations that would flower in the baroque keyboard music that was to follow. (Other pieces here, including the amazing "Fantasia," are downright stark, with sudden stops and mood changes, and very little in the way of extra notes.) This disc, which features harpsichord specialist Gustav Leonhardt, contains some of Byrd's most engaging themes, music that endures in part because it once upon a time represented a new direction, and in part because it's just plain beautiful.

GENRE:  Classical. **RELEASED:** 2005, Alpha. **KEY TRACKS:** "Fantasia," "Que Passe for My Lady Nevell," "Pavan and Galliard in B-flat Major." **NEXT STOP:** Giovanni Palestrina: *Twenty-nine Motets for Five Voices, From Cantico Canticorum,* Cambridge Singers (John Rutter, cond.). **AFTER THAT:** J. S. Bach: *The Well-Tempered Clavier, Book 1,* Glenn Gould Edition.

Voices Flying in New Formations

Mr. Tambourine Man

The Byrds

Lurking inside *Mr. Tambourine Man* are DNA maps not only for everything the Byrds would do, but an entire genre of rock music. The album, the first from the five-piece group, overflows with the runaway idealism of folk-rock. Bits of its twang would define the group's 1968 Nashville foray *Sweethearts of the Rodeo*—which would later become a key text for the alt-country movement. It's got hints of the psychedelia that erupted on the single "Eight Miles High" the following year. Its chiming guitars and dusty vocal harmonies form the blueprint for the California folk-rock of the early 1970s. The "jangle" that came to define Tom Petty and later R.E.M. in the '80s first reared its head here.

The Byrds had been together eight months when they began working on *Mr. Tambourine Man.* They'd caused a stir playing Bob Dylan covers in Los Angeles nightclubs, so it was probably inevitable they'd record some—after "Mr. Tambourine Man," which became the first Byrds single, the group recast "All I Really Want to Do," "Spanish Harlem Incident," and,

The Byrds' *Mr. Tambourine Man* peaked at #6 on the U.S. charts.

most thrillingly, "Chimes of Freedom." The originals, particularly the stark confessionals of Gene Clark, are hardly a step down: "You Won't Have to Cry" stands among the great love songs of rock, while its alter ego, the bitter "I'll Feel a Whole Lot Better," endures not just for its crystalline harmonies, but for the wandering guitar lines that provide counterpoint underneath.

When *Mr. Tambourine Man* dropped, it was embraced primarily for its novel vocal approach, the way it grafted Dylan's message onto Beatle-buoyant refrains. The voices of David Crosby, Gene Clark, Jim (later Roger) McGuinn, and Chris Hillman combined for a windblown sound that's about wide-open nature vistas, not show business. This was communal singing that emulated the orderly resolutions of Bach and the crankiness of folk raconteurs; when situated within the nest of twelve-string guitar strumming and chiming electric leads, the chorale blossomed into something utterly new. Since then that sound has been endlessly deployed by documentarians to evoke the idealism of the '60s—the moment when popular music stirred souls, cried down injustice, and lifted, really lifted, people up.

GENRES: 🎸 Rock 🪕 Folk. **RELEASED:** 1965, Columbia. **KEY TRACKS:** "I'll Feel a Whole Lot Better," "Chimes of Freedom." **CATALOG CHOICES:** *Younger than Yesterday; Sweetheart of the Rodeo.* **NEXT STOP:** Buffalo Springfield: *Retrospective* (see p. 129). **AFTER THAT:** The Eagles: *Desperado.*

Homemade Sounds of the Future

My Life in the Bush of Ghosts

David Byrne and Brian Eno

When David Byrne, the lead singer of Talking Heads, and Brian Eno, the producer and conceptual artist (see p. 258), began work on *My Life in the Bush of Ghosts* in 1980, they had little of the technology musicians take for granted today. There was no easy way to sample prerecorded sounds. No pitch correction. No Pro Tools software. The sonic collages on this album were created with multiple tape recorders, which contained the voices of radio talk show hosts, Arabic singers, and other "found" material dropped in "on the fly," at strategic points. As Byrne explained in an essay, "If the gods willed, there would be a serendipity and the vocal and the track would at least seem to feel like they belonged together and it would be a 'take.'"

Grafting the passionate voices from one audio artifact onto the rhythms of another, Byrne and Eno created a sound environment like none before it, a low-budget aria defined by jarring juxtaposition. *Bush of Ghosts* remains a pivotal vision, one that has had lasting influence on adventurous hip-hop producers (including Public Enemy's production team, the Bomb Squad) and served as a catalyst for countless audio grab-bag pop experiments.

Despite the zooming advance of technology since its release, *Bush of Ghosts* does not sound dated. It does, at times, have a primitive quality, but that's intentional: Spinning textured tape-loop wonderfulness over African drums, Byrne and Eno conjure an at once ancient and futuristic framework for the sermons of TV evangelists and the entreaties of Lebanese mountain singers. On "New Feet," a track left off the initial LP but added to a 2006 CD version, the whip-cracking tribal pulse is augmented by what sounds like an oboe choir, offering solemn *om* tones in the background. Heavily processed voices sit at the margins of the mix, their wobbly calls and nearly out-of-tempo responses creating friction with everything else. This never resolves: The whole track feels fitful, out of phase, dance music that impedes flow. Which, of course, was the idea. Yes, new feet were needed to dance to these sonic provocations. But *Bush of Ghosts* equipped alert listeners with something that would prove even more crucial: new ears.

GENRE: 🎸 Rock. **RELEASED:** 1981, Sire. (Reissued 2006, Nonesuch.) **KEY TRACKS:** "America Is Waiting," "The Jezebel Spirit," "Very Very Hungry," "New Feet." **NEXT STOP:** DJ Shadow: *Endtroducing* (see p. 229). **AFTER THAT:** Public Enemy: *Fear of a Black Planet.*

Café Tacuba ✦ Uri Caine ✦ Camarón de la Isla ✦ Can ✦ Nati Cano's Mariachi los Camperos ✦ Captain Beefheart and His Magic Band ✦ The Caravans ✦ James Carr ✦ Elliott Carter ✦ The Original Carter Family ✦ Martin Carthy (with Dave Swarbrick) ✦ Cartola ✦ Enrico Caruso ✦ Pablo Casals ✦ Cascabulho ✦ Neko Case ✦ Johnny Cash ✦ Dorival Caymmi ✦ Emmanuel Chabrier ✦ Manu Chao ✦ Tracy Chapman ✦ Ray Charles ✦ Marc-Antoine Charpentier ✦ Hariprasad Chaurasia ✦ The Chemical Brothers ✦ Clifton Chenier ✦ Don Cherry, Dewey Redman, Charlie Haden, and Ed Blackwell ✦ Vic Chesnutt ✦ Chic ✦ Chicago ✦ The Chieftains ✦ Sonny Chillingworth ✦ Frédéric Chopin ✦ Charlie Christian ✦ The Clancy Brothers and the Dubliners ✦ Clannad ✦ Guy Clark ✦ Sonny Clark ✦ The Clash ✦ Van Cliburn ✦ Jimmy Cliff ✦ Patsy Cline ✦ The Coasters ✦ Eddie Cochran ✦ Joe Cocker ✦ Codona ✦ Leonard Cohen ✦ Nat King Cole and His Trio ✦ Ornette Coleman ✦ John Coltrane ✦ John Coltrane and Johnny Hartman ✦ The Comedian Harmonists ✦ Ry Cooder ✦ Sam Cooke ✦ Alice Cooper ✦ Aaron Copland ✦ Chick Corea and Return to Forever ✦ Cortijo y Su Máquina del Tiempo ✦ Elvis Costello and the Attractions ✦ Cream ✦ Creedence Clearwater Revival ✦ Regine Crespin ✦ Bing Crosby ✦ Crosby, Stills, Nash, and Young ✦ George Crumb ✦ Celia Cruz and Johnny Pacheco ✦ The Cure ✦ Cypress Hill

C

A Crowded Crossroads

Cuatro caminos

Café Tacuba

D uring the opening moments of "Puntos cardinales," Café Tacuba can be heard flailing away in several different time signatures at once. The percussion instruments offer faint outlines of possible beat patterns—

what might be a downbeat in one scheme is an afterthought (or a red herring) in another. Meanwhile, vocalist Rubén "Elfego Buendía" Albarrán sings in a rolling 6/8 meter that crosses the percussion at odd angles. The contrasting elements all float in space until, at 1:26, the refrain kicks in. Then everything abruptly locks into a steady house rhythm, a pulse that gathers the cerebral metric stuff onto a streamlined train and sends it shuttling down the tracks.

That transition is the essence of Café Tacuba, the Mexico City quartet whose albums routinely inspire outsized superlatives from the rock press. Conversant in the rich heritages of Mexican folk and Jamaican ska as well as some of rock's more obscure back pages, Café Tacuba creates exploratory music that's too defiantly danceable for any ivory tower.

Rubén Albarrán (aka "Elfego Buendía") wears one of his signature masks.

Cuatro caminos isn't the trippiest Café Tacuba—that prize goes to the 1999 *Reves/Yo soy.* But it is the most consistently astounding and, curiously, the most accessible. First, focus on the impossibly catchy refrains, which equal (and often better) the hookcraft of any Anglo rock band. Then listen for the subversive stuff underneath—the churning polyrhythms, brazen detours into dissonance, and explosions of instrumental fury that make this some of the most adventurous stuff in the great wide world of rock.

GENRE: 🌐 World/Mexico. **RELEASED:** 2003, MCA. **KEY TRACKS:** "Eo," "Mediodía," "Que pasara." **CATALOG CHOICE:** *Reves/Yo soy.* **NEXT STOP:** Bloque: *Bloque* (see p. 100). **AFTER THAT:** Los Fabulosos Cadillacs: *Los fabulosos calavera.*

A Meta-Mahler Mash-Up

Urlicht/Primal Light

Uri Caine

T he funeral march from Gustav Mahler's Fifth Symphony as an ersatz tango? A bit of lieder juiced by a manic jazz piano trio? The third movement from Mahler's First Symphony as a klezmer set-closer?

In the hands of pianist and conceptualist Uri Caine, what seems destined to sound like novelty or sacrilege becomes something else—a revelatory "opening" up of the music of Mahler to some late-twentieth-century urban air.

On this, the most successful of Caine's many multidisciplinary exploits, the pianist and his ensemble of downtown New York City improvisers retain the sense and the spirit of Mahler, the master of somber and deep nineteenth-century moods, even as they wrangle new miracles from his works. Listen for the way violinist Mark Feldman handles the scene marked "Primal Light" from Symphony No. 2, which Mahler subtitled "Resurrection." At first, he slices through the music with jazzbo disregard and brusque strokes. Then, as the piece goes on, he seems warmed if not overcome by the theme. He treats it with admiration, reverence. His impassioned, well-informed reading fulfills Caine's grand design—it magically

Blurring boundaries, Caine has explored Brazilian music, jazz, classical chamber works, and funk/fusion on his many recordings.

enlivens the original without trampling its distinctive melodic contours.

This is meta-Mahler, interpreted by resourceful musicians conversant in the taunts of hip-hop and the flip contentiousness of jazz. There's room for quirky postmodern mash-ups, but also passages of disarming tenderness. Check out "I Often Think They Have Merely Gone Out!" from *Songs on the Death of Children.* Here Caine and vocalist Arto Lindsay slither, bossa nova–like, in a way that gently universalizes its tragic subject.

GENRE: 🎷 Jazz. RELEASED: 1997, Winter and Winter. KEY TRACKS: "I Often Think They Have Merely Gone Out!," "Primal Light," "The Drunkard in Spring," "Funeral March." CATALOG CHOICES: *Live at the Village Vanguard; The Philadelphia Experiment.* NEXT STOP: Dave Douglas Tiny Bell Trio: *Constellations.* AFTER THAT: Gustav Mahler: *Symphony No. 4* (see p. 468).

The Flamenco Sgt. Pepper

La leyenda del tiempo

Camarón de la Isla

When the enormously popular singer Camarón de la Isla (real name: José Monge Cruz) died at age forty-one after battling lung cancer, the government of Spain grieved along with its people. "The flamenco has been orphaned" went the 1992 governmental decree. Camarón, as he was known, had captured hearts in his early twenties by singing flamenco—the form associated with the Gypsy troubadours of southern Spain that incorporates traces of Indian raga, Gregorian chant, and Andalusian folk song—with fierce passion and almost supernatural poise.

The recordings Camarón made with guitarist Paco de Lucía when both men were in their early twenties remain some of the most riveting examples of the flamenco tradition. But the singer didn't coast on that initial success. With the experimental *La leyenda del tiempo*, he achieved an overhaul of the long-entrenched (and seemingly unmovable) flamenco tradition, bringing it into the rock era while avoiding the cheese factor that trapped so many castanet-wielding would-be Mick Jaggers. The songs here use spry electric piano and squiggly Moog synthesizer solos, and sometimes feature an electric guitar roaming freely in the background. Some pieces have odd and unconventional orchestrations (the sitar-and-voice essay "Nana del caballo grande," one of several featuring the poetry of Federico García Lorca), while others thrive on polyrhythms that suggest Brazilian samba.

Camarón's vocal style is well matched to the diverse settings. He sings loping, extended melodies that wriggle and wail to communicate love's torments. Buoyant and reflective at the same time, he delivers flamenco's tragic narratives without laying it on too thick. In his book *Misterios del arte flamenco*, historian Ricardo Molina explains that "flamenco is the primal scream in its primitive form, from a people sunk in poverty and ignorance." Camarón took that traditional style, and by being a bit of a daredevil, made it relevant again.

GENRE: ⊕ World/Spain. RELEASED: 1979, MercuryPolygram Iberica. KEY TRACKS: "Volando voy," "La leyenda del tiempo," "Nana del caballo grande." CATALOG CHOICE: *Con la colaboración especial de Paco de Lucía.* NEXT STOP: Gipsy Kings: *Gipsy Kings.* AFTER THAT: Various Artists: *The Rough Guide to the Music of the Balkan Gypsies.*

Anything but Canned Avant-Rock

Tago Mago

Can

Tago Mago, the 1971 adventure from Germany's Can, is one of the very few essential albums to come out of rock's tiny avant-garde boomlet of the early 1970s. It is steeped in the experimental ethos and electronic sound-mangling that was happening throughout Europe at the time (check out Van der Graaf Generator, and PFM), but it's got a more assertive sense of rhythm. It shows a willingness to let the music be spacey for minutes on end; several of the tracks stretch out for close to fifteen minutes; they're riveting even when the Jackson Pollock sound splotches (and primal-scream vocal spasms) become grating. One selection, the nineteen-minute "Halleluhwah," is a psychedelic riff on a New Orleans parade,

This album was named after Isla de Tagomago, an island off the Spanish coast.

dotted with intricate improvised solos.

In 1971, what passed for radicalism in rock was either determinedly odd sonics, or unorthodox structures. Can, a five-piece then organized around the talk-singing (or shrieking) of Japanese vocalist Damo Suzuki, specialized in both. Its sonic palette included the glinting rhythm guitars that would later turn up in punk, and swirling synthesizers; on the tempoless "Aumgn," most of the sounds arrive shrouded in languid echoes and reverberations.

Tago Mago was Can's third album, and its best. Its daring aligns it with the Velvet Underground, while its sense of grandeur influenced such progressive rockers as Genesis. And the dense textures, which Can pursued more avidly on subsequent albums, became a key component of Krautrock (the Germanic progressive school) and noise-rock (its '80s derivation). With this album, Can proves that experimentation doesn't have to be impenetrable or indulgent: In the hands of musicians intent on exchanging ideas both silly and profound, it can be a thing of wonder.

GENRE: 🎸 Rock. **RELEASED:** 1971, Spoon/Mute. **KEY TRACKS:** "Mushroom," "Halleluhwah," "Aumgn." **CATALOG CHOICE:** *Future Days.* **NEXT STOP:** Velvet Underground: *White Light, White Heat.* **AFTER THAT:** The Soft Machine: *Third.*

Add Salt and Lime

¡Viva el mariachi!

Nati Cano's Mariachi los Camperos

When Linda Ronstadt went searching for musicians to help with her Mexican folk song project *Canciones de mi padre*, she sought the services of Nati Cano, the leader of the Los Angeles–based Mariachi los Camperos. Cano has been a force in mariachi music for more than forty years—both as a one-man preservation society honoring mariachi tradition, and an innovator on the bandstand striving to give age-old Mexican folk songs a contemporary jolt.

Cano proved indispensable to the Ronstadt project. And, as he acknowledges in the liner notes of this fantastic recording, he benefited in return: The album and successful tour furthered his quest to bring concert-hall respect to mariachi, a sound regarded by many in the U.S. merely as pleasant accompaniment to quesadillas and salsa.

¡Viva el mariachi!, a crisply recorded compilation of Cano's recordings from the 1990s, is a perfect way to encounter mariachi head-on. It showcases Cano's suave band playing songs that are standards of the repertoire—"Ojitos verdes," "Paloma negra"—as well as lesser known *boleros*, *rancheras*, and tunes derived from the Cuban *son*.

The *ranchera* songs hail from the Mexican countryside and, as interpreted by Cano, exude the feeling of open space, along with the desolation felt by those who have lots of time to ponder a vanished love. The *boleros*, which are typically even more sentimental, come across as forlorn confessions—check Luis Damian's vocal on "La malagueña" to hear falsetto singing at a keening, carefully controlled peak.

Many of the tracks revolve around intricate three- and four-part harmony, and wistful accordion. They're musical expressions of gallantry, and in the hands of a master like Cano, they take mariachi from the back room at a Mexican restaurant to the concert hall, revealing all the deepest, most profoundly soul-stirring aspects of the music along the way.

GENRE: 🌐 World/Mexico. **RELEASED:** 2002, Smithsonian Folkways. **KEY TRACKS:** "Ojitos verdes," "Paloma negra," "La malagueña." **CATALOG CHOICE:** *Llegaron los Camperos: Concert Favorites of Nati Cano.* **NEXT STOP:** Linda Ronstadt: *Canciones de mi padre.* **AFTER THAT:** Mariachi Vargas de Tecatitlán: *Ultimate Collection.*

Now Leaving Frownland

Trout Mask Replica

Captain Beefheart and His Magic Band

T he wise and sometimes visionary Captain Beefheart (Donald Van Vliet) opens this extended adventure in surrealism with a wonderfully candid confession: "My smile is stuck, I can't go back to your Frownland."

Consider these words a territorial marker, indicating the point where conventional notions of rock music end and enchanted Day-Glo electric preposterousness, piled high and served with extra sauce, begins. Atop a foundation of relatively normal blues guitar riffs, the Magic Band parades all sorts of non sequiturs in sound—screeching jazz-gone-awry dissonance followed by Delta blues howls followed by thunkety-thunk cartoon rhythms followed by radio-drama gibberish ("a squid eating doe in a polyethylene bag is fast and bulbous!"), all delivered by characters who sound like they long ago stopped questioning life down this *Alice in Wonderland* rabbit hole.

Released in 1969—a year of many revolutions, musical and otherwise—*Trout Mask Replica* is Beefheart's finest hour. It's a circus-sideshow exhibition, made possible in part by producer and champion Frank Zappa, who, in a classic inmates-running-the-asylum move, gave Beefheart full creative control. Its settings of slightly unhinged poetry against rampaging guitarist-as-spearchucker backdrops can challenge even the most open-minded listener—if at first the irregular rhythms of tunes like "Dachau Blues" and "My Human Gets

On *Late Night with David Letterman* in 1982, Van Vliet said his pseudonym referred to "a beef in my heart against this society."

Me Blues" seem intentionally off-putting, give them a second chance. As your ears become accustomed to Magic Band logic, you'll discover astounding instrumental juxtapositions and delightful melodic ripples beneath the often impenetrable surface.

Trout Mask didn't make Beefheart a star, but it did establish him as one of rock's great eccentrics. In this role, he's influenced generations of artists; Tom Waits and Beck, to name two, snatched Beefheart's strategies for nonlinear storytelling, while countless punk and postpunk acts borrowed the abrasive, needling attack of the Magic Band. Those worshippers might have started out over in Frownland. But they ended up smiling, in spite of themselves, at Beefheart's delectable absurdities.

GENRE: 🎸 Rock. **RELEASED:** 1969, Bizarre/Straight. (Reissued 1995, Reprise.)
KEY TRACKS: "Frownland," "Hair Pie, Bake 2," "Dachan Blues," "Moonlight on Vermont," "My Human Gets Me Blues." **CATALOG CHOICES:** *Safe as Milk; Doc at the Radar Station.* **NEXT STOP:** Frank Zappa: *Joe's Garage.* **AFTER THAT:** Eugene Chadbourne: *End to Slavery.*

Check Your Pulse If You Don't Feel the Spirit Here

The Best of the Caravans

The Caravans

Every musical style has kingmakers, those keen-eared scouts who spot talent and trends way ahead of everybody else. In gospel, one of the most important is Albertina Walker, singer and leader of the long-lived Chicago-based singing group the Caravans. Founded in 1952, the group cranked out hits and led huge revivals through the mid-'60s. Its torrid close-knit harmonies were one draw, but just as important were the peerless soloists Walker showcased—Bessie Griffin (see p. 328), Dorothy Norwood, Cassietta George, Inez Andrews, Shirley Caesar, and others, many of whom had successful solo careers after leaving the group. Walker also developed some of gospel's great songwriting instrumentalists, including James Herndon and James Cleveland.

The Caravans recorded over 150 albums. For a while in the late '50s—the period covered by this anthology—the group was a fixture on religious radio, performing originals and reworking classic gospel songs. "I Won't Be Back," the fast-moving opening track, shows the basic Caravans strategy: The soloist is Shirley Caesar, and as she launches into what soon becomes scalding testimony, the others snap out response lines with the precision of master drummers. Their repartee happens at breakneck speed and feels too freewheeling to have been prearranged: The women are following the call of that higher power, and by the end, their intensity spurs Caesar to abandon all restraint and shout.

The Caravan singers were experts at this type of head-spinning exchange. Of special note is Inez Andrews, whose unshakable contralto powers a slow, restrained reading of "Mary Don't You Weep" and the resolute "I'm Not Tired Yet." Hearing her deliver line after intense line, you might begin to wonder whether this faith of hers has miracle properties. Less sanctified souls would be spent after singing just one of those intense choruses.

GENRE: ✝ Gospel. **RELEASED:** 1977, Savoy. (Recorded between 1958 and 1962.) **KEY TRACKS:** "I Won't Be Back," "Mary Don't You Weep," "I'm Not Tired Yet." **CATALOG CHOICE:** *Freedom.* **NEXT STOP:** Sam Cooke and the Soul Stirrers: *Sam Cooke with the Soul Stirrers* (see p. 186).

Those Regrets That Mess with Your Mind

You Got My Mind Messed Up

James Carr

James Carr devotes the twelve songs of this lost 1966 classic to a detailed account of what happens to a man consumed by love. It takes him about thirty seconds into the first song, "Pouring Water on a Drowning Man," to establish credibility on the subject, and from there the underappreciated Memphis singer delivers noble and heartfelt elaborations that rank among the most intense in all of soul. He confesses that the water in his eyes isn't raindrops. He recalls, in a mood of enveloping regret, those delicious moments he and the long-gone girl spent at "The Dark End of the Street." (This stands as the definitive performance of the song.) By the time he reaches the title proclamation—which foreshadows his own bouts with mental illness—Carr has pretty much mapped out that place where obsessed lovers go to live quietly with their bitterness.

For most of his life, Carr struggled with bipolar disorder, which often got in the way of his career.

You Got My Mind Messed Up (and the several subsequent albums) should have made Carr (1942–2001) a star; at the time he was ascending, he was overshadowed by such titans as Wilson Pickett and Otis Redding, who were in their prime. After his records failed to find an audience, he disappeared for nearly a decade. Though his late-career recordings exhibit polish, the material isn't nearly as strong as the songs here. The "comeback" did help bring some old work back into circulation: The CD version of this must-own classic has twelve surprisingly strong bonus tracks, several of them previously unreleased.

GENRE: 🎵 R&B. **RELEASED:** 1966, Goldwax. (Reissued 2005, Vivid Sound.) **KEY TRACKS:** All of them. **CATALOG CHOICE:** *The Complete Goldwax Singles.* **NEXT STOP:** Otis Redding: *Otis Blue* (see p. 636). **AFTER THAT:** Howard Tate: *Get It While You Can* (see p. 763).

A Playful American Composer

Symphonia: Sum fluxae pretium spei; Clarinet Concerto

Elliott Carter

BBC Symphony (Oliver Knussen, cond.)

Whenever Elliott Carter is on an orchestra's program, the percussion section can count on being busy: The American composer, born in 1908 and still working well into the twenty-first century, writes in grand contentious tussles, and he punctuates his thoughts with carefully timed clanks, pops, and rattles. Sometimes the percussion "plays along" with a melodic phrase, helping clarify its outline; early in the final movement of the Symphonia, when the strings finish a particularly beautiful sustain, Carter breaks the spell with a simple two-note tap on the woodblocks.

Carter's emphasis on percussion isn't unique—many twentieth-century composers of classical music used kettle drums and other toys from the orchestra's back row to emulate the clatter of the machine age. Carter's music is built on the juxtaposition of contrasting elements, the creation and dissipation of chaos. These two vivid pieces show that Carter doesn't rely on a "system" of rules or fixed devices—he simply sets up contrasts of tone and color and then writes little episodes, passages in which the initial juxtaposition leads somewhere terrifying, or wonderful. The final movement of the Symphonia is an excellent example of this: After four minutes of string reverie, there come birdcalls from the high winds, and rumbles from a marimba, and splashes of cymbal that nearly overtake everything else.

These pieces, along with his four string quartets (two of which earned Pulitzer Prizes), form the core of Carter's contribution, and follow the general trajectory of the New York–born composer's music. They begin with the most intense bursts of harmony and then settle down, a strategy one critic has described as Carter scaring off the faint of heart. Further, both the spry seven-movement clarinet piece and the Symphonia end with stunning effects, flourishes that seem to reward the listener for having made it through the audio land mines Carter has set.

GENRE: 🎵 Classical. **RELEASED:** 1999, Deutsche Grammophon. **KEY TRACKS:** Clarinet Concerto: Scherzando; Largo. Symphonia: Partita; Allegro Scorrevole. **CATALOG CHOICE:** *The Four String Quartets/Duo for Violin and Piano,* Juilliard String Quartet. **NEXT STOP:** Alban Berg: *Violin Concerto* (see p. 80). **AFTER THAT:** György Ligeti: *Edition 1: String Quartets and Duets,* Arditti String Quartet.

The Carter Family: 1927–1934

The Original Carter Family

This should be required listening for anyone who wants to understand the American experience. In some ways it *is* the American experience— the songs of the Carter Family tell about the hardships of rural Appalachian life, the tragic deaths of young children, the vastness of the Virginia mountains, the scramble to feed a large and hard-working brood. There's faith and determination, too, and inspirational songs full of a mystic reverence. But perhaps the Carter Family's most impressive contribution is this: They sang all kinds of songs, blues and gospel, murder ballads, hymns and old British folk songs. They were the living embodiment of the American idea of the "mixing bowl."

The group was first heard outside of its southern Virginia home in 1927, when Alvin Pleasant Carter took his then wife Sara and Maybelle Addington, her cousin, to Bristol, Tennessee, to audition for the talent scout and early music-business impresario Ralph Peer.

(Johnny Cash once called the 1927 session "the single most important event in country music history.") The legendary Peer was impressed— at the time, much rural music was instrumental, made by string bands—and the Carter Family's recording career began immediately. Sara had a transfixing voice, Addington strummed the guitar with a schoolmarm's precision, and A.P. found songs by traveling the countryside, taking notes as strangers shared their favorites. He taught his family these pieces that had often been handed down for generations, making slight adjustments that, in the early record business, were enough to earn him composer credit. (He did write several key songs, including "My Clinch Mountain Home" on this compilation.) But he was mainly an aggregator: By the time the family band fizzled, in the early 1940s, he'd preserved a treasury of American song, black and white, sacred and secular, like no other.

The five-disc *1927–1934* contains impressively cleaned-up versions of the important early recordings, and these show the family's extraordinary range: The Carters were incandescent singing chirpy two-steps ("Keep on the Sunny Side") and sweet love odes ("I'm Thinking Tonight of My Blue Eyes") and yet completely believable telling about treachery and callousness ("Forsaken Love"). The legacy has been maintained by subsequent generations of country music's First Family. Addington, who'd married A.P. Carter's brother,

became known as "Mother Maybelle," and her daughters, Helen, Anita, and June, rose to prominence as the Carter Sisters. Solo success followed for June Carter Cash, her husband, Johnny Cash, and his daugher, Rosanne Cash. Together they didn't merely keep the circle unbroken, they expanded it.

GENRE: ◍ Country. **RELEASED:** 2000, Columbia Legacy. **KEY TRACKS:** "River of Jordan," "Can the Circle Be Unbroken," "Cannon Ball Blues." **CATALOG CHOICE:** *Keep on the Sunny Side.* **NEXT STOP:** Ralph Stanley: *Saturday Night/Sunday Morning.* **AFTER THAT:** Rosanne Cash: *The Wheel.*

The Best from a Folk Catalyst

Byker Hill

Martin Carthy (with Dave Swarbrick)

It doesn't take much in the way of musical acumen to get by as a folk performer. The basic guitar-strumming techniques can be acquired in a matter of hours—even if, as with all things, mastery takes longer. It isn't even

necessary to have a pleasing voice. For a while there in the early '60s, if you could sorta tell the story about the woman who pines for the seafaring two-timer with a drinking problem, you were ready for the coffeehouse.

That's why it's good to have a copy of *Byker Hill*, the third album from the British guitarist and singer Martin Carthy, and the third to feature Dave Swarbrick on mandolin and violin. A few minutes with this will prove to skeptical friends that in the right hands, folk can be a virtuoso thrill. Acknowledged for "modernizing" folk and lending encouragement to such important bands as Fairport Convention (see

Carthy prefers a Martin guitar for his percussive picking style.

p. 268) and Steeleye Span (see p. 738), Carthy is a multitasking marvel here, singing breathless extended melodies and plucking out fast counterlines in the background. These sad tales of murder and marital infidelity are shadowed, and often elaborated upon, by the wily Swarbrick, whose improvised lines are so elaborate they could have been written out, note for note, beforehand.

Though this was fairly early in his career, Carthy was already emerging as a folklorist— he was known to scour obscure references (among them the field recordings of British composer Percy Grainger) in search of "definitive" lyrics or music, and was not only equipped to compare each one, but inclined toward profound rearrangements. Here, Carthy shows a healthy respect for tradition while constantly pushing at its confining aspects—he's doing folk on a technically astute plane, with an intellectual vitality worlds away from the aw-shucks simplicity that often defines the form.

GENRE: 🌐 Folk. **RELEASED:** 1967, Topic. **KEY TRACKS:** "The Man of Burnham Town," "Byker Hill," "John Barleycorn." **CATALOG CHOICE:** *Second Album.* **NEXT STOP:** Fairport Convention: *Unhalfbricking.* **AFTER THAT:** Albion Band: *The Prospect Before Us.*

The Heart of the Samba

Cartola

Cartola

It took Angenor de Oliveira (1908–1980), known to Brazilians as Cartola, quite a while to develop a recording career. He first came to prominence in 1928, when he put together what became an enormously influential Carnaval organization, the Samba School of Mangueira. A self-taught guitarist and singer, he wrote many of the group's pieces, and is credited as the first in Brazil to use samba as the musical foundation for lavish pre-Lenten parades. Incredibly, his first record under his own name didn't appear until 1974; it was made when he was sixty-five, after several decades in artistic (and alcoholic) exile. This album, the follow-up, came two years later.

Cartola (left) composed hundreds of songs over his career.

Cartola is the heart of the samba, with no bells, whistles, or celebrity distractions. Its twelve simply arranged songs have been played by the massive percussion-based Mangueira ensemble in parades and competitions—some are considered by Brazilians to be almost folk songs, with them since childhood. This setting casts them in different light; pieces that can seem thunderous on the streets emerge in subtle shades, with percussion serving as one spice among many.

In the "samba de morro" (samba of the hills), as Cartola's style was known, shattered love affairs are mourned in words that suggest he'll never recover; yet at the same time, his themes carry hints of optimism, a cautious belief that brighter days lie ahead. That mixture of disappointment and hope is a Cartola trademark. It saturates the melodies. It permeates the beats. It makes just about every tune—the slippery up-tempo "As rosas não falam," the more contemplative "O mundo é um moinho," and the bassoon (!) feature "Preciso me encontrar"—seem like the heroic journey of one who's gone deeply into the dance of love, gotten hurt more than once and yet remains ready, even eager, to dance again.

GENRE: 🌐 World/Brazil. **RELEASED:** 1976, Melopea. (Reissued 2000.) **KEY TRACKS:** "As rosas não falam," "Preciso me encontrar," "O mundo é um moinho." **CATALOG CHOICE:** *Serie Aplauso.* **NEXT STOP:** Marisa Monte: *Memories, Chronicles, and Declarations of Love.* **AFTER THAT:** Edu Lobo: *Sergio Mendes Presents Lobo.*

The First Singing Superstar

Twenty-one Favorite Arias

Enrico Caruso

I n the liner notes accompanying this collection of Enrico Caruso's cherished arias, there's a story about the beginnings of his recording career. Possessing a tenor more robust than any other at the time, Caruso was already a sensation

when a representative from London's Gramophone and Typewriter Company sought him out in 1902. His offer was for Caruso to sing ten arias in an afternoon (try getting an opera singer to do that today!), at a fee of a hundred pounds total—about fifty dollars per aria. Caruso agreed, but suddenly the home office wasn't happy with this arrangement, cabling the representative F. W. Gaisberg: "Fee exorbitant. Forbid you to record." Gaisberg defied his employer and recorded Caruso anyway.

Caruso in one of his signature roles, Canio from *Pagliacci*.

The rest is history. Caruso (1873–1921) became the first major recording artist, and his approach to singing—a chesty bravado that sought to thrill rather than charm—became the ideal for subsequent generations. Caruso was a powerful voice, and also a singer attuned to the peculiarities of opera. He had exquisite breath control, smoothness in all registers, and a keen sense of character. This compilation, drawn from 78-RPM originals, begins with his iconic turn as Canio, the tragic clown of *Pagliacci*, singing "Vesti la giubba" in 1907. It's super-dramatic but somehow not excessive, a study in the careful management of volatile emotion.

It's a minor miracle that modern listeners can discern any subtlety in Caruso's recordings. All were made before the invention of the recording microphone in 1925, and they have

undergone extensive "cleaning" via computer-aided audio restoration. Though the signal is at times muffled or otherwise marred, Caruso's clarion tone prevails—at times during the Act 1 excerpt from Verdi's *Aida*, it's possible to forget that this is a historical document, because there's such richness and dimension in the voice. That vocal tone is something to marvel at, and even the cool heads at the *Grove Dictionary of Music* are effusive when talking about Caruso: "The exceptional appeal of his voice was, in fact, based on the fusion of a baritone's full, burnished timbre with a tenor's smooth, silken finish. . . . This enabled him in the middle range to achieve inflections of melting sensuality, now in caressing and elegiac tones, now in outbursts of fiery, impetuous passion." Those traits survive on these recordings, which, even after all these years, still have the power to amaze.

GENRE: 🎻 Classical. **RELEASED:** 1990, RCA. (Recordings made before 1920.) **KEY TRACKS:** *Pagliacci:* "Vesti la giubba." *Aida:* "Se quel guerrier io fossi . . . Celeste Aida." *Otello:* "Ora e per sempre addio." **NEXT STOP:** Luciano Pavarotti: *Amore: Romantic Italian Love Songs.* **AFTER THAT:** Plácido Domingo: *Very Best Of.*

A Worldly Cellist Goes One-on-One with Bach

J. S. Bach, Suites for Cello, Vols. 1 and 2

Pablo Casals

T he world's most celebrated cellist got his start playing dinner music: When he was twelve, growing up in the town of Vendrell near Barcelona, Pablo Casals worked as part of a trio in a popular café, playing three hours nightly for not much money. At age thirteen, he stumbled onto the manuscript for the Bach suites for unaccompanied cello. As he recalled later, the music had a massive impact.

He worked on the six pieces for nearly twelve years before venturing to play them in public. When he finally did, at age twenty-five, he didn't simply focus on one of the many dances in each suite, as his peers did. Instead, he played the suites whole, with all the repeats, to preserve what he called "the cohesion and inner structure of each movement."

Casals's interpretations were finally recorded in the 1930s, and they sound like pieces he's lived inside for years. The cellist captures Bach's vaunted structure, and uses an array of articulations to illuminate the multitiered logic of the themes. As with much baroque music, there are lots of notes; Casals plows through the connective phrases in a way that isolates—and brings to the fore—the less-obvious extended melodies. The interpretations are stunningly nuanced yet unified: Casals told students that he approached each suite based on Bach's written indications for its introductory prelude. "Suite 1" is labeled "optimistic," and in his hands that's exactly how it comes across—brisk and assured, always on the lookout for new horizons. Each suite receives a similarly empathetic reading, which is one reason these recordings are so revered; they catch Casals flowing through the music, going beyond technique to uncover a visceral dimension of Bach often hidden behind the fancy notes.

GENRE: 🎻 Classical. **RELEASED:** 1988, EMI. **KEY TRACKS:** No. 5 (C Minor), No. 2 (D Minor). **CATALOG CHOICE:** *Casals Edition: Beethoven Complete Cello Sonatas.* **NEXT STOP:** *Dvořák Cello Concerto, Haydn Concerto in C,* Jacqueline du Pré, Chicago Symphony Orchestra (Daniel Barenboim, cond.).

Mangue Beat Manifesto

Hunger Gives You a Headache

Cascabulho

M ost of Brazil's rich regional folk styles have remained just that—well-preserved heritage music with little international aspiration. There are, however, exceptions—like the music coming from Recife, in northeast

Brazil. Since the early 1990s, a group of younger musicians equipped with samplers jolted the folk music they've known since childhood (styles called *coco* and *forro* among others) with wicked dashes of funk and psychedelic electronica. While the catalyst of this "mangue beat" scene was Chico Science, who died in 1997, the most accomplished followers were the intense (if short-lived) Cascabulho.

The album's title alludes to the suffering of Brazil's poor.

Hunger Gives You a Headache is dedicated to Jackson do Pandeiro, an accordionist and composer of the 1950s who was one of Brazil's first hybridizers; his trick was to merge traits of the accordion-based *forro* with samba and other modern styles. Cascabulho reinterprets several of the legendary Pandeiro's compositions ("17 na corrente," "Xodó do sanfoneiro") as well as other well-known traditional songs. Alongside them are originals by singer Silvério Pessoa

and these are the gems—spirited, celebratory tunes that carry cries of social injustice along with the occasional sampled Charlie Parker riff or P-Funk bass line. Pessoa writes in bite-sized catchy bursts, and relies on call-and-response with backing singers to give his refrains their staying power. The songs embrace samba, African Candomblé ritual, and down-tempo funk, a divine mix that Cascabulho shares with gypsy collage artist Manu Chao (see p. 154) and other open-minded purveyors of world groove.

GENRE: ⊕ World/Brazil. **RELEASED:** 2000, Piranha. **KEY TRACKS:** "Boi catimbó," "Xodó do sanfoneiro," "Vovó Alaíde." **CATALOG CHOICE:** Silvério Pessoa: *Silvério Pessoa.* **NEXT STOP:** Jackson do Pandeiro: *Cinqüenta Anos de Carreira.* **AFTER THAT:** Banda Black Rio: *Best of Banda Black Rio.*

Great Vignettes-in-Progress, Endings Optional

Fox Confessor Brings the Flood

Neko Case

Booker T. Washington once defined excellence as "doing a common thing in an uncommon way." The act of telling stories in song certainly qualifies as a common thing—the world is full of singer-songwriters, would-be poets armed with guitars and the desire to share their deepish innermost thoughts.

Very few practitioners, however, offer tales as uncommon—and vividly wrought—as those found on Neko Case's fourth studio album *Fox Confessor Brings the Flood.* Case writes in snapshots, not full narratives. Her vignettes-in-progress follow carefully wrought characters into a brief and often pivotal moment, only to disappear before telling "what happened."

Hardly any of the songs have endings, happy or otherwise, and that openness can be unsettling to those accustomed to conventional resolutions. It can also be quite liberating. Case tells of schoolgirl rivalry ("Margaret vs. Pauline") in the singsong lilt of overheard gossip. She sketches a neighborhood reacting to a tragedy ("Star Witness") as a series of fleeting, disconnected details that might have been gleaned from the newspaper. In many cases, her images feel more like detours than plotlines. "Lion's Jaws" is an account of a lover's treachery, but it begins with Case's awed appreciation of a natural vista: "How can people not know what beauty this is, I've taken it for granted my whole life . . . since the day I was born."

Until this album, Case's reputation rested largely on her stripped-down Americana songs and her sturdy "classic-country" singing voice, which has earned comparisons to Patsy Cline (see p. 175). The voice remains the same—not many singers can do both the harrowing swoops of "Maybe Sparrow" *and* the gospel-roadshow shouting on "John Saw That Number." But Case changed everything else. The songs got spookier, the lyrics more

opaque, resembling hastily scrawled first drafts; in fact, she told interviewers, she intentionally did little fussing over the lyrics. And she cultivated an often desolate atmosphere closer to Joni Mitchell's *Hejira* than anything country. The setting suits these songs: Like a fortune-teller casting runes, Case scatters an array of glittering fragments and then walks away, leaving listeners to cobble the story together. Or not.

GENRE: 🎸 Rock. **RELEASED:** 2006, Anti. **KEY TRACKS:** "Star Witness," "Hold On, Hold On," "That Teenage Feeling," "Dirty Knife." **CATALOG CHOICE:** *Blacklisted.* **NEXT STOP:** Joni Mitchell: *Hejira.* **AFTER THAT:** Laura Veirs: *Year of Meteors.*

Cash, With Captives

At Folsom Prison

Johnny Cash

I t's one thing to sing about killing a man "just to watch him die" for an audience of upstanding paying customers. It's quite another to spin that tale inside a prison. From the moment he introduces himself on this, the first of

his legendary prison-concert records (it was also his first million-seller), Johnny Cash (1932–2003) makes it clear that he appreciates the uniqueness of his position—that to this assembly he's not a temporary escape from the drudgery of the pen, but a living symbol of the rebel road. He's got to convey empathy with the treacherous impulse and somehow avoid glorifying it outright.

Cash's handling of this dynamic makes *Folsom Prison* riveting. Opening with his already iconic "Folsom Prison Blues"—the song that includes that unsettling

Johnny Cash at Folsom Prison on the day of recording.

confession, "I shot a man in Reno, just to watch him die"— the Man in Black clippety-clops through grim story-songs about love and revenge and justice, allegories in which remorseful men ponder the consequences of their actions ("Twenty-five Minutes to Go," "I Got Stripes") or contemplate the inevitable ("The Long Black Veil"). As on all of his best live performances, Cash never lays anything on thick: He leaves room for the listener's own reckonings, and implies emotional undercurrents without stating them. Cash connects with this rough crowd not by being a cartoon tough, but by spinning stories about what it means to be human, and to struggle with the mistakes no amount of hard time can undo.

GENRE: 🌑 Country. **RELEASED:** 1968, Columbia. **KEY TRACKS:** "The Long Black Veil," "Folsom Prison Blues." **CATALOG CHOICE:** *Live at San Quentin.* **NEXT STOP:** Merle Haggard: *Honky-Tonkin'.* **AFTER THAT:** Waylon Jennings: *Waylon Live.*

More than a Comeback

American Recordings

Johnny Cash

Very few figures in American music have had second lives as rich as that of Johnny Cash (1932–2003). The legend whose 1960s recordings inspired waves of outlaw country endured a long period of what might charitably be described as "artistic decline" in the 1970s and '80s—issuing a string of thin, ill-conceived albums. And then, in storybook fashion, along came a producer and worshipper with indie cred to burn, Rick Rubin, who was determined to help Cash regain his voice.

Cash recorded this album in his living room, with only a guitar.

"I think in many ways he felt like he was done, and that nobody cared about what he was doing anymore," Rubin recalled shortly after Cash died. "He had no motivation around him." The producer of Slayer and the Beastie Boys prevailed upon Cash to try record-making again, and encouraged him to be who he was at that moment—a man confronting old age, looking back on scores left unsettled.

In this way, *American Recordings* is more than a comeback—it's a rare glimpse of a legend in the late innings. Cash is no longer invincible, but he's still got that mojo, and man, does he use it. The sepulchral voice holds the spotlight almost by default, standing apart from Rubin's minimal, unobtrusive accompaniment. The songs include several Cash originals on familiar themes (murder ballads, train songs), as well as covers of rock-era compositions. Nick Lowe's "The Beast in Me" sounds like it was written with Cash in mind, while Leonard Cohen's "Bird on a Wire" becomes almost hauntingly poetic.

American Recordings introduced Cash to a new generation, and served as the blueprint for a series of subsequent albums, which included unlikely but stupendous covers of songs by Nine Inch Nails and others. The last of them, *American V: A Hundred Highways,* was completed just before Cash's death. The storied voice is heartbreakingly wobbly, and sickness haunts every note like the train he sings of on his lugubrious "The 309," but the mighty Cash spirit rolls on.

GENRE: 🌑 Country. **RELEASED:** 1994, American. **KEY TRACKS:** "Delia's Gone," "Bird on a Wire," "The Beast in Me." **CATALOG CHOICES:** *Hymns by Johnny Cash; American V: A Hundred Highways.* **NEXT STOP:** Nick Cave and the Bad Seeds: *The Boatman's Call.* **AFTER THAT:** Mark Lanegan: *Whiskey for the Holy Ghost.*

Clues to the Elusive Brazilian Soul

Caymmi e seu violão

Dorival Caymmi

The songs of Dorival Caymmi's 1959 solo voice-and-guitar masterpiece *Caymmi e seu violão* celebrate man's deep connection to the sea. The swaying, simple melodies sound like they've been hanging around the shoreline forever, just waiting to attach to a sympathetic ear. The narratives talk directly about the ocean ("O mar") and those who depend on it ("Promessa de pescador"), and though in some of the more turbulent ballads he portrays the water as a threatening malevolent presence, just as often it's a friend, welcoming with open arms.

Caymmi came by his affinity for nature early on—he was born in Salvador da Bahia, the region of Brazil known for its spectacular beaches and West African culture. Though he appears to have been attached to Bahia, after he moved to Rio de Janeiro (to study law) he never again lived in his home city. He began recording in the late 1930s, and quickly earned reverence for his rustic,

Caymmi's career spanned 50 years.

plainspoken songs, which have been interpreted by virtually every major Brazilian star from Carmen Miranda forward. The Caymmi songbook, like that of Antonio Carlos Jobim (see p. 397), offers clues about the distinctly "Brazilian" soul. But where Jobim worshipped beautiful people, Caymmi shines light on ordinary folks and their daily preoccupations—food, lore, the weather. His songs seem simple, yet like the sea, there's turbulence below the gently undulating exterior.

GENRE: 🌐 World/Brazil. **RELEASED:** 1959, EMI Brazil. **KEY TRACKS:** "O mar," "O vento." **CATALOG CHOICE:** *Caymmi.* **NEXT STOP:** Baden Powell: *Os Afro Sambas.*

A "Comic Opera with Elaborate Underwear"

Le roi malgré lui

Emmanuel Chabrier

Chorus of Radio France, New Philharmonic Orchestra of Radio France (Charles Dutoit, cond.)

French composer Emmanuel Chabrier once described *Le roi malgré lui*, his most famous work, as "a comic opera with elaborate underwear." That's an accurate characterization of a piece that often operates on two distinct levels at once. There's the confusing libretto about a reluctant French noble who's elected king of Poland (a rough translation of the title: "The King, In Spite of Himself"). Beneath that, there's the "underwear"—chord sequences that resolve in sly, snakelike fashion and structures (including, in Act 2, an elaborate chase-scene fugue) that are more intricate than most plot-moving devices. It's an enchanting piece in spite of its operatic baggage.

Luckily for the opera-averse, Chabrier (1841–1894) offers unobstructed views of his main themes in the wonderful orchestral "preludes" to each act. These demonstrate his knack for the unexpected. The "Venice" melody is heard in the Act 2 duet marked "Barcarolle" between Henri (the King, sung by Gino Quilico) and Alexina (Isabel Garcisanz), and returns in the prelude to Act 3. That "restatement" makes the compositional ingenuity easier to hear: After a few merry elaborations on the A-section theme, the woodwinds usher in a contrasting melody that sends the music sailing off a cliff, harmonically speak-

ing. Nothing resolves the way you expect it to, and somehow, after a round of swerves and swoops, Chabrier manages to return to the main theme. Which feels calm and orderly, as if the preceeding interlude was something of a dream.

This opera isn't performed regularly, in part because of its dense libretto, which has been rewritten several times. This version, recorded with a French orchestra and chorus, benefits from the steadying presence of conductor Charles Dutoit, who savors Chabrier's expansive lines while emphasizing the jagged rhythmic upheaval the composer embedded below the surface.

GENRE: 🎭 Opera. **RELEASED:** 1985, Erato. **KEY TRACKS:** Act 1: "Romance," "Duo"; Act 2: "Introduction," "Barcarolle"; Act 3: "Entr'acte." **ANOTHER INTERPRETATION:** Janine Micheau: *French Opera Arias.* **NEXT STOP:** Jacques Offenbach: *Les contes d'Hoffman,* Orchestre de la Société des Concertos du Conservatoire (Andre Cluytens, cond.).

The Street Music of the Twenty-first Century

Clandestino

Manu Chao

*C*landestino is scraps and castoffs and tribal beats, the nickels and dimes that add up to culture. It is not traditional, but instead blends traditions from Europe and Latin America together, into a melting-pot swirl of global

electronic groove music. There's been a ton of that stuff since the 1990s, and much of it is generic—tabla beats looped with hip-hop bass and bits of vaguely ethnic sounds to make a "small world" collage. French-born Manu Chao knows better.

His first international music adventure was with the Paris-based group Mano Negra in the early 1990s. A large and sometimes unruly ensemble known for impromptu performances

in train stations and docks, the group became a sensation throughout Europe for its energetic gypsy dance music cut with elements of punk and hip-hop. Arguments over money drove some of the core musicians away, and by 1995 Chao (real name Oscar Tramor) moved to Madrid and formed Radio Bemba Sound System. His plans for the new group were more ambitious: A rock band that reflected the world's great street cultures. The band spent several years touring

South America, soaking up folk styles and recording as it went, often collaborating with local musicians.

Clandestino is an outgrowth of Chao's global-nomad phase. It's less overtly party-oriented than Mano Negra—Chao begins with South American folk tunes strummed on acoustic guitar, then adds dub-style bass lines, Afro-Cuban rhythms, and odd sonic artifacts (including samples of speeches by members of the Zapatista movement, the left-leaning Chao's political heroes). Some of his refrains carry sociopolitical messages—on the electrifying "Mentira," he sings about the escapist nature of urban life—and some, including his reworking of the Mano Negra

Clandestino is Manu Chao's first full-length solo album.

hit "King of the Bongo" here titled "Bongo Bong," are downright silly. Even in its most absurd moments, *Clandestino* represents a different, more culturally sensitive take on the mix-and-match world of electronic music. If this resonates, it's because Chao knows, loves, and respects his source material. Where others hear scattered scraps, he hears a symphony.

GENRE: 🌐 World. **RELEASED:** 1998, Virgin. **KEY TRACKS:** "Mentira," "Lagrimas de oro," "Dia Luna . . . Dia Pena." **CATALOG CHOICE:** *Proximo Estación: Esperanza.* **NEXT STOP:** Mano Negra: *Patchanka.* **AFTER THAT:** Ozomatli: *Ozomatli.*

Taking That Ride to Anyplace Better

Tracy Chapman

Tracy Chapman

66 "Fast Car," the song that first brought Tracy Chapman national attention, belongs alongside "We Gotta Get Out of This Place" and "Born to Run" on the short list of great escape songs. Its narrative follows

the conventions of the form: Singing in the voice of a convenience store worker, Chapman longs to get away from the mundane and actually begin living. "You got a fast car, I want a ticket to anywhere," she sings. "Maybe we can make a deal, maybe together we can get somewhere." By the last verse, a sense of urgency grips her. She gives her coconspirator an ultimatum: "Leave tonight or live and die this way."

Tracy Chapman began playing the guitar and writing songs when she was only 11 years old.

"Fast Car" proved the perfect entrée for a student of Tufts University who was in almost every way going against type. At a time when most African American women in music set out to be R&B divas, the Cleveland-born Chapman sang quietly and thoughtfully about the lives of the disadvantaged. Her songs portrayed poverty in human terms, telling about dignified people pushed to the breaking point.

(One song, "Mountains o' Things," was an inventory of a poor girl's materialistic dreams.) Without raising her voice or sounding alarms, she found ways to address long-deferred issues of race and class; track one, "Talkin' 'bout a Revolution," envisions a time in the near future when the long oppressed seize a moment to change the world.

Chapman doesn't overload her straightforward songs with "message" either: All she has to do is put some heat into her urgent, almost trembling voice and a despairing situation sprouts possibilities.

GENRE: 🎸 Rock. **RELEASED:** 1988, Elektra. **KEY TRACKS:** "Fast Cars," "For My Lover," "Mountains o' Things." **CATALOG CHOICE:** *New Beginning.* **NEXT STOP:** Odetta: *At Carnegie Hall.* **AFTER THAT:** Ani DiFranco: *Dilate.*

The Early Peak of the Genius

The Best of Ray Charles: The Atlantic Years

Ray Charles

The singles Ray Charles recorded for Atlantic Records beginning in 1955 are often described as the "birth" of soul. The pianist and vocalist was the first to refine up-tempo gospel, blues, and boogaloo into a highly combustible, era-defining sound—see his superheated "I Got a Woman," as galvanizing an experience as any in popular music. That's where Charles *started.* Over the next several years, he took the basic notion of soul much further: This collection covers soul in its toddler years ("Hallelujah, I Love Her So"), soul in its heady tumultuous adolescence ("Night Time Is the Right Time"), and soul as the expression of a wise man torn apart by his love for a woman ("Drown in My Own Tears").

Ray Charles is "the only true genius in the business."
—Frank Sinatra

focusing on the key charting hits and choice B sides (including "Greenbacks") of Charles's first phase. These outline his development from jump-blues shouter into the architect of undeniably propulsive, quintessentially American music. To hear the Genius at absolute peak, check out the massive "What'd I Say," the tune that spread his brand of infectious, exultant musical enthusiasm all over the world.

This anthology was released after Rhino carefully remastered Charles's catalog for a comprehensive boxed set; sonically, it's a huge improvement over previous collections. The only gripe is that it doesn't include any of the jazz, big band, or studio orchestra recordings that dominated Charles's long-playing Atlantic

Charles's singles have been endlessly repackaged, sometimes in shoddy and incomplete ways—even the three-disc *Birth of Soul* box has a few holes in it. This twenty-track single disc provides an excellent introductory lesson, albums. Those who find themselves in need of more Ray Charles music (and really, don't we all need more?) might seek out *The Genius of Ray Charles* (1959), his breakthrough with studio orchestra, which includes an authoritative "Come Rain or Come Shine"; then *Genius + Soul = Jazz* (1960), which finds Brother Ray fronting a big band. To fully appreciate Charles's formidable range, listen to all of these. But start here—these electrifying Atlantic singles remain Charles's most significant legacy.

GENRE: 🎵 R&B. **RELEASED:** 1994, Rhino/Atlantic. **KEY TRACKS:** "What'd I Say," "Hallelujah, I Love Her So," "I Got a Woman," "Night Time Is the Right Time," "Sticks and Stones," "Drown in My Own Tears." **CATALOG CHOICES:** *The Genius of Ray Charles; Genius + Soul = Jazz; Ray Charles and Betty Carter.* **NEXT STOP:** Solomon Burke: *Rock 'n' Soul.* **AFTER THAT:** Van Morrison: *Too Late to Stop Now.*

Genius of Soul Does Country

Modern Sounds in Country & Western, Vols. 1 and 2

Ray Charles

Shortly after Ray Charles died in 2004, the songwriter and musicologist Tom Waits gauged the blind pianist and singer's contribution this way: "Your collection could be filled with nothing but music made by Ray Charles and you'd have a completely balanced diet."

These two forays into what Charles called "hillbilly music" support that contention. If it began as a lark (or a way to test whether he really did have "artistic freedom" at new label ABC-Paramount), Charles's country exploration quickly became something else—a kind of cultural dynamite. Not only was this black man serious about a music often considered crude—or even racist—by intellectuals and denizens of soul, he was interpreting it in profound, starkly beautiful ways: His delivery caught the emotions underneath those tales of cheating hearts, and transformed trite lyrics into personal-sounding confessionals. He found the tenderness in Hank Snow's spitting-

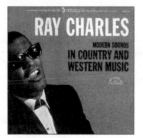

Modern Sounds stayed at #1 on the *Billboard* pop album charts for 12 weeks.

nails classic "I'm Movin' On." He sang Hank Williams's "You Win Again" with disarming directness. He brought a devastating sincerity to the hit "I Can't Stop Loving You," singing in a way that even overcame the sappy studio chorus.

The success of *Modern Sounds*, Vol. 1 practically ensured there would be a sequel, and amazingly, Vol. 2 is nearly as poignant as the original. Taken together, these two groundbreaking sets are prime-genius Ray Charles, doing what he did best: erasing artificial divisions between musical genres to uncover the common heart and soul lurking underneath. As Charles himself told music historian Peter Guralnick: "You take country music, you take black music, you got the same goddamn thing exactly."

GENRE: ⚫ Country. RELEASED: 1962, ABC-Paramount. KEY TRACKS: "You Don't Know Me," "Worried Mind," "Careless Love," "I Can't Stop Loving You." CATALOG CHOICES: The Genius After Hours; O Genio, Live in Brazil 1963. NEXT STOP: Van Morrison: Pay the Devil.

Crazy Lady Wants Revenge

Médée

Marc-Antoine Charpentier
Lorraine Hunt, Les Arts Florissants (William Christie, cond.)

The tragic story of Medea, the sorceress and murderess of myth known here as Médée, involves characters of royal standing doing lowdown things and treachery on an unfathomable scale—standard opera fare. Curiously, the music that baroque composer Marc-Antoine Charpentier (1643–1704) wrote for this deep five-act work sounds like it was intended not for the stage, but rather for some tightly structured church service. There are reverent cascading vocal chorales, and soaring melodies in the manner of Bach's St. Matthew Passion.

In a perverse way, the pious tones provide a moral "anchor" for the story of this ruthless woman—who, as immortalized in a play by Euripides, steals the golden fleece and scatters bodies as she and her lover Jason escape to Corinth. There, King Creon gives the couple shelter but soon schemes to have the warrior Jason marry his daughter. Angered and exiled, Médée (played marvelously by Lorraine Hunt) goes for revenge: She kills Creon and his daughter, then stabs her children to death to spite their father.

These brutal exploits are conveyed through music of striking beauty—highlights of this work include lavish instrumental passages written to accompany brisk onstage dances, recitatives that move the plot along in clever ways, and sparkling vocal themes that occasionally recur to delightful effect. Charpentier understood French opera's requirements for visual spectacle (at one point Médée takes flight on her pet dragon). But the more elaborate moments indicate he was also tuned to the lyricism that defines Italian opera. *Médée*, which was rediscovered in the 1980s, presents Charpentier as a crucial bridge between those distinct styles.

This performance showcases the early-music ensemble Les Arts Florissants, considered one of the best in the world at revitalizing old music. Even when the singers are venting rage, the precision of the playing makes it possible to focus on small details and odd pairings that give the work its richness (listen for the way an active bassoon part aligns with the harpsichord in Act 1). The recording is also notable because it presents Hunt in one of her first roles as a mezzo-soprano. Her dark, smoky hue turns out to be perfect for Médée, yet she never relies on mere tone: Shaping lengthy phrases into bursts of visceral emotion, she gives listeners an up-close view of Médée's twisted mind.

GENRE: ⚫ Opera. RELEASED: 1995, Erato. KEY TRACKS: Act 1, Scene 4: "L'Allégresse en ces lieux"; Act 2, Scene 1: "Aufritt: 'Il est temps de parler.'" CATALOG CHOICE: Te Deum, Esteban Cambre, Arcadia Ensemble. NEXT STOP: Claudio Monteverdi: Vespers (see p. 515). AFTER THAT: Francesco Cavalli: La calisto, Concerto Vocale (René Jacobs, cond.).

Be Centered Now

Raga Darbari Kanada

Hariprasad Chaurasia

T he English poet Samuel Taylor Coleridge once said, "What comes from the heart goes to the heart." Music is an illustration of that circuit in action. Sounds travel fast between hearts; when a musician like the flutist Hariprasad Chaurasia sends out the animated whispers that begin the hour-long *Raga Darbari Kanada*, it is difficult to remain unaffected. His woody breathy tone is a direct transmission from tranquility central. He makes no demands, does not expect you to instantly become "centered." Yet he vibrates on a frequency that puts contentment right in front of you, and shows that it is attainable.

Chaurasia's mastery of the *bansuri* bamboo flute is one lure of this spacious and wonderfully warm recording—which begins as a nocturnal meditation, and gradually builds intensity as the melodic arcs grow longer and more involved. A raga is not a fixed score; it's more like a seed, a set of notes and instructions about how they should be ordered, and it's often intended to dwell in a particular mood or time of day. (This one is intended for performance just before midnight.) Recognizing that any dissonance mucks up the transmission of heart energy, Chaurasia shapes each phrase with slight yet deliberate strokes.

Chaurasia is considered among the greatest Indian flutists, and here, he alternates between astounding flights and long sustained tones. Often he'll recede into the background to bring the crisp percussive work of tabla player Fazal Qureshi to the forefront. That happens memorably on the final section of the raga, entitled "Medium Tempo Gat in Ektal," when Chaurasia's flitting caprices are underpinned by a recurring drone plucked on the sitarlike *tampura*. The movement lasts nearly seven minutes, and from its very first taps, the significant challenges of raga form take a back seat to the conversation, a communication between hearts.

GENRE: ⊕ World/India. **RELEASED:** 1993, Nimbus. **KEY TRACKS:** "Medium Tempo Gat in Ektal," "Dhun in Maga Mishra Pilu," "Alap and Jar." **CATALOG CHOICES:** *Flying Beyond: Improvisations on Bamboo Flute; Remember Shakti.* **NEXT STOP:** Ram Narayan: *The Master.*

Block Rockin' Beats, Indeed

Dig Your Own Hole

The Chemical Brothers

E lectronica is easily lampooned as the revenge of the nerds, knob-twiddling obsessives who spend hours in the studio getting just the right oomph out of the kick drum. That characterization applies to Ed Simons and

Tom Rowlands, better known as the Chemical Brothers. The duo's albums offer exceptionally crisp renderings of instruments both real and imagined. Drums are rendered with dental-drill precision, each tick locating a different raw nerve. Guitars stab with serial-killer menace. The bass thuds like Satan's dungeon door slamming shut.

The Chemical Brothers got the name of this album from graffiti outside their London studio.

These (and other) sounds prove crucial to the dance floor–rattling adventures of *Dig Your Own Hole*, which integrates the pulse of hardcore techno with elements of hip-hop and rock, then blows the whole crazy collage up larger-than-life. The first example of "arena electronica," it's an involving swirl of sound, with terse back-beats exploding into dizzying outbreaks of cacophony. The opening roar, "Block Rockin' Beats," centers on a hip-hop sample (from rapper Schoolly D); in the Chems' conception, the hook provides the only relief from a raw and abrasive attack. The pulse itself is so savagely serrated it's impossible to tell whether it started out as something "hip-hop" or "big beat" (the tag some gave to the Chemicals' approach) or really any discrete style. It's coalesced into one densely packed multihued roar.

From there, the duo engages in intensely creative era-mangling: "Electrobank" is a mutant soul revue that got lost in some faraway galaxy. This groove has the vibrant throttling intensity of a live band, and is punctuated by what sounds like a horn section. (Listen closely, because it's really a bit of turntable wizardry.) Even the overt attempt at pop crossover is daring: "Setting Sun," which features vocals by Oasis songwriter Noel Gallagher, exists in a languid dream state, its lovely melody accentuated by oozing, subterranean instrumental embellishments. *Dig Your Own Hole* was released in 1997, alongside similarly spirited works like the Prodigy's *Fat of the Land* and Daft Punk's *Homework*. Of those three bold, new-horizons-in-dance-music titles, *Dig* is the most thrilling. And the one that best transcends its moment.

GENRE: 〰 Electronica. **RELEASED:** 1997, Astralwerks. **KEY TRACKS:** "Block Rockin' Beats," "Electrobank," "Setting Sun." **CATALOG CHOICES:** *Exit Planet Dust; Come with Us.* **NEXT STOP:** The Prodigy: *The Fat of the Land.* **AFTER THAT:** Daft Punk: *Homework.*

Les Bon Temps Roulez with the King!

Bogalusa Boogie

Clifton Chenier

Here's knee-buckling hard-swinging boogie, the kind that feels like it could easily last all night but might exhaust you well before that. Clifton Chenier, the undisputed King of Zydeco, was known for sweeping whole dance floors into a cyclonic swirl of motion. He and his Red Hot Louisiana Band could groove, mercilessly and relentlessly, in live performance. *Bogalusa Boogie*, recorded in a day, is one of the very few studio records to capture that intensity.

Chenier (1925–1987) was the primary architect of zydeco, the Southern Louisiana delectation that combines elements of French Cajun music with the blues. Not only is he responsible for the style's basic rhythms, he built a repertoire of hot-pepper jabs and stabs that made the accordion a rhythm instrument. These have been used by virtually every consequential zydeco band that followed.

Most of Chenier's records celebrate the rollicking push-pull of zydeco, its intricate alchemy of endless propulsion. But this one has a little extra Tabasco in it, and some ferocious back-and-forth exchanges—on the brisk "Allons à Grand Coteau" (Let's Go to Grand Coteau), Chenier swaps ideas with boisterous saxophonist John Hart and the rhythm section until their exchanges grow into hurtling big band–style shout choruses.

Clifton Chenier was known for decades as the "King of Zydeco."

Producer Chris Strachwitz writes in the liner notes that Chenier insisted during the recording session that the band just keep playing, not even allowing a pause to listen back to what they'd just done. "The band ripped through one number after another without second takes, as if they were playing a hot dance and were enjoying every moment of it." That enjoyment, central to (and maybe the key X factor in) great zydeco, is inescapable here.

GENRE: 🔵 Blues.
RELEASED: 1975, Arhoolie.
KEY TRACKS: "Ride 'Em Cowboy," "Ti Na Na," "Allons à Grand Coteau," "Bogalusa Boogie." **CATALOG CHOICES:** *Louisiana Blues and Zydeco; Bayou Blues.* **NEXT STOP:** Buckwheat Zydeco: *Buckwheat's Zydeco Party* (see p. 128). **AFTER THAT:** Beau Jocque: *Pick Up On This!*

Ornette Alums Revisit the Master's Teachings

Old and New Dreams

Don Cherry, Dewey Redman, Charlie Haden, and Ed Blackwell

The sage tenor saxophonist Joe Lovano keeps a list of often-overlooked records that he believes are vital to the understanding of jazz history. This 1979 gathering of veterans of Ornette Coleman's groups is on it.

"The people on this record are not playing together all the time," Lovano said in a 2002 interview. "They sorta have to switch back into the Ornette way of looking at music, which is pretty different from everything else. You can tell their minds are engaged the whole time—Dewey [Redman, the tenor saxophonist] plays these long melodies that have a beautiful shining heart inside them."

Lovano (see p. 456) might have been thinking about Redman's solo on the gorgeous Don Cherry tune "Guinea." Just as the sing-song melody is winding down, Redman makes a scrambling, not entirely graceful lunge into the tenor saxophone's upper register. He's been itching to break away, and now, after Cherry's done his trumpet thing, Redman sees his chance. He begins with big single notes, played just so—he's a man stepping carefully around some bad memories. His playing would be great with just bass and drums (the setting for most of the solos with this quartet), but just as Redman is starting, Cherry switches to piano, providing a firm anchor. Redman responds with a wail. He cries a bit. His phrases—utterly logical yet oddly shaped—swell with such life that they threaten to burst apart.

Old and New Dreams emphasizes the lyrical side of the Ornette Coleman group. The quartet mellows the strident harmonic palette of such path-finding records as *Free Jazz* (1960), making their flashes of subversion a part of the discourse, rather than the entire conversation.

GENRE: 🅙 Jazz. **RELEASED:** 1979, ECM. **KEY TRACKS:** "Lonely Woman," "Guinea," "Togo," "Song for the Whales." **CATALOG CHOICE:** Dewey Redman: *The Struggle Continues.* **NEXT STOP:** Ornette Coleman: *In All Languages.* **AFTER THAT:** Art Ensemble of Chicago: *Urban Bushmen* (see p. 28).

"A Question in Your Nerves Is Lit . . ."

Is the Actor Happy?

Vic Chesnutt

Vic Chesnutt has been confined to a wheelchair since surviving a car crash in 1983, when he was eighteen years old. Since then, through a series of wild and revelatory albums, he's developed into the great "outsider" artist of singer-songwriterdom, the rare storyteller capable of enchanting listeners with fanciful and far-flung imagery in one verse, and shrewd, caustic, devastatingly blunt assessments of human nature in the next.

In the songs of *Is the Actor Happy?*, Chesnutt's best work, the normal order of things is twisted around until a benign idea becomes eerie, unsettling and chillingly uncomfortable settings come to seem perfectly normal. He sings in curious tones that at times seem intentionally off-putting—he'll whine like a child, lingering over some syllables until the words become grossly elongated, their very meanings distorted.

Chesnutt starts with subjects cherished by countless strumming-and-humming cof-

Chesnutt lives in Athens, Georgia, where he frequently collaborates with other members of the city's vibrant music scene, including R.E.M. and Widespread Panic.

feehouse troubadours—musings on the costs and dangers of commitment, the sting of betrayal, what it means to give up. Then, through sheer idiosyncratic will, he pushes these subjects toward the macabre and the surreal. At times his own experience seems to inform the narratives—one gem here, "Free of Hope," turns on the caustic refrain "Free of hope, free of the past, thank you God of Nothing, I'm free at last." It's a despairing moment, a "man curses the fates" diatribe, and also a perversion of the oft-heard gospel refrain. Chesnutt doesn't take it to church, however: He rises over the majestic anthem-rock backing, his voice defiant and fiery, making no attempt to disguise his bitterness.

Chesnutt's discography includes thrashing punk explorations and more sedate, image-rich writing—his calmer songs reflect the influence of such Southern Gothic storytellers as Flannery O'Connor and William Faulkner. *Is the Actor Happy?* captures those (and other) extremes, and presents Chesnutt at his most engaging as a singer. On the beautifully harmonized country-rocker "Gravity of the Situation" and the vengeful "Guilty by Association" (which features vocals from R.E.M.'s Michael Stipe), Chesnutt restrains his freakish impulses, allowing the startling and disarmingly wistful beauty of his music to shine through.

GENRE: 🎸 Rock. **RELEASED:** 1995, Texas Hotel. **KEY TRACKS:** "Gravity of the Situation," "Free of Hope," "Guilty by Association." **CATALOG CHOICES:** *The Salesman and Bernadette; West of Rome; Ghetto Bells.* **F.Y.I.:** Chesnutt once aptly said, "Other people write about the bling and the booty. I write about the pus and the gnats." **NEXT STOP:** Daniel Johnston: *Fun.* **AFTER THAT:** Mark Eitzel: *60 Watt Silver Lining.*

C'est le Best Disco Album Ever

C'est Chic

Chic

Most musicians heard disco and sneered. The slick band called Chic found joy in its repetitions, and with this album created a blueprint for a tonier, upmarket disco style that depended upon serious musicianship.

Chic could play the same four-measure vamp for an hour and keep it riveting. That's because it was, above all, a real band. Guitarist Nile Rodgers fitted Memphis-style chicken-scratching rhythm guitar to disco rhythms. Bassist Bernard Edwards popped his way up and down the fretboard, often handling the melodies (check the opener "Chic Cheer" for a hint of how powerful he could be in this role). Drummer Tony Thompson's patterns were as effective as those from a drum machine, but infused with heart. It didn't matter what else was happening—elaborate string parts, layers of keyboards—because the core locomotion was so strong. (Rappers got it right away:

Bassist Bernard Edwards (above) played a Music Man StingRay, which he bequeathed to Duran Duran's John Taylor after his death.

The Sugar Hill Gang appropriated the rhythm loop of Chic's 1979 hit "Good Times" for its signature "Rapper's Delight.")

That flamboyant locomotion is the reason to seek *C'est Chic*, the band's second album. It's got the massive hit "Le Freak," and several equally exciting tracks, including "Savoir Faire" and "I Want Your Love," which might just be the grabbiest dance floor anthem ever.

GENRE: 🎵 R&B. **RELEASED:** 1978, Atlantic. **KEY TRACKS:** "Chic Cheer," "I Want Your Love," "Savoir Faire," "Le Freak." **CATALOG CHOICE:** *Risqué.* **NEXT STOP:** David Bowie: *Let's Dance.* **AFTER THAT:** Prince: *Lovesexy.*

These Guys Really Knew What Time It Was

The Chicago Transit Authority

Chicago

You can't tell it from the milquetoast power-ballads they dished out in the 1980s, but Chicago was once among the elite experimental outfits in rock. The band's early recordings—this 1969 debut and the five or six efforts that follow—contain musically astute explorations that just happened to become hits. The later efforts, typified by bonbons like 1984's "You're the Inspiration," are impeccably produced cuddle toys. Compare the two, and what you hear is two fundamentally different bands, with contrasting objectives and philosophies.

In fact, from the very beginning the Chicago Transit Authority—the name was shortened to Chicago after the success of the first album, under threat of legal action from the municipal transit agency—depended on multiple personalities. The anchor was a savage R&B-revue-style rhythm section, which first attracted attention with this album's tightly wound version of the Spencer Davis hit "I'm a Man." There were three main singers, each with a distinct tone and approach, who happily alternated between lead and backing-vocal duties. On top was a horn section, but not the squaresville horns associated with Vegas: These guys wrote elaborate lines with an uptown dazzle that eluded the other brassy rock bands of the day.

Chicago was born around the time free-form FM radio took off, and became linked to (and benefited from) its expansiveness. Too sophisticated to jam endlessly, these

The Chicago Transit Authority stayed on the *Billboard* charts for 171 weeks.

musicians instead wrote sprawling, suite-like pieces that borrowed backbeats from Southern soul and organizational ideals from the symphonic repertoire (the stately rallentandos of "Questions 67 and 68," which give each approaching chorus a sense of portent). Some tunes had long, elaborately scored instrumental passages in the middle, and others were technically demanding pop dusted with a touch of hippie ideology. Holding these extremes together was guitarist Terry Kath, who died in a gun accident in 1978. Kath's dissonant chords and scampering fretboard inventions (which once impressed Jimi Hendrix) give many pieces here a needed edge. Kath is everywhere at once, except in the spotlight: Like everyone affiliated with this large ensemble, he was more interested in contributing to the band's fancy colors than grabbing solo glory.

GENRE: 🎸 Rock. **RELEASED:** 1969, Columbia. **KEY TRACKS:** "Beginnings," "Questions 67 and 68," "Does Anybody Really Know What Time It Is?," "I'm a Man." **CATALOG CHOICES:** *Chicago; Chicago III; Chicago V.* **NEXT STOP:** Blood, Sweat & Tears: *Child Is Father to the Man.* **AFTER THAT:** Chase: *Chase.*

The Early Peak of an Irish Powerhouse

The Chieftains 4

The Chieftains

Well before the Chieftains began organizing recording endeavors around guest pop stars, the Irish sextet was the world's most dependably rousing purveyor of Irish jigs and reels. Nothing against the commercially successful later stuff—it's occasionally super-inspired (see Mick Jagger's version of "The Long Black Veil" on the album of the same name) and often beautiful, with the delicate instrumentation making pop vocalists feel comfortable.

But the first cluster of Chieftains titles—made from roughly 1965 until the late 1970s—exhibit a pure delight, and a spry rhythmic sense, that eluded the group as it tried to cross over. You could listen to fifty recordings of Irish traditional music and never hear a more delirious, masterfully synchronized reel than the "Drowsy Maggie" that opens *Chieftains 4*. Uilleann pipe master Paddy Maloney and his crew play it with an audible smirk and a pubgoing rowdiness. The ensemble, which gained a serious textural dimension with the addition of harpist Derek Bell just before this was recorded, is the star throughout: Listen for the way Peadar Mercier (tenor bodhrán) and Sean Potts (bass bodhrán) spin off each other on the picturesque "The Morning Dew."

There are, though, spotlight numbers. One is the fascinating multipart suite "The Battle of Aughrim," which finds Maloney using the pipes to "describe" via music a battle. Maloney renders it with a storyteller's patience. As he moves from one theme to the next, his playing evokes the tense buildup as forces gather, then the braying chaos of the battle itself, and finally the desolation and grief felt by those who survive. This final "Lament" section finds Maloney playing an eerie, heart-heavy theme, as though he's the last living soul on the battlefield, and it's all he can do to send his comrades to their eternal rest.

GENRE: 🌐 World/Celtic. **RELEASED:** 1973, Atlantic. **KEY TRACKS:** "Drowsy Maggie," "The Battle of Aughrim," "Cherish the Ladies," "The Morning Dew." **CATALOG CHOICES:** *Another Country; The Long Black Veil; Irish Heartbeat.* **NEXT STOP:** Clannad: *Macalla* (see p. 170). **AFTER THAT:** Van Morrison: *Hymns to the Silence.*

Music for a Hawaiian Sunset

Endlessly

Sonny Chillingworth

The guitar was brought to Hawaii in the 1830s by Spanish and Mexican cowboys. It quickly became part of the indigenous culture, and over time natives developed their own distinct way of playing it. In the local style known as "slack key" guitar, some strings are tuned lower than on a typical guitar. The bass parts are played with a lazy thumb while the harmony is finger-picked in stricter rhythm.

The masters of the slack key style—pioneers like Gabby Pahinui (see p. 572), Leonard Kwan, and Chillingworth—all retained some of the Spanish/Mexican influence, though in differing degrees. Chillingworth, the most worldly of them despite growing up in a rural area, can sound like a cowboy or a wandering singer of romantic love odes. He interprets age-old Hawaiian songs with a straightforward sincerity, and his vocals have a wistful aspect that's closer to a Spanish love song (or woebegone country ballad) than the music tourists associate with the islands. The title track of this posthumously released set, a version of the Brook Benton R&B hit, shows that he knew how to make his commanding baritone haunt a song.

Chillingworth's guitar playing, swift and assured yet the farthest thing from showboating, lifts his music from the realm of the pleasant into something approaching transcendence. *Endlessly*'s instrumental songs can sometimes cast a contemplative New Age spell; he always approaches them with fastidious precision, transforming idle thoughts into flashes of serene Hawaiian soul.

GENRE: 🌐 World/Hawaii. **RELEASED:** 1999, Windham Hill. **KEY TRACKS:** "Endlessly," "Keiki Slack Key," "Moana Chimes/ Pa'ahana." **CATALOG CHOICE:** *Sonny Solo.* **NEXT STOP:** Gabby Pahinui: *The Gabby Pahinui Hawaiian Band,* Vol. 1.

Secrets Come Spilling from the Piano

Ballades and Scherzos

Frédéric Chopin
Arthur Rubinstein

Many musicians have a central composer who serves as a "home base," the lens through which they see all the others. For pianist Arthur Rubinstein, this was Frédéric Chopin. The Polish-French composer wrote volumes of music for the piano, some of it rococo and grand, and some graced with a pensive, inward-looking character—a private musing. With Chopin (1810–1849), there's often music waiting behind the music, and when played with the Polish-born Rubinstein's innate sensitivity, his works seem to spill secrets from the piano.

Usually in art, a "ballad" refers to a storylike narrative. Not in Chopin. These pieces

Taken in 1849, this is the only known photograph of Frédéric Chopin.

have no greater sense of narrative than any number of other Chopin works in various forms. They're tightly written, and although they hew to an ABA-type structure, they seem predominantly lyrical, more preoccupied with expansive melody than carefully observed form. Reaching the conclusion of the fourth Ballade, listeners often marvel at the vast distances Chopin journeyed in one ten-minute piece.

Rubinstein (1887–1982)

approaches the Ballades as excuses to play rhapsodically. Though blessed with great technique, his hallmark was his musical personality—his warm touch, and an enviable ability to slide ever so slightly away from standard practice. When Chopin repeats an idea for cumulative effect, Rubinstein never phrases it the same way—it's like he's viewing the same idea from a different angle. He's a master of shading, and at times on the third and fourth Ballades, it seems he's delivering each melodic unit at its own tempo, gently pulling back from the pulse to wring every drop of meaning from the line.

A titan of twentieth-century piano, Rubinstein recorded Chopin constantly throughout his career, often revisiting the same pieces several times. Early recordings, made during the 78-RPM era, have a rollick-ing and at times headstrong aspect; later ones are steadier. Rubinstein once claimed that some of his best performances happened late in his career, and this disc, recorded during his third go-around with Chopin in the early days of stereo, is rich with that accumulated wisdom.

GENRE: 🎹 Classical. **RELEASED:** 1959, RCA. **KEY TRACKS:** Ballades Nos. 1 and 4. Scherzos Nos. 2 and 3. **ANOTHER INTERPRETATION:** Vladimir Horowitz: *Horowitz Plays Chopin Ballades, Nocturnes, Preludes.* **CATALOG CHOICE:** *Nineteen Nocturnes* (Vol. 49 of the Rubinstein Collection). **NEXT STOP:** W.A. Mozart: *Piano Concertos Nos. 20 and 21,* Mitsuko Uchida. **AFTER THAT:** Claude Debussy: *Preludes for Piano, Books 1 and 2,* Paul Jacobs.

The Piano Concerto as Improvisational Platform

Piano Concertos Nos. 1 and 2

Frédéric Chopin
Krystian Zimerman, Polish Festival Orchestra (Krystian Zimerman, cond.)

These strange and unorthodox works were begun in 1829, when Frédéric Chopin was nineteen. He was still living in Poland, hadn't yet ventured to seek his fortune in Paris, and was apparently not interested in following established concerto form. The result is appealing youthful wildness. The orchestra and piano take turns stating the themes, and they rarely work together. The pianistic episodes bubble with the grand (improvised-sounding) harmonic schemes that made Chopin's piano music so revelatory.

Only the fussiest scholar listens to the cresting explorations of the first movement of Concerto No. 1 and faults their lack of structure. The rest of us hear Chopin's inventions as genius, deftly sketched melodies sent through unexpected chordal slaloms. These sound logical even as they veer off for brief detours into other tonal centers. Writing in 1850, the pianist and composer Franz Liszt appreciated Chopin's music this way: "His inspirations were powerful, fantastic, impulsive; his forms could be naught but free."

This recording, by the Polish pianist Krystian Zimerman, captures that aspect of Chopin. It's a labor of love. Though he'd recorded both pieces in his youth (at roughly the same age Chopin was when he composed them), the pianist and conductor took a more obsessive approach in 1999. He assembled his own orchestra, one willing to rehearse extensively without union overtime concerns interfering with the creative atmosphere. Once he had the pieces tweaked to his liking, Zimerman then took the group on a world tour.

The obsessiveness paid off: These are frequently astounding interpretations, blessed with subtle touches, like the halting hairsbreadth pauses in Concerto No. 1's second movement. Conducting from the piano, Zimerman puts his group, and his listeners, in touch with the impetuousness of Chopin, and shows how the composer's impulsive initial phrase can blossom into a purposeful, extensively elaborated motif. Zimerman plays freely, as though singing some epic, never-repeated melody, treating it as though it's something Chopin improvised on the fly.

GENRE: 🎵 Classical. **RELEASED:** 1999, Deutsche Grammophon. **KEY TRACKS:** All of them. **ANOTHER INTERPRETATION:** Martha Argerich: *Chopin Panorama.* **CATALOG CHOICE:** *The Complete Nocturnes and Impromptus,* Claudio Arrau. **NEXT STOP:** Leoš Janáček: *Piano Works* (see p. 391).

Antidote for Anxiety

Nocturnes

Frédéric Chopin
Maria João Pires

The next time you find yourself running late in bumper-to-bumper traffic, turn off whatever revving music is playing and slip in Portuguese pianist Maria João Pires's rendition of the Chopin Nocturnes, the composer's short and often wistful inventions for solo piano.

At first the murmuring chords may seem all wrong, especially for the vigilant alertness that's necessary in stop-and-go driving. But embrace the counterintuitive and see what happens. As Pires uncovers Chopin's ruminative themes, the rhythm of the road shifts ever so slightly. Her touch at the piano suggests fleetness and calm all at once, a powerful alternative to road rage. And even when some of these pieces pass through stormy environs, they exude an enveloping serenity—a quality Pires plays up with invisible skill.

These pieces, which cemented the composer's reputation in the salons of late-eighteenth-century Paris, are totally unhurried complete

Maria João Pires performed her first piano recital at age 5.

thoughts that depend equally on steely logic and quick wits. (Traits, not incidentally, that are vital to safe driving.) Played with Pires's sensitivity to slight fluctuations of tempo and shading, the Nocturnes cut to the chase while seeming to meander casually. You might not get where you're going any faster, but you will have been transported, profoundly, along the way.

GENRE: 🎵 Classical. **RELEASED:** 1995, Deutsche Grammophon. **KEY TRACKS:** The three from Opus 15. **ANOTHER INTERPRETATION:** Arthur Rubinstein. **CATALOG CHOICE:** *Ballades and Scherzos* (see p. 166). **NEXT STOP:** Erik Satie: *Piano Works,* Yuji Takahashi.

The First, and One of the Best

The Genius of the Electric Guitar

Charlie Christian

One of the first jazz musicians to explore the possibilities of the electric guitar, Charlie Christian forged an identity for the instrument and established many of its enduring qualities. His brief career is an illustration of how, even in the 1930s, sound traveled fast. An Oklahoma kid who grew up hearing country music, the guitarist with the crisp, heavy-handed attack auditioned for Benny Goodman's band in 1939 at the behest of talent scout John Hammond. Christian got the gig, and from his sideman's perch immediately began rearranging the furniture in the parlor of jazz. Through recordings with Goodman and several under his own name, Christian became one of the most talked-about (and copied) musicians of the age. He started fires with just his ringing tone, and when he took the spotlight (see his signature "Solo Flight"), he swung with such force it didn't matter how timid the other musicians were—he and his Gibson carried them.

"He had that ability to take a note . . . and just pound it into your head until it was the greatest note you ever heard," recalled the guitarist Les Paul, another pioneer, who considered Christian a friend.

By 1941, Christian was a star. The next year he succumbed to tuberculosis—at the age of twenty-five. He left behind a pile of recordings, collected on the four-disc *The Genius of the Electric Guitar*, that displays both irrepressible creativity and an enviable command—Christian's playing established a long-unchallenged technical standard for the instrument. His solos foreshadow bebop, and his furious and exacting chording style was emulated decades later by many rock and blues guitarists. In fact, his fingerprints are all over much of the music that came after him—he's audible in Wes Montgomery and Jimi Hendrix, Leslie West and Stevie Ray Vaughan, and countless others. It's a mind-boggling legacy even before you consider this: Christian's entire discography was recorded in just three years.

GENRE: 🎷 Jazz. **RELEASED**: 2002, Sony Legacy. **KEY TRACKS**: "Solo Flight," "What's New." **NEXT STOP**: Tal Farlow: *Tal Farlow's Finest Hour.* **AFTER THAT**: Wes Montgomery: *Boss Guitar.*

What'll It Be?

Irish Drinking Songs

The Clancy Brothers and the Dubliners

Lots of cultures respect a good libation, but few can outdo the Irish in terms of pure and heartfelt worship. Pub songs speak in reverential tones about the animating powers of whiskey and beer—the way these magic elixirs lighten the burdens of the troubled and give courage to the meek. To the sober, these tunes can seem silly, or evidence of moral decay. To those in the middle of a Saturday night bender, they're a kind of lifeline, connecting generations.

The Clancy Brothers garnered huge success after being on *The Ed Sullivan Show* in 1961.

This compilation features spirited songs about spirits, recorded in the 1960s by two of the most prominent Celtic music acts—the Dubliners and the Clancy Brothers with Tommy Makem. The bearded Dubliners began making music in Dublin pubs in the 1960s, and quickly acquired a reputation for raucous, hard-drinking performances. Here, they dust off an old Australian tune, "The Pub with No Beer," and re-create a communal exhortation, "Drink It Up Men," just right for closing time.

The Clancy Brothers with Tommy Makem started as struggling New York actors; they switched to harmonizing when the folk revival took hold in the late '50s. Their trick was to expand on the traditional Irish ballads they'd heard growing up; they used five-string banjo

and guitar (then an exotic instrument in Celtic music), and made elaborate vocal arrangements of tunes usually handled by a solo singer. Their contributions to the drinking-song canon range from extreme jollity ("Beer, Beer, Beer") to foreboding ("Whiskey, You're the Divil") to somber—this collection closes with "The Parting Glass," a salute to drinking buddies at last call. "Oh, all the money that e'er I spent, I spent it in good company," goes one line. "So fill to me the parting glass, goodnight and joy be with you all."

GENRE: 🌐 World/Celtic. **RELEASED:** 1997, Columbia/Legacy. **KEY TRACKS:** "Beer, Beer, Beer," "Mountain Dew," "The Moonshiner," "Tim Finnegan's Wake," "The Parting Glass." **CATALOG CHOICES:** The Dubliners: *Spirit of the Irish, The Ultimate Collection.* The Clancy Brothers with Tommy Makem: *In Person at Carnegie Hall.* **NEXT STOP:** The Pogues: *Rum, Sodomy, and the Lash.* **AFTER THAT:** Altan: *Horse with a Heart.*

Not Your Typical Jigs and Reels

Macalla

Clannad

In the '80s, the Brennan family of Gweedore, County Donegal, was responsible for two of the most successful Celtic music acts ever—the pop-leaning band Clannad (Gaelic for "family") and the solo career of Clannad keyboardist Enya, who transformed the vapors of the Irish bogs into keening New Age gold.

Clannad, formed in the pub where Papa Brennan was the proprietor, was just beginning to break out of the traditional Celtic mold when Enya left her three siblings in 1982 to

pursue a solo career. By this 1985 album, Clannad had developed a sound that linked the earthy mysticism of traditional Irish music to the airbrushed guitar pop and soothing harmonies of Fleetwood Mac. *Macalla* shows how rich this territory is: The album's rapt ballads and stately medium-tempo anthems are among the most inventive contemporary music to come from Ireland.

Clannad recorded the rhythm parts for *Macalla* in England, and then moved to Dublin's Windmill Lane Studios to do the vocals. After struggling with the melody to one song written by Ciaran Brennan, the band sought refuge at the local pub. There they encountered members of U2. In storybook fashion, days later Bono was in the studio, singing on and helping to develop what became the Top 20 1986 hit "In a Lifetime."

The song, which intertwines Bono's brawny voice with Moya Brennan's more fragile, ribbonlike instrument, is not the only highlight.

Macalla means "echo" in Gaelic, and that's one unifying idea: Each little bubble of melody arrives with lots of space around it. Even when there's a backbeat, Clannad makes room for faintly reverberating waves of sound that eventually circle back around. Out of those delicate mists comes a deep sense of Celtic tradition, a music of great fervor that floats with feathery grace.

GENRE: 🌐 World/Celtic. **RELEASED:** 1985, RCA. **KEY TRACKS:** "In a Lifetime," "Caislean Oir," "Closer to Your Heart," "Blackstairs." **CATALOG CHOICE:** *Clannad 2*. **NEXT STOP:** Enya: *Watermark*. **AFTER THAT:** Loreena McKennitt: *The Visit* (see p. 489).

The Arrival of a Major Songwriter

Old No. 1

Guy Clark

When Guy Clark's debut rolled out in 1975, it looked like the start of a promising career. One original song, "L.A. Freeway," had already been a big hit for Jerry Jeff Walker. The personnel included a cluster of fast-rising performers, among them Emmylou Harris and Rodney Crowell, both of whom considered Clark's wry storytelling to be part of the Nashville future.

Despite critical raves, *Old No. 1* didn't connect with a sizable audience—the liner notes to a reissued edition speculate that Clark didn't receive the blessing of country radio airplay because "his voice was too rough and gravelly to appease the commercially minded radio stations."

That weathered voice is, of course, integral to Clark's sharply observed vignettes, which follow the not necessarily noble exploits of wandering souls. The singer and songwriter grew up in the small West Texas town of Monahans, and was raised by his grandmother, who operated a hotel. Clark said later that sev-

eral of these songs were inspired by characters who passed through—most likely the wildcat oilman of "Desperados Waiting for a Train," and the good-time gal "Rita Ballou." Unlike many of the facile one-hit-plus-filler albums Music City was cranking out at the time, *Old No. 1* is genius from beginning to end, with each sketch offering sharply observed, short-story glimpses into human nature.

GENRE: 🔵 Country. **RELEASED:** 1975, RCA. **KEY TRACKS:** "Rita Ballou," "She Ain't Goin' Nowhere," "Like a Coat from the Cold," "Desperados Waiting for a Train." **CATALOG CHOICE:** *Texas Cookin'*. **NEXT STOP:** Willis Alan Ramsey: *Willis Alan Ramsey* (see p. 632). **AFTER THAT:** Townes Van Zandt: *Live at the Old Quarter* (see p. 801).

Cool Struttin'

Sonny Clark

One of seven albums pianist Sonny Clark recorded under his own name between 1957 and '58, *Cool Struttin'* is a master class in the (nearly lost) art of jazz accompaniment. Clark's piano solos are cogent and calm, a thoughtful amalgam of Bud Powell blitheness and Red Garland poise cut with a touch of Thelonious Monk's harmonic impulsiveness. But the late-night looseness of this session springs from what Clark and the rhythm section play in the background, behind saxophonist Jackie McLean and trumpeter Art Farmer. Concentrating on providing apt rejoinders (as opposed to conjuring brand-new horizons),

Cool Struttin' is an "enduring hard-bop classic."
—*New York Times*

Clark frames the solos using tidy chordal jabs. His accompaniment nicks the fine edges of the beat, syncopations caught (and deftly reinforced) by master drummer Philly Joe Jones. At times during McLean's enthusiastic romp through "Sippin' at Bells," the solo lines are the direct outgrowth of this rhythm section's active teasing and prompting.

The knack for goading soloists made Clark (1931–1963) a favorite of musicians and one of the first-call pianists of the Blue Note roster, despite the fact that his own recordings were rarely big sellers. In the original liner notes, Farmer, an astute jazz appreciator, tells critic Nat Hentoff that Clark's approach has "no strain in it." That's key. Like Philly Joe Jones and all the great jazz support players, Clark knew that his cohorts would sound good if everything around them felt good. And this certainly does.

GENRE: 🎷 Jazz. **RELEASED:** 1958, Blue Note. **KEY TRACKS:** "Cool Struttin'," "Blue Minor," "Sippin' at Bells." **CATALOG CHOICE:** *Sonny's Crib.* **NEXT STOP:** Wynton Kelly: *Kelly Blue.* **AFTER THAT:** Red Garland: *At the Prelude.*

London Calling

The Clash

Punk in late '70s London is often portrayed as an all-stops housecleaning in which everything venerable and old gets the heave-ho. The Clash is usually held up as a prime mover of this insurrectionist moment—the title track of this classic, a thrumming military march with a bad attitude, proclaims, "London calling, now don't look to us, all that phony Beatlemania has bitten the dust."

Yet these four working-class kids didn't loathe that old-time rock and roll. Like other bands associated with the revolution of 1977, the Clash revered the trailblazers of early rock, R&B and reggae, and for this third album, the band repurposed stray sparks from vintage records into a roiling, careening sound that enchanted safety-pin-sporting punk scenesters as well as those too old for the mosh pit. Songwriters Joe Strummer and Mick Jones conjured clever tunes based on creepy-crawly "Monster Mash" rhythms. They rejiggered the blues ("Brand New Cadillac"), built a jangling classic out of old Buddy Holly scraps ("Train in Vain"), and cast the jitters of ska in a new light ("Lover's Rock"). Even the cover of *London Calling*—which borrows the layout of Elvis Presley's first long-player—reflects an awareness of history. It's as though somebody dared to open a window in the House of Punk, letting in bits of the outside world for the first time in too long.

These scavengings provide the perfect

On the cover: Paul Simonon smashing his Fender Precision Bass.

springboard for front man Strummer, whose caustic, ever-skeptical perspective gives *London Calling*—the rare double album sold for a single-album price—its rebel edge. Strummer's a classic crank: As he rails against entrenched powers and decries poverty and the evil doings of the British government, he comes across not as a narcissitic punk, but an engaged citizen who actually cares about what's happening. This riled-up idealism is a Clash trademark; it's in full cry here and on the subsequent *¡Sandinista!* When they really get on the high horse, Strummer and his mates—blistering guitarist Jones, bassist Paul Simonon, and drummer Topper Headon—can make you believe they've gathered all the outrage ever expressed in the name of rock and roll, and are, right at this instant, fomenting a new revolution with it.

GENRE: 🎸 Rock. **RELEASED:** 1979, Epic. **KEY TRACKS:** "London Calling," "Brand New Cadillac," "Spanish Bombs," "The Guns of Brixton," "Revolution Rock," "Train in Vain." **CATALOG CHOICE:** *Sandinista!* **NEXT STOP:** Gang of Four: *Entertainment!* (see p. 298). **AFTER THAT:** The Specials: *The Specials*.

The Concert Pianist as Rock Star

Rachmaninoff: Piano Concerto No. 3
Prokofiev: Piano Concerto No. 3

Van Cliburn

Van Cliburn arrived at Carnegie Hall on May 19, 1958, as the classical-music equivalent of a rock star. The Fort Worth, Texas–based pianist had recently won the first Tchaikovsky competition in Moscow, besting his hosts at their national music during a tense moment of the cold war. Upon his return, he was greeted with a ticker tape parade in New York City (he remains the only classical figure to receive one), and shortly after became the first classical musician to sell a million copies of a recording.

At Carnegie Hall, Cliburn, then twenty-three, performed one of the most demanding pieces in the classical repertoire—Rachmaninoff's Piano Concerto No. 3 in D Minor, a work of dazzling interlocked melodies and sudden mood changes. He caught every curve of it: Throughout this live performance, Cliburn has a sparkle in his touch and a rare knack for making the intricate fingerwork sound like an impulsive caper. The accompanying Symphony of the Air, the New York ensemble that rose from the ashes of the NBC Symphony Orchestra, picks up his slight changes of emphasis. At times during the folk songs of the first movement, the ensemble seems to sway behind Cliburn, leaning into the supporting passages with exactly the same amount of elbow grease the pianist applies. The result is a transfixing, unified reading.

While the pace of the Rachmaninoff requires Cliburn to scamper, the Prokofiev

Van Cliburn began learning to play the piano when he was just 3 years old.

Piano Concerto No. 3, the most frequently heard Prokofiev piano music, demands more drama. The pianist delivers the phrase that becomes the primary theme with a precise articulation that remains the industry standard—to this day, few snap off chords the way Cliburn does on this performance, which was recorded in 1960 with the lively Chicago Symphony Orchestra.

These recordings catch Cliburn at a lyrical peak. Alas, the adulation apparently got to him: Critics who'd heard him early on complained that his later interpretations never went anywhere different, that he essentially stopped growing as an artist. Which makes this recording all the more essential: It shows Cliburn at a moment when he was more than the culture's latest unlikely "It" boy. He was a musician in full control of his art.

GENRE: 🎵 Classical. **RELEASED:** 1960, RCA. **KEY TRACKS:** Rachmaninoff: first movement (Allegro ma non tanto). Prokofiev: first movement (Andante). **ANOTHER INTERPRETATION:** Martha Argerich: *The Great Pianists Series*. **CATALOG CHOICE:** *Piano Concertos by Beethoven and Schumann*. **NEXT STOP:** Richard Goode: *Beethoven: The Late Piano Sonatas*.

Reggae Rises Here

The Harder They Come

Jimmy Cliff

Jimmy Cliff was already established as a singer and songwriter in Jamaica when filmmaker Perry Henzell heard his 1969 hymn to perseverance, "Many Rivers to Cross." Sensing that Cliff's song was the perfect anthem for his tale about the class and socioeconomic struggles of a rural roustabout in the city of Kingston, Henzell invited him to contribute other songs that advanced the narrative, and soon after cast Cliff as the film's leading man. The movie and its stirring soundtrack gave much of the world its first taste of reggae music, and it made Cliff an international star and the first reggae crossover artist.

Cliff's songs prove ideal for export: They're built on the effortless push-pull of reggae rhythm, while embracing the upbeat exuberance of American soul music (especially "You Can Get It if You Really Want It," which echoes the vocal intensity of early Stax-Volt). Other compositions hint at Southern gospel: "Many Rivers" and "Sitting in Limbo" are solemn, hymnlike expressions of faith. And though the lyrics are simple, they are powerfully inspirational. Several of the songs have culture-specific meanings: Though "Many Rivers" sounds like a plainspoken sermon of persistence, it was heard in Jamaica as a rallying cry of rude-boy culture, a bold street kid talking

Rolling Stone named "The Harder They Come" one of the "500 Greatest Songs of All Time."

openly about grabbing what he could.

The soundtrack includes other shining early-reggae moments: The frenetic "Pressure Drop," which was the first Toots and the Maytals hit; the Melodians' "Rivers of Babylon"; the Desmond Dekker hit "007 (Shanty Town)." Disc 2 of the 2003 Deluxe Edition collects other notable reggae crossover attempts from the fertile moment, roughly from 1968– 1972, before Bob Marley exploded on the scene. Among these are Cliff's disillusioned war cry "Viet Nam," the Johnny Nash classic "I Can See Clearly Now," and the Maytals' "54-46 (That's My Number)."

GENRE: 🌐 World/Jamaica. **RELEASED:** 1972, Island. (Reissued 2003.) **KEY TRACKS:** "Sitting in Limbo," "Many Rivers to Cross." **CATALOG CHOICE:** *Struggling Man.* **NEXT STOP:** Toots and the Maytals: *Live.*

A Complete View of a Legend

The Patsy Cline Collection

Patsy Cline

Patsy Cline (1932–1963) possessed one of the most arresting voices in all of music, a soft-yet-firm clarion call that was suited not just to the torch songs that made her famous but rockabilly and gospel (the very

last song she recorded, before dying in a plane crash at age thirty, was "Just a Closer Walk with Thee").

This versatility is generally ignored by the hundreds of compilations of Cline's hits. But it is key to appreciating her art. Cline recorded for several years before generating any attention; she spent this time learning the

subtle arts of inflection and persuasion. Some of the material she did for the Four Star label (which had control of her song choices) doesn't fit her well at all, and yet she makes it transfixing—as the 1955 reading of "Turn the Cards Slowly" and "Try Again" (1957) demonstrate, Cline had the rare ability to fill a slight song with personal overtones, until it mattered.

This four-disc chronological box is the only comprehensive choice for those wishing to collect Cline. Its first two discs, devoted to the pre-stardom years, chronicle an artist's search for the most effective platforms for her immense talent. Discs 3 and 4 show what happened after she'd found it—when she poured that wistful tone into such rocking-chair country-pop classics as "Crazy," "Walkin' After Midnight," and others. Cline's gift to love-song singing was her gentleness. She could let you know that she was aching inside without overt gestures or flamboyant drama (a lesson often lost on other female country singers of the 1960s). Though the arrangements around her got more elaborate, somehow Patsy Cline never did any showboating. With her, falling to pieces was a matter of little things crumbling, one by one. Not a demolition.

GENRE: ◷ Country. **RELEASED:** 1991, MCA. **KEY TRACKS:** "Walkin' After Midnight," "Crazy," "When Your House Is Not a Home," "Your Cheatin' Heart." **CATALOG CHOICE:** *Patsy Cline and Kitty Wells.* **NEXT STOP:** k.d. lang: *Shadowland.* **AFTER THAT:** Brenda Lee: *This Is . . . Brenda.*

"Patsy Cline is and perhaps will always be the standard bearer for all female country singers."
—Tammy Wynette

Don't Talk Back to the Court Jesters of Rock and Roll

"Yakety Yak"

The Coasters

The clever teen-centered songwriting team of Jerry Leiber and Mike Stoller found its perfect mouthpiece in the Coasters. Five West Coast (hence the name) guys with a knack for cracking wise, the group wasn't the flashiest or anywhere near the most vocally impressive of the doo-wop outfits. But it always had fun. And through that zillion-watt brightness, the Coasters helped prepare the world for rock and roll: "Yakety Yak" and the group's subsequent singles stand as key bridges between doo-wop and rock.

"Yakety Yak," the classic soundtrack of parents hassling their teenagers to help around the house, is the first song the Coasters released after following Leiber and Stoller to the East Coast. It's a three-minute theatrical production that stands among the towering achievements of early rock: The beat is wild, and the saxophone (from R&B honker King Curtis) sends things almost out of control with every break. And yet the Coasters assume their various roles with Broadway poise; their winking irreverence gives the teen complaints a dimension of knowing maturity.

Leiber and Stoller would repeat the "Yakety Yak" formula on the string of subsequent Coasters hits, from the confessions of a class clown named "Charlie Brown" to the jumping "Speedo" to "Poison Ivy." Any decent Coasters anthology will include all the aforementioned, as well as a few singles that show the group wasn't some sort of novelty act—seek out the gorgeously sung "Searchin'" from 1957, and its flip side, "Young Blood."

GENRE: 🎸 Rock. **RELEASED**: 1958, Atlantic. **APPEARS ON:** *The Very Best of the Coasters* (1993, Rhino). **NEXT STOP:** The Drifters: *Save the Last Dance for Me.* **AFTER THAT:** Clyde McPhatter: *Clyde McPhatter.*

"Gonna Raise a Fuss . . ."

"Summertime Blues"

Eddie Cochran

Anyone who ever had to work on a sunny day in the middle of the summer knows the anguish of "Summertime Blues," Eddie Cochran's rock evergreen. The young man just wants to have fun, but life keeps getting in the way—his boss tells him he's got to work late, then his parents aren't happy because he skipped out on work, and when he appeals to his congressman for help, the wise elder says, "I'd like to help you son, but you're too young to vote."

Written by Cochran and his manager Jerry Capehart, the tune took off like wildfire shortly after it was released, in early June 1958. "There had been a lot of songs about summer, but none about the hardships of summer," Capehart told *Rolling Stone*, adding that the duo knocked the tune out in forty-five minutes the night before it was recorded. The recording helped establish Cochran as a leader of the hard-rocking wing of rockabilly, and stands as an early example of the crafty use of multitracking: Cochran doubled both the acoustic and electric guitars for a thicker sound than was common at the time. Also notable is the presence of Earl Palmer, the great New Orleans session drummer, whose easygoing pulse makes the tune crackle and jump. Though "Summertime Blues" has been covered endlessly, most nota-

Cochran wasn't just a musician, he also starred in two movies.

bly by the Who (see p. 858) and Blue Cheer, nobody has improved upon the snap of the original.

The song reached number 8 on the *Billboard* Hot 100 singles chart in late September 1958, and though Cochran had subsequent hits, the singer and guitarist from Minnesota didn't reach his full potential: He was killed at age twenty-one in a car accident while touring England in the spring of 1960. *Somethin' Else: The Fine Lookin' Hits of Eddie Cochran* makes a case for Cochran as an underappreciated early visionary—an accomplished guitarist and magnetic vocalist whose straight-shooting singles (not just "Summertime Blues" but the equally electrifying "C'mon Everybody" and "Nervous Breakdown") rev with the hot-rodding essence of rock and roll.

GENRE: 🎸 Rock. **RELEASED**: 1958, Liberty. **APPEARS ON:** *Somethin' Else: The Fine Lookin' Hits of Eddie Cochran.* **NEXT STOP**: The Who: *Live at Leeds.* **AFTER THAT:** Gene Vincent: *The Screaming End.*

Another "Only in the Early '70s" Artifact

Mad Dogs and Englishmen

Joe Cocker

Joe Cocker has said that when this project began in 1970, he didn't know most of the musicians assembled by songwriter/arranger Leon Russell for what turned out to be his most important U.S. tour. It's easy to believe that, because there were some thirty-six people involved on stage—horn players, strings, backing singers, and an extra-large rhythm section with multiple drummers and keyboard players. Their nightly exploits were documented by a film crew that traveled coast-to-coast, and recorded by Cocker's label, A&M Records, at several stops. (This double album was recorded at New York's Fillmore East.)

If such an endeavor around a not-yet-huge artist seems wildly extravagant, chalk it up to the times: This was how they rolled in the early '70s. And Cocker, another of the artists whose profile jumped after appearing at Woodstock in August 1969, looked like a safe bet. Russell, then a Svengali to several artists, believed that the grind-it-out British belter with the Ray Charles obsession could be huge if presented in the right context. So he wrote screaming arrangements of songs Cocker had been singing for years, and positioned the singer at the center of a constantly moving (and frequently gaudy) revue.

Bigger isn't usually better in rock. But *Mad Dogs* works, in part because the ensemble pushes Cocker in ways few rock singers are ever pushed. He sings Traffic's "Feelin' Alright" as a series of boxing maneuvers, slipping his ad-libs into the (few) open spaces. He feeds off the campy vaudeville backing for the Beatles' "She Came In Through the Bathroom Window." And though he enjoys the power of Russell's ensemble on the full-throttle rock numbers, Cocker is most persuasive when the heat isn't full force: This steady-rolling version of "Cry Me a River" deserves a spot in the hall of fame, as does the sultry version of Russell's "Delta Lady" that closes the program.

GENRE: 🎸 Rock. **RELEASED:** 1971, A&M. **KEY TRACKS:** "Cry Me a River," "Delta Lady," "Blue Medley," "Feelin' Alright." **CATALOG CHOICE:** *Joe Cocker.* **NEXT STOP:** Ray Charles: *Genius + Soul = Jazz.* **AFTER THAT:** Blood, Sweat & Tears: *Blood, Sweat & Tears.*

Listen to This While Traveling at Night

Codona 3

Codona

No genre labels adequately describe the music made by the trio of trumpeter Don Cherry, sitar and dulcimer master Colin Walcott, and hand percussionist Naná Vasconcelos. It is largely improvised, but light-years removed from jazz. It has riveting, beautifully recorded ethnic percussion conversations that are too open, too transparent, to fall under the catchall term "world music."

Codona, simply, is its own universe. When it started, in 1978, trumpeter Cherry was busy making solo records, Walcott was leading his band Oregon through some of the most ambitious music it ever made, and Vasconcelos was beginning his solo career, focusing on the bow-shaped Brazilian instrument known as the *berimbau.*

On this third album, the three continue to explore the connections between ethnic music and the questing spirit of free jazz. They've evolved an entire vocabulary, a fantasy world in which Brazil meets India. The groove that erupts six minutes into "Goshakabuchi" is characteristic: Everything leading up to this has been calm and tempoless, with each musician offering an expansive, free-associative

lark. Suddenly Vasconcelos crashes into a downbeat and keeps going, churning out a clatter of metallic percussion that sounds like a rainstorm hitting a tin roof. Within seconds, Walcott is banging an SOS on the strings, and Cherry is tossing out squabbling little provocations. "Travel by Night," the third track, hits a more intense groove, and sustains it brilliantly. Its multitextural and unclassifiable music doesn't hit you over the head with weighty themes. Instead, it's journeying music, forever unfolding and evolving.

GENRES: 🅐 Jazz 🌐 World. **RELEASED:** 1982, ECM. **KEY TRACKS:** "Travel by Night," "Lullabye," "Clicky Clacky," "Goshakabuchi," "Inner Organs." **CATALOG CHOICES:** *Codona 1, Codona 2.* **NEXT STOP:** Pat Metheny and Lyle Mays (featuring Naná Vasconcelos): *As Falls Wichita, So Falls Wichita Falls.* **AFTER THAT:** King Crimson: *Lark's Tongues in Aspic.*

A Poet of the Vicissitudes of Love

Songs of Leonard Cohen

Leonard Cohen

Nothing is absolute in the cosmology of Leonard Cohen. The Canadian songwriter and poet dwells in the deep shadows of the heart, where things slide in all directions, ambiguity reigns, and rational thought no longer serves. A black-humored troubadour of love, he's prone to expressing undying admiration and withering disdain for the same person, often in the same verse, sometimes in the same line or the same word. He specializes in dirges and processionals, and begins them when hope is nearly lost. From there, he goes chasing the longest of long shots, spurred on by a rogue's faith. He's busted up that the Marianne of "So Long, Marianne," one of several muses occupying center stage here, has flown. He laments this bygone love not just with the expected bitterness but overwhelming affection; his

past-tense descriptions of intimate moments are so vividly wrought, they reveal him all but consumed by the memory.

Cohen was past thirty before he started writing music and recorded this, his first album. He'd already made an impression as a poet and novelist in his native Montreal, and he carried the literary devices into his earnest troubadour phase. His tales don't always unfold in linear sequence—at times, Cohen's songs are like novels with key chapters missing. In them, love is portrayed as a dizzying dance that sends participants to peaks of exaltation and valleys of torment and back again. As he painstakingly itemizes his own shortcomings and reflects on the steps that led to his present despair, his resigned tone of voice makes the snags and snarls of an affair seem almost heroic.

Leonard Cohen, seen here during the early days of his career, poses for a portrait in a New York City diner.

Cohen's fixation on the alternating currents of love sets him apart from the singer-songwriters sometimes mentioned as his peers. On this album and two exquisite subsequent ones, *Songs from a Room* and *Songs of Love and Hate*, he transforms a common songwriter conceit—romance as a path to enlightenment, if not redemption—into an urgent, revelatory, all-consuming epic quest.

GENRE: 🎸 Rock.
RELEASED: 1967, Columbia.
KEY TRACKS: "So Long, Marianne," "Suzanne," "Sisters of Mercy," "Hey, That's No Way to Say Goodbye." **F.Y.I.:** Several of these songs turn up in Robert Altman's anti-Western *McCabe and Mrs. Miller.* **CATALOG CHOICES:** *Songs from a Room; Songs of Love and Hate; The Future.*
NEXT STOP: Kris Kristofferson: *Kristofferson.*
AFTER THAT: Damien Rice: *O.*

The Teddy Bear Swings

The Complete After Midnight Sessions

Nat King Cole and His Trio

Nat King Cole (1919–1965) went to swankyville gracefully, in a way that made musical sense. The Alabama native started his career as a jazz pianist, and despite the beauty of his warm-cocoa baritone, took to singing slowly. When he eventually stepped out front of big studio orchestras, on such themed records as *Sings for Two in Love* (1954), Cole retained his knack for sculpting phrases, and the ability to offset schmaltzy surroundings with the subtlest wink of irreverence.

Still the hipsters groaned. Here was a really smart jazz musician "wasting" his talent by singing garishly, and leaving jazz behind. The polite entertainer picked

The Trio was originally called the King Cole Swingsters.

up on the derision; this album, which featured his trio joined by several jazz soloists, was a response to those who claimed he'd sold out. It's a great way to appreciate one of the most enchanting voices of the twentieth century.

The conceit is obvious: Here's the Cole trio doing its own thing after the paying customers have gone home. The spotlight is on the group's unperturbed, and seemingly effortless, sense of swing—when Cole sings jazz, he's not the marquee star but just part of the band. That doesn't mean he tears off wildly for points unknown; rather, he just takes it easy, taking time to poke around in the margins, dabbling rather than outright making declarations. His treatments of "Just You, Just Me" and "I Know That You Know" glide with the blithe, devil-may-care irreverence that vanished from popular music by the late '50s, never to return.

And even though he's off duty, Cole never stops being an entertainer. The solos are short and to the point, framed by the taciturn piano chords. The tunes include pieces Cole performed regularly and jazz treats like "Caravan," which features a spirited trombone solo from its composer, Juan Tizol. To discover why Cole remains unforgettable, cue up the shapely "Blame It on My Youth" or any of the ballads here, and relax, because that's what everyone involved is doing.

GENRE: 🎤 Vocals. **RELEASED:** 1957, Capitol. **KEY TRACKS:** "Just You, Just Me," "Blame It on My Youth," "Caravan," "Sweet Lorraine." **CATALOG CHOICES:** *Love Is the Thing; The Christmas Song.* **NEXT STOP:** Shirley Horn: *Here's to Life.* **AFTER THAT:** Chet Baker: *Let's Get Lost: The Best of Chet Baker Sings* (see p. 40).

The First Great Wail of the Jazz Avant-Garde

The Shape of Jazz to Come

Ornette Coleman

C ue this up whenever you want to be transported back to a time when radicalism was on the loose in America. These days, it's pretty much in the deep freeze. The culture that once revered the brave frontier explorer and the cranky outsider has become wary, reluctant to change, conservative in the most basic sense.

It wasn't always thus. When this album appeared in 1959, sparks were in the air, and there was growing receptivity to alternative views in art and society. Ornette Coleman, an alto saxophonist from Texas, seized the opening; through sheer force of will and a bit of press-agent moxie, he loudly created space for what became known as the jazz avant-garde. *The Shape of Jazz to Come* amounts to his founder's manifesto. It features no piano—and doesn't rely on the predetermined chord sequences

Ornette Coleman was awarded a Pulitzer Prize for music in 2007.

that had defined jazz since the 1920s. Instead, he and his group seek out open, mutable harmonies that can change with the melodies, acquiring new colors and characteristics with each note. Coleman called this approach "Harmolodics," and his accomplices get right into it: As Coleman and trumpeter Don Cherry play questioning melodies and asymmetrical provocations, bassist Charlie Haden and drummer Billy Higgins interject jabbing, slashing rejoinders as the discussion evolves. (Among the many examples of Coleman defying expectations is the ballad "Lonely Woman," a plaintive theme that bears no traces of insurrection.)

Even some jazz hipsters weren't ready for "Congeniality" and the other winding, winningly melodic agitations on *The Shape of Jazz to Come*. And they sure weren't ready for *Free Jazz* (1961), which featured two fierce quartets playing at once, an étude for sirens in stereo. Somehow, though, a few bold souls responded to Coleman's shape-shifting music right away, and by the end of 1961, free jazz was in full cry, changing everything in its path.

GENRE: Jazz. **RELEASED:** 1959, Atlantic. **KEY TRACKS:** "Peace," "Congeniality," "Lonely Woman." **CATALOG CHOICES:** *Free Jazz; Dancing In Your Head; In All Languages.* **NEXT STOP:** Archie Shepp: *Four for 'Trane.*

A Roaring Hard-Bop Express

Blue Train

John Coltrane

T hose who knew John Coltrane (1926–1967) speak of him as a principled man who kept his word and tried—even through an extended addiction to heroin, which he finally conquered in the late '50s—to do the right thing. This incandescent set might be cited as proof. It came about when, in 1956, Coltrane paid a visit to the offices of Blue Note records looking for recordings by the soprano sax pioneer Sidney Bechet (it would be a few years before Coltrane himself would pick up the soprano). While conversing with Alfred Lion, cofounder of the label, Coltrane agreed to record for Blue Note, and received a small advance. Then, in 1957, Coltrane signed with Prestige Records, and though Blue Note had apparently forgotten about the handshake deal, Coltrane hadn't. He honored the commitment with this album—recorded in a day—of electrifying originals and a mellow reading of Jerome Kern's "I'm Old Fashioned."

This is a jazz thrill not to be missed, with Coltrane and his cohorts sounding like they've been chasing hard-bop bliss together for years. Pivoting and shouting and shooting stingers out of his trumpet, the nineteen-year-old Lee Morgan makes the most of each

In 1960, Coltrane called *Blue Train* the favorite of his albums.

stop-time phrase (there are many); after he grabs listeners on "Locomotion" or "Moment's Notice," he doesn't let go until he's dashed off a screaming, career-best solo. The same goes for trombonist Curtis Fuller, and pianist Kenny Drew, whose turn on "Lazy Bird" neatly summarizes the leader's harmonic ideas. And then there's Coltrane. He's not yet into the exhaustive (and exhausting) "sheets of sound" approach, but he's getting there; each of these improvisations has a touch of the beat-the-clock panic that would define such later works as *Giant Steps*.

GENRE: Jazz. **RELEASED:** 1957, Blue Note. **KEY TRACKS:** "Moment's Notice," "Blue Train," "I'm Old Fashioned." **CATALOG CHOICES:** *Coltrane's Sound; Coltrane Plays the Blues.* **NEXT STOP:** Lee Morgan: *Search for the New Land* (see p. 521). **AFTER THAT:** Miles Davis and John Coltrane: *Live in Stockholm, 1960.*

Devotional Music of the Highest Order

A Love Supreme

John Coltrane

Approach this with what yogis call "beginner's mind," and prepare to enter a state of radiant calm. A place where the abstraction associated with jazz clarifies into stillness and great humility, yet through it comes the sound of striving—not for a better car or higher-grade libations, but a purer soul. This is John Coltrane's grown-up symphony to God (or whatever spirit-entity), which aims to bring listeners to a higher state of consciousness. (A church in San Francisco, the St. John Will-I-Am Coltrane African Orthodox Church, believes it can; *A Love Supreme* is among its core sacred texts.)

When Coltrane recorded it, on a December day in 1964, it was his attempt, as a reformed junkie, at spreading the news that human transformation is not just desirable, but possible. In the liner notes, Coltrane explains, "During the year 1957, I experienced, by the grace of God, a spiritual awakening which was to lead me to a richer, fuller, more productive life. At that time, in gratitude, I humbly asked to be given the means and privilege to make others happy through music."

A Love Supreme is an act of evangelical ardor and a lunge in the direction of the eternal. Coltrane intentionally didn't give pianist McCoy Tyner, bassist Jimmy Garrison, and drummer Elvin Jones much time to prepare, and as a result they follow him into the unknown with tender acolyte steps. The work's four sections ("Acknowledgement," "Resolution," "Pursuance," and "Psalm") are set to a Coltrane-penned prayer reprinted in the notes. Each is built on massive, enveloping drones that inspire a feeling of reverence. As happened on Coltrane's less overtly spiritual works, the players get right inside the saxophonist's thoughts, adding supportive gestures that send Coltrane higher. All involved know they're in the company of a great animating force, who's pushing toward a deeper understanding and pulling them along. It is the sense of shared pursuit that makes *A Love Supreme* the most devout jazz work ever.

GENRE: 🅙 Jazz. **RELEASED:** 1965, Impulse. **KEY TRACKS:** "Acknowledgement," "Psalm." **CATALOG CHOICE:** *Meditations.* **NEXT STOP:** Archie Shepp and Horace Parlan: *Goin' Home* (see p. 694).

The Art of the Ballad

John Coltrane and Johnny Hartman

John Coltrane and Johnny Hartman

Johnny Hartman's baritone calls from the bar Billy Strayhorn was writing about in "Lush Life," the once-glamorous place offering "jazz and cocktails" to a clientele of slightly frayed regulars. His voice is slippery and warm, as inviting as the leather banquette where couples sit for hours, gazing in a love trance. Its warm timbre evokes other pleasures, too—the breeze on a seaside veranda, butter melting on a homemade biscuit.

In terms of sheer smooth sound, no jazz singer ever got in the same ballpark. Hartman's voice transports you inside the songs almost involuntarily, and keeps you transfixed with an almost magical shorthand—he sings jazz with no shooby-doo whatsoever. On this, the most important record he ever made, Hartman's tone is complemented by another, equally elemental sound: the glinting metallic cry of John Coltrane's tenor saxophone.

Recorded in a single day in 1963, this six-song collection finds the unlikely tandem working over some tender saloon songs—in addition to "Lush Life," there's a definitive "My One and Only Love," and a melancholy treatment of "They Say It's Wonderful." Hartman (1923–1983), a balladeer in the Billy Eckstine mold, hadn't made a record of

his own since 1956, but there's no evidence of rust: His edge-free voice glides regally along, not asserting authority but being authoritative nonetheless. The same goes for Coltrane. Here and on the equally rhapsodic *Ballads*—arguably the most beautiful set of torch songs ever recorded by a jazz instrumentalist—he tugs at the edges of music, gliding through the contours of the melodies until he arrives at the most telling and poignant notes. Lots of jazz musician-singer collaborations offer more tunes than the six featured here; few, though, contain more music.

GENRES: 🅙 Jazz 🅥 Vocals. **RELEASED:** 1963, Impulse. **KEY TRACKS:** "Lush Life," "They Say It's Wonderful," "My One and Only Love." **CATALOG CHOICES:** Hartman: *I Just Dropped By to Say Hello.* Coltrane: *Ballads.* **NEXT STOP:** Frank Sinatra and Duke Ellington: *Francis A. and Edward K.* **AFTER THAT:** Bill Evans and Tony Bennett: *The Tony Bennett–Bill Evans Album* (see p. 78).

Lighthearted, Yet More than Comic

The Comedian Harmonists

The Comedian Harmonists

Think of the Comedian Harmonists as an American barbershop quartet that spiffs up campy and quaint old-timey tunes with persnickety German precision. The group—three tenors, one baritone, and one bass singer,

plus pianist Erwin Bootz—was formed by tenor Harry Frommermann in Berlin in 1928, and by the early '30s had become a sensation throughout Europe. The group specialized in transforming old beer hall tunes and American pop songs into dazzling entertainments. While most barbershop groups employed the same tight harmony throughout a tune, the Harmonists changed theirs from line to line; on this compilation, the elaborate vocal arrangements include jazzy solos and

intentionally exaggerated, almost corny group swoons.

At times this craftily choreographed music sounds as if it's designed to accompany the nonstop action in early *Tom and Jerry* cartoons. The Harmonists sing everything with an impressive paranormal unity—listen to the winking panache they bring to the cowboy song "The Last Roundup." Three of the singers were Jewish, and eventually fled to Austria after the government asked the group to stop singing "Jewish melodies" (even though "ethnic" tunes were only a part of the Harmonists' repertoire). Highlights of this anthology of early 78s include a spry romp through "Happy Days Are Here Again" and a treatment of Duke Ellington's "Creole Love Call" in which the voices, using a wordless scat-singing style, replicate the chittering of big band brass and the growly muted trumpet of soloist Cootie Williams. Throughout, there's a sense of worlds colliding. As they frame the fizzy exuberance of American song in an exacting European context, the Harmonists arrive at a sound that's odd, and engrossing, and unexpectedly wonderful.

GENRE: 🌐 World/Germany. **RELEASED:** 1999, Hannibal. **KEY TRACKS:** "Creole Love Call," "The Last Roundup," "Tea for Two." **FURTHER INQUIRY:** The 1997 biopic *Comedian Harmonists* tells the group's story in a lively, engaging way. **NEXT STOP:** The Revelers: *Breezin' Along with the Revelers*. **AFTER THAT:** Los Zafiros: *Bossa Cubana*.

A Greasy Serving of Americana

Paradise and Lunch

Ry Cooder

The Band was into big myths and war stories. Dylan spouted truth so obvious it scolded you for missing it. And Ry Cooder, perhaps the most criminally overlooked auteur of the early '70s, chased plain-folks wisdom, the stories and songs swapped after family dinner in rural America.

The big idea with Cooder is that the source material can come from anywhere. He seizes on an ordinary children's song or churchy hymn, some needlepoint-sampler artifact of lost Americana, and with nothing more than a shot of electrifying rhythm guitar, jolts it alive. His previous albums find him goosing Appalachian folk, dust-bowl balladry, old-time jazz, and Tejano songs, each time shaping those patchwork instrumentals around his rambling narratives. *Paradise and Lunch*, his masterwork, goes for the backwoods and the swamp: The multi-instrumentalist resurrects durable Deep South church marches and wildcat blues as bawdy entertainments, and transforms a Bobby Womack soul anthem ("It's All Over Now," better known as a Rolling Stones hit) into a loping, wicked New Orleans stomp.

Each of the nine selections has the air of something fantastical (and at times preposterous) to it, as though Cooder and his excellent accomplices (which include, on a boisterous "Ditty Wah Ditty," the legendary jazz pianist Earl "Fatha" Hines) find themselves in an odd, utterly pleasurable barroom tableau, and they intend to keep rollicking along until things clarify. Cooder's knack for conjuring atmosphere served him well later on the '70s—particularly on a series of haunting film scores, including *Paris, Texas* and *Crossroads*. But no visuals are necessary to appreciate the gruff and greasy medicine show that is *Paradise and Lunch*.

GENRE: 🎸 Rock. **RELEASED:** 1974, Reprise. **KEY TRACKS:** "Jesus on the Mainline," "It's All Over Now." **CATALOG CHOICES:** *Boomer's Story; Chicken Skin Music*. **NEXT STOP:** Little Feat: *Dixie Chicken*. **AFTER THAT:** John Prine: *John Prine* (see p. 614).

The Flip Side of Sam Cooke

Sam Cooke with the Soul Stirrers

Sam Cooke and the Soul Stirrers

Gospel was Sam Cooke's rock. It provided the inspiration for his most awesome vocal performances and furnished the structure of his most significant compositions, from "Touch the Hem of His Garment" to "A Change Is Gonna Come." Cooke (1931–1964) began singing with the Soul Stirrers in 1950—this collection opens with his first recording, "Peace in the Valley," from the following year. Over the next six years, he created a magnificent canon of modern songs of devotion, each sparked by his intently focused, world-changing ad-libs. Where most gospel groups put the empha-

Between 1957 and 1965 Sam Cooke had 29 U.S. Top 40 hits.

sis on the sonorous harmonies and the canted repetition of key phrases, Cooke shaped the Soul Stirrers around more personal declarations; his work really begins when he finishes with the verses. Throughout this collection, on the imploring "Nearer to Thee" and the more woeful "Mean Old World," Cooke shows a profound understanding of life and spirituality without ever trying to sound "deep." That's almost a magic trick, and it places these vocal performances among the most carefree, wondrous, life-affirming, graceful, awe-inspiring, and galvanizing ever directed to the heavens.

GENRE: ✝ Gospel.
RELEASED: 1991, Specialty. **KEY TRACKS**: "Touch the Hem of His Garment," "Be with Me Jesus." **CATALOG CHOICE**: *The Rhythm and the Blues*. **NEXT STOP**: Aretha Franklin: *Amazing Grace* (see p. 289). **AFTER THAT**: The Rance Allen Group: *A Soulful Experience*.

As Sam Cooke Says, "Don't Fight It, Feel It"

Live at the Harlem Square Club

Sam Cooke

A powerful singer with an impossibly sweet voice, Sam Cooke began and ended his career in gospel. In between he helped invent soul music, showed a generation of African American performers the importance of taking control of their own business affairs, and wrote charming love ditties and "A Change Is Gonna Come," a song that stands as the defin-

ing statement of the civil rights movement.

The history of postwar popular music is not the same without him. A soulman with smooth-as-silk phrasing, Cooke placed an incredible twenty-nine singles in the Top 40 during his short secular run. They're all precious diamonds, and are gathered on countless anthologies (*Portrait of a Legend 1951–1964* is the best). Since Cooke recorded for several labels, the greatest-hits route is a logical starting point. Step two is this astounding document, which shows just how persuasive Cooke could be in live performance. A natural entertainer, he transforms stock pop conceits into urgent imperatives, and lifts tunes known for bubbly innocence ("Cupid") to breathtaking emotional heights.

Recorded in January 1963 but not officially released until 1985, *Live* shows why Cooke was revered by so many artists: His show begins at a roaring peak and gets hotter from there. Every song, even the ones where he gets the crowd to sing along, exposes a different facet of his genius. Drop in anywhere—the beseeching secular ballad "Bring It On Home to Me" (the template for "A Change Is Gonna Come") or the raucous "Somebody Have Mercy," which showcases his devastating ad-libs—and be amazed.

GENRE: 🎵 R&B. **RELEASED:** 1985, RCA. (Reissued 2006.) **KEY TRACKS:** All of them. **CATALOG CHOICES:** *Portrait of a Legend, 1951–1964; Keep Movin' On.* **NEXT STOP:** Otis Redding: *Otis Blue* (see p. 636). **AFTER THAT:** Al Green: *Let's Stay Together.*

"Well, We Got No Class . . ."

"School's Out"

Alice Cooper

H ere, in heavy rock form, is the euphoria that spreads through schools everywhere when the final bell rings and the long-awaited summer vacation begins. Reckless and brazen, it's audio wildfire, the feeling

of running full-tilt through the halls and raising hell, feeling invincible. "Well, we got no class," singer Vincent Damon Furnier (who later changed his name to Alice Cooper) yells proudly, anticipating unstructured days ahead. "And we got no principles, and we got no innocence. . . . We can't even think of a word that rhymes."

That last line offers a clue about the enduring appeal of Alice Cooper. Unlike many of its emulators, this prototypical early '70s "shock rock" band exhibited a winking self-awareness, a sense that the

"The last three minutes of the last day of school . . . if we can catch that three minutes in a song, it's going to be so big."
—Alice Cooper

heart-attack clanging chords and the parent-baiting refrains were, in fact, just show business. It helps, too, that Alice Cooper's songwriting brain trust had killer hook sense: "School's Out" is a parade of addictive melodies, each one grabbier than the last, interspersed with one spectacular "bridge" section. That's when the abrasive guitars recede, and the band veers into a miasma of vocal harmony and sound-warp wizardry that still, even after all these years of heavy classic-rock radio play, has a riveting power.

"School's Out" was a summer song of 1972—it spent weeks in the Top 10, and helped the album of the same name become Alice Cooper's first platinum seller. Listen to it alongside some of the band's other singles produced by the amazing Bob Ezrin—the stomp-anthem "I'm Eighteen," "Elected," "No More Mr. Nice Guy," "Under My Wheels," all collected on *The Best of Alice Cooper*—and discover that Alice Cooper wasn't just among the first heavy rock bands, but one of the best ever.

GENRE:  Rock. **RELEASED:** 1972, Warner Bros. **APPEARS ON:** *School's Out; The Best of Alice Cooper.* **CATALOG CHOICES:** *Killer; Love It to Death.* **NEXT STOP:** Nine Inch Nails: *Pretty Hate Machine.* **AFTER THAT:** Marilyn Manson: *Antichrist Superstar.*

A Truly American Symphony

Symphony No. 3

Aaron Copland
New York Philharmonic (Leonard Bernstein, cond.)

Aaron Copland wrote some of the most quintessentially "American" concert music of the twentieth century. His broad-shouldered themes ("Fanfare for the Common Man," which defines the fourth movement of this symphony) glorify hard work, determination, and grit in ways that make such things heroic, not corny. His tone poems hint at either the majestic vastness of the untamed West or, in the case of the amazing "Quiet City" appended to this disc, the desolation of urban life. His dances—the ballet *Appalachian Spring*, which interpolates the Shaker song "Simple Gifts," is the most famous—recast folk material in imaginative flourishes.

Aaron Copland is often called "the dean of American composers."

The Brooklyn-born Copland (1900–1990) was trained in Paris, in the studio of the legendary Nadia Boulanger. His early works flirt with jazz (a craze for many composers, including Stravinsky, in the '20s and '30s), but by the late '30s he arrived at his own "sound," in which plainspoken aw-shucks themes are supported by rhythmic stutter-steps and orchestral washes in sunset hues. The broad Symphony No. 3 is full of characteristic Coplandisms. Its first movement is a kind of prelude, with little fixed tempo. Here and in the subsequent sections, the declarative "Fanfare for the Common Man" theme appears in refracted form; one of Copland's gifts is his ability to assemble his melodies into tricky, yet easily identifiable, intervallic caprices. By the time the actual "Fanfare" melody arrives, early in the fourth movement, its elements have been swirling in the air for nearly thirty minutes.

The compositional scheme is heightened by this interpretation: Conductor Leonard Bernstein, whose own works were influenced by Copland, plays up the less showy underpinnings of the piece. This reading, the second of two recorded by Bernstein with the New York Philharmonic, bubbles with the wild American exuberance Copland intended. But Bernstein spends as much energy on the unglamorous nuts and bolts, which he brings to life with a cool, evenhanded competence.

GENRE: 🎻 Classical. **RELEASED:** 1986, Deutsche Grammophon. **KEY TRACKS:** Third

movement (Andantino quasi allegretto); fourth movement (Fanfare). **CATALOG CHOICE:** *Bernstein Century: Billy the Kid, Appalachian Spring, and Rodeo,* New York Philharmonic (Leonard Bernstein, cond.). **NEXT STOP:** John Adams: *Violin Concerto/Shaker Loops,* Gidon Kremer, London Symphony Orchestra (Kent Nagano, cond.). **AFTER THAT:** Charles Ives: *Sonata No. 2,* Gilbert Kalish.

Featherweight Fusion

Light as a Feather

Chick Corea and Return to Forever

*L*ight as a Feather joined jazz pianist Chick Corea and the then husband-and-wife team of vocalist Flora Purim and percussionist Airto in a clash of potentially opposing ideologies. Corea, a veteran of Miles Davis's

electric bands, was known for his squabbling, extroverted virtuosity, particularly on the electric piano. The Brazilians, meanwhile, approached everything with characteristic serenity and deep understatement.

What could have been a catastrophic mess became one of the shining moments of jazz fusion, an aptly titled work of gentle breezes and free spirits soaring over hidden (or at least partially obscured) compositional complexities. Everyone involved is in pursuit of lightness: Corea's "You're Everything" moves at an almost jittery samba clip yet never feels hurried. The title track, written by Purim and bassist Stanley Clarke, requires this alert band to transition between several tempos, and they do so casually, without thinking, as though sauntering between rooms at a party.

The peak expression from the first of three completely different Return to Forever bands,

Chick Corea calls this album's song "You're Everything" his favorite among the vocal songs he has written.

Light as a Feather had immediate impact on jazz. It triggered interest among musicians in Brazilian forms beyond bossa nova and foreshadowed the more cerebral European jazz of the later 1970s. Its Corea originals "Spain" and "500 Miles High" became standards, the rare jazz pieces with ethereal lyrics well matched to the sounds. Most important, its uncluttered atmospheres took listeners out of a conventional jazz headspace and lifted them to that lofty stratosphere above the tree line, where it's possible to get some perspective on things.

GENRE: 🎷 Jazz. **RELEASED:** 1973, Verve. **KEY TRACKS:** "You're Everything," "Spain," "500 Miles High." **CATALOG CHOICES:** *Now He Sings, Now He Sobs; Children's Songs.* **NEXT STOP:** Weather Report: *Black Market.* **AFTER THAT:** Opa: *Goldenwings.*

La Máquina del Tiempo

Cortijo y Su Máquina del Tiempo

When he recorded this, the *timbale* master Rafael Cortijo was already regarded as a key catalyst of Puerto Rican music, a veteran known for his revitalization of the traditional *bomba* and *plena* rhythms as well as the outright fire breathed by his combo. Cortijo (1928–1982) knew how to make people dance, but he was also an adventurer, and for this project he teamed up with young musicians (many from the University of Puerto Rico) who were intent on taking the island nation's folklore rhythms to previously unexplored plateaus.

The result is one of the most imaginative cross-genre eruptions in Latin music history. From the opening "Carnaval," it's clear the rhythm is going to be anything but conventional: It's set in *plena* pulse, but with a river of samba running through it. Somehow Cortijo's rhythm team synchronizes the two styles, to the point where the focus is on the heat generated by the various soloists and not the astonishing novelty of the mash-up. Highly recommended for: anyone who's had enough conventional *son*, salsa, or *plena;* those curious about how Latin musicians responded to the new horizons of jazz fusion; any and all thrill seekers.

GENRE: 🌐 World/Puerto Rico. **RELEASED:** 1974, Musical Productions. **KEY TRACKS:** "Carnaval," "Gumbo," "De coco y anís." **CATALOG CHOICE:** *Bueno, y que?* **NEXT STOP:** Ismael Rivera: *Sonero no. 1.* **AFTER THAT:** Eddie Palmieri: *La perfecta* (see p. 573).

Armed Forces

Elvis Costello and the Attractions

Elvis Costello made one of rock's all-time great entrances. The songs of his debut, *My Aim Is True* (1977), established a curious new persona for rock, that of an "avenging geek" whose vocabulary gives his withering contempt a refined expression. Within months of its release, the album's cover photo and its songs—spastic ones like "Less than Zero," tender ones like "Alison"—became part of essential hipster discourse on both sides of the Atlantic. The follow-up, *This Year's Model,* showed Costello's considerable dexterity as a songwriter, and knack for pumping up innocent hooks into expressions of anger, if not outrage. *Armed Forces,* which followed less than a year later, lashes Costello's acerbic wit to slightly more elaborate production from pub rock kingpin Nick Lowe, author of the album's enduring anthem

"(What's So Funny 'Bout) Peace, Love, and Understanding?"

Armed Forces was written when Costello was twenty-four, after he and the Attractions had finished a long tour of the U.S. by van. It is the bridge between Costello the "punk singer-songwriter" and Costello the unabashed romantic of rock's New Wave. In the liner notes of the expanded edition, Costello recalls that while on the road, the band listened to cassettes of Conway Twitty and Loretta Lynn, Cheap Trick, and ABBA. And it's possible to hear the influence of those polished productions in *Armed Forces*'s specific details (the whomping piano-studded refrain of "Accidents Will Happen" and the nattily harmonized "Moods for Moderns"). This is the record where Costello realizes that the doors are wide open, and he can make any kind of snarly (or idealistic) noise he wants. So he makes all kinds of noise—songs that thrum with Springsteen-like idealism ("Peace, Love, and Understanding") or express disdain ("Goon Squad") or go to

Born Declan MacManus, Costello was inspired to combine the names of Elvis Presley and his great-grandmother for his stage name.

great lengths to draw parallels between cultural and personal upheavals ("Two Little Hitlers"), an idea underscored by Costello's original working title for the album, *Emotional Fascism.*

Since this awakening, of course, Costello has taken full advantage of those open doors, writing ambitious works for string ensemble and collaborating with Paul McCartney and Burt Bacharach on snappy tradition-minded pop songs. Virtually everything in his discography is smart, and though Costello has since disparaged some of his *Armed Forces* lyrics—he writes that "some of the highly charged language may now seem a little naive"—few records in rock nail the details, musical *and* emotional, the way *Armed Forces* does.

GENRE: 🎸 Rock.
RELEASED: 1979, Columbia.
KEY TRACKS: "Accidents Will Happen," "Goon Squad," "Moods for Moderns," "(What's So Funny 'Bout) Peace, Love, and Understanding?"
CATALOG CHOICES: *My Aim Is True; This Year's Model; King of America; The Delivery Man.* **NEXT STOP:** Graham Parker: *Squeezing Out Sparks* (see p. 579). **AFTER THAT:** Nick Lowe: *Jesus of Cool.*

When Clapton Really Was God

Disraeli Gears

Cream

Cream crammed a lot into three years. Though it started as a blues-rock band—guitarist Eric Clapton formed the group in 1966 after leaving John Mayall's Bluesbreakers—it evolved quickly, first as a purveyor of imaginative singles ("I Feel Free"), then a leading exponent of psychedelic rock (British division). Cream's configuration—Clapton's guitar alongside Jack Bruce's bass and Ginger

Baker's drums—established the idea of the "power trio," a lean machine in which every musician had a specific role. Its penchant for extended instrumental explorations made it the jam band; Cream's epic journeys inspired similar trips by acts including the Grateful Dead and Santana, and obliterated the rules governing the structure and length of rock songs. Before Cream, rock was mostly about verse, chorus, and eight bars of guitar. After Cream, which sold fifteen million records during its run, it could be almost anything.

Disraeli Gears (1967), the band's second album, is the best snapshot of this multifaceted beast. Recorded just after the Beatles' *Sgt. Pepper* (see p. 60) shifted the emphasis to full albums rather than singles, it contains one of the all-time great rock riffs ("Sunshine of Your Love"), several enduring blues distillations ("Strange Brew" and "SWLABR," an acronym for "She Walks Like a Bearded Rainbow"). Crucially, it catches Clapton at his least affected. When he steps up to play, he is not the guitar god—as he'd been anointed during his time with the Bluesbreakers—but an open-minded melodist, intent on finding unexpected truths within the three-chord crunch.

Disraeli Gears was recorded in six days. It began under the direction of Atco president

The *Disraeli Gears* cover art was designed by Australian artist Martin Sharp.

Ahmet Ertegun, who initially deemed "Sunshine of Your Love" to be "psychedelic hogwash," but after two days Ertegun ceded the production job to Felix Pappalardi. Instantly the tenor of the sessions changed: Pappalardi got the band to loosen up, added piles of guitar distortion, and helped Cream transform the blues standard "Lawdy Mama" into the heady "Strange Brew."

The expanded edition is worth hearing for the powerful original mono mixes and nine tracks recorded live at the BBC. These show that the trio, later known for long detours down the road marked Indulgence, could take wild swings and, at the same time, maintain enough discipline to honor the song.

GENRE: 🎸 Rock. **RELEASED:** 1967, Atco. (Expanded edition, 2004, Polydor.) **KEY TRACKS:** "Sunshine of Your Love," "Strange Brew," "Tales of Brave Ulysses." **CATALOG CHOICES:** *Wheels of Fire; Cream Live.* **NEXT STOP:** Blind Faith: *Blind Faith* (see p. 98). **AFTER THAT:** Jimi Hendrix Experience: *Are You Experienced* (see p. 355).

The Dirty South

Willy and the Poor Boys

Creedence Clearwater Revival

Among the many musical miracles happening in northern California in 1969 was a scrappy East Bay band called Creedence Clearwater Revival. That year, the group cranked out not one, not two, but three albums that form a unified extended portrait of life in the molasses-slow, sometimes sinister South. The specific miracle is this: These records— *Bayou Country, Green River,* and *Willy and the Poor Boys*—were made before singer and songwriter John Fogerty and his steaming locomotive of a rhythm section ever visited the American South. Fogerty told NPR's *Fresh Air* in 1998 that ever since childhood, he had been drawn to the "mythicized and romanticized territory" around the bayous and the Mississippi Delta, the area where the blues took root. It was, he thought, more interesting than writing about Main Street in El Cerrito.

The first Creedence record, which contains the quartet's remake of Dale Hawkins's swamp classic "Suzie Q," became a minor hit in 1968. Immediately Fogerty's label began pressuring him to crank out more music. He did this with great speed, writing tight radio songs and thoughtful album tracks in dizzying succession. *Bayou Country* and *Green River* establish the basic topography and set the stage for this album, which brings the disjointed elements of Creedence's trick bag—the gospel group-sings, the bored-kid hand-jive, the tremolo blues guitar shimmering like asphalt in the heat—into purposeful alignment. *Willy* might be regarded as Fogerty's shining hour just for the eternal class-warfare truths of "Fortunate Son," but there's also the slightly ominous "Don't Look Now" and the cowbell-studded moment of

From left: Tom Fogerty, Doug Clifford, John Fogerty, and Stu Cook.

block party giddiness, "Down on the Corner." The covers aren't shabby, either: The vocal chorale of "Cotton Fields" takes the Leadbelly theme into the revival tent, while "The Midnight Special," a staple of Hank Williams's shows, is rendered so passionately it sounds like a Creedence original.

The band digs into everything as though they know there's only one chance to escape the hellhounds, so they'd better get things right. They're totally committed to the music and remarkably unified, and though other records from Fogerty's hot streak have longer jams (notably "Heard It Through the Grapevine"), none maps out the shadowy realm of rural psychedelia as thoroughly as this one.

GENRE: 🎸 Rock. **RELEASED:** 1969, Fantasy. **KEY TRACKS:** "Fortunate Son," "Down on the Corner," "The Midnight Special." **CATALOG CHOICES:** *Green River; Cosmo's Factory.* **NEXT STOP:** The Georgia Satellites: *The Georgia Satellites.* **AFTER THAT:** My Morning Jacket: *It Still Moves* (see p. 537).

The Anti-Soprano, on a Greatest Hits Program of French Song

Crespin Sings Berlioz and Ravel

Regine Crespin
L'Orchestre de la Suisse Romande (Ernest Ansermet, cond.)

Some music comes out just fine through earbuds or the small speakers that sit alongside desktop computers. This recording of the sublime French soprano Regine Crespin, who retired in 1989, isn't among them. Sure, you'll get the notes that way. But to fully be "with" her voice, which was far warmer and more voluptuous than that of most French sopranos, there's no substitute for decent equipment.

Crank this up to encounter a truly great, almost miraculous instrument. Most singers have noticeable "breaks" between registers, points in the scale where their tone changes, and they have to finesse things. Not Crespin. Her singing voice is seamless. As she moves from pitch to pitch, the predominant quality is liquidity; there's no point at which extra "massaging" happens. Ascending to the upper register, Crespin never seems to be taxed in any way. She doesn't push, doesn't ask for spotlights, doesn't make too much of the words; the voice just seems to gather mass, and grace, as it moves.

Only because Crespin failed her college entrance examinations was she permitted by her father to study voice.

This program of French song from several eras is a great showcase for Crespin, and one of her most revered recordings. It begins with Berlioz's *Les nuits d'été*, six melodies with rich orchestral accompaniment, each striking a sharp emotional impression. Some are simple and declarative ("Villanelle"), with hints of the futuristic later Berlioz lurking in the orchestrations; others (the Wagner-influenced "Au cimetière") are moodier, defined by long strands of restive melody. These seem written for Crespin, as does the Ravel "Shéhérazade" and Poulenc's light, cabaretlike songs that close the program. Crespin sings them all with a childlike delight, as if she's off on an afternoon stroll and fully confident that the beautiful string textures will magically follow her every turn.

GENRE: 🎻 Classical. RELEASED: 1963, Decca. KEY TRACKS: Berlioz: "Le spectre de la rose," "Au cimetière." Ravel: "Asie." Poulenc: "Hotel," "La reine de coeur." CATALOG CHOICE: *Italian Opera Arias*. NEXT STOP: *The Very Best of Victoria de los Angeles*.

Bing: Not Just for White Christmas Anymore

A Centennial Anthology of Decca Recordings

Bing Crosby

66 **T**he thing you have to understand about Bing Crosby," the jazz clarinetist and bandleader Artie Shaw once said, is that he was "the first hip white person born in the United States."

That's hard to fathom now. Crosby (1903–1977) is the picture next to the word "milquetoast" in the modern dictionary, a singer whose overriding feyness is remembered more than his agile baritone, whose association with a tame age of popular music overshadows the fact that he phrased with a jazz musician's control of nuance. That's what Shaw was responding to: Instrumentalists listened closely to Crosby, because unlike just about every other singer of the 1930s, the proto-crooner from Spokane, Washington, came across as one cool customer, forever relaxed. He was one of the first recording artists to communicate subtlety on tape, to not merely sing a song but impart a mood.

This excellent two-disc overview of Crosby's peak career years is full of those moods—thoughtful renditions of standards, ballads that melt into thin air. To lose your

Crosby preconceptions, cue up one of his early soundtrack performances, "Pennies from Heaven." Though he's supported by a huge orchestra, Crosby outlines a very slight pulse, setting a pace that is subtle yet unfailingly steady. His verses have a musing way about them, and later, at the point where the song crests, Crosby doesn't pour on extra emotion. Instead, he hums a bit of the tune, endearingly, as though envisioning a trailing shot in a film. There are plenty of other selections—from the perennial "White Christmas" to offbeat island exotica ("Blue Hawaii") to songs celebrating a carefree life ("I've Got a Pocketful of Dreams")—that could, in a moment of generous revisionism,

In 1962, Crosby was the first person to receive the Grammy Lifetime Achievement Award.

bolster Bing's hipness quotient. But when you really listen to this graceful singer, it's clear he didn't care about hipness. The truly hip never do.

GENRE: 🎤 Vocals. **RELEASED:** 2003, Decca/ MCA. **KEY TRACKS:** "Stardust," "Pennies from Heaven," "Blue Skies," "White Christmas," "I've Got a Pocketful of Dreams." **F.Y.I.:** Crosby had thirty-eight #1 hits, more than the Beatles (twenty-four) and Elvis Presley (eighteen). **CATALOG CHOICES:** *Bing Sings Whilst Bregman Swings; Fancy Meeting You Here* (with Rosemary Clooney). **NEXT STOP:** Frank Sinatra: *Swingin' Session!* **AFTER THAT:** Madeline Peyroux: *Careless Love.*

A Last Gasp of '60s Idealism

Déjà vu

Crosby, Stills, Nash, and Young

Different music was needed in the aftermath of Woodstock. To grossly oversimplify: The nation of flower children woke up from the trip, found Nixon still in power and things trending badly in Vietnam and elsewhere, and came face-to-face with the grown-up disillusionment that the heady previous years had kept at bay. It was a harsh morning after. An idealism hangover.

Ready with the salves and smelling salts was this carefully lawyered supergroup, built around a three-way of rock refugees—David Crosby (ex-Byrds), Stephen Stills (ex-Buffalo Springfield), and Graham Nash (ex-Hollies). Their first collaboration had given the world the doot-dootling "Suite: Judy Blue Eyes" the year before. For its second effort the trio added Neil Young (ex-Buffalo Springfield), and immediately sought cultural relevance by singing Joni Mitchell's you-are-there postscript "Woodstock." Both a last reprise of '60s idealism and a prayer for inner peace, *Déjà vu* applies reassuring colorburst harmonies to songs about controlling the few things a rainbow child could—the length of one's hair (Crosby's still-dramatic "Almost Cut My Hair"), the values you impart to your kids (Nash's "Teach Your Children"), the order of one's home (Nash's domesticity curio "Our House").

Incredibly, the four participants didn't often function as a band while recording this hotly anticipated (and instantly successful) effort, which allegedly took eight hundred studio hours to finish. Each brought in a few originals, and recorded them independently. Only when it was time to do vocals did the four come together, and it is those soaring, precision-formation harmonies that remain the focal point. Young's hymnlike "Helpless" simply isn't the same song without the distinctive colorations of this choir; the same can be said of his three-part "Country Girl" or the mystical Crosby title track, which proclaims, "We have all been here before." To really appre-

In 1970, *Déjà vu* hit #1 on the *Billboard* 200 album chart.

ciate what this contentious group did when it was united, however, just start with the Stills-penned opener "Carry On." This is the essence of CSNY—impossibly gorgeous cascading vocals that urge everyone leaving the farm to continue in faith, because "love is coming to us all." It might have been a last gasp. But it doesn't sound like one.

GENRE: 🎸 Rock. **RELEASED:** 1970, Atlantic. **KEY TRACKS:** "Helpless," "Woodstock," "4+20," "Carry On." **CATALOG CHOICE:** *Crosby, Stills, and Nash.* **NEXT STOP:** Joni Mitchell: *Blue.* **AFTER THAT:** Buffalo Springfield: *Retrospective* (see p. 129).

Lingering Echoes of War

Black Angels

George Crumb
The Kronos Quartet

During the heyday of the classical music "avant-garde" in the 1960s and '70s, composers believed they had a mandate to reinvent music from the ground up. George Crumb was one of the very few who actually managed to do it. His works—pieces like "Black Angels" written for string quartet in 1970, the centerpiece of this astounding disc by the Kronos Quartet—are perverse and often startling constellations of sound that challenge conventional notions of how music should be organized.

In this and other Crumb pieces, for example, one doesn't detect clear beginnings or endings; instead, the music is a procession of episodes, dazzling textures, and extreme chords that rarely seem to lead into or connect with one another. The Kronos dives in, and

within a minute or so of the first movement, gets deep into Crumb's punishing soundscape—the knotted, crying chords were inspired by the Vietnam war, but the piece conjures any place from which there is no clearly marked exit. The four string players gnaw and chatter as if they're reenacting an aerial attack, yet the juxtapositions of sound register with the force of body blows. Crumb relies heavily on percussion (his scores require players to strike a cymbal with a double bass bow). Though he does notate his work, parts of this piece suggest that the "score" might be a collage. He asks musicians to think in broad shapes, not notes, and the effects he generates can be awesome. They can also be terrifying.

David Harrington, the first violinist and conceptual force behind the Kronos Quartet, once said that he initially formed the group to play pieces like "Black Angels." Crumb's challenging piece, which is in some ways closer to the howling dissonance of heavy metal than string quartet music, aligns perfectly with

His interest in numerology led Crumb to structure "Black Angels" around the numbers 13 and 7.

the group's sensibility. Keen interpreters of the traditional repertoire, the four musicians are determined to escape its confines, and do this by applying a rock-auteur sensibility to recording projects. Kronos has commissioned notable contemporary classical works, but just as often goes outside of that world. Its concept albums include *Monk Suite*, devoted to the works of jazz composer-pianist Thelonious Monk, and the terrific *Pieces of Africa*, which gathers propulsive and often polyrhythmic work from contemporary African composers.

The theme of *Black Angels* might be broadly described as "disillusionment with humanity occasioned by war." The Kronos complements Crumb's piece with Dmitri

Shostakovich's String Quartet No. 8, a woeful, sometimes forbidding testament to the victims of fascism. Also here is a striking interpretation of Thomas Tallis's motet "Spem in alium," and a scratchy recording of a Charles Ives song to which the Kronos fashioned apt accompaniment.

Where Crumb wants listeners to wander over barren lands and share the agony of battle, Shostakovich, whose work closes the disc, describes something less visual but no less visceral—a soul-ravaging brutality, the kind that's accomplished without bullets.

GENRE: 🎸 Classical. **RELEASED:** 1990, Nonesuch. **KEY TRACKS:** "Black Angels": Part One: Departure: "Sounds of Bones and Flutes" (second movement); Part Three: Return: "God-music." String Quartet No. 8: Largo (first movement), Allegretto (third movement). **CATALOG CHOICES:** Crumb: *Ancient Voices of Children,* Contemporary Chamber Ensemble (Arthur Weisberg, cond.). Kronos: *Pieces of Africa; Monk Suite.* **NEXT STOP:** Uri Caine: *Urlicht/Primal Light* (see p. 138). **AFTER THAT:** Harry Parch: *Enclosure 7.*

The Best Showcase for the Queen of Salsa

Celia y Johnny

Celia Cruz and Johnny Pacheco

Johnny Pacheco is one of the very few recording artists to shape an entire genre of music—both through his own records and as the cofounder and artistic visionary behind Fania Records. Along with his partner,

an attorney named Jerry Masucci, the Dominican-born flutist and percussionist helped develop the sound and the stars of New

York salsa. His productions were tight, and notable for exacting percussion foundations. From its inception in 1964, the label earned a reputation as a haven for artists, and Pacheco was one reason why: He had great instincts matching singers with songs, and then assembling constellations of specific talents around them.

When the Cuban singer Celia Cruz began working with Fania in the early '70s, she'd gone a while without a hit. Pacheco recognized that she'd done her best work in front of small bands, notably the late '50s gems she recorded in Cuba with the Trio Matamoros. He also sensed that on her subsequent U.S. recordings, the fiery singer was sometimes overwhelmed by the orchestra. For this, her first "starring" production at the label, he designated his band, which at the time featured the dazzling pianist Papo Lucca and *tres* master Charlie Rodriguez, as the backing foil. Pacheco requested material from the songwriters regularly contributing to Fania, explaining that he wanted room for Celia Cruz to shine. What came back was pure explosive groove music.

Celia y Johnny topped the charts and went gold.

Celia y Johnny opens with "Quimbara," a chattering rumba that remains a dance-floor classic. Then comes the slightly less frantic "Toro mata," which finds Pacheco and his musicians luring Cruz into some of the most heated ad-libbed "inspirations" she ever recorded. (Indeed, just these two tracks provide a comprehensive argument for Cruz as the "Queen of Salsa.") The album's success led Fania to repeat the "stars-in-collaboration" formula (there's even a follow-up featuring Cruz and Pacheco). But this one remains the benchmark. It's the recording that spread the sweet magic of Celia Cruz the farthest.

GENRE: 🌐 World/Latin. **RELEASED:** 1974, Fania. **KEY TRACKS:** "Quimbara," "Toro mata," "Canto a La Habana." **CATALOG CHOICE:** *Azúcar: The Very Best of Celia Cruz.* **NEXT STOP:** The Fania All Stars: *Commitment.* **AFTER THAT:** Rubén Blades and Willie Colón: *The Good, the Bad, the Ugly).*

Taking the Mope to the Dance Floor

The Head on the Door

The Cure

Some bands evolve in logical, stepwise fashion, so that when they finally hit the big time, early believers are still on board. Others lurch ahead, sacrificing key elements of their sound in pursuit of a bigger audience.

With this disciplined album, the Cure found an artistically credible middle path.

The Head on the Door followed a series of grim dirge records, among them the critically acclaimed *Pornography* (1982) and *The Top* (1984). These earned the British five-piece a devoted following of mascara-wearing goth

youth, and a one-way ticket to the rock-cliché pasture: How many times can a singer groan, at great length and agonizingly slow tempo, about the direness of one's circumstances and still sound relevant? Perhaps recognizing this dead end, frontman Robert Smith set out to broaden the group's palette. He copped some of the bouncy synthesizer cues then powering New Wave pop. He wrote short songs, and didn't shy away from singable refrains. He and the rhythm section generated irresistible—and surprisingly funky—grooves, and augmented them with flamenco guitar and other exotica. So as not to completely startle the faithful, he sang this more buoyant stuff in the same distraught voice that had been the Cure's most identifiable trademark. And he retained some of the despairing narratives of mope music.

The Cure's lineup has changed over the years, but goth frontman Robert Smith has been a constant presence.

This juxtaposition—gloomy lyrics set against music that says, "Come out and play!"—triggered a new era for the Cure. The band takes swings at bubbly styles it couldn't have pulled off before (notably the Latin beat of "The Blood"), recasts existential torment in grabby Eurobeat trappings ("In Between Days"), and generally stops fretting about every little thing. The stylistically similar subsequent album *Kiss Me Kiss Me Kiss Me* was the commercial breakthrough, but *The Head* is the moment when sunshine first entered the dungeon, throwing light on possibilities the Cure pursued, with great gusto and much success, for years afterward.

GENRE: 🎸 Rock.
RELEASED: 1985, Elektra.
KEY TRACKS: "Sinking," "The Blood," "Kyoto Song," "Close to Me," "In Between Days." **COLLECTOR'S NOTE:** The 2006 reissue includes an entire disc of alternate takes and previously unreleased material. **CATALOG CHOICES:** *Pornography; Kiss Me Kiss Me Kiss Me.* **NEXT STOP:** Depeche Mode: *Violator.* **AFTER THAT:** Bauhaus: *Swing the Heartache.*

The High Point of Stoner Rap

Black Sunday

Cypress Hill

R ecording artists dread the "sophomore slump." After having years to develop the songs (and the sonic identity) of their first efforts, many find themselves paralyzed as they attempt a worthy follow-up.

Careers have been derailed, lives turned upside down, in pursuit of the second course to properly complement the first.

The Los Angeles rap outfit Cypress Hill seemed a likely candidate for the slump. The group's taut 1991 debut was instantly embraced by the hip-hop elite for its slowed-down beatbox funk and its multilingual discussions of the illuminating virtues of marijuana. When it came time to return to the studio, Cuban-born brothers Sen Dog and Mellow Man Ace, along with L.A. rappers B Real and DJ Muggs, radically altered the formula. They added repetitive acoustic-bass phrases that could have been lifted from jazz records, heavy metal guitars, and a touch of Public Enemy's sound-effects anarchy. What had been a typical boom-bap attack suddenly acquired a bongload of sonic possibility.

Atop this dark sound, the rappers of Cypress Hill dispense audacious rallying cries and cutting-contest taunts that are infintely more clever than typical hip-hop confrontations. No matter the subject, be it mental instability ("Insane in the Brain") or the laws of karma ("What Go Around, Come Around, Kid"), sooner or later these guys find their way back to rhapsodic discourse on the almighty buzz. The pot references grew tiresome on subsequent releases, but here they're part of the DNA, a point of commonality that, along with the whomping rhythm, helped make *Black*

Selling 3.25 million copies, *Black Sunday* went triple platinum in the U.S.

Sunday a crossover success. No surprise, really. After all, the good high is something that disaffected emo-obsessives, snarling metalheads, and hip-hop kids—all members of the Cypress tribe thanks to this disc—can agree on.

GENRE: 🎤 Hip-Hop.
RELEASED: 1993, Ruffhouse.
KEY TRACKS: "I Ain't Goin' Out like That," "Insane in the Brain," "Hits from the Bong."
CATALOG CHOICE: *Cypress Hill.* **NEXT STOP:** Dr. Dre: *The Chronic* (see p. 236).
AFTER THAT: Ultramagnetic MCs: *Critical Beatdown* (see p. 794).

I. K. Dairo and His Blue Spots ✦ Dick Dale and His Del-Tones ✦ Karen Dalton ✦ D'Angelo ✦ Danger Mouse ✦ Bobby Darin ✦ Rev. Gary Davis ✦ Miles Davis ✦ Miles Davis and Gil Evans ✦ Sammy Davis Jr. ✦ Claude Debussy ✦ The Decemberists ✦ De Danann with Mary Black ✦ Deep Purple ✦ De La Soul ✦ Sandy Denny ✦ Derek and the Dominos ✦ Paul Desmond with Jim Hall ✦ Toumani Diabaté **D** and Ballake Sissoko ✦ Neil Diamond ✦ Manu Dibango ✦ Bo Diddley ✦ Digital Underground ✦ Dion ✦ The Dixie Chicks ✦ The Dixie Hummingbirds ✦ Dizzee Rascal ✦ Djavan ✦ DJ Shadow ✦ Eric Dolphy ✦ Antoine "Fats" Domino ✦ The Doors ✦ Thomas A. Dorsey ✦ Michael Doucet and BeauSoleil ✦ Dave Douglas ✦ Nick Drake ✦ Dr. Dre ✦ Dr. John ✦ Doris Duke ✦ Vernon Duke and Ira Gershwin ✦ Jacqueline du Pré ✦ Henri Dutilleux ✦ Antonín Dvořák ✦ Bob Dylan

Before King Sunny Ade, There Was I. K. Dairo

Definitive Dairo

I. K. Dairo and His Blue Spots

To many consumers of American pop, "world music" is code for esoterica—the audio equivalent of a museum diorama about the customs of people in far-off lands. That's a shame, because musicians from Africa and elsewhere are tuned to the irresistible melodies and infectious syllabic combinations that Madonna worshippers know as the pop hook.

Case in point: Nigerian guitarist I. K. Dairo, whose band the Blue Spots was one of the most popular outfits in Africa during the 1970s. Dairo (1930–1996) is mostly remembered as an early pioneer of juju music, and one of the first to utilize the talking drum, key to centuries-old Yoruba ceremonies, in an entertainment context. But he deserves attention as a master of the repetitive catchphrase. Just about every track on this compilation erupts in a recurring, easily sung, two- or four-measure motif. Dairo establishes a theme and the backing singers crank it out endlessly, leaving room for the leader to create variations and embellishments with his voice or guitar.

Upon Dairo's death, Nigerian radio stations played nothing but his music, and musicians honored him by not performing in public.

These bright motifs become a powerful form of uplift—even if you don't get the words, it's hard to miss the spirit of praise that drives "Baba Ngbo Ti Wa" (Father Hears Us) and others on this set. They are far shorter than the usual juju marathons, which can last more than thirty minutes. Dairo later told people that these tunes were all recorded in a single day. That seems hard to believe, in part because it can take Western pop acts years to come up with one hook as riveting as the twenty or so on display here.

GENRE: 🌐 World/Nigeria. **RELEASED:** 1996, Xenophile. **KEY TRACKS:** "Okin Omo Ni," "Baba Ngbo Ti Wa," "Ta Lo Ba Mi Ri."
NEXT STOP: Ebenezer Obey: *Juju Jubilee.*
AFTER THAT: Amadou and Mariam: *Wati.*

Riding the Waves with the . . .

King of the Surf Guitar

Dick Dale and His Del-Tones

The rapid-fire staccato blasts and careening slides that electrify these songs were not in the guitar vocabulary until a surfer kid of Polish and Lebanese descent, Richard Monsour, put them there. Monsour, rechristened Dick Dale by a music-biz impresario, created the first surf-guitar instrumental in 1961 ("Let's Go Trippin'") and during the subsequent "craze" proved to be the key trailblazer in terms of tricks and techniques to make the guitar go *zoom*. His repertoire of sounds and crazy wipeouts have been emulated by guitarists ever since.

"King of the Surf Guitar" is Dick Dale's performance nickname.

Dale got his start in California, playing at a Newport Beach ballroom, the Rendezvous, after his father obtained the proper permits to allow teens to congregate and dance (one stipulation: the boys had to wear ties). The guitarist acquired a reputation for playing at extreme volumes, and putting on a show that drove kids crazy. Dale was an avid wave rider, and when he began to connect those passions—writing music that emulated the charging rush of waves in motion—he hit upon a sound that, along with the songs of the Beach Boys, mythologized surf culture.

This collection begins with Dale's early trailblazing singles, as well as adaptations that are far from surf music. Using half-step melodies and exotic Middle Eastern scales that he heard growing up, the guitarist and his band, the Del-Tones, conjure a world where everything, even "Hava nagila," can be amped way up. Country fans won't want to miss his treatment of "(Ghost) Riders in the Sky," while anyone who loves a good chase should seek out "Miserlou," Dale's galloping masterpiece.

GENRE: 🎸 Rock. **RELEASED:** 1995, Rhino. **KEY TRACKS:** "Miserlou," "Let's Go Trippin'," "Surf Beat." **CATALOG CHOICE:** *Surfer's Choice.* **NEXT STOP:** The Ventures: *Walk, Don't Run: The Best of . . .* **AFTER THAT:** Jan & Dean: *The Little Old Lady from Pasadena.*

How Did the World Miss Her?

It's So Hard to Tell Who's Going to Love You the Best

Karen Dalton

Karen Dalton (1938–1993) was a denizen of the Greenwich Village folk scene in the early '60s. A singer and guitarist, she made two records late in the decade and then promptly vanished, becoming a footnote figure remembered only by the few who were captivated by her intense, room-hushing performance style. One of those was Bob Dylan. In the first volume of his memoir *Chronicles*, he writes, "Karen had a voice like Billie Holiday's and played the guitar like Jimmy Reed and went all the way with it."

This, Dalton's debut, falls in the rather large cracks between folk, jazz, and blues. It is an oddly perfect listening experience. A singer of uncommon emotional control, Dalton writes gut-level direct songs that prefigure the genre-blurring efforts of Lucinda Williams and the Americana songwriters of the 1990s. Yes, the half-Irish, half-Cherokee singer has a timbre and tone that echo

Holiday, but she's got her own ideas about how to develop a mood. Phrasing in detached bursts, she creates a zone of placidness, a quiet little world in which her interpretations flourish on their own schedule. At times she sounds like she's being coy about the blues—as though she recognizes just how far toward the form's flatted thirds and outright moans she can go before sounding like an imitator.

Dalton didn't write her own songs—some have suggested that her lack of original material, coupled with a deep apprehension over recording, hin-

"She was the only folk singer I ever met with an authentic 'folk' background."
—Peter Stampfel of the Holy Modal Rounders

dered her career. But her interpretations stand: Here (and to a lesser degree on the follow-up album *In My Own Time*), Dalton transforms everyday songs into wrenching events.

GENRE: 😊 Folk.
RELEASED: 1969, Capitol. (Reissued 2003, Koch.) **KEY TRACKS:** "Little Bit of Rain," "Ribbon Bow," "In the Evening (It's So Hard to Tell Who's Going to Love You the Best)." **CATALOG CHOICE:** *In My Own Time.* **NEXT STOP:** Fred Neil: *Bleecker and MacDougal.* **AFTER THAT:** Nick Drake: *Pink Moon.*

An Early Shot of Neo-Soul

Brown Sugar

D'Angelo

When he first appeared, with the slinky single "Brown Sugar" in 1995, the keyboard player and singer D'Angelo talked like a man on a mission. Though certifiably part of the hip-hop generation, this unknown commodity proclaimed himself bored with the entrenched urban music formula—moderately funky repetitive hooks with a rap interlude in the middle. He wanted a different kind of revolution, he said. One powered by live instruments (not sampled grooves) and a respect for the titans of vintage R&B.

In a way, the Richmond, Virginia, native was the R&B equivalent of jazz traditionalist—a loud advocate for the music's frequently discarded core values. But he wasn't a scold; in fact, he

Brown Sugar sold over 2 million copies.

oozed pure honey. Singing in a restrained way that earned him comparisons to Sam Cooke and Marvin Gaye, D'Angelo, who was twenty-one at the time, made persuasion—not some muscle-flexing supremacy—his primary goal. Within a year of its release, *Brown Sugar* was widely acknowledged as a catalyst of the neo-soul movement.

The rapture-seeking whoos and ahhhs are not the whole story, however. In the middle of "Brown Sugar," where a hit-minded producer would likely drop in the rap cameo, D'Angelo tucks in eight delicious bars of skating-rink organ. It's hardly assertive enough to be called a solo—really, this is the son of a Pentecostal minister, just pawing around on the keys—but it allows the music to breathe. Virtually every one of the tracks has a similar instrumental touch or some slight rhythm section punch that sends things a tad outside the ordinary. One shining example is "Me and Those Dreamin' Eyes of Mine": Atop a bomping syncopation, D'Angelo multitracks his voice into a choir, then rolls through a series of choreographed vocal ad-libs in the style of Marvin Gaye. Understated and devastatingly funky, this restrained vocal performance is one for the ages.

After the success of *Brown Sugar,* D'Angelo took five years to release a follow-up.

There's lots to admire about *Voodoo*—the sound is richer, the grooves are mercilessly tight, the harmony vocals intensely ornate. But the album suffers from the modern urban-music plague: They're great jams waiting for a song to show up. This album has the songs, too.

GENRE: 🎙 R&B. **RELEASED:** 1995, EMI. **KEY TRACKS:** "Cruisin'," "Brown Sugar," "Me and Those Dreamin' Eyes of Mine." **COLLECTOR'S NOTE:** When this was released, a very limited number of vinyl pressings were circulated to club DJs. The vinyl version offers a much fuller mix than is available on CD. **CATALOG CHOICE:** *Voodoo.* **NEXT STOP:** Van Hunt: *Van Hunt.* **AFTER THAT:** Omar: *For Pleasure.*

Sound Mangling Taken to Marvelous Extremes

The Grey Album

Danger Mouse

Don't bother looking for this one in stores—it's not there, and never was. Because it violates copyright laws, DJ and producer Brian Burton's unlikely sampled mash-up of rapper Jay-Z's *The Black Album* and the Beatles' *White Album* exists only as an illegal download. It became one of the most talked-about bootlegs in history, and started a media firestorm—both because of its unorthodox use of "sacred" pop texts, and its argument that profoundly new music could be pulled from the wreckage of a collision. It represents a pinnacle of sample-manipulation art.

Burton, who goes by the stage name Danger Mouse, got the idea when Jay-Z released a DJ-only disc of a cappella rapping from *The Black Album* to club DJs. After measuring the tempo of Jay-Z's raps,

Entertainment Weekly named the *The Grey Album* the best album of 2004.

he scoured *The White Album* for isolated drum attacks and percussion sounds, and then painstakingly fashioned instrumental backdrops from carefully snipped and rejiggered sections of the Beatles' performances. "A lot of people just assumed I took some Beatles and, you know, threw some Jay-Z on top of it or mixed it up or looped it around, but it's really a deconstruction," Burton told MTV News.

Once he had the basic sounds, Burton used music software to process them—sometimes changing the pitch, or adding effects. He took bits from several Beatles songs and meshed them together: "Change Clothes" uses guitar parts of "Piggies" and the bass line from "Dear Prudence," creating an odd and sometimes disorienting listening experience in which the source material is profoundly warped.

Burton completed his experiment in a two-week marathon of activity in his bedroom. Within weeks, it became an Internet phenomenon; during the "Downhill Battle" campaign against restrictive major-label digital rights policies, over 100,000 people downloaded it in a single day. Since then, the mash-up has become an official genre in itself, often embraced by major-label marketing types as a way to increase sales. *The Grey Album* stands apart from those cash-grabs. It's a creative benchmark, a high-concept feat of musical integration that, in the process of scrambling its sources, totally revitalizes them.

GENRE: 🎧 Hip-Hop. **RELEASED:** 2004, on the Internet. **KEY TRACKS:** "What More Can I Say" (utilizes "While My Guitar Gently Weeps"), "99 Problems" (utilizes "Helter Skelter"). **CATALOG CHOICE:** Danger Doom: *The Mouse and the Mask.* **NEXT STOP:** Gorillaz: *Demon Days.* **AFTER THAT:** Solex: *Low Kick and Hard Bop.*

Oh, the Shark Bites . . .

That's All

Bobby Darin

Although he's often portrayed as a Junior Sinatra nightclub entertainer who knew how to work the celebrity game, Bobby Darin was above all a singer. Blessed with the ability to propel a big band or croon confidingly

in intimate settings, Darin (1936–1973) was curious about all kinds of music, and gamely experimented with unusual material (in the mid-'60s his live show included a "folk" set). He first appeared as an upmarket teen idol; in 1958, his Top 10 hits included "Splish Splash" and "Queen of the Hop." By the release of this second album the following year, he put himself in a completely different orbit: *That's All* not only features his signature hit, that swaggering mob-don version of the *Threepenny Opera* song "Mack the Knife," but shapely, seemingly effortless versions of "It Ain't Necessarily So" and "Softly, as in a Morning Sunrise."

Bobby Darin wanted "to be remembered as a human being and as a great performer."

Darin trod lightly on songs that others crushed to death, and his irreverence—which becomes distracting on the chatty *Darin at the Copa*, recorded shortly after this date—makes these studio renditions magnetic. He flips his way through the swinging big-band barnstormer "I'll Remember April," then turns around and sings the beautiful title track and "Beyond the Sea," another Top 10 hit, with a coy caginess. "Mack the Knife" topped the singles charts for nine consecutive weeks, won the Record of the Year Grammy, and helped Darin take home the Best New Artist trophy as well. Heard decades removed from the frenzy he created (and cultivated), it stands as the most fetching statement Darin ever made. It's a snapshot of a star just before he hits warp speed, at perhaps the last moment he can afford to play fast, loose, and casual.

GENRE: 🔵 Vocals. **RELEASED:** 1959, Atco.

KEY TRACKS: "Mack the Knife," "It Ain't Necessarily So," "Beyond the Sea," "I'll Remember April." **CATALOG CHOICE:** *Darin at the Copa.* **NEXT STOP:** Dion: *Lovers Who Wander.* **AFTER THAT:** Jamie Cullum: *Twentysomething.*

Zealousness, with a Shot of Blues

Harlem Street Singer

Rev. Gary Davis

The voice on this recording belongs to a sixty-four-year-old man. Someone who, after a life of hard work, might have expected to be able to take life easy by this point. The Reverend Gary Davis (1896–1972) began performing professionally in the 1920s, and spent much of the '40s and '50s singing on Harlem street corners—in all kinds of weather, no doubt facing daily indifference. Though there's gruffness in Davis's voice, there's also great vigor, and a sense of mission. To hear him is to marvel at how someone who sang for so long under such less-than-perfect conditions was able to be persuasive—and at times utterly charming—well into his advancing years.

Rev. Davis had a unique guitar-playing style, using only his thumb and index finger.

Davis grew up in Laurens, South Carolina, and taught himself guitar. By age twenty, he'd developed techniques that were eventually copied by many other so-called ragtime guitarists—Blind Lemon Jefferson and Blind Willie Johnson (see p. 400). Drawn to religion, Davis became an ordained minister in 1937, and that changed his repertoire: From then on he stayed away from secular blues and adapted gospel songs and spirituals with his own blues-tinged guitar touches.

His rediscovery during the '50s folk revival led to a stack of recordings. This one, made in three hours by the esteemed jazz engineer Rudy Van Gelder, features Davis solo. Whenever he reaches the end of his verses, he simply switches into a finger-picking style for spry guitar interludes. Among the lesser-known pieces tucked between gospel-blues standards is a wondrous expression of faith, "I Belong to the Band," and a song that sums up Davis's exemplary work ethic, "Lord, I Feel Just like Goin' On." He did that, for far longer than most would have. And we are richer for it.

GENRES: ✝ Gospel 🔵 Blues. **RELEASED:** 1960, Prestige/Bluesville. **KEY TRACKS:** "I Belong to the Band," "Twelve Gates to the City," "Lord, I Feel Just like Goin' On," "Tryin' to Get Home." **CATALOG CHOICES:** *From Blues to Gospel; If I Had My Way (Early Home Recordings).* **NEXT STOP:** Blind Willie Johnson: *Sweeter as the Years Go By.* **AFTER THAT:** Son House: *The Original Delta Blues.*

All Shades, All Hues

Kind of Blue

Miles Davis

O f life's great paradoxes, there's a special place for the Zen thought that "Less is more." It is a simple enough idea: Load up a novel or a piece of music with too much information, and the effort can wind up overwhelming the essential inspiration. On an intellectual level this principle is easy enough to understand. And yet it's always amazing to encounter art that embodies the less-is-more impulse—the finely filtered piano works of Erik Satie (see p. 675), the strung-out stillness of Chet Baker singing a ballad (see p. 40), the crystalline perfection of Miles Davis's *Kind of Blue.*

This collection, the most famous jazz album of all time, tells what happens when thoughtful jazz musicians pursue ideas across a profoundly uncluttered canvas. The rhythms are basic swing. The melodies, typified by the ambling ascending-scale motif of "So What," are simple linear exercises. The harmony, though, is downright radical: Where much jazz before it is ruled by fast-moving chordal schemes, the *Kind of Blue* songs slow things down—they're organized around droning single chords, known as "modes," that can last for a long time. A single shift of the harmony—on "So What," for example, the tonality moves up just a half step—changes the weather, making it feel like galaxies are realigning. The genius of Davis's structures is that immediately after such power surges, the cycle begins again.

Each time, the pathways are wiped clean. The soloists—trumpeter Davis, saxophonists Cannonball Adderley and John Coltrane, and pianists Bill Evans and (on one track) Wynton Kelly—have room to find new ways to explore, aided by the rhythm team of bassist Paul Chambers and drummer Jimmy Cobb.

Modal music requires an improviser to conceptualize and organize ideas differently. The pianist Bill Evans, whose open-ended chord voicings are key to *Kind of Blue*, wrote in the liner notes that the musicians arrived at the sessions completely unprepared: They each encountered Davis's music only after they'd entered the studio. To him, this enhanced the session's magic: "Aside from the weighty technical problems of collective coherent thinking, there is the very human, even social need for empathy from all members to bond for the common result." Unlike many jazz records, *Kind of Blue* is defined by that sense of common purpose. It's the sound of musicians honoring the simplicity of a setting by listening closely, playing less, and saying more.

GENRE: 🎷 Jazz.
RELEASED: 1959, Columbia.
KEY TRACKS: "So What," "Freddie Freeloader," "All Blues." **CATALOG CHOICES:** *In a Silent Way; ESP; Miles Smiles.* **NEXT STOP:** Herbie Hancock: *Maiden Voyage* (see p. 338). **AFTER THAT:** John Adams: *Hoodoo Zephyr.*

"I prefer a round sound with no attitude in it."   —Miles Davis

A Milestone of Studio Orchestra Jazz

Sketches of Spain

Miles Davis and Gil Evans

Miles Davis learned to play the trumpet in public, during the frantic mid-1940s outbreak known as bebop. For much of the 1950s, his development happened on two parallel tracks—his many small group sessions, and this and other large ensemble works arranged by Gil Evans.

The small groups encouraged Davis (1926–1991) to develop his technical facility, while the work with Evans forced him to pare things down to an essence of what needed to be said. Eventually, he jettisoned the glib bebop runs in favor of more isolated, often quixotic melodies. *Sketches*, the most ambitious of Davis and Evans's collaborative projects, was a key turning point in the trumpeter's development—in an interview decades later, Evans argued that the long sustained notes of *Sketches* forced Davis to "get his thing together."

The engrossing, unapologetically romantic music on this album demands extreme discipline—particularly the adaptation of Spanish composer Joaquín Rodrigo's *Concierto de Aranjuez* and Evans's original "Saeta," which asks Davis to emulate the extended incantations of a Muslim prayer leader, or *muezzin*. "'Saeta' was the hardest thing for me to do on *Sketches*," Davis recalled in his autobiography. "To play

parts on the trumpet where someone was supposed to be singing. Because you've got all those Arabic music scales in there, black African scales that you can hear. And they modulate and bend and twist and snake and move around."

Davis does his share of twisting through these lavish tone poems, which match his perpetually yearning expression with some of the most beautifully orchestrated large-ensemble writing in all of jazz. To prepare for the session, Evans studied flamenco and Spanish folk music. His lush and inviting backdrops provide Davis with all the "vibe" he needs to pull listeners out of the everyday grind and into a shadowy and surreal Andalusian landscape where the smallest gesture can seem heroic.

GENRE: 🎵 Jazz. **RELEASED:** 1960, Columbia. **KEY TRACKS:** "Saeta," "Will o' the Wisp," "Adagio." **CATALOG CHOICE:** *Porgy and Bess.* **NEXT STOP:** Duke Ellington: *The Far East Suite* (see p. 253). **AFTER THAT:** Wayne Shorter: *Alegria.*

The Art of the Possible

Highlights from the Plugged Nickel

Miles Davis Quintet

This is excellent music for getting unstuck. Follow along closely, and you may find that the ongoing conversations rippling through the music can lure you into less literal ways of thinking. That's essentially what the five musicians here are doing—using all kinds of untapped resources to change the dimension of the canvas. In motivational-speaker parlance, they're "thinking outside the box," working minute by minute and note by note to create an atmosphere in which happy accidents happen.

Saxophonist Wayne Shorter, pianist Herbie Hancock, bassist Ron Carter, and drummer Tony Williams had been with Miles Davis a little more than a year when they arrived at the Chicago club called the Plugged Nickel for an extended engagement in December 1965. Though the material is basic club fare—a typical set would include a blues, a ballad, standards like "Stella by Starlight" and "Yesterdays," and one of Davis's *Kind of Blue* tunes—the five approach each as a new chance to create. After the melody has been stated, they move in a flow of rapidly shifting ideas, sparring at an awesome high level some have described as "telepathic." Williams, particularly, senses where the points of emphasis should be; his dancing cymbal patterns and "Hail Mary" bombs coincide perfectly with Hancock's curtly snipped chords.

This part–free-form and part-structured environment brings out the best in these soloists. Davis sends out pouty lost-little-boy long tones, Hancock tugs and pulls the time apart, and Shorter makes intense lunges that are deeply passionate and cerebral at the same time.

Columbia captured just about every set of the engagement on tape—it's available on eight CDs as *The Complete Plugged Nickel,* an unparalleled trove of great improvisations. This single-disc *Highlights* is an excellent introduction to the inner workings of the most important acoustic jazz group of the era, which within a few years created equally mindblowing studio sides (*ESP, Miles Smiles, Nefertiti*). Once you're unstuck, stick around to experience a collaborative intensity that remains unique in all of music.

GENRE: 🎵 Jazz. RELEASED: 1965, Columbia. (Reissued 1997.) KEY TRACKS: "Walkin'," "Yesterdays," "So What." CATALOG CHOICES: *Miles Smiles; ESP; Nefertiti.* NEXT STOP: Wayne Shorter: *Speak No Evil.* AFTER THAT: Herbie Hancock: *Speak like a Child.*

The Milestone Before Bitches Brew . . .

The Complete In a Silent Way Sessions

Miles Davis

In a Silent Way is among the most significant transitional works in the history of jazz, and one of the least appreciated. It is the step Miles Davis took before *Bitches Brew* (see next page), the album that became the urtext of jazz-rock

fusion. It is the first work to pull the maverick trumpeter fully into the world beyond jazz, while drawing on all the vibe-cultivating tricks he'd developed earlier in the 1960s. By this time, Davis was well-known for anticipating sea changes in jazz. After learning his craft

in bebop, he took the music in new directions with astounding frequency—first pioneering cool jazz (*Birth of the Cool,* 1949), then hard bop (*Workin',* 1956), then the modal inventions of *Kind of Blue* (1959), then the radical harmonies and free-jazz adventuring that defined his '60s quintet (*ESP*, 1965). As he moved away from strict jazz context with this project, Davis sought a fundamentally new sound—there's no old-school "swing" in its two extended tracks, but no explicit "rock," either. It is freedom and openness, the pursuit of an idea not fully hammered out and quite possibly too spacey to pin down. It sits apart from any genre classification, except for the one marked "Astoundingly creative music."

In the early 1990s, when Columbia Records began cataloging Davis's master tapes for reissue, its discoveries included the original session tapes from which *Silent Way* was drawn, as well as several pieces recorded at the time that were rejected. (Like *Bitches Brew*, it was spliced together by Davis and producer Teo Macero; one section is actually used twice.) These were released on the three-CD *The Complete In a Silent Way Sessions*, and they're eye-opening whether or not you know the original work. The extended jams show how ideas coalesced around short electric piano phrases or rhythmic motifs, and how Davis drew perfectly formed pearls of melody out of thin air. Of particular note is the stark "Splash" and its doppelgänger, "Splashdown," two haunting seafaring explorations kept on track by the dual electric pianos of Chick Corea and Herbie Hancock. For any other artist, these would have been key pieces; in the scheme of *Silent Way*, they were just more invention than one album could hold.

GENRE: Jazz. **RELEASED:** 2004, Sony. (Recorded 1969.) **KEY TRACKS:** "Shhh/Peaceful," "It's About That Time." **CATALOG CHOICES:** *Bitches Brew* (see below); *Jack Johnson*. **NEXT STOP:** Mahavishnu Orchestra: *Birds of Fire*. **AFTER THAT:** Weather Report: *I Sing the Body Electric*.

The Headiest Brew

Bitches Brew

Miles Davis

If there's such a thing as night music, this is it: a beat like a resting pulse, steady and shallow. Lugubrious bass clarinet rattling around in the cellar. Long expanses of no melody whatsoever, where nothing much happens.

Appearing now and then is Miles Davis, spearing trumpet lonesomeness into the abyss. The musicians travel from light ethnic jazz to deep rock backbeats, and exchange thoughts as though they're involved in a marathon late-night dorm room conversation, where the pressure's off and any outlandish idea gets serious consideration.

The shadows and ripples of *Bitches Brew* are not, how-

Bitches Brew's psychedelic cover art was created by painter Mati Klarwein.

ever, entirely organic—they're the result of an unusual studio sleight-of-hand. Like its brooding predecessor *In a Silent Way*, *Bitches Brew* was put together in the editing room. To arrive at the "final" compositions, Davis and producer Teo Macero sifted through hours of jamming, organizing individual solos and transitional lulls into an after-the-fact cosmic order. At times this approach, the reverse of typical jazz record-making, imposes structure where none was evident; at other times, thematic ideas are inserted, to contrast with the interplay.

Bitches Brew retains the feeling of spontaneous exchange between members of an astounding band (whose three keyboardists were Chick Corea, Joe Zawinul, and Keith Jarrett), while retrofitting those exchanges with a minimal framework. The 2003 expanded edition, which includes the previously unreleased source jams in their wandering entirety, shows how the editing was integral to the final product: The jams could be endless and drifty, but the tracks of the "finished" *Bitches Brew* somehow feel like a cogent whole. It became a staple of nighttime programming on free-form FM radio (tales of DJs slapping on Side One, which contains the twenty-minute "Pharoah's Dance," and then sneaking out for a toke are

legion), and its deep moods set the tone for much of the jazz-rock fusion that followed.

The editing isn't the only studio sleight-of-hand involved in *Bitches Brew*: Amazingly, this music of nocturnal emotions was recorded during the day. Keyboardist Corea, whose distorted electric piano is one spark plug among many, recalls that the sessions began every morning, promptly at ten. "I remember several of us grumbling about having to get up so early to make the session. What's amazing to me now is the mood. If I didn't know, I'd say this went down at three in the morning."

GENRES: 🅙 Jazz 🅚 Rock. **RELEASED:** 1969, Columbia. (Expanded edition, 2003.) **KEY TRACKS:** "Pharoah's Dance," "Spanish Key," "Miles Runs the Voodoo Down." **CATALOG CHOICES:** *In a Silent Way; Jack Johnson; Tutu.* **NEXT STOP:** Weather Report: *Black Market.*

Mr. Entertainment as a Singer

I Gotta Right to Swing

Sammy Davis Jr.

The conventional assessment of Sammy Davis Jr. presents him as a Swiss Army knife type of performer—a skilled impressionist, fantastic dancer, and effortless comic whose shows never centered on any one thing, least of

all his singing. That's a slight, because though he lived in Sinatra's shadow and released lots of goofy records, Davis (1925–1990) had an innate knack for deepening and personalizing the songs sung by every other saloon singer. *I Gotta Right to Swing* is among the best showcases for Davis, and one of the unfairly overlooked gems of the vocal swing era. Recorded with an uncredited Count Basie Orchestra (minus

Sammy Davis Jr. was part of the Rat Pack during the 1960s.

pianist Basie), it finds Davis executing blues, jazz, and R&B (one of the hottest tracks is his version of Ray Charles's "I Got a Woman") with a blithe panache, and an enviable sense of timing. Davis couldn't escape the Sinatra influence—virtually everyone making vocal records from the late '50s forward borrowed something from the Chairman—but here, before entering what might charitably be called his schmaltz phase, Davis swings in his own sweet way. At once coy and exultant, he delivers Duke Ellington's "Do Nothin' till You Hear from Me" with a rough-and-tumble sense of rhythm. Though he occasionally panders to the Vegas showroom faction of his audience (check out "The Lady Is a Tramp"), Davis compensates with an agility and exuberance that cranks the already hot band up a few notches. Put this on whenever you want to demolish the argument that swing singing begins and ends with Sinatra.

GENRE: 🎵 Vocals. **RELEASED:** 1960, Decca/MCA. **KEY TRACKS:** "Get on the Right Track, Baby," "I Got a Woman," "Till Then," "This Little Girl of Mine." **COLLECTOR'S NOTE:** The 1999 reissue includes the 1957 Davis record, *It's All Over but the Swingin'*. **CATALOG CHOICE:** *Sammy Davis Jr. Sings and Laurindo Almeida Plays.* **NEXT STOP:** Tony Bennett: *Basie Swings, Bennett Sings.* **AFTER THAT:** Dean Martin: *This Time I'm Swingin'!*

A Meeting in the Woods . . .

Pelléas et Mélisande

Claude Debussy

*Irene Joachim, Jacques Jansen, Henri Etcheverry,
Yvonne Gouverne Symphony Orchestra (Roger Désormière, cond.)*

What comes to mind when somebody mentions Claude Debussy? Much of the French impressionist's output is devoted to nature in its undisturbed glory—his pieces evoke contemplative lakes and

swirling ocean waves, fawns peering through the forest in the afternoon sun. And when somebody says "opera"? We conjure statuesque divas emoting loudly, in almost unnatural exaggerated phrases, accompanied by grand and often overwrought musical fanfares.

So, Debussy opera? It's not quite as nature-show idyllic as one might expect. With this somewhat surreal adaptation of a play by French symbolist Maurice Maeterlinck, Debussy took the French approach to opera—works best described as frothy comedies of manners—into the swollen crescendos and sudden jolts associated with Wagner. The plot follows several average Joes as fate carries them from everyday existence into tense, human drama. Set in an ancient,

Claude Debussy began playing piano at age 7 and entered Paris Conservatoire the same year.

unspecified rural culture, it opens with a hunter lost in the woods (Golaud, sung by Henri Etcheverry), who encounters a weeping Mélisande (Irene Joachim). She gives Golaud no details of her traumatic past but agrees to follow him home, and that's when trouble begins. There are subplots involving jealousy, infidelity, and all manner of suspicion, and to accentuate them, Debussy generates music that surges and simmers, eventually breaking into the heated shouting matches operagoers expect.

Like Wagner, Debussy uses the orchestra to fill in emotional contours in the story—anytime you want to know what a character is feeling, check what the string section is doing in the background. That's where Debussy rocks.

To accompany the flowing, structurally unconventional arias he's written for the singers, he conjures an often oppositional musical narrative, of sinister shadows and subtexts.

This version, recorded in Paris during the Nazi occupation, throws bright light on these rippling backdrops. The singers are at career peak, but the ensemble, led by Roger Désormière, deserves equal admiration for its attention to Debussy's slight changes in shading and sudden bursts of color. At times the instrumental passages (particularly the orchestral prelude) offer moods that are richer and more nuanced than the vocal lines.

GENRE: ☻ Opera. **RELEASED:** 1941, EMI. **KEY TRACKS:** Prelude; Act 2: Scene 1. **ANOTHER INTERPRETATION:** Frederica von Stade, Berlin Philharmonic (Herbert von Karajan, cond.). **CATALOG CHOICE:** *Nocturnes Nos. 1–3; Prélude à l'après-midi d'un faune,* Julius Baker, L'Orchestre National de Radiodiffusion, France (Leopold Stokowski, cond.). **NEXT STOP:** Gaetano Donizetti: *L'elisir d'amore,* Joan Sutherland, Luciano Pavarotti, English Chamber Orchestra (Richard Bonynge, cond.). **AFTER THAT:** Richard Wagner: *Die Walküre* (see p. 839).

Impressionism, at the Piano

Preludes

Claude Debussy
Krystian Zimerman

Debussy titled his piano studies the way painters do—to suggest specific images and general points of inspiration. Among these short, richly imagined pieces are renderings of a girl with flaxen hair, "Footprints in the Snow," "The Sunken Cathedral," and the "Gateway to the Alhambra Palace," one of several sketches sent from a shadowy gothic netherworld.

Debussy transfers his distinct symphonic "sound"—lulling orchestrations that suggest calm water—to a lone piano. It's possible to listen to an elegant version of the Preludes, like this one from Polish pianist Krystian Zimerman, and forget that it's coming from eighty-eight keys and three deftly manipulated foot pedals—there are light, hardly pianistic pastels here. Though the music is technically demanding, it rarely sounds that way. The notes almost bend. The chords ooze, leaving no trace of the firm initial attack. Even the few gaudy moments—like "Minstrels," a jazz fantasy inspired by street musicians Debussy wrote in 1905 during the time he was scoring *La mer*—find the composer working to balance the extroverted theme with more solemn motific elaborations.

In each case Zimerman gets at the composer's intent, and then some. He reads Debussy not note-by-note but shape-by-shape, and inside his contoured interpretations there is, at times, the slightest professorial nudge, as if he's saying, "Listen right here, do not miss the plain and astonishing beauty of this phrase."

GENRE: ♫ Classical. **RELEASED:** 1994, Deutsche Grammophon. **KEY TRACKS:** "Voiles," "Brouillards," "Gateway to the Alhambra Palace." **ANOTHER INTERPRETATION:** *The Debussy Album,* Katia and Marielle Labèque. **CATALOG CHOICE:** *La mer* (see p. 634). **NEXT STOP:** Frédéric Chopin: *Nocturnes:* (see p. 168). **AFTER THAT:** Ernesto Lecuona: *Ultimate Collection* (see p. 441).

A Great Work of Rock Summation

The Crane Wife

The Decemberists

The Decemberists are the band to have around whenever one of your classic-rock-obsessed friends starts groaning about how nobody writes melodies anymore. Throughout *The Crane Wife,* the Oregon five-piece led by singer and songwriter Colin Maloy offers elaborate, heights-scaling themes that celebrate (and blur) various fixed points on the rock time line. Like the Arcade Fire (see p. 24), the Decemberists summarize lots of what's come before while striking out in brazen, unlikely directions. The story-songs on *The Crane Wife* could almost be answers to what-if questions: What if a band fluent in art rock and early Pink Floyd augmented that upheaval with floral Beach Boys vocal harmonies? What if the psychedelic mysticism of the Zombies was surrounded by stuttering jazz-fusion polyrhythms? What if the hushed folk introspection of Simon and Garfunkel melted into long instrumental journeys that furthered the spirit of the vocals?

The Crane Wife was inspired by a Japanese folk tale and Shakespeare's *The Tempest.*

The Crane Wife offers answers to these and other questions, but not in an elitist "our collection is bigger than yours" way. Maloy specializes in themes that are so simple they feel eternal. But being a bit of a contrarian, he'll juxtapose athletic church-organ arpeggios around those tunes, and nudge them just a few steps away from the expected. To hear Maloy's schemes at peak quirkiness, check out "The Perfect Crime #2" and parts of "The Island," two standouts on an album of many, in which the effusive refrains go places rock bands rarely visit anymore.

GENRE: 🎸 Rock. **RELEASED:** 2006, Capitol. **KEY TRACKS:** "The Crane Wife 1 & 2," "The Perfect Crime #2," "The Island," "Sons & Daughters." **CATALOG CHOICE:** *Picaresque.* **NEXT STOP:** Doves: *The Last Broadcast.* **AFTER THAT:** The Arcade Fire: *Funeral.*

A Love Letter to a Celtic Home

Song for Ireland

De Danann with Mary Black

The goddess Danu and her people, the Tuatha De Danann, hold a special place in Irish-Celtic mythology. Considered a race of Irish "gods," they perfected magic for their own use, and allegedly traveled on a big cloud to settle the land that became Ireland.

The band De Danann, catalysts in the evolution of traditional Irish music, became popular for their own kind of magic—the ability to conjure a lost (and possibly mythical) Ireland through jigs and reels and lachrymose songs of despair. The band started at Sunday morning jam sessions in the early 1970s at the Hughes Pub in Spiddal, a small County Galway town. Organized by the fiddler Frankie Gavin and guitarist Alec Finn (still the only constant members), these informal sessions grew into a thriving hub of traditional music, through which have come important Irish singers—Dolores Keane, Maura O'Connell, and, most consequentially, Mary Black.

Song for Ireland features Black, whose cool detachment is a perfect complement to the athletic and gregarious Gavin. De Danann is known for transforming stock pub entertainments into pieces that are exceedingly vivacious; the lively excursions here are offset by more somber tunes that allow Black to shine. Though the album was recorded shortly after Black joined up with De Danann, it sounds as if they've been playing together for years. When Black hits her stride—on "Hard Times" and "Mulqueen's Reels," among others—she shows a heavy Celtic heart and a deep love for the land that inspired the project, which feels like the longing reflections of one who's far away from home.

GENRE: ⊕ World/Celtic. **RELEASED:** 1983, Sugar Hill. **KEY TRACKS:** "Hard Times," "Turkey in the Straw," "Mulqueen's Reels." **CATALOG CHOICES:** De Danann: *The Mist-Covered Mountain.* Mary Black: *By the Time It Gets Dark.* **NEXT STOP:** Altan: *Harvest Storm.*

The Deepest Heavy Rock from England

Machine Head

Deep Purple

Deep Purple's "Smoke on the Water" lives wherever guitars are sold. Like its obvious model, Cream's "Sunshine of Your Love," it's an insanely memorable riff that boils rock and roll down to an easily mastered (and endlessly repeatable) four-bar code. It still crawls regularly from the din of amateur hour in the guitar department, an easy shortcut to cool for misfit kids.

It's also the rare rock song that describes the circumstances of its creation—"Smoke" tells how the five-piece Deep Purple, then just beginning to attract attention, had its recording plans derailed by a fire. Under pressure to create its seventh album quickly, the band had rented the famous Casino in Montreux, Switzerland, and the Rolling Stones' mobile studio. The night before the recording was to start, an audience member ("some stupid" in the song) fired a flare gun into the ceiling during a performance by Frank Zappa and the Mothers of Invention. The resulting fire sent smoke all over the coastal area, ruined the venue, and forced Deep Purple to scramble for an alternate location. They landed in the vacant Grand Hotel, where they set up in corridors and had to walk through a mazelike series of rooms and balconies to reach the recording equipment.

Though the arena-rattling "Smoke on the Water" was the band's breakthrough (and the reason the album hit the top five in the U.S. and sold over two million copies in a year), it's perhaps the least musically substantial offering on *Machine Head*. The other tracks show Deep Purple differentiating itself from the heavy-rock heavyweights (Black Sabbath, Led Zeppelin) then ruling England: The opener, "Highway Star," scoots along, sleek and almost jazzlike, a caterwauling groove that inspires one of the most demonically intricate solos in the hard rock canon. Each track is rendered with steady-handed precision, and is spiked by head-swiveling solos that all but taunt aspiring axmen: "Sure, you can cop the riff, but let's see you do *this*!"

GENRE: 🎸 Rock. **RELEASED:** 1972, Warner Bros. **KEY TRACKS:** "Highway Star," "Space Truckin'." **CATALOG CHOICE:** *Who Do We Think We Are.* **NEXT STOP:** Black Sabbath: *Paranoid* (see p. 92). **AFTER THAT:** Cream: *Live Cream.*

Peace and Love Rap

Three Feet High and Rising

De La Soul

Kings of a head-nodding approach to groove that embraced all kinds of musical expression, De La Soul went from zero to 90 miles per hour faster than any other group in hip-hop history. One minute in 1988 they were

Long Island unknowns with a penchant for nonsensical live performances. Months later they were being called the "future of rap."

Three Feet High and Rising is the album responsible for that change—twenty-four songs about flowers and peace and sex and body odor intercut with silly game show skits, with spontaneous raps offset by easygoing, thrown-together chanted refrains. Crucial to its sound is DJ Pasemaster Mase

Critic Robert Christgau called *Three Feet High and Rising* "unlike any rap album you or anybody else has ever heard."

(Vincent Mason). Where most DJs capture a distinct slice of an old record and repurpose it for use as a backdrop, this deep thinker, with encouragement from producer Prince Paul (of Stetsasonic), gives the samples a starring role. He uses them as brief punch lines, wry counterpoints to the narratives, or as split-second "drop-ins" designed to change the mood. The snippets come fast and furious—sometimes

MC Posdnous (Kelvin Mercer) will be running some idea down, and he'll stop, seemingly in mid-phrase, to let some surreal, seemingly incongruous old record finish his thought. These sounds include obscure disco singles, a longtime rap standby, as well as vintage jazz titles and hits by the Turtles, Steely Dan, and Johnny Cash. (The Turtles' "You Showed Me," which was used on "Transmitting Live from Mars," eventually got De La Soul into trouble; the band sued the rappers, in one of several cases that established the current precedent known as "sample clearance," in which the owner of the recording must grant permission before it is sampled.)

For all the psychedelic sound-twisting, De La Soul's breakthrough, which topped the *Village Voice*'s annual Pazz and Jop critics' poll after its release, remains even more notable for its stances. Running alongside the inevitable (and often funny) rap-prowess proclamations are anti-drug messages and be-yourself anthems. De La Soul's embrace of nonconformity, on "Me, Myself, and I" and other tracks, may be its biggest contribution: *Three Feet High and Rising* made it supremely cool to be a hip-hop iconoclast.

GENRE: Hip-Hop. **RELEASED:** 1989, Tommy Boy. **KEY TRACKS:** "Me, Myself, and I," "Ghetto Thang," "Say No Go." **CATALOG CHOICE:** *De La Soul Is Dead.* **NEXT STOP:** A Tribe Called Quest: *The Low End Theory* (see p. 786). **AFTER THAT:** Mos Def: *Black on Both Sides.*

The Lost Art of Making Time Stand Still

Sandy

Sandy Denny

T he British folk goddess Sandy Denny (1947–1978) was obsessed with time. On the first song she ever wrote, she wondered, "Who Knows Where the Time Goes?" She posited an answer, musing in a tone

of distanced, daydreaming ambivalence, with stanzas about time as a great unknowable. This, her second solo album, opens with an anthem of patience, "It'll Take a Long Time," a thought she extends a few selections later with a wise cover of Bob Dylan's "Tomorrow Is a Long Time." Among the unreleased songs that surfaced after her death is a wispy, totally stunning meditation on life's passages entitled "Now and Then."

In 1971, Sandy Denny did a duet with Robert Plant on Led Zeppelin's "The Battle of Evermore."

Toussaint), and pointed rock guitar ("It'll Take a Long Time" features Richard Thompson— see p. 775—and pedal steel player "Sneaky Pete" Kleinow in an animated conversation).

The songs are plenty interesting to start with, and Denny gives them extra richness. Her phrasing is easy and casual—at times she seems to muse over an idea for a while before letting it go, giving each note slow consideration. This makes for quite a contrast: As she laments the ceaseless rush of time, her lovely, languid voice makes time stand still.

Denny was a key figure in three British folk institutions—her voice graced the heyday of Fairport Convention (see p. 268) as well as Strawbs and Fotheringay. She managed, along the way, to wander from the traditional bent of the bands long enough to investigate slightly more accessible pop-leaning music. *Sandy* is the most successful of these projects—a series of graceful odes appointed with shimmering string ensembles ("Listen, Listen"), festive horns ("For Nobody to Hear," arranged by Allen

GENRE: Folk. **RELEASED:** 1972, A&M. **KEY TRACKS:** "It'll Take a Long Time," "Listen, Listen," "Quiet Joys of Brotherhood." **CATALOG CHOICE:** *Who Knows Where the Time Goes* (a box set that includes "Now and Then"). **NEXT STOP:** Fotheringay: *Fotheringay.* **AFTER THAT:** Judee Sill: *Heart Food.*

When Eric Met Duane . . .

Layla and
Other Assorted Love Songs

Derek and the Dominos

In 1970, the recording engineer Tom Dowd brokered one of the most auspicious meetings in rock history—between guitarist Eric Clapton and the slide-guitar master Duane Allman. Clapton was working with Dowd at Miami's Criteria Studios, attempting to shake off the bitter demise of Blind Faith with a new group that included keyboardist and singer Bobby Whitlock. After a few days of what Dowd describes as "getting sounds and breaking ice," Allman called, curious to see the British guitar legend in person. Clapton's group went to watch the Allman Brothers play instead, and after the concert, the musicians partied all night, eventually repairing to the studio the next afternoon.

Clapton's collaboration with Duane Allman is revered as a pinnacle of rock guitar.

Dowd: "We turned the tapes on, and they went on for fifteen, eighteen hours like that. I went through two or three sets of engineers."

Those jams—furious marathons based loosely on blues songs (Howlin' Wolf's "Killing Floor") and simple riffs—set the stage for *Layla and Other Assorted Love Songs*, a multidimensional rock landmark. Clapton was, according to legend, at loose ends during this time: He'd fallen in love with Patti Boyd, the wife of his best friend George Harrison, and was deeply troubled—a pain evident not just on the celebrated title track he wrote with Jim Gordon, but also such apt covers as Freddie King's sorrowful blues about messing with a friend's wife, "Have You Ever Loved a Woman."

Fueled by cocaine, heroin, and Johnny Walker ("It was scary," Whitlock recalls, because "we didn't have little bits of anything. . . . We had these big bags laying out everywhere"), the group went from open jamming to developing actual songs, among them the beseeching "Bell Bottom Blues." The basic concept was rock, pitched at the whiplash frequency of Memphis soul. The band worked up nontraditional approaches to old blues (this "Key to the Highway" has a searing energy that far outstrips Clapton's more scholarly later blues), and then recorded the masterpiece "Layla" as a suite, in stages.

Inspired by the Persian poet Nizami's romantic fable *The Story of Layla and Majnun*, Clapton wrote lyrics that expressed a worshipful devotion, and surrounded the verses with a guitar phrase, authored by Allman, that endures as a rock and roll national anthem. Then, when things can go no higher, comes the postcoital cigarette—in the form of a reflective elegy, written on piano by Gordon, that allows Allman and Clapton to have a more leisurely discussion. Their combined mojo takes everyone to church, where the impassioned whirling-dervish embrace of two swooning, imploring guitars leads to a state of illuminated bliss. Transcendence-wise, this is as close as rock gets to Coltrane's quartet collectively hitting the rafters at the Village Vanguard, or Nusrat Fateh Ali Khan singing in an unshakable trance, or . . .

GENRE: 🎸 Rock. **RELEASED:** 1971, Polydor. **KEY TRACKS:** "Layla," "Why Does Love Got to Be So Sad?" "Have You Ever Loved a Woman," "Key to the Highway." **CATALOG CHOICE:** *The Layla Sessions* (three discs, contains the studio jams). **NEXT STOP:** John Coltrane Quartet: *Live at the Village Vanguard.* **AFTER THAT:** J. J. Cale: *Troubadour.*

Take More than Five

Take Ten

Paul Desmond with Jim Hall

The jazz police will tell you that the Dave Brubeck Quartet's *Time Out* (1959), which features the Paul Desmond–penned hit "Take Five," is one of the most important jazz records of all time. It's mostly pleasant and bold at times (see particularly "Blue Rondo à la Turk"), but it suffers from a fatal flaw: Brubeck's piano playing. The esteemed leader is revealed as something of a musical clod on *Time Out*, his awkwardness marring much of what's great about the record. Brubeck favored odd time signatures and disjointed grooves, perhaps counting on those complexities to mask his shortcomings playing straight swing.

"I have won several prizes as the world's slowest alto player."
—Paul Desmond

No such troubles exist on this, Desmond's "follow-up." "Take Five" was the first jazz instrumental to sell a million copies, so naturally there were attempts to re-create the magic. This quartet date, featuring guitarist Jim Hall, was recorded four years later; it begins with a knock-off of "Take Five" that's far more easygoing. Hall approaches the rhythm as a series of glancing karate chops, allowing Desmond to float and flirt with exotic scales. The alto solo, which is really more like a chatty conversation with Hall, lifts "Take Ten" to a place where sensitivity matters.

From there, Desmond and Hall breeze through a program of bossa novas and standards played to glorify the melodies, not their egos. Both soloists tread lightly, stringing together thoughtful phrases that aspire to the lyricism and concision of great poetry. A key part of Desmond's appeal comes from his alto tone, which is tart like a gin and tonic but offers shades and hues that linger like a great burgundy. He's been easy to deride—another cool-school white dude—but because of recordings like this, impossible to dismiss. Anthony Braxton (see p. 114), the firebrand of the avant-garde alto, loved Desmond. This album makes it easy to understand why.

GENRE: 🎷 Jazz. **RELEASED:** 1963, RCA. **KEY TRACKS:** "Take Ten," "Alone Together," "Black Orpheus." **CATALOG CHOICES:** *Easy Living; From the Hot Afternoon.* **NEXT STOP:** Jim Hall: *Concierto.* **AFTER THAT:** Stanley Turrentine: *Salt Song.*

Twenty-One Strings? Sounds like Thousands

New Ancient Strings

Toumani Diabaté and Ballake Sissoko

Here's an illustration of how the past operates in African music. Back in the late 1960s, Sidiki Diabaté and Djelimadi Sissoko—two Mali-born masters of the twenty-one-string African *kora* who were related by marriage—got together for an album of duets. The result, *Ancient Strings*, spotlights the *kora*'s wondrous, dancing sound on a set of mostly traditional Malian songs. This collaboration, which became a classic, inspired younger African musicians who were then turning away from tradition, to reconsider the versatile *kora*.

Toumani Diabaté with his *kora,* a twenty-one-string harp-lute.

The sons of both musicians grew up to learn the demanding instrument, and in 1999 reprised their fathers' duet on the magnificent *New Ancient Strings*. The second-generation meeting benefits from an open worldview: The two engage in fiery jazz-like back-and-forth exchanges, and transform the hypnotic quality of Malian instrumental music into a springboard for skittering hard-rocking ad-libs. Diabaté and Sissoko sustain an intense conversation throughout, trading solo and accompaniment roles seamlessly, generating spiderwebbed clusters of notes that, despite all the finger wizardry, communicate on a pure spirit level.

This is one of several amazing collaborations engineered by Diabaté. *Songhai*, his 1989 meeting with the Spanish flamenco group Ketama and British folk-rock bassist Danny Thompson, transforms an improbable gathering into an album-length expression of pure joy. Another gem is the 2005 duet with guitarist Ali Farka Touré, *In the Heart of the Moon.*

GENRE: ⊕ World/Mali. **RELEASED:** 1999, Hannibal. **KEY TRACKS:** "Bi Lambam," "Kora Bali." **CATALOG CHOICES:** *Songhai; In the Heart of the Moon.* **NEXT STOP:** Herbie Hancock and Foday Musa Suso: *Village Life.* **AFTER THAT:** Various Artists: *Jali Kunda: Griots of West Africa and Beyond.*

You're the Words, He's the Tune, Play Him

Hot August Night

Neil Diamond

A soft rocker whose strong suit is bombast, Neil Diamond cuts a maddening figure through pop music: He's responsible for some of the most infectious odes to joy ever to grace an AM radio ("Cherry Cherry," "I'm a Believer"), and the mastermind behind a boatload of bloated, pretentious, manipulative tuneage ("I Am . . . I Said").

Can't have one without the other. But you *can* focus on a moment before the songwriter and guitarist became mired in unmitigated sap: This 1972 concert at the Greek Theatre in Los Angeles, which finds Diamond's alter ego, "Brother Love," gathering the diffuse strands of his musical personality into an exuberant, roof-rattling revue, amazingly, avoids schmaltz.

"My voice is unadorned. . . . I try to be honest and truthful and soulful with the voice I have."
—Neil Diamond

Diamond was already an expert in the studio; *Tap Root Manuscript* and his other acclaimed recordings are built around crisp acoustic guitar, with layers of harmony vocal and just the right specks of instrumental "seasoning"—you don't have to love the songs to respect the craft behind them. For Diamond, putting those songs across live was another matter: He'd been touring with a typical small rock combo, and began to realize that some of his material— epic-sounding songs like "Girl, You'll Be a Woman Soon" and "Sweet Caroline"—could benefit from a thicker sound. So he augmented the arrangements, wrote snazzy horn charts, and added grand orchestral swells and fanfares. Remarkably, the extra musicians don't goop things up. They match the pomp of Diamond's big-tent themes, and jolt everything with palpable electricity, making this the rare live album that improves, in some cases dramatically, on the studio versions.

GENRES: ✪ Pop 🅗 Rock. **RELEASED:** 1972, MCA. **KEY TRACKS:** "Cherry Cherry," "Red Red Wine," "Kentucky Woman," "Holly Holy." **CATALOG CHOICES:** *Tap Root Manuscript; Beautiful Noise.* **NEXT STOP:** John Mayer: *Room for Squares.* **AFTER THAT:** Maroon Five: *Songs About Jane.*

A Groove for the Ages

"Soul Makossa"

Manu Dibango

The vocal chant from this 1972 dance floor classic—which goes something like, "mama se, mama-sa, mama-koss-sa"—is best known as the chorale from Michael Jackson's 1981 hit "Wanna Be Startin' Something." Though the rhythms are slightly different, the vocal cadences are nearly identical; when Jackson's song appeared, there was enough direct appropriation for the Cameroon-born saxophonist and composer Manu Dibango to threaten a copyright infringement lawsuit. (The parties settled out of court, with Jackson paying Dibango an undisclosed sum but not offering any songwriting credit.)

Just one time through the Dibango original—which was introduced to the West by New York DJ Frankie Crocker, and is sometimes identified as the first disco song—and it's easy to see why Jackson had it in his head. Everything about the track is addictive, from the initial two-note saxophone theme to the burbling bass line to the twice-famous refrain. Even though there are no solos, this is one totally enchanting jam, spurred, in spots, by Dibango's Isaac Hayes–like deep-baritone spoken comments.

Dibango was already a veteran when he recorded "Soul Makossa." In the '60s, he played jazz in Paris, Brussels, and the Congo (with the group Africa Jazz), and later led a band that specialized in a hybrid of African music and hard Southern soul. This track, his biggest hit, is available on several career anthologies. Of them, *Africadelic: The Very Best of Manu Dibango* is choice: It's got some

In 2004, Dibango was appointed a UNESCO Artist for Peace.

terrific forays into boogaloo ("Wouri") as well as later collaborations with great African singers and a clever DJ Flex "Soul Makossa" remix that makes Jackson's borrowing totally clear.

GENRE: 🌐 World/Cameroon.
RELEASED: 1972, Unidisc.
APPEARS ON: *Africadelic: The Very Best of Manu Dibango.*
CATALOG CHOICE: *Wakafrica.* **NEXT STOP:** Fela Kuti: *Coffin for Head of State.*
AFTER THAT: Tony Allen: *Lagos No Shaking.*

The Rock Heartbeat

Bo Diddley

Bo Diddley

If Bo Diddley (1928–2008) had received a dollar every time some act borrowed his distinctive beat—that bouncing *chank, a-chank-chank, chank chank,* with maracas shaking right alongside—he'd have been the richest man in rock.

The Rolling Stones would have had to pay up several times. Bruce Springsteen would owe for "She's the One." Buddy Holly for "Not Fade Away." The Strangeloves' 1965 "I Want Candy" was a direct copy, as was the Who's "The Magic Bus."

Diddley didn't get diddley for inspiring all that music. Virtually everybody in rock used his beat, but not everybody gave him props. This left the Mississippi native, who'd moved to Chicago as a teenager, a bit bitter: In an interview in the early 1990s, Diddley (real name: Ellas McDaniel) railed against record labels

and managers, but said he was equally hurt that artists didn't make their sources clear: "I wish they would just let the people know where it comes from. That's all."

Diddley had an impact as soon as he was signed to the Chess subsidiary Checker in the mid-'50s—he told people that other artists around Chess viewed him as a threat, because he was capable of singing both the blues and rock and roll. His debut single, "Bo Diddley," went to the top of the R&B charts in July 1955, and for the next few years Diddley served up variations on its basic strategy, which borrowed from blues and early rock but wasn't aligned with either.

This album, his first, remains the best single-disc account of Diddley's

Bo Diddley with his signature Gretsch guitar, nicknamed the "Twang Machine."

sly genius. It suggests that as his namesake beat spread like wildfire, it overshadowed other, equally potent aspects of his art—notably his songwriting, which combines blues phraseology with a deep understanding of human nature. Diddley explored a diverse array of rhythms over the years, but that bankable beat remains his most important contribution. And this record is the best way to hear it—in its most elemental state, as pounded out by Diddley on his trademark rectangular guitar. It's a hot-wired code for the ages, accompanied by just tribal drums and vocal taunts and maybe some party-time maracas to keep things swinging. No matter how technology-happy rock gets, it's still all you need.

GENRE: 🎸 Rock. **RELEASED:** 1958, Checker. **KEY TRACKS:** "Bo Diddley," "Mona," "Before You Accuse Me," "Who Do You Love." **CATALOG CHOICE:** *Rare and Well Done.* **NEXT STOP:** The Rolling Stones: *Out of Our Heads.* **AFTER THAT:** Bruce Springsteen: *Born to Run* (see p. 733).

"We Won't Be Rockin' Bells That Go a-Ding and a-Dong"

Sex Packets

Digital Underground

The extra-large Oakland, California, crew Digital Underground was hardly the first hip-hop act to sample the music of '70s funk pathfinders Parliament-Funkadelic. But with this near-delirious debut,

it became the first to fully update the P-Funk vision for hip-hop heads. The Underground assimilated the teachings of P-Funk—the taunting refrains, the rumbling bass lines, the chaotic onstage antics—into surreal party music. Hip-hop hasn't been the same since.

Meant to be enjoyed more than dissected, *Sex Packets* begins with "The Humpty Dance," which answers the musical question, "What would

Selling over 1 million copies, *Sex Packets* reached platinum status.

P-Funk have sounded like in a rap context?" This seemingly slight bonbon is all elastic grooves and squiggly lines and the horny wordplay of leader Gary "Shock G" Jacobs—who appears as Humpty Hump, one of his many alter egos. This dude is the perfect rap buffoon: He looks like a hapless loser in a Groucho Marx getup, but rhymes like a hired assassin, dispensing one-liners like he's getting paid by the dagger. The term "Sex Packets" refers not to condoms, but an imaginary space-age pill that, according to the lyrics, helps induce and accelerate sexual fantasies. Whenever a brother's having trouble with the ladies, a packet is prescribed. As a result, much of what follows "The Humpty Dance" is a hot-and-bothered discussion of getting it on, with detours that allow various Underground members to explain their tactics ("The Way We Swing") or explore witty repartee at a fast-break pace ("Freaks of the Industry"). Countless MCs have yammered at length and in graphic detail about the sex they want and the sex they need. Digital Underground does something else entirely: Casting sex as a blessed event (as opposed to a predatory game), this crew takes the desire that powers the funk, and uses it to power hip-hop that's fresh, frolicsome, and, even after all these years, still a little freaky.

GENRE: 🎧 Hip-Hop. **RELEASED:** 1990,

Tommy Boy. **KEY TRACKS:** "The Humpty Dance," "The Way We Swing," "Underwater Rimes" (remix), "Doowutchyalike." **NEXT STOP:** Jungle Brothers: *Straight out the Jungle.* **AFTER THAT:** The Beastie Boys: *Licensed to Ill.*

Mapping the Journeys of . . .

"The Wanderer"

Dion

With or without his street-corner harmonists the Belmonts, Bronx-born Dion DiMucci was, for many, the early embodiment of rock and roll cool. He looked great in leather, sang in a voice that simultaneously conveyed toughness and empathy, and showed generations of performers the importance of creating a persona to accompany the music. This song, one of a handful of singles to reach the Top 10 after Dion went solo in 1960, became his calling card.

"The Wanderer" is a durable rock and roll archetype—the teenager in love who's shed his letter-sweater innocence, and won't be tied down. Everything about him is twitchy, elusive. Having learned the hard way about love's consequences and tribulations, he's the type of guy who doesn't get too cuddly, and as he advises prospective lovers about this, his forthrightness becomes a virtue—he's doing the gals a favor by warning them of his roving ways.

For a jukebox-targeted song circa 1960, "The Wanderer" is a surprisingly developed character study. That's only half of it. As with his other singles from the period—especially the sunkissed "Runaround Sue" and the cover of the Drifters' "Ruby Baby"—Dion's exuberant refrains have their own magnetic pull; if you ever need to explain the wildcat energy of rock and roll to a Martian, these untroubled songs would

Dion's "The Wanderer" reached #2 on the U.S. *Billboard* charts.

be an excellent place to start.

"The Wanderer" first appeared on the album titled *Runaround Sue* (1961), which includes mature pop gems (the entrancing "Lonely World") as well as sparkling teen-idol treatments of "Dream Lover" and "In the Still of the Night." "The Wanderer" turns up on just about every decent hits collection; the most comprehensive survey of Dion is the three-disc *King of the New York Streets.*

GENRE: 🎸 Rock. **RELEASED:** 1960, Laurie. **APPEARS ON:** *Runaround Sue; The Essential Dion; King of the New York Streets.* **CATALOG CHOICES:** *Born to Be with You* (produced by Phil Spector, U.K.-only release); *Bronx in Blue.* **F.Y.I.:** Dion and his group the Belmonts were on tour with Buddy Holly and others in January–February 1959. After the show in Clear Lake, Iowa, Dion decided he couldn't afford the $36 plane fare to the next gig; the plane crashed, killing Holly, Ritchie Valens, and the Big Bopper. **NEXT STOP:** Del Shannon: *Greatest Hits.* **AFTER THAT:** The Wood Brothers: *Ways Not to Lose.*

Thinking Girl's Country Pop

Wide Open Spaces

The Dixie Chicks

O n the title track of this multiplatinum breakthrough, Dixie Chicks lead singer Natalie Maines champions the dreams and aspirations of young American women. Defending a girl's right to dream (while at the same time voicing concern about the vanishing wilderness), she proclaims "She needs wide open spaces, room to make her big mistakes."

In the staid world of mid-'90s country, when high-gloss Shania Twain was the closest thing to a "rebel" girl, this stance was a bit unusual. The three Chicks—Maines, Emily Robison, and Martie Maguire—did things their own way, and sang proudly about it. They railed against the sexist expectations of Nashville, which they knew well (Maines's father is Lloyd Maines, the veteran pedal-steel guitarist and record producer). They wrote their own songs (half of this album is original material). And eventually they made their own trouble, by questioning President Bush's conduct of the war in Iraq.

But it's the sound of the Chicks that makes these declarations of independence so unshak-

Wide Open Spaces won a Grammy for Best Country Album.

able. Whether sharing man trouble or affirming the rebellious impulse, the three singers braid their voices together into breathtaking harmonies that shift around, on a quest for new loveliness. It's a stunning, shimmering sound, and it enlivens songs written by the Chicks, and those penned by a small crew of California tunesmiths in the Jackson Browne mold—this version of J. D. Souther's "I'll Take Care of You" is definitive. And, in another refreshing departure from Nashville practice, there's no filler: Each of the twelve songs on *Wide Open Spaces* is stunning.

GENRE: 🌐 Country. **RELEASED:** 1998, Monument/Sony. **KEY TRACKS:** "I'll Take Care of You," "There's Your Trouble," "You Were Mine." **CATALOG CHOICE:** Home. **NEXT STOP:** Gretchen Wilson: *Here for the Party.*

The Best from Enduring Soldiers in the Gospel Army

Thank You for One More Day

The Dixie Hummingbirds

W hen his group the Dixie Hummingbirds celebrated its seventy-fifth anniversary in 2003, lead singer Ira Tucker Sr. was asked about the life of an African American singing group traveling the church and revival tent gospel circuit of the 1940s and '50s. "There was a time when we were happy to split four dollars between us," he recalled. "We were discriminated against, people called us names. We went through what we did because we loved to share our music. When you compare it to now, there's no way that a group would start out and suffer like we did." But he's not sure he'd trade any part of the experience: "When you start low, and you don't let it get you down, you bring those things with you when you come up."

That's not all the Dixie Hummingbirds brought. The group—with Tucker's emotional lead vocals supported by a traditional quartet backing—used a snappy, interactive style of singing to interpret spirituals and hymns. Its wide-wingspan harmonies and solo vocal declarations (which influenced secular stars like Jackie Wilson) attain the fulminating fervor of an epic sermon. Even in its lone "crossover" moment—the 'Birds sing with Paul Simon on

The Dixie Hummingbirds accompanied Paul Simon on his single "Loves Me like a Rock."

his gospel shuffle "Loves Me like a Rock"—the group did its work without straying far from what a churchgoer might expect to hear on Sunday morning.

Formed originally in South Carolina and relocated to Philadelphia in the 1940s, the Dixie Hummingbirds toured with Sister Rosetta Tharpe, Mahalia Jackson, and others, and recorded for a variety of labels. This collection, released in conjunction with their seventieth anniversary in 1998, shows why the Hummingbirds were one of the most spirited groups ever to travel the gospel highway.

GENRE: ✝ Gospel. RELEASED: 1998, Peacock/MCA. KEY TRACKS: "Loves Me like a Rock," "Ezekiel Saw the Wheel," "Two Little Fishes and Five Loaves of Bread." CATALOG CHOICE: *Gospel at Newport.* NEXT STOP: The Blind Boys of Alabama: *Atom Bomb.* AFTER THAT: Louis Armstrong: *Louis Sings the Good Book.*

A Fresh Hip-Hop Voice from London

Boy in da Corner

Dizzee Rascal

D izzee Rascal wouldn't have become a recording artist were it not for a tolerant high school music teacher in a working-poor East London neighborhood. Young Dylan Mills grew up on the streets in the '90s,

and spent time running drugs and doing other mischief, even though his friends considered him a sharp MC with a special knack for the dance subgenre called "garage." He often skipped classes, but one day, on a whim, he wandered into his school's music room. There he found a computer loaded with music-making software. After some brief instruction, he began

making beats and backgrounds to go with his rhymes. He was hooked.

Those beats became the catalyst for *Boy in da Corner*, Dizzee Rascal's high-strung and intensely individual debut, which was recorded in 2002 when he was eighteen and went on to win the U.K.'s prestigious Mercury Music Prize the following year. Where many British rappers seek to "Americanize" their delivery, Mills spews a steady stream of London slang, and peppers his tales of brotherhood and romantic conquest with the insider lingo of his posse. The narratives are concerned with making the best of bleak surroundings; they're propped up by category-defying music that incorporates techno drum programming and electro squiggles. The variety alone is stunning: Where most commercial hip-hop sits in a reliable medium tempo, Dizzee Rascal lives up to his moniker with fast-paced caterwauling freak-outs and

"Finally, the Mercury Music Prize judges pick a real winner."
—*Planet Sound*

jarring blasts of dissonance. Every track is wound tight, to the point of being hyper, if not harsh. The density of the sound, coupled with Mills's spitfire delivery, helped establish the brash Dizzee Rascal as the rare hip-hop MC with an instantly identifiable, and totally original, concept.

GENRE: 🎧 Hip-Hop. **RELEASED:** 2003, XL Recordings. **KEY TRACKS:** "I Luv U," "Wot U On," "Fix Up, Look Sharp." **NEXT STOP:** The Streets: *Original Pirate Material* (see p. 751).

The Peak of a Master Melodist

Luz

Djavan

Computers are generally considered to be a positive evolutionary step in the production of popular music—they make it possible to move ideas around quickly, to try different sound combinations without endless rerecording. But there's a downside: Computers have induced several generations of pop songwriters to think of melodies as little more than repeatable patterns. Quincy Jones, the producer responsible for Michael Jackson's *Thriller* (see p. 386) and other smash hits, considers this a problem: "What you hear nowadays are these little bitty phrases, two measures or four measures, that wind up being the whole melody . . . but they don't really take you anywhere."

To encounter more expansive themes, ideas that swerve around sharp corners and take flying leaps and generally don't end up in expected places, check out *Luz*, the career peak of Brazilian singer and songwriter Djavan. Recorded in Los Angeles in 1982 and sung entirely in Portuguese, this is a shining example of compositional ideas that wander far from, and happily elude, repetitive two-measure loops on the grid. Djavan's songs here—particularly "Sina" and "Capim"—are like winding paths through a forest, with each verse pulling you closer to a clearing. Splayed out over long and lazy phrases, Djavan's music registers as the opposite of numbing repetition. Instead it unfolds like a breathtaking vista.

Djavan enhances this feeling by the way he sings—with a breezy irreverence. He's got that Brazilian understatement working, and though he knows these melodies are plenty compelling, he doesn't deliver them straight. Moving with gymnastic dexterity and a great sense of flow, he massages the original themes into improbable, astoundingly musical shapes. Needless to say, none of them fits into a two-measure spot on anybody's grid.

GENRE:  World/Brazil. **RELEASED:** 1982, Sony. **KEY TRACKS:** "Petala," "Sina." **CATALOG CHOICE:** *Seduzir.* **NEXT STOP:** Lô Borges: *Lô Borges* (see p. 106). **AFTER THAT:** Tribalistas: *Tribalistas.*

Cut-Paste to the Nth Power

Endtroducing

DJ Shadow

This recording is built entirely from fragmented pieces of other records. When it was released, in late 1996, sampling had been part of hip-hop production for a long while, but few in the genre approached it the way Josh Davis (aka DJ Shadow) did: He collated scores of tiny audio "events" into recurring rhythms, then surrounded that beat with ephemeral odds and ends, including dialog from movies and assorted bits found on '60s sound-effects records. His drums are often not drums at all, but fragments of sounds played backward, heavily processed, and choreographed into intricate patterns.

DJ Shadow at work.

The California-born Davis developed a reputation years before this debut appeared, as part of a small coterie of underground DJs specializing in instrumental hip-hop. He could make radically funky sounds out of literally any source material, from Tangerine Dream to Nirvana to old jazz records. And on top of that funky music he layered lushly textured audio that suggested ominous doings ahead.

It is the slashing stuff around the beats that sets this influential album apart: Davis approaches each piece the way a pop songwriter would, seeking to communicate specific ideas or foster introspection, while transporting listeners into astonishing detailed soundscapes. His "Midnight in a Perfect World" aspires to an idealized vision of place. His multipart "What Does Your Soul Look Like" ponders that big question across a sumptuous open canvas.

And while the center of attention is often the quick-stepping and sometimes fitful beats, *Endtroducing* is arguably more significant for its color palette. These are rich multidimensional collages, with doomy chords that hover like mushroom clouds, and shimmering textures that are layered into a total-immersion listening experience. That's the genius of DJ Shadow: Though it's painstaking work manipulating old records into new sounds, he never seems stuck in some laboratory. He's out on the streets, soaking up life as it rushes past.

GENRE:  Electronica. **RELEASED:** 1996, MoWax/Universal. (Reissued 2005.) **KEY TRACKS:** "Best Foot Forward," "What Does Your Soul Look Like," "Organ Donor," "Midnight in a Perfect World." **COLLECTOR'S NOTE:** *Endtroducing* was reissued with a disc of bonus material in 2005. The highlight is a twelve-minute live DJ Shadow performance. **NEXT STOP:** Dr. Octagon: *Dr. Octagonecologyst.* **AFTER THAT:** DJ Spooky: *Songs of a Dead Dreamer.*

Freedom, Swinging

Out to Lunch

Eric Dolphy

The rare multitasker with an instantly identifiable sound on several instruments (flute, bass clarinet, alto saxophone), Eric Dolphy made free jazz that was filled with laughter and contentious arguments and lively expressions of humanity. Early experience playing with Charles Mingus, John Coltrane, and others (and listening to the work of Ornette Coleman, a free pioneer who'd grabbed the spotlight just ahead of him) taught the Los Angeles–born Dolphy that avant-garde jazz had the potential to alienate even a hipster audience. So on his originals, he made sure that the music could lure ordinary listeners—his sound was heady avant-garde cut with a touch of child's play.

In 1964, Eric Dolphy was post-humously inducted into the *Down Beat* Jazz Hall of Fame.

Dolphy (1928–1964) spent much of his career as a sideman. His break came when he joined the Charles Mingus Quartet in 1959; from there he made irreverent contributions to records by Ornette Coleman (see p. 181), Booker Little (see p. 450), and, most notably, John Coltrane (see p. 182). Dolphy participated in Coltrane's groundbreaking Village Vanguard recordings in late 1961. Dolphy recorded under his own name beginning in 1960, but it's *Out to Lunch* (1964) that best illustrates his thinking. The five tunes incorporate recurring riffs and winding-road melodies, and Dolphy enlists a top-shelf ensemble (trumpeter Freddie Hubbard, bassist Richard Davis, drummer Tony Williams, vibraphonist Bobby Hutcherson) to help him pursue ideas that are intricately interconnected. Saying in the liner notes that he knew he wanted "a free date to begin with," Dolphy explains that this rhythm section pointed him toward a new notion of freedom. "They can play different kinds of ways, like Tony does here—different ways, but you can still count it."

While Williams's choppy metric agitations keep everyone on edge, Hutcherson, who went on to make dazzling records on his own (see p. 375)—is the date's true catalyst. The vibraphone has a more transparent sound than the piano, and Hutcherson makes the most of it—his crisp chording creates open vistas, and Dolphy fills these up with animated flute solos that suggest ladies gossiping over tea ("Gazzelloni") or foreboding bass clarinet excursions ("Hat and Beard" might be the instrument's shining jazz moment). When Dolphy really wanted to have fun, however, he picked up the alto saxophone. On the title track, he alternates between outlining the harmony when he darts "inside" to play a bluesy phrase, and obliterating it with squawks and squeals that head for the outer limits. Where, it seems, he can get away with almost anything.

GENRE: 🎷 Jazz. **RELEASED:** 1964, Blue Note. **KEY TRACKS:** "Straight Up and Down," "Hat and Beard," "Something Sweet, Something Tender." **CATALOG CHOICE:** *At the Five Spot,* Vol. 1. **NEXT STOP:** John Coltrane: *Live at the Village Vanguard.* **AFTER THAT:** Rahsaan Roland Kirk: *The Inflated Tear.*

An Early Domino in the Game of Rock

They Call Me the Fat Man: The Legendary Imperial Recordings

Antoine "Fats" Domino

Between 1955 and 1963, Fats Domino sent thirty-six songs onto *Billboard*'s Top 40 singles chart. These include some of the enduring flames of early rock—"Blueberry Hill," from 1956,

is the most famous, and alongside it are the timeless confections "Walking to New Orleans," "Whole Lotta Loving," "Ain't That a Shame," "I Hear You Knocking," "My Blue Heaven," and one of Domino's personal favorites, "Blue Monday." ("Anybody that works can appreciate the words in that song," he once said.)

The string of chart successes is remarkable—Domino was the top-selling African American rocker of the 1950s, and second only to Elvis Presley overall. But even more remarkable is this: During that same eight-year run, when the

Over his fruitful career Fats Domino had 66 U.S. Hot 100 chart hits.

New Orleans pianist and singer was recording for Imperial Records and collaborating with arranger Dave Bartholomew, Domino created a stack of lesser-known works that are every bit as interesting as the singles. These are the reason to spring for the four-disc *They Call Me the Fat Man* over any single-disc hits collection: Here, it's possible to discover the Domino backstory, written in heady, hardswinging jump blues, the core repertoire of New Orleans R&B ("Lil' Liza Jane," "Mardi Gras in New Orleans"), and a handful of ballads ("What Will I Tell My Heart") that

display a sense of drama missing from some of the good-time radio songs.

Domino had the great fortune to fall in with Bartholomew, a trumpet player and arranger whose band was the Crescent City's swingingest post World War II. Those musicians—including the peerless drummer Earl Palmer and tenor saxophonist Alvin "Red" Tyler—followed Bartholomew into the recording studio. They established the multifaceted "Domino" sound, which blended parade-beat rhythms with the catcalling zaniness of jump blues. And they left just enough room for the unmistakable pounding of the man who helped make the piano a rock and roll instrument.

GENRE: 🎸 Rock. **RELEASED:** 1991, EMI. **KEY TRACKS:** "If You Need Me," "My Blue Heaven," "Ain't That a Shame," "Lil' Liza Jane." **FURTHER INQUIRY:** *Blue Monday: Fats Domino and the Lost Dawn of Rock 'n' Roll,* by Rick Coleman, is a compelling, comprehensive biography. **NEXT STOP:** Huey "Piano" Smith: *This Is Huey "Piano" Smith* (see p. 717). **AFTER THAT:** Professor Longhair: *New Orleans Piano* (see p. 616).

The Most Slamming Doors

The Doors

The Doors

O n side one, track one of this still astounding debut, a slightly disturbed Jim Morrison repeatedly bellows the phrase "Break on through to the other side." He sounds like he's found passage to a promised land, and is determined to help others make the journey. His invitation also happens to summarize the Doors' guiding idea: This is rock music for and about transcendence.

Lots of what was great about the Doors has to do with Morrison breaking through—mentally, physically, spiritually. He sings from inside a dream state; even on a song about the search for the next

The Doors has gone platinum 5 times.

whiskey bar, the former UCLA film student sounds as if he's drinking to pursue enlightenment. Casting himself as the romantic poet hungry for fresh experience, Morrison (1943–1971) tells what he's seen in torrents of grandiose images, using a trick bag of howls and shouts to enhance the scenes. When Morrison begs to sleep all night in the "Soul Kitchen," his rhythm section makes it a place of sensual bliss and also psychic refuge. When he seeks a love spark, on the Farfisa organ–kissed "Light My Fire" that became the defining Doors single, the group's questing propulsion keeps that ember alive through a long instrumental interlude that has the feeling of an epic journey. (There's another, even more psychedelic one on "The End.")

This album is one of those perfect one-sitting listening experiences, with no wasted notes and no extraneous poetry. Even decades after the druggy moment of its creation, *The Doors* somehow retains its mystique, and feels greater than the sum of its parts. Much of that has to do with Morrison, who transforms rather ordinary urgings—when you think about it, "Come on baby, light my fire" is pretty banal as refrains go—into lofty-sounding sentiments that were cherished by millions. Implicit in all of Morrison's invitations is the notion, often unstated but clearly audible, that something better awaits on the other side. He believes this, in a way that makes others believe, too—that's one reason Morrison went from being relatively unknown to the king of the rock mystics, then a cynical star, and finally a victim of the Dionysian excesses associated with his trade. The whole arc only lasted a few years, but it couldn't have happened without this album, made by Morrison and three adventure-minded musicians at a time in their lives when breaking on through was all that mattered.

GENRE: 🎸 Rock. **RELEASED:** 1967, Elektra. **KEY TRACKS:** "Break On Through (to the Other Side)," "Soul Kitchen," "Twentieth Century Fox." **CATALOG CHOICE:** *Morrison Hotel.* **FURTHER INQUIRY:** Fans of Morrison's lyrics will be captivated by his first book of poetry, *The Lords and the New Creatures,* published in 1971. **NEXT STOP:** Love: *Forever Changes* (see p. 457). **AFTER THAT:** Nine Inch Nails: *Pretty Hate Machine.*

The Mother Lode of Gospel

Precious Lord

Thomas A. Dorsey

Just about everyone who ever sang gospel interpreted the music of Thomas Dorsey, so there's no shortage of amazing renditions of his individual songs. But to obtain a primer in the prolific and profound Dorsey, whose standards include "Peace in the Valley" and "If We Never Needed the Lord Before," this compilation is hard to beat. It showcases some of the most compelling voices in modern gospel bringing life to songs they cherished.

Dorsey (1899–1993) began playing blues and jazz piano, and recorded with, among others, the Chicago legend Big Bill Broonzy (see p. 117) and Ma Rainey (see p. 628). In the early '30s he dedicated himself to church music, with little immediate success. He sent out five hundred copies of his song "If You See My Savior" to churches nationwide, and it took three years before a single order, earning him exactly a dime, came back. In 1932, his first wife died in childbirth, an experience that shook him: "I wanted to go back to blues," he recalls in the liner notes, but instead, in his grief he wrote his signature song, "Take My Hand, Precious Lord" (sung here by Marion Williams). The extended lament of one who's been shaken and no longer has strength to go on, the song became a kind of African American national anthem, a part of many mourning rituals and civil rights rallies.

Dorsey didn't just write hymns; his repertoire includes more hopeful, expectant visions ("Peace in the Valley," sung here by Texas native Rebert Harris), expressions of pure devotion ("Search Me Lord," a platform for the dizzying Bessie Griffin), and tunes that revitalize the conversational cadences of spirituals and field songs ("Hide Me in Thy Bosom," made magical by the Dixie Hummingbirds). Every one sparkles, and even if you're not a churchgoer, you'll probably recognize these reassuringly sturdy tunes, which have a way of affirming all that is good in the world.

GENRE: 🎵 Gospel. **RELEASED:** 1994, Sony Legacy. **KEY TRACKS:** "Hide Me in Thy Bosom," "It's a Highway to Heaven," "I Don't Know Why." **NEXT STOP:** *Say Amen Somebody!* Original Soundtrack Recording. **AFTER THAT:** *The Gospel at Colonus,* 1985 Cast Recording.

A New Spin on the Cajun Two-Step

Bayou Deluxe

Michael Doucet and BeauSoleil

In the late 1960s, when Louisiana's traditional Creole and Cajun culture was in seemingly irreversible decline, fiddler Michael Doucet traveled all over the bayou looking for musicians to teach him the tunes bands once played at dances. The project began as an official one—he'd been awarded a Folk Arts Apprenticeship from the National Endowment for the Arts—but after Doucet met and studied with the old-timers, it became something of a personal crusade. He absorbed the techniques of the great instrumentalists, among them fiddler Dewey Balfa (see p. 41), and helped a few of his mentors return to performing. His efforts sparked what has been described as the "Cajun Renaissance" of the 1970s, in which younger musicians of Acadian descent began to embrace a heritage that had been neglected for several generations.

The National Endowment for the Arts awarded Doucet a National Heritage Fellowship in 2005.

career, and includes several pieces Doucet picked up during his apprenticeship days. "Tasso/McGee's Reel," for example, interpolates a dance popularized by Cajun fiddler Dennis McGee in the 1950s, while other pieces look back at earlier greats, including the legendary accordionist Joseph Falcon and his guitarist wife, Cleoma, who began recording in the late 1920s. Doucet's folk-heritage discoveries are offset by crossover-minded later experiments, several of which lit up film soundtracks. And because BeauSoleil can't resist subverting the established order, there are delightfully unusual treatments of familiar songs—like "Les bon temps rouler" played as a waltz. Everything crackles with the giddy feeling of a Friday night at a festive dance hall, and that's no accident: This band learned from watching masters move a crowd. They lean into the off-beats, jolt dancers with all sorts of unexpected syncopations, and create the sound of lusty let-the-good-times-roll abandon—music so vital and engrossing it's hard to imagine it was ever in danger of disappearing.

What started as a cultural preservation project ended up as something else entirely—a joyous, rollicking sound that holds onto tradition while opening windows on the modern world. As a result of his fiddling studies, Doucet knew how to play the brisk two-steps and grand waltzes as they'd been heard for generations. But as a child of the rock era, he was inclined to experiment. He formed BeauSoleil in 1975, and within a few years, the band grew into cross-culture-collision specialists. The best BeauSoleil music incorporates bits of funk, Caribbean calypso, Irish reel, and blues into an invigorating swirl that demands dancing.

This collection plays like a dream live set. It gathers highlights from BeauSoleil's long

GENRE: 🔵 Blues. **RELEASED:** 1993, Rhino. **KEY TRACKS:** "La chanson de Mardi Gras," "J'ai été au zydeco." **CATALOG CHOICE:** *L'amour ou la folie.* **NEXT STOP:** Iry LeJeune: *Cajun's Greatest, The Definitive Collection.*

The Best from a Prolific New Jazz Composer

Charms of the Night Sky

Dave Douglas

The pianist Paul Bley tells young musicians that no matter what else they do, it's important to record themselves at least every six months. In his estimation, documenting one's music regularly is not simply useful for charting progress, but as a way to systematically foster the creation of new ideas.

The discography of composer and trumpet player Dave Douglas is an illustration of this wisdom. Since the late 1980s, the New York–based musician has written and recorded at a blinding rate. He's done ambitious full-length suites for large ensemble, multiple records with several innovative small groups (including his quintet and the Tiny Bell Trio), and explored comminglings of jazz, funk, ethnic music, and electronic loops. Almost all these feature original Douglas compositions, and many of them place him in contexts that are far from what a jazz player would consider a "comfort zone." *Charms of the Night Sky* is among his most unusual concoctions, a series of roaming meditations for trumpet, violin (Mark Feldman), accordion (Guy Klucevsek), and bass (Greg Cohen).

Calm and unabashedly romantic, *Charms* is a chamber jazz exploration of the most ethereal sort. Some of the music happens at a languid, stately tempo; "Dance in Thy Soul," dedicated to bassist Charlie Haden, finds Douglas and Feldman trading broad-toned ad-libs between the lines of a questioning theme. Klucevsek's accordion provides instant wistfulness, a quality Douglas exploits on tunes like "Sea Change," which is a slow waltz you might imagine hearing outside a Paris café. As with other Douglas projects, the combination of instruments and textures provides a general framework. From there, it's up to the other musicians to fill in the details. This they do not as scientists mapping the positions of the stars, but as impressionist painters seeking to convey, in delicate and almost imperceptible shades, the awesome aura of the night sky.

GENRE: 🅐 Jazz. **RELEASED:** 1998, Winter & Winter. **KEY TRACKS:** "Sea Change," "Little One," "Dance in Thy Soul." **CATALOG CHOICES:** *Strange Liberation; Freak In.* **NEXT STOP:** Uri Caine: *Live at the Village Vanguard.* **AFTER THAT:** Pachora: *Unn.*

"You Find the Darkness Can Give the Brightest Light"

Five Leaves Left

Nick Drake

In his treatise *A Defense of Poetry*, Percy Bysshe Shelley likens the poet to "a nightingale who sits in darkness and sings to cheer its own solitude with sweet sounds." That eloquently describes the enterprise of the British singer, songwriter, and guitarist Nick Drake (1948–1974). On three albums that were almost completely ignored during his lifetime, Drake developed music uniquely suited to solitude. His voice an otherworldly, hollowed-out half whisper, his guitar outlining unusual hypnotic patterns, Drake created a sound-world that stands apart from "folk" or "rock." From that place he wrote spare, wrenching songs unlike anything else in popular music.

Drake struggled with mental illness—he died after an overdose of antidepressants, an apparent suicide. He wasn't afraid to explore his conflicted interior world, but he didn't dwell there all the time: This album includes tales of strange oracles ("River Man"), vision-quest journeys ("Three Hours"), philosophical musings on fame ("Fruit Tree"), and luminous portraits of women ("The Thoughts of Mary Jane"). Many are distinguished by a strange confluence: They're woeful and almost resigned, steeped in the enveloping melancholy characteristic of British romantics like Shelley. But at the same time, they contain shrewd, levelheaded appraisals of human nature.

Five Leaves Left is Drake's first statement. Its ruminating songs left those in his circle (which included Fairport Convention guitarist Richard Thompson) awed, and inspired predictions of fame. Its riches are almost infinite—the austere guitar finger-study inventions; the strings (arranged magnificently by Robert Kirby) providing a somber, funereal aura; the melodies that tremble yet manage to cut through the thickest armor.

From here, Drake turned toward more upbeat, Van Morrison–influenced pop (*Bryter*

The album title is thought to be a reference to a warning in Swan cigarette paper packets—only "five leaves left."

Layter), and when that failed to draw a sizeable audience, he wrote the stark troubled blues incantations of *Pink Moon.* It took a VW ad campaign in the 1990s to bring his music to wide attention, triggering more interest than he'd ever experienced in his lifetime. Drake would have approved: On his intense, prophetic "Fruit Tree," he sings, "Safe in your place, deep in the earth, that's when they'll know what you were really worth."

GENRES: 🅒 Folk 🅡 Rock. **RELEASED:** 1969, Hannibal. **KEY TRACKS:** "Time Has Told Me," "River Man," "Three Hours," "Cello Song." **CATALOG CHOICES:** *Pink Moon; Bryter Layter.* **NEXT STOP:** John Martyn: *Solid Air* (see p. 480). **AFTER THAT:** Joni Mitchell: *Blue.*

Arguably the Most Important Gangsta Rap Ever

The Chronic

Dr. Dre

At one point during this album's phenomenal run, the producer, MC, and newly minted Death Row Records Svengali Dr. Dre proclaimed, "I can take a three-year-old and make a hit record with him."

That's not as wild a boast as it initially appears. After all, the most consequential rapping on this record comes from a nasal-sounding newcomer then named Snoop Doggy Dogg (that's him on the single "Nuthin' but a 'G' Thang"), and the assorted stanzas from other MCs have a touch of playground taunt in them. By the time he made this, the resourceful doctor, aka Andre Young, had spent years as part of the L.A. hardcore group N.W.A., where his job was to redeem extremely violent lyrics by situating them within sophisticated musical accompaniment.

With *The Chronic*, Dr. Dre's potion attains perfection. His productions are often set in minor keys, unusual for hip-hop, and feature creeping Parliament-style bass lines, squiggly high-pitched synthesizer phrases, and undulating low-key beats. Even when the subject matter is intended to shock—and *The Chronic* has raps that glorify violence and the mistreatment of women while celebrating the extremely potent marijuana that gives the album its title—Dre's music counters with a calm, poised demeanor. Other hard-core hip-hop producers slam listeners; Dre gets heads bobbing with grooves that sit just below a boil, threatening to erupt at any moment. His backdrops serve as a kind of neutral territory, against which all sorts of excessive behavior goes down. (The foreboding "The Day the Niggaz Took Over," for example, is built around a four-note ringtone taunt that's repeated so frequently it becomes menacing all by itself.)

The title *The Chronic* is a slang term for high-grade marijuana.

The Chronic sold more than three million copies in its first year and drew a steady stream of rap wannabes to Dr. Dre's door. Among those influenced by the album was a young white kid from Detroit named Marshall Mathers, who was discovered at an L.A. rap contest in 1997. After getting over his amazement that Mathers, better known as Eminem, was white, Dre agreed to produce what became *The Marshall Mathers LP*, the first hip-hop album after *The Chronic* to generate multiplatinum sales.

GENRE: 🎙 Hip-Hop. **RELEASED:** 1992, Death Row. **KEY TRACKS:** "Let Me Ride," "Nuthin' but a 'G' Thang," "Rat-Tat Tat-Tat." **CATALOG CHOICE:** *Dr. Dre Presents the Aftermath.* **NEXT STOP:** Eminem: *The Slim Shady LP.* **AFTER THAT:** 50 Cent: *Get Rich or Die Tryin'.*

Potions from the Good Doctor

Gris-Gris

Dr. John

The next time you sense evil spirits at the door, light the candles and cue up this spooky and beautiful slice of New Orleans ritual hoodoo. Concocted in 1968 just as psychedelic rock was bubbling over,

it is the first appearance of Dr. John the Night Tripper, a cagey alter-ego character of R&B pianist Mac Rebennack, who explains on "Gris-Gris Gumbo Ya-Ya," that he's "got remedies of every description" for assorted ills, from a mean boss to a cheating lover.

Rebennack drew inspiration from his city's voodoo priests and Mardi Gras Indian tribes, but wasn't interested in anything folkloric. Instead, he conjured a swampy, drug-tinged approximation of a voodoo initiation ritual, complete

The name "Dr. John" came from a Louisiana voodoo practitioner of the early 1800s.

with solemn processional funk, Afro-Cuban percussion, and mesmerizing chants. Some pieces seem derived from established African dances— "Danse Kalinda Ba Doom" moves at a careening 6/8 clip—and others, most notably "Mama Roux," carry traces of Cuban mambo from the 1950s. Despite Rebennack's talk-growled verses and the air of mysticism, *Gris-Gris* is hardly an aimless ramble. When the Night Tripper and his band get good and revved, as they do on the steady-rolling "Walk on Gilded Splinters," they transform a simple phrase into head-nodding ritual music. All of the elements click together perfectly—the exotic beats, the trippy echoing vocal ad-libs, and Dr. John's name-checks of his favorite street characters combine into a sound with strange hypnotic powers. It's music that could only have come from New Orleans, that outpost of the spirit world, the only place in America where a greasy-fingered pianist with

frogs in his mouth can become a truth bringer, a healer, and a high priest of soul.

GENRE: 🌀 R&B. **RELEASED:** 1968, Atco. **KEY TRACKS:** "Mama Roux," "Walk on Gilded Splinters." **CATALOG CHOICES:** *Dr. John's Gumbo; Dr. John Plays Mac Rebennack.* **NEXT STOP:** The Neville Brothers: *Fiyo on the Bayou.* **AFTER THAT:** James Booker: *New Orleans Piano Wizard Live!* (see p. 104).

Pure Soul from a Strong and Unsung Voice

I'm a Loser

Doris Duke

On the big Periodic Table of Soul, Doris Duke's *I'm a Loser* occupies a tiny spot near the footnotes, well removed from the classics of Aretha Franklin and such potent lesser lights as Irma Thomas. That says more about the music industry circa 1970 than it does about Duke's pealing series of scorned-woman songs: Here you will find some of the most riveting nonhits ever filed under the broad and often vague classification of "soul."

Variously identified as a "deep soul" or "Southern soul" singer, Georgia-born Duke had a coarse, hard-times voice and a sense of pace that came from singing in church. Her career was spent mostly singing backup—she toiled at the Apollo Theater in Harlem for a time, and did session work with producers Gamble and Huff in Philadelphia. Duke spends much of this set mulling over the stormy ends of various romances, via dramatic confrontation scenes written by Gary U.S. Bonds and produced by the perfectly maniacal guitarist and multi-instrumentalist Jerry "Swamp Dogg" Williams.

This album showcases the whiplash-inducing guitar work of Jerry "Swamp Dogg" Williams.

But like all the greats, Duke knows how to build her testimony, one line at a time. Particularly effective are the songs where she's somehow jolted by love: "Feet Start Walking" tells of her surprise when she arrives at her man's house, and lo and behold, he's not alone. The awkwardness of that encounter is replayed on the even more strident "To the Other Woman (I'm the Other Woman)." Duke gives each vignette its own grease—she's an incredibly confident singer who can reach down and cry when necessary, but is inclined to just add hummed affirmations and let bubbling bass lines and the locked-down grooves say it all.

GENRE: 🌀 R&B. **RELEASED:** 1970, Kent/ Ace. (Reissued 2005.) **KEY TRACKS:** "Feet Start Walking," "Ghost of Myself," "To the Other Woman (I'm the Other Woman)." **F.Y.I.:** At the same time he was creating these Duke singles, Jerry "Swamp Dogg" Williams was recording his own subversive hard-soul opus *Total Destruction to Your Mind,* which has yet to appear on CD. **NEXT STOP**: Bettye La Vette: *Souvenirs*. **AFTER THAT**: Carla Thomas: *Carla.*

Experience the Follies as the Locals Did

The Ziegfeld Follies of 1936

Vernon Duke and Ira Gershwin

Broadway Encores! Revival with Christine Ebersole, Howard McGillin

In the opening number of this revue, the narrator proclaims that this Follies will be different. His audience in 1936 was probably not too thrilled about that, as the Ziegfeld Follies were known for beautiful girls (who appeared topless but stood stock-still, in observance of a city ordinance that allowed nudity but not nude dancing) and madcap comedy sketches. The shows were the *Saturday Night Live* of their day, full of wry topical references and songs that winked at (or derided) current events and celebrities. One little-heard line written by lyricist Ira Gershwin for the standard "I Can't Get Started" proclaims: "I've been consulted by Franklin D., and Greta Garbo's had me to tea. Yet I'm broken hearted, because I can't get started with you."

The Ziegfeld Follies were inspired by the Folies Bergères of Paris.

the starpower of the original, which included Josephine Baker, Bob Hope, Fanny Brice, and others. But the revival offers something genuinely rare in Broadway history: those original orchestrations. Conventional Broadway front-office wisdom holds that audiences expect the music to be "updated." As a result, original scores have been neglected, and sometimes lost. The original orchestrations for *Ziegfeld* are amazing. At every turn the pit orchestra supplies the nervy embellishments and responses the songs need, as well as unexpectedly powerful counterlines (see "I Can't Get Started") that fling already pristine melodies into rarefied air. Those who know the Great American Songbook will recognize many of these tunes, and appreciate hearing them the way they were originally conceived.

Unlike other revues, this show, which was revived for the Broadway Encores! series in 2001, has aged well. Vernon Duke's music has that affable Broadway luster; it's universal without pandering, and rich with harmonic twists. Ira Gershwin adds racy wit and an overactive imagination (sample rhyme: "pulchritudinous" with "the lewd in us"). There are torch songs and songs that mock torch songs, romantic ballads and a surprisingly durable tropical fantasy ("Island in the West Indies").

The cast of this revival includes Christine Ebersole and Howard McGillin; it can't match

---

GENRE: 😊 Musicals. **RELEASED**: 2001, Decca. **KEY TRACKS**: "I Can't Get Started," "Island in the West Indies," "Gazooka," "That Moment of Moments." **NEXT STOP**: *The 1934 Recording of the Ziegfeld Follies*, Original Broadway Cast.

A Vivid Performance from a Wild Child

Elgar: Cello Concerto

Jacqueline du Pré
BBC Symphony Orchestra (John Barbirolli, cond.)

An audacious wild child of a performer several decades before attitude became a common ploy in the marketing of classical music, Jacqueline du Pré (1945–1987) made the cello an instrument of dramatic extremes. Under her control it could sing with a robust sweetness. Or, as happens in the solo passage that begins the second movement of Elgar's Cello Concerto, it could become a throttling and threatening weapon. Slicing through convention to get to raw, exposed nerve.

Du Pré was inclined to veer from the notes and indications on the page. This fiery, less literal interpretation of the Elgar finds her using an assortment of devices to amplify what she most cherishes in the score. She delivers some of the legato lines as magnificent smooth arcs of glasslike sound, then attacks the pizzicato passages like a drill sergeant barking orders. The piece, composed in 1919,

Jacqueline du Pré started playing the cello when she was just 4 years old.

somewhat distorted biopic *Hillary and Jackie*). She first recorded the piece in 1965, with conductor John Barbirolli and the London Symphony Orchestra. This version was recorded live in Prague two years later, and here she seems even less inhibited—the rare concert soloist who's embracing the upheaval associated with the Summer of Love. She's not worrying about flawless execution—she's seeking core truths. And she finds them within Elgar's sturdy themes, uncovering moments of breathtaking beauty followed, inevitably, by equally moving expressions of soul turmoil.

is Elgar's last completed work. Less a formal concerto than a soliloquy for solo cello with orchestral accompaniment, it offers inventive winding-path melodies, and motifs that at times feel like personal confessions. Du Pré, who is credited with reviving interest in the piece, stretches these out, savoring their unusual shapes.

The fiery cellist's career was shortened by multiple sclerosis (her story is told in the

GENRE: 🎻 Classical.
RELEASED: 2006, Testament.
KEY TRACKS: Second movement; fourth movement. **CATALOG CHOICE:** *Favorite Cello Concertos*. **FURTHER INQUIRY:** Elizabeth Wilson's authoritative biography *Jacqueline du Pré: Her Life, Her Music, Her Legend* was researched in cooperation with the cellist's husband, the musician and conductor Daniel Barenboim. **NEXT STOP:** Antonín Dvořák: *Cello Concerto,* Mstislav Rostropovich, Berlin Philharmonic (Herbert von Karajan, cond.).

The Cello Concerto Goes Modern

Cello Concerto
"Tout un monde lointain"

Henri Dutilleux

Mstislav Rostropovich, Orchestre de Paris (Serge Baudo, cond.)

The subtitle "Tout un monde lointain" (A Whole Remote World) says it all about Henri Dutilleux's mystical, slow-to-congeal Cello Concerto. Commissioned by one of the most colorful figures of classical music of the '60s and '70s—Russian cellist and conductor Mstislav Rostropovich, who emigrated to the West in 1974—it transports listeners into an atmosphere that's unusually spooky for classical music. In this place, the wise-owl "voice" of the cello speaks of vague poetic rapture.

Dutilleux spent nearly a decade writing this piece, which has five movements rather than the conventional three. Each movement is "inspired" by a quote from French poet Charles Baudelaire, and occupies a distinct mood—the murkiest (and most entrancing) is the often tempoless fourth, which asks the string section to conjure a dense forest of shadows, with hints of danger lurking. It's one of the rare works for soloist and orchestra that doesn't state overt themes, but instead uses recurring rhythmic and melodic motifs to lure you into the process of theme-building. You listen as it is being born, so to speak, and if you're waiting for the romantic-era neon-sign "important" declaration, you'll be disappointed.

The writing forces the cello into demanding and sometimes unnatural positions—heart-rending melodies at the top of the instrument's range, and cluttered tangles of pizzicato notes near the bottom—and yet Rostropovich never sounds taxed. His spirited, surging interpretation overcomes the convolutions Dutilleux has loaded into the score: Rostropovich doesn't just master the considerable technical challenges, he makes this knotty music sing.

The other contemporary work on this collection was also written for Rostropovich—Polish composer Witold Lutosławski's Cello Concerto. This piece adheres to the general ethos of concerto form—it has three movements and revolves around the oppositional dynamic between soloist and orchestra, with the lone voice tossing out radical ideas that are eventually embraced by the group. But like Dutilleux, Lutosławski (1913–1994) is determined to push the established structures a bit, by introducing experimental harmonies and longish themes that don't repeat. Particularly striking are the outlandish exchanges and dramatic tussles of the final movement, which features the soloist at times brazenly taunting the group. Some have said that the piece is an essay on conformity, and that makes it a perfect vehicle for the mighty Rostropovich, who as a young man in the Soviet Union crusaded for free speech and eventually defected, settling in the United States in 1974. His authoritative readings of these two strikingly different pieces have helped both to become modern classics.

GENRE: 🎼 Classical. **RELEASED:** 1970, EMI Classics. **KEY TRACKS:** Dutilleux: first movement, fourth movement. Lutosławski: second movement. **CATALOG CHOICE:** Dutilleux: *Symphony No. 2, Metaboles,* Orchestra National Bordeaux Aquitaine (Hans Graf, cond.). Lutosławski: *Concerto for Piano and Orchestra,*

Krystian Zimerman, BBC Symphony Orchestra (Witold Lutosławski, cond.). **NEXT STOP:** Franz Liszt: *Piano Sonata in B minor,* Krystian

Zimerman. **AFTER THAT:** Pierre Boulez: *Répons,* Ensemble InterContemporain (Pierre Boulez, cond.).

A Czech in New York Sends Home a Series of Postcards

Symphony No. 9

Antonín Dvořák

Royal Concertgebouw Orchestra (Mariss Jansons, cond.)

This piece is often identified as the "New World Symphony," but composer Antonín Dvořák, from Czechoslovakia, actually gave it a different subtitle—"From the New World," connoting less a comprehensive summation of a vast place than quick repertorial dispatches from it. Beginning in 1892, Dvořák spent a few years living in New York City, working to establish a music school. Like other European musicians, he found himself enchanted. But he was also homesick, and that contradiction drives the piece. This dizzying, craftily integrated celebration of spirituals, Native American folk songs, and other ethnographic elements was put together by someone who couldn't wait to get back to the old country.

Dvořák (1843–1904) was curious about folk music. But unlike the composers who followed him, most notably the Hungarian genius Béla Bartók (see p. 46), he did not go into the field searching for the authentic. Instead, he was content to learn the folk styles from published anthologies, and this gives some of his appropriated themes a smoothed-over, almost genteel air. Still, the fast-moving chord sequences of the opening movement make clear that Dvořák has absorbed essential bits of the character

"I am convinced that the future music of this country must be founded on what are called Negro melodies. . . . They are the folk songs of America and your composers must turn to them." —Antonín Dvořák

of New York, and by extension America: Underpinning his themes is a deep restlessness, a sense of unresolved striving.

Often his harmonies follow elaborate cycles, making sideways lunges into neighboring keys the way a jazz hipster might toy with Bach. The first movement ends in a transfixing pastoral air with touches of Aaron Copland, and that's followed by a languid second movement in which Dvořák grapples with the earthy, deeply rooted tones of African American spirituals. (In a particularly wry twist, he calls upon the English horn, a double reed instrument not known for soulfulness, to handle the theme.)

The final movement begins with the brassy, bold declaration that is the piece's calling card. This is one of those moments that challenges an orchestra: Dvořák expects the ensemble to summon an overgrown American exuberance, and anything less can cast ugly shadows on the subtle music that's come before. Led by Latvian Mariss Jansons, Amsterdam's legendary orchestra brings plenty of brawn to the task, but also provides the necessary leavening touches; more than once, the luminous, perfectly proportioned strings send the whole group ascending to skyscraper heights.

This piece can play like a parade of disconnected clichés, and Jansons, who believes that musical epiphanies in performance are the product of exacting rehearsals, won't have that: He reads Dvořák's score as an awed testament to a once-exotic place, and guides the performance so the colors on top change like a prairie sunset, and the underlying rhythms move with the bustle of the city streets.

GENRE: 🎸 Classical. **RELEASED:** 2004, RCO Live. **KEY TRACKS:** First and fourth movements. **CATALOG CHOICE:** Symphonies Nos. 7 and 8, Cleveland Orchestra (Christoph von Dohnányi, cond.). **NEXT STOP:** Pyotr Ilyich Tchaikovsky: *Symphony No. 6,* Oslo Philharmonic (Mariss Jansons, cond.). **AFTER THAT:** Maurice Ravel: *Piano Concerto in G,* Arturo Benedetti Michelangeli (see p. 25).

"Well I Started Out on Burgundy, but Soon Hit the Harder Stuff . . ."

Highway 61 Revisited

Bob Dylan

This is a mile marker. Starting here, the vocabulary of rock music undergoes significant expansion. New ideas about words and music and their relationship are loosed into the air, to be puzzled over and endlessly analyzed. Before this, the folk musicians in Dylan's milieu sorta tiptoed through the blues, avoiding complete overhauls of the source code. Bob Dylan swoops in, complaining to the chamber of commerce (about Samson and Delilah), taunting that square Mr. Jones because he doesn't know what's happening, and suddenly it's a new day. The blues can be anything—especially when Mike Bloomfield is playing them. The guitars speak the folkie chords, but they're electric and howling and they jangle nerves in a very different way. Suddenly everybody's hitting the harder stuff.

And you're going to need harder stuff to figure out what the hell Dylan is talking about. Who's the target of all this ire, the scorn of

Bob Dylan has won an Oscar, a Grammy, a Golden Globe, and, in a first for a rock musician, a Pulitzer Prize.

"Just Like Tom Thumb Blues" and the derision of "Queen Jane Approximately"? From the very beginning of the first song, "Like a Rolling Stone," the words arrive by the boxcar, forming a portrait of what Dylan sees as smug bohemian arrogance. Possibly the most vituperative song ever to become a hit, this one signals how drastically the game has changed. Everything that follows—the cryptic callouts to former lovers, the grave warnings about assorted vanities, and especially the harangues at the self-important characters stalking on the fringes of folk—aims not so much for a "story" with a "point," but a more general scene-setting of a chaos in progress.

Scholars have done exhaustive etymologies of these lyrics, tracing every reference and every possible living person who pops up. It's safe to say this has not brought them closer to understanding the songs, which unspool like epic foreign films. This is a key aspect of the enduring allure of *Highway 61 Revisited*: Its conjoining of word and blues is so delirious and convoluted and evasive, it cannot be pinned down. The eleven-minute finale, "Desolation Row," catches the great contrarian seeing how far he can go, how much memory he can erase ("Don't send me no more letters, no, not unless you mail them from Desolation Row"), how much distance he can put between himself and

the staid trappings of troubadourdom. Dylan lets rage take a turn behind the wheel, and when he looks into the rearview mirror, those strumming-and-humming days are far back in the distance, and fading fast.

GENRE: 🎵 Rock. **RELEASED:** 1965, Columbia. **KEY TRACKS:** "Like a Rolling Stone," "Tombstone Blues," "Queen Jane Approximately," "Desolation Row." **CATALOG CHOICE:** *Bootleg Series Vol 6: Live 1964— Concert at Philharmonic Hall.* **NEXT STOP:** You've arrived at the next stop.

One of the Greatest Albums of the Rock Era

Blonde on Blonde

Bob Dylan

By virtually any measure—hallucinatory insights per minute, raucous reworkings of the blues, rambling tales of transcendence—*Blonde on Blonde* stands among the greatest works of the rock era. Its ever-shifting

combinations of intense roots music and sweeping narrative represent storytelling on an extraordinarily high level; some consider it the closest thing in rock to classic literature. It's not the single defining work of Dylan's career, but it's among them. Any record that contains such endlessly beguiling verse-chorus epics as "Sad-Eyed Lady of the Lowlands," "Visions of Johanna," "Just Like a Woman," "Absolutely Sweet Marie," and "Stuck Inside of Mobile with the Memphis Blues Again" has to be.

On the Dylan time line, this record follows *Highway 61 Revisited* (see previous page). In terms of temperament, it's some distance from that earlier landmark. Dylan replaces the

In 1999, *Time* magazine named Dylan one of the "100 Most Influential People of the 20th Century."

frantic word-torrent lunges of old with an unhurried swagger, the cadence of a man who knows what he wants. A sense of assurance permeates everything: Where he once allowed himself long stretches of idle speculation, Dylan now seems more purposeful, attuned to the world, his conversation rooted in the present moment.

Blonde was recorded in Nashville, and its howling hard-rock stomps and easy-going shuffles feel like they were captured quickly, with the rough edges preserved. The unflappably steady band is key to this—it includes Al Kooper (whose creeping organ defines "Sad-Eyed Lady of the Lowlands") and Robbie Robertson (credited as "Jaime Robertson," whose questioning guitar animates "One of Us Must Know"). The musicians bring plenty of energy, but it's their cool competence and unerring sense of timing that Dylan has been missing.

As he unwinds the novelistic narratives of his ballads, Dylan lingers just a bit over each carefully wrought image, taking his time sketching the magnificent "Visions of Johanna." And when he breathes fire into the harmonica to launch the last verse of "Most Likely You Go Your Way (and I'll Go Mine)," Dylan sounds like a veteran bandleader prodding his crew for the evening's last big push. (That harmonica interlude might boil down to two notes, but it's some of the most fervent needling riffage in the bard's discography.)

Like *Highway 61*, *Blonde on Blonde* is somewhat inscrutable. It's packed with rogues and schemers and tender-hearted lovers caught in tense situations. Sometimes these vignettes play out in such surrealistic ways you wonder if Dylan put them there just to confuse those who cobble together biographies based on song lyrics. Of course, these verses are more than that now. They're part of the soul of American music.

GENRE: 🅑 Rock. RELEASED: 1966, Columbia. KEY TRACKS: "Rainy Day Women #12 & 35," "Sad-Eyed Lady of the Lowlands," "Visions of Johanna," "Just Like a Woman," "Absolutely Sweet Marie." CATALOG CHOICES: *John Wesley Harding; Desire.* NEXT STOP: The Band: *Music from Big Pink.* AFTER THAT: Warren Zevon: *Warren Zevon.*

"Like It Was Written in My Soul"

Blood on the Tracks

Bob Dylan

Shortly after initial test pressings of this album began to circulate in November 1974, Bob Dylan had a change of heart. The sessions, which took place in New York in September, had been arranged quickly, and in characteristic fashion, Dylan gave the musicians (from Eric Weissberg's band, Deliverance) little instruction. The singer and songwriter expected them to simply follow what he was doing. Listening to the results, Dylan decided that several of the key songs—including "Tangled Up in Blue," "Idiot Wind"—needed more. He hastily assembled a band in his native Minnesota, and over two days in late December recorded versions that were more to his liking. The originals became a bootlegger's bonanza—a few of them were eventually released on Volume 3 of the authorized *Bootleg Series.* Meanwhile, the sleeve notes printed at the time of the initial pressings refer to several lines that Dylan excised in rerecording.

There's nothing wrong with the originals, of course. These songs of disillusionment, many inspired by the rocky end of Dylan's marriage to Sara Lownds, are sturdy enough to withstand all sorts of interpretation. But in the rerecording, Dylan summons a raw, overtly wounded tone that magnifies the feeling behind the words; there's no misunderstanding the vulnerability that saturates "Tangled Up in Blue," or the veiled fondness behind "If You See Her, Say Hello."

And really, the slightly desperate shouts of the Minnesota versions help make *Blood on the Tracks* an ultimate breakup album. Though it's filled with allegories and cryptic riddles, somehow the basic plotline—she's gone, he's overcome with sadness—is inescapable. Virtually everything has that energy: The nine-minute odyssey "Lily, Rosemary, and the Jack of Hearts" and the feral rant "Idiot Wind" form an eerie self-portrait of a man who's been blindsided, knocked flat by that "Simple Twist of Fate," and is gradually beginning to apprehend where, exactly, he stands.

GENRE: 🎵 Rock. RELEASED: 1975, Columbia. KEY TRACKS: "Tangled Up in Blue," "Simple Twist of Fate," "Idiot Wind," "Shelter from the Storm." CATALOG CHOICES: *Blonde on Blonde* (see p. 244); *Planet Waves; Oh Mercy.* NEXT STOP: Joni Mitchell: *Blue.* AFTER THAT: Beck: *Sea Change.*

The Great Bard at His Loosest

Love and Theft

Bob Dylan

Even the most irrationally optimistic among Bob Dylan's faithful couldn't have predicted his late-career exploits. Before the 1994 MTV *Unplugged* appearance that introduced him to a new generation, the great songwriter was pulling dwindling crowds (and tepid reviews) on the road. He wasn't writing songs. By some accounts, he wasn't even trying to honor the terms of his recording contract. Something happened around that time to inspire Dylan to begin creating again; when *Time out of Mind* appeared in 1997, it was widely hailed as a reawakening, his first strong album since *Oh Mercy* (1989).

Full of foreboding images, twilight ballads, and dire warnings, *Time* felt very much an elder statesman's statement. What followed it, *Love and Theft,* is another thing entirely—a joyous, rollicking trip along the forgotten American back road, with Dylan as half-crazed tour guide. Driving fast and shouting over the wind, the iconic singer and songwriter seems determined to put everything mundane and mass-produced behind him.

This is Dylan doing low-tech, pre-Internet time travel. His stanzas reach back and forth across generations, seating bluesman Charley Patton next to songwriter Hoagy Carmichael at some dream cocktail party where the bands play old-time soft-shoe music and the blues and torchy jazz. His lines apply quaint old-school notions of civility (and chivalry) to modern problems. Still an expert harvester of regret, Dylan writes lyrics that sound like they were chewed on during marathon highway drives. But the narratives are only a part of Dylan's late-career evolution. At least as important has been his awakening as a musician. During his tours of the 1990s, he became interested in the guitar and guitar solos. This instrumental energy flares up on *Time out of Mind*—see "Cold Irons Bound"—and becomes integral to *Love and Theft,* particularly on the rippling blues "Honest with Me" and the romantic "Moonlight" and "Sugar Baby." The musical touches aren't always extreme, but they give Dylan's words a jolt. And that jolt is all it takes for Dylan to shake that "oracle of a generation" baggage he's been carrying around since the '60s.

GENRE: 🎵 Rock. RELEASED: 2001, Columbia. KEY TRACKS: "Mississippi," "High Water (for Charley Patton)," "Honest with Me," "Sugar Baby." CATALOG CHOICES: *Oh Mercy; Time out of Mind; Bootleg Collection,* Vols. 1–3. NEXT STOP: Tom Waits: *Swordfishtrombones.* AFTER THAT: Joe Henry: *Trampoline.*

The Eagles ✦ Snooks Eaglin ✦ Steve Earle ✦ Earth Wind & Fire ✦ Edward Elgar ✦ Duke Ellington ✦ Missy Elliott ✦ Ramblin' Jack **E** Elliott ✦ Emerson, Lake, and Palmer ✦ Eminem ✦ Brian Eno ✦ Eric B. and Rakim ✦ Alejandro Escovedo ✦ ESG ✦ Estrellas de Areito ✦ Bill Evans Trio ✦ Bill Evans and Jim Hall ✦ The Everly Brothers ✦ Cesaria Evora

What a Difference a Personnel Change Makes

Hotel California

The Eagles

T he hit-making operation known as the Eagles was riding the biggest album of its career, the pleasant (if molasses-slow) *One of These Nights,* when guitarist and songwriter Bernie Leadon announced in December 1975 that he was leaving the group. Normally, personnel changes for bands of this stature are cataclysmic. This one was different: Replacing Leadon, who wrote the group's single "Witchy Woman," was guitarist Joe Walsh, whose banshee wail and theatrical solos sparked the James Gang and such solo singles as "Rocky Mountain Way."

"This is a concept album, there's no way to hide it."
—Don Henley

Almost overnight, the band known for peaceful easy feelings acquired a pronounced rock swagger. The timing was perfect: The Eagles had pretty much exhausted the cactus-and-tequila iconography of country rock as practiced by the Byrds and the Flying Burrito Brothers. Walsh's biting guitar—and the hard, edgy sound favored by his producer Bill Szymczyk—put principal writers Don Henley and Glenn Frey in touch with a rock-star audacity they'd been missing. Together and separately, they came up with a confluence of muscular music and acidic lyrics that are unlike anything else the Eagles had done to that point. Henley later said that the album, released during the U.S. bicentennial celebration, was the band's comment on American decadence.

Hotel California begins with the premise that all of America is interested in what happens at the SoCal fantasy factory; its songs invite listeners inside the never-ending music business bacchanal, which was at a particular high point in the mid-'70s. And then, as they chronicle dark appetites and dependencies, the Eagles poke holes in all the cherished backstage myths. Here's addiction viewed from the perspective of a brutal morning after ("Life in the Fast Lane," the album's super-energized rock moment) and celebrity excess drawn with such skill it becomes a surreal grotesque.

The album, which stands as the Eagles' überstatement, belongs to a long line of conceptual works about the perils and perks of rock stardom. Though others are more intense (see Pink Floyd's *Wish You Were Here*), few have offered such detailed portraits of dissipation in progress, right down to the pink champagne on ice. Being entertainers, the Eagles offset these caustic observations with more accessible material—the gently sung ballad "New Kid in Town," the retro "Victim of Love," and a plaintive country-rock ode that's the album's often-neglected masterstroke, "Try and Love Again."

GENRE: 🎸 Rock. **RELEASED:** 1976, Asylum. **KEY TRACKS:** "Life in the Fast Lane," "Try and Love Again." **CATALOG CHOICE:** *Desperado.* **NEXT STOP:** Gram Parsons: *GP/Grievous Angel* (see p. 581). **AFTER THAT:** Pink Floyd: *Wish You Were Here.*

On the Street with Snooks, the Human Jukebox

New Orleans Street Singer

Snooks Eaglin

Much of what's essential about Snooks Eaglin, the blind New Orleans street singer who had a brief run as an R&B barnstormer in the 1960s, is contained within "Careless Love" from this disc of 1958 solo recordings.

It's stone simple—like many buskers, Eaglin transforms nursery-rhyme ditties into sneakily profound statements. The song sits in that gentle side-to-side shuffle that underpins so much music from New Orleans—though he liked to perform with a band, all Eaglin really needs to get things rocking is his own steady-handed guitar accompaniment.

And "Careless Love" typifies a distinctly New Orleans singing style you don't hear very often. Eaglin is a master of the woe-is-me whimper—he sounds pitiable as he tells of being tied to a lover's apron strings. When he realizes this paramour has been lying ("You said you love me, didn't mean a thing"), the phrase comes with such fresh bitterness, the relationship might have dissolved moments before. There's no shouting and no showbiz here—Eaglin's preferred discourse is blues intimacy, and his slight Louis Armstrong inflections give each repetition (the song is essentially three lines) new wrinkles.

New Orleans Street Singer was recorded after folklorist Harry Oster heard Eaglin busking on the streets of the French Quarter. "Careless Love" and assorted other gems established Eaglin as an acoustic bluesman, and because it was released by Folkways during the height of the folk revival, many music lovers believed this was Eaglin's only trick. In fact, Eaglin cut a number of hot R&B sides with bandleader Dave Bartholomew in 1961. New Orleans natives knew, but it took a series of electric-blues records for Black Top in the 1980s to round out that first impression: Eaglin's one of those people who can play anything.

GENRE: 🔵 R&B. **RELEASED:** 1959, Folkways. **KEY TRACKS:** "See See Rider," "Mean Old World," "Rock Island Line," "Careless Love." **CATALOG CHOICES:** *Teasin' You. The Spirit of New Orleans: The Genius of Dave Bartholomew* also offers a nice sampling of Eaglin's R&B work. **NEXT STOP:** Earl King: *Sexual Telepathy.* **AFTER THAT:** Joseph Spence: *Good Morning Mr. Walker.*

A Honky-Tonk Texan Makes like Emerson

Transcendental Blues

Steve Earle

A note introducing these fifteen songs from Steve Earle begins: "I have spent most of my life (like most people) avoiding transcendence at all costs." After looking for loopholes and easy escapes, he explains, he concludes that transcendence is "being still enough long enough to know when it's time to move on." These songs reflect his change in attitude. In them, he confesses to large (and petty) jealousies, weighs the moral repercussions of running away from problems, and ponders devotion and betrayal and all manner of romance-related suffering.

Transcendental Blues is Steve Earle's ninth studio album.

Earle knows a bit about rough patches. After taking the music world by storm with the unexpected combination of Texas grit and Springsteen myth that marked his debut *Guitar Town* (1986), the singer, songwriter, and guitarist, who's been married six times, became addicted to heroin and cocaine. At one point, after *The Hard Way*, he stopped recording for five years, and spent some time in jail. Following rehab, he became more aggressive about musical exploration, releasing a series of albums that are loaded with tales of sin and redemption, and are musically eclectic to a fault.

Range-wise, *Transcendental Blues* is as ambitious as any of them—there are Celtic songs and bluegrass rambles and hard rockers.

Yet unlike the earlier efforts, it's remarkably integrated, a series of finely wrought compositions that draw from rock and country, psychedelic folk, and Sufi mystic music as needed. The lyrics are sharp and often self-recriminating, in the manner of Earle's mentor, friend, and sometime songwriting partner Townes Van Zandt (see p. 801). But the musical frameworks are snappy and bright, with the sonic punch of the Beatles circa *Rubber Soul*. If you ever wondered what a sweet little British Invasion pop tune would sound like surrounded by serrated grunge guitar and sung by a scrapper on the run from inner demons, check out "Everyone's in Love with You."

GENRE: 🎸 Rock. **RELEASED:** 2000, E-Squared/Artemis. **KEY TRACKS:** "Everyone's in Love with You," "I Can Wait," "The Boy Who Never Cried," "The Galway Girl," "When I Fall." **CATALOG CHOICES:** *Guitar Town; Copperhead Road.* **NEXT STOP:** Son Volt: *Trace.* **AFTER THAT:** Townes Van Zandt: *Live at the Old Quarter* (see p. 801).

A Long-Player Every Bit as Intense as the Group's Singles

All 'n' All

Earth Wind & Fire

Easily the most intense three minutes ever committed to tape by '70s hit-makers Earth Wind & Fire is "Sing a Song," the tightly wound but never fully erupting essay in funk lavishness that was a hit single from the band's 1975 album, *Gratitude*. Next on the list might be "Reasons," the ballad showcase for the skyscraping falsetto of vocalist Philip Bailey from *That's the Way of the World,* which was also released in '75. In the time-compressed shorthand of pop, those are the must-have moments.

But they're not the whole story. At the time of these successes, the Memphis-based band, led by drummer, producer, and part-time mystic Maurice White, was attempting to move beyond singles. *All 'n' All,* which came out in 1977, was EWF's first and best attempt at developing a wholly satisfying album experience, a cycle in which every song mattered. The unifying thread was Brazilian rhythm. "We'd been hanging out for a month in Argentina and Brazil, especially Rio," White recalled in the liner notes. "Man, we heard stuff that blew our minds, opened our heads up wide. I wanted some of it in our music." After studying the progressive funk of Banda Black Rio and the arty songs of Milton Nascimento, White and his core group wrote pieces that embraced undulating samba and chants heard at Carnaval, and integrated elements of Brazilian rhythm into the EWF lockstep funk. The wordless vocal "Runnin'" with its *ba-bee-da-boo-whees*, turned up on jazz radio, and several album tracks, including the jittery "Jupiter," were easily catchy

All 'n' All's "Runnin'" won a Grammy Award for Best Instrumental in 1978.

enough to follow the high-gloss "Serpentine Fire" onto the radio.

White connected the tunes with a series of interludes built on the African thumb piano known as *kalimba* and street percussion; one, "Brazilian Rhyme," was based on a Nascimento song. Though brief, these pieces unified the album, and gave it a cosmopolitan sound that, like the music that inspired it, opened heads up wide.

GENRE: 🔵 R&B. **RELEASED:** 1977, Columbia. **KEY TRACKS:** "Serpentine Fire," "Runnin'," "Magic Mind," "I'll Write a Song for You." **CATALOG CHOICE:** *The Best of Earth Wind & Fire*, Vol. 1. **NEXT STOP:** George Duke: *A Brazilian Love Affair*. **AFTER THAT:** Kool and the Gang: *Live at the Sex Machine*.

Conducted by the Composer, Smashingly

Symphony No. 1

Edward Elgar
London Symphony Orchestra (Edward Elgar, cond.)

Y ou'd think that the guy who wrote the tune would be uniquely qualified to lead others through it. But it doesn't always work out that way. Sometimes when they're on the podium, composers linger over details that seem slight,

or take things too slowly so they can show off the splendor of the orchestrations—Igor Stravinsky was sometimes derided for that.

The British composer Edward Elgar (1857–1934) conducted frequently, and here, leading the London Symphony Orchestra through his first symphony, he suggests that the composer need not be an overzealous tour guide to bring the music to life. Elgar presents himself as a cut-to-the-chase dude who leads by getting

out of the way. He sets up brisk businesslike tempos, and trusts that the group will bring out the colors embedded in the score.

This is obvious right from the piece's ostentatious opening march. It's a big, honking, self-conscious way to open a symphony, along the lines of "here we come striding in to save the day!" Elgar was expert at processionals—he wrote "Pomp and Circumstance," after all—and is exceedingly careful choosing the pace.

Biographer Jerrold Northrop Moore describes Elgar's performance here as "not rushed, but quicker than most conductors have taken it since. . . . It moves with a certain stir but without the weight of hindsight."

The piece does exude the enveloping air of nostalgia—some hear it as a requiem for pre–World War I England, the moment just before the last shreds of innocence vanished. Elgar's conception for the orchestra emphasizes that—his Scherzo second movement is crisp and militaristic, his third movement is a feast of deep, plush tones that have a ruminative air. There's a distinct ruefulness to it, and a sadness. As the long-toned themes unwind, these qualities intensify. It's as though Elgar's

"The trees are singing my music.
Or have I sung theirs?"
—Edward Elgar

gestures pull the musicians into the parlor of a grieving war widow who, having suffered through the parades, is finally letting go of that stoic British stiff upper lip.

GENRE: 🎵 Classical.
RELEASED: 1930, EMI.
KEY TRACKS: First and third movements. **ANOTHER INTERPRETATION:** London Philharmonic (Georg Solti, cond.). **CATALOG CHOICES:** Symphony No. 2; Symphony No. 3, London Symphony Orchestra (Colin Davis, cond.). **NEXT STOP:** Ralph Vaughan Williams: Orchestral Works, various orchestras and conductors. **AFTER THAT:** Frederick Delius: Orchestral Works, BBC Symphony (Andrew Davis, cond.).

A Cornerstone of American Music

Never No Lament:
The Blanton-Webster Band

Duke Ellington and His Orchestra

These three discs contain many of the most enduring compositions of the greatest American composer, Duke Ellington, as recorded by the most personable and multidimensional big band of all time, the Duke Ellington Orchestra. Blithe dances, rubato tone poems, and multipart suites, these towering pieces embody the carefree grace of great swing while hiding Ellington's enormous musical sophistication, which revs gently under the hood of a limo ready to spirit you to a swank soiree. Ellington (1899–1974) built his scores not part by part, but according to the strengths and idiosyncrasies of his individual musicians, many of whom stayed with him for decades. He wrote to take advantage of their musical personalities, and gave those personalities room to shine—for proof, look no further than "Concerto for Cootie," a tour de force of trumpet mannerisms popularized by the unmistakable Cootie Williams. Listen to anyone else play it, and you realize that the notes Ellington wrote are a starting point; Williams's spirit *makes* the tune.

Ellington's recorded legacy spans six decades. Like any enduring institution, the band experienced highs and lows; this compilation, which highlights the period 1940–1942, represents one golden age—when Ellington's most economical, incandescent writing was brought to life by characters determined to catch every little ripple lurking in the scores. Part of the magic can be attributed to an influx of new talent that began in 1939. The first addition was young bassist Jimmy Blanton, who anchored the Ellington sound with agile, harmonically advanced walking lines that anticipate bebop. Then there was Ben Webster, the thick-toned tenor saxophonist, who could deliver hot shout choruses ("Cotton Tail") as effectively as buttery ballads ("Sepia Panorama"). Also at this time, Ellington brought composer and arranger Billy Strayhorn into the fold; among his early pieces here is one that became the band's express-shuttle glide of a theme song, "Take the A Train."

Duke Ellington received a Grammy Lifetime Achievement Award in 1966.

Ellington wrote to capture moments of life as he knew it—he once described his "Harlem Air Shaft," which pushes the band to soft and loud extremes, as a tour of the sounds and smells you'd pick up leaning out the window of a tenement apartment building. That sense of humanity, the rare ability to lift ordinary scenes into wondrous sonic abstractions, permeates everything Ellington.

GENRE: 🅙 Jazz. **RELEASED:** 2005, RCA. (Recordings made in the early '40s.) **KEY TRACKS:** "Ko-Ko," "Harlem Air Shaft," "Cotton Tail," "Concerto for Cootie." **CATALOG CHOICE:** *Ellington at Newport, 1956.* **NEXT STOP:** The Thad Jones/Mel Lewis Orchestra: *Opening Night at the Village Vanguard, February 7, 1966.*

The Composer as Tourist

The Far East Suite

Duke Ellington

D uke Ellington thrived on the road. He wrote songs and scored arrangements in the backseat of a car while traveling from city to city, and was known to make pilgrimages to interesting places while the musicians in his employ slept. Like many composers before him, Ellington let his adventures as a tourist inform his work, writing a series of "musical snapshots" to celebrate places he'd been. This suite, recorded in 1966 after extensive tours of the Middle East and Asia, is the most invigorating of them. It's also one of Ellington's late-career high points, a piece that stands among his last great contributions, next to the even more ambitious *Sacred Concerts*.

The Far East Suite includes pieces by Ellington and his alter ego, composer Billy Strayhorn, and relies on some of the most personable soloists in the band's long history. These musicians don't exactly have it easy, because many of the pieces are built on exotic scales and harmonies far from the typical jazz framework. The musicians rise to these challenges: Alto saxophonist Johnny Hodges begins his solo on "Isfahan" with cautious phrases, and as he gets comfortable he uncorks impressive blasts of swooping and pitch-bending invention.

Not every tune is exotic: Though named for a majestic sight, "Mount Harissa" is a hard-swinging boogaloo enlivened by a bouncing Paul Gonsalves tenor solo; it could just as easily have been titled "Greens and Gravy." That tune and a few others are examples of Ellington's unsurpassed genius—his ability to load a novel's worth of poignancy into the limiting structure of a three-minute song. They show that Ellington was hip to the rhythmic innovations happening in jazz in the early '60s. Yes, he was intent on sharing the exotic thrills he

Far East Suite was recorded over 3 days in December 1966.

picked up in the Far East. But that didn't mean Ellington was going to stop swinging.

GENRE: 🅙 Jazz. **RELEASED:** 1967, RCA. (Reissued 2003.) **KEY TRACKS:** "Mount Harissa," "Isfahan," "Blue Pepper (Far East of the Blues)," "Tourist Point of View." **COLLECTOR'S NOTE:** The 2003 edition contains seven previously unreleased alternate takes. **CATALOG CHOICES:** *The Third Sacred Concert; Anatomy of a Murder; Afro-Bossa.* **NEXT STOP:** John Coltrane Quartet: *Africa/Brass.* **AFTER THAT:** Stan Kenton and His Orchestra: *Cuban Fire.*

Respect Earned

Respect M.E.

Missy Elliott

From the minute she arrived in 1996, rapping and cowriting several songs on Aaliyah's second album, *One in a Million,* Missy "Misdemeanor" Elliott made clear that she intended to travel her own path. A bellicose rapper with an extraordinary gift for catchy phrasing, Elliott dismissed annoying rivals with withering putdowns dispensed at 120 beats per minute. And yet, on her trailblazing debut, *Supa Dupa Fly* (1997), she seemed equally interested in having a good time: Unlike gangstas and underground urban prophets, she approached hip-hop as dance music, sensual music, a prelude to getting it on. She didn't conform to the typical male rapper's notions about sex, either: On some of her most memorable tracks, Elliott presented

herself as a woman in control, talking up her physical attributes ("I'm Really Hot") in ways both explicit and assertive.

Elliott's singles, gathered on this excellent collection that for some reason hasn't been released in the U.S., define the state of the art in commercial hip-hop from the 1990s forward. Just about every singer, rapper, and producer aiming for a hit on urban radio has copped something from these highly addictive productions, which marry Elliott's incisive running commentary to razor-sharp rhythm programming.

Elliott dishing it in year 2004.

Key to Elliott's enterprise is Timbaland, the beatmaker whose concept, honed through his work with Elliott, propelled him into the top tier of in-demand producers. On the Bengal-influenced "Get Ur Freak On" and others, he establishes a hypnotically simple pulse, then surrounds it with burbling "incidental" sounds and hand-percussion blips. As with much of his work, the final result is so streamlined it feels wholly spontaneous, as if he just sat down at the sampler and banged the thing out in minutes. And that sets the tone for Elliott's contributions. From the opening verse of "The Rain," the big single from *Supa Dupa Fly*, she dishes lines that seem too crazy to be premeditated, interrupting the free association every so often to deliver one of those radio-ready catchphrases. The result: a synergy of groove and message rare in the assembly-line world of contemporary urban music.

GENRE: 🎙 Hip-Hop. **RELEASED:** 2006, Goldmind/Atlantic. **KEY TRACKS:** "Get Ur Freak On," "We Run This," "Gossip Folks," "The Rain (Supa Dupa Fly)." **COLLECTOR'S NOTE:** This compilation also features several dance remixes, most notably the amped-up Basement Jaxx treatment of "4 My People." **CATALOG CHOICE:** *Supa Dupa Fly.* **NEXT STOP:** Mary J. Blige: *No More Drama.* **AFTER THAT:** Salt-n-Pepa: *Blacks' Magic.*

The Musings of a Character Just Outside the Folk Spotlight

The Essential Ramblin' Jack Elliott

Ramblin' Jack Elliott

How lucky we are that people like Ramblin' Jack Elliott were on the scene way back when, sharing bottles with folk pioneers like Woody Guthrie and picking up the stories of train-hopping hobos and other outsized characters of the American road. His music is the diary those figures never kept.

A pretension-free performer with a gruff voice, Elliott was drawn to the drifting life early: At age fifteen, he ran away from home to join a traveling rodeo. Though he eventually returned home and finished high school, his course was set. He spent his adult life mostly on the road, often in the company of Guthrie and other strong-willed types, and when he began singing professionally he borrowed the cagey demeanor of some of the outcasts he'd met along the way.

Born in Brooklyn, Elliott was Guthrie's long-serving (and last) road companion. Elliott applied what he learned to his performances in the small coffeehouses and clubs in Greenwich Village—where among those who heard his mixture of vintage songs and stories was the young Bob Dylan. Once, in an interview with a British newspaper, Elliott described feeling humbled by Guthrie's output: "I used to look over his shoulder as he'd sit there at the typewriter and knock off these songs just as quick as you could blink. And each time they'd be perfect and needed no correcting. . . . I realized there was no way I was gonna top that. And I decided it would be better to just . . . find the songs and interpret them the way they suited me."

That's what Elliott has done for the last half century—his songbook, which is well represented on this anthology, contains old folk, gospel, and blues standards as well as the odd sheepherding song. When he performs live (several tracks here are taken from a 1965 concert), Elliott prefaces the tunes with long yarns that digress into other yarns—Odetta nicknamed him "Ramblin'" for that reason. Thing is, that arcane stuff in his head is culturally significant, a part of American history that has escaped the books. Just by singing his simple songs, Elliott pulls listeners into that earlier time—when personality mattered, when entertaining meant telling a story and not endless smoke and mirrors and fireworks. His characters don't exist anymore—they've been obliterated by televi-

sion and the media-entertainment complex. But they did once, and that's why we need guys like Ramblin' Jack to pass along what they knew about the world, before it's gone forever.

GENRE: Ⓕ Folk. **RELEASED:** 1976, Vanguard. **KEY TRACKS:** "Sadie Brown," "Will the Circle Be Unbroken," "Black Snake," "Talkin' Columbia," "Blind Lemon Jefferson," "Don't Think Twice, It's All Right." **CATALOG CHOICE:** *Hard Travelin' (Songs of Woody Guthrie and Others).* **NEXT STOP:** Fred Neil: *Bleecker and MacDougal.* **AFTER THAT:** Lightnin' Hopkins: *Lightnin' Hopkins* (see p. 367).

Rampant Three-Way Virtuosity

Brain Salad Surgery

Emerson, Lake, and Palmer

Show-offs, these guys were. Technically obsessed geeks in artists' clothing. Led by Keith Emerson, demonic overlord of organ and synth, the trio, which included drummer Carl Palmer and bassist Greg Lake, cooked up a heavy music that, even in the prog-happy early '70s, was exotic. First, ELP bludgeoned listeners with dense chords and drums like cannon fire. And then it blew them away with regrooved bits of symphonic music pumped to larger-than-life grandeur.

Formed in 1970 when Lake left the imploding King Crimson, the trio hit paydirt on its first try: Among the songs on the band's debut was the wistful "Lucky Man," which

According to Greg Lake, the group talked with Jimi Hendrix about a collaboration shortly before the guitarist died.

became a staple of album rock radio. That emboldened the three, and over the next few records ELP would create highly dramatic renditions of classical pieces (Aaron Copland's "Hoedown," Modest Mussorgsky's "Pictures at an Exhibition") and originals built on intricate, if sometimes bombastic, syncopations ("Tarkus"). The fourth effort, *Brain Salad Surgery,* stands as the most fully realized—and still decidedly brazen—ELP statement.

The album opens in a mood of great import, with Lake singing William Blake's poem "Jerusalem." Then comes another appropriation—this time of twentieth-century Argentine composer Alberto Ginastera's Piano Concerto No. 1, which Emerson retooled into the intense and episodic "Toccata." That's followed by a Lake ballad, "Still . . . You Turn Me On," perhaps the most graceful music these three ever made together.

The centerpiece is a sprawling four-movement futuristic keyboard fantasia, "Karn-Evil 9," which opens in a blaze of up-tempo rock, then travels through mystical sci-fi settings so that Emerson can show off his electrifying Moog synthesizer creations. Listen as they navigate the fast-moving rapids of the opening section of "Karn-Evil 9" and the knotty polyrhythms of the suite's "Third Impression," and you'll first be stunned by the fitful, thrashing, jaw-dropping technique involved. Hang out a little longer, and you'll pick up the intellect and sensitivity behind the technique. Lots of progressive rock bands played hard and loud. The power audible in ELP at its peak comes from the trio's extraordinary unity and cohesiveness, not volume.

GENRE: 🎸 Rock. **RELEASED:** 1973, Atlantic. **KEY TRACKS:** "Karn-Evil 9," "Still . . . You Turn Me On," "Toccata." **CATALOG CHOICE:** *Tarkus*. **NEXT STOP:** Genesis: *The Lamb Lies Down on Broadway* (see p. 305). **AFTER THAT:** PFM: *Photos of Ghosts*.

He Is Whoever You Say He Is

The Marshall Mathers LP

Eminem

From his very first utterances, the rapper born Marshall Mathers III presented himself as a street urchin and a kingpin, a victim and a perpetrator, a sensitive soul and a paranoid brute. His discography charts the development of not just his art, but the large walk-in closet where he kept his dramatis personae, the alter egos that help define poor misunderstood Em. He spends lots of time on the microphone talking about who he is, who you say he is, how he knows who the culture thinks he is, why that's wrong, how guys like you can't hope to fathom trickster souls like him.

Eminem got to be a bully with the identity politics bait-and-switch, but it was a good trick, and he took it to impressive extremes on this, his best (and darkest) album. Backed by Dr. Dre's most menacing slasher-film beats, Eminem dispenses blow-by-blow violence and withering dismissals with a verbal dexterity that has no equal in hip-hop. On the first single, "The Real Slim Shady," which bor-

Eminem's second album sold 1,760,049 copies in its first week.

rows its tagline from the game show *To Tell the Truth*, Eminem dishes on the exploits of various celebrities (notably Christina Aguilera) while tossing out lines intended to taunt and confuse those trying to divine whatever his "real" identity might be. He changes everything else as well: While some rappers rely on the same cadence and tone for every caper, Eminem alters his flow, his voice, his word choices, his entire character, from verse to verse.

Just how extreme are these transformations? Compare "The Real Slim Shady" with another single, entitled "Stan," which shares letters from an obsessed (and seemingly unbalanced) fan. Backed by a brooding sample from the singer Dido, Eminem muses on fame (and how ordinary folks just can't understand its pressures) while the earnest and increasingly desperate "Stan" plans to kill himself and his pregnant wife in twisted homage to Eminem's "97 Bonnie and Clyde" from *The Slim Shady LP*. It's unsettling and extreme, and also gripping—a combination that distinguishes much of the rapid-fire wordplay here.

Not surprisingly, controversy followed Eminem throughout the promotion of this effort and the subsequent tour. He weathered the various firestorms like a combative champ, using the accusations as fresh evidence about how seriously he'd been misunderstood. In fact, many of these tunes find Eminem offering

cagey responses in anticipation of the media reaction—making *The Marshall Mathers LP* a perfect Möbius strip of audacious statements followed by aggrieved reactions from Eminem's various alter egos. None of whom are exactly who you think they are.

GENRE: 🎤 Hip-Hop. **RELEASED:** 2000, Aftermath/Interscope. **KEY TRACKS:** "Stan," "The Real Slim Shady," "Kill You," "The Way I Am," "I'm Back." **CATALOG CHOICES:** *The Slim Shady LP; The Eminem Show.* **NEXT STOP:** 50 Cent: *Get Rich or Die Tryin'.* **AFTER THAT:** Busta Rhymes: *When Disaster Strikes.*

Another World, for Real

Another Green World

Brian Eno

Prepare to enter the Enosphere. In this place, the everyday trappings of pop music—clock-punching rhythm guitars, hammering drums—operate according to a different logic. The composer, producer, conceptualist,

and contrarian Brian Eno has his own philosophies of sound and the spatial relationships between sounds; his music is lush, layered, yet throughout clarity is prized over clutter. Eno has explored these notions of sound on a series of slow-moving instrumental records he describes as "ambient" (he's often credited with coining that term; one example is *Music for Airports,* see next page). He's refined them through his productions for David Bowie, U2, and others. On *Another Green World,* one of his most influential "pop" collections, he shows how these concepts can spark shadowy, rivetingly unusual music. It's Eno in digest form.

Eno music feels like it was created in all-

Among the musicians who contributed to this album: guitarist Robert Fripp, violist John Cale, and drummer Phil Collins.

consuming dream states—it doesn't assault as much as envelop its listeners, swirling around like mist. In the soundscapes of this classic, Eno positions ritualistic hand-drum patterns next to eerie wind-blown synths, then lets them drift along, until their coexistence seems somehow natural. Some pieces seem inspired by surreal visual images, à la Magritte; on the vivid "Sky Saw" and "In Dark Trees," each instrumental event, right down to the last stray chime, is placed exactingly to enhance Eno's overall effect.

It's not easy to lure people into such an abstract place, and even more difficult to keep them there. A secret of *Another Green World* is its captivating sequence: The majestic instrumentals evoke areas of vast oceanic beauty, and just when Eno's fully exhausted them, they fade away, eclipsed by tightly focused, if not always overtly catchy, songs with words. This flowing structure gives the album a pleasant journeying quality, as Eno provides listeners not just with outright thrills, but moments of deep soothing calm to recover from them.

GENRE:  Rock. **RELEASED:** 1975, EG. **KEY TRACKS:** "In Dark Trees," "Sky Saw," "Little Fishes," "St. Elmo's Fire." **CATALOG CHOICES:** *Before and After Science; Here Come the Warm Jets.* **NEXT STOP:** Peter Gabriel: *Passion: Music for The Last Temptation of Christ.* **AFTER THAT:** Jon Hassell: *Power Spot.*

The Way Station as a Place Itself

Ambient 1: Music for Airports

Brian Eno

Inside the vast enveloping tones and isolated melodic events that make up Brian Eno's *Music for Airports* is a serenity distinctly missing from the experience of air travel. There's none of the frantic scramble for the gate or the jostle of queuing humans. There isn't even much discernible pace, or rhythm. Instead, these airy audio "environments" are designed to counter the constant motion of transit with a monastic stillness. Calm radiates from the deep background. Vast enveloping textures, as still as desertscapes, are the primary lure. Contemplatively plinked piano notes pop out from the drones, each one representing a fragment of melody that rarely coalesces into what could be considered a "theme."

"As soon as I hear a sound, it always suggests a mood to me."   —Brian Eno

Eno developed *Music for Airports*, the first in a series of ambient projects, in the late '70s while working as a producer on the Talking Heads' decidedly un-ambient *More Songs About Buildings and Food.* Eno wasn't the first to explore the concept of music as palliative or "background," but he was ahead of his time recognizing the psycho-acoustic properties of sound, and the ways various tones could help shape the experience of being in a particular space or situation. As he wrote in the liner notes: "Ambient music must be able to accommodate many levels of listening attention without enforcing any one in particular; it must be as ignorable as it is interesting."

By that measure, *Airports*, which has actually been used in the passenger waiting areas of some airports, is an unusual success. It's as ignorable as drapery, like much of the music classified as New Age that followed it. Yet if you bring full awareness to it, you may discover unexpected riches waiting inside. Both the piano-based sixteen-minute opening track "1/1," which was cocomposed by former Soft Machine drummer Robert Wyatt, and the more impressionistic drones of "2/2" cast a captivating spell. It's possible to be drawn deep into these "environments" without intellectually processing them at all.

GENRE:  Electronica. **RELEASED:** 1978, EG/Astralwerks. **KEY TRACK:** "1/1." **CATALOG CHOICES:** *Fourth World*, Vol. 1:

Possible Music (with Jon Hassell); *My Life in the Bush of Ghosts* (with David Byrne; see p. 136). **NEXT STOP:** Jean-Michel Jarre: *Oxygene.* **AFTER THAT:** Mark Isham: *Tibet.*

You Know They Got Soul

Paid in Full

Eric B. and Rakim

Paid in Full is the old-school hip-hop handbook, a mother lode that inspired countless other classics while establishing some of the form's standard practices. It taught subsequent generations tactics for massaging sound (by using effects, chopping samples into discrete bits, etc.), and showed countless producers ways to vary the boom-bap.

Start by paying attention to the elaborate beat schemes. Eric B. (full name Eric Barrier) wasn't the first hip-hop DJ to find treasure in the James Brown catalog, but he was among the first to do radical creative things with his gleanings—as Stetsasonic, another

On the cover: Erik B. (left) and Rakim (right).

great New York group, once observed, "Tell the truth, James Brown was old 'til Eric and Rakim came out with 'I Got Soul.'" On that track, the turntablist massages tiny bits of familiar records—sometimes just a snare drum hit, or a touch of Brown's vocal foil Bobby Byrd, or one of Brown's trademark "Good Gawd" grunts—into an undulating, totally original mosaic. Then, he steps up to scratch sonic mayhem over the pulse; cue up the last few minutes of "My Melody" to hear one of the most deliriously inspired turntable improvisations in hip-hop history.

Most of the time, however, the rhythms are austere and streamlined, and this gives rapper Rakim (full name Rakim Allah) room to spin through rhymes like "You scream I'm lazy, you must be crazy, thought I was a donut, you tried to glaze me." Rakim's an improviser, too—while other MCs proffer unbroken streams of boasting, he packs his ideas into dense clusters, sometimes cramming several improbable internal rhymes into the same line. Even more impressive is his command of syncopation; landing hard on offbeats, and varying points of emphasis, he transforms ordinary rhyme cadences into choppy bursts of greatness.

The deluxe edition of *Paid in Full* is essential just for Cold Cut's remix of "Paid in Full," which is accurately subtitled "Seven Minutes of Madness." This reimagining has been nearly as influential as the original text, and stands as one of the great hip-hop remixes of all time.

GENRE:  Hip-Hop. **RELEASED:** 1987, Fourth and Broadway. (Reissued 2003, Island.) **KEY TRACKS:** "My Melody," "I Know You Got Soul," "Move the Crowd," "Paid in Full," "Eric B. Is President." **CATALOG CHOICE:** *Follow the Leader.* **NEXT STOP:** EPMD: *Business Never Personal.* **AFTER THAT:** Eminem: *The Slim Shady LP.*

As in, Heaviness

Gravity

Alejandro Escovedo

A lejandro Escovedo began his career fronting two hard-hitting, often-thrilling rock bands in the 1980s, Rank and File and the True Believers. Neither caught on, and after the Believers packed up in 1987, Escovedo began looking for different outlets. Then his first wife committed suicide, and that changed everything: Suddenly Escovedo found himself writing inward-looking songs of grief and loss. These came in many forms—somber ones colored by a novelist's sense of human nature, philosophical ones that draw life lessons out of tense and tangled situations.

Gravity, Escovedo's first solo album, gathers these songs. It's quite different from most singer-songwriter records, partly because of the circumstances of its creation, partly because of its brilliantly scored string-quartet backing, and partly because Escovedo is prone to understatement. His voice has a natural coarseness; the jarring realization "She Doesn't Live Here Anymore" comes as much from the texture of voice—which is broken apart, halting, unsure—as the narrative itself.

Gravity's songs unfold slowly, and usually wind up in a listless, all-cried-out, numb-from-pain zone. This is where Escovedo is most comfortable. Though he put rock behind him to record this, he retains a rock frontman's sense of drama, and the ability to detach from the deeply troubling situations he's describing. He sings sad, regal songs like "Five Hearts Breaking" as if he's resigned to the long trudge forward, and no matter how reluctant he is, he has to keep on keeping on. Gravity, indeed.

GENRE: 🎸 Rock. **RELEASED:** 1992, Watermelon. (Reissued 2002, Lone Star). **KEY TRACKS:** "Broken Bottle," "By Eleven," "Five Hearts Breaking," "She Doesn't Live Here Anymore." **COLLECTOR'S NOTE:** The 2002 reissue appends a second disc of live performances of some *Gravity* songs. **CATALOG CHOICES:** *Thirteen Years; The Boxing Mirror.* **NEXT STOP:** Lucinda Williams: *Sweet Old World* (see p. 864). **AFTER THAT:** Richard Buckner: *Devotion and Doubt.*

A Funky Family Affair

A South Bronx Story

ESG

F ifty-five seconds into "Tiny Sticks" by the minimalist groove band ESG, there's a moment when the tune seems to fall apart. It's been pumping along, an up-tempo percussion festival with a thumping Bronx hip-hop bass line, when suddenly drummer Valerie Scroggins attempts a halting little fill. It doesn't quite work. Even though it feels like a glitch, her sisters, Renee, Deborah, and Marie, and percussionist Tito Libran follow her, in almost telepathic synchronization. Then they snap back into tempo and suddenly you realize this is one tight groove.

ESG went aboveground with the release of this album.

That's an extreme example of the kind of rhythmic lock that made ESG almost famous within New York's "No Wave" scene of the late 1970s. The South Bronx family band got good at pumping out a relentless beat all the way live, in the era just before drum machines and samplers became commonplace. This wasn't fancy rhythm, sometimes just a four-on-the-floor drums and a simple bass line, but as it went on (and on), it became hypnotic. And ESG worked it, interpolating thumps from disco and stuttering, DJ-style breaks from early hip-hop. The band's extended tracks became a DJ's best friend; singles like "UFO" and others packed the floor, and have been endlessly sampled by such hip-hop luminaries as LL Cool J and Big Daddy Kane. (At one point the group issued a single in protest, entitled "Sample Credits Don't Pay Our Bills.") Maybe ESG was threatened by sampling, but it was hardly rendered obsolete. That's because the group played every little offbeat and attack together. And as any connoisseur of James Brown, Funkadelic, and other great music made before computers can tell you, a band that can hunker down and groove like this is a rare and precious thing.

GENRES: 🔵 R&B 🔴 Hip-Hop 〰 Electronica. **RELEASED:** 2005, Soul Jazz/Universal Sound. **KEY TRACKS:** "You're No Good," "UFO," "Come Away," "Tiny Sticks." **CATALOG CHOICE:** *Step Off.* **NEXT STOP:** Liquid Liquid: *Liquid Liquid.* **AFTER THAT:** Luscious Jackson: *Fever in Fever Out.*

A Jam Session for the Ages

Los Heroes

Estrellas de Areito

A decade before the Buena Vista Social Club (see p. 805) put a spotlight on the precious jewels among Cuba's underemployed older musicians, the state-run label undertook an ambitious cultural experiment: In 1979, it gathered musicians from several generations to jam together, in the spirit of the Cachao *Descargas* (see p. 454) of the 1950s. Participants in the weeklong sessions included future Buena Vista pianist Rubén González and members of the jazz-fusion band Irakere. Arrangements were generated on the fly, solos were extended, and the vocalists traded places constantly to rain catcalls on each other. The five (!) records that resulted didn't connect with a Cuban audience—some believed they were too modern—and were shelved, lost among the many undervalued treasures at Havana's Egrem Studios.

Although they sometimes wander a bit, the Estrellas sessions—in the two-disc form now available—catch musicians working together to extend the heritage of Cuban dance music.

Disc one offers spirited modernizations of the timeless Cuban *son* root—*guaguancó, guajira, charanga,* among others. These exist on multiple layers. The percussionists observe every spec of the tradition, playing the way dance bands did in the '50s. On top of that, the soloists interject all sorts of modern dissonances, exploring at a breezy, conversational pace. Although disc two goes a bit more show-biz, there's plenty of substance beneath the

Estrellas de Areito includes over 30 notable Cuban musicians.

eruptions, and a fire—the by-product of the collision between heritage and irreverent musicianly hipness—that could only have happened in Cuba.

GENRE: 🌐 World/Cuba.
RELEASED: 1999, Nonesuch.
KEY TRACKS: "Llora timbero," "Yo si como candela," "Guajira guantanemera." **NEXT STOP:** Cachao y Su Orquesta: *Cuban Jam Session,* Vol. 2.
AFTER THAT: Various Artists: *Havana Jam.*

One Magic Sunday

Sunday at the Village Vanguard/ Waltz for Debby

Bill Evans Trio

Time moves differently on Sundays. The pressure to "do" slacks off, and it's possible to let your mind wander, at least a little. This gravitational shift is so strong it even affects musicians, known to be impervious to the rhythms of the working week. For proof see *Sunday at the Village Vanguard* and *Waltz for Debby,* two contemplative discs recorded by the Bill Evans Trio on a single day of alleged rest (and reissued in 2005 as *The Complete Village Vanguard Recordings, 1961).*

Evans believed that the trio should be a meeting of equals.

Here is the most harmonically astute pianist in jazz, Bill Evans, working for the last time with his most attentive accomplices—the drummer Paul Motian, and the bassist Scott LaFaro, who would die in a highway accident ten days later. The material is standard Evans Trio fare—Gershwin's "My Man's Gone Now," Miles Davis's "Solar"—and

as always Evans seems eager for an adventure. But the feeling he cultivates is one of naptime serenity, an idle daydream at the piano. His cohorts pick that up right away; sometimes the trio swings together, and sometimes they circle around three tempos at once, committing to nothing. Though Evans was by this time associated with the impressionistic colors he brought to Davis's 1959 landmark *Kind of Blue* (see p. 208), his less-appreciated but perhaps more important weapon—an assured, endlessly subtle sense of swing—is in full effect here.

Part of the low-keyness could be attributed to simple fatigue: The trio had played a full evening (including the Vanguard's customary late show) on Saturday, and began the first of five (!) sets at 4:30 the following afternoon. Riverside recorded nearly every set on that Sunday, splitting the highlights into two albums equally groaning with greatness. (There's now a three-disc "complete" box that offers all the sets in their entirety.) Even Evans's pet phrases—the hairpin turns and the glib dancing triplets he slipped into countless studio sessions and late-night jams—resonate differently in this context, radiating a pensive, reflective mood that you don't encounter in jazz clubs every day.

GENRE: 🎧 Jazz. **RELEASED:** 1961, Riverside. (Both albums reissued together 2005.) **KEY TRACKS:** "My Man's Gone Now," "Waltz for Debby," "My Foolish Heart." **CATALOG CHOICE:** *Conversations with Myself.* **NEXT STOP:** Miles Davis Quintet: *In Person Friday and Saturday at the Blackhawk.* **AFTER THAT:** Ahmad Jamal: *Cross-Country Tour.*

Summit Meeting, No Grandstanding

Undercurrent

Bill Evans and Jim Hall

What happens to jazz when the drummer and the bass player take five? Does the music go all gooey and formless, a balladic tone painting? In the case of *Undercurrent,* one of the most famous piano-guitar conversations in music history, the opposite occurs: Pianist Bill Evans and guitarist Jim Hall discover just how intense jazz rhythm can be when it is implied (and danced around) rather than overtly stated.

The two start with "My Funny Valentine," which is usually played as a slow ballad but here moves at a demandingly brisk medium swing. The opening chorus features Hall. Instead of providing conventional backing, Evans throws Hall a series of short stop-time chordal jabs, each landing on a jarring offbeat. Hall responds with sentence fragments that bounce off the syncopations yet somehow maintain the tempo. Then the tasks are reversed, and Hall takes a different approach in the supporting role—he uses florid, open-ended chords to lure the pianist into a more contemplative state. Again the tempo isn't

Undercurrent is a collaboration between two modern jazz giants.

strictly followed. But it's always there—as a steady undercurrent, the driving taskmaster of a drummer who's felt but not heard.

Evans and Hall both have unflappably solid notions of time, and they behave like dancers freed from the tyranny of a chorus line. They're also expert listeners, and unlike most summit meetings of jazz heavyweights, this collection (and a 1966 postscript, *Intermodulation*) is a lesson in restraint. On each of these extended conversations, from the syrup-slow "I Hear a Rhapsody" to the yearning "I'm Getting Sentimental Over You," the two slide between soloist and accompanist roles, taking turns extending and reinventing the themes. Theirs is jazz interaction at its most elemental, stripped of gratuitous razzle-dazzle.

GENRE: 🎷 Jazz. **RELEASED:** 1962, Blue
Note. **KEY TRACKS:** "My Funny Valentine"

(both takes), "I Hear a Rhapsody." **CATALOG
CHOICE:** *Intermodulation.* **NEXT STOP:**
Steve Lacy and Mal Waldron: *Sempre amore.*

The Sweet Side of Early Rock

Cadence Classics:
Their Twenty Greatest Hits

The Everly Brothers

Rock and roll was busting out all over when Archie Bleyer, the honcho of Cadence Records, gave "Bye Bye Love" to his new act the Everly Brothers in 1957. He wasn't, however, expecting a rock and roll single. He considered the song, which was written by the enormously gifted husband-and-wife team of Boudleaux and Felice Bryant, a fairly straightforward post-breakup ditty in the style of Hank Williams. It didn't turn out that way: Don and Phil Everly added forcefully strummed acoustic guitars and a crackling up-tempo beat. And then they sang "Bye Bye Love" together, in a honeyed close harmony that recalls the family bands of a much earlier time.

The Everly Brothers hold the record for the most *Billboard* Top 100 singles by a duo.

Sweeter and slightly more reserved than the roaring music coming from Sun Records in Memphis, "Bye Bye Love" was the rare early rock hit song with multigenerational appeal: Kids dug it, and even those adults averse to rock were eventually won over by its catchiness. The tune reached number 2 on the pop charts, stayed at number 1 on the country charts for seven weeks, and established the basic Everlys approach: Heartbreak songs that seek out little glimpses of sunshine, and hold onto hope in the midst of the pain. Much of the lightness depends on the duo's telepathic vocal connection: Moving in lockstep, their voices usually pitched a third apart, Phil and Don Everly sing in a way that redeems typically overwrought teen-romance odes.

This collection features all of the consequential Everlys hits for Cadence. After "Bye Bye Love" came "Wake Up Little Suzie," "All I Have to Do Is Dream," and Roy Orbison's "Claudette." Even the lesser-known B sides are first rate: To hear pure anguish set to music, cue up "I Wonder If I Care as Much." In three delicious, dejected minutes, it pretty much explains why major musical figures of the 1960s—the Beatles, Simon and Garfunkel, and many more—considered the Everlys to be rock and roll royalty.

GENRE: 🎸 Rock. **RELEASED:** 1990, Rhino.
KEY TRACKS: "Bye Bye Love," "All I Have to Do Is Dream," "Claudette," "I Wonder If I Care as Much," "When Will I Be Loved." **CATALOG CHOICE:** *Two Yanks in England.* **NEXT STOP:** The Righteous Brothers: *You've Lost That Lovin' Feelin'.* **AFTER THAT:** The Hollies: *Evolution.*

An Idyllic Masterwork from the Barefoot Diva

Cesaria

Cesaria Evora

G eographically, the island nation of Cape Verde sits near the halfway point between Portugal and Brazil. It's close to Africa, but its music—and particularly the swooning *morna* that is the chosen style of Cesaria Evora,

the island's most evocative singer—is strikingly European, soaked with the bittersweet regret the Portuguese call *saudade,* and the tremble of French chanson circa Edith Piaf (see p. 598).

Morna has, for over 150 years, expressed the soul of Cape Verde. It has much in common with the heart-heavy Portuguese fado—they share a sense of vague yearning. Its love songs for a distant sweetheart are disarmingly poetic, rich with imagery and far-flung metaphors.

Evora's ribbonlike voice, which can sound serene and troubled at the same time, is the perfect conduit for *morna.* It took her a while to exploit it: The woman known as the "barefoot diva" (she performs without shoes in tribute to the poor of her homeland) made several recordings as a young woman. But she soon retired from music because she was a single mother and couldn't support her children by singing.

Then, when she was in her forties, Evora was invited to Portugal to record two songs for

Cesaria Evora, the world's most famous practitioner of Cape Verdean morna music.

an anthology devoted to Cape Verdean music. That led to more recordings, and eventually, after her austere *Miss Perfumado* became an unlikely café hit, Evora began touring in Europe. Many consider that 1992 acoustic record, which contains the bedrock of her repertoire, the pure Evora experience. But far more interesting, both sonically and musically, is the follow-up *Cesaria.* This features a more substantial (yet still acoustic) ensemble of several guitars and an accordion. It captures Evora's lazily sauntering phrases and transparent, otherworldly tone in full idyllic glory, beckoning from a remote island vista where stillness reigns, and there is time to be alone with your thoughts.

GENRE: 🌐 World/Cape Verde. **RELEASED:** 1995, RCA. **KEY TRACKS:** "Petit pays," "Areia de Salamansa," "Tudo tem se limite." **CATALOG CHOICE:** *Miss Perfumado.* **NEXT STOP:** Bebel Gilberto: *Tanto tempo* (see p. 310). **AFTER THAT:** Mercedes Sosa: *Misa Criolla.*

John Fahey ✦ Fairport Convention ✦ Manuel de Falla ✦
Tal Farlow ✦ Fatboy Slim ✦ Gabriel Fauré ✦ Faust ✦ Cheo
Feliciano ✦ Jose Feliciano ✦ Narvel Felts ✦ Bernarda Fink
✦ Sergio Fiorentino ✦ Fishbone ✦ Ella
Fitzgerald and **F** Louis Armstrong
✦ Roberta Flack ✦ The Flaming Lips ✦
Lester Flatt, Earl Scruggs, and the Foggy Mountain Boys ✦
Fleetwood Mac ✦ Frank Emilio Flynn ✦ The Four Freshmen
✦ The Four Tops ✦ Franco and TPOK Jazz ✦ Aretha Franklin
✦ Lefty Frizzell ✦ Fugazi ✦ The Fugees ✦ Funkadelic

Transfiguration, Indeed

The Transfiguration of Blind Joe Death

John Fahey

Here's a rarity: Music for solo guitar that can function as calm and relaxing background fodder and yet, if you go deep enough inside it, reveals a roiling, surprisingly turbulent netherworld. Throughout his fifth album, the mercurial John Fahey (1939–2001), one of the great musical scavengers of the 1960s, references the blues and folk and ragtime, yet keeps the influences at some distance. His songs employ traits of those styles in unexpected ways, enlivening instrumental death chants ("I Will Be Changed") and picturesque landscapes ("On the Sunny Side of the Ocean").

Central to the scenes is Fahey's guitar prowess, which is built on a similar feat of translation. He was one of the first to apply the fingerpicking techniques of traditional country and blues steel-string playing to less-traditional settings. Then, he added complex tunings and tightly clustered voicings of his own derivation. Fahey found a way to simultaneously affirm the riches left by his musical forefathers and express his own soul: Even at this album's bluesiest moment, the swerving pitch-bends of "How Green Was My Valley,"

it's possible to hear echoes of Fahey's heroes Mississippi John Hurt and Charley Patton while knowing that those patriarchs would never have written anything remotely like this. Though Fahey made other crucial contributions to music—his label, Takoma, gave the world Leo Kottke, as well as his own explorations of Indian raga and Native American music—the expert filtrations of *Blind Joe Death* stand apart, proof that even the most entrenched forms can be transfigured in dazzling ways.

GENRE: 🎵 Folk. **RELEASED:** 1965, Takoma. **KEY TRACKS:** "Orinda-Moraga," "On the Sunny Side of the Ocean." **CATALOG CHOICE:** *Death Chants, Breakdowns, and Military Waltzes.* **NEXT STOP:** Leo Kottke: *6- and 12- String Guitar* (see p. 432). **AFTER THAT:** Bonnie "Prince" Billy: *I See a Darkness* (see p. 102).

The Reimagining of British Folk

Liege and Lief

Fairport Convention

To appreciate how far Fairport Convention took British folk, cue up its version of the traditional murder ballad "Matty Groves," one of several groundbreaking reworkings of old tunes on the band's exquisite

Liege and Lief. It starts as a relatively conventional yarn, with vocalist Sandy Denny retelling how a cheating wife met a violent end. As the tale winds down, guitarist Richard Thompson steps out of the shadows. He doesn't immediately assert himself; instead, he picks up Denny's sense of tragedy and incorporates it into what becomes a guitar epic. What follows, over the next four minutes, is not folk and not rock; it's more like an instrumental treatise on honor and betrayal offered by a shrewd student of human nature.

Fairport Convention formed in April 1967.

Liege and Lief, the group's fourth album, was substantially different from its earlier folk-rock efforts; the band started out emulating American folk-pop combos such as the Mamas and the Papas, and its previous album, *Unhalfbricking,* contains spirited Dylan cov-

ers. Here, the band seems fully engaged in all that 1969 had to offer, from prog-rock to Celtic jousting to those substantially reimagined murder ballads. Historical accounts of Fairport suggest that the band was imploding during these sessions—Denny and bassist Ashley Hutchings would depart immediately after its completion. But it's impossible to tell that from the music, which exhibits an almost telepathic group cohesion.

GENRE: 🎧 Folk. **RELEASED:** 1969, A&M. **KEY TRACKS:** "Matty Groves," "Tam-Lin," "Come All Ye." **CATALOG CHOICE:** *Unhalfbricking.* **NEXT STOP:** Martin Carthy and Dave Swarbrick: *Byker Hill* (see p. 146). **AFTER THAT:** Richard and Linda Thompson: *Shoot Out the Lights* (see p. 775).

Non-Stop to Madrid Now Boarding

El sombrero de tres picos

Manuel de Falla

L'Orchestre de la Suisse Romande (Ernest Ansermet, cond.)

The Spanish composer Manuel de Falla (1876–1946) originally intended the music of *El sombrero de tres picos* (The Three-Cornered Hat) to accompany a pantomime. The hat in the title is worn by the local magistrate, and the piece tells of a love triangle involving the politician, a local miller, and his unfaithful wife. The work was commissioned by Sergei Diaghilev, whose Ballets Russes premiered Stravinsky's *The Rite of Spring.* As it evolved, it became more of a traditional ballet score, with two songs sung in flamenco's "cante-jondo" style. It premiered in London in 1919, with sets by Pablo Picasso.

Falla isn't nearly as famous as his esteemed collaborators, but when you hear his vivid, imagistic writing, you'll understand how he earned a place in their midst. He's the closest thing in Spanish music to someone like Béla Bartók, a proud nationalist whose compositions invoke generations-old folk themes. *El sombrero de tres picos* begins in a restive mood, with impressionistic swirling strings offset by flutes imitating birdsong (Falla's most dazzling inspirations are often carried by the high woodwinds). A few minutes into the second section, a grandiose jousting dance erupts. That's when the composer hauls out artifacts from his ongoing search for the Andalusian soul, including a deeply moving, heroic melody that returns bigger than ever in the final scene. The piece is organized into six sections, and the music for each is largely episodic. When a theme recurs, it usually comes back profoundly changed, hinting at new narrative wrinkles waiting in the wings. (That's a frequent Falla trick: During the "Ritual Fire Dance" from his short opera *El amor brujo*, included here, the composer twists ceremonial voodoo melodies into surreal configurations.)

This recording is guided by Ernest Ansermet, who conducted the piece's London premiere. A mathematician who came to music late in life, Ansermet founded this ensemble, L'Orchestre de la Suisse Romande, and recorded regularly at Geneva's acoustically lush Victoria Hall—his discography is revered by audiophiles for its pristine sound quality. Throughout *El sombrero de tres picos* and *El amor brujo*, Ansermet is extremely attentive to the details of Falla's orchestrations, particularly the flashes of tense harmony that lurk below the main themes. Unlike those who turn Falla's picturesque scenes into tourist music, Ansermet shines precise light on the less showy aspects. In his conception, the expected bravado is countered by moments of doubt, yielding a complex, detailed mosaic.

GENRE: 🎸 Classical. **RELEASED:** 2000, Decca. (Originally recorded between 1955 and 1961.) **KEY TRACKS:** *El sombrero:* "Dance of the Miller's Wife," "The Corregidor's Dance." *El amor brujo:* "Ritual Fire Dance." **CATALOG CHOICE:** *Night in the Gardens of Spain* (piano concerto), Arthur Rubinstein, Rubinstein Collection, Vol. 18. **NEXT STOP:** Isaac Albéniz: *Echoes of Spain*, John Williams. **AFTER THAT:** Agustín Barrios: *Guitar Music, Vol 1.*

After This, He Became a Sign Painter

The Swinging Guitar of Tal Farlow

Tal Farlow

The jazz life wasn't for Tal Farlow (1921–1998). The self-taught guitarist didn't begin to play until he was twenty-one, but he learned fast, and by 1950 he was a part of vibraphonist Red Norvo's acclaimed trio. This led to a series of records as a leader and a demanding travel schedule. And then, less than a year after recording this drummerless barrage of bebop in 1958, Farlow abruptly quit touring, settled in New Jersey, and became a sign painter. Over the next few decades, he performed sporadically, and his reclusiveness only enhanced his legend as one of the most lyrical jazz guitarists, and the rare musician who'd forged his own language. Other guitarists were better known (the overrated Joe Pass is one), but within the six-string brotherhood, Farlow was one who inspired genuine awe.

The Swinging Guitar shows why. Farlow plays "Taking a Chance on Love" (and other tunes) by tapping or brushing past the strings. He renders every note crisply, even when the music's flying by at ultrafast tempos. Every note is exactingly placed, and still Farlow manages to sound like he's "singing" on the instrument—even the technical slaloms of "I Love You" or the chamber-jazz arrangement of "Yardbird Suite" show him attending closely to the overall shape of his lines, forming complete complex thoughts out of what would be, in other hands, jumbles of notes. Farlow's easygoing demeanor permeates everything—his own spearing lines, the Django Reinhardt–style percussive chording he plays behind pianist Eddie Costa. Those little things put this record in the vicinity of true jazz mastery: There's enormous technical skill involved in the conversations,

Tal Farlow is nearly as famous for his reluctance to play as for his top-notch abilities.

yet they sound serene and casual, like idle chitchat over coffee.

GENRE: 🎷 Jazz.
RELEASED: 1959, Verve.
KEY TRACKS: "Taking a Chance on Love," "You Stepped out of a Dream," "Like Someone in Love." **CATALOG CHOICE:** Red Norvo Trio: *The Red Norvo Trio with Tal Farlow and Charles Mingus at the Savoy.* **NEXT STOP:** Jim Hall: *Jazz Guitar.* **AFTER THAT:** Jimmy Raney: *A.*

Staggeringly Creative Groove Constructions

Better Living Through Chemistry

Fatboy Slim

Like many DJs, Norman Cook—the journeyman former rocker who makes dance music under the name Fatboy Slim—builds fine, wiggly grooves out of tiny bits of old records. Equally important to the beats on on this breakthrough, though, is his sense of drama. Consider his tune "Everybody Needs a 303," which uses the bass line and vocal hook from Edwin Starr's "Everybody Needs Love." After it's been percolating for a few minutes, the drums nearly vanish into an oceanic wave of white noise. Then, slowly, the sounds clarify—we hear a chanting crowd in a stadium, followed by a bubbling synthesizer figure that morphs from a round blob to a knife-edge as it repeats. When the vocal sample returns, it's chopped into ever-smaller pieces as a rumble intensifies beneath it. Then the snare drum barrels in, surging

Fatboy Slim performing in Australia in 2000.

and rolling with such power it threatens to explode the speakers as it crests.

That little episode lasts over a minute, and changes everything. When the groove finally returns, it travels at a different velocity. The drums seem bigger and better than before. Experience this crescendo (or one of the many others on *Better Living*) on a dance floor, and you may feel it as a timed-release drug, spreading a sudden wave of euphoria.

Cook first attracted attention as the bassist of the (very smart) British jangle-pop band the Housemartins. Applying the tricks of the songwriter trade to his club incarnation, he creates instrumental passages that are riveting in ways much repetitive dance music is not, studded with interesting chord changes and other sound-collage manipulations. Along with its follow-up, *You've Come a Long Way, Baby,* this record influenced much of the popular electronica of the 1990s. The rippling "Give the Po' Man a Break" sounds like the template for every track on Moby's hit *Play* (1999), while "Going out of My Head" finds Cook showing how even harsh rock power chords (courtesy of the Who's "I Can't

Explain") can, with the proper sorcery, wind up feeling groovy.

GENRE: 🎧 Electronica. **RELEASED:** 1996, Astralwerks. **KEY TRACKS:** "Santa Cruz," "Going out of My Head," "Everybody Needs a 303," "Give the Po' Man a Break." **CATALOG CHOICES:** *You've Come a Long Way, Baby.* The Housemartins: *London 0 Hull 4.* **NEXT STOP:** The Chemical Brothers: *Dig Your Own Hole* (see p. 159). **AFTER THAT:** Prodigy: *The Fat of the Land.*

A Different Sort of Impressionist

Requiem, Pelléas et Mélisande, Pavane

Gabriel Fauré

Montreal Symphony Orchestra and Chorus (Charles Dutoit, cond.)

Gabriel Fauré (1845–1924) was an innovator who had nothing against the past. His music goes its own moody way, gently and sneakily and with great sensitivity to what's come before. Operating with much less fanfare than his more famous contemporary countryman Claude Debussy, Fauré created music that is unfailingly demure; pleasantness covers every external surface, almost obscuring the emotions underneath. His pieces rarely venture to extremes, and you have to pay close attention to their inner workings—like the serpentine melody lines of the *Pavane,* which glance momentarily at different keys, then turn back—before the core of his art is revealed.

Fauré's central medium was song. His notion of art song conforms to classic ABA structure, but with simple, direct melody lines. Even his Requiem, among the most "songful" such works of all time, leans in that direction: It was intended to be a concert piece, not part of a church service, and has little of the counterpoint heard in the sacred music of Germanic composers. Check out the

Pius Jesu movement, for example, where the lines spun so lovingly by Kiri Te Kanawa bear the faint hint of a parlor song, or a cabaret piece. Those looking for sobering piety may be disappointed; the rest of us can enjoy a stirring rhapsody, complete with those garish harp arpeggios that French composers couldn't seem to resist.

This version of the Requiem, with the Swiss-born Charles Dutoit conducting the Montreal Symphony Orchestra and Chorus, honors Fauré's composerly demeanor while magnifying the reassuring beauty of his melodies. The *Pavane,* which is often programmed with Fauré's Requiem, is rendered methodically but not with a heavy hand. Also here is the incidental music Fauré wrote for the play *Pelléas et Mélisande;* it's the story Debussy adapted for his opera of the same name (see p. 213), and as such provides an interesting comparison of temperament. Debussy, the pioneering impressionist, insists on the primacy of music among the arts. Fauré's task is to simply provide atmosphere for the theatrical proceedings; it's a humbler job, and Fauré does it as though he's happy to exist somewhere in the mix, an equal among writers, poets, and painters.

GENRE: 🎻 Classical. **RELEASED:** 1990, London. **KEY TRACKS:** Requiem: Sanctus, Libera Me. *Pélleas:* Andantino. *Pavane.* **CATALOG CHOICE:** *Piano Quartets,* Yo-Yo Ma et al. **NEXT STOP:** Claude Debussy: *La mer* (see p. 634). **AFTER THAT:** Maurice Ravel: *Complete Works for Piano* (see p. 635).

Germanic Progressive Rock

Faust/So Far

Faust

T he first thing to know about Faust, the pioneering German noise-rock band, is that it was put together by a music journalist. Acting as a producer and conceptualist, Uwe Nettlebeck managed to get a bunch of players to buy

into his vision for a different kind of rock band, one oriented around clashing dissonances and improvisation and the ethos of experimental electronic music. Said band didn't sell tons of records, but became one of the more influential outfits in progressive rock history.

The first clue that there's new thinking going on: The band's self-titled debut opens in a swirl of noisy static.

"Faust" is German for "fist," seen here on the cover in X-ray form.

Underneath it, way in the background, are trace snippets of the Rolling Stones' "(I Can't Get No) Satisfaction" and the Beatles' "All You Need Is Love," as well as early examples of tape manipulation. Then comes a circus march, which is first played straight, then as a trumpet-and-guitar figure with a bit of rock savagery in it. This theme recurs several times, eventually swelling into a lusty cause célèbre played with a jazz anarchist's swagger.

Faust—whose claims to fame include the first coinage of the term "Krautrock"—doesn't stay in any one environment for long. The three

extended pieces on this debut are all journeys, with agitated grooves rising up and then fading into an entirely different atmosphere. Many times the transitions and linkages between motifs are more interesting than the motifs themselves; in Faust's best moments, the musicians move between time signatures and tempi as though following a detailed score. Included on the same disc is Faust's second album, *So Far.* It's slightly more conventional, but here too the band's renegade streak prevails: Even working within recognizable song forms, Faust winds up with jarring and episodic music that doesn't simply expand the existing playing field. It creates a new one.

GENRE: 🎸 Rock. **RELEASED:** *Faust:* 1971, Virgin. *So Far:* 1972, Virgin. (Reissued 2000, Collector's Choice.) **KEY TRACKS:** "Why Don't You Eat Carrots?," "It's a Rainy Day, Sunshine Girl." **CATALOG CHOICE:** *Faust IV.* **NEXT STOP:** Neu!: *Neu!* (see p. 546).

The First and Best Expression of Salsa Romántica

Cheo

Cheo Feliciano

alsa romántica was celebrated as a major development when it broke out in the late 1980s. But those who'd been following Latin dance music for decades saw past the hype: Those smooth rhythms and nonthreatening loverman melodies—the tropical equivalent of bedroom soul—had been a part of the music forever. Or at least since this first solo album by *sonero* Cheo Feliciano, the Puerto Rican master who is the patron saint of suave, low-key salsa.

The first lure is Feliciano's magnificent voice—a wine connoisseur might describe it as having a rich mahogany core, with traces of cotton candy around the edges. But this velvety album, made with the A-list musicians of Fania Records, showcases other skills, among them Feliciano's ability to knit together a story through short, often ad-libbed phrases. Where other salsa singers strive for rhythmic exactitude, Feliciano can seem deceptively lazy. Cue up "Anacaona," the dance floor classic that begins the album, to hear him singing in a casual way, willfully disregarding the beat. He tugs against the forward surging salsa rhythm introducing an unexpected tension into the lines.

Every instrumental sound serves to cradle and enhance Feliciano's delivery. There are no horns—instead, the counterpoint comes in the form of clean unisons by vibraphonist Louie Ramirez and electric guitarist Vinnie Bell, with pianist Larry Harlow (see p. 343) sneaking jazz-influenced subversions into the margins.

Feliciano had just finished heroin rehab when he recorded *Cheo*, one of the most consistent albums in the Fania catalog. It became a hit, and was followed by a series of gaudier musical experiments. Those who fall under Feliciano's gentle spell should investigate the string-heavy *Sentimiento, tu*, which contains his huge bolero hit "Amada mia." Like all of this record, it's plenty romantic, even if it's not considered *salsa romántica*.

GENRE: ⊕ World/Puerto Rico. **RELEASED:** 1972, Fania. (Reissued 2006.) **KEY TRACKS:** "Anacaona," "Piensa en ti," "Mi triste problema," "Medianoche y sol." **CATALOG CHOICES:** *Sentimiento, tu; Estampas.* **NEXT STOP:** Roberto Roena y Su Apollo Sound: *4.* **AFTER THAT:** Marc Anthony: *Contra la corriente.*

The Prehistory of a Master Vocalist

El sentimiento, la voz, y la guitarra

Jose Feliciano

rom his earliest performing opportunities, the blind singer and guitarist Jose Feliciano sought crossover success. While attending high school in the Bronx, the Puerto Rico–born musician spent his evenings sitting in at

Greenwich Village folk clubs (such as Gerde's Folk City, where he was discovered). He eventually dropped out of school, signed with RCA Records in 1964, and on his first recordings, he sings the gimmicky "Hi-Heeled Sneakers" and "Everybody Do the Click" and other pop songs, in English.

Shortly after that, Feliciano changed course, focusing on the pathos-filled ballads and folk songs he'd heard as a youngster. He made a series of recordings aimed at the Latin market, sung in Spanish, which are not his best-known titles—but in terms of pure vocal expression, works like *El sentimiento, la voz, y la guitarra* rank among his finest. Where the early novelty hits feel forced (if not totally contrived), these tunes show an exquisite sense of timing. After the slow, shoe-gazing tempo of "Sin luz" settles in, for example, Feliciano uses slight inflections and curlicue turns to conjure an idyllic courtship scene—he's the ardent young man cooing

Feliciano was born blind because of congenital glaucoma.

softly to [...] guitar in t[...]

Felic[...] fortable si[...] the maste[...] [...] language: All he has to do is launch a pained line, and the choked-up tone of his voice amplifies the feeling. *El sentimiento* suggests Feliciano was wise to seek his roots: Once he got control of the unhurried boleros and undulating *son montuno* rhythms that are the cornerstones of Latin pop, he became the rare singer who could transform any old song of seduction (like the Doors' "Light My Fire," his biggest hit) into a captivating, highly personal plea.

GENRE: 🎵 Vocals. RELEASED: 1967, RCA. KEY TRACKS: "La copa rota," "Lagrimas negras." CATALOG CHOICE: *Alive Alive O,* Vol. 1. NEXT STOP: Beny Moré: *Y hoy como ayer.* AFTER THAT: Sergio Mendes: *Sergio Mendes and Brasil '66.*

Narvel the Marvel

Drift Away:
The Best of Narvel Felts, 1973–1979

Narvel Felts

66 "When Your Good Love Was Mine," one of the early hits on this collection of gems from unjustly forgotten country singer Narvel Felts, starts out mildly enough—with a kicky little Nashville beat, and some dancing pedal-steel guitar from veteran Lloyd Green. The first eight bars of the verse are nothing special either: It's another song about a guy looking back, remembering a sweet love that's gone. And then, right around bar ten, the band starts to stir. Felts gives his silvery voice some wings, and suddenly we're inside a big reverb-laden Righteous Brothers production—the urgent sound of classic pop circa the mid-'60s. The beat gets more insistent, and by the time he hits the song's apex, Felts has transported his listeners from the lunch-bucket normalcy of Nashville into an exalted pop place.

n the string of (mostly dium-sized) hits represented here, Felts—whom Dolly Parton once called "the greatest voice in country music"—manages this trick repeatedly. Alternating between an authoritative baritone and a surprisingly agile falsetto (which he uses to great effect on "Reconsider Me"), the Missouri-born singer lifts up ordinary little clichés just by the emphasis he puts on some words. Felts was comfortable doing Elvis Presleyish rockabilly, humble gospel, and was particularly compelling singing soul. The great pleasures of this set include renditions of the Jackie Wilson smash "Lonely Teardrops" and the Dobie Gray

Narvel Felts is a member of the Rockabilly Hall of Fame.

title track. Felts drifted away in the late '70s after his backup band went on to become the supergroup Alabama. Since then, he's devoted himself to religious music and touring on the oldies circuit, where his still formidable voice can be heard singing these just plain great songs.

GENRE: 🌑 Country.
RELEASED: 1996, Bear Family. **KEY TRACKS:** "Drift Away," "When Your Good Love Was Mine," "Until the End of Time," "Lonely Teardrops," "To Love Somebody." **NEXT STOP:** Roy Orbison: *Mystery Girl.* **AFTER THAT:** Charlie Rich: *Behind Closed Doors* (see p. 644).

The World's Greatest Lullaby, and Then Some

Brahms: Lieder

Bernarda Fink

To see if these often-overlooked Brahms songs are your thing, start at the very end. That's where Argentine soprano Bernarda Fink interprets the most famous song the German composer ever wrote, "Wiegenlied," better known as the Brahms Lullaby. Though it's not technically demanding, the piece is nonetheless a formidable challenge to perform—that music-box theme is so fragile, the slightest extravagant gesture can yank it right out of the nursery.

Fink, who was initially discouraged by her family from pursuing a performance career, understands this. She treats "Wiegenlied" as a song, not a showpiece. Her radiant, smooth voice sets the tone, and she sails forth on calm seas, maintaining a mood of soothing intimacy. There are no opera-diva eruptions here—or, for that matter, anywhere on this set, which features Fink accompanied

by her frequent collaborator, pianist Roger Vignoles. Rather, Fink creates drama out of gentle, understated hues: Listening to "Old Love," for example, it's possible to pick up all sorts of mixed emotions in her reading of the line "There's a knock at my door but no one is outside." She begins with a tone of apprehension, which morphs into expectation, then a kind of wild hope. As on many of these pieces, Fink is theatrical in a sly, understated way.

A contemporary of the late Lorraine Hunt Lieberson (see p. 372), Fink is well equipped to bring Brahms's often demanding songs to a wider audience. The composer is known mostly for his hefty symphonies and instrumental works, but according to the *Grove Dictionary*, Brahms led a women's choir for a time, and between 1851 and 1886 published thirty-one volumes of songs—including 196 solo songs, duets, and small-scale choral works. Much of that material has been neglected by modern singers, who gravitate to his late *Four Serious Songs* or his lighter fare. With this collection, Fink gathers some of the most expansive pieces in Brahms's book—to hear the protean melodist at peak, cue up the haunting "Wie Melodien zieht es mir" and

"Von ewiger Liebe." Through her measured readings, Fink makes these feel as familiar, and as beautiful, as that ubiquitous lullaby.

GENRE: 🎼 Classical. **RELEASED:** 2007, Harmonia Mundi. **KEY TRACKS:** "Wiegenlied," "Wie Melodien zieht es mir," "Von ewiger Liebe." **ANOTHER INTERPRETATION:** *Deutsche Volkslieder,* Elisabeth Schwarzkopf. **CATALOG CHOICE:** *Canciones Argentinas.* **NEXT STOP:** Frida Leider: *Lebendige Vergangenheit.* **AFTER THAT:** Lorraine Hunt Lieberson: *Handel Arias.*

The Zen of Bach

J. S. Bach, Volume 1

Sergio Fiorentino

A few minutes into the Allemande movement of J. S. Bach's Partita No. 4 in D, Italian pianist Sergio Fiorentino deliberately slows things down. He's been moving in relatively orderly fashion through the chord sequence, dutifully visiting different keys in the cyclic fashion of so much great Bach music. Then, as if seized by a subversive thought, Fiorentino pauses ever so slightly. The next few lines creep along. They're more stately than what's come before as the pianist savors the shape of the line as well as individual glistening notes within it.

Fiorentino (1927–1998) was a master of Bach Zen, the ability to illuminate particularly beautiful parcels without losing the thread—and, crucially, the lyricism—of the overall theme. Similar exhibitions light up the two dance suites, or partitas, on this disc, which was recorded in 1996, shortly before Fiorentino's death.

In the Sarabande of Partita No. 1 in B Flat, there's a moment when the pianist, who's again been moving at a contemplative crawl, plays a magical sustained trill in the right hand while his left hand takes up what has

become an epic melodic quest. Fiorentino's bass notes have the same pearly fullness as his work in the higher registers, and when the hands switch back you find yourself almost sad that the bass, with its marvelous liquid legato, didn't get to lead the expedition a bit longer.

It is a minor miracle that recordings like this one exist. Fiorentino began his career in the 1950s, making his Carnegie Hall recital debut in 1953. The next year, he nearly died in an airplane crash; during his recovery he put his career on hold, and began teaching in his native Naples. Then, at age seventy-six he stopped teaching, and began concertizing again. This period yielded recordings of astonishing clarity and purpose, in which the understated pianist, true to Zen form, "sells" Bach without shouting, luring listeners into the microchip detail that makes Bach's picture so beautiful.

GENRE: 🎻 Classical. **RELEASED:** 1998, APR. **KEY TRACK:** Partita No. 4 in D. **CATALOG CHOICE:** Chopin Sonata No. 3, Schubert Sonata No. 21. **NEXT STOP:** Ludwig van Beethoven: Symphony No. 5 (transcribed for piano by Franz Liszt), Glenn Gould. **AFTER THAT:** Leif Ove Andsnes: *Horizons.*

Too Mind-Blowing for Alternative Rock Hipsters

Truth and Soul

Fishbone

A party band with a pronounced political streak, Fishbone came blazing out of South Central Los Angeles in the early 1980s with an audacious blend of funk, ska, R&B, and punk specially designed to jolt stoned suburban teens from their stupor. The six-piece was initially regarded as a wacky novelty—what else could a group of African American kids mixing hardcore punk and skittering island rhythms be? But after a few years of legendary performances, the Fishbone mind-meld took hold, and others started sniffing the possibilities. The band became pioneers of a new kind of rock, its frenzied double-time jitters and hazy ska paving the way for No Doubt and countless less imaginative skate-punk bands.

Spin magazine named *Truth and Soul* one of the most influential alternative rock albums of all time.

None of Fishbone's followers got anywhere near the warp-speed delirium evident on *Truth and Soul*, the band's second album. Referencing jolly circus-sideshow tunes, Sun Ra horn squalls, and utopia-minded psychedelic rock refrains, Fishbone tossed previously isolated musical ideas together, and used the resulting musical combustion as fuel. To hear this in action, check out "Bonin' in the Boneyard." It begins with a ripping up-tempo funk pulse that gets looser as it goes along, until the chorus erupts. And what a chorus: This gleeful sundazed "yeah, yeah" vocal chant carries the very DNA of rock and roll inside it. When the funk returns, there's no pronounced transition—instead the music just glides into the next gear and keeps rolling.

Truth and Soul begins with a cover of Curtis Mayfield's cautionary drug tale "Freddie's Dead." Every subsequent track visits a new locale, and each seems to draw on a different kind of renegade creativity: Sometimes Fishbone's overpowering musical muscle helps focus outrage about persistent racism ("Subliminal Fascism"), and sometimes a buoyant beat is used to lighten up a heavy subject like divorce ("Ma and Pa"). Fishbone was never able to transition from being the alt-rock daily special to headlining act, another instance of a great band being too hip even for hipsters.

GENRE: 🎸 Rock. **RELEASED:** 1988, Columbia. **KEY TRACKS:** "Ma and Pa," "Freddie's Dead," "Bonin' in the Boneyard," "Subliminal Fascism," "Ghetto Soundwave." **CATALOG CHOICE:** *The Reality of My Surroundings.* **NEXT STOP:** The Roots: *The Roots Come Alive.* **AFTER THAT:** Los Amigos Invisibles: *Arepa 3000* (see p. 19).

The Start of Ella's Songbook Legacy

Ella Fitzgerald Sings the Cole Porter Songbook

Ella Fitzgerald

Ella Fitzgerald was already the preeminent voice in the jazz world when she began what became her signature project in 1956: a series of recordings devoted to works by each of the great stage and screen composers of postwar America. The first of these, *Sings the Cole Porter Songbook,* is a dream pairing of singer and song. Not only does it bubble over with the lucid phrasing and childlike playfulness that made Fitzgerald so beloved, it presents Porter's songs (from such musicals as *Can Can; Red, Hot, and Blue;* and *Anything Goes*) as a compelling body of work, to be appreciated apart from the narrative of a show. The songbooks were hits collections, in a sense, teaching millions about the legendary musical theater composers.

Norman Grantz, the jazz impresario who spearheaded the project, explained in the liner notes to a Fitzgerald boxed set that "the concept of the songbook required that the songs and the performance had to have equal weight. Ella was of course the best singer. But the songs had to be just as important." All thirty-two selections on the Cole Porter set fulfill Grantz's vision.

"Lady Ella" was awarded 13 Grammys over the course of her career.

Fitzgerald illuminates the shapely contours of Porter's melodies with understated elegance, and a technique that's almost transparent. She leans into Porter's inventive secondary themes as they float into different keys and moods, and approaches the tunes not as a jazz showoff but as a faithful interpreter. As on the many songbooks that followed this one, Fitzgerald varies the backing: She sings with just piano accompaniment on "Miss Otis Regrets"; works with guitarist Barney Kessel and a rhythm section for "I Concentrate on You"; fronts a big band, arranged by Buddy Bregman, for several jaunty, whirling toe-tappers (among them a definitive reading of "Easy to Love"); and somehow manages to keep schmaltz at bay when singing with a studio orchestra on "I Love Paris."

GENRES: 🎤 Vocals 🎵 Jazz. **RELEASED:** 1956, Verve. **KEY TRACKS:** "I Concentrate on You," "I Get a Kick out of You," "Easy to Love." **CATALOG CHOICES:** *Ella Fitzgerald Sings the Jerome Kern Songbook; Sings the Duke Ellington Songbook.* **NEXT STOP:** *Sarah Vaughan Sings the George Gershwin Songbook,* Vol. 1.

Ella and Louis

Ella Fitzgerald and Louis Armstrong

L egend has it that Louis Armstrong pioneered scat singing when, during a recording session in the late 1920s, he dropped a page of sheet music and insisted on continuing. Without the score, he ended up dishing impromptu vocal phrases in the general vicinity of the melody. Armstrong's accidental innovation became a cornerstone of jazz, a way for singers to participate in its on-the-fly invention.

Armstrong might have been the first, but Ella Fitzgerald was arguably the best of the scat singers. Her sly approach to phrasing—that poised, balletic grace, the impetuous streak that kept accompanists guessing—became the standard for vocal improvisation. No matter how technically tricky Fitzgerald's ideas were (if transcribed, some would look downright daunting), they sail out as breezy, off-the-top-of-the-head ramblings.

This 1956 meeting, which features the Oscar Peterson Trio, catches both singers in peak form, with the gravel-voiced Armstrong ambling

Ella and Louis: two of the most influential jazz singers of the 20th century.

as Fitzgerald flits around, birdlike and carefree in the upper atmosphere. The deliciously slow tempos allow each singer to stretch such familiar melodies as "The Nearness of You" well beyond the routine. Neither strives to impress. Nobody tries to reinvent the wheel. Instead, Fitzgerald and Armstrong banter and jive delightfully, enjoying what happens when everyone in the studio is locked into that pure joy frequency: The magic just emerges, all by itself.

GENRES: 🎤 Vocals 🎵 Jazz. **RELEASED:** 1956, Verve. **KEY TRACKS:** "Tenderly," "The Nearness of You," "Stars Fell on Alabama." **CATALOG CHOICE:** *Ella and Louis Again.* **NEXT STOP:** *Ray Charles and Betty Carter.*

"The First Time Ever I Saw Your Face"

Roberta Flack

T he canvas is almost blank when Roberta Flack begins "The First Time Ever I Saw Your Face." There's barely a discernible tempo—activity, such as it is, comes from idling acoustic guitar chords. A bass creeps in, and Flack drops little sprinklings of piano ornamentation on top. The lullaby mood changes when she begins to sing: Suddenly what had been a neutral atmosphere is flipped into something stately, pensive, almost regal. Flack captures Scottish songwriter and playwright Ewan MacColl's recollection of love with a quiet, and very internal, lucidity. It's as if she's talking to herself, remembering, with a kind of awed reverence, someone extraordinary.

A former junior high school teacher, Flack recorded "The First Time" on her debut, *First Take.* The album drew positive notices from jazz critics—Flack was "discovered" by organist Les McCann, and the album included a sassy reading of his "Compared to What" as well as two Donny Hathaway songs. But it sold little until Clint Eastwood put "The First Time" into his film *Play Misty for Me.* That essentially

Roberta Flack's "The First Time . . ." reached #1 on the *Billboard* Hot 100.

kick-started Flack's career: The song hit number one in early 1972, lifting the album to the top of the charts for five weeks. Flack then made several strong albums, each with at least one transfixing ballad—the best known is "Killing Me Softly with His Song," a monster hit in 1973. The subsequent recordings are pleasant showcases for Flack's serene easygoingness, her ability to improvise without relying on showbiz dazzle. But "The First Time" stands apart: So slow it'd never get a chance on the radio today, it's the rare song that makes time stand still.

GENRE: 🎙 R&B. **RELEASED:** 1969, Atlantic. **APPEARS ON:** *First Take* and all her hits collections. **CATALOG CHOICES:** *Roberta Flack and Donny Hathaway; Killing Me Softly.* **NEXT STOP:** Anita Baker: *Rapture* (see p. 39). **AFTER THAT:** The Fugees: *The Score* (see p. 292).

A Spoonful Weighs a Ton

The Soft Bulletin

The Flaming Lips

On "The Spiderbite Song," one of fourteen symphonic pop triumphs on *The Soft Bulletin,* singer Wayne Coyne speculates about poison traveling through the body after a toxic bite. It's odd and fantastical, and like many

earlier Flaming Lips songs, more than a touch preposterous. It's also based on a true story: Lips drummer Steven Drozd suffered from exactly this sort of bite, and was facing amputation when medication finally got the reaction under control.

The reality-bites bent of that song prevails throughout *The Soft Bulletin,* which is quite possibly the most beautiful pop record of the 1990s. In the past, Coyne was known for his far-

flung high-concept tales of space travel. This time, he goes there only once or twice, choosing instead to tackle real-life stuff—the need for love, ordinary folks struggling and triumphing over adversity, the human desire to make some sense of existence. The Lips had been through a rough patch before embarking on this record. Guitarist Ronald Jones went off on a spiritual journey and never came back. And bassist Michael Ivins had been in a bizarre hit-and-run accident that required a long recuperation. (Coyne wrote about that, too, in another verse of "The Spiderbite Song.")

Though rooted to the earth, the songs of *The Soft Bulletin* are nonetheless lavishly dressed, and meticulous in their details. Most unfold at a methodical, majestic pace, with a sense of grandeur that recalls Pink Floyd circa *Wish You Were Here*. The basic trio is bolstered by an active orchestra, which frequently serves as a character or another "voice" rather than nondescript backdrop. Unlike most alt-rockers, Coyne and his crew think in sprawling floor-to-ceiling mosaics, and when that bigness surrounds Coyne's yearn-

The Soft Bulletin's cover art is an altered version of a 1966 *Life* magazine photo from an article on LSD.

ing voice, as happens on the anthemic "What Is the Light?," the beatifically dazed "Suddenly Everything Has Changed," and the glorious confection "Race for the Prize," it's a sound as magical as any in music.

GENRE: 🎸 Rock.
RELEASED: 1999, Warner Bros. **KEY TRACKS:** "Race for the Prize," "A Spoonful Weighs a Ton," "The Spiderbite Song," "What Is the Light?," "The Observer," "Waitin' for a Superman." **CATALOG CHOICE:** *Yoshimi Battles the Pink Robots.* **NEXT STOP:** Pink Floyd: *Wish You Were Here.* **AFTER THAT:** Frank Zappa and the Mothers: *Overnight Sensation.*

If You Like the Beverly Hillbillies *Theme, You'll Love This*

Foggy Mountain Jamboree

Lester Flatt, Earl Scruggs, and the Foggy Mountain Boys

Lester Flatt (1914–1979) and Earl Scruggs (born 1924) were the great evangelists of bluegrass. Guitarist and singer Flatt and banjo picker Scruggs wrote brisk, accessible tunes in the style of former employer and bluegrass patriarch Bill Monroe (see p. 513). After leaving Monroe in 1948, they developed a more extroverted, upbeat approach to the music, and with the help of a crack band they called the Foggy Mountain Boys, set out to take bluegrass to a wider audience. The group recorded a series of singles first for Mercury and then Columbia that spotlight Flatt's guileless voice complemented by fleet instrumental interplay. They became regulars at the Grand Ole Opry and on radio, exposure that helped the group's profile grow over several generations. Flatt and Scruggs were there when the folk revival of the late '50s increased interest in roots styles. Then in 1962, they were heard (and

seen) on network television, when they were hired to write "The Ballad of Jed Clampett," the theme of *The Beverly Hillbillies*. They made occasional appearances on the show, playing themselves.

This album, the first Flatt and Scruggs title for Columbia, collects singles recorded between 1951 and 1955 and produced in Nashville by veteran Don Law. These feature several Foggy Mountain lineups that are now considered "dream teams" of bluegrass: bassist Jody Rainwater, mandolinist Curly Seckler, fiddlers Paul Warren and Chubby Wise, and several guitarists (including, for a short time, the young Chet Atkins).

Jamboree alternates between vocal and instrumental tracks; it begins with "Flint Hill Special," one of several examples of a Flatt and Scruggs trademark, that controlled quick-stepping pace anchored by staggeringly complex banjo patterns. There are, naturally, more contemplative moments—the sad ballads that were a Monroe specialty, as well as songs of praise (more of these are available on the equally amazing *Foggy Mountain Gospel*). Seek this out to hear one of bluegrass's most unified ensembles tearing through barn burners and sorrowful laments, each brought to life with reverence, and no extra fanfare.

GENRE: ◯ Country. **RELEASED:** 1957, Columbia. **KEY TRACKS:** "Flint Hill Special," "It Won't Be Long," "Foggy Mountain Special," "Your Love Is Like a Flower," "Reunion in Heaven." **COLLECTOR'S NOTE:** The 2005 reissue, which has a much cleaner remastering job than previous CD versions, also includes three bonus tracks, including the great "Dear Old Dixie." **CATALOG CHOICE:** *Foggy Mountain Gospel.* **NEXT STOP:** Bill Monroe: *The Music of Bill Monroe* (see p. 513). **AFTER THAT:** Nashville Bluegrass Band: *Waitin' for the Hard Times to Go.*

British Chamber Blues

Then Play On

Fleetwood Mac

A case can be made for Fleetwood Mac as the most important band in rock history. The quintet led by drummer Mick Fleetwood and bassist John McVie made an impact in two distinct eras, first as one of the leading acts of the British blues-rock explosion of the 1960s, and then, with a different lineup, as purveyors of sun-kissed California pop in the mid-'70s. That second period, epitomized by *Rumours*, was when the band hit commercial paydirt; its several hit albums brought joy to millions, and bankrolled experiments *(Tusk)* that pushed pop toward a grandeur few have attempted. Between these two towering peaks are a handful of near-classics, like the gloomy and downcast *Bare Trees* or the pop-leaning *Heroes Are Hard to Find.* Think about other rock bands who've had productive second acts: Very few have left this much rewarding—and remarkably varied—music behind.

Then Play On is the last Fleetwood Mac album featuring founding member Peter Green.

The elegant *Then Play On* is one masterpiece of the early, blues-leaning incarnation of Fleetwood Mac. But it's hardly a typical blues record. It's more like chamber music with blues undertones, played by white Brits who walk in the shadow of the Beatles and understand that their version of the blues will not have the rhythmic drive of, say, anything on Chess records. At times, this music does strive for the urgent propulsion of great blues—on guitarist Peter Green's "Show-Biz Blues," it takes only hand claps and tambourines to get the revival tent rocking. "Rattlesnake Shake" is even more minimal—just a serrated-edge rhythm guitar triggers each vocal eruption. But it's not all party time, as there's a deep vein of contemplative music here: Danny Kirwan's tunes are cast in lachrymose tones, which invoke the blues as more a feeling than a sound. Among Kirwan's contributions is a stately instrumental, "My Dream," that unfolds like a series of secretive diary entries.

Some critics say *Then Play On* missed reaching its potential audience because it didn't swagger enough, didn't go where other blues-rockers (notably John Mayall's *Blues Breakers;* see p. 484) were going. But that's also its strength. These are thoughtful, often fragile songs. They're governed by understate-ment, filled with taciturn gestures played by a group of musicians who are more intent on creating a collective effect than a great solo. In a way, *Then Play On* is a last gasp of hippie idealism. Not long after this, the Me Decade pursuit of individual glory began.

GENRE: 🎸 Rock. **RELEASED:** 1969, Warner Bros. **KEY TRACKS:** "Closing My Eyes," "Show-Biz Blues," "My Dream," "Oh Well." **CATALOG CHOICES:** *Bare Trees; Heroes Are Hard to Find.* **NEXT STOP:** Ten Years After: *Shhhh.* **AFTER THAT:** Savoy Brown: *Raw Sienna.*

The Steps That Led to Rumours

Fleetwood Mac

Fleetwood Mac

The Meeting, as it is known in Fleetwood Mac lore, took place over margaritas. Drummer Mick Fleetwood and bassist John McVie had been kicking around Los Angeles in search of a new guitar player, and had invited a young guitarist and songwriter, Lindsey Buckingham, and his then-girlfriend Stevie Nicks to have a drink. Fleetwood had been listening to *Buckingham Nicks,* the duo's sparkling debut, and he wanted to hire Buckingham as a guitarist. He sensed that Buckingham could take Fleetwood Mac away from the vaguely spacey music (see *Bare Trees,* from 1972) that the band had made with just-departed guitarists Bob Welch and Danny Kirwan.

Buckingham was interested, but insisted that Nicks be included as well; Nicks joined Christine McVie, then John's wife, in a vocal blend that became the

Fleetwood Mac's most commercially successful lineup: clockwise from left—Lindsey Buckingham, Mick Fleetwood, Christine McVie, John McVie, and Stevie Nicks.

Mac's new trademark. The group singing wiped away any lingering blues traces from previous Mac incarnations, replacing them with California sunshine. After revamping "Crystal" from *Buckingham Nicks,* the individual members wrote new songs with the expansive harmonies in mind. The hit-making incarnation of Fleetwood Mac was born.

The history books say that this band peaked with *Rumours,* the 1975 internecine romance chronicle that became one of the top-selling albums of all time. Certainly *Rumours* is accomplished. It's also a tad too straightforward—the refrains are pleasant in a nondemanding way, the rhythms patter unobtrusively around in house-coat and slippers. *Fleetwood Mac*, by contrast, burns a little bit. "World Turning" surrounds an ageless blues cry with crackling banjo lines, while "I'm So Afraid" and "Landslide" look at vulnerability from different angles. "Rhiannon," the best of Nicks's witch-goddess odes, moves through time with paranormal grace.

Also well worth tracking down is *Buckingham Nicks*. In some ways a template for *Fleetwood Mac*, it's filled with low-key ruminations featuring two people who find thrills singing in close harmony. The album's performances are intimate, yet as is true of everything Buckingham touches, poised and methodical—qualities not usually associated with debut records made on shoestring budgets. Despite petitions from devoted fans, it has never been issued digitally in the United States. That's wrong: This is one quiet gem that deserves to see daylight again.

GENRE: 🎸 Rock. **RELEASED:** 1975, Warner Bros. **KEY TRACKS:** "Crystal," "Landslide," "World Turning," "I'm So Afraid." **BUYER BEWARE:** In recent years, unscrupulous sellers have flooded the Internet with noisy vinyl-to-CD transfers of *Buckingham Nicks*. **CATALOG CHOICES:** *Bare Trees; Rumours*. **NEXT STOP:** Steely Dan: *Can't Buy a Thrill*. **AFTER THAT:** Bread: *The Best of Bread*.

The Piano Map of Cuban Music

Musica original de Cuba

Frank Emilio Flynn

In 1959, the blind pianist Frank Emilio Flynn (1921–2001) recorded a collection of *danzóns*, the Afro-Cuban adaptation of classical dance styles (minuet, waltz, mazurka) brought to Cuba by the French in the early nineteenth century. The Cuban government funded the sessions, and the album, *Danzas y danzóns de Cuba*, on the esteemed Sonotone label, became a part of the permanent collection of the Cuban History Museum. Although it was forgotten in the political upheaval happening at the time of its creation, it returned to circulation with additional material in 2006, as *Musica original de Cuba*.

Danzas was just another session for Flynn, the classically trained pianist whose career path winds through most of the consequential music of modern Cuba. But it's a key puzzle-piece, clarifying the con-

Frank Emilio Flynn taught himself to play the piano when he was 10.

nection between the lovely melodies of the *danzón* and the more exploratory dance styles—*son*, rumba, etc.—that evolved from it. As an integral part of Ignacio Piñeiro's Septeto Nacional and the band of *sonero* Miguel Matamoros, Flynn learned to satisfy demanding Cuban dancers, and when he struck out on his own in the late 1950s, he maintained the same attention to steady, delicately swinging rhythm. His bands were, however, bent on exploration; their understated yet remarkably vital rhythm helped establish the tone and aesthetic perimeters of Cuban jazz.

This set captures Flynn's sprightly pianistic style, which assimilates ragtime chords and Cuban folklore and French dances into something timeless and uniquely Cuban. It's piano-bar music for a detective caper set in Old Havana—wistful and vaguely sad, defined by tenderness but informed by an awareness of the world's evils.

GENRE: 🌐 World/Cuba. **RELEASED:** 1959, Sonotone. (Reissued 2005.) **KEY TRACKS:** "Tres lindas Cubanas," "Virgen de Regla," "La belleza," "El canon." **CATALOG CHOICE:** *Tribute to Ernesto Lecuona.* **NEXT STOP:** Noro Morales: *His Piano and Rhythm.* **AFTER THAT:** George Shearing: *Latin Lace/Latin Affair.*

Harmony So Square It Was Hip

The Four Freshmen and Five Trombones

The Four Freshmen

Anything can be hip, anything can be square. Consider, for example, this curiously great document from the Four Freshmen. To one generation, it's nice easy listening. To another, it's a creamed-corn stain on an expensive white linen shirt. One jazzer might think "squaresville," and another might hear these limpid, empathetic vocals as pure quiet sophistication, the gentle and confiding empathy sought by such memorable singers as Chet Baker (see p. 40).

There may never be a cure for rampant hipsterism, but the next time you want to try to tame the arrogant smugness within, put this on and see if you might find something valid in it. There's certainly lots going on: sumptuous vocal blends running the gamut from well-scrubbed unisons to neatly pressed four-part harmonies, conveying tightly drawn and highly specific emotions. On this program of standards and show tunes, the four voices slide and weave, changing the chordal character of the tune as the interior voices resolve. (To hear a particularly agile example, listen to the lively, shape-shifting reharmonization of the oft-neglected "I Remember You.")

This album is one of several the group did with specific themed backing (one CD reissue pairs this with the more blaring *Five Trumpets* effort). It's the best of them, and one of the great underappreciated records of the transitional period during the middle '50s when pop and rock were on opposite trajectories. Brian Wilson, the songwriter and architect of the Beach Boys' sound, has often acknowledged borrowing ideas for his group's vocal blend from the Freshmen. You don't have to listen closely to pick up that connection, but if you do listen closely, you'll hear dazzlingly choreographed vocals, delivered with a swooning sincerity that seems almost alien in this age of machine-gun brashness. Which, to one way of thinking, might qualify the Frosh as "hip."

GENRE: 🎤 Vocals. **RELEASED:** 1956, Capitol. (Reissued 1998, Collector's Choice.) **KEY TRACKS:** "I Remember You," "Angel Eyes," "Speak Low," "Guilty." **CATALOG CHOICE:** *The Four Freshmen in Person.* **NEXT STOP:** The Hi-Lo's: *And All That Jazz.* **AFTER THAT:** The Mills Brothers: *The Anthology.*

The Tops of the Tops

Anthology

The Four Tops

According to one axiom of the middle 1960s, if you listened to the radio long enough, sooner or later a Four Tops song would come on. Since the dawn of satellite radio in 2001, that wait time has been significantly reduced. On an average summer Saturday in 2005, the great pleading Tops single "Bernadette" appeared at least three times within six hours on Sirius—in the music mix of a classic soul channel, an interview with rocker Graham Parker on an alt-rock station, and during Kid Leo's show on the Underground Garage.

That says plenty about the Tops, the most exuberant of Motown hit-makers. The Detroit quartet—which retained the same personnel for four decades—made drop-dead incredible singles, and totally underwhelming filler-filled albums. The rousing and galvanic "Same Old Song," "I Can't Help Myself (Sugar Pie Honey Bunch)," and "Bernadette" can't be labeled "soul" or "pop" or "rock"— they're an amalgamation of all that and more, set to hot-rodding four-on-the-floor rhythm. Key to the enterprise is singer Levi Stubbs,

From left: Lawrence Payton, Levi Stubbs, Abdul Fakir, and Renaldo Benson.

whose urgent declarations have inspired critical rhapsodies, and at least one great song of homage, Billy Bragg's "Levi Stubbs' Tears."

Recalling the Four Tops' heyday, songwriter Brian Holland—part of the Holland/Dozier/Holland team responsible for many Four Tops hits— said that after "I Can't Help Myself" was finished in 1965, he and a girlfriend listened to a test pressing of the song "three to four hundred times" in the course of a weekend. That's one amazing thing about the Tops: You can hear the same old song over and over again, and never get tired of it.

GENRE: 🎙 R&B. **RELEASED:** 2004, Motown. **KEY TRACKS:** "Same Old Song," "Bernadette." **NEXT STOP:** The Supremes: *Anthology*. **AFTER THAT:** Isley Brothers: *3+3*.

Enter OK, Leave KO'd

The Rough Guide to Franco

Franco and TPOK Jazz

The fleet-fingered Congolese guitarist and singer known as Franco (1938–1989) released over 150 albums in his four-decade career, and was said to have written over a thousand songs. Despite the fact that Franco (real name:

François Luambo Makiadi) was one of the biggest African stars in the world from the early 1970s until his death, very little of the music he made with his band OK Jazz (later called TPOK Jazz, for "Tout Puissant," meaning "Almighty") is consistently available in the U.S. That's an outrage, because this extra-large three-hundred-pound-plus "Sorcerer" has much to offer the six-string obsessed. And his band, which in the 1980s swelled to over thirty musicians, is essential listening for those even casually interested in African dance music.

Franco played with a hard, metallic attack, and an almost physical force—at times it sounds like he's shoving people out of the way, or pushing his musicians deeper into the groove. And yet his wiry and agile melody lines rarely dominate the spotlight. They're more like sidecars, running along in tandem with and occasionally jabbing at the vocal themes sung in Lingala. Franco does solos—notably on "Mario," a parable about a gigolo in Europe—but he's also a master of arpeggio patterns, one of the rare guitarists who can mesmerize by playing the same thing over and over.

Given the limited offerings, the twelve-song *Rough Guide to Franco* is a great place to start exploring. A career survey, it starts with early recordings from the late 1950s and early '60s—which show Franco gamely re-Africanizing Cuban rumba, then the rage in much of West Africa. The band gets good at smoothing and animating that pulse, until, by the middle '70s, the groove becomes wholly African. The later works are even more interesting, as they show Franco leading his massive, well rehearsed band through marathon commentaries on social problems. (A characteristic tune, "Beware of AIDS," warns listeners of the disease that would eventually kill him.)

Several of the extended pieces contain a pivot-point known in Congolese music as *sabene*. It's the moment when the allegory is finished and the emphasis shifts to the dance floor, and Franco makes the most of it. He pushes his band ever higher, creating tension by repeating verses, and then he and the other guitarists erupt, rewarding the anticipation with shimmering, elegant guitar conversations. These last for glorious minutes on end. Churning and spinning toward rapture, the band makes its hyperbolic motto—"Enter OK, leave KO'd"—a reality.

GENRE: 🌐 World/Congo. **RELEASED:** 2001, Rough Guides/World Music Network. **KEY TRACKS:** "Mario," "Aya la' Mode," "Tailleur," "Attention Na Sida." **CATALOG CHOICE:** *Live en Hollande.* **NEXT STOP:** Pepe Kalle: *Gigantafrique!* (see p. 417). **AFTER THAT:** Various Artists: *Guitar Paradise of East Africa.*

The Queen of Soul

I Never Loved a Man the Way I Love You

Aretha Franklin

The beginning of Aretha Franklin's "Respect" is one of those pop-culture moments that's been played so often it barely registers anymore. Pay attention next time, because it remains a head-swiveling hall-of-fame entrance. Before she even utters a word, you can feel Franklin rearing back, gathering momentum for the knockout punch. When she actually delivers the challenge of that first line—"What you want, baby, I got it"—she connects with devastating force. The urgency in her voice serves notice to all that someone special has arrived.

Propelled by the gritty Muscle Shoals rhythm section (and her own terse piano chording), Franklin is out to flatten all doubt about her prowess as a lover while, crucially, collecting her "propers" as a woman. It takes her about half a verse to accomplish that; for the rest of this three-minute throwdown, she sings at the top of her range, stringing together jaw-droppingly brilliant ad-libs like a boxer who doesn't know when to stop hitting.

"Respect" was written and originally sung by Otis Redding (see p. 636). Franklin's version, recorded during her first sessions for Atlantic Records, leans a bit harder on the message—she sings it both as a broad affirmation of self-worth and a warning. Woe to the man who does not appreciate this woman. The song not only hit the top of the R&B and pop charts, it became a cultural touchstone,

Franklin performing at New York's Madison Square Garden in 1968.

invoked by feminists and those involved in the civil rights movement, among others.

"Respect," track one on Franklin's Atlantic Records debut, is the song that propelled her to the throne marked "Queen of Soul." The remaining material on this album, which is often described as the greatest soul album of all time, helped her stay there. Franklin follows the radioactive hit with a steady, remarkably poised version of Ray Charles's "Drown in My Own Tears," then personalizes the confessional title track and several Southern soul standbys ("Do Right Woman, Do Right Man") before closing with Sam Cooke's prayerful "A Change Is Gonna Come." All of it vibrates with the heady intensity Franklin summons in the opening seconds of "Respect."

GENRE: 🎤 R&B.
RELEASED: 1967, Atlantic.
KEY TRACKS: "Respect," "A Change Is Gonna Come," "Drown in My Own Tears," "Do Right Woman, Do Right Man."
CATALOG CHOICE: *Lady Soul.* **NEXT STOP:** Ruth Brown: *Miss Rhythm* (see p. 123).
AFTER THAT: Candi Staton: *I'm Just a Prisoner.*

Sunday Morning with the Queen

Amazing Grace

Aretha Franklin

Aretha Franklin grew up in church, and from her earliest torch-song recordings (collected on Columbia's excellent *Jazz to Soul* anthology) through hits like "Respect" and "Spanish Harlem," she sang as though trying to rouse listeners from a Sunday-services slumber. This was no accident: Her father, the celebrated Detroit churchman Reverend C. L. Franklin, brought home such friends as Sam Cooke, who began his career in gospel before crossing over to soul stardom. Franklin told biographer David Ritz that she learned the secrets of phrasing sitting in the family room.

Aretha Franklin at a press conference on March 26, 1973.

In 1972 after a string of hits, Franklin took the first of many detours, putting her pop career on hold to make *Amazing Grace*, a two-disc live compendium of gospel classics. Following Cooke's example, the fiery mezzo-soprano doesn't change anything about her delivery, applying the formidable lung power she displayed on "Respect" to songs of faith, gratitude, and praise. Franklin's steady, authoritative phrasing galvanizes her accomplices: On the choir warhorse "How

I Got Over," Franklin sends the members of the Southern California Community Choir into a euphoric overdrive they somehow sustain throughout this two-hour affair. Her father, known in his day as the "Million Dollar Voice," is on hand to provide benedictions, but it's daughter Aretha's billion-dollar voice—an instrument that's both steely in its resolve and Silly-Putty supple—that does most of the rousing. This is still the best example of an R&B singer going back to her "roots" to sing gospel.

GENRE: ✝ Gospel. RELEASED: 1972, Atlantic. KEY TRACKS: "How I Got Over," "Amazing Grace." CATALOG CHOICE: *Live at the Fillmore West.* NEXT STOP: Elvis Presley: *Ultimate Gospel.* AFTER THAT: Sam Cooke and the Soul Stirrers: *The Gospel Soul of Sam Cooke with the Soul Stirrers.*

These Are the Songs That Made Honky-Tonk Mainstream

Look What Thoughts Can Do

Lefty Frizzell

William Orville "Lefty" Frizzell (1928–1975) entered a recording studio for the first time in 1950, to cut a carefree tune he'd written called "If You've Got the Money, I've Got the Time." The version was intended as a demo, to show Frizzell's skills, but Columbia Records liked the performance enough to put it out as a single, and by October of that year it reached number 2 on the country charts. This began an incredible couple of years in which Frizzell generated a string of hits. At one point in October 1951, the son of a traveling oil driller, who grew up in boom-and-bust oil towns, had four singles in the country Top 10 at the same time.

Frizzell sang with no affectation, and made no attempt to hide (or play up) his drawl—he sounded like an ordinary guy and wrote ordinary-guy songs, many of them about having a good time on a Saturday night. These established him as a poet of the honky-tonks, someone who could even make the grooming involved in getting ready for a date sound enchanted. When he wasn't painting the town, Frizzell also sang convincingly about home, and the redeeming love of a devoted woman. These pieces, which depend on his steady guitar accompaniment, are not always as straightforward as they seem: The early "I Love You a Thousand Ways" is mostly an earnest expression of devotion, with traces of guilt and regret creeping into the narrative as it goes along.

This anthology collects all of Frizzell's early singles, including the essay in brooding magnificence entitled "Always Late (With Your Kisses)," one of the radio standbys from his peak year of 1951. These singles reached just about every kid with a Nashville dream; they're mentioned by such luminaries as Merle Haggard, George Jones, Willie Nelson, and Keith Whitley as important early influences. Frizzell faded from the front

Lefty with his signature guitar, a Paul Bigsby–customized 1949 Gibson J-200.

lines of country music after 1954, and though he continued to record had very few chart successes. He once attributed this to the common problem of "too much success too soon," a hard-luck tale that's all too familiar in the realm of honky-tonk country.

GENRE: ◉ Country.
RELEASED: 1997, Columbia.
KEY TRACKS: "If You've Got the Money, I've Got the Time," "Always Late (With Your Kisses)," "I Love You a Thousand Ways," "Look What Thoughts Will Do." **CATALOG CHOICES:** *Listen to Lefty; Songs of Jimmie Rodgers; Saginaw, Michigan.* **NEXT STOP:** Merle Haggard: *I'm a Lonesome Fugitive.* **AFTER THAT:** Willie Nelson: *To Lefty from Willie.*

Steady Diet of Ideology

Repeater

Fugazi

Like many self-styled punks of the late 1980s, Ian MacKaye of the seminal Washington, D.C., bands Minor Threat and Fugazi talked the ideological talk, railing about the evils of corporate music and the soul-rotting effects of consumer culture. But unlike many of his peers, who eventually went into business with major labels and compromised their values, MacKaye actually walked the walk. As both a musician and a label owner, he used all available business leverage to advocate what he thought best for his audiences. He insisted on cheap tickets (at the height of Fugazi's popularity, admission was usually $15, with no service charge) and cheap CDs, and no liquor or tobacco advertising.

MacKaye became more of a hero for his thinking—he pioneered the clean-living approach that came to be known as "straight-edge" within the hardcore punk community—than for the music his bands made. That's unfortunate, because when future generations look beyond the MacKaye media profile, they'll discover an iteration of punk that was both intelligent and thrilling, and far more original than many scenesters at the time recognized. Named for Vietnam-era GI slang (Fucked Up, Got Ambushed, Zipped In), Fugazi built an abrasive attack from two disciplined overlapping guitars (played by MacKaye and Guy Picciotto) and chanted taunts expressing varying levels of outrage. "Merchandise" is typical: Over an almost Neanderthal, gleefully mangled ska beat, MacKaye and company imagine themselves as evil shopkeepers, yelling the refrain, "We owe you nothing, you have no control."

Repeater was the first of 7 studio albums Fugazi released.

Repeater, the band's full-length debut, is American hardcore with energy to burn. Though the lyrics do tend to hit MacKaye's pet themes over and over (could that explain the title?), the music moves all over the place—as they progress, these wound-too-tight tunes touch dub reggae and island polyrhythm as well as scalding free jazz and four-on-the-floor rock. All of it feels guided by a strong sense of purpose, which might be the X factor missing from so much hardcore: When every other punk band was selling out and cashing in, Fugazi stayed true to its ideals. It didn't cave when it easily (and profitably) could have. Even in the soul-sucking music business, that oughta count for something.

GENRE: 🎵 Rock. **RELEASED:** 1990, Dischord. **KEY TRACKS:** "Turnover," "Merchandise," "Greed," "Sieve-Fisted Find." **CATALOG CHOICES:** Fugazi: *Steady Diet of Nothing*. Minor Threat: *Out of Step*. **NEXT STOP:** Rage Against the Machine: *Rage Against the Machine*. **AFTER THAT:** Bad Brains: *I Against I* (see p. 37).

Nudging Hip-Hop a Step or Two Toward Bob Marley Idealism

The Score

The Fugees

The Fugees came along during hip-hop's reign of thugs in the mid-'90s, and with the zingy, unapologetically accessible songs on this album offered respite from the steady diet of fantasy confrontations and senseless killings. This was overdue. And, at least to Lauryn Hill, Pras Michael, and Wyclef Jean, vitally important. The three New Jersey rappers saw firsthand the trickle-down effect happening in gangstaland: In songs suffused with sadness, the three imply that hip-hop's glorification of violence led to further waves of real-life violence. With great eloquence, they lament how

The Score, the Fugees breakthrough, has sold over 6 million copies in the U.S.

people—smart young black people who should know better—become dazzled by the glamour of gangsta life, and then, inevitably, find themselves in too deep.

This cycle of violence is just one topic of *The Score*, which is built on head-bobbing reggae, chopped-up beatbox syncopations, and unusual island rhythms. The Fugees talk black heritage and African identity, castigate police over racial profiling, and imagine a reasonable urban world where people sit and talk through their differences. Such notions don't sound so far-fetched when delivered by Lauryn Hill, whose trembling and easily outraged voice seems hell-bent on change. Wherever she is in the mix (and at times she's in the background), Hill nudges listeners in the direction of the moral high road, and like her hero Bob Marley (whose "No Woman No Cry" is covered passionately here), helps those prone to violence recognize their brutality.

The Score, which sold over six million copies, didn't change hip-hop. But its success did open up bandwidth for alternative viewpoints, and proved that rap devoted to subjects other than bloodlust could be viable. It helped create a climate in which enlightened ideas about race and education and the issues of urban America could get a hearing. Incredibly, it did this while entertaining people, its diatribes carried by irresistibly danceable music.

GENRE: 🎤 Hip-Hop. **RELEASED:** 1996, Ruffhouse. **KEY TRACKS:** "Fu-Gee-La," "Ready or Not," "The Beast," "Family Business," "No Woman No Cry." **CATALOG CHOICES:** Wyclef Jean: *Wyclef Jean Presents the Carnival.* Lauryn Hill: *The Miseducation of Lauryn Hill* (see p. 360). **NEXT STOP:** The Roots: *Rising Down.* **AFTER THAT:** De La Soul: *De La Soul Is Dead.*

The First Great Post-Hendrix Guitar Thang

Maggot Brain

Funkadelic

Every serious music collection needs at least one guitar solo that can stop a party in its tracks. Eddie Hazel's epic journey on the title track of this, the first great Funkadelic record, will do the trick. After an initial eruption of feedback and some ominous words about the maltreatment of Mother Earth, there's a gently plucked electric-guitar arpeggio reminiscent of the background part in "The House of the Rising Sun." Against this backdrop, Hazel enters with a pure single note, as though he's sending out sonar to see how deep the water goes. A few other isolated tones follow—Hazel is in no hurry, he maxes out every pitch-bending cry, fashioning an elegy. The quest lasts more than ten minutes, and by the end it feels like Hazel has

Maggot Brain starts with the line, "Mother Earth is pregnant for the third time, for y'all have knocked her up."

just delivered some profound and possibly majestic truth, a rousing sermon that affirms (and then subverts) everything worth cherishing about the ritual known as the rock guitar solo.

Maggot Brain was recorded in 1971, a period when many musicians were still grieving Jimi Hendrix, who'd died the previous year. Hazel, a veteran of George Clinton's various ensembles, was often described as a "Hendrix disciple." With this solo and his contributions to the rest of this album, Hazel steps away from that influence to claim his place among the greats. He makes the guitar speak his language, and presents a highly individual refinement of the teachings of Jimi. Hazel doesn't eclipse Hendrix, but instead shows that the great one's inspiration could mutate in countless potent ways.

The rest of *Maggot Brain* isn't exactly lightweight. There's a scalding bit of gospelized funk ("Can You Get to That") that shows how persuasive George Clinton could be as a singer. Also here is one of the great songs about interracial romance ("You and Your Folks, Me and My Folks"), a showcase for the hot-footed rhythm section ("Super Stupid"), and another extended romp ("Wars of Armageddon") that contains the seeds of the marathon Funkadelic jams to follow, most notably *One Nation Under a Groove* (1978). Created at a time when superlong jams were common, these Funkadelic workouts push the possibilities to the edge: If you follow Hazel's fitful and twisted path on "Maggot Brain," by the end, you will be a different person.

GENRE: 🎤 R&B. **RELEASED:** 1971, Westbound. **KEY TRACKS:** "Maggot Brain," "Wars of Armageddon," "Super Stupid." **CATALOG CHOICES:** Funkadelic: *One Nation Under a Groove*. Hazel: *Games, Dames, and Guitar Thangs*. **NEXT STOP:** Miles Davis: *Tribute to Jack Johnson*. **AFTER THAT:** Sonny Sharrock: *Ask the Ages* (see p. 693).

Peter Gabriel ✦ Serge Gainsbourg ✦ Rory Gallagher ✦
Gang of Four ✦ Jan Garbarek and Ralph Towner ✦ Carlos
Gardel ✦ Judy Garland ✦ Erroll Garner ✦ Djivan Gasparyan
✦ Marvin Gaye ✦ Genesis ✦ George Gershwin ✦ Stan Getz
and João Gilberto ✦ Gilbert and Sullivan ✦ Bebel Gilberto
✦ João Gilberto ✦ Dizzy Gillespie and His Orchestra ✦
The Jimmy Giuffre   Three ✦ Philip Glass
✦ Osvaldo Golijov   **G**   ✦ Gong ✦ Benny
Goodman and His   Orchestra ✦ Dexter
Gordon ✦ Henryk Górecki ✦ Gothic Voices with Emma
Kirkby ✦ Glenn Gould ✦ El Gran Combo de Puerto Rico
✦ The Grateful Dead ✦ Al Green ✦ Grant Green ✦ Green
Day ✦ Edvard Grieg and Robert Schumann ✦ Bessie Griffin
and the Gospel Pearls ✦ Juan Luis Guerra y 440 ✦ Guided
by Voices ✦ Guns N' Roses ✦ Woody Guthrie ✦ Buddy Guy

Peter Gabriel 3

Peter Gabriel

T he pop world wasn't quite ready to confront the inhumanity of apartheid in 1979, when Peter Gabriel wrote "Biko." Telling the story of South African journalist and activist Steve Biko, who died after sustaining head injuries during an interrogation, Gabriel helped change the climate a little—and in the process revived the then-moribund notion of the protest song. Under a steady martial drum cadence and a majestic, easily sung melody that linked arena rock spectacle and African spirituality, "Biko" became one of the first truly global political anthems. And it remains one of the best.

"Biko" is also the most humane, empathetic moment on *Peter Gabriel 3*, the third consecutive self-titled album from the British art-rocker. The album opens with a sirenlike shriek called "Intruder." That's followed by a mechanical cry of desperation, "No Self-Control," that has Gabriel, who first drew attention as a member of Genesis, making like a freaked-out robot whose circuits are frying. Lyrics throughout hint at simmering anger and despair under the surface of everyday interactions, and they bubble up in fractured bits of gibberish. One characteristically jarring piece, "Games Without Frontiers," transforms playground taunts into an extended metaphor about

geopolitical tension. The nine songs preceding "Biko" are as close to psychodrama as pop music gets, all sharp angles and heightened, sometimes terrifying moods. Then "Biko" kicks in, and its ceremonial grandeur offers a welcome respite. Shedding his arty obfuscations, Gabriel shares his vision for the end of apartheid with a bracing directness: "You can blow out a candle, but you can't blow out a fire," he sings. "Once the flame begins to catch, the wind will blow it higher." His passionate indignation caught on and became part of the global pressure on the racist South African government, eventually contributing to its demise.

GENRE: 🎸 Rock. **RELEASED:** 1980, Mercury. (Reissued 1983, Geffen.) **KEY TRACKS:** "Biko," "Not One of Us," "Games Without Frontiers." **CATALOG CHOICES:** *So; Passion: Music for* The Last Temptation of Christ. **NEXT STOP:** Sigur Rós: *Agætis Byrjun* (see p. 700). **AFTER THAT:** Waldemar Bastos: *Pretaluz* (see p. 51).

Histoire de Melody Nelson

Serge Gainsbourg

A concept album about taboo love, *Histoire de Melody Nelson* puts everything interesting about French pop sensualist Serge Gainsbourg (1928–1991) in one place. If the cover photo of a teenager clutching a doll is any indication, the object of his affection is a young beauty. The sound is orchestral, but there's also an intensely cooking, vaguely psychedelic rock rhythm section underneath. Its vocal schemes are the typical Gainsbourg pillow talk: He whispers through rambling, semierotic dreams of the girl, and she appears every now and then just to wistfully state her name—an audio apparition haunting his thoughts.

Serge Gainsbourg, born Lucien Ginsburg, didn't achieve success until his mid-30s.

The follow-up to Gainsbourg's biggest hit—the 1969 duet with Jane Birkin, "Je t'aime, moi non plus," a marvel of talk-singing with some heavy breathing thrown in—*Melody Nelson* is at once explicit and intentionally opaque, an inscrutable, multihued bedroom reverie that also glances at darker themes of obsession and drug abuse. It's brilliantly arranged, with the orchestra's contours muted just enough so that Gainsbourg's purring voice remains the focus. In the liner notes to a Gainsbourg compilation, the L.A. singer and songwriter Beck described the album as

"one of the greatest marriages of rock band and orchestra I've ever heard."

Beck was among the many pop scavengers bitten by the Gainsbourg bug in the 1990s. Hip-hop producers and electronic cut-and-paste wizards seized Gainsbourg's scenes, sometimes just to nab a suggestive phrase like "sixty-nine année erotique." Others, notably Stereolab and the electronic duo Air, emulated Gainsbourg's thick atmosphere, picking up on his ability to subsume all kinds of music (funk, rock, chanson, bossa nova) into a sound that's infinitely alluring and at the same time just slightly sleazy.

GENRES: 🎸 Rock 🎤 Vocals. **RELEASED:** 1971, Mercury. **KEY TRACKS:** "Melody," "Ballade de Melody Nelson." **CATALOG CHOICE:** *Love and the Beat,* Vols. 1 and 2. **NEXT STOP:** Stereolab: *Emperor Tomato Ketchup* (see p. 739). **AFTER THAT:** Air (French electronic duo): *Moon Safari.*

An Irish Blues-Rocker at His Apex

Irish Tour 1974

Rory Gallagher

Those who think they've heard it all in the realm of electric guitar are referred to the first two minutes of this album. Rory Gallagher comes onstage to raving applause—he was already a star in his native Ireland, and one of the few brave souls willing to tour the country during the bitter civil strife of the 1970s. He tunes his instrument quickly, sends out a few test signals, and then jumps into his original "Cradle Rock." What follows is solo-guitar machismo—ninety seconds of crowbar-like single-note attacks and flamboyant lunging

pitch-bends, followed by a Delta blues taunt that lets the band know it's time to go to work.

Even if you're immune to daredevil rock-guitar tricks, this is jaw-dropping stuff. Gallagher (1948–1995) was one of the few virtuosos who kept his considerable technical mastery in his back pocket, for emergency use only. When he lets loose, it's a real eruption, not stagecraft. On "Cradle Rock," "As the Crow Flies," and other songs on *Irish Tour 1974*—this uniformly thrilling collection drawn from concerts in Belfast, Dublin, and elsewhere—Gallagher's rhythm guitar has a strutting Aerosmith quality. Just when *that* seems to be his stock-in-trade, he'll turn around and drop a stupendous melody line that sounds like it was beamed from rock and roll heaven. And then he'll deliver another one until these phrases gather into an epic fable.

Gallagher built several originals on the blues, and was equally comfortable reaching back to a standard or two—this set features a steamrolling cover of Muddy Waters's "I Wonder Who" and a sorrowful reading of J. B. Hutto's "Too Much Alcohol." Where other rockers seize the blues as a chance to show off, Gallagher positively sings on the guitar, to the point where you wonder whether his fingers are even on the strings.

GENRE: 🎸 Rock. **RELEASED:** 1974, Buddah. **KEY TRACKS:** "Cradle Rock," "I Wonder Who," "Walk on Hot Coals," "Back on My Stompin' Ground (After Hours)," "As the Crow Flies." **CATALOG CHOICE:** *Live in Europe.* **NEXT STOP:** Peter Green: *The Peter Green Anthology.* **AFTER THAT:** Albert King: *Live.*

Highly Concentrated Punk Polemic

Entertainment!

Gang of Four

Scores of bands followed the Sex Pistols–led punk revolution. Very few of them ever made a record that's simultaneously as informed and enraged as Gang of Four's debut *Entertainment!* Here are essays on post-Marxism and materialism ("Damaged Goods" makes the case that accumulating stuff ends up killing the soul), as well as angry tirades against ruling-class society and withering critiques of nationalism ("Not Great Men"). Heard from the cushy confines of consumer culture thirty years on, some of the songs are downright prescient: "Natural's Not in It" begins with "The problem of leisure, what to do for pleasure."

"There has always been a misconception that we were just a bloody-minded bunch of miserable socialists intent on overturning society," bassist Dave Allen says in the liner notes of an anniversary edition. Instead, he argues, Gang of Four was really looking for alternatives. "We were questioning the herd mentality."

That questioning can be overt, but it often functions like a stealth bomb within the songs of *Entertainment!*—it's possible to enjoy the ragged forward thrust of the music without getting hung up on its rhetoric. That's because the four former Leeds University students embrace more musical diversity than many of their anarchy-minded peers. The rhythm section pumps out proud, unironic snatches of disco, dub reggae, and deep funk. They're hardly genius musicians, but as a group use worldly, slightly off-kilter rhythms to propel the commentary along. You might find yourself disagreeing with the Gang's polemics, but it's hard to argue with them when you're dancing.

GENRE: 🎸 Rock. **RELEASED:** 1979, EMI. **KEY TRACKS:** "Natural's Not in It," "Damaged Goods," "I Found That Essence Rare," "At Home, He's a Tourist." **CATALOG CHOICE:** *Solid Gold.* **NEXT STOP:** The Clash: *London Calling* (see p. 172). **AFTER THAT:** Wire: *Pink Flag.*

Music to Gaze at Fjords By

Dis

Jan Garbarek and Ralph Towner

In the 1970s, when the improvisation-oriented German label ECM hit its creative stride, critics complained that some of its offerings were glacially slow—music to gaze at fjords by. But in fact, ECM documented vivacious European chamber jazz and the sparkling early work of Pat Metheny, in addition to those wandering sound-sculpture-at-3-A.M. titles cherished by heavy-lidded progressives. *Dis*—a collaboration between Norwegian saxophonist Jan Garbarek, guitarist Ralph Towner, and a foreboding brass ensemble—is among the most beautiful.

The music begins a distance away, with otherworldly bells and chimes. It's the kind of drone you'd hear in winter, and by the time Garbarek enters, prospects for sunshine are almost nil; everything has the feeling of heavy clouds and deep portent. The "theme" of the first piece doesn't appear until seven minutes in—it's a gorgeous ascending phrase that hangs in the air, like an unexpected and uncomfortable question. Other compositions are more traditionally songlike: "Krusning," with Garbarek on soprano, is a pensive meditation set against a faraway brass section, while "Yr" is a spinning dance that relies on Towner's agile, skittering accompaniment style.

Much of the richness, and the tension, comes from the glancing exchanges between Garbarek's brooding long tones and Towner's more animated guitar pirouettes. But part is attributable to sheer sound: Like many similar ECM dates, this was recorded in Oslo, Norway, by engineer Jan Erik Kongshaug, who captured everything with an obsessive, almost photographic detail. The result is something both chilling and chilly; yet instead of keeping you at a distance, this record lures you deep into the vast dronescapes, where it's hard not to feel a rush of awe at the majesty of the mountains or whatever natural wonder is nearby.

GENRE: 🎷 Jazz. **RELEASED:** 1977, ECM. **KEY TRACKS:** "Yr," "Vandrere," "Viddene." **CATALOG CHOICES:** Garbarek: *Officium* (with Hilliard Ensemble). Towner: *Solstice* (see p. 783). **NEXT STOP:** Eberhard Weber Colours: *Silent Feet.* **AFTER THAT:** Terje Rypdal: *Odyssey.*

Amor at 78-RPM

The Best of Carlos Gardel

Carlos Gardel

The French-born singer and composer Carlos Gardel (1890–1935) took the street music he heard growing up in the poor sections of Buenos Aires, and transformed it into a national treasure—not to mention some of the most evocative singing of all time. The suave Gardel single-handedly pioneered *tango-canción*, or tango song, and his singing had such allure that it helped "legitimize" tango. Before him, the Argentine elite regarded tango as a diversion of the lower classes; after him, the general population fell under the spell of tango's brazen sensuality.

Gardel recorded regularly for more than a decade, acted in several movies, and became an international celebrity; at the time of his death, in a plane crash in Colombia, his friends included Charlie Chaplin and other luminaries. Those around the singer, including several guitarist collaborators, admired his agile baritone as well as his stamina, his ability to churn out one memorable performance after another. Six of the songs on this collection, including Gardel's dramatic original "El dia que me quieres" were recorded in a single day in 1935.

A fedora hat was one of Carlos Gardel's signatures.

These recordings were transferred from original 78-RPM singles. That means there's some surface noise, and the audio isn't as crystalline as that made in the digital age. Still, it's impossible to miss Gardel's gift—his smoldering tone, the way he casually shares inner feelings. Gardel defines the soul of tango not as particular notes or tricks but as a kind of reverie: Lost in the memory of an incredible woman he'll never dance with again, he sings so that others might understand this particular type of sadness, and maybe get lost in it too.

GENRE: 🌐 World/Argentina. **RELEASED:** 1998, EMI. **KEY TRACKS:** "Silencio," "El dia que me quieres," "Volver." **NEXT STOP:** Frank Sinatra: *Sings for Only the Lonely* (see p. 707). **AFTER THAT:** Astor Piazzolla: *Tango: Zero Hour* (see p. 599).

The Return of a Beloved Voice

Judy at Carnegie Hall

Judy Garland

When Judy Garland began rehabbing her career in the late 1950s, she had few options. She was overweight, addicted to uppers and downers, and battling hepatitis (in the process of recovery, she eventually weaned herself off drugs). She couldn't get much going in Hollywood, where movie musicals were out of fashion. So she turned to recording, and beginning in 1955, made an album a year—among the highlights of this "recording artist" phase is *That's Entertainment!*, which features her with a small jazz group.

To solidify her comeback, Garland followed a strategy used by countless other entertainers on the rebound, and performed to rave reviews in London, Paris, and Amsterdam. These ditched the lavish productions (and costumes) of her previous live shows, and put the emphasis on the singing—on Garland's crisp diction and knack for reshaping a theme. This two-disc set comes from 1961, and is one of the first shows Garland did upon returning to the U.S. It is uniformly enchanting, with rhapsodic ballads done in patient rubato and snazzier up-tempo numbers that flatter Garland's still movingly idealistic voice.

The orchestra, conducted by Mort Lindsay, helps the former Dorothy make the most of her material: On "Almost Like Being in Love" and several other songs, the musicians slow things to a crawl for the final verse, encouraging Garland to fashion a dramatic finish. At one point on disc 2, Garland wisecracks about singing all night, but she had too

Reporter Gordon Cox called this concert the "greatest night in show business history."

much showbiz sense for that: She was smart to finish the evening while she was still bringing these tunes to dazzling peaks.

GENRE: 🎙 Vocals.
RELEASED: 1961, Capitol.
KEY TRACKS: "Stormy Weather," "Almost Like Being in Love." **CATALOG CHOICE:** *That's Entertainment!* **NEXT STOP:** Barbra Streisand: *The Broadway Album.* **AFTER THAT:** Rufus Wainwright: *Does Judy at Carnegie Hall.*

Refined Piano Trio

Concert by the Sea

Erroll Garner

I t's rare to hear applause break out in the middle of a jazz solo, but that's what happens after a particularly spry chorus from Erroll Garner on "I'll Remember April," the opening track on this famous live recording from 1955.

The Pittsburgh-born pianist begins with a beboppy flourish of single lines, followed by sixteen bars of crashing chords, the kind that require both hands playing together. Then, suddenly, he turns down the volume. The audience strains to hear where Garner's trio will go; delighted applause breaks out when, after the music's been whispering, Garner drops a series of carefully placed pokes and boxer jabs, phrases that have a taunting hide-and-seek quality. These, inevitably, lead to some circus-sideshow razzle-dazzle.

A self-taught musician who played entirely

Because of his small size, Garner had to sit on a telephone book while performing.

by ear, Garner (1921–1977) was prone to such exaggerated manipulations—which some detractors considered keyboard stunts. An easygoing performer (one Garner biography is titled *The Most Happy Piano*), he understood that while audiences expected feats of musical daring, they also wanted to be entertained. His performances here are a touch more "scripted" than those of most jazz headliners, but that's not necessarily a fault: Through abrupt loud-soft contrasts and mood swings, Garner creates riveting episodes. One minute he's conjuring the wry blues of old-time stride players and the next he's in a modern mode, chopping through angular, severe-sounding chords. Though he skips around through several decades, the ride is Cadillac smooth, and extraordinarily assured.

The only downside to *Concert by the Sea*, one of the best-selling jazz piano albums of all time, is its sound quality. Though the auditorium, a converted church in Carmel, California, is known to offer sparkling acoustics, the recording is generally dim. The piano sounds as though it's been captured at a distance—muffling Garner's precise attack on the up-tempo numbers.

GENRE: 🎷 Jazz. **RELEASED:** 1955, Columbia. **KEY TRACKS:** "I'll Remember April," "It's All Right with Me," "Where or When," "Teach Me Tonight." **CATALOG CHOICES:** *Solo Flight; The Original Misty.* **NEXT STOP:** Ahmad Jamal: *But Not for Me* (see p. 387).
AFTER THAT: Art Hodes: *Art Hodes' Hot Five.*

One Lonely Instrument Takes On Heartache

I Will Not Be Sad in This World

Djivan Gasparyan

In his caustic comment on humanity, *Notes from the Underground*, Russian novelist Fyodor Dostoyevsky's bitter and sometimes mean main character asserts that "suffering is the sole origin of consciousness."

If that's true, then music can be a primary means of altering consciousness. Across cultures and continents, people seek in music a temporary refuge from suffering, a way to quickly change one's mind-set, if not one's circumstances. The Armenian Djivan Gasparyan, whose instrument is the oboe-like *duduk*, plays with an awareness that his listeners need to shake off a burden or two. He doesn't bully them with jolly jigs or any forced frivolity. Instead, he offers deeply felt, heavyhearted sounds for contemplation.

These turn out to be a counterintuitive form of uplift. This album features Gasparyan performing mostly solo, with another *duduk* supplying a drone background. Despite the title, sadness is definitely here to stay—his lithe, fragile themes have a feeling of enveloping grief, the kind that won't lift by will alone. Gasparyan plays from deep inside that feeling, and is determined to understand its various dimensions. He makes the *duduk* sound like a woman's muffled sobs, or, when he wants to be superemphatic, his attacks take on the breathy chuffing of a wooden flute.

Often erroneously filed under "New Age," this disc offers the most "traditional" way to encounter Gasparyan, who's also featured in the soundtrack to *The Last Temptation of Christ* and has collaborated with the Kronos Quartet and guitarist Michael Brook. Those varied projects offer traces of the sensitivity that sits center stage here: He plays valiantly, knowing that he can't wipe out sadness with the magical flickering notes of his *duduk*. But he can try to transcend it.

GENRE: 🌐 World/Armenia. **RELEASED:** 1989, Opal. (Originally recorded 1983.) **KEY TRACKS:** "Little Flower Garden," "Brother Hunter," "A Cool Wind Is Blowing." **CATALOG CHOICES:** *Black Rock* (with Michael Brook); *Heavenly Duduk.* **NEXT STOP:** David Torn: *Cloud About Mercury.* **AFTER THAT:** Claudio Monteverdi: *Vespers of the Blessed Virgin* (see p. 515).

A Mega Single in Many Forms

"I Heard It Through the Grapevine"

Marvin Gaye (and others)

A t Motown's weekly "Quality Control" meetings, held every Friday in the early years, a small committee of staff producers, executives, and songwriters would vote on the recordings under consideration as singles.

According to legend, the first time Norman Whitfield and Barrett Strong brought in this song, which they wrote for Smokey Robinson and the Miracles, it was rejected. Same thing happened to the version they worked up featuring the Isley Brothers. The third attempt was for Marvin Gaye (1939–1984); the duo pitched it slightly higher than Gaye's range, which gave his vocals a pleading, almost desperate quality. That didn't click either. A fourth version of the song, set in a brisk gospel rhythm and sung by Gladys Knight and the Pips, met with Quality Control approval and became a hit in 1967.

Strong and Whitfield still weren't satisfied. Something about the slower, more tribal pulse of Gaye's unreleased version haunted them, and the duo persuaded label honcho Berry Gordy to include it, at the last minute, on a 1968 Gaye album called *In the Groove*. It wasn't designated as the single, but within weeks Gaye's "Grapevine" became the most requested song from the album at radio stations. Motown was eventually forced to release it, and Gaye's version hit the top of the *Billboard* singles

"Grapevine" was Marvin Gaye's first #1 hit single.

chart in December 1968 and stayed there for seven weeks. *In the Groove* was eventually renamed—in Gaye's official discography, it's called *I Heard It Through the Grapevine*.

As pervasive as that single was, it's hardly the last word on "Grapevine," which unlike many big hits thrives in all kinds of surroundings. The account of the rumor mill that swirls around a cheating lover has been reimagined as a swaggering soul revue romp (Ike and Tina Turner), a bomping-and-honking instrumental (King Curtis), a glinting rhythm-guitar-fueled punk frenzy (the Slits), a campy commercial (the California Raisins), and a spooky eleven-minute epic of swamp psychedelia (Creedence Clearwater Revival), to name just a few versions. All of them tell the same story. And all of them tell different stories. And that, right there, is the glory of pop music.

GENRE: 🔵 R&B. **RELEASED:** 1968, Motown. **APPEARS ON:** *I Heard It Through the Grapevine.* **ANOTHER INTERPRETATION:** Check out the Creedence Clearwater version on *Cosmo's Factory.* **NEXT STOP:** Smokey Robinson and the Miracles: *The Ultimate Collection* (see p. 650). **AFTER THAT:** Martha and the Vandellas: *Dance Party!*

Message Music on a Higher Level

What's Going On

Marvin Gaye

In the two years before he began work on this, his magnum opus, Marvin Gaye struggled with writer's block, depression, and addiction—while still recording at a relentless pace. So when, in 1970, he announced to executives at Motown Records that he'd be producing his next album himself, he faced a degree of skepticism. No artist, not least an infirm one, rejected Hitsville's famed assembly line.

Gaye eventually prevailed, and the rest is history—*What's Going On* is a radical miracle of pop music, an alignment of talent and message unlike anything before or since. Using his formidable powers of seduction, Gaye spoke about the Vietnam war, conditions in the inner cities, and the environment in a way that gently led listeners to greater awareness. "Something happened with me during that period," Gaye said later. "I felt the strong urge to write music and to write lyrics that would touch the souls of men."

He did that first with the title song, which rises from the sounds of a party in progress—an emotional homecoming for a Vietnam veteran. The song acquired its distinctive sound, with several different layers of Gaye's lead vocals, through a happy studio accident: As an engineer played back a practice track he'd recorded earlier, Gaye, sitting at the piano in the famous Motown studio nicknamed the "Snakepit," began singing along, echoing and embellishing the existing vocal. His overlapping voices, locked in an urgent, internal conversation, surprised everyone in the room—and from that moment became a distinguishing feature of *What's Going On*.

When Motown executives heard the track, they flatly refused to release it—saying it was too political, not hit material. A standoff ensued: Gaye vowed he wouldn't do anything else for the label until "What's Going On" came out, and in January 1971, six months after it was recorded, the song was issued. It became an immediate hit, reaching the top of *Billboard*'s soul chart and the number two position on the pop charts. Motown wanted an album to follow immediately, and during a feverish ten-day marathon, Gaye and a crew of writer/producers knocked it out, with the house rhythm section, the Funk Brothers, establishing the basic accompaniment and members of the Detroit Symphony providing the sweet, questioning strings. The album reached stores in May, and its album tracks and subsequent singles—"Mercy Mercy Me (The Ecology)" and "Inner City Blues (Make Me Wanna Holler)"—coalesced into one riveting whole, a commentary somehow greater than the sum of its (stellar) parts. Through these persuasive songs, Gaye took the frustrations of a heated wartime moment and made them eternal: *What's Going On* resonates wherever there is conflict and misunderstanding, touching the souls of men by calling to the highest within them.

GENRE: 🎙 R&B. **RELEASED:** 1971, Motown. **KEY TRACKS:** "What's Going On," "Inner City Blues (Make Me Wanna Holler)."

F.Y.I.: Smokey Robinson, Gaye's Motown peer, once called this "the greatest album of all time."

CATALOG CHOICE: Here, My Dear. **NEXT STOP:** Stevie Wonder: *Innervisions* (see p. 872). **AFTER THAT:** Sly and the Family Stone: *There's a Riot Goin' On.*

The Big Neon Sign over the Bedroom Door Says . . .

Let's Get It On

Marvin Gaye

66 "H ave your sex," Marvin Gaye writes in the liner notes of this landmark of bedroom soul. "It can be very exciting . . . if you're lucky." And if you're really lucky, that sex will feel a bit like this album

sounds—slippery and heated and all-consuming, governed equally by urgency and tenderness. An essay on carnal delight in eight parts, *Let's Get It On* is one for the ages not just because of its plush backgrounds (particularly the wah-wah guitar of Melvin Ragin, a key player on the L.A. Motown sides) or its melodies (largely improvised), but because of Gaye's needy-man delivery, the way he transforms "please baby" into a

Let's Get It On was Gaye's bestselling album during his lifetime.

bouquet of beautifully arranged pleas. He's just a few years removed from *What's Going On* (see previous page), his comment on society, but he's really worlds away: Sharing his formidable repertoire of bended-knee incantations, Gaye wants to stay in the bedroom as long as it takes to celebrate every last sacred ritual of love.

This album triggered an enormous outbreak of slightly salacious bedroom soul, much of it the equivalent of play-by-play coverage from ringside. Gaye's endeavor is different: Singing in that sly, delighted way, he brings listeners into his need, shares the pleasure and the torment, makes raw desire sound almost noble and immediate. When Gaye talks about getting it on, you are there.

GENRE: 🎵 R&B. **RELEASED:** 1973, Motown. **KEY TRACKS:** "Let's Get It On," "You Sure Love to Ball," "Distant Lover," "Just to Keep You Satisfied." **CATALOG CHOICE:** *Midnight Love.* **NEXT STOP:** Teddy Pendergrass: *Love Songs.* **AFTER THAT:** Astrud Gilberto: *Finest Hour.*

Gotta Get In to Get Out

The Lamb Lies Down on Broadway

Genesis

T his sometimes talky art-rock epic is more than two hours long. That's a significant time investment, considering that the primary lyricist, Peter Gabriel, intended audiences to follow his tale of a half–Puerto Rican juvenile delinquent on the loose in New York from start to finish. Inevitably, you lose something by parachuting in somewhere in the middle.

Still, by parachuting in, you can quickly determine whether you're temperamentally disposed toward *Lamb,* one of the towering peaks of progressive rock. Cue up the eight-minute "In the Cage," on disc 1. Listen to its mad-hatter keyboard arpeggios and thrashing tilt-a-whirl rhythms. Check out the manic edge in Gabriel's voice. If the fitful, sometimes suffocating, trapped-in-a-psychodrama feeling of the tune makes you curious about what happens next, go back to the beginning and settle in for a rare treat. If, however, you're not completely enthralled, stay away. (Instead seek out the less demanding Genesis album *Trick of the Tail.*)

While *Lamb's* lyrics overflow with visions of majestic grandeur (practically a prerequisite for British art-rock), the music exhibits a grind-it-out grittiness, with muscular, at times even funky, polyrhythms. It's possible to love *Lamb* and not care at all about the story: The band's

During their 1974 tour, Genesis played this album in its entirety 102 times.

cohesive attack is intriguing enough to atone for any stray moments of overblown pageantry.

When *Lamb* was released in 1974, drummer Phil Collins told an interviewer that "It's about a schizophrenic." Gabriel called his primary character, Rael, a "split personality." Attempting to rescue his brother John, Rael finds himself swept underground, where he encounters grisly video game–style fantasy figures that impede his progress. As the work goes on, the real and subterranean worlds interconnect in odd, hallucinatory ways. By the end, it seems that Rael is on a youth's quest to discover himself, not his sibling. Cosmic? Yes. Go down that rabbit hole. All will become clear.

GENRE: 🎸 Rock. **RELEASED:** 1974, Atlantic. **KEY TRACKS:** "In the Cage," "The Lamb Lies Down on Broadway." **CATALOG CHOICES:** *Selling England by the Pound; Trick of the Tail; Genesis.* **NEXT STOP:** Supertramp: *Crime of the Century.* **AFTER THAT:** Syd Barrett: *The Madcap Laughs.*

A Spangly Celebration of the Great American Cityscape

Complete Works for Piano and Orchestra, with Rhapsody in Blue

George Gershwin
Michael Boriskin, Eos Orchestra (Jonathan Sheffer, cond.)

T he relentlessly optimistic, Manhattan skyline–evoking *Rhapsody in Blue* actually exists in several different forms. The original work was commissioned by bandleader Paul Whiteman and intended for a big band. Gershwin composed it in three weeks on an upright piano, and the piece premiered in February 1924 to instant acclaim. The success led to a more florid full-orchestra version, scored by Ferde Grofé—this is the one the big symphonies play when they're trying to woo new subscribers. Grofé also wrote a less sentimental score for a (smaller) theater orchestra, and that's the one found here, in a 1998 recording.

It's a perfect middle ground—the Whiteman version has its moments of Guy Lombardo–esque runaway schmaltz, and the full orchestra version sometimes hits Gershwin's skyscraping themes with an anvil. The smaller group gets everything across, with colors far more interesting than those possible with a brassy big band—note the way the French horns, down low, get Gershwin's slow-to-crest crescendos started. The Eos Orchestra, from New York, is fleet—bringing the animated gestures to life in a way that leaves pianist Michael Boriskin lots of room. Boriskin wisely understates the piece's familiar declarative themes, and yet his solo passages, particularly the galloping accelerando that erupts shortly after the ten-minute mark on the CD, are executed with a mix of showbiz panache and jazzbo brazenness.

The remaining works on this disc aren't nearly as famous as the iconic *Rhapsody*, but they're well worth hearing. The Concerto in F, which Gershwin orchestrated himself, shows the composer exploring thematic development more deeply (the entire Adagio second movement is a caprice that elaborately intertwines two or three small, initially disconnected melodies), and offers several moments of challenging fingerwork for the piano. The "Variations on 'I Got Rhythm'" takes Gershwin's classic tune to the concert hall, where it seems out of place, a jazzman slumming in a tux.

GENRE: 🎶 Classical. **RELEASED:** 1998, BMG. **KEY TRACKS:** *Rhapsody in Blue.* Concerto in F: Adagio. **ANOTHER INTERPRETATION:** *Gershwin: Concerto in F with Ravel: Concerto in G,* Pascal Rogé, Vienna Radio Symphony (Bertrand de Billy cond.). **NEXT STOP:** Herbie Hancock: *Gershwin's World.* **AFTER THAT:** Audra McDonald: *Way Back to Paradise.*

"Folk Opera" for the Ages

Porgy and Bess

George Gershwin

Glyndebourne Festival Opera (Sir Simon Rattle, cond.)

L ike many a tunesmith associated with Tin Pan Alley and the heyday of Great American Song in the 1930s, George Gershwin (1898–1937) wished to be considered a "legitimate" composer. This piece, which stretched

nearly four hours at its 1935 premiere, brought him that recognition. It's an all-stops-out opera (Gershwin described it as a "folk opera") filled with broad, quintessential Southern melodies, hymns of devotion, and jazz-tinged songs of yearning that swell to grand proportions. It's been hailed among the great works of the twentieth century, and reviled as racist (because some of its sharply drawn characters behave according to white stereotypes of African Americans

during that time) by such eminent figures as Duke Ellington and Harry Belafonte.

Above dispute: the expansive, breathtakingly beautiful songs Gershwin used to tell the story, which is set in an impoverished community in Charleston, South Carolina. The Brooklyn-born composer and pianist visited the region several times while adapting DuBose Heyward's play *Porgy,* and spent time around Folly Beach, where the Gullah Negroes worked, lived, and worshipped. Those who know Gullah culture credit Gershwin with capturing its idiosyncratic speech patterns and vocal inflections.

The plot involves a crippled man (Porgy, sung here by Willard White) and his struggle to extract a young girl (Bess, sung by Cynthia Haymon) from the clutches of drug dealers and pimps. It's a story of unconditional devotion that unfolds through scenes of hardship and adversity. Even the minor characters are richly drawn, and Gershwin gives each tight emblematic songs, with memorable recurring melodies. Through these frameworks, a character's nuances emerge: The drug dealer Sportin' Life is a fairly marginal presence when he steps up to sing "It Ain't Necessarily So," one of many songs from the show to become a standard. As the song unfolds, we learn about his code of ethics, his thought process, and values. We get a "feel" for him that's borne out later.

This production, from the Glyndebourne Festival in 1988, relies on previous stagings, notably the Houston Grand Opera 1976 production that restored nearly thirty minutes of music cut in 1935. It has a team of smooth singers

Gershwin died of a brain tumor just 2 years after *Porgy and Bess* premiered.

led by the exuberant conductor Sir Simon Rattle, who understands drama (note the terrorized rape scene on Kittiwah Island) and is attentive to the small touches Gershwin embedded within the orchestrations—even those who know the work well may discover new riches and oddities here.

Rattle encourages his soloists to savor Gershwin's graceful gliding arcs of melody, and why not? These pieces—"Summertime," "I Loves You Porgy," "My Man's Gone Now," "It Ain't Necessarily So," "A Woman Is a Sometime Thing," and on and on—are each towering accomplishments, gathering bits of local color and the heavy sigh of the blues into a deeply affecting and universal sound.

GENRE: 🎭 Opera. **RELEASED:** 1989, EMI. **KEY TRACKS:** "Summertime," "I Loves You Porgy," "My Man's Gone Now," "It Ain't Necessarily So," "A Woman Is a Sometime Thing." **ANOTHER INTERPRETATION:** Miles Davis and Gil Evans: *Porgy and Bess.* **NEXT STOP:** Ella Fitzgerald: *Sings the Gershwin Songbook.* **AFTER THAT:** Duke Ellington: *Sophisticated Ladies.*

A Breeze of Brazil

Getz/Gilberto

Stan Getz and João Gilberto

In the hard-bop middle '50s, the leading saxophonists devoted considerable energy to perfecting an instantly identifiable "sound"—John Coltrane brandished a glinting, metallic sheen, Sonny Rollins a much darker,

enveloping mahogany. Stan Getz went in a different direction. His sound was diffuse, distinguished by pillowy puffs of air. Everything

he did was dinner-hour smooth, genteel, seemingly designed to not startle anyone.

Yet Getz did startle the jazz world with

this recording, a collaborative effort involving some of the leading lights of Brazilian music. In the steady, undulating guitars of the bossa nova beat, Getz found an ideal cradle for his almost meek tone. *Jazz Samba*, an exploration with guitarist Charlie Byrd recorded in an afternoon in 1962, was a hit, as was the mostly cheesy follow-up, *Big Band Bossa Nova*. Getz's idea this time was for a more intimate setting built around the bossa supernova, composer Antonio Carlos Jobim, and the form's most skilled interpreter, João Gilberto. At the sessions, Getz asked Gilberto's then-wife Astrud to translate "The Girl from Ipanema" and other songs; although Jobim and Gilberto thought that Astrud was not ready to record, Getz was impressed with her singing, and insisted she be a part of the date. The stars aligned. She remembered later, "After we listened to the finished take, Stan looked at me and said very

emphatically, 'That song is gonna make you very famous.'"

Getz was prophetic. "Ipanema" became a worldwide smash, and the rare jazz song to turn up on jukeboxes. The album remains one of the most successful jazz releases of all time. Not coincidentally, it's also one of music's most thoughtful cross-cultural exchanges. João Gilberto sings in a way that defies time. Getz, recognizing the spell could be broken with too many notes, leaves lots of room. With just his lullaby tone, he makes these sweet, sad songs sweeter and sadder.

GENRE: 🎵 Jazz. **RELEASED:** 1963, Verve. **KEY TRACKS:** "The Girl from Ipanema," "Desafinado." **CATALOG CHOICE:** *Jazz Samba*. **NEXT STOP:** Toots Thielemans: *The Brazil Project*, Vol. 2. **AFTER THAT:** Wanda Sa: *Vagamente*.

The Most Inventive Operetta from the Powerhouse British Tandem

The Mikado

Gilbert and Sullivan

Orchestra and Chorus of the Welsh National Opera
(Sir Charles Mackerras, cond.)

Before *The Mikado* came to be, the collaboration between William Gilbert (the wry wordsmith whose training was in law) and Arthur Sullivan (the composer whose early concert works marked him as a great hope for

"serious English music") was on the rocks. Having created some of the most memorable musical theater works of the day—the light operas (or operettas) *The Sorcerer, H.M.S. Pinafore*, and *The Pirates of Penzance* among them—the two hit an impasse when Sullivan rejected a Gilbert premise for a play about a magic pill. Stung, Gilbert insisted this was the only plot he'd develop;

The Mikado was Gilbert and Sullivan's ninth opera.

Sullivan maintained that the idea too closely resembled that of *The Sorcerer*. Several months later, in the spring of 1884, a trade expo triggered a wave of interest in things Japanese among Londoners, and Gilbert was inspired to concoct a new story. Nominally about the villagers of Titipu and their method of punishing transgression, *The Mikado* is really a universal tale of lust and manners—with running commentary on the social and political mores of contemporary England.

The operetta contains some of the most inspired music in the Gilbert and Sullivan book—these hearty full-ensemble choruses, and stem-winding solos sprinkled with unexpected intervallic challenges, influenced George Gershwin, Irving Berlin, the Kinks' Ray Davies, and many others. This production, featuring the operatic voices of Donald Adams (as the Mikado), Anthony Rolfe Johnson (as Nanki-Poo), and Marie McLaughlin (as Yum-Yum), makes the most of each effusive moment, transforming sometimes twee "patter songs" into revealing star turns. Gilbert and Sullivan use these yammering verses, which are occasionally bawdy and not at all politically correct, to establish the characters. When we first encounter Nanki-Poo, on the "A Wandering Minstrel I," he appears as a human jukebox ("If you call for a song of the sea, we'll heave the capstan 'round"), and a lively satiric foil for the more conventional leading man Mikado.

Recorded in Wales over three days in 1991, this *Mikado* isn't the work of the troupe most often associated with Gilbert and Sullivan—the D'Oyly Carte Ensemble. The D'Oyly interpretations, which are widely available, sometimes have the air of an inside joke to them, a feeling of "we all know the work so let's have fun, shall we?" No such smugness is evident here, as British conductor Sir Charles Mackerras attends to the nuts and bolts of the piece, showing off the tense orchestrations Sullivan used to support his declarative melodies. Mackerras's clear, ostentation-free reading offers newcomers a way to encounter Gilbert and Sullivan on musical terms, without any excessive effusiveness. Any glibness in the lavish Act 1 finale, or the Act 2 scenes where the principals argue about who among them is worthy of prosperity, is in the score. Also in the score, of course, is some of the most lively, head-swivelling, wonderfully irreverent music ever written for the music-theater stage.

GENRE: 🌑 Opera. RELEASED: 1992, Telarc. KEY TRACKS: Act 1: "A Wandering Minstrel I," "Finale"; Act 2: "A More Humane Mikado Never . . ." ANOTHER INTERPRETATION: D'Oyly Carte Opera Company. CATALOG CHOICE: *H.M.S. Pinafore,* D'Oyly Carte Opera Company (Isidore Godfrey, cond.). NEXT STOP: George Gershwin: *Porgy and Bess* (see p. 307). AFTER THAT: The Kinks: *Village Green Preservation Society* (see p. 427).

Next-Generation Sultriness from Brazil

Tanto tempo

Bebel Gilberto

It took an electronica-savvy producer from Yugoslavia named Mitar Subotić (1961–1999) to help Brazil get its groove back in the 1990s. Suba, as he was known, came to Brazil in 1990 on a UNESCO scholarship. Enchanted with the country's music, he hoped to become a DJ or a studio remixer. He wrote songs and theater works, and quickly wormed into the arty São Paulo underground. Word of his intricate percussion loops and electronic adaptations of bossa nova spread, and within a few years he was collaborating with an elite circle of artists including Bebel Gilberto, daughter of the legendary singer and guitarist João Gilberto. Suba had nearly finished his work on this album when, in November 1999, a fire broke out in his home studio; he died trying to rescue a briefcase full of master tapes and computer files.

Suba's sleek backdrops suggested a way for Brazilian music to move forward, or at least take a step beyond the prison of '60s kitsch. Of the many singers he worked with, Bebel Gilberto was the best equipped to fully realize and extend the inspiration—she's got cool restraint in her DNA. The combination of his cosmopolitan rhythms and her sultry, classically coy Brazilian voice makes *Tanto tempo* one of the most intensely pleasurable listening experiences to emerge during the year 2000.

Gilberto is no radical—a spin through her sleepy, wistful rendition of Antonio Carlos Jobim's "Summer Samba (So Nice)" will confirm that. But she's not a Luddite, either. She's conversant in the choppy rhythms of clubland, and able to connect its undulating pulses to old-school bossa nova and other not-so-distant rhythmic relatives. And regardless of the deri-

Tanto tempo was Gilberto's first album to be released in the U.S.

vation of the groove, Gilberto maintains, throughout, a kind of nature-preserve serenity: When things are really cooking, as on the acoustic-guitar samba "Sem contenção," Gilberto seems to float lazily along, removed from the frenzy. She sings everything as though deep in contemplation, and this gives tunes like "Alguem" rich contrast: The beat has its share of jarring syncopations while the wispy overlapping layers of vocals suggest a surreal dream sequence in a film.

GENRE: 🌐 World/Brazil. **RELEASED:** 2000, Six Degrees. **KEY TRACKS:** "Tanto tempo," "Sem contenção," "Alguem." **CATALOG CHOICE:** *Bebel Gilberto.* **FURTHER INQUIRY:** For more Suba, check out both *São Paulo Confessions* and *Tributo,* which features a percussion-plus-loops performance with drummer João Parahyba. **NEXT STOP:** Morelenbaum2/Sakamoto: *Casa.* **AFTER THAT:** Moreno Veloso: *Music Typewriter.*

The Other White Album

João Gilberto

João Gilberto

Those who know Antonio Carlos Jobim's "Aguas de Marco" may think something's wrong with their equipment when they hear the version that opens this enchanting João Gilberto masterpiece. Rather than follow the theme's elegantly spaced phrases, Gilberto runs them together, skipping over the beats and pauses every other Jobim-worshipping singer observes. The effect is at once exhilarating and disorienting—it's as though this master is toying with expectations, intentionally jumping ahead to vex listeners.

Gilberto, known to Brazilians as O Mito ("the legend") for his languid interpretations of bossa nova, is usually more subtle about the changes he makes, and on the rest of this set, he uses tiny inflections and hairline shadings to rejigger the themes of Jobim and other post–bossa nova composers. Virtually everything in Gilberto's superlative catalog benefits from his attention to the little details, but this record, with its pattering percussion, wordless vocal caprices ("Undiu"), and steady acoustic guitar, is definitive. Listen to it with headphones to fully appreciate a singer whose control comes with no apparent effort, whose serene art is most devastating at a whisper.

João Gilberto is credited with furnishing bossa nova with its insistent beat.

GENRE: 🌐 World/Brazil. **RELEASED:** 1973, Verve/ Universal. **KEY TRACKS:** "Aguas de Marco," "Undiu," "Eu quero um samba," "Eu vim da Bahia." **CATALOG CHOICES:** *Amoroso/Brazil; Live in Montreux; Getz/Gilberto* (see p. 308). **NEXT STOP:** Antonio Carlos Jobim: *Wave.* **AFTER THAT:** Maria Bethania: *Alibi.*

Mambo Kings at Work Here

Afro

Dizzy Gillespie and His Orchestra

Dizzy Gillespie's exploration of Latin jazz began in the middle '40s, just after bebop broke from the hipster underworld to startle mainstream listeners. Gillespie was suddenly in demand, and to capitalize he put together a fearsome big band built around Cuban conga player Chano Pozo. The pair wrote a song, "Manteca," that established a new hybrid—brassy, rhythmically terse big-band catcalls over clipped Latin rhythms. The song became a dance floor hit, and on the strength of just a handful of recordings for RCA, Gillespie won major acclaim as a pioneer, if not the primary architect, of Latin jazz.

The trumpet player with the inflated jowls, perhaps the most beloved entertainer in jazz history, returned to Latin jazz many times over the years, most notably on this record. After signing with Verve Records in 1952, Gillespie enlisted Cuban composer Chico O'Farrill to create a longer piece patterned

Gillespie played a modified "bent" horn, which contributed to his signature sound.

after O'Farrill's trailblazing *Afro Cuban Jazz Suite,* first recorded by percussionist Machito's orchestra in 1950. The *Manteca Suite* begins with the famous "Manteca" theme, and then follows a winding path through several other rhythmic styles before ending in a mighty jazz blowing session. In his arrangements for Gillespie, O'Farrill celebrates the snapping vitality of the Afro-Cuban pulse, trusting that if the underlying rhythm is hot, the soloists will eventually start cooking too. Sure enough, the crisply chopped ensemble parts give way to blazing trumpet hijinks, and there are moments when several horn players trade ideas round-robin style.

The second side features a smaller ensemble playing some of Gillespie's most evocative pieces—"A Night in Tunisia," his bustling arrangement of "Caravan." Though less ambitious, these display Gillespie not merely as a master of the specific idiomatic quirks of jazz and Latin music, but among the very few who could combine them into a single coherent language.

GENRE: 🅙 Jazz. **RELEASED:** 1954, Norgran/Verve. **KEY TRACKS:** Afro Cuban Jazz Suite, "A Night in Tunisia." **F.Y.I.:** An excellent overview of the origins of Latin jazz is available on the single disc *The Original Mambo Kings*. **CATALOG CHOICE:** *The Complete RCA Victor Recordings*. **NEXT STOP:** Chico O'Farrill: *Cuban Blues*.

A Quiet Moment that Anticipates Several Storms

1961

The Jimmy Giuffre Three

In the liner notes of his 1956 album *The Jimmy Giuffre Clarinet*, the multi-instrumentalist and composer put forth a then-radical sense of the subtle timbral possibilities of jazz: "It has been said that when jazz gets soft, it loses its gusto, its funkiness. It is my feeling that soft jazz can retain the basic flavor and intensity that it has at a louder volume and at the same time perhaps reveal some new dimensions of feeling that loudness obscures."

After starting in big bands (he wrote the Woody Herman tune "Four Brothers" and played in the band for a while), Giuffre (1921–2008) devoted much of his recording career to putting that notion into practice.

Jimmy Giuffre called his music "blues-based folk jazz."

He was temperamentally drawn to the "cool school" of West Coast jazz musicians, and yet approached it on his own terms—his albums of the 1950s sometimes reach boisterous levels. Likewise, these two records he made for Verve in 1961, *Fusion* and *Thesis*, practically overflow with gusto. But they do so at a whisper—without drums, without big shout choruses, without fanfare. Working with pianist Paul Bley and bassist Steve Swallow, Giuffre delves into structurally challenging music as though determined to avoid the deferential quality of cool. He replaces it with a firm, sure sense of theme—a curt boldness that Bley, one of the most attentive accompanists ever, exploits with pinpricks and sledge-hammering chords, as appropriate.

A key to the particular feeling of this is the clarinet—in Giuffre's hands it's a completely different instrument than the shrill one played by those swing-era cats. Giuffre doesn't use much vibrato or other ornamentation, and he doesn't squawk. He stays close to the instrument's rich-mahogany lower register, and operates stealthily, seeking out tonal complexities other clarinetists miss. Out of that softish sound comes highly attentive exchanges and melodies of resounding power that do exactly as Giuffre says: uncover dimensions of feeling that louder jazz rarely visits.

CATALOG CHOICES: *Free Fall; The Jimmy Giuffre Three.* **NEXT STOP:** Paul Bley: *Tears.* **AFTER THAT:** John Surman: *A Biography of the Rev. Absalom Dawe.*

GENRE: 🅙 Jazz. **RELEASED:** 1961, Verve. (Reissued 1992, ECM.) **KEY TRACKS:** "Emphasis," "Carla," "Flight," "The Gamut."

Riff/Swirl/Riff/Swirl/Repeat

Einstein on the Beach

Philip Glass

hilip Glass didn't invent the arpeggio—the series of notes played in succession that usually outline a chord. It's common currency in music. He holds no proprietary stake in endless repetition, either. Nonetheless, the New York composer has built a completely idiosyncratic musical signature just by manipulating those two devices. Virtually anywhere you visit in a Glass work (*Einstein on the Beach* is one of what he calls his "portrait" operas), you'll encounter short arpeggiated motifs looping around each other, like interconnected spirograph circles. He is the "Riff/Swirl/Riff/Swirl/Repeat a zillion times" guy.

PHILIP GLASS / ROBERT WILSON
EINSTEIN ON THE BEACH

Einstein on the Beach premiered in 1976.

and his longest, usually clocking in around five hours without intermission. It's not "about" anything in the traditional sense, though there are times during this recording when it sounds as if important events are unfolding. The namesake luminary is referenced occasionally, the chorus chants meaningful-sounding sets of numbers (the code for an atom bomb? a waitress's phone number?), but there's no central narrative.

At times during "Train 1," from the first act of *Einstein on the Beach*, Glass's unorthodox ensemble (which includes saxophones and electronic keyboards) has two or three of these interlocking phrases going. Just when the pattern clarifies, Glass will shorten it by a few beats. This sends everything into a slightly different orbit, as he explained in the liner notes to this edition: "A simple figure can expand and then contract in many different ways, maintaining the same general melodic configuration but, because of the addition or subtraction of one note, it takes on a very different rhythmic shape." This amounts to Glass's trade secret, a scheme that informs much of his composition. A plotless series of marathon riffs and short connective episodes dependent on Robert Wilson's visuals, *Einstein* is Glass's first opera,

As a result, those looking for "story" usually come away from this marathon underwhelmed. Those in search of an all-consuming musical experience, on the other hand, find themselves mesmerized by *Einstein*. The most elaborate of Glass's major works, it's a triumph of arpeggio mangling and arpeggio management, an excellent example of how small recurring units can be massaged into music of dazzling and often hypnotic intricacy.

GENRE: ⬛ Opera. **RELEASED:** 1993, Nonesuch. **KEY TRACKS:** "Train 1," "Night Train," "Dance 1." **CATALOG CHOICE:** *Koyaanisqatsi.* **NEXT STOP:** Steve Reich: *Different Trains.* **AFTER THAT:** Steve Roach: *Dreamtime Return* (see p. 649).

An Opera for the Operaphobic

Ainadamar

Osvaldo Golijov
Atlanta Symphony Orchestra and Women's Chorus (Robert Spano, cond.)

The rat-a-tat of gunfire that opens a crucial late scene of Osvaldo Golijov's boundary-breaking *Ainadamar* signals the murder, by fascist soldiers, of this opera's protagonist, Spanish playwright Federico García Lorca.

The deed is long anticipated—the piece is a series of sorrowful remembrances of Lorca by his muse, Margarita Xirgu. But this isn't a typical three-shots-and-then-tranquility episode. Using a device favored by hip-hop producers, Golijov aligns the gunfire into a beat. What starts as random violence becomes a series of staccato jabs, echoed by hand drummers, that crackles with the energy of street rhythm.

Osvaldo Golijov has won two Grammy awards, one for *Ainadamar*.

The thunder is characteristic of the transfixing, often sad *Ainadamar*, which means "fountain of tears" in Arabic. An Argentine composer of Eastern European Jewish descent, Golijov has a deep understanding of pulse; just about everything consequential in *Ainadamar* happens at a crisply defined gait. The piece, which premiered in 2003, begins with the rapid clicks of a manual typewriter, pounding out a triple-meter rhythm that echoes Afro-Cuban religious rituals. It's a moment to be cherished, a union of acoustic and electronic sounds so alien to opera, it seems destined to rattle the rafters of staid halls. If the rhythms themselves don't floor you, Golijov's orchestrations—somber Van Gogh–like swirls of color in which one tonality "bleeds" into the next—probably will. Even when the vocal line sits solidly in one key, the accompaniment often seems to slide around, describing a destabilized world where nothing is exactly as it seems.

Later, Golijov provides compact songs based upon tango, methodical derivations of heartsick bolero, and guitars strummed with the fire of flamenco. The role of Xirgu is sung powerfully by Dawn Upshaw, who emphasizes the mystical and/or religious superstitions that underpin daily life in many Latin cultures; at times her despairing tones resemble those of the great Portuguese fado singer Amália Rodrigues (see p. 654). Some of these evocations follow the structural dictates of the borrowed styles, and others don't—as Golijov explained in an interview after the premiere, "When I use flamenco, for instance, it's because I need to evoke a certain emotion, not because the music is 'flamenco.' I modulate between cultures. I use them in the same way that other composers use tonal areas or modulate from key to key."

Golijov's assimilation of diverse musical "worlds" gives this piece a surprising universality; it has also helped establish him as a talent to watch. In a sense, he's doing the same kind of folk-song rescue that Béla Bartók (see p. 46) and others did in the first half of the twentieth century, but intergrating recovered material into intricate mosaics resembling those of electronic pop artists. In Golijov's work, the collage lures listeners into a grand, swirling tableau—where the extravagant keening melodies have the power to haunt you long after the shots stop ringing and the pulse fades.

GENRE: 🌐 Opera. **RELEASED:** 2006, Deutsche Grammophon. **KEY TRACKS:**
"Lamento por la muerte de Federico," "Mariana, tus ojos," "A la Habana." **CATALOG CHOICE:** *Ayre.* **NEXT STOP:** Astor Piazzolla: *The Vienna Concert.* **AFTER THAT:** Lorraine Hunt Lieberson: *Sings Peter Lieberson: Neruda Songs.*

A Prog-Rock Gas

Gazeuse!

Gong

Choppy, hiccuping grooves? Check. Endlessly long solos from a flamboyant guitarist? Check. Vaguely exotic sounds? Check. Yup, it's jazz-rock fusion all right. Yet somehow Gong's finely-tuned *Gazeuse!* neatly sidesteps the clichés associated with the form. It's a totally engrossing journey, one of the few fashion records that's plenty verbose yet doesn't get tangled up in its own discourse.

Gong began, in the early '70s, as an exceptionally versatile band intent on exploring new amalgamations of jazz and rock. *Camembert Electrique* (1971), masterminded by the Australian guitarist, vocalist,

The original U.S. version of the album was called *Expresso*.

and mythmaker Daevid Allen, told of life on Planet Gong, and introduced a cast of whispering gnomes and Pothead Pixies who hung around for three similarly spacey subsequent albums. Then came a huge shake-up. Allen and others left, and the band ditched the interstellar conceits to emphasize muscular, hard-driving, super-intense instrumental music.

Virtuoso drummer Pierre Moerlen, the band's new leader, put together a frontline consisting of two mallet players, on vibraphone and marimba—they sometimes play together, but often their lines overlap and interlock, connecting ancient (the wood of marimba) with modern (the metallic ping of the vibraphone), tribal ritual with subway ride. Into that lattice-work steps Allan Holdsworth, a demonically inventive guitar soloist whose approach changes depending on the atmosphere. He lunges and snarls like a heavy-metal god, and then, when the rhythm's more funky, plays a twisted melody that sounds like the aural representation of a calculus equation.

When Holdsworth's playing, this band sounds like it's on a purposeful quest. A notoriously technical musician, he may have a ton to say, but doesn't feel compelled to say it all at once. He moves over these percolating soundscapes with the patience of a great storyteller, and as you follow his thoughts on the swervy "Night Illusion" and the booty-shaking "Ensnuria," you can't help wondering how fusion ever got such a bad name. This bubbly stuff sure doesn't deserve it.

GENRE: 🎸 Rock. **RELEASED:** 1976, Virgin. **KEY TRACKS:** "Night Illusion," "Percolations." **CATALOG CHOICE:** Allan Holdsworth: *Metal Fatigue.* **NEXT STOP:** Brand X: *Missing Period.* **AFTER THAT:** Jean-Luc Ponty: *King Kong.*

The Complete 1938 Carnegie Hall Concert

Benny Goodman and His Orchestra

Tickets for admission into Carnegie Hall on January 16, 1938, cost $2.75, a steep charge at the time. But this was no ordinary event. It was the first-ever jazz concert at the storied hall, and it featured not just the most popular swing band in the land, the Benny Goodman Orchestra, but the clarinetist's trio and quartet and members of the bands led by Count Basie and Duke Ellington.

This was swing's "coming out" party, and as is audible on the (alas, noisy) surviving tapes, the crowd was in the mood, to say the least. When Goodman and crew finish "Sing, Sing, Sing," the barnstorming showcase for drummer Gene Krupa that was a favorite of swing dancers, the response is thunderous. The same thing happens on Goodman's bobbing-and-weaving hit "Don't Be That Way," and an extended jam through "Honeysuckle Rose." Swing, as practiced by Goodman's "hot" band, easily warms up the rarefied setting. At least one reason is Goodman's own facility; his classical chops are audible here, as are his instincts for finding—and sometimes leaning on—the blue notes.

By the time he stepped on the Carnegie stage, the clarinetist, born in Chicago to Hungarian Jewish immigrants, had already made an even more important contribution to jazz—by employing qualified musicians and arrangers regardless of color. In 1934, Goodman was hired to provide music for the NBC radio series *Let's Dance;* in search of an authentic swing sound, Goodman retained arranger Fletcher Henderson (see p. 354), whose exuberant scores gave Goodman hit after hit. The next year, with his big band in demand, Goodman put together a trio (and later a quartet) to play during the band's breaks; this group was built around pianist Teddy Wilson, the first African American to appear regularly with a white band. (Anticipating trouble in the Deep South, where Jim Crow laws enforced racial segregation, Goodman simply skipped touring in the region.) Later additions to Goodman's groups included vibraphonist Lionel Hampton and the innovative electric guitarist Charlie Christian (see p. 169), who added a welcome dose of modernity. Goodman's moves, which came ten years before Jackie Robinson would integrate Major League Baseball, were not just headline-grabbing publicity stunts: They helped him develop and spread a suave, color-blind sense of swing that for a long time had no peer.

Originally conceived as a publicity stunt, the Carnegie Hall concert turned out to be a huge success.

GENRE: 🅙 Jazz. **RELEASED:** 1992, Columbia. **KEY TRACKS:** "Sing, Sing, Sing," "Don't Be That Way," "One O'Clock Jump." **CATALOG CHOICE:** *The Complete RCA Victor Small Group Recordings.* **NEXT STOP:** Lionel Hampton: *Hamp and Getz.* **AFTER THAT:** Artie Shaw: *The Centennial Collection.*

Behind the Beat, and Right on Time

Go!

Dexter Gordon

Every jazz musician has a different approach to time. Some play exactly on the beat, some push ahead like commuters afraid to be late for work, and some, like the tenor saxophonist Dexter Gordon (1923–1990), hang a mile back, forever threatening to grind the music to a crawl.

The L.A.-born tenorman knew that it took only that threat—the hint of a work slowdown—to keep things interesting. On his wonderful career highlight *Go!*, Gordon zozzles through a swinging original called "Cheese Cake" at a perfectly serene pace that almost disregards the tempo. He does the same thing on the medium bounce "Second Balcony Jump," and the ballad "Guess I'll Hang My Tears Out to Dry." The music might be galloping, but Gordon just pokes along, timing his phrases to create tension with his precision-minded rhythm section, which includes pianist Sonny Clark and drummer Billy Higgins. Having played with Gordon some, they came to this date prepared: They let him ramble, and reinforce his allusions to nursery rhymes and pop songs while doing everything they can to keep the train running on time.

Go! was recorded in August 1962, just before Gordon, who'd already done time on drug-related charges and mounted at least one "comeback," left the U.S. to live the expatriate jazz life in Europe, which he did for the next fifteen years. Although his stated intention for leaving was to reach a wider audience, he also managed to miss the social upheaval of urban America in the 1960s. The isolation had an interesting impact on his art: The music Gordon made after this date, including such well-respected works as *Our Man in Paris*, has a time-capsule quality, as though he's willfully clinging to the sounds of a long vanished bebop moment. Jazz changed dramatically, but Gordon stayed put. This worked to his advantage when, upon returning to the States in the late '70s, he began another comeback—reinventing himself as a ballad-playing elder statesman. He capped his career acting and playing in *'Round Midnight,* the 1986 film about the lives of expatriate jazzers; Gordon proved convincing in the starring role, hitting the notes of determination and dissipation that defined his own career while staying, as always, just a shade behind the beat.

GENRE: 🎵 Jazz. **RELEASED:** 1962, Blue Note. **KEY TRACKS:** "Second Balcony Jump," "Cheese Cake." **CATALOG CHOICES:** *Our Man in Paris; Sophisticated Giant.* **NEXT STOP:** Johnny Griffin: *A Blowin' Session.* **AFTER THAT:** Red Garland Quintet: *Soul Junction.*

Gordon's 6'5" stature earned him the nickname "Long Tall Dexter."

Believe the Subtitle

Symphony No. 3, Op. 26: Symphony of Sorrowful Songs

Henryk Górecki

Dawn Upshaw, London Sinfonietta (David Zinman, cond.)

Nothing much happens in the first few minutes of this work. We open in a pool of low-strings murk, and we stay there, stewing. It's as though the Polish composer Henryk Górecki is clearing his throat, insisting on a certain quality of attention. Or, perhaps, he's making sure the whole room reaches the proper gloomy frequency.

This stasis has an effect. When the sonorities do change, they have cataclysmic impact. Górecki organized the extended first movement as a series of overlapping "canons," or rounds, in which slow-moving motifs are layered over each other to create a counterpoint. It's a cerebral technique sometimes used by minimalists, but Górecki lets the ideas emerge so gently, it hardly seems like a device at all—the dissonances that result carry their own emotional surges. The chords swell up one by one, gusts of wind announcing a gathering storm. When the voice enters, after thirteen minutes, things have swirled to a head; the grieving mother at the center of the work is finally heard. What had been indistinct atmosphere becomes jabbing weaponry behind her.

As the subtitle suggests, the texts are concerned with sorrow. Some are shrouded in religious pleas: The prayer in the second movement was found written on the wall of a Gestapo prison cell in Poland. When Dawn Upshaw, as the grief-stricken mom, digs into it on this recording, her request for help from

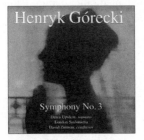

Górecki himself was surprised by the commercial success of this piece.

the Blessed Virgin seems both desperate and futile, a necessary exercise in the long quest for "closure." The final movement again hits the somber tone of an ancient chant, even though this text appropriates a folk song for the mother's lament: "He lies in a grave, I know not where."

Górecki's masterwork premiered in 1976, and was well received though hardly a sensation. This recording became an unlikely global phenomenon in the early 1990s—selling so well it reached number 6 on the British pop albums chart. One theory about the decades-delayed response is that the world wasn't ready for such a dose of sad music in the middle '70s. But certainly some credit goes to this coloristic reading from conductor David Zinman, who lets the festering chordal schemes decay spectacularly, sweeping all within earshot into deep, inescapable sorrow.

GENRE: 🎼 Classical. **RELEASED:** 1994, Nonesuch. **KEY TRACK:** Second movement: Lento y Largo. **CATALOG CHOICE:** *String Quartets Nos. 1 and 2,* Kronos Quartet. **NEXT STOP:** Arvo Pärt: *Tabula rasa* (see p. 582). **AFTER THAT:** Louis Andriessen: *De Staat.*

The Work of a Pre-Renaissance Renaissance Woman

A Feather on the Breath of God: Sequences and Hymns by Abbess Hildegard of Bingen

Gothic Voices with Emma Kirkby

During a life of almost wanton creativity that was radical for the twelfth century, the individualistic Abbess Hildegard of Bingen wrote plays and poems, studied medicine, painted (one of her works adorns the cover of this CD), and spent a decade documenting her paranormal visions in a book called *Scivias.*

Feather is one of the bestselling collections of pre-classical music ever.

Those pursuits all required a certain boldness. In her compositions Hildegard alters the rigid conventions of sacred music to express the sound inside her soul. Her tunes can be appreciated as a derivation of Gregorian chant, the mostly anonymous religious melodies that are forever seeking harmonious resolution. But where chant can feel dutiful, Hildegard wrote gentle spiral-staircase melodies that sway and swerve and suggest what it's like to be seized with religious fervor. Some of them, like "O ecclesia," are imbued with an almost erotic yearning, as the voice attempts ever more unlikely intervallic leaps to unite with the spiritual source.

To modern listeners, this may seem an obvious pursuit—aren't most artists seeking that communion, that higher plane, when they begin? But in the Middle Ages, one didn't "compose": Music was seen primarily as a way to give religious texts a hallowed framework. Hildegard is significant for the ardor and the beauty of her melodies: This woman was obviously transported by devotion, and long before it was standard practice, she found a language that enabled her to share that devotion with others.

Released well before the *Chant* craze of the 1990s, this disc was among the first to show that early music could be commercially viable. Credit for this goes to Christopher Page, the director of Gothic Voices, who stripped away most of the instrumental accompaniments (which often merely double the vocal line) in order to focus on the strangely stirring modal melodies. And to English soprano Emma Kirkby, whose renderings of "Columba aspexit" and "Ave, generosa" exude a calmed, centered beauty. Sliding into her wondrously luminous upper register, she makes it easy to imagine what these themes might have sounded like when Hildegard, the firebrand abbess, first divined them.

GENRE: 🌐 Classical. **RELEASED:** 1981, Hyperion. **KEY TRACKS:** "Columba aspexit," "O ecclesia," "O ignis spiritus," "Ave, generosa." **CATALOG CHOICE:** *The Marriage of Heaven and Hell.* **NEXT STOP:** Karlheinz Stockhausen: *Stimmung* (see p. 744).

A Double Take on Bach from a Musical Maverick

A State of Wonder: J. S. Bach's Goldberg Variations

Glenn Gould

Before Glenn Gould, pianists usually approached the Goldberg Variations with great reverence, observing Bach's notions of structure and pace, while adding little of themselves. As a result, most recordings were kind of snoozy—fitting for a piece that, according to Bach legend, was commissioned by the insomniac Baron von Keyserling for his court harpsichordist, named Goldberg, to play in the wee hours.

A twenty-two-year-old Canadian prodigy, Gould (1932–1982) transformed this often-overlooked also-ran of the piano repertoire into a platform for thoughtful, ecstatic, intensely personal playing. On his 1955 recording debut, Gould completely gooses Goldberg. But he's never merely a brash youth. He finds singing flourishes within Bach's transitional melodies. He makes the connective tissue that links major themes almost float along. Seizing upon little bits of counterpoint that other pianists obscured, he calls attention to the almost cryptic multilayered logic Bach embedded in the initial aria and the thirty subsequent variations, which are presented in ten groups of three. Among the most illuminating of Gould's treatments are the showy, impulsive 5th Variation and the 25th Variation (sometimes referred to as "Black Pearl"), which is saturated with a feeling of introspection.

This recording established Gould as an important pianistic thinker, and launched a career that ballooned to rock-star proportions. He became a mythic figure, a situation his willfully odd demeanor (he was known to mumble audibly or chuckle to himself during performances) did little to dispel. And though he was usually reluctant to revisit pieces he'd recorded in the past, Gould returned to the Goldberg shortly before his death from a massive stroke in 1982. He allegedly didn't like the liberties he'd taken with the variations as a young man, and in the liner notes to the new treatment said he wanted to consider the work's "thirty very interesting but independent-minded pieces" in terms of the "arithmetical correspondence between theme and variation."

Sure enough, the later recording—on the second disc of this double-feature—is more contemplative. The tempos are stately—when he comes upon a small idea that delights him, Gould slows down just a hair to savor it. He's still focusing on Bach's interior subtleties, but he refrains from letting his own impulses wash over them quite as often, and this detachment allows the magnificent orderliness of the work to shine through.

GENRE: ⚅ Classical. **RELEASED:** 2002, Sony Classical. **KEY TRACKS:** From 1955: Variation 3, Variation 25. From 1981: Aria, Variation 9, Variation 10. **COLLECTOR'S NOTE:** A bonus disc includes a fifty-minute Gould interview discussing the differences between the early and late treatments. **CATALOG CHOICE:** J. S. Bach: *The Art of the Fugue* (Gould on church organ). **NEXT STOP:** E. Power Biggs: *The Great Preludes and Fugues,* Vol. 1. **AFTER THAT:** Jacques Loussier Trio: *The Brandenburgs.*

Highlights from a Long Career of Driving People Wild on the Dance Floor

30 Aniversario

El Gran Combo de Puerto Rico

When Latin musicians speak of "swing," they're talking about a rhythmic propulsion that's akin to—but not quite the same as—the swing associated with jazz. It's a feeling that's elusive, and impossible to notate. As in jazz, swing in salsa has to do with the emphasis on certain parts of the beat, and the spaces between the beats. But it also connotes the ways the various percussion parts fit together, and a rhythm section's ability to spin repetitive figures into a pulse that floats along organically. "Either you have it or you don't," the pianist Eddie Palmieri once said. "It can't be taught."

Latin swing carries important regional differences—the Puerto Rican variety is tighter and more exact than the more open, loping Cuban swing, yet not nearly as jittery as the Dominican version. One of the most distinctive rhythmic approaches of any modern group belongs to El Gran Combo de Puerto Rico, which has, for more than forty years, cranked out incredibly upbeat music for dancing, all of it blessed with a signature swing feel. This band isn't concerned with blazing new trails; it makes music to be enjoyed. Few outfits equal its knack for spreading positive vibes across a dance floor.

This compilation, issued to mark the band's thirtieth anniversary in 1992, is a parade of energetic contagions. There are early chant-based hits from the band's first album, *Acangana*, and more elaborate arrangements from the smoother *salsa romántica* of the '90s. Incredibly, no matter the musical fashion, the core values of the Combo—which was formed by pianist and arranger Rafael Ithier in 1962, when he and several musicians left the esteemed Cortijo y Su Combo to create a sassier band—remain the same. All share the relentless swing that makes every refrain (the best include "El menu," "Brujeria," and "Timbalero") sound like an invitation to an amazing party.

GENRE: 🌐 World/Puerto Rico. **RELEASED:** 1992, Combo. **KEY TRACKS:** "El menu," "Son de Santurce," "Brujeria," "Un verano en Nueva York." **CATALOG CHOICE:** *Acangana.* **NEXT STOP:** Sonora Ponceña: *Fuego en el 23.* **AFTER THAT:** Batacumbele: *Con un poco de songo* (see p. 52).

Look Through Any Window . . .

American Beauty

The Grateful Dead

There are many portals through which to begin an exploration of the Grateful Dead. You could start at the beginning, with the 1967 self-titled debut, to hear the San Francisco group trying to shake its jug-band roots while serving up suitably weird blues designed to accompany the storied countercultural acid tests.

Or you could start near the end, with *In the Dark* (1987), the Dead's last studio work of consequence, which yielded the commercial success "Touch of Grey" and other songs lit with the wisdom of grizzled road vets. Some Deadheads would advise that the only reasonable first recorded encounter with the mythic band that rose from San Francisco hippie culture is a live concert recording—and thanks to an aggressive archive program, there are plenty available.

Sooner or later, though, anyone seeking to understand the Dead needs to hear *American Beauty*, the crown jewel of the band's studio efforts. Recorded in August and September 1970, this collection documents the Dead before jamming became its raison d'être. The tunes are simple, kindhearted rambles through American folk, country two-step, and appropriations of Appalachian hymns. The performances are reverent, with little soloing and nothing getting in the way of the songs. And what songs: For decades after this release, the presence of its highlights "Sugar Magnolia," "Truckin'," "Box of Rain," or "Friend of the Devil" on a set list was known to send hempnecklaced Deadheads into rapture. That's partly because the tunes are so life-affirming, and partly because in the years of touring, the

Guitarist Garcia reportedly picked the band's name when he came upon the phrase in a dictionary.

songs evolved tremendously— from disciplined three-minute miniatures into jaw-dropping twenty-minute odysseys.

The Dead wasn't temperamentally suited to the studio. But around the time of this album, the musicians and primary lyricist Robert Hunter were writing at a fever pitch, building a songbook that was revolutionary and patchwork-quilt quaint at the same time. Just as Hunter appropriated the plainspoken language of old folk songs, guitarist Jerry Garcia, who'd played banjo in jug bands, brought that instrument's crisp articulation to the electric guitar. Everyone else follows that folkloric bent without seeming too worried about details; the performances are sometimes ragged and the vocals stray off-key. Yet somehow the scruffiness becomes part of the charm, helping to speed the trip back to the sounds and folklore of an earlier time while underscoring the Dead's great alchemy trick—transforming the rustic into the revelatory.

GENRE: 🅑 Rock. **RELEASED:** 1970, Warner Bros. **KEY TRACKS:** "Sugar Magnolia," "Truckin'," "Box of Rain," "Friend of the Devil." **CATALOG CHOICES:** *Live Dead; Workingman's Dead; Dick's Picks,* Vol. 4. **NEXT STOP:** The Band: *Music from Big Pink.* **AFTER THAT:** Jerry Garcia Band: *Live.*

The Apex of Soul Singing

Call Me

Al Green

Thanks to the enormous popularity of TV's *American Idol*, the ideal of singing in this great land has devolved into a kind of extreme sport— empty athletic expressions, bombastic shows of brutal lung power.

Al Green does not sing this way. He's gonna sneak in. He's gonna slide over until he's inches from your ear. He's hardly gonna open his mouth, just enough to give you one of those patented "Hmmm baby" lines that go right down to your knees. *Have you been makin' out OK?*

This works better.

This is singing of such subtlety and control it makes anything showy seem incredibly coarse by comparison. Starting with *Gets Next to You* (1971) and continuing through five releases over the next three years, Green, producer Willie Mitchell, and a crew of tuned-in Memphis musicians created not just a stack of hits, but a deeper shade of soul, in which nuance matters more than shouting. The "sound" that helped make Green one of the greats is minimal. Skeletal guitar, creeping organ, pattering drums set the table. Then Green slinks in and whips up a gourmet feast.

Though it wasn't the breakthrough (that would be *Gets Next to You*) and doesn't have the hugest hits (that would be *Let's Stay Together*), *Call Me* is Green's first totally cohesive statement. It's the moment when everything clicks, and the moment just before Green and Mitchell are aware of everything clicking: Later works have just a hint of self-consciousness.

Green became a minister in '76 and in the '80s recorded mostly gospel.

Call Me also sports two of the most compelling covers in Green's songbook—the Hank Williams chestnut "I'm So Lonesome I Could Cry" and Willie Nelson's "Funny How Time Slips Away." These are as significant as the loverman originals—in part because they remind you of how the great voices of the South, white and black, moved their listeners beyond stereotypical notions about race.

With Green, all considerations of style and genre, the twang of Williams and all the rest, become insignificant next to the intense and perpetual seduction in progress. Green does his beautiful thing without clobbering anyone over the head. If everyone in America listened to him once a week, *American Idol* would quickly seem meaningless.

GENRE: 🎤 R&B. **RELEASED:** 1973, Hi Records/The Right Stuff. **KEY TRACKS:** "Call Me," "Have You Been Makin' Out OK?," "I'm So Lonesome I Could Cry," "Here I Am (Come and Take Me)." **CATALOG CHOICES:** *Let's Stay Together; I'm Still In Love with You.* **NEXT STOP:** Donny Hathaway: *These Songs for You, Live.* **AFTER THAT:** Tyrone Davis: *Turn Back the Hands of Time.*

The Spirit Moves

Feelin' the Spirit

Grant Green

Dig deep enough into the past lives of jazz musicians, and somewhere along the way you'll arrive at a church. Often that dimension is dormant, but every now and then the influence of long-ago Sunday mornings emerges, as happens on the charged *Feelin' the Spirit.*

The guitarist Grant Green, one of the

most important soul-jazz bandleaders of the 1960s, began his professional career at thirteen, accompanying choirs at his St. Louis church. Although he quickly moved on to blues and jazz (and had the typical jazzman battles with addiction), he never lost the zealousness or the sense of unshakable optimism that underpins spirituals and other religious music. In his hands, even a greasy soul mambo or a sullen blues could take on the characteristics of prayer.

During a prolific period of recording in 1962, Green put together a Latin-themed album, then a country set, and then convinced Blue Note to let him do this album of spirituals—those descended-through-generations expressions of pain, like "Nobody Knows the Trouble I've Seen," that have roots in slave culture, the blues, and work songs. Green got young Herbie Hancock to

Green has been called "one of the great unsung heroes of jazz guitar."

play piano, a crucial choice: Throughout *Feelin' the Spirit*, the two sustain a reverent running discussion, trading ad-libs that are nearly as memorable and thoughtfully considered as the original themes. They're members of the congregation who, having just heard a life-changing sermon, are still mulling its ramifications. Needless to say, these are ideal conditions for the ever-elusive spirit to move freely around the room.

GENRE: 🎵 Jazz. **RELEASED:** 1962, Blue Note. **KEY TRACKS:** "Go Down Moses," "Joshua Fit de Battle of Jericho." **CATALOG CHOICES:** *Born to Be Blue; Idle Moments.* **NEXT STOP:** George Benson: *It's Uptown.* **AFTER THAT:** Wynton Marsalis: *In This House, On This Morning.*

High-Concept Brat Rock

American Idiot

Green Day

A story headlined "New Rock Is Passé on Radio" in *The New York Times* arts section of April 28, 2005, noted that all across America, the big radio conglomerates were moving away from the "modern rock" genre, and abruptly flipping their formats to talk, urban music, or even classic rock.

The story featured rock industry types lamenting this demise, but from a musical standpoint it was long overdue. Ever since the wickedly smart 1994 Green Day album *Dookie*, released just before Nirvana's Kurt Cobain committed suicide, modern rock (also tagged "alternative" rock or "alt" rock) had been overrun by aggrieved boys. These artists (Creed, Blink 182, and others) seized on the bratty adenoidal whine of Green Day singer

Billie Joe Armstrong but missed his accompanying wink, and as a result their self-obsessed musings mattered mainly to other adolescent males in similar alienated states.

With the barbed *American Idiot*, Green Day takes aim at all the self-indulgence that surrounds modern rock culture as well as the presidency of George W. Bush and the media. Armstrong is still wryly self-aware, but as he follows the character called "St. Jimmy" around a soulless suburban dystopia, there's palpable disgust in his voice. And alarm. He rants about consumer culture and the worship of false idols in severe tones; he talks about the search for "realness" in a way that makes you wonder whether anything is worth believing in. *American Idiot* catches the applecart-upsetting anarchy that fueled the first iteration of punk and the withering social critiques associated with the Who and the Clash, but it cushions those blows with addictive, diabolically hooky refrains. Green Day's jittery sing-alongs operate on several different levels at once: They're strident warnings about

This was the first Green Day album to reach #1 in the U.S.

the fragile mental makeup of the disaffected American Everykid, and at the same time they sound like victory dances for those conniving enough to reach the upper echelons of *Grand Theft Auto* on the PlayStation.

GENRE: 🎸 Rock.
RELEASED: 2004, Reprise.
KEY TRACKS: "Jesus of Suburbia," "Boulevard of Broken Dreams," "Whatsername."

CATALOG CHOICE: *Dookie.* **NEXT STOP:** Ramones: *Ramones* (see p. 631). **AFTER THAT:** Godsmack: *Awake.*

Delicate and Poetic, Like a Song

Lyric Pieces

Edvard Grieg
Emil Gilels

Lullabies, dances, and caprices on such subjects as homesickness and memory, Edvard Grieg's *Lyric Pieces* are delicious miniatures. The Norwegian composer is known for his piano concerto, which is, on one level, similarly compact—a series of motifs that are cannily strung together into perfectly proportioned phrases. Here, there's no stringing—these brief investigations, which were published between 1867 and 1901, capture a moment and then move on. These pieces are not as dependent on structure as, say, Mendelssohn's *Songs Without Words*—they don't always follow AB song form. In Grieg, a terse expression of theme might be followed by a detour into a related tonal center, then a recapitulation. Just as often, though, Grieg doesn't even bother to circle around to the original theme. He simply finishes his thought and moves on.

To get an idea of Grieg's evocative compositional style, cue up the opening "Arietta,"

the most famous of the *Lyric Pieces*, and then its echo at the end of the disc, "Remembrances." The first expression is spry, and the later one is wistful, almost sad. Russian pianist Emil Gilels renders both with almost superhuman restraint, taking pains to make the common melody signify in vastly different ways.

Gilels understands the compactness of Grieg (1843–1907), who devoted much of his career to writing Norwegian art music inspired by folk forms. In these renderings, the compositions are beautiful and at the same time earthy, spiked with a zest for the tiny slivers of life. Claude Debussy once derided Grieg's music as "bonbons filled with ice," but in Gilels's clean passages there is also great warmth—an affection for the lyrical bent of the pieces, and overriding respect for the shards of poetry scattered inside the music.

GENRE: 🎵 Classical. **RELEASED:** 1973, Deutsche Grammophon. **KEY**

TRACKS: "Melodie," "Homesickness," "Arietta," "Remembrances." **ANOTHER INTERPRETATION:** Walter Gieseking. **NEXT STOP:** Felix Mendelssohn: *Songs Without Words,* Andras Schiff. **AFTER THAT:** Irén Marik: *From Bach to Bartók.*

Two Heavyweights of the Piano Repertoire

Grieg, Schumann Piano Concertos

Edvard Grieg and Robert Schumann
Leif Ove Andsnes, Berlin Philharmonic (Mariss Jansons, cond.)

While a student in Leipzig, young Norwegian Edvard Grieg heard Clara Schumann perform her husband's then-recent piano concerto, which was premiered in 1856. It was a eureka moment, and it inspired Grieg to work on a piano piece of his own. When he completed it, in 1870, Grieg took it to Franz Liszt, the reigning king of the Germanic piano, who according to legend played through it flawlessly, and made suggestions. The similarities between the two works made it a logical pairing on concert programs and recordings.

The two pieces are in the same key. They both start with a sudden orchestral flourish, then a descending piano figure that establishes the primary rhythmic motif of the opening movement. But as Norwegian pianist Leif Ove Andsnes observes in the liner notes of this crisp reading, the two pieces have vastly different resonances. "The Schumann is emotionally very complex—at times even schizophrenic, as if it's trying to pull you in different directions simultaneously. The Grieg, on the other hand, is passionate, extroverted, and childlike. It's more of a young man's piece."

Andsnes brings a discernible wonder—and a heart tuned to the romantic—to

Edvard Grieg has been called the "Chopin of the North."

both works. The Grieg, which was recorded in a studio, finds him amplifying the composer's origins by riffling through the folk-dance themes (and extended fantasias built upon them) with a youthful spring in his step. The Schumann, recorded live, is more lyrical: An exchange between piano and oboe near the end of the first movement finds both musicians savoring the theme, while the rhapsodic second movement has a dreamy, unhurried air. This carries over into the finale, an extended power surge that requires the pianist to alternate between floral harplike runs and lines that are much more technically challenging. Andsnes simply eats these up.

The Berlin Philharmonic is exacting, as usual, and Andsnes counts on that. His darting flashes sometimes test the prevailing tempo, as if he's trying to see how far he can pull away before sending the orchestra off the track. This creates moments of exhilarating tension, but happily, no derailments.

GENRE: 🎧 Classical. RELEASED: 2003, EMI. KEY TRACKS: Grieg: second movement. Schumann: first movement. ANOTHER INTERPRETATION: Murray Perahia: *Great Pianists Series*. CATALOG CHOICE: Schumann: *Piano Works*, Wilhelm Kempff. Grieg: *Lyric Pieces for Piano* (see p. 326). NEXT STOP: Leoš Janáček: *A Recollection*, Andras Schiff.

Pure Exalting Joy

Recorded Live at "The Bear" in Chicago

Bessie Griffin and the Gospel Pearls

O f the many fire-breathing gospel women working in Mahalia Jackson's shadow, Bessie Griffin (1922–1989) was the one most likely to send a congregation into rapture. Her voice was big and authoritative, a supple yet sturdy instrument that one student, the singer and songwriter Neko Case (see p. 150), esteems as "the greatest singing voice North America has ever produced." Griffin used that gift to send pure exalting joy through time-tested warhorses of gospel, and when supported by the five Gospel Pearls, who were more vigorous than most backing chorales, the sound they produced together is awesome. You hear Griffin do anything—"Wade in the Water," "Didn't It Rain"—and you're ready to join her congregation.

A native of New Orleans, Griffin managed to record for over four decades. Although she was frequently cited as a major force in gospel, and appears on many key compilations, she never attained superstar status. Compounding that slight is this: Many of her best works, including *Swing Down Sweet Chariot* and the conceptual *Portraits in Bronze*, have not been issued on CD. As a result, this live date, which is a bit heavy on the upbeat jubilee zeal, is the best way to encounter Griffin. Put it on, and prepare to be converted.

GENRE: ✝ Gospel. RELEASED: 1963, Epic. (Reissued 1998.) KEY TRACKS: "Wade in the Water," "Same Train," "Move Up a Little Higher." CATALOG CHOICE: *Even Me: Four Decades of Bessie Griffin*. NEXT STOP: Mavis Staples: *We'll Never Turn Back*. AFTER THAT: Various Artists: *The Great Gospel Women*.

Carefully Planned Collisions

Fogaraté!

Juan Luis Guerra y 440

A ll recording artists struggle with stereotyping, but those who make tropical Latin music perhaps suffer the most: The minute a Latin band has a hit built on a specific regional rhythm, like say Colombian *cumbia*, it is expected to churn out similar *cumbia*s, if not exact facsimiles, forevermore. The charismatic Juan Luis Guerra has openly defied this marketing constriction. He's from the Dominican Republic, and though his early hits were associated with the country's brisk dance style known as merengue, he's insisted on exploring lots of distantly related musics, including funk and salsa and, on several sumptuously arranged tracks on this set, African *soukous*.

Guerra, who studied at the Berklee School of Music in Boston, isn't interested in putting the whole world-in-a-blender approach: He brings a respect for tradition, and a craftsman's sense of detail, to his carefully managed collisions. The tracks enlivened by *soukous* catch the subtleties of both styles without blurring their distinctive features; Guerra's precision makes this new pulse seem utterly organic, like it should have been there all along. When,

on "La cosquillita," Guerra's mighty band 440 welcomes the legendary accordionist of traditional merengue, Francisco Ulloa (see page 794), they play things by the book, perfectly placing every last tick of the mercilessly fast rhythm so old-time sticklers will appreciate it.

The album's highlight is the straightforward "Oficio de enamorado," a suave salsa adventure that moves at two speeds simultaneously: As the band punches out a razor-sharp, exacting rhythm, Guerra trades the Dominican punctuality for a looser, more Cuban approach to time, singing about the thrills and torments of love like he's got all day.

GENRE: 🌐 World/Dominican Republic. **RELEASED:** 1994, RCA International. **KEY TRACKS:** "Oficio de enamorado," "El farolito." **CATALOG CHOICE:** *Bachata rosa.* **NEXT STOP:** Pedro Luis Ferrer: *Rustico.* **AFTER THAT:** Milly Quezada: *Tesoros de mi tierra.*

Record Geek Makes Good

Bee Thousand

Guided by Voices

As a young man, Guided by Voices singer and songwriter Robert Pollard lived the record-geek rock and roll dream. He was the kid who knew every note of the rock canon (right down to the rare British B sides), the type who'd spent his entire youth and young manhood in the garage, writing songs openly derived from those of his heroes. Then, after years of this, his songs suddenly stopped being so derivative. They acquired a disarming catchiness, a cocktail of familiar elements that somehow ends up tasting exotic anyway. Through several lineup changes, GBV was never a commercial force. But it became something even

Bee Thousand was recorded on a four-track in the basements and garages of the band members.

rarer: the cult act propelled by critics and the cognoscenti into a rare position of influence.

Bee Thousand is the first album on which Pollard's rock worship fully coalesces. In his best songs, the guitar-pummeling intensity of the Who bumps into the melodic finery of the Beatles, creating a musical delirium that atones for Pollard's cryptic lyrics. Just the song titles hint at the willful obfuscation in store: "Gold Star for Robot Boy," "Her Psychology Today," and "Kicker of Elves." On those songs and others, though, Pollard's words are secondary to his vocal melodies: "Tractor Rape Chain," one of several tunes that echo the anthem era, finds him singing behind a thick curtain of guitars, an obliterating drone that nearly drowns him out.

When *Bee Thousand* appeared, Pollard was making his living teaching grade school and playing Dayton, Ohio, clubs on weekends. Within a year, he became a full-time rocker, and as the band began attracting national attention, he acquired a reputation as an onstage wildman. The antics helped "sell" Guided by Voices, but the songwriting is Pollard's lasting legacy—virtually every GBV album that has followed this one, and there have been many, contains flashes of drop-dead hook-happy greatness.

GENRE: 🎸 Rock. **RELEASED:** 1994, Scat/Matador. **KEY TRACKS:** "Hardcore UFOs," "Tractor Rape Chain," "Hot Freaks," "Gold Star for Robot Boy," "Kicker of Elves." **CATALOG CHOICES:** *Half Smiles of the Decomposed; Alien Lanes.* **NEXT STOP:** Sebadoh: *Sebadoh III.* **AFTER THAT:** Dinosaur Jr.: *Where You Been.*

"Welcome to the Jungle, We Got Fun and Games"

Appetite for Destruction

Guns N' Roses

Never in rock has such a shrill little peashooter of a voice done so much damage. Axl Rose blazed into the otherwise tame consciousness of 1987 sounding like he was in the grip of some hernia-inducing martial-arts lock. His voice seemed stuck in "panic" mode, and though it wasn't the most artful sound, his scream was exactly what rock needed at the time. It located the menace that had gone missing. It romanticized the pull of heroin and other lurid dangers. It could clean out your cobwebs.

Naturally Rose had some help—in the form of laughably cartoonish characters that might have been sent from Central Casting to play dissipated rockers on some cop show. There was the lead guitarist named "Slash," who did just that, a stoned looking bassist named Duff, and a leering rhythm guitarist named Izzy Stradlin. Later, ego-related com-

Appetite is the bestselling debut album in rock history.

plications soured the enterprise, but during the making of this album these guys were blood brothers, down together for whatever debauchery was on the menu and into playing hard rock with maximum impact.

Appetite opens with an invitation to go behind the scenes into GN'R world, via the come-on "Welcome to the Jungle," since used for countless scenes of drug-addict desperation in feature films. Then comes a rapid attack of abrasive three-chord rock, each selection taking advantage of Rose's rusty needle of a singing voice. On several other drug trips, notably the frenzied "Mr. Brownstone," GN'R shows both cohesion and dexterity, the ability to switch between pile-driving backbeats and less tethered, often mystical, reflections.

The Guns' vision of hard rock—which introduced a touch of hip-hop gangster menace into the classic rock stomps of the '70s—broke big immediately. And then, true to the *Behind the Music* script, success became the band's undoing. There were subsequent releases, though the truly great songs of the two-disc *Use Your Illusion I* and *II* could have easily fit on a single EP. After that came the outright madness that only descends on the most indulged rock stars: public feuding, nasty lawsuits, endless rumors. Rose, owner of the GN'R trademark, mounted ill-fated tours and then spent over ten years recording the fifth studio album, *Chinese Democracy*, with a band of hired guns. As of this writing, it remains unreleased.

GENRE: 🎸 Rock. **RELEASED:** 1987, Geffen. **KEY TRACKS:** "Welcome to the Jungle," "Mr. Brownstone," "Paradise City," "Rocket Queen." **CATALOG CHOICE:** *Use Your Illusion I* and *II.* **NEXT STOP:** The Black Crowes: *Shake Your Money Maker.* **AFTER THAT:** Velvet Revolver (featuring the original GN'R rhythm section): *Velvet Revolver.*

Dust on the Tracks, in the Wind, Everywhere

Dust Bowl Ballads

Woody Guthrie

With this series of vivid story-songs, Woody Guthrie made the dust storms that roiled the Southwest in the 1930s a part of the American experience. People in other parts of the country heard news about them, of course, but Guthrie's accounts brought the devastation to human scale, where the suddenness and terror, and the lingering aftereffects, could be fully felt. They gave the dust dimension.

Guthrie was born in Okemah, Oklahoma, and like so many fleeing the dust in the 1930s, moved to California. These songs chronicle the hardships faced by the victims of the drought there, and the pain they felt having to abandon their homes. When he recorded this set in New York in 1940, his voice held traces of the dust, mixed, warily, with indignation. "Tom Joad, Part 2" tells about the trials of dust-bowl refugees, among them a preacher who can't take it anymore. "Vigilante Man" explores the

Dust Bowl Ballads was Guthrie's first commercial release.

inevitability of violence—and the all-too-human men who inflict it—in forsaken places.

Guthrie, who later in 1940 wrote his most famous song "This Land Is Your Land," isn't much of a showman here—he emphasizes the hearts and souls of the people he's met—people who had no time to worry about the fine points of craft. He plays rudimentary guitar, and sings with little affectation save a parched dryness in his voice.

Dust Bowl Ballads remains Guthrie's most successful record, both in terms of sales and influence. Bob Dylan made these songs the backbone of his early repertoire, and wrote countless verses that follow Guthrie's outlines. Bruce Springsteen's *The Ghost of Tom Joad* looked at the descendants of the dust bowl, the victims of the same type of economic dislocation in a different time. These and other acolytes aspire to what came naturally to Guthrie here—narratives in which specific trials and tribulations offer insight into that elusive set of qualities sometimes called "the American character."

GENRE: 🌀 Folk. RELEASED: 1940, RCA. (Reissued 2000, Buddha.) KEY TRACKS: "Talking Dust Bowl Blues," "Pretty Boy Floyd," "I Ain't Got No Home," "Vigilante Man." CATALOG CHOICE: Library of Congress Recordings, Vol. 1. NEXT STOP: The Almanac Singers: Complete General Recordings (see p. 17).

No, Really, He Has Them

Damn Right, I've Got the Blues

Buddy Guy

Buddy Guy begins several songs here where most bluesmen end up— belting at the very top of his range. From the first notes of "Five Long Years," for example, he can be heard snarling as though he's been singing this particular song for ten minutes. Rage fills his voice, and shoots through his guitar. He's been wronged, and complains bitterly about how he worked two jobs for years, bringing home all his pay to an ungrateful woman who's taken advantage of him.

Starting at such a fever pitch can be risky. But Guy— the Chicago guitarist and singer who was present at the creation of important blues works in the 1960s, '70s, and '80s—somehow finds new places to take the pain. Curiously, though, when it's time for him to take a guitar solo, he goes in the other direction. He hushes the band down to a whisper, and then sneaks in all quiet-like. Having set the scene with those neon-lit verses, Guy's now going to take you deeply into this feeling, to places only the guitar can go. Note for stabbing note, he makes sure you appreciate the full dimension of what he's been talking about.

This record—which is sometimes referred

Guy has been known to play the guitar with his teeth.

to as a "comeback" even though Guy never went away—offers stupendous guitar solos, sometimes two in the same song. They're compact survey courses in blues feeling, covering everything from the *sotto voce* moan to the highly sexualized pitch-bending tirade to the full-on Muddy Waters roar he learned from playing alongside the master. A born entertainer, Guy has all kinds of crowd-pleasing tricks at his disposal. He turns out a solo on "Early in the Morning" that's so ferocious it humbles guests Jeff Beck and Eric Clapton, then blazes through "Five Long Years" like he's out to rekindle that classic Chicago blues fire all by himself.

GENRE: 🔵 Blues. RELEASED: 1991, Silvertone. KEY TRACKS: "Damn Right, I've Got the Blues," "Black Night," "Five Long Years." CATALOG CHOICE: The Complete Chess Studio Sessions. NEXT STOP: Otis Rush: The Classic Cobra Recordings (see p. 664).

Charlie Haden ✦ Merle Haggard ✦ Bill Haley and His Comets ✦ Tom T. Hall ✦ Oscar Hammerstein II and Jerome Kern ✦ Herbie Hancock ✦ George Frideric Handel ✦ Larry Harlow ✦ Joe Harriott Double Quintet ✦ Emmylou Harris ✦ George Harrison ✦ PJ Harvey ✦ Clara Haskil ✦ Donny Hathaway ✦ Coleman Hawkins ✦ Ted Hawkins ✦ Franz Josef Haydn ✦ Isaac **H** Hayes ✦ Ofra Haza ✦ Jascha Heifetz ✦ Fletcher Henderson ✦ Joe Henderson ✦ Jimi Hendrix ✦ Jerry Herman ✦ Bernard Herrmann ✦ Andrew Hill ✦ Lauryn Hill ✦ Roscoe Holcomb ✦ Billie Holiday ✦ Dave Holland ✦ Buddy Holly ✦ Gustav Holst ✦ John Lee Hooker ✦ Sol Hoʻopiʻi ✦ Lightnin' Hopkins ✦ Shirley Horn ✦ Vladimir Horowitz ✦ Son House ✦ Whitney Houston ✦ Howlin' Wolf ✦ Freddie Hubbard ✦ Lorraine Hunt Lieberson ✦ Mississippi John Hurt ✦ Hüsker Dü ✦ Bobby Hutcherson ✦ Huun-Huur-Tu

Bolero Laid Bare

Nocturne

Charlie Haden

The boleros that were popular in Cuba during the 1940s and '50s walk a fine line between romance and schmaltz. Depending on who's singing, these songs of unfulfilled passion can seem totally natural—or seriously overwrought. Bassist Charlie Haden had a typical jazzman's instinct about ways to shed new light on these tunes: Ditch the vocals. Or, more specifically, allow instrumentalists to "sing" these yearning themes. His *Nocturne* explores the hidden meanings and undercurrents of the form.

It's bolero laid bare, and reconstituted as an existential quest for understanding. A veteran of the innovative bands led by Ornette Coleman (see p. 181), Haden's forte is "opening up" rigid verse-chorus structures. Here, he, Cuban pianist Gonzalo Rubalcaba, and percussion wizard Ignacio Berroa do exactly that, adding interesting pauses and momentary detours that give the music a languid, floating aura. The musicians use the themes to deliberate about love and its cruelties anew, in a way that is open to the whims of the moment. Rubalcaba is an unlikely one to lead this charge: Until *Nocturne*, he was known mostly for his blistering 200-mph displays of technique. This project requires something much more tender from him. He approaches these stoic, sturdy melodies as though playing them for his children at bedtime.

Nocturne begins with "En la orilla del mundo," a haunting theme that connects the smoldering pulse of tango to the harmonic adventurousness of Claude Debussy. That casts the spell, and incredibly, the ten subsequent tracks sustain it. One of the many triumphs of this record is its enveloping aura of respectful quiet: Whether playing old tunes or like-minded originals, Haden and his accomplices (including guest guitarist Pat Metheny and saxophonists Joe Lovano and David Sanchez) fixate on the spirit of the bolero, and discover that even without the words, it has much to teach about life.

GENRE: 🅙 Jazz. **RELEASED:** 2001, Verve. **KEY TRACKS:** "Tres palabras," "Yo sin ti," "En la orilla del mundo," "El ciego." **CATALOG CHOICES:** *Folk Songs; The Ballad of the Fallen.* **NEXT STOP:** Gonzalo Rubalcaba: *Solo.* **AFTER THAT:** Frank Emilio Flynn: *Musica original de Cuba* (see p. 285).

Yes, Mama, You Were Right

Mama Tried

Merle Haggard

Country singers love their mamas. Country singers also love whiskey, and when they love whiskey too much, they get into trouble. When they get into trouble, they let mama down. This makes them feel worse, so they find their way back to whiskey.

Such is the cycle of life Merle Haggard sketches on his inspired *Mama Tried*. Not all the songs talk about running afoul of what mama taught was right—"In the Good Old Days" fondly remembers a hardscrabble youth spent walking miles to school carrying lunch in the bib of his overalls, and "Run 'Em Off" is the directive of a man worried about his wife being too friendly with the milkman.

But many of the originals are set in prison cells, with the young Haggard, who'd only been recording for four years when he made this, looking back. In the straightforward, affectation-free singing style that remains his trademark, he recalls nights of drinking that went sour and the horrible deeds that ensued, lamenting how, as his mama well knew, "I Could Have Gone Right." Even before the cover of Johnny Cash's "Folsom Prison Blues" (see p. 151), Haggard has laid out a detailed profile of the roughneck rogue—who only now, with the benefit of hindsight, has regret about what he's done.

"Mama Tried" is one of Haggard's 38 #1 singles.

The songs of *Mama Tried* are drawn, at least partly, from experience. Haggard's family fled the dust bowl of Oklahoma in the 1930s and settled in Bakersfield, California. His father died when he was nine; the trauma propelled young Merle to a life of petty crime that landed him in prison several times. He returned to Bakersfield (from San Quentin) in 1960, and began performing—aligning himself with the assertive, honky-tonk sound then blossoming in the region. This and other recordings for Capitol—including the hit "Okie from Muskogee"—established Haggard as an articulate and passionate torch carrier for traditional country and its working-folks values.

GENRE: ○ Country. **RELEASED:** 1968, Capitol. (Reissued 2006.) **KEY TRACKS:** "Mama Tried," "In the Good Old Days," "Teach Me to Forget." **CATALOG CHOICES:** *A Working Man Can't Get Nowhere Today; Lonesome Fugitive.* **NEXT STOP:** Waylon Jennings: *Honky Tonk Heroes* (see p. 395). **AFTER THAT:** George Strait: *Strait from the Heart.*

The Dawn of the Rock Era

"Rock Around the Clock"

Bill Haley and His Comets

The song many consider the one to permanently establish "rock and roll" in American culture began as a B side. After Bill Haley and His Comets were signed to Decca in 1954, producer Milt Gabler convinced Haley to release a futuristic little song called "Thirteen Women" as a first single. "(We're Gonna) Rock Around the Clock" was an afterthought, recorded hurriedly at the end of the session. Neither track electrified a huge audience ("Rock Around the Clock" peaked then at twenty-three), and Haley went on to record other singles—including a spirited version of Joe Turner's "Shake, Rattle, and Roll."

Almost a year later, the film star Glenn Ford was working on a teen movie called *Blackboard Jungle*. The producers asked if anyone knew a good song to open the film. Ford brought in a stack of 45-RPM singles owned by his son, Peter, including Haley's minor hit. The producers liked its brash, buoyant feel, and grabbed it immediately. After the film's premiere, "Rock Around the Clock" went berserk. It became the first rock and roll song to top the *Billboard* charts, and it stayed at number 1 for eight weeks in the summer of 1955. And it was one of the first rock songs to incite riots: In both the U.S. and England, there was chaos among teenagers in theaters when the song played before the film started. Since then, Haley's little tune has figured prominently in all kinds of pop-culture artifacts—notably the film *American Graffiti* and the TV series *Happy Days*, renewing its popularity over several generations.

Because the song has so much rhythm and blues in it, Haley has been lumped in with Pat

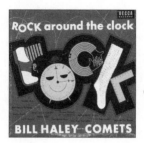

"Rock Around the Clock" stayed at the top of the charts for 8 weeks.

Boone and others as just another white appropriator of African American styles. The comparison has merit (Haley was crazy for R&B), but is unfair in one respect: Unlike Boone, who diluted every rhythm, Haley and his hard-charging crew understood the music well enough to execute it respectfully, right down to the careening solos and whomping stop-time breaks. Some credit for this goes to producer Gabler, who'd worked with Louis Jordan and others, and communicated to the Comets the fine points of the danceable backbeat. They obviously learned quickly, burning this high-spirited jump blues—recorded before Elvis Presley ever registered a chart hit—into the very source code of rock and roll.

GENRE: 🎸 Rock. **RELEASED:** 1955, Decca. **APPEARS ON:** *Rock Around the Clock*. **NEXT STOP:** Jerry Lee Lewis: *Twenty-five All-Time Greatest Sun Recordings*. **AFTER THAT:** Eddie Cochran: *Somethin' Else! The Fine-Lookin' Hits of . . .*

A Storyteller Goes Roaming

In Search of a Song

Tom T. Hall

By the time Tom T. Hall began making records, in the late '60s, most of the basic themes of country songs—cheating hearts and brawls and sad girls left alone at the bar—had been well explored. This did not deter the sharp-eyed singer, songwriter, and guitarist, who grew up in Olive Hill, Kentucky. First he wrote about morality and manners—his best-known song is the Jeannie C. Riley hit about hypocrites, "Harper Valley PTA." Then, after a few years of mid-level success, Hall set out on long solo drives, searching for the truths known only to residents of small-town America. He found characters and song ideas by the bushel, and these he harvested for several years, earning the moniker "The Storyteller."

This album, Hall's fifth, plays like a rambler's road diary, or a novel filled with larger-than-life characters. It begins with "The Year that Clayton Delaney Died," a portrait of Hall's childhood hero Floyd Carter, a hard-drinking musician. Then come tales of love in vain ("Tulsa Telephone Book" is a great one) and journalistic accounts of tragedies ("Trip to Hyden" visits the scene of a mining accident).

Every now and then Hall, whose straightforward singing style is bolstered by equally unaffected arrangements, shares his own experiences. "Kentucky, February 27, 1971," is his account of a pilgrimage he made to a wise and weary farmer. He was, as the album title implies, in search of a song. Instead he gets an earful about why kids don't hang around the unforgiving hills, and then an apology from the farmer: "Guess there ain't no song here after all."

Another gem, "The Little Lady Preacher," sounds as if it might be autobiographical; it finds the narrator, a drifter who fits Hall's general profile, playing bass for a weekly

Hall's songs have been recorded by Johnny Cash and Loretta Lynn, among many others.

religious radio show. Hall describes the guitarist next to him as a good musician with a penchant for drink and reckless living, and over several verses describes how the guitarist and the pious lady preacher become friendly. One week Hall shows up for work and they've vanished. Together. Stunned because he's unemployed, and because he will miss that attractive preacher, he can't help but wonder "who it was converted whom." They just don't write songs like that anymore.

GENRE: 🌑 Country. **RELEASED:** 1971, Mercury. **KEY TRACKS:** "The Year That Clayton Delaney Died," "Tulsa Telephone Book," "Trip to Hyden," "The Little Lady Preacher." **COLLECTOR'S NOTE:** The most recent CD release combines this album with Hall's 1973 *The Rhymer and Other Five and Dimers.* **NEXT STOP:** Johnny Cash: *At Folsom Prison* (see p. 151). **AFTER THAT:** Bobby Bare: *Sleep Wherever I Fall.*

The First Hot-Topic Hammerstein Musical

Show Boat

Oscar Hammerstein II and Jerome Kern
Frederica von Stade, Jerry Hadley, 1988 Studio Cast

*S*how Boat, which premiered in 1927, is the first work by Oscar Hammerstein to directly address social issues—it features an interracial marriage, heated discourse on racism and its evils, and a tragic, alcoholic heroine

in Julie, a light-skinned African American who, after "passing" as a white entertainer, is discovered and forced by police to leave the boat. It is sometimes considered the *Gone with the Wind* of Broadway, a tale of the passing of eras in the Deep South that touches on still-sensitive sub-

jects. That alone made it a rare thing in 1927, in a medium then dedicated to escapism.

The score, by Jerome Kern, helped Hammerstein greatly. Carefully avoiding caricature, Kern caught the slow stateliness of Southern life—both in its blues inflections ("Ol'

Man River," which became Paul Robeson's signature tune) and its romantic wistfulness ("Can't Help Lovin' Dat Man"). The lyricist took full advantage of the setting—the action happens in the world of hired entertainers on a riverboat—to have characters break into song at will. (The show's most famous ballad, "Bill," blossoms during a rehearsal scene. Trivia buffs will note there are no characters named Bill; the piece was written for an earlier Kern show.)

Before his career as a lyricist took off, Oscar Hammerstein attended Columbia University Law School.

There have been countless revivals of *Show Boat*, and several film versions. This three-disc studio extravaganza ranks among the most complete versions of the show—it includes the

beautiful "I Have the Room Above Her," which was added to the 1936 film version, and offers the chance to hear temperamental opera star Teresa Stratas sing Julie, in what some consider her best recorded performance.

GENRE: 😊 Musicals.
RELEASED: 1988, EMI/Angel.
KEY TRACKS: "Can't Help Lovin' Dat Man," "Ol' Man River," "I Have the Room Above Her." CATALOG CHOICES: Hammerstein: *Oklahoma!*, Original 1943 Broadway Cast. NEXT STOP: Ella Fitzgerald: *Sings the Jerome Kern Songbook.* AFTER THAT: Paul Robeson: *Live at Carnegie Hall, May 9, 1958.*

A True Voyage

Maiden Voyage

Herbie Hancock

One way to think about jazz is as a protracted conversation. A musician tosses out a radical new idea on a record, and then, months or years later, another artist will pick up the same device and take it someplace else. For example, after Miles Davis's *Kind of Blue* (see p. 208) appeared in 1959, many young jazzers embraced its unorthodox harmonic schemes, which replaced the mile-a-minute chords of bebop with slower-moving and more contemplative "modes."

Of the many recordings built on the ideas of *Kind of Blue*, Herbie Hancock's *Maiden Voyage* stands among the very best. It's a return volley of the long-distance sort, as it was recorded six years

Hancock recorded this album while still a member of Miles Davis's "second great quintet."

after Davis's groundbreaking work. But the influence is unmissable. When he recorded *Maiden Voyage*, pianist and composer Hancock was in Davis's band, and thus intimately familiar with the song strategies. He put them to use in interesting fashion, writing a five-song suite about the ocean. Hancock explains in the liner notes that his intent was to capture the "vastness and majesty" of the sea, and his songs evoke the ebb and flow of open water, with periods of modal calm followed by cresting tumult. The title track is a direct descendent of Davis's "So What," with chords that change so slowly they become major events. But through most of *Maiden Voyage*, and particularly on tunes like the deceptively tricky "Dolphin Dance," Hancock uses modality to create moments of pause, places to take a brief rest before diving in again. A sophisticated expansion of the *Kind of Blue* idea and at the same time a showcase for Hancock's ear-stretching chords, *Maiden Voyage* is one of the great pensive pleasures of jazz.

GENRE: 🎷 Jazz. **RELEASED:** 1965, Blue Note. **KEY TRACKS:** "Dolphin Dance," "The Eye of the Hurricane," "Maiden Voyage." **CATALOG CHOICE:** *Empyrean Isles.* **NEXT STOP:** Wayne Shorter: *Speak No Evil.* **AFTER THAT:** McCoy Tyner: *The Real McCoy* (see p. 792).

Out of the Shadow of Sly Comes the Funkiest Fusion

Head Hunters

Herbie Hancock

Herbie Hancock did lots of soul searching in the early '70s. After pursuing heady jazz expression as part of acoustic and electric jazz ensembles led by Miles Davis, he concluded, as many of his contemporaries did, that his destiny lay elsewhere. In one interview, he remembered thinking at the time that he'd never reach Charlie Parker status. The keyboardist said he needed to "forget about becoming a legend and just be satisfied to create some music to make people happy."

That philosophical shift led him to Head Hunters, the band built around bassist Paul Jackson, drummer Harvey Mason (later Mike Clarke), percussionist Bill Summers, and reedman Bennie Maupin. And *that* led to an album that opened up worlds even the visionary Hancock didn't foresee. Four extended jams built on simple recurring rhythm figures modeled after the hits of then-massive Sly and the Family Stone, *Head Hunters* represented a leading edge of electric funk exploration then. It remains a landmark still.

The opening track "Chameleon" is an

"Chameleon," this album's single, reached #42 on the *Billboard* Hot 100.

instant firestarter: Built on a Sly-like motif (Hancock once said these songs came to him after he visualized what it would be like to play in Stone's band), it's wound much tighter than most fusion. The revolving-door loop practically forces the soloists to reach beyond typical blues-based riffing, and Hancock responds with shimmering, at times impressionistic electric piano colors that float over the timekeeping agitations. All of the solos are cool and cosmopolitan—to experience an absolute peak of electric jazz, check Hancock's up-tempo romp on "Sly." Against a squabbling clavinet part that is jaw-dropping all by itself, Hancock drops a series of syncopated electric piano figures that are every bit as cogent and adventurous as his memorable turns with Davis's '60s quintet. *Head Hunters* became the bestselling jazz album of all time and made Hancock a legend. Naturally, it happened immediately after he stopped worrying about being a legend.

GENRE: 🅘 Jazz. **RELEASED:** 1973, Columbia. **KEY TRACKS:** "Chameleon," "Sly," "Watermelon Man." **CATALOG CHOICES:** *Mr. Hands; Sound System; Village Life* (with Foday Musa Suso). **NEXT STOP:** Weather Report: *Black Market.* **AFTER THAT:** Billy Cobham: *Dreams.*

"Et Tu, Brute?" in Song

Giulio Cesare

George Frideric Handel

Magdalena Kožená, Anne Sofie von Otter, Les Musiciens du Louvre (Marc Minkowski, cond.)

Opera of the late baroque period usually goes like this: A distraught character enters the scene, with an aria that details his or her particular circumstance. After sharing, that singer totters off and a new one, with a new set of concerns, appears. Often, the connections between "scenes" aren't so clear—personalities emerge slowly, one episode at a time, and listeners have to stitch the details together.

This diffuse approach can be taxing, especially when the opera is about some mythical god or goddess. *Giulio Cesare*, which is among a handful of Handel's operas to dramatize the life of a genuine historical figure, is less abstract, and more engrossing as a result. In the great Roman leader, Handel has a character whose exploits—and motivations—were known to the learned in his audience. He takes advantage of this, painting a deeply human portrait of a leader, a love affair, a tense time in world history. When, for example, Cleopatra realizes her man is about to be killed by conspirators, her melody grows heavy under the weight of this accumulating dread. As readers of history we know what's going to happen; Handel provides the familiar narrative with rich emotional undercurrents. As listeners, we can't help but feel it.

On one level, *Giulio Cesare*—considered among Handel's very best work in any genre—is an extended meditation on grief. Though there are arias that express triumph and heroism ("Va tacito e nascosto"), and a few devoted to delicious seductions (Cleopatra's quietly lyrical "V'adoro, pupille," sung as a rhapsody by Magdalena Kožená), much of the music is deeply doleful, addressing various states of emotional devastation. The principals involved in this 2003 version manage to "round out" the temperaments of their characters while hewing to the rigid outlines of Handel's score. There are several jaw-dropping performances—Kožená is a scene-stealing Cleopatra, while Anne Sofie von Otter brings sparkle to the lesser role of Sesto. The ensemble, under the direction of Marc Minkowski, executes Handel's flowing themes with such open, affectionate spirit, it's easy to forget that this is a story of betrayal.

GENRE: 😊 Opera. **RELEASED:** 2003, Deutsche Grammophon. **KEY TRACKS:** "Svegliatevi nel core," "Va tacito e nascosto," "V'adoro, pupille." **ANOTHER INTERPRETATION:** Beverly Sills, New York City Opera. **CATALOG CHOICE:** *Operas, Arias, and Overtures,* Emma Kirkby. **NEXT STOP:** Marc-Antoine Charpentier: *Médée* (see p. 158). **AFTER THAT:** Giuseppe Verdi: *Rigoletto,* Joan Sutherland, Luciano Pavarotti, London Symphony Orchestra (Richard Bonynge, cond.).

Sing Hallelujah Here

Messiah

George Frideric Handel
Gabrieli Consort and Players (Paul McCreesh, cond.)

Back in Handel's day, being a composer meant entertaining aristocracy, delighting the children, and (often in the very same piece) honoring higher powers. A majority of commissions were for works intended to overtly glorify God—for many composers, stirring up devout feelings was a routine assignment, rather like jingle writing today. As a result, there are plenty of run-of-the-mill religious pieces, with dutiful hymnlike themes recounting familiar biblical stories. The lively *Messiah* is not one of those. For this plotless three-part work (with sections focusing on Christ's birth, crucifixion, and resurrection), Handel drew on a staggering array of musical devices, and used them in smart, surprisingly dramatic, ways.

Consider the piece's most recognizable theme, the "Hallelujah" chorus from part two. Heard out of context, it's a fearsome, whiplash-inducing ride, all exaltation overdrive. But part of its power comes from the way Handel sets it up: The section begins with the composer at his darkest, with murmuring low notes and a recurring phrase, "He was despised," that functions as a meditative koan, repeating as Handel follows the idea through to its conclusion. Then, after the "Hallelujah" chorus, the canvas changes completely: The third section opens with a single declaration, "I know that my Redeemer liveth," which has a deep and purposeful simplicity, in contrast to the busy flag-waving processionals that precede it.

This recording, by conductor Paul McCreesh's Gabrieli Consort, offers a steady stream of riches. Among them: McCreesh's brisk tempi; the deft harpsichord playing, which often lurks in the middle of the orchestra; the fine ensemble singing; and stupendously smooth turns from Dorothea Röschmann and Bernarda Fink. These soloists don't simply replicate the elaborate curlicue ornamentations singers used during this period—they create unusual and sometimes daring inventions that are never so flowery as to obscure the pulse.

Handel revised his works constantly (for those keeping score, this version is the "Foundling Hospital" version from 1754). He was also known to recycle his ideas. There's evidence of that in this piece: A theme from one of his early Italian cantatas forms the basis of the startling and majestic "For unto Us a Child Is Born." Instances of such repurposing have raised some scholarly eyebrows, but the outrage is misplaced and overlooks the reality of the composer's situation: He had a good stirring theme that he knew many hadn't heard. In reappropriating it, he rescues it from obscurity, gives it a second life. Some melodies are too precious to be sacrificed to semantics.

GENRE: 🎵 Classical. **RELEASED:** 1996, DG Archiv. **KEY TRACKS:** Part 1: "Every Valley Shall Be Exalted," "Behold the Lamb of God/He Was Despised"; Part 2: "Hallelujah."
ANOTHER INTERPRETATION: Jerome Hinds, Philharmonia Chorus and Orchestra of London (Otto Klemperer, cond.). **NEXT STOP:** J. S. Bach: *St. Matthew Passion,* Dietrich Fischer Dieskau. **AFTER THAT:** Gustav Mahler: *Symphony No. 2 "Resurrection,"* Bavarian Radio Symphony Orchestra (Otto Klemperer, cond.).

Baroque Sounds to Accompany Lavish Celebrations

Water Music
Music for the Royal Fireworks

George Frideric Handel
Le Concert Spirituel (Hervé Niquet, cond.)

George Frideric Handel got some weird assignments in his day, including these two pieces designed to accompany public spectacle. In 1717, England's King George I was seeking to bolster his sagging popularity, and ordered up a festival featuring a royal fleet of barges to patrol the Thames. To complement this, he commissioned music from Handel, a celebrity who'd just arrived in England from his native Germany. One of the ships had an estimated fifty musicians stationed aboard, and they played Handel's *Water Music* even though, in those pre-amplification days, it might have been difficult for anyone on shore (or, for that matter, on nearby barges) to hear it. (Some musicologists theorize that the suites, comprising mostly dances like the minuet, gavotte, and English country dances, were intended to be played indoors, at a feast following the festivities.)

The monarch was delighted with the music; according to newspaper accounts, he asked that the pieces be repeated several times. It's easy to understand why: Handel's melodies have a surging, bursting-with-life quality. They're at times grand and florid, but more often move with a fleet, ballet dancer's sense of animation. This recording, by the French period-music ensemble Le Concert Spirituel, heightens the interplay between instruments built into the score: At times the strings respond

Handel was born in Germany but lived much of his adult life in England.

to the stately brass declarations with snickering rejoinders, like ladies gossiping.

Each of the three suites has its own structure (the first contains ten sections of dances and more expansive song-like "airs"; the second, which contains the famous "Alla Hornpipe," only five), but all are considered precursors to the symphonic form that would take root after Handel's death. Further proof of the success of the *Water Music* came in 1749, when King George II enlisted Handel to write music to accompany a fireworks demonstration. The fanfare-rich *Royal Fireworks Music* is esteemed as another pre–symphonic era gem, but it didn't exactly have a smooth premiere: A storm broke out, causing unintended fires instead of fireworks.

GENRE: 🎵 Classical. **RELEASED:** 2003, Glossa. **KEY TRACKS:** *Water Music:* "IV (Andante)," "VI (Air)." *Royal Fireworks Music:* "I (Overture)," "V (Minuets I and II)." **CATALOG CHOICE:** *Concerti Grossi, Opus 6,* Academy of Ancient Music (Andrew Mauza, cond.). **NEXT STOP:** W. A. Mozart: *Symphonies Nos. 35–41,* Berlin Philharmonic (Karl Böhm, cond.).

Not Typical Tipica

Salsa

Larry Harlow

Every musical style has its moments of reckoning with the past, when its active practitioners circle around to acknowledge the masters who came before. This happened in an unusual way in New York City's Latin music community in the mid-'70s. Although the Fania label was riding high with hit after dance floor hit, a small group of its musicians began looking to vintage Cuban *son*, rural *guajira*, and *conjunto* music, dusting off the compositions of the *tres* master and bandleader Arsenio Rodríguez (see p. 655).

Larry Harlow's sparkling *Salsa*, recorded in 1974, belongs to that moment. A tribute of sorts to Rodríguez, it's an early example of what came to be called *tipica*—hard-driving arrangements built on the rhythms and structures of Cuban dance music of the 1950s. The pianist Harlow, who was part of a small group of Jewish musicians who'd become accepted on the Latin scene, understood the streamlined allure of Rodríguez's group. He also knew that in 1974, dancers expected more sound. So he grafted energetic horn charts and tricky jazz-like compositional interludes onto the vintage *conjunto* rhythms, and got the members of his orchestra, a top-shelf Fania ensemble featur-ing trumpeter Ray Maldonado and bassist Eddie "Guagua" Rivera, to attack the music with the lusty abandon of Rodríguez's legend-ary bands.

From the opening "No quiero," one of four hits from this set, it's clear Harlow is on to something: The angular brass catcalls are thoroughly modern, while the relaxed ad-libs of singer Junior Gonzalez, particularly on the age-old *son montuno* "Popo pa mi," hark back to a more gracious age of Latin dance music. It's a rare generational push-pull, and throughout it Harlow manages to tip his hat to the regal Rodríguez while blasting out a party underneath.

GENRE: 🌐 World/Latin. **RELEASED:** 1974, Fania. **KEY TRACKS:** "No quiero," "La cartera," "Sueltame." **CATALOG CHOICE:** *Hommy: A Latin Opera.* **NEXT STOP:** Tipica '73: *Tipica '73.* **AFTER THAT:** Manny Oquendo y Libre: *Ritmo, sonido y estilo.*

East Meets West

Indo-Jazz Suite

Joe Harriott Double Quintet

Oh, those kooky '60s, when the experimental impulse was in the air, and every little ripple in the culture seemed to tell of a new bohemia on the rise. *Indo-Jazz Suite* is a product of that ethos, a meeting of five European jazz players, three classical Indian musicians, and violinist and composer John Mayer, who was dedicated to the idea that the strict structures and droning, static harmonies of raga can inspire boundary-busting improvisation. Mayer, who moved to Britain from Calcutta in 1952, was inspired by the then-burgeoning jazz scene of his new home. He wrote four ragas that follow (at least in a general way) the scale patterns that underpin traditional Indian music; several of them, including the brisk "Raga Gaud-Saranga," are built on a recurring bass line that's a distant cousin of the walking jazz bass. Mayer showed the members of alto saxophonist Joe Harriott's quintet the corresponding scales, and encouraged them to experiment over the pattering rhythms. Harriott, the Jamaican-born conceptualist who was often compared to Ornette Coleman, tyrannizes the placid setting with hissing and wailing post-bebop, while others in his band, particularly trumpeter Kenny Wheeler, dabble in shorter, more furtive bursts. The jazzers are plenty interesting and all, but sitar player Diwan Motihar, who uses conventional Indian ad-lib strategies, is among the most dexterous soloists.

There are astonishing moments here, splashed over rhythms that rock intensely yet maintain an outward air of cool. A summit that's far more sensitive than the usual cross-cultural smashup, *Indo-Jazz Suite* suggests that Rudyard Kipling was a beat behind when he declared that East was East and West was West and "never the twain shall meet." Here, the distant realms meet, converse, and find utterly hypnotic common ground.

GENRE: 🅙 Jazz. **RELEASED:** 1966, Atlantic. (Reissued 1999, Koch.) **KEY TRACKS:** "Raga Gaud-Saranga," "Contrasts." **CATALOG CHOICE:** Kenny Wheeler: *Gnu High* (see p. 855). **NEXT STOP:** L. Subramaniam: *Conversations.* **AFTER THAT:** Naná Vasconcelos: *Saudades.*

The Emergence of a Country Iconoclast

Pieces of the Sky

Emmylou Harris

Even before she recorded on her own, the young Emmylou Harris turned heads with some of her first trips to the recording studio: She was the haunting and haunted female voice accompanying Gram Parsons

on his galvanizing 1972 solo debut *GP* and its follow-up *Grievous Angel* (see p. 581), works that forged a profound connection between country and rock. After Parsons died from a drug overdose in September 1973, Harris's star rose. This album, released in 1975, was her major label debut, and its amiable blend of pop and traditional tunes

Harris was discovered by members of Gram Parsons's band.

became the blueprint for many of her subsequent works.

Even if she hadn't been associated with Parsons, Harris would have emerged sooner or later: Hers is among the most arresting voices in all of popular music. It's reedy and small, a fragile crystalline miniature that tells of emotional wounds in the least demonstrative tones possible. On this consistently inspired set, she sings such durable melodies as the Beatles' "For No One" as if she's gliding along, trying to be untroubled. Every heavy phrase is bathed in calm; even when she mourns deeply, as on her tribute to Parsons, "Boulder to Birmingham," a slight tremble in her voice is the primary way she signals heartache. The restraint gives Harris's interpretations a special one-two punch: They sound effortless at first, but on closer scrutiny become devastating. Let pop singers uncork extravagant me-so-hurt testimonials; Harris soldiers stoically onward, meting out despair as a subtle spice rather than the main ingredient.

GENRE: ◐ Country. **RELEASED:** 1975, Reprise. **KEY TRACKS:** "If I Could Only Win Your Love," "For No One," "Boulder to Birmingham." **CATALOG CHOICES:** *Wrecking Ball; Roses in the Snow.* **NEXT STOP:** Gillian Welch: *Revival.* **AFTER THAT:** Iris DeMent: *Infamous Angel.*

On the Devotional Path

All Things Must Pass

George Harrison

T he unspectacular squabbling end of the Beatles yielded three profoundly different attempts at crawling out from under the wreckage. John Lennon shared his experience with primal-scream therapy on the harrowingly raw *Plastic Ono Band.* Paul McCartney trended predictably gooey, with an inconsistent album (*McCartney*) that is redeemed by one of his forthright love songs, "Maybe I'm Amazed."

George Harrison confronted the breakup head-on, with the graceful, philosophical *All Things Must Pass.* A series of elegies, dream sequences, and thoughts on the limits of idealism, it is arguably the most fully realized solo statement from any of the Beatles.

Though Harrison began writing for this album while the Beatles were dissolving, several tunes—including the oft-covered "Isn't It a Pity"—were written earlier, and initially offered to the group. Harrison conceived *All Things* as a diverse amalgam: There are short études that resemble those on side two of *Abbey Road* (see p. 62); feisty impromptu jams (on the supplemen-

All Things Must Pass **was the first triple album by a solo artist.**

tal disc entitled "Apple Jam") that feature Eric Clapton, Jim Gordon, Billy Preston, and others; and yearning, high-spirited pop productions like the majestic first single "My Sweet Lord."

Just about every track offers a different type of ecstasy: The meditative "Beware of Darkness" follows a halting, patient path toward illumination, while "Apple Scruffs" zooms around unencumbered, an explosive peak-experience refrain that comes direct from heaven's songbook. On the upbeat single "What Is Life" and others, Harrison grabs what he needs from his old band—that insinuating hook sense—and uses it to frame an utterly comfortable metaphysical discourse. Later Harrison's music would turn inward, becoming preoccupied with the imponderable questions of spirituality. But here, in the company of "wall of sound" producer Phil Spector

...nue of amazing musicians, Harrison attains (and sustains) a state of radiant grace.

GENRE: ⏻ Rock. **RELEASED:** 1970, Apple/EMI. **KEY TRACKS:** "Beware of Darkness," "Isn't It a Pity," "If Not for You." **CATALOG CHOICE:** *Brainwashed.* **NEXT STOP:** John Lennon: *Plastic Ono Band.* **AFTER THAT:** Paul McCartney and Wings: *Venus and Mars.*

The Culmination of a Long Journey

Stories from the City, Stories from the Sea

PJ Harvey

By the time she got to this album, her sixth, British rocker Polly Jean Harvey had traveled to great extremes in search of a sound. She'd attracted attention right off the bat, with the sirenlike wail of *Dry,* her 1992 debut, and then *Rid of Me* (1993). Soon, though, she abandoned the abrasion of that period to cast herself as a postmodern blues shouter (*To Bring You My Love,* 1995). Then she went arty, singing against a backdrop of torch-song spookiness (*Is This Desire?,* 1998). Each lunge came complete with brazen, hypersexual lyrics that earned her comparisons with Patti Smith (see p. 719) and the loyal admiration of critics. Commercial success, though, was another story. Still is.

Harvey eventually stopped trying to develop elaborate new settings, and that's when her great music happened. *Stories from the City, Stories from the Sea* pulls together salient characteristics from her various experiments, and channels them into messy and supremely attitudinal rock and roll. It's a work of summation and assimilation; though several of the previous albums occasionally reach higher heights, this one is where her varied musical interests come together.

Harvey was raised on a small sheep farm in England.

The line from *Stories* that got the most ink—"I can't believe life is so complex, When I just want to sit here and watch you undress," from "This Is Love," one of the blues-tinged numbers—offers a clue about Harvey's mind-set. She's as blunt as any man when talking about what she's lusting for, and quite happy to set off on her own to go get it. *Stories* is a chronicle of those journeys, many of which happen in New York. Sometimes she tears off and finds love, or lust; sometimes she stumbles into profound insights, and sometimes she winds up in a drunken rage, wandering the downtown streets in the wee hours, beset by lingering disappointments and not quite able to sort out the mess she's in. This, it turns out, makes for entrancing music.

GENRE: ⏻ Rock. **RELEASED:** 2000, Island. **KEY TRACKS:** "This Is Love," "Beautiful Feeling," "The Whores Hustle and the Hustlers Whore." **CATALOG CHOICE:** *To Bring You My Love.* **NEXT STOP:** Cat Power: *The Greatest.* **AFTER THAT:** The Breeders: *Pod.*

Galloping at the Piano

Mozart: Piano Concerto No. 20 in D Minor
Scarlatti: Eleven Sonatas

Clara Haskil
Winterthur Symphony Orchestra (Henry Swoboda, cond.)

This bracing and thoughtful rendition of Mozart's Piano Concerto No. 20 in D Minor was recorded in 1951, after Romanian pianist Clara Haskil (1895–1960) had suffered her share of travails. A student of the legendary French pianist Alfred Cortot, she'd survived surgery to remove a brain tumor, and developed advanced curvature of the spine, which forced her to play in an awkward hunched position. The handicap inevitably became part of her public profile, as she wrote around this time: "My way of presenting myself to the public, of bowing, my physical posture at the piano, all this apparently produces disastrous impressions. I didn't know it was that bad . . . but all the critics mention it."

She might not have looked like your average Central Casting concert pianist, but as this recording demonstrates, Haskil was a mighty warrior. She plays Mozart, her specialty, as though each phrase is crucial to an ongoing argument, and needs to be shaded a certain way to be fully appreciated. Everything about her music feels carefully considered, even when she's scampering through Mozart's boisterous passages. The opening Allegro movement reveals much about her approach: Mozart begins the piece by having the orchestra play a network of themes, ideas that define where the piece will go. The first piano entrance, which is one of the most famous in the concerto literature, glances at those themes while moving in a completely different and even more compelling direction. Haskil glides into the opening phrase, a heart-leaping ascending interval, and gets to allegro gradually, gathering the force of the orchestra behind her in a way that makes the transition almost imperceptible.

The program continues with a second, equally essential treat: Haskil's interpretation of eleven sonatas by Domenico Scarlatti. The prolific Italian composer moved to Lisbon in 1719 and found a "voice." He fell in love with the tense chords of the Iberian guitar, and wrote 555 piano sonatas that incorporate those sounds into inventive miniatures. While most piano sonatas are organized into multi-movement works, Scarlatti conceived them as single-movement studies, usually lasting five or six minutes. The eleven here have elaborate arpeggio schemes and stormy two-hand eruptions. Haskil executes them with delight, galloping through the most technically challenging moments like a racehorse, with an abandon she may well have only experienced when playing the piano.

GENRE: 🎼 Classical. **RELEASED:** 1951, Deutsche Grammophon. (Reissued 2001). **KEY TRACKS:** Mozart: Allegro, Romance. Scarlatti: Sonata in C Minor, Sonata in F Minor, Sonata in C Major. **CATALOG CHOICE:** *Clara Haskil Plays Mozart and Beethoven* (with Arthur Grumiaux). **NEXT STOP:** Alfred Cortot: *The Master Classes.*

Proof that Part of Singing Is Innate, Not Learned

Everything Is Everything

Donny Hathaway

Donny Hathaway (1945–1979) never set out to be a singer. A keyboard player and gifted arranger, he began his career playing on Curtis Mayfield sessions. Hathaway then briefly worked with the R&B saxophonist King Curtis, who urged him to sing. That didn't do the trick. Nor did the entreaties of his wife, a trained vocalist, and Roberta Flack (whom he met at Howard University).

This reluctance is almost impossible to fathom when you hear Hathaway slide dramatically between pitches on the original "Je vous aime," from his stunningly varied and beautifully sung debut. He is

Hathaway's first of three studio albums was a modest hit in 1970.

completely comfortable in his own skin, singing to communicate, not to show off. He has a highly personal vocabulary drawn from plaintive gospel declarations and Ray Charles–style ad-libbing. His suave phrases emerge perfectly formed, each framed by his aggressive piano chords or plusher musical accoutrements (at times even French horns!) he designed as counterpoint to the simply stated melodies.

Hathaway went on to have great commer-

cial success on a series of duets with Flack. But *Everything Is Everything*, with its churchy 12/8 devotional "Thank You Master" and its thrilling jazz-combo version of "Misty," remains the most vibrant (and complete) picture of his talent. It's also one of the most influential debuts in all of pop. Hathaway wasn't a household name when he committed suicide in 1979, but has become one since, as an impressive list of luminaries, including Alicia Keys and D'Angelo, strive to re-create his utterly effortless approach to singing. Needless to say, nobody's even come close.

GENRE: 🎵 R&B. **RELEASED:** 1970, Atlantic. **KEY TRACKS:** "Je vous aime," "Misty," "Thank You Master." **CATALOG CHOICE:** *These Songs for You, Live.* **NEXT STOP:** D'Angelo: *Brown Sugar* (see p. 204).

The Greatest Jazz Ballad Ever

"Body and Soul"

Coleman Hawkins

This performance by tenor saxophonist Coleman Hawkins (1904–1969) is one of the rare moments in jazz where you can actually feel the goalposts moving. It's a dividing point, marking the limits of swing and the beginnings of modernity, a record so striking most musicians remember exactly where they were when they first heard it. Sonny Rollins, a Hawkins disciple, recalled his first encounter this way: "It was on a cheap radio, and Coleman's sound still came through."

Many jazz musicians of the 1930s interpreted "Body and Soul," a then-popular swooning love song with a challenging chord sequence. None of them come near what the Missouri-born Hawkins, who'd performed in the big bands of Fletcher Henderson (see p. 354) and others, did with it in just two choruses and a brief coda. Recorded in New York after Hawkins returned from five years in Europe, this solo, his debut for RCA, established him as an important voice on the tenor saxophone, and a beacon of the new. For starters, there's his sound—big and husky, with a tightly measured vibrato. Then there are his dexterous, almost-glib lines: Unlike most everyone in jazz of the day, Hawkins doesn't simply vamp on the blues, or arpeggiate to outline the harmony. Instead, he conjures grand pirouetting melodies that move with a dignified,

"When I heard Hawk, I learned to play ballads." —Miles Davis

almost ghostly grace. These spontaneous ad-libs venture far from the original theme, yet retain a sense of the tune's framework, forming a running commentary to it. Hawkins's solo, a first take, has since been fitted with lyrics, and studied and deconstructed by generations of instrumentalists. And though he rerecorded "Body and Soul," which became his theme song, several times, the original, with its pattering tempo and delicate chords from pianist Gene Rodgers, has never been improved upon.

Rollins believes that this hugely popular solo, along with Hawkins's subsequent work, greatly expanded the public's notion of the jazz musician: "He showed that a black jazz musician could depict all emotions with credibility, even a beautiful ballad that represented the peak of civilization."

GENRE: 🎷 Jazz. **RELEASED:** 1940, RCA. **APPEARS ON:** Coleman Hawkins: *Body and Soul.* **CATALOG CHOICE:** *The Hawk Flies High.* **NEXT STOP:** John Coltrane: *Ballads.* **AFTER THAT:** Gene Ammons: *Gentle Jug.*

An Incredible Busker Finally Gets His Shot

The Next Hundred Years

Ted Hawkins

Ted Hawkins (1936–1995) spent most of his "career" sitting on a milk crate on Venice Beach, playing a beat-up acoustic guitar and singing for spare change. Patterning his phrases after Sam Cooke, he'd do soul standards and well-known blues tunes to enchant passersby. Occasionally, he'd slip in one of his own hard-luck songs, which referred, obliquely, to his tough upbringing, his struggles with alcoholism, and various

trips to prison. Among his regular visitors were people who worked in the music business; after being primed for stardom by unscrupulous types, Hawkins grew wary and bitter. As he complained in a 1994 interview, "Seemed like every week somebody would come along and tell me how I was going to be rich."

Tony Berg, a Geffen Records executive, managed to win Hawkins's trust, and in 1993 convinced the singer, who'd already recorded several solo efforts, to go into a studio and record with a top-flight band. *The Next Hundred Years* brought Hawkins his first real critical acclaim; months later, before the first royalty check could come his way, he suffered a stroke and died.

That sense of misfortune defines not just Hawkins's career, but the songs he loved to sing. One, "There Stands the Glass," shares the thoughts of a man who's haunted and seduced by alcohol; it's gripping because Hawkins, whose voice has the texture of coarse sandpaper, clearly empathizes. The original

An anonymous street performer in the States, Hawkins had modest success in Europe.

"Strange Conversation," meanwhile, showcases Hawkins's stylistic blendings—his ability to apply a folkie's philosophical perspective to a dispiriting blues tale, while singing like a wounded soul angel. Incredibly, Hawkins never sounds like he's out to smash borders when he sings. This unique artistic place his songs evoke, a world he developed over years on the boardwalk, was simply where he lived.

GENRE: ⬤ Blues. **RELEASED**: 1994, Geffen. **KEY TRACKS**: "Strange Conversation," "There Stands the Glass," "Groovy Little Things," "Ladder of Success," "Long as I Can See the Light." **CATALOG CHOICE**: *Watch Your Step.* **NEXT STOP**: Ben Harper: *Diamonds on the Inside.* **AFTER THAT**: Taj Mahal: *The Natch'l Blues* (see p. 760).

Papa and His Not-So-New Bag

Twelve London Symphonies

Franz Josef Haydn

London Philharmonic Orchestra (Eugen Jochum, cond.)

Josef Haydn (1732–1809) is often referred to as "Papa" Haydn, the father of the symphony. Others working at the same time wrote for large groups of strings and winds, but through gradual experimentation and refinement over many years, Haydn arrived at a four-movement format that became the enduring standard—a framework embraced by his student, Ludwig van Beethoven, as well as Gustav Mahler and many of the world's great composers. Haydn is probably more famous for his structural contribution than for any particular symphony out of the more than one hundred he created.

Cue up the magnificent Symphony No. 102 to appreciate what a shame this is. The "London" symphonies, written near the end of Haydn's life, represent a culmination of his work. They're bustling and bold, with a pulse-quickening sense of forward motion that prevails even in slower, more reflective sections (see the fantastically lyrical cello solo in the second movement). Throughout this piece and the others on this two-disc set, Haydn holds fast to his basic structure—there's a first movement with several contrasting themes and a "development" section, a slow second movement, a minuet or some other dance form for the third, followed by a busy final movement that often follows the outline of a rondo. But beneath that overall form, Haydn works to "loosen" things up, through extended reworkings of the themes. These passages, particularly in No. 104, his final symphony, transform plummy, pleasant melodies into thoroughly engaging and sometimes marathon journeys.

It's perhaps fitting that a British orchestra should interpret Haydn's London Symphonies, which were inspired by a visit the composer made after his patron died in 1790. Yet much credit for the vibrancy of this reading goes to Eugen Jochum, a German conductor who led the Hamburg Symphony during World War II and later founded the Bavarian Radio Orchestra. Jochum specialized in Bruckner and regularly recorded Brahms and Beethoven; he tackled Haydn late in his career, and that turns out to be a plus. Rather than whip up a frenzy from the podium, he patiently lets Haydn's wizardry unfold. Jochum seeks nothing less than an elusive "golden mean," and he gets it—his balancing of murmuring winds and airborne strings is perfect, his tempos judicious. There are lots of recordings of these prototypical works. These performances, crackling with life, are among the very best.

GENRE: 🎼 Classical. RELEASED: 1973, Deutsche Grammophon. (Reissued 1993.) KEY TRACKS: No. 93: second movement. No. 104: first movement. No. 101 "The Clock": second movement. ANOTHER INTERPRETATION: New York Philharmonic (Leonard Bernstein, cond.). CATALOG CHOICE: Piano Sonatas, Marc-André Hamelin. NEXT STOP: Ludwig van Beethoven: Symphonies Nos. 5 and 7, Vienna Philharmonic (Carlos Kleiber, cond.). AFTER THAT: Robert Schumann: Das Paradies und die Peri, Orchestre Revolutionnaire et Romantique (John Eliot Gardiner, cond.).

Can You Dig It?

Shaft

Isaac Hayes

Original Motion Picture Soundtrack

Hot Buttered Soul, the 1969 album that established the Memphis producer-arranger Isaac Hayes, contains just four tracks. One is a nine-minute showcase for the endlessly interesting backing ensemble the Bar-Kays; another is an ornate orchestral reimagining of the 1964 Burt Bacharach classic "Walk On By" that lasts for twelve minutes.

Such long expanses of instrumental vamping became Hayes's trademark—they're the cornerstone of this 1971 project, the soundtrack to the blaxploitation film Shaft. While others working at Memphis's Stax label concentrated on terse three-minute songs, Hayes gave listeners the long cinematic tour. He approached music as though he were expected to provide a full evening's worth of material. On his most successful recordings, grooves simmer for minutes before anything as overt as a melody appears.

The "Theme from Shaft," a groove étude built on expertly manipulated wah-wah guitar, became a cultural phenomenon. It spread from the big screen to the pop charts (the title song, featuring Hayes's talky narration, was a huge hit) to marching band halftime routines. The song helped bring Hayes (whose deep baritone became known to a later generation as the voice of Chef on *South Park*) an Oscar for best score. He was the first African American to receive that honor.

The original *Shaft* theme (and, indeed, much of the soundtrack) still sizzles. Hayes utilizes the many colors of the orchestra—a single low piano note, a noirish, shadowy flute, a hissing cymbal that kicks things off—to set a mood, and then cooks up musical chase

Shaft is the bestselling album ever to be released by Stax Records.

scenes so tense, no visuals are necessary.

GENRE: 🎙 R&B.
RELEASED: 1971, Stax.
KEY TRACKS: "Do Your Thing," "Soulsville," "Theme from *Shaft*." **CATALOG CHOICE:** *Hot Buttered Soul.*
NEXT STOP: Curtis Mayfield: *Superfly.* **AFTER THAT:** Booker T. and the MGs: *Melting Pot* (see p. 105).

A Trailblazing Rethinking of Devotional Music

Fifty Gates of Wisdom: Yemenite Songs

Ofra Haza

Israel-born Ofra Haza (1957–2000) began this project knowing that the material she'd chosen—traditional Yemenite *diwan* songs that Haza, the youngest of nine children, heard growing up—would, given ongoing

Israeli-Palestine tensions, be considered radical for a Jew to sing. So why stop there? To the devotional poetry, much of it written by sixteenth-century rabbi Shalom Shabazi, she added electronic percussion used as part of *diwan* celebrations and loops similar to those found in techno and other dance music.

It was a mash-up made in heaven, a confluence of ancient wisdom and dance floor escapism that singlehandedly triggered the genre sometimes called "ethnotechno." Among those who owe Haza and producer Bezalel Aloni a debt: Afro Celt Sound System, Sheila Chandra, Banco de Gaia, Bebel

Haza became an international superstar in the '80s, finding an unlikely audience in the U.K. club scene.

Gilberto (that's not including the pop artists who sampled Haza's voice and textures, among them Eric B. and Rakim and the dance collective M.A.R.R.S.).

While many have followed the *Fifty Gates* idea in pursuit of similarly unlikely fusions, the original has several distinctive—that is, uncopyable—traits: The texts, which are published in English in the accompanying liner notes, are rhapsodic expressions of love ("no bandages will heal the wounds inflicted upon my longing heart") that are conducive to singing. Then there's Haza's silky siren of a voice. She delivers long, maze-like trails of melody with an almost noble air—

all alone, just through her demeanor, she makes clear that the textures swirling around her are as righteous as anything traditional ever was.

GENRE: 🌐 World/Middle East. **RELEASED:** 1985, Shanachie. **KEY TRACKS:** "Galbi," "Im nin'alu," "Ash'alech." **CATALOG CHOICE:** *Shaday.* **NEXT STOP:** Ekova: *Heaven's Dust.* **AFTER THAT:** Márta Sebestyén: *Muzsikás* (see p. 686).

A Master Instrumentalist, a Polarizing Figure

Brahms, Tchaikovsky Violin Concertos

Jascha Heifetz
Chicago Symphony Orchestra (Fritz Reiner, cond.)

People talk about the coldness of masters. How someone who has consummate command of an instrument can come off haughty, or disdainful, or otherwise unimpressed with the music he's bringing to life. In recent years this charge has been leveled at several classical performers of the mid-twentieth century, including Jascha Heifetz, the peerless (and polarizing) violinist. The logic goes like this: Listen to these Calamity Jane tempos! The flashy displays of technique! What a snob!

This recording is often held up as an example of this coolness—particularly the Brahms, which has lots of high-register hijinks. Sure enough, in the first movement Heifetz seems detached, and more than a little haughty. But check out what happens when the tempo slows down, at the start of the second movement: Here the shimmering Heifetz tone warms up, begins to glow. The violinist, who was born in Russia and became an instant sensation after his Carnegie Hall debut in 1917, goes from note to note with great caution. Heifetz pays attention to the placement of notes and their emphasis in a way that suggests the care of a rock climber stretching just a bit beyond arm's length to find secure footing. And like a master climber, he brings all of his skill, as well as his instincts as a human being, to the task. He's never going to be confused with a sappy romantic, but he knows how to set Brahms's flowing thoughts free.

Heifetz studied with Leopold Auer, the noted Russian teacher for whom the Tchaikovsky Violin Concerto was written. As on the Brahms, Heifetz plays the Tchaikovsky like a chase scene, though he adds slight ornamentations to the first movement that help him stamp the piece as his own. The remainder of the concerto is rendered with a cool, evenhanded, maybe even dispassionate precision—exactly the type of authoritative execution that some find thrilling and some find soulless. Follow Heifetz through these meticulous, carefully shaped lines, and you may come to appreciate his mastery as an end in itself, the klieg light that brings clarity to every corner of the music.

GENRE: 🎻 Classical. **RELEASED:** 1957, RCA. **KEY TRACKS:** Brahms: second movement. Tchaikovsky: first movement. **ANOTHER INTERPRETATION:** Tchaikovsky: David Oistrakh, Dresden Staatskapelle (Franz Konwitschny, cond.). **CATALOG CHOICE:** Beethoven: *Violin Concerto,* Boston Symphony Orchestra (Charles Munch, cond.). **NEXT STOP:** *Beethoven, Sibelius Violin Concertos,* David Oistrakh.

The First Great Big Band

A Study in Frustration

Fletcher Henderson

letcher Henderson (1897–1952) sits near the top of the list of jazz trailblazers who never received adequate props—hence the title of this career overview. The pianist and arranger started his band in 1923, and almost immediately it became a sensation—its tight execution and jumping rhythm, honed during a decade-long run as the house band at Roseland Ballroom, established the standard for big-band jazz. Duke Ellington emulated the Henderson band's panache, and clarinetist Benny Goodman was so impressed by the detail of the arrangements (by saxophonist Don Redman and later Henderson himself) that in 1934 he purchased some for his own swing outfit, which was just getting started.

Fletcher Henderson intended to be a chemist before starting his career as an arranger.

That's where the frustration comes in: Goodman had hit after hit with tunes Henderson did first—and often better. In a 1961 interview, legendary record executive John Hammond explained Henderson's frustration this way: "He made great recordings of his own compositions which sold a minimal number, only to have the same tunes and arrangements cut by Benny Goodman with astronomical sales."

Thankfully, sales figures aren't the whole story. The versions of "King Porter Stomp," "The Dicty Blues," "Moten Stomp," and other tunes on display here argue for Henderson's sleek band as one of the all-time-great catalysts of jazz. Acknowledged as the primary inspiration for Goodman, the Henderson band influenced other outfits as well: Bandleader and pianist

Count Basie once said, "If it hadn't been for [Henderson's] music, I don't know where we would have been."

Henderson's notion of jazz involves intricate scoring for the brass and saxes, and hinges on a key contrast: The ensemble plays with tremendous finesse, setting the stage for Henderson's not-so-secret weapons: incendiary soloists. Henderson had a keen ear for talent, and at various times during his heyday, he made room for irreverent improvisations from trumpeter Louis Armstrong and saxophonists Coleman Hawkins and Benny Carter, among others who went on to become stars. The melding of sharp ensemble unity with sparkling solos results in swing with an extra shot of go-juice: No big band in the history of jazz dishes shimmies, shakes, and shout choruses quite like Henderson's does here.

GENRE: 🎷 Jazz. RELEASED: 1994, Columbia/Legacy. KEY TRACKS: "King Porter Stomp," "Raisin' the Roof," "Moten Stomp." CATALOG CHOICE: Duke Ellington Orchestra: *Ellington at Newport, 1956.* NEXT STOP: Benny Goodman: *The Complete 1938 Carnegie Hall Concert* (see p. 317). AFTER THAT: Jimmie Lunceford: *Lunceford Special, 1939–1940.*

Power, in All Its Forms

Power to the People

Joe Henderson

I f it were music, what would a slogan like "Power to the people" sound like? Would it be a flash of anger demanding an end to oppression? Or would it be a ringing melody, affirming the highest ideals of equality and democracy, gently inducing reflection? Would it be the rock singer Patti Smith braying "People Have the Power" or Marvin Gaye lamenting "Make Me Wanna Holler"?

The phrase was heard often during the civil rights movement, and by the time the wily tenor saxophonist Joe Henderson seized it, in 1969, it was probably headed to the rhetorical graveyard. Yet this isn't one of those "topical" album titles jazz musicians slapped on instrumental works in hopes of instant relevance. Henderson (1937–2001) had thought about what "power" is, and his originals focus on quintessential jazz manifestations of it—what happens when five musicians unite in pursuit of one goal, and then what happens when, as on the boogaloo "Afro-Centric," a lone renegade splinters away off on an individual power grab.

Although never a "name" like Sonny

This album features Herbie Hancock playing piano.

Rollins, Henderson had a huge impact on saxophone jazz in the late '60s—because of both his angular compositions ("Isotope," a geometry problem in blues form) and his musing, idiosyncratic playing style. On *Power*, Henderson improvises like a sculptor, patiently chipping at the block while envisioning the final form. His solos are mazelike knots borne out of a highly developed sense of order. When he gets going, Henderson suggests that an individual's power is less about brute force than elasticity, the ability to reshape difficult circumstances on the fly.

GENRE: 🎷 Jazz. **RELEASED:** 1969, Milestone. **KEY TRACKS:** "Black Narcissus," "Isotope," "Power to the People." **CATALOG CHOICES:** *Inner Urge; Double Rainbow.* **NEXT STOP:** Herbie Hancock: *Speak like a Child.*

The Rules of Rock Guitar Rewritten

Are You Experienced

The Jimi Hendrix Experience

T hink of the most superhuman superlative, a word for the most exalted achievement, the best of the best. Hold it in your mind as you cue up Jimi Hendrix jangling through "Hey Joe" from this enduring collection.

Does the honorific match the sound? Does it even come close?

Of course not. Because words do not satisfactorily capture what Hendrix (1942–1970) did on, to, and with the electric guitar. Throughout this most essential rock document, the Seattle native who got his start with the Isley Brothers plays as though handling fire. It's right on his fingertips, pulsing through his wrists, and as long as he keeps moving, he won't get burned. His lines sear the wires that carry them. His rhythm playing doesn't merely dictate a pulse—it suggests an almost savage way of keeping time. Inside his playing is a concentrated expression of abandon, freedom seeking, the embodiment of every psychedelic desire.

Hendrix is the single most important instrumentalist in rock history, and this debut album by the Jimi Hendrix Experience is

The Experience formed in 1966.

the most succinct introduction to his work. Already, the group has perfected its potent combination of brute force and bittersweet melody, which Hendrix bolsters by singing in a slouchy, don't-bother-me way. It's almost as though singing is an afterthought for Hendrix; he's more concerned with the big picture, the awesome unrestrained feeling he's pouring into "Purple Haze" and the other classics here. Get inside his vision of rock and roll, this all-encompassing experience that has awed generations, and pretty soon everything else begins to feel a little bit timid.

GENRE: 🎸 Rock. **RELEASED:** 1967, MCA. **KEY TRACKS:** "Purple Haze," "Manic Depression," "Foxey Lady." **CATALOG CHOICES:** *Jimi Plays Monterey; BBC Sessions.* **NEXT STOP:** Jeff Beck: *Blow by Blow.*

A New Sound Being Born

Band of Gypsys

Jimi Hendrix

Recorded at the Fillmore East in New York on New Year's Eve—the last night of the 1960s—this is Jimi Hendrix tearing out toward a bold new kind of mind-warp. He'd exhausted the possibilities of the conventional

verse-chorus song context (see *Are You Experienced,* above), and as the new decade dawned, the former paratrooper and his newly assembled "black" band—the drummer Buddy Miles and bassist Billy Cox—sought different horizons. This trio was not tiptoeing to get there: It was into the hard and the harsh. The group's wide-open vamps were often built on static single chords, some leaning toward the shadowy landscapes of Miles Davis's *Bitches Brew,* some with the kinetic thump of Sly Stone funk.

With Hendrix, the starting point doesn't matter much—a few minutes into any of these pieces, he's off in the ether, giving guitar clinics for contortionists. *Band of Gypsys* just might be the heaviest explosion of electric guitar prowess ever caught on tape—these writhing, screaming, bent-over-backward solos are works of herculean imagination. At the same time, the album is one of the most thrilling glimpses of a new sound being born. Hendrix wasn't exactly sure where he was going, and neither were his cohorts. They knew the general terrain, and knew how to support Hendrix when he stepped into the spotlight, but the "form" was mostly free. Hendrix being Hendrix, there were no road maps, and the group hadn't been playing together enough to have developed protocol. That created its own blank-slate energy: Listen as the stuttering funk of "Machine Gun" progresses, and you'll hear the band follow Hendrix first at close range, then with less note-by-note attention. As he builds up steam, the pulse behind him becomes brutally physical, a whomp that registers in the gut.

Band of Gypsys contains material that Hendrix was just working up at the time—these are the definitive recordings of "Who

One of Hendrix's guitars, a left-handed Fender Stratocaster with sunburst finish, fetched $168,000 at auction in 2006.

Knows," "Message to Love," and "Machine Gun," among others. It's the only live album Hendrix authorized, and though the Band itself was short-lived (Hendrix dissolved it several weeks after this show), *Band of Gypsys* remains a once-in-a-lifetime explosion of cosmic guitar.

GENRE: 🎸 Rock.
RELEASED: 1970, Capitol.
KEY TRACKS: "Message to Love," "Machine Gun," "Who Knows," "Power of Soul."
F.Y.I.: Hendrix produced this album under the pseudonym "Heaven Research." **CATALOG CHOICE:** *Axis: Bold as Love.* **NEXT STOP:** Mahavishnu Orchestra: *Birds of Fire.* **AFTER THAT:** The Allman Brothers Band: *At Fillmore East (*see p. 16).

Still Looking Swell

Hello, Dolly!

Jerry Herman
Original Broadway Cast

Hello, Dolly! is your basic Broadway show with few artistic pretensions. A classic tale of two love interests (one a mature couple, the other a pair of teenagers), it's got broad, anthemic tunes, caprices that rise out of nowhere to animate whatever's happening on stage, and songs catchy enough to stand apart from the plot, which is derived from Thornton Wilder's play *The Matchmaker.*

Formula isn't bad when it's executed by a master like Jerry Herman, who was young and relatively untested at the time. Herman wrote several of the songs in a weekend as part of an audition for producer David Merrick. His gift for fetching, durable melodies quickly became

impossible to miss: Louis Armstrong's version of the title theme was a Top 40 hit before the show even opened on Broadway.

Herman was also adept at developing his characters: The personas of *Hello, Dolly!* acquire dimension gradually, in offhand ways. Until the Act 1 finale, "Before the Parade Passes By," Dolly has functioned as a purveyor of blithe songs and comic moments. Here, although the music is lighthearted, she deepens unexpectedly as she sings about moving beyond the ghost of her deceased first husband. She's thinking of herself as an individual, and the plucky way she vows to rebuild her identity makes the moment stirring.

Hello, Dolly! was written with Ethel Merman in mind. After Merman, then at the height of her fame, demurred, Carol Channing got the part. It became Channing's first hit since *Gentlemen Prefer Blondes* in 1949, and it's easy to hear why: Channing is a fireball, drawing on internal fortitude and determination

Carol Channing as Dolly in *Hello, Dolly!*

to jolt these endlessly tuneful songs into unexpected emotional terrain.

GENRE: 😊 Musicals.
RELEASED: 1964, RCA.
(2003, expanded edition.) **KEY TRACKS:** "Hello, Dolly," "Before the Parade Passes By." **COLLECTOR'S NOTE:** The expanded edition includes several tracks from a 1965 all-black cast version featuring Pearl Bailey and Cab Calloway. **CATALOG CHOICE:** *Mame*, Original Broadway Cast. **NEXT STOP:** Sarah Vaughan: *The Rodgers and Hart Songbook.*

The Score that Showed Everyone How to Heighten Horror

Psycho

Bernard Herrmann
Royal Scottish National Orchestra (Joel McNeely, cond.)

The opening moments of Bernard Herrmann's score for *Psycho* are defined by two contrasting musical entities: The slightly ominous staccato pulsing of cellos and basses, and the serene lyrical swirls of the upper strings as they play a simple scale-like theme. When these ideas intersect, late in the "Prelude" that serves as the music for the opening titles, the effect is stunning: It's the moment before panic totally sets in, when there's still the possibility of some clarity of thought. Our sensory awareness is heightened, but the "terror" button has not yet been pushed.

This canny extended setting is just the first example of Herrmann's genius in *Psycho*, one of the many instances where the New York composer adds something profound to Alfred Hitchcock's cine-

The eerie structure of the Bates Motel graces *Psycho*'s album cover.

matic marvel. A conductor with the CBS Symphony Orchestra in the 1930s, Herrmann began his film career with *Citizen Kane*, scored many of Hitchcock's thrillers, and died the night he completed work on *Taxi Driver* (1976). For *Psycho*, he uses only strings—a move that forces him to embrace multiple styles of composition and juggle several divergent musical personalities. Some of the music is typical bad-man-lurking-in-the-shadows stuff, with the murmuring sustained notes and desperate yelps from the violins used to death in less imaginative slasher fare. But there are only a few such gratuitous moments in a score that virtually defined horror-film music. Whenever the pace needs to quicken, Herrmann snaps into a different gear, dashing off short repeating patterns and themes that scamper furtively around, defined by the shivering chill that runs through them.

Unlike many orchestral "adaptations" of film music, this version follows Herrmann's original score to the note. It's the rare film music experience that is engrossing all the way through on its own, from the elaborate tension-mounting trickery of the opening moments to that dizzyingly intense shower scene, where it sounds like a thousand violins are each screaming at a slightly different pitch. According to the lore surrounding *Psycho*, Hitchcock wanted the action in the shower to stand alone, without music. Herrmann defied him, conjuring an accompaniment so suited to one of filmdom's most unforgettable scenes, it's impossible to imagine the visuals without it.

GENRE: 🎸 Classical. **RELEASED:** 1997, Varèse Sarabande. **KEY TRACKS:** "The Shower," "The Rainstorm," "Prelude/The City." **BUYER BEWARE:** Danny Elfman's reworking of *Psycho* adds nothing to, and in fact detracts from, Herrmann's score. **CATALOG CHOICES:** The scores to *Vertigo; Taxi Driver; Fahrenheit 451.* **NEXT STOP:** Alfred Newman: *The Razor's Edge,* Original Motion Picture Score.

Now Departing, Destination Unknown

Point of Departure

Andrew Hill

Unlike most jazz musicians involved in the hard bop scene of the 1960s, pianist Andrew Hill (1931–2007) didn't take every job that came along. In fact, he turned down almost everything—unless it involved playing his own music. A deep thinker who'd spent years developing his compositional style, Hill was steadfast about this, even if it meant hardship. At one point he wrote a letter to *Down Beat* magazine explaining his position. He invited those who wanted him to continue making music to send money. Years later, after his contract with Blue Note Records expired, he sought grant funding for his compositions and taught.

As a teenager, Hill played with Charlie Parker and Miles Davis.

Listening to *Point of Departure*, which lets a top-shelf ensemble loose on Hill's intricate, suitelike compositions, reveals why the pianist was so determined to avoid compromise: He was immersed in developing new strategies, platforms that would spark musical conversations far more interconnected than the blithe chatter that prevails at jam sessions. For Hill, who'd studied with the classical composer Paul Hindemith, spending an evening playing "My Funny Valentine" and other such standards was counterproductive. Better to be at home, refining his defiantly knotty unconventional tunes.

Point of Departure is one of five albums Hill recorded for Blue Note between November 1963 and June 1964. It's startlingly inventive—extended, wandering melodies give way to outbreaks of skittering "free bop" time-shifting that recall the Miles Davis '60s quintet (that group's drummer, Tony Williams, is on board). But there are also passages that demand fleet fingerwork: The twelve-minute "Refuge" contains themes that tax the significant abilities of saxophonists Eric Dolphy (alto) and Joe Henderson (tenor); Dolphy's solo is one blurred, impossible-to-transcribe run-on sentence. When it's his turn, Hill moves through odd, irregular clumps of pianistic notions like he's turning the earth over for new planting.

In a sense, that's what Hill did as a composer: He took common ideas and turned them over, until they became newly fertile. And

beyond cliché. Alas, his future-jazz sound never caught on outside the community of musicians and a few enlightened listeners. It was an iconoclastic vision far different from anything else happening in 1964, and it remains that way today—a point of departure, with many possible outcomes.

GENRE: 🎵 Jazz. **RELEASED:** 1964, Blue Note. **KEY TRACKS:** "Refuge," "Spectrum," "Flight 19." **CATALOG CHOICES:** *Passing Ships; Judgment.* **NEXT STOP:** Herbie Nichols: *The Complete Blue Note Recordings* (see p. 550). **AFTER THAT:** Greg Osby: *Banned in New York.*

Not Exactly Book Learning Here

The Miseducation of Lauryn Hill

Lauryn Hill

"**H**ow you gonna win if you ain't right within?" Lauryn Hill wants to know. So she asks again. And again. The phrase, from a single called "Doo Wop (That Thing)," turns out to be the defining question of

The Miseducation of Lauryn Hill. Concerned with such quaint old-school notions as character and integrity, Hill begins this song cycle by observing that these qualities are absent in hip-hop as she knows it. This is cause for lament, and on the reggae-tinged opener "Lost Ones" and several other tracks, the Fugees singer speaks eloquently on how the creators of urban music could use a moral compass. She castigates rappers who "gained the whole world for the price of your soul." Later, on the ominous "Final Hour," she warns about the karmic implications of greed: "You could get the money, you could get the power, but keep

Hill's only studio album has sold 18 million copies worldwide.

your eyes on the final hour."

This was not the type of message many who enjoyed Hill's melismatic vocals on the Fugees hit *The Score* could have predicted. But it was right on time, a passionately sung plea for reason that arrived after the commercial peak of gangsta rap, and served as a cleansing counterpoint to that style's low-road luridness.

Here's serious Aretha Franklin–caliber vocal daring on songs that split the difference between hip-hop and R&B without cheating either side. It's a suite laid out by a sharp observer who, like Stevie Wonder, could be indignant about injustices while appealing to the best within her listeners. Poised enough to chant down hotheads and somehow keep things light, Hill doesn't just rant: Tucked between the consciousness-raising songs are trembling personal dramas, ballads like "Ex-Factor" that catch Hill phrasing in fitful bursts, delivering moments of passionate, jaw-dropping singing that have no contemporary equal.

GENRES: 🌀 R&B 🎤 Hip-Hop. **RELEASED:** 1998, Ruffhouse/Columbia. **KEY TRACKS:** "Ex-Factor," "Doo Wop (That Thing)," "Final Hour." **CATALOG CHOICE:** Fugees: *The Score* (see p. 292). **NEXT STOP:** Jill Scott: *Who Is Jill Scott?* (see p. 681). **AFTER THAT:** Erykah Badu: *Mama's Gun* (see p. 38).

Backwoods Purity

The High Lonesome Sound

Roscoe Holcomb

Roscoe Holcomb's voice is an acquired taste. It is thin and reedy, scratched and scraggly, with hints of desperation around the edges. Some have described him as a prototypical "mountain man"—singing in wild "get off my land!" bursts, his voice coming across thorny, unapologetic, tetchy, and mean. Before you write him off, however, consider those who have been captivated by his work—among them Bob Dylan, Eric Clapton, and Ralph Stanley.

The folklorist John Cohen, who helped bring attention to Holcomb (1911–1981) during the folk revival of the early '60s, characterized his singing style as "the high lonesome sound."

Bob Dylan described Holcomb as having an "untamed sense of control."

That description, which later was attached to Bill Monroe and other bluegrass singers, comes close to catching Holcomb's eerie tone, his faintly otherworldly presence.

This album gathers recordings made in 1961, 1964, and 1974, and shows Holcomb as a singer with zero performance affectation—when he tells a tale like that of "Trouble in Mind," he conveys a completely open, unvarnished humanity. Hear him sing anything and you can tell he's a man who has come to his wisdom one hardship at a time.

Holcomb lived in Daisy, Kentucky, in the Appalachian Mountains, and worked in coal mines and on construction jobs for most of his life. A guitarist who played excellent banjo, Holcomb didn't have a professional career, and during long spans of his life he made music only for himself. His specialties included the blues, hymns (his falsetto style comes from the Old Regular Baptist tradition), and allegorical ballads. His singing isn't smooth; usually he phrases in irregular fits and starts. But if you listen a while, you might well find his music entrancing—the haunted and haunting sound of an America that's a long time gone.

GENRE: 🎵 Folk. **RELEASED:** 1998, Smithsonian Folkways. **KEY TRACKS:** "Moonshiner," "Trouble in Mind," "Willow Tree." **NEXT STOP:** Dock Boggs: *Folkways Years, 1963–1968* (see p. 101). **AFTER THAT:** Ralph Stanley: *Saturday Night and Sunday Morning*.

There's Billie Holiday, and There's Everyone Else

The Ultimate Collection

Billie Holiday

Billie Holiday (1915–1959) started out singing with big bands in the 1930s, and for those gigs, her vocabulary was the shooby-doodling happy talk of swing, then the coin of the realm. Over the next two decades, through struggles with heroin addiction and other personal ordeals, Holiday developed an idiosyncratic performance style that separated her from every other singer on the planet. This first-ever career retrospective compresses that evolution into two discs, and includes spry early singles, dramatic ballads, and excerpts from her last studio set, *Lady in Satin*, which she croak-sings in a wobbly, poignantly devastated voice.

Lester Young gave Holiday the nickname "Lady Day."

Holiday slowed jazz singing down to a crawl, and with help from the pianist Teddy Wilson and others, brought it to a place of great intimacy. She shaped familiar melodies into a language of alluringly fractured half-sentences and mewling, vaguely discontented sighs. And she dared to bring her own life experience into her interpretations, infusing a generic lyric like "Good Morning Heartache" with a palpable appreciation for all manner of love trouble. In her hazy world, heartbreak is a given, poise is constantly being tested, and every phrase reveals new cracks in an already precarious emotional state.

As her profile grew, the Baltimore-born singer ventured beyond the torch song. With a forthrightness that was radical for the time, Holiday brought her listeners face-to-face with the legacies of racial hatred ("Strange Fruit," 1939) and poverty ("God Bless the Child," 1941). In a sense, the protest music of the 1960s has roots in her work.

This two-CD, one-DVD set amounts to the best "first encounter" with Billie Holiday. It includes definitive versions of "You Go to My Head," "Willow Weep for Me," and "I Thought About You," among others, performances that show her singing in a way that effortlessly coaxed greatness from her surrounding musicians. Holiday was the type of singer who kept musicians on their toes; check out the version of "Fine and Mellow," taped for Robert Herridge's *Seven Lively Arts* TV show in 1957, to see her casting a spell over saxophonists Lester Young and Coleman Hawkins. Both the audio and video spotlight the delicate balances that define Holiday's art. She's barely there and at the same time all the way there, singing with the heavy eyelids of last call and a hyperalert awareness of pain, conjuring a soul's anguish that cannot be adequately captured in words.

GENRES: 🎵 Jazz 🎤 Vocals. **RELEASED:** 2006, Verve. (Originally recorded between 1933 and 1958.) **KEY TRACKS:** "Fine and Mellow," "Don't Explain," "Good Morning Heartache," "God Bless the Child," "Strange Fruit," "You Go to My Head." **CATALOG CHOICES:** *Lady Day: The Complete Billie Holiday on Columbia, 1933–1944; Songs for Distingué Lovers.* **NEXT STOP:** There is none.

Conference of the Birds

Dave Holland

A frequent knock on the jazz avant-garde is that the music doesn't swing. That may be true of some free-jazz classics, but right from the opening bars of "Four Winds," this agile quartet assembled by British bassist Dave Holland pretty much demolishes the charge. Over a twisting, skating, medium-brisk pulse, tenor saxophonist Sam Rivers rips out wickedly inventive lines that are two steps and one sharp corner removed from hard bop.

This is swing unmoored. Swing strung from different pillars, freed of its guy wires. Swing taken at leaps across buildings. Swing without the historical baggage.

In the years just before this, Holland had been working with saxophonist Anthony Braxton, pianist Chick Corea, and drummer Barry Altschul in the group known as Circle. *Conference of the Birds* transplants some of Circle's rhythmic venturing to a pianoless context, and shows how the absence of governing harmony can open up all sorts of possibilities. Holland's originals force the players to explore

The album is named after an epic poem by Farid al-Din Attar.

distinct textures and moods: One piece, "Q & A," involves all four musicians in rapid-fire interchanges, while the more somber flute duet "Now Here (Nowhere)" exists in a comforting zone of introspection.

Conference of the Birds doesn't always turn up on the short list of great avant-garde records—it was completely ignored by Ken Burns in his multipart TV documentary *Jazz.* Within the community of jazz musicians, however, the reverberations from this *Conference* are still being felt—not much jazz made in the 1970s breathes with the moods, textures, and ferocious freewheeling interaction available here.

GENRE: 🎵 Jazz. **RELEASED:** 1972, ECM. **KEY TRACKS:** "Four Winds," "Conference of the Birds." **CATALOG CHOICE:** *The Razor's Edge.* **NEXT STOP:** Circle: *Paris Concert.*

The Buddy Holly Collection

Buddy Holly

B uddy Holly is one of several key rock figures to fall victim to "biopic" syndrome: Thanks in part to *The Buddy Holly Story,* the 1978 movie starring Gary Busey, the legacy of the bespectacled rocker from Lubbock,

Texas, has been reduced to a handful of well-known songs ("Peggy Sue"), his clean-cut image of fey innocence, and the tragic circumstances of his death. (Along with the Big Bopper and Ritchie Valens, Holly died in the February 1959 plane crash that's often cited as "the day the music died" and was the subject of Don McLean's 1971 hit "American Pie.")

Critic Bruce Eder describes Holly as "the single most influential creative force in early rock and roll."

Holly's career did only last eighteen months—heck, he only released two albums during his lifetime. But the soundbite version misses key elements of his contribution. Here, in two discs that include intermittently interesting early demos, is a fuller picture of an artist whose musical ideas were embraced by scores of rockers and became standard practice.

Holly's architectural refinements to early rock are most obvious in his guitar playing. Where most of his peers were following the blues-riff outline established by Chuck Berry, Holly supported tunes like "Rave On" with intricate instrumental counterlines, étude-like scales that the Beatles later turned into high art (see songs like "Day Tripper"). Just his deployment of two guitars moving in different, often oppositional orbits was revolutionary.

Then there are the songs themselves. In 1957, rock and roll was still primarily about performance, with most of the early stars relying on others—often the skilled song-merchants of the Brill Building—for material. Not Holly. He and his band the Crickets came up with a surprising number of signature tunes, from "Peggy Sue" to "That'll Be the Day" to "I'm Looking for Someone to Love." These are full of hot-rodding energy and highly concentrated rock and roll exuberance that really did disappear the day the music died.

GENRE: 🎸 Rock. **RELEASED:** 1990, MCA. **KEY TRACKS:** "Midnight Shift," "Brown Eyed Handsome Man," "That'll Be the Day," "Not Fade Away," "Maybe Baby," "(You're So Square) Baby, I Don't Care." **NEXT STOP:** The Beatles: *Meet The Beatles!* **AFTER THAT:** Marshall Crenshaw: *Marshall Crenshaw.*

Movie Music Wthout the Movie

The Planets

Gustav Holst

Boston Symphony Orchestra (William Steinberg, cond.)

The seven movements of *The Planets* correspond to the seven planets of the solar system (besides Earth) known to humanity when British composer Gustav Holst finished this, his most famous orchestral piece, in 1916. Not only was recently demoted Pluto still undiscovered (that happened in 1932), but there wasn't any satellite photography. So to evoke the faraway realms that have intrigued so many through the centuries, Holst (1874–1934) relied on his formidable imagination, with an assist from Greek mythology. Each of the movements is named for a planet, and subtitled according to its attributes—Mars, for example, is the "Bringer of War."

Don't expect any celestial Space Mountain tinkling here. Using unlikely combinations of instruments and odd open-ended chords splayed out across the ensemble, Holst describes vast fantastical horizons, emphasizing tone and temperament. "Mars" is tense, with a march cadence bubbling under the surface and hell breaking loose above it. "Saturn, the Bringer of Old Age," is even more ambiguous; low brass in its nearly ten-minute Adagio offer intimations of great portent against the faint tick from a faraway clock. "Mercury" spreads an eerie theme over high-pitched woodwinds and celeste to suggest the sounds you'd hear in an upper atmosphere very different from that of Earth.

William Steinberg's reading of *The Planets* plays up the sense of abstract exploration—he moves with the steadiness of an aerial photographer, surveying lots of territory, guiding the pliant orchestra over grandiose hills and valleys. It might seem like folly to expect people who grew up in an age of space exploration to be wowed by Holst's interplanetary daydreaming—after all, we know what these planets look like now. But Steinberg and the Boston celebrate the mysteries, transporting listeners to a time when space was the great unknown, and humans, even ones like Holst with colossal imaginations, mere flyspecks.

GENRE: 🎻 Classical. **RELEASED:** 1971, Deutsche Grammophon. **KEY TRACKS:** "Mercury," "Saturn," "Mars." **ANOTHER INTERPRETATION:** Leonard Bernstein: *Bernstein Conducts Holst, Barber, Elgar.* **CATALOG CHOICE:** *Choral Symphony,* Royal Philharmonic Orchestra (Hilary Davan Wetton, cond.). **NEXT STOP:** Hector Berlioz: *Symphonie fantastique* (see p. 82).

The Growl of the Blues

John Lee Hooker
Plays and Sings the Blues

John Lee Hooker

John Lee Hooker (1917–2001) didn't have the most polished pipes in the blues business, nor the most graceful delivery. He had something more important: a voice that caught all the struggle and trouble, late-night treachery, and double-crossed dealings commonly loaded into blues narratives.

Hooker made music as though lives, including his own, were on the line. He could sound as smooth as aged bourbon, or as roughed-up as gravel under the wheels of a getaway car. He put years of hurt behind the most clichéd blues declaration. The early singles collected on *Plays and Sings the Blues,* most from 1951 and '52, show that well before he was a blues legend, Hooker was an uncommon method actor—a master of inflection whose tools were a weary, fed-up tone and sandpapery timbre. Several of these songs, including "Mad Man Blues," are examples of his perpetually moving boogie style, in which a shuffling rhythm underpins spirited call-and-response between voice and guitar. The sound, which Hooker developed playing Detroit clubs in the 1940s (while working at Ford Motor Company during the day), galvanized British rock musicians in the 1960s, including the Rolling Stones and John Mayall and the Bluesbreakers. It made Hooker one of the darlings of the U.K. "blues revival" and helped introduce authentic blues to subsequent generations.

Hooker's catalog includes over one hundred titles, cut for every consequential blues label, often under such pseudonyms as Birmingham Sam and Delta John. Only a few, like *Plays and Sings*, are consistently rewarding. Most were recorded quickly, in keeping

"I don't play a lot of fancy guitar. . . . The kind of guitar I want to play is mean, mean licks."
—John Lee Hooker

with one of his core beliefs about the music: "Once you start thinking too much about the blues," he told an interviewer in 1997, "you can wear yourself down and lose it."

GENRE: Blues.
RELEASED: 1961, Chess.
KEY TRACKS: "Baby Please Don't Go," "Worried Life Blues."
CATALOG CHOICES: *Hooker 'n' Heat*; *The Real Folk Blues*; *Alone*. **NEXT STOP:** Howlin' Wolf: *Moanin' in the Moonlight* (see p. 371).

Far Hipper than Most Luau Music

Master of the Hawaiian Guitar, Vols. 1 and 2

Sol Ho‘opi‘i

The jittery jazz jump of the Roaring Twenties converges with blues and the sanguine calm of Hawaiian folk song in the powerful music of steel guitarist Sol Ho‘opi‘i. While most Hawaiian musicians were entertainers, Ho‘opi‘i—who appeared in a number of films before having a religious awakening in 1938—considered himself primarily a musician. He developed several innovative tunings for steel guitar that endure to this day. His sweet arching lines and crisp rhythmic chords influenced many Western swing and country players, among them Don Helms, a member of Hank Williams's group.

You have to listen carefully to get the Ho‘opi‘i magic: On these two volumes of his best singles, he slips polished little pearls of wisdom into maddeningly brief eight-bar solos and inventive restatements of the themes. The first set, a collection of recordings made between 1926 and 1930, is heavy on adaptations of ragtime and blues—his version of "Stack o' Lee Blues" has a surprisingly modern pulse, while his "I Ain't Got Nobody" echoes and amplifies the zesty camp of the original. The second is more eclectic, containing brisk rambles and rococo Hawaiian folk unified by Ho‘opi‘i's technically challenging—and extraordinarily lyrical—guitar improvisations.

GENRE: World/Hawaii. **RELEASED:** 1991, Rounder. **KEY TRACKS:** Vol. 1: "I Ain't Got Nobody," "Stack o' Lee Blues." Vol. 2: "Na ali'i," "Ten Tiny Toes." **NEXT STOP:** Sonny Chillingworth: *Endlessly* (see p. 165). **AFTER THAT:** Lonnie Johnson: *Steppin' on the Blues*.

A Quiet Rebuke to Life in the Fast Lane

Lightnin' Hopkins

Lightnin' Hopkins

People today don't have the patience for music that moves at the snail's pace of "Penitentiary Blues," the first track on this 1959 solo gem from Texas bluesman Sam "Lightnin'" Hopkins (1912–1982). It lumbers slowly along, and those who expect concision from their blues troubadours may find themselves exasperated by the weary-sounding Hopkins, who began recording in the late '40s. He wanders. He digresses. He doesn't stick to blues form—in the great tradition of Son House and others, Hopkins stretches out the chords of the blues, changing them at his whim. That's even true of the somber

Hopkins is revered as a pioneer of rural Texas blues.

instruction "See That My Grave Is Kept Clean," a key tune in the solo blues repertoire, which Hopkins alters in sly, subtle ways.

This short set—just nine songs plus Hopkins's reminiscence about Blind Lemon Jefferson—was recorded in Hopkins's Houston apartment by musicologist Sam Charters. Hopkins had spent several years lying low; after recording steadily for small labels, he'd pawned his guitar and was barely involved in music.

Charters got the guitar, and convinced Hopkins to record by bringing along a bottle of gin. In the liner notes, Charters explains that he held the microphone in his hand, positioning it near the guitar's tone hole during solos and moving it when Hopkins began singing. He captured an intimate, unadorned slice of the blues, a glimpse of "Lightnin'" moving with glacial slowness, rebuking everything fancy and highfalutin about the form.

GENRE: 🎵 Blues. **RELEASED:** 1959, Folkways. **KEY TRACKS:** "Penitentiary Blues," "Bad Luck and Trouble," "See That My Grave Is Kept Clean." **CATALOG CHOICES:** *Mojo Hand; Blues Kingpins.* **NEXT STOP:** Son House: *Martin Scorsese Presents the Blues: Son House* (see p. 369). **AFTER THAT:** Blind Lemon Jefferson: *King of the Country Blues.*

The Best from the Least Showy Jazz Singer of All Time

Close Enough for Love

Shirley Horn

There are lots of prerequisites for being a jazz diva; playing an instrument isn't one of them. Spend an hour listening to the magnificent singer and pianist Shirley Horn, however, and you'll understand why it helps. When she sings, the husky-voiced Horn is all about understatement—her little brushed-off phrases and breathy undertones bring an almost other-worldly luster to standards. Her voice seems to float along, an illusion she creates by the way she accompanies herself on the piano, with economical chords and carefully measured phrases. She carves out a cozy space where her voice goes, and makes sure that space remains completely uncluttered. Where most singers (and, for that matter, pianists) rush to fill every second, her genius happens inside vast openness.

Horn (1934–2005) had the most unusual career path of any great jazz singer. A native of Washington, D.C., she made a few records with Quincy Jones for Mercury, beginning in 1963. Among those enchanted by her delivery was Miles Davis, who heard some of his own austere tactics in her work and became a loud champion. But at the very moment she seemed poised for stardom, Horn dropped out of sight to raise a family, continuing to perform, occasionally, in D.C. clubs.

Horn never lost her knack for spinning miniature dramas from the standard repertoire. Amazingly, when she was rediscovered in the mid-'80s, her gift had deepened. This album is the most entrancing of a series of solid records she made for Verve, and it's got all the hallmarks of her style—ballads that move at a transfixing crawl and polite mid-tempo swingers dotted with brilliant ad-libs. The spotlight always finds Horn's calm, affect-free voice, which is plenty intoxicating all by itself. But it's her behind-the-scenes work at the piano—the thick moods she draws from simple, almost still chords—that lifts *Close Enough for Love* to the realm of the sublime.

GENRES: 🎵 Jazz 🎤 Vocals. **RELEASED:** 1988, Verve. **KEY TRACKS:** "Once I Loved," "I Got Lost in His Arms," "It Could Happen to You," "But Beautiful." **CATALOG CHOICE:** *You Won't Forget Me.* **NEXT STOP:** Abbey Lincoln: *Abbey Sings Billie,* Vol. 1. **AFTER THAT:** Norah Jones: *Feels like Home.*

Piano Perfection Happened Here

Horowitz at the Met

Vladimir Horowitz

Every music collection needs examples of unassailable mastery, recordings that capture technical perfection. This is one. The pianist Vladimir Horowitz (1903–1989) was perhaps the most technically accomplished of all the great pianists of the mid-twentieth century, a fastidious musician who made clarity his calling. Even when delivering great thundering outbursts—check out the climactic moments of Franz Liszt's Ballade No. 2 on this 1981 solo recording—his groupings of notes and clusters are distinct. If such moments in the pianistic repertoire are hailstorms, Horowitz makes sure we can pick out the part each pebble plays.

Born in Kiev, Horowitz debuted in 1922 and first performed at Carnegie Hall in 1928; of that occasion, the reviewer for *The New York Times* wrote, "It has been years since a pianist created such a furor with an audience in this city." After his 1965 "comeback" performance at Carnegie Hall, Horowitz got more finicky about his music making. He would perform recitals only at 4 P.M. on Sundays. He demanded his own piano, which according to legend had heavily lacquered hammers and supersensitive keys; to accommodate him, the instrument was lifted by crane out of the second story of his Manhattan townhouse.

This recording, on that piano, is enthralling. It begins with Domenico Scarlatti's Six Sonatas, a series of melodic inventions Horowitz interprets gingerly, embellishing little. The Liszt, which is as dense as Wagner in spots, finds Horowitz maintaining several pulses at once, and shows that he could summon brute force when needed. Chopin's Ballade No. 4 is its inverse—rather than sounding all the notes of a chord simultaneously, Horowitz fans them out, in brisk, metrically perfect arpeggiations that expand the shape of Chopin's lines. Like so much great Horowitz, the enhancements are rarely intended as showstoppers—they're just unassuming inventions, made dazzling by his calm, low-key delivery.

GENRE: 🔂 Classical. **RELEASED:** 1981, RCA. **KEY TRACKS:** Liszt: Ballade No. 2. Rachmaninoff: Prelude, Op. 23, No. 5. **CATALOG CHOICES:** *Horowitz in Moscow; Favorite Chopin.* **NEXT STOP:** Chopin: *Twenty-four Preludes,* Arthur Rubinstein. **AFTER THAT:** J.S. Bach: *The Well-Tempered Clavier Book 1,* Sviatoslav Richter.

A Near Complete Tour of One Haunted House

Martin Scorsese Presents the Blues: Son House

Son House

In his 1993 memoir, *The Land Where the Blues Began,* folklorist Alan Lomax, who recorded Son House (1898–1988) at Klack's general store in Lake Cormorant, Mississippi, in 1941, described House at work this way:

"With him the sorrow of the blues was not tentative, or retiring, or ironic. Son's whole body wept, as with his eyes closed, the tendons in his powerful neck standing out with the violence of his feeling and his brown face flushing."

That description is echoed in accounts from blues scholars and other slack-jawed witnesses to House's incantatory performances, and it reveals the essential truth about Son House. He vibrated blues feeling, and beamed it out to the world with such force that his intentions could not be misread.

A running partner of blues pioneer Charley Patton and a major influence on Robert Johnson

The grandfather of the blues, House's disciples include Muddy Waters and Robert Johnson.

and Muddy Waters (who once said, "Where I come from, Son House is the king!"), House wrote a stack of compositions that form the core repertoire of the rural blues—"Levee Camp Blues," "Special Rider Blues," "Death Letter," "Grinnin' in Your Face," and others. He first recorded, with Patton's help, in 1930, a harrowing session that yielded the initial few songs on this career-spanning overview.

House's next major recordings were the Lomax Library of Congress works in 1941 and 1942. These include the impassioned "Special Rider Blues," which showcases his incendiary slide guitar techniques. Listen closely on "Walking Blues," from that session, to hear a train rumbling by in the distance.

Like so many bluesmen, House was "rediscovered" in the 1960s; the last selections here come from 1965, and include his classic arrangement of "John the Revelator" and his original "Death Letter," one of the most poignant love songs of all time. After receiving a letter telling him his lover has died, House tells of going to see her, laid out on the "cooling board." That's when he begins to realize his loss, which he expresses in the anguished final shout: "I didn't know I loved her, 'til they laid her in the ground."

GENRE: 🔵 Blues. RELEASED: 2000, Columbia/Legacy. KEY TRACKS: All of them. CATALOG CHOICE: *Complete Library of Congress Recordings, 1941–1942.* NEXT STOP: Blind Willie Johnson: *The Complete* (see p. 400). AFTER THAT: Mississippi Fred McDowell: *Amazing Grace.*

The Debut of a Powerhouse

Whitney Houston

Whitney Houston

It's not often that a record designed down to the last breath to be commercially accessible ends up changing the rules. Whitney Houston's debut did exactly that. Discovered and launched by legendary record executive Clive Davis,

Houston came out of nowhere in early 1985, and within two years virtually everything on urban radio sounded like an echo of this album—producers shamelessly borrowed the beats, the string sounds, and the plush padded keyboards, while a school of singers (Toni Braxton, the members of TLC, Janet Jackson) emulated Houston's writhing phrases and demanding-diva delivery.

Whitney Houston **peaked at #1 and stayed there for 14 weeks.**

Houston was, to be sure, something special. The daughter of gospel dynamo Cissy Houston, she grew up in Newark, New Jersey, singing in church. Her early career included jingle dates and appearances in clubs—her first recording was with producer Bill Laswell's experimental rock band Material. From the start, Houston had an unusual combination of skills: the timing of a jazz singer and the range—and indomitable vocal power—of a

gospel soloist. This enchanted Davis, who spotted her one night when she was singing in a club, offered her a contract on the spot, and was largely responsible for pairing her with the various producers who provided the material.

Although some songs lean into vapid "adult contemporary," this stunning success (for over a decade it was the bestselling debut from a female artist) establishes Houston's command of nuance. She's a singer confident enough to turn out a sweeping ballad ("Saving All My Love for You") without getting too showy, and a playful presence who can whip an ordinary hook ("How Will I Know") into an occasion for high-energy belting. Houston went on to have other big hits, as did many of the followers who hijacked her formula. Most of that music is exceedingly competent and boring. This has fire in it.

GENRE: ⊙ R&B. **RELEASED:** 1985, Arista. **KEY TRACKS:** "How Will I Know," "Saving All My Love for You," "The Greatest Love of All."

CATALOG CHOICE: *The Bodyguard,* Original Motion Picture Soundtrack. **NEXT STOP:** Toni Braxton: *Toni Braxton.* **AFTER THAT:** Mariah Carey: *Butterfly.*

The Howl of the Wolf

Moanin' in the Moonlight

Howlin' Wolf

❝ **W**hen I heard Howlin' Wolf," Sun Records founder Sam Phillips recalled, "I said, 'This is for me. This is where the soul of man never dies.'" The singer, songwriter, and blues harmonica master

Wolf, né Chester Burnett, who didn't begin his recording career until the age of forty-one, had that effect on people. He used his voice as a harrowing instrument—his favorite devices included a wounded animal cry and a mumbled, guttural growl. Each amply demonstrated how he earned his stage name. His repertoire of primal expressions drew equally on anger and pain, and were completely convincing: This singer wasn't trying to simulate some abstract feeling—he was chasing it down, delivering it whole. His feral lunges on stage and his dogged pursuit of emotional truth were known to scare people.

Rolling Stone ranked *Moanin'* #153 on the magazine's list of the 500 greatest albums of all time.

Phillips heard him in 1951, when Burnett, from small-town Mississippi, was still making his living as a farmer and playing juke joints on the side. Phillips persuaded the singer to do some sessions at the Memphis Recording Service—the small studio Phillips ran while launching Sun Records. The first dates yielded several regional hits—among them "Moanin' at Midnight" and "All Night Boogie," which both appear on the first Howlin' Wolf "album," *Moanin' in the Moonlight.*

Pretty soon, word of this singular talent spread. Chess Records snapped Wolf up, and convinced him to move to Chicago in 1953. From then on, the recordings combined the raggedness of rural blues— Wolf claimed that as a boy, he'd been taught by the pioneering Charley Patton—with the rhythmic sophistication of hard-swinging Chicago blues.

The combination, exemplified on this collection by snarly tracks from Memphis and several with a snapping Chicago bomp, remains devastating. No blues singer swaggers the way Wolf does: He might not be polished, his phrases might not be pretty, but he's completely committed to them. He believes with an intensity that simply can't be dismissed. It doesn't take long with *Moanin'* to realize Phillips was right: This is where the soul of man never dies.

GENRE: ⊕ Blues. **RELEASED:** 1959, Chess. **KEY TRACKS:** "Smokestack Lightning," "All Night Boogie." **CATALOG CHOICE:** *The Back Door Wolf.* **NEXT STOP:** Robert Johnson: *The Complete Recordings* (see p. 404). **AFTER THAT:** Various Artists: *The Real Folk Blues.*

Expansive and Daring Electric Jazz

Red Clay

Freddie Hubbard

Red Clay is one of those records that mucks up the neat evolution narrative of jazz. It was recorded in 1970, several years after its star pianist Herbie Hancock and others had begun using the electric piano, and during the time when bandleaders like Miles Davis were experimenting with high-wattage rock rhythms. But it's the creation of veteran hard bop trumpeter Freddie Hubbard, whose open and inquisitive solos instantly separate it from more pedestrian jazz-rock comminglings.

Hubbard believed he could reach the "acoustic" and "electric" jazz audiences without alienating either. *Red Clay* is one of a handful of records to manage that trick. Its compositions, all by Hubbard, are centered on the blues and *Kind of Blue*–style modality—except for the title track, which borrows its chord sequence from the pop hit "Sunny." Hubbard's tunes encourage showboating, and all here rise to the challenge: Saxophonist Joe Henderson navigates "The Intrepid Fox" as though trying to show what "stealth" might

Hubbard plays his distinctive, soulful trumpet.

sound like, and Hancock animates "Suite Sioux" with utterly sweet lines and crisp staccato bursts of chording that become their own kind of melody.

Red Clay became a jazz touchstone. It brought the trumpeter's daring, bellicose style to a wider audience, and then, inevitably, created demand for follow-ups. Hubbard obliged, and while some of his subsequent efforts are pleasant, they're slight when compared with the dazzling color bursts that prevail here.

GENRE: 🎷 Jazz. **RELEASED:** 1970, CTI. **KEY TRACKS:** "The Intrepid Fox," "Suite Sioux," "Red Clay." **CATALOG CHOICE:** *Backlash.* **NEXT STOP:** Stanley Turrentine: *Salt Song.* **AFTER THAT:** Donald Byrd and the Blackbyrds: *City Life.*

Bach, Beamed from the Netherworld

Bach: Cantatas

Lorraine Hunt Lieberson
Orchestra of Emmanuel Music (Craig Smith, cond.)

In the most famous of Peter Sellars's staged versions of these Bach cantatas, Lorraine Hunt Lieberson appeared as a frail patient, hooked up to medical tubes, wandering around singing words found in Luke 2 ("Ich habe genug") about being ready to die. The piece, performed at Lincoln Center in 2002, stayed with people—partly because of her radical appearance and partly because of the singing, which on this recording exhibits a luminous, glimpse-of-the-netherworld quality.

That cantata, written for the Feast of Purification, and another, written for the eleventh Sunday following Trinity, are for solo voice. They're anomalies in Bach's work: Most of the more than three hundred cantatas he wrote call for a full chorus and often elaborate musical accompaniment. The two offered here are more spare. They depend on the sensitive accompaniment of a small orchestra, and showcase the attention-grabbing powers of Hunt Lieberson (1954–2006), who began her career as a soprano but by this time had grown into a mezzo-soprano.

From the first aria, "Ich habe genug," Hunt Lieberson demonstrates unusual attention to the "small" aspects of vocal delivery, as well as a deep appreciation for the way Bach created music to cradle and complement text. She keens in a way that makes her voice sound

LORRAINE HUNT LIEBERSON

"Few artists have brought such emotional vulnerability to their work." —Anthony Tommassini, *New York Times*

like a magical glasslike instrument played at supersoft volume (she was an accomplished violist). She measures out the emotion of her phrases with great care, mirroring the tones Bach intended. One example comes on that opening aria: After hovering in a wistful mood most of the way, Hunt Lieberson's tone changes when she reaches the phrase "the hope of the righteous." It's as though the words have triggered a flash of optimism, allowing the singing to take flight. Though these treatments of Bach became famous for their staging, these recordings—particularly the porcelain-pure lullaby "Schlummert ein"—don't need any extra imagery. Hunt Lieberson provides it all.

GENRE: 🎻 Classical. **RELEASED:** 2003, Nonesuch. **KEY TRACKS:** Cantata 82: "Ich habe genug," "Schlummert ein." Cantata 199: "Auf diese Schmerzensreu." **CATALOG CHOICES:** *Handel Arias; Sings Peter Lieberson: Neruda Songs.* **NEXT STOP:** Igor Stravinsky: *Les Noces,* Musikfabrik NRW (Daniel Reuss, cond.).

The Mellow Bluesman of Mississippi

Today!

Mississippi John Hurt

The tale of Mississippi John Hurt (1893–1966) is typical—he was one of many bluesmen to be rediscovered during the Folk Revival of the early '60s, and like others, he experienced a decades-delayed career renaissance. But his sound is worlds away from ordinary blues—accompanying himself with precise fingerpicked guitar, Hurt made quiet, old-timey music that's closer to the temperament of a coffeehouse troubadour than a roaring Chicago-style bluesman.

Hurt first recorded in 1928, in sessions for Okeh Records that included the legendary

Lonnie Johnson. After a few years plying his trade with intermittent success (Okeh dissolved during the Depression), Hurt went back to Avalon, Mississippi, where he'd grown up, to work as a sharecropper. Decades later, two of his early songs were included on Harry Smith's *Anthology of American Folk Music* (see p. 803), and that inspired several musicologists to go looking for him. Once found, he was encouraged to relocate to Washington, D.C., where he restarted his performing career. His appearance at the 1963 Newport Folk Festival drew raves, and Hurt spent the last three years of his life performing and recording most of his songbook, on three stellar albums.

Today! is the first of the three, and only a hair more enjoyable than his final statement, *Last Sessions*. Both are easygoing affairs organized around the steady boom-chink of Hurt's guitar, which carries strong echoes of ragtime piano.

Hurt spent most of his life working as a sharecropper in Avalon, Mississippi.

His singing is oddly magnetic: Hurt exudes a kind of wide-eyed sweetness, as though he's just now discovering something awesome about songs he's been performing for years. Hurt's singing and the varied accompaniment patterns he uses on "Make Me a Pallet on Your Floor" and other pieces have been endlessly scrutinized by young blues aspirants. One student, the guitarist Stefan Grossman, marveled at how his simple backing fit perfectly with the songs of hardship, deception, and murder: "He was incredible, the storybook grandfather full of wise tales and wonderful stories."

GENRE: 🔵 Blues. **RELEASED:** 1966, Vanguard. **KEY TRACKS:** "Candy Man," "Make Me a Pallet on Your Floor," "Corinna, Corinna." **CATALOG CHOICES:** *1928 Sessions; Last Sessions.* **NEXT STOP:** Taj Mahal: *The Blues.* **AFTER THAT:** Sleepy John Estes: *Brownsville Blues.*

A Roar from the American Rock Underground

Zen Arcade

Hüsker Dü

A loose concept album about a runaway kid who encounters unpleasantness out in the unforgiving real world, *Zen Arcade* is among the most thrilling, musically radical documents to emerge from the American rock underground of the 1980s. A highly pressurized tour of the adolescent turmoils, it's got the requisite indie-rock elements, including rototilling guitars, and lacerating, possessed-by-demons backbeats and vocal wails so besieged that words seem superfluous.

Yet more than thrash attitude is on display here. The Minneapolis-based Hüsker Dü—guitarist and singer Bob Mould, drummer and singer Grant Hart, and bassist Greg Norton—developed a rare cohesion, an all-for-one ensemble attack that made the music sound larger than the sum of its parts.

These guys really *play:* Tucked inside some *Zen Arcade* tunes are outbreaks of lurching prog-rock fury, off-kilter guitar constructions, and blistering up-tempo slaloms far more intricate than most speed-metal. That's not to overlook the candy song-writers Mould and Hart (who usually wrote separately, and often fought about the band's direction) put there: A stagger-ing number of the songs rely on honest-to-goodness hooks. These rarely occupy the prime spotlight—Mould's wall of dense lo-fi guitar sludge sits at the forefront—but they're there all the same, leavening the otherwise scalding "Indecision Time," bringing momentary sweetness to the timeless shrug "Whatever."

"The closest hardcore will ever get to an opera."
—David Fricke, *Rolling Stone*

According to the liner notes, the twenty-three songs of *Zen Arcade* were recorded in a forty-five-hour frenzy of activity; the recording cost just $3,200. Many of the tunes are first takes, and while previous and future Hüsker Dü records contain mostly straightforward guitar-based rockers, this album has strange song fragments built on piano, haunted space-jam instrumentals, acoustic guitar ballads, and even blurry-sounding tape experiments.

Not every one of these will make the Hüsker hall-of-fame reel, but some, including the bitterly acidic "Never Talking to You Again," deserve a spot. Like many of the strong moments here, "Never Talking" plays like a transcript of some contentious confrontation, a moment when the emotional temperature of a conversation suddenly escalates into the red zone. That's where Hüsker Dü likes to be—at the ragged edge, torn up and ready to rage but not so far gone that things lurch out of control.

GENRE: 🎸 Rock. **RELEASED:** 1984, SST. **KEY TRACKS:** "Never Talking to You Again," "Something I Learned Today," "Indecision Time," "Pink Turns to Blue," "Turn On the News." **CATALOG CHOICES:** *New Day Rising; Warehouse: Songs and Stories.* **NEXT STOP:** Meat Puppets: *Too High to Die.* **AFTER THAT:** The Replacements: *Let It Be* (see p. 643).

Good Vibes for Days

Components

Bobby Hutcherson

During his tenure at Blue Note Records, which lasted from 1964 to 1977, Bobby Hutcherson managed to change the jazz conception of the vibraphone all by himself. Before him, the instrument was associated with pleasant percussive swing, à la Lionel Hampton. Hutcherson tore off in other direc-tions, using the bell-like clarity of his instru-ment to create open atmospheres tailor-made for seeking. From the start of his recording career, Hutcherson presented himself as a student of hard bop determined to get beyond Art Blakey's sound; his best recordings, like this 1965 date, aspire to the adventurous, har-monically advanced concepts of his frequent collaborator, pianist Herbie Hancock.

Hutcherson was among the first Blue Note artists to recognize that hard bop and free jazz needn't be strangers; his composi-tions here create an important bridge between open-vista frontiering and hard bop's more formalized structures. The tunes, some writ-ten by Hutcherson and others by drummer

Joe Chambers, are tricky and rigorous, but never so cerebral they can't accommodate a singing melody. (Hutcherson is really good at sneaky lyricism: On the waltz "Little B's Poem," he strings patient lines into a rhapsody.) Using warm prodding plinks and wide-open chords, Hutcherson clears out lots of space. His goal is to inspire true tonality-shifting exploration, and he recognizes that to get that going, the

Hutcherson with his vibraphone set.

atmosphere—the *vibe*, if you will—is as important as the compositional framework.

GENRE: 🅱 Jazz. **RELEASED:** 1965, Blue Note. **KEY TRACKS:** "Components," "Little B's Poem," "Movement." **CATALOG CHOICES:** *The Kicker; Mirage.* **NEXT STOP:** Joe Henderson: *Black Narcissus.* **AFTER THAT:** Stefon Harris: *A Cloud of Red Dust.*

Eerily Peaceful Singing

The Orphan's Lament

Huun-Huur-Tu

You're forgiven if, when you first hear Huun-Huur-Tu, you think this "throat singing" thing is a gimmick. The singers of the most popular group from Tuva, near Russia's Mongolian border, manipulate the air in their throats and windpipes to sing several tones simultaneously. And not just any notes—croaking low drones, flute-like high register wisps, and myriad tonal colors in between. When put in the service of folk songs (about the role of ancestors and the beauty of the Tuvan steppe), these voices give off an oddly celestial resonance. Or they can sound like the flatulence of pond-dwelling creatures. No matter where Huun-Huur-Tu go, the disconcerting sounds follow: Though enormously skillful, this isn't your typical relaxing-by-the-fire kind of singing group.

Although the four members of Huun-Huur-Tu sing gently and often quietly, some quality inside the voices suggests urgency. Using techniques similar to those Tibetan Buddhists and North American Inuit employ, the singers rarely need much instrumental support: On the faster tunes, the voices outline the tempo, with help from frame drums and their own percussion

instruments (one rattle is made from bull's scrotum and sheep's kneebones). The long, enveloping drones are riveting in a different way—here the singing moves slowly, in almost microtonal shifts that can become quite abrasive.

And though throat singing is probably an acquired taste, at several moments on HHT's second international release those trembling glottal sounds totally define a mood—see the despairing title cut "The Orphan's Lament," or the more impulsive "Borbanngadyr," which both display an alarming beauty that requires no translation.

GENRE: 🌐 World/Russia. **RELEASED:** 1994, Shanachie. **KEY TRACKS:** "The Orphan's Lament," "Eki attar," "Borbanngadyr." **CATALOG CHOICE:** *Live 1.* **NEXT STOP:** The Bulgarian Women's National Radio and TV Chorus: *Le mystère des voix bulgares* (see p. 130).

Abdullah Ibrahim Trio ✦ Iggy and the Stooges ✦ Ilê Aiyê ✦ The Incredible String Band ✦ The Isley Brothers ✦ Burl Ives ✦ Charles Ives ✦ Joe Jackson ✦ Mahalia Jackson ✦ The Jackson Five ✦ Michael Jackson ✦ Ahmad Jamal ✦ Elmore James ✦ Etta James ✦ Rick James ✦ Skip James ✦ Leoš Janáček ✦ Jane's Addiction ✦ Keith Jarrett ✦ Eddie Jefferson ✦ Waylon Jennings ✦ The Jesus and Mary Chain ✦ Flaco Jiménez ✦ Antonio Carlos Jobim ✦ Antonio Carlos Jobim and Elis Regina ✦ Elton John ✦ Little Willie John ✦ Blind Willie Johnson ✦ James P. Johnson ✦ Linton Kwesi Johnson ✦ Lonnie Johnson ✦ Robert Johnson ✦ Tommy Johnson ✦ Freedy Johnston ✦ Joi ✦ Fern Jones ✦ George Jones ✦ Norah Jones ✦ Rickie Lee Jones ✦ Janis Joplin ✦ Scott Joplin ✦ Louis Jordan ✦ Josquin des Prez ✦ Joy Division

I, J

Jazz Composition, South African Style

Yarona

Abdullah Ibrahim Trio

W hen asked about his favorite musicians, Duke Ellington frequently mentioned the South African jazz pianist and composer Abdullah Ibrahim, whom he first heard at a nightclub in Zurich. Known in the '60s and '70s as "Dollar Brand," Ibrahim is one of the few international jazz musicians to develop his own "language," a sound that casts the prayerful melodies of his homeland in a harmonically hip jazz context. His tunes are simple, graceful, and cautiously celebratory—it's easy to imagine a children's choir singing them.

Yarona was recorded live at Manhattan's Sweet Basil nightclub in 1995.

Ibrahim has scored some of his compositions for large ensembles, but his music, which he has said is inspired by South Africa itself, is ideally suited to intimate jazz exploration. On this trio CD, he begins his "Nisa" in a Keith Jarrett–like zone, purposefully stating and restating an opening gambit. Then he wanders off, carried by the sauntering pulse to a land of longer, more complicated ideas. When, after several minutes, Ibrahim returns to his original phrase, it reverberates with unexpected force.

Yarona contains playful updates of songs Ibrahim has been playing for decades—including the serene "Cherry/ Mannenburg" (which was originally titled "Cape Town Fringe") and "African Marketplace"— as well as newer material. As Ibrahim takes them apart, he locates troubled undercurrents and tiny side ideas, little things that enhance his compositional intent. Like so much art from Africa, Ibrahim's music sounds simple, but there is always more—much more—lurking beneath the surface.

GENRE: 🎵 Jazz. **RELEASED:** 1995, Enja.
KEY TRACKS: "Cherry/Mannenburg," "African River," "Tintinyana," "African Marketplace."
CATALOG CHOICES: *African Space Program; Duke Ellington Presents the Dollar Brand Trio.*
NEXT STOP: Bheki Mseleku: *Meditations.*

Rock as Social Menace Starts Here

Raw Power

Iggy and the Stooges

T his album, the third from Detroit rockers Iggy and the Stooges, was released in 1973. Hardly a commercial success at the time, it has, nonetheless, had an extraordinarily active afterlife. It was a primary inspiration for the punk rockers in London and New York who were just starting to make noise in 1975, and the West Coast punks who followed a few years later. In his posthumously released journal, Nirvana singer and songwriter Kurt Cobain, the avatar of grunge, mentions *Raw Power* as his all-time favorite album. The bands associated with the second and third iterations of punk that followed grunge, the Blink 182s of the world, copied it in some cases note for note. John Frusciante, the guitarist of the Red Hot Chili Peppers, summed up the album's stature this way in a 2001 interview: "When you think about all the ways bands these days try and expand rock and roll, most of them look pretty silly next to *Raw Power*. That is a definitive statement."

Iggy Pop is referred to by many as the "Godfather of Punk."

It's also got curious origin stories. Plagued by various addictions, the Stooges lapsed into an extended limbo after the band's second album, *Funhouse*, flopped in 1970. David Bowie, then flying high in his Ziggy Stardust (see p. 109) guise, encouraged Iggy Pop to try again. Pop—known to *New York Times* readers as Mr. Pop and to his mom as James Newell Osterberg—agreed to a deal brokered by Bowie, which gave the star control over the final product. (Bowie mixed most of the album, attempting to correct what he heard as sonic flaws; Pop did the wilder mix on "Search and Destroy.")

To most rock ears, the initial version was plenty edgy for a rock record in 1973—its torrents of distorted buzzsaw guitar, from newest Stooge James Williamson, proved the perfect counterpoint to Pop's howling, proudly lewd declarations. But Pop and the Stooges knew that the original tracks held more sonic mayhem—elements Bowie's mix didn't exactly optimize. Fans of the record knew it too, as bootlegged versions of Pop's initial mixes circulated widely.

So when Columbia invited Pop to remix *Raw Power* in 1997, he seized the chance to right an old wrong, as he explains in the liner notes: "This is a wonderful album but it's always sounded fragile and rickety, and that band was not fragile and not rickety." Sure enough, the new version expands the smudgy guitar distortion into an enveloping roar, and amps up the rhythm section so that even when it's playing things straight, on a genius song like "Shake Appeal," it sounds like it's blowing rock convention to bits. This, of course, was Pop's guiding vision all along—music so brutal, it carries a physical jolt. Mission accomplished, Mr. Pop.

GENRE: 🎸 Rock. **RELEASED:** 1973, Columbia. (Reissued 1997.) **KEY TRACKS:** "Search and Destroy," "Shake Appeal." **CATALOG CHOICES:** *Funhouse.* Pop solo: *Skull Ring.* **NEXT STOP:** Richard Hell: *Blank Generation.* **AFTER THAT:** Nirvana: *In Utero.*

Thundering Groove Ecstasy from More Than 100 Drummers

Canto negro

Ilê Aiyê

*C*anto negro puts listeners inside the drum corps, or *blocos afros*, that rule the annual Carnaval celebrations in Brazil's coastal Salvador de Bahia region, one of the most "African" areas of Brazil. These community groups build from the drum up—some of the big ones boast over 100 percussionists working in tight synchronization, united in pursuit of what sounds like mass groove ecstasy.

The thundering sounds of "Caminho" and other tracks here reflect a rare confluence of ancient and modern inspiration. The basic beats and chants are drawn from Candomblé, a centuries-old derivation of African religion in which specific rhythms are used to appeal to particular deities for assistance. The singers (most pieces contain lively exchanges between solo singers and the ensemble) slip comments on current politics and conditions in the neighborhoods into their petitions, connecting ritual mantras to the concerns of the day. Add in the element of competition—during the parades, the groups vie against rival neighborhoods—and

Members of Ilê Aiyê have been playing together since 1974.

suddenly this already energetic music becomes a rallying point and proving ground. Cultural and community pride are on the line.

This samba is markedly different from the samba associated with Brazil's cities: The pace ambles along at a sultry gait that's positively lazy and much less jittery than Rio samba. Teams of cross-sticking snare drummers converge on a strong polyrhythmic heartbeat, then beam their collective wisdom straight at the feet and hips of everyone within earshot, transforming ordinary street corners into dance floors.

GENRE: 🌐 World/Brazil. **RELEASED:** 1995, Interra. **KEY TRACKS:** "Que bloco es esse," "Caminho," "Havemos de voltar." **NEXT STOP:** Portela Passado de Glória: *A Velha Guarda da Portelo.* **AFTER THAT:** Olodum: *Pela vida.*

Fanciful Stories Designed to Enchant . . .

The Hangman's Beautiful Daughter

The Incredible String Band

Conceived by Incredible String Band songwriters Mike Heron and Robin Williamson as a series of stories designed to amuse (and, in a roundabout way, educate) an adolescent girl growing up in simpler times,

The Hangman's Beautiful Daughter is a psychedelic trip through the tilt-a-whirl of hippie culture. The third album from the inventive British folk-rock band bubbles with odd allegories and the exotic sounds of dulcimer, harpsichord, and oud. In this unpredictable sonic realm, children are confronted with witches and Minotaurs and cosmic fairy tales told in couplets like "Earth, water, fire and air, met together in a garden fair."

But tucked into wordy invocations of mythology ("The Minotaur's Song") and microbiology ("A Very Cellular Song") are redeeming prog-rock instrumental forays; some of these are interrupted by wriggling vocals from Williamson, who'd recently returned from Morocco and was obviously under the influence of that country's hypnotic singers. Like many music makers of this era, the band has a short attention span, abandoning one rhythm to shift, unexpectedly, into another; there are little tunes inside of bigger tunes, and at times the band goes soldiering off, never to return to the original theme.

ISB deserves credit for loosening British folk from its roots; this album aligns with similarly spirited efforts by Pentangle and Fairport Convention that helped expand folk in more progressive, less literal directions. But its influence goes beyond that. *The Hangman's Beautiful Daughter* encouraged

ISB's founding members Robin Williamson (left) and Clive Palmer (right).

scores of rockers (notably Led Zeppelin) to take wild leaps into the mystic unknown, where even jaded types could reconnect with their inner druid.

GENRE: 🎵 Folk.
RELEASED: 1968, Elektra.
KEY TRACKS: "Koeeoaddi There," "A Very Cellular Song." **CATALOG CHOICE:** *Changing Horses.* **NEXT STOP:** Mike Heron: *Smiling Men with Bad Reputations.* **AFTER THAT:** Steeleye Span: *Below the Salt.*

The Best Shot from a Dynasty

The Heat Is On

The Isley Brothers

The Isley Brothers turn up in the most unlikely chapters of pop history. The Cincinnati, Ohio, family band had success right out of the box, with the frenzied frat-house staple from 1959, "Shout," and its "follow-up" from 1962, "Twist and Shout." Later in the '60s, the group created several enduring radio classics, including "It's Your Thing" and "That Lady (Parts 1 and 2)." Rock fans revere the group for giving a young guitarist named Jimmy James (aka Jimi Hendrix) his first employment experience. And though the band's profile dimmed in the 1990s, its lead singer Ronald Isley reinvented himself in 2001 as the boudoir-bound Mr. Bigg, crooning alongside R&B hitmaker R. Kelly on the smash "Contagious."

The Heat Is On was the Isley Brothers' first #1 album.

To hear the Isleys at their most blistering, look for the early '70s titles *3+3* (1973) and this follow-up, which offer thumping party jams

and sensitive-guy romance in equal measure. *The Heat Is On* starts with "Fight the Power," one of the great rallying cries of 1970s pop. The lyrics give voice to a boiling-point exasperation—"I tried to roll with the punches, I got knocked on the ground"—but in typical Isley Brothers fashion, the music is totally under control. The rhythm section, which by this time had inspired Sly and the Family Stone and others seeking funk-rock utopia, starts with an elastic two-chord vamp. Then guitar and keyboard parts are added, and before long, these interlocking cogs become a mighty machine that seems forever on the verge of levitating. Sometimes, as happens on the title track, the band's disciplined timekeeping rises up and demands center stage. And sometimes, just one passionate single part becomes the catalyst: Listen to the way Ernie Isley's tantalizing lead guitar, a screaming arrow of tone, powers "Hope You Feel Better Love."

This album is one of many from the 33⅓-RPM era to be organized thematically: Side one offers the up-tempo stuff, while side two is the "chillout" set. A master of reflective romance balladry, Ronald Isley deploys a slight but discernible tremble to sing of all-consuming devotion on the late-night-radio staple "For the Love of You," then uses his supple, invitingly warm voice to create the feeling of "Sensuality" in sound.

GENRE: 🌀 R&B. **RELEASED:** 1975, T-Neck/Epic. **KEY TRACKS:** "Fight the Power," "Hope You Feel Better Love," "For the Love of You," "Sensuality." **CATALOG CHOICE:** *3+3; Harvest for the World.* **NEXT STOP:** DeBarge: *All This Love.* **AFTER THAT:** The Brothers Johnson: *Look Out for #1.*

Songs Picked Up on the Lonely Road

The Wayfaring Stranger

Burl Ives

After a few years of college, Burl Ives set out to discover America. He hitchhiked from town to town, supporting himself by busking on street corners. He picked up songs along the way, and by the late '30s had fashioned himself into a quintessentially American wandering troubadour—a banjo-playing roughneck familiar with train-jumping hobos and kindly farmers, a rogue who would sing mournful Irish ballads with a bit of bootlegger whimsy.

Ives turned this restless spirit into a media persona. Beginning in 1940, on his own radio show, and continuing through a decades-long career in music and film, Ives was the Wayfaring Stranger. This barebones voice and guitar album, his first for Columbia, shows why he was considered a catalyst for the folk revival: Ives retained the raconteur demeanor that endeared him to radio audiences, the rare folk singer who could tell wild stories of men meeting terrible fates with a twinkle in his eye.

Despite successful children's albums and the seasonal hit "Have a Holly Jolly Christmas," *The Wayfaring Stranger* remains Ives's best shot. A hit shortly after it was released, its almost-too-commonplace songs were embraced by younger folk singers, who picked up the basic melodies and his affection for the old tunes, even if they missed Ives's characteristic wryness. Ambling through "Cowboy's Lament" (better known as "Streets of Laredo"), Ives found a sense of tragedy lurking behind the familiar. And because he was comfortable moving from one region to another, *The Wayfaring Stranger* is a rambler's grab bag of wisdom picked up from many journeys.

GENRE: 🎵 Folk. **RELEASED:** 2000, Collectables. **KEY TRACKS:** "Roving Gambler," "Cowboy's Lament," "Cotton-Eyed Joe," "Pretty Polly." **COLLECTOR"S NOTE:** The 2000 reissue (now the only way to purchase this on CD) offers a bonus not included on the original LP: Ives's rapt rendition of the bluegrass standard "Pretty Polly." **CATALOG CHOICE:** *Chim Chim Cheree & Other Children's Choices.* **NEXT STOP:** Pete Seeger: *The Bitter and the Sweet.*

A Wild and Beautiful Imagining of America

Symphony No. 2, Symphony No. 3

Charles Ives

New York Philharmonic (Leonard Bernstein, cond.)

Here, in audio form, is the American "melting pot" they talk about in grade school social studies. A patchwork quilt of not-quite-complementary sonorities, Charles Ives's five-movement Symphony No. 2 contains traces of the nineteenth-century patriotic march "Columbia, the Gem of the Ocean" played by screeching brass, alongside bits of "The Battle Hymn of the Republic" and "Turkey in the Straw." Sometimes these references occur in isolation, and sometimes all at once, boisterous collisions that seem to lampoon the very idea of "patriotic" music. In this piece and others by Ives, the impact comes not from the reconfigured themes themselves, but in the ways they're juxtaposed against each other—in a spectacular, not at all random but sometimes random-sounding cacophony.

As Leonard Bernstein once noted, Ives can be considered our "musical Mark Twain, Emerson, and Lincoln all rolled into one." At the same time, Ives (1874–1954) created music that looks ever forward: His startling collage approach became a guiding idea for the American avant-garde of the 1960s. (Less enamored observers have likened Ives to Grandma Moses, an expert at popularizing folk art rather than creating from whole cloth.)

Ives acquired his unusual notions about music as a child. He grew up in Danbury, Connecticut, and his early musical experiences include hearing his father, a local bandleader, playing two contrasting pieces on the family piano at the same time. This engendered a lifelong love for simultaneity and is one inspiration for the clashing sounds that define his signature works. Ives's schemes aren't always graceful, and at times the results have an unruly quality (especially compared with the work of another quintessentially "American" composer, Aaron Copland), but they are always entirely *his*.

The New York Philharmonic, with Bernstein at the helm, treats Ives as a visionary whose renegade jumbles signify something central to the American soul. Bernstein senses the danger in making too much of the familiar tunes of Symphony No. 2, and as the piece evolves he tends to emphasize its outsized contrasts, notably the trembling chord clusters Ives wrote for strings and the rollicking piano accompaniments, which require the performer to use fists and forearms. Also here is the more reserved Symphony No. 3. Writing for a string orchestra, Ives appropriates mostly hymns and religious songs, engendering a mood of reflection that's surprising given the uproars of Symphony No. 2. Those intrigued by the rattle and hum of Ives might seek the composer's most challenging piece, Symphony No. 4, next.

GENRE: 🎵 Classical. **RELEASED:** 1958, 1965, Sony Classical. (Reissued 1998.) **KEY TRACKS:** Symphony No. 2: second and fifth movements. Symphony No. 3: second movement, "Children's Day." **CATALOG CHOICE:** *Symphony No. 4,* San Francisco Symphony (Michael Tilson Thomas, cond.). **NEXT STOP:** Elliott Carter: *Symphony No. 1, Piano Concerto,* Mark Wait, Nashville Symphony (Kenneth Schermerhorn, cond.). **AFTER THAT:** John Corigliano: *Of Rage and Remembrance: Symphony No. 1,* National Symphony Orchestra (Leonard Slatkin, cond.).

Jackson's High-Stepping City Tour

Night and Day

Joe Jackson

When this album appeared in the thick of New Wave frenzy in 1982, most pop people knew Joe Jackson as a scrawny Englishman with a bratty voice (see "Is She Really Going Out with Him?," his then-biggest hit) and a penchant for ersatz up-tempo swing.

It's safe to say that no one was prepared for the cinematic *Night and Day*—a cosmopolitan swirl of taunting rhythm and big, chomping piano chords that ranks among the great pop valentines to New York City. The album is split into two distinct temperaments—the "Night" side suggests the frantic bustle of clubland, while the subsequent "Day" side is more reserved, with tender ballads ("Breaking Us in Two"), thoughts about life's downers ("Cancer," with its paranoid refrain "Everything gives you cancer"), and outbreaks of bombast (most notably, "Real Men").

Even within these polarities, Jackson rarely stays in the same part of town for more than a few minutes. The brilliantly sequenced Night side begins in a surreal Hell's Kitchen gloom, and just as the ears get used to its abrasion,

The album's title comes from the famous Cole Porter song.

Jackson goes off in search of "Chinatown." He seeks a mindset as much as a neighborhood, and his faux-Asian dissonances are so skillfully wrought that you hope he doesn't find it. Just when *that* starts to seem normal, Jackson puts on his two-tone shoes for "Steppin' Out," a whirring vision of a gleaming, idealized cityscape. Despite overexposure on the radio, this hurtling theme still works. It's maybe what Gershwin would be cranking out were he a Jackson contemporary and obsessed with the wizardry of techno—music that's futuristic and at the same time utterly romantic, a collision a lot like Manhattan itself.

GENRE: 🎸 Rock. **RELEASED:** 1982, A&M. **KEY TRACKS:** "Steppin' Out," "Target," "Breaking Us in Two." **CATALOG CHOICE:** *Big World.* **NEXT STOP:** Squeeze: *Argybargy.*

Early Genius from a Gospel Legend

The Apollo Sessions: 1946–1951

Mahalia Jackson

Mahalia Jackson set a high bar for herself when, at the age of thirty-five, she went into New York's tiny Apollo studios to record her first consequential singles. Just about everything she did for

Apollo is definitive—from her fulminating "Said He Would" to her oft-recorded "In the Upper Room" to what is easily the most energized recording of Herbert Brewster's "I Will Move On Up a Little Higher." Some of these intimate and refreshingly loose sides were captured on the cheap, at 3 A.M., with just a pianist providing accompaniment. They show Jackson testing the waters, figuring exactly how much blues fire and other secular traits she could slip into her gospel.

The spine-chilling contralto who became a cultural icon (she sang on the Mall in Washington, D.C., just before the Reverend Martin Luther King gave his "I Have a Dream" speech) was born in a poor section of New Orleans. She moved around as a teenager; in Chicago, she met the composer Thomas Dorsey, who encouraged her to integrate blues feeling into her interpretations of spirituals. One treat of the Apollo sessions is hearing Jackson ad-lib far more brazenly than most of her gospel counterparts dared.

Several of these selections became hits, and led to her signing with Columbia Records in 1954. That's when Jackson took off: The label's vast distribution network meant that her recordings could travel beyond the gospel circuit, and she quickly became a crossover star, performing in concert halls for adoring crowds of all races. (According to legend, the young Elvis Presley used to sneak in to hear her sing.) Although Jackson's Columbia output contains drop-dead classics (notably *Bless This House* and *Live at Newport, 1958*), the Apollo sessions catch the moment when her zealous blues-tinged singing solidified into the mighty sound that changed gospel forever.

GENRE: ⊕ Gospel. **RELEASED:** 1994, Pair. **KEY TRACKS:** "In the Upper Room," "Didn't It Rain," "Said He Would." **CATALOG CHOICE:** *Live at Newport, 1958.* **NEXT STOP:** Marion Williams: *My Soul Looks Back.* **AFTER THAT:** The Clara Ward Singers: *Take My Hand, Precious Lord* (see p. 845).

The Prototypical J5 Single

"I Want You Back"

The Jackson Five

A bubbly song of contrition, "I Want You Back" established the lucrative recipe the Jackson Five would follow for its entire hit-making run: Take one jittery, impossibly caffeinated beat. Add some strings, classic Motown harmonies, a singsong refrain so simple it sounds like a playground taunt. Mix it hot, so the vocals are inescapable. Then add some bite—in the form of a single electric guitar note that threads, Morse code–like, throughout the entire tune. That instrumental urgency, coupled with a scat-sung "breakdown" that recalls Sly and the Family Stone's exuberant tag-team vocalizing, makes "I Want You Back" the apex of the J5.

And of course the song, which unseated B. J. Thomas's "Raindrops Keep Fallin' on My Head" at the top of the chart in January 1970, has Michael Jackson singing lead. Then age eleven, Jackson pleads with a grown-up's notion of how the script of love is supposed to go, talking about how he dismissed the girl prematurely and is now full of (painfully audible) regret. This performance stands among the most passionate vocals from any pop artist—not just those in the child-star division—and as a result has become an endlessly emulated benchmark. One could argue that the various generations of boy bands—from Jodeci in the '80s to Hanson and 'NSync in the '90s—derived their entire repertoire of wheedling and begging tactics from this track.

The Jackson Five was, in classic Motown fashion, a singles operation; the album carrying this song, *Diana Ross Presents the Jackson Five*, is otherwise unexceptional. The best way to experience "I Want You Back" and

The Jackson Five originally hail from Gary, Indiana.

the other radio blasts that followed is on any of the available anthologies.

GENRES: 🟤 R&B ⭐ Pop.
RELEASED: 1969, Motown.
APPEARS ON: *Diana Ross Presents the Jackson Five; The Jackson Five Anthology.*
CATALOG CHOICE: Michael Jackson: *Off the Wall.* **NEXT STOP:** Sly and the Family Stone: *Stand!* (see p. 713).
AFTER THAT: 'NSync: *Celebrity.*

Pop Music's Wizard of Oz Moment

Thriller

Michael Jackson

T hose effervescent Jackson Five singles notwithstanding, Michael Jackson's artistic peak didn't begin until "Don't Stop 'til You Get Enough," the disco-strings fantasia that was the first single from *Off the Wall* (1979).

It ended somewhere around "Man in the Mirror," the inspirational trinket from the intermittently bad *Bad* (1987). After that, the artist the tabloids called Wacko Jacko continued to generate hits (and grab headlines, first for his facial transformations, then the notorious pajama parties with preteen boys at his Neverland Ranch), but something fundamental about his enterprise changed. If he started out easing down the yellow brick road, he wound up the fearful little man behind the curtain, a "King of Pop" desperate for loyal subjects.

Between those mileposts sits *Thriller*, a confluence of craft and inspiration that sent shockwaves through popular culture. The

Thriller spent 80 weeks in the Top 10 of the *Billboard* chart, 37 of them at #1.

sounds on this record expanded the palette of the pop hit. The dances became stock elements of music presentation—except for the moonwalk, which only Jackson could do anyway. *Thriller*'s stylized visuals established the basic "language" of music videos. The clothes changed street fashion. And on and on.

How deep is this record? Seven of its nine tracks were Top 10 hits. As of late 2007, the album had sold over sixty million copies. When it came time to put out the "comprehensive" Jackson career overview boxed set, Sony left off one of *Thriller*'s gems, "Human Nature," perhaps because it would have been the seventh of the album's nine tracks to appear on the set.

One revisionist take on *Thriller* says it's really producer Quincy Jones's baby, that the orchestral lushness he provided would have been successful no matter who was singing. The 2003 Special Edition, a significant sonic upgrade, reveals Jones's strings and horns as catalysts and complementary forces, always providing exactly the right amount of fairy dust. But the hooks are Jackson's doing, as is the ambitious songwriting, which takes him from his dance floor comfort zone into rock and slithery post-disco and even caramel-cream balladry. Jackson turns every selection into high

drama, punctuating his lines with fitful sighs and grunts and that squeaky "whee-hee" that soon grew irritating. Heck, *he* soon grew irritating. But before he crossed that line, before he was the king of anything, he made a record you wanted to hear again and again and again. And after those zillions of spins, it's thrilling still.

GENRE: ⭐ Pop. **RELEASED:** 1982, Epic. **KEY TRACKS:** All of them. **CATALOG CHOICE:** *Off the Wall.* **NEXT STOP:** Stevie Wonder: *Songs in the Key of Life* (see p. 873). **AFTER THAT:** Prince: *Lovesexy.*

Carefree Jazz Piano

But Not for Me: Live at the Pershing

Ahmad Jamal

Jazz piano took a radical swerve with Ahmad Jamal. Before the Pittsburgh native became a phenom with this 1958 live date, his third album, the instrument had been at the center of an escalating arms race:

It was populated by speed demon beboppers (Bud Powell, Tommy Flanagan) striving to impress with ever more formidable technique and by more conceptual thinkers (Dave Brubeck) incorporating harmonies used in classical music.

Jamal's approach is completely different. He has plenty of dazzle in his fingers, but he rarely shows it. Instead, he projects a serene, unhurried, lyrical swing—even on his most heated lines, he plays as though the keys have been doused with warm butter. He uses silence, putting oceans between his phrases. He makes the piano sing. On "But Not for Me," the Gershwin classic, Jamal transforms sweet-nothings blues phrases—the kind associated with another jazz minimalist,

Ahmad Jamal at the piano during a 1959 rehearsal.

Count Basie—into sparkling, slippery gems of ad-libbing.

Jamal's restraint proved a serious lure. The album's "single," a sly little Latin-rhythm fantasia entitled "Poinciana," appeared on jukeboxes and became Jamal's signature tune. Its success propelled *But Not for Me*, recorded in a small Chicago club where Jamal's trio was the house band, to number 3 on *Billboard*'s album chart—it remained on the charts for 107 weeks, unusual for a jazz record even then. Its success brought Jamal to the peak of jazz fame—Miles Davis became one vociferous champion—but the pianist's later albums failed to replicate the low-key ethos of this one. Though he sometimes got close, *But Not for Me* stands as his masterwork, the moment when Jamal short-circuited rampant jazz abstraction with music that just plain feels good.

GENRE: 🎷 Jazz. **RELEASED:** 1958, MCA.

KEY TRACKS: "Poinciana," "There Is No Greater Love." **CATALOG CHOICE:** *Ahmad's Blues.* **NEXT STOP:** Miles Davis: *Friday Night at the Blackhawk.* **AFTER THAT:** The Three Sounds: *Black Orchid.*

A Shadow History of Rock Guitar

The Sky Is Crying

Elmore James

When a long-gone blues legend is name-checked by rockers as an influence, the connection can sometimes be vague or hard to discern. That's not the case with Elmore James (1918–1963):

Put on this high-revving collection, and the connections become impossible to ignore. That's because James's recorded legacy amounts to a shadow history of rock guitar. His rich tone (he was among the first bluesmen to understand the visceral bite of the electric guitar) and expressive command of the bottleneck slide hit just about everybody who followed. James is a primary source for the incendiary boogie of the Allman Brothers (see p. 16), and the harrowing leads of Stevie Ray Vaughan (see p. 826), not to mention Eric Clapton's crying solos circa Derek and the Dominos (see p. 219) and the rowdy '80s work of George Thorogood and the Destroyers.

James is known as the "King of the Slide Guitar."

For most of his life, James was known for his 1951 hit recording of "Dust My Broom," his update of the Robert Johnson tune. As he bounced around to different labels, the guitarist and singer was encouraged to record thinly veiled knockoffs. He did this willingly at first, but soon enough began to emphasize his own writing, exploring beyond hot-stepping boogie. This collection, which gathers important singles made between 1951 and 1961 for such small regional labels as Trumpet, Flair, and Chief, features most of his enduring originals—including campy struts shot full of excitable guitar ("Sunny Land"), and driving shuffles like "I Can't Hold Out" that you can imagine romping forever in a club.

In fact that's what James often did: After serving in the Navy during World War II, he moved to Chicago and put together his high-intensity band, the Broomdusters, with pianist Johnny Jones. A cohesive unit, this group jolts familiar Delta riffs with reckless abandon. Like the rockers who would later copy them, these guys aren't just broomdusters, they're thrillseekers.

GENRE: 🎵 Blues. **RELEASED:** 1998, Rhino. **KEY TRACKS:** "The Sky Is Crying," "Please Find My Baby," "I Can't Hold Out," "Shake Your Moneymaker." **CATALOG CHOICE:** *Original Folk Blues.* **NEXT STOP:** Willie Dixon: *I Am the Blues.* **AFTER THAT:** J. B. Hutto: *Hawk Squat.*

Definitive Southern Soul

Tell Mama

Etta James

Conventional discographical wisdom holds that the best way to encounter Etta James, the soul singer with the gilded bullhorn of a voice, is through her Chess debut *At Last!* (1960). That album does contain her biggest hit (the title track), but focuses mainly on her skill as a ballad interpreter. It's marred, a bit, by the overactive studio orchestra; after a few selections you might find yourself wanting to pull those sappy strings out of her way.

Tell Mama, recorded in Muscle Shoals in 1967, tells a richer story. It's got a smoldering ballad, "I'd Rather Go Blind," that ranks among the very best things James ever cut. The rhythm section is the Fame Studios crew that helped refine Southern soul, and much of the music is up-tempo and propulsive. The chance to hear James in front of a great band, having to work to keep the heat turned up, is not to be missed. She tears into the title track determined to enjoy (and then exploit) the tightly wound groove. She sings "Don't Lose Your Good Thing" like a big sister giving advice—there's nothing fancy about her phrasing, yet it carries worldly wisdom. And after starting the Otis Redding–penned soul-revue stomp "Security" unexceptionally, James finishes the tune in a flourish of scalding, merciless, for-the-ages ad-libs.

The 2001 reissue augments the twelve original tracks of *Tell Mama* with ten more tunes cut during the same sessions. Often such bonus material is inferior, but not here: James undertakes several forays into rock and pop (a surprisingly credible "I Got You, Babe," and a torrid "You Took It") that anticipate and actually overshadow her later projects. Not long after *Tell Mama* appeared, James began an epic struggle with substance abuse, working intermittently through much of the '70s. Comeback recordings of the 1980s spotlight her mighty and remarkably well-preserved voice. They're well mannered and pleasant; *Tell Mama* is the essence of soul.

GENRE: 🎵 R&B. **RELEASED:** 1968, Chess. (Reissued 2001.) **KEY TRACKS:** "Tell Mama," "I'd Rather Go Blind," "Security," "Don't Lose Your Good Thing," "You Took It." **CATALOG CHOICE:** *At Last.* **NEXT STOP:** Dusty Springfield: *Dusty in Memphis* (see p. 732). **AFTER THAT:** Doris Duke: *I'm a Loser* (see p. 238).

The Best Way to Work Out That Disco Karma

Street Songs

Rick James

Disco was in its drab, faceless twilight when *Street Songs* came along and superfreaked all over 1981, reminding Village People victims how thrilling music played by live musicians could be.

The timing was pure genius: Recognizing that disco had pushed the live-band funk that defined the '70s—Earth Wind & Fire, Parliament—to the deep margins, Motown songwriter/producer Rick James styled himself as a leering, winking ringmaster of a hard-funking revue. He cranked out thumping rubber-band backbeats that sounded like they could roll all night. His lyrics, such as they were, told of disco-era debauchery in the codes of cocaine clubland. And he sang

Rick James in his heyday, sporting his signature curls.

them in a me-so-horny whine that oozed risqué outlandishness.

For all the attitude and period accoutrements (this is one of the first "urban" records to utilize the buzzy analog synths then swarming new wave pop), *Street Songs* is surprisingly strong on the hit-making fundamentals. The album's monster singles—"Give It to Me," "Super Freak"—are both built on succinct, endlessly repetitive two-measure bass phrases,

ordinary vamps that scoot along in a hypnotic groove. The album tracks aren't as potent, but in one case, a smoldering ballad with Teena Marie entitled "Fire and Desire," James suggests that as much as he wants to be the next funk bad boy, he can't completely shake that Motown sweetness.

In 1990, lightweight rapper MC Hammer appropriated elements from "Super Freak" for what became his breakthrough song, "U Can't Touch This." It was another reminder, a generation removed, of the potency of these tunes: Without James's sirens-wailing hookcraft, Hammer's derivative rapping would never have hit the big time.

GENRE: 🎵 R&B. **RELEASED:** 1981, Motown. **KEY TRACKS:** "Give It to Me," "Super Freak," "Fire and Desire." **NEXT STOP:** The Mary Jane Girls: *The Mary Jane Girls*. **AFTER THAT:** Prince: *Dirty Mind*.

A Primary Root of the Blues

The Complete Early Recordings of Skip James

Skip James

Buyer beware: As listening experiences, the early recordings of the 1930s-era blues greats are almost all crude. Like similar collections of Charley Patton, this set is drawn from original 78-RPM singles, which have lots of surface noise and distortion. And that's under the best of circumstances.

Still, the music comes through, a ghostly beam from a bygone age. And what music: The frail falsetto of Skip James is primal. Even when he delivers a straight old blues line, there's fire

inside his voice, telling of troubles he can't undo. James borrows the incantations of preachers for some of his inspirational numbers ("Jesus Is a Mighty Good Leader," "Be Ready When He Comes") and gooses more typical "straight" blues with a sense of abject desperation.

James grew up on a plantation in Bentonia, Mississippi, where his mother was the cook; he was known to resent the Jim Crow South, and that frustration turns up in some of his music. "In Skip James you hear a lot of sorrow, but also a lot of anger," the guitarist and blues scholar John Fahey once observed. To hear this, cue up the dejected, openly frustrated "Devil Got My Woman," which is among the spookiest declarations in all of recorded blues.

Tempering his raw emotional edge is James's deceptive instrumental skill. These early sides, recorded in 1931 at the request of the Jackson, Mississippi, impresario H. C. Speir, feature James on both guitar and piano. The guitar tracks have a spry, easygoing air, particularly "I'm So Glad," a James original covered by Cream in the '60s that brought the bluesman the biggest payday of his career. And though James does play the blues straight, several tunes, like the amazing "Special Rider Blues," find him darting impulsively away from the form. He's even more fanciful on piano, interrupting "22-20 Blues" with lavish glissandos and jolly rhythmic phrases that catch the wildcat temperament of boogie-woogie. In spite of the sound problems, these early recordings are more interesting than the handful of solid, less chilling, records he made after being rediscovered in the early '60s. Unlike many bluesmen who grew more powerful with age, Skip James seized the full force of blues expression as a young man and pushed it as far as he could right then. That—and the eeriness of his voice—makes these early James sessions unique. Nobody in blues, not the superstars or the rockers who imitated them, stands above him.

GENRE: 🎵 Blues. **RELEASED:** 1994, Yazoo. **KEY TRACKS:** "Devil Got My Woman," "Special Rider Blues," "I'm So Glad," "Jesus Is a Mighty Good Leader." **NEXT STOP:** Charley Patton: *Complete Early Recordings*. **AFTER THAT:** Son House: *Delta Blues*.

Dreamlike Reverie at the Keyboard

Piano Works

Leoš Janáček
Rudolf Firkušný

In his ruminative piano music, the Moravian composer Leoš Janáček (1854–1928) takes a pronounced delight in confounding expectations. He states a simple motif, then modulates into a related key, and at the very moment when things seem to be moving toward an inevitable Brahms-style resolution, the bottom drops out and Janáček plunges into a much darker mood. In several of his pieces here, written between 1901 and 1908, it takes only a second for the music to go from a sense of conventional order to a sound suggesting utter soul devastation.

That tactic of bait-and-switch chordal surprise aligns Janáček with Mahler and his Hungarian counterpart Béla Bartók (as well as rock bands like Radiohead). Janáček uses it expertly, leading listeners through innocuous arpeggios for some time before lowering the boom. Even if you know them well, his most beautiful piano works—image-rich stream-of-consciousness suites like the fourteen-section "On an Overgrown Path" and the shorter but no less evocative "In the Mists"—remain disarming. Janáček's big idea seems to be to avoid the linearity and repetition of the romantics, and he does this by writing themes that travel like babbling brooks, then stop in idle repose, and eventually clear through tangled underbrush to reprise, distantly, the original inspiration. (The eleventh section of "On an Overgrown Path," marked "Andante," vividly follows this scheme.)

This 1972 recording is about as close to Janáček's intention as any could be: The pianist, Rudolf Firkušný, was one of the composer's students, and often played from scores that incorporated Janáček's handwritten changes. Firkušný has a patient, delicate touch that aligns perfectly with the suspense Janáček slipped into these elusive, magical pieces.

GENRE: 🎼 Classical. **RELEASED:** 1972, Deutsche Grammophon. **KEY TRACKS:** "On an Overgrown Path," "In the Mists." **CATALOG CHOICE:** *Glagolithic Mass.* **NEXT STOP:** Erik Satie: *Gymnopédies* (see p. 675). **AFTER THAT:** Radiohead: *Kid A.*

An Alt-Rock Catalyst

Ritual de lo Habitual

Jane's Addiction

The Los Angeles quartet Jane's Addiction blazed into alternative rock consciousness in 1988, with songs that suggest a teenage riot in progress, sung by a concept-minded lead singer, Perry Farrell, whose default singing voice is a strident banshee wail.

That first salvo (on the band's major-label debut, *Nothing's Shocking*) prepared the cool-hunting segment of the rock audience for *Ritual de lo Habitual*, a feast of glinting guitar collisions and hurtling, almost frantic rhythms. Of the many mile markers in the history of alternative rock, this stands among the most significant. Although it would be another year before the alt-rock nation became a commercial force with the release of Nirvana's *Nevermind* (see p. 553), *Ritual* helped create the conditions for change. It proved that an extreme version of rock rebellion, one built on ear-splitting dissonances, could sell lots of copies. Most of *Ritual* either starts at the sound of panic or ends up there, but the music is rarely just agitation for its own sake. The journeys involve jarring changes in meter and mood: "Three Days" evolves from drifty lethargy into backbeats of lacerating intensity.

Although Farrell attracted the lion's share of the attention—rarely has such an abrasive voice been so seductive—his delivery depended on the sure support of Jane's rhythm section. Most musicians who aligned themselves with punk avoided bringing much of the past into their attack, but not guitarist Dave Navarro: On the band's biggest hit, "Been Caught Stealing," he generates a tightly wound rhythm guitar line that descends directly from "Sex Machine"–era James Brown. Those canny connections to the past went largely undetected in the frenzy, but they're one reason *Ritual* remains an all-consuming experience.

GENRE: 🎸 Rock. **RELEASED:** 1990, Warner Bros. **KEY TRACKS:** "Three Days," "Been Caught Stealing," "Then She Did . . ." **CATALOG CHOICE:** *Nothing's Shocking.* **NEXT STOP:** Smashing Pumpkins: *Siamese Dream.* **AFTER THAT:** Mercury Rev: *Boces.*

An Evening of Spontaneous Creation

The Köln Concert

Keith Jarrett

Maybe Keith Jarrett wanted to clear the jazz fusion he'd made with Miles Davis out of his system. Maybe he was tired of the rigid rituals of standard jazz. Maybe he was just restless. Whatever the motivation, in the mid-1970s, Jarrett devoted a chunk of his performance schedule to curious and captivating solo piano recitals. He'd enter the hall, soak up the ambience of the room and its inhabitants, and, with allegedly nothing prepared, play whatever popped into his head. Sometimes he'd drift through ethereal vapors, and discover enchantingly wistful, lace-thin themes. Sometimes he'd go off searching for a lost melody and get lost himself. Sometimes he'd hammer so hard he'd pound the life out of an idea.

Jarrett has been known to stop playing if crowd noise disturbs his concentration during a performance.

The solo concerts opened a window into Jarrett's thought process. When the Pennsylvania native was cooking, as he was during this 1975 performance at the Köln Opera House in Germany, what streamed out was utterly unclassifiable—a few bars of rowdy rock chords interrupted by a fitful blues invention or the music accompanying Sunday services at a backwoods Baptist church. Jarrett would follow the smallest motif until its secrets had been exhumed and spun him elsewhere. Several sections of *Köln* have subsections, governed by their own thematic logic; part of the wonder of this recording is hearing him develop organizational frameworks on the fly. In real time. Unedited.

The Köln Concert became Jarrett's breakthrough and biggest hit. Its success enabled him to do solo gigs steadily, and for some years, until the formation of his standards trio in 1981, they were his primary performance outlet. Then, in the '90s, Jarrett contracted an immune-system virus, and was unable to perform for several years. Upon his return, he resumed solo concerts; the most moving of the later ones is *La Scala*, which has a nightmarish quality, like he's recalling the darkest days of his illness.

When Jarrett recalls *Köln*, however, it is not with fondness. "The wrong instrument was rented," he said in a 2004 interview. For him, the tone of the piano was much too bright. "We ended up with a tape of terrible sounding bad harpsichord. . . . Everybody wanted to get that sound for a while. I can tell you this: I never wanted to get that sound." Despite Jarrett's misgiving, what happened on that piano that night is spontaneous creation. Of the highest order.

GENRE: 🎷 Jazz. **RELEASED:** 1975, ECM. **KEY TRACKS:** "Part IIa," "Part IIb." **CATALOG CHOICE:** *La Scala*. **NEXT STOP:** Bill Evans: *Conversations with Myself*. **AFTER THAT:** Paul Bley: *Tears*.

Songs with a Singing Heart

My Song

Keith Jarrett

This is the record to play for your pop-obsessed friends who think they don't like jazz. There's no spang-a-langing swing. No happy brass. Not even so much as a shout chorus. Instead, pianist Keith Jarrett leads three quiet Europeans through a series of unassailably beautiful, bravely romantic rhapsodies. *My Song* is chamber music—its restive themes are stated plainly and then elaborated on by four empathetic musicians. At the same time, *My Song* is also rhythmic music, in its own meandering way—the title track is built around a steady lilting piano phrase, while "Questar" moves at an ambling, fractured flamenco backbeat. (Steely Dan interpolated bits of the melody and the rhythm of "Questar" into "Gaucho.")

At the center of this record are Jarrett's winding-road themes, tunes with a singing heart. These exude the straightforward earnestness of children's music—everything beneath the melodies is there to glorify and amplify them. The simplicity inspires gallant long-tone solos from saxophonist Jan Garbarek, and slippery, effortlessly liquid lines from Jarrett, who is in an unbelievable zone here. The tunes give off plenty of light by themselves, and as Jarrett wanders through them, he somehow locates more sources of illumination, expanding these heartbreakingly direct, emotionally open themes as he goes. The result is unlike anything else ever filed under "Jazz."

GENRE: 🅙 Jazz. **RELEASED:** 1978, ECM. **KEY TRACKS:** "Questar," "Country," "Tabarka," "My Song." **CATALOG CHOICES:** *Arbour Zena; Facing You; Belonging.* **NEXT STOP:** Ralph Towner: *Solstice* (see p. 783).

Jazz Mythology, in Words and Music

The Jazz Singer

Eddie Jefferson

This record offers insight into the larger-than-life personalities of the great jazz instrumentalists. The Pittsburgh-born singer Eddie Jefferson learned solos from famous recordings note for note, and then wrote riffs featuring the musicians in key roles. His version of "So What," which opens this album, transforms Miles Davis's solo from *Kind of Blue* (see p. 208) into an essay about jazz manners, referring to the trumpet player's penchant for leaving the bandstand after finishing his turn.

Jefferson's paraphrase of Lester Young's "Paper Moon" imagines the hip tenor saxophonist leading an interplanetary expedition. "That hummin' and hummin' and hummin' and hummin' you hear is just the motor of my rocket, dear," he sings at one point, adding "have no fear." And his "Body and Soul" immortalizes Coleman Hawkins, using the squiggly shapes the saxophonist set down on the legendary original (see p. 348): To Jefferson, he "sounded like a band of angels in the sky, and I have never ever heard a sweeter tone."

Jefferson (1919–1979) was among the first to use this approach, which came to be known as "vocalese." Though he's got a decent voice and an animated manner, his key contribution is his lyrics, with their expertly turned evocations of club life and wild onomatopoeic flights. A tap dancer at the start of his career, Jefferson's first break came when he wrote words to James Moody's recording of "I'm in the Mood for Love," which became a monster hit. (One of several versions Jefferson did is included here.) The jazz world took notice: Jefferson's narratives have, in

Jefferson invented the vocalese singing style.

some cases, become the primary jazz-vocal texts.

Most of *The Jazz Singer* was recorded in 1959, with a few dates in 1960 and '61. This was a time of exploding creativity in jazz. The music was evolving rapidly, and clubgoers were treated to feats of astounding instrumental dexterity on a regular basis. Jefferson's adroit wordplay captures that sense of possibility, and the feeling of pure slackjawed awe that went along with being on the scene when it was happening.

GENRES: 🎵 Jazz 🎤 Vocals. **RELEASED:** 1965, Inner City. (Reissued 1993, Evidence.) **KEY TRACKS:** "So What," "Moody's Mood for Love," "Lester's Trip to the Moon." **CATALOG CHOICE:** *Letter from Home.* **NEXT STOP:** Lambert, Hendricks, and Ross: *The Hottest New Group in Jazz* (see p. 438).

The Beginnings of Outlaw Country

Honky Tonk Heroes

Waylon Jennings

It's somehow fitting that this set, which busted open the Outlaw Country movement and remains one of its sacred texts, came about as the result of an argument. It happened in a recording studio, when then-unknown songwriter Billy Joe Shaver interrupted Jennings's work, claiming that the singer had once promised to record an album of his songs. With musicians and others watching, Shaver threatened Jennings with bodily harm. Jennings agreed to listen to a few tunes. What he heard became the backbone of *Honky Tonk Heroes*—simple odes that told tales of devotion, bitterness, and lessons learned living paycheck-to-paycheck.

The first album Jennings (1937–2002) produced himself, *Honky Tonk Heroes* is the opposite of the prettified Nashville Sound. Its defining guitars are rough—even the typically sweet pedal steel seems brusque—and the surrounding instruments, particularly the harmonica and fiddle, carry the hint of rebellion. In this ethos, Jennings doesn't have to put on any airs: His gruff voice makes every phrase seem as lived-in as a frayed old couch on the front porch. The album includes at least one Jennings concession to the times. "We Had It All," the only song not written by Shaver, features a heavy, swooning string arrangement; it became a Top 30 single. (Of the Shaver songs, the one that fared the best commercially was "You Ask Me To," which reached the country Top 10).

The commercial success of *Honky Tonk Heroes* is secondary to its influence: This became a rallying point for everyone who ever wanted to break free of the Nashville system, and has inspired generations of songwriters and performers to heed their ornery inner voices.

GENRE: ◎ Country. **RELEASED:** 1973, Buddah. **KEY TRACKS:** "Old Five and Dimers (Like Me)," "You Ask Me To," "Low Down Freedom," "Omaha." **CATALOG CHOICE:** *Lonesome, On'ry, and Mean.* **NEXT STOP:** Joe Ely: *Honky Tonk Masquerade.* **AFTER THAT:** Shooter Jennings: *Electric Rodeo.*

C'mon, Feel the Candy . . .

Psychocandy

The Jesus and Mary Chain

The year 1985 was a big year for Madonna ("Like a Virgin"), Phil Collins ("Sussudio"), and Foreigner ("I Want to Know What Love Is"). It was also the year of *Psychocandy*, the debut of the Jesus and Mary Chain,

which is one of the most defiantly different rock records of the decade. Though it didn't sell anywhere near Madonna numbers, this was a hipster must, a record that, like the similarly spirited works by the Velvet Underground, wound up influencing a whole subdivision of rock activity for years to come.

The Jesus and Mary Chain innovation was simple: Fronting a loud rhythm section, the guitar playing and singing brothers William and Jim Reid, of East Kilbride, Scotland, blasted out fuzztone roars that were almost impenetrable—thick with distortion, and at times packing a brutal, feel-it-in-your-gut punch. Then, deep inside this squall-of-sound, far enough in the background so they'd never be labeled "pop," they slipped in seriously upbeat melodies—shapely and incandescent lines that a pop aesthete raised on Phil Spector would recognize.

Though not perfectly balanced between

The Reids cite Phil Spector and the Beach Boys as major influences.

darkness and light (darkness, of course, wins), *Psychocandy* is a near-perfect record. The guitars are like no guitars Foreigner knows—some fire off like assault weapons, some only operate in the key of dental drill (see "In a Hole"), and some are there to just add a cloud of pitchless fuzz. The Reids have their fun too: On "Never Understand," after they've surrounded a typically sweet vocal theme with the usual forbidding drones, one guitar breaks from the pack, as though an extremely rare solo is about to begin. Only it's not a guitar. It's a human male. Wailing. In an unfaked agony that puts a little extra psycho in *Psychocandy*.

GENRE: 🎸 Rock. **RELEASED:** 1985, Warner Bros. **KEY TRACKS:** "In a Hole," "Just like Honey," "Never Understand." **CATALOG CHOICE:** *Twenty-one Singles.* **NEXT STOP:** The Velvet Underground: *White Light, White Heat.*

Around the World with Flaco

Squeeze Box King

Flaco Jiménez

F laco Jiménez has pushed *norteño* (or, as it's known north of the border, Tex-Mex) music as far as it might ever go without sacrificing its plaintive and earthy aura. He's played the traditional polkas and waltzes in an old-world *conjunto* group featuring his accordion, along with bass, drums, and the twelve-string *bajo sexto* guitar. He's collaborated with rock stars and been an integral part of the genre's first and only supergroup, the Texas Tornados, featuring Freddy Fender, Doug Sahm, and Augie Meyers.

But it took Jiménez until this delightful 2003 release to make an overt lunge for total world domination. The album opens with "En el cielo no hay cerveza" (In Heaven There Is No Beer), the polka standard, sung in English, Spanish, and Dutch. While the multiple languages are a novelty, the music underneath them is anything but: Jiménez plays the polka straight, cultivating a chipper party-time atmosphere that transcends words. Then he saunters into a playful Colombian *cumbia*, "Tan solo," executed with an offhand mastery of the journeying, horse-and-buggy syncopations. Those who've never been inclined to dance to *cumbia* might give this tune a try: It's almost impossible to stand still while it's playing. (The same goes for just about everything on this set, which gently gooses *norteño* tradition.)

Even the slow-dance songs are transfixing. Jiménez's gentle, patient covers of Cuban boleros and durable rancheras like "La tormenta" (The Storm) and "La rosa negra" (The Black Rose) tell sorrowful stories about the loss of love, set at a deliberate pulse that heightens the bittersweetness of the lyrics.

GENRE: 🌐 World/Mexico. **RELEASED:** 2003, Compadre. **KEY TRACKS:** "En el cielo no hay cerveza," "Tan solo," "La tormenta." **CATALOG CHOICES:** *Texas Tornados; Ay te dejo en San Antonio.* **NEXT STOP:** Vicente Fernández: *The Living Legend.* **AFTER THAT:** Freddy Fender: *Twentieth Century Masters: The Best of Freddy Fender.*

The World's Greatest Sensualist Plays . . .

The Composer of "Desafinado" Plays

Antonio Carlos Jobim

A lways in the music of Antonio Carlos ("Tom") Jobim, there's a beautiful, unreachable woman standing just outside the frame. The Brazilian composer of so much bossa nova was one of the world's great musical sensualists; he made marathon longing seem sublime, even noble.

Jobim's melodies move with supreme feminine sleekness; as he watches that girl from Ipanema go by, he's a worshipper of beauty who precisely emulates the sway of her gait. As he ponders the end of a great love, his murmuring "How Insensitive" catches not just the expected twinge of melancholy, but an abiding (and possibly irrational) reverence for the one whose bed he will no longer share.

Things seem fragile in Jobim's music. The melodies are threadbare wisps kept airborne by unrequited desire. The harmonies are of a molecular structure that is unique to him—rich with elaborate sliding chordal schemes and yet as fleeting as sand sculpture. Although many dismiss Jobim as dentist-office music, the instrumental Verve sides (this and the equally entrancing *Wave*), with their modest piano declarations and cascading strings, are the living essence of the notion that less is more. It takes a while to appreciate how much more. Go past the surface beauty, past the dinner-dress slink of the bossa rhythm, and there discover a cool quiet place near the shore, where you can go to meditate on the great vanished love. Alone.

GENRE: 🌐 World/Brazil. RELEASED: 1963, Verve. KEY TRACKS: "Desafinado," "Once I Loved," "The Girl from Ipanema." CATALOG CHOICE: *Wave*. NEXT STOP: João Gilberto: *Au vivo en Montreux*. AFTER THAT: Egberto Gismonti: *Sol do melo dia*.

A Pairing of Subtle Sensibilities

Elis & Tom

Antonio Carlos Jobim and Elis Regina

This summit meeting features songs written by the king of the sidewinding half-step melody, sung with reverence by the queen of disconsolate yearning. Recorded over two days in Los Angeles in 1974, *Elis & Tom* arrived more than a decade after the "bossa nova craze" swept America. Antonio Carlos Jobim was known worldwide for his lithe and strikingly beautiful melodies ("Wave," "Triste," etc.), which had been endlessly reimagined by singers and jazz players. Likewise, Elis Regina was well established as a quintessentially Brazilian voice, a singer whose languid phrasing described emotions too fragile to be attached to specific words.

Though she'd been through the Jobim songbook more than once, Regina is hardly on autopilot. Quite the opposite: She sings Jobim as though tasting exotic fruit for the first time—somewhat cautiously, and with curiosity. "What I hear in this," says the jazz singer Jane Monheit, "is someone claiming songs that have been done too often, restoring a bit of the quietude that was inside them originally."

Regina flourishes within the spare atmosphere. Tunes like the opening duet "Aguas de Marco" are built around a simple rhythm section, with strings and other embellishments deployed judiciously. The selections include several of Jobim's lesser-known gems, including the rhapsodic "So tinha de ser com você." Regina approaches these pieces intending to shine gentle light on the melodic details Jobim has loaded inside. There are many. She finds them all. And she lifts them up on her fingertips and gives the melodies wings, spreading wonder the way Jobim does—effortlessly.

GENRE: 🌐 World /Brazil. RELEASED:

1974, Verve. **KEY TRACKS:** "Aguas de Marco," "Triste," "Modinha," "So tinha de ser com você." **CATALOG CHOICES:** Jobim: *Jobim.* Regina: *Como & porque* (see p. 639).

Toots Thielemans and Elis Regina: *Aquarela do Brazil.* **NEXT STOP:** Gilberto Gil and Jorge Ben: *Gil & Jorge.* **AFTER THAT:** Ella Fitzgerald and Louis Armstrong: *Ella and Louis* (see p. 280).

The Most Elaborate Elton

Goodbye Yellow Brick Road

Elton John

Elton John's first double album begins in a dark and stormy mood. The wind is howling. A lone church bell chimes in the distance, ushering in an eleven-minute faux-goth suite, "Funeral for a Friend/Love Lies Bleeding," that's galaxies away from the blithe "Crocodile Rock" or, for that matter, any previous hits. It's as though the prodigiously talented pianist and his longtime lyricist, Bernie Taupin, mean to bust out of the radio-bonbon business. So they've put together a series of willfully weird and wonderful vignettes about biker-bar poseurs and exotic lesbians—not to forget the heavy-metal groupie immortalized in "Bennie and the Jets," who engages in ritualistic animal sacrifice.

In other words, *Goodbye* is an Art Statement. Its seventeen selections showcase John's criminally under-appreciated band, and are note-for-note more musically ambitious than anything he attempted previously. And despite its extravagant leaps, it's the rare Elton John record (*Honky Château* is another) where the album cuts are as strong or stronger than the singles. *Goodbye* marks the moment when Taupin's snarling outsider cynicism collides most spectacularly with John's questioning melodies and dizzy-

Goodbye Yellow Brick Road is Elton John's biggest hit, with 20 million copies sold.

ing étude-book piano arpeggios. It's not a "concept" album in the strictest sense, but *Goodbye* does have a recurring theme—disillusionment. The title track tells of a boy stung by the city he once viewed as an Oz. "Candle in the Wind" follows a fan as he tries to reconcile the myths and legends attached to Marilyn Monroe.

While it generated four singles and cemented John's superstar status, *Goodbye* was an end, of sorts. After it, John zoomed with full ardor toward the flamboyant and the rococo. He continued to crank out hits—in fact, he's the only artist to have notched at least one song in the Top 40 every year from 1970 through 1995. But the later ones have all the nuance of the Disney films they sometimes accompany, especially when compared with the phantasmagoric oddities found here, along John's yellow brick road.

GENRE: ⊗ Pop. **RELEASED:** 1973, MCA. **KEY TRACKS:** "Grey Seal," "Goodbye Yellow Brick Road," "Harmony." **CATALOG CHOICE:** *Captain Fantastic and the Brown Dirt Cowboy.* **NEXT STOP:** Todd Rundgren: *Something/Anything?* (see p. 622). **AFTER THAT:** Ben Folds Five: *Whatever and Ever Amen.*

Big Things from Small Packages

The Very Best
of Little Willie John

Little Willie John

In the mid-1950s, just as James Brown and Jackie Wilson were getting started, Little Willie John came along and defined what a soul singer could do. He swerved into sweetness, shouted with earthshaking feeling, transformed phrases like "Talk to Me" into desperate cries for help. The diminutive Arkansas native had the nuance of a jazz singer and the emotional focus of a blues belter, traits that made him a key connecting point between musical worlds that were at that time isolated from each other. He showed everybody who followed how to draw on different realms, as James Brown acknowledged later, explaining why he was moved to record a tribute a month after John died in prison in 1968, while serving time on a murder charge. "Willie John was a singer that could take you places," Brown said in Gerri Hirshey's 1984 book *Nowhere to Run.* "I did not want this fact to be lost to man."

John's recordings have not been lost. But they haven't exactly been enthusiastically rediscovered, either—even his most famous song, "Fever," is best known for recordings by Peggy Lee and Elvis Presley, which are both virtual note-for-note copies of John's still-definitive original. But it's the other singles that remain John's best legacy: The bended-knee plea "Need Your Love So Bad," the rough "Suffering with the Blues," and "Leave My Kitten Alone" are the work of a singer who always got himself immersed in the emotional netherworld of a song. One reason to seek this Collectables set over the Rhino anthology *Fever* is "A Cottage for Sale," a dreamy ballad that presents John as a master of perfectly timed persuasion.

GENRE: 🎵 R&B. **RELEASED:** 2001, Collectables. **KEY TRACKS:** "A Cottage for Sale," "Fever," "Need Your Love So Bad," "Leave My Kitten Alone." **NEXT STOP:** James Brown: *Messing with the Blues.* **AFTER THAT:** Wynonie Harris: *The Best of.*

The Lamp Is Still Burning

The Complete
Blind Willie Johnson

Blind Willie Johnson

On the very first day Blind Willie Johnson recorded professionally, in a makeshift Dallas studio in December 1927, the Texas singer and guitarist rattled off a mournful song called "It's Nobody's Fault but Mine."

Decades later, it was modified by Led Zeppelin, and became one of the group's signature hits. That day Johnson also recorded a song called "Mother's Children Have a Hard Time," which has been recorded by Eric Clapton and others. And Johnson sang "Jesus Make Up My Dying Bed," which Bob Dylan turned into "In My Time of Dying." The gospel-bluesman also did "If I Had My Way I'd Tear the Building Down," which has been covered by the Grateful Dead, among others.

But that's not all: Johnson's big day included a song that stands as his defining moment—"Dark Was the Night, Cold Was the Ground," an account of the crucifixion of Christ. It's a hymn, and when sung in church, it involves the preacher and congregation in somber call-and-response exchanges. He wrings out the main theme in measured tones sliding across the strings using a pocket knife instead of bottlenecks or more conventional implements. He then sings or hums, in croaky voice, the wordless vocal "responses," which are often little more than the typical parishioner variations on "uh-huhhmmm." It's a dark, disconsolate, deeply moving masterpiece. Ry Cooder, who used the tune as a model for his film soundtrack *Paris, Texas,* once called it "the most soulful, transcendent piece in all American music."

Those same superlatives might apply to many of Johnson's recordings, which were made between 1927 and 1930 and are collected on this startling two-disc set. Johnson didn't consider himself a bluesman, and concentrated on material with a spiritual message. Yet because he had the ability to make the guitar talk so vividly, his ideas spread quickly through the blues world, becoming common performance practice. Johnson never got the credit for that—he's another of the major figures who's been nearly lost in the back pages of American musical history. Yet because of that first day in the studio, everyone who cares about rock and roll and blues and gospel is at least distantly acquainted with the Blind Willie Johnson mojo. Go back to the source to discover just how powerful that mojo can be.

GENRES: ✝ Gospel ⛨ Blues. **RELEASED:** 1993, Columbia. **KEY TRACKS:** "It's Nobody's Fault but Mine," "Dark Was the Night, Cold Was the Ground," "Keep Your Lamp Trimmed and Burning." **NEXT STOP:** Sister Rosetta Tharpe: *The Gospel of the Blues.* **AFTER THAT:** Rev. Gary Davis: *Harlem Street Singer* (see p. 207).

The Father of Stride Struts His Stuff

The Original James P. Johnson

James P. Johnson

In stride-style piano, the left hand leaps wildly between bass notes and chords plinked in the center of the keyboard. Meanwhile, the right hand is busy doing cartwheels and backflips and triple-lutz reverses. The masters of the form, including father and self-proclaimed "dean" of stride James P. Johnson, make this juggling act sound like the most natural thing in the world.

Johnson (1894–1955) brought stride to a rococo peak in the late 1920s. He wrote fanci-ful inventions streaked with childlike optimism and an irreverent sense of humor—one characteristic tune is "The Charleston." He also wrote intricate "suites," like "Yamekraw: A Negro Rhapsody," in which he contrasts brief episodes of improvisation with more elaborate composed-in-advance themes. He could play lightning-fast tempos—jazz historian Marshall Stearns once described a Johnson performance this way: "It was as if Franz Liszt had discovered ragtime."

A native of New Brunswick, New Jersey, Johnson first attracted attention in 1913, playing small clubs in the Hell's Kitchen neighborhood of New York. He began recording in 1920, often performing original tunes like "Harlem Strut" and "Jingles." He attracted a coterie of worshippers and students, including Fats Waller and Duke Ellington, and within a few years, he was among the city's celebrated instrumentalists, backing Bessie Smith (see p. 715) and Ethel Waters. Johnson also found himself in demand as a composer—he wrote for nightclub revues and Broadway musicals. The writing took over his schedule, and Johnson didn't perform regularly again until the early 1940s, during a resurgence of interest in "traditional" jazz.

These recordings, made between 1942 and 1945, demonstrate Johnson's ability to rock the keyboard. Though his approach is a touch more refined, he's still gunning through demanding pianistic agility trials. His left hand doesn't always stride steadily—sometimes he'll sneak in an unexpected pause, or break the flow of a melody like "Sweet Lorraine" with unusual offbeat syncopations. These are kinetic. As he moves up the keyboard from the bass line, through the clipped chords, and into the delicious top octaves of the piano, Johnson pirouettes like a ballerina, making every note seem perfect.

GENRE: 🎵 Jazz. **RELEASED:** 1996, Smithsonian Folkways. **KEY TRACKS:** "Liza," "Jersey Sweet," "The Dream," "St. Louis Blues," "Twilight Rag." **CATALOG CHOICE:** *King of Stride Piano, 1918–1944.* **NEXT STOP:** Willie "The Lion" Smith and Luckey Roberts: *Harlem Piano.* **AFTER THAT:** Dick Wellstood: *Live at the Sticky Wicket.*

Poetry in Dub

Dread Beat an' Blood

Linton Kwesi Johnson

"People know me as a reggae artist," Linton Kwesi Johnson once complained. "They don't know me as a poet. But I began with the word." And with words, the Jamaican-born Johnson, who was raised in England, made a huge contribution to music: He's among the first to deliver his poetry over the beats of Jamaican reggae. He is often hailed as the father of the style he called "dub poetry." This album, his 1978 debut, finds Johnson hammering out dub's essential structure: Rants about race and prejudice, poverty and injustice, wrapped in vivid imagery (lots of bloodshed and martyrdom) and surrounded by warm, open, deceptively serene music.

Dread Beat an' Blood, which like many subsequent LKJ projects, was aided by multi-instrumentalist Dennis "Blackbeard" Bovell, uses the sunny atmosphere of reggae as a kind of Trojan horse. Johnson's not blunting any realities, just trying to cultivate sympathetic ears; he recognizes that his message has a better chance of getting through if it is supported by undulating bass lines and echoey rhythms. The lazy atmosphere provides a contrast to Johnson's formidable intellect—he majored in sociology at Goldsmiths College, University of London, and has published several acclaimed volumes of poetry.

But as he talks of being black, struggling economically, and suffering through brutality and violence, Johnson rarely gets up on the soapbox. Instead, he scatters traces of dismay and discouragement between the lines, in smooth, endlessly syncopated phrases. Lots of rappers and spoken-word artists have studied (and imitated) Johnson's intricate cadences; few have packed as much concern and outrage into what sounds, from a distance, like party music.

GENRE: ⊕ World/Jamaica. **RELEASED:** 1978, Front Line/Caroline. **KEY TRACKS:** "Song of Blood," "Five Nights of Bleeding." **CATALOG CHOICE:** *LKJ in Dub.* **NEXT STOP:** Mutabaruka: *Any Which Way . . . Freedom.* **AFTER THAT:** The Last Poets: *The Last Poets.*

The Johnson Who's Nearly as Important as Robert

The Original Guitar Wizard

Lonnie Johnson

New Orleans–born Lonnie Johnson (1894–1970) was the first consequential guitar improviser, the first instrumentalist to connect the blues and jazz (performing with Louis Armstrong's Hot Five and the Duke Ellington Orchestra), and one of the first great songwriters of the blues.

Johnson's "firsts" are only part of his story. As this budget-priced four-disc box makes clear, he was also one of the best guitarists of the early twentieth century, a firebrand who could play rings around his peers. His command of the guitar is almost freakish for the period. On most recordings from the 1920s, guitarists are usually heard strumming chords and doing little else. As Johnson's 1928 solo "Savoy Blues" proves, he was thinking melodies. And not just obvious ones: Johnson dances around, plucking out sweet perfectly formed thoughts that leap decades ahead. His tone is warm, his attack precise, and his ideas staggeringly inventive—he's really a harbinger of future electric guitar dazzle.

This box contains most of Johnson's crucial recordings made before 1951, including his duets with guitarist Eddie Lang (notably "Guitar

Lonnie Johnson revolutionized the one-string guitar solo.

Blues" and "Blue Guitars," recorded on successive days in 1929). Despite his reputation among musicians, Johnson wandered in and out of music jobs during the 1940s and '50s. He was working as a janitor when he was rediscovered in 1959, and returned as a mythic figure, drawing large audiences on the then-booming folk blues circuit. Though he recorded several solid albums after his comeback, the material from his early career is of greater musical consequence—these crisply remastered recordings contain nothing less than the building blocks of modern guitar music.

GENRE: ⊖ Blues. **RELEASED:** 2006, Proper (U.K.). **KEY TRACKS:** "Guitar Blues," "Savoy Blues," "Misty Mornin'" (with Ellington), "You Done Lost Your Good Thing Now." **CATALOG CHOICE:** *The Complete Folkways Recordings.* **NEXT STOP:** Robert Johnson: *The Complete Recordings* (see next page).

Hear the Hellhounds

The Complete Recordings

Robert Johnson

The complete recordings of singer, composer, and guitarist Robert Johnson include tales of fast and mean-spirited women, drifter-on-the-lonesome-road laments, a utopian sketch of a place called "Sweet Home Chicago,"

and, most notably, a suite of haunted songs about the ominous doings of the Devil. Taken together, the forty-one performances form the backbone of the blues, and are among the most influential artifacts in all of twentieth-century music: Virtually everyone who followed Johnson—the electric bluesmen of the 1940s, Eric Clapton, and countless rock guitarists—copped something from his trick bag.

Eric Clapton called Johnson "the most important blues musician who ever lived."

But nobody got all of it. Johnson was the first bluesman to give his narratives about hard luck and trouble a correspondingly troubled—harrowing, actually—sound. And he remains the all-time champ. Rattling off ice-pick lead lines and expertly clustered guitar chords at the same time, Johnson treats the blues not as entertainment, but as a kind of metaphysical Emergency Broadcasting System, cautioning all who will listen about the evils waiting just up the road. He shouts in his songs but he trembles too, and when he slides into that keening, armor-piercing upper register, you can't miss the sense that this is someone who's been spooked, rattled to the core. In his accounts of the badass apparition he encountered at the mythic crossroads ("Cross Road Blues"), or the woman who sprinkled hotfoot powder at his door ("Hellhound on My Trail"), or the daily vexations of life on the run ("Me and the Devil Blues"), the circumstances become

secondary to the chilling, terrified delivery. The vocals align perfectly with Johnson's guitar playing. A master of microtones that fall between the cracks of the tempered scale, the bluesman combines sure-handed four-on-the-floor rhythm with impossibly nimble leads—when Rolling Stone guitarist Keith Richards first heard Johnson, he wanted to know who the second guitarist was. There isn't any—everything you hear is Johnson, solo, playing live.

Johnson's career was tragically short—he died in 1938 at age twenty-seven, a little more than a year after the second of two (!) recording sessions that make up *The Complete Recordings*. He left behind many legends, none more powerful than the one about that fateful midnight meeting with the Devil at the crossroads of Highways 61 and 49 in Clarksdale, Mississippi. There, he supposedly swapped his soul in exchange for guitar prowess. Let these astounding performances worm into your subconscious, and that deal starts to seem plausible, even worth its eternal price.

GENRE: 😊 Blues. **RELEASED:** 1990, Columbia. (Recordings made in 1936 and 1937.) **KEY TRACKS:** "Ramblin' on My Mind," "Cross Road Blues," "Last Fair Deal Gone Down," "Hellhound on My Trail." **NEXT STOP:** Son House: *Library of Congress Recordings*.

The Chilling Sounds of a Nearly Forgotten Bluesman

Complete Recorded Works in Chronological Order

Tommy Johnson

Tommy Johnson drank regularly with Charley Patton, one of the patriarchs of the blues, and swore he'd met the Devil at the crossroads years before Robert Johnson (no apparent relation) did. Much of his brief career—he recorded only from 1928 to 1930—was spent either trying to score a drink in dry Southern towns or singing in the streets to earn money for the next round. The obsession with alcohol impaired Johnson's professional prospects—although he lived until 1956, his performances at house parties and clubs were notoriously erratic. But during the brief time Johnson did record, the bottle helped bring chilling realism to his art. *Complete* shows him as a rip-roaring entertainer whose agitated Delta guitar phrases and guttural, almost unhinged-sounding vocal shouts were galvanizing. One legend has him shout-singing for hours on end, and hearing the energy he pours into "Alcohol and Jake Blues," which commemorates a wicked bender, or "Morning Prayer Blues," which tells about the consequences, it's easy to imagine Johnson as a relentless performer who didn't know when to stop.

Heard decades later, Johnson's tales can seem like strings of commonplace blues conceits. But his delivery—the way he'd change his voice from a low moan to a ghostly high whine, all while locked into an assured, steady guitar accompaniment—was hugely influential, an inspiration for Howlin' Wolf (see p. 371), Otis Spann, and many others. Johnson never made a "definitive" record, yet his legend lives on as one of those rousing, almost scary figures who left an impression on everyone who heard him.

GENRE: 🎵 Blues. **RELEASED:** 2000, Document. **KEY TRACKS:** "Cool Drink of Water Blues," "Maggie Campbell," "Canned Heat Blues," "Alcohol and Jake Blues." **NEXT STOP:** Howlin' Wolf: *Moanin' in the Moonlight* (see p. 371). **AFTER THAT:** Blind Willie McTell: *The Definitive* (see p. 492).

Thirteen Flying Leaps, Each Different, All Perfect

Can You Fly

Freedy Johnston

This album starts with Freedy Johnston making a confession: "Well I sold the dirt to feed the band." He sounds unsteady, and maybe a little upset, as he shares this thought, which turned out to be autobiographical.

The reedy-voiced Johnston actually sold part of his inherited family farm, in Kinsley, Kansas, to pay for the recording sessions that yielded *Can You Fly*.

Talk about putting things on the line. Here's a guy who sounds like a cross between a forlorn slacker and Jimmy Stewart, literally betting the farm on a longshot rock and roll dream. Spend a little while with these fine songs, sung with winsome looseness, and you will be grateful for Johnston's determination. At first *Can You Fly* seems simply pleasant and easygoing—too easygoing, in fact, to be carrying any big ideas. Go deeper, and you discover that Johnston's songs are loaded with details that insinuate themselves into your subconscious.

Though he's no jack-of-all-trades, Johnston is compelling whether he's twitching like a '60s rocker, or doing a revival-tent stomp in the Hank Williams tradition ("Remember Me"), or moving solemnly through the grim chores that

Johnston has been described as a "songwriter's songwriter."

go along with being an adult ("Tearing Down This Place").

Can You Fly was acclaimed as soon as it was released and led Johnston to a major-label recording contract. Though he followed it with one near-great record (*This Perfect World*), Johnston never connected the same way again. Those who subscribe to the "necessity is the mother of invention" theory of creativity have suggested that Johnston stumbled because, subsequently, the stakes weren't the same; having sold the dirt and fed the band, he never quite had that make-or-break motivation again.

GENRE: 🎸 Rock. **RELEASED:** 1992, Bar None. **KEY TRACKS:** "The Lucky One," "Tearing Down This Place," "Responsible." **CATALOG CHOICE:** *This Perfect World.* **NEXT STOP:** Badly Drawn Boy: *The Hour of Bewilderbeast.* **AFTER THAT:** Bright Eyes: *I'm Wide Awake, It's Morning* (see p. 115).

A Potent Message from the Asian Underground

We Are Three

Joi

It started as a test-kitchen experiment: Take elements of traditional Indian classical music, add beats prepared on samplers and drum machines, slip in a hit or two of Ecstasy, and serve in a warm club environment. Lots of musicians and DJs experimented with variations on this recipe in London during the 1990s, where the "Asian Underground" first took root. Amon Tobin, Talvin Singh, and others created a kind of suave backbeat pastiche, a mingling of cultures you'd never expect to hear together.

When this got into the hands of musicians with a conceptual bent—like Joi, brothers Haroon and Farook Shamsher—the dish became a little more gourmet. Joi's approach was cinematic, with lots of murky stuff happening in the background and odd, keening vocals in English and Bengali swerving through the mix.

The first Joi album, *One and One Is One*, generated buzz in London and beyond. Encouraged, the Shamshers—two DJs who'd studied tabla and traditional Indian percussion—set out to make a much more elaborate follow-up. Haroon Shamsher was in Bangladesh recording snippets of native instrumentalists and singers when he suffered a heart attack and died. Farook took the material on his older brother's hard drive, and, after a four-month period of mourning, used it to fashion *We Are Three*, arguably the most rousing, musically intricate album to emerge out of the Asian Underground.

While it's designed for clubs, this is dance music that's also perfect for listening—or driving. The beats are straightforward, and, at times, as relentlessly repetitive as house music. On top of them is a multitracked smorgasbord of sound—buzzing flutes, synthy strings, and guitars all vie for the spotlight, but often lose out to the tastefully synched tabla drums, and the amazing vocal samples. (The sidewinding

"Prem," for example, is built around a melody sung by a fourteen-year-old girl who, happily, doesn't have much use for the tempered scale.) In interviews to promote this album, Farook explained that his brother had left lots of tape, but few written notes. This meant he had to intuit what his brother intended for each snippet, a job he found to be second nature. "I almost always knew where he wanted to go.... I feel in some ways that his hand is in all parts of this album."

GENRE:  World Electronica.
RELEASED: 2000, Real World. **KEY TRACKS:** "Prem," "Journey," "Don't Cha Know That." **CATALOG CHOICE:** *One and One Is One.* **NEXT STOP:** Amon Tobin: *Supermodified.* **AFTER THAT:** Talvin Singh: *OK.*

A Treasure Lost on the Gospel Highway

The Glory Road

Fern Jones

Until this 2005 reissue, the unclassifiable singer and songwriter Fern Jones was destined to be the tiniest of footnotes, as the author of one lone gospel hit. Back in the '50s, when she and her husband, Raymond Jones, were

working the Pentecostal revival-tent circuit in the South, the *Grand Ole Opry* star (and ex–Louisiana governor) Jimmie Davis heard her song "I Was There When It Happened." Jones sold him the rights, Davis claimed half the songwriting credit, and when the song became something of a standard (Johnny Cash recorded it on his Sun debut), Jones seemed poised for more widespread success.

Things didn't turn out that way. The Arkansas native recorded one album for Dot

Fern Jones was only 16 when she and her husband married and began touring together.

Records, *Singing a Happy Song*, in 1959. She had help from a Nashville-based all-star rhythm section that had backed Elvis Presley the previous year: Guitarist Hank "Sugarfoot" Garland, pianist Floyd Cramer, bassist Joe Zinkan, and drummer Buddy Harman created what was, at that time, a radical mixture of jumping rockabilly and toe-tapping gospel. The music was as twitchy and alive as the rock and roll that was then exploding, but Jones, who had a touch of Wanda Jackson fire in her, kept the emphasis on straight-and-narrow declarations of praise. Her plain voice twinkled in a way that connected the spirit of the revival tent with the sweat of the roadhouse—she was perhaps the only white gospel artist with the confidence to even attempt the hot arrangements of the guitar-playing whirlwind Sister Rosetta Tharpe, whose "Didn't It Rain" is interpreted with great zeal here.

Singing a Happy Song vanished not long after it was released, when Dot shuttered its gospel operation. Jones retired from performance in 1960, leaving that one album and several 78-RPM singles, which are included on *The Glory Road*. Every track is wonderful.

From the simple originals that share advice Jones got from her mother ("Be Thankful You're You") to the songs of abiding faith she'd sung for years (the Tindley hymn "By and By"), Jones's amalgam of early rock, country, and gospel was a kind of cultural dynamite, and way ahead of its time.

GENRES: ✝ Gospel ☕ Country.
RELEASED: 2005, Numero. **KEY TRACKS:** "I Was There When It Happened," "Didn't It Rain," "Take My Hand, Precious Lord," "Be Thankful You're You." **NEXT STOP:** Sister Rosetta Tharpe: *Soul Sister*. **AFTER THAT:** Wanda Jackson: *Queen of Rockabilly*.

"There's the Bed"

The Grand Tour

George Jones

This album opens with George Jones, known to some fans as the "King of the Broken Hearts," offering a guided tour of a house that used to be home. As you might expect, the place is loaded with bitter memories.

Every room triggers some different recollection of the woman, the good times, the child she ripped from his life. Jones sounds at once shattered and determined to move stoically on; he's audibly haunted by the place and what it represents.

Country records (even George Jones records) that start out so vividly usually devolve into filler pretty quickly. Not this one. Produced by Billy Sherrill and featuring swooning strings and surprisingly delicate rhythm section work, *The Grand Tour* goes from one stunning Jones showpiece to the next. Many are concerned with little treacheries in the margins of the book of love: Jones summons a gentlemanly respect to tell about his last lover ("Once You've Had the Best"), and strikes the cautious pose of one who doesn't want to be hurt again ("Pass Me By if You're Only Passing Through"), and in

each case, seems to completely live inside the emotion of the song.

Jones sings in a plainspoken and unassuming way, and as his songs evolve, his delivery slyly enhances the troubles described in the lyrics. The emotional shades come through little gestures—he'll chuckle halfheartedly, or give a dejected sigh, or shrug his way through a line, letting the inflections tell the story.

When this album was made, Jones was in the grip of serious alcohol addiction, but you can't detect that from the firm, resolute performances. Along with Jones's comeback effort of 1980 *I Am What I Am*, which contains his hall-of-fame single "He Stopped Loving Her Today," this album stands among the most memorable vocal performances not just in Jones's storied career, not just in country music, but in all of music.

GENRE: ● Country. **RELEASED**: 1974, Epic. **KEY TRACKS**: "The Grand Tour," "Darlin'," "Once You've Had the Best," "Borrowed Angel," "She Told Me So." **CATALOG CHOICES**: *I Am What I Am; Heartaches and Tears; In a Gospel Way.* **NEXT STOP**: Conway Twitty: *She Needs Someone to Hold Her.*

An Anti-Diva Debut

Come Away with Me

Norah Jones

To fully appreciate the revolution that was Norah Jones, consider the moment she made her entrance. It was the spring of 2002, and the women ruling the pop charts—Britney Spears, Jessica Simpson, et al.—were getting over by selling a laddie-mag ideal of sex appeal. With a few exceptions, these shrill sirens weren't singers so much as huge marketing operations, outfitted with songs designed to extend the "brand." The music didn't have to be killer, just danceable and suggestive in a skanky "leave nothing to the imagination" way.

Norah Jones's debut album sold 20 million copies worldwide.

Come Away with Me is a whole different kind of come-on. Jones, the out-of-wedlock daughter of Indian music master Ravi Shankar, snuck in all catlike, and her quietude suggested a way of orienting oneself to the world that was far different from the pop diva approach. Tone mattered: Where just about everything pushed by major labels at the time had the subtlety of a sledgehammer, Jones made music with soft edges, and a breezy, open-window wistfulness. The folks at her label had modest expectations; the record, which blends earthy country and torch-song sophistication, seemed destined for a place in the back of the store near "Easy Listening."

What happened next was the rare triumph of quality over celebrity skin. Word spread quickly. When you walked into a boutique and this was playing (and for a while it seemed like it was always playing), the sweetly sad, almost list-less songs invited you to linger, the antithesis of a high-pressure sell. Through these unassuming songs, many written by Jesse Harris, Jones positioned herself as an alternative to the prevailing ethos of pop-music hype, even refusing to appear in music videos. The public was hungry for an artist like this: Her album, which won eight Grammy awards, sold nearly ten million copies in its first year.

Come Away (and its equally sublime follow-up *Feels like Home*) both depend on a little-appreciated secret weapon: Jones's instantly identifiable pianistic touch. In much the way Ahmad Jamal does, she conjures an aura of contemplative calm with just a handful of carefully massaged notes. These invite listeners into a kind of refuge. By paying such close attention to the instrumental atmospheres of her songs, Jones creates ideal conditions for her husky and fascinatingly complex voice. All she has to do is whisper and it's devastating.

GENRE: ● Vocals. **RELEASED**: 2002, Blue Note. **KEY TRACKS**: "Don't Know Why," "Come Away with Me," "Feelin' the Same Way." **CATALOG CHOICE**: *Feels like Home.* **NEXT STOP**: Nina Simone: *Four Women.*

Life, in Bittersweet Fits and Restless Starts

Pirates

Rickie Lee Jones

Rickie Lee Jones will probably be forever associated with the talky boho-girl scenes of "Chuck E's in Love" and "Last Chance Texaco" from her 1979 debut, songs that cast the schemes of the down-and-out in tones of romantic hipsterdom. But her most important contribution came when she refused to make an easy-money sequel, and instead concocted the far more ambitious *Pirates*—a multihued gem that lifted singer-songwriter introspection to the realm of art music.

Here Jones trades the hallowed street corner for a long sojourn in the mythic desert. She swaps the acoustic-guitar earthiness of her debut for expansive piano-based textures, and from this loftier perch follows street toughs and "sad-eyed Sinatras" as they angle, often in vain, for momentary bliss. Her characters are desperate to break away from drudgery, and she chronicles their doomed attempts the way Springsteen did in *Born to Run* (see p. 733)—breathlessly, and with an acute sense of destiny. But where *Born to Run* revs mostly on that busting-out urge, Jones's odes are riddled with ambivalence and conflicting emotions. They're stories told in bittersweet fits and restless starts.

There are eight songs on *Pirates*, and

Jones brings a slightly different vocal characterization to each one. She sings "Living It Up" in a voice that hides deep disappointment behind stoic bravado. She trembles through each line of the tragic "Skeletons," emulates a lonesome bird on "Traces of the Western Slopes," and cops a hint of junkie dissipation for the gorgeously harmonized "A Lucky Guy." Each inflection becomes central to its narrative, and that's one way to tell how completely Jones changed the game: Lots of singers do credible interpretations of songs by Leonard Cohen or Joni Mitchell, but it's impossible to conceive of these songs rendered properly by any other voice.

GENRE: 🎸 Rock. **RELEASED:** 1981, Warner Bros. **KEY TRACKS:** "Living It Up," "We Belong Together." **CATALOG CHOICES:** *Flying Cowboys; The Magazine.* **NEXT STOP:** Fiona Apple: *When the Pawn . . .* (see p. 23). **AFTER THAT:** Joan Armatrading: *Joan Armatrading.*

The Precious Last Testament of a Belter

Pearl

Janis Joplin

Janis Joplin had recorded most of the vocals for this album before she died, from a heroin overdose in a Hollywood hotel, on October 4, 1970. But it wasn't finished: She was scheduled to return to the studio the day after she died, to do the vocals on at least one more song. The song appears on *Pearl* as an instrumental. It's called "Buried Alive in the Blues."

The sentiment of "Buried Alive" is typical blues woe—one verse goes, "All caught up in a landslide, bad luck pressing in from all sides, just got knocked off my easy ride, buried alive in the blues." It's tempting to hear the tune as an eerie epitaph. But that overlooks one key Joplin trait: Though she poured everything into the blues, she never let herself get swallowed up by it.

By her last year, the belter from Port Arthur, Texas, had grown into a devastatingly original voice, the rare white interpreter of African American music who resisted the ready cliché. She treated old Delta songs and '50s R&B ballads as theatrical platforms, ripe for large-scale rethinking. Her blues woe was never typical blues woe. Matching paint-peeling power with an uncanny sense of dramatic timing, she could turn out a plea that

Janis Joplin was just 27 when she died.

made listeners feel like they were part of a fateful make-or-break moment happening right then.

This album contains her only chart-topping single (the posthumously released "Me and Bobbie McGee") and several of her most compelling covers ("Get It While You Can," "Cry Baby"). More significantly, it captures the astounding repertoire of vocal mannerisms Joplin discovered singing with her old band Big Brother and the Holding Company and perfected with this ensemble, which she called the Full Tilt Boogie Band. The 1999 reissue contains four previously unreleased live bonus tracks, recorded in the summer of 1970 on a Canadian tour, all showcasing the mighty Joplin at the peak of her powers.

GENRE: 🎸 Rock. **RELEASED:** 1971, Columbia. **KEY TRACKS:** "Cry Baby," "Move Over," "Me and Bobby McGee," "Try (Just a Little Bit Harder)." **CATALOG CHOICE:** *Cheap Thrills* (with Big Brother and the Holding Company). **NEXT STOP:** Bonnie Raitt: *Green Light.* **AFTER THAT:** Ronee Blakley: *Welcome.*

The Rag Legend's Rolls

Elite Syncopations

Scott Joplin

The artist listed on this collection, and a corresponding one called *The King of Ragtime Writers,* is Scott Joplin. Alert historians will argue that this can't be: The famous pioneer of ragtime did most of his work between 1899 and 1917, the era before recording, even before electricity. To supplement his publishing income, Joplin did, however, document several of his famous rags on piano rolls designed for player pianos. A few of the six surviving original Joplin rolls—which capture only the sequence of notes, not nuances of performance or dynamics—appear on each of these recordings; the remaining selections on each disc are taken from piano rolls made by other musicians, who followed Joplin's original notation.

The lure isn't the performances—they're as dry and mechanical as you'd expect from an ancient technology. It's the tunes themselves, sweeping and joyous pieces that show Joplin as a composer for the ages, the man who laid several cornerstones in the foundation of jazz. The chords move at a boom-chinking clip, but there are also stark, disarmingly lyrical melodies on display, many of which carry a sweetly sad undercurrent that expands the jovial stereotype of ragtime. Joplin always wanted to move beyond rags—he wrote several unsuccessful operas, and other "legitimate" pieces, but the ragtime sheet music paid the

bills. He's been rediscovered many times over the years, most notably when Marvin Hamlisch interpreted "The Entertainer" and "Maple Leaf Rag" in the 1973 period film *The Sting*. What's nice about this disc is there's no extra gauze of nostalgia, no period kitsch; all that's here is the gleeful good-timey style Joplin created.

GENRE: 🎵 Jazz. **RELEASED:** 1987, Shout Factory/Biograph. **KEY TRACKS:** "Maple Leaf Rag," "A Real Slow Rag."
CATALOG CHOICE: *The King of Ragtime Writers.* **NEXT STOP:** Dick Hyman: *Some Rags, Some Stomps, and a Little Blues.* **AFTER THAT:** James P. Johnson: *Carolina Stomp.*

No Jump Blues Jumped Harder or Higher

The Best of Louis Jordan

Louis Jordan

Louis Jordan (1908–1975) gave hipster highlife a suitably swinging soundtrack. Together with his band the Tympany Five (which frequently numbered more than five musicians), the alto saxophonist and singer turned the irrational exuberance of a Saturday night into a cause célèbre, and went to great lengths to immortalize its pleasures. With flip, lingo-laced lyrics, he romanticized the house party and the fish fry, and during an incredible run (more than fifty singles on *Billboard*'s R&B chart) that began in 1942 and ended nearly a decade later, Jordan's brisk hotfooting music helped lighten up the hard times. His jump blues and boogie established the basic framework of rock and roll; Bill Haley, Ray Charles, and others mentioned Jordan's group as a primary inspiration.

Louis Jordan is often called the "King of the Jukebox."

Born in Arkansas, the son of a bandleader, Jordan understood the American need for escape, especially among those who lacked the funds to party. During World War II, he worked for the Armed Forces Radio network and appeared in short "soundie" films. Eventually Jordan was featured in Hollywood films, including *Follow the Boys* and the musical *Beware,* one of the few with an all–African American cast. (A 1980s Broadway musical, *Five Guys Named Mo,* was built on, and extended, the Jordan myth.)

For all his skill as an entertainer, Jordan

was no slouch behind the saxophone, and as the twenty jukebox-rocking career highlights here demonstrate, he maintained a band that could really play. The material hits spots along the spectrum between kitschy ("Ain't Nobody Here But Us Chickens") and sublime ("Don't Let the Sun Catch You Cryin'"); all of it is powered by that steamrolling Louis Jordan rhythm, which spreads pure joy as it clackety-clacks down the tracks.

GENRE: 🎵 R&B. **RELEASED:** 1975, MCA. **KEY TRACKS:** All of them. **BUYER BEWARE:** There are over a dozen Jordan anthologies, including several that contain rerecordings Jordan made in the '60s. The more desirable versions were recorded in the '40s and '50s and originally issued by Decca. **NEXT STOP:** Big Joe Turner: *Boss of the Blues*. **AFTER THAT:** T-Bone Walker: *Shotgun*.

Church Music to Spark an Internal Renaissance

Missa pange lingua, Motets

Josquin des Prez

*A Sei Voci, with Maîtrise des Pays de Loire Children's Choir
(Bernard Fabre-Garrus, cond.)*

In this sacred choral work by Renaissance composer Josquin des Prez (c. 1440–1521), the grouped voices do more than merely state the text of the hymn. They generate a stilled and shining sound of awe, a profoundly otherworldly tone that is suited to the savoring of mysteries, be they sacred or secular. No religious affiliation is required to enter into this reverence. Josquin takes his listeners there, via celestial voices. Give him a few minutes and he will elevate you, or make you a believer. Or, at the very least, induce calm.

The Mass, recorded here by the French ensemble A Sei Voci with a children's choir, is a fantasy on the *pange lingua* hymn pertaining to the Feast of Corpus Christi, with words from Thomas Aquinas. The chant is found in its most complete form in the very beginning and very end of the Mass; elsewhere, it's embedded, broken up and slowed down into a series of long-held whole notes that anchor the composer's contrapuntal fantasy. You're not necessarily supposed to be able to pick out the hymn at any given point, and it can be equally tricky to discern where one part of the Mass stops and another begins.

Josquin and his contemporaries composed under the belief that the words themselves had holy power and therefore didn't need to be "sold" to the listener (after all, many of the pieces were based on the same Mass text they heard week in and week out in church). This might explain the piece's unusual ending: There's no big culminating statement, no finale. Having appealed to man's "higher" self so effectively, the Mass merely dissipates into thin air, leaving listeners in a state of awed contemplation.

GENRE: 🎵 Classical. **RELEASED:** 2000, Astrée/Naïve. **KEY TRACKS:** Kyrie, Gloria, Sanctus. **COLLECTOR'S NOTE:** A Sei Voci does not perform the entire Mass, only the parts composed by Josquin. This allows the inclusion of several breathtaking motets, among them the "De profundis clamavi." **ANOTHER INTERPRETATION:** *Missa pange lingua*, Ensemble Clément Janequin. **NEXT STOP:** The Hilliard Ensemble: *Pérotin*.

An Early Antithesis of Punk

Unknown Pleasures

Joy Division

When the musicians of Joy Division first met in 1977, at a Sex Pistols show in Manchester, punk was everything cool, the prevailing expression of disaffected youth. Two years later, singer Ian Curtis (1956–1980) and his three musicians presented this astonishing counterargument, which amounts to the beginnings of a new rock and roll language.

Joy Division seized the blunt expressions and me-first narcissism of punk, then filtered them through restrained, and at times elegant, melodies. Its tunes build from pulsating war-drum tom-toms, and share grim narratives that describe deep and inescapable existential quagmires. Most punk productions are a poke in the eye with a sharp stick; Joy Division hovers in a predatory stance, the menacing stalker in the background.

Curtis's baritone emerges out of the blanket of fog, spreading dread before he even gets started on his tales of urban isolation and romantic betrayal. Like Jim Morrison and very few other rock singers, Curtis—who hanged himself shortly before the release of Joy Division's second and final album, *Closer*—commands the spotlight with just his presence, his weighed-down tone. The musicians and producer Martin Hannett seize on

The album's cover art is a transcription of signals emitted by an exploding star.

this, and through skillful use of reverb and other sound-shaping effects position that foreboding voice at the center of music that broods and oozes, yet remains several sizes larger than life.

The thick and at times impenetrable wash of sound wasn't exactly a huge hit right away. But it resonated with an extraordinary number of musicians who became rock stars in the '80s and '90s, among them the Smiths, U2, the Cure, Depeche Mode, and Nine Inch Nails. Just about any rock that carries more than a veneer of darkness owes some debt to Joy Division and this still-surprising album, which makes despair and other dire emotional straits seem frighteningly alluring.

GENRE: 🎸 Rock. **RELEASED:** 1979, Factory. **KEY TRACKS:** "Disorder," "She's Lost Control," "New Dawn Fades," "I Remember Nothing." **CATALOG CHOICE:** *Closer.* **NEXT STOP:** Bauhaus: *Mask.* **AFTER THAT:** Echo and the Bunnymen: *Heaven Up Here.*

Henry Kaiser and David Lindley with Musicians from Madagascar ✦ Kayhan Kalhor, Shujaat Husain Khan, Swapan Chaudhuri ✦ Pepe Kalle ✦ Oum Kalthoum ✦ John Kander and Fred Ebb ✦ Salif Keita ✦ Khaled ✦ Ali Akbar Khan ✦ Nusrat Fateh Ali Khan and Party ✦ Junior Kimbrough ✦ King Crimson ✦ Albert King ✦ B.B. King ✦ Carole King ✦ The Kinks ✦ Rahsaan Roland Kirk ✦ Kiss ✦ Gladys Knight and the Pips ✦ Kodo ✦ Konono No. 1 ✦ Leo Kottke ✦ Kraftwerk ✦ Lili Kraus ✦ Alison Krauss ✦ Fela Kuti and the Afrika 70

Long Way to Go for a Jam Session

A World Out of Time

Henry Kaiser and David Lindley with
Musicians from Madagascar

This is the first of five (!) records that the guitarists Henry Kaiser and David Lindley recorded on a two-week trip to Madagascar in 1991. Both musicians have a healthy sense of adventure—Kaiser has recorded free jazz and tributes to the Grateful Dead, and Lindley made key contributions to Jackson Browne's best records—but for this project, they behaved more like culturally sensitive treasure hunters. Rather than snatching elements of the island nation's exotic music for their own purposes, they sought collaboration and discovered what happens when worlds collide. First they learned native songs and musical customs,

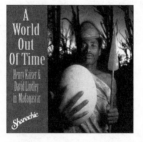

Kaiser and Lindley blend the folk music of San Francisco with traditional Malagasy.

which are drawn from both Indonesian and African sources. Then they turned the tape recorder on, capturing spirited traditional folk songs and extended jam sessions.

This approach opens a window into the rich musical world of Madagascar, the island which lies off the southeast coast of Africa. Kaiser and Lindley regarded the artists they collaborated with as teachers and guides, and as this record shows, became "fluent" enough in the musical details to make contributions without derailing the grooves. On "Ambilanao zaho," the high-energy electric band led by Rossy (Paul Bert Rahasimanana) seems to come alive when Lindley's searing slide guitar appears; later comes a solo by Kaiser in which he (unintentionally, apparently) imitates the cry of a native lemur. Key to the enterprise are the fluttering, defiantly ethereal voices: On the rivetingly dejected "Kobata," Dama Mahaleo,

one of the country's most popular singer-songwriters, gathers elements of music from South Africa, the Middle East, and India into a swirl of emotion that nearly overwhelms the visiting Westerners. Another Mahaleo track, "Dihy," begins with a caprice by Rakoto Frah, the master of the *sodina* flute, and then evolves into a spry dance, with lyrics about a very old woman dancing with a young woman symbolizing the circle of life.

Other highlights include "Vavarano," which finds young guitarist D'Gary translating the motifs of traditional Malagasy instruments to fingerpicked acoustic guitar. This first volume, the best of the five, triggered a wave of international interest in music from Madagascar. Several of the featured musicians wound up with their own record contracts, and have continued to explore the cross-cultural possibilities they chased with such spirit here.

GENRE: 🌐 World/Madagascar.
RELEASED: 1992, Shanachie. **KEY TRACKS:** Ramilison: "Kabary." Mahaleo: "Dihy," "Kobata." Tarika Sammy: "Hana." Sylvestre Randafison: "Izahay sy i malala."
CATALOG CHOICE: *A World Out of Time*, Vol. 3. **NEXT STOP:** Tarika Sammy: *Balance*. **AFTER THAT:** Rossy: *Island of Ghosts*.

A Lost Language of Soul Mates

Ghazal: Lost Songs of the Silk Road

Kayhan Kalhor, Shujaat Husain Khan, Swapan Chaudhuri

The "silk road" refers to the extended overland routes that crisscrossed Eurasia and China, linking Persia and India and helping the spread of commerce. Between the fourteenth and eighteenth centuries, during Pathan and Mongol dynastic invasions, many cultures, including those of India and Persia, brushed against each other on the road. This is audible in these countries' music: Though the basic foundations of Indian raga and Persian *dastgah* are different, instrumentalists in both strive for the same thing—to replicate the writhing, heart-tugging sounds made by human voices.

The connection between these geographically separated styles is celebrated on the hypnotic *Lost Songs of the Silk Road*, a collaboration that has the sweep of an epic journey and the transporting power of trance music. Using microtonal clusters, exotic scales, and extravagant pitch-bending swerves, Kayhan Kalhor (the Iranian-born master of the Persian violin *kamancheh*), Indian sitarist Shujaat Husain Khan, and tabla drummer Swapan Chaudhuri create music that makes these distantly linked traditions seem like they belong organically together.

Lost Songs can be appreciated for its grand melodic gestures, with instrumentalists swooning like women swept up in the rapture of love. It's also an intense lesson in improvisation—Kalhor and Khan trade explosive rhetorical declarations while staying within a general mood. In this music, an ad-libbed phrase can call for abrupt changes in tempo, bursts of lashing stringed fury, or outright cries of agony. One vivid example comes near the end of the nineteen-minute "Saga of the Rising Sun," when the three gradually shift from a brisk pulse to a slow one. They've been cruising along on a delicately interlocked rhythm and suddenly hit some traffic, so they gradually slow things up, into a majestic, carefully coordinated processional that defies notation. It's stunning.

GENRE: 🌐 World/India, Iran. **RELEASED:** 1998, Shanachie. **KEY TRACKS:** "Saga of the Rising Sun," "Come with Me." **CATALOG CHOICE:** *The Rain.* **NEXT STOP:** Yo-Yo Ma and the Silk Road Ensemble: *When Strangers Meet.*

The Towering Giant of Soukous

Gigantafrique!

Pepe Kalle

As he tells his listeners on the staggering nine-minute dance "Pon moun paka bouge," Pepe Kalle (1951–1998) developed his singing style as a very young man: His first experience with music was singing hymns in the choir of the Catholic primary school he attended in Léopoldville, Zaire (now Kinshasa, Democratic Republic of the Congo). Then, in high school, he "apprenticed" with the father of modern Zairean music, Joseph Kabasele, who taught him how to treat a melody with great care and humility. By the time Kalle was twenty, he'd had more training than most African singers ever get.

Pepe Kalle is also known by his nickname, "The Bombe Atomique."

"Pon moun paka bouge" suggests that Kalle is aware of and grateful for the unusual properties of his voice, which is distinguished by its commanding power as well as an inescapably woeful twinge. On the refrain, Kalle—a big man with a massive baritone—cautions dancers to stay where they are, because he and guitarist Diblo Dibala and the rest of the Empire Bakuba band intend to blow their minds. The final three minutes or so find them making good on the promise: The music is an eruption of carefully threaded electric guitar arpeggios, vocal chants, and keening

Kalle entreaties, each one more riveting than the previous.

Kalle's voice is a marvel—the brief, wriggling prayer that opens "Tiembe raid pa moli" will tell you that—but his reputation rests as much on the surging rhythmic intensity of his band, which takes the calypso-like dance style called *soukous* to high levels, and keeps it there. This recording combines material from two sessions with two sets of musicians; the three tracks featuring Dibala, the great genius of guitar as embroidery, rank among the all-time great examples of effortless loose-limbed African dance music.

GENRE: 🌐 World/Congo. **RELEASED:** 1990, Afro Rhythms/Ace. **KEY TRACKS:** "Tiembe raid pa moli," "Bilala-lala," "Pon moun paka bouge." **CATALOG CHOICE:** *Larger than Life.* **NEXT STOP:** Tabu Ley Rochereau: *Babeti soukous.* **AFTER THAT:** M'bilia Bel: *Bameli soy.*

The Star of the East

Legend of Arab Music

Oum Kalthoum

One persistent and unproven legend about Egyptian singer and songwriter Oum Kalthoum (1904–1975) has to do with the scarves she held and waved around during her performances. Some contend that she was able to sing so passionately for such duration—a typical concert might contain three or four tunes and last six hours—because the scarves were doused with opium or hashish.

These writhing, sobbing phrases invite that kind of speculation; they seem divinely inspired, barely connected to earthly concerns. Kalthoum began performing at age twelve, when her father, an imam, disguised her as a boy so she could be part of his troupe. Her professional career began in the late 1920s, and within a decade she was a star, with a popular radio show, film roles, and a reputation for stirring deep emotions within her listeners. More than once, Bob Dylan has mentioned her among his favorite singers.

Legend contains recordings made in the 1950s and '60s, when Kalthoum was at the peak of her improvisatory powers. The pieces, most concerned with love and longing, each last at least twenty minutes, and for much of that time Kalthoum can be heard repeating key phrases and contorting her voice into improbable shapes, in pursuit of the ecstatic state known in Arabic music as *tarab*. The path she takes is not a straight line—sometimes she executes half-step trills and tricky turns with fastidious precision, and sometimes her lines float along, all wiggly-worm loose. When Kalthoum really gets riffing, her listeners respond with loud shouts or applause, and the interaction inspires even more adventurous leaps. On and on it goes, until what began as a simple declaration of love becomes an extraordinary journey, epic in scope and spine-chilling in its intensity.

GENRE: 🌐 World/Egypt. **RELEASED:** 2007, Retro/Proper. (Recorded between 1952 and 1967.) **KEY TRACKS:** "Gadet hobak leih," "Hadeeth al rouh." **CATALOG CHOICE:** *Inta Omri*. **COLLECTOR'S NOTE:** Kalthoum's name is spelled many different ways—as Om Koultoum, Om Kalthoum, Oum Kalsoum, Oum Kalthum, Omm Kolsoum, Umm Kolthoum, Um Kalthoom. **NEXT STOP:** Nusrat Fateh Ali Khan: *In Concert in Paris* (see p. 422). **AFTER THAT:** Fairuz: *Legendary Fairuz.*

All That Jazz, with Extra Fizz

Chicago

John Kander and Fred Ebb
Bebe Neuwirth, Ann Reinking, James Naughton, Joel Grey,
1996 Broadway Cast

Sometimes a Broadway show doesn't quite sync up with the times. That was the fate of the original *Chicago*, which bowed in 1975. Though many biographers of director Bob Fosse consider it his best all-around show, it wasn't an instant hit. *A Chorus Line* took the major Tony Awards that year.

The rare production with two female leads equal in stature, *Chicago* struck a different nerve when it returned in 1996. Its portrayal of the rampant backroom corruption of Chicago in the 1920s resonated with those following the ongoing murder trial of O.J. Simpson and other scandals.

Lyricist Fred Ebb's songs are a series of vividly sketched character studies, brought to life with composer John Kander's period pastiche, which incorporates campy vaudeville and the vivaciousness of early jazz. Each member of the ensemble gets to the essence of his or her role quickly—Bebe Neuwirth is chilling as the murderess Velma Kelly proclaiming her innocence in "The Cell Block Tango," Joel Grey (as Roxy Hart's husband) employs an almost ghostly malaise to sing "Mister Cellophane," and James Naughton cops some crooner feckless-ness for sleazy lawyer Billy Flynn's first big

The 1996 production of *Chicago* is the longest-running revival on Broadway.

number, "All I Care About." Great songs no matter who's singing them, they're rendered with a fizzy flair, and a sense of nuance missing from the much-acclaimed 2002 film adaptation.

GENRE: 😊 Musicals. RELEASED: 1996, RCA. KEY TRACKS: "All That Jazz," "Mister Cellophane," "The Cell Block Tango." ANOTHER INTERPRETATION: Original Motion Picture Soundtrack. CATALOG CHOICE: *Cabaret*, Original Broadway Cast. NEXT STOP: Richard Rodgers and Lorenz Hart: *Pal Joey*, Original Broadway Cast.

African Royalty Sings

Moffou

Salif Keita

Ever since his first international album *Soro* (1987), albino singer Salif Keita has combined elements of his Malian heritage with the trappings of Western pop. A griot whose ancestors include the warrior kings who founded the Mandingo empire, Keita nearly hit a golden mean right away with the critically acclaimed *Soro*, a relentlessly energetic set that proved he was capable of entertaining thousands in his homeland one night and revelers in Paris the next.

Soro was something special at the time—mostly because of Keita's keening, infinitely expressive vocals. The album hasn't aged well: Its liberal use of synthesizers and a loud, too-busy horn section interfere with its outbreaks of vocal genius. Unfortunately, those same high-gloss Western pop sounds have defined many of Keita's follow-up efforts. Though he's got one of the world's truly special voices, Keita—who as an albino youth was ostracized by his family and later disowned by his father for becoming an entertainer—has not used it with discretion, at times chasing a global-party ethos that exists mainly on Putumayo compilations.

Somewhere along the way Keita evidently realized he was squandering his gift, and not doing the griot's work of carrying on the stories

Keita recorded *Moffou* after spending time in Paris.

of his people. *Moffou* (2002) represents a huge course correction: It's a stripped-down affair built on hand percussion and acoustic instruments, with moody expanses that inspire some of Keita's most stirring improvisations. First he sings the melodies of "Yamore" and "Moussoldu" as though they were hymns. Then, as the music loosens up, he begins to embellish the stories he's telling with his voice—adding troubled sighs, or soaring leaps into his clarion (and seemingly endless) upper register. These have very little in common with Keita's earlier attempts at crossover. They're wise and often sad laments that find Keita abandoning Afro-pop showbiz in order to share, griot-like, the heritage of his people.

GENRE: 🌐 World/Mali. RELEASED: 2002, Decca. KEY TRACKS: "Yamore," "Moussoldu," "Katolon," "Koukou." CATALOG CHOICE: *Soro*. NEXT STOP: Youssou N'Dour: *Egypt.* AFTER THAT: Oumou Sangare: *Ko sira* (see p. 670).

The Crossover Move of a Rai *Rebel*

N'ssi, N'ssi

Khaled

When Khaled, the Algerian singer, songwriter, and accordionist who bills himself as the "King" of his country's *rai* music, began his campaign to reach a Western audience in the early 1990s, he did what many world music acts have done: He hired a hotshot producer. Often that's a strategy for failure—virtually every artist, from youngsters to such veterans as Youssou N'Dour, has stumbled when releasing slicked-up productions designed to enchant Western ears.

Khaled released his first album at age 14.

This project is different. Khaled wisely selected Don Was, coleader of the esoteric pop band Was (Not Was). The producer's mission is to pull disparate musical worlds into sympathetic orbit. As Khaled sings the wriggling, gymnastic lines that are common currency in Algerian dance music, Was slips a pedal steel guitar into the mix. It's a slightly perverse choice—a "let's see what happens if we put cowboys into the picture" kind of thought—but it works. Without diminishing the steady rhythmic undercurrent, Was creates a poignant frame for Khaled's vocals.

Was never goes too far with his adornments. He recognizes that *rai* rocks hardest when there's not much to goop it up. The music visits bobbling funk and more slithery atmospheres, but the emphasis remains on Khaled. In the liner notes, Was characterizes Khaled as a rock-style rebel—years before this release Khaled and other *rai* stars were attacked by Algerian fundamentalists as unsavory influences. The incendiary music here explains the concern. It carries hints of revolution the way James Brown's music does, its rhythm fierce enough to steamroll any status quo.

GENRE: 🌐 World/Algeria. **RELEASED:** 1992, Cohiba/Mango. **KEY TRACKS:** "Serbi serbi," "Chebba," "Alech taadi," "Zine a zine." **CATALOG CHOICE:** *Kutche* (with Safy Boutella). **NEXT STOP:** Cheb Mami: *Meli meli.*

A Dazzling Example of Hindustani Classical Raga

Traditional Music of India

Ali Akbar Khan

During the early moments of these traditional Hindustani ragas, Ali Akbar Khan plays the twenty-five-string *sarod* with light brushstrokes and gentle pitch-bending melodies. His sitar-like instrument, whose body is carved from a single block of wood, handles both melody and rhythm, and as a result he can control the "mood" of the music all by himself.

Eventually, the ragas—pieces built on intricate asymmetrical recurring beat patterns—evolve into fierce and agitated peaks. To make them happen, Khan's repertoire (and musical personality) expands. He attacks the instrument, which is played using a bow, with thrashing strokes. He repeats single notes emphatically, placing them at odd angles against a rhythm tapped on two tabla drums and the drone-producing stringed tampura. As he strikes and lunges, Khan's serene composure goes on the back burner. He becomes an improvising dynamo, swept into the pursuit of an all-encompassing euphoria.

That gradually escalating shift of tone is central to Indian classical music, and a particular specialty of Khan's. Once called "an absolute genius, the greatest musician in the world" by violinist and conductor Yehudi Menuhin, Khan began studying music at age three with his father, the legendary teacher

Ali Akbar Khan is the master of the *sarod*.

Ustad Allauddin Khan—whose other pupils included Ravi Shankar. Most of the younger Khan's childhood was spent practicing (one account says he practiced eighteen hours daily) and learning the intricate governing structures of the music. The first raga here, the seventeen-minute "Raga Chandranandan," is his own creation. Khan was responsible for the first Western recording of Indian classical music, and though Shankar became more visible through associations with the Beatles and others, Khan (who appeared with Shankar on George Harrison's *Concert for Bangladesh*) was the one who awed musicians. Follow the wizard along these winding, ever-illuminating paths to hear why.

GENRE: 🌐 World/India. **RELEASED:** 1965, Prestige. **KEY TRACKS:** "Raga Chandranandan," "Raga Malika." **CATALOG CHOICE:** *Signature Series, Vol. 2: Three Ragas.* **NEXT STOP:** Ravi Shankar: *Three Ragas* (see p. 692). **AFTER THAT:** John McLaughlin: *Remember Shakti.*

Utterly Magical Vocal Spontaneity

In Concert in Paris

Nusrat Fateh Ali Khan and Party

Like many of the rock stars who borrowed from him, Nusrat Fateh Ali Khan (1948–1997) was in search of ecstasy when he sang. He'd make single phrases sound like heroic journeys, stringing together long melismatic lines that would climb methodically toward heaven. Then he'd follow these with shuddering dips and pitch-swerving curls that would plunge his listeners into unexpected terrain.

But unlike most rock stars, Khan—the most visible figure to emerge from the Pakistani devotional singing style known as *qawwali*—was never in a particular hurry to reach the ecstatic state. His performances, including these recorded in Paris in the 1980s, were marathons. It could take more than fifteen minutes for a poem (many written by the ancient Sufi mystic Rumi) to unfold.

The first disc of this mountainous, career-best five-disc set amounts to an overdose of Khan's shape-shifting vocal contortions, ad-libs that feel charged with paranormal inspiration. "Naat" begins restlessly, with furtive scattered phrases. Khan gathers the members of his "Party" into a processional, and after seven minutes or so, his improvisations evoke a fast-moving, thundering river. Then, suddenly, he begins singing like a worried old lady tottering along on her heels. Then like a sea creature wriggling on the shore. With each characterization, it's clear that Khan is hardly thinking about the notes, or the lengths of his phrases, or even how he'll respond to the somber chants of his accompanying singers. He's

focusing on something more sweeping—an enduring, lasting bliss, rare and elusive, a state that must be actively sought. And when the nimble Khan—whose name translates roughly as "the king of the opening to success"—gets close to it, he savors and tries to sustain this state. He treats it as a seeker's reward, the pleasure that comes after the long stair-stepping quest, the gateway to previously hidden realms of consciousness.

GENRE: 🌐 World/Pakistan. **RELEASED:** 1988, Ocora. **KEY TRACKS:** "Naat," "Manaqib Ali," "Kafi." **F.Y.I.:** Ocora also released the concerts documented here on individual discs, as *Live in Paris,* Vols. 1–5. **CATALOG CHOICE:** *Mustt mustt* (with Michael Brook). **NEXT STOP:** The Sabri Brothers: *Ya habib.* **AFTER THAT:** Jeff Buckley: *Grace* (see p. 126).

Live from a Juke Joint, the Beginning and End of Music

All Night Long

Junior Kimbrough

The blues as it's practiced in the Mississippi hill country is what folklorists call "social music"—it only really comes alive when there are listeners to respond to it, by dancing or hollering or whatever.

It doesn't lend itself to the air-conditioned isolation of recording studios. This may be one reason it took so long for the guitarist and singer Junior Kimbrough (1930–1998) to get a hearing: For more than thirty years, Kimbrough performed at weekly house parties and a juke joint he ran in Mississippi. There, he built a reputation for harrowing, trance-inducing electric blues performances. Backed by a bunch of top-shelf musicians

Kimbrough was born and raised in Hudsonville, Mississippi.

who called themselves the Soul Blues Boys, Kimbrough tossed out primordial cries and Memphis soul riffs, hard-chomping funk, and marathon wandering drones that one student, the rockabilly pioneer Charlie Feathers, heard as "the beginning and end of music."

Kimbrough's rep didn't spread from the hill country until he was sixty-one, when he and fellow bluesman R. L. Burnside were featured in the 1991 film *Deep Blues*. This long-overdue debut was recorded in an afternoon at Kimbrough's second juke joint, a former Sanctified church in Holly Springs, Mississippi (the first one burned down); according to the album's producer, music critic Robert Palmer, lightning struck the building during the session, inspiring the rueful "Slow Lightnin'." The first disc issued by the forward-thinking Fat Possum label, *All Night Long* is a clawing and clattering roar that expands the definition of electric blues. It's scrappier and more introspective than, say, the strutty Chicago style, and illuminated by snakelike guitar lines that wander restlessly along, rarely ending in neat or tidy ways. A glimpse of an iconoclast in as relaxed a "studio" setting as possible, this warm and resonant recording is essential listening for those in search of blues power, undiluted.

GENRE: 🌀 Blues. **RELEASED:** 1992, Fat Possum. **KEY TRACKS:** "Work Me Baby," "Done Got Old," "All Night Long." **CATALOG CHOICE:** *Sad Days, Lonely Nights.* **NEXT STOP:** Mississippi Fred McDowell: *Mississippi Delta Blues*, Vols. 1 and 2. **AFTER THAT:** Otha Turner: *And the Afrossippi Allstars.*

A Progressive Rock Manifesto

In the Court of the Crimson King

King Crimson

This record effectively decimates the argument that progressive rock of the late '60s and early '70s was little more than the babbling technical feats of overamped nerds. Guitarist Robert Fripp and his band certainly had chops to burn when they recorded this—the opening track, "Twenty-first-Century Schizoid Man," contains a long-distance lunge of an improvisation that makes most rock guitar solos sound like nursery rhymes. But from there, Fripp and his crew, which includes future Emerson, Lake, and Palmer bassist/vocalist Greg Lake, seek meaningful music in more placid atmospheres. Their conversations wander far from any expected "rock" context, into extended suites. "Moonchild" opens as a tender love song, with Fripp's long-tones hovering in the background. That evolves into an ambient rubato ("The

Pete Townshend called this album an "uncanny masterpiece."

Dream" segment), which is eventually eclipsed by a guitar-and-percussion exchange ("The Illusion") that uses the spirit of free jazz to explore spacy open vistas.

This album resonated with those predisposed to progressive rock of the Pink Floyd variety. But King Crimson never developed a fan base commensurate with its talent. Personnel changed regularly around Fripp over the years, and though these subsequent ensembles made great records—check out the dense thrill ride called *Lark's Tongues in Aspic* from 1973, or the decidedly funkier *Discipline* from 1981—there remains something special about this first crusading journey, an example of greatly nuanced music in a genre where nuance is often in short supply.

GENRE: 🎸 Rock. **RELEASED**: 1969, Atlantic. (Reissued 2004, Caroline.) **KEY**

TRACKS: "Twenty-first-Century Schizoid Man," "I Talk to the Wind," "Moonchild." **CATALOG CHOICES**: *Lark's Tongues in Aspic; Discipline.* **NEXT STOP**: Pink Floyd: *Piper at the Gates of Dawn.* **AFTER THAT**: Yes: *The Yes Album* (see p. 881).

A Classic from a King of the Blues

Born Under a Bad Sign

Albert King

File this under "Change does a bluesman good." For the early part of the 1960s, Albert King (1923–1992) recorded fairly conventional electric blues for regional labels in St. Louis and Chicago, with little success.

In 1966, he was invited to cut a few singles for the Stax label in Memphis, and that's when lightning struck. Backed by the überconfident band known as Booker T. and the MGs—organist-pianist Booker T. Jones, guitarist Steve Cropper, bassist Donald "Duck" Dunn, drummer Al Jackson Jr.—King found himself at the center of an earthier, less-traditional attack, one informed by rock and rhythm and blues. In this context, his lusty blues-guitar boilermakers resonate with devastating force, separating him from the other "Kings" of the blues, B.B. King and Freddie King.

Albert King plays the guitar left-handed, without restringing the instrument from the typical right-handed configuration.

Born Under a Bad Sign collects these first singles, several of which reached into the Top 40 on *Billboard*'s R&B chart. Usually such compilations are unsatisfying hodge-podges, but these singles make a strikingly coherent package, one that feels as though it was planned as an album sequence. Every track is demonically inspired, and funky in ways lots of electric blues is not. Each features the left-handed guitarist King, whose broad, gut-wrenching

sound has no peer in the world of guitar; so powerful is his solo on "Personal Manager," British blues disciple Eric Clapton plays chunks of it, note-for-note, on Cream's "Strange Brew."

After he's blown convention to smithereens, King throws a curve with the final track—a version of the Ray Noble torch song "The Very Thought of You." The mighty King, who was known as the "Velvet Bulldozer," has evidently decided that it's quitting time. He's done all the heavy lifting, and now he's gonna sit back and swing easy, and prove to all doubters that a blues belter who's not even particularly respected for his singing can, in the right atmosphere, turn a song like this *out*.

GENRE: 🎵 Blues. **RELEASED**: 1967, Stax. **KEY TRACKS**: "Born Under a Bad Sign," "Crosscut Saw," "The Hunter," "The Very Thought of You." **CATALOG CHOICE**: *Live Wire/Blues Power.* **NEXT STOP**: Freddie King: *Let's Hide Away and Dance Away with Freddie King.* **AFTER THAT**: B.B. King: *Lucille.*

A King-Sized Helping of Blues History

Live at the Regal

B.B. King

T he first clue that this isn't a typical evening of blues is the screaming. After the first two songs, the crowd at Chicago's Regal Theater sounds like it's responding to the Beatles on *The Ed Sullivan Show*—shrieks

King had **74** entries on the *Billboard* R&B charts between 1951 and 1985.

of elation erupt every time B.B. King plays. It's not an applause-meter contrived sound, either: This is a direct circuit between performer and audience, and it's running hot.

The second clue comes from the guitar of the mighty King himself. He's plenty flashy when he wants to be, but on this night he lights up the disconsolate "How Blue Can You Get?" with some of the most exquisitely restrained note-bending ever heard in the blues. Most guitarists make wild slurping arcs, of a minor third or more, when they bend a string. King thinks mostly in carefully controlled microtones here. He swerves in such a way that when he reaches the desired note—at, of course, the exact millisecond he intended—it feels like the end of a long journey. The expression seems greater because it's accomplished within such a narrow range.

With these slight-yet-significant gestures and his charming song introductions, King keeps listeners glued. Culled from a week of performances in November 1964 at the theater, this disc stands among the best in King's extra-large discography. Listen to King and the band open up and roar, and it becomes impossible to settle for the perfunctory, punching-the-clock blues that has, sadly, become the status quo.

GENRE: 🔵 Blues. **RELEASED:** 1965, Chess/MCA. **KEY TRACKS:** "Every Day I Have the Blues," "Help the Poor." **CATALOG CHOICE:** *Live in Cook County Jail.* **NEXT STOP:** Muddy Waters: *At Newport 1960* (see p. 848). **AFTER THAT:** Little Milton: *Grits Ain't Groceries.*

Still Capable of Moving the Earth

Tapestry

Carole King

T he copyright date on nine of the twelve songs of Carole King's *Tapestry* reads 1971, the year the album was released. Theoretically, it's possible that some of these accounts of frazzled road-damaged romance were written years before and kept on the shelf. But the prolific King—who in the '60s cowrote such incandescent blasts as Little Eva's "The Loco-Motion" and the Aretha Franklin hit "(You Make Me Feel like) A Natural Woman" with her then-husband Gerry Goffin—had issued her first solo album, the erratic *Writer*, the year before. She probably wouldn't have held back anything great on purpose.

Tapestry sold 13 million copies in 1971 alone.

That means the core songs of the biggest-selling album of the '70s, and the East Coast's best answer to all the singer-songwriter strumming California was exporting at the time, came together quickly, in a matter of months. That might not seem so terribly impressive until you stop to really savor the songs in question: "I Feel the Earth Move," "So Far Away," "It's Too Late," "Home Again," "Beautiful," "Way Over Yonder," "You've Got a Friend," "Where You Lead," "Smackwater Jack," and "Tapestry." Individually, these are delicate, sophisticated, and effortlessly beautiful pop odes. Each is rich in backstory and loaded with interpersonal tension. Each has at least one sturdy, splendid melody (often several). And each is brought to an aching place by King's matter-of-fact delivery. Any one of them would make a normal tunesmith's year. So many, in such close proximity, qualifies *Tapestry* as one of the most extravagant bundles ever dropped by a generous muse.

GENRE: 🎙 Pop. **RELEASED:** 1971, Ode. **KEY TRACKS:** "I Feel the Earth Move," "So Far Away," "Beautiful," "You've Got a Friend." **CATALOG CHOICE:** *Rhymes and Reasons.* **NEXT STOP:** Bread: *The Best of Bread.* **AFTER THAT:** Norah Jones: *Not Too Late.*

A Kinks View of Pastoral England

The Kinks Are the Village Green Preservation Society

The Kinks

For more than thirty years, the Kinks have been one of the most misunderstood bands in rock, beloved by an elite few while being ignored by the masses. Musicians heap on the highest praise—the Who's Pete Townshend described this album as Ray Davies's *Sgt. Pepper*, a work that "makes him the definitive pop poet laureate." And yet, in America at least, the Kinks' profile is a notch above "cult curiousity."

One explanation: The group was a moving target, evolving at lightning speed. From its early incarnation as an R&B-influenced bar band ("All Day and All of the Night") through a brief psychedelic phase through the period of almost perverse British nostalgia epitomized by *Village Green*, the Kinks created great music that was a bit (and sometimes a lot) ahead of the curve. *Village Green* is the most extravagant example of this: After developing a following for brash, tightly jabbing guitar pop, Davies and his cohorts went profoundly acoustic here, replacing terse hooks with pub sing-alongs and wordy evocations of an imagined simpler time. There are oompah refrains and dashes of music-hall finery, odes to strawberry jam and sounds you might encounter in a prim English village square of yesteryear.

Some have conjectured that Davies felt the need to respond to the conceptual works created by the Beatles and the Rolling Stones in 1967 and '68, yet was determined not to follow along too closely. His solution was to conjure an idealized place, a town not unlike Fortis Green, the one where he grew up. Davies's characters wax nostalgic over old photographs and lost friends, then look outward, on tracks like the idyllic perspective exercise "Big Sky" or a throaty lament about "The Last of the Steam-Powered Trains."

Ray Davies (top left) and the band in 1970.

And as is true of all of Davies's best work, the brilliantly developed characters exhibit more shades of emotional gray than most pop-song protagonists. The music might suggest that these poor souls just walked out of some nostalgic Charles Dickens tableau, but the sharp, caustic descriptions speak eerily and effectively about the plight of modern man.

GENRE: 🎸 Rock. RELEASED: 1970, Reprise/Earmark. KEY TRACKS: "Do You Remember Walter," "Big Sky," "Picture Book." CATALOG CHOICES: *Muswell Hillbillies; Misfits; Something Else.* NEXT STOP: Big Star: *Radio City* (see p. 88). AFTER THAT: Death Cab for Cutie: *Transatlanticism.*

Three Instruments Simultaneously, One Amazing Sound

Volunteered Slavery

Rahsaan Roland Kirk

Blind multi-instrumentalist Rahsaan Roland Kirk brought several big ideas to jazz—he was among the first (and best) at playing multiple wind instruments at once, and during the social upheaval of the 1960s, he laced his music with consciousness-raising chants and provocations.

One of a handful of amazing records Kirk (1936–1977) made for Atlantic in the late '60s, *Volunteered Slavery* argues that Kirk was at the same time also a detail guy, attuned to the galvanic power of small ideas. Lighting onto an up-tempo gospel rhythm, he nudges it just enough to subvert the expected amen cadences.

Kirk shows off his unique talent.

Whether riffing on an early-jazz parade beat or playing totally free, Kirk's command of the entire jazz language is astounding. In the course of a single solo, he can sound like a well-oiled horn section playing esoteric harmonies or three different musicians squabbling. To underscore his point that people of all races willingly volunteer for subjugation, Kirk interpolates the utopian closing theme to the Beatles' "Hey

Jude" into the title track, a wry comment on universalism.

This album is divided between short pieces recorded in the studio and highlights from Kirk's appearance at the Newport Jazz Festival in 1968. Every track sparkles—the studio selections turn on brash horn-section arrangements that keep the music tightly focused, while the live stuff is more expansive and improvisation-oriented. Make sure not to miss the spirit-summoning "A Tribute to John Coltrane," which finds Kirk transforming the inspiration he gets from the jazz legend into captivating, passionately original torrents.

GENRE: 🅙 Jazz. **RELEASED:** 1969, Atlantic. (Reissued 2002, Collectables.) **KEY TRACKS:** "Volunteered Slavery," "I Say a Little Prayer," "Search for the Reason Why," "A Tribute to John Coltrane." **CATALOG CHOICES:** *Blacknuss; The Inflated Tear.* **NEXT STOP:** Yusef Lateef: *The Blue Yusef Lateef.*

And, as Homer Simpson Once Said, Party Every Other Day

"Rock and Roll All Nite"

Kiss

66 "Y ou drive us wild, we'll drive you crazy." That's one of several insanely catchy refrains on this defining Kiss hit. It's also the karmic law of live rock, and for a time in the middle 1970s nobody worked it better than Kiss. The four remarkably average musicians from New York wore superhero costumes and painted their faces (in a style they went so far as to trade-mark) to look like horror-film castoffs. The band understood that if music alone wouldn't drive listeners wild, they'd have to haul out some high-concept theatrics. Kiss shows channeled the alienated roar of metal into cartoonish poses and garish

The band members sporting the signature Kiss look.

pyrotechnics, several involving the distinctively protruding tongue of bassist Gene Simmons. The music itself was almost always second-ary—except, that is, when the band was playing a song like "Rock and Roll All Nite."

Written by Simmons and guitarist Paul Stanley, the song was a response to a record-company executive who heard the third Kiss album *Dressed to Kill* and decided the band needed an anthem. He got one. "Rock and Roll All Nite" is the frenzy of great rock and roll in highly concen-trated form. From the first note, Kiss seemed poised to erupt. The "definitive" version of the song is on the band's commer-cial breakthrough *Alive!*, from 1975. There's some debate about how much post-concert "sweetening" was involved in *Alive!*—Simmons says in his autobiography that the band couldn't have spent much time, because the label was nearly broke at the time—but the end result is undeniable. The crowd's already wild when the song starts up. And Kiss, true to its word, drives them crazy.

GENRE: 🅡 Rock. **RELEASED:** 1975, Casablanca. **APPEARS ON:** *Dressed to Kill; Alive!* **NEXT STOP:** Thin Lizzy: *Live and Dangerous.* **AFTER THAT:** Various Artists: *Dazed and Confused* (see p. 809).

A Peak of Call-and-Response Soul

Imagination

Gladys Knight and the Pips

T he great vocal groups of R&B function at times the way the choruses did in Greek theater: Between choreographed steps, the backing singers comment on the unfolding story—adding amen-style punctuation, or

moans of sympathy, or the aural equivalent of a raised eyebrow.

Consider "Midnight Train to Georgia," the chart-topping hit by the Atlanta group Gladys Knight and the Pips. In a voice that has the coarseness of crushed velvet and the slightest knife-edge of fresh hurt, Knight tells the story of her man, an unlucky drifter who's fleeing his problems. When she recalls how "he kept dreaming that someday he'd be the star," the

Imagination **was the group's first album after leaving Motown Records.**

three suave supporting singers known as the Pips never break stride with their dismissal: "A superstar? But he didn't get far."

Similar exchanges enliven all of *Imagination*, the 1973 effort that's a quiet wonder of '70s soul. Where "Midnight Train," written by Jim Weatherly originally as "Midnight Plane to Houston," finds the Pips tempering Knight's enthusiasm, the title track, a rollicking

Temptations-style single, has the Pips providing pep talks. Their banter sounds effortless—Knight launches her solo flights out of the Pips' terse but effective harmony—and it makes virtually every track, even a lush ballad like "Best Thing That Ever Happened to Me," seem like a story retold by a circle of friends. Knight brings the drama when necessary, but most of the time she's coy and reserved, listening in as the Pips transform the backing-singer's worn repertoire of whoo-hoos into something much more engaged, a sly running commentary.

GENRE: 🎵 R&B. **RELEASED:** 1973, Buddah. **KEY TRACKS:** "Midnight Train to Georgia," "Best Thing That Ever Happened to Me." **CATALOG CHOICE:** *Neither One of Us.* **NEXT STOP:** TLC: *CrazySexyCool.*

Your Neighborhood Drum Circle Wishes It Sounded Like This

Live at Acropolis, Athens, Greece

Kodo

" A kabanar," the final selection on this live recording, begins with ordinary everyday pounding, like someone knocking on a front door. The crowd picks up the rhythm, and begins clapping along, only to be left in the dust by this troupe of expert Japanese drummers as they quicken the pace to a gallop. After that frenzy dies down, there's a duet between flute and the drums, each playing its own repetitive pattern. More drums enter, and pretty soon what had been a calming meditation balloons into another, equally thrilling chase.

Whether the members of this nine-piece troupe are maintaining a steady pulse or chopping it into bite-sized bits, they transform the *taiko* style of ceremonial drumming into riveting, and wholly complete, music. These pulses are overpowering not simply because they're loud (listen on good speakers to hear drums make an animalistic roar) but because the musicians are so thoroughly attentive to every attack. They're locked together in pursuit of a kind of groove ecstasy, and their sensitive interplay can lure a casual listener deep into the rhythm.

The group considers its mission to be at least partly spiritual—according to the group,

Kodo can be translated as "heartbeat," but also as "children of the drum." That second meaning is an indication of the group's sensibility: Though the music is often complex, it is suffused with a spirit of childlike openness.

In the years since it began touring internationally, Kodo, which hails from the Japanese island of Sado, has engaged in cross-cultural experiments with electronica producers as well as drum luminaries like the Grateful Dead's Mickey Hart. These collaborations are pleasant, but this crisp live recording, captured at one of the world's most hallowed ancient sites, is drumming on a whole different level.

GENRE: 🌐 World/Japan. RELEASED: 1995, TriStar. KEY TRACKS: "Akabanar," "Zoku," "Miyake." CATALOG CHOICE: *Ibuki.* NEXT STOP: Mickey Hart: *Planet Drum.* AFTER THAT: Mongo Santamaria: *Drums and Chants* (see p. 671).

From Junkyard Car Parts and Megaphones Comes . . .

Congotronics

Konono No. 1

At first it sounds like some late-night carousing happening a mile away: There's the steady clatter of metallic percussion and the happy plinking of three *likembé* thumb pianos. Taunting voices crackle through antique megaphones known as "voice throwers," their cries answered by an insistent police whistle.

There's fuzz all around the sound, and when it's coupled with the call-and-response chanting, the music of the Kinshasha band Konono No. 1 seems almost surreal, a riveting balance of the ancient and the ultramodern. The beats are descended from the trance

Before founding the group in the 1970s, leader Mingiedi was a truck driver.

music of the Bazombo region on the Congolese/Angolan border, the chants are those used in rituals that have been handed down for generations. But those thumb pianos, one supplying bass lines and the other two creating a chordal patchwork, are intriguingly distorted. Bandleader Mawangu Mingiedi, who formed Konono No. 1 in the late '70s, developed a way to make the *likembé* louder using magnets and homemade amplifiers powered by car batteries. When paired with percussion made from junkyard scraps, the sound of the *likembé* becomes odd and exotic.

Konono's music thrives on interplay: The more there is going on, the more it feels as though the rhythm could roll forever. The three thumb pianos sometimes crisscross like bike messengers threading a busy intersection, and sometimes line up together for a hard-crunching attack closer to heavy metal than anything African. *Congotronics* would be captivating even if it were somehow rendered cleanly, but it's the coarseness, and the deft but not quite perfect synchronization of contrasting ideas, that makes it irresistible. Get inside this recording, which works really well loud, and what seemed at first to be an odd street-carnival curiosity becomes utterly hypnotic trance music.

GENRE: 🌐 World/Congo. **RELEASED:** 2004, Crammed Discs. **KEY TRACKS:** "Kule Kule," "Paradiso." **CATALOG CHOICE:** *Congotronics 2.* **NEXT STOP:** Fela and Egypt 80: *Beasts of No Nation.* **AFTER THAT:** Various Artists: *Centrafrique: Musique Abaya/ Chants a penser.*

Quietly Radical Solo Guitar

6- and 12-String Guitar

Leo Kottke

The next time you hear a gorgeously recorded acoustic guitar, with every tick of finger against strings sounding like a whisper meant only for you, give a small prayer of thanks for Leo Kottke. And for this debut record,

a marvel from 1969 that opened up new ways of thinking about the guitar.

The front-porchy *6- and 12-String Guitar* doesn't scream "revolution"—Kottke's compositions often follow the straight-forward logic of folk songs. But dotting the periphery are intricate arpeggios and slippery jazz flourishes, hints of blue-grass rambles and homespun strumming. The tricky passages amble blithely by: Kottke might be a technical wizard, but he's more interested in gentle shadings than full-spotlight derring-do. He treats the guitar as a source of texture and, to accentuate that, positions the microphone in close proximity to the fretboard. This gives these instrumentals an astounding intimacy. You feel

Kottke used a polyphonic finger-picking style on the steel-string acoustic guitar for this album.

the clicks and the breaks and the sparks that fly from the steel strings, and when he gets going, as on the precise attacks of "Vaseline Machine Gun" or the woodsy "The Tennessee Toad," the result is something more than just sound—it's a palpable texture.

Kottke was twenty-four when he recorded this. His father, a wandering golf pro, moved the family constantly, and Kottke later said he soaked up regional songs and styles as a result. He spent less than eight hours in the studio to get the thirty-eight minutes of *6- and 12-String Guitar.* "All I had to do," he recalled, "was sit down and play everything I ever knew." The finished product, released by John Fahey on his Takoma label, established Kottke as a preeminent guitar thinker and set his career in motion—these songs, all originals save a luminous version of Bach's "Jesu, Joy of Man's Desiring," remain the backbone of his performances.

The album's recording technique spread like wildfire. Its simplicity of sound and approach made it a key inspiration for New Age music (the guitarists on the Windham Hill label all had Kottke on the brain). And though many have copied Kottke's devices, none have used them quite this way, to explore the legends of backwoods America through six (or twelve) shiny unassuming strings.

GENRE: Ⓓ Folk. **RELEASED:** 1969, Takoma/Fantasy. **KEY TRACKS:** "The Driving of the Year Nail," "The Sailor's Grave on the Prairie," "The Tennessee Toad." **CATALOG CHOICE:** *A Shout Toward Noon.* **NEXT STOP:** Michael Hedges: *Aerial Boundaries.* **AFTER THAT:** Alex de Grassi: *Southern Exposure.*

An Early Electronica Milestone

Trans-Europe Express

Kraftwerk

K raftwerk's hypnotic 1974 smash "Autobahn" took machine worship to new heights. One of the first hit singles made entirely with synthesizers, it put listeners on the German highway system of its namesake, where cars whoosh past at superhigh speeds, and, through the magic of the Doppler effect, blur into a symphony of ever-changing sound as they streak by.

In the aftermath of "Autobahn," it was probably inevitable that the German keyboard quartet would progress from cars to more sophisticated machines. Sure enough, this hugely influential follow-up finds Kraftwerk romancing

Kraftwerk's name translates to "Power Station."

hypercompetent robots and cyborgs with loose circuits, bullet trains, and other big rigs controlled by oddly impassive humans. On "Showroom Dummies," a chilly voice repeats the phrase "We are showroom dummies" in affectless English about a zillion times. The verses tell what happens when the dummies decide to rise up and seize the day: They abandon their posts and head for a nightclub. Where, of course, they dance.

As with much Kraftwerk music, "Showroom Dummies" can be appreciated on several levels. It's a *Twilight Zone* episode, or a caustic comment on the disconnectedness of modern life (even mannequins long for fellowship). It's also electrifying dance music. Kraftwerk's drum machine patterns map out a symmetrical grid, and everything that goes on top of it—recurring synth blips, shimmering washes of digital-pastorale chords—lines up to the millisecond, a triumph of mechanistic precision. This method of music-making, radical in the mid-'70s, has become commonplace since. Virtually everyone producing hip-hop or electronic dance music has drawn inspiration from these visionary blasts—including Afrika Bambaataa, whose 1982 single "Planet Rock" famously interpolates the "Trans-Europe

Express" theme. The tune's the same, but the differences are striking: Bambaataa uses it to beckon listeners to his electro-funking dance floor, where the party never ends. In Kraftwerk's conception there is no party, just an eerie barren ecosystem, frozen under ice.

GENRES: 🕃 Rock 𝄢 Electronica.
RELEASED: 1977, Capitol. **KEY TRACKS:**
"Europe Endless," "Showroom Dummies," "Trans-Europe Express." **ANOTHER INTERPRETATION:** The synthesized melody of "Trans-Europe Express" was sampled by Afrika Bambaataa for his futuristic single "Planet Rock," one of many hip-hop appropriations of Kraftwerk. **CATALOG CHOICE:** *Autobahn.* **NEXT STOP:** Jean-Michel Jarre: *Oxygene.* **AFTER THAT:** Tangerine Dream: *Phaedra.*

Not Tickling, but Caressing, the Ivories

Mozart Piano Sonata No. 11, Piano Concertos Nos. 12 and 18

Lili Kraus

Boston Symphony Orchestra (Pierre Monteux, cond.)

Describing the middle (Minuet) movement of Mozart's Piano Sonata No. 11, musicologist Eric Blom singles out its "frail, wistful quality," which he says "makes it as haunting a piece of romantic piano music as anything one can think of in Schumann or Chopin." That's quite an accomplishment, considering that Mozart wrote this well before the dawn of the Romantic era, and about fifty years before those guys began composing.

To experience every disconsolate breath of Mozart's forward-looking marvel, seek out this recording made in the 1950s by Hungarian pianist Lili Kraus (1903–1986). Of the gazillions of pianists who have recorded Mozart, few possess the sensitivity of phrasing and touch that's on display here. Kraus establishes herself from the very beginning of the sonata, with a breezy and unfussy statement of the opening music-box theme that seems to waft from the piano, leaving just the faint outline of a firm attack. Later, as the piece unfolds, the passagework becomes the pianistic equivalent of the hundred-yard dash; even here Kraus doesn't seem to be laboring—her touch is so light, her phrases so crisply turned out, all that hangs around is the music itself. Kraus's transparent approach is fully on display in the middle movement, where the pace slows and there's less clever ornamentation. As she winds through thickets of bunched-up notes, she caresses each just a bit, coaxing from it directions to the next one. In this methodical way, she uncovers the rhapsodic qualities of the piece.

Kraus's unassuming tone defines the two concertos, which are from Mozart's torrid earlier years. These pieces are both striking for their focus: Where later works explore nuances and shades of gray, these are fixated on a single emotion, which Mozart sets out in the initial theme and then develops in the variations. That forces the pianist to provide the colorations and points of emphasis, and Kraus doesn't disappoint: Using sparkling articulations, she illuminates small details in imperceptibly slight, sometimes miraculous, ways. She plays with supreme confidence, treating Mozart as a puzzle master, a keeper of secrets. Her job is to find them, and when she does, she shines light on them and slinks gracefully out of the way, so that listeners can be as awed by Mozart's genius as she is.

GENRE: 🎼 Classical. **RELEASED:** 2004, Urania. (Recorded 1953, 1954.) **KEY**

TRACKS: Sonata No. 11: second movement. Concerto No. 12: first movement. Concerto No. 18: second movement. **ANOTHER INTERPRETATION:** *The Piano Sonatas,* Mitsuko Uchida. **CATALOG CHOICE:** Kraus: *Mozart Solo Keyboard Works.* **NEXT STOP:** Arcadi Volodos: *Volodos Plays Liszt.*

A Vitalizing Shot of Bluegrass

I've Got That Old Feeling

Alison Krauss

Child prodigy Alison Krauss probably didn't intend to transform bluegrass when she put together her first band. But then, she was only ten years old—and already a championship fiddler. By fourteen, Krauss, who also sings beautifully, began recording under her own name, and within a few projects, she'd single-handedly brought a wild-eyed youthful vigor to the style known for its staid adherence to tradition.

Krauss won hearts quickly because of the plaintive directness of her voice and the parallel terseness of her fiddle. On this, her third album, the native of Champaign, Illinois, proves

Krauss cites Dolly Parton as one of her major influences.

that youthfulness does not equal recklessness: The up-tempo songs move with authority, the ballads with grandmotherly patience. Just when she finishes some heartbreaking verse, along comes a quietly dazzling instrumental caprice—led sometimes by Krauss's fiddle, but just as often by the dobro (played by the master Jerry Douglas, who also produced the album) or mandolin (both Sam Bush and Stuart Duncan). Like all the great ensembles of country music, her band Union Station is dazzling when it's moving at a disciplined gallop, just keeping time.

The album isn't exclusively bluegrass.

There are country weepers ("That Makes One of Us"), folk-leaning songs ("Endless Highway"), and tunes that use rock-era devices to update bluegrass themes ("Winter of a Broken Heart"). Krauss's skillful meshing of styles foreshadows the more ambitious genre-jumbling efforts she initiated later—most notably *Raising Sand,* her stupendous 2007 collaboration with Led Zeppelin frontman Robert Plant. *I've Got That Old Feeling,* which won the 1990 Bluegrass Album Grammy, marks the moment Krauss sneaks away from tradition, and discovers that the core bluegrass values she assimilated so well have prepared her to play anything.

GENRE: 🌎 Country. **RELEASED:** 1990, Rounder. **KEY TRACKS:** "I've Got That Old Feeling," "Wish I Still Had You," "Winter of a Broken Heart." **CATALOG CHOICES:** *Lonely Runs Both Ways; Raising Sand.* **NEXT STOP:** Patty Loveless: *Mountain Soul.* **AFTER THAT:** Bela Fleck: *Bela Fleck and the Flecktones.*

The Worldly Afro-Beat

Confusion/Gentleman

Fela Kuti and the Afrika 70

Fela Kuti built one of the mightiest grooves ever to come out of Africa—which is saying something. The Nigerian singer, social commentator, keyboardist, and saxophonist called his sound "Afro-Beat," but it really was global music—deeply elastic funk spiced with African syncopation and R&B horns, and enlivened by storytelling soloists. Like James Brown, Fela (as he was universally called) knew how to repeat a simple riff until it became a perpetual-motion machine. Sometimes he'd let a rhythm percolate for ten or fifteen minutes, and only when he was sure his listeners were properly tenderized by the groove would he open his mouth. To preach. Or sing. Or harangue. Then, using one of several dialects (including pidgin English), Fela would decry the corruption of Nigeria's military government or the class system or, on "Confusion," what he saw as the "colonial" mind-set of some Africans. (These pointed comments more than once led to his arrest, and in 1977, after one scathing song attacking the Nigerian military, Fela's commune, the Kalakuta Republic, was raided by soldiers, his studio destroyed.) Carried by the relentless pulse, the slogans wormed from the dance floor into Nigeria's political discourse—among the most famous are "Teacher, Don't Teach Me No Nonsense," "Black President," "Coffin for Head of State," and "Expensive Shit."

Fela (1938–1997) recorded more than fifty albums, and almost all of them contain music worth hearing. *Confusion* (1975), which was combined with the more subdued *Gentleman* for reissue, is one of the very best, a demonstration of just how rousing Afro-Beat's deftly interlocked rhythms can be. Atop them, Fela and his band ping-pong between the routine and the radically experimental. Drop in early in the twenty-five-minute title track, and it's a reverb-y prog-rock conversation between Fela, on keyboards, and drummer Tony Allen; six or seven minutes later, it's primo Afro-Beat played by a supremely confident rhythm section that regularly sustained this crackling intensity for hours. On a tour of Nigeria in 1970, the members of James Brown's band were floored when they heard Fela: "We were telling them they're the funkiest cats we ever heard in our life," recalls bassist William "Bootsy" Collins. "I mean, this is the James Brown band, but we were totally wiped out!" Essential just for its surging and striding grooves, *Confusion/Gentleman* is an excellent way to begin an exploration of one of African music's most incandescent acts.

GENRE: 🌐 World/Nigeria. **RELEASED:** *Confusion*: 1975, EMI; *Gentleman*: 1973, EMI. (Reissued 2000, MCA.) **KEY TRACKS:** "Confusion," "Fefe Naa Efe," "Gentleman." **CATALOG CHOICES:** *Original Suffer Head; Zombie; Beasts of No Nation.* **NEXT STOP:** Thomas Mapfumo: *The Chimurenga Singles* (see p. 473). **AFTER THAT:** Tony Allen: *Lagos No Shaking.*

Kuti developed his own approach to playing the saxophone, trumpet, and keyboards.

Steve Lacy and Mal Waldron ✦ Lambert, Hendricks, and Ross ✦ Héctor Lavoe ✦ Leadbelly ✦ Ernesto Lecuona ✦ Led Zeppelin ✦ Peggy Lee ✦ Michel Legrand ✦ John Lennon ✦ Alan Jay Lerner and **L** Frederick Loewe ✦ Jerry Lee Lewis ✦ Dinu Lipatti ✦ Franz Liszt ✦ Booker Little ✦ Little Richard ✦ Los Lobos ✦ Julie London ✦ Israel "Cachao" López y Su Ritmo Caliente ✦ The Louvin Brothers ✦ Joe Lovano ✦ Love ✦ Lyle Lovett ✦ Loretta Lynn ✦ Lynyrd Skynyrd

Hot House

Steve Lacy and Mal Waldron

This chess match belongs on the top shelf where the great jazz dialogues—between Louis Armstrong and Earl Hines, Bill Evans and Jim Hall—are kept. It's a conversation between soprano saxophonist Steve Lacy (1924–2004), who began his career playing Dixieland and evolved into one of the genre's most compelling "free" players, and pianist Mal Waldron (1926–2002), who specialized in bebop and just about everything after. Starting at specific points in jazz history—they play an underappreciated Thelonious Monk tune, "Friday the Thirteenth," and "Petite fleur," a lovely piece by early jazz trailblazer Sidney Bechet. Moving through tricky melodies, they blur elements of traditional jazz into the gnarled harmonies brandished by the "out" players of the 1960s. Lacy and Waldron are as mindful of jazz tradition as the young lions claiming jazz headlines at the time of this recording were, but not nearly as worshipful: they concatenate ideas into a delightfully breezy and defiantly unchronological survey—any rejoinder from any era can be pressed into service, and usually winds up enriching the moment.

One example of this is Duke Ellington's "The Mooche." Waldron establishes a zombie march rhythm, exaggerating the thudding footfall of some terrible apparition. Lacy, who can sound like he's blowing the keys right off of the soprano, scampers around leaving bebop trills everywhere, an impish sprite who simply won't be intimidated. Chasing in the frantic romping style of early Tom and Jerry cartoons, the two hurl everything they've got at each other, their volleys an oddly perfect combination of high-level thinking and low-down conniving. They're so well matched as adversaries that nobody ever emerges a clear victor. And that's just fine.

GENRE: 🎷 Jazz. **RELEASED:** 1991, RCA Novus. **KEY TRACKS:** "House Party Starting," "Hot House," "Friday the Thirteenth," "The Mooche." **CATALOG CHOICES:** Lacy: *The Straight Horn of Steve Lacy*. Waldron: *The Quest*. **NEXT STOP:** Bill Evans and Jim Hall: *Intermodulation*. **AFTER THAT:** Joe Lovano: *Joyous Encounter*.

The Hottest New Group in Jazz

Lambert, Hendricks, and Ross

Jazz scholars will tell you that the vocal trio Lambert, Hendricks, and Ross made its biggest contribution in vocalese—the vocal technique in which instrumental jazz solos are transformed into crazy torrents of words that somehow become a story. In fact, this trio translated *all* elements of instrumental jazz into vocal music—the solos, the bigband shout choruses, the lovely chord voicings.

For example, when the group performs "Summertime" on this breakthrough album, it replicates Gil Evans's unusual scoring for the Miles Davis landmark *Porgy and Bess*: The supporting voices sing recurring phrases like "Summertime is on the way" to mimic the background lines Evans wrote. The same strategy defines the swing-era staple "Caravan." Behind the keening melody, the unified voices of Dave Lambert, Jon Hendricks, and Annie Ross make like a busy saxophone section, repeating the line "through the desert and over the sands" incessantly.

Hendricks masterminded most of these adaptations, which vaulted the group to nearly instant stardom. His lyrics carry multiple messages about jazz, communicating awe at the music's possibilities as well as admiration for the lonely quest of the jazz musician. In wry,

The group won a Grammy Hall of Fame Award in 1998.

hipster language, Hendricks captures a wide spectrum of jazz culture, from the seedy club to the rollicking late-night house-party jam. Those who are baffled by the codes of bebop might check Hendricks's brisk and blithe feature "Cloudburst" here: Through choruses taken at breakneck speed, he rattles off crazed, not-quite-nonsense syllables that romanticize, and also humanize, the feats of the music's great instrumentalists. As with much of the music these three highly simpatico singers made, it brightens the corners of a rarefied style, making its wonders accessible to all.

GENRES: 🅑 Jazz 🅥 Vocals. **RELEASED:** 1960, Columbia. **KEY TRACKS:** "Cloudburst," "Summertime," "Caravan." **COLLECTOR'S NOTE:** The two-disc 1999 edition includes two subsequent albums by the trio, *Sing Ellington* and *High Flyin'*. **CATALOG CHOICE:** *Sing a Song of Basie.* **NEXT STOP:** Eddie Jefferson: *The Jazz Singer* (see p. 394). **AFTER THAT:** King Pleasure: *King Pleasure Sings/Annie Ross Sings.*

El Cantante de los Cantantes

De ti depende

Héctor Lavoe

Puerto Rican singer Héctor Lavoe (1946–1993) led a tragic life graced with moments of artistic greatness. After coming to New York in 1967, and quickly causing a sensation with Willie Colón's orchestra, Lavoe encountered a steady stream of trouble. He lost his brother (car wreck) and his seventeen-year-old son (gun accident), suffered through a fire at his home, the murder of his mother-in-law, and then the death of his father. He became addicted to narcotics and alcohol, contracted AIDS, and struggled to make it to gigs on time. Once, during a particularly bad patch, he jumped from the ninth floor of a hotel in an apparent suicide attempt. And lived.

Lavoe's bad luck tends to color, if not overshadow, his reputation as a singer. It takes only a few minutes with *De ti depende*, his second solo effort, to appreciate how unfair that is: Sure, the dude had problems. But as he moves with foxlike stealth through the opener "Vamos a reir un poco," and dashes off delirious vocal animations on the theme of "Periódico de ayer," he sounds like someone who knows what it feels like to dance to a great band and is determined to spread that feeling.

Héctor Lavoe was nicknamed "El Cantante" (the singer).

Part of that skill can be attributed to his background: Unlike many Puerto Rican singers, Lavoe (born Héctor Pérez) was proud to call himself a "jibaro," the island nation's equivalent of a rural hayseed. He considered this heritage (which he sang about on the single "Mi gente") to be a crucial element in his music: Not only are Puerto Rico's "country" singers among the loudest and most powerful, they're also capable of stirring deep emotion without sounding melodramatic. Lavoe coupled that earthy approach

with a jazz singer's knack for bold improvisation. When he's "on," as he is here, nobody in salsa gets near him. His chattering, quick-witted ad-libs don't just cover up whatever he was suffering through offstage; they sail right over it, to a utopia far away from the daily struggles. Which, of course, is one measure of a true artist.

GENRE: 🌐 World/Puerto Rico. **RELEASED**: 1975, Fania. (Reissued 2006.) **KEY TRACKS**: "Vamos a reir un poco," "Periódico de ayer," "Hacha y machete." **FURTHER INQUIRY:** Lavoe's life was the inspiration for the 2007 biopic *El Cantante,* starring Marc Anthony and Jennifer Lopez. **CATALOG CHOICE:** *Comedia.* **NEXT STOP**: Ismael Quintana y Papo Lucca: *Mucho talento.* **AFTER THAT:** Rubén Blades y Seis del Solar: *Escenas.*

The Best of an American Griot

Where Did You Sleep Last Night?

Leadbelly

Some musicians are born composers. Some are hunter-gatherers, soaking up old songs and styles and repopularizing, if not rescuing, them. Huddie Ledbetter, the guitarist and singer who performed as Leadbelly,

was a bit of both. He wrote or substantially rewrote several enduring pieces—"Goodnight Irene," which he performed just as "Irene," was a hit for the Weavers shortly after he died nearly penniless. But he's equally revered for renditions of folk songs he picked up while in prison, including odes to trains like "Rock Island Line" and work songs like "Cotton Fields."

Leadbelly is the "King of the 12-String Guitar."

The son of a sharecropper, Leadbelly (1888–1949) was born in Louisiana and first began to play guitar at age seven. He drifted as a young man, and found himself in jail more than once. He won notoriety in 1924 when he petitioned Texas governor Pat Neff for early release and won by writing and singing a song. In 1933, Leadbelly was "discovered" in Louisiana's

Angola prison by folklorist John Lomax and his son Alan, who'd come to the prison to document folk songs. Leadbelly performed "Irene," a song he said his uncle taught him, for the Lomax tape recorder, and upon his release went to work with the Lomaxes as a chauffeur and assistant on field recording trips. Eventually (after more troubles with the law), Leadbelly left the Lomaxes, and in 1936 took up residence in New York, where he was embraced by a group of activist folk and blues artists, including Woody Guthrie, Pete Seeger, Sonny Terry, and Brownie McGhee.

Leadbelly recorded off and on during the 1930s, but it wasn't until 1941, when he joined up with Moses Asch, the founder of Folkways records, that he documented decent representations of his signature pieces. This disc, compiled from the original masters, features many Leadbelly classics as well as the waltz-meter title track, one of the most harrowing pieces in his songbook. These show why Leadbelly is so revered: His voice is authoritative and bracingly clear, and his playing has the drive of a fearsome rhythm section even when, as per his custom, he is playing alone. All its songs, both originals and covers, reveal Leadbelly as one of the few figures in American music to function the way griots do in Africa—preserving the heart and the essential narratives of a people by passing along, and, crucially, reanimating, their songs.

GENRES: 💿 Folk 🎵 Blues. **RELEASED:** 1996, Smithsonian Folkways. **KEY TRACKS:** "Where Did You Sleep Last Night?," "Rock Island Line," "Good Morning Blues." **CATALOG CHOICE:** *King of the 12-String Guitar.* **NEXT STOP:** Woody Guthrie: *Dust Bowl Ballads* (see p. 331). **AFTER THAT:** Blind Boy Fuller: *Truckin' My Blues Away.*

Won't You Pour Me a Cuban Breeze . . .

The Ultimate Collection: Lecuona Plays Lecuona

Ernesto Lecuona

Sometimes described as the "Cuban Gershwin," Ernesto Lecuona (1896–1963) wrote film scores and expansive pieces for a symphony orchestra he led, along with piano études and pop-song miniatures. Of these, it is the miniatures—songs that include "Malaguena," "Siboney," and "Andalucia (The Breeze and I)"—that had the widest circulation as staples of the 1950s-era easy-listening orchestras led by Ray Coniff, Percy Faith, and Mantovani.

Normally, that would be reason to stay away. But Lecuona is bulletproof: No matter how sentimental the orches-

Lecuona enjoyed both popular and critical success.

trations, his themes exude a quiet dignity, celebrating in the supremacy of a sturdy melody. Seek him out whenever you're dreaming of mojitos at a breezy old Havana café.

This two-disc set gathers Lecuona's solo piano performances of his primary works. Most were recorded in the 1950s, and show off his unique skill set: He was trained as a classical pianist, yet he was conversant in the popular musical forms that have enchanted Cubans since the 1920s. Specifically, Lecuona was adept at translating Afro-Cuban dance rhythm to the piano. Pieces like "Danza lecumi" turn on a lively ostinato figure in the bass, and atop that foundation Lecuona communicates crisp two-hand constructions that outline his chord sequences. Like Gershwin, Lecuona specializes in wistful, lyrical melodies that need no window dressing; their shapely slopes say it all. The spareness of these perfor-

mances sometimes gives them cocktail-hour connotations, but that's okay: Calm, regal, and perfectly proportioned, Lecuona's themes completely transcend schmaltz, offering a window into the Cuban soul.

GENRES: 🌐 World/Cuba 🎼 Classical.
RELEASED: 1997, RCA. **KEY TRACKS:** "Malaguena," "Andalucia," "La comparsa," "Noche azul," "La brisa y yo." **NEXT STOP:** Bola de Nieve: *Y su piano.* **AFTER THAT:** Noro Morales: *His Piano and Rhythm.*

If You Don't Know This, You Need Schoolin'

Led Zeppelin II

Led Zeppelin

Led Zeppelin II is an example of how, in the rock and roll business, necessity really can be the mother of invention. Led Zeppelin (singer Robert Plant, guitarist Jimmy Page, bassist John Paul Jones, and drummer John Bonham) erupted out of England in January 1969, with a hard-edged record that suggested much of the preceding activity in British blues-rock had been child's play. The debut generated intense demand for the band to tour *and* to record again—a problem since Zeppelin hadn't written much new material. A make-do solution was brokered: The band would record intermittently, at stops during tours scheduled for January through August.

Rather than compose entirely new songs, Plant recast lyrics and melodic ideas from old blues standards—the opening track, "Whole Lotta Love," drew several lawsuits asserting that it was a thinly veiled copy of Willie Dixon's "You Need Love/Woman You Need Love," a tune often associated with Muddy Waters. These suits were settled out of court; subsequent pressings credit Dixon as a co-composer. But even the most diehard blues apologist has to recognize that Led Zeppelin did something totally different with the source material—

transforming often-appropriated blues tropes into a startlingly visceral, grab-you-by-the-throat sound that changed rock forever.

The hard-rocking tunes on *II* foreshadow the basic guitar attack of heavy metal—as well as the campier blues riffage of bands like Aerosmith. The lighter, folk-tinged tunes, such as "What Is and What Should Never Be," anticipate the mystical airs Zeppelin would pursue later, most successfully with the epic "Stairway to Heaven" (from *IV*). Even the other blues "borrowings" are notable for their audacious steps: "The Lemon Song," which interpolates Howlin' Wolf's "Killing Floor," lifts the flatted-third "moan" that is common currency in the blues to a level of sublime invention.

As both a soloist and creator of dense guitar textures, Page is tremendous here; his playing may be a personal best in a career with many candidates. He gets help, of course, from the rhythm section, which follows him closely and is audibly energized by what he's doing. They didn't write all the songs, but on this monumental work the members of Led Zeppelin come to fully "own" them. Following in the tradition of generational borrowing that defines the blues, they radically revamp the outlines of the music until it speaks with a bold, sometimes brutal fury. An attack that could only have happened in the heady times of 1969, it's plenty startling, still.

GENRE: 🎸 Rock. **RELEASED:** 1969, Atco. **KEY TRACKS:** "Whole Lotta Love," "Heartbreaker," "What Is and What Should Never Be," "The Lemon Song." **CATALOG CHOICES:** *Physical Graffiti; IV.* **NEXT STOP:** Black Sabbath: *Paranoid* (see p. 92). **AFTER THAT:** The Yardbirds: *Live Yardbirds (Anderson Theater New York, March 30, 1968).*

Zep Live, at Peak

How the West Was Won

Led Zeppelin

It was, to paraphrase one overused Led Zeppelin lyric, a sound like the hammer of the gods. When Zep played live, the boogie that stomped plenty hard in the studio suddenly took on an air of terrifying menace. Sludgy,

torturously slow rock beats were thwacked with bone-crushing power. Even the quiet songs felt like they were designed to rip out the jugular. Delicate acoustic guitar meditations dissolved into pure electric thunder, alternating currents of power and finesse executed for maximum drama.

For much of the last quarter-century, you really did have to have been at a show to fully appreciate Zep: Its lone live album, *The Song Remains the Same*, is erratic and unsatisfying. The band rectified this in 2003, with a two-disc release culled from two 1972 West Coast shows. Here, guitarist Jimmy Page and frontman Robert Plant, along with bassist John Paul Jones and drummer John Bonham, chew up a songbook that, in the decades since Zep's demise, has become a sacred rock and roll text. The version of "Dazed and Confused"

Led Zeppelin (from left to right): Jones, Page, Bonham, and Plant.

lasts twenty-five transfixing minutes; "Whole Lotta Love," which lasts twenty-three minutes, finds Plant linking its refrain with bits of '50s rock classics.

In an interview shortly after *West* was released, Page said that in compiling the set, he sifted through hours of live shows, reliving many of the band's best nights. "As much as we played them, I don't think we did 'Rock and Roll' or 'Heartbreaker' the same way twice. . . . Robert would just . . . go in crazy directions depending on how everybody was feeling. Each piece kind of acquired multiple personalities."

Page came away from his vault research with one realization about Led Zeppelin, which disbanded after Bonham's death in 1980: The band never peaked, never suffered the usual quality-control lapses that come with middle age. Even the very last shows, he says, were scary. "God, what an urgent machine it was."

GENRE: 🎸 Rock. **RELEASED:** 2003, Atlantic. **KEY TRACKS:** "Whole Lotta Love," "Black Dog," "What Is and What Should Never Be." **CATALOG CHOICES:** *IV; Physical Graffiti; BBC Sessions.* **FURTHER INQUIRY:** The two-disc simultaneously released *DVD* contains footage from several tours and is the best visual account of the band live. **NEXT STOP:** Cream: *Live Cream*, Vol. 1. **AFTER THAT:** Soundgarden: *Superunknown* (see p. 726).

Bitter and Strong and Hot

Black Coffee

Peggy Lee

In its monthly "Blindfold Test" feature, *Down Beat* magazine asks prominent jazz people to identify and talk about great records without providing them any information about the artists. Shortly after this album appeared, the bandleader Raymond Scott participated, and when the editors played him the desultory blues "Black Coffee," he figured he was hearing Billie Holiday: "It must be Billie Holiday, but it is so accurate, precise, and artistic that I can't believe it."

Scott wasn't the only one intrigued by the low-key Lee, whose collection of sullen breakup songs remains a high point of the 1950s "golden age" of singing. Billed, erroneously, as a "concept" album, *Black Coffee* is more like a dream nightclub set from a pouty performer well acquainted with the art of the small gesture. For proof, check "I Didn't Know What Time It Was" or the equally compelling "Easy Living," which Lee sings with the gliding grace of a soaring bird.

Initially issued as eight songs on a set of 78-RPM singles in 1953, *Black Coffee* was so popular Decca invited Lee to expand the

record so it could be reissued as a long-player. Four songs were added in 1956, and though the instrumentation is different and Lee had already tuned into rock and roll (her chart-topping single "Fever" would erupt in 1958), these purring performances defy time: She puts herself right back into the atmosphere of the original, bringing a light, cocktail-hour melancholy to "You're My Thrill" and "There's a Small Hotel." On her subsequent works, Lee lost the Billie Holiday resemblance.

But here, on these great songs about busted-apart romance, she sings from such a deep emotional place she easily earns those Lady Day comparisons.

GENRE: 🎤 Vocals. **RELEASED:** 1956, Decca. **KEY TRACKS:** "Black Coffee," "Easy Living," "I Didn't Know What Time It Was." **CATALOG CHOICE:** *Beauty and the Beat* (with George Shearing). **NEXT STOP:** Julie London: *At Home/Around Midnight* (see p. 454). **AFTER THAT:** Dinah Washington: *Miss D After Hours.*

Duke Ellington once said, "If I'm the Duke, then Peggy's the Queen."

Three Great Jazz Days in New York

Legrand Jazz

Michel Legrand

In early June 1958, the French composer, arranger, and pianist Michel Legrand came to New York on a heady mission. Just beginning to make a name for himself with film scores, Legrand intended to gather some of the biggest names in jazz and have them play his unconventional interpretations of tunes associated with specific moments in the music's history. He wrote the charts in three weeks, and spent time corralling stars like Miles Davis, Dizzy Gillespie, John Coltrane, and Ben Webster—as well as lesser-known young players who went on to have impact later, trumpeters Donald Byrd and Art Farmer and saxophonist Phil Woods among them.

Legrand was one of the first Europeans to work with jazz innovators such as Dizzy Gillespie and Stan Getz.

Exactly how Legrand convinced the luminaries is unclear. One possibility is that, since his other gigs at the time included conducting for French crooner Maurice Chevalier, he likely could afford to pay decently. What matters is he assembled three separate "dream team" bands to record on three different days, and walked away with one of the greatest all-star sessions in jazz history. *Legrand Jazz* is the rare summit of titans that is engrossing all the way through: These arrangements inspire thoughtful, expansive, anything-but-typical-big-band solos.

Starting with a shifting-meter treatment of Fats Waller's "The Jitterbug Waltz," Legrand reimagines jazz from the Louis Armstrong era ("Wild Man Blues") to bebop. In each case, he honors the original melodic shapes, but places them in strikingly modern frameworks—the beautiful "Nuages" features four trombones playing wide Stravinsky-like chords, while the arrangement of "A Night in Tunisia" pumps up the original theme into a multilayered fanfare.

Just about every selection features a different soloist (or several), and it's clear that Legrand, who went on to make his name with such film scores as *The Thomas Crown Affair* and *Summer of '42,* thought deeply about the background textures surrounding these solo passages. Emphasizing colors rather than riffs, he creates settings that coax spellbinding solos from his hired guns— among the best are Davis's disconsolate muted-trumpet turn on "'Round Midnight" and tenor saxophonist Ben Webster's rhapsodic swirl through "Nuages," which is saturated with smoky romance. Legrand might have been an outsider, but he understood something about jazz that eluded many of its full-time practitioners: The mood of the music can be as powerful a lure as the notes.

GENRE: 🎷 Jazz. **RELEASED:** 1958, Philips. **KEY TRACKS:** "The Jitterbug Waltz," "'Round Midnight," "A Night in Tunisia," "Don't Get Around Much Anymore." **NEXT STOP:** Gil Evans: *Out of the Cool.* **AFTER THAT:** The Thad Jones–Mel Lewis Big Band: *Consummation.*

Music to Change the World By

Imagine

John Lennon

By the time he got to *Imagine*, John Lennon (1940–1980) had pretty much exhausted the narrative devices of the rock and roll song. As a member of the Beatles, he'd explored rock as pure hedonistic escape, a means of grappling with cosmic mysteries, and many points in between. On his own, with *Plastic Ono Band*, rock became an outlet for the jarring subconscious secrets revealed by primal scream therapy, a window into the harrowing and the surreal. (*Mind Games* itself came later.)

Imagine, Lennon's most consistent solo work, can be seen as an attempt to get back to basics and to reengage with the world that Lennon had kept at some distance since his band's demise. Throughout songs that howl about war,

Lennon called *Imagine* "chocolate-coated for public consumption."

seek open communication, and dare to dream of utopia, Lennon maintains two seemingly contradictory perspectives: He's the somewhat jaundiced, cynical citizen who, despite knowing better, isn't willing to completely abandon his idealism.

The result is music defined by confrontation and conflict—yet at its core it retains a hint of touching schoolkid earnestness. Lennon makes sweeping demands ("Gimme Some Truth") that voice deep impatience and bitterness, and he derides war in unequivocal terms ("I Don't Wanna Be a Soldier"). But he's also a frail human, not some diatribe machine: Another highlight of this album is the aching confessional "Jealous Guy." Then, of course, there's the title track. A

lilting private moment at the piano, "Imagine" exists in a place entirely apart from everyday concerns—it's an idyllic afternoon daydream that makes time stand still. In a calm and centered voice, Lennon implies that any seemingly unattainable goal (whether global unity, or peace) begins within each of us—with attitude change, with belief change. The caustic Beatle expects to get slammed ("You may say I'm a dreamer," he muses, taking comfort in the fact that he's "not the only one"). He knows that simply by sending out such a message, he's beginning to move the energy around. And by reclaiming the right to dream big, Lennon makes an idealistic notion seem somehow possible—not simply within our reach but worth reaching for. Put this on the next time you need to be reminded that a song really can change the world.

GENRE: 🎸 Rock. **RELEASED:** 1971, Apple/EMI. **KEY TRACKS:** "Imagine," "Jealous Guy," "I Don't Wanna Be a Soldier," "Gimme Some Truth." **CATALOG CHOICES:** *Plastic Ono Band; Mind Games; Rock 'N' Roll.* **NEXT STOP:** Harry Nilsson: *Nilsson Schmilsson* (see p. 551). **AFTER THAT:** The Apples in Stereo: *Fun Trick Noisemaker.*

A Fairly Delightful Musical

My Fair Lady

Alan Jay Lerner and Frederick Loewe
Rex Harrison, Julie Andrews, Original Broadway Cast

Most original-cast albums of the 1950s were recorded in a single day. Producers tried to schedule the sessions as close to the opening of the musical as possible, thinking that the nuances of the work would be fresh in the performers' minds. That strategy sometimes backfired: The frenzy of getting a show off the ground meant performers hadn't yet settled into the songs. And were often exhausted besides.

Amazingly, there's no fatigue in the zippy readings of this Lerner and Loewe masterpiece, which was recorded in one marathon fourteen-hour session on March 25, 1956. *My Fair Lady* is an update of George Bernard Shaw's update of the story of Pygmalion, the mythic Greek figure who falls in love with his sculpture. Both leads, Rex Harrison and Julie Andrews, are beyond lively, and the supporting cast—which, as was often the case with Lerner and Loewe, got the meatiest songs—positively sparkles. Seek out "On the Street Where You Live," sung by John Michael King in the smallish role of Freddy Eynsford-Hill; his flip, understated rhapsody oozes charm, and avoids the stiltedness that often accompanies musical theater.

Set in pre–World War II London, *My Fair Lady* is a drawing-room tale of class distinctions animated by Loewe's relentlessly sunny melodies. The show yielded an astounding number of songs that became standards,

Critic Mark Steyn called *My Fair Lady* the "perfect musical."

including the luminous "I Could Have Danced All Night" and "I've Grown Accustomed to Her Face." Harrison, as Henry Higgins, enjoys every wink of his ironies: When he describes himself, in "I'm an Ordinary Man," his exaggerated demeanor suggests his character is anything but ordinary. That Harrison caught this specific dynamic so early in what became a historic extended run is remarkable. In a vivid illustration of how precarious these inflections can be, by the time of the 1959 London cast recording, he lost that gleam—he's no longer in on the joke—making the iridescent 1956 version the clear choice.

GENRE: 😊 Musicals. **RELEASED:** 1956, Columbia. **KEY TRACKS:** "I Could Have Danced All Night," "On the Street Where You Live." **COLLECTOR'S NOTE:** This 1956 original cast version includes interviews with the show's stars, taped at the conclusion of the recording session. **ANOTHER INTERPRETATION:** Jeremy Irons, Kiri Te Kanawa, London Symphony Orchestra (John Mauceri, cond.) **NEXT STOP:** Ella Fitzgerald: *Ella Sings Broadway.* **AFTER THAT:** Cole Porter: *Kiss Me Kate,* Original Broadway Cast.

Live at the Star Club, Hamburg

Jerry Lee Lewis

When he stepped onto the stage at the Star Club in April 1964, Jerry Lee Lewis was essentially washed up in the U.S. The self-described "old country boy, mean as hell," was several years past the golden moment in 1957 when he shot to stardom with his second single, a barn-burner called "Whole Lotta Shakin' Goin' On." The song introduced the high-energy Lewis, who along with Elvis Presley and others helped make the Sun Records roster the most potent in rock and roll. Then in December of that year, things changed when Lewis married his thirteen-year-old cousin. After riding

Lewis gives one of his famous rousing performances.

high, he was suddenly as cold as ice, shunned by radio. Over the next few years, nothing Lewis tried brought back the love.

So the Hamburg show should be just another night in the long and seemingly futile comeback campaign of an early rock also-ran. It sure doesn't sound that way. The pianist and singer, a rebel among the rebels at Sun, plays like a house afire, barreling through his ornery rockabilly—he knows that lesser acts are succeeding with tepid reworkings of his 1957 hits, and, of course, can't help but feel the Beatles breathing down his neck. Lewis throws himself into the show as though he's still a huge star, and, incredibly, he's treated that way: The devoted audience can be heard chanting "Jer-ry!" between songs and roaring approval when he roars.

Lewis pounds the piano as though intent on punishing it, and sings with rip-snorting intensity here. He's one of the few rock pioneers who, on any given night, can re-create the electrical charge of the moment when rock and roll was exploding for the first time, and he brings the patrons of the Star Club into that excitement. Virtually everything levitates—his hits and covers of others ("Hound Dog," "Good Golly Miss Molly") are bawdy and raucous. The band's wound as tight as a Swiss watch, but the old Lewis swagger, that droll and flip irreverence, keeps everything loose, and makes this one of the very best live albums in rock history.

GENRE: 🎸 Rock. **RELEASED:** 1964, Philips (Reissued 1994, Bear Family). **KEY TRACKS:** "Mean Woman Blues," "What I'd Say," "Hound Dog," "Long Tall Sally." **CATALOG CHOICE:** *Eighteen Original Sun Greatest Hits.* **BUYER BEWARE:** Lewis rerecorded his hits for the 1989 movie *Great Balls of Fire,* which starred Dennis Quaid; these versions are considerably less powerful than the originals. **NEXT STOP:** The Million Dollar Quartet (Lewis, Elvis Presley, Carl Perkins, Johnny Cash): *The Million Dollar Quartet.* **AFTER THAT:** Chuck Berry: *The Great Twenty-eight.*

Softness Through Strength

Besançon Festival, 1950

Dinu Lipatti

In a sense, Dinu Lipatti (1917–1950) was the James Dean of the classical piano world: A towering figure who burst on to the scene, blazed brightly for a minute, and disappeared just after attaining widespread fame. Originally from Romania, Lipatti emerged after World War II as a major pianist, but was diagnosed with leukemia and only managed a few years of solid recording before he died. (His entire recorded output fits on five CDs.)

This is a live recording of his farewell recital, recorded in 1950 when he was seriously ill. Lipatti selected pieces that were among his favorites—and then performed them as though renewing long-lost friendships and flirtations. Though he was unable to attempt the last of the fourteen Chopin waltzes, there's no trace of illness in these performances, nothing compromised about Lipatti's execution. Rather, it's possible to hear the characteristics of his playing that inspired reverence: the springwater clarity of his tone, the distilled simplicity of his phrasing. His Bach partita shows a gentleness that prefigures much modern pianistic interpretation. To play Mozart (the Piano Sonata No. 8 is here),

Lipatti brings both boundless energy and a great rhythmic reserve. The lines seem to bubble up from deep within the piano, and Lipatti's long fingers (a trait that gave him enviable control when playing widely spaced chords) do the rest.

Lipatti remains one of the world's pianistic marvels, thanks to this disc and the others the legendary EMI executive Walter Legge documented during Lipatti's brief lifetime. Legge once described Lipatti's gift as "softness through strength." That's an excellent summation of an artist who, in a short run, set a standard for sensitivity that few recitalists ever reach.

GENRE: 🎷 Classical. **RELEASED:** 1957, EMI. (Reissued 2004.) **KEY TRACKS:** Mozart: Piano Sonata No. 8. Chopin: Waltzes. **CATALOG CHOICE:** *Piano Concertos.* **NEXT STOP:** Claude Debussy: *Complete Works for Piano,* Aldo Ciccolini.

The Daredevil Show-Off of the Romantic Era

The Two Piano Concertos, The Piano Sonata

Franz Liszt

Sviatoslav Richter, London Symphony Orchestra (Kiril Kondrashin, cond.)

It's possible that Hungarian-born Franz Liszt (1811–1886) began composing just so he'd have something dazzling to play in concert. These pieces uphold that theory. The first rock star of classical music, Liszt was a piano demon from a young age, known for performances during which he'd dispatch difficult music at breakneck speed. His first two Concertos and the work many consider his greatest achievement, the Sonata in B minor, are daredevil works that aim, first, to thrill listeners, then seduce them with jaw-dropping melodies.

For these reasons, Liszt is tricky to play. He asks pianists to maintain composure while navigating Tony Hawk–style reverse spins and somersaults; the minute his lines start to sound "hard" or in any way calculated, the composer's spell is broken. Russian pianist Sviatoslav Richter understands this. He reads Liszt as a study in flickering lights and feathering runs, and breezes nonchalantly through the knottiest phrases. Recognizing that the material is plenty showy, Richter interprets the two Concertos with a minimum of flash. His steadiness, particularly during the intricate thematic reinventions of the Second Concerto, gives these pieces the gravitas they need.

When he gets to the Sonata, however, Richter pretty much puts Liszt on another level. The piece is a single continuous work, divided into four distinct sections; Richter treats the second one as a precious breakable jewel, treading lightly on the initial theme statement and bringing rapt attention to the extended pianissimo passage in the middle. It's as though Richter means to change the common perception of Liszt, suggesting that in choice moments, this composer known as a reckless risk-taker can actually communicate with a poet's tenderness.

GENRE: 🎼 Classical. **RELEASED:** 1988, Philips. (Concertos recorded in 1961, Sonata in 1988.) **KEY TRACKS:** Sonata in B Minor. Concerto No. 1: first movement. Concerto No. 2: second movement. **CATALOG CHOICE:** *Faust Symphony,* Kenneth Riegel, Boston Symphony Orchestra (Leonard Bernstein, cond.). **NEXT STOP:** Frédéric Chopin: *Études,* Maurizio Pollini. **AFTER THAT:** Olivier Messiaen: *Vingt regards sur l'enfant-Jésus* (see p. 498).

Little Known but Lots Amazing

Out Front

Booker Little

It's 1961. Ornette Coleman has just kicked the doors down with what hipsters are calling the "new" jazz. Guys like Eric Dolphy and Max Roach are playing high-profile bebop gigs, and then the next week find themselves mixing it up with insurrection-minded musicians in freer contexts. Of course, they're the rare birds who can go both ways: Camps and cliques are coalescing around ideologies. The older bebop-schooled guys scorn the free players as undisciplined. The free-jazz camp thinks the old guard is corny.

Into this contentious moment walks Booker Little, a young trumpet player with a warm, assured tone and a penchant for torrents of not-quite-bop that dodge and weave with great elegance. He's a composer, too, and that's where the real psych-out is: At a time when many around him are choosing sides, Little is seeking a musical accommodation, an approach that borrows wisdom from both camps. The songs on this provocative set seek wide-open vistas, and at the same time present the musicians with serious harmonic challenges, à la hard bop. They inspire solos of pure abandon and also much more carefully considered statements. (Listen to Little carve up the tempo changes he's loaded into the original "We Speak.")

The tunes are all stellar, but of particular note is "Man of Words." It's a tempoless contemplation Little wrote for the critic Nat Hentoff, who at the time ran the Candid label that issued this record, and it features some of Little's most searching, dramatic declarations.

Little's life story is tragically short. Born in Memphis, Tennessee, in 1938, he studied at the Chicago Conservatory, then moved to New York in 1958. His playing with Roach's group established him as one to watch—many considered his fleet, technically adept

Booker Little · Out Front

Booker Little and his Quintet featuring Max Roach

While attending the Chicago Conservatory, Booker Little shared a room at a YMCA with Sonny Rollins.

style to be the first new approach to the trumpet since Clifford Brown. Little recorded frequently as a sideman, and made only four records under his own name before he died, suddenly, of kidney failure in October 1961. He was twenty-three.

GENRE: 🅱 Jazz.
RELEASED: 1961, Candid.
KEY TRACKS: "We Speak," "Quiet, Please," "Moods in Free Time," "Man of Words."
CATALOG CHOICE: *Booker Little and Friend.* **NEXT STOP:** Lee Morgan: *Search for the New Land* (see p. 521). **AFTER THAT:** Wayne Shorter: *Speak No Evil.*

The First Rock and Roll Whirlwind

The Georgia Peach

Little Richard

Before popular music became a forum for deep thoughts about the human condition, it was mainly about *a-whop-bop-a-lu-bop.* It *was* Little Richard. Peeping and sliding and pounding the piano,

transmitting on a frequency of pure electric sensation, Richard embodied the spirit of rock and roll like nobody else. On his stage, rock was twitchy and irresistible, a highly addictive potion with no known antidote. You had to be ready for his blend of frenzied gospel, jump blues, and R&B, because with just a lurch into that heaven-bound falsetto, the diminutive Richard Penniman from Macon, Georgia, skipped the ramp-up and took you straight to the higher ground.

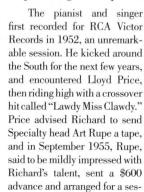

In his high school yearbook, Bob Dylan said his ambition was "to follow Little Richard."

The pianist and singer first recorded for RCA Victor Records in 1952, an unremarkable session. He kicked around the South for the next few years, and encountered Lloyd Price, then riding high with a crossover hit called "Lawdy Miss Clawdy." Price advised Richard to send Specialty head Art Rupe a tape, and in September 1955, Rupe, said to be mildly impressed with Richard's talent, sent a $600 advance and arranged for a session in New Orleans. Legend has it that after a frustrating morning spent recording blues songs,

Richard entertained the musicians at lunch with an impromptu romp through the explicit "Tutti Frutti Good Booty," which impressed the executive Bumps Blackwell so much he asked a local songwriter, Dorothy LaBostrie, to craft less explicit lyrics. The song, revised as "Tutti Frutti" and recorded in a flash, launched Little Richard. Over the next couple of years, Richard would define—and then exhaust—a singular rock and roll sound. His amazing string of singles, all represented on this comprehensive anthology, includes "Long Tall Sally," "Slippin' and Slidin' (Peepin' and Hidin')," and "Good Golly Miss Molly," as well as updates of pieces made famous by Louis Jordan ("Keep a Knockin'") and Jerry Lee Lewis (Richard does an absolutely blazing version of "Whole Lotta Shakin' Goin' On"). The explosion of interest led to appearances in movies (*The Girl Can't Help It*), and Richard blossomed into an international star—the Beatles opened for him in the U.K.

The ride ended as quickly as it began. In late 1957, Richard experienced a religious awakening that prompted the first of several "retirements." He attempted comebacks throughout the '60s, continued to be a powerful live performer, and eventually recorded several memorable gospel albums. Usually such a long period of "decline" is cause for lament. But with Little Richard—whose influence on Prince, James Brown, Michael Jackson, and others is unmissable—the initial contribution was so huge, it seems almost inevitable that his prime would be abbreviated. Nobody burns that brightly for long.

GENRE: 🎵 R&B. **RELEASED:** 1991, Specialty. **KEY TRACKS:** "Tutti Frutti," "Keep a Knockin'." **CATALOG CHOICES:** *Little Richard Is Back; God Is Real.* **NEXT STOP:** Esquerita: *Vintage Voola.* **AFTER THAT:** Jerry Lee Lewis: *Eighteen Original Sun Greatest Hits.*

A Closer Walk with a Rock Legend

Sings the Gospel

Little Richard

Gospel was more than the musical foundation for rock dynamo Little Richard—it also served as a refuge, sheltering him when the music business got too intense. Several times during his career, the illustrious Richard Penniman announced that he was "retiring" to make religious music. The first happened on the heels of the height of his popularity in 1957, another in the early '60s, which led to this, the best of his gospel collections. It's incandescent. Backed by a tight rhythm section (and a hand-clapping chorus on the jubilee numbers), the pianist and singer sails through gospel standards he probably

During his period of evangelism, Richard said that rock music was of the devil.

sang as a child—"Just a Closer Walk with Thee" and "Coming Home," which he begins with a preacherly sermon—as well as less familiar affirmations like "Every Time I Feel the Spirit." The minimal production shows off Penniman's roof-rattling and always authoritative voice, and even the tempoless devotionals rock with the fire Penniman poured into "Tutti Frutti." Only now, he's aiming at the heavens.

GENRE: 🎵 Gospel. **RELEASED:** 1964, 20th Century. (Reissued 1996, Prime Cuts.) **KEY TRACKS:** "I'm Tramping," "Every Time I Feel the Spirit," "Coming Home," "God Is Real." **NEXT STOP:** Louis Armstrong: *Louis and the Good Book.* **AFTER THAT:** Andrae Crouch: *The Best Of.*

A Party Band Goes Deep

Kiko

Los Lobos

To recover from the huge success of their remakes of "La Bamba" and "Come On, Let's Go" that were featured in a 1987 Ritchie Valens biopic, the East Los Angeles rock band Los Lobos tore off in extreme directions.

First they tried snarly loud rock, then quaint Mexican folk song. Eventually they wound up in the slightly spooky netherworld that is *Kiko*.

A loosely interlaced set of dream sequences dedicated to stolen pleasures and the challenges of living "on the short side of nothing," *Kiko* is the crowning achievement in the Los Lobos oeuvre, the record that balances the rowdy barrio attitude of their early music against deeper, more reflective elegies. When work on it began, the members of Los Lobos had a single goal: to create music that was fundamentally different from anything they'd done before. The first move was to hire producers Mitchell Froom (who brought along vintage tape-loop keyboards and other odd noisemakers) and Tchad Blake, who'd been part of a Lobos side project, the Latin Playboys. Drummer Louis Perez recalled that Froom and Blake "were coming off a giant hit with Crowded House, and wanted to do something new, too. So we threw away the formulas and surrendered to intuition."

The songs of *Kiko* were not prepared in advance, as had been the band's custom; they were written in the studio. Rather than build

Los Lobos translates to "the Wolves."

everything around a steady beat, Froom cultivated thick atmospheres, and encouraged the Los Lobos primary songwriting team, Perez and guitarist David Hidalgo, to use those as a starting point. As a result, some slower songs float along, wrapped in haunting shrouds of heavy-tremolo electric guitar, and even the barreling goodtime stomps, like "That Train Don't Stop Here," carry a shadowy undertone. Inspired by the less-restrictive settings, the songwriters came up with imagerich songs, three-minute shots of magic realism. These are made compelling by the utterly amazing guitarist and singer Hidalgo, whose weeping leads and wincing vocals speak the universal language of the blues—with none of the blues clichés.

GENRE: 🎸 Rock. **RELEASED:** 1992, Slash/Warner Bros. **KEY TRACKS:** "Angels with Dirty Faces," "Wake Up Dolores," "Kiko and the Lavender Moon," "That Train Don't Stop Here." **CATALOG CHOICE:** *How Will the Wolf Survive?* **NEXT STOP:** The Latin Playboys: *The Latin Playboys.* **AFTER THAT:** X: *Wild Gift* (see p. 878).

Music for That Swanky Cocktail Party

At Home/Around Midnight

Julie London

Jazz needs its sex kittens—the gals like Julie London, perpetually coy vocalists who don't break new ground, but instead offer an irresistible form of pillow talk. When instrumental jazz was evolving at a dizzying rate in the 1950s, singers like London—who, at the time, were not even considered jazz singers—provided necessary contrast, offsetting the instrumentalists' herculean feats with less abstract, playful treatments of familiar songs.

Perhaps best known as the foxy nurse on TV's *Emergency!* in the '70s, London spent much of the '50s as a chanteuse, recording a series of LPs with covers that presented her as an upmarket nightclub ingenue. Two of the most satisfying—*At Home*, which was recorded with a small jazz group in her living room, and *Around Midnight*, which showcases London with a large studio orchestra—were reissued on a single disc in 1996, and they offer an ideal way to appreciate this tempestuous talent. London knew how to sing sweet and low,

London recorded 32 albums.

and how to use the microphone to make it seem as though she were right beside you; her version of "You've Changed," from *At Home* (1959), is a series of whispers punctuated by the alert chords of guitarist Al Viola. Surprisingly, she conveys the same casual air when backed by a larger ensemble— see the breathy "Lush Life," with strings. No matter what's going on around her, London always maintains her sultry cool, slipping in half-step implications and flirty flourishes that gently expand these familiar songs.

GENRE: 🎵 Vocals. **RELEASED:** 1996, EMI. **KEY TRACKS:** "You've Changed," "Lush Life." **CATALOG CHOICE:** *Julie Is Her Name.* **NEXT STOP:** Anita O'Day: *Anita Swings the Most.*

The Long Lost DNA of Latin Jazz

Descargas: Cuban Jam Sessions in Miniature

Israel "Cachao" López y Su Ritmo Caliente

If you happened to wander into the forlorn downstairs bar of South Miami Beach's Waldorf Hotel in the early 1980s—before the Deco-architecture revival got going, and years before South Beach hit the fashionista party circuit—you might have encountered a non-descript trio playing "Guantanamera" and Latin-tinged lounge classics. This was music for chatting, not listening, and like countless other patrons, you probably wouldn't have paid much attention to the musicians. Mistake: On the bass there, working in an unassuming, almost invisible way, was one of the all-time legends of Cuban music—Israel "Cachao" López (1918–2008), whose résumé includes the invention of the mambo (1937), and the *descarga*, an informal structure for jamming, in 1957. This giant wasn't slumming, and his gig wasn't a case of how the mighty have fallen; López preferred playing to just about anything else, and, being a bass player, he was accustomed to a certain anonymity.

The backstory: Revered for his role anchoring some of the most exciting records ever made in Cuba, López left the country in 1962, three years after Fidel Castro rose to power. López settled first in New York, and played with some of the top Latin acts of the day—including Tito Rodriguez and Charlie Palmieri. He moved to Miami and planned on slowing down, but after a decade of mostly unheralded service in the Waldorf and other lounges, López was "rediscovered" in 1992 by the actor Andy Garcia, who spearheaded a

documentary. The film, *Como su ritmo no hay dos* (There Is No Rhythm like His), led to new music (the inspired *Master Sessions*, Vol. 1) and triggered a full-scale reappraisal of the quiet man known to musicians simply as Cachao.

This new interest eventually prompted a wave of CD reissues, including this trailblazing session and several other records made in Cuba in the late '50s. These are archival paydirt, superhot tracks recorded cleanly and with great care. López encourages an exceptionally tight Cuban rhythm section (featuring bongo master Yeyo Iglesias) to converse in the rapid-fire back-and-forth ethos associated with jazz; the term *descarga* also connotes sexual release, and there are plenty of eruptions here. Starting with just a skeletal frame, the players work together, in an "old world" atmosphere of mutual respect, to make the forays memorable. They do that and something more significant besides, catching the swaggering assertiveness and deep sense of romance that drives so much Cuban music.

GENRE: 🌐 World/Cuba. **RELEASED:** 1957, Panart. **KEY TRACKS:** "Oye mi tres montuno," "El manisero," "Trombone criollo." **CATALOG CHOICES:** *Master Sessions*, Vol. 1; *Jam Session with Feeling*. **NEXT STOP:** Las Estrellas del Arieto: *Los heroes* (see p. 262).

The Higher Power Has His Hands Full

Satan Is Real

The Louvin Brothers

Between verses of "Satan Is Real," the mandolin player and singer Ira Louvin offers a spoken allegory about the guy with the pitchfork. He knows that his listeners believe in God; his concern on this day is that they understand just how dangerous Satan is. "I grew selfish and unneighborly," the reverent man from the Alabama mountains confesses. "My friends turned against me, and finally my home was broken apart."

Even given the melodramatic bent of entertainment in the 1950s, such a caution-ary tale seems transparent, the cheap ploy of a radio preacher. But Ira Louvin makes it work. A mandolin player with a distinctive keening tenor voice and a reputation as a mean drunk (he died in a car accident after drinking), he projects concern for not just his audience but all of humanity. Each time he starts up a new verse, he sounds more determined to affect change in the lives of his listeners. He's not judging anyone's choices, just trying to make sure that the lost have all the facts, which he and his brother Charlie, one of the most formidable brother harmony groups of all time, deliver with galvanizing force.

Critics call this one of "the greatest iconic album covers of all time."

Everything on *Satan Is Real*—from the country weepers to the hillbilly rambles to the do-right songs cautioning against sin—has the air of true-believer righteousness. Split between songs the Louvins wrote for the occasion ("There's a Higher Power," "Are You Afraid to Die?") and pieces written by Nashville tunesmiths, *Satan*

Is Real is resolute country gospel pure and simple. Extolling the wonders of a caring God, the Louvins bring theology to the front porch in a way anybody who's strayed can understand.

GENRE: 🌑 Country.
RELEASED: 1960, Capitol.
KEY TRACKS: "There's a Higher Power," "Satan Is Real," "The Kneeling Drunkard's Plea."
F.Y.I.: For the album's all-time camp-classic cover, Ira Louvin built a twelve-foot-tall devil out of plywood and sprayed rocks with kerosene. By the time of the final snap, Charlie Louvin recalls, the duo was in some danger: "Those rocks, when they get hot, they blow up." **NEXT STOP:** Johnny Cash: *Hymns by Johnny Cash*. **AFTER THAT:** The Everly Brothers: *The Fabulous Style of the Everly Brothers*.

Two Bands, One Leader, Worlds Apart

Quartets:
Live at the Village Vanguard

Joe Lovano

Personality is crucial to jazz. Everything about the music can change, drastically, depending on the players involved, their curiosity, their inclination to connect with each other, and the vibe in the room.

This live two-CD set amounts to a primer on those dynamics, showing how a masterful improviser will adjust his approach to fit the surroundings. Each disc is devoted to a different band, with saxophonist Joe Lovano leading two different rhythm sections he played with regularly during the mid-1990s. One group, with the trumpeter Tom Harrell, hangs out at the far edges of modernism, utilizing elements of "free jazz" in crafty ways. The other, with

pianist Mulgrew Miller, is more rooted in the bebop tradition; its repertoire includes uptempo romps and tricky tunes by Thelonious Monk and John Coltrane.

Lovano doesn't completely change his stripes, but his playing does take on the character of each group. On the more agitated disc one, the rhythm section cultivates a careening, applecart-upsetting mode of discourse; this inspires Lovano to fits of phenomenal dexterity and fluttering, impossible-to-transcribe phrases. With the more traditional group on disc two, he trafficks in big beefy phrases that snag every offbeat and fleeting rhythmic permutation. And at the same time, he's a warm soul just singing through the horn: His solo on disc two's "Lonnie's Lament" is a typically endearing statement, full of broadly lyrical lines.

Lovano studied at the Berklee College of Music.

Lovano is one of the few soloists of his generation to gain training in the touring big bands (he spent time with Woody Herman). When he's really running hot, Lovano brings jazz history to life. In the same solo, he can sound like a growly barnstormer from the Basie band of the 1930s, or an effete avant-garde experimentalist whose art is all about "shapes and colors."

Each band reaches astonishing peaks. Listening to the two documents back-to-back, it's impossible to miss Lovano's sharp instincts and extraordinary flexibility, characteristics crucial to the dynamic of jazz. The music's moving in one direction, and then out of nowhere Lovano gets a wild idea. The scenery changes, and suddenly the music's on a different continent.

GENRE: 🅙 Jazz. **RELEASED:** 1996, Blue Note. **KEY TRACKS:** "Fort Worth," "Uprising," "Lonnie's Lament," "Reflections," "This Is All I Ask." **CATALOG CHOICES:** *Celebrating Sinatra; Joyous Encounter; On Broadway,* Vol. 3 (with Paul Motian and Bill Frisell). **NEXT STOP:** Dexter Gordon: *Go!* (see p. 318). **AFTER THAT:** Eric Alexander: *New York Calling.*

The Underside of the Summer of Love

Forever Changes

Love

There's the official historical record of the Summer of Love, available in countless documentaries. And then there's the alternative idea L.A.-based songwriters Arthur Lee and Bryan MacLean proffer on *Forever Changes*—

this one trades rampant hippie idealism for paranoia, portrays drug use as both illuminating and pathetic ("Live and Let Live" opens with an addict's realization, "Oh, the snot has caked against my pants"), and suggests that widespread mayhem, if not full societal breakdown, is right around the corner.

Somehow this cycle, written during an extended drug binge in a Hollywood mansion

Now considered a masterpiece, *Forever Changes*'s reception in 1967 was lukewarm.

where Bela Lugosi once lived, expresses these dark thoughts without becoming totally morose. Its apocalyptic scenarios come wrapped in lush strings, skittering harpsichords, and whimsical extended melodies. Years later, Lee recalled that when Love was working on these songs, he was convinced these words would be his last. That perhaps explains why *Forever Changes* feels so radical, it was made under a "nothing left to lose" cloud. At the same time, the gentlemen of Love still valued song structure: MacLean, who wrote the gorgeous opening track "Alone Again Or," once said that his background in musical theater impacted his mercurial partner Lee: "What you have (in Love) is a black guy from L.A. writing show tunes." But that's not all he (or Love) wrote: This album offers top-flight blues, folk-rock trippier than that of the Byrds, classic rock balladry, orchestral pop, and on and on.

It's hard to believe that such a diverse array of caustic, lavishly arranged, and often opaque songs grew out of the cultural moment of 1967. Love is profoundly out of step with the times, a brave (some would say necessary) counterpunch to the prevailing peace/love ethos. Not surprisingly, *Forever Changes* didn't fare well commercially. But over the years, it has become almost a sacred text. Inside these songs are ideas about guitar soloing that Lee's friend Jimi Hendrix rode into the stratosphere; hints of the mysticism and transcendence that became the calling card of the Doors; and the seeds of goth, orchestral pop, and other sub-genres. Few records of the era cast such a wide (and still lengthening) shadow.

GENRE: 🎸 Rock. **RELEASED:** 1967, Elektra. **KEY TRACKS:** "The Red Telephone," "A House Is Not a Motel," "Alone Again Or." **CATALOG CHOICE:** *Da Capo.* **NEXT STOP:** The Doors: *The Doors* (see p. 232). **AFTER THAT:** Syd Barrett: *The Madcap Laughs.*

An Epic of God, Country, and Cornbread

Joshua Judges Ruth

Lyle Lovett

Anyone who's ever endured a marathon sermon with a grumbling stomach will relate to Lyle Lovett's "Church." Over a sauntering-down-the-aisle beat, the smooth-talking Texan with the cockeyed pompadour tells of a preacher so caught up in the spirit he refuses to release his congregation. Eventually Lovett's hunger overtakes him, and he rises up with a prayer of his own: "To the Lord, let praises be, it's time for dinner now, let's go eat."

There's just a hint of desperation in Lovett's voice, which often has a stricken bewildered tone. But also there is an audible twinkle, and that's the key to Lovett's art. Like an urbane Mark Twain, Lovett pokes at self-obsessed fatuousness and assorted other human foibles. He's a parodist ever ready with the ironic wink (something genuinely new

Lovett's wild hair is almost as iconic as his music.

for roots music when he first appeared, and still extremely rare today). At the same time he's an incurable romantic, the rare storyteller capable of seizing all the possibilities within a song called "She's Leaving Me Because She Really Wants To." Yes, it's a high-irony critique of Nashville cliché. But it's also a disarmingly honest look at where a love went wrong. Much of Lovett's writing here—the extravagantly spiffy production numbers ("Since the Last Time") and the sullen landscapes ("North Dakota")—works in that wry way, on multiple levels. Get tired of Lovett the wisecracking country *enfant terrible*, and pretty soon Lovett the balladeer will show up, hat in hand, singing something that might make you cry.

GENRE: ◒ Country. **RELEASED**: 1992, MCA. **KEY TRACKS**: "She's Already Made Up Her Mind," "North Dakota," "You've Been So Good up to Now," "Church." **CATALOG CHOICES**: *Pontiac; And His Large Band.* **NEXT STOP**: Randy Newman: *Twelve Songs* (see p. 549). **AFTER THAT**: Robert Earl Keen Jr.: *No Kinda Dancer.*

Sign the Guest Book at the Church of Loretta

The Definitive Collection

Loretta Lynn

The teachings of the Church of Loretta: Respect women. Know exactly what you're doing in a moment of cheating flirtation. Don't demonize women who've gone through divorce. Take good care of the kids, even if you don't talk about 'em much. Most of all, love each other.

These and other lessons await in the plainspoken songs of Loretta Lynn, the singer who rose from poverty in a Kentucky coal town to become a country music legend. Most well known for her autobiographical song "Coal Miner's Daughter" (which spawned an autobiography and a feature film), Lynn is the first country feminist and one of the genre's great champions of ordinary people. She came along at a time when country lyrics were obsessively coy and offered a take-no-crap alternative—her blunt lyrics cut to the chase about those who sneak around. One of her big hits, "You Ain't Woman Enough (To Take My Man)," offers a withering appraisal of a floozy, while "Don't Come Home A-Drinkin' (With Lovin' on Your Mind)" takes an equally scornful view of a hard-partying man.

Lynn lived a full life before her recording career got started. The second of eight children, she's part Cherokee and grew up on land that was traversed in the forced migration of Native Americans known as the "Trail of

Lynn has had more banned songs than any other artist in the history of country music.

Tears." She was married a few months before her fourteenth birthday, and gave birth to four children in rapid succession— she became a grandmother by age twenty-nine. Her family moved to Nashville in the early '60s, and with help from Patsy Cline's producer Owen Bradley, Lynn's career took off in 1964 (when she was twenty-nine) with three Top 10 hits, including an indelible cover of "Blue Kentucky Girl." From there, she went on a tear, recording a series of megahits (she was the first woman to register fifty Top 10 singles) that sometimes landed her in hot water. Several of her original songs— "Rated X" and "The Pill"—were banned by country radio stations, but as Lynn observes in the liner notes of this anthology, the attention didn't exactly hurt: "They went to number 1 and sold more than the others."

This one-disc career overview contains most of Lynn's best-known songs and several of her ripped-from-real-life duets with Conway Twitty. Every one tells of some trying situation or reveals some dimension of character, some lesson Lynn picked up just living day to day. She shares them with you like a sympathetic big sister, so you don't make the same mistakes she did.

GENRE: ⊙ Country. **RELEASED:** 2005, MCA. **KEY TRACKS:** "Blue Kentucky Girl,"

"Rated X," "Coal Miner's Daughter," "Don't Come Home A-Drinkin' (With Lovin' on Your Mind)." **CATALOG CHOICE:** *Van Lear Rose* (produced by Jack White of the White Stripes). **NEXT STOP:** Conway Twitty: *She Needs Someone to Hold Her.* **AFTER THAT:** Reba McEntire: *My Kind of Country.*

"Turn It Up"

"Free Bird"

Lynyrd Skynyrd

The cry goes up whenever a rock show hits a slow patch. Somebody shouts "Free Bird," and all within earshot understand the message: This band better take things up a notch, and pronto. The natives are restless.

If only Skynyrd were here to show these pikers how to rock out properly.

A hit that became an all-purpose parody of rock excess, Lynyrd Skynyrd's 1973 "Free Bird" remains a polarizing artifact. Depending on whom you ask, it's either the dumbest contrivance to ever thrill an arena or the perfect rock odyssey, an instant cliché or a Southern stoner jam par excellence. Some have even argued that the nine-minute song is the American answer to Led Zeppelin's "Stairway to Heaven."

The band derived its name from members' high school gym teacher Leonard Skinner.

or the boogie-blues foundation of ZZ Top, so they keep the groove locked on a sturdy, dependable three-chord attack. This creates the perfect setting for guitar solos of epic proportion, and the band's three (!) lead players don't disappoint: The instrumental passages are a feast of harpooning long tones and whammy-bar hijinks that overlap into a torrid three-way conversation. Hearing the studio original and the even longer jam on *One More from the Road*, it's easy to dismiss the charge that Skynyrd traveled the same road to rowdy every night. But when the route's as engrossing as this one is, why mess with detours?

Underpinning the rebel-rock abandon is a fairly conventional build-to-the-climax song structure. "Free Bird" begins with a weepy and almost grand guitar melody; it takes several verses for the rhythm section to dislodge the ballad and start kicking ass. It's in this second episode where the musicians of Lynyrd Skynyrd (several of whom would die in a 1977 airplane crash) show their resourcefulness: They don't have the jazz dexterity of the Allman Brothers

---

GENRE: 🎸 Rock. **RELEASED:** 1974, MCA. **APPEARS ON:** *Pronounced Leh-Nerd Skin-Nerd; One More from the Road.* **NEXT STOP:** The Allman Brothers Band: *At Fillmore East* (see p. 16). **AFTER THAT:** .38 Special: *Wild-Eyed Southern Boys.*

Baaba Maal with Mansour Seck ✦ Guillaume de Machaut ✦ Madonna ✦ Madredeus ✦ Magic Sam ✦ The Magnetic Fields ✦ The Mahavishnu Orchestra with John McLaughlin ✦ Mahlathini and the Mahotella Queens ✦ Gustav Mahler ✦ The Mamas and the Papas ✦ Henry Mancini ✦ Thomas Mapfumo and the Blacks Unlimited ✦ Irén Marik ✦ Bob Marley and the Wailers ✦ The Mars Volta ✦ Martha and the Vandellas ✦ Pat Martino ✦ Bohuslav Martinů ✦ John Martyn ✦ Jules Massenet ✦ Johnny Mathis ✦ The Dave Matthews Band ✦ Nicholas Maw ✦ John Mayall with Eric Clapton ✦ Curtis Mayfield ✦ Les McCann and Eddie Harris ✦ Eugene McDaniels ✦ MC5 ✦ Kate and Anna McGarrigle ✦ Loreena McKennitt ✦ Sarah McLachlan ✦ Carmen McRae ✦ Blind Willie McTell ✦ Brad Mehldau ✦ M83 ✦ The Mekons ✦ Memphis Minnie ✦ Yehudi Menuhin ✦ Olivier Messiaen ✦ Metallica ✦ The Meters ✦ The Pat Metheny Group ✦ Arturo Benedetti Michelangeli ✦ The Mighty Diamonds ✦ Mighty Sparrow and Lord Kitchener ✦ Charles Mingus ✦ Ministry ✦ The Minutemen ✦ The Mississippi Sheiks ✦ Joni Mitchell ✦ Hank Mobley ✦ The Modern Jazz Quartet ✦ The Modern Lovers ✦ Juana Molina ✦ Thelonious Monk ✦ The Thelonious Monk Quartet with John Coltrane ✦ Bill Monroe ✦ Gabriela Montero ✦ Claudio Monteverdi ✦ Wes Montgomery ✦ Tete Montoliu ✦ Moondog ✦ Douglas Moore and John Latouche ✦ Jason Moran ✦ Beny Moré ✦ Lee Morgan ✦ Alanis Morissette ✦ Ennio Morricone ✦ Van Morrison ✦ Jelly Roll Morton ✦ Mos Def and Talib Kweli ✦ Mother Love Bone ✦ Paul Motian ✦ Wolfgang Amadeus Mozart ✦ Maria Muldaur ✦ Hugh Mundell ✦ Los Muñequitos de Matanzas ✦ Modest Mussorgsky ✦ Os Mutantes ✦ My Bloody Valentine ✦ My Morning Jacket

M

Pure Singing, from the Spirit Center

Djam Leelii

Baaba Maal with Mansour Seck

I f you close your eyes while listening to this, it's possible to imagine a solitary man, walking at a measured pace over vast plains. Maybe he's on a long journey, and to pass the time he sings to himself—for companionship, for strength,

for endurance. His words sound like prayers lit by a serene sense of reverence. There is no look-at-me ego in his game. He might be wandering, but he never loses contact with his spirit, never gets sidetracked by mankind's schemes and contrivances.

When he first emerged in the 1980s, Senegalese singer Baaba Maal sounded like he'd walked out of just such an African pastoral, carrying wisdom from earlier times. His first recordings (this one, which was recorded in 1984 but not released in the U.S. until 1989, is the best) display a fierce determination, the singing of a man on a mission. The musical surroundings are spare—often just Mansour Seck's acoustic

"Maal opened his mouth and beautiful pearls and lilies and songbirds came flying out."
—Michael Stipe

and electric guitars, and percussion—which leaves room for Maal's impossibly beautiful voice. It's at once calming and explosive, drawing equally on leonine strength and delicate beauty. Unlike some of his funk-leaning later works, these gently imploring declarations strike tones of humility, reserve, and passion in perfect measure.

GENRE: 🌐 World/Senegal. **RELEASED:** 1989, Island/ Mango. **KEY TRACKS:** "Lam tooro," "Muudo hormo," "Salminanam." **CATALOG CHOICE:** *Live at the Royal Festival Hall.* **NEXT STOP:** Youssou N'Dour: *Egypt.* **AFTER THAT:** Cheikh Lô: *Bambay Gueej.*

A Marvel of Medieval Music

Motets

Guillaume de Machaut
The Hilliard Ensemble

T he next time you find yourself numbed by the lockstep hammering of contemporary music, slip into this medieval marvel. Within seconds, you'll be transported 650 years into the past, to an echoey place where

five male voices sing in overlapping "parts" that are often in different languages, in a

church that gives every perfectly rounded vocal utterance special resonance. There's no modern frame of reference for this ancient form of blues, which is built on long, low, hollowed-out tones that seem to sustain indefinitely.

Guillaume de Machaut lived in fourteenth-century France. He was one of the few medieval composers who left detailed instructions about how his work was to be performed—most music of his time was transmitted orally. He had talent as a poet and these pieces utilize his words, which chronicle thoughts on love and spiritual questing through contrasting vocal parts. In the motet form, one elongated line states the basic "story" using a melody that would be recognizable to churchgoers. On top are two other texts—the "triplum" is a florid and usually verbose elaboration, and the "motetus" provides the story's moral lesson. As these texts align, they form a kind of meditation on the specific emotional state: The luminous "He Who Loves Most" tells about the anguish of unrequited love; beneath

the plot are deep tones of resignation, in such repeated phrases as "Thy will be done."

This 2004 recording of the Motets features England's Hilliard Ensemble, one of the most accomplished vocal groups devoted to early music. The words are often heated and intense, but the Hilliard voices are set at a cooler temperature—the singers don't embellish, delivering their lines with eerie detachment. This allows Machaut's often melancholy intent to glide right past the modern listener's external armor, and straight into the soul.

GENRE: 🌐 Classical. **RELEASED:** 2004, ECM. **KEY TRACKS:** "With Sighing, Suffering Heart," "Because Pity Does Not Wish," "He Who Loves Most." **NEXT STOP:** Hilliard Ensemble with Jan Garbarek: *Officium.* **AFTER THAT:** The Bulgarian Women's National Radio and TV Chorus: *Le mystère des voix bulgares* (see p. 130).

The Road from Naughty to Namaste

Ray of Light

Madonna

Once she stopped being the Material Girl and the transgressive wayward Catholic school student, after she'd exhausted every tricked-out voguing move and played every sex-taboo card available to a media-exploiting mythmaking superstar, Madonna got saved. By yoga.

Ray of Light is the account of her awakening. Or, depending on the perspective, her atonement.

It presents la diva Ciccone at her most reflective: Where in the past, her lyrics were extensions of whatever image-manipulation ploy she had in play, she's suddenly spouting

Ray of Light debuted at #2 on the *Billboard* Top 200 Albums chart.

cosmic truths—about devotion to higher ideals, about love as a redeeming force, about the merciless boomerang of karma. In these songs, love is something far loftier than the horny obsession she so expertly glorified on early singles, something precious and almost noble. She signals this change of heart, which allegedly grew out of her two-hour daily yoga practice, in the album's opener, which talks about how she confused the trappings of fame for love: "[I]t all became a silly game, some things cannot be bought."

With that, Madonna neatly flips the narcissism of club music into a soundtrack for the solo-journeying, ever-seeking higher self. She's aiming for the realm of the exalted, and amazingly, she hits the mark. The hustling loops, blipping electronic textures, and warm synthy strings created by electronic pioneer William Orbit (and others) cushion some of the most beguiling hooks she's written, among them "Nothing Really Matters" and the samba-tinged "To Have and Not to Hold." *Ray*

of Light stands alone in Madonna's catalog, largely because the contrivances are kept to a minimum. And because for the first time since her debut, she comes across as fully immersed in the possibilities of the music, not the marketing tricks she'll use to sell it.

GENRE: ✪ Pop. RELEASED: 1998, Maverick/Warner Bros. KEY TRACKS: "To Have and Not to Hold," "Ray of Light." CATALOG CHOICE: *The Immaculate Collection.* NEXT STOP: Sarah McLachlan: *Surfacing* (see p. 490). AFTER THAT: Krishna Das: *Breath of the Heart.*

Reflecting-Pool Calm

O espírito da paz

Madredeus

There are times in this information-overload culture when the bitstream of "news" becomes relentless and the signals grow irrevocably tangled, when nothing makes sense and the only solution seems to be to sit in a dark room and try to regain some measure of internal peace.

For those moments, there is Madredeus.

If ever songs of epic longing had healing properties, these do. They're remarkably centered short pieces, and though they bask in the melancholy quality the Portuguese call *saudade*, they communicate in uncluttered tones, radiating a calm missing from urban life. The mostly minor-key odes of *O espírito da paz* are based loosely on the Portuguese fado—that traditional pub music of endlessly mushrooming romantic disappointments. Here, the fado's confessions are surrounded by pensively plucked acoustic guitars, solemn cellos, and the occasional New Age synthesizer.

Though derided by some as "fado lite," these songs are deeply affecting because they are sung by a master of understatement, Teresa Salgueiro. Her luminous voice so captivated filmmaker Wim Wenders that he created a film, the 1994 *Lisbon Story*, around it. Salguiero uses little vibrato and no ornamentation, even in her weepy upper register. Rather than parading disappointments around, she simply leaves hints, and lets the laments speak for themselves. For whole stretches of this engrossing record, she's up there at seagull altitude where troubles are supposed to disappear, still carrying all kinds of hurt but sailing onward.

GENRE: 🌐 World/Portugal. RELEASED: 1994, Metro Blue. KEY TRACKS: "Silencio," "O mar," "Ajuda." CATALOG CHOICE: *Ainda* (the soundtrack to *Lisbon Story*). NEXT STOP: Mariza: *Fado Curvo.* AFTER THAT: Amália Rodrigues: *The Art of Amália Rodrigues* (see p. 654).

Chicago Blues, West Side Division, Defined

West Side Soul

Magic Sam

Guitarist and singer Magic Sam Maghett (1937–1969) began his career in Chicago in the late 1950s, a period of intense competition within the city's impossibly talent-rich blues scene. Not only were established masters like Muddy Waters and Willie Dixon in their prime, but younger rebels from the West Side, notably Buddy Guy and Otis Rush, were beginning to draw attention. You had to be wicked good or otherwise magical, just to get a gig.

To differentiate himself, Magic Sam developed a distinctive, treble-heavy guitar tone. He used a tightly controlled tremolo to add emphasis, and phrased in a way that made everything he played feel like a harpoon to the heart. His singing was similarly

Sam was Mississippi-born.

raw, with a touch of high-revving R&B attitude, à la Otis Redding. This combination defines *West Side Soul*, one of the most electrifying blues records of all time. It begins in a Memphis mood, with the slippery "That's All I Need," then visits John Lee Hooker–style hypnotic boogie ("I Feel So Good"), pure uptight agitation ("I Don't

Want No Woman"), painfully slow blues ("All of Your Love"), and a hard-shuffling version of Robert Johnson's "Sweet Home Chicago."

West Side Soul grows more intense as it goes along—after eight tracks, Magic Sam launches the whiplashing instrumental "Lookin' Good," three minutes and eleven seconds of locked-tight rhythm-guitar groove that reveals a whole new aspect of his art. He died the year after this came out, leaving behind a legacy of jaw-dropping club performances and just two radiant records.

GENRE: 🔵 Blues. **RELEASED:** 1967, Delmark. **KEY TRACKS:** "Sweet Home Chicago," "I Don't Want No Woman," "Lookin' Good." **NEXT STOP:** Buddy Guy: *Damn Right, I've Got the Blues* (see p. 332).

Looking at Love from Every Possible Angle

Sixty-nine Love Songs

The Magnetic Fields

This is one of those high-concept ideas that seems totally awesome at first. But then when you think about it, the prospect of hearing sixty-nine songs, all on the subject of love, has all the allure of three hours at a poetry reading. In a folding chair.

Here the chamber-pop band the Magnetic Fields, led by the wobbly voiced auteur (and occasional music critic) Stephin Merritt, examines love the way Melville looked at the ocean—with wariness and admiration, with a compulsive need to account for every ripple, with all precious metaphors and far-flung images at the ready.

On these three well-stuffed CDs, there are grand long-winded verses in the Gilbert and Sullivan tradition. There are eerie electronic studies in desolate disaffection. There are Gershwinesque affirmations of love's redeeming power and bitter, scowling torch songs about how romance is just not good for you. And, oh, yes, there are more than a few confessions of black-hearted souls who are deeply and irreversibly obsessed, among them a country rocker called "I Don't Want to Get Over You" and an eerie meditation called "Love Is like a Bottle of Gin" that muses on the illusory comfort both provide. Often, one song "answers" another: "(Crazy for You But) Not That Crazy" is the voice of the hangover, when reason takes over after love's gotten to be too much like gin.

"*69 Love Songs* is . . . an album about love songs, which are very far away from anything to do with love." —Stephin Merritt

You'd think that so many variations on the same theme would become tiresome after a while. Quite the opposite. Merritt is a sucker for romance in all its seasons, and as he travels from dance-floor flirtations to statements of serious devotion to tearful accounts of breakups (one of the best of these is titled "The Cactus Where Your Heart Should Be"), he catches stray, often touching insights into human nature. He's also enough of a musician to recognize that in order to sell his pithy wares, he needs to present them in a range of colors, textures, and sizes. The diversity of sounds rescues *Sixty-nine Love Songs* from High Concept Overdrive, and gives it an amorphous musical identity, the sound of lives lived in the real world. You might not want to take on this megadose in one sitting. But you could.

GENRE: 🎵 Rock. **RELEASED:** 1999, Merge. **KEY TRACKS:** "I'm Sorry I Love You," "If You Don't Cry," "I Don't Want to Get Over You," "Very Funny." **CATALOG CHOICE:** *i* (each song begins with the letter *i*). **NEXT STOP:** Sufjan Stevens: *Illinoise* (see p. 742). **AFTER THAT:** Jack Logan: *Bulk*.

A Flame Undimmed by Time

The Inner Mounting Flame

The Mahavishnu Orchestra with John McLaughlin

If Jimmy Page's guitar attack made Led Zeppelin the "Hammer of the Gods," then John McLaughlin's work with Mahavishnu Orchestra is the "Devil's Needlepoint." A cool Brit with Eastern spiritual leanings and seemingly limitless six-string technique, McLaughlin plays as if running an agility course, nailing small details while engineering statements that can take your breath away. His majestic lines, both the "written" melodies and the improvised derivations, come blazing across the soundscape. More than once you may hear one of these lurching riffs, which usually chug along in some odd time signature, and wonder "What kind of a mind thinks up stuff like this?"

Answer: A restless one. By the time he formed this group, McLaughlin had established himself as part of the rapidly coalescing jazz-rock-fusion movement, first with Miles Davis during the famed *Live/Evil* sessions, then as part of the Tony Williams Lifetime (see p. 866). On his website, McLaughlin recalls that after playing a gig with Davis in a Boston club in 1970, Davis told him it was time to form his own band. The guitarist listened: "If he says it, it must be true." The first incarnation of Mahavishnu was in place by Feburary 1971; this recording was made after just two weeks of live performances. It's clear that everyone's on the same mission: They crank the fusion rhythms that Davis pioneered up faster and louder, creating a whiplash-inducing pulse that seems forever on the verge of exploding.

Two adjacent tracks on this consistently amazing debut, "Noonward Race" and "A Lotus on Irish Streams," reveal Mahavishnu's

Bandleader and guitarist John McLaughlin composed all of the songs on *The Inner Mounting Flame.*

range. The former is a panicky up-tempo whirlwind powered by virtuoso drummer Billy Cobham. It features solos by McLaughlin, who frequently relies on a double-neck guitar for extra textural possibilities, as well as violinist Jerry Goodman and keyboardist Jan Hammer, whose electric piano positively crackles.

The tune lasts six minutes, and after its tricky passages and all-out intensity, the tempoless "A Lotus" seems almost too tranquil. But this beautiful theme is demanding in a different way; it requires the five musicians to bring the cohesion of the up-tempo stuff to delicate, slowly unraveling themes. This they do with great care. Having established that they can play virtually anything, the group discovers that a different kind of profundity blossoms when they play nearly nothing.

GENRE: 🎷 Jazz. **RELEASED:** 1971, Columbia. **KEY TRACKS:** "Meeting of the Spirits," "Noonward Race," "A Lotus on Irish Streams," "You Know You Know." **CATALOG CHOICE:** *Birds of Fire.* **NEXT STOP:** King Crimson: *Larks' Tongues in Aspic.* **AFTER THAT:** Tortoise: *TNT.*

A Groaner Goes Global

Paris/Soweto

Mahlathini and the Mahotella Queens

It's impossible to overstate the impact Paul Simon's *Graceland* had on African music. The artists who were prominently featured on the album became celebrities, and even talents who weren't directly involved –suddenly found themselves with bookings in Europe and the United States. Among the most unusual cases was the man known as the Lion of Soweto, a bass-voiced "groaner" who'd

been on the scene when South African township jive, aka *mbaqanga* music, was just getting started: Simon "Mahlathini" Nkabinde (1937–1999).

Mahlathini, whose showbiz name translates as "jungle on his head" (a reference to his warriorlike presence), has a voice that's so coarse you don't expect much entertainment from it. He sings in a straightforward, declarative manner, with no pretense at all—he's a teller of truths, not some artiste. Halfway through the shimmering opener "Kazet," he hums, almost to himself, a gravelly response to the carefree airborne refrain sung by his three background singers, the Mahotella Queens. It's just a monosyllabic grunt, so low it blends in with the bass and is easily missed. Once you pick it up, you realize how important it is to the overall sound: This unusual animalistic tone contrasts powerfully with the sweetness of the surroundings.

This album was recorded in Paris (the European locus of African music) in 1989, after the ensemble finished its first post-*Graceland* international tour. With the exception of one ill-advised Art of Noise experiment, its songs are relentlessly springy township jive, with shining vocal refrains in several languages and elastic, gravity-defying rhythms. For all Mahlathini's overt and covert scene-stealing, this potent music depends on an array of forces, most definitely including the band led by saxophonist West Nkosi and the three Mahotella Queens. These women, known for their intricate dance steps, sing the hooks of these songs in waves of pure uplift—the next time you need music that affirms the human spirit, check out "Melodi ya lla" or "Re ya dumedisa," and prepare to smile.

GENRE: 🌐 World/South Africa.
RELEASED: 1987, Celluloid/Polydor. **KEY TRACKS:** "Kazet," "Safa indlada," "Melodi ya lla," "Re ya dumedisa." **CATALOG CHOICE:** The Lion of Soweto. **NEXT STOP:** Ladysmith Black Mambazo: Shaka Zulu. **AFTER THAT:** Various Artists: Guitar Paradise of East Africa.

A Child's View of Heaven

Symphony No. 4

Gustav Mahler

Royal Concertgebouw Orchestra (Willem Mengelberg, cond.)

When this recording of a 1939 performance was first issued, in 1960, some scholars derided conductor Willem Mengelberg's elastic, shapeshifting interpretation. They charged that even though Mengelberg knew Mahler (and had been present at rehearsals for the piece, which was completed in 1901), the conductor let the tempos slide around, and took other liberties with the work that closes Mahler's *Wunderkind* phase. Later, as musicians revisited the score, it became clear that Mengelberg was not sensationalizing, but instead following Mahler's instructions. To the letter.

This was easy to do, because the Austrian composer didn't take anything for granted—he was a micromanager, notating slight changes (of tempo and emphasis) to ensure that every desired effect happened as he intended. Throughout this piece, which explores the unique insights and perceptions of children, Mahler (1860–1911) creates animated lines defined by sudden impulses—a lyrical theme will dart ahead, only to freeze momentarily before the chase begins anew.

By following Mahler's intentions, Dutchborn Mengelberg uncovers nuances lost in the "straight tempo" readings of conductors like Herbert von Karajan. Consider the astounding third movement. Where others render the theme with militaristic precision, Mengelberg concentrates on Mahler's curiosity about the "paranormal"—he works the strings into a celestial body that hovers above the ground, floating from one transcendent state to another without bothering with questions of tempo or meter. The Fourth is sometimes dismissed as "Mahler lite," and to be sure, it's more approachable than the stormier symphonies that followed. Partly inspired by a book of folk poems entitled *Das Knaben Wunderhorn*, it's also among Mahler's most beautiful creations. To zoom in on that aspect, locate the unconventional final movement, which features a solo soprano voice (on this recording, Jo Vincent) singing about a child's vision of heaven. It's a fairy-tale place—with abundant food and unlimited time for play—and yet, Mahler being Mahler, the fantasy is wrought with exquisite details. And, naturally, it comes with less-sugary undercurrents, hints of the tragic, the gloomy, and the bittersweet.

In addition to composing, Mahler was a successful conductor.

GENRE: 🎵 Classical. **RELEASED:** 1960, Philips. (Recorded 1939.) **KEY TRACK:** Third movement. **ANOTHER INTERPRETATION:** Berlin Philharmonic (Herbert von Karajan, cond.). **CATALOG CHOICES:** Symphony No. 8, Chicago Symphony Orchestra (Georg Solti, cond.); Symphony No. 2, New York Philharmonic (Bruno Walter, cond.). **NEXT STOP:** Dimitri Shostakovich: Symphonies 1 and 7, Chicago Symphony Orchestra (Leonard Bernstein, cond.). **AFTER THAT:** Maurice Ravel: *Daphnes et Chloë*, Montreal Symphony Orchestra (Charles Dutoit, cond.).

A Master Ponders Ways to Say Good-bye

Das Lied von der Erde

Gustav Mahler

Christa Ludwig, Fritz Wunderlich,
Philharmonia Orchestra (Otto Klemperer, cond.)

A s every Tin Pan Alley tunesmith knows, there are a million ways to say good-bye. The Austrian composer Gustav Mahler offers one of the most deeply affecting with his late set of symphonic songs *Das Lied von der Erde*

(The Song of the Earth). "The Farewell," which lasts around thirty minutes, follows a melancholy soul as he makes his long passage into the Next World.

It starts at dusk, with the sun sinking behind mountains. The protagonist, sung here by mezzo-soprano Christa Ludwig, draws attention to different nature images ("see how the moon above floats like a silver ship"); the orchestra diminishes correspondingly, until it's possible to hear the low strings of the harp, and the whisper of a flute. The lyrics focus on interior thoughts until, around fourteen minutes in, there's a pronounced shift—into a black-overcoat funeral march. The final moments of the piece suggest a transition to the afterlife, with the voice eerily trailing off as it reports that "horizons are blue and bright!"

Written during a feverish final creative burst that also yielded his massive Symphony No. 9 (see below) and the unfinished Symphony No. 10, this is one of the world's great elegies—German conductor and composer Bruno Walter once called it "the most personal utterance among Mahler's creations, and perhaps in all music." It's also among Mahler's more direct personal statements, music he wrote as he confronted his own demise. Ludwig and tenor Fritz Wunderlich both sound as if they're right in the middle of the conflict Mahler imagines, torn between life on earth and the quiet seductions of the afterlife.

The conductor, Otto Klemperer, was in a position to know what the composer intended—for a while during his early career, he served as Mahler's assistant. He conducts Mahler with a deep understanding, emphasizing certain sonorities so that the earth (or death) nearly assaults our senses. More than mere knowledge of Mahler is in play; this performance glows with a genius that transcends earthly concerns.

GENRE: 🎸 Classical. **RELEASED:** 1967, EMI. **KEY TRACKS:** "Von der Jugend," "Der Abschied" (The Farewell). **ANOTHER INTERPRETATION:** Kathleen Ferrier, Julius Patzak, Vienna Philharmonic (Bruno Walter, cond.). **CATALOG CHOICE:** Symphony No. 8, Staatskapelle Berlin (Pierre Boulez, cond.). **NEXT STOP:** Richard Strauss: *Four Last Songs* (see p. 750). **AFTER THAT:** Sergey Rachmaninoff: *All-Night Vigil* (see p. 625).

Nine Was Enough

Symphony No. 9

Gustav Mahler

Berlin Philharmonic (Herbert von Karajan, cond.)

Even the mighty Gustav Mahler couldn't escape the Ninth Symphony curse. He was well aware, as he began work on this epic, that many of the world's great composers (Beethoven, Bruckner, Schubert, and Dvořák among them) died before they could finish a tenth symphony, so when his choral work *Das Lied von der Erde* (see previous page) was premiered, Mahler initially declared it his Ninth so that this gargantuan piece, well under way, could be Number Ten. Just one problem: *Das Lied* isn't a symphony. Mahler completed the Ninth and was halfway through the follow-up when his heart gave out.

Though it doesn't start out that way, the Ninth most definitely is conceived as a full-throttle Big Orchestra experience. It also is generally considered a milestone, the last great work of the Romantic era. Mahler inverts the customary emotional topography of the four symphonic movements: His opening and closing segments are cast in slow and ruminative moods, while the middle two movements are brisk, and full of animated dancelike episodes. This can puzzle those expecting the typical arc of an orchestral work, but it suits Mahler's aims: The languid, surprisingly lyrical initial motifs lure listeners in, establishing a hypnotic state that carries through the caprices that follow. By the time the swollen chords of the final movement roll in, there's no need for a sirens-blazing finale—a more modest invitation to thought and reflection will suffice.

The shimmer coming from the string section during the fourth movement, one of Mahler's finest, is reason enough to seek out this live recording, which was made near the end of Herbert von Karajan's tenure with the Berlin. The group was deservedly famous for its depth of tone, and while that's evident here, even more remarkable is the ensemble unity; on the stupendous Molto Adagio, the musicians lock into a vibrato pattern that carries from the lowest voice to the highest. This knits the threads of the piece together in a remarkable way—it sounds like the whole ensemble is breathing together. Karajan cultivated that group dynamic, and uses it brilliantly in the symphony's final moments, when Mahler several times pushes things to the edge of tension. Some conductors read Mahler's manipulations literally, creating in the final movement a constant ricochet between peaks and valleys. Karajan, never a composer's errand boy, concerns himself more with the ramp-up and the cooldown, and by taking his time between extremes, celebrates the full magnificence of Mahler's schemes.

***

GENRE: 🎼 Classical. **RELEASED:** 1983, Deutsche Grammophon. **KEY TRACKS:** Fourth movement: Molto Adagio; second movement: Poco piu mosso subito. **CATALOG CHOICE:** Symphony No. 5, Chicago Symphony Orchestra (Georg Solti, cond.). **NEXT STOP:** Anton Bruckner: Symphony No. 4, Berlin Philharmonic (Simon Rattle, cond.).

***

Homesickness, Spun Sweetly

"California Dreamin'"

The Mamas and the Papas

Written by John Phillips on a frigid Manhattan night in the winter of 1962, when his girlfriend, Michelle, was homesick for Southern California, "California Dreamin'" is one of the all-time great songs of

longing. Phillips came up with its chord structure in the wee hours and woke up Michelle before dawn to get help with the lyrics. In an NPR interview decades later, Michelle remembered telling him about visiting a church when she was out for a walk: "I just loved going into churches. And that's where we got the lyric for the second verse." That verse begins: "Stopped into a church I passed along the way/Well, I got down on my knees, and I pretend to pray."

The group, from left: Mama Cass Elliot, Denny Doherty, Michelle Phillips, and John Phillips.

The song became the group's first single. Released in November 1965, it hit the Top 10 in January '66, even though radio stations in the group's adopted hometown of Los Angeles rejected the song. It wasn't until a Boston station began playing it that the Mamas and the Papas' smooth, folk-influenced harmonies caught on. While it never reached the top spot, the song stayed on the charts for seventeen weeks and propelled the group into stardom.

Another measure of the song's incandescence are the distinctly different interpretations it has inspired over the years: Jose Feliciano's 1968 version played up the song's melancholy, while Funkadelic guitarist Eddie Hazel made it a platform for wriggling improvisation on *Games, Dames, and Guitar Thangs*. Queen Latifah, meanwhile, sang it as a brassy production number on *The Dana Owens Album.* The original remains a marvel: The Mamas and the Papas were studio newbies when they recorded "California Dreamin'," but they knew how their four beautifully meshed voices lift a simple feeling—homesickness—to the realm of great art.

GENRE: 🌑 Rock. **RELEASED:** 1965, Dunhill. **APPEARS ON:** *If You Can Believe Your Eyes and Ears.* **NEXT STOP:** Fleetwood Mac: *Rumours.* **AFTER THAT:** The Grass Roots: *The Grass Roots Greatest Hits.*

An Instant Classic

Breakfast at Tiffany's

Henry Mancini

For a time in the 1960s, Henry Mancini (1924–1994) was the grand master of the iconic theme song. His pulse-quickening motif for *Peter Gunn,* the early television crime show, inspired a wave of copycats, and his slinky music for *The Pink Panther* provided the film series with an instantly familiar musical signature—hear two measures and you know who's about to enter the picture.

Mancini's most decorated work, though, is the music he wrote for the 1961 adaptation of Truman Capote's novel *Breakfast at Tiffany's,* which starred Audrey Hepburn as the young New York socialite Holly Golightly. Almost overnight, its title waltz "Moon River," with lyrics by Johnny Mercer, became a standard, reinterpreted by countless singers and musicians; there are now over a thousand recordings of it. The score brought Mancini two Oscars and five Grammy Awards.

"Moon River" is just plain beautiful, even when reimagined, somewhat improbably, as a big-band cha-cha. (Both the original and the Latin versions are included on this suite of selections from the score, which was recorded after the film's release and remains the best representation of its music.) Just as impressive, though, are the less-celebrated tunes Mancini

Audrey Hepburn called her role as Holly Golightly "the jazziest of my career."

wrote for the film. From his first professional opportunities, the composer displayed a knack for sweet, enduring melodies. *Breakfast* offers a staggering array of those, in styles ranging from lounge bossa nova ("Sally's Tomato") to cha-cha ("Latin Golightly") to brisk and showy big-band jazz ("The Big Blow Out"). Don't be surprised if, after hearing these tunes a few times, you find yourself humming them. That's the "Mancini magic" at work.

GENRE: ✴ Pop. **RELEASED:** 1962, RCA. (Reissued 1986.) **KEY TRACKS:** "Moon River," "Sally's Tomato," "The Big Blow Out," "Hub Caps and Tail Lights." **CATALOG CHOICE:** *The Pink Panther,* Original Motion Picture Soundtrack. **NEXT STOP:** Quincy Jones: *The Pawnbroker,* Original Motion Picture Soundtrack. **AFTER THAT:** Burt Bacharach: *Butch Cassidy and the Sundance Kid,* Original Motion Picture Soundtrack.

The Lion of Zimbabwe Roars Here

Chimurenga Singles, 1976–1980

Thomas Mapfumo and the Blacks Unlimited

Hearing Thomas Mapfumo's passionately sung missives one after the other is a little like watching a film montage of newspaper headlines flashing across the screen. They chronicle the tumult in Zimbabwe during the 1970s: The singer and songwriter grew up in an area where revolution against the white minority government was coalescing. Mapfumo began recording songs that spoke about governmental corruption and neglect. Eventually, with sharp-tongued missives like "Mothers, Send Your Sons to War," his rhetoric escalated into direct calls for violent action.

Before long, Mapfumo's music became a key part of the revolution—he called the sound "chimurenga," which means "struggle" in the Shona language—and used his songs to rally a growing revolutionary movement. Much of what he talks about on these singles became part of (or echoed) ideas in public discourse, and when Robert Mugabe was elected in 1980, Mapfumo went from being an enemy of the state to a folk hero, sharing the stage at a celebratory concert with Bob Marley. (He's since been critical of the Mugabe government.)

Mapfumo's music is modern, often utilizing a Western-style drum kit and (occasionally) a horn section. But it carries distinct traces of traditional Shona songs—on some pieces here, the electric guitar outlines the cyclical patterns of the Shona *mbira* (a *kalimba*-like instrument with forged metal keys). The rhythms just simmer along, a steady mesmeric backing that contrasts with Mapfumo's riveting gut-level exhortations. The revolution that inspired these songs is in the past. But Mapfumo's sense of indignation, and his knack for speaking truth to power, makes the music eternal—the rare case where a musician starts out trying to galvanize a specific audience and winds up with something strong enough to hit everybody.

GENRE: 🌐 World/Zimbabwe. **RELEASED:** 1989, Shanachie. (Recorded between 1976 and 1980.) **KEY TRACKS:** "Kwaedza mu Zimbabwe," "Nyarai," "Munhu mutema." **NEXT STOP:** Salif Keita: *Soro.*

A Talent Preserved by Private Recordings

Bartók in the Desert: The Art of Irén Marik

Irén Marik

The story of Hungarian pianist Irén Marik (1905–1986) starts out seeming fairly typical. She emigrated to the U.S. in 1946 when the Soviets moved into Hungary, one of many European musicians who fled Europe to either escape the Nazis, the war, or its unnerving aftermath. Like others who were similarly displaced, she abandoned hopes of a concert career in favor of a stable, and much less visible, existence as a piano teacher. She settled in the desert, near Death Valley, California.

But Marik did not stop playing the piano. A product of Budapest's Liszt Academy and one of the very few students of composer Béla Bartók, she simply pursued music for herself. She continued to practice, often seven hours a day, and had a habit of giving informal concerts for friends. Some of these were recorded, by Marik or others, for purposes of study—legend has it that she threw away ones she felt were inferior, only to have them rescued from the trash bin by neighbors. *Bartók in the Desert* gathers some of her greatest home-recorded hits. Just the range of repertoire is impressive: Marik spins blithely through Bartók's Rondo No. 1 on Folk Themes, devours Beethoven's Piano Sonata No. 30, and plays Liszt's "Apparitions" in bursts of hyper-

After defecting to the U.S., Marik never returned to her homeland of Hungary.

clarity, as if she's trying to pin down an elusive ghost.

Marik told people she didn't learn much from Bartók. But she clearly absorbed some things by being in his orbit— she was part of a serious music culture in Budapest, and that culture informs the interpretations of her later years, which have the severity often associated with Hungarian pianists (notably Annie Fischer) and at the same time a more visceral streak. Discovered by Allan Evans, the founder of Arbiter Records, a label that specializes in obscure pianists, Marik symbolizes something truly rare: an artist pursuing music not for fame or fortune or other external rewards, but for the all-consuming love of it.

GENRE: 🎵 Classical. **RELEASED:** 2004, Arbiter. **KEY TRACKS:** Bartók: "Romanian Folk Dances," Rondo No. 1 on Folk Themes. Beethoven: Piano Sonata No. 30. **CATALOG CHOICE:** *From Bach to Bartók.* **NEXT STOP:** Simon Barere: *The Last Recording Sessions.*

Marley's Breakthrough Moment

Natty Dread

Bob Marley and the Wailers

The original Wailers were first poised to explode in 1973, with the international release of *Catch a Fire,* which had been remixed and sonically enhanced to appeal to rock fans. Despite a tour featuring

one of the most awesome Jamaican bands ever, with Bob Marley (1945–1981) alongside the contrasting voices of Bunny Livingston (aka Bunny Wailer) and Peter Tosh, success didn't come. Six months later, despite another strong record (*Burnin'*), the Wailers still didn't erupt—if anything, the band was barely oozing

into pop consciousness. Not until Eric Clapton covered the *Burnin'* track "I Shot the Sheriff" did reggae reach worldwide consciousness.

With "Sheriff" clearing a path, Island Records seized the moment. It put Marley's name out front—suddenly the band was known as "Bob Marley and the Wailers"—and the frontman and principal songwriter did his part, delivering what is arguably the most tuneful reggae album of all time, *Natty Dread.*

Recorded after the Wailers' first extensive tours outside Jamaica, *Natty Dread* combines the grinding rhythms of the band's early sides with a sweet, one-love sensibility calibrated to enchant pop ears. The Wailers had undergone radical change—both Tosh and Livingston departed just before this recording, replaced by a trio of female singers called the I-Threes. Marley seems emboldened by the new possibilities; he loosens up and adds more aphorisms to his lyrics, and through songs like "Lively Up Yourself" invites listeners to join him in a place where the dance floors are made of rubber.

The album became a hit, propelling Marley toward legend status. Among the unexpected consequences: Thousands of American and British kids newly addicted to reggae went searching for anything by the Wailers. As a result, the group's stupendous early albums (*African Herbsman*, which contains rougher versions of "Lively Up Yourself" and "Duppy Conqueror") and the titles immediately preceding *Natty Dread* finally got the attention they deserve.

GENRE: ⊕ World/Jamaica. **RELEASED:** 1974, Tuff Gong/Island. **KEY TRACKS:** "No Woman No Cry," "Them Belly Full but We Hungry," "Talkin' Blues," "Bend Down Low." **CATALOG CHOICES:** *African Herbsman; Catch a Fire.* **NEXT STOP:** Peter Tosh: *Legalize It.* **AFTER THAT:** Toots and the Maytals: *Funky Kingston* (see p. 778).

Movement of Jah People

Exodus

Bob Marley and the Wailers

A s his international stature grew in the late 1970s, Bob Marley became an engine of idealism, using his music to talk about deplorable situations and daring to dream of societies where all are equal. His consciousness-raising works—particularly this album and the Africa-centered *Survival*, which is nearly as good—are never sanctimonious, but so rich with humanity and compassion that they stir those same qualities in listeners.

Exodus is Marley's best studio album—*Time* magazine once named it the "album of the century." It was recorded in London, where Marley relocated after being injured in a 1976 murder attempt at his

In 1978, Bob Marley, by then internationally renowned, was awarded the Peace Medal of the Third World from the United Nations.

home in Jamaica. The opening songs (for vinylheads, "side one") find Marley turning away from the day-to-day struggle, his customary subject, and instead addressing metaphysical concerns, mixing the lofty language of a spiritual seeker with the urgent tones of an insurrectionist. The second "half" comes back down to earth, via a collection of sweet and worshipful love songs ("Three Little Birds") and dance-party reggae (the springy "Jammin'"). The Wailers here are in rare form—

streamlined, supertight beats are bolstered by rumbling, elastic funk, and the serenely steady rhythm guitar of Junior Marvin.

By the time this album appeared, lots of music people outside Jamaica revered reggae; it had moved beyond exotic novelty to become almost a social movement, a communal spiritual experience. You can detect that throughout *Exodus*, particularly on the closing medley, which finds Marley connecting his utopian original "One Love" to the classic Curtis Mayfield hymn "People Get Ready." This is one of those tracks all humanity should hear—a prayer for love and understanding from a voice of pure idealism, whose every utterance is an affirmation. Listen, and believe.

GENRE: 🌐 World/Jamaica. **RELEASED:** 1977, Tuff Gong/Island. **KEY TRACKS:** "Jammin'," "So Much Things to Say," "Three Little Birds," "One Love/People Get Ready." **CATALOG CHOICES:** *Survival; Legend.* **NEXT STOP:** Steel Pulse: *Earth Crisis.* **AFTER THAT:** The Heptones: *Night Food.*

A Transmission from the "Other Side," in Scream-o-Vision

The Bedlam in Goliath

The Mars Volta

Acccording to Mars Volta guitarist and songwriter Omar Rodriguez-Lopez, the spirit world deserves some credit for his band's fourth album, *The Bedlam in Goliath*. The story: Lopez found a Ouija board in a Jerusalem curio shop, and bought it for his bandmate, singer and lyricist Cedric Bixler-Zavala. On tour, the game they nicknamed The Soothsayer became part of the post-show relaxation routine, until the same characters began turning up night after night. Bixler-Zavala took notes, incorporating some of the messages into his book of lyrics. Rodriguez-Lopez describes what happened next as a "haunting"—a period of tumult and terror that impeded work on the album, and ended only when the terrified band buried the game board.

Even from the Mars Volta, one of the most imaginative forces in the progressive wing of rock, this origin tale seems preposterous, a desperate play for media attention. Until you hear the music. From the first jaw-dropping outburst, *Bedlam* could be what's playing as the unquiet dead plot revenge on the living. Scintillating and pulse-quickening, it's a distinctly different brand of troubled-kid psychodrama, more chilling than anything labeled "rock" that's surfaced in the new millennium. Its challenging, heaving rhythms are wound supertight, its dissonances have a slap-across-the-face stridency, and the vocals tear through the spectrum in scream-o-vision: At key moments Bixler-Zavala reaches into a wondrous falsetto to share a woman's fright, or multitracks his voice into a ghost choir whose harmonies are pitched in the key of existential dread.

Just as notable are the luminaries from Music Heaven haunting the periphery of suites like the eight-minute "Metatron." In the course of this one stupendous track, the Mars Volta credibly exhumes elements of the music of Frank Zappa (the hiccuping odd-meter hijinks), Charles Mingus (the prayer-meeting 6/8 gospel blues interlude), Charles Ives (the jarring polytonal collisions of guitar and organ), and Kurt Cobain (the sweet yet abrasive hooks). When the Mars Volta brings those spirits together to jam, the outcome is mind-bending and terrifying—a thrill ride with Satan at the wheel.

GENRE: 🎸 Rock. RELEASED: 2008, Republic/Universal. KEY TRACKS:

"Metatron," "Tourniquet Man," "Wax Simulcra." CATALOG CHOICE: *Francis the Mute*. NEXT STOP: Frank Zappa: *Hot Rats*. AFTER THAT: Nine Inch Nails: *The Downward Spiral* (see p. 552).

The Quintessential Summer Single

"Dancing in the Street"

Martha and the Vandellas

This is the ultimate summer single, two minutes and thirty-eight seconds of heat in audio form. Hear just a few seconds of the introduction, a fanfare for soul-revue horns, and pretty soon that school's-out-let's-party state of mind takes hold. Then the vocals start, and Martha Reeves, the former Motown secretary with the commanding voice, issues an "invitation across the nation, a chance for folks to meet." The lure? "Swinging and swaying and records playing." Of course.

Perhaps the most magical part of the song, though, is the list of cities where Reeves expects dancing to break out. Lots of hits from the era contain references to specific locales, but few convey the sense of purpose Reeves brings to this. She makes you feel that if you're not out there, you're really missing something. Each city gets a little shot of love ("can't forget the Motor City") that registers as totally sincere; even some of pop's greatest voices, like Mick

Jagger and David Bowie (who collaborated on a version in 1985), can't match Reeves's energetic roll call.

"Dancing in the Street" was cowritten by Marvin Gaye, producer Mickey Stevenson, and Ivy Jo Hunter, and was originally intended for another Motown singer, Kim Weston, who passed on it. Recorded in two takes and featuring Hunter playing a crowbar for percussion, the tune became a smash hit for Reeves in the summer of 1964, and has been included on countless hits compilations since. Still, the Vandellas album issued by Motown in the spring of 1965, entitled *Dance Party,* arguably remains the best. It's got "Dancing in the Street" and the scarifyingly good subsequent single "Wild One," several smart B sides and covers, and a thrilling   Supremes-like

Martha and the Vandellas are, from left to right, Rosalind Ashford, Betty Kelly, and Martha Reeves.

tune called "Nowhere to Run," making it one of the few consistently strong long-players from singles-obsessed early Motown.

GENRE: 🔘 R&B. RELEASED: 1964, Gordy. APPEARS ON: *Dance Party*. OTHER INTERPRETATIONS: Mick Jagger/David Bowie; Dusty Springfield; Van Halen. NEXT STOP: Aretha Franklin: *Lady Soul*. AFTER THAT: Bettye LaVette: *Souvenirs*.

An Original Jazz Guitar Voice Steps Out

Consciousness/Live!

Pat Martino

Whenever you're feeling lethargic, unable to get anything done, cue up "Sunny" from Pat Martino's famed *Live!* disc, and prepare to have your clock cleaned. Here, in a solo that lasts more than four minutes,

the guitarist motors from one peak to the next with such determination he seems less a jazz musician than a superhero charged with saving Planet Earth. On his first chorus, he forms long phrases out of dizzyingly intricate post-bebop lines, and guides each one to a brink that is utterly satisfying. At this point you'd expect him to chill for a minute, but Martino starts all over again, manufacturing even more ambitious ideas, pushing them up yet another mountain, toward yet another exhilarating culmination.

Martino came up playing with Philadelphia organ groups in the mid-'60s, and began recording under his own name in 1967. By the early '70s his records were being dissected by guitarists from all corners of music, for both his monstrous technique and his warm lyrical way. This release pairs *Live!* with a studio date from 1974, *Consciousness*, that is equally inspired: Beginning with a spry romp through Coltrane's "Impressions," *Consciousness* offers blindingly bright—yet never glib—Martino solos, each a marvel of structure. To hear an improviser in full control of his resources, check

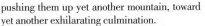
Pat Martino began playing professionally when he was only 15 years old.

out the curvy bossa nova "Along Came Betty," then a pensive solo guitar reading of Joni Mitchell's "Both Sides Now."

Martino is a kind of superhero in real life. In 1980, he had lifesaving brain surgery to correct an aneurysm, and discovered afterward that he'd completely forgotten how to play the guitar. He spent years relearning the instrument, in part by listening to his old records, and began recording again in 1987. Interestingly, Martino didn't simply recover his formidable technique, he developed a patient and highly personal melodic style that wasn't so obvious on his early works. Of the later recordings, the electrically charged *Live at Yoshi's*, with organist Joey DeFrancesco, is among the best.

GENRE: 🎷 Jazz. RELEASED: 1997, 32 Jazz. (*Consciousness* was originally issued in 1974, *Live!* in 1972, both on Muse.) KEY TRACKS: "Impressions," "Along Came Betty," "Both Sides Now," "Sunny." CATALOG CHOICES: *East!*; *Live at Yoshi's*. NEXT STOP: John Abercrombie: *Timeless*. AFTER THAT: Bill Frisell: *Lookout for Hope*.

Just Another Dream About a Woman

Julietta

Bohuslav Martinů
Maria Tauberova, Ivo Zidek, Orchestra and
Chorus of the National Theater, Prague (Jaroslav Krombholc, cond.)

If this opera about dream merchants were ever adapted by Hollywood, the folks responsible for Jim Carrey's *The Truman Show* would be a logical production team. Like that disconcerting depiction of a would-be utopia, *Julietta*

looks at the elaborate construction of fantasy, in this case the myths a man builds around a woman he thinks he met years before. He travels to a quaint seaside town to find her, and discovers that none of the villagers have memory function—including Julietta, who sometimes pretends to know him and at other times slips up. In the final act, we learn that everything Michel, the male lead, thinks about is an illusion—the girl Julietta, the town where their romance is growing, everything. He's purchased the "Julietta" package from a dream agency. Of course he'd better be careful: If clients stay too long in the dream, they can't come back. They end up shuffling around in gray pajamas, mentally locked in Juliettaland.

The prolific Martinů wrote nearly 400 pieces.

Czech composer Bohuslav Martinů (1890–1959) wrote the music and the libretto after a play by Georges Neveux that premiered in Paris in 1930. Martinů began writing his operatic adaptation before obtaining the rights; Neveux, who'd initially granted permission to Kurt Weill, took it back after hearing the music Martinů had written for *Julietta*. The work premiered in 1936, in Prague.

The story's delightful, the music full of rhapsodic flourishes that scream "Paris," including the prominent use of accordion coursing through

the orchestra in some scenes. Still it's rarely mounted. What explains this neglect? It's sung in Czech, for one thing. And its melodic streams are demanding and dense—this is not a heat-and-serve work. Martinů expects his main characters to share complex inner thoughts via correspondingly complex music. Amazingly, leads Maria Tauberova and Ivo Zidek render the challenging pieces with a light, songlike flow. They make *Julietta* enchanting whether you follow the narrative or not.

Another problem could be Martinů's profile. Though *Julietta* is captivating, much of his output sounds less distinguished now. So Martinů is low on the Great Composer Leaderboard and therefore not top-of-mind when opera companies look for a sexy "name." That shouldn't be a strike against the playful and surreal *Julietta*.

GENRE: 🎵 Opera. **RELEASED:** 1965, Supraphon. (Remastered 2002.) **KEY TRACK:** Act 2, scene 3: "The Key to Dreams." **CATALOG CHOICE:** Symphony No. 6, Czech Philharmonic (Jiří Bělohlávek, cond.). **NEXT STOP:** Antonín Dvořák: Symphony No. 9. (see p. 242). **AFTER THAT:** Georges Bizet: *Carmen Highlights,* Kiri Te Kanawa, London Philharmonic (Georg Solti, cond.).

Out of Mists and Haunted Shadows Comes . . .

Solid Air

John Martyn

Not much is terribly "solid" about *Solid Air,* one of the most inventive (and criminally overlooked) recordings of the early '70s. John Martyn floats through his shadowy originals, singing slurry, slip-sliding melodies like a jazz crooner who's one drink past his limit. He accompanies these with tinkling keyboard asides that sometimes have the wispy character of wind chimes. Often the closest thing to a pulse comes from Martyn's guitar, which provides "May You Never" (later covered by Eric Clapton) with a pensive and gentle governing rhythm.

Born in Scotland, Martyn began his career obsessed with the blues of the rural Mississippi Delta, and he brought that influence into the British folk scene of the late '60s, where his circle included Richard Thompson and Nick Drake. This album, Martyn's peak, certainly reflects the creativity that was flourishing at the time—the strumming patterns sometimes resemble those Drake used to hypnotic effect on *Pink Moon,* and the lead guitar declarations (some from Martyn, some from guest Thompson) share the exploratory quality of the great Fairport Convention records.

But Martyn is no follower. Throughout this spellbinding set, he creates an ethereal, placid soundscape, a place that seems untouched by earthbound cares. And then from that serenity, he grapples with all sorts of real problems—among them Drake's

Over his 40-year career the influential Martyn has released more than 20 studio albums.

apparent suicide, which inspired the anguished title track. The contrast reaches a riveting pinnacle on bluesman Skip James's "I'd Rather Be the Devil/Devil Got My Woman." Here Martyn fractures and then reassembles familiar blues phraseology until it becomes his own language. Listen to the way his snarling ad-libs rise from the delicate textures of this tune, or "Go Down Easy," and you can't help but wonder how Martyn attracted only a cult following.

One explanation could be the times: Given the outpouring of greatness in the early '70s, it's perhaps inevitable that some genius works would get lost. Still, to the hippie-folk-revivalists (Devendra Banhart, Sufjan Stevens) who emerged in the late 1990s, *Solid Air* is a key text, a little like *Revolver* and *Sticky Fingers* and *Pet Sounds* rolled into one.

GENRES: 🎵 Folk 🎸 Rock. **RELEASED:** 1973, Island. **KEY TRACKS:** "Solid Air," "I'd Rather Be the Devil/Devil Got My Woman," "Go Down Easy," "May You Never." **CATALOG CHOICES:** *Bless the Weather; Sunday's Child.* **NEXT STOP:** Nick Drake: *Pink Moon.* **AFTER THAT:** Fairport Convention: *Unhalfbricking.*

"My Heart Was Frivolous and Fickle"

Manon

Jules Massenet

Victoria de los Ángeles, Henri Legay, Chorus and Orchestra
of the Théâtre National de l'Opéra-Comique (Pierre Monteux, cond.)

This work, the jewel in the otherwise ordinary output of French composer Jules Massenet (1842–1912), is considered a high point of *opéra comique*. That's not because it's funny: The form takes its name from a particular theater in Paris (the Opéra-Comique), which is smaller than the city's main houses. Because of its size, works written for that venue had the option of spoken dialogue. Massenet skillfully took full advantage of that possibility, using rich orchestral underscoring to soften the transitions between spoken and sung portions of the narrative.

Manon is based on a popular French novel about an attractive young woman fresh from the convent (Manon, sung here by the divine Victoria de los Ángeles) who falls in love with a young man, des Grieux (Henri Legay), from a high-born family. They run off together, and are happily living in poverty when the man's family intervenes, offering Manon a sizable quantity of money to allow them to kidnap him. This sets up the rest of the action, a series of mishaps and foibles embedded with allegorical lessons on love and greed. The couple is split up, and after she has some high-living years, she goes to the seminary and lures des Grieux back. The fourth act finds the couple in a casino, desperately gambling to maintain their lifestyle. Caught cheating, they're sent to prison. As Manon dies in poverty, she sings about how foolish she's been, and how she always loved him.

Tour several of *Manon*'s spectacular arias, and you may grow curious to experience the entire opera. The first (and perhaps most memorable) moment happens in Act 2, when Manon, having agreed to the abduction, reflects on the broken romance while gazing at the small table where she and des Grieux took their meals. "Adieu, notre petite table" is like a frozen moment in a film—Massenet slows down the action long enough to let his heroine explore her conflicted emotions, and all that the table represents.

Manon's last big aria, in Act 5, is more intense. Through her shadings and inflections, Victoria de los Angeles communicates the upheavals and setbacks her character endures. Earlier in the work, she plays Manon to accentuate femininity, moving from her natural lyric-soprano voice into a coquettish, rapid coloratura. By the final aria, the circumstances have completely changed, and de los Angeles modulates her singing accordingly. She's resigned and sad, moving with heavy heart toward the key climactic notes. The conductor Thomas Beecham once said he'd "happily give up all the Brandenburg Concertos for *Manon*." This performance can help you understand why.

GENRE: 😊 Opera. **RELEASED:** 1955, EMI. (Reissued 2000, Testament.) **KEY TRACKS:** "Adieu, notre petite table," "Quelle éloquence!" **CATALOG CHOICE:** *Werther*. **NEXT STOP:** Georges Bizet: *Carmen* (see p. 89). **AFTER THAT:** Giuseppe Verdi: *Il trovatore*, Maria Callas, Chorus and Orchestra of La Scala (Herbert von Karajan, cond.).

Oh, the Flickering Firelight

Open Fire, Two Guitars

Johnny Mathis

The back cover of *Open Fire, Two Guitars* shows Johnny Mathis standing in front of a microphone in the recording studio, a cardigan sweater hanging from his thin frame. A coffee cup sits on the floor in the corner. His eyes are closed. He's seeking that singer's brand of truth. Without hearing a note, you know what's inside: A warm and cozy program of familiar songs in an intimate setting.

Yet *Open Fire* was a bold move for Mathis in 1959. At the time, he was just a few years into his recording career, and he'd developed a reputation for carefully preened large orchestra productions. For this session, he seeks a polar opposite. The

Open Fire, Two Guitars is certified gold in the U.S.

backing, provided by guitarists Al Caiola and Tony Mottola (bolstered occasionally by jazz bassist Milt Hinton), forces Mathis fully into the spotlight, where his famously gorgeous vocal instrument—and every decision he made about how to deploy it—is on display.

From the opening bars of "Bye Bye Blackbird," Mathis is careful in this threadbare setting not to step on the gas too quickly: He starts off sounding forlorn, and as "Blackbird" evolves, he fills in slightly different shades of blue, giving the song some portent jazz singers miss. On other pieces, like "When I Fall in Love" and "In the Still of the Night," Mathis methodically deepens the mood, one sparrowlike verse at a time. The tempos are mostly slow—another challenge for a pop singer—but Mathis luxuriates in them, savoring the liberties he can (but doesn't always) take. Anyone looking for a starter lesson on the fine art of phrasing could spend a few semesters with this and still not catch all the romance Mathis slips between two serene guitars.

GENRE: 🎵 Vocals. **RELEASED:** 1959, Columbia. **KEY TRACKS:** "In the Still of the Night," "Bye Bye Blackbird," "I'll Be Seeing You." **CATALOG CHOICE:** *Heavenly.* **NEXT STOP:** Shirley Horn: *I Thought About You.*

One Great Live Document Among Many from These Road Warriors

The Gorge

The Dave Matthews Band

For perspective on the particular mojo the Dave Matthews Band has going, check out "Drive In, Drive Out" from this 2002 live set recorded at the Gorge in Washington State. It's a song that's been a staple at frat house keggers for years, a vaguely jammy copacetic ideal of rock and roll that also works great on an amphitheater lawn. Like much DMB music, it seems to ask very little from listeners.

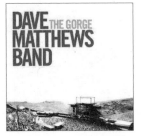

Matthews put together his band in the early '90s while working as a bartender.

Get closer, though, and "Drive In, Drive Out" is a different story. The pulse is fitful, studded with jerky syncopations. Exacting drummer Carter Beauford's notion of rhythm is less a straight line than an array of choices; he lunges into wild tangents as the mood strikes him, maintaining just enough backbeat to sustain the booty-shake. Everyone on stage responds with lunges of his own; some eventually lead to frenzied, unexpectedly dissonant freak-outs.

This multilevel approach—it's party music! it's egghead music!—has, from the start, defined the Dave Matthews Band. The musicians assembled by singer, songwriter, and former bartender Matthews in the early 1990s were veterans of bar bands in the college town of Charlottesville, Virginia, serious players with respect for bluegrass and Frank Zappa and everything in between. By the first official studio album *Under the Table and Dreaming*

(1994), they had developed an approach that remains unique in rock: music that can thunder like great metal, while at the same time thriving on the collective spirit of jazz—with elements of funk and folk in the margins. (Matthews, the only guitarist, plays primarily acoustic.) All of that is evident on the two-CDs-plus-DVD *The Gorge*, which was recorded over three nights and features whiplashing versions of the band's concert staples. Rarely has rock music of such intricacy reached, and thrilled, so many listeners.

GENRE: 🎸 Rock. RELEASED: 2004, RCA. KEY TRACKS: "Two Step," "Drive In, Drive Out," "Pantala Naga Pampa/Rapunzel," "Gravedigger," "Ants Marching" (DVD only). COLLECTOR'S NOTE: The accompanying DVD offers a whole different slate of songs. CATALOG CHOICES: *Under the Table and Dreaming; Crash; Before These Crowded Streets*. NEXT STOP: Phish: *Live at Madison Square Garden, New Year's Eve 1995*. AFTER THAT: The Jerry Garcia Band: *Lunt-Fontanne, NYC, 10/31/87*.

Contemporary Music, Settling Scores with the Old Masters

Violin Concerto

Nicholas Maw

Joshua Bell, London Philharmonic (Roger Norrington, cond.)

Among the challenges the contemporary classical composer faces is the nagging issue of how to deal with the past. For much of the twentieth century, at least within the academic circles that gave us twelve-tone music, the composer was expected to avoid anything that worked previously. Those edicts relaxed toward the end of the century, as figures like British composer Nicholas Maw

and the American John Adams took steps away from modernism, openly incorporating devices from the Romantic era and elsewhere to create new, and profound, music.

A few years after this wondrous concerto premiered, Maw—whose most notorious piece, the one-movement Odyssey Symphony, lasts one hundred minutes—summed up his relationship with the music of the past this way, in an interview with the *Financial Times*: "It's one of the arrogances of the twentieth century that art has to contain only the new. Previously it contained something people knew and something they didn't know—and I suppose that's what I'm aiming at."

The Violin Concerto achieves that balance. It's tonal, and organized so that a student of the classic showpiece concertos can follow the action. Yet it makes unusual demands on both the soloist and the orchestra. Six and a half minutes into the Scherzo second movement, for example, Maw writes an extended passage for pizzicato strings. It's not terribly tricky, but it needs to be executed so that each attack registers cleanly. Bell and the London Philharmonic nearly exaggerate these in pursuit of a stunning effect: For a minute or so, it feels like your brain is being repeatedly clawed and picked

Joshua Bell won a Grammy for Nicholas Maw's Violin Concerto.

at by some powerfully hungry creature.

The piece was written for Bell, who has alternated between crossover-minded projects (*The Red Violin*) and serious repertoire since breaking out as a golden boy in the early '90s. Revered for his broad tone, the violinist keeps Maw's lines on the slacker side of nerdy, and by generally resisting any oversized flourishes, he allows the somewhat unmoored third movement to float rhapsodically along. There and elsewhere, Bell plays with great relaxed ease, treating the new and familiar elements inside Maw's score with the same steady hand.

GENRE: 🎙 Classical. **RELEASED:** 1999, Sony Classics. **KEY TRACKS:** Scherzo; Finale: Allegro Moderato e Grazioso. **CATALOG CHOICES:** *Odyssey Symphony,* City of Birmingham Symphony Orchestra (Simon Rattle, cond.). **NEXT STOP:** *Concertos,* Joshua Bell, Cleveland Orchestra (Vladimir Ashkenazy, cond.). **AFTER THAT:** Osvaldo Golijov: *La Pasión Segun San Marcos.*

Truth, at Age Twenty-one

Blues Breakers

John Mayall with Eric Clapton

Eric Clapton was twenty-one years old when he made these recordings with British blues titan John Mayall. Think about that: Though there are exceptions (Janis Ian famously sang about learning the truth at seventeen),

most people spend their late teens and early twenties groping and moping, or chasing the next buzz, not knowing much about the ways of the world. As Goethe said: "Every one believes in his youth that the world really began with him, and that all merely exists for his sake."

At least with the guitar in his hands, Clapton was different. When he leans into one of the disciplined guitar solos on this disc, he's not a headstrong kid with something to prove, or a student parroting back received blues wisdom. He is a new iteration of the blues, a harbinger of the next level. He brings a working knowledge of the form's guitar masters, but also a language of his own, a feeling and a way of moving through rhythm that didn't exist quite this way before him.

Clapton's appearance with Mayall (his recording debut came several years before, with the Yardbirds) is a key document of British blues-rock. It's also one of the most significant titles in his extensive discography, a succession of crying leads and brilliantly snarled bunches of ideas over unshakable Chicago blues backbeats. In terms of melodic invention, none of the blues music Clapton made later, as an elder statesman, touches it. For proof, compare any of Clapton's 1990s blues homages with the coruscating solo at the center of "Have You Heard" and his equally assured turn on "Ramblin' on My Mind," a

On the cover: from left, Mayall, Clapton, John McVie, Hughie Flint.

laid-back blues that features his first recorded vocal.

Subsequently, Clapton has returned to the blues as a touchstone, or, perhaps, a means of recovering his lost youth. The only person to be inducted three times into the Rock and Roll Hall of Fame, he might be yearning for the sparks-flying energy that marks this record, a moment when, just by playing what he was feeling, Clapton changed things.

GENRES: 🎸 Rock 🎵 Blues. RELEASED: 1966, Decca. (Reissued 2001, Deram.) KEY TRACKS: "Ramblin' on My Mind," "Little Girl," "All Your Love," "It Ain't Right." CATALOG CHOICE: *Blues from Laurel Canyon.* NEXT STOP: The Yardbirds: *Over Under Sideways Down* (see p. 880). AFTER THAT: John Lee Hooker/Canned Heat: *Hooker 'n' Heat.*

No Place like It Back Then, Either

There's No Place like America Today

Curtis Mayfield

Curtis Mayfield's fingerprints are on some of the most stirring and significant popular music ever made. During the Motown explosion of the mid-'60s, the singer, songwriter, guitarist, and producer developed his own

take on Temptations-style group harmony, by way of smooth swaying singles ("Gypsy Woman") and mountains-moving calls to consciousness ("People Get Ready," a hymn of the civil rights movement). When message music began to infiltrate the pop charts, Mayfield served up the subversive soundtrack to *Superfly,* which counters the blaxploitation film's message with sorrowful, gritty sketches

of inner-city poverty and violence. When funk began getting freaky in the early '70s, Mayfield put together one of the era's tightest bands (see *Curtis/Live!*), and with his weeping wah-wah leads and chicken-scratching rhythm guitar, he showed subsequent generations the fine points of groove production.

No single album fully captures the contribution of Mayfield, the perpetually underestimated genius who was paralyzed in 1990 when a lighting truss struck him on a concert stage in Brooklyn. This ironically titled 1975 gem might just be the best appetizer from the enormous Mayfield menu. Though it offers no big hits, it's got stellar examples of his primary song types—from abiding affirmations of faith (the proud gospel-tinged "Jesus," "Love to the People") to celebrations of romance ("So in Love") to laments about poverty and violence ("Hard Times," "Billy Jack"). Each is sung from a perch slightly above the scrounging streets, and most feature at least a bit of Mayfield's trembling falsetto, which knits anger and empathy into a unified expression, the thoughts of an uncle dismayed by a wayward nephew.

In 1999, Curtis Mayfield was inducted into the Rock and Roll Hall of Fame.

Of the songwriters who made it their business to testify about the brutality of America's inner cities, Mayfield is the most effective. His songs are educations in themselves. Anyone seeking perspective on the African American experience from the 1960s onward should know about this rare poet, who speaks powerful truth even as the music around him drips with sweetness, grace, and compassion.

GENRE: 🎶 R&B. **RELEASED:** 1975, Curtom. **KEY TRACKS:** "Billy Jack," "So in Love," "Hard Times." **CATALOG CHOICES:** *Curtis/Live!; Superfly.* **NEXT STOP:** Donny Hathaway: *Everything Is Everything* (see p. 348). **AFTER THAT:** Outkast: *Speakerboxxx/The Love Below.*

Live Jazz Thrills, Made by Near-Strangers

Swiss Movement

Les McCann and Eddie Harris

For his slot on the final night of the 1969 Montreux Jazz Festival, the pianist (and sometime singer) Les McCann invited two horn players he'd heard earlier in the festival, the saxophonist Eddie Harris and trumpeter Benny Bailey, to join him. According to the liner notes, the two had not played McCann's high-wattage, soul-influenced tunes before. There wasn't time for a proper rehearsal; Bailey recalled later that he asked Harris and McCann to call out chord changes as the songs went along.

Such impromptu cameo appearances, a fixture of jazz festivals, rarely yield consequential music—more often they become wandering ego-driven jam sessions. The live *Swiss Movement* is different. For nearly an hour, Harris and Bailey pretend they know the Les McCann songbook well, and follow the pianist through a set that attains a rare golden mean between jazz, rock, and soul. The grooves pulsate with a purposeful electricity, but the soloists maintain a jazz focus—Bailey spits out intricate bebop inventions over the blues vamp "The Generation Gap," while on the gospel-tinged "You Got It in Your Soulness," Harris pushes to the outer limits of the harmony, in much the way he did on his own experimental records of the period.

The tone is set from the first notes of the opening track, "Compared to What," which became the unlikeliest of hits. A showcase for McCann's gruff shouted vocals, it's a litany of complaints about decaying American society and the Vietnam war ("The President, he's got his war, / Folks don't know just what it's for / Nobody gives us rhyme or reason, / Have one doubt they call it treason"). McCann sustains a tone of fresh outrage throughout, and the musicians reinforce it by whipping through harsh, taunting inventions between verses. Inside this one extended seven-minute power surge is an essence of jazz, the notion that thrilling for-the-ages music can be created by near-strangers, on the fly, with very little advance preparation.

GENRE: 🎷 Jazz. **RELEASED:** 1969, Atlantic. (Reissued 1996, Rhino.) **KEY TRACKS:** "Compared to What," "Cold Duck Time," "You Got It in Your Soulness." **CATALOG CHOICES:** Les McCann: *Much Les.* Eddie Harris: *The Electrifying Eddie Harris.* **NEXT STOP:** Gene Ammons: *Boss Tenors.* **AFTER THAT:** Ornette Coleman: *In All Languages.*

A Radical Approach to Consciousness-Raising

Headless Heroes of the Apocalypse

Eugene McDaniels

"No amount of dancing is going to make us free," Eugene McDaniels proclaims on "Freedom Death Dance," a call to action on his alternately suave and politically charged 1971 solo record. Tired of the lofty rhetoric of the civil rights movement, McDaniels—who went on to write hits for Roberta Flack and others—tries to mobilize an opposition, all the while castigating those who have become zombified by drugs (or popular culture). At times McDaniels seems totally unhinged: The last few minutes of a lament about the treatment of Native Americans, "The Parasite (for Buffy)," is given over to eerie wheedling screams.

This cover features McDaniels screaming between two warring samurai.

McDaniels might have believed his proclamation about the futility of dancing, but that didn't stop him from creating a visionary amalgamation that takes funk, jazz-fusion, blues, and rock to new places. The rhythm section, helmed by McDaniels on keyboards, is the star here: On track after track, they achieve an easygoing yet totally engaged backbeat that helps assuage McDaniels's erratic vocals. That cohesive rhythm has made the album indispensable to subsequent generations: Some of the best minds in hip-hop have copped bits of *Headless Heroes,* including A Tribe Called Quest (which utilized "Jagger the Dagger"), and Pete Rock and CL Smooth, whose hit "Act like You Know" begins with the riff from "Freedom Death Dance."

Headless Heroes didn't exactly meet with universal appreciation when it was released, however. According to several accounts, then–Vice President Spiro Agnew called Atlantic Records to complain about the album, which was getting some airplay in Washington, D.C., and other urban centers. Shortly after that, in what might have been either capitulation or coincidence, Atlantic stopped promoting the album, and it quickly disappeared. It was finally issued on CD in 2001.

GENRE: 🎙 R&B. **RELEASED:** 1971, Atlantic. (Reissued 2001, Water.) **KEY TRACKS:** "Freedom Death Dance," "The Lord Is Back," "The Parasite (for Buffy)." **NEXT STOP:** Gil Scott-Heron: *Pieces of a Man* (see p. 684). **AFTER THAT:** A Tribe Called Quest: *The Low End Theory* (see p. 786).

A Record Too Far Ahead of Its Time

Kick Out the Jams

MC5

Not many rock and roll bands make their first foray into the big world with a live album. But hearing the ragged and proudly belligerent *Kick Out the Jams,* it's clear that's what MC5 had to do: It would have been difficult to get this kind of roar, built on the ballistic twin guitars of Fred "Sonic" Smith (later Mr. Patti Smith) and Wayne Kramer, under laboratory conditions.

According to legend, it didn't happen to the MC5 all that often in clubs, either: Many who saw them around the time of these dates at Detroit's Grande Ballroom, in late October 1968, say that *Kick Out the Jams* catches a night when all the feedback howls and razoring noise (not to mention a sprinkling of acid-radical White Panther Party rhetoric) came together perfectly, with enough power to suggest a new area of rock and roll pursuit. It took years for others to follow the MC5's lead, however, and when punk broke out in the middle '70s, the Detroit faithful had reason to shrug and go, "What took you guys so long?"

Listening to these eight songs now, after several generational iterations of punk, what is most impressive is the way this band sustained the feeling of near-delirium for as long as it did. The rhythm section attack is pulverizing,

MC5 (which stands for Motor City Five) formed in 1964 while they were in high school in Lincoln Park, Michigan.

perfectly suited to frontman Rob Tyner's charged, edge-of-anarchy screeds. By the time the MC5 gets to the eerily dissonant set-closing appropriation of Sun Ra's "Starship," these guys seem to have grown more fearless. They sound like they could do anything. That sense of threat is what many would-be punk rockers took from the battle cry "Kick Out the Jams," and the MC5 in general. Wilco's Jeff Tweedy explains that allure this way: "Part of what's amazing about this record is the feeling of danger that runs through it. . . . I mean, the audience is there, totally having their brains taken out of their skulls, and they're receiving it."

GENRE: 🎸 Rock. **RELEASED:** 1969, Elektra. **KEY TRACKS:** "Kick Out the Jams," "Rocket Reducer No. 62 (Rama Lama Fa Fa Fa)," "Starship." **CATALOG CHOICE:** *Back in the USA.* **NEXT STOP:** The New York Dolls: *Too Much Too Soon.* **AFTER THAT:** Ramones: *Ramones* (see p. 631).

The Debut of a Should-Be Dynasty

Kate and Anna McGarrigle

Kate and Anna McGarrigle

Canadian sisters Kate and Anna McGarrigle make quiet, beautifully crafted singer-songwriter records that few outside of a devoted coterie of fans, many of them recording artists, have heard. Since the '70s—when Linda Ronstadt covered this album's "Heart like a Wheel"—successive waves of singer-songwriters have seized on the McGarrigles' blunt and sometimes acidic humor, the wide harmonies and eccentric perspectives that define their songs. Such influence should, at the very least, make the McGarrigles' music easy to find; in fact, several important albums have fallen out of print over the years. Everything the duo did in the 1970s is worth hearing; rarely have simple, plaintive songs been graced with such tightly bound sisterly vocals, a swooning siren sound with more power than either McGarrigle could achieve alone.

Kate McGarrigle (left), Anna McGarrigle, (right).

The key, though, is the songwriting: There's true daring, and a willful eccentricity, driving these explorations of modern love's minefields and barren ruins. Anna's haiku "Heart like a Wheel" belongs among the great metaphors about romance and devotion; Kate's "(Talk to Me of) Mendocino" catches a yearning for place that's as profound, and vividly sketched, as the yearning for love. The quaint, old-timey sounds (fiddle, accordion, banjo) aren't there to take listeners back to another era; instead, they provide contrast and color, framing the porcelain-pure harmonies. Swirled together, these elements combine for oddly revelatory folk music that registers as a wrenching feeling in the gut even before you're able to appreciate it intellectually.

GENRES: 🎧 Folk 🎸 Rock. **RELEASED:** 1975, Hannibal. **KEY TRACKS:** "Heart like a Wheel," "Jigsaw Puzzle of Life," "(Talk to Me of) Mendocino." **CATALOG CHOICE:** *Heartbeats Accelerating.* **NEXT STOP:** The Story: *The Angel in the House.*

Life-Affirming Lamentations

The Visit

Loreena McKennitt

The Canadian songstress Loreena McKennitt is known mostly for her evocations of Celtic rituals—her catalog contains updates of ancient melodies (she does a version of "Greensleeves" here). Yet one of the highlights of *The Visit*, her breakthrough, has strikingly modern inspiration: "Bonny Portmore" tells of a grand tree that stood on the grounds of Portmore Castle until it was felled by loggers. McKennitt describes the environmental devastation and the loss of a powerful symbol in the same graceful voice she uses to sing lullabies. Like the great singers of English ballads, she makes this one loss resonate across time and space, testifying for all of humanity, quietly asking for forgiveness in the face of countless environmental tragedies.

McKennitt has that rare knack for giving a specific image (or folktale) broad universal resonance. You can be lying on a massage table (this disc is a favorite with those who do bodywork) and hardly paying attention, and there's something about her calm reserve, her ability to assert herself at a whisper, that conveys more than comforting pleasantries. This gift prevails throughout *The Visit*, on the picturesque evocation of a languid paradise, "Tango to Evora," and just as stirringly on narratives like the eleven-minute "The Lady of Shalott," her adaptation of a Tennyson poem.

Regardless of her subject, McKennitt remains serene while expressing despair or outrage—she just winds her way through the ethereal mist that seems to envelop every record by female Celtic artists, trusting that her silver ribbon of a voice will convey the fullness of her thoughts. Somehow it does.

GENRE: 🌐 World/Celtic. **RELEÁSED:** 1991, Quinlan Road/Verve. **KEY TRACKS:** "Bonny Portmore," "The Lady of Shalott," "Tango to Evora," "The Old Ways." **CATALOG CHOICE:** *The Book of Secrets.* **NEXT STOP:** Phil Coulter: *Sea of Tranquility.* **AFTER THAT:** Katell Keineg: *O Seasons, O Castles.*

Mysteries Built, One Sigh at a Time

Surfacing

Sarah McLachlan

Before this megasuccess, it was possible to dismiss Sarah McLachlan as another Enya-influenced peddler of vague mystic allegories. *Surfacing* changed that. It established the Canadian singer and songwriter as a master of the moody confessional and the soft-focus ethereal atmosphere, who knew to put enough backbeat in her tunes to get them on the radio.

On a nuts and bolts level, the songs of *Surfacing* are not exactly earth-shattering— McLachlan proffers fervent U2-style anthems, lilting piano ballads, and methodical medium-tempo rockers that move with the steadiness of ticking clocks. Familiar stuff, in other words. Though structur-

Surfacing has sold over 11 million copies worldwide.

ally slight, the songs become revelatory as McLachlan develops them. She sings with no affectation and very little inflection, and her detachment forces the melodies, like the almost-too-common weeping line of "Angel," to stand on their own. When she reaches the chorus of "Adia," McLachlan's controlled demeanor makes the brave and stately theme, which carries a thought about lost innocence, more devastating. Elsewhere, she's almost too coy—it might take a couple of spins to pick up the derision in "Building a Mystery," her sketch of a lost soul caught up in New Age quackery.

Production (by McLachlan and Pierre Marchand) is central to the appeal of *Surfacing*—a case can be made for this album as one of the most sonically alluring works of the 1990s. Each selection comes with its own thick and carefully cultivated aura designed to enhance the specific shades of melancholy McLachlan seeks. The surroundings are shrouded in mist while the themes are needle-direct—a contrast that welcomes you into this calm place of refuge again and again, and shows you something different each time you visit.

GENRE: Rock. RELEASED: 1997, Arista. KEY TRACKS: "Building a Mystery," "Sweet Surrender," "Adia," "Angel." CATALOG CHOICE: *Fumbling Towards Ecstasy.* NEXT STOP: Tori Amos: *Little Earthquakes.* AFTER THAT: Heather Duby: *Post to Wire.*

A Tall Order for a Singer

Carmen Sings Monk

Carmen McRae

The music written by jazz pianist Thelonious Monk really isn't for vocalists. Though Monk's melodies have an open, singing quality, their jagged leaps and unlikely contours are forbidding to singers accustomed to smooth, serene lines. Monk wrote intricate, architectural music that demands so much in the execution, a singer is lucky to just hit the right notes, let alone embellish them successfully.

None of this stopped Carmen McRae. At age sixty-eight, the jazz vocalist known for her winking sense of humor and sly phraseology tackled the Monk songbook, drawing on lyrics written by Jon Hendricks, Abbey Lincoln, and others. She emerged with the most engaging vocal tribute to Monk ever, a performance that makes these challenging works sound walk-in-the-park easy.

Recorded with a small group in the studio (there are also two live performances, with different backing, from the same year), *Carmen Sings Monk* offers versions of some of the master's well-known jam-session tunes, including the blues "Straight No Chaser," as well as crystalline

Carmen McRae recorded more than 60 albums during her career.

readings of less-heard pieces like "Ugly Beauty." McRae and Monk were friends, and the singer's admiration comes through not just in her clear rendering of his themes, but in small details like tempo: She takes rhapsodic ballads like "Ruby My Dear" at a languid pace, magnifying the poignancy of the line. An interesting corollary to Monk's own recordings (see p. 511), this is a great way to encounter one of the compositional geniuses of the twentieth century.

GENRES: Jazz Vocals. RELEASED: 1988, RCA Novus. KEY TRACKS: "Straight No Chaser," "Ruby My Dear," "Ugly Beauty," "I Mean You." CATALOG CHOICE: *Here to Stay.* NEXT STOP: Cassandra Wilson: *Blue Skies.* AFTER THAT: Norma Winstone: *Somewhere Called Home.*

The Works of an Archetypical Blues Legend

The Definitive Blind Willie McTell

Blind Willie McTell

Think of Blind Willie McTell as Central Casting's dream composite of blues folklore. The Atlanta-based singer and guitarist was blind, which puts him in the crowded fraternity of blind blues singers of the 1930s—alongside Blind Boy Fuller, Blind Willie Johnson, and others. McTell was no stranger to whiskey and barroom violence, and sang about those things in vivid detail, sometimes giving roadhouse story-songs the feeling of tragedy. Like John Lee Hooker, the guitarist and singer born Samuel McTell recorded for several different labels at once by using various pseudonyms—among them Blind Willie, Georgia Bill, and Hotshot Willie. And like too many of his brethren, his 1959 death, after a brain hemorrhage, went largely unnoticed; not until reissues began in the 1970s (and Bob Dylan wrote a song immortalizing him) did the music world begin to appreciate his contribution.

The story might be typical; Blind Willie McTell's music is not. He was one of the first true virtuosos of the blues guitar; virtually everything he recorded, from the early "Statesboro Blues" on Victor Records through these more focused Okeh/Columbia sides, exhibits a crisp sense of rhythm and a gift for making the guitar "talk." His chosen instru-

ment was the twelve-string acoustic, and where many of his peers just rattled out big chords on it, he plucked and picked, weaving in delicate melodies that echoed the dazzle of ragtime. On the chilling "Death Room Blues" when he groans about his imminent demise in a nasal, endlessly troubled voice, McTell embodies all the dread associated with 1930s blues. And when he and his frequent accompanist Curley Weaver get going, the two sound like four or more guitarists caught up in a cutting contest, playing with all their might just to be noticed.

Blind Willie McTell recorded music for nearly 30 years.

GENRE: 🔵 Blues. **RELEASED:** 1993, Columbia Legacy. **KEY TRACKS:** "Lord Send Me an Angel," "Love Makin' Mama," "My Baby's Gone." **CATALOG CHOICE:** *The Complete Victor Recordings, 1927–1932.* **NEXT STOP:** Blind Willie Johnson: *Dark Was the Night.* **AFTER THAT:** John Lee Hooker: *Alone.*

A Jazz Thinker Discovers Orchestral Textures

Largo

Brad Mehldau

Jazz hit the skids in the late '90s. The establishment, represented by Jazz at Lincoln Center artistic director Wynton Marsalis and his many disciples, cranked out scholarly but inconsequential rehashes of music made decades before. Rejecting this mind-set, a bunch of younger players attempted to overthrow orthodoxy by, among other things, covering songs by such rock bands as Black Sabbath and Radiohead. The most musical of these new thinkers: the pianist Brad Mehldau.

An intense young man who read German philosophy and early in his career struggled with heroin addiction, Mehldau and his trio savored the lyrical, often rhapsodic side of pop. With *Largo* he continues an investigation of Nick Drake and the Beatles that he'd begun on earlier records, transforming the familiar themes into platforms for open-ended questioning. These journeys, along with Mehldau's doctrine-free original compositions, suggest jazz that feels profoundly contemporary, not a pale echo of 1957.

The material on *Largo*, which was produced by Jon Brion (Fiona Apple, etc.), is moody-to-maundering stuff, with subterranean melodies calling from the shadows. Brion augments the trio with odd combinations of horns, guitar synth, and choppy rhythm loops—fashioning a tasteful, sometimes ethereal collage that practically manufactures mystery. The setting shows off Mehldau's graceful way with a melody—a trait that's eluded many of his contemporaries, including the trio known as the Bad Plus. And it puts him in a zone that's closer in temperament to Chopin's *Nocturnes* than any jazz proving ground. Mehldau touches the piano delicately, sweetly, until he draws out elements of his "sound" that he would never have encountered doing ordinary jazz repertory work.

GENRE: 🎷 Jazz. **RELEASED:** 2002, Warner Bros. **KEY TRACKS:** "Paranoid Android," "Dear Prudence," "Wave/Mother Nature's Son." **CATALOG CHOICES:** *Anything Goes; Live in Tokyo* (solo piano). **NEXT STOP:** E.S.T.: *Seven Days of Falling.* **AFTER THAT:** Jon Brion and Various Artists: *Eternal Sunshine of the Spotless Mind,* Original Motion Picture Soundtrack.

Shimmering Triumphs of Texture

Dead Cities, Red Seas & Lost Ghosts

M83

Two young musicians, bored with techno, sneak into the workshop of French electronic pop pioneer Jean-Michel Jarre. They're not criminals, just clubbers looking for kicks. They power up the massive synths and the odd vintage beat machines. They play cautiously at first, not wanting to mess with equipment that sounds like it's still set up for Jarre's grandiose 1977 hit *Oxygene*. Gradually they grow bolder, seeking swirls of synthesized strings and oscillating organ chords way too psychedelic for a rave. Pretty soon they've got an aural portrait of a barren cityscape still smoldering in the aftermath of some cataclysmic event.

M83. DeadCities, RedSeas&LostGhosts

The duo parted in 2004; Gonzalez continues to record as M83.

The twelve-track epic *Dead Cities* wasn't actually created in Jarre's studio, but it might have been. Antibes-born Nicholas Fromageau and Anthony Gonzalez utilize many of the French electronic pop pioneer's favorite pre-digital sounds, and share Jarre's notion of the majestic. One key difference has to do with perspective: This duo approaches everything from a distance, as though filming a wonder of nature. The wide-angle panoramic views give the music an Eno-ambient aura and a Pink Floyd spaciness. It transforms what would, in other hands, be slow-to-congeal ambient music into shimmering triumphs of texture.

Since the two multi-instrumentalists live in the techno world, the music hums along at a hyperefficient clip, the pace of an urban rush hour. Yet there's nothing frantic going on here. Throughout, M83 tries to loosen up the deadening assembly-line grind associated with post-millennium electronica—sometimes weaving sleepy female voices into the atmosphere, sometimes abandoning rhythm entirely to conjure placid pools of still water. These guys are thinking about the world beyond the dance floor, and their organic, deeply engrossing sequences unfold into music that's strikingly picturesque, a soundtrack in search of a movie.

GENRE: 🎵 Electronica. **RELEASED:** 2003, Gooom Disque. (U.S. release 2004, Mute.) **KEY TRACKS:** "America," "Cyborg," "Beauties Can Die." **CATALOG CHOICE:** *Before the Dawn Heals Us.* **NEXT STOP:** Jean-Michel Jarre: *Oxygene.* **AFTER THAT:** Four Tet: *Rounds.*

A Caustic Comment on the Wonders and Absurdities of . . .

Rock 'n' Roll

The Mekons

In the jaundiced songs of the Mekons, rock and roll appears as a corrupter of youth and a path to salvation, an empty exercise and a possibly threatening cultural force. Sometimes it's all that at once: On "Club Mekon," Sally Timms proudly sings, "When I was just seventeen, sex no longer held a mystery/I saw it as a commodity to be bought and sold, like rock and roll."

Elsewhere on this state-of-rock missive released in 1989, the British band comments wryly on the messianic tendencies of rock stars ("Blow Your Tuneless Trumpet" wickedly skewers U2's Bono), and on rock as a form of imperialism. There's an indignant rant about the escapist excesses of America, "Empire of the Senseless," and a haunting little ditty called "Amnesia" that invokes Elvis Presley with its refrain "Bless my soul what's wrong with me, I forgot to forget to remember." ("I Forgot to

Remember to Forget" is a classic Elvis title.)

The Mekons rely on the usual rock tools to serve up this delirium—guitars pushed to the melting point by Jon Langford, the group's sonic architect, and drums that pound like they're heralding imminent apocalypse. Also on hand are violins, which sometimes shred bluegrass fiddle style and sometimes bolster the guitar counterlines. The textures generally enhance the haranguing from Timms and Langford, who shout caustic dire rants knowing that the large ensemble is pumping out redeeming sweetness behind them.

The Mekons began in Leeds in the late 1970s; the group was part of the same sociopolitical punk underground that gave the world Gang of Four (see p. 298). But unlike most every other band of its milieu, the Mekons evolved in dramatic fashion: After forays into punk and danceable synth pop, the band delivered the

Rock 'n' Roll is the Mekons' seventh album.

astonishing *Fear and Whiskey* (1985), which approached Hank Williams–style country with the wild abandon of punk, and is generally credited with sparking the subgenre known as "alt-country." *Rock 'n' Roll* came next. It sold poorly, and was the only Mekons album made for a major label; its follow-up, the nearly-as-good *Curse of the Mekons*, was rejected by executives. That now looks like a blessing. The Mekons were—and are—too intense to thrive for long under any corporate thumb.

GENRE: 🎸 Rock. **RELEASED:** 1989, A&M. **KEY TRACKS:** "Club Mekon," "Only Darkness Has the Power," "Cocaine Lil," "Amnesia," "Blow Your Tuneless Trumpet." **CATALOG CHOICES:** *Fear and Whiskey; Curse of the Mekons.* **NEXT STOP:** Gang of Four: *Entertainment!* (see p. 298). **AFTER THAT:** Meat Puppets: *Too High to Die.*

One of the Great Female Guitarists

Hoodoo Lady, 1933–1937

Memphis Minnie

Memphis Minnie was a blues shouter and an entertainer, one of the early masters of double entendre who could make a commonplace greeting sound like a risqué invitation. She's not remembered enough these days, and, when she is, too often it's only for her showbiz singing style. But an equally consequential legacy is evident on this compilation: The Mississippi-born Lizzie Douglas, the oldest of thirteen children, rocked the acoustic guitar.

She kept wicked time, for starters, had a lusty, distinctive sense of swing, and was able to tear out surprisingly substantial solos. Her three husbands were all musicians and collaborators, and in the course of those marriages she established the basic dynamic of small-group blues that became commonplace in postwar Chicago. One legend says that she beat two prominent early bluesmen, Big Bill Broonzy (see p. 117) and Tampa Red, in a guitar contest, and hearing her deft work on "Ice Man (Come On Up)," that seems totally plausible. She might not have been the flashiest player, but Douglas had a knack for cutting to the chase with apt single-line inventions and hard-hitting chords.

Hoodoo Lady collects her entertaining 1930s recordings, widely considered her best. These show that she was a key link between rural blues and the more disciplined, uniform twelve-bar blues form that Broonzy and others popularized later. Among the gems are "Down in the Alley," "I'm a Bad Luck Woman," and a slow confession called "Caught Me Wrong Again." On that one, her man discovers her cheating,

Memphis Minnie was discovered singing in a Beale Street barbershop.

but Minnie, mindful of the decorum of the age, describes it differently: "You caught me makin' friends," she acknowledges, with an unmistakable wink in her voice.

GENRE: 🌐 Blues.
RELEASED: 1991, Columbia/ Legacy. **KEY TRACKS:** "Down in the Alley," "I'm a Bad Luck Woman," "Ice Man (Come On Up)," "Caught Me Wrong Again." **NEXT STOP:** Big Mama Thornton: *Hound Dog* (see p. 776). **AFTER THAT:** Sister Rosetta Tharpe: *Gospel Train*.

Two of the Four Great German Violin Concertos

Beethoven Violin Concerto
Mendelssohn Violin Concerto

Yehudi Menuhin

Beethoven: Philharmonia Orchestra and Mendelssohn: Berlin Philharmonic (Wilhelm Furtwängler, cond.)

At a celebration of his seventy-fifth birthday in 1906, the renowned violinist Joseph Joachim, who'd known and worked with Brahms and Mendelssohn, observed that Germany had given the world four essential violin concertos. He esteemed Beethoven's to be the greatest, regarded the Brahms as nearly its equal in terms of seriousness, and described Max Bruch's concerto (see p. 740) as the "most seductive." But, Joachim continued, "the most inward, the heart's jewel, is Mendelssohn's."

This recording contains two of the four magnificently interpreted by the virtuosic Yehudi Menuhin—the mighty Beethoven work, a rousing triumph of the composer's "heroic" period, and the Mendelssohn, which is nearly its equal in terms of melodic riches. New York–born Menuhin (1916–1999), a one-

time child prodigy revered for his porcelain-smooth tone and control of expressive nuances, recorded these in 1952 and 1953. They're clean, authoritative, and vividly wrought, with no grandstanding hijinks to obstruct either composer's intent.

The Beethoven was written in 1806, around the time of the composer's Fourth Symphony and Fourth Piano Concerto. When it premiered, it was the longest work of its kind. The piece is built around two distinct themes—the first is rhythmic and has some distant relationship to the opening of the Fifth

Symphony, while the other is a legato singer's line, a linear ascending phrase that grows more epic as the work evolves. Menuhin approaches this precious theme expansively, and keeps on "singing" through tricky solo cadenza passages that might have been cribbed from the Devil's Finger Exercise folio. If you're not awed by the strong alternating currents of Beethoven—the cool math-teacher logic that gives way to blood-boiling emotional peaks—as brought to life by Menuhin, you might just have Freon running through your veins.

As Joachim noted, the Mendelssohn is an intimate, inward-turned work, with brooding folk-song themes rising from lush orchestrations. It's an equally strong showcase for Menuhin, who shapes the extended rhapsodies of the Andante middle movement as though the composer were whispering in his ear. Despite the tricky fingerings and the unusual intervals, there is no strain in this music-making. Menuhin catches Mendelssohn's meditative undertone, and with great calm, goes about illuminating the many facets of this "heart's jewel."

GENRE: 🎻 Classical. **RELEASED:** 1953, EMI. (Reissued 1999.) **KEY TRACKS:** Beethoven: Second and fourth movements. Mendelssohn: Second movement: Andante. **ANOTHER INTERPRETATION:** Beethoven: Itzhak Perlman, Berlin Philharmonic (Daniel Barenboim, cond.). **CATALOG CHOICE:** J. S. Bach: *Sonatas and Partitas for Solo Violin*, Yehudi Menuhin. **NEXT STOP:** Felix Mendelssohn: *Songs Without Words*, Andras Schiff. **AFTER THAT:** Edouard Lalo: *Symphonie espagnole*, Isaac Stern (see p. 740).

Written in a Prison Camp Bathroom

Quartet for the End of Time

Olivier Messiaen

Gil Shaham, Paul Meyer, Jian Wang, Myung-Whun Chung

French composer Olivier Messiaen (1908–1992) wrote most of the *Quartet for the End of Time* while in a German prison camp. The composer's tale of its genesis is understandably dramatic—he said that the only place he could write was the bathroom, and that he was forced to use the rather unusual (but extremely evocative) combination of violin, clarinet, cello, and piano because that's all that was available. In recent years, Messiaen's associates, including several musicians who served time with him, have disputed some of these assertions—the cellist who played the premiere, which was held in the Silesian camp in January 1941, says that though the composer remembers a rickety three-stringed cello, his instrument had the usual four strings, and he needed all four to play the tricky piece.

The circumstances of this piece's creation, along with its title, make this quartet in eight movements seem apocalyptic. In fact, Messiaen intended it to describe the passage of time in more of a metaphysical, Millennium Clock sense. The composer, who was Roman Catholic and served as the organist of Paris's La Trinité cathedral, once explained that the eight movements reflected the seven days of creation, plus an eighth day representing "everlasting light . . . eternal peace."

Hints of the quest for that light lurk throughout—in the capricious birdsong (a

Messiaen obsession) that animates the third movement, and the restless extended cello meditation of the spectacular fifth movement, which plays out against entrancing repetitive piano chords. Messiaen's greatest passages don't rely on typical harmonic schemes of tension and release; instead, they're defined by vast plateaus and unexpected key changes.

The quartet on this 2000 recording, led by Korean pianist Myung-Whun Chung, brings plenty of energy to the piece, and a respect for Messiaen's mystical leanings. While some composers shine only under note-perfect execution, Messiaen comes alive when the musi-cians are guided by common intuition rather than just the printed score. By participating in Messiaen's search for illumination, they bring listeners along with them.

GENRE: 🎼 Classical. **RELEASED:** 2000, Deutsche Grammophon. **KEY TRACKS:** Movements 3, 5, and 8. **CATALOG CHOICE:** *Turangalila,* Bastille Opera Orchestra (Myung-Whun Chung, cond.). **NEXT STOP:** Krzysztof Penderecki: *Threnody to the Victims of Hiroshima,* Katowice Polish Radio Orchestra and Chorus. **AFTER THAT:** Karlheinz Stockhausen: *Stimmung* (see p. 744).

Looking at Jesus from All Sides

Vingt regards sur l'enfant-Jésus

Olivier Messiaen
Pierre-Laurent Aimard

An evening-long series of vignettes for solo piano, *Vingt regards* is Olivier Messiaen's meditation on the infant Jesus, and, by extension, spirituality itself. Written in Paris in 1944, shortly after the trailblazing composer was released from prison camp (where he'd composed *Quartet for the End of Time,* see previous page), it begins with deliberate chords played in unwavering rhythm—the solemn march of the pious. From there, Messiaen explores different perspectives on the miracle birth, sorting through the symbology that's accumulated over centuries. There are episodes imagining the thoughts of "God the Father," and the reactions of the prophets and the angels. Messiaen (1908–1992) was a devout Catholic; his pieces mix ritual aspects of the Mass with hints of mysticism and outbursts that equate religious devotion with sensual bliss. The titles and brief descriptions Messiaen wrote to "explain" the sections draw on Biblical images—the preface to the third section reads "Descending in a spray, rising in a spiral, the terrible trade between humans and God, God made man to make us gods." But words are limiting; this music ventures far from any fixed programmatic narrative. Each section finds its own source of light, its own tonal signature: In the "Noel," for example, the Christmas bells carry menacing, dissonant overtones. The otherworldly mists of the nineteenth section, "Je dors, mais mon coeur veille," suggest Erik Satie puzzling over the jet age, while the big bruising chords that begin the final section could be Messiaen's simulation of the inferno down below.

The vast temperamental range of the piece has been known to vex those who attempt to perform it. French pianist Pierre-Laurent Aimard studied with Messiaen and his interpretation is notable for its clarity, as well as its obvious affection for the composer's quirks. Without sensationalizing, Aimard points out the piece's more outlandish effects. He brings a fanciful touch to the surreal birdsongs, then executes the superfast ascending and descending lines with precision, allowing them to unfold like metaphysical chase scenes, never demanding tidy resolution. As he seizes on Messiaen's fantastical details, Aimard approaches the work less as a literal representation of one storied "miracle birth," and more like a celebration of miracles, celestial and otherwise.

GENRE: 🎻 Classical. **RELEASED:** 2000, Teldec. **KEY TRACKS:** I."Regard du Père"; X. "Regard de l'esprit de joie"; XVI. "Regard des prophètes, des bergers et des mages"; XX. "Regard de l'église d'amour." **CATALOG CHOICES:** *Catalogue des Oiseaux,* Anatola Engorski. **NEXT STOP:** György Ligeti: *Ligeti Edition 3, Works for Piano,* Pierre-Laurent Aimard. **AFTER THAT:** Keith Jarrett: *La Scala.*

This Heavy Machinery Requires Skill

Master of Puppets

Metallica

Those whose diet consists of "heavy" orchestral fare—Mahler, Wagner—will find much to appreciate in Metallica. Through its many stylistic changes, the Bay Area heavy rock quartet has expanded metal's ritualistic pummeling with music of impressive, even daunting, intricacy. Its dense textures establish connections between metal's Sturm und Drang and the percussive string ensemble passages of major symphonic works. Metallica's crowd-revving anthems (for years, Yankees reliever Mariano Rivera was introduced with its "Enter Sandman") exhibit a Wagnerian sense of pageantry.

Master of Puppets has sold over 6 million copies in the U.S.

This is the album where Metallica fully recasts metal as thinking-person's music. In some ways a formal restatement of the innovations found on the previous *Ride the Lightning* (1984), it's the band's first consistent set of songs, with doom-laden lyrics (about mind control, leprosy, and sanitarium living) propelled by hiccuping odd-meter syncopations and other devices, all wound up tight and played a touch faster than safe speed.

Constantly threatening to career out of control, *Master* shows how thrilling metal can be when its fully torqued. Drummer Lars Ulrich plays like a technical demon whose job is to irritate the others. And lead guitarist Kirk Hammett pushes right back, giving the up-tempo thrash of "Damage, Inc." its outsized (but never gratuitously theatrical) menace. There are plenty of highlights in the band's catalog, but *Master of Puppets* unites the fury and the finesse in a bludgeoning attack that is viscerally thrilling, and at the same time really smart. Kinda like Wagner.

GENRE: 🎸 Rock. **RELEASED:** 1986, Elektra. **KEY TRACKS:** "The Thing That Should Not Be," "Damage, Inc.," "Master of Puppets." **CATALOG CHOICE:** *Metallica.* **NEXT STOP:** Anthrax: *Among the Living.* **AFTER THAT:** Richard Wagner: *Götterdämmerung* (see p. 840).

"The best . . . band in the world"—Mick Jagger

Look-Ka Py Py

The Meters

Break down the deceptively simple recordings of the Meters, and you will find the essential DNA of hypnotic groove music. On the New Orleans quartet's own titles and the many pop records the group played on (including

the LaBelle smash "Lady Marmalade"), the key characteristic is restraint. Nobody works too hard on Meters records. The rhythm is built on a loose-tight axis, with some elements (usually Zigaboo Modeliste's snappish drumming) pushing forward and other forces (the carefully articulated guitar lines of Leo Nocentelli or spare jabs from Art Neville's B3 organ) pulling back.

The Meters formed in 1967.

The result is James Brown–style funk with a little Bourbon Street shuffle in its step. Most of the songs on this satisfyingly greasy second album are just riffs, simple recurring phrases that expose the inner workings of the pulse—a marvel built on precisely interlinked parts. Bassist George Porter recalled that the title track was inspired by a problematic piston in the band van: "It kept going 'ooka-she-uh, ooka-she-uh,' over and over." The musicians began pounding

and singing along, and wrote the song on the spot.

The Meters did this and two other albums for the small Josie label before moving to Reprise. Their later works are slick productions that helped connect this important band to a wider audience. While powerful, that music feels slight compared with the sizzle of the early Meters, works that gather funk, Mardi Gras Indian chants, and the sauntering swing of New Orleans backbeats of the highest order.

GENRE: 🔵 R&B. **RELEASED:** 1970, Josie. (Reissued 1999, Sundazed.) **KEY TRACKS:** "Look-Ka Py Py," "Oh, Calcutta!," "Funky Miracle," "Dry Spell," "Yeah, You're Right." **CATALOG CHOICES:** *Funkify Your Life; The Original Funkmasters* (UK). **NEXT STOP:** The JBs: *A Funky Good Time.* **AFTER THAT:** Little Feat: *Waiting for Columbus.*

"The Wind Through the Trees in Heaven . . ."

The Pat Metheny Group

The Pat Metheny Group

With the pinpoint-precise guitar arpeggios that open "Phase Dance," the Pat Metheny Group blows years of jazz fusion excess to smithereens. Then, having cleared the air, the quartet led by the Missouri-born guitarist Pat Metheny goes off in search of open-sky vistas not typically associated with jazz—its songs evoke idyllic shorelines and pastel-shaded landscapes and snow drifts on a mountainside. One review of Metheny during this period described his music as "the wind through the trees in heaven."

STEREO 825 593-2 ℗
PAT METHENY GROUP
LYLE MAYS
MARK EGAN
DAN GOTTLIEB

ECM

The Pat Metheny Group reached #5 on *Billboard*'s Jazz Albums chart.

If not that, it is, at the very least, the sound of possibilities multiplying. The compositions on this, the Metheny Group's first foray, are organized around buoyant, irrepressibly optimistic melody lines and tunes that unfold slowly, as episodic journeys. The Group was often described as jazz-fusion, but one trip through the brisk "Lone Jack" or "San Lorenzo" reveals how incomplete that designation is: These beautiful crystalline atmospheres are unlike anything else in music. They have touches of samba, require a skill set far different from most jazz, and use a language for improvisation that draws as much from the rich harmonies of Maurice Ravel as from bebop.

This album established the basic palette of the Metheny Group, an uncluttered sound centered around Metheny's rounded, reverb-soaked tones. Though later albums are more thoroughly choreographed, they still offer stirring atmospheres and breathtaking climactic moments. Equally significant is the music Metheny has made apart from the group, in collaboration with such jazz luminaries as Ornette Coleman (*Song X*), Roy Haynes (*Question and Answer*), and others. These projects have helped Metheny grow as a composer, and perhaps because they exist in the shadow of the Group titles, are among the most underappreciated in recent jazz history.

GENRE: 🎷 Jazz. **RELEASED:** 1978, ECM. **KEY TRACKS:** "Phase Dance," "Jaco," "San Lorenzo." **CATALOG CHOICES:** *Offramp; Letter from Home.* Pat Metheny: *80/81; Song X; Rejoicing; Question and Answer.* **NEXT STOP:** Keith Jarrett: *My Song* (see p. 394). **AFTER THAT:** Pedro Aznar: *Contemplation.*

Impressive Tone in Every Note

Ravel: Piano Concerto in G
Rachmaninoff: Piano Concerto No. 4

Arturo Benedetti Michelangeli
Philharmonia Orchestra (Ettore Gracis, cond.)

O n the great big spectrum of sound, how many points are there between the pianissimo of a butterfly's fluttering wings and the triple forte of a subway screaming into the station? Are these split into discrete increments, as on a guitar amplifier where "1" is quiet and "10" (or in the case of Spinal Tap, 11) is loud? Or is volume better understood as an unbroken, continuous arc?

These two concertos showcase a pianist whose art grapples with (and, indeed, depends upon) such considerations. The Italian pianist Arturo Benedetti Michelangeli (1920–1995) was respected for his technical command; but he was revered for his precise attention to volume and shading, the ability to illuminate key phrases just by changing the tone ever so slightly.

Both pieces are late masterworks by their respective composers, and both offer Michelangeli lots of chances to engineer marathon shifts. His entrances on the Ravel start out reserved, as though he's choosing a level that will allow him to maximize the music to come. The piece, which Ravel wrote around the same time as his *Concerto for the Left Hand,* is one of the wildest rides in the orchestral repertoire: After the pastoral calm of the second movement, the third shuttles brazenly into the bustle of a jazz-age city. The Rachmaninoff has similar flashes, and here Michelangeli's technique is the catalyst, knitting the composer's small and frequently isolated melodic "cells" into a fast-moving and highly satisfying whole.

Michelangeli fought in the Italian army during World War II. His career took off after the war, and though he developed a following in Europe, he didn't perform frequently in the U.S. and remains significantly less known here. These lovingly recorded performances were captured during Michelangeli's late-1950s peak, and they helped establish him among the world's great soloists, alongside Arthur Rubinstein and Vladimir Horowitz. They are also considered among the best-ever concerto discs (perhaps out of respect, no other pianist has paired these two works on the same recording). Michelangeli's performances earn that respect, not only because the lines themselves arrive so well polished, but because he enlivens them with such vivid contrasts. You almost wonder whether there's a volume knob hidden somewhere on the piano.

GENRE: 🎵 Classical. **RELEASED:** 1958, EMI. (Reissued 2000.) **KEY TRACKS:** Ravel: second movement. Rachmaninoff: first movement. **CATALOG CHOICE:** *Michelangeli Plays Grieg and Debussy.* **NEXT STOP:** Vladimir Horowitz: *At the Met* (see p. 368). **AFTER THAT:** Monique Haas: *Plays Debussy, Ravel, and Bartók,* Orchestre National de l'ORTF (Paul Paray, cond.).

The First from the Temptations of Trenchtown

Right Time

The Mighty Diamonds

One often overlooked aspect of reggae in its "roots" heyday of the 1970s is harmony singing. Before Bob Marley and the Wailers went international, successful acts needed both charismatic leaders and supporting singers fluent in the choreographed group singing associated with doo-wop and Motown. The original Wailers were outstanding in this regard: Check *African Herbsman* or any of the records made for the Trojan label to hear a curious kind of harmony featuring three distinctive lead voices.

The Mighty Diamonds represent another less star-driven reggae harmony apex. On the smash 1976 debut *Right Time,* three principal singers—founder and harmony singer Lloyd Ferguson, lead singer Donald Shaw, and harmony singer Fitzroy Simpson—wrap messages of concern in a sheath of gossamer vocal sweetness. The songs start out plenty smart (among the highlights is a plea entitled "Africa," and the self-explanatory "I Need a Roof") and acquire a stirring resonance as they unfold, in large part because of the way the singers interact. The Diamonds might have planned every note of these clustered three-part schemes, which often take them to the top end of their ranges. But the singing never feels scripted. Quite the opposite: Often the three voices seem to stumble into each other like kids horsing around; they casually toss off call-and-response quips and reggae's more devout declarations as though singing the first thing that pops into their heads. Which is perhaps why *Right Time* feels so right.

GENRE: 🌐 World/Jamaica. **RELEASED:** 1976, Virgin. (Reissued 1984, Shanachie.) **KEY TRACKS:** "Right Time," "Africa," "Have Mercy." **CATALOG CHOICE:** *Deeper Roots.* **NEXT STOP:** The Heptones: *Party Time.* **AFTER THAT:** Los Zafiros: *Los Zafiros.*

Step Out with the Caribbean Parade Masters

Sixteen Carnival Hits

Mighty Sparrow and Lord Kitchener

For a time in the 1950s and '60s, calypso was the hottest ticket to bliss in the Caribbean. Built on a propulsive, carefully calibrated dance rhythm, its upbeat vibe spread through the streets of Trinidad and Tobago, then to England and the U.S. (where, in 1956, Harry Belafonte had a huge hit with a record called *Calypso*). This collection, which gathers Carnival hits from two prolific legends, shows how diabolical calypso was at its peak. It can be appreciated as soaring, irrepressibly joyful party beats, but if you listen closely you'll pick up social and political messages, incendiary calls to consciousness that prefigure the similar bent of reggae.

The album's cover features both Lord Kitchener (left) and Mighty Sparrow (right).

The songs here represent some of the modern era's grabbiest "Road Marches" created for the annual Carnival parades and competitions. Lord Kitchener (real name: Aldwyn Roberts) emerged in the late '40s, the Mighty Sparrow (Slinger Francisco) followed in the mid-'50s, at the moment when the basic outlines of calypso were solidifying. Rival bandleaders and singers, they'd compete to create the tune that would be "the" hit of each year's festivities—to win, a composer had to have a singable theme and at least a glance at current events. The set begins with Sparrow's endlessly catchy 1956 entry, "Jean and Dinah," and moves through hits from the next two decades; in addition to being an excellent introduction to calypso, it shows how the style changed with the times, absorbing the jaunty horns of Louis Jordan in the '50s and a bit of Motown exuberance in the '60s. (Calypso changed again in the late '70s, with the intense vocals of what was called "soca," or soul-calypso; cue up "Sa sa yea" to hear an early example of that.)

The personalities of the artists come through vividly: Kitchener, who was established when Sparrow arrived on the scene, is affable and genteel, a showman who relaxes everyone while exhorting his rhythm section to do the hard work. Sparrow, who earned his nickname for flitting around the stage (most calypsonians plant themselves in front of the mic when they sing), is more risqué and also more daring musically. Both sound like they're smiling almost all the time, and though the lyrics refer to the concerns of the poor and the struggling, when you listen to these Carnival songs, you begin to believe it's possible to saunter through any hardship.

GENRE: 🌐 World/Trinidad. **RELEASED:** 2000, Ice. **KEY TRACKS:** "Jean and Dinah," "May may," "Mama dis Is mas," "Sa sa yea." **CATALOG CHOICES:** Mighty Sparrow: *Hot and Sweet.* Lord Kitchener: *Klassic Kitchener,* Vol. 1. **NEXT STOP:** Various Artists: *Calypso Awakening.* **AFTER THAT:** Duke Ellington: *A Drum Is a Woman.*

The Whole Time Line of Jazz, in Forty Minutes

Mingus Ah Um

Charles Mingus

The crowded and cacophonous time line of jazz comes alive in the music of Charles Mingus. The bassist and thinker, one of the most erudite of bandleaders, had the rare ability to channel ghosts from long ago—the

jumps of Jelly Roll Morton, the tirades of bebop—into music that couldn't have been born a second earlier.

Mingus made music that was so joltingly alive it scared people. This album, his first for Columbia Records, is described by one record guide as an "extended tribute to ancestors," and that's certainly part of what's going on: There are nods to tenor saxophonist Lester Young ("Goodbye Pork Pie Hat") and Duke Ellington ("Open Letter to Duke") and Jelly Roll Morton ("Jelly Roll"). But Mingus doesn't freeze his sources in their historical moment. Situating them inside his group's rowdy irreverence, he brings them into the present, makes them part of *his* story.

By 1959, Mingus, forever interested in the world beyond jazz, had developed a sound that bubbled with blues and the fervor of gospel. These are key ingredients in *Ah Um.* The opening wail "Better Git It in Your Soul," arguably

In 2003, *Mingus Ah Um* was one of 50 recordings added to the National Recording Registry.

the single piece that sums up Mingus best, is built on a boisterous prayer-meeting gospel vamp. Its fast-moving call-and-response volleys are punctuated by saxophone honks and vocal exclamations as things heat up, giving the piece the feeling of a happening. That's what Mingus wanted. He taught his musicians by singing and playing the parts on piano, providing just enough guidance to get his twisting themes across—and trusting that the musicians would take it from there, contributing exuberant outbursts of their own.

GENRE: 🎷 Jazz. **RELEASED:** 1959, Columbia. **KEY TRACKS:** "Better Git It in Your Soul," "Goodbye Pork Pie Hat." **CATALOG CHOICES:** *Blues and Roots; Money Jungle; Pithycanthropus Erectus.* **NEXT STOP:** George Russell: *The Jazz Workshop.* **AFTER THAT:** Air: *Air Lore* (see p. 13).

Putting the Klang *in Industrial Music*

The Mind Is a Terrible Thing to Taste

Ministry

At the two-minute mark of "Thieves" and several times later in the song, Ministry's pulse is bolstered by what sounds like a whirring pneumatic drill. It's not a gimmick—it functions almost like a solo guitar, adding punctuation. As it pops out of nowhere, the drill sound (one website speculates it's actually an auto-rewind camera) adds just a touch of extramusical menace to the proceedings. Not that extra menace is needed: Ministry's second major-label album stands as one of the great works of industrial music, a skillfully managed noise assault that just happens to have some arena-worthy hooks. And backbeats too.

Ministry started in 1981 as a New Wave synth band on the Chicago club scene. With his band's first few albums, Cuba-born leader and multi-instrumentalist Al Jourgensen proffered dark, heavily synthetic moods. But after hearing rock bands like Big Black integrate drum machines and other unlikely instruments, Jourgensen reconfigured Ministry as a noise collage experiment. *The Land of Rape and Honey* (1988) is the band's first fully realized work, with terrifying sampled voices, supermangled guitar, and sputtering, slashing beats. Aggressive yet danceable, it became the blueprint for all of what was tagged "industrial" dance music.

The Mind Is a Terrible Thing to Taste furthers that general scheme, except the loud, metalish guitars are positioned further forward in the mix, and the songs are more disciplined. And every stray sound—a dental drill, a clanking crowbar—enhances the assault.

The Mind was way ahead of its time and remains one of the most influential heavy-rock efforts of all time: The kicking hip-hop experiment "Test" puts the major practitioners of rap-rock to shame; the dramatic "Breathe" shows where Trent Reznor of Nine Inch Nails (see p. 552) shopped for ideas. He picked up some key ones, but there's plenty more inside this mesmeric, delightfully warped, mile-a-minute assault. Go on, have a taste.

GENRE: 🎸 Rock. **RELEASED:** 1989, Sire. **KEY TRACKS:** "Thieves," "Burning Inside," "Breathe." **CATALOG CHOICE:** *The Land of Rape and Honey.* **NEXT STOP:** Nine Inch Nails: *The Downward Spiral* (see p. 552). **AFTER THAT:** Skinny Puppy: *Too Dark Park.*

Revving Toward Land Speed Records with Every Song

Double Nickels on the Dime

The Minutemen

The Minutemen seized punk as a platform for wild, free, impossibly rangey art music. Where most punk bands on the independent circuit of the early '80s were lucky to bang out five chords, the trio fronted by guitarist and singer D. Boon could really play, with lively wit and intelligence besides. The Minutemen put renegade energy into tricky jazz freak-outs, twisted *norteño* polkas, and pummeling parodies of hair bands—and knew enough about those styles to conjure them respectfully before smashing them to bits. The San Pedro, California, band had a freight-train sense of forward motion. Its music would leap out at you, barreling relentlessly down the tracks, and sometimes if you blinked during a performance, you missed a song. (Hence the band's name.)

On the cover, Mike Watt is driving at exactly 55 mph ("double nickels" in trucker slang).

The head-spinning *Double Nickels on the Dime* is the Minutemen manifesto, forty-three songs—several clocking in around ninety seconds—that explore gonzo abandon at breakneck speed. At times Boon, who emphasized the treble frequencies of the guitar over everything else, plays like he's creating some sort of postmodern art installation. Or he uses flailing, ice-picking stabs to trigger a pogo epidemic. Or he plays crazy flamenco-influenced chords ("Cohesion"). Or he veers into some spazzy skronky space sounds ("It's Expected I'm Gone"). His staccato rhythm attack is instantly identifiable, a calling card that many guitarists tried, unsuccessfully, to copy.

Amazingly, despite the abundance of songs, there isn't an outright stinker in the bunch. Even a decidedly lo-fi track like "Don't Look Now," which captures the band ripping in front of a mostly indifferent club audience, has its charms. Alas, there are only a few other great Minutemen titles to investigate: Boon was killed in a van accident just weeks after the follow-up to *Double Nickels*, *Three-Way Tie (for Last)*, was released. It's impossible to know where this band would have gone next. It would have been interesting.

GENRE: 🎸 Rock. **RELEASED:** 1984, SST. **KEY TRACKS:** "Cohesion," "It's Expected I'm Gone," "God Bows to Math," "Corona," "Dr. Wu." **CATALOG CHOICE:** *Three-Way Tie (for Last)*. **NEXT STOP:** Mike Watt: *Contemplating the Engine Room.* **AFTER THAT:** Queens of the Stone Age: *Rated R.*

String-Band Country Blues

Honey Babe Let the Deal Go Down

The Mississippi Sheiks

If there were such a thing as a music dynasty in the deep South of the 1920s, the Chatmon (or, sometimes, Chatman) family from the hill country near Jackson, Mississippi, would be it. Patriarch Henderson Chatmon, a fiddle player, was responsible for an estimated two dozen children; his son Sam once told an interviewer that at times the family band included "about nine of us full brothers and seven half-brothers, from Charley Patton on back." (The early blues pioneer Patton's family history is the subject of much speculation.)

The Chatmons recorded in various combinations and under different names (the Mississippi Mud Steppers, the Mississippi Blacksnakes), and in some cases worked solo (brother Bo Carter was the most prolific, with over a hundred sides, many of them risqué, to his credit). The most famous of the groups was known as the Mississippi Sheiks. Their repertoire included square dances, folk songs, and country blues, usually played on guitar and fiddle, with vocals—the so-called "string band" configuration. The group was already established when it first recorded in February of 1930, for the race label Okeh Records. At that first session, captured by a mobile unit in Shreveport, Louisiana, the Sheiks recorded two tunes that would become famous, "Sitting on Top of the World" and "Stop and Listen Blues No. 2."

In 2008, "Sitting on Top of the World" was inducted into the Grammy Hall of Fame.

Over the next two years, the group—usually Carter and Lonnie Chatmon on violins, with Walter Vinson on guitar and vocals—created a series of sweetly played and sometimes hauntingly sung singles, many of them collected here. These are key documents of country blues, and arguably the most important string band records of all time. Though less intense than the work of solo guitarists like Patton (see p. 584), Robert Johnson (see p. 404), and Skip James (see p. 390), they're arrestingly passionate, full of spite, and wise about the world in a way that presages the guitar-based Delta blues that followed. This anthology captures most of the group's important work, and includes several sides the Sheiks cut with popular blues singer Texas Alexander (including the beautifully played "Seen Better Days"). A big bonus is this edition's careful audio restoration, which renders once blurry instrumental touches with startling clarity.

GENRE: 🔵 Blues. **RELEASED:** 2004, Columbia/Legacy. (Original recordings 1930–1931.) **KEY TRACKS:** "Sitting on Top of the World," "Stop and Listen Blues No. 2," "Seen Better Days." **CATALOG CHOICE:** *Stop and Listen.* **NEXT STOP:** Charley Patton: *Founder of the Delta Blues* (see p. 584). **AFTER THAT:** Skip James: *The Complete Early Recordings* (see p. 390).

A Sound Painter Expands Her Palette

Court and Spark

Joni Mitchell

Joni Mitchell's second album gave the world a little koan called "Both Sides Now," which became a huge hit for Judy Collins. Mitchell's third included "Woodstock," a skeptical travelogue that Crosby, Stills, Nash, and Young turned into a counterculture anthem. The album after that, *Blue,* is often referred to as a "pioneering classic of singer-songwriter music" for its painstaking accounts of romance's riptides.

Blue is plenty wrenching. It's also monochromatic. After it, the restless Canadian singer-songwriter and guitarist (she's also an accomplished painter) began expanding her notion of what a song might be. She hired a band (the ace studio musicians known as the L.A. Express), and sought both watercolor hues and bold splashes of instrumental color, setting her sharply observed lyrics against clarinets and icy muted trumpets and snarling treble-heavy electric guitars. This emphasis on texture coalesces on Mitchell's magnificent sixth album, *Court and Spark*—a series of inward-looking confessional odes whisked along on the breezy, forever untroubled buoyance of California pop.

With a rhythm section on board, Mitchell is no longer tethered to the steady guitar strumming that defined previous works. That's a huge shift, and it loosens up everything else. Her tunes are dotted with abrupt pauses and shadowy interludes, and dramatic moments when the anchoring rhythm evaporates completely. Where she once sought to give blow-by-blow accounts of romance messes, Mitchell here dashes off impressionistic sketches—of music-biz types chasing "the star-maker machinery behind the

Mitchell was a catalyst of the Southern California singer-songwriter revolution of the early '70s.

popular song" ("Free Man in Paris") and disconsolate teens "breaking like the waves at Malibu" ("Trouble Child") and snooty types with "passport smiles" ("People's Parties"). The music's fast-changing nuances force Mitchell to become a more expansive vocalist—she sings these lithe long-distance melodies with a wriggling freedom, swooping and lunging like a bird who's just escaped captivity and is discovering new ways to fly.

GENRE: ⭐ Pop. **RELEASED:** 1974, Asylum. **KEY TRACKS:** "Trouble Child," "Car on a Hill." **CATALOG CHOICES:** *Hejira; Mingus; Shadows and Light.* **NEXT STOP:** Rickie Lee Jones: *Pirates* (see p. 410). **AFTER THAT:** José González: *Veneer.*

A Superlatively Swinging Session

Soul Station

Hank Mobley

During the jazz heyday of the late '50s and early '60s, when the crisp swing of "hard bop" poured from small cafés and shadowy clubs, the majority of recording projects were like *Soul Station*: "blowing" dates recorded in a single day by a cluster of journeymen. These easygoing sessions, often centered on rearrangements of standards or blues-based originals, were intended as snapshots of great players in action, doing their thing in unguarded, low-pressure situations.

By the time he recorded *Soul Station*, Hank Mobley, a gruff-toned tenor saxophonist from Philadelphia, had been involved in scores of such dates as both a leader and a hired-gun sideman—common practice at Blue Note Records, the de facto home of hard bop, during

this era. For what became his ninth Blue Note release, Mobley nabbed pianist Wynton Kelly and bassist Paul Chambers from the Miles Davis band, as well as drummer Art Blakey, the esteemed leader of the Jazz Messengers. He got ready for the session by writing a couple of tunes, including the spry blues "Dig Dis," and sketching out slightly altered standards.

Despite (or likely because of) the minimal prep, Mobley caught some pure jazz poetry on February 7, 1960. Everybody involved in the recording is having fun: Blakey's dancing, effortlessly pinging ride-cymbal patterns set the tone, and the other rhythm players, particularly pianist Kelly, fall right into the pocket, delivering crisp and totally attentive accompaniment with no wasted effort. This inspires Mobley, who was known to move at a leisurely pace, to take some chances; his solos here are among the most animated in his entire discography, with intricate paragraph-length thoughts punctuated by sharp hairpin-turn spinouts. And even when he's roaring, or when Kelly is rattling the piano apart, the atmosphere is all convivial lightness, a mood no amount of advance planning could have sparked.

GENRE: 🅙 Jazz. **RELEASED**: 1960, Blue Note. **KEY TRACKS**: "Dig Dis," "If I Should Lose You." **CATALOG CHOICE**: *Workout.* **NEXT STOP**: Art Blakey and the Jazz Messengers: *Moanin'* (see p. 95).

The Jazz Embodiment of Individual and Collective Poise

European Concert

The Modern Jazz Quartet

Not a hair is out of place in the music of the Modern Jazz Quartet. No tie crooked, no cuff unlinked. Yet listen attentively to these purveyors of genteel dinner-jacket jazz and a different impression emerges: On this

sparkling concert recording from 1960, the group pulls off the unlikely parlor trick of dishing great improvisational feats while minding its manners.

The MJQ began in 1951, and performed steadily, with several hiatuses, into the '90s. Its personnel remained mostly constant—the drummer Kenny Clarke was replaced by Connie Kay in 1955. This performance was relatively early in the group's history, but it doesn't

Known for their reliability and manners, the MJQ never missed a gig and was never late.

sound like it: Already it has the cohesion often associated with veteran string quartets. The group was forever being compared to classical ensembles, in part because of the crystalline magic combination of piano and vibraphone, and in part because of the tight discipline of its pieces. While other jazz groups sought wide-open vistas, the MJQ choreographed its music down to the last countrapuntal riffs.

This program opens with "Django," a wistful Lewis original that pays homage to Gypsy guitarist Django Reinhardt. The tune, the group's biggest "hit," has several distinct sections that shift from expansive baroque-style chord sequences to hunkered-down blues vamps. Each soloist interprets the road map differently. Jackson plays elegant, questioning lines that yearn for more freedom, while Lewis, a crafty scene-setter who deploys the harmony of bebop and Debussy-style impressionism with equal facility, uses short, furtive phrases to encrypt the blues into his own code. The pianist's solo ends with a gradual rallentando, as the four musicians downshift from a vibrant swing pulse into something almost tempoless. This change is plenty dramatic but feels completely smooth, the imperceptible gearshifts of a luxury sedan. That's teamwork, at a high level, and there's lots and lots of it on display here.

GENRE: 🎷 Jazz. **RELEASED:** 1961, Atlantic. **KEY TRACKS:** "Django," "I Should Care," "Bag's Groove," " 'Round Midnight."

CATALOG CHOICES: *Fontessa; The Complete Last Concert.* **NEXT STOP:** The Dave Brubeck Quartet: *Time Further Out.* **AFTER THAT:** Cal Tjader: *The Monterey Concert.*

The First Punk Record?

The Modern Lovers

The Modern Lovers

The first nine songs of this supercharged album were recorded in 1972 and 1973, but not released until 1976. That's significant, because in the intervening years, the sound that songwriter/guitarist Jonathan Richman and his Boston-based band developed—a wiry, stretched-tight, three-chord rock with emphasis on guileless lyrics—resembled the music later known as punk. "Roadrunner," the rampaging chant that opens this record, is often cited as the "first" punk song; it's been covered by the Sex Pistols and Joan Jett, among others.

The delay can be attributed to typical music-business machinations—and Richman's artistic evolution. According to the liner notes of this reissue, once the record was finished, the songwriter told his label, Warner Bros., that he'd grown sick of the songs and wouldn't perform them live. The label then refused to release the album, and the band, which included future Talking Head Jerry Harrison and future Car David Robinson, broke up. *The Modern Lovers* was rescued by an enterprising small label, Beserkley, which reportedly bought the masters for $2,300 and put the recordings out, to considerable critical acclaim, in the heated punk explosion of 1976. By then, however, Richman had renounced rock, focusing on the insightful pop that has distinguished his subsequent career.

Jonathan Richman, far right, wrote all the songs on *The Modern Lovers.*

He might have changed horses too soon. *The Modern Lovers* is a thrilling slice of rock and roll, informed by equal parts suburban-kid anxiety and three-chord cool. Regardless of its place in the history of punk, this set of deliberately blunt songs produced by John Cale (The Velvet Underground was a huge influence on Richman) remains a delightful listening experience—too smart for its own good sometimes, and just dumb enough to describe raging hormones in heroic terms. Among Richman's great gifts is the ability to deliver wry appraisals of human nature while sounding like a kid who's just looking for the next thrill: When he sings "Some people try to pick up girls and get called asshole, this never happened to Pablo Picasso," there's admiration in his voice, and a little bit of wonder too.

GENRE: 🎸 Rock. **RELEASED:** 1976, Beserkley. (Reissued 2003, Castle.) **KEY TRACKS:** "Pablo Picasso," "Road Runner." **CATALOG CHOICE:** *Rock and Roll with the Modern Lovers.* **NEXT STOP:** Talking Heads: *Talking Heads 77.*

The Best from an Argentine Original

Segundo

Juana Molina

In interviews after this astounding record appeared in 2003, Juana Molina said she'd never studied Brian Wilson's late Beach Boys music, hadn't checked out too much pop-electronica, and only had a passing knowledge of Björk.

She explained that she'd grown up around Brazilian music (her father was a poet and lyricist) and spent much of her adult life working in Argentine television—eventually hosting a popular weekly sketch comedy series. Only after she walked away to pursue music did she begin to take in the wide world of pop.

That's hard to believe listening to "Mantra del bicho feo," one of several pieces that revolve around gorgeous cascading waterfalls of multitracked Molina vocals. Though there are lyrics, she sings most of the song in a repertoire of *bwees* and *bah-bah-bahs* that recall the Beach Boys, except with spry post–bossa nova guitar patterns and hand drums bubbling underneath. Her music has a tranquil air, but every now and then Molina, who recorded this by herself at home, mostly at night, lets the har-

In 2003, *Segundo* was named Best World Music Album by *Entertainment Weekly*.

monies drift into dissonance, or brings in an odd squiggle from a detuned synthesizer. When that happens, the music feels as if it's being slowly pulled into a more sinister zone, a trip with Captain Beefheart at the wheel and Björk navigating.

Those unpredictable flareups give Molina's songs—which tell of misunderstandings and missed connections—an undercurrent of vague disquiet. One gets the sense that Molina, an artist with little tolerance for the status quo and an ear for adventure, likes it that way.

GENRE: 🌐 World/Argentina. **RELEASED:** 2003, Domino. **KEY TRACKS:** "Martin Ferro," "La visita," "Quiero," "Mantra del bicho feo." **CATALOG CHOICE:** *Son.* **NEXT STOP:** Beth Orton: *Central Reservation* (see p. 568). **AFTER THAT:** Savath and Savalas: *Apropa't.*

The Most Melodious Thunk

The Unique Thelonious Monk

Thelonious Monk

Thelonious Monk had enough personality for ten jazz musicians, and over the course of his career it brought him equal helpings of fame and scorn. Some bebop musicians of the '40s derided his intricate tunes as gibberish, and for a time in the late '40s and early '50s he had trouble working as a pianist because his approach—he'd jab at the piano in fits of pointillistic fury that one wag described as a "melodious thunk"—was so alien to the prevailing ideal (embodied by Bud Powell) of smooth, unflappable technique. Then, in the mid-'50s, the tide turned: Suddenly Monk's iconoclastic ways won favor. He became a celebrity, his compositions hailed as a vision of the jazz future.

Monk started playing the piano when he was 9 years old.

Maybe the world had finally caught up with this defiant individual, or maybe the tipping point was this and a few other sizzling records he made for Riverside in the mid-'50s. Monk began his association with Riverside by doing an album of Ellington tunes, and then this sparkling trio date, which is devoted to standards.

Jazz historians consider the record that followed this one, *Brilliant Corners*, to be the must-have. It does showcase Monk's scissoring originals, and each is a marvel. But for sheer impulsive delights, *Unique* is hard to beat, largely because of the authoritative gait of his supporting musicians—bassist Oscar Pettiford and drummer Art Blakey, perhaps the most adroit backing tandem Monk ever had. Applying himself to songs other jazzers would consider trite—"Tea for Two," "Just You, Just Me"—Monk emerges as a subversively lyrical soloist, a trickster capable of keeping listeners on edge with jabbing chords, then seducing them with gloriously romantic melodies. Blakey's presence means that nothing's frantic—when, on "Just You," Monk sets off a rattling series of chordal repetitions, Blakey saunters serenely, his ride cymbal pointing the way to calm waters.

There are signs that Monk recognized his contrary nature. In the notes to *The Complete Thelonious Monk on Riverside*, producer Orrin Keepnews recalls overhearing the pianist preparing a sideman for a recording session. "Don't pay too much attention to what I'm playing behind you," Monk cautioned. "Because when we record I'll probably be playing something completely different, and it'll only confuse you." Which, of course, is exactly why you should pay attention.

GENRE: 🄹 Jazz. **RELEASED:** 1956, Riverside. **KEY TRACKS:** "Just You, Just Me," "Tea for Two." **CATALOG CHOICES:** *Brilliant Corners; Solo Monk.* **NEXT STOP:** Andrew Hill: *Point of Departure* (see p. 359). **AFTER THAT:** Jason Moran: *The Bandwagon* (see p. 519).

A Lost Chapter of Jazz Found

At Carnegie Hall

The Thelonious Monk Quartet with John Coltrane

Because so much jazz happened live, some slivers of its history are sketchy or incomplete. We know, for example, that John Coltrane spent much of 1957 (around eight months) playing with pianist Thelonious Monk's group; though a few assorted studio dates and off-quality live tapes exist, there's a shortage of recordings devoted to what musicians remember as a fiery, groundbreaking band.

So when a tape of this November 1957 Carnegie Hall benefit concert was unearthed during a vault cleanout in early 2005, it was as if the Dead Sea Scrolls had turned up on 57th Street. Produced by Voice of America radio for overseas broadcast, this pristine recording fills in a key bit of the Monk legacy: The pianist, who first emerged during the birth of bebop, had by this time assembled the most iconoclastic songbook in jazz—tunes that jabbered in a hinky, halting language all their own, each governed by an intricate internal logic. Not every soloist could contend with Monk, because where other composers provided easy chairs, he put sharp tacks down. The ever-restless Coltrane was, in many ways, Monk's perfect foil—like Monk, he was interested in elucidating a song's underlying architecture.

This performance features Coltrane and a crack rhythm team working through some of Monk's lively, mazelike music. Coltrane sounds like he's fully absorbed the intricacies of it; he

thelonious monk quartet
with john coltrane at carnegie hall

"[The] musical equivalent of the discovery of a new Mount Everest."   —*Newsweek*

slips genius flirtations into the yearning cries of "Monk's Mood," and storms through the choppy "Evidence" at tripletime, savoring the friction of the pianist's clustered supporting chords. Monk's solos are the huge surprise: Though usually resistant to anything too accessible, he's positively garrulous here, tossing out a mixture of scare-tactic melodies and jabbing, pointillist, rhythmic catchphrases like he knows he can't be caught. Off in the deep margins, you can sometimes hear Coltrane playing long tones behind Monk, to outline the harmony. It's a simple thing, something horn players did often as counterpoint in clubs, but it's electrifying all the same hearing the mighty 'Trane lifting the pianist's intense inventions just a little bit higher.

GENRE: 🅰 Jazz. **RELEASED:** 2005, Blue Note. **KEY TRACKS:** "Epistrophy," "Monk's Mood." **CATALOG CHOICE:** *Monk's Dream.* **NEXT STOP:** Miles Davis: *Miles in Tokyo.* **AFTER THAT:** John Coltrane: *Coltrane's Sound.*

The Father of Bluegrass

The Music of Bill Monroe

Bill Monroe

Isaac Stern, the great classical violinist, once said that a great musician doesn't take his music to people—he plays and the people eventually come to him. One illustration of this is Bill Monroe (1911–1996). A swift-fingered mandolinist, Monroe developed the folk songs and unassuming mountain music he heard growing up in Rosine, Kentucky, into what we now know as bluegrass. He's the one who first called it bluegrass, and the one who developed its attack, the florid fiddle lines anchored by crisp guitar and mandolin picking.

Monroe was working at an oil refinery and playing music with his brother Charlie in a string band at night, when the duo began attracting the interest of record companies. Beginning in 1936, the Monroe Brothers cut over sixty songs for RCA/Bluebird, including the splendid "What Would You Give in

Exchange for Your Soul," but by 1938 the brothers parted ways. Bill Monroe spent the rest of his career as a solo bandleader. Though he had a reputation for being difficult, he was also a gifted teacher: His band, the Blue Grass Boys, included most of the significant figures of '50s and '60s bluegrass, including fiddler Vassar Clements, the wizardlike guitar-and-banjo duo Flatt and Scruggs (see p. 282), and singer Mac Wiseman.

In 1966, Bill Monroe was made an honorary Kentucky colonel.

Monroe recorded for decades. This anthology, produced by the Country Music Foundation, is the first to draw material from his output for Columbia, RCA, and Decca. As a result, it offers a full picture of Monroe, from the rambunctious early rambles that left listeners stunned ("Bluegrass Breakdown") to mournful ballads ("You'll Find Her Name Written There") to later works, like the tightly harmonized "I'm Going Back to Kentucky,"

that had rock stars like Jerry Garcia volunteering to be one of the Blue Grass Boys. The sound quality improves over the years, but little else changes. That's because Monroe didn't try to "sell" bluegrass; in the liner notes, he's quoted as saying, "I thought I'd touch the country people—the farm people—and that would be as far as it would ever get." Through musical fads and cultural tumults, Monroe played his same steady truth-telling music. And people came to him.

GENRE: ◉ Country. **RELEASED:** 1994, MCA. **KEY TRACKS:** "I'm Sittin' on Top of the World," "Bluegrass Breakdown," "Lonesome Moonlight Waltz," "John Henry." **CATALOG CHOICE:** *Off the Record, Vol. 1: Live Recordings 1956–69.* **NEXT STOP:** Flatt and Scruggs: *Foggy Mountain Gospel.* **AFTER THAT:** Jerry Garcia and David Grisman: *Jerry Garcia/David Grisman.*

Beyond the Notes, a New Window onto Bach

Bach and Beyond

Gabriela Montero

Classical music is often treated as a fixed entity: The score is absolute, to be followed with reverence, and the interpreter is expected to go only so far to embellish a piece. These are awesome works of genius, goes the thinking, and they must be treated with kid gloves.

That's a strange modern notion. Bach, Mozart, and Liszt, great improvisers all, wrote with the expectation that future interpreters would cut loose a little and reconfigure as the occasion demanded. To facilitate that, Bach conceived his music in orderly cycles and steps. Any musician who understands his general

harmonic logic—the scheme of chords moving in sequence, sometimes threaded together by a corresponding melody—can take Bach far from the page. (And many have, including jazz pianists Keith Jarrett and Jacques Loussier.)

To experience a journey that's based on Bach but doesn't follow him note for note, check out Argentine pianist Gabriela Montero's rendition of "Jesu, Joy of Man's Desiring." She begins with a fairly conventional statement of the theme, but soon enough plunges into different key centers—first, the relative minor, then a minor key a few doors down. Her lines glance at the general trajectory of the original text, and somehow manage to slide just enough into the exotic to prompt a rethinking: Your ear knows how the chords are supposed to resolve, and yet Montero is pulling someplace else, into a less expected and more emotionally expansive zone.

Gabriela Montero
BACH AND BEYOND

"I have rarely come across a talent like Gabriela's. She is a unique artist."   —Martha Argerich

Montero makes her living as a concert pianist. In the liner notes she explains that she kept her improvisational musings to herself until she played for the legendary pianist Martha Argerich (see p. 25), who encouraged Montero to develop this dimension of her talent.

That was a blessing. Here's a thoughtful and exceedingly alert musician who's tethered to Bach and rebelling against him at the same time, whose murmuring approach opens a new window into his music, whose shadings and whims and melodic leaps stray from the score just enough to call attention to the awesome architecture embedded deep within it.

GENRE: 🎹 Classical.
RELEASED: 2006, EMI. **KEY TRACKS:** "Jesu, Joy of Man's Desiring," Adagio, Prelude in C. **CATALOG CHOICE:** *Gabriela Montero.* **NEXT STOP:** Keith Jarrett: *Shostakovich: The Twenty-four Preludes and Fugues, Op. 87.* **AFTER THAT:** Jacques Loussier Trio: *The Brandenburgs.*

Choirmaster Seeks New Job, Has Original Material . . .

Vespers of the Blessed Virgin 1610

Claudio Monteverdi

Concerto Italiano (Rinaldo Alessandrini, cond.)

Somewhere around 1610, Claudio Monteverdi (1567–1643) hit the wall. After serving for years as choirmaster to the Duke of Mantua and occupying himself writing innovative books of madrigals, he realized he needed a better job. The twenty-five-section *Vespers of the Blessed Virgin,* designed for varying musical accompaniments, was an attempt to address this situation. Some scholars believe part of Monteverdi's motivation was to "advertise" his skills, and if so, the *Vespers* did the trick. In 1612, he was appointed *maestro di cappella* at Venice's basilica of St. Mark, a position he held until his death.

The piece, performed with gusto by the early music ensemble Concerto Italiano, is an unconventional, thoroughly captivating sacred choral work. Alternating between intricate overlapping chorales and demanding passages for solo singers, it presents Monteverdi as an inventive and independent-minded melodist—and cements his legacy as the primary "bridge" between Renaissance and baroque music.

In Monteverdi's time, vespers were not like Masses—they weren't nearly as formal, and often consisted of whatever leftover music happened to be lying around. These are different. Monteverdi envisioned the piece as a whole, and wrote magisterial chorales and exultant solo turns. Though he did some repurposing (the opening sequence is borrowed from his 1607 opera *L'Orfeo*), he composed the majority from scratch, sometimes relying on psalms as text. This gives the piece an unusual unity; broad thematic ideas turn up in several places, helping Monteverdi connect the cool ethereal tones of Renaissance polyphony to the florid spiraling phrases that characterize baroque music. Even as he employs these diametrically opposed techniques, Monteverdi sustains a questing, crusading, uplifting spirit throughout. He doesn't skimp on the "glory hallelujah" stuff. But he doesn't suffocate listeners with excess piousness either. Thrilling.

GENRE: 🎼 Classical. **RELEASED:** 2004, Naïve. **KEY TRACKS:** "Ave maris stella," "Psalm 109/Dixit Dominus." **ANOTHER INTERPRETATION:** The Scholars Baroque Ensemble. **CATALOG CHOICES:** *Madrigals*, The Consort of Musicke; *L'Orfeo*, Anne Sofie von Otter, Anthony Rolfe Johnson, English Baroque Soloists (John Eliot Gardiner, cond.). **NEXT STOP:** *La rocque 'n' roll: Popular Music of Renaissance France*, The Baltimore Consort. **AFTER THAT:** J. S. Bach: *Mass in B Minor* (see p. 36).

Live Jazz from a Guitar Titan

Smokin' at the Half Note

Wes Montgomery

Here's yet another woeful example of how the barons of the record industry haven't always been the best caretakers of music. When Creed Taylor, the producer and executive then working at Verve Records, heard these recordings made by Wes Montgomery and the Wynton Kelly trio at New York's Half Note in June of 1965, he told the musicians that only two tracks were worthy of release—"No Blues" and "If You Could See Me Now." Taylor booked studio time for September, and captured several more songs, which were added to the live cuts and released as the (misnamed) original *Smokin' at the Half Note*.

At the time, Montgomery was an established star, responsible for several snapping records that revolutionized jazz guitar, among them *Boss Guitar* and *Full House*. And though the Half Note sessions caught him in

"Wes had a corn on his thumb, which gave his sound that point. . . . That's why no one will ever match Wes."
—George Benson

peak form, playing with one of the most accomplished rhythm sections of the day—his friend and pianist Kelly, drummer Jimmy Cobb, and bassist Paul Chambers—Montgomery didn't fight Taylor. Not long after this date Montgomery and Taylor embarked on a series of successful, if largely saccharine, instrumental pop records. Then in 1968 the guitarist suffered a heart attack and died suddenly.

That's when the original misjudgment about the Half Note material was compounded: In the rush to offer the public anything by the late Montgomery, the label went back to the Half Note session, and added brass and woodwinds to several tracks, releasing it on an album called *Willow Weep for Me*. Talk about a clunker: The sizzling, never-before-heard live Montgomery was muddled up with excessive, utterly pointless arrangements. Not until 2004 were these recordings available without the appended orchestra.

They're essential listening—for the knifing clarity of Montgomery's lines and the rapid rejoinders of his accompanists, for the way he plucks ideas out of thin air, for the palpable texture of his blocky trademark octaves and elegant whiplash chords, for the flash of inven-

tion that is "Impressions" and the dolorous, questioning spirit that propels "What's New?" No matter what any executive says, this is one no-nonsense, never-to-be-improved-upon document of live jazz.

GENRE: 🅐 Jazz. **RELEASED:** 1965, Verve. (Reissued 2004.) **KEY TRACKS:** "Impressions," "No Blues," "If You Could See Me Now." **CATALOG CHOICES:** *Full House; Boss Guitar*. **NEXT STOP:** Wynton Kelly: *Kelly Blue*. **AFTER THAT:** Jim Hall: *Concierto*.

Spanish Keyboard Magic

Solo Piano

Tete Montoliu

J azz history is filled with characters like Tete Montoliu, the Spanish pianist who was a favorite of musicians (he played with Rahsaan Roland Kirk and others) yet never quite connected with a wide audience. Blind since birth,

Montoliu (1933–1997) didn't tour a lot. Though he recorded frequently, most of his titles were put out by small European labels; as far as chain-store America is concerned, he doesn't exist.

Still Montoliu was a major talent. He had all the technique a piano player ever needs, and a gift for accompanying horn players with spunky, unusually clustered chords. Where some pianists set out to dazzle, Montoliu was mostly into making up sweet lines. He was also an expert at mimicking styles—he could quickstep through bebop like Bud Powell, or play pastel shades à la Bill Evans. Still, Montoliu always sounded like himself.

This CD brings together two of Montoliu's strongest albums, each representing a distinct facet of his musical personality. *Yellow Dolphin Street*, recorded in February 1977, is mostly standards. Reworking "You've Changed" and "If You Could See Me Now" with altered harmonies, Montoliu reveals himself, phrase by shining phrase, as a bold jazz intellect who's also a

romantic. *Catalonian Folksongs*, cut later the same year, is one of Montoliu's many attempts to view the music of his heritage through a jazz prism. The songs, many by Spanish singer-songwriter Joan Manuel Serrat, are simple, earnest odes. Rather than take them straight to beboptown, Montoliu honors the proud shapes of the melodies, throwing special light on what he hears as poignant. His elaborations are guided by pure delight, rewrites that expand mightily on the wistful original themes. These have lots of jazz in them. It's just not of the tiresome "Look at me!" variety.

GENRE: 🅐 Jazz. **RELEASED:** 1989, Timeless. **KEY TRACKS:** "You've Changed," "Yellow Dolphin Street," "If You Could See Me Now," "Manuel," "Una gitarra." **CATALOG CHOICES:** *Boleros*, Vol. 1; *The Music I Like to Play*, Vol. 1. **NEXT STOP:** Chick Corea: *My Spanish Heart*. **AFTER THAT:** Gonzalo Rubalcaba: *Solo*.

An Introduction to a True Original

The Viking of Sixth Avenue

Moondog

This is the first decent anthology devoted to the zany multi-instrumentalist Louis Hardin, who called himself Moondog and was happiest performing his "symphonies" and strange fusions of jazz, classical, and Native American chant on the streets of New York. In a Viking suit. In all kinds of weather. He was one of Manhattan's most famous and enigmatic street fixtures, and over the decades his acquaintances and champions included Charlie Parker, Igor Stravinsky, Janis Joplin, and Frank Zappa.

As a child growing up in Arkansas and then Wyoming, Moondog (1916–1999) went with his father to an Arapaho Sun Dance ceremony. This left a deep impression; much of his music is set to the steady thrumming of the tom-tom, an integral part of Native American music. Moondog also incorporated the ritual chanting patterns of ceremonial music from around the world, and after moving to New York in the late '40s, began integrating elements of jazz—though he told an interviewer that some of his esteemed solos, like the one on "Lament I: Bird's Lament," were actually written out note for note.

A happy outsider who largely disdained traditional performance outlets like clubs and concert halls, Moondog did manage to document his ideas on records for several labels (Joplin, who recorded his madrigal "All Is Loneliness" on the debut album by her band, Big Brother and the Holding Company, helped get him a contract with Columbia). His compositions have the wild inventiveness of music made by a child: There are trancelike explosions of interconnected rhythm, and catcalls from bleating and shouting saxophones, and fantastical cartoon-music whiz-bangs. Most of the time Moondog overdubbed all the parts himself, re-creating the slightly wacky house band he heard in his head. It's some of the most inventive music the New York streets ever produced.

GENRE: 🎷 Jazz. **RELEASED:** 2006, Honest Jon's. **KEY TRACKS:** "Lament I: Bird's Lament," "All Is Loneliness." **CATALOG CHOICES:** *Moondog I* and *II*. **NEXT STOP:** Harry Partch Ensemble: *The Music of Harry Partch*. **AFTER THAT:** The Residents: *God in Three Persons*.

An Oft-Neglected Great American Opera

The Ballad of Baby Doe

Douglas Moore and John Latouche
Beverly Sills, Walter Cassel, New York City Opera (Emerson Buckley, cond.)

This great American opera tells the true story of Baby Doe Taber, the trophy wife of a Colorado mine prospector and U.S. senator, Horace Taber. Their premarital relationship was an open secret in the town of Leadville, and

and when they finally married, the couple lived lavishly until a devaluation of silver made their holdings essentially worthless. After Horace died, in 1899, Baby Doe retreated to a cabin on the property of the "Matchless mine," and undertook repeated attempts to make it profitable while scribbling increasingly delusional notes to herself. She was found frozen to death on the floor of her cabin in 1935; by that time, her story had inspired a stage play, a musical, a one-woman show, and several books.

Douglas Moore wrote music for more than 40 years.

The plot devices are fairly common. As ever, the genius is in the telling: Composer Douglas Moore (1893–1969) spends much of the first act establishing the mores and manners of the day, via broad-shouldered music that has the sweep (but, happily, not the clip-clopping clichés) of the American West. Then, early in the second act, the music grows deeper, throwing the characters into sharper relief; suddenly what had been a conventional morality play grows into a more nuanced human drama. The work ends with a quiet aria that telescopes time: Baby Doe, played by Beverly Sills, sheds her hood to reveal that she's grown old and gray, and then continues singing about her incredibly sad circumstances.

This was Sills's first major role, and it remains one of her best. A child prodigy, she toured regularly as "the youngest diva in cap-tivity." She married a wealthy man and was able to pick her engagements. She was living in Cleveland when *Baby Doe* was being cast, and heard through the diva grapevine that composer Moore considered her too tall to play Baby Doe. She auditioned anyway, wearing her highest heels and singing the arias from memory; she got the part.

What she does with it is tremendous acting: Rather than play up the trophy wife aspect of Baby Doe, which would turn most women in the audience against her, Sills instead approaches Baby Doe as an innocent, cultivating empathy for the character. Her wonderfully proportioned and radiant voice does the rest, emulating the gentle sway of the weeping willow ("Willow Song"), capturing the nervousness that runs beneath polite conversation ("I Beg Your Pardon"). Even if you're somehow not rooting for Baby Doe, it's impossible to deny Sills's moving, ever effortless singing. This is what people mean when they talk about a star-making performance.

GENRE: 🎭 Opera. **RELEASED:** 1961, Deutsche Grammophon. **KEY TRACKS:** "Willow Song," "The Fine Ladies," "The Cattle Are Asleep," "Always Through the Changing." **NEXT STOP:** Jules Massenet: *Manon* (see p. 481). **AFTER THAT:** Renée Fleming: *Bel canto*.

Chinese Stock Reports, Taped Phone Conversations, Radical Jazz

The Bandwagon

Jason Moran

" Ringing My Phone (Straight Outta Istanbul)," one of six originals on this electrifying 2002 live date, might be the first piece written for jazz trio and one side of a phone conversation. When he was performing in Istanbul, Moran became friends with a tour guide hired to show him the city. With her permission, he recorded her talking with her parents on the phone, and then, borrowing editing techniques from hip-hop and William Burroughs, refashioned the audio to repeat some phrases and chop up others. Around that fixed audio, he composed a sprawling piano "theme."

The Bandwagon was recorded live at New York City's Village Vanguard.

The result is a topsy-turvy dream sequence. The woman, speaking Turkish, is lighthearted and playful; Moran, one of the most provocative thinkers in jazz, surrounds her irregular phrases with intrepid stair-step runs and stormy "responses." His longtime rhythm section, bassist Tarus Mateen and drummer Nasheet Waits, reinforces that fractured feeling. That, Moran said later, was the whole idea. "I wanted to make something where none of us could use the things we rely

on all the time. We had to play differently."

Such brain-teaser challenges are a Moran hallmark. *The Bandwagon* also features his fractured take on Afrika Bambaataa's early hip-hop anthem "Planet Rock," a musical fantasia built around a radio stock report in Chinese, a bit of Brahms, and a zealously reharmonized version of the '30s standard "Body and Soul." An outgrowth of the pianist's curiosity and his determination to subvert neo-traditional jazz doctrine, these pieces argue that there's profound music hiding inside the most ordinary conversations.

GENRE: 🅙 Jazz. **RELEASED:** 2003, Blue Note. **KEY TRACKS:** "Planet Rock," "Ringing My Phone (Straight Outta Istanbul)." **CATALOG CHOICE:** *Same Mother.* **NEXT STOP:** Greg Osby: *Banned in New York.*

The Best Introduction to a True Original

Cuban Originals

Beny Moré

In his heyday during the late 1950s, bandleader and singer Beny Moré (1919–1963) was known as "el Barbaro del Ritmo," the wild man of rhythm, due to his penchant for up-tempo dance numbers. His family (he was born to

former slaves in Cienfuegos, on Cuba's southern coast) practiced Santeria, the Cuban religion derived from the deities of Africa's Yoruba people. As "Francisco Guayabal" and other tracks on this compilation demonstrate, Moré was a singer who embraced the African elements of Cuba's heritage.

But Moré was also the most suave ballad singer south of Nat King Cole, a natural persuader who linked the cool of postwar crooners

to the wistful longing essential to bolero. Moré's interpretations were dramatic, marked by wild swings of mood—among the trademarks displayed on "Mucho corazón" are unexpected forays into his falsetto range. Everybody who cares about the fine art of singing should know Beny Moré.

Fiercely loyal, Moré regarded the musicians of his Banda Gigante as his "tribe"; he intentionally sought dark-skinned Cuban musicians to combat the racism of Havana's nightclub owners. Though he didn't read music, he was known to create arrangements on the fly, by singing the motifs he wanted his horn section to play; sure enough these arrangements have a blithe, lighthearted quality that's worlds away from the blaring trumpets some mambo bands used like weapons.

Cue up "Manigua" for a crash course in the many facets of Moré: One minute he's the wild man of rhythm, the next he's the swooning lounge don. As the singer Compay Segundo, a

Moré learned to play guitar as a child, making his first instrument from a board and a ball of string.

Cuban legend who followed in Moré's footsteps, once put it: "He was a showman and he was the greatest of them all. No one else came near."

GENRE: 🌐 World/Cuba. **RELEASED:** 1999, RCA. **KEY TRACKS:** "La culebra," "Bonito y sabroso," "Que bueno baila usted." **CATALOG CHOICE:** *Complete Recordings 1953– 1960.* **NEXT STOP:** Compay Segundo: *Calle Salud.* **AFTER THAT:** Ibrahim Ferrer: *Buena Vista Social Club Presents . . . .*

A Soul-Jazz Icon's Most Daring Expedition

Search for the New Land

Lee Morgan

Two months before he made this album, one of the most inventive of the hard bop era, the trumpet player Lee Morgan recorded a career-defining hit called "The Sidewinder." A kicky boogaloo filled with slurry late-night solos, "The Sidewinder" stood apart from everything happening in jazz in 1964. It became one of the first crossover records of the 1960s, showing countless jazz musicians a (soon to be worn-out) path toward commercial viability marked "soul jazz" or some such.

During the brief period before "The Sidewinder" reached the marketplace, before anyone could have anticipated its impact, the twenty-four-year-old Morgan turned up at engineer Rudy Van Gelder's New Jersey home (and studio) with a different band to record this gem. Compared with "The Sidewinder,"

Lee Morgan recorded over 25 albums as bandleader.

Search for the New Land is an "art" statement—the solemn title suite alternates between a tempoless rubato and a broken African rhythm, and his other originals are loaded with characteristically tricky hard-bop challenges, explorations guided by the inquisitive interplay of pianist Herbie Hancock and guitarist Grant Green.

After "The Sidewinder" exploded, Morgan's career changed. He was persuaded to make a series of less interesting soul-jazz titles, among them the patently derivative blues *The Rumproller*. He was murdered (by his mistress) on the bandstand in

1972, leaving behind a stack of "Sidewinder"-style crowd-pleasing recordings, and the much more vigorous music he found, briefly anyway, on this *Search*.

GENRE:  Jazz. **RELEASED:** 1964, Blue Note. **KEY TRACKS:** "Search for the New Land," "The Joker," "Mr. Kenyatta." **CATALOG CHOICES:** *The Sidewinder; Live at the Lighthouse.* **NEXT STOP:** Wayne Shorter: *Speak No Evil.* **AFTER THAT:** Freddie Hubbard: *Backlash.*

Somebody's a Little Upset

Jagged Little Pill

Alanis Morissette

J*agged Little Pill* refutes your mother's wisdom about how anger is not a terribly constructive emotion. On most of these riveting, fulminating songs, Alanis Morissette snarls, at the top of her formidable lungs, about egregious slights—from parents who suffocate with their expectations ("Perfect"), from lovers who've become too needy and dependent ("Not the Doctor"), or the ones who sent her into a prolonged spinout ("You Oughta Know").

There's lots of music powered by anger. What sets this hugely influential album apart is Morissette's knack for bringing listeners into the center of her storm. She doesn't merely recount assorted setbacks, she offers a minute-by-minute tour of them, sparing no detail to describe raw and often uncomfortable emotions. Morissette's taunting voice sits right at the front of the mix, and though she starts out delivering the simple yet devastating melodies straight, she eventually hauls out an impressive array of wounded bleats and bellowing screams to deliver her stories. These wild flashes feel truly wild, too unruly to have been plotted beforehand.

Throughout *Jagged*, Morissette does the high-drama stuff while the band, which includes ace alt-rock guitarist Dave Navarro

Jagged Little Pill has sold over 30 million copies worldwide.

(Jane's Addiction), provides steady, unflappable support. The album's most memorable songs aspire to the swaggering confidence of U2's big-tent anthems, and have similarly broad sing-along refrains. These give Morissette's self-absorbed lyrics—particularly the litany of betrayal that is "You Oughta Know"—a sense of righteousness. The melodies are deceptively simple and thoroughly ingratiating, and as they repeat, they become rallying cries strong enough to empower the disheartened. Morissette frequently sounds like she's totally lost in pursuit of catharsis, but that's just showbiz: No matter how heavy the subjects or how much fire she breathes, she knows that at the end of the day, she's selling pop songs. Not transcripts of therapy sessions.

GENRE:  Rock. **RELEASED:** 1995, Maverick/Reprise. **KEY TRACKS:** "You Oughta Know," "All I Really Want." **CATALOG CHOICE:** *Supposed Former Infatuation Junkie.* **NEXT STOP:** Avril Lavigne: *Let Go.* **AFTER THAT:** Paula Cole: *This Fire.*

The Sauce in the Spaghetti Western

A Fistful of Film Music

Ennio Morricone

A lonesome, troubled hero rides into the frame. We know he's lonesome by the whip-poor-will off in the distance, and from the trebley electric guitar that clippety-clops along in dusty isolation. A showdown looms, and as the storm clouds gather, the bad guys march in, accompanied by foreboding snare drums rattling away.

These techniques are part of the prolific Italian film composer Ennio Morricone's enduring contribution to music in film. Over a twenty-year career that began in the slap-dash world of low-budget spaghetti Westerns, Morricone has developed an aural short-hand of specific moods and atmospheres, a lexicon that's been copied by virtually everyone in film—both in outright imitation and in campy send-up. But as this career survey argues, Morricone's film scores are more than an endless parade of predictable sonic cues. From his early films (*A Fistful of Dollars*) through more nuanced ones (*The Good, the Bad and the Ugly*) to contemplative later projects (*The Mission*), Morricone starts with these mood-setting devices then slips in deeply felt and surprisingly affecting melodies.

The composer, whose first instrument was the trumpet, orients everything in his scores around singable motifs; even the pastoral scenes where the music serves as pure plush backdrop push, sometimes with glacial slowness, toward an overarching theme. Disc one is heavy on the campier moments in Morricone's filmography. The second disc showcases his more mature work, and it's uniformly stunning—a series of invitingly lush scenes and precise orchestrations that are grand and stirring. Without any visuals.

GENRE: 🎷 Classical. **RELEASED:** 1995, Rhino. **KEY TRACKS:** "The Ecstasy of Gold," "Navajo Joe," "March of the Beggars." **NEXT STOP:** Bernard Herrmann: *Music from the Great Hitchcock Movie Thrillers.*

The Way Young Lovers Do

Astral Weeks

Van Morrison

V an Morrison was not yet the mystic healer or revered rock troubadour of the spiritual when he and a group of skeptical jazz musicians gathered to make this album, his second solo effort. He wasn't an entirely unknown quantity either: He'd authored one rattling classic of garage rock ("Gloria," recorded by his group Them), and one long ranting tragic blues ("T.B. Sheets"). Despite those flashes of success, the Irish singer was already mired in music business trouble. He was living in Cambridge, Massachusetts, doing a boho thing, playing gigs with just a bass player. Prospects were not exactly bright.

According to bassist Richard Davis, who'd worked with such luminaries as Eric Dolphy, the Irish bard played the outline of his songs on guitar, and expected the others to follow him. He encouraged some improvisation, and to facilitate that, gave very little guidance. This turns out to be key to *Astral Weeks*: Rather than pursuing a fixed idea, this ensemble is out in the mists, listening for anything solid to grab, moving tentatively so as not to shatter the airy atmosphere. Much of the album drifts along without a fixed tempo, with the musicians swirling strains of folk melody or boppish riffage around Morrison's lover-as-hero character. (The sweet and somber sounds of a string quartet were added later.)

Astral Weeks doesn't come at you straight. A song cycle that loosely follows the desperate

Astral Weeks was inducted into the Grammy Hall of Fame in 1999.

thoughts of a young man who's consumed by an unattainable woman, its lyrics sometimes seem so loaded with meanings and allusions they make your brain hurt. And then, when you least expect it, Morrison's idle dreaming odes, like "Cyprus Avenue" and "Beside You," sneak up and explode—images you missed last time suddenly feel significant. Later, Morrison got downright haughty about his quests, singing obtuse dark-night-of-the-soul ramblings like a Joyce scholar slumming in the pubs. But here he's just a seeker, somebody who's been torn apart. Lost in the reverie of her touch, he salvages what pleasure he can from the memory.

GENRE: 🎸 Rock. **RELEASED:** 1968, Warner Bros. **KEY TRACKS:** "Cyprus Avenue," "The Way Young Lovers Do," "Sweet Thing." **CATALOG CHOICES:** *Moondance; His Band and Street Choir; Tupelo Honey; Too Late to Stop Now.* **NEXT STOP:** Nick Drake: *Bryter Layter.* **AFTER THAT:** Grant Lee Buffalo: *Fuzzy.*

The Best from the First Great Jazz Composer

Birth of the Hot

Jelly Roll Morton

Jelly Roll Morton claimed that he single-handedly invented jazz in 1902, one example among many of his inclination toward grandiose mythmaking. In several of the spry, ragtime-influenced songs he wrote later, the Creole pianist from New Orleans loudly touted his own talent: "His melodies have made him Lord of Ivories," goes one original song. "Just a simple little chord, now at home as well as abroad, they call him Mr. Jelly Lord."

Morton (1885–1941) might have been a braggart, but he could back it up at the piano. He developed a wildcatting style that had elements of ragtime and his city's parade rhythms, and he wrote a stack of tunes that are both marvelously sweet and alive with rhythm. His legend began in the opulent bordellos of New Orleans's

Storyville neighborhood, where he'd play for ladies of the evening and their clients. After bouncing around a bit (and taking work with minstrel shows), Morton arrived in Chicago in 1926, and began recording with a group he called the Red Hot Peppers. These zippy, boundlessly joyful performances— "Black Bottom Stomp," "The Pearls," "Wild Man Blues," "Wolverine Blues" and others included on this excellent single-disc survey—established Morton as the first great jazz composer.

Rumor has it Morton's business card referred to him as the "Originator of Jazz."

Morton was also an innovative arranger. Rather than assign an entire melody to a single instrument, Morton would divide his themes into little sections punctuated by stop-time breaks and brief solos. By the end of one of his tightly choreographed tunes, which usually last under three minutes because of the limitations of recording equipment, he's taken listeners through fantastic jubilees and complex duet passages, with, naturally, some hot jazz soloing on the side.

Morton recorded for Victor until 1930, when the rise of the swing big bands shoved him to the sidelines. Unprepared for such a turn, he toiled, mostly unknown, in piano bars. When musicologist Alan Lomax tracked him down in 1938, Morton was working as bartender, cook, and pianist at the Jungle Inn in Washington, D.C.

Lomax got him to reminisce, for a series called the *Library of Congress Recordings*, about the origins of his tunes as well as the way he transformed a ragtime piano piece like "Tiger Rag" into jazz. Though he'd fallen far, old Jelly Lord sounds plenty animated as he recalls, with characteristic bravado, how he created jazz.

GENRE: 🎷 Jazz. RELEASED: 2000, RCA/Bluebird. (Original recordings made between 1926 and 1930.) KEY TRACKS: "Black Bottom Stomp," "Wolverine Blues," "Dead Man Blues," "Grandpa's Spells." CATALOG CHOICE: *Kansas City Stomp: The Library of Congress Recordings*, Vol. 1. NEXT STOP: Louis Armstrong: *The Complete Hot Fives and Hot Sevens* (see p. 26). AFTER THAT: Eubie Blake: *Early Rare Recordings*, Vol. 1.

An Antidote to Bling Culture

Mos Def and Talib Kweli Are Black Star

Mos Def and Talib Kweli

O f the many changes that roiled hip-hop after the violent deaths of Tupac Shakur (see p. 789) and the Notorious B.I.G. (see p. 555), the most dismaying was the rapid rise of bling culture. MCs and entrepreneurs like Sean Combs (then known as Puff Daddy) who'd been affected by those murders began aggressively name-checking brands of expensive Champagne and luxury cars, as though living large was the best way to escape the genre's multiplying tragedies. One could argue that this wave of narcissistic materialism contributed to the general erosion of persuasive wordplay: Where Tupac's raps, for example, waxed philosophical, the third-generation gangster like 50 Cent seized exclusively on the bullying gunplay.

Not everyone rolled that way. The New York–based Native Tongues collective, which spawned A Tribe Called Quest and others in the 1980s, promoted alternatives to the prevailing gangsta-rap viewpoints. This 1998 album, the only collaboration between agile thinkers Mos Def and Talib Kweli, is among the best.

They arrive at the microphone bursting with ideas—about the meaning of blackness ("black like the planet that they fear, why they scared?"), about the decline of the rhyming art ("some people think MC is shorthand for misconception"), about the rampant spread of violence ("Hater Players"). But they don't

The album's title refers to a shipping line founded by Marcus Garvey.

overwhelm listeners with verbiage. The thirteen tracks on this debut, named after the shipping line run by the Universal Negro Improvement Association founder Marcus Garvey, work first as music—the DJ Hi-Tek creates deep rhythmic pockets and thick atmospheres, and the two MCs just saunter through them. Those looking for polyrhythmic slice-and-dice rapping spiked with sticky melodic refrains (and narratives that don't involve loaded firearms) will find much to admire here.

GENRE: 🌐 Hip-Hop. RELEASED: 1998, Rawkus. KEY TRACKS: "Astronomy (Eighth Light)," "Definition," "Brown Skin Lady," "K.O.S. (Determination)." CATALOG CHOICES: Mos Def: *Black on Both Sides.* Talib Kweli: *Reflection Eternal.* NEXT STOP: Common: *Like Water for Chocolate.* AFTER THAT: Blackalicious: *Blazing Arrow.*

Before and After a Rock Tragedy

Apple

Mother Love Bone

This is the tale of yet another rock drug-abuse tragedy, and the astonishing music that came in its aftermath. Mother Love Bone's singer Andrew Wood was one of the most promising figures on the Seattle music scene of the pre-grunge late 1980s. Just after his band finished recording its major-label debut, *Apple,* Wood checked himself into rehab to battle a recurring heroin problem. Upon his release, he promptly overdosed and died. When *Apple* appeared shortly thereafter, rock lovers everywhere had the bittersweet experience of encountering a sizable talent never to be heard from again. Wood (1966–1990) sang with the Dionysian determination of T. Rex's Marc Bolan, and imbued his phrases with the mysticism that is one lingering legacy of Led Zeppelin. He got away with songs that had a nonsensical streak—among them, "Stardog Champion," "Captain Hi-Top," and the funky "This Is Shangri-La"—not least because he had a voice made to rattle arenas. It didn't hurt that his band, which included future Pearl Jam founders Stone Gossard on guitar and Jeff Ament on bass, more than equaled his power output.

Stunned by Wood's death, the Seattle music community grieved in public. One ad hoc group, featuring Gossard and Ament backing Soundgarden singer Chris Cornell, called itself Temple of the Dog (after a Wood lyric). They began recording Wood's songs, and soon added originals inspired by his sound (the agitated "Pushing Forward Back") or his death ("Say Hello 2 Heaven," "Reach Down"), and invited others to collaborate on what became *Temple of the Dog*. Among those was Eddie Vedder, whose

Rolling Stone said this album "succeeds where countless other hard rock albums have failed."

"Wooden Jesus" is one highlight; this project led directly to the beginning of Pearl Jam. Blessed with some of Cornell's most impassioned singing, *Temple of the Dog* is a series of severe, beseeching entreaties built on the Mother Love Bone sound, and one of the very few rock-era salutes to not merely celebrate but to extend the spirit of its subject.

GENRE: 🎸 Rock.
RELEASED: 1990, Universal. **KEY TRACKS:** "This Is Shangri-La," "Bone China." **NEXT STOP:** Temple of the Dog: *Temple of the Dog*. **AFTER THAT:** Pearl Jam: *Yield*.

Lullabies of Broadway, Like You've Never Heard Them Before

On Broadway, Vol. 1

Paul Motian

By the time drummer Paul Motian and his group began recording the Broadway songbook in 1988, jazz musicians had pretty much trampled it. At that time, the Wynton Marsalis tradition-first revolution was in full swing; among young jazzers, knowing the work of the Gershwins and Rodgers and Hart was considered basic literacy. Unfortunately, when given the chance to play these sturdy old reliables, they frequently treated them as platforms for mindless run-at-the-mouth technique, steamrolling over the rhapsodic possibilities.

Motian and his remarkable group went the other way. They loosened up the fibers of the garments, to the point where the familiar cadences of the tunes took exotic turns. Often during Jerome Kern's "They Didn't Believe Me" and other gems, guitarist Bill Frisell patiently pulls the harmony apart strand by strand, like a bewildered dad untangling Christmas tree lights. The others—Motian, saxophonist Joe Lovano, and bassist Charlie Haden—wait to see where Frisell hangs the things, and then cautiously step in, one revealing tone at a time. The result is a conversation that unfolds in a kind of procedural slow motion, with each statement gently shading what comes next.

Motian, a key part of the celebrated Bill Evans Trio (see p. 263), is one of the world's great colorists. In this group, his arsenal of cymbal splashes and artful brushstrokes provide a kind of alternate melody: He bathes Lovano's reading of "Someone to Watch Over Me" in swirls of pattering triple-time rhythms. As the tune evolves over nine minutes, his inventions provoke knotty group discussions that wander happily away from any one fixed tempo—in much the same way Frisell's original compositions, on his own gorgeous albums, do. Gershwin's enduring theme is there, hovering and echoing around the perimeter, sounding startlingly more vital in these destabilized surroundings than it does on more conventional readings.

GENRE:  Jazz. **RELEASED:** 1989, JMT. (Reissued 2003, Winter and Winter.) **KEY TRACKS:** "Liza," "They Didn't Believe Me," "I Concentrate on You," "Someone to Watch Over Me." **CATALOG CHOICES:** *On Broadway*, Vol. 3; *Misterioso*. **NEXT STOP:** Bill Charlap: *Written in the Stars*. **AFTER THAT:** Bill Frisell: *Before We Were Born*.

An Upstairs/Downstairs Comic Opera

The Marriage of Figaro

Wolfgang Amadeus Mozart

Veronique Gens, Patrizia Ciofi, Angelika Kirchschlager, Simon Keenlyside, Concerto Köln (René Jacobs, cond.)

Georges Bizet, the French composer of *Carmen*, once drew an emotional distinction between Beethoven and Mozart. When listening to the *Eroica* symphony, Beethoven's Third, he wrote, "I am moved and surprised, and my eyes, ears, and intelligence are inadequate to admire them. But when I hear *The Marriage of Figaro* . . . I am altogether happy, I experience a feeling of well-being, a complete satisfaction."

That's a telling distinction; Mozart's more formal theater works, like this *opera buffa* (comic opera) are rhapsodic swirls of evocative consonance. As much as you might try to intellectualize them, you can't help but feel them. The young master doesn't try too hard to dazzle; his control of form and harmony are such that he can impart changes of tone and mood with a grace note, or a glance. Everything is in its right place in Mozart; the only deviation from expected form here is the long finale to the second act, a farcical fantasia in which deception is piled on deception for nearly twenty minutes.

Mozart wrote over 600 musical compositions.

Figaro is a sequel of sorts. It's based on the second of three plays by Pierre Beaumarchais about the romantic lives of the French upper crust. The first play was adapted by Rossini into the hit Italian opera *The Barber of Seville*, and the second catches up with the same characters years later, on a single "crazy" day when the Countess Almaviva realizes her marriage is a sham. Rather than stray, she makes the Count fall in love with her again, by pretending to be someone else. There are flirtations between the royalty and the servants, and attempts to expose the infidelities lead to moments of humor and humiliation.

Opera in Mozart's day was usually thin soup, both in terms of music and message. This one beats that rap, because its inventive themes and scurrying interstitial passages—what Richard Strauss described as the work's "heavenly frivolities"—are so fully developed, they're capable of standing apart from the narrative. This production, which features instruments in common usage during Mozart's time, is less string-heavy than modern interpretations; the winds provide shadings that bring out the luster in Mozart's vocal lines. With the exception of a too-blustery Count, every role enjoys great singing.

GENRE: 🕮 Opera. **RELEASED:** 2004, Harmonia Mundi. **KEY TRACK:** Act 2: Finale. **CATALOG CHOICE:** *Don Giovanni,* Elisabeth Schwarzkopf, Joan Sutherland, Philharmonia Orchestra (Carlo Maria Giulini, cond.). **NEXT STOP:** Gioachino Rossini: *The Barber of Seville,* Maria Callas, Philharmonia Orchestra and Chorus (Alceo Galliera, cond.).

Wolfgang Finds His Symphonic Voice

The Late Symphonies

Wolfgang Amadeus Mozart
Vienna Philharmonic (Karl Böhm, cond.)

It took Mozart practice to write meaningful works for symphony orchestra. The scholars list forty-one finished works, with some additional bits and sketches. Of those, some of the early ones are small, rather juvenile studies.

Slightly later works adhere almost too closely to the early symphonic templates used by Haydn and others; they show Mozart as the good student, not yet the great composer.

Near the end of his life, though, Mozart found his orchestral "voice." Beginning with No. 35 (the "Haffner," which was written in 1782) and continuing with the three symphonies (Nos. 39, 40, and 41) he wrote in the summer of 1788, Mozart developed an authoritative style notable for symmetry and logic—each event, right down to the tympani in the slow introductory passages of No. 38, functions as part of the melodic framework.

These seven symphonies are high points in the history of music. They're notable for their wildly exuberant dances, their floral colors, and the way Mozart links seemingly disconnected four-to-six-note motifs into larger thematic groups. Some of his writing feels densely packed: By the end of the first movement of No. 38, you feel as if you've lived through a year or two of musical experience. Striking in a different way is No. 40,

in G minor, which displays a thicker sense of orchestration and stormier, tempestuous proto-Beethoven moods; some believe this hints at the type of music Mozart might have made had he lived longer.

As in all of his composition, Mozart is extremely attentive to form. The basic outline of a symphonic work hadn't been codified all that long when Mozart began, and most of the late Mozart symphonies follow the accepted blueprint. The first movement is written in "sonata allegro" form, with two themes of contrasting character going through elaborate exposition, then a development "jam" in the middle, then a recapitulation. The second is a reflective, moodier songlike piece; one deeply moving example happens in Symphony No. 38, when after nearly five minutes of a gossamer melody in major key, Mozart moves into minor, broods a bit, and then brings the theme back into the major-key sunlight. The third is usually a dance or a march; the fourth, a blazing finale. These final movements make lots of "That's All, Folks" wrapping-up noises, and of them, No. 41 is beloved for its melodic gyrations, set at a torrid gallop.

These performances, led by the Austrian Karl Böhm, have all the colors of a big modern orchestra and the agility of the small ones prevalent in Mozart's time. Lately much effort has been expended by music historians trying to re-create exactly the instruments, orchestral configurations, and tempi that Mozart and his peers would have used. Hearing these modern renditions, which have that aristocratic high-classical precision but also a brisk dancing-in-the-streets animation, you wonder if academics make too much of the niggling details. When executed with the instinctive feeling Böhm engenders throughout the rapt and responsive Vienna Philharmonic here,

Mozart's intentions seem not only honored, but furthered.

GENRE: 🎻 Classical. **RELEASED:** 1967, Deutsche Grammophon. **KEY TRACKS:** Symphony No. 38: first and second movements. Symphony No. 41: second and fourth movements. **ANOTHER INTERPRETATION:** Vienna Philharmonic (Leonard Bernstein, cond.). **CATALOG CHOICE:** *Symphonies Nos. 25, 26, 27, 29, and 32,* Academy of St. Martin in the Fields (Neville Marriner, cond.). **NEXT STOP:** Ludwig van Beethoven: *Symphony No. 3, Egmont Overture,* Berlin Philharmonic (Herbert von Karajan, cond.). **AFTER THAT:** Robert Schumann: *The Four Symphonies,* Vienna Philharmonic (Leonard Bernstein, cond.).

A Different Kind of Music for the Morning After

Requiem

Wolfgang Amadeus Mozart
La Chapelle de Québec (Bernard Labadie, cond.)

If this version of Mozart's storied Requiem has a little something extra, that may be because it was recorded on September 20, 2001, nine days after the terrorist attacks on the World Trade Center and the Pentagon. Performing

at the acoustically splendid Troy Savings Bank Music Hall in Troy, New York, Canadian ensemble La Chapelle de Québec channeled the grief and disbelief many felt during that time into the searching, slow-simmering Requiem, the sprawling religious work that Mozart (1756–1791) left unfinished when he died.

From the very start, this Requiem is defined by a marrow-deep sense of loss, the ache that comes with realizing someone you love is gone forever. People all over the U.S. were feeling something

Requiem was Mozart's last composition.

like that during those shell-shocked days. The Troy program, planned a year before, proves stunningly suited to this moment. From the somber opening through the whispery and fragile "Lacrimosa" and beyond, Mozart's Requiem brings abstract notions about suffering into the here and now. The stirring, life-affirming melodies, which join voice and orchestra in a crusade toward the hereafter, remember the departed and at the same time offer quiet, solid consolation to survivors.

Though the moment of this performance is auspicious, the players avoid overdramatizing. Throughout, the soloists and ensemble err on the side of understatement, trusting that Mozart's themes are sufficient lure. Even the exalting "Rex tremendae" is handled with care: Where others punch it out like a showy fanfare, this group, under the direction of Bernard Labadie, seeks a more muted, rhapsodic reading. They emphasize the inner workings of Mozart's choral writing, bringing the magic he trusted to the subsidiary voices into the open.

More generally, this version does something rare in music. It shows how a composer's meditations on life, death, and spirituality can come hurtling through his-

tory to resonate, almost eerily, in the tumultuous present.

GENRE: 🎼 Classical. **RELEASED:** 2002, Dorian. **KEY TRACKS:** "Kyrie," "Rex tremendae," "Lacrimosa," "Confutatis." **OTHER INTERPRETATIONS:** Berlin Philharmonic, St. Hedwig's Cathedral Choir (Rudolf Kempe, cond.); Boston Early Music Festival Orchestra and Chorus. **F.Y.I.:** The Requiem figures prominently in the film *Amadeus,* which implies, incorrectly, that the piece was commissioned by Mozart's "rival," Antonio Salieri. **CATALOG CHOICE:** *Piano Concertos Nos. 20 and 21,* Rudolph Serkin, London Symphony Orchestra (Claudio Abbado, cond.). **NEXT STOP:** Giuseppe Verdi: *Requiem* (see p. 832).

A Sly Sliver of the '70s

Maria Muldaur

Maria Muldaur

Maria Muldaur's solo debut appeared in 1973, during a moment of great openness in popular music. How open? The onetime folksinger gathered a Jimmie Rodgers country tune ("Any Old Time"), an introspective pop ballad (Ron Davies's "Long Hard Climb"), a saucy bit of cabaret ("Don't You Make Me High"), an evocation of old-timey entertainment ("Vaudeville Man"), and some sly passionately sung funk ("Three Dollar Bill"). And she put them all together, side by side, on the same album. And that album became a hit. Today, such a prospect might not survive ten minutes in a major label conference room.

Of course a big part of the allure was "Midnight at the Oasis," the album's surprise single. Added after everything else was recorded, the tune is a flirty

Muldaur's hit "Midnight at the Oasis" reached #6 on *Billboard*'s Hot 100.

invitation to forbidden pleasure, set in an Arabian Nights desert. A breezy concoction, it falls somewhere between jazz, pop, and cocktail hour. Muldaur sings it like she's goofing around; she delivers lines like "Let's slip off to a sand dune and kick up a little dust" with a knowing wink. The musicians around her pick up on that pleasure-chasing vibe: After one of Muldaur's verses, guitarist Amos Garrett sneaks into the front of the mix with coy, pitch-bending chords and tasteful intimations of the blues. Many students of record-making, including Stevie Wonder, consider this one of the great instrumental breaks in all of pop.

The album is strong all the way through, and considering how many styles it visits, feels remarkably unified. Some credit for that goes to producers Joe Boyd and Lenny Waronker and the band, which includes pianist Mac Rebennack (Dr. John), mandolin wiz David Grisman, jazz bassist Dave Holland, and guitarist Ry Cooder. That's not to underplay Muldaur's role: She slides into these plush, easygoing surroundings, and in a voice that's warm and untroubled and free of contrivance, spreads sunshine. While kicking up a little dust.

GENRES: ⊛ Pop ⓚ Rock. **RELEASED:** 1973, Reprise. **KEY TRACKS:** "Any Old Time," "Midnight at the Oasis," "My Tennessee Mountain Home," "Mad Mad Me." **CATALOG CHOICE:** *Waitress in a Donut Shop.* **NEXT STOP:** Norah Jones: *Not Too Late.* **AFTER THAT:** Nina Simone: *Anthology* (see p. 705).

The Passionate Declaration of a Teenager

Africa Must Be Free by 1983

Hugh Mundell

Most child prodigies are technical whiz-kids, masters at executing sophisticated musical ideas. But usually those ideas are composed by someone else—the prodigy's art is an interpretive one. Which is why the late Jamaican singer and songwriter Hugh Mundell was so exceptional: When he was sixteen, he wrote this set of purposeful roots-reggae songs that express a cogent, forceful, activist worldview.

Hugh Mundell recorded his first single when he was only 13.

At an age when most kids spend their time scheming ways to party, Mundell was channeling thoughts about the world's troubles into the elemental *Africa Must Be Free by 1983*, his first record. The hymnlike odes talk about brotherhood and racial exploitation, and express resignation about the reality of black-on-black violence. In the title track, the sparrow-voiced Mundell cautions his Jamaican brothers about the lessons of Ethiopia. Another song, "Day of Judgment," includes a line about the role of the media as society's watchdog: "The press must [be] free so we all can see your wrongdoing and your brutality."

For all these astute observations, and the calm minimalism of the backing tracks, Mundell still sounds like a kid. That's one of the reasons *Africa*, which was produced by reggae don Augustus Pablo, has such resonance. Mundell is not a trained singer; what starts as an earnest, straightforward declaration sometimes tips into appealing wildness. His sincerity struck a chord in Jamaica, where the title track became a hit and the album—one of the most zealous collections released during the explosive mid-'70s period of reggae creativity that included landmarks by Bob Marley and Peter Tosh—was hailed as a classic.

Mundell made other records, none as compelling. He was shot and killed in (of all years) 1983 while sitting in a car with a protégé, Junior Reed. Pablo, a master of dub, created a light, tasteful dub treatment of Mundell's masterwork that was released in the early '80s, and has been appended to the CD release ever since.

GENRE:  World/Jamaica. **RELEASED:** 1978, Message. (Reissued 1989.) **KEY TRACKS:** "Book of Life," "Run Revolution a Come," "Day of Judgment." **CATALOG CHOICE:** *Blackman's Foundation.* **NEXT STOP:** Augustus Pablo: *King Tubbys Meets Rockers Uptown* (see p. 572). **AFTER THAT:** Cedric Im Brooks: *Cedric Im Brooks and the Light of Saba.*

Calling African Spirits Long Distance, from Cuba

Ito Iban Echu:
Sacred Yoruba Music of Cuba

Los Muñequitos de Matanzas

This music was created to appease, praise, enchant, or request help from the deities, known as orishas, of the African Yoruba tradition. As Yoruba beliefs have evolved in Cuba, the entreaties have been set to unique rhythms, and are dependent on the tones produced by specific drums (the *bata* drum, played by hand, figures prominently).

That's what happens on *Ito Iban Echu*, an electrifying set of musical offerings to the orishas by Los Muñequitos de Matanzas. The group was founded in 1952, and became one of the island nation's most important preservers of not just traditional folklore,

"Los Muñequitos" means Little Dolls. Matanzas is a Cuban city.

but rumba and Afro-Cuban dance music. The CD's title comes from a phonetic Spanish interpretation of a Yoruba phrase meaning "It came out well"—it's often spoken when a *babalu*, or diviner, finishes consulting with an oracle. But it's a fitting description of these live tracks, which exude a deep sense of mission.

The drums guide everything—the pace of the chants, the intensity of the singing, the rough "structure" of the pieces. A set of *bata* drums has six heads, each of a different size; the resulting pitches are thought to speak directly to the orishas. As rendered by the veteran group, the chants become hypnotic cycles of declaration, affirmation, and elaboration. Among the most intense are "Chango eyeleo," for the flamboyant deity of thunder and lighting, and "Yemaya (seco)," for the water goddess who governs motherhood and fertility. All of the chants affirm something crucial about life—or the afterlife. With deep passion Los Muñequitos show how simple phrases can become a conduit for communication with the spirit world.

GENRE:  World/Cuba. **RELEASED:** 1996, Qbadisc. **KEY TRACKS:** "Eleggua (con guira)," "Babalu aye," "Yemaya (seco)," "Chango eyeleo." **FURTHER INQUIRY:** The producer of this album, Ned Sublette, is the author of an authoritative history, *Cuba and Its Music: From the First Drums to the Mambo.* **CATALOG CHOICE:** *Rumba Calienta 88/77.* **NEXT STOP:** Mongo Santamaria: *Drums and Chants* (see p. 671). **AFTER THAT:** Lazaro Ros: *Songs for Elegua.*

The Baddest Russian Opera

Boris Godunov

Modest Mussorgsky
Kirov Opera and Orchestra (Valery Gergiev, cond.)

Early in the first act of this massive Russian opera, there's a scene in a courtyard outside a monastery. News of the death of a child tsar has gripped the populace, and the boyars—the Russian equivalent of senators—are urging calm as they crown a new leader. The crowd, somewhat browbeaten by the police, responds in cascading waves that alternate between grief and outrage. Though the plotline involving the new leader, the evil Boris who murdered the child to take power, hasn't yet become clear, the tone of the voices tells you there's something nasty afoot. Soon after, there are entreaties to the heavens to help poor Russia.

From there, *Boris Godunov* becomes a *Macbeth*-like tale of treachery and deception. The tale sprawls, and Modest Mussorgsky (1839–1881), the most harmonically daring of Russian composers, pumps it up further, writing scenes for brawny male voices supported by towering orchestral chords. The music is distinctly Russian and loaded with brio—it's among a handful of operatic works to successfully use ethnic sounds and styles.

Mussorgsky wrote two versions of *Boris Godunov*. The first, from 1869, was deemed unfit for performance because it didn't contain such requisite operatic elements as a romantic aria. The composer thoroughly changed it for the premiere in 1872, adding characters and folk song themes, as well as the so-called Polish act, which was designed to satisfy those who believe even historic dramas must have a love duet.

This recording offers both Mussorgsky scores, performed by the Russian Kirov Opera under studio conditions in the Netherlands. It's the rare opportunity to hear the progression of an opera. While many fans prefer the longer, somewhat more conventional later edition, there's something amazing about the more focused earlier one, which lays out the duplicities in the story more clearly. Both treatments feature the deep Russian bass voices, who, like athletes priming for a worthy adversary, approach *Boris Godunov* with keen alertness. They aim to do these heated melodies justice, and they do.

GENRE: 🎵 Opera. **RELEASED:** 1998, Philips. **KEY TRACKS:** Act 1: "For Whom Dost Thou Forsake Us?"; Act 2: "I Have Achieved Supreme Power"; Act 3: "A Humble, Simple Pilgrim." **ANOTHER INTERPRETATION:** Vienna Philharmonic (Herbert von Karajan, cond.). **CATALOG CHOICE:** *Night on Bald Mountain*, USSR Symphony Orchestra (Evgeny Svetlanov, cond.). **NEXT STOP:** Osvaldo Golijov: *Ainadamar* (see p. 315).

The opera's title character.

A Doomsayer, Unexpurgated

The Nursery; Sunless; Songs and Dances of Death and Other Songs

Modest Mussorgsky

Boris Christoff, L'Orchestre National de la Radiodiffusion Française (Georges Tzipine, cond.)

Of all the amazing pieces written by Russian composer Modest Mussorgsky—the opera *Boris Godunov*, piano suites like *Pictures at an Exhibition*—the ones that reveal most about him are his songs.

Mussorgsky (1839–1881) struggled with mental instability and was known to be an alcoholic, and as a result, he didn't always complete his scores; in many cases, his original sketches were "refined" posthumously, by such well-meaning fellow composers as Nikolai Rimsky-Korsakov.

The songs underwent no such filtering—they're Mussorgsky unexpurgated, sharing what's going on in his head. That explains the grim and sometimes disturbing notions, the melodies that dwell in murky darkness, the absence of pleasantries. The austere *Sunless*, for example, explores depression and sleeplessness; its talky themes, sung here with appropriate solemnity by Boris Christoff, could be the babbling internal conversation of a troubled soul. As on the other songs and cycles here, form is often mutable and difficult to discern—Mussorgsky uses free-flowing melodies, with few repeating anchor phrases, to frame the narratives.

Though its six parts offer more fanciful melodic window-dressing, *The Nursery* is, on the whole, even scarier. Most composers treat children as fairy-tale innocents, but Mussorgsky (who wrote the words for this one himself) depicts children here as cunning proto-adults, cute on the surface but with grown-up talent for lying and manipulating.

The most intense music here is found in the *Songs and Dances of Death*, a series of haunted episodes that might as well have been written for Christoff's thick voice-of-doom baritone. Christoff brings consummate control to the music, and also an actor's sense of intonation that transforms the songs into little dramas. The songs themselves are focused in ways that suggest isolated emotions; whenever a tune gets lachrymose, Christoff sings as though his eyes are welling up in tears. The first song presents Death as a gentle sort, helping relieve the earthly burdens of a drunk peasant in a snowstorm. The "Cradle Song" finds Death singing a lullaby to a sick child, while in the final song, Death appears as battle general, out to claim an army. Christoff sings this one with Russian gusto and a slight hint of a raised eyebrow: Where the previous pieces characterize Death as a force of nature, this one makes Death seem greedy and creepy. It's almost as if the composer has resigned himself to that old adage: If Death doesn't get you one way, it'll get you another.

GENRE: 🎵 Classical. **RELEASED:** 2003, EMI Classics. (Recorded 1955–1957.) **KEY TRACKS:** *Sunless*: Song 1: "Within Four Walls." *The Nursery*: Song 5: "On the Hobbyhorse." *Songs and Dances of Death*: Song 2: "Lullaby." Song 4: "The Field Marshal." **CATALOG CHOICE:** *Boris Godunov* (see previous page). **NEXT STOP:** Richard Strauss: *Four Last Songs* (see p. 750). **AFTER THAT:** Jussi Björling: *Great Operatic Arias*.

The Sound of a Sunshine Insurrection

Mutantes

Os Mutantes

Mutantes is the second album from one of the most important cult bands in the world, the resourceful Brazilian trio that blended samba, rock, funk, and psychedelia into playful and idealistic mongrel art that screams "everything is possible."

The members of Os Mutantes really believed that. Along with compatriots Caetano Veloso and Gilberto Gil, they were part of the radical *tropicália* movement in Brazil that began in 1967. Though centered on music, *tropicália* endeavored to challenge the country's military dictatorship—both overtly and through subversive lyrics and rock-influenced musical trappings, considered heresy by proud nationalists. *Tropicália*'s creators sought to move beyond the mellow pleasantries of the bossa nova, Brazil's treasure, using distorted guitars and psychedelic exotica. Each *tropicálista* did things differently: Os Mutantes were experts at juxtaposition, setting a kicky mod cha-cha beat against heavy-metal power chords, or interrupting an undulating samba with buoyant flower-power refrains. Now, such collisions are routine; then, before the dawn of cut-and-paste culture, they were radical.

The first Os Mutantes effort was written and recorded in 1968, just as *tropicália* was coalescing. This second was made in a week and a half, when the movement was in full upheaval mode. The music reflects that energy—there are irreverent attempts at country and western ("Não va sé perder por aí") and moments of textured collage that echo the solemnity of religious ritual ("Dios mil e um"). Singer Rita Lee and brothers Sérgio Dias (guitar and voice) and Arnaldo Baptista

In 2006, the band reunited, playing together for the first time since 1978.

(keyboards and voice) grew up listening to British and American rock via shortwave radio, and by this time had built their own effects devices to emulate what they heard. Not only did they get pretty close—check out the oddly watery vocals on "Dia 36" or the sizzling cymbals of "Fuga No. 2," made by recording a can of bug spray—the gadgets gave them a distinct signature. "We didn't have the equipment the rock musicians had," Sérgio Dias said before the band's first-ever U.S. performance, on a reunion tour in 2006. "We had to make our own sounds."

It took decades for other musicians to fully fathom the band's diabolical mixings, but through reissues, the cult of Os Mutantes—which includes Beck, Stereolab, Cibo Matto, and others—continues to grow. It should forever: This sunny, defiantly ad hoc music is still way ahead of its time.

GENRE: 🌐 World/Brazil. **RELEASED:** 1969, Polydor. (Reissued 1999, Omplatten.) **KEY TRACKS:** "Dia 36," "Fuga No. 2," "Dios mil e um," "Não va sé perder por aí." **CATALOG CHOICE:** *Os Mutantes.* **BUYER BEWARE:** Later Os Mutantes efforts and compilations have titles similar to those of the first few records but are much less interesting. **NEXT STOP:** Stereolab: *Emperor Tomato Ketchup* (see p. 739). **AFTER THAT:** Suba: *São Paulo Confessions.*

Noise, Redefined

Loveless

My Bloody Valentine

Those who spend their days applying hairsplitting genre distinctions to rock bands had a devil of a time with My Bloody Valentine. The Irish-British band, whose *Loveless* is regularly voted one of the ten most important rock records of the 1990s, was initially described as noise-rock, for the layers of menacing feedback purveyed by guitarist Kevin Shields. Then, the four-piece became the leading avatar of a sound described as "shoegazing" rock, because the musicians had a tendency to look at the floor. Later, with this album, some critics called My Bloody Valentine, which drew its name from a Canadian horror film, "bliss pop."

If those tags seem a bit arbitrary, that's because this music, which is defined by guitar-orchestra lushness and abrasive grandeur, is nearly impossible to pin down. Shields told interviewers he was influenced by the Velvet Underground, the Jesus and Mary Chain, and the Beach Boys—yet no matter how you triangulate these sources, they don't necessarily lead to the sweeping sounds of *Loveless*. By this, his band's second full-length effort, Shields had developed a daunting arsenal of sound. Its thick towers of guitar distortion move in waves like heat radiating from the pavement; odd slurpy pitch-bends that suggest tape-recorder malfunction; vocals that hide behind extravagant chordal yowls. Each of the eleven songs attains a dense orchestral roar; on those that have vocals, either by Shields or rhythm guitarist Bilinda Butcher, the refrains come across serene, kissed with celestial sweetness.

When he made this, Shields—who's something of a perfectionist, and hasn't released much music since—was thinking less like a rock guitarist than an irreverent sound mangler, in the tradition of Anthony Braxton, or Public Enemy. In his fantastical and sometimes off-putting creations, murk enhances the mystery, and beauty comes wrapped in the guitar equivalent of barbed wire.

GENRE: 🎸 Rock. **RELEASED:** 1991, Sire. **KEY TRACKS:** "Only Shallow," "When You Sleep," "Soon." **CATALOG CHOICE:** *Isn't Anything.* **NEXT STOP:** Jesus and Mary Chain: *Psychocandy* (see p. 396). **AFTER THAT:** Sonic Youth: *Daydream Nation* (see p. 725).

Blissed-Out Melodies That Rock

It Still Moves

My Morning Jacket

Jim James's impossibly lovely voice beckons from a parallel universe where rock and roll singing has not devolved into banshee screams or cartoon-superhero posturing. In this place, no bands wear spandex. Melody still counts for something. Being earnest, or believing in someone or something, is not an automatic liability.

The lead singer and songwriter of Kentucky's My Morning Jacket, James is a child of the '90s, and thus born far too late to be part of the great flowering of American rock of the late '60s and early '70s (the Doors, Buffalo Springfield, Neil Young, the Allman Brothers). This doesn't stop him from attempting to get back. His voice is usually bathed in warm echoes that make him seem far away, and openly yearns for that earlier era—in his music are traces of Young's weeping-willow refrains and Led Zeppelin's transcendence-seeking epics, not to mention the Doors' dark otherworldliness (or is that otherworldly darkness?). Crucially, he's not a revivalist, or some kind of nerd scholar: For all the vintage sonics (accomplished using old-school echo machines and other sound-shaping gizmos) James fronts a scrappy, ornery rock band that can throw down a slick groove and cruise with the best of the post-Phish noodlers. And then, unlike those bands, My Morning Jacket can astound listeners almost at will, just by circling back to one of its plaintive, unexpectedly stirring hooks.

The band's particular alchemy—gritty backbeats supporting vocals that float along in a metaphysical haze—reaches a strong peak on its third effort, *It Still Moves*. Some songs, like the opener "Mahgeetah," amount to a nonstop parade of blissed-out guilty-pleasure melodies, while the nine-minute "I Will Sing You Songs," traces a longer arc, with meditative verses erupting into spectacular cascades of vocal harmony. Virtually every song here (even the superdisciplined short ones) crackles with a sense of motion, endless seeking, restless travel. That's another way My Morning Jacket aligns with the classic rock legends: Its best songs are journeys, not destinations.

GENRE: 🎸 Rock. **RELEASED:** 2003, ATO. **KEY TRACKS:** "Mahgeetah," "Master Plan," "I Will Sing You Songs." **CATALOG CHOICES:** *At Dawn; Evil Urges.* **NEXT STOP:** The Flaming Lips: *The Soft Bulletin* (see p. 281). **AFTER THAT:** M. Ward: *Transistor Radio.*

Nas ✦ Milton Nascimento with Lô Borges ✦ Fats Navarro and Tadd Dameron ✦ Youssou N'Dour ✦ Oliver Nelson ✦ Ricky Nelson ✦ Willie Nelson ✦ Neu! ✦ Aaron Neville ✦ Phineas Newborn Jr. ✦ Randy Newman ✦ Herbie Nichols ✦ Harry Nilsson ✦ Nine Inch Nails ✦ Nirvana ✦ Nitty Gritty Dirt Band ✦ No Doubt ✦ The Notorious B.I.G. ✦ Les Nubians ✦ N.W.A. ✦ Laura Nyro ✦ Paul Oakenfold ✦ Phil Ochs ✦ Sinéad O'Connor ✦ Odetta ✦ The O'Jays ✦ King Oliver and His Creole Jazz Band ✦ Remmy Ongala and Orchestre Super Matimila ✦ Roy Orbison ✦ Orchestra Baobab ✦ Orishas ✦ Orquesta Casino de la Playa ✦ Beth Orton ✦ Shuggie Otis ✦ Outkast ✦ Buck Owens

N, O

An Against-the-Grain Hip-Hop Debut

Illmatic

Nas

In the early '90s, West Coast gangstas ruled hip-hop. The feisty Ice Cube, formerly of N.W.A., released three straight million-selling albums describing the brutality in South Central Los Angeles. MCs from everywhere were still parsing producer Dr. Dre's 1992 magnum opus *The Chronic* (see pg. 236), and among that hit's young stars was the redoubtable Snoop Doggy Dogg, whose *Doggystyle* topped the charts in 1994.

Into this moment walked Nasir Jones, a perceptive New York kid who'd dropped out of school and earned his street cred in the then-volatile neighborhood near the Queensboro Bridge. ("When I made *Illmatic*," Nas told MTV later, "my soul was trapped in the Queensbridge projects.") The son of jazz trumpeter Olu Dara, Nas hooked up with producers from the alternative rap underground—Pete Rock, Q-Tip, and DJ Premier—and began making hip-hop that used sophisticated, often jazz-influenced loops to support his cagey poetics. Lacing trace amounts of bitterness into his cadences, Nas sounded supremely calm venting about how he'd been betrayed by women, his friends, and the educational system. On the somewhat ironic "One Love," he realizes that some of the people he's been running with aren't trustworthy, observing exasperatedly, "When we start the revolution, all they'll probably do is squeal."

Nas understood that he had to project a certain toughness just to get heard, but he wasn't interested in glorifying violence—one distinguishing characteristic of *Illmatic* is the way resolute optimism serves as an antidote to the bleak surroundings, an idea overtly expressed on "The World Is Yours," but also evident on "One Time 4 Your Mind" and "Represent." The album, which features exactly one guest star (radical for a hip-hop debut), lasts under forty minutes. That's all the time it takes Nas to separate himself from the pack: While some MCs brutalize listeners, Nas relies on finesse and verbal dexterity to make the narratives not simply "real," but gut-wrenching.

GENRE: 🎤 Hip-Hop. **RELEASED:** 1994, Columbia. **KEY TRACKS:** "N.Y. State of Mind," "The World Is Yours," "Life's a Bitch." **CATALOG CHOICE:** *Street's Disciple.* **NEXT STOP:** Jay-Z: *Reasonable Doubt.*

The "Corner Club" That Could

Clube da esquina

Milton Nascimento with Lô Borges

Milton Nascimento probably has to make some conscious "effort" when he sings. Listening to this magical record from 1972, it's impossible to detect any at all. The Brazilian singer and songwriter glides above the streets, aware of (but never encumbered by) human problems. In an edge-free falsetto, he swoops down, drops a phrase, and then poof! He's gone. On to the next bit of loveliness.

Nascimento has had this aptitude, unique among humans, from the very start of his career. *Clube da esquina*, a double-album collaboration with songwriter and multi-instrumentalist Lô Borges (see p. 106), is a series of fragile melodies and cascading chorales that show-cases the trembling beauty of Nascimento's voice. Its brief étude-like rock songs aligned Nascimento with the Musica Popular Brasileira (MPB) movement; like other recordings of the era, it was threatened with censorship by the military dictatorship. (The threat inspired the duo: A 1978 sequel is loaded with even more double entendres and political comment.)

Nascimento met Borges in Belo Horizonte, the mystical landlocked city that is the capital of Minas Gerais, a province north of Rio.

As the cover indicates, this album was trying to overcome many divisions in Brazilian society.

The two, along with Borges's brother and several others, called themselves a "street-corner gang" (hence the album title, which means the "Club on the Corner"), and developed a collaborative working style that drew on their varied talents, à la the Beatles. These pop curios and heartbroken ballads have an introspective, almost spiritual character common to music from the heavily Catholic Minas Gerais region. Many were later covered with great success by other artists. But the versions here are undeniable: This is one of the most staggeringly beautiful collections of pop songs in any language, from any era.

GENRE: 🌐 World/Brazil. **RELEASED:** 1972, EMI. **KEY TRACKS:** "O trem azul," "Caravo e canela," "San Vicente," "Nada sera como antes." **CATALOG CHOICES:** Milton Nascimento: *Milton*. Lô Borges: *Lô Borges* (see p. 106). **NEXT STOP:** Tribalistas: *Tribalistas*. **AFTER THAT:** Chico Buarque: *Construcão*.

When Tadd Met Fats . . .

The Complete Blue Note and Capitol Recordings

Fats Navarro and Tadd Dameron

This compilation documents the brief, extraordinary collaboration of two woefully overlooked jazz geniuses. The material comes from the pen of pianist and composer Tadd Dameron (1917–1965), whose tricky yet supremely logical tunes balance bebop macho against a warm-hearted lyricism. Taking these pieces to the next level is the trumpeter Fats Navarro (1923–1950), a fireballer with a radiant tone and technique to burn, whose recording career only lasted four years.

Not every speed demon could handle Dameron's compositions, which are far more demanding than the typical heat-and-serve jam-session riffs. Navarro, who first attracted attention in 1945 when he replaced Dizzy Gillespie in the Billy Eckstine band, makes them seem easy. He begins his turn on Dameron's bebop agility course "Our Delight" with clipped single notes, then broad and effusive lines that carry the distant hint of taunting blues. His solo ends with an ascending series of perfectly placed triplets that's so precise it seems to startle the rhythm section. That's not the only "how'd he do that?" stunner either: The alternate take of "Our Delight" features an even more blistering Navarro solo, one of several here that have been taken apart, note for note, by generations of jazz trumpeters.

These small group recordings were made in the late 1940s, for Blue Note. Even though Navarro could literally play anything, he did his best work contending with the unconventional minefields Dameron loaded into these tunes. To hear that happening at a dizzyingly high level, check out "Focus" and any of the several versions of "Bouncing with Bud." These pieces have all the Dameron trademarks—the off-center chords and backdoor resolutions, the loping lines that wander a step or two away from the conventional. Dameron's music is challenging stuff, in part because it demands more than the razzle-dazzle technique that defined so much jazz of the 1940s: It asks soloists to dig deep and share something of their souls as well.

GENRE: 🎵 Jazz. **RELEASED:** 1995, Blue Note. **KEY TRACKS:** "Our Delight," "Focus," "What's New," "Bouncing with Bud," "Boperation." **CATALOG CHOICES:** *Fats Navarro with Tadd Dameron Live; The Magic Touch of Tadd Dameron.* **STOP:** Freddie Hubbard: *Backlash.* **AFTER THAT:** Charles Mingus: *Blues and Roots.*

A Glimpse of Early N'Dour

Immigrés

Youssou N'Dour

For years, the magnetic singer and songwriter Youssou N'Dour has been involved in two completely different recording industries. At home in Senegal, N'Dour and his Super Étoile de Dakar band make sweaty and

passionate (and often live) *mbalax*, the rhythmic music he pioneered. N'Dour, who since the early '80s has been mentored and championed by British rocker Peter Gabriel, also creates entirely different music for export. These works are aimed at a cosmopolitan crowd and are notable for their funky, slightly more accessible beats, and follow pop-song verse-chorus outlines. Many aspiring African stars pursue similarly bifurcated strategies; N'Dour is

N'Dour began performing when he was 12 years old.

among the few to make compelling records in both spheres.

This 1984 album, arguably his best, was recorded before N'Dour started dividing his output. Its title track was inspired by N'Dour's first visit to Paris, where he encountered many Senegalese people drawn to the city's opportunities. He was moved by the fact that these émigrés were disconnected from their African home; one lyric pleads, "Don't forget where you belong, don't cut yourselves off."

The four extended tracks of *Immigrés* have plenty of snappy instrumental sections, forays in which the two guitarists and multiple drummers create a combustion engine of groove. These are plenty intense by themselves, and become incandescent when N'Dour sings. His voice has been described as "angelic," but it's also got a reedy almost shrill texture, and a touch of grandmotherly worry to it. N'Dour understands its effects. He doesn't oversing, doesn't try to showboat. Whether the rhythm's running hot or moving at a more measured, ceremonial gait, he times his declarations perfectly, so that what registers is not just the words, but an otherworldly urgency. This is a voice big enough—and strong enough—to carry many dreams of Africa inside it.

GENRE: 🌐 World/Senegal. **RELEASED:** 1984, Virgin. (Reissued 2002, Sterns Music.) **KEY TRACKS:** "Pitche mi," "Immigrés/Bitim rew," "Taaw," " Badou." **F.Y.I.:** N'Dour's "breakthrough" in the West came on Peter Gabriel's 1986 hit "In Your Eyes," which makes great use of his keening vocals. **CATALOG CHOICE:** *Egypt.* **NEXT STOP:** Salif Keita: *Soro.* **AFTER THAT:** Cheikh Lô: *Bambay Gueej.*

Some of the Most Vivid Imagery in All of Jazz

The Blues and the Abstract Truth

Oliver Nelson

O liver Nelson started out as a jazz saxophonist in the 1950s and grew into a formidable composer-arranger with his own distinctive sound. By 1967 he developed an entirely different career, writing music for film and TV. His vibrant scores—which include *Death of a Gunfighter, It Takes a Thief, Ironside,* and *The Six Million Dollar Man*—are filled with attitude, cop-show chases, and splashes of dizzying brass drawn from his jazz experience.

The Hollywood stuff is accomplished and exciting, but this album, Nelson's zenith, is a landmark of jazz orchestration. When he recorded it in 1961, he was already thinking in terms of drama; the arrangement on this set has some of the most vivid imagery in all of jazz. His "Hoedown" takes place at a country fair, where square-dance reels collide with amen cadences from the revival tent. The scurrying "Cascades," the most cerebral of Nelson's originals, plays like a ramble through a thick forest.

And then there is "Stolen Moments," nine minutes of noir jazz bliss that sounds like it was beamed from a wood-paneled lounge in the Los Angeles of James Ellroy novels. Nelson has the horns doing a swaying counterpoint to his primary theme, played by trumpeter Freddie Hubbard. They're like a miniature big band, but the music feels as wide open as the Miles Davis small groups. The soloists bring a restless, questioning quality to the tableau; every chord change is another invitation into a hipster underworld. One after another, the soloists clear a space at the bar for you, set down a generous highball, and say: Go ahead. Steal a minute. No one will know.

GENRE: 🎷 Jazz. **RELEASED:** 1961, Impulse. **KEY TRACKS:** "Stolen Moments," "Teenie's Blues," "Cascades." **CATALOG CHOICE:** *Afro-American Sketches.* **NEXT STOP:** Jimmy Smith and Wes Montgomery: *The Dynamic Duo.* **AFTER THAT:** Dave Douglas: *Strange Liberation.*

Wise Men Never Fall in Love, So How Are They to Know?

Greatest Hits

Ricky Nelson

In 1963, Ricky Nelson (1940–1985) sang "Fools Rush In" with the besotted rashness of a teenager in love. A galloping ballroom samba tricked out with electric guitars, "Fools" is one of Nelson's most accomplished singles.

Its lead vocal arrives bursting with promise, yet as it goes along, Nelson introduces little shrugs of sadness. He communicates the self-consciousness of one who has been the fool before, is happy to be the fool for this wonderful girl, and knows that, inevitably, he will be again.

In 1972, this same singer, now billed as Rick Nelson, had his last chart hit with a song he wrote himself, called "Garden Party." It's his recollection of a 1971 oldies show at Madison Square Garden, where he was booed off the stage. The incident apparently rattled him: All youthful exuberance is drained from his voice, and in its place is barely disguised bitterness. The former showbiz kid, who as the son of Ozzie and Harriet appeared weekly on national television, has arrived at a life lesson: "You can't please everyone, so you've got to please yourself."

There are lots of points on the spectrum between the wild passion of "Fools Rush In" and the jaded awareness of "Garden Party." In the years after his 1957 debut—"I'm Walkin',"—a song he recorded to impress a date who was an Elvis Presley fan—Nelson visited many

Ricky Nelson had more than 50 *Billboard* Hot 100 Hits.

of them. His singles share the anxious musings of hormonal teenagers ("Hello Mary Lou"), as well as more mature thoughts on devotion ("Everlovin'"), ponder the overwhelming hurt of a romance's end ("Lonesome Town"), and the heart-racing feeling of a flirtation that's just beginning ("Waitin' in School").

As these became hits, Nelson grew into a pop star whose runaway fame eclipsed the musicality of his records. That's a shame, because Nelson's work easily towers over that of other media-driven teen idols. His records are musically smart and sonically expansive, with carefully manicured rhythm tracks and just a hint of sweetening. And many of them are greatly enhanced by the presence of James Burton, the guitarist whose sparkling leads are part of classics by Elvis Presley, Dale Hawkins, and others. This anthology catches all the big hits, and arranges them in a nonchronological, musically logical sequence—a nice touch.

GENRE: 🎸 Rock. **RELEASED:** 2003, Capitol. **KEY TRACKS:** "Hello Mary Lou," "Travelin' Man," "Fools Rush In," "Garden Party." **CATALOG CHOICE:** *Ricky Sings Again.* **NEXT STOP:** The Everly Brothers: *Cadence Classics: Their Twenty Greatest Hits* (see p. 265). **AFTER THAT:** Chris Isaak: *Heart Shaped World.*

A Country Concept Album

Red Headed Stranger

Willie Nelson

When Columbia Records signed Willie Nelson in 1974, the label thought it was in business with a proven commercial-country hit-maker, the author of Patsy Cline's "Crazy" and Faron Young's "Hello Walls."

The executives had no idea this restless spirit, then associated with the ascendant "outlaw" wing of country, would immediately take advantage of the terms of his contract: As Nelson recalled, "It was the first time that I had quote artistic control end quote." His response: a twisted tale of a troubled preacher who murders his wife and her new lover, then hits the road.

The songs are short, seemingly disconnected drifter laments arranged into a ragtag travelogue. Often a single guitar provides the only accompaniment to Nelson's grandfatherly warble, and the "story" sometimes gets lost inside the character sketches. In the liner notes for the 2000 expanded edition, Nelson remembers the label as being "shocked" by this unconventional album, and then-president Bruce Lundvall concurs. At the time, Lundvall told label staffers "it may not be an important commercial album by Willie" but predicted it would become a significant part of the singer and songwriter's legacy.

Red Headed Stranger confounded those sales projections. It sold three million copies and established Nelson as a uniquely uncompromising crossover figure in country music, one of the few capable of massaging its enduring myths into newly compelling narratives. The album's interpretations of vintage songs sparkle like gold dust, while Nelson's connective-tissue originals, particularly "Time of the Preacher," update Hank Williams with a shot of wry. The expanded edition includes four eyebrow-raising tracks, including a dusty cover of Williams's "I Can't Help It (If I'm Still in Love with You)" and Nelson's reworking of Bach's Minuet in G as, of all things, a ragged country waltz. Why this bit of delirium was snipped from the original remains a mystery.

GENRE: Country. **RELEASED:** 1975, Columbia. (Reissued 2000.) **KEY TRACKS:** "Time of the Preacher," "Just As I Am," "Blue Eyes Crying in the Rain." **CATALOG CHOICE:** *Teatro.* **NEXT STOP:** Johnny Cash: *American Recordings* (see p. 152). **AFTER THAT:** George Jones: *Cup of Loneliness.*

A Croaker Does Standards

Stardust

Willie Nelson

Willie Nelson is one great fake-out artist. A few minutes with that craggy voice on the stereo, and the logical conclusion is that he's not much of a singer. And then a few more minutes go by, and you're captivated—this grizzled dude knows how to get his voice into a zone where his intentions can't be misread, where the warts and the flaws work for him. He sings through what would be deal-breaking disadvantages for others; you follow along in part because you wanna see if the old coot can make it.

In a career that spans over 50 years, Nelson has won 10 Grammys.

Some in the Nashville Establishment hooked into Nelson's oddly compelling style early on. It took this album of standards to establish Nelson as a singer with a disarming, logic-defying knack for vocal persuasion.

Produced by organist Booker T. Jones (of Booker T. and the MGs fame), *Stardust* catches Nelson in a chilled-out easygoing-grandpa mood. He's singing stuff that he grew up with—old torch songs ("Someone to Watch Over Me"), tunes he heard Ray Charles sing ("Georgia on My Mind"), and hushed ballads including "Moonlight in Vermont," a marvel of nonrhyming prose imagery that Nelson names in the liner notes as his all-time favorite song. The small band follows his moves at close range, veering between country, soul-ballad tricks, and jazz turnarounds in a way that blurs genres while making perfect musical sense.

One example: On the dramatic ending of "Blue Skies," after he and the band have sauntered through a few bouncy, optimistic choruses, he shifts gears into half time, and then, after a few bars, slows things even further. It's a rallentando that suggests the bittersweet feeling that sometimes descends at the end of a beautiful day. The blue sky is darkening. Dusk is approaching. And Nelson, in a rare turn as Mr. Softie, is wistful, not quite ready to let go of the light just yet.

GENRE: ◑ Country. **RELEASED:** 1978, Columbia. (Reissued 1999.) **KEY TRACKS:** "Blue Skies," "Enchanted Melody," "Moonlight in Vermont," "Someone to Watch Over Me." **COLLECTOR'S NOTE**: The 1999 remastered version is a sonic upgrade, and includes two bonus tracks: "Scarlet Ribbons" and "I Can See Clearly Now," the latter of which foreshadows Nelson's 2005 reggae covers set *Countryman*. **CATALOG CHOICE:** *You Don't Know Me: The Songs of Cindy Walker*. **NEXT STOP:** Nat King Cole: *Love Is the Thing*.

This Was New Then, and Still Is Now

Neu! '75

Neu!

Formed by two musicians who left Germany's Kraftwerk (see p. 433) because the group wasn't taking enough chances, Neu! (pronouced "noy") developed—and perfected—sound-mangling ideas that turned up, years later, in all kinds of electronic dance music. One of the most widely imitated tricks happens on "E-Musik," when multi-instrumentalists Michael Rother and Klaus Dinger put drum sounds through an effects device called a phase shifter. This gadget changes the pitch of the drums, and their tone: One minute the beat sounds like it's coming from little bitty microchips, the next it becomes deeper and heavier—the sound of some monster trudging up the stairs in a horror film. Oscillating back and forth across that spectrum, Neu!'s processing gives the drums a sense of sweep and distinct melodic arcs. Nowadays virtually every rave DJ uses this trick to ramp up the intensity on the dance floor.

This album, the duo's third, is notable for the diversity of its experiments. The pieces on side one occupy an otherworldly, Eno-ish ambient mood, with lush synthesizer textures and noise manipulations draped over crisp, minimalist backbeats. Those are followed by a tune that shows Neu! at its noisiest (the rattling "Hero") and the ten-minute "E-Musik," which

Neu! '75 was recorded between December 1974 and January 1975.

contains a series of unexpectedly lyrical guitar solos. Even at the peak of sonic uproar, Neu! keeps everything streamlined—this is rock that has the serene orderliness of music for meditation. At least that's how John Frusciante of the Red Hot Chili Peppers hears it: On a sticker plastered to the remastered version of *Neu! '75*, he raves "I love it when people glorify space and simplicity."

GENRES: 🎸 Rock 🌀 Electronica.
RELEASED: 1975, Astralwerks. **KEY TRACKS:** "E-Musik," "Isi," "See Land."
CATALOG CHOICE: *Neu!* **NEXT STOP:** Brian Eno: *Another Green World* (see p. 258).
AFTER THAT: Faust: *Faust/So Far* (see p. 273).

A '60s Soul Classic

Tell It like It Is

Aaron Neville

On one of his first trips to a recording studio in 1965, the New Orleans singer Aaron Neville transformed an ordinary doo-wop slow dance called "Tell It like It Is" into a platform for some of the most heartfelt vocalizing ever to grace a jukebox. The folks at Par-Lo Records, a small local label, knew they had something special. They talked up the song to R&B stations in the South (and then the nation) and within months, the song became a national number 1 hit.

Neville maintains that this success never did him much good financially: When he returned from his first big tour, he discovered that Par-Lo had gone bankrupt. Like so many other young artists who were exploited at the time, he found himself in a tight money situation. He began painting houses, and driving a delivery truck around New Orleans. Though

he recorded intermittently (including, alas, several pale rerecordings of "Tell It like It Is"), it took more than a decade for Neville to support himself fully through music again.

Incredibly, this all-time-great single isn't the only thing worth hearing on the long-neglected album of the same name. Like many New Orleans entertainers, Neville grew up singing blues and up-tempo stuff as well as ballads, and the original songs commissioned for this date showcase his versatility. Highlights include a cannily harmonized bit of up-tempo soul, "A Hard Nut to Crack," a sultry ballad in the style of Bacharach and

David, "You Think You're So Smart," and a grooving blues called "Jailhouse" that approaches the intensity of the great Sam Cooke's R&B hits. Though not every tune is stunning, several of them stand as missed opportunities, hits that should have been. The happy ending: After playing informally at Mardi Gras parties for years, the members of Neville's family got serious about making music together, and since the mid-1970s, the Neville Brothers have become a kind of national treasure. They're the only family outfit whose nightly repertoire includes New

"Tell It like It Is" reached #1 on the *Billboard* R&B charts.

Orleans parade marches and ridiculously funky jazz and, of course, the poignantly quavering voice of Aaron Neville singing "Tell It like It Is."

GENRE: 🎙 R&B.
RELEASED: 1965, Par-Lo.
KEY TRACKS: "Tell It like It Is," "She Took You for a Ride," "Bet You're Surprised," "Hold On, Help Is on the Way."
CATALOG CHOICE: The Neville Brothers: *Fiyo on the Bayou.* **NEXT STOP:** Sam Cooke: *Live at the Harlem Square Club* (see p. 186). **AFTER THAT:** James Hunter: *People Gonna Talk.*

A World, Indeed

A World of Piano!

Phineas Newborn Jr.

Not many pianists could get away with the Liberace-style flourish that is Phineas Newborn Jr.'s opening statement here. The song is the bebop blues "Cheryl," and after a brisk romp through the theme, Newborn begins a series of perfect triplets that ascend, gradually, from the middle of the keyboard. Up and up he climbs, his fingers tracing a tornadolike whirl that doesn't stop until he runs out of keys.

It's pure showmanship, the kind of thing that makes casual listeners in the clubs sit upright and pay attention. But as is often true with the prodigiously gifted Newborn, there's more going on—underneath it, deep in the basement of the piano, the Memphis jazzman's left hand supplies an earthy blues melody. That's this often-ignored pianist's killer

In addition to piano, Newborn studied trumpet and both tenor and baritone saxophone.

app, the ability to slip profound inventions between flashes of jaw-dropping technique.

A fixture of the New York hard bop scene in the early '60s, Newborn struggled with mental illness and disappeared for years at a time. Though his command of the piano rivaled that of Oscar Peterson, to whom he was frequently compared, Newborn never won widespread acclaim the way Peterson did.

One reason: Where Peterson is forever conscious of pleasing his crowd, Newborn chases his own bliss. He shoots wildly intelligent, iconoclastic ideas into otherwise nondescript mid-tempo swing, rippling and roaring where other pianists would be content to prance. Newborn's placid introduction to "Lush Life" is a work of great inward-looking meditation, while his solo on "Daahoud" is its polar opposite—its reckless curiosity sends the rhythm team of bassist Paul Chambers and drummer Philly Joe Jones into an effortless overdrive. Newborn's dynamic playing made him a favorite among musicians, and

though his subsequent works don't sustain the zing that distinguishes *A World of Piano!*, he's heard in full roar on Roy Haynes's *We Three*, which was recorded the following year.

GENRE:  Jazz. **RELEASED:** 1962, Contemporary. **KEY TRACKS:** "Cheryl," "Oleo," "Lush Life," "Daahoud." **CATALOG CHOICE:** *Harlem Blues.* **NEXT STOP:** Roy Haynes: *We Three.* **AFTER THAT:** Wynton Kelly: *Kelly Blue.*

The Early Work of Dr. Sardonic

Twelve Songs

Randy Newman

Arguably one of the smartest songwriters of the rock era, Randy Newman has several different, and seemingly contradictory, areas of expertise and claims to fame. The singer and pianist first attracted attention through

hooky, dramatic pop songs that were picked up by a variety of artists. (He wrote "I Don't Want to Hear It Anymore," one of the riveting moments on Dusty Springfield's *Dusty in Memphis*, see p. 732.)

When he began making his own records, a different Newman emerged—that of a skeptical raconteur with a rapier wit. His songs of the early '70s skewer self-absorbed urban sophisticates, trailer park vixens, backwoods bigots, and short people, among many others; in each case, the withering insights come wrapped in a sound that's inviting and deceptively warm, almost affectionate. Then, in the 1980s, Newman followed three of his paternal uncles into the film music business, shelving satire in favor of squishy feel-good tunes. These were featured prominently in such blockbusters as

Randy Newman has won an Academy Award, 2 Emmys, and 5 Grammys.

Toy Story and *A Bug's Life.*

This, Newman's second album, is his most rocking, musically focused affair. Where his self-titled debut and a later concept album about life in the South, *Good Old Boys*, rely on elaborate orchestration, these tunes depend on rock-band chemistry and that mysterious elixir known as boogie. Running things from his piano, Newman turns out Tin Pan Alley melodies and easygoing New Orleans barrelhouse piano riffs, collapsing several generations of music into one sound. The guitarists (including Ry Cooder) respond with tangy blues asides that lead to the wrong side of the tracks, which, it turns out, is where Newman is most comfortable singing. (Or growling, as some have described it; Newman grew up in New Orleans, and can affect the sauntering demeanor of Louis Armstrong.) His delivery makes even potentially preposterous characterizations believable: Few pop songs have described loneliness with more precision than "If You Need Oil," the rambling thoughts of a bored gas station attendant.

Newman's songwriting strategies crystallize on *Twelve Songs*. If you only know his film music, don't miss these at once greasy and entertaining rambles, which are loaded with blunt portrayals of human nature and some of the most acidic satire ever tucked into three-minute pop songs.

GENRE: 🅡 Rock. **RELEASED:** 1970, Reprise. **KEY TRACKS:** "Have You Seen My Baby?," "Mama Told Me Not to Come," "Lover's Prayer," "If You Need Oil." **CATALOG CHOICES:** *Sail Away; Good Old Boys.* **NEXT STOP:** Mose Allison: *Allison Wonderland* (see p. 15). **AFTER THAT:** Warren Zevon: *Excitable Boy* (see p. 888).

Inside a Brilliant (and Neglected) Compositional Mind

The Complete Blue Note Recordings

Herbie Nichols

E ven in jazz, where tragic stories are a dime a dozen, the career of Herbie Nichols (1919–1963) stands out. The pianist and composer was around during the early days of bebop; his approach solidified

at the same jam sessions where Thelonious Monk threw down. But Nichols, a loner, had bills to pay, and spent most of his time working in Dixieland and traditional jazz groups around New York, rarely performing his own music. He recorded three trio albums for Blue Note in 1955 and 1956 and was quickly dropped—due to the fact that hardly anyone bought his records. After a few scattered other projects, including another trio date for Bethlehem Records, Nichols pretty much gave up. He died at age 44, suffering from leukemia.

Only after his death did jazz musicians begin to appreciate the crystalline logic of his compositions. *The Complete Blue Note Recordings* argues for Nichols as a lost major figure—the author of some of the most thoughtful, unorthodox piano trio music of the '50s.

Herbie Nichols first performed with the Savoy Sultans in 1937.

Nichols wrote an estimated 170 tunes. Most of them are highly ordered sets of short motifs, with phrases that acquire power as he moves them around the keyboard. Nichols had his own language, drawn from percussive outbursts (he favored the hard attack possible on upright pianos), complex sequences, and fast-moving harmony. His pieces follow elaborate winding paths. Though a technical wizard, he never used facility as a crutch; he prized melodic development far more than whiz-bang soloing.

The Biographical Encyclopedia of Jazz describes Nichols's career as "plagued by bad luck and obscure groups." True enough. But those who discover Nichols usually treasure him—for the spry intellectual challenges and whimsical nature of his music. He's the rare instance where the contribution is actually more compelling than the Hollywood tale of its tragic creator.

GENRE:  Jazz. **RELEASED:** 1997, Blue Note. **KEY TRACKS:** "House Party Starting," "Double Exposure," "Blue Chopsticks." **FURTHER INQUIRY:** The excellent *Four*

Lives in the Bebop Business by A. B. Spellman profiles altoists Jackie McLean and Ornette Coleman, and pianist Cecil Taylor as well as Herbie Nichols. **CATALOG CHOICE:** *Love, Gloom, Cash, Love.* **NEXT STOP:** Sonny Clark: *Cool Struttin'* (see p. 172). **AFTER THAT:** Andrew Hill: *Point of Departure* (see p. 359).

Tart, Smart Songs from a True Rogue

Nilsson Schmilsson

Harry Nilsson

Between the demise of the Beatles and the explosion of California folk-rock in the early '70s, there was a brief period when storytellers like Harry Nilsson and Randy Newman became the locus of thinking-person's pop music. Newman (see p. 549) was already esteemed as a genius tunesmith. Nilsson (1941–1994) was a slightly wilder character, a renaissance rogue determined to rescue pop from the straightlaced and the feckless.

Nilsson Schmilsson represents a particular peak of that arty era. A work of sheer swooning-strings opulence, it sits in the shadow of the Beach Boys' *Pet Sounds* (see p. 55), Brian Wilson's then-abandoned *Smile,* and the Beatles' *White Album* (see p. 61). It's also a series of preposterous leaps designed to work on many levels at once: Nilsson's songs include inscrutable oompah marches, craftily arranged dime-store exotica (on the spooky "Coconut," he plays a potion-brewing island medicine man), and outbreaks of vaudeville camp.

These would be novelty numbers were it not for Nilsson's voice, which trembles, constantly, with an inner-demon anguish. Having built his songs into towering mountains of sound,

On many of his recordings, this Grammy winner is credited only as Nilsson.

Nilsson sings them in a way that melts every contrivance of the accompaniment. His take on the then-popular Carpenters-style lilting love ode, "Without You," flirts dangerously with crooner bathos, yet somehow winds up sounding like the confessions of a ripped-apart romantic. His agitated rock anthem "Step into the Fire," a Doors knockoff, is similarly facile at first, yet blossoms into a platform for angry ranting. Nilsson's irreverence, coupled with the plain and gorgeous arcs of his melodies, put him in a class by himself. Often unjustly dismissed as a stylist or a mere eccentric, he was the rare auteur who, on this record at least, made circus-sideshow songs strike a nerve the way torch ballads usually do.

GENRE: 🎸 Rock. **RELEASED:** 1971, RCA. **KEY TRACKS:** "Without You," "Coconut." **CATALOG CHOICE:** *Nilsson Sings Newman.* **NEXT STOP:** Randy Newman: *Twelve Songs* (see p. 549). **AFTER THAT:** R.E.M.: *Up.*

An Audio Song Cycle from the Dark Side

The Downward Spiral

Nine Inch Nails

So this is what it's like inside a blast furnace. Or, perhaps, the cauldron of one's deepest fears. It's impossible to turn away from the terror. A voice from the dark side of hell taunts you, preying on every insecurity, mocking your needs.

Trent Reznor, the auteur behind Nine Inch Nails, has created this "environment" because he wants you to know how such a predicament, possibly *his* predicament, feels. During the harrowing opening moments of "March of the Pigs," he throws you in headfirst. The overdriven, serrated-edge guitars and equally distorted vocal shouts bring you to a place where the order of things means nothing, where "God is dead and no one cares," where your most cherished ideals melt in the heat. You can't escape the whomp of these highly tactile sounds, and when, at the end of each verse, things get blissfully quiet so that Reznor can ask the musical question, "Doesn't it make you feel better?," the momentary tenderness brings no relief. Because off in the distance there's the ominous sense that the big machines are cranking up again. More punishment awaits.

The Downward Spiral is an amazing bit of rock and roll psychodrama, a series of tense and often troubling scenes pumped up to Pink Floyd–esque grandeur. The songs connect the cudgel-like bluntness of industrial rock (such as Ministry, see p. 505) to more ornate—and sometimes surprisingly beautiful—orchestrations. Its narratives follow disturbed characters as they attempt to extract themselves from

"I don't know why I want to do these things, other than my desire to escape from Small Town, U.S.A., to dismiss the boundaries, to explore."
—Trent Reznor

the grip of various psychosis; when, on "I Do Not Want This," a sociopath expresses the desire to "do something that matters," he could be referring to anything from rape to a random act of heroism.

The distinguishing characteristic of many of these songs is dissonance. But it's never exclusively noise: Reznor is fluent in King Crimson (see p. 424), knows death metal and the more philosophical metal of the late '80s, can do a wicked power-ballad guitar solo when necessary (see "Ruiner"), and, surprisingly, has a healthy admiration for the droning synths of '80s mope-rock. When swirled together, these elements become a towering sound that pushes to extremes in the belief that pain serves a cathartic purpose. As he sings on the disarming "Hurt" (which was covered with astonishing clarity by Johnny Cash years later), "I hurt myself today, to see if I still feel."

GENRE: 🎸 Rock. **RELEASED:** 1994, Nothing/Interscope. **KEY TRACKS:** "March of the Pigs," "Ruiner," "Hurt," "Closer." **CATALOG CHOICE:** *Pretty Hate Machine.* **NEXT STOP:** Ministry: *The Mind Is a Terrible Thing to Taste* (see p. 505). **AFTER THAT:** Johnny Cash: *American IV.*

"I Feel Stupid and Contagious"

Nevermind

Nirvana

During the decade before this album arrived in 1991, rock was mostly puffy shirts and pouffy hair, a tyranny of unimaginative major-label pseudo-metal (Poison, Mötley Crüe) hyped by the unquestioning pop-culture toadies at MTV. After "Smells like Teen Spirit"—which boils the restlessness of a generation down to the all-purpose bored-kid shout "Here we are now, entertain us"—just about everything was different. Including MTV.

Singer and songwriter Kurt Cobain found himself hailed as the kid with the lock on the Gen X zeitgeist, and suddenly a rather large contingent of bands and their flannel-wearing fans were disciples in the First Church of the Perpetually Distressed Kurt. Among the ironies of this trendlet: "Smells like Teen Spirit" borrows its rhythm pattern from Boston's 1975 corporate-rock anthem "More than a Feeling" and its chord progression from the 1963 party classic "Louie Louie," bits of history grunge scenesters no doubt disdained. As far as Nirvana is concerned, grunge is cobbled from refurbished parts, made relevant by its caged-animal, sick-of-it-all attitude.

On one level, *Nevermind* is an elaborate psych-out: There's Cobain, dispensing disconnected brain droppings ("I'm so ugly, that's OK cause so are you") like some kind of unkempt street lunatic, while underneath, he and his accomplices, bassist Krist Novoselic and drummer Dave Grohl, punch out the rock with the cool precision of assembly-line workers. The rhythm guitars of "Come as You Are" or "Lithium" are, by themselves, a quintessence—brutal codes

"He had a lot of charisma from a very young age."
—Cobain's Aunt Mari

that are pumped up to larger-than-life size by producer Butch Vig and mixer Andy Wallace. The guitars are the catalysts for Cobain's jarring soft-then-loud contrasts, in which eerie verses are followed by a bases-clearing eruption on the refrain. Other rock bands did this (some say Cobain picked it up from the Pixies; see p. 602), but few made it so compelling, even when it sounded like Nirvana was smushing two disconnected songs together.

Cobain committed suicide in 1994, after struggling publicly with fame (and various addictions). He resented all vaunted appraisals of what Nirvana did. He knew he'd written great tunes—*Unplugged in New York*, recorded live, shows that the *Nevermind* songs are structurally as straightforward as the Beatles' "Eight Days a Week"—but he didn't want to be enshrined as any kind of cultural avatar. Cobain thrived on a malcontent's outsiderness, and from that perch, gave a whole bunch of people reason to believe in rock and roll again.

GENRE: 🎸 Rock. **RELEASED:** 1991, Geffen. **KEY TRACKS:** "Smells like Teen Spirit," "Come as You Are," "Breed," "Lithium." **CATALOG CHOICES:** *Unplugged in New York; In Utero.* **NEXT STOP:** The Melvins: *Houdini.* **AFTER THAT:** Soundgarden: *Superunknown* (see p. 726).

A Cross-Generational Summit Meeting

Will the Circle Be Unbroken

Nitty Gritty Dirt Band

Just before starting "The Precious Jewel," one of the dusted-off standards on this unusual cross-generational summit meeting, veteran singer Roy Acuff tells his younger accompanists, the Nitty Gritty Dirt Band, about a long-standing policy he follows in the recording studio. "Once you decide you're going to record a number, don't say, 'Oh, we'll take it over and do it again,'" Acuff says in one of several moments of priceless studio chat between tracks. "Because every time you go through it, you lose a little something."

It's unlikely that all of the thirty-seven tracks on this triple album were first takes. But an astonishing number of them have that first-take feeling. In one of the most unusual musical apprenticeships of the rock era, the Nitty Gritty Dirt Band invited country and bluegrass legends to spend time in the studio, sharing songs and traditions. The guests included Mother Maybelle Carter (who plays "Keep on the Sunny Side" on autoharp!), Merle Travis, banjo master Earl Scruggs, Acuff, and others. Also invited were younger, lesser-known musicians—this record established Vassar Clements as a profoundly melodic (and surprisingly versatile) fiddler.

The host band was attentive to the veterans—unlike the many rock figures then grafting country earnestness onto electric backdrops, these guys wanted to do the songs the "right" way, and they sought not just the lines but the magical little embellishments between them. The reverence is audible. Respect flows in both directions, as the mythic "circle" that stretches back to the Carter Family remains unbroken.

GENRES: ◐ Country ⊛ Rock.
RELEASED: 1972, Capitol. **KEY TRACKS:** "Keep on the Sunny Side," "Wreck on the Highway," "I Saw the Light," "Orange Blossom Special." **CATALOG CHOICE:** *Alive.* **NEXT STOP:** Various Artists: *O Brother, Where Art Thou?* (see p. 817).

No Misery Here

Rock Steady

No Doubt

Jim Dickinson, the producer who helped create enduring records by Big Star, the Replacements, and others, has a simple theory about recording: "Misery sticks to the tape." There may be no better illustration of this than the discography of SoCal ska-punk popularizers No Doubt. After breaking through with a tart, playful album called *Tragic Kingdom* in 1995, the quartet fronted by singer/pop culture savant Gwen Stefani spent more than two years working on the follow-up. The band later described some of that marathon birthing process as difficult, and though the resulting album *Return of Saturn* did sell, its elaborate sonic schemes and mature pop-star-as-grownup themes at times felt labored, if not tortured.

Somewhat desperate for a remedy, Stefani and crew did what rock stars do: They called up big-name producers from all over the map. Then they booked time for rest and research in Jamaica. Within weeks, No Doubt was immersed in the then-thriving dance hall culture, collaborating with the fast-rising duo Steely and Cleavie and others on terse, urgent-sounding rhythm riffs. Pretty soon the legendary production team of Sly and Robbie was involved. The duo put some grit into the sirenlike single "Hey Baby" (which includes the strident Stefani's hall-of-fame line, "I'm just sipping on chamomile,

Frontwoman Gwen Stefani performing in 2002 at the Jackson Square Park in New Orleans.

watching all the girls with their sex appeal") and the down-tempo "Underneath It All," which was written by Stefani and Eurythmics producer Dave Stewart. Hip-hop kingpins the Neptunes turned in a buzzy New Wave stomp, "Hella Good," that became a club anthem, and the groove machine known as Prince contributed the stealth classic "Don't Let Me Down."

The result is a hot 2 A.M. party record, one of the grabbiest to emerge in the new millennium. Not only is there no misery on *Rock Steady*, there's barely any reflection at all. Stefani's simple lyrics are concerned with being alive in the moment, having a good time, and leaving worries behind. It's not the heaviest thing ever, but those positive vibrations are contagious.

GENRES: 🎸 Rock ⭐ Pop. **RELEASED:** 2002, Interscope. **KEY TRACKS:** "Hella Good," "Hey Baby," "Start the Fire," "Don't Let Me Down." **CATALOG CHOICE:** *Tragic Kingdom.* **NEXT STOP:** Prince: *Parade.* **AFTER THAT:** Red Hot Chili Peppers: *Blood Sugar Sex Magik.*

"Honeys Play Me Close, Like Butter Play Toast"

Ready to Die

The Notorious B.I.G.

T he Brooklyn-born rapper and self-styled don Notorious B.I.G. was murdered in 1997 at the height of his popularity, a crime that echoed the graphic rapped accounts of violence that made him an icon. Born Christopher Wallace, B.I.G., or Biggie Smalls, established himself with this chilling debut record, which is the first credible East Coast response to the gangsta rhetoric of N.W.A. (see p. 557) and other Los Angeles hardcore rappers. In early cameos, Wallace came off as a jokester, but here he blossomed into the hip-hop epitome of brutal elegance, an imposing figure with a quick temper and great play-by-play skills. Wallace came from the streets, and knew the aspirational script shared by many of his brothers there; like other rappers (Tupac Shakur et al.) he worked it into overblown tales of cruelty toward women, gang-member insecurity, and thug life under the constant threat of death.

Notorious B.I.G. in New York City in 1996.

But the narratives of *Ready to Die*, one of the most creative gangsta rap albums of all time, aren't just devoted to the daily realities. There are also dream-sequence fantasies of a life spent enjoying opulence, the spoils of a drug-dealing superhero. Recognizing that they couldn't offer a whole album of nonstop killing sprees, Wallace (and his Svengali, Sean Combs) added upbeat pop-leaning cuts, and more introspective narratives that find Wallace reflecting on cruelty. The best of these, the title track and the closer, "Suicidal Thoughts," both wallow in a foreboding deathly gloom.

Wallace was a deceptively skillful lyricist.

Unlike many of his peers, his delivery is the opposite of agitated—at times here he sounds lazy, like he's rapping with a big wad of gum in his mouth. There's a touch of self-awareness in his lines, not to mention a sly wit in the consistently inventive rhymes. He glorifies gangsta values and sounds positively gleeful plotting violence. Yet somehow, in subtle ways, Wallace communicates that no matter how grisly things get, there's a human with a heart behind the Glock. Even if that side appears only briefly, to comment on the condition of a potential victim's underpants.

GENRE: 🎤 Hip-Hop. **RELEASED:** 1994, Bad Boy. **KEY TRACKS:** "Ready to Die," "Things Done Changed," "Big Poppa." **CATALOG CHOICE:** *Life After Death.* **NEXT STOP:** 2Pac: *All Eyez on Me* (see p. 789). **AFTER THAT:** Snoop Dogg: *Doggystyle.*

Fetching from a Distance . . .

Princesses Nubiennes

Les Nubians

There is no such thing as background music. Only inattentive listeners. Even the most wallpapery music holds secrets, and can be appreciated on its own—not as a carefully chosen room accent or a distant accompaniment to your restaurant meal. All the same, there are times when we turn to music for nothing more than a vibe transfusion—you know, after a dinner party, when everyone needs to move around a little. When the ambient, far-off hint of a sexy backbeat is enough.

This album, the debut of two beautiful sisters who call themselves Les Nubians, is perfect for such moments. Hélène and Célia Faussart, whose father is from France and mother from Cameroon, sing mostly in French. But they're into globe-hopping. This album anticipates the world-aware beats of the Black Eyed Peas' will.i.am and other new-millennium urban stars.

At times the Nubian vocal harmonies echo those found on Sade records (there's a cover of "Sweetest Taboo" here), then get slightly wilder, pushing toward a vague psychedelia. The beats follow a similar trajectory: Though set in a basic, earthy hip-hop zone, they're enriched by African hand-drum rhythms, spacey chanted refrains, and the duo's coy, gently pleading vocals. The result is music that speaks in the universal language of the mellow groove, effortlessly melting elements from world music and clubland together. On the surface *Princesses Nubiennes* makes few demands, but it offers unexpected riches when you take the time to encounter it up close.

GENRE: 🎙 R&B. **RELEASED:** 1998, Virgin. **KEY TRACKS:** "Demain," "Makeda," "Bebela," "Voyager." **NEXT STOP:** Zap Mama: *Adventures in Afropea.* **AFTER THAT:** Soul II Soul: *Keep On Movin'.*

The First Great Gangsta Rap Record

Straight Outta Compton

N.W.A.

With his 1985 declaration "Park Side Killers is makin' that green/ One by one I'm knockin' 'em out," the Philadelphia rapper Schoolly D (Jesse Weaver Jr.) pushed hip-hop in the lucrative new direction that came to be known as gangsta rap.

When this brusque incendiary track reached the West Coast, and particularly South Central Los Angeles, it was all the kindling necessary to start a craze. Within a year, Ice-T had released "Six in the Morning," which borrowed directly from Schoolly D, and a loose-knit collective called N.W.A. (Niggaz Wit Attitude) was creating music that described, in graphic detail, a reality much of white America never encountered up close.

Newsweek said *Straight Outta Compton* "introduced some of the most grotesquely exciting music ever made."

Two years later, N.W.A.'s second album, *Straight Outta Compton,* tore the genre wide open. Writing in *Rolling Stone,* comedian Chris Rock called it "the British Invasion for black people," an apt analogy considering how much subsequent hip-hop was directly inspired by it.

Straight Outta Compton opens with an assertion: "You are about to witness the strength of street knowledge." That's no empty boast. In the course of thirteen tightly wound tracks, MCs Ice Cube, Easy-E, and Ren tear, round-robin style, through descriptions of turf wars, revenge fantasies, sour drug deals, and late-night street-corner confrontations that turn into bloodbaths. These are more than just inventories of violence and cruelty: They're an insider's dissection of ghetto socioeconomics, highlighting the desperation and futility felt by those who see few opportunities on the horizon.

This album sparked enormous controversies—one song, which denigrated the police, drew the ire of the FBI, while others were denounced for their lack of respect for women. Some of the raps are difficult to defend, but not the musical backdrops: The assault-rifle drum machine rhythms concocted by Dr. Dre remain an industry standard. Though they lack the menacing adornment of later Dre productions (notably his own *The Chronic,* see p. 236), the destabilized, eerie unsettled feeling he creates here makes it easy for the rappers to let their inner thugs loose.

GENRE: 🎤 Hip-Hop. RELEASED: 1988, Priority. KEY TRACKS: "Gangsta Gangsta," "Straight Outta Compton," "Express Yourself."

CATALOG CHOICE: Ice Cube: *AmeriKKKa's Most Wanted*. NEXT STOP: Dr. Dre: *The Chronic* (see p. 236). AFTER THAT: Public Enemy: *Fear of a Black Planet*.

A New York Amalgam like None Other

Eli and the Thirteenth Confession

Laura Nyro

Listening to these perfectly sculpted, constantly surprising pop miniatures, it's possible to imagine Laura Nyro (1947–1997) soaking up inspiration by walking around New York. A musical omnivore, the singer, songwriter, and pianist gathered gospel refrains and soul shouts into a glorious street-level sound. One of her supercollider concoctions, "Eli's Comin'," spins conga-heavy Latin boogie into a music-theater second-act showstopper. Another, "Stoned Soul Picnic," immortalizes the beatific, spaced-out vibe of flower children in the park.

Nyro's second album (and easily her best), *Eli,* reminds that pop songwriting was a different game in the late 1960s. Without making a big deal of the mechanics, Nyro created maze-like songs that change tempo, key, and mood frequently. Often the music slows when she reaches the end of a verse, shifts to an entirely new pulse for the hook, and eventually circles back to the original groove in grand and satisfying fashion. Nyro guides these changes from the piano, providing an anchor with persistent lilting chords, a signature. Her music is sophisticated without sounding elite—each instrumental touch becomes somehow essential to the tale. Nyro never had the success others did with her material (songs from this album were big hits for the Fifth Dimension and Three Dog Night), but that doesn't diminish her contribution: Like no one before her, Nyro gathered the tangled and often contradictory sounds running through her city, and wove them into riveting and wholly original music.

GENRE: ✪ Pop. RELEASED: 1968, Columbia. KEY TRACKS: "Lu," "Eli's Comin'," "Stoned Soul Picnic." CATALOG CHOICE: *New York Tendaberry*. NEXT STOP: Fiona Apple: *When the Pawn . . .* (see p. 23). AFTER THAT: Nellie McKay: *Get Away from Me*.

Fasten Seat Belts, Get Ready For . . .

Tranceport

Paul Oakenfold

On *Tranceport,* British DJ Paul Oakenfold offers a high-revving tour through the techno offshoot known as "trance." The style is distinguished by what can seem like endless repetition—detractors say it's well suited to the mental reprogramming of those who've escaped the clutches of religious cults.

But as with other electronic dance subgenres, there's more to it. In the hands of a skilled practitioner, trance can be a totally absorbing sensory journey, with rippling waves of texture and ultrastreamlined grooves. Oakenfold starts with slivers of well-known European club hits, fractures them into cellular bits, and then methodically puts them together in novel ways. Once he's locked a few rhythm patterns into a loop, he'll add contrasting rhythms on top, building a tight, and dazzlingly interdependent, pulse that changes texture as elements are added and subtracted. Sometimes these beat constructions sound like they're coming from a tiny transistor radio speaker. Then, through the magic of sound-shaping effects, they'll swell up into an obliterating, almost symphonic roar.

Tranceport is Oakenfold's fifth album.

As massaged and manipulated by a keenly musical DJ like Oakenfold, those extremes exert a hypnotic pull. *Tranceport* captures this, condensing the perpetual-motion club experience into a satisfying CD-length adventure. Though it's not the kind of art you typically learn about in a conservatory, there is, undeniably, art in its filter sweeps and cresting beats—the kind best experienced on a crowded dance floor, or in a fast car on an open highway at night, when the momentum of the music and the momentum of the machine become one.

GENRE: 🅦 Electronica. RELEASED: 1998, Kinetic. KEY TRACKS: "Purple," "Café del Mar," "El Niño." CATALOG CHOICE: *A Voyage into Trance; Creamfields.* NEXT STOP: Paul van Dyk: *The Politics of Dancing.* AFTER THAT: Basement Jaxx: *Remedy.*

A Folksinger, Torn Asunder by Rock

There and Now: Live in Vancouver 1968

Phil Ochs

Somewhere around 1967, the folksinger Phil Ochs caught the rock and roll bug. This afflicted lots of people, but he was hit particularly hard. He'd made a name for himself with thoughtful protest anthems and journalistic songs that rambled on seas of endless verses (one, "When in Rome" on *Tape from California,* lasts thirteen minutes). After his rock awakening, Ochs became interested in recording with more than just a guitar. Starting in 1967 with *Pleasures of the Harbor,* his records grew ornate, with strings and lush production supporting his image-rich (sometimes too rich) lyrics.

These records weren't as stirring as his folk works—the material's more erratic, and at times Ochs tries a bit too hard to be arty. Thankfully, it took several years for Ochs to make the change as a live performer. When he toured in 1967 and 1968, he still appeared solo, accompanying himself on guitar. This concert recording, which wasn't released until 1990, comes from that "between" period. It was recorded shortly after the violent protests of the 1968 Democratic National Convention in Chicago—where Ochs appeared—and features Ochs's significant songs from both the "folk" and "rock" sides of his catalog.

Between the first two selections, Ochs asks his crowd for its indulgence, explaining that he hasn't performed much since the convention and may forget some lyrics. He needn't have worried: These interpretations are deeply felt, and intense, highlighting Ochs's fervor as often as his wry wit. While his commentary

Ochs played the clarinet before taking up guitar.

on American apathy, "Outside of a Small Circle of Friends," is plenty sharp on *Pleasures,* here it grows almost savage, a withering appraisal of a culture in denial.

GENRE: 🎵 Folk.
RELEASED: 1990, Rhino.
KEY TRACKS: "There but for Fortune," "Outside of a Small Circle of Friends," "Crucifixion."
F.Y.I.: Ochs's telling of the Edgar Allan Poe classic "The Bells" features none other than Allen Ginsberg chiming in on bells. **CATALOG CHOICE:** *Pleasures of the Harbor.* **NEXT STOP:** Tom Paxton: *Outward Bound.*

You Do Want What She's Got Here

I Do Not Want What I Haven't Got

Sinéad O'Connor

With this bracing album, Sinéad O'Connor expanded the notion of what a female singer-songwriter could be. A wild child with a shaved head, a voice like a siren, and knack for audacious media hijinks

(among them ripping up a picture of Pope John Paul II on *Saturday Night Live*), O'Connor came along at a time when demand for journal-scribbling Joni Mitchell intellectual types was waning. O'Connor, who is Irish, went for something much more visceral: flinty, quick-to-anger songs powered by outrage and indignation—and, significantly, a touch of the hip-hop backbeat.

Most of the songs on this, O'Connor's biggest success, deal with the topics favored by countless sensitive gals—stormy

Sinéad O'Connor was named after Sinéad de Valera, wife of Irish President Éamon de Valera.

relationships with parents, friends, and uncaring lovers. The difference is in the stance: O'Connor approaches each tune like she's poised for a confrontation. Or recovering from one. "Three Babies" begins in a mood of naptime-in-the-nursery reflection, but as it unfolds, O'Connor gathers up considerable fury, reaching into her pained and plaintive upper register for a series of devastating cries.

This album is essential listening just for O'Connor's dramatic turn-on-a-dime vocal performances. Among the best: a deep, almost religious incantation featuring just her voice and drums ("I Am Stretched Out on Your Grave"), a scathing comment on British racism ("Black Boys on Mopeds"), and a wounded treatment of Prince's "Nothing Compares 2 U," her massive hit. This is arguably the most dramatic exhibition of O'Connor's volatile gift: One minute she's hissing with rage at the lover who's fled, the next minute she offers up a conciliatory phrase, something that's so fragile and disarm-ingly forthright, you wonder if it's coming from the same person.

GENRE: 🎸 Rock. **RELEASED:** 1990, Ensign/Chrysalis. **KEY TRACKS:** "Black Boys on Mopeds," "Nothing Compares 2 U," "Feel So Different," "Three Babies," "I Am Stretched Out on Your Grave." **CATALOG CHOICE:** *Throw Down Your Arms.* **NEXT STOP:** Alanis Morissette: *Jagged Little Pill* (see p. 522). **AFTER THAT:** Tori Amos: *Little Earthquakes.*

A Record of Incalculable Influence

Odetta Sings Ballads and Blues

Odetta

This is allegedly the record that inspired a young Bob Dylan to trade in his electric guitar for an acoustic model; years later, he said Odetta was "the first thing that turned me on to folk singing." He was not alone.

Many folk-revival artists cited this 1956 document and the several that followed as primary catalysts.

The fierce Odetta, who was born in Birmingham, Alabama, started out wanting to be an opera singer. That was a daunting challenge in the segregated 1950s, so she pursued musical theater, and at eighteen became part of a touring production of *Finian's Rainbow.* When the tour got to San Francisco, she heard folk music and was hooked: She learned to play guitar and began singing the mix of work songs, spirituals, and blues that would, in a few years, make her famous.

Odetta recorded several times before she was signed to the Tradition label, but *Sings Ballads and Blues* is her first fully realized statement. Its songs associated with Leadbelly ("Easy Rider," "Muleskinner Blues") show how

"If only one could be sure that every 50 years a voice and a soul like Odetta's would come along . . ." —Maya Angelou

authoritative Odetta was as a guitarist; her timing is flawless. And they present her as a riveting singer, particularly in her fulminating lower register (her high notes still have a touch of operatic affectation here). Of special note are the spiritual songs, among them "Joshua" and the closing medley that includes "Oh Freedom," "Come and Go with Me," and a resolute "I'm on My Way." These have a spine-chilling directness, a sense of hard-won knowledge that the more collegiate folkies couldn't match.

Sings Ballads and Blues has been reissued many different ways. The most rewarding package is the two-disc *The Tradition Masters,* which includes the stirring *At the Gate of Horn,* recorded live in a Chicago club. This time, Odetta isn't alone: She's accompanied by bassist Bill Lee, filmmaker Spike Lee's father, a steadying (and underappreciated) presence on many great folk records.

GENRE:  Folk. RELEASED: 1956, Tradition. KEY TRACKS: "Muleskinner Blues," "Joshua," "Deep in the Pen," "Jack o'

Diamonds." From *At the Gate of Horn:* "Midnight Special," "Take This Hammer." CATALOG CHOICE: *At Carnegie Hall.* NEXT STOP: Karen Dalton: *It's So Hard to Tell Who's Going to Love You the Best* (see p. 203). AFTER THAT: Oscar Brown Jr: *Sin and Soul* (see p. 122).

Suave Soul with a Mission

Back Stabbers

The O'Jays

The first great album of '70s Philadelphia soul, *Back Stabbers* took the best impulse of the era's pop music—that inclination to celebrate love as something precious—and bathed it in the studio-orchestra opulence that became the defining characteristic of the "Sound of Philadelphia."

This was a potent combination, and a gold mine. On the opening track, lead singer Eddie Levert proclaims the album's guiding philosophy: "Love is not a state of mind, love's a fact of life." Nine songs later, on the massive hit "Love Train," the singer sends an urgent, idealistic appeal to others who might feel the same way: "People all over the world, join hands, start a love train." In between are accounts of love trouble ("992 Arguments"), fear of commitment ("Time to Get Down"), and a trenchant cautionary tale about deceitful friends ("Back Stabbers").

The songs are all great, but the arrangements—far more lavish than anything else on the radio—makes them undeniable classics. Producers Kenny Gamble and Leon Huff assembled a team of arrangers who conceived of pop on an orchestral level. The Philly Sound is distinguished by active, often tricky string parts that snake around the vocal lines, offset with jazz guitar and vibraphone and other sophis-

This record hit #10 on the *Billboard* Top 40 Albums chart.

ticated touches. The arrangers—and the musicians of what became known as the MFSB (Mother Father Sister Brother) Orchestra, which included moonlighting Philadelphia Orchestra members—do the hard work. All the O'Jays' Levert (and Teddy Pendergrass and the other Philly-soul stars) had to do was slide their vocals into a sumptuous, instantly sensual mix.

Back Stabbers contains most of the key O'Jays tracks (one exception is the ambitious seven-minute masterpiece "For the Love of Money," issued on the subsequent *Ship Ahoy*). Its message of tolerance cut across barriers of race and radio formats, proving that, in the early '70s anyway, there really was room on the Love Train for everybody.

GENRE:  R&B. RELEASED: 1972, Epic. KEY TRACKS: "Back Stabbers," "Love Train," "992 Arguments." CATALOG CHOICE: *Ship Ahoy.* NEXT STOP: Harold Melvin and the Blue Notes: *Wake Up Everybody.* AFTER THAT: The Stylistics: *Round Two.*

The First Great Band of Early Jazz

Off the Record: The Complete 1923 Jazz Band Recordings

King Oliver and His Creole Jazz Band

The tales about Joe "King" Oliver (1885–1938) usually have to do with showmanship. Oliver started performing in 1908, and in the early days of his career in New Orleans the cornet player and bandleader was sometimes seen playing solo while walking the streets of Storyville, the city's red-light district. According to legend, when he'd get to clubs and honky-tonks where the bands led by Buddy Bolden and other established names were employed, he'd play extra loud, luring patrons to the street with his antics. Like an early jazz pied piper, he'd get people to follow him to his own gig at the Aberdeen Cafe.

Oliver was one of the first to appreciate the entertainment aspects of jazz. He was also the music's first great bandleader. These 1923 recordings were made with the group he brought with him to Chicago in 1919, which included the young Louis Armstrong, pianist Lil Hardin (Armstrong's future wife), and the Dodds brothers, drummer Warren "Baby" Dodds and the marvelously inventive clarinetist Johnny Dodds. Together, this group virtually defined what would be called "Hot" jazz. Its intricate arrangements, played with snappy instrumental panache, transformed jittery ragtime into deeper music brushed with blues feeling. The band was cohesive in startling (and strikingly modern) ways: Cue up the second version of "Snake Rag" on this anthology to hear the musicians landing on, and holding, a delicious flatted third interval in hyperdramatic fashion.

From left to right: Honore Dutrey, Baby Dodds, Louis Armstrong, King Oliver, Lil Hardin, Bill Johnson, and Johnny Dodds.

The musical legacy of Oliver's Creole Jazz Band—which includes his crafty early use of brass mutes to produce wah-wah-like warbling sounds—nearly didn't survive into the CD era. These recordings were made at the Gennett studio in Indiana with primitive, pre-electric methods, including the old-fashioned "recording horn." Most reissues have been terribly noisy, to the point where individual instruments are indistinct. This two-disc collection was done by a Maryland-based label specializing in the restoration of early audio artifacts. Though not spotless, it does offer a crisp, surprisingly vivid picture of one of the great bands of early jazz at its peak.

GENRE: 🎶 Jazz. RELEASED: 2006, Off the Record. KEY TRACKS: "Dippermouth Blues," "Snake Rag," "Zulus Ball," "Workingman Blues." F.Y.I.: In his autobiography, Louis Armstrong says that the man he called "Papa Joe" was his biggest influence: "I still think that if it had not been for Joe Oliver, jazz would not be what it is today." NEXT STOP: Louis Armstrong: *The Complete Hot Fives and Hot Sevens* (see p. 26). AFTER THAT: Duke Ellington Orchestra: *Early Ellington: The Complete Brunswick Recordings 1926–1931*.

Passionately Sung Odes to Heal the Soul

Songs for the Poor Man

Remmy Ongala and Orchestre Super Matimila

O f all the qualities necessary for a healer, compassion is the foundation. This is perhaps why the Zaire-born, Tanzania-based singer Remmy Ongala is known as The Doctor. It's not for his medical skill—he has none—but for songs that speak, with great empathy, about suffering and poverty, trials he knew from personal experience.

Ongala lost his mother when he was nine, and from then on was responsible for the care of his younger siblings. He recalled that, growing up, "I lived in trouble, food was a problem. I picked up bread that others had thrown away. All the songs I sing result from the difficulties I had in the past." His break in music came when an uncle called him to Dar es Salaam to be part of Orchestra Makassy. He later joined the Matimila band, which was "owned" by a local businessman. Eventually he formed his own group, which he called Orchestre Super Matimila.

With the elegies and sorrowful laments of *Songs for the Poor Man*, Ongala transforms his experiences into music of fierce resolve. Every piece is based on the interlaced guitar arpeggios that define *soukous*, the shimmery Afro-pop dance style. But where conventional *soukous* is brisk and almost uptight, Super Matimila broadens the backbeats, slows them down, gives them a processional swagger and a touch of East African funk. The rhythm is entrancing without being overpowering, and that's ideal for Ongala, who in some ways is just singing lullabies. Whether his weathered voice is praising the steadfastness of women, or reckoning with death (the amazing "Kifo"), Ongala sounds like one who knows what it's like to be down, and knows, also, that he will not give up.

GENRE: 🌐 World/Tanzania. **RELEASED:** 1993, Real World. **KEY TRACKS:** "Kifo," "Pamella." **CATALOG CHOICE:** Orchestra Makassy: *Legends of East Africa.* **NEXT STOP:** Geoffrey Oryema: *Exile.* **AFTER THAT:** Tabu Ley Rochereau: *The Voice of Lightness* (see p. 651).

The Unearthly Voice

For the Lonely: Eighteen Greatest Hits

Roy Orbison

I nducting Roy Orbison (1936–1988) into the Rock and Roll Hall of Fame in 1987, Bruce Springsteen contrasted the exuberance of early rock with the tender musings of one shy bespectacled kid. "Roy's ballads were always the best when you were alone and in the dark. Because they addressed the underside of pop romance. They were scary. His voice was unearthly."

Of all the figures on the scene during the first decade of rock, the shy, Texas-born Orbison was the one focusing on the cold hours after the sock hop, when the ardent young lover found himself alone, contemplating that unrequited romance. "You walked away, the pain began, I knew I'd never love again," Orbison sings on "I'm Hurtin'," one of the more symphonic of his singles. Other late-night confessions are, of course, more familiar: the dejected "Blue Bayou," perhaps the most achingly vulnerable of Orbison hits; the perpetual sigh that is "In Dreams"; the worshipful "Oh, Pretty Woman." These are not just craftily produced showcases for a trembling voice that ranged three octaves and featured a wondrously controlled

After several lean decades, Orbison returned to the charts in 1989, with his posthumous release, *Mystery Girl*.

falsetto—they're also maps to a world of pent-up longing.

As happened with many of his contemporaries, Orbison's primary singles have been reissued in countless configurations—there are so many hits albums featuring the same set of songs, you might expect a sticker on the outside claiming "Available for the first time in this sequence!" Of them, *For the Lonely* offers clean sound quality, with none of the gimmicky "enhancements" that often mar recordings from the 1950s and '60s.

GENRE: 🎸 Rock. **RELEASED:** 1988, Rhino. **KEY TRACKS:** "Only the Lonely," "Running Scared," "Dream Baby," "Blue Bayou," "Oh, Pretty Woman." **CATALOG CHOICES:** *Authorized Bootleg Collection* (4 CDs); *Mystery Girl*. **NEXT STOP:** Eddie Cochran: *Somethin' Else! The Fine Lookin' Hits Of*. **AFTER THAT:** Chris Isaak: *Heart Shaped World*.

Cuba to Africa, and Everywhere in Between

Pirates Choice

Orchestra Baobab

For the first three minutes, "Utrus horas" is just another sultry, syrup-slow Cuban groove played with reverence by African musicians. And then, at 3:42, guitarist Barthelemy Attisso creeps into the spotlight. Working

methodically, he cobbles together a solo that is at once conversational and majestic, an extended, sweeping journey that deserves a spot in the Electric Guitar Hall of Fame.

In a coy, incredibly patient way, Attisso issues a desolate cry, then another, followed by a few Claptonesque pitch-bending declarations. Then he elongates his lines, emulating the bravura swagger of a trumpet player lighting up

a Havana nightclub. As he globe-trots, he pulls languid phrases out of thin air, and punctuates them with crisp chords. At times he veers into free-jazz dissonance, but there is absolutely nothing overheated or even extroverted about this solo. Or, for that matter, the equally stupendous ones throughout.

Among the first of many bands to explore Cuban rhythm, Orchestra Baobab—a force in

African music for a long stretch of the 1970s and '80s—became a sensation in Senegal for its fusion of drumming from the country's Casamance region with Cuban syncopations. This beautiful album circulated widely outside of Africa, and is generally credited with sparking interest in what became known in the U.S. as "world music."

Ironically, the attention didn't help Baobab: In Senegal, the more assertive pulse of *mbalax* was spreading quickly, propelled by the singer Youssou N'Dour (see p. 542). The group disbanded in 1987; Attisso stopped playing to make his living as a lawyer in his native Togo. Then, in 2001, *Pirates Choice* was reissued with many extra tracks, triggering demand for new Baobab music. When the band reformed

The group got its name from a nightclub, Baobab, in Dakar where it played regularly.

later that year, Attisso had to be sent a guitar so he could teach himself to play again. It's impossible to tell that this band has been dormant when you hear *Specialist in All Styles*, which was recorded in 2003. The poised groove is still there, and as they reconnect with it, Attisso and his mighty group find some new magic too.

GENRE: 🌐 World/Senegal. **RELEASED:** 1982, Virgin. (Reissued 2001, Nonesuch.) **KEY TRACKS:** "Utrus horas," "Ray M'Bele," "Soldadi," "La rebellion." **CATALOG CHOICE:** *Specialist in All Styles.* **NEXT STOP:** Bembeya Jazz National: *The Syliphone Years* (see p. 76). **AFTER THAT:** T.P. Orchestre Poly-Rythmo: *The Kings of Benin Urban Groove, 1972–1980.*

Music That Overcomes the Politics of Isolation

Antidiotico

Orishas

For a while in the 1990s, international hip-hop—made by MCs rapping in languages other than English—seemed poised to explode. As has happened with jazz and blues and other indigenous American musics, hip-hop attracted followers from around the world, many of whom didn't get past wooden imitations of the cadences that came easily to American rappers. Some, however, had original ideas: In France, the exuberant MC Solaar developed a reputation for witty, intricate narratives fired off over twinkly beats familiar to young Parisian clubgoers.

And from Cuba came Orishas, brandishing elements of that country's folklore as a killer retro-nuevo, back-to-the-future weapon. Here, on a series of singles the group made beginning in 1999, is inventive urban music that inte-grates the familiar boom-bap of the Bronx with the nimble *son* and rumba pulses that have kept Cuban dance floors busy for generations. It's an incendiary mix, aligning seemingly opposed rhythmic ideas into one galvanizing and highly danceable sound. It's also an example of how musical ingenuity transcends politics: These MCs developed their hybrid approach individually in high school, learning rap by listening to American radio. They met in Europe while on student exchange programs, and decided to flee Cuba to pursue the hip-hop dream. They're now based in France; each of the group's four critically acclaimed albums comment (often sardonically) on Cuban politics while expressing solidarity with the island nation's people.

Named for the deities of the Afro-Cuban Santeria faith, Orishas bring distinct Cubanness into every backbeat, whether those beats are made on machines or involve traditional percussion instruments. Or both, as in the clever improvement on reggaeton entitled "Hay un son" and "5.3.7 Cuba," which hinges on the chorus of the Cuban evergreen "Chan Chan." The tune starts tersely, with a beat a thug like 50 Cent might dig, and grows more intense as rappers Ruzzo and Yotuel launch

syncopated fast-breaking outbursts of free-style. These dexterous ad-libs suggest that Orishas aren't merely fluent in several languages. They're the rare children of hip-hop who've become expert at interpolating music from several generations into a dizzying rhythm matrix unlike anything else on the planet.

GENRE: 🎤 Hip-Hop. **RELEASED:** 2007, Universal Latino. **KEY TRACKS:** "Hay un son," "A lo Cubano," "5.3.7 Cuba." **CATALOG CHOICE:** *El kilo*. **NEXT STOP:** MC Solaar: *Prose Combat*. **AFTER THAT:** Calle 13: *Residente o visitante*.

The Incubator of Modern Cuban Music

Memories of Cuba

Orquesta Casino de la Playa

This Havana ensemble, one of the cornerstones of Latin dance music, didn't start out as an all-star band. But within ten years of its founding in 1937, many of its original musicians had become either stars on their

own or in-demand sidemen—among them the fiery vocalists Cascarita (Orlando Guerra) and Miguelito Valdés, pianist and arranger Pérez Prado, and percussionist Mongo Santamaria.

And during its first few years as a band, Casino played a key role in modernizing Cuban music. While other dance bands in Havana were dishing quaint, faintly rhythmic parlor music, this group emphasized the pulse, let the singers cut loose, and even left room for instrumental solos (check out Prado's demonic turn on the opener "Llora"). Its arrangements, many written by future Mambo King Prado, put the brassy swagger of American big bands through more rhythmically strenuous workouts.

This anthology covers Casino's most fruitful years, 1937–1944 (the group moved to Mexico City in 1948, and became less of an artistic force). Its first ten tracks feature Cascarita; among them is the heated "El

caballo y la montura," built on *guajira*, the Cuban equivalent of "country" music, which showcases Cascarita's flippant phrasing. There are fewer Valdés tracks, but they're all classics. Whether he's slithering around doing a nightclubbish evocation of Cuban Santeria ritual (the solemn "Babalu," which inspires some powerful ad-libs) or finding poignance in the plaintive vendor's calls of "El manicero," Valdés's lazy, languid phrases have a way of tugging you by the heartstrings, into an elegant musical world that vanished a long time ago.

GENRE: 🌐 World/Cuba. **RELEASED:** 1991, Tumbao. **KEY TRACKS:** "Llora," "Babalu," "El caballo y la montura." **CATALOG CHOICE:** Miguelito Valdés: *Algo nuevo*. **NEXT STOP:** Beny Moré: *The Most from Beny Moré*. **AFTER THAT:** Ritmo Oriental: *Historia de la Ritmo*, Vol. 1.

Cracked and Pleading and Perfect . . .

Central Reservation

Beth Orton

Beth Orton's second album *Central Reservation* is haunted by death, rejection, and regret. It tells about a wandering and deceitful lover, and of a vanished romance so encompassing, the "Stars All Seem to Weep" when it ends. One song, the ambling waltz "Pass in Time," shares advice Orton's mom gave on her deathbed: She wanted her daughter to lighten up and enjoy life because "you're here just a little while."

Despite the bleak subjects, *Central Reservation* is the opposite of a downer. It's the perfect audio for a slow-moving Sunday morning. Like Billie Holiday, Orton sings without holding anything back—she's throwing open the windows of her heart, holding up her imperfections while seeking a more complete understanding of life. Her cracked and pleading voice (a touch of Holiday there, too) draws you in, and though she's still in the everything-hurts phase of breakup, she sounds determined to learn, heal, move on. The surroundings—questioning strings, jazz vibraphone, forcefully strummed acoustic guitar—offer a lush cushioning, and

there's a great duet ("Pass in Time") with the underappreciated jazz singer Terry Callier, whom Orton regards as a major influence. Even when Orton's lyrics speak in general terms about heartache, there is no ambiguity or generalized formless gloom in her delivery. Every emotional wrinkle is rendered with stunning precision. Like a mapmaker plotting exact coordinates, Orton uses that perpetually shook-up, melancholy voice to pull listeners into the thick of a feeling—and then she stays there, describing it in tones as much as in words.

GENRE: 🎸 Rock. **RELEASED:** 1999, Arista. **KEY TRACKS:** "Pass in Time," "Stars All Seem to Weep," "Stolen Car," "Central Reservation." **CATALOG CHOICE:** *Trailer Park.* **NEXT STOP:** Dido: *No Angel.* **AFTER THAT:** Terry Callier: *First Light.*

A Lost Classic of Psychedelic Soul

Inspiration Information

Shuggie Otis

Sophisticated and gently sung, dotted with jazzy interludes and psychedelic detours, Shuggie Otis's fourth album *Inspiration Information* belongs in the "Should Have Been Huge" file. When *Inspiration* was released in 1974, a small circle of critics and musicians began talking about Otis as a next big thing. Part of their awe can be explained by Otis's production style: He played almost all the instruments, including a primitive drum machine, himself. His primary instrument is the guitar, and many of the great *Inspiration* tracks depend on a "guitar orchestra" of sorts, with cleanly plucked rhythm sharing the spotlight with tasteful wah-wah pedal work and easygoing, almost languorous leads. The songs range from sunny afternoon daydreams ("Island Letter") to gentle Weather Reportish Latin fusion ("XL-30") to colorful, idealistic funk in the Sly Stone mold ("Aht Uh Mi Hed").

Otis began performing when he was just 12.

Incredibly, the love never materialized for *Inspiration.* The album disappeared after a few weeks on the lower rungs of the charts. But *Inspiration* had an afterlife: Several years later, it inspired George Johnson of the Brothers Johnson to explore Otis's other, equally obscure efforts. He was transfixed by a taunting singsong number on the previous album, *Freedom Flight,* entitled "Strawberry Letter 23" that Otis wrote when he was fifteen. The Brothers Johnson covered "Strawberry" and it became one of the biggest hits of 1977.

For the next several decades, *Inspiration* existed mainly in the private stashes of hipsters and DJs. It was finally reissued in 2001, on a package that included Otis's original "Strawberry Letter 23." This time, the album drew fawning coverage in the press and prompted a long-overdue reappraisal of the singer and guitarist, who'd spent decades in a semi-spotlight on the West Coast blues circuit. It's easy to understand why contemporary urban musicians, whose art is built on endless repetition, would revere the loose, resolutely iconoclastic *Inspiration*: It calls from a time before the loop was king, before everybody followed the same worn-out playbook.

GENRE: 🎵 R&B. **RELEASED:** 1974, Epic. (Reissued 2001, Luaka Bop.) **KEY TRACKS:** "Island Letter," "Aht Uh Mi Hed," "XL-30." **CATALOG CHOICE:** *Shuggie's Boogie: Shuggie Otis Plays the Blues.* **NEXT STOP:** Sly Stone: *Fresh.* **AFTER THAT:** Graham Central Station: *Release Yourself.*

Putting the Stank Right on Ya

Stankonia

Outkast

The funky genre-blind freshness of Outkast's *Stankonia* grew out of a conscious decision. When singer and conceptualist André 3000 (André Benjamin) and the rapper and sound sleuth Big Boi (Antwan Patton)

began work on this, the most critically lauded release of 2000, they stopped listening to hip-hop. "That music was starting to sound real comfortable," Benjamin explained. "There wasn't any adventure to it."

Stankonia took care of that. Stretching outside of hip-hop for its vocabulary (as well as its samples), Outkast created a mind-boggling

intergalactic amalgam, a place where old soul and new street rhymes mix together, becoming highly concentrated. *Stankonia* isn't just for hip-hop heads—it engages the whole wide world. It's got hippie music interludes and singer-songwriter stanzas. It talks poignantly about unintended pregnancy ("Ms. Jackson") and corporate greed ("Gasoline Dreams").

It delves into electronica (the jungle "B.O.B."), but also has room for a drum machine samba ("Humble Mumble"). Its explosive rhythms and character-actor vocals sync up in spasms of gonzo invention that are appealing, whether Outkast aims for the far future or trips back to update '70s P-Funk with the lewdly winking "I'll Call Before I Come."

Though Outkast has had a bigger hit since (*Speakerboxxx/The Love Below*), musicians are still grappling with

Stankonia peaked at #2 on the *Billboard* 200 chart.

Stankonia—which, like Stevie Wonder's *Songs in the Key of Life* and a handful of other records, manages to not simply define a moment in pop history, but look far beyond it.

GENRE: 🎙 R&B.
RELEASED: 2000, LaFace/Arista. **KEY TRACKS:** "B.O.B," "Gasoline Dreams," "Ms. Jackson," **CATALOG CHOICES:** *Speakerboxxx/The Love Below; Aquimini.* **NEXT STOP:** Goodie Mob: *Soul Food.* **AFTER THAT:** Prince: *3121.*

A Dozen Gems Featuring the Young Buck

Buck Owens Sings Harlan Howard

Buck Owens

Harlan Howard's 1960s songs are the country-radio equivalent of postgraduate work in Interpersonal Dynamics. A student of the cruelties and comforts of love, Howard writes in dramatic fashion about how romances unravel, the little ways healthy couples affirm their devotion to each other, and (of course) the woeful state of the lover who finds himself left behind. Many in the Nashville song factory have famously covered this territory, but Howard's detail-rich tunes simply ring differently—his characters are real folks suddenly unafraid to be sensitive.

When it was issued in 1961, *Buck Owens Sings Harlan Howard* was the first full-length exploration of Howard, who struggled for much of the 1950s before placing songs with Owens, Kitty Wells, and others. Though there have been several "songbooks" of Howard classics since, this one remains the best, in large part thanks to Owens. The singer and guitarist (and future star of TV's *Hee Haw*) intuits that the best way to sing Howard is to be forthright, if not brutally honest, about heartache. He's hurting, but in a stoic, big-screen-cowboy way, and he finds an injured tone that makes "Foolin' Around" and the almost too chipper "Heartaches for a Dime" and others supremely riveting.

Along with Merle Haggard, Owens helped establish the rough-hewn honky-tonkin' "Bakersfield" sound. Though he's widely revered for that more animated music, his treatments of these Howard ballads deserve equal respect. Not many singers can make a seemingly innocent offhand phrase from a lover (or an ex) resonate with such a mighty sting.

GENRE: 🌑 Country. **RELEASED:** 1961, Capitol. **KEY TRACKS:** "Foolin' Around," "Let's Agree to Disagree," "Keys in the Mailbox." **CATALOG CHOICE:** *I've Got a Tiger by the Tail.* **NEXT STOP:** Harlan Howard: *All-Time Favorite Country Songwriter.*

Augustus Pablo ✦ Gabby Pahinui ✦ Eddie Palmieri ✦ Pantera
✦ Ivo Papasov and His Orchestra ✦ Parisa ✦ Charlie Parker
✦ Graham Parker and the Rumour ✦ Parliament ✦ Gram
Parsons ✦ Arvo Pärt ✦ Dolly Parton ✦ Hermeto Pascoal ✦
Charley Patton ✦ Billy Paul ✦ Les Paul with Mary Ford ✦
Pavement ✦ Johnny Paycheck ✦ Pearl Jam ✦ Dan Penn
and Spooner Oldham ✦ Pentangle ✦ Art Pepper ✦ Pere
Ubu ✦ Carl Perkins ✦ Itzhak Perlman ✦
Lee "Scratch" Perry ✦ Peter, Paul and
Mary ✦ The Oscar

P

Peterson Trio ✦ Liz
Phair ✦ Sam Phillips ✦ Washington Phillips ✦ Edith Piaf ✦
Astor Piazzolla ✦ Wilson Pickett ✦ Pink Floyd ✦ Pixies ✦
The Pogues ✦ The Police ✦ Charlie Poole ✦ Cole Porter ✦
Portishead ✦ Baden Powell ✦ Bud Powell ✦ Elvis Presley ✦
The Pretenders ✦ The Pretty Things ✦ Louis Prima ✦ Prince
and the Revolution ✦ John Prine ✦ Procol Harum ✦ Professor
Longhair ✦ Sergey Prokofiev ✦ Propellerheads ✦ Public
Enemy ✦ Giacomo Puccini ✦ Tito Puente and His Orchestra

King Tubbys Meets Rockers Uptown

Augustus Pablo

Dub arrives at its magic by subtraction—removing vocals and other elements exposes the hypnotic stuff underneath. The Jamaican style began when, in the late '60s, the engineer and sound system operator King Tubby scrapped the lead vocal tracks from a reggae single he was mixing. The spare sound caught on with dancers, and pretty soon artists were doing dub versions for the B sides of singles. On these, the basic rhythm section would be put through all kinds of sound effects, until the building blocks of reggae were rearranged. Sometimes clattering percussion would be the "star"; sometimes the only thing going would be the steady thud of deep bass.

Among the followers of King Tubby was young producer Augustus Pablo, whose chosen instrument was the wind-powered child's keyboard known as the melodica. Pablo brought his projects to Tubby for final mixdowns, sessions where the two would "deconstruct" the songs, part by part, until something entirely new emerged.

This mostly instrumental collaboration began when King Tubby heard Pablo's production of "Baby I Love You So" by Jacob Miller. Weaving tiny bits of Miller's vocal between Pablo's percussive chords, Tubby created, in an afternoon, what became "King Tubbys Meets Rockers Uptown," a slithering minor-key piece with transfixing mystical overtones. The rhythm section, whch includes the esteemed bassist Robbie Shakespeare, becomes the star, rattling off head-nodding and endlessly danceable dub variations. Dub's earthy minimalism has enchanted many pop artists—see No Doubt's *Rock Steady* (p. 554), which was partly inspired by this and other Pablo efforts. If you've never quite gotten dub, don't give up until you try this record. It's one of the form's few sacred texts.

GENRE: 🌐 World/Jamaica. **RELEASED:** 1976, Shanachie. **KEY TRACKS:** "Keep On Dubbing," "Young Generation Dub," "Stop Them Jah." **CATALOG CHOICE:** *East of the River Nile.* **NEXT STOP:** Lee "Scratch" Perry: *Arkology* (see p. 594). **AFTER THAT:** No Doubt: *Rock Steady* (see p. 554).

Best of the Gabby Band 1972–1977

Gabby Pahinui

Just a few notes from Gabby Pahinui's guitar, and a feeling of perfect-sunset serenity spreads over the room. A master technician who is one of several responsible for refining the Hawaiian "slack key" guitar style, Pahinui

(Pa-ha-newy) plays in a way that's beyond laid-back. There's no contrivance or manipulation in his game—on these simple folk songs and originals, he strives for and attains an ideal of beauty. No matter how stressed you are when you start listening, he has a way of softening the cares of the world.

Pahinui mastered the guitar without learning to read music.

After several apprenticeships, Pahinui (1921–1980) began recording in 1946. His works drew attention to Hawaii's long heritage of stringed-instrument innovation—ever since Portuguese laborers brought the four-string *braguinha*, a precursor to the ukulele, to Hawaii in the 1870s, local musicians have tweaked the instruments and changed the playing styles to suit their needs. Slack-key guitar might be considered the most extreme example: Its otherworldly swooping is produced by carefully slackening and tightening the tension of guitar strings. The result is a sound that's a bit like the bluesman's pitch-bending, but over longer intervals.

Some slack-key masters play with the exaggerated manner of lounge musicians trying to wow tourists. Pahinui's recordings, particularly the ones he made with this band in the 1970s, are much more subtle. The emphasis is on the way each of the parts fit together—often a strumming acoustic guitar coexists with a ukulele, a wandering steel-string lead, and some distant slack-key melody picking up the bittersweetness of the vocal. These recordings feature several of Pahinui's sons, as well as his protégé Sonny Chillingworth (see p. 165) and longtime friend Atta Isaacs. Some tracks also include guest Ry Cooder, who became enchanted after hearing a Gabby Band record in a Honolulu gift shop. It's easy to hear what caught Cooder: This band sways in a way that's both mighty and delicate, embodying a grace that seems to come naturally in Hawaii.

GENRE: 🌐 World/Hawaii. **RELEASED:** 1990, Panini. **KEY TRACKS:** "Ku'u pua lei mokihana," "Aloha ka nanini," "Lei nani." **CATALOG CHOICE:** The Pahinui Brothers: *The Pahinui Brothers.* **NEXT STOP:** Sonny Chillingworth: *Endlessly* (see p. 165). **AFTER THAT:** Ray Kane: *Punahele.*

The Daredevil of Latin Piano Tears Up the Dance Floor

La perfecta

Eddie Palmieri

When Eddie Palmieri made *La perfecta*, his first solo record, in 1962, he'd spent years paying dues in New York's finest mambo big bands, serving the needs of discerning dancers. The pianist and composer borrowed ideas from those bands, added dashes of jazz irreverence, and convinced an unflappable young singer (Ismael Quintana) and a bunch of precision-minded instrumentalists to join what he envisioned as a high-energy combo. The group quickly evolved into a perfectly proportioned rhythmic juggernaut; its aptly titled debut endures as one of the most exciting in the history of Latin music.

It's also one of the most influential. Palmieri's terse arrangements feature trombones as often as trumpets, frequently with a flute on top. That alignment, which makes the seven-piece horn section seem as robust as a big band, was borrowed by countless salsa stars of the late '60s and '70s, among them Willie Colón (see p. 93) and Héctor Lavoe (see p. 439).

As often as it's been copied, there's lots about *La perfecta* that remains untouchable. The ensemble executes everything with unsurpassed unity, and when one musician steps out for a solo—in addition to electrifying turns from Palmieri, this album contains swaggering hall-of-fame ad-libs by trombonist Barry Rogers—the others provide assured, steadying support. No tune here lasts more than three minutes, and as a result, the solos are usually abbreviated. That doesn't mean they're not potent: Cue up "Conmigo" or "Ritmo caliente" to hear Palmieri, the jazz daredevil, dispensing jolting, syncopated chords as though he's trying to give dancers conniptions. On later records, Palmieri would elaborate at much greater length; the solos here offer thrills and spills in short, super-concentrated bursts.

GENRE: 🌐 World/Latin. RELEASED: 1962, Alegre. (Reissued 2007, Fania.) KEY TRACKS: "Conmigo," "Mi pollo," "Tema la perfecta," "Ritmo caliente." CATALOG CHOICES: *The Son of Latin Music; Harlem River Drive.* NEXT STOP: Sonora Ponceña: *Determination.* AFTER THAT: Conjunto Libre: *Ritmo, sonido, y estilo.*

Salsa, Expanded for Full Orchestra

Eddie Palmieri

Eddie Palmieri

E ven in its experimental moments, Afro-Cuban music doesn't usually stray far from the dance floor. The truly great bands consider keeping dancers happy to be their primary mission. They hew to the familiar song forms and follow the example of Tito Puente, the don of Latin music, who believed in swinging and not going too kooky on people.

Curious musicians eventually chafe under such restrictions. Among those who found ways to rebel was Eddie Palmieri, the pianist and composer who became a major figure in New York Latin music in the '60s. A student of everything from bebop to Stravinsky and twentieth-century composition, Palmieri showed early in his career that he was capable of suppressing his anarchic instincts long enough to play it straight. But after a few critically hailed dance projects, he'd take a hard left—exploring a Latin-jazz full of upheaval, or, in the case of this self-titled, magnificent 1982 release, writing suites for orchestra that radically expand conventional salsa form.

There are just five pieces, and each takes a different winding path to arrive at its formidable dance pulse. Palmieri wrote fanfares that reach back to the quaint Cuban ceremonial style of the 1920s, *danzón*, and introspective tempoless passages unlike anything in the canon. He left space for long improvisations—among the most memorable is Barry Rogers's bluesy trombone solo on the swaggering "No me hagas sufrir."

Palmieri didn't use the orchestra simply for backgrounds: He conceived of the project as an extended conversation between orchestra and rhythm section, and his score contains plenty to keep the studio musicians busy. On the elaborate "El día que me quieras," for example, the theme is first stated by oboe, then a rococo woodwind ensemble. When vocalist Cheo Feliciano finally enters, his lines float along, with the same baroque winds providing a cushion. Recalling the arduous sessions, Palmieri said years later that what amazed him was the ways Feliciano and the other featured vocalist, Ismael Miranda, seized and exploited the massive arrangements: "No matter what was going on, and at times that orchestra was loud, when the singing started everything hit a higher level."

GENRE: 🌐 World/Latin. **RELEASED:** 1982, Fania. **KEY TRACKS:** "No me hagas sufrir," "El día que me quieras." **CATALOG CHOICES:** *Lo que traigo es sabroso; La perfecta* (see p. 573). **NEXT STOP:** Orchestra Harlow: *The Best of Orchestra Harlow with Ismael Miranda.* **AFTER THAT:** Malavoi: *Matebis.*

Vulgar, in a Good Way

Vulgar Display of Power

Pantera

Perhaps Ovid was a headbanger. The ancient Roman poet and philosopher, who wrote long rhapsodies about love, women, and mythological transformations, once observed that "A safe pleasure is a tame pleasure."

By that logic, he likely would have enjoyed Pantera's *Vulgar Display of Power*, a romping stomping blast that exposed the softness and pomposity of 1980s hair metal.

The power on display here isn't all vulgar—an awesome precision guides these jackhammering guitars and pulverizing backbeats. This is metal with much of the artifice stripped away, with emphasis on sheer crushing force rather than inflated audaciousness.

Pantera formed in Arlington, Texas, in 1981.

The band's previous experience might have had something to do with that: Pantera spent the '80s trying to sell itself as a glam-metal band, and met mostly with indifference. When the Arlington, Texas, four-piece went back to the drawing board, it rethought metal from bottom to top, rejecting standard practice. *Vulgar Display* is the result. Its rhythms lumber

majestically; at times Pantera sounds like a speed-metal band that's shifted into low gear. Its lyrics express an undisguised hostility; screechy vocalist Phil Anselmo could, in his most ferocious moments, easily be mistaken for a psychopath. Equally impressive is the furious rule-breaking lead guitar of Darrell Abbott, aka Dimebag Darrell, whose extended solos, often performed with no rhythm guitar support, are marvels of dastardly unhinged intensity. Dimebag was murdered in 2004 while performing onstage with the band he formed after Pantera dissolved in 2000; his death prompted vigils on satellite radio metal channels, and left a gaping hole in the genre. Very few guitarists—in any genre—had Dimebag's flair for dramatic solos.

Vulgar Display was a career-making

huge commercial success, but it is equally notable for the shock waves it sent through heavy rock. Virtually all of the "groove metal" and rap-metal bands of the '90s (Korn, etc.) copped some of the caterwauling menace and the massive sonics that define this work. It's not all vulgar. It's not all pretty. But it consistently hits extremes of one sort or other, and that is enough. As Ovid also wrote: "Be patient and tough; one day this pain will be useful to you."

GENRE: 🎸 Rock. **RELEASED:** 1992, Atco. **KEY TRACKS:** "Mouth of War," "Rise," "Live in a Hole," "Hollow." **CATALOG CHOICES:** *Cowboys from Hell; Far Beyond Driven.* **NEXT STOP:** Tool: *Aenima.* **AFTER THAT:** System of a Down: *Toxicity* (see p. 758).

Like No Wedding Band Anywhere

Balkanology

Ivo Papasov and His Orchestra

The clarinet player is charging along at breakneck speed, like he's climbing stairs three at a time. The accordion is scampering right behind. The pace is so fast you can't imagine anyone actually dancing to this clattering giddiness. But at weddings and other gatherings in Bulgaria, that's what happens when clarinetist and bandleader Ivo Papasov shows up.

A strange cross between Lawrence Welk and Johnny Rotten, Papasov is beloved across generations in his homeland, in part for his rashness on the bandstand, not just at weddings but all sorts of communal gatherings. He selects tempos that most mortals can't handle, and then dishes twirling, head-spinning phrases that are so demanding it's a wonder the band stays together. And yet never is his music just flash for its own sake: Papasov and his polished ensemble treat traditional tunes of Turkey and Greece (as well as their homeland) first with reverence. Then, as the pieces go along, they shift into instrumental adventures that move with the madcap intensity of a high-speed chase. (One could argue this is

Clarinetist Papasov was born in Kardzhali, Bulgaria, in 1952.

a good way to prepare young lovers for the turbulence of marriage.)

Balkanology shows a wide range of material, including a few pretzel-twist ballads ("Istoria na edna lyubov," with pitch-bending vocals from Maria Karafezieva) and a reggae-tinged "Mladeshki Dance." The zesty up-tempo songs, though, are the primary lure—showcases for Papasov's delightfully fleet solos, and ensemble passages that keep those on the dance floor in perpetual motion.

GENRE: 🌐 World/Bulgaria. **RELEASED:** 1991, Hannibal. **KEY TRACKS:** "Istoria na edna lyubov," "Mominsko horo," "Ivo's ruchenitsa." **CATALOG CHOICE:** *Orpheus Ascending.* **NEXT STOP:** Márta Sebestyén and Muzsikás: *Márta Sebestyén and Muzsikás* (see p. 686). **AFTER THAT:** Matisyahu: *Live at Stubb's.*

Persian Music at Its Most Persuasive

Baz Amadam:
Parisa at Royal Festival Hall

Parisa

The "songs" of much Iranian classical music aren't fixed arrangements of words and melodies and rhythms, as in the West. Rather, the repertoire of a singer like the stunningly inventive Parisa is made up of modal entities called *gushe*. Each of these has a distinct tonal center but not a fixed theme; the melodic and rhythmic formulas serve as the starting point for improvisation.

So when Parisa begins "Chant Accompanied by Quanoon" in this concert recorded at London's Royal Festival Hall, she must summon the mind-set of a jazz musician. She knows the outline of the tune, and has some idea of the path she'll travel. But she doesn't know each stop along the way, and neither do her accompanists, who are, for the most part, hand drummers.

United in pursuit of the mystical ecstatic state known to Sufis as *hal*, Parisa's fellow musicians begin "Chant" with simple pattering rhythms that chatter and laugh, emulating a lively discussion between women. Parisa enters after a few minutes, and immediately the contentiousness of the instruments transforms into a purposeful, journeying stride. Her vocals are a mix of rapid glottal shakes and yodeling swoops, and they're positively galvanizing: Before long the *quanoon*, a dulcimer-like stringed instrument, is running alongside her, mimicking her spry phrases underscoring the hope in her voice as she repeats the chant of "zood" ("soon" in Farsi). These exchanges may not be the dictionary definition of ecstatic trance, but beware: They have the power to lift you a few inches off the ground.

Remarkably, so do the instrumental pieces—alone, without the dazzle of Parisa's improvisations, the focus shifts to the whipsaw interplay of the drummers. Which is plenty engrossing by itself.

GENRE: 🌐 World/Iran. **RELEASED:** 1995, PlayaSound. **KEY TRACKS:** "Chant Accompanied by Quanoon," "Reng shahr ashub." **NEXT STOP:** Nusrat Fateh Ali Khan: *In Concert in Paris* (see p. 422). **AFTER THAT:** DJ Cheb I Sabbah: *Shri Durga*.

First Flights of the Bird

A Studio Chronicle, 1940–1948

Charlie Parker

Charlie "Yardbird" Parker once told an interviewer that to him, music was about "just playing clean and looking for the pretty notes." The saxophonist's pursuit of those pretty notes, which gathered fast-moving streaks of impossible lyricism into jaw-dropping solos, stands as one of the most rousing quests of the twentieth century. Bebop, the music Parker and a close group of cohorts created, is a paradox: Although it can sound like an unencumbered spirit stream of pure technique, it's actually a highly persnickety language, with its own codes and protocols. The recordings Parker and the other charter members of bebop's exclusive club (Dizzy Gillespie, Max Roach, and Thelonious Monk) made for Dial and then Savoy Records show each soloist handling the slalom-like challenges of form and blindingly fast rhythm with a hipster's competitive cool. The music demands quick-witted resourcefulness: On the leaping intervallic exercise "Moose the Mooche," Parker and company take apart the harmony of "I Got Rhythm" until it sounds like an entirely different piece.

Until recently, bebop aesthetes had to go to several sources to hear the best of Parker's work for Dial and Savoy during the crucial

Parker began playing the saxophone when he was 11.

incubating phase of the bebop style. Now, there are a number of comprehensive surveys of the period, including the two-disc "overview" *Yardbird Suite* and this exhaustive yet inexpensive five-disc box, which begins with Parker's days as a sideman (his early Jay McShann sides are here) and includes every significant studio date, including several with young vocalist Sarah Vaughan. The digital transfers are crisp (considering the often deteriorated quality of the source tapes), and the sound of Parker's saxophone, muffled on previous releases, becomes a luminous flash of light as it lands with astonishing consistency on the pretty notes.

GENRE: 🎷 Jazz. **RELEASED:** 2003, JSP. **KEY TRACKS:** "Bloomdido," "Donna Lee," "Scrapple from the Apple." **CATALOG CHOICE:** *The Complete Savoy Live Performances.* **NEXT STOP:** Dizzy Gillespie and His Orchestra: *Afro* (see p. 312). **AFTER THAT:** Sonny Stitt: *Kaleidoscope.*

A Renegade Goes Uptown

Charlie Parker with Strings

Charlie Parker

Charlie Parker didn't just help invent the torrid jazz style known as bebop in the 1940s. The fast-living alto saxophonist, a notorious junkie who pawned his horn regularly, made an even more significant contribution:

He taught often insulated jazz musicians to expand their thinking. He was a modernist, a curious citizen of the world who let his obsessions—Stravinsky and Bartók and Gypsy scales, not to mention Bach—inform his art. Through projects like the very popular *Charlie Parker*

with Strings, which is among the first recordings to feature a jazz soloist with studio orchestra, Parker showed all who followed that it was possible to modify the vocabulary of jazz, that bebop's intricate codes could spread beyond its contentious small-group breeding grounds.

Though it now sounds almost quaint, *Charlie Parker with Strings* was a radical notion in 1949: It put the most technically adept improviser on the planet in a less rhythmically boisterous, almost plush setting. As Parker said in an interview, he'd been angling to record with an orchestra since the early 1940s. "I was looking for new ways of saying things musically. New sound combinations." That search led him to the arranger Jimmy Carroll, whose active, unschmaltzy charts provide the impulsive saxophonist with just enough structure. The album spawned several hit singles (including "Just Friends") and became Parker's biggest seller.

As Parker anticipated, the studio orchestra atmosphere compelled him to change his tactics as an improviser: He plays more lyrically, with an almost heartbreaking tenderness. The darting and dashing that distinguishes earlier works remains, however, and as Parker blows through the silky string counterlines and harp glissandos, he delights in confounding expectations. He's the ballroom renegade playing pretty for the dancers, just to show he can. Until that moment when pretty no longer cuts it, and the irreverent Parker steps on the gas to take everyone, including the unsuspecting string players, for a thrill ride.

GENRE: 🎷 Jazz. **RELEASED:** 1949, Verve. (Reissued 1995.) **KEY TRACKS:** "Everything Happens to Me," "Dancing in the Dark." **CATALOG CHOICE:** *Charlie Parker Collection.* **NEXT STOP:** Clifford Brown: *Clifford Brown with Strings.* **AFTER THAT:** Miles Davis: *Birth of the Cool.*

A Curmudgeon Rocks

Squeezing Out Sparks/Live Sparks

Graham Parker and the Rumour

Positioning himself somewhere between "angry young man" (as he was often described) and "wise philosopher," Graham Parker spends much of the tart *Squeezing Out Sparks* talking soul. He ponders the challenges of remaining human in trying situations, the importance of keeping passion alive, the ways love gets you twisted. Such weighty themes were not exactly dominating rock discourse in 1979, and that tells you something about Parker: He's the prototypical acerbic outsider, happiest when at odds with prevailing fashion.

Parker's songs are tightly disciplined affairs modeled on classic R&B (or a Van Morrison–style distillation of it), with the verses telling a story and the choruses summarizing a

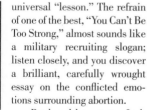

Most critics call *Squeezing Out Sparks* the best album of Parker's career.

universal "lesson." The refrain of one of the best, "You Can't Be Too Strong," almost sounds like a military recruiting slogan; listen closely, and you discover a brilliant, carefully wrought essay on the conflicted emotions surrounding abortion.

Produced by veteran Jack Nitzsche, *Squeezing Out Sparks* is leaner and meaner than previous Parker releases—there's no horn section, and the rhythms slapped out by the Rumour hew closer to a driving, gritty ideal of pub-rock, with fewer excursions into reggae. Everything feels pumped up and agitated except for Parker's vocals. As he navigates melodies designed to flatter his limited range and nasal tone, Parker sings with a surprising agility, if not grace; his performance on "Passion Is No Ordinary Word" stands among the great rock vocals of the 1970s.

The latest reissue combines the ten tracks of the original release with *Live Sparks*, a promo-only release sent to radio stations to show how devastating Parker and his crew could be on stage. The *Sparks* songs display an incredible zinging energy, as do the addi-tional pieces—including "Mercury Poisoning," Parker's withering assessment of circumstances at his old record label, and a spirited cover of the Jackson Five's "I Want You Back."

GENRE: 🎸 Rock. **RELEASED:** 1979, Arista. **KEY TRACKS:** "Discovering Japan," "Local Girls," "Nobody Hurts You," "You Can't Be Too Strong," "Passion Is No Ordinary Word." **CATALOG CHOICES:** *Heat Treatment; Howlin' Wind; The Mona Lisa's Sister.* **NEXT STOP:** Brinsley Schwarz: *Nervous on the Road.* **AFTER THAT:** Eggs over Easy: *Good 'n' Cheap.*

A Real Type of Thing Going Down

Mothership Connection

Parliament

Naturally the singer and ringmaster George Clinton deserves credit as the mastermind of this space-funking cowboy trip. Give Bootsy Collins some love, too, for the subsonic rumble in the bass that gets people moving before they even know it. But there are always unsung heroes where Parliament is concerned, and one is Glenn Goins, the sweet-voiced singer and guitarist who was one of this collective's many secret weapons. After the main chorus of the title track has been churning for a while, Goins leans in with a counterline for the ages: "Swing down sweet chariot and let . . . me . . . ride!" With this one old-time gospel invocation, Goins changes what had been a mildly campy intergalactic groove into a spiritual quest.

That's Parliament in a nutshell: Funk as a pathway to physical bliss, and at the same time, metaphysical understanding. The long-running revue began in the mid-'60s

Clinton formed Parliament when he was doing hair at a New Jersey barber shop.

as a soulful doo-wop group (the Parliaments, whose first hit, in 1967, was called "I Wanna Testify") and became one of the most influential and creative collectives of the 1970s—influencing hit-makers like Earth Wind & Fire as well as virtually everyone connected to hip-hop.

Mothership Connection begins with what was a stock P-Funk device (heard on the preceding album *Chocolate City* and others), later co-opted for countless hip-hop skits: The smooth talk of a DJ from the mock radio station WEFUNK, whose patter amounts to an inventive elaboration on sister group Funkadelic's famed line, "Free your mind and your ass will follow." From there, Clinton and crew do everything they possibly can to loosen up any lingering rigidity in your pelvic region.

Each track is unassailable individually; heard in sequence, *Mothership Connection,* which is one of nine albums the group released between 1974 and 1980, becomes almost overwhelming. Its grooves are hard-hitting yet as loose as the jellied limbs of basketball stars. Its chants treat funk as a path to enlightenment, melding the idealism of the late '60s (best embodied by Sly and the Family Stone) with Me Decade escapism. Put it all together,

and you have a cosmic revival meeting of the highest order.

GENRE: 🎵 R&B. **RELEASED:** 1975, Casablanca. **KEY TRACKS:** "Mothership Connection (Star Child)," "Unfunky UFO," "Give Up the Funk (Tear the Roof Off the Sucker)." **CATALOG CHOICE:** *Funkentelechy vs. the Placebo Syndrome.* **NEXT STOP:** Funkadelic: *One Nation Under a Groove.* **AFTER THAT:** Eddie Hazel: *Game, Dames, and Guitar Thangs.*

Cosmic American Music

GP/Grievous Angel

Gram Parsons

After helping the Byrds go country with *Sweetheart of the Rodeo,* and then founding the short-lived but brilliant Flying Burrito Brothers, Gram Parsons (1946–1973) went under the radar for a while in the late '60s. A free spirit who struggled with addiction—he died after overdosing on morphine and tequila in the desert near California's Joshua Tree National Park—Parsons lost a year or more partying. He spent time hanging out with the Rolling Stones during the making of *Exile on Main Street,* and performed occasionally, but wasn't inclined to write or record his own work until 1972, when he heard Emmylou Harris singing at a Washington, D.C., folk bar called Clyde's. Her sturdy, unaffected voice hit something in him: "I found a chick singer who's real good who I want to sing with," Parsons told an interviewer in the spring of 1972. "If you get a really good chick, it works better than anything because you can look at each other with love in your eyes."

Love, along with longing and a loner's

Grievous Angel was released after Parsons's death in 1973.

isolation, defines what Parsons did next—*GP,* one of the most quietly visionary debuts of the 1970s. Parsons hated the term "country-rock." He described his patchwork of weepy country ballads, careening blues, and up-tempo rambles as "cosmic American music," and he worked to heighten those mystic elements, particularly when singing with Harris. On the two-stepping "That's All It Took" and "A Song for You," the duo sounds like veterans of the country road show; one soars while the other keeps a foot on the earth.

GP is the mother lode of Parsons's songwriting, a series of sketches from a wide-open stylistic frontier that would soon, with the arrival of the Eagles, become one of the defining sounds of the '70s. Though the follow-up *Grievous Angel* contains several originals, including the haunting closer Parsons and Harris wrote together, "In My Hour of Darkness," it primarily shows Parsons's knack for personalizing other people's music. Among its killers: a wrenching rendition of Boudleaux Bryant's "Love Hurts" (a song memorably cut by the Everly Brothers) and a raucous treatment of Tom T. Hall's "I Can't Dance."

GENRE: 🎸 Rock. RELEASED: 1990, Warner Bros. (GP originally issued 1972, Grievous Angel 1973.) KEY TRACKS: GP: "That's All It Took," "A Song for You," "Streets of Baltimore," "Kiss the Children." Grievous Angel: "Love Hurts," "Return of the Grievous Angel," "I Can't Dance." COLLECTOR'S NOTE: The three-CD 2006 The Complete Reprise Sessions offers upgraded sonics and alternate takes and demos. NEXT STOP: George Jones and Tammy Wynette: Sixteen Biggest Hits. AFTER THAT: Jackson Browne: Saturate Before Using.

The Triad-Twirling Mystic of Estonia Confronts the Blank Slate

Tabula rasa

Arvo Pärt

A rvo Pärt took a long, winding, and noisy path to discover his singularly quiet "voice" as a composer. Born in Estonia in 1935, Pärt began by imitating Prokofiev and other neoclassicists. Then he embraced dissonant serialism on a cluster of pieces that brought little success. In 1968, Pärt said good-bye to all that and withdrew into a study of medieval music. That lasted a decade. When he returned, his compositions were completely different—he'd pared his ideas down to a cellular level, devoting himself to kernels of ancient-sounding melody set into steadily pulsating rhythms.

The result is often termed minimalism, but where Steve Reich and others strive for an ultramodern rhythm-based grid, Pärt burrows into extended repetitions of simple tones, seeking a mystical calm. Pärt termed this operating idea "tintinnabulation," which is fancy talk for "the ringing sound of bells." This is literally a fixture of his pieces (listen for the tolling bells of "Cantus in Memory of Benjamin Britten"), and also a description of his approach to the humble triad—hit the chord repeatedly and hang in long enough, goes his thinking, and that sound will whisk you into an enveloping trance.

Elsewhere Pärt uses triads differently—on the title track, featuring violinist Gidon Kremer, he fractures them into fantastic arpeggios that swirl around like planets in a tight orbit. Each piece utilizes different instrumentation, and one, "Fratres," is heard two ways—first with just piano and violin, then as played by twelve cellos, a truly magnificent sound. The chord sequence is the same for both, but the music moves in strikingly different ways. In the duo setting, the repeated triads inspire extended mystical variations that register as silvery shimmers. In the larger group, those same chords unleash darker and more foreboding tones, a primal, slow-motion groan emanating from oceanic depths.

GENRE: 🎼 Classical. RELEASED: 1984, ECM New Series. KEY TRACKS: "Tabula rasa," "Fratres," "Cantus in Memory of Benjamin Britten." CATALOG CHOICES: Passio; Miserie. NEXT STOP: Henryk Górecki: Symphony No. 3 (see p. 319). AFTER THAT: John Tavener: Darkness into Light, Chilingirian Quartet and Anonymous 4.

Pure Country Parton

Coat of Many Colors

Dolly Parton

With "Coat of Many Colors," an autobiographical recollection of her hardscrabble girlhood, Dolly Parton made a huge leap. She'd been well known for years, as the duet partner of hit-maker Porter Wagoner.

But this song—and really the entire album—cast her in a different light: It revealed the bubbly entertainer as a sharp-eyed country auteur, a gifted storyteller who, without dropping a beat, could set a vivid scene, quote relevant Scripture, and gossip a little bit, too.

Parton was the fourth of twelve children born in a one-room cabin in the east Tennessee foothills. When she

Dolly Parton has had 42 Top 10 country albums.

was young, her mother sewed her a coat made from hand-me-down rags. She wore it to school, and as she recalls in the song, the kids made fun of her. Yet she never stopped being proud of her mother's resourcefulness: "I know we had no money, but I was as rich as I could be/ In my coat of many colors my mama made for me."

The song became Parton's signature. It reached the Top 10 on the country charts in 1971, and it paved the way for a series of pure

country albums that are all worth hearing, especially when compared with the high-gloss country-pop crossover Parton pursued later in the '70s. The stylistic range is itself impressive: "Traveling Man," a steamy account of a young girl's flirtations with an older man, chugs along like a ripping Texas-roadhouse rocker, while "She Never Met a Man (She Didn't Like)" is a weepy hymnlike ballad. Parton wrote seven of the songs (Wagoner the other three), and though subsequent records yielded bigger hits (*Jolene*, from 1974), none quite match the poignant stories and fervent feeling Parton put into *Coat*.

GENRE: Country. **RELEASED:** 1971, RCA. **KEY TRACKS:** "Coat of Many Colors," "Traveling Man." **CATALOG CHOICE:** *Jolene*. **NEXT STOP:** Emmylou Harris: *Luxury Liner*.

Boundary-Breaking Music from a Brazilian Thinker

Slaves Mass

Hermeto Pascoal

The Brazilian multi-instrumentalist and composer Hermeto Pascoal believes that music springs from traffic noise and farmyard squalling and people's everyday speech; he calls this the "Sound of the Aura," a concept that aligns him, sensibility-wise, with such provocative musical thinkers as Sun Ra, John Cage, and Ornette Coleman. In Pascoal's universe, an utterly beautiful piano phrase will suddenly morph into growls and grunts and gales of laughter that, amazingly, don't obliterate the beauty of what's come before. It's Pascoal's way of reminding listeners that the most precious moments are fleeting. Reality can intrude anytime.

Pascoal has been recording since the 1960s. He was a part of Miles Davis's *Live/Evil* band—contributing two songs, "A ingrejinha" and "Nem um talvez," that were incorrectly credited to others—and shortly after began incorporating jazz into his projects. *Slaves Mass*, from 1977, encompasses jazz fusion and languishing waltz ("Aquela valsa," which dissolves into a deliciously airborne samba). Between its disarmingly tuneful themes are ritual chants, drum-circle polyrhythms, and outbreaks of heated, daring improvisation.

A key aspect of Pascoal's genius is his understanding of the forms and conventions of Brazilian music. Several pieces here begin as ordinary declarative themes, the kind you might hear on a bossa nova record, but before they get too cozy, Pascoal will transpose the same phrase up a step, then another, then another, until the quaint original thought becomes unsettling, if not terrifying. Adding to the destabilized feeling is Pascoal's ability to communicate on a variety of instruments. He makes his choices according to what color or texture a particular moment needs, and if the daring, logic-leaping virtuosity of his piano solo "Escuta meu piano" doesn't startle you, his fluttering spasms of flute on "Cannon" certainly will.

GENRES: 🌐 World/Brazil 🎵 Jazz.
RELEASED: 1977, Warner Bros. **KEY TRACKS:** "Aquela valsa," "Escuta meu piano," "Tacho," "Missa dos escravos." **CATALOG CHOICE:** *Only If You Don't Want It.* **NEXT STOP:** Lô Borges: *Lô Borges* (see p. 106). **AFTER THAT:** Irakere: *Misa negra.*

An American Original, Screamin' and Hollerin' the Blues

Founder of the Delta Blues

Charley Patton

T he first blues celebrity, Charley Patton (1891–1934) was also one of the most important "Johnny Appleseed" figures in American music. Traveling from town to plantation in the Deep South, raising hell at every stop, Patton spread the catharsis of the blues to people who probably didn't realize how much they needed it until he showed up. He reached them first with sheer power: One follower, Sleepy John Estes, estimated that Patton's voice could be heard clear across a five-hundred-yard field without any help.

Once Patton had an audience, he would sing about riverboats and disasters, ponies (his signature song was "Pony Blues") and mean old black cats, the joys of female companionship and the dread of death. Piling verse atop intense verse, Patton made these tales resonate with sharp vocal inflections, and exaggerated emphasis on certain words. Virtually every other consequential blues singer picked up tricks from him—some, like Son House, learned directly, by following the entertaining whirlwind around, watching him alternate between rousing spirituals and bawdy blues. (Others heard the 78-RPM singles he recorded for Paramount, represented here.)

Founder of *the Delta Blues* and its companion, *King of the Delta Blues*, capture the highlights of Patton's brief recording career. The sound is compromised—because Paramount sold the masters (allegedly for scrap!), all that survives are the poor-quality 78s—and still Patton comes booming through. He's a fierce presence, a master of exhortation whose ideas spread in part because he did more than shout and holler. He persuaded.

Charley Patton, who grew up in Mississippi, is regarded as "Father of the Delta Blues."

GENRE: 🔵 Blues.
RELEASED: 2001, Yazoo.
KEY TRACKS: "High Sheriff Blues," "Screamin' and Hollerin' the Blues," "It Won't Be Long," "High Water Everywhere."
CATALOG CHOICES: *King of the Delta Blues; The Complete Recordings 1929–1934.* **NEXT STOP:** Son House: *Blues from the Mississippi Delta.* **AFTER THAT:** Howlin' Wolf: *Moanin' in the Moonlight* (see p. 371).

This One Goes Out to Cheating Hearts Everywhere

"Me and Mrs. Jones"

Billy Paul

O n one level, this 1972 single is just another page in the overstuffed cheating hearts songbook—that sad tome filled with accounts of ordinary folks falling victim to forbidden desire. But unlike many of those songs, it's the chronicle of a transgression that doesn't stand in judgment of anybody. Quite the opposite: Billy Paul sings "Me and Mrs. Jones" as one who's trapped in a situation that's escalated way beyond his imagining, and finds himself powerless inside its illicit lure. One verse in, and Paul is saying how "we both know that it's wrong," presenting his case in such a way that empathy is the natural reaction. He makes you feel the seductive pull of the situation—and really, everything about "Me and Mrs. Jones" is a seduction. The guitars give off a cognac-and-candlelight richness. The music beckons from some opulent lounge, where an orchestra plays music sneaky lovers can grind to. Then there's Paul, who came up in jazz. He translates the torture of the situation into engrossing ad-libs, torn-apart twists, and turns so powerful they can be understood in any language.

This song remained on the top of the *Billboard* singles chart for three weeks despite the fact that some stations wouldn't play it because it "glorified" adultery. In some ways "Me and Mrs. Jones" was the first great cheating song of a duplicitous decade, that time of Watergate dirty tricks and cover-ups. Paul's confessional hit transcends its era—while also sidestepping the clichés of the sneaking-around genre. Other tunes examine adultery in greater detail, but none make the vast gray area between "right" and "wrong" sound so alluring.

GENRE: 🔴 R&B. **RELEASED:** 1972, Philadelphia International. **APPEARS ON:** *360 Degrees of Billy Paul.* **NEXT STOP:** Teddy Pendergrass: *The Best of Teddy Pendergrass.* **AFTER THAT:** Luther Vandross: *The Ultimate Luther Vandross.*

The Best of the Capitol Masters: Ninetieth Birthday Edition

Les Paul with Mary Ford

Les Paul first previewed his far-out notion of a guitar "chorale" at a party he and his wife and singer, Mary Ford, held at their Los Angeles home in 1947. The guests were Hollywood types, and in the liner notes of this anthology, Paul recalls slipping his homemade wax disc of "Lover" onto the turntable, just to see how the revelers would react. "They'd never heard anything like it, had no idea what or who it was," Paul writes. "But Mary quickly made the connection. . . . She threw her arms around me saying, 'Wow! So that's what you've been doing out in the garage.' "

Les Paul was born in 1915 in Waukesha, Wisconsin.

Wow is right: "Lover" is the first-ever multitrack recording. It was accomplished by the careful stacking of individual parts, one atop another. More than a jaw-dropping parlor trick, this tune begins the modern recording era.

Driven by the dream that one man could emulate an orchestra without hiring extra hands, Paul had been working on the recording for several years. He gave each of the eight different guitar parts on "Lover" a specific mission: Some offered sparring and parrying counterpoint to the melody; some of the guitars were recorded at half-speed so that when played at regular speed, they sounded impossibly fast; some served as a kind of "bass line." (Paul played his own drum parts on many of these hits.) Don't be put off by the tame, easy-listening initial verses: After a break, "Lover" erupts into a quick-stepping sprint

that is utterly delightful. Other selections find Paul applying his multitracking tricks to Ford's vocals: Check out "How High the Moon" to hear a lush, wonderfully harmonized Mary Ford chorale.

Paul was the classic garage tinkerer made good. In addition to inventing multitracking (and developing commercial eight-track recorders used in studios), he is responsible for the solid body electric guitar (the storied "Les Paul" model), as well as homemade contraptions that helped him create echo and reverb and muted plucking sounds. This collection, which includes spry versions of standards, jumping blues, and indelible songs like "Vaya con Dios," suggests that Paul's gadget-making was always purposeful. He built these devices to help him realize the music—deep and surprisingly futuristic music—he had bouncing around in his head.

GENRES: 🅙 Jazz 🅥 Vocals. **RELEASED:** 2005, Capitol. **KEY TRACKS:** "Lover," "Vaya con Dios," "How High the Moon," "Tennessee Waltz." **CATALOG CHOICE:** *Chester and Lester* (see p. 29). **NEXT STOP:** Speedy West and Jimmy Bryant: *Stratosphere Boogie* (see p. 854). **AFTER THAT:** Paco De Lucia, Al DiMeola, John McLaughlin: *Guitar Trio*.

Rock Geekdom, Immortalized

Crooked Rain, Crooked Rain

Pavement

There were certain things you had to do to appear cool in the alternative rock scene of the 1990s. You had to maintain the look of above-it-all contempt, a slacker aloofness that actually took some practice to pull off. You had to tromp around in eroded Doc Martens, proffering an elitist's disdain for corporate rock (and the mindless lemmings who worshipped it).

On his band Pavement's second full-length outing, songwriter and singer Stephen Malkmus took this contempt to a new level, made it a part of his art. Sounding less interested in communicating with an audience than gossiping with a few friends, Malkmus devoted long stretches of his songs to stream-of-consciousness chatter. His lyrics can seem like a sustained sneer, with puzzling non sequiturs and insider putdowns interrupted every so often by startlingly cogent insights.

Crooked Rain, Crooked Rain, Malkmus's magnum opus, is a cockeyed song cycle about rock geekdom. It starts with a disaffected suburban youth wanting to make some noise in his rec room. From there it looks at fandom and its discontents ("Cut Your Hair"), lampoons then-huge arena powerhouses Stone Temple Pilots and Smashing Pumpkins ("Range Life"), and

parodies rock's backstage excesses ("They pull out their plugs and they snort up their drugs," goes one line on the withering "Fillmore Jive").

Malkmus talk-sings like a suburban rock gawker, in spasms of unruly off-keyness. He plays with the same abandon, and that's one reason *Crooked Rain, Crooked Rain* endures—this at times savage attack represents a pinnacle of alt-rock guitar. The guitars communicate in a language of sideways lurches and dorky skinned-knee dissonances, and their (inevitable) collisions feel too harrowing to have been planned. Primitive and perfectly apt, they're the skronks an Indie Kid might come up with minutes after getting his first guitar, and they keep Pavement away from anything remotely resembling holier-than-thou rock-star posturing.

GENRE: 🎸 Rock. **RELEASED:** 1994, Matador. **KEY TRACKS:** "Cut Your Hair," "Silence Kit," "Elevate Me Later." **CATALOG CHOICE:** *Slanted and Enchanted.* **NEXT STOP:** Sonic Youth: *Goo.*

Singles That Should Have Been Huge

On His Way

Johnny Paycheck

Before Johnny Paycheck (1938–2003) hit paydirt with his 1977 version of the rebel anthem "Take This Job and Shove It," he was a Nashville singer and songwriter with a honky-tonk heart and a penchant for recalling relationships that dissolved in dimly lit bars.

You can hear this on the (mostly unsuccessful) singles for the Little Darlin' label, which Paycheck founded with producer Aubrey Mayhew in the mid-'60s. One early session yielded a zippy celebration called "The Lovin' Machine." Another paired Paycheck with George Jones's rhythm section, the Jones Boys, and

Paycheck began playing the guitar when he was 6 years old.

featured a Hank Cochran jukebox song, "A-11" ("if you push A-11, there'll be tears") that had recently been a hit for Buck Owens. The Paycheck version, which is a touch grittier, reached the Top 20 on the country singles charts, and launched his career. Over the next several years the Ohio-born singer issued an "A-11" follow-up, "The Meanest Jukebox in Town" and a tongue-in-cheek plea to Cochran for more great songs ("Help Me Hank, I'm Falling").

Those songs form the backbone of this anthology, which collects all the singles that sent Paycheck "on his way," many of which never appeared on any album. One, a dismaying account of addiction entitled "The Wheels Fell off the Wagon," was (until recently) totally unreleased—a major loss, considering the way Paycheck's nuanced, deeply affecting vocal redeems a too-common country narrative. As "Take This Job" and his other later successes make clear, that was Paycheck's enduring gift—the ability to render some low-rent, heard-it-all-before, cheating-heart ode as the saddest song in the world.

GENRE: ⬤ Country. **RELEASED:** 2005, Koch/Little Darlin'. **KEY TRACKS:** "The Wheels Fell off the Wagon," "A-11," "The Lovin' Machine," "I'd Rather Be Your Fool." **F.Y.I.:** Born Donal Eugene Lytle, Paycheck first recorded as Donny Young. **CATALOG CHOICE:** *The Gospel Truth: The Complete Gospel Sessions.* **NEXT STOP:** Merle Haggard: *Mama Tried* (see p. 334). **AFTER THAT:** Bobby Bare: *The Best of Bobby Bare.*

"Thoughts Arrive like Butterflies"

Ten

Pearl Jam

Reading the lyrics of the middle section of "Alive," one of the eleven great rock songs on Pearl Jam's debut *Ten*, you might think they're from a dark existential play by Albert Camus:

Is something wrong she said
Well of course there is
You're still alive she said
Oh do I deserve to be?
Is that the question?
And if so, if so,
Who answers? Who answers?

Eddie Vedder, Pearl Jam's singer and lyricist, wrote "Alive" when he was pumping gas in San Diego, and had time to reflect. The song was inspired by his own life: When he was a teenager, his mother told him that the man he thought was his father was actually his stepfather, and that his biological father had died years before. The interlude is Vedder's attempt to capture the waves of conflicting feelings that hit him that day: He said later that the song's protagonist is "still dealing with the death of [his] father." And, Vedder added, he feels puzzled and burdened by the knowledge that "I'm still alive."

That refrain was widely misheard as an inspirational message—not the first time that would happen to this staggeringly creative five-piece from Seattle, which followed Nirvana to stardom in the wake of the grunge explosion.

Eddie Vedder wrote many of the lyrics for *Ten* for his Pearl Jam audition.

"Alive," and virtually everything else, on this rousing debut, goes straight for the jugular—Pearl Jam's rhythm section links the majestic brawn of Led Zeppelin to the righteous fervor of the Who to the visceral, distorted, frayed-nerve guitar attack that made Seattle famous. Vedder, meanwhile, isn't nearly that straightforward: He favors obtuse, encrypted lyrics, and though it's easy enough to parse the general subjects of "Jeremy" (the meanness of kids) or "Once" (guns), his stories don't always unfold in linear fashion or end with a tidy summary. This is one reason *Ten*—and much of the band's subsequent work—remains so captivating: It's just cryptic enough to get you thinking and not so brainy that it forgets to rock.

GENRE: 🎸 Rock. **RELEASED:** 1991, Epic. **KEY TRACKS:** "Even Flow," "Jeremy," "Alive," "Why Go." **CATALOG CHOICES:** *Vs.; Yield.* **NEXT STOP:** Screaming Trees: *Dust* (see p. 685). **AFTER THAT:** Days of the New: *Days of the New.*

A Soul Songwriter Steps Out of the Shadows

Live from This Theater

Dan Penn and Spooner Oldham

Music history is full of characters like Dan Penn, the Memphis-based singer, songwriter, and record producer whose profile is nowhere near commensurate with his talent. Responsible for cowriting James Carr's signature hit "Dark End of the Street," the Aretha Franklin classic "Do Right Woman," and other tormented classics of low-key soul, Penn is one of the most gifted (and least known) white soul singers ever, a master of the well-placed groan and slight but telling inflection. Those who have heard his original 1960s-era demos, private working tapes used to showcase new songs, consider them a type of sacred text.

You would have to be an obsessive fan to discover Penn's vocal gift, however. He's stepped from the shadows only a few times over the years—most persuasively in 1972, for a long out-of-print album called *Nobody's Fool.* Which is why this live set, recorded in 2004 in Europe, is so valuable: Working alongside his songwriting partner, the keyboard player and harmony singer Spooner Oldham, Penn rolls through his classics with captivating understatement, emphasizing the gentle slopes of the melodies over the ad-libbed swoops that often clutter up a great soul song. His readings are a songwriter's readings, designed to help listeners appreciate the architecture of a drop-dead genius song like "I'm Your Puppet," which is taken at a poignant slow crawl, or "It Tears Me Up," which acquires its power one perfectly proportioned line at a time.

There isn't a weak moment on *Live*, which celebrates those Southern staples of church and chicken, while exhibiting an irreverence (and easygoing humor) often missing from the comeback efforts of once-greats. That might be because Penn—who was once described by Elvis Costello as "what Elvis Presley could have been"—has never gone away. He just hung out in the background, scribbling songs filled with truth, and singing them only occasionally.

GENRE: 🔵 R&B. **RELEASED:** 2005, Proper. **KEY TRACKS:** "It Tears Me Up," "I'm Your Puppet," "Ol' Folks." **CATALOG CHOICE:** *Nobody's Fool.* **NEXT STOP:** Otis Redding: *Otis Blue* (see p. 636). **AFTER THAT:** James Carr: *The Essential James Carr.*

Inventive Music, Woven from Sturdy Folk Stock

Basket of Light

Pentangle

Pentangle came together in 1967, at a time when cross-genre experimentation was rampant in rock and cherished traditional musics were routinely being upended. Even so, the quartet's collages of swaying blues, British folk song, hard-swinging jazz, and psychedelic guitar tapestries seemed, to some, preposterous. It was, to be sure, a radical lunge: No act had blended styles (or philosophies) together quite so brazenly before. Just the notion of opening up a sea chantey for renegade jazz soloing was exotic.

By the time of this third effort, *Basket of Light*, Pentangle had distilled its various influences into a clear, potent brew. The focal point is vocalist Jacqui McShee, who doesn't merely sing lead; she adds multitracked harmony parts, creating vocal cascades that have a willowy, sometimes haunting grace. Behind her are subtle, and surprisingly volatile, musical conversations—"Once I Had a Sweetheart," for example, is enlivened by a trippy transatlantic-blues exchange between John Renbourn on sitar and Bert Jansch on the guitar. An entirely different musical extreme is reached on "Light Flight," the nominal single, which juxtaposes jerky odd-meter instrumentals against McShee's placid singing.

The half-live, half-studio *Sweet Child*, which features bold reimaginings of songs by jazzman Charles Mingus and blues singer Furry Lewis, is often named as the pinnacle of Pentangle. But *Basket of Light* is the group's most fully realized statement—a journey in which hallowed traditional material is reborn in a tangle of wild and wondrous sounds.

GENRE: 🔵 Folk. **RELEASED:** 1969, Transatlantic. **KEY TRACKS:** "Once I Had a Sweetheart," "Light Flight." **CATALOG CHOICES:** *Sweet Child.* John Renbourn and Bert Jansch: *John Renbourn and Bert Jansch.* **NEXT STOP:** Fairport Convention: *Liege and Lief* (see p. 268). **AFTER THAT:** Ruthann Friedman: *Constant Companion.*

A Paragon of Cool Gets Hot

Art Pepper Meets the Rhythm Section

Art Pepper

This date began as a kind of rescue mission. In January 1957, Lester Koenig, president of the small Contemporary label, hired Miles Davis's rhythm section to lure alto player Art Pepper, who was then struggling with heroin addiction and hadn't played in weeks, out of a self-imposed exile. The rhythm section—pianist Red Garland, bassist Paul Chambers, and drummer Philly Joe Jones—was coming off a feverish burst of work, having just finished recording four albums *(Relaxin', Steamin', Workin', Cookin')* to fulfill Davis's contract with Prestige.

According to the liner notes, Koenig deliberately surprised Pepper (1925–1982), telling him about the session only hours in advance to avoid panicking the fragile musician. Pepper's horn was in disrepair. The rhythm section had been out late the night before. Despite seemingly long odds, the session clicked—the combination of this steady-simmering band and Pepper, a master of tart and measured phrasing, made for low-key jazz magic.

Pepper is clearly inspired by his all-star sidemen—he plays with an uncharacteristic abandon, alternating between boppish runs and slippery, pitch-bending swerves. Garland counters the alto player's furtive lines with compact chordal rejoinders that are the jazz equivalent of the skeptical raised eyebrow. And Jones, who had no peer at this type of businesslike swing, guides the session with a feathery wrist, using just a crisp ride-cymbal pattern to keep all hands focused on the beat. History regards this as the date that got Pepper back on track, and while that's true, it overlooks the main reason why: This vibrant, steady, uncluttered backing could make *any* decent soloist shine.

GENRE: 🎷 Jazz. **RELEASED:** 1957, Contemporary. **KEY TRACKS:** "Straight Life," "You'd Be So Nice to Come Home To," "Star Eyes," "Birk's Works." **CATALOG CHOICE:** *Saturday Night at the Village Vanguard.* **NEXT STOP:** Miles Davis: *Steamin'.* **AFTER THAT:** Paul Desmond: *Easy Living.*

This Is What the Cool Kids Were Listening To

Dub Housing

Pere Ubu

On its spartan website, the Cleveland "avant-garage" band Pere Ubu once proclaimed that it "is not now nor has it ever been a viable commercial venture." The note, written by lead singer and chief conceptualist

David Thomas, goes on to crow a bit about this: "We are the longest-lasting, most disastrous commercial outfit to ever appear in rock 'n' roll. No one can come close to matching our loss-to-longevity ratio."

That might be true, but it doesn't tell the whole story. Thomas overlooks the fact that from the band's very early homemade singles—"Thirty Seconds over Tokyo" (1975) and its follow-up "Final Solution"—Pere Ubu managed to catch the attention of a high proportion of Listeners Who Mattered, several generations of highly successful rock provocateurs (including Joy Division, Hüsker Dü, R.E.M., and the Talking Heads) who couldn't help stealing a conceit or two from the Pere Ubu playbook. This made the band a kind of hidden-in-plain-sight phenomenon: While the "avant-garage" thing blew right over the heads of civilians, the cognoscenti were avidly following the odd audio spectacles cooked up by Thomas and his instrumentalists.

Pere Ubu (named for a character in the French play *Ubu roi* by Alfred Jarry) wields noise as both a punishment and an utterly delightful thing, sometimes in the same stanza. The musicians of Ubu think of themselves as noisemakers in the French *musique concrète* tradition, engineers of wild juxtapositions. But where the French guys cloistered in the academy, Pere Ubu ventures into the lands of surf-rock and film noir. Its songs turn on all kinds of different destabilizing devices—from dental-drill guitar whine to spasmodic, lurching rhythms to synthesist Allen Ravenstine's spooky textures.

Though plenty dense, the music is never so thick as to completely overwhelm the gleeful (and often absurdist) mutterings of frontman Thomas. His incantations ride the noise in what was then a totally new way. It's been imitated endlessly since, but none of the Ubu wannabes, even the famous ones, have quite equaled the spectacularly surreal thrill that is *Dub Housing*.

GENRE: 🎸 Rock. **RELEASED:** 1978, Rough Trade. **KEY TRACKS:** "Codex," "Caligari's Mirror," "Navvy." **CATALOG CHOICES:** *The Modern Dance; The Tenement Year.* **NEXT STOP:** Wire: *Pink Flag.* **AFTER THAT:** The Feelies: *Crazy Rhythms.*

The First from Mr. Blue Suede Shoes

Dance Album

Carl Perkins

Guitarist, singer, and songwriter Carl Perkins made just this one record for Sun during the early days of rock and roll. But he was on the scene at label headquarters in Memphis, a sly catalyst whose fingerprints are all over the music of the label's giant-sized stars. Perkins's crisply articulated guitar lines formed the cool strut that came to be called "rockabilly," and the attitude he put into them made every track he played on explode.

Perkins liked to tell people his first guitar was made from a cigar box and a broom handle, with baling wire for strings. His song sense wasn't quite so primitive: He's best known as the author of "Blue Suede Shoes," one of rock's all-time-great jumps. His 1956 version of the song, included here, became a smash hit, one of the few rock-era songs to reach the Top 10 of the pop, R&B, and country charts simultaneously. (It was also Sun's first million-seller.) Just as Perkins's star was rising, bad luck descended. On the way to an appearance on TV's *Perry Como Show,* he was injured (and his brother was killed) in a car crash. Unable to perform, Perkins lost the face time on TV (other bookings had included the *Ed Sullivan Show*), and shortly after that, momentum around his record dried up. Then Presley did a rollicking version of "Blue Suede Shoes" that ballooned into an even bigger hit. Recalling the twist of fate, Perkins said he didn't resent Presley: "Elvis was not to be denied the top spot. He had . . . the looks and the moves and everything that the world was waiting on."

Still, Perkins's agile, spiderwebbed runs continued to define rock guitar; in the early days

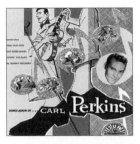

"Carl Perkins's songs personified the Rockabilly Era."
—Charlie Daniels

only Chuck Berry and Presley guitarist Scotty Moore had commensurate influence on six-string-wielding kids. And his songs—"Honey Don't," "Movie Magg," and "Everybody's Trying to Be My Baby," all on this album—endure, still, as rock standards.

GENRE: 🎵 Rock. **RELEASED:** 1958, Sun. **KEY TRACKS:** "Honey Don't," "Blue Suede Shoes," "Only You." **NEXT STOP:** Elvis Presley: *Sun Sessions.* **AFTER THAT:** Rockpile: *Seconds of Pleasure.*

Klezmer Gone Kwazy

Live in the Fiddler's House

Itzhak Perlman

This disc offers traditional Yiddish klezmer played by one of the great classical violin soloists of modern times, Itzhak Perlman, alongside some of the most imaginative ensembles of the 1990s klezmer revival—among them Andy Statman's Klezmer Orchestra, the Klezmer Conservatory band, and the Klezmatics. In the course of an hour, Perlman and the various bands pursue a robust revitalization of klezmer, easily handling the music's technical demands (those seesawing themes played at superfast tempos) while celebrating its irrepressible zest.

"Meron Nign/In the Sukke," the first selection featuring clarinetist Statman (see p. 737), is perhaps the best place to start. As the tempo accelerates toward the frantic, Perlman and Statman create a kind of chase-scene klezmer, scattering joyous melodic shards in their wake. Perlman doesn't take up too much of the spotlight, but when he does step out, you know it: He plays with such command, even the careening themes sound like warm-up exercises.

The klezmer renaissance had been going on for at least a decade when this was recorded, and even though the performers' styles and areas of concentration differ, they understand each other. Their shared language comes in handy on the finale, which involves musicians from all the groups. What could be a cast-of-thousands mess becomes, instead, an unstoppable dance, with many voices sharing the same mirth.

GENRE: 🌐 World/Klezmer. **RELEASED:** 1996, Angel. **KEY TRACKS:** "Meron nign/In the Sukke," "Doina naftule," "Klezmer Suite." **CATALOG CHOICE:** *Paganini: Twenty-four Caprices.* **NEXT STOP:** Don Byron: *Plays the Music of Mickey Katz.*

A Treasure Trove of Dub from a Brazen Renegade

Arkology

Lee "Scratch" Perry

I f King Tubby was the "father" of the reductionist sound-mangling/remix style known as dub, then Lee "Scratch" Perry is the wayward son. Perry's ideas took Jamaican music down strange alleys and expanded the horizons of many

recording artists, including Bob Marley (whose *Trojan Sessions* feature Perry's rhythm team) and Junior Murvin (whose classic falsetto elegy "Police and Thieves" is here in several forms).

In addition to leading his own laid-back band, the Upsetters, the 4'11" Perry is a prolific composer and producer. He opened his Black Ark studios in the early '70s and began assembling one of the larg-

Perry has released more than 50 albums during his career.

est (and, alas, most disorganized) catalogs in Jamaican music—in his heyday, he was known to rework performances he'd just recorded by adding echo or eliminating lead vocals or dropping in odd, startling extra sounds. He often did not label the "originals" or differentiate them from his reworked versions. Sometimes Perry reached well beyond Jamaican culture for material: "In These Times," which was a hit for Errol Walker, craftily interpolates the theme of

Gershwin's "Summertime."

Split between his own work and productions he did for other artists, the three-disc *Arkology* only scratches the surface of Perry's contribution. But it includes many of the electrifying dub tracks that reverberated throughout the Jamaican music community and, later, the world of electronic music. Today's remixing hotshots might own every digital gadget, but somehow they miss the earthy flow and juxtapositional ingenuity of this lo-tech *riddim* master.

GENRE: 🌐 World/Jamaica. **RELEASED:** 1997, Island. **KEY TRACKS:** "In These Times," "Grumblin' Dub," "Curly Locks." **CATALOG CHOICE:** *Super Ape.* **NEXT STOP:** Augustus Pablo: *King Tubbys Meets Rockers Uptown* (see p. 572). **AFTER THAT:** DJ Shadow: *Endtroducing* (see p. 229).

Folk's First Pop Moment

Peter, Paul and Mary

Peter, Paul and Mary

O f the many ripples emanating from the 1950s "folk revival," Peter, Paul and Mary were perhaps the most inevitable—an enterprising singing group that brought the heady righteousness of folk to a pop audience.

Starting with this charming, contrivance-free 1962 debut and continuing for a run of seven hit albums, the New York trio created consciousness-raising music that was well scrubbed and appealing enough to land on the radio. Although the group's very first single was the crisply sung "Lemon Tree," many of its other songs got people thinking about the times they were living in: Hedy West's wistful "500 Miles," an earnest rewrite of Sister Rosetta Tharpe's "This Train," and two Pete Seeger classics, "Where Have All the Flowers Gone" and "If I Had a Hammer."

From top to bottom, Paul Stookey, Mary Travers, and Peter Yarrow.

"Hammer" was the group's breakthrough hit, and a big reason this album stayed on the charts for 185 weeks. When he looked back on it years later, Peter Yarrow described it as the song that defined the trio's mission: "It was an attempt to use music to create community . . . to address social injustice or for gathering spirit."

Subsequent efforts furthered that mission. Guided by the savvy manager Albert Grossman, Peter, Paul and Mary successfully championed songs written by Grossman's other client, Bob Dylan: Among the great PPM singles are rousing three-part-harmony versions of "Blowin' in the Wind" and "Don't Think Twice, It's All Right." As rock ascended and the cultural climate changed, Peter, Paul and Mary issued singles that were less strident (see "Leaving on a Jet Plane," from 1967). But by then, they'd made a serious mark, showing a generation that shouting down injustice and crafting grabby hit songs were not mutually exclusive endeavors.

GENRE: 🎵 Folk. **RELEASED:** 1962, Warner Bros. **KEY TRACKS:** "500 Miles," "If I Had a Hammer," "Lemon Tree," "This Train." **CATALOG CHOICE:** *Album 1700.* **NEXT STOP:** Joan Baez: *Any Day Now.* **AFTER THAT:** Odetta: *At Carnegie Hall.*

A Ride into Jazz Mythology

Night Train

The Oscar Peterson Trio

When the Canadian jazz pianist Oscar Peterson tackled this set of familiar jam-session tunes in 1962, he was already being mentioned in the same breath as Art Tatum, and regarded as one of the most technically adept pianists ever to play jazz. He could be an overpowering dynamo, tearing through ultra-fast, almost jittery tempos as though he thought of bebop as a personal endurance test.

Peterson's relentlessly technical approach had its detractors—some jazz fans complained that his records were soulless technical exhibitions. *Night Train* is one persuasive counterargument, the moment when Peterson let a more reserved side of his genius emerge.

A relaxed, late-night-swinging session, it finds Peterson (1925–2007) less interested in dazzling than exploring the infinite nuances of jazz rhythm. When, for example, he digs into Duke Ellington's "C-Jam Blues," he starts out with a series of coy, Count Basie–like phrases in the middle of the keyboard, each isolated by several measures of open space. Then comes a stop-time passage, in which the rhythm section cuts out and Peterson is left to finish his thoughts alone. That prompts a fantasia of more intricate, dancing bebop, and then, when things get good and hot, a recurring riff in the style of a barn-burning big-band shout chorus. By this point Peterson is swinging so hard it hurts, and just about every phrase elicits a crisp rejoinder from drummer Ed Thigpen. One pleasure of this recording is hearing Peterson's intimate interaction with his accompanists.

The album brought Peterson his biggest

fame to date—"Happy Go Lucky Local (aka Night Train)" was a substantial jukebox hit—and made him a jazz celebrity. He and his trio began playing concert halls rather than clubs, the drums were replaced by guitarist Herb Ellis, and shortly thereafter, the recordings got showy. That makes *Night Train* all the more precious, the rare glimpse of Peterson trying to move listeners with casual, devil-may-care swing rather than astound them with babbling virtuosity.

GENRE: 🎵 Jazz. **RELEASED:** 1962, Verve. **KEY TRACKS:** "C-Jam Blues," "Band Call," "Bag's Groove." **CATALOG CHOICE:** *At the Concertgebouw*. **NEXT STOP:** Bud Powell: *The Amazing Bud Powell*, Vol. 1 (see p. 607). **AFTER THAT:** Herbie Nichols: *The Complete Blue Note Recordings* (see p. 550).

The Indie Rock Exile

Exile in Guyville

Liz Phair

iz Phair's lo-fi debut *Exile in Guyville* got lots of attention for its forthright lyrics—on one song she advises a lover that she wants to be his "blowjob queen," on another she casually mentions that she's been getting rough

treatment from boys since she was twelve. Phair used this luridness to give her relationship snafus an uncomfortable level of detail. The words helped draw the initial attention, but it was the music that ultimately set her apart from everything else in indie rock: This eighteen-song cycle is overstuffed with sweet, insinuating melodies, and offhand remarks that blossom into breathtaking gorgeous refrains.

Liz Phair majored in art history at Oberlin College.

rockers—Phair once claimed, somewhat preposterously, that her album was a track-by-track "response" to *Exile on Main St.* These are offset by giddy pop confections like "Never Said," which masks its bitterness behind an exuberant harmony chorus, and trembling, tentative waltzes that catch Phair singing in a kind of swan-diving free fall. At once elegant and primitive, *Exile* is that rare debut

The mostly homemade *Exile* sprays Phair's musings across an ambitious range of music. There are several grinding Rolling Stones–style

loaded with such a dizzying range of leaps and zingers, you begin to wonder whether all of them came from the pen of the same artist.

Exile was all Phair, and it made her more than a star—she became a spokesperson and symbol for countless struggling female rockers. Ten years later, after a series of erratic follow-ups, Phair did an artistic spinout: She hired the Matrix, the L.A. pop production team that created immense hits for Avril Lavigne and others. The result was the awkward *Liz Phair*, which attempted to graft *Exile in Guyville*'s brazenness onto polished Lavigne-like girl-pop—exactly the kind of inane stuff Phair would have ridiculed during the *Exile* era.

GENRE: 🎸 Rock. **RELEASED:** 1993, Matador. **KEY TRACKS:** "Johnny Sunshine," "Never Said," "Stratford on Guy," "Flower." **CATALOG CHOICE:** *Whip-Smart*. **NEXT STOP:** PJ Harvey: *Rid of Me*. **AFTER THAT:** Hole: *Live Through This*.

Daring Detour from an Underappreciated Singer-Songwriter

Fan Dance

Sam Phillips

Back in the 1990s, before the illegal copying of music via the Internet triggered widespread record-industry panic, the barons of the big labels were quite content to spend millions promoting 'NSync and Britney Spears, the pop equivalent of instant pudding. Even though label rosters at the time included such magnificent talents as the singer and songwriter Sam Phillips, the executives devoted most of their resources to the acts most likely to hit it big, a "winner-take-all" model that prized the quick sensational buck over the long-term career. Then one day they woke to find cases of Ashlee Simpson CDs in the warehouse and hardly any promising newcomers in the pipeline. Oops.

The artists were there. They'd just been marginalized. Among them was Phillips, a tunesmith whose forte is intricate, high-gloss post-Beatles pop with a sour twist. Since the 1980s, Phillips has plowed past label indifference to cobble together one of the most varied and interesting discographies in contemporary music. She started out as Leslie Phillips, making contemporary Christian music (the shadow classic *The Turning*), then went secular and earned a following for her smart, opulent song (*Martinis and Bikinis*). Then, despite a string of critical successes, she was dropped from her label.

Fan Dance, which was produced by Phillips's then-husband T-Bone Burnett, came after a five-year hiatus. It represents another shift—it pulls Phillips away from lavish arrangements, and into a shadowy, mysterious, torch-song ethos. Each of the twelve tracks calls from a specific locale; one ("Edge of the World") uses a rattling upright piano to evoke the sounds of a long-deserted vaudeville hall, another ("Below Surface") sends distress signals from murky depths. Phillips writes tightly compressed verses and declarative refrains, but in these noirish dream sequences the "hooks" rarely clobber you over the head. Instead, the eerie images and haiku melodies worm slowly into your subconscious, firing the imagination in ways that pop music, adrift in the age of Ashlee Simpson, rarely does anymore.

GENRE: 🎸 Rock. **RELEASED:** 2001, Nonesuch. **KEY TRACKS:** "Edge of the World," "Soul Eclipse," "Love Is Everywhere I Go," "Below Surface." **CATALOG CHOICES:** *The Turning; Martinis and Bikinis*. **NEXT STOP:** The Beatles: *Abbey Road* (see p. 62).

The Complete Works of a Gospel Powerhouse

The Keys to the Kingdom

Washington Phillips

Like many in the rural South in the early decades of the twentieth century, Washington Phillips (1880–1954) didn't consider singing and playing music any kind of job. The East Texas gospel pioneer—whose complete works, recorded between 1927 and 1929, are collected on this single disc—was a farmer, a tinkerer, and a traveling preacher welcomed by Methodist and Church of God congregations. In the years after his musical career, he was said to lead a "solitary" life; he lived with his mother, selling homemade syrup he made from sugarcane. When he performed, which was rarely, it was on street corners.

Only 16 of Phillips's songs were recorded.

Under slightly different circumstances, however, Phillips could have been a full-time musician; the world would have been a richer place. He sings hymns with a grandfatherly warmth, his tone plaintive but free of torment. Phillips sounds devout without putting on airs; when he proclaims "I Am Born to Preach the Gospel," it's impossible to question his sincerity. Phillips accompanies himself on a zither-like instrument (sometimes two, playing one with each hand) that he modified himself, and this enhances his delivery: At times the strings are positively celestial, and yet they can produce a gritty, urgent sound when attacked with force (cue up "Denomination Blues"). The sound, which influenced such solo performers as Sister Rosetta Tharpe, is a world unto itself, an utterly original offshoot of gospel and blues that stays with you long after the last track ends.

GENRE: 🕈 Gospel. **RELEASED:** 2005, Yazoo. **KEY TRACKS:** "Lift Him Up That's All," "Denomination Blues." **NEXT STOP:** Sister Rosetta Tharpe: *Gospel Train.* **AFTER THAT:** Rev. Gary Davis: *Harlem Street Singer* (see p. 207).

The Little Sparrow of a Zillion Myths

The Voice of the Sparrow

Edith Piaf

The details seem fantastical, the stuff of myth. Edith Piaf (1915–1963) was allegedly born under a streetlamp in a poor section of Paris, was blind from age three to seven, and recovered her sight by a miracle petitioned for by the prostitutes in her grandmother's brothel. She grew up mostly on the streets, and after suffering neglect by her father (a street acrobat) and her mother (an aspiring cabaret singer), she cut out on her own at age fifteen. A few years later, she was discovered busking by nightclub owner Louis Leplée. He gave her the nickname that would stay with her—La Môme Piaf (the Little Sparrow)—and helped arrange for her to record.

Piaf's life was chronicled in the 2007 film *La vie en rose*.

Piaf mined that street-urchin upbringing throughout her career: The songwriters drawn into her orbit would write songs based on the stories she'd tell, and all sorts of myths attached themselves to her. The facts might not have always added up, but it hardly mattered: Piaf had a persuasive way about her, singing with a blend of fluttery vulnerability and brute force. Piaf used her wide, intense vibrato to push already sad songs to the breaking point. Most comfortable singing about tragedy and pain, she virtually defined French chanson, and later helped launch the careers of others who followed her approach, including Charles Aznavour.

Piaf became famous before World War II. She cowrote her signature song, "La vie en rose," during the German occupation of Paris. Piaf recorded constantly through the 1950s—one hit, the nearly overwrought "Non, je ne regrette rien," came in 1960, three years before she died. By then, she was more than an entertainer: Her swooning voice had become the de facto sound of France, a symbol and source of pride. No other singing star in the world can claim such a lock on national identity.

GENRE: 🎤 Vocals. **RELEASED:** 1991, Capitol. **KEY TRACKS:** "La vie en rose," "Toujours aimer," "C'est l'amour," "Non, je ne regrette rien." **CATALOG CHOICE:** *Live at Carnegie Hall.* **NEXT STOP:** Charles Aznavour: *Aznavour Live.* **AFTER THAT:** Yves Montand: *Montand chante Prévert.*

Music for the Hours Between Midnight and Dawn

Tango: Zero Hour

Astor Piazzolla

hen the Argentine composer and master of the accordion-like *bandoneón* Astor Piazzolla looked back on his career, which he'd devoted to a radical re-imagining of his country's staid ceremonial tango, he focused on this 1986 project with his New Tango Quintet. "This is absolutely the greatest record I've made in my entire life," the man sometimes referred to as the Argentine Duke Ellington said. "We gave our souls to [it]."

Through Piazzolla's trembling and lamenting melodies, these five musicians share what they know about life. They spin ordinary lines into great romantic swirls that are easygoing and generous, and not always tethered to tango. They're secret sharers, these players, and they slip their wisdom into your back pocket without your even knowing. Every melody depends on soul; it's audible in the nose-diving violin glissandos and the promenading beats, in the way forward-marching pulses melt into stillborn softness, and in Piazzolla's upper register, which seems forever on the verge of tears.

Piazzolla composed a lot of music in his nearly fifty-year career. Some of it was sultry bordering on bawdy, some distinguished by intricate ensemble passages, some devoted to sad laments over lost youth. *Tango: Zero Hour* distills all of Piazzolla's compositional tricks into music that is achingly beautiful and totally demanding, equally dependent on the spring-loaded precision of his band and pure emotion. Moving as one, the ensemble follows Piazzolla past the notes on the paper and into the magic hours between midnight and dawn, where they can freely give their souls.

GENRE: 🌐 World/Argentina. **RELEASED:** 1986, American Clavé. (Reissued 1998, Nonesuch.) **KEY TRACKS:** "Milonga del Angel," "Michelangelo '70." **CATALOG CHOICE:** *The Vienna Concert.* **NEXT STOP:** Dino Saluzzi: *Rios* (with David Samuels).

Wicked Pickett Sings for You

The Exciting Wilson Pickett

Wilson Pickett

Wilson Pickett is the embodiment of hard-hitting, gutsy Memphis soul. A charming shouter, the man known as "Wicked Pickett" didn't have the finesse of Otis Redding or the sweet-talking suave of Al Green.

But Pickett (1941–2006) knew how to express himself. He had the gift of directness. Where others showered listeners with ornamental prettiness, Pickett simply spoke his mind.

As on so many of the city's storied records, everything here depends on the backing band, an A-list crew that includes guitarist Steve Cropper, bassist Duck Dunn, and drummer Al Jackson Jr., all veterans of hundreds of Southern soul sessions. Just by keeping time, the players get Pickett going; by the second verse of "Land of 1,000 Dances," one of several oldies-radio staples here, the singer is taunting and gritting his teeth through the theme, seeking ways to turn up the heat.

This album, Pickett's second for Atlantic, offers a balanced diet of familiar songs and lesser known ones. In a happy discographical quirk, it contains the same recording of "In the

Pickett grew up singing in Baptist choirs.

Midnight Hour" that appears on his first Atlantic release; the single was his breakthrough hit in 1965 and remains his most enduring contribution to the jukeboxes of the world. That's the only overlap: *The Exciting* contains the additional hits "Land of 1,000 Dances" and the equally fervent shout-out "634-5789," as well as hard-working covers of "Something You Got" and "Barefootin'." All show why so many singers still revere Wilson Pickett: No matter how tricked-out the song, he doesn't do fancy cartwheels. He just tells the story straight. And that's enough.

GENRE: 🔴 R&B. **RELEASED:** 1966, Atlantic. **KEY TRACKS:** "In the Midnight Hour," "Land of 1,000 Dances," "Something You Got." **CATALOG CHOICE:** *The Wicked Pickett.* **NEXT STOP:** Rufus Thomas: *Walking the Dog.*

One Giant Step for Space Rock

Dark Side of the Moon

Pink Floyd

Sometime in the mid-'90s, people began gathering in living rooms to share a curious mixed-media experience: watching *The Wizard of Oz* while listening to Pink Floyd's *Dark Side of the Moon,* the enormously popular space-rock classic that stayed on the *Billboard* charts for more than a decade. If, the urban legend goes, you start the music precisely when the MGM lion roars for the third time, all sorts of unlikely coincidences happen. Roger Waters utters the phrase "look around," and Dorothy looks around. The chimes that usher in Floyd's "Time" coincide with the appearance of the Wicked Witch of the West on her bike, then stop when she gets off. And so on.

Dark Side of the Moon has sold over 40 million copies.

Such synchronicities can be interesting. But the *Oz* visuals are ultimately a distraction, because *Dark Side,* which spent 741 consecutive weeks (fourteen years) on the *Billboard* 200 top-selling album chart, is an engrossing movie all by itself. Make that several movies: Depending on where you drop in, it can seem a dour *Eraserhead*-style psychodrama ("Brain Damage"), or a riddling art film about existentialism ("Us and Them"), or a morality tale on greed ("Money").

Each song is a fully realized self-contained statement, but also functions within Pink Floyd's larger scheme: The album is an integrated suite, an extended listening experience with no pauses. The pieces drift along and float into each other, linked by plush instrumental atmosphere. Textures throughout are as soft as a padded cell; this is art rock that makes good use of multitracking to create layers of sound. The vocals are delivered with total stoner detachment—except, that is, for guest Clare Torry's tornado-like wordless gyrations, which define "The Great Gig in the Sky." And though much of the album moves at a crawl, it all feels thrilling. More than partial credit for this goes to guitarist David Gilmour, whose solo passages are filled with elegantly sustained notes. Where other guitarists look to stun, Gilmour rarely steps out of slow motion, and his exquisitely shaped phrases lift the music to plateaus of breathtaking grandeur. (A career best in this regard comes on the follow-up to *Dark Side, Wish You Were Here,* and the majestic twenty-six-minute "Shine on You Crazy Diamond.")

By the time *Dark Side* culminates in the sweeping cosmic koan "Eclipse," it becomes clear that Pink Floyd has managed a neat trick: Its grandiose journey just so happens to conform, at least loosely, to a familiar Hollywood storytelling arc. You know the one: We start out in a place kinda like Kansas. And wind up somewhere else entirely.

GENRE: 🎸 Rock. **RELEASED:** 1973, EMI. **KEY TRACKS:** "Us and Them," "Money," "Breathe in the Air," "Eclipse." **CATALOG CHOICE:** *Wish You Were Here.* **NEXT STOP:** Radiohead: *OK Computer* (see p. 627). **AFTER THAT:** Moody Blues: *Seventh Sojourn.*

Gnashing Guitars, Melodies of Unexpected Loveliness

Doolittle

Pixies

Thank (or blame) the Pixies for the fitful temperament of alternative rock in the 1990s. The Boston four-piece, fronted by singer Black Francis and anchored in every sense by bassist-vocalist Kim Deal, emerged in 1986. By this, its third release, it had perfected an unusually influential sound: Broken-glass guitars set in spectacular jagged arrays, disarmingly sweet vocal refrains delivered at a full bellow, tunes that take seconds to jolt listeners from nap-time serenity to the pogoing maelstrom of the mosh pit. Kurt Cobain, the leader of Nirvana (see p. 553), loved the Pixies; his band's notions about dynamic contrast can be traced back to the whiplash-inducing "Gouge Away" and other gems on this album.

None of the moods of *Doolittle* last long; furious outbreaks of squalling noise and gnashing guitars abruptly dissipate, giving way to melodies of unexpected loveliness. In this way, the album is different from the previous Pixies effort, *Surfer Rosa*, which was produced by noisemeister Steve Albini to be much more of a steady roar. It's as though the band finished touring *Surfer Rosa* and realized that it was taxing work to bludgeon people for an entire evening. Hence, the next batch of Pixies songs come with quiet, needling interludes between the thunderclaps. The menace is still there—Francis sings the savant lines of the opening track "Debaser" like he's a lunatic who's being pushed to the brink, and the band plays as though this one song is its only shot at a manifesto. (Guitarist Joey Santiago has said that this is the best single-song distillation of the Pixies experience.)

Doolittle wasn't a commercial success immediately. But it became one of those buzzed-about landmark records that traveled far on word of mouth. If you cared about rock noise in 1989, you needed to hear it. That's still true.

GENRE: 🎸 Rock. **RELEASED:** 1989, 4AD/ Elektra. **KEY TRACKS:** "Debaser," "I Bleed," "Wave of Mutilation," "Here Comes Your Man." **CATALOG CHOICE:** *Surfer Rosa*. **NEXT STOP:** Nirvana: *In Utero*.

A Pub Band Grows Up

If I Should Fall from Grace with God

The Pogues

At first the Pogues didn't care much about falling out of God's favor, or anyone else's. On its international debut, the Elvis Costello–produced *Rum, Sodomy, and the Lash*, the seven-piece group that began in the

London streets gave traditional Irish music a gleeful punk makeover. Emulating the dissonant squall of bands like the Clash, the Pogues—the name is a shortened version of the Gaelic phrase *pogue mahone*, or "kiss my ass"—transformed age-old chanteys and sing-alongs into music of extreme rowdiness. It was a match made in pub heaven, even if the band's erratic live shows reinforced every stereotype of the stumbling sloppy-drunk Irishman.

The Pogues began playing together in London in 1982.

After *Rum* generated considerable next-big-thing hype and became a hit, singer and songwriter Shane MacGowan developed an introspective side. Once a happy lout, he was suddenly sprinkling sharp observations about class politics and privilege, belonging and alienation, into his songs, giving dimension to what had been party music. On *If I Should Fall from Grace with God*, still slurring his words, MacGowan hits some political ideas head-on ("Birmingham Six"), but more often slips stealthy insights into jolly-sounding up-tempo numbers (like the title track). MacGowan's more nuanced lyrics also demand that the band slow down now and then; one pleasure of *If I Should Fall*, which is easily the Pogues' creative zenith, are sullen pieces like "Fairytale of New York," a wistful novel of a song that features singer Kirsty MacColl. Even in these tender moments, MacGowan sounds like a reluctant observer of life's cruelties. He's put down his beer long enough to jot down a few thoughts that won't let go of him, but intends to resume his carousing as soon as possible.

GENRE: 🎸 Rock. **RELEASED:** 1988, Island. (Reissued 2006, Rhino.) **KEY TRACKS:** "If I Should Fall from Grace with God," "Bottle of Smoke," "Fairytale of New York," "Turkish Song of the Damned." **CATALOG CHOICE:** *Rum, Sodomy, and the Lash.* **NEXT STOP:** Black 47: *Fire of Freedom.* **AFTER THAT:** Dexy's Midnight Runners: *Searching for the Young Soul Rebels.*

"Take the Space Between Us, Fill It Up Some Way"

Synchronicity

The Police

"Synchronicity I" hurtles along at a hundred miles an hour, carrying word of "a connecting principle" and strange occurrences happening far away. It's a Police version of a pattern-pulse exercise, a Steve Reich outtake played by spiked staccato guitars. Its finale is two or so minutes of deliciously pulverizing rhythm unlike anything in rock, the snapping backbeat of a gospel jubilee gone haywire.

Thus begins one of the more curious multi-platinum successes in rock history, a tense and challenging work that is a million miles away from "Roxanne, turn on the red light." Inside its twelve tracks are worries of apocalyptic doom ("Walking in Your Footsteps"), tales of power and betrayal ("Wrapped Around Your Finger"), Carl Jung's ideas about coincidence and the undetected connections between people and events ("Synchronicity I" and "II,"

"Tea in the Sahara"), and the vows of an obsessive stalker ("Every Breath You Take").

Though it shares some of the dark tone and the fluid, jazzlike rhythms the Police used on its previous album, *Ghost in the Machine* (1981), *Synchronicity* is more revved, more volatile. Even at sedate tempos, the band seems inclined to see what happens when things career out of control. The big bangs in the songs are triggered by zooming fly-by guitars, or drummer Stewart Copeland's skillfully knotted polyrhythms, or vocal harmonies that are searing and strident.

From its beginnings as a New Wave trio in 1977, the Police—Copeland, bassist and singer Sting, and guitarist Andy Summers—did things differently. The band's first two albums hit upon a reggae-pop sound that spread like wildfire, and over the next four years, the contentious trio crafted albums that offered insanely addictive radio songs as well as darker experimental

The Police are, from left, Andy Summers, Sting, and Stewart Copeland.

journeys. Unlike so many rock successes, the Police evolved creatively at each step. As Sting's writing matured, reggae became a spice rather than the main groove, and the musical textures broadened. And then, after the extensive *Synchronicity* tour, the trio, at that moment the biggest band in the world, concluded it had exhausted the artistic possibilities. So it walked away. But not before proving that it's possible for a rock band to pursue challenging, defiantly noncommercial musical ideas and still thrill an awful lot of people.

GENRE: 🎸 Rock. **RELEASED:** 1983, A&M. **KEY TRACKS:** "Synchronicity II," "King of Pain," "Every Breath You Take," "Miss Gradenko," "Tea in the Sahara." **CATALOG CHOICES:** *Zenyatta Mondatta; Ghost in the Machine.* **NEXT STOP:** XTC: *Skylarking* (see p. 878). **AFTER THAT:** Oysterhead: *The Grand Pecking Order.*

The Collected Musings of a Pioneering Country Wanderer

You Ain't Talkin' to Me: Charlie Poole and the Roots of Country Music

Charlie Poole

A millworker and moonshiner, Charlie Poole spent most of his adult years wandering the South, raising hell. He and the band he called the North Carolina Ramblers would leave home for weeks at a time, playing for barn dances and on street corners. Through that piecemeal work, his spry sound spread, influencing countless musicians. It later became a core component of bluegrass.

Poole (1892–1931) played the banjo with three fingers. He'd damaged his right hand in a drunken wager (he claimed he could catch a baseball without a glove no matter how hard it was thrown, and lost), and taught himself to play in what was called a "clawhammer" style. His time was flawless: On this anthology of his 78-RPM recordings, Poole taps out a tempo so strong it carries his accomplices (usually a guitarist and a fiddler) right along with it. Poole's nimble group favored brisk tempos that kept people dancing. The band's repertoire included Civil War ballads, woebegone drifter laments ("May I Sleep in Your Barn Tonight Mister" is one of the highlights on this three-disc set), early blues, mountain dances, and vaudeville numbers.

Poole's drinking binges and renegade exploits made him a legend in the Piedmont hills of Virginia and North Carolina, where he sold most of his records. He continued to record until 1930, and when Columbia records canceled his contract, Poole went back to millwork,

suffering from depression. He died at age thirty-nine, after a thirteen-week bender. His records survived, however: Several famous bluegrass banjo stars, including Don Reno, learned their craft listening to Poole. But it wasn't until Harry Smith's 1952 *Anthology of American Folk Music* (see p. 803) that those outside the Piedmont region appreciated the fiery sounds of country music's first renegade.

GENRE: 🔘 Country. **RELEASED:** 2005, Columbia. **KEY TRACKS:** "The Girl I Left in Sunny Tennessee," "Don't Let Your Deal Go Down Blues," "May I Sleep in Your Barn Tonight Mister." **NEXT STOP:** Bill Monroe: *The High Lonesome Sound of Bill Monroe.* **AFTER THAT:** Flatt and Scruggs: *Foggy Mountain Jamboree* (see p. 282).

Get Another Kick Out of Cole

Anything Goes

Cole Porter
1987 Broadway Revival Cast

Kiss Me Kate is often mentioned as the quintessential Cole Porter musical, but in terms of sheer compositional invention, *Anything Goes*, from 1934, shines just a bit brighter. This is the show that gave the world

"I Get a Kick Out of You," that famous treatise on the giddiness of romance. It's also where to find "Easy to Love," the most sweeping and least corny of Porter's ballads; "You're the Top"; and, of course, "Anything Goes." Just about every composition has a tart Porter observation (often on class and social status) or withering retort—to go along with melodies strong enough to support the wordiest lyrics.

This 1987 production, mounted by Lincoln Center, ushered in the

In 1988, *Anything Goes* won Tony Awards for Best Revival and Best Choreography.

era of "revisicals"—elaborate revivals from the golden age of Broadway. Set on board a luxury liner, the show was, from set design to costumes, an opulent Deco throwback. As has happened with other revisited musicals, the producers pulled in hit songs from other Porter shows. (These include "De-Lovely" and "Friendship," both well utilized in this context.)

To those who have learned Cole Porter songs listening to Sinatra or jazz singers, the more exacting music-theater approach may seem a bit stiff. These singers do lay the vibrato on thick—at times Patti LuPone, whose turn here made her into a bankable star, sings so passionately that the lyrics become garbled. But she also knows how to deliver Porter's athletic, not-always-obvious rhymes: Her "I Get a Kick Out of You" contains several nods to the role's originator, Ethel Merman.

GENRE: 😊 Musicals. **RELEASED:** 1988, RCA. **KEY TRACKS:** "Anything Goes," "I Get a Kick Out of You," "Easy to Love," "It's De-Lovely." **ANOTHER INTERPRETATION:** Original Broadway Cast. **CATALOG CHOICE:** *Kiss Me Kate,* Original Broadway Cast. **NEXT STOP:** Ella Fitzgerald: *Ella Fitzgerald Sings the Cole Porter Songbook* (see p. 279). **AFTER THAT:** Jerry Herman: *Hello, Dolly!* (see p. 357).

Trip-Hop on Permanent Smolder

Dummy

Portishead

When this album of lushly turned-out melancholy tiptoed into pop consciousness in 1994, there wasn't a category for it. Music snobs and critics noticed the drum programming and the swooshing filter sweeps, and concluded it was some new offshoot of dance music—"trip-hop," they called it, aligning Portishead with its neighbors from Bristol, Massive Attack. In the U.K., the dance community embraced Portishead first; in the U.S., it was the alternative rock crowd, who heard Beth Gibbons's fragile, dream-state vocals and decided Portishead was indie-girl angst at a slower speed.

Portishead exploited this in-betweenness—at times *Dummy* feels like a listless background drone, the audio wallpaper that envelops patrons of swanky restaurants. But behind that cabaret noir mood is something more: Fragmented stories that rise out of deep sadness and spread heavy vibes all over the room. Gibbons sings like she's shrouded in mist. She pouts like a starlet, and projects a drifty, anything-but-centered persona that's essential to "Sour Times" and "Numb," two (of many) doleful, slow songs that became unlikely singles.

Dummy won the prestigious Mercury Music Prize for 1994 (the U.K. equivalent of the Album of the Year Grammy) and grew into a hit on both sides of the Atlantic. Gibbons and multi-instrumentalist Geoff Barrow's stroke of genius was the realization that the same nuts and bolts of electronic music, which most DJs were using to create pulse-pounding excitement, could be repurposed to serve gentler, spookier ends. They conjure not just beats but an atmospheric world, often just out of the hovering wails from overdriven guitars. Then Gibbons tells about what it's like to live inside such a place—where you walk around in a disconsolate daze, and life moves slowly, and there's always the chance for further reflection.

GENRE: 🎸 Rock. **RELEASED:** 1994, Go! Discs. **KEY TRACKS:** "Sour Times," "Strangers," "It Could Be Sweet." **CATALOG CHOICE:** Beth Gibbons and Rustin Man: *Out of Season.* **NEXT STOP:** Beth Orton: *Central Reservation* (see p. 568). **AFTER THAT:** Solex: *Low Kick and Hard Bop.*

The Best of a Bossa Nova Refugee

O universe musical de Baden Powell

Baden Powell

S oon after American interest in Brazilian bossa nova erupted in the early '60s, many of the music's budding stars traveled to the U.S. to spread the word. There, they made the music a phenomenon by collaborating with jazz musicians (*Getz/Gilberto*—see p. 308—is among the collaborative triumphs from this period).

The guitarist, singer, and composer Baden Powell went to Paris instead. It was a radical thing to do at the time: The French were indifferent to bossa nova, and Powell wasn't yet a known entity. But Powell immediately found work in nightclubs, and within months began recording for the Barclay label. A conservatory-trained guitarist and the most musically gifted of any of the bossa clan, Powell reworked Jobim's tunes into ethereal, dream-sequence caprices. His early works for Barclay (represented here on the early tracks) are brushed with a feeling of starry nights and Parisian romance.

Powell considered himself more a musician than a singer, and several of his instrumentals, including an exploration of Thelonious Monk's "'Round Midnight," exhibit a rare combination of intense lyricism and enormous technical facility. Powell was equally versed in classi-cal music: His original "Samba em Prelúdio" craftily interweaves elements from Heitor Villa-Lobos's "Prelúdio das Bachianas brasileiras, No. 4." The beauty of his playing sometimes overshadows Powell's other great gift—his wondrous compositions, which are defiantly joyful and harmonically adventurous in ways even Jobim's music was not. This anthology gathers many of Powell's significant works, though as with Jobim, these graceful songs became better known when they were recorded by others—perhaps most transfixingly by Elis Regina (see p. 639).

GENRE: 🌐 World/Brazil. **RELEASED:** 2002, Universal South America. **KEY TRACKS:** "Xango," "Samba do Avião," "Dora," "Asa branca." **CATALOG CHOICE:** *Os Afrosambas de Baden e Vinicius*. **NEXT STOP:** Luiz Bonfá: *Live in Rio 1959*. **AFTER THAT:** Elis Regina: *Em pleno verão*.

The DNA of Bebop on Piano

The Amazing Bud Powell, Vol. 1

Bud Powell

B ud Powell (1924–1966) brought bebop to the piano. The New York native assimilated the glib, eddying lines created by the genre's pioneers, saxophonist Charlie Parker and trumpeter Dizzy Gillespie, and from them fashioned a parallel pianistic vocabulary of slippery phrases that took others years to apprehend. His playing, in his best years, is a highly caffeinated, cram-packed essay on bebop's possibilities.

Alas, Powell's best years were few. This disc, his third as a leader, gathers recordings he made starting in 1949, when he was twenty-four years old. By then he'd suffered a racially

Admirers call Powell "the Charlie Parker of the piano."

motivated beating that gave him recurring headaches, and had spent time in mental institutions; still, according to the musicians who gathered at his Harlem apartment during this period, he was relatively stable and writing lots of music. The album opens with a quintet identified as "Bud Powell's Modernists," featuring trumpeter Fats Navarro (see p. 541) and saxophonist Sonny Rollins (see p. 659) playing Powell's aptly named "Bouncing with Bud" and the bebop standby "52nd Street Theme." It also includes recordings made in May 1951, after Powell was released from Creedmore Sanitarium, where he'd received shock treatment. Drummer Roy Haynes, who appears on the early tracks, recalls in the liner notes that Powell's experiences had cost him something: "That's when you started thinking of Bud as having two periods, before

and after. Before, he was much sharper."

Still, all of *The Amazing*, Vol. 1 (and parts of Vol. 3, which includes a torrid fantasia in the style of Bach keyboard music, "Bud on Bach") is essential listening. There are three versions of Powell's crowning compositional achievement, "Un poco loco," two in a trio setting that inspires some of his most robust, intellectually vibrant improvisation. Among several breathtaking ballads, there's an ambling version of "You Go to My Head" that starts at cocktail hour and winds up well past midnight. The takes with the fiery and very young Navarro and Rollins show Powell's gift for goading accompaniment: Even when other piano players caught up to his galloping run-on bebop sentences, nobody could touch his exquisite sense of timing.

GENRE: 🎷 Jazz. **RELEASED:** 1951, Blue Note. (Reissued 2001.) **KEY TRACKS:** "Un poco loco," "Dance of the Infidels," "Bouncing with Bud," "Ornithology," "You Go to My Head." **CATALOG CHOICE:** *Bud! The Amazing Bud Powell*, Vol. 3. **NEXT STOP:** Red Garland: *A Garland of Red*. **AFTER THAT:** Hank Jones: *The Trio*.

The Big Bang

Elvis at Sun

Elvis Presley

Nearly a year after he'd walked into Memphis Recording Service as a paying customer to cut "My Happiness" as a gift for his mother, eighteen-year-old Elvis Presley was summoned back to the studio. The honcho, Sam Phillips, had a new song his assistant thought would be right for "that boy with the sideburns."

Presley (1935–1977) didn't do much with the song, "Without You." But Phillips and guitarist Scotty Moore heard *something* in Presley and were intrigued enough to book another session, for July 5, 1954. That night they worked through many of the tunes Presley knew, mostly middle-of-the-road pop like "Harbor Lights." And then, according to legend, the young singer started riffing on Arthur Crudup's "That's All Right." It was late, but the sparks made Phillips sit up and listen. He encouraged Presley to do it again while the tape was rolling.

Nothing in American music was quite the same after that. The question of Presley's "poaching" of R&B and other African American styles is a real one, best left to the academics. But this much is beyond dispute: The kid with the sideburns understood—and respected—his source material. From the start, he connected the rhythmic gait of rock and roll directly to that of jump blues and R&B, and made the result sound like the most natural thing in the world.

For all the rebel lore that attached to Presley later, this album, along with his eponymous debut for RCA, amount to the big bang, the crucial brazen moment when the impulse to "rock" transcended notions of race, and style, and ownership. The Sun material has

Presley is the only performer to be inducted into 4 music halls of fame.

been reissued endlessly; *Elvis at Sun* is a sparkling, nicely remastered representation of the groundbreaking early Presley sides. Here you'll find not only "That's All Right" but its influential flip side, "Blue Moon of Kentucky," the signature Bill Monroe tune that Presley transforms into hellfire rockabilly. Also here is the iconic "Good Rockin' Tonight" and both fast and slow versions of "I'm Left, You're Right, She's Gone."

By November 1955, Presley had moved to RCA, bringing with him the mix of rockabilly, country, blues, and pop songs that would make him a legend. *Elvis Presley* has been augmented with extra tracks, but it's arguable whether any vault tidbit can improve on a set that includes "Blue Suede Shoes," "I Got a Woman," and "Money Honey."

GENRE: 🎸 Rock.
RELEASED: 2004, RCA.
KEY TRACKS: "Harbor Lights," "That's All Right," "Good Rockin' Tonight."
CATALOG CHOICES: *Elvis Presley; Elvis.* **NEXT STOP:** Various Artists: *The Sun Story.*

The Finest from the Choirboy King

How Great Thou Art

Elvis Presley

Some speculate that Elvis Presley's sedate performance of "Peace in the Valley" on the *Ed Sullivan Show* in January 1957 was a type of media atonement, to make up for his incendiary hip-swiveling appearances the year before. That may be true—who knows what calculations were going on in those frenzied days when the Memphis rocker was just becoming a star—but it shortchanges the devout Presley's sense of himself as an artist. The future icon had an abiding love of gospel and a keen sense of how to make it his own. The sacred works stand among the most stirring, plainly beautiful material in his massive catalog.

Presley (1935–1977) once boasted, "I know practically every religious song that's ever been written," and, beginning with an EP connected to the Sullivan appearance, began documenting a songbook of hymns, spirituals, and up-tempo

This album won a 1967 Grammy for Best Sacred Performance.

jubilees featuring traditional gospel quartet singing. *How Great Thou Art* is his second full gospel collection, and it covers quite a range: Supported by pianist Floyd Cramer and the vocal groups the Imperials and the Jordanaires, Presley does a few brisk revival-meeting tunes ("So High," "Run On"), several pieces set in a medium-tempo rocking-chair pulse ("Farther Along," "Where Could I Go but to the Lord," both enriched by Cramer's plinking asides),

and the obligatory trembling rubato hymns (the title track, one of Presley's all-time best).

Presley was completely at home singing religious songs. The warm, full voice that launched rock and roll grows bigger and fuller as it glides effortlessly through these expressions of faith. There's no hype, no sales pitch. Just a servant sharing the glory of what God gave him.

GENRES: 🪧 Gospel ⭐ Pop. **RELEASED:** 1967, RCA. **KEY TRACKS:** "How Great Thou Art," "Run On," "Where Could I Go but to the Lord." **F.Y.I.:** Presley's four Grammy awards were all connected to his religious records. **CATALOG CHOICE:** *He Walks with Me.* **NEXT STOP:** Sam Cooke: *Sam Cooke with the Soul Stirrers* (see p. 186). **AFTER THAT:** Louis Armstrong: *Louis Sings the Good Book.*

Out of Tragedy Comes . . .

Learning to Crawl

The Pretenders

Rock bands sometimes evolve by blundering their way forward. Then there are those, like the Pretenders, forced to evolve by a ghastly type of attrition. When the band of three Brits and Ohio-born singer Chrissie Hynde first arrived, in 1980, its sound was a spring-loaded siren, with unconventional guitars going haywire and a driving rhythm that was somewhere between punk and an amphetamine-abusing '60s soul revue. The band's self-titled debut, one of the great opening chapters in rock, gave the world such enduring gems as "Precious" and "Brass in Pocket."

It couldn't last. In 1982, just after the band finished touring for their second album (*II*), bassist Pete Farndon was fired. Two days later,

guitarist James Honeyman-Scott died of a drug overdose. (Farndon would die the same way the following year.) Though key elements of her band were gone, Hynde returned to the studio a month later to record "Back on the Chain Gang." After the song charted, in January 1983, Hynde rebuilt the band around original drummer Martin Chambers and guitarist Robbie McIntosh. The reconstituted Pretenders substituted a sleek, highly efficient streamlined rhythm for the spiking attack of the debut. Hynde modified her vocal approach accordingly, singing in a more detached, conversational style. If she'd once courted frenzy, she was now cool, diffident, haughty. And she used her experience as fuel for her songs: About "Watching the Clothes" Hynde once explained: "My flatmate Kevin Sparrow died on Christmas Day of 1979. I took some of his clothes to the launderette and sat there and watched them spinning 'round in the dryer, sadly knowing he'd never wear them again. Sometimes you can dump your grief in a song."

Learning to Crawl was certified platinum in the U.S. in 1984.

For all the tragedy that surrounded its creation, *Learning to Crawl* is hardly a foreboding rumination on death. Its pleasures include a withering critique of American timidity ("Middle of the Road"), a commentary on the gutting of the American city in the wake of Reaganomics ("My City Was Gone"), and one of rock's most beautiful songs about Christmas ("2,000 Miles"). Some fans of the debut still hold it up as the most significant Pretenders statement, but Hynde's handling of what happened to her—the way she transformed sad circumstances into music of great wisdom and poignancy—puts *Learning to Crawl* on another level entirely.

GENRE: 🎸 Rock. **RELEASED:** 1984, Sire. **KEY TRACKS:** "Middle of the Road," "Back on the Chain Gang," "2,000 Miles." **CATALOG CHOICE:** *Pretenders*. **NEXT STOP:** Blondie: *Parallel Lines* (see p. 99). **AFTER THAT:** The Runaways: *The Runaways*.

A Lost Classic of the British Invasion

Get the Picture?

The Pretty Things

The Pretty Things are the British Invasion group that never invaded. Formed at London's Sidcup Art College in 1963, the quintet developed in close proximity to the early Rolling Stones; guitarist Dick Taylor was briefly a Stone, and Keith Richards was a classmate. Both bands discovered Bo Diddley and Chuck Berry around the same time, and both openly emulated the maracas-shaking whomp of big-beat Chicago blues. One went on to world domination, and somehow the Pretty Things, whose name was drawn from a Diddley lyric, became the answer to a rock-trivia question.

Here's where we sing that old song about how life isn't fair: Even on this, their second release, the Pretty Things manifest the surly, cocksure irreverence that later became a Stones trademark. They had the hard swing, the R&B road-show swagger, and, in Jagger look-alike Phil May, a singer who favored the raw edges of the music. Listening to this trove of neglected gems, it's clear this band also had a Stonesian sense of rock's possibilities, its capacity to startle, threaten, and soothe. The Pretty Things could be as surly as anyone in the game (see "Buzz the Jerk") and as downright exciting, too ("You Don't Believe Me").

Of the many theories to explain the Pretty Things' footnote status, the most plausible is that the group wasn't nearly as prolific, songwriting-wise, as its competition. The group's first enduring original, "Midnight to Six Man," was written by guitarist Taylor in 1965, and it's more an intense rhythm riff than a great composition. May came up with several distinctive songs for the set, among them "You Don't Believe Me" and the title track. Despite several distinctive subsequent singles and a crazy psychedelic trip (*S.F. Sorrow*), by the late '60s the group had been totally eclipsed by the Stones. This still sizzling record argues that the Pretty Things deserved better.

GENRE: 🎸 Rock. **RELEASED:** 1965, Fontana. **KEY TRACKS:** "You Don't Believe Me," "Midnight to Six Man," "Come See Me." **CATALOG CHOICE:** *S. F. Sorrow.* **NEXT STOP:** The Yardbirds: *Having a Rave-Up.* **AFTER THAT:** Love: *Forever Changes* (see p. 457).

The Happiest! The Showbizziest!

The Wildest!

Louis Prima

If you only know the cheeky David Lee Roth cover of "Just a Gigolo/I Ain't Got Nobody" from 1985, do yourself a favor and seek out *The Wildest!*, a slice of '50s showbiz delirium that includes the more madcap Louis Prima original.

Though paced a bit slower than the rock remake—it's almost a vaudeville bounce—Prima's "Gigolo" swings much harder, with a hipster's controlled giddiness. From his first entrance, Prima (1911–1978) drops alternately woeful and exuberant Louis Armstrong–inspired scatting, and his entreaties are matched by shoop-shoopy band-vocal catcalls and the honking saxophone of Sam Butera.

The Wildest! was reissued in 2002, with 4 additional tracks.

as if it's chasing a scoundrel. Along the way, the rhythm shifts from typical lounge-act 4/4 to a New Orleans parade romp (complete with a reference to "When the Saints Go Marching In") to a barn-burning big-band shout-chorus finale.

This collection marked the end of several years of studio frustration for the New Orleans–born singer of Italian ancestry: Prima felt his recordings didn't get close to capturing the rollicking magic of his live act. According to the liner notes, when he heard *The Wildest!*, Prima knew he'd taken a big step forward. "This is it. This is three o'clock in the morning at the Sahara."

That song's combination of jazz and jive sent Prima's career into overdrive. Literally every track of *The Wildest!* sparkles with the combination of mugging-for-the-crowds irreverence and seriously disciplined execution that was his signature. You'll find "Nothing's Too Good for My Baby," a duet with Keely Smith that's notable for its choreographed wordless vocal tandems, and a jittery "You Rascal You" that is a showstopper. As Prima's vocals fall lazily off the beat, the rhythm section sounds

GENRE: 🎤 Vocals. **RELEASED:** 1957, Capitol. **KEY TRACKS:** "Just a Gigolo/I Ain't Got Nobody," "The Lip." **NEXT STOP:** Keely Smith: *I Wish You Love.* **AFTER THAT:** Perez Prado: *Havana 3 AM.*

The Commercial Apex in the Reign of Prince

Purple Rain

Prince and the Revolution

Compared with the horny escapades of Prince's white-hot early works *For You* and *Controversy*, the line from *Purple Rain* that provoked outrage from politicians and religious leaders—about a girl named Nikki caught "in a hotel lobby masturbating with a magazine"—seems downright tame. Its crime was really about market penetration: The scandalously funky early Prince works circulated among a marginalized freak element in clubland. *Purple Rain*, a triumph-over-family-troubles Hollywood film, hit everybody.

Vanity Fair called *Purple Rain* the best soundtrack of all time.

As a movie, *Purple Rain* is campy and clichéd and somehow, unlike subsequent Prince movies, roguishly charming. The accompanying music is something else again. It comes hot on the heels of the Minneapolis multi-instrumentalist's two biggest singles, "Little Red Corvette" and the visionary blast of premillennium tension entitled "1999," and like both of those, it is funk and rock in the same instant. It's last-set-in-the-club party music and baby-making music, brash guitar power chords bumping sweet soul refrains, post-disco shoop-shoop twirling into up-tempo gospel jubilee. Among its pleasures are a single built around nothing but guitar and drums ("When Doves Cry") and a beatific '60s anthem ("Take Me with U") that depends on passionately strident, practically microtonal vocal harmonies. That's not to overlook the title track, a majestic rock anthem that inspires some of the most glorious power-ballad guitar soloing of all time.

GENRES: R&B Rock. **RELEASED:** 1984, Warner Bros. **KEY TRACKS:** "When Doves Cry," "Baby I'm a Star," "Take Me with U." **CATALOG CHOICE:** *Parade*. **NEXT STOP:** D'Angelo: *Brown Sugar* (see p. 204). **AFTER THAT:** Terence Trent D'Arby: *Symphony or Damn*.

Many Signs, All Pointing Up

Sign o' the Times

Prince

Beginning in 1980, with the risqué *Dirty Mind*, Prince went on an exceptional decade-long tear, issuing a series of albums that regularly sent everybody else in pop and R&B back to school. The year 1981 brought *Controversy* followed by the rousing 1982 double album *1999*. Then in 1984 came his commercial breakthrough *Purple Rain* (see previous page), followed in '85 by the psychedelic *Around the World in a Day*. The next year brought *Parade*, the seriously underrated soundtrack to his second film, *Under the Cherry Moon*. This album came next, in the middle of 1987, and it was followed a few months later by the lascivious, intended-for-fans-only *Black Album*. After that came the ornate *Lovesexy*, in 1988. The *Batman* soundtrack, released in 1989, was the decade's first sign that Prince might be mortal after all.

In 2004, Prince was inducted into the Rock and Roll Hall of Fame.

Compare this track record to that of anyone else making music at the time, and Prince emerges as not just one prolific hombre, but the only artist whose ideas went right from his own records into wide circulation. The long arm of Prince is evident in the big Janet Jackson singles of the '80s, the new jack swing of Teddy Riley, the rock leanings of Terence Trent D'Arby, and the list goes on. And so does the influence: Just about every Outkast album has at least one Prince moment.

On this record, Prince taunts those who would copy him, with rhythmically intricate songs that are so willfully idiosyncratic, gymnastic in their vocal contortions, and musically dense that they elude easy classification. Disc one is notable for its beatbox manglings—in particular "Housequake" and the title track. Disc two opens with a ballistic rocker ("U Got the Look") and stays hot the rest of the way—first with the oversexed meditation on gender roles, "If I Was Your Girlfriend," featuring a sped-up voice he calls "Camille," and then with the live "Gonna Be a Beautiful Night." This instant party shows just how deep Prince goes: It puts snazzy Ellington horns and James Brown rhythm guitar in the service of a timeline-defying jam that's as irreverent as the best Funkadelic. He and the band destroy that groove so thoroughly on that track, it's a surprise when a slow ballad, "Adore," rises up out of the applause. Don't turn it off: It finds Prince screaming like Jim Morrison and twittering in his falsetto range like jazz diva Sarah Vaughan. As with just about everything here, it's amazing. And impossible to imitate.

GENRES: 🔵 R&B 🔴 Rock. **RELEASED:** 1987, Warner Bros. **KEY TRACKS:** "U Got the Look," "Housequake," "If I Was Your Girlfriend," "Adore." **CATALOG CHOICES:** *Parade; 3121.* **NEXT STOP:** Anywhere you go after this is going to seem tepid.

A Priceless First Peek at . . .

John Prine

John Prine

The Vietnam vet is home, and struggling. Money's running out. He doesn't exactly have employable skills. The mood of John Prine's "Sam Stone" is one of quiet and vague desperation, until Prine drops in a single line: "There's a hole in daddy's arm where all the money goes."

That's Prine: Blunt and casual and chilling all at once. His songs seem to be ambling along, radiating simplicity, and then wham, Prine shares a single telling detail, in this case a heroin habit, that gives his narrative urgency. Like an old-time raconteur, he's got a stealthy, well-honed sense of the dramatic. Unlike most songwriters who were commenting on the effects of war in 1971, the former mailman and army mechanic didn't align himself with any cause—as he recalled in an anthology, "all the other Vietnam songs were basic protest songs. . . . I don't remember any other songs that talked about the soldiers at all."

This record would be an essential bit of American songwriter lore just for "Sam Stone." But it also includes several pieces that are just

as acutely observed—including the prayerlike "Angel from Montgomery," which is practically a standard, and the austere "Hello in There," which should be one. These and several other barbed commentaries established Prine as a songwriter's songwriter. Once you digest this chilling, carefully wrought gem, there are a bunch of equally pointed (and almost as great) Prine records waiting.

GENRES: 🌞 Folk 🎸 Rock. **RELEASED:** 1971, Atlantic. **KEY TRACKS:** "Hello in There," "Sam Stone," "Angel from Montgomery." **CATALOG CHOICES:** *The Missing Years; Great Days: The John Prine Anthology.* **NEXT STOP:** Willis Alan Ramsey: *Willis Alan Ramsey* (see p. 632). **AFTER THAT:** Guy Clark: *Old No. 1* (see p. 171).

A Rock Processional for the Ages

"A Whiter Shade of Pale"

Procol Harum

Lindsey Buckingham of Fleetwood Mac once told an interviewer he considers this processional-tempo megahit a "classical soul song." John Lennon said it made great listening for an acid trip. Brian Wilson thought he was hearing the music to his own funeral when it was playing. Even its lyricist, Keith Reid, has fessed up to not knowing what it's about—his lyrics are a series of abstract images and sailing metaphors, with appearances by the "vestal virgins" and revelers who "trip the light fandango."

The first song that British band Procol Harum ever recorded, "A Whiter Shade of Pale" is four minutes and three seconds of utterly breathtaking beauty—part affirmation of life and part appeal to an oth-

The band's manager named Procol Harum after a friend's Burmese cat.

erworldly presence. Framed by creeping church-organ counterpoint, it carries traces of well-known works by Johann Sebastian Bach—the chord sequence written by keyboardist and singer Gary Booker emulates Air on a G String, and in a few places the melody echoes Bach's Cantata 140, also known as "Wachet auf" (Sleepers Awake). But Booker goes in another direction with his singing—he's spent and weary, almost overcome with resignation.

A massive hit upon its release in 1967

(some consider it *the* single of the Summer of Love), "Whiter Shade" has sold millions, been covered by countless artists (including Willie Nelson) and used in movies and advertising. And still the original has the power to stop time.

GENRE: 🎸 Rock. **RELEASED:** 1967, Deram. **APPEARS ON:** *Procol Harum; Greatest Hits.* **NEXT STOP:** Moody Blues: *Seventh Sojourn.* **AFTER THAT:** Electric Light Orchestra: *Eldorado.*

The Notes of a Wily Professor

New Orleans Piano

Professor Longhair

The mighty New Orleans pianist Henry Roeland Byrd (1918–1980), better known as Professor Longhair, had a tireless left hand, an ingratiatingly besieged voice, and the rare ability to get a room going all by himself.

That's what Atlantic Records founder Ahmet Ertegun discovered when he made a pilgrimage to hear the man called "Fess" in 1949: "We came upon a nightclub—or, rather, a shack—which like an animated cartoon appeared to be expanding and deflating with the pulsations of the beat," Ertegun recalled in producer Jerry Wexler's memoir of the Atlantic years. "Instead of a full band, I saw only a single musician—Professor Longhair—playing these weird wide harmonies, using the piano as both a keyboard and a bass drum."

Fans call Longhair the "Bach of Rock and Roll."

Ertegun, blown away, recorded Byrd playing his originals backed by a full band in 1949 and 1953. These sessions, collected on this blazing disc, codified the tricks of the piano trade as practiced in the Crescent City—usually a syncopated rumba-style bass line supporting wild boogie-woogie meanderings. The Atlantic sides, considered by some historians to be a crucial spark in the development of rock and roll, made Byrd a local legend, though not a star. After a long period of dissolution in the 1960s, when for a time he swept the floors of a record shop, he was rediscovered in the early '70s and embraced by a generation that was just beginning to discover the city's rich rhythm and blues heritage. Byrd began recording again; among his best later works are such electrifying live records as *Big Chief.*

One of the great entertainers, Fess delighted people with his confident stride style and relentless, rollicking sense of swing. His originals "Tipitina" and "Hey Little Girl" push toward an elation that goes beyond words, a conflagration of boogie and jump blues and his own island-tinged "rum boogie" that is as close to pure groove nirvana as most humans ever get.

GENRE: 🎵 Blues 🎤 R&B. **RELEASED:** 1972, Atlantic. **KEY TRACKS:** "Tipitina," "Ball the Wall," "Hey Little Girl," "Mardi Gras in New Orleans." **CATALOG CHOICE:** *Big Chief.* **NEXT STOP:** James Booker: *New Orleans Piano Wizard Live!* (see p. 104). **AFTER THAT:** Dr. John: *Dr. John's Gumbo.*

Ill-Fated Lovers Go for a Spin

Romeo and Juliet, Op. 64

Sergey Prokofiev
The Cleveland Orchestra (Lorin Maazel, cond.)

For a piece that's considered one of the most visionary ballet scores, Sergey Prokofiev's *Romeo and Juliet* didn't get off to a promising start. When he was first approached about a ballet based on the Shakespeare play, the Russian composer demurred, noting that fourteen composers had already written operatic versions of the piece.

Convinced to go ahead, Prokofiev finished the piece in 1936. It was initially rejected by the choreographers, who said its quick shifts of meter made it impossible to dance to. The Leningrad premiere in 1937 was canceled. Instead, the work premiered in Czechoslovakia the following year, where it met with raves. Similar praise greeted the 1940 Russian premiere.

It's easy to hear why the dancers were challenged: Prokofiev's syncopations are tricky, at times even clumsy. They're not oriented around the obvious repetitions favored by ballet dancers, but oddly shaped ideas that are hard to count rhythmically. And though the melodies are often arresting, at times the love story gets subsumed under agitated outbreaks of fighting.

Prokofiev adapted the piece for orchestra, but the original ballet version—with its fifty-two discrete "scenes"—is more interesting. It shows the composer's playful approach to storytelling, his embrace of unconventional sounds (several sections use the mandolin), and his knack for character development. The scenes, particularly Juliet's frenzied scheming early in Act 3, are strikingly rendered by the brawny Cleveland Orchestra, here conducted by Lorin Maazel. The Clevelanders get the colorful flourishes and the composer's calisthenic swirls, and treat the piece as a series of dramatic provocations—music that, despite Prokofiev's initial misgivings, provides new perspective on the plight of those familiar ill-fated lovers.

GENRE: 🎻 Classical. **RELEASED:** 1973, Decca. **KEY TRACKS:** All of Act 3. **CATALOG CHOICE:** *David Bowie Narrates Peter and the Wolf*, Philadelphia Orchestra (Eugene Ormandy, cond.). **NEXT STOP:** Maurice Ravel: *Daphnis et Chloë, Suite No. 2*, St. Louis Symphony Orchestra (Leonard Slatkin, cond.).

Making Big Beat a Little Bigger

DecksandDrumsandRockandRoll

Propellerheads

The next time you find yourself in the tiresome argument about how music made with samplers and computers doesn't have any heart, cue up "Bang On!" on this doozy of a debut disc from a duo associated with the electronica style called Big Beat. Turn it up and let it play for a minute. Watch as this mind-bending tour de force takes control of the room— a wine connoisseur might describe the groove as having faint James Brown notes with a Memphis soul foundation, and occasional hints of glam guitar. And then excuse herself to get a spot on the dance floor.

After overhearing the term "propellerhead" (slang for a nerd), Gifford and White knew it was the perfect name for their band.

"Bang On!" is a post-modern construct—like much electronica of the '90s, it's built entirely from old records. But as assembled by Propellerheads (Will White and Alex Gifford, from Bath, England), this precise combination of source material becomes even better than any one "real" thing. The beat is huge, and filtered to sound hyperreal, and though there are clavinets popping and guitars slashing and even some (well hidden) turntable pyrotechnics, it's the revue-style rumble of the bass and drums that rules this. It's a sound strong enough to steamroll over everything in your brain, make you write bad checks, send you into one-night stands you'll regret before dawn.

That track and several others approach the caterwauling frenzy of great rock and roll, and the consistently delirious *DecksandDrums* doesn't stop there. Its adventures include lushly appointed fantasies on hip-hop themes and kitschy spy-movie chase scenes. "History Repeating" features a sassy cameo from British vocalist Shirley Bassey. "Why ask your head when it's your hips that are swinging?" the imploring Bassey wants to know. It's a question that applies to everything Propellerheads.

GENRE: ⊗ Electronica. RELEASED: 1988, Wall of Sound. KEY TRACKS: "History Repeating," "Bang On!," "Spybreak!," "360 Degrees (Oh Yeah?)." NEXT STOP: The Chemical Brothers: *Dig Your Own Hole* (see p. 159). AFTER THAT: Fatboy Slim: *Better Living Through Chemistry* (see p. 271).

Believe the Hype

It Takes a Nation of Millions to Hold Us Back

Public Enemy

Public Enemy showed it was possible to wring revolution from two turntables and a microphone. And, oh yeah, a boatload of samples, too. The New York collective, built around rapper Chuck D and his idiot-savant comic foil Flavor Flav, brought social commentary to street rhyming, which had been mostly apolitical. That was one revolution. Then, the rappers and the producers who called themselves the Bomb Squad developed a completely original means of conveying those ideas. Starting with a massive menu of siren squalls and stray audio artifacts, they pumped up basic beats into a terrifying and unprecedented noise assault. While Chuck D, who once described hip-hop as "black America's CNN," was dispensing blunt and incisive attacks on hypocrisy, the Bomb Squad did whatever it took to make his words nuclear—often surrounding him with dense, nearly indecipherable torrents of sound.

Hank Shocklee, the founder of the Bomb Squad, told *Musician* magazine that creating this accompaniment was, in the pre–computer music age, incredibly time-consuming: He and his cohorts would put together short rhythm loops from various sources, and then juxtapose them. "You'll hear three different kick drums, three snares, three high hats, and each has its own time frequency." Atop those beat constructions the Bomb Squad added layers of staticky noise. More than once during the making of this album, the group's equipment crashed, sending the entire production, which could involve sixty or seventy tiny slivers of audio, back to the drawing board.

Public Enemy's *It Takes a Nation* ... was the first hip-hop album to top the *Village Voice*'s Pazz and Jop poll.

It Takes a Nation features Chuck D fulminating (in the stentorian baritone he patterned after sportscaster Marv Albert) about conditions in urban America, and what he sees as veiled racist double-talk. And then it flips the script, on tracks that catch him and Flavor Flav riffing like a comedy team, softening the bitter missives with irreverent playground taunts. The blend of tactics—on this and the equally intense *Fear of a Black Planet*—is the miracle of Public Enemy. Though they see themselves as messengers, they love hip-hop too much to reduce everything to a lecture.

GENRE: 🎵 Hip-Hop. **RELEASED:** 1988, Def Jam. **KEY TRACKS:** "Bring the Noise," "Don't Believe the Hype," "Black Steel in the Hour of Chaos." **CATALOG CHOICE:** *Fear of a Black Planet*. **NEXT STOP:** Rage Against the Machine: *Rage Against the Machine*. **AFTER THAT:** The Last Poets: *This Is Madness*.

The Stirring Escapades of Starving Artists

La bohème

Giacomo Puccini

Luciano Pavarotti, Mirella Freni, Berlin Philharmonic (Herbert von Karajan, cond.)

Opera began in the 1600s as an attempt to revive Greek tragedy, and it's been a tug-of-war between words and music ever since. The opera world has suffered through works at both extremes—recklessly wordy narratives in search of musical anchor, and gorgeous music lacking plot lines. Italy's Giacomo Puccini (1858–1924) achieved a very happy medium with this, a breakthrough work considered his "perennial youthful" opera. Throughout his voyeuristic tour of Paris's starving-artist bohemia in the nineteenth century, Puccini sprinkles genuinely memorable melodies, songs that would be deeply affecting independent of any narrative. All of his musical decisions were informed by the necessities of the drama, and timed to last exactly as long as needed to advance the story, and no more.

The opera, the basic outlines of which were hijacked for the '90s musical *Rent*, begins on Christmas Eve in Paris's Latin Quarter. The year is 1830, and the painter Marcello (sung by Rolando Panerai) and his roommate, the poet Rodolfo (Luciano Pavarotti), are shivering because there's no fuel to heat the fire. Rodolfo burns a manuscript he's been writing, there's a confrontation with the landlord, and after several other unemployed bohemians traipse through on their way to make merry at Café Momus, Rodolfo finds himself alone with neighbor Mimi, who's looking for a light for her candle. By the end of Act 1, which culminates in Rodolfo's beautiful aria, they've fallen in love. The three subsequent acts pick up melodic threads of the first, and sometimes evolve entirely new themes. The best of these, in the second act, is the aria of Musetta, a vixen whose appearance at the café is intended to make former lover Marcello jealous. In the third, an extended discussion finds Rodolfo explaining why he's no longer hot for Mimi, a position that later fills him with remorse; in the fourth, the dying Mimi (the sopranos seem to perish at the end of many Puccini operas)

Puccini was inspired to be an opera composer after seeing a performance of Verdi's *Aida*.

hallucinates a glimpse into the hereafter, aided by florid string counterlines.

This 1973 recording revolves around two of the premier Italian voices of recent times, the richly hued and effortlessly resonant tenor Pavarotti (heard here at a golden moment before he became a brand) and the perpetually-in-motion Mirella Freni, who makes a bewitching Mimi. A key player here is conductor Herbert von Karajan, who was, according to musicians, himself an extremely gifted actor. When he demonstrated a phrase to a singer, he was able to completely embody the nuances of the character—so much so that even the minor players seem to spring to life when they make their entrances. Of course Karajan has help in this regard—the coloristic splendor and firm gestures of the mighty Berlin Philharmonic.

GENRE: 🎭 Opera. **RELEASED:** 1973, London. **KEY TRACKS:** Act 1: "O soave fanciulla"; Act 2: "Quando men vo"; Act 4: "Sono andati?" **ANOTHER INTERPRETATION:** RCA Symphony Orchestra (Thomas Beecham, cond.). **CATALOG CHOICE:** *Turandot* (see below). **NEXT STOP:** Vincenzo Bellini, *Norma* (see p. 75)

Puccini's Last (Unfinished) Stand

Turandot

Giacomo Puccini

Joan Sutherland, Luciano Pavarotti, London Philharmonic Orchestra (Zubin Mehta, cond.)

There are operas that chronicle heroic struggles against fate or the elements. And then there are those like *Turandot*, in which the terror comes in human form—in this case a cruel, petty, vindictive ruler. Giacomo Puccini's last opera is the story of a frigid princess who beheads suitors who can't answer her three riddles. The plot is ghastly at times; the title character a nasty tyrant. And yet *Turandot* contains some of the most sweepingly lyrical, arrestingly beautiful music in all of opera.

A brief tour of the musical highlights includes the animated singing of the three ministers Ping, Pang, and Pong early in Act 2 as they recall what life was like before they entered the anxious environs of Turandot's court. Further into Act 2, check out the moment when Turandot poses her riddles—singing with the delighted glee of a known villain, Joan Sutherland amplifies the taunts and insinuations of the text. And then cue up "Nessun dorma," the grave and resolute aria for Calaf (Luciano Pavarotti) in Act 3, to see if his determined, petitioning vocals can melt the cold heart of the princess. In this, one of Pavarotti's most famous performances, you can feel trembling, pent-up resentment bubbling beneath the surface.

This 1967 studio recording features several singers who probably weren't the most obvious choices for their roles at the time. The title character typically had been played by Wagnerites, singers prone to oversized delivery. Sutherland wasn't that—her calling card is finesse. Somehow, though, conductor Zubin Mehta draws an almost animalistic, instinct-driven performance from her. The entire work feels shot full of energy—Mehta gets the singers to attend to the specifics without neglecting the motives (and warped mores) of their characters.

Puccini didn't finish *Turandot*, which some have speculated drew on his own experience (his wife was known to be a cold, jealous type). He had trouble with the resolution of the story, the moment in the third act when Turandot realizes her meanness and becomes a good wife to Calaf. He'd orchestrated the entire work, and made numerous attempts at endings, but was stymied by the final scenes. The opera was finished by Franco Alfano, and many musicians find its conclusion unsatisfactory: At the 1926 premiere, more than a year after Puccini's death, conductor Arturo Toscanini stopped where he thought the composer's input ended, and left the orchestra and singers to finish the opera without him.

GENRE: 🎭 Opera. **RELEASED:** 1967, London. **KEY TRACKS:** Act 2: "Olà Pang, olà Pong"; "O tigre! O tigre"; "In questa reggia." Act 3: "Nessun dorma." **ANOTHER INTERPRETATION:** Birgit Nilsson, Franco Corelli, Rome Opera Theater Orchestra and Chorus (Francesco Molinari-Pradelli, cond.). **CATALOG CHOICE:** *Tosca,* Maria Callas, La Scala Chorus and Orchestra (Victor de Sabata, cond.). **NEXT STOP:** Joan Sutherland: *BBC Recitals, 1958, 1960, 1961.*

The Most Powerful Puente

Dance Mania!

Tito Puente and His Orchestra

Though his forays into Latin jazz were explosive, and his support of singers legendary, *timbale* master Tito Puente (1923–2000) made his most important contribution leading a dance band. He understood what dancers needed—as a child, he'd won several dance competitions—and during the 1950s heyday of the big Latin bands in New York, his rock-steady ensemble delivered exactly what dancers dancing needed, set after dazzling set of sultry cha-cha and screaming mambo played without a whisker out of place.

Dance Mania!, one of more than a hundred albums in Puente's catalog, is among the first titles that show the leader attempting to replicate in the studio what his band did nightly in performance. It's strikingly simple—verses followed by exchanges with a chorus of backing singers, followed by exciting, roof-raising instrumental mambos that make good use of then-novel stereo separations. Within that basic structure Puente and his musicians open up new worlds: On "Mi chiquita quiere bembe," the verses are in typical cha-cha rhythm, but when they're finished, the band lunges into a riveting African-style triple-meter gallop. Every selection here jumps— there are eloquent solos (see Puente's marimba feature "Hong Kong Mambo") and moments of starched-shirt ensemble execution. Just hearing the introduction to "Llego mijan," you can imagine couples racing to the dance floor and staying there, locked in motion, as long as the music continues. While Puente's Latin-jazz titles in the '70s and '80s offer glossy big-band passages and jaw-dropping percussion fireworks, those isolated displays can't match the steamrolling intensity that defines Puente in his prime. Which is here.

GENRE: 🌐 World/Latin. **RELEASED:** 1958, RCA. **KEY TRACKS:** "Llego mijan," "Mambo gozon," "Hong Kong Mambo." **CATALOG CHOICE:** *Night Beat.* **NEXT STOP:** Tito Rodriguez: *Live at the Palladium* (see p. 656). **AFTER THAT:** Eddie Palmieri: *La perfecta* (see p. 573).

Queen ✦ Sun Ra and His Arkestra ✦ Sergey Rachmaninoff ✦ Radiohead ✦ Ma Rainey ✦ Bonnie Raitt ✦ Jean-Philippe Rameau ✦ Ramones ✦ Willis Alan Ramsey ✦ Ernest Ranglin ✦ Maurice Ravel ✦ Otis Redding ✦ Jimmy Reed ✦ Lou Reed ✦ Elis Regina ✦ Steve Reich ✦ Django Reinhardt ✦ R.E.M. ✦ The Replacements ✦ Charlie Rich ✦ Nikolai Rimsky-Korsakov ✦ Minnie Riperton ✦ Ismael Rivera con Kako y Su Orquesta ✦ Max Roach ✦ Steve Roach ✦ Marty Robbins ✦ Smokey Robinson and the Miracles ✦ Tabu Ley Rochereau ✦ Jimmie Rodgers ✦ Richard Rodgers and Oscar Hammerstein II ✦ Amália Rodrigues ✦ Arsenio Rodríguez y Su Conjunto ✦ Tito Rodriguez ✦ The Rolling Stones ✦ Sonny Rollins ✦ Linda Ronstadt ✦ The Roots ✦ Roxy Music ✦ Todd Rundgren ✦ Run-DMC ✦ Otis Rush ✦ Tom Rush ✦ Arthur Russell ✦ Mitch Ryder and the Detroit Wheels

Q, R

The Campiest Rock Concept Album Ever

A Night at the Opera

Queen

"Is this the real life? Is this just fantasy?" With these questions, Queen frontman Freddie Mercury leaves behind the run-of-the-mill jive talk of rock to embark on the epic quest for enlightenment known as "Bohemian Rhapsody." It's six delirious minutes of *opera buffa* outlandishness, a series of music-theater scenes that borrow everything but the powdered wigs from opera. The show begins with aria-like voice-and-piano passages that catch Mercury in full tragic-hero swoon, and lively exchanges between the lead singer and a thundering, hectoring chorus. Then, just when the geegaws get a little too twee, along comes Brian May with his laser-beam guitar, boogie-stomping all over the stage, determined to purge all pomposity.

The "Rhapsody," immortalized in the comic film *Wayne's World*, is not the only moment of rococo tongue-in-cheek brilliance that Queen loaded into *A Night at the Opera*. Fully half of the album tends toward camp—there are seafaring sing-alongs ("'39") and vaudeville-style soft-shoe tunes ("Seaside Rendezvous") and a few themes that might have been inspired by a toy calliope ("Lazing on a Sunday Afternoon"). Delivered with sly winks and high-gloss dazzle, these put Queen closer, sensibility-wise, to the theatrical entertainments of a bygone age than anything on pop radio.

Yet Queen does also manage to kick it. Tucked between the kitschy, amazingly detailed period pieces are several conventional pop songs—conventional at least in terms of structure, as the four-piece can't resist pumping up simple themes into tottering spectacles. These include the zooming, cleverly harmonized confession "I'm In Love with My Car" and the savage "Death on Two Legs," which turns on a dizzying multilayered guitar attack. Modest in scale when compared to "Bohemian Rhapsody," these are just as head-spinningly intricate, illustrations of Queen's ability to conjure music of preposterous flamboyance that somehow still manages to flat-out rock.

GENRE: 🎸 Rock. **RELEASED:** 1975, Elektra. **KEY TRACKS:** "You're My Best Friend," "'39," "Bohemian Rhapsody." **CATALOG CHOICE:** *Sheer Heart Attack*. **NEXT STOP:** Sweet: *Desolation Boulevard*.

An Early Interplanetary Voyage of the Arkestra

Jazz in Silhouette

Sun Ra and His Arkestra

Of all the earthlings bitten by the space exploration bug that took hold in the late 1950s, the bandleader and pianist Sun Ra was the trippiest. He claimed to have been born on Saturn (records for Herman "Sonny" Blount list his place of birth as Birmingham, Alabama, in 1914), and over more than fifty full-length recordings, developed a cosmic philosophy in which jazz helps to link scattered notions about paranormal phenomena, the wonders of ancient Egypt, and astral mumbo jumbo (in one chant, the band repeatedly proclaims: "We travel the spaceways, from planet to planet"). The Arkestra was Sun Ra's sound source and traveling vessel; when really flying, as

Sun Ra takes his name from Ra, the Egyptian god of the sun.

on this 1958 recording, the group could send elements of jazz hurtling at warp speed toward several possible futures.

Sun Ra migrated quite a bit in search of ideal conditions for his exploits. The pianist, who'd been part of Fletcher Henderson's bands in the 1940s (see p. 354), formed the Arkestra in the mid-'50s, in Chicago; he moved to New York in 1961, and then to Philadelphia in 1970. At each stop, the sound of the band changed at least a little. The early recordings are, predictably, the most conventional; later the band went much further out. *Jazz in Silhouette*, from the Chicago period, contains straight-up bebop blues (Ra's "Blues at Midnight") and sadistically tricky ensemble lines ("Enlightenment") as well as a solemn processional, "Ancient Aiethopia,"

with vague Middle Eastern overtones.

No single record can capture the full greatness of the Sun Ra Arkestra. Still, of the early sides, this one offers heated solo outbursts and amazing two- and three-way conversations betweem soloists. It catches the band swinging hard and already thinking about jazz in futuristic ways. To hear another peak of Ra and the Arkestra check out the droning, chanting *Space Is the Place*, one of the epic journeys from the early '70s. Many of the records the group made on Ra's Saturn label and other small imprints have been rereleased; the best advice for those curious about this iconoclast is to try several things. Just don't forget to buckle your seat belt: With Ra, turbulence can occur at any moment.

GENRE: 🎵 Jazz. **RELEASED:** 1958, Saturn. (Reissued 1991, Evidence.) **KEY TRACKS:** "Enlightenment," "Saturn," "Ancient Aiethopia," "Hours After," "Blues at Midnight." **CATALOG CHOICES:** *Bad and Beautiful/We Travel the Spaceways; Fate in a Pleasant Mood/When Sun Comes Out.* **NEXT STOP:** Captain Beefheart and His Magic Band: *Safe as Milk.* **AFTER THAT:** Cedric Im Brooks: *Cedric Im Brooks and the Light of Saba.*

Pulling an All-Nighter, Old-School Style

All-Night Vigil, Op. 37

Sergey Rachmaninoff

Estonian Philharmonic Chamber Choir (Paul Hillier, cond.)

ith this piece for unaccompanied chorus, composer and pianist Sergey Rachmaninoff transformed centuries-old chants from the Russian Orthodox Church service into bold (and timeless) spirit music.

It was written in 1914, during the years of the Great War and just before the Russian Revolution of 1917, a period of major upheaval in Russia and throughout the world. Though he was in what historians now see as his composing prime, Rachmaninoff spent much of that year touring as a performer. Some suggest that the *All-Night Vigil* was his response to the hardships of war, his way of seeking solace in chaotic times.

Each of Rachmaninoff's legendarily large hands covered the interval of a thirteenth on the piano.

The piece is, to be sure, far more contemplative than the great Russian's other works from around the same time. For ten of the piece's fifteen sections, Rachmaninoff (1873–1943) starts with the liturgical chants that underpin the Orthodox service; the other five follow chant structure more loosely, with orchestral shadings and moments when the voices approximate bells or trumpets. Then, breaking with church style, he uses multiple layers of harmony to enhance the fervent emotional tones. Rachmaninoff created shapely melody lines that resemble liturgical chant and at the same time reach well outside the rigid prescriptions of church music. Listen for the passages for tenor and mezzo-soprano soloist, which are saturated with a rhapsodic lyricism.

There is something almost mystical about Paul Hillier's version of the *All-Night Vigil*. Hillier emphasizes the inward turn of the piece, and under his direction the ensemble sings in a way that's gently stirring. Though the singers recognize the "hybrid" nature of Rachmaninoff's composition, they treat it as spiritual music, reflecting both the influence of the Lutheran church and the ancient pagan beliefs that still prevail in modern Estonian society. This is true of the gilded sopranos and the quintessential Russian basses; to experience the bone-rattling power of low notes, check the Nunc Dimittis, which shows off the rich hues of this Estonian choir. They're deep. Like the work itself.

GENRE: 🎼 Classical. RELEASED: 2006, Harmonia Mundi. KEY TRACKS: "Lord, Now Lettest Thou," "O Gentle Light," "The Six Psalms," "My Soul Magnifies the Lord." CATALOG CHOICE: *The Bells/Symphonic Dances,* Russian State Symphony Orchestra (Valery Polyansky, cond.). NEXT STOP: Giuseppe Verdi: *Requiem* (see p. 832).

The Composer as Performer

His Complete Recordings

Sergey Rachmaninoff

S ergey Rachmaninoff wrote most of his major works for piano before fleeing the Russian Revolution in 1917, and devoted much of his energy after immigrating to the U.S. to performing them. This was out of necessity:

He had to earn a living somehow, and though his melancholic rhapsodies (particularly the Second Piano Concerto) were beloved, his place in the pantheon was anything but assured. So he barnstormed, playing not just in New York and the expected cultural capitals, but also in smaller cities across the country. He became, quietly, an evangelist for his compositions.

The tall, dour-looking Russian had this much going for him: He was a monster at the piano. Rachmaninoff was revered by world-class pianists, like Arthur Rubinstein, as a godlike figure able to transport listeners into the "heart" of a piece, whether or not he wrote it. This ten-disc set was recorded between 1925 and 1942, during the age of 78-RPM (rarely does a selection last more than four minutes). It catches Rachmaninoff grappling with Chopin, Beethoven, and others in a muscular and completely authoritative way, as though he's appraising these giants at eye level, as a peer and not a worshipful student. That perspective makes a difference: Rachmaninoff organizes the main threads of Beethoven's Sonata No. 3, Op. 30, into stupendous legato lines that leave room for Fritz Kreisler's equally smooth violin. Together they lift a pretty piece into the realm of a rare delicacy. Rachmaninoff did this "essentializing" thing when he performed solo as well—check his utterly tempoless reading of Chopin's Nocturne No. 2, Op. 9, another triumph of slowness and patience. Playing Schumann's "Carnival," Rachmaninoff makes sure that his listener knows exactly when the piece is heading toward its culminating point.

Rachmaninoff's own works are as melodically rich as those he interpreted; though classical music has had its share of composers who performed (Stravinsky is another), very few have been able to shine light on the intricacies of their compositions the way Rachmaninoff does here.

These recordings are not noted for their digital clarity, but they're remarkably listenable given their age. Those seeking a less exhaustive dose of Rachmaninoff might seek out the four concertos with the Philadelphia Orchestra represented here, which are also sold separately, or Vladimir Horowitz's rightly revered 1951 recording of Concerto No. 3, which exposes more popular latter-day readings of the piece—like, oh, David Helfgott's version in *Shine*—as extremely shallow.

GENRE: 🎼 Classical. **RELEASED:** 2006, RCA. **KEY TRACKS:** Concerto No. 2. Concerto No. 3. Symphony No. 3. **ANOTHER INTERPRETATION:** *Horowitz Plays Rachmaninoff: Concerto No. 3, Sonata No. 2,* RCA Victor Symphony (Fritz Reiner, cond.). **CATALOG CHOICE:** *Symphonic Dances,* Minnesota Orchestra (Eiji Oue, cond.). **NEXT STOP:** Robert Schumann: *Piano Concerto,* Sviatoslav Richter.

"For a Minute There, I Lost Myself"

OK Computer

Radiohead

Maybe Radiohead had a crystal ball when, back in 1996, it began developing this dystopian essay on the darker implications of technology. At the time, there wasn't much public awareness about the sinister

applications of data mining. The big identity theft scares were just beginning. The terrorist attacks of 9/11 hadn't happened, so it was well before the Bush administration's secret program of high-tech surveillance on its citizens.

Yet oozing through the substrata of "Let Down" and "Paranoid Android" and other fragile compositions is a vague sense of dread, and a touch of Big Brother foreboding that bears strong resemblance to the constant disquiet of life on Security Level Orange, post-9/11. Casting himself as a dazed character from a Camus play, singer and lyricist Thom Yorke ponders what it means to be plugged in and at the same time profoundly disconnected. Everywhere he turns, he confronts suspicion and mistrust, as well as new demands on his fast-withering soul. When, on the grand processional that is the album's most dramatic moment, he bumps into the "Karma Police," he's given the existential rough-up, along with a warning: "This is what you get when you mess with us."

OK *Computer* reached #1 on the U.K. albums chart.

OK Computer is notable for more than its prescient theme. Throughout, the instrumentalists, particularly guitarist Jonny Greenwood, find jarring ways to underscore the lyrics—on "Exit Music (for a Film)" and others, the intricately layered electric guitars multiply the horror inside Yorke's voice—and head—by a factor of ten. With subsequent albums, the British five-piece has refined and expanded this basic approach; the troubled elegies of *Kid A*, the snarling *Hail to the Thief*, and the austere meditations of *In Rainbows* continue the journey of the lost soul who made his debut on the 1993 single "Creep." Awesome listening experiences all, they map a riveting and unexpectedly coherent journey, a progression through various states of darkness. If most rock is an expression of limitless possibility, Radiohead's oeuvre is the sinister flip side, a tour of the soul-sucking psychic traps waiting just ahead on the hi-def digital horizon.

GENRE: 🎸 Rock. **RELEASED:** 1997, Capitol. **KEY TRACKS:** "Paranoid Android," "Karma Police." **CATALOG CHOICES:** *Kid A; In Rainbows.* **NEXT STOP:** Pink Floyd: *The Wall.* **AFTER THAT:** Coldplay: *Parachutes.*

The Mother of the Blues at Her Best

Ma Rainey's Black Bottom

Ma Rainey

Ma Rainey comes through louder and clearer than any other blues singer of the 1920s. Though her recordings have the staticky veneer that plagues everything from the era, Rainey somehow pierces the noise.

A veteran who'd been belting for more than twenty years before her voice was captured for posterity, she dispenses risqué notions and wronged-woman blues with wry and worldly inflections, a mixture of growls and shouts that just about everyone after her copied.

Rainey (1886–1939) matters because she was among the first blues artists to develop more than a regional following: Through grueling roadwork as a part of circuses and minstrel shows, she and her husband—who billed themselves as the "Assassinators of the Blues"—became well-known performers throughout the South. This made Ma Rainey a powerful influence: Bessie Smith, the so-called Queen of the Blues, heard (and openly imitated) Rainey. (According to one legend, Smith took lessons from her.)

Rainey is also significant because of the joy on display here—she's one of the few early recording artists whose personality comes through. Where others froze when the primitive machines started up, she camped and hollered the same way she would in a nightclub. Her tunes recorded between 1924 and 1928 are distinguished by a cheeky irreverence and great spirit. Her big voice bellowing, she tells stories about those crazy men who've let her down, enjoys the double-entendre talk about her "Black Bottom"—which,

Ma Rainey (center) was billed as the Mother of the Blues.

of course, is a dance. Her delight is more than contagious—it's a part of the animating force

handed down through generations as the blues.

GENRE: 🎵 Blues.
RELEASED: 1975, Yazoo.
KEY TRACKS: "Ma Rainey's Black Bottom," "Don't Fish in My Sea," "Stack O'Lee Blues." **CATALOG CHOICE:** *Complete Recorded Works,* Vol. 4. **NEXT STOP:** Bessie Smith: *The Essential Bessie Smith* (see p. 715). **AFTER THAT:** Ida Cox (with Coleman Hawkins): *Blues for Rampart Street.*

The First Flicker of Raitt Greatness

Give It Up

Bonnie Raitt

All the qualities that made Bonnie Raitt's *Nick of Time* (1989) a multi-Grammy-winning smash hit—the sneaky slide-guitar asides, the confiding relationship odes, the stoic, slightly troubled vocals—are present, in more concentrated form, on her second album, *Give It Up* (1972).

Both offer joyful, effortless-sounding pop songs and uncommonly touching ballads—the last song on *Give It Up*, the plaintive "Love Has No Pride," has been a cornerstone of Raitt's live shows ever since. And both depend on Raitt's deeply felt yet pretension-free vocals—she's part wise blues

In 2000, Raitt was inducted into the Rock and Roll Hall of Fame.

belter and part '70s earth mama, with a pinch of Ma Rainey and a dash of Janis Joplin.

But there's a key difference between the works, and it has to do with recording methodology: *Nick of Time* was made in the Age of Overdubs, when record makers with

substantial budgets hunkered down for months in the studio, assembling songs by layering instruments one atop another. It's unassailably polished, if a tad numb-sounding when compared with the loose *Give It Up*, which was made with a small group of musicians huddled together in pursuit of a groove, in real time.

Here's Bonnie Raitt before stardom came calling, when she could cut loose with a mean and greasy rhythm section, adding little quips of tasty guitar to the proceedings. Her spare, barbed-wire lines sit perfectly inside the beat, coaxing out greatness from all around her. Beneath Raitt's words, there's a rich parallel musical dialogue under way, lively exchanges of little ideas and happy accidents that demonstrate what can happen when everyone locks into the same musical frequency in the same moment. It's not an exotic approach—thousands of records share the *Give It Up* give-and-take—but in the age of music assembled on computers, it sure can feel that way.

GENRE: 🎸 Rock. **RELEASED:** 1972, Warner Bros. **KEY TRACKS:** "Love Me like a Man," "Give It Up or Let Me Go," "Too Long at the Fair," "Love Has No Pride." **CATALOG CHOICES:** *Green Light; Nick of Time.* **NEXT STOP:** J.J. Cale: *Troubadour.* **AFTER THAT:** Shelby Lynne: *I Am Shelby Lynne.*

A Luscious Bonbon of French Baroque

Platée

Jean-Philippe Rameau
Opéra National de Paris (Marc Minkowski, cond.)

As recently as the 1960s, Jean-Philippe Rameau (1683–1764) was regarded as a music theorist who wrote important books on harmony and happened to compose, often for harpsichord, on the side. Turns out that's not the whole story. This figure from the far reaches of music history has attracted new interest in the last decade or so, as musicians have discovered that some of his works—including this comic opera—are easily as creative (and sometimes much bolder) than those of Charpentier, Lully, and other big names of French baroque.

A fable about an ugly swamp creature, *Platée* was written midway through Rameau's opera career, and premiered in 1749. It borrows devices from his primary operatic forms (opera ballet and lyric tragedy) without fully conforming to either. The lead, Platée, is a she—a tenor in drag, sung here by Paul Agnew—who doesn't know how ugly she is. On this DVD shot live in Paris in 2004, the creature is convincingly hideous, in an Evil Muppet way. Much of the action and the dancing plays up the comic aspects of Platée's plight: Like countless characters from myths and fables, she longs for human contact yet has no idea of the effect her ghastly appearance has on others—in a sense, she's the opposite of the Little Mermaid.

The story, which plays out in three acts and a clever prologue, offers Rameau lots of chances to flaunt the prevailing musical conventions of his day. At the same time he shows off his advanced notions of rhythm (which anticipate Hector Berlioz) and harmony (which, in the piece's calm moments, glance toward Debussy-style impressionism). From the first forward-charging ascending lines, Rameau gives the characters melodies that have palpable heat and considerable emotional energy. These themes are so powerful they transcend their historical context—when you hear this surging yet easygoing music, you don't immediately think of the baroque, with its distanced, fussy formality. You just think "beautiful music."

GENRE: 🎭 Opera. **RELEASED:** 2004, Kultur DVD. **KEY TRACKS:** Prologue; Act 1: "Que ce séjour est agréable"; Act 2: "Air pour les fous gais et tristes"; Act 3: "Amour, amour." **CATALOG CHOICE:** *Harpsichord Music,* Vol. 1, Gilbert Rowland. **NEXT STOP:** Marc-Antoine Charpentier: *Médée* (see p. 158).

The First Great Blast of Punk

Ramones

Ramones

Made for $6,000 by a group of misfit kids from Queens who could barely play their instruments, *Ramones* is the first, best, and most unlikely manifesto of punk rock. It's also a kind of antistandard, the record that

decimates all the academic theorizing that gathered around punk as cultural watershed. Later punk became a "movement," a study in stance and calculation that could be endlessly reappropriated. But in 1976, when the four leather-jacket-wearing Ramones regularly terrorized New York's CBGBs with twenty-minute shows, punk was Joey Ramone (1951–2001) uttering the immortal words "Now I wanna sniff some glue" in a dire monotone.

The Ramones toured practically nonstop for 22 years, performing 2,263 concerts.

Ramones is cheap thrills sped up to breakneck speed and played as though the four musicians (who, in a marketing ploy, each took the last name Ramone even though they were not related) were racing to see who could finish first. Most of the songs depend on three chords, and last less than two minutes—the basic Ramones strategy is run, gun, and done. In an interview in *Please Kill Me*, an oral history of punk, bassist Dee Dee Ramone (1952–2002) recalls that when the band began, the musicians "didn't know how or what to play. We'd try some Bay City Rollers and we absolutely couldn't do that. We didn't know how. So we just started writing our own stuff and put it together the best we could."

The songs the Ramones concocted for this album (and subsequent ones) work because they're so simple. Anyone could play them—even though the Ramones had a relent-

less energy that was hard to duplicate. The Everyman quality proved critical to the spread of punk: Two of the significant U.K. punk bands, the Clash (see p. 172) and the Damned, began performing within days after seeing the Ramones' London debut, which happened on July 4, 1976.

The Ramones' punk was a spastic lurch, a homemade contraption that seemed at any minute on the verge of spinning out of control. Yet unlike many who followed in their footsteps, the Ramones were inclined to embrace (and, in their own skronky way, celebrate) the joyous touchstones of early rock—running through "I Wanna Be Your Boyfriend," "Judy Is a Punk," and (later) "Rockaway Beach" is an echo of the crazed-surfer-kid abandon of the 1950s. But it's just an echo: By the time the Ramones are finished, they've mangled the optimism of early rock into jaundiced, diffident, maniacal rallying cries of the disaffected that could only have risen from the post-Watergate 1970s.

GENRE: 🎸 Rock. **RELEASED:** 1976, Sire. (Reissued 2008, Rhino.) **KEY TRACKS:** "Now I Wanna Sniff Some Glue," "53rd and 3rd," "Blitzkrieg Bop." **CATALOG CHOICE:** *Rocket to Russia.* **NEXT STOP:** Gang of Four: *Entertainment!* (see p. 298). **AFTER THAT:** Patti Smith: *Horses* (see p. 719).

The One (and Only) Record from a Visionary

Willis Alan Ramsey

Willis Alan Ramsey

This, the lone album by enigmatic Texas singer-songwriter Willis Alan Ramsey, gave the world one of the most poignant songs ever written about Woody Guthrie (the pedal-steel drenched "Boy from Oklahoma") as well as "Muskrat Love," the whimsical hit for the soft-rock group the Captain and Tennille (here titled "Muskrat Candlelight"). That spread tells something about the Alabama-born tunesmith, whose works have been memorably covered by Jimmy Buffett ("The Ballad of Spider John") and Waylon Jennings ("Satin Sheets"). A storyteller with a quick wit and a penchant for catchy melodies, Ramsey helped develop the sound and the sensibility of "progressive" or "alternative" country associated with everyone from Lyle Lovett to Son Volt. And then he went underground.

Lyle Lovett called this "one of the greatest records of all time."

Recorded quickly for a small label in 1972, Ramsey's debut has acquired mythic status over the years, in part because he's been so stingy with his work. He cowrote a few songs with Lovett in the 1990s, but has yet to release a follow-up. One website claims he moved to the British isles to study Celtic balladry.

The genius of *Willis Alan Ramsey* lies in his vocals. Ramsey's songs are salt-of-the-earth stuff, with zero pretension—no cornpone wizardry needed. Ramsey sings with a slightly bemused affect, a raconteur who counts on his slight drawl to keep his story at least plausible. This unassuming delivery makes you want to follow Ramsey's characters around and be there when the title character of "Watermelon Man," who's been awaiting the arrival of the sweet fruit for months, gets that first juicy bite.

GENRE: ⏺ Country. **RELEASED:** 1972, Shelter. (Reissued 1999, Koch.) **KEY TRACKS:** "Boy from Oklahoma," "Muskrat Candlelight." **NEXT STOP:** Townes Van Zandt: *Live at the Old Quarter* (see p. 801).

Getting Down . . .

Below the Bassline

Ernest Ranglin

This is a gathering of journeymen who, over several decades, have been present at the creation of world-altering groove music. The leader, guitarist Ernest Ranglin, developed the syncopated style of ska and reggae guitar, and participated in literally hundreds of important records from Jamaica, including early works by Bob Marley (to whom he taught guitar) and Toots and the Maytals. Pianist Monty Alexander, also from Jamaica, earned his reputation mostly in jazz, recording frequently with alums from Oscar Peterson's groups. Saxophonist Roland Alphonso is known for his pioneering ska band the Skatalites. Drummer Idris Muhammad provided the lean and mean pulse that helped define soul-jazz; his records for the CTI label in the '70s showed many jazz musicians how to credibly interpret funk.

Ranglin played ukulele as a child.

Ranglin hired these musicians (along with young bassist Ira Coleman and keyboardist Gary Mayone) to help him execute a hybrid of reggae and jazz. Such a stylistic merger might seem far-fetched on paper, but as practiced by these veterans, it becomes the most natural combination in the world—a thick trance-like groove with lots of air around it, the perfect setting for interpreting the Abyssinians' prayerful "Satta Massagana" and the Toots Hibbert early hit "54-46 (Was My Number)."

Ranglin's gentle, understated presence sets the tone: Everything he plays arrives a shade behind the beat, and like a Caribbean Wes Montgomery, he quickly sends his melodies soaring, then plucks beautiful octaves and unlikely chords out of thin air. The languidness doesn't equal sleepiness, however: Just when he seems to have settled into a copacetic vibe, Ranglin will slip in a frighteningly fast how'd-he-do-that? phrase, like he's checking to see if people are paying attention. Those momentary flights are as close as these groove masters get to flexing their muscles; hearing them converse on classics of the roots reggae repertoire is like getting reacquainted with a long lost friend who's as enthusiastic as you remember, and still bursting with new ideas.

GENRES: 🌐 World/Jamaica 🅙 Jazz. **RELEASED:** 1996, Island. **KEY TRACKS:** "King Tubby Meets the Rockers," "Satta Massagana," "54-46 (Was My Number)." **CATALOG CHOICE:** *Memories of Barber Mack.* **NEXT STOP:** Idris Muhammad: *House of the Rising Sun.* **AFTER THAT:** Bheki Mseleku: *Beauty of Sunrise.*

A Double Shot of Operatic Ravel

L'heure espagnole
L'enfant et les sortilèges

Maurice Ravel

Orchestre National de la R.T.F., Berlin Philharmonic and Berlin Radio Symphony and various soloists (Lorin Maazel, cond.)

Maurice Ravel, master orchestrator, wrote two operas in his life—one as a relatively young man still developing his signature (*L'heure espagnole*, which premiered in 1911), the other (*L'enfant et les sortilèges*), which debuted in 1926 when he was at the peak of his powers, in control of unconventional textures and daring colorations.

Both are enormously entertaining works, particularly as rendered by Lorin Maazel on this definitive two-disc set, which was recorded in 1958 and 1965 and features a who's who of French opera talent of the 1960s—Jane Berbié, Jean Giraudeau, Gabriel Bacquier. Hewing to French opera tradition, these singers value a precise rendering of text over subtleties of tone. They execute some of the more outlandish touches, like the Four Freshman–ish vocal harmonies near the climax of *L'heure espagnole*, with exaggerated vivacity.

The early opera is a lusty farce. It follows a woman who's desperate to have an extramarital dalliance during the one hour of the week her clockmaker husband is out adjusting the village clocks. Various suitors find themselves hidden inside grandfather clocks and subjected to all sorts of comic trials; in the end, the workman hauling the clocks gets the girl. Ravel (1875–1937) matches the lightheartedness of the story with equally capricious, furtive music that suggests perpetually thwarted lust.

L'enfant et les sortilèges (The Child and the Spells) is much more fantastical—its improbable dialogues and surreal pastiches show how Ravel's palette expanded over the years. The story of a naughty child who is suddenly terrorized by the household objects he's abused, this opera begins with a hypnotic woodwind-and-upper-strings figure that suggests the motion of a wobbling top. The libretto, by celebrated author Colette, takes the young boy through all sorts of phantasmagoria (including a haunting riff on multiplication tables) before he acquires the sensitivity of a grown-up. Among the most intense scenes is an exchange between an English coffee mug and a Chinese teacup, in which stereotypical national traits balloon into magnificent and improbable aural fantasias. Though it can be effectively staged, this is one of those imagistic works that's actually more powerful when the visuals are left to the imagination.

GENRE: 🎭 Opera. **RELEASED:** 1988, Deutsche Grammophon. **KEY TRACKS:** *L'heure*: Scene 1: "Señor Torquemada"; Scene 21: "Un financier." *L'enfant:* "Ding Ding Ding Ding," "How's Your Mug?" **CATALOG CHOICE:** *Daphnis et Chloë*, Suite No. 2, St. Louis Symphony Orchestra (Leonard Slatkin, cond.). **NEXT STOP:** Cecilia Bartoli: *Chant d'Amour.* **AFTER THAT:** Frederick Delius: *Orchestral Works*, BBC Symphony (Sir Andrew Davis, cond.).

More than Just Crowd Pleasers

Boléro, La mer, Pictures at an Exhibition

Maurice Ravel, Claude Debussy, Modest Mussorgsky

Berlin Philharmonic (Herbert von Karajan, cond.)

e come to music to "see" pictures the human hand can never paint, vistas no camera can capture. The composers represented here, on this monster of a symphonic disc, were experts at this: Press play, close your eyes, and prepare for three strikingly different visual experiences.

French composer Claude Debussy (1862–1918) begins with the same tools that everyone since Mozart used, and then hangs a big left turn. In his music, the harmonic schemes that underpin centuries of Western composition are gently uprooted or suspended. His chords don't pull toward an inevitable orderly resolution—they just sit there and shimmer, inviting contemplation. This unorthodox approach to harmony defines Debussy's three-part seascape *La mer*, which is often cited as a high point of impressionism, the style that borrowed its aesthetic from Monet and other painters of the late nineteenth century. In Debussy's version, vast oceanic surges substitute for formal melodic declarations, and slow-moving orchestral swells serve as the piece's underlying organization. It's a journey unlike any other in music.

The same can be said for *Pictures at an Exhibition*, the unusual "collaboration" between Russian composer Modest Mussorgsky (1839–1881) and Frenchman Maurice Ravel. Mussorgsky wrote the work, a tribute to painter Victor Hartmann, for piano in 1874; Ravel orchestrated it in 1922, after peering deeply into Mussorgsky's brief, pastiche-like scenes. Ravel understands the Russian's vocabulary—and Hartmann's vocabulary, as well. The music moves along briskly, encompassing episodes of childlike playfulness ("The Gnome") and also breathtaking grandiosity—the final picture, "The Great Gate of Kiev," finds Ravel using widely spaced block-style chords to bolster the imposing Russian theme.

Ravel himself was capable of wild effects, devices that only reveal their genius after they've been playing for a while. So it is with *Boléro*, a perpetually unraveling study that became a hit of sorts after it was used in the movie *10* (1979) to accompany scenes of bikini-clad Bo Derek cavorting on a beach. Ravel intended it as a ballet; its rhythm is a muted march-like processional that can, if played with the sense of deliberation von Karajan employs here, suggest slow motion. The theme wanders, yet has its own logic—it's like an elaborate musical labyrinth. In some orchestral pieces, this type of repetition makes the theme more familiar. Not in *Boléro*: Thanks to Ravel's unusual scoring and the circular structure, the melody becomes more elusive as the piece progresses. In this way, *Boléro* resembles great works of visual art: Look once and you think you "get" it. Look again, and you realize how little of it you actually took in.

GENRE: 🎷 Classical. **RELEASED:** 1966, Deutsche Grammophon. (Reissued 1996.) **KEY TRACKS:** *La Mer*: second movement. *Pictures at an Exhibition*: "The Great Gate of Kiev." *Boléro*. **NEXT STOP:** Fireballet: *Night on Bald Mountain*.

Flowers Blooming Out of Chairs

Complete Works for Piano

Maurice Ravel
Alexandre Tharaud

In a letter to his friend Louis Lalay, French composer Claude Debussy acknowledged that his rival impressionist Maurice Ravel was extraordinarily gifted, then wrote: "What annoys me is the attitude he adopts of being a 'conjurer' . . . casting spells and making flowers burst out of chairs. . . . The trouble is, a conjuring trick always has to have a build-up, and after you've seen it once, you're no longer astonished."

Accurate description or jealousy? The Ravel piano works, played with extraordinary sensitivity by French pianist Alexandre Tharaud, may help with an appraisal of this most elusive genius. Often, when a composer offers keyboard versions of orchestral pieces, the reductions are obvious—hollow shells waiting for the muscle (and the colors) of an orchestra to complete them. That's not the case with Ravel: His writing for piano is so vivid, and so unlike anything else in music, that it often reveals more than the scored versions. Consider the climax of "Ondine," the first movement of "Gaspard de la nuit": Tharaud has been leaving the theme to hang, and nearly drift away, in the middle of the piano. At about five minutes and forty-five seconds, there's a long pause, longer than necessary. Then comes what we expect—the crashing chord. And then comes something we don't expect: Tharaud gradually slows the theme to a crawl. He plays

Ravel's estate reportedly earns more royalties than that of any other French composer.

like he's pulling apart an interlocked puzzle, sometimes following a tempo and sometimes just hesitating to savor a pearly single note.

This two-disc set collects everything Ravel wrote for piano, as well as pieces he wrote on the piano and later worked up for orchestra. Almost everything is sublime. Tharaud plays the suite of dances, "Valses nobles et sentimentales," with many changes of tempo and meter, as though calling attention to facets of Ravel's writing that the orchestras plow right over. Equally revealing is his reading of the famous "Pavanne for a Dead Princess," a solemn, stoic tune that might as well be the dictionary definition of elegiac music. There are no gimmicks, no conjuring tricks. It's just one unbroken sob of a melody, and that's all Ravel needs to cast a spell.

GENRE: 🎸 Classical. **RELEASED:** 2003, Harmonia Mundi. **KEY MOMENTS:** "Gaspard de la nuit," "Sonatine," "Pavanne for a Dead Princess." **CATALOG CHOICE:** *La valse,* Berlin Philharmonic (Pierre Boulez, cond.). **NEXT STOP:** Claude Debussy: *La mer* (see p. 634).

He Doesn't Just Sing Soul, He Redefines It Right Here

Otis Blue

Otis Redding

The catchall term "soul" means different things to different people. Otis Redding, everyone can agree on. The most emotional singer ever to utter the ubiquitous plea, "Can I get a witness?," Redding (1941–1967) came along after Ray Charles and Sam Cooke had established the basic perimeters of soul music; to their outlines he added a sense of happening-this-instant urgency. The life problems in his songs are not idle abstract ones; they are wounds and sores that need attention *right now.* When he sings the Cooke prayer "A Change Is Gonna Come," Redding replaces the idealism of the original with a desire so deep it sounds like no amount of radical change will satisfy it.

Otis Blue is Redding's singing clinic, a compendium of soul devices nobody used more persuasively. It features several Redding originals—including the hot-wired "Respect," the number 1 hit for Aretha Franklin—as well as astonishingly individual interpretations of songs then recent to the charts. "My Girl," the 1965 Temptations hit written by Smokey Robinson, is typically redrawn: Though he follows the melody, Redding heats up the opening line with a fast vibrato, the first signal that we're not in Motown anymore. After that, on the chorus, Redding drops in slight inflections and raw asides that express reverence for womanly loveliness on a level far deeper than the original. He does the same thing with Solomon Burke's "Down in the Valley" and three songs associated with Cooke—"A Change Is

In 1994 Redding was inducted into the Songwriters Hall of Fame.

Gonna Come," "Shake," and "Wonderful World." Perhaps the most eyebrow-raising lunge is Redding's version of "(I Can't Get No) Satisfaction," in which he schools the Rolling Stones in the fine art of expressing frustration.

Redding died in a plane crash in December 1967, shortly after recording the mournful "(Sittin' on) the Dock of the Bay," a song cowritten with guitarist Steve Cropper that became his biggest hit. The corresponding album, released in early 1968, is not quite the all-stops-out Redding showcase that this one is, but it's a marvel all the same.

GENRE: 🎵 R&B. **RELEASED:** 1965, Atco. **KEY TRACKS:** "Ole Man Trouble," "Respect," "A Change Is Gonna Come," "Shake." **CATALOG CHOICES:** *Live at the Whiskey-A-Go-Go; The Dock of the Bay.* **NEXT STOP:** Solomon Burke: *Rock 'n' Soul.* **AFTER THAT:** Wilson Pickett: *The Exciting Wilson Pickett* (see p. 600).

The Big Boss Man of the Blues

The Very Best of Jimmy Reed

Jimmy Reed

Jimmy Reed (1925–1976) turns up on the Rock and Roll Hall of Fame's list of 500 Songs That Shaped Rock and Roll—for his loping, swaggering 1960 hit "Big Boss Man." But the illiterate Mississippi-born bluesman, who

got his break in Chicago in the early 1950s, probably deserves to be there for "Honest I Do," which was one of the first tunes the Rolling Stones ever recorded. Or for "I Ain't Got You," a hit for the Yardbirds. Or for "Baby What You Want Me to Do," a sexy slow strut that's been covered by countless acts, including Elvis Presley and Neil Young.

Reed's gut-level anthems feel eternal; it's hard to imagine the blues without them. Their simplicity made it easy for Reed, who was a notorious alcoholic, to remember the words even when he was half crazed. It also makes them perfect for rock and roll: Billy Vera, the rock songwriter and historian, once noted that "anybody with a range of more than six notes could sing Jimmy's tunes."

Still, Reed's original versions have something extra—a smooth sense of flow, a buoyant and irrepressible rhythm. Indeed, none of the covers completely captures the effortless swing that Reed and his longtime rhythm guitarist (and secret weapon) Eddie Taylor made a signature—if other bluesmen clomped around, Reed and Taylor moved in a perpetual slink, like tomcats prowling. This anthology offers a healthy sampling of Reed's great original tunes and a few lesser-known works, like the instrumental "Odds and Ends." Listen closely, because on several of the tracks,

Reed had 14 singles near the top of the *Billboard* R&B charts during his career.

it's possible to hear Reed's wife, Mary "Mama" Reed, singing gently along, keeping her often-inebriated man on the beat. From time to time, she actually whispers the words he's supposed to sing next. That's true love right there.

GENRE: 🔵 Blues. **RELEASED:** 2000, Rhino. **KEY TRACKS:** "Baby What You Want Me to Do," "Bright Lights Big City," "Shame, Shame, Shame," "I Ain't Got You." **CATALOG CHOICE:** *Live at Carnegie Hall.* **NEXT STOP:** Otis Rush: *The Classic Cobra Recordings* (see p. 664). **AFTER THAT:** Peter Green: *Man of the World.*

A Sociology in Sound

New York

Lou Reed

Nobody in rock romanticizes the flinty, unsettled, perpetually on-edge dynamic of New York City quite the way Lou Reed does. The guitarist, poet, and singer—who as architect of the Velvet Underground

(see p. 830) influenced generations of musicians—treats the city not just as an endless source of pitiable characters, but a place where great minds and lunatics are neighbors. His wide-eyed *Transformer* (1972) paints a debauched insider's portrait of the World of Warhol that was then happening downtown; as he follows drag queens and art savants through assorted passion plays, Reed arrives at his biggest hit ("Walk on the Wild Side") and

In the liner notes to this album, Reed instructs the listener to hear *New York* in one sitting, "as though it were a book or a movie."

one of his most enduring songs ("Satellite of Love").

To fully get Reed, start with *Transformer* (well, at least a chunk of it; like many of Reed's projects, it is erratic), then move to his most consistent work, *New York* (1989), which Reed once described as "as good as I get." On this talky, character-filled record, he returns to the sociology of *Transformer* and subsequent albums, updating it to reflect the brutality of the age of AIDS.

(One lament, "Halloween Parade," plays like a shell-shocked roll call of the downtown departed, and the survivors who grieve for them.) The songs are caustic, informed by a metro columnist's sense of the interconnectedness of the city: When, on "Dirty Blvd.," Reed tells of people who've fallen through the social safety net and turned to prostitution, he also looks at the well-heeled customers whose lust fuels this particular economy. His diatribe about political correctness, "Good Evening Mr. Waldheim," castigates the pope, Jesse Jackson, and others who take cover behind rhetorical phrases like "common ground."

The pictures Reed paints here are often bleak, and it's a measure of his artistry that New York isn't a total downer—there is, amazingly, a sense of hope glimmering through, and at times great humor. His inventory of souls who are about to snap under the pressure, "Sick of You," contains this choice couplet:

"The ozone layer has no ozone anymore, and you're gonna leave me for the guy next door? I'm sick of you."

Reed and his accomplices seize on these sparks—this band delivers fury on demand, and uses it to bolster music that's agitated one minute and elegiac the next. Howling at the limousine class about tragedies happening just blocks away, Reed bears witness to the indifference and uncaring running rampant in his beloved city, snapping eye-opening candids at a moment when New York was particularly unfeeling, and hard to love.

GENRE: 🎸 Rock. **RELEASED:** 1989, Sire. **KEY TRACKS:** "Romeo Had Juliette," "Halloween Parade," "Sick of You," "Busload of Faith." **CATALOG CHOICES:** *Transformer; Rock 'n' Roll Animal; Songs for Drella* (with John Cale). **NEXT STOP:** Mott the Hoople: *Mott.* **AFTER THAT:** New York Dolls: *New York Dolls.*

The How and Why of Greatness

Como & porque

Elis Regina

E lis Regina arrived at the first ever Brazilian Popular Music Festival in 1965 as a new sensation, the winner of a televised song competition. She'd just begun collaborating with composers Baden Powell, Caetano Veloso,

and others affiliated with what became the Musica Popular Brasileira movement. By the end of her performance of Edu Lobo's "Arrastão," Regina had tears streaming down her cheeks, her arms held out in a crucifix position—a not-so-subtle comment on Brazil's military dictatorship. That's all it took to propel her to stardom.

Regina was showbiz and art and political theater all

Regina was beloved for her interpretations of songs by Brazil's most renowned composers.

rolled up into one devastating, impossible-to-deny voice. She had the ability to tiptoe through bombast, and at times conveyed, through the glasslike transparency of her singing, much more than whatever the words said. In her life choices Regina (1945–1982) reminded some of Janis Joplin; she had a volatile temper, and like Joplin struggled with addiction—she died of an overdose weeks after marrying for the third time. (In Brazil her death registered as a national loss: Over 100,000 people turned up to mourn, and sing songs she made famous, at her memorial service, which was held in a soccer stadium.)

The spry *Como & porque* is among the best of a stack of classic albums—those smitten with Regina have a journey of at least a dozen truly sublime discoveries ahead. This one is notable for her completely untroubled singing and the similarly light arrangements, sometimes with just a trio and sometimes with sweeping orchestral backing. Handling tricky melodies with deceptive ease, Regina shows different aspects of her vocal personality on each one. She multitracks her voice

into a chorale for the cascading fantasy "Casa forte," demands answers to basic questions (like "How?" and "Why?") of a mystical deity on "Canto de ossanha," and breezes through Milton Nascimento's "Vera Cruz" as though surveying the breathtaking landscape from a low-flying plane.

GENRE: 🌐 World/Brazil. **RELEASED:** 1968, Verve/Universal. **KEY TRACKS:** "Vera Cruz," "Casa forte," "Watch What Happens." **CATALOG CHOICES:** *Aquarela do Brasil* (with Toots Thielemans); *Elis & Tom* (see p. 398). **NEXT STOP:** Gal Costa: *Gal Tropical*. **AFTER THAT:** Maria Rita (Regina's daughter): *Maria Rita*.

Trance Magic

Music for 18 Musicians

Steve Reich
Ensemble Modern

The rhythm that underpins *Music for 18 Musicians* approximates the nervous second hand of a ticking clock. It's played first by a constellation of mallet instruments, and once the relentlessly rigid *ditditditdit* pulse

is established, it becomes the canvas on which the rest of this fifty-eight-minute experience unfolds. Its tightly wound rhythm evokes the relentless pace of modern urban life, and also suggests something of its inhabitants—people who might be victims of a dehumanizing mechanization, or those who valiantly struggle against it.

Reich helped pioneer minimalism, a compositional style dominated by repetitive phrases arranged in a kind of grid and offset by slow-to-congeal, often hidden, melodies. In minimalism, the harmonic ripples are few and far between. And they don't always resemble those of most classical music—when chords change in Reich's works, it feels like a massive ocean liner is slowly changing course. Originally

a Cornell philosophy major, Reich became intrigued by tape manipulation while he was in college. His early works utilized multiple tape machines to explore the concept of "phasing," in which sounds that start out together gradually drift out of sync, forming unexpected polyrhythms. Soon after, Reich began to work with live instruments. He studied drumming in Africa, wrote a piece for four hands clapping, and eventually developed the juxtaposed patterns and crystalline sonic scheme (mallets against flute and bass clarinet, vocal percussion against strings against piano) of *Music for 18 Musicians*, which premiered in 1976.

Sometimes built around a single instrument and sometimes made of interlocking parts, the entrancing rhythm of *18 Musicians* is its primary attraction. But this pulse isn't the only thing happening. On top of it, Reich places incongruous, oddly placid textures—sustained notes that hover in a glacial choreography of slow-motion collisions. These give the piece its remarkable contours, moments when the relentless computer-code staccato is transformed by slight but unmistakable traces of messy humanity.

Reich intended the piece for his own ensemble, and never wrote an official note-by-note score. A graduate student at Cornell assembled one, and it served as the "text" for this version, which is more fanciful than Reich's initial ECM recording.

GENRE: 🎼 Classical. **RELEASED:** 1999, RCA Red Seal. **ANOTHER INTERPRETATION:** The 1976 ECM recording, with Reich's ensemble, was the first. **CATALOG CHOICE:** *Different Trains.* **NEXT STOP:** John Adams: *Hoodoo Zephyr.*

The Best from Europe's First Jazz Ensemble

The Classic Early Recordings in Chronological Order

Django Reinhardt

When the French writer Jean Cocteau said that "Legend is flesh on the bones of fiction," he might have been thinking about Django Reinhardt, the Gypsy guitarist who became the first European jazz musician of any consequence. From the time Reinhardt (1910–1953) was a child, stories swirled around him—about his amazing musical memory, his ability to play the banjo, his first instrument, with dizzying dexterity. Cocteau claimed to have "discovered" Reinhardt playing on the street, and described his sound as a "guitar which laughs and weeps, guitar with a human voice."

Reinhardt was exposed to jazz in 1931, when he and his brother were taken in by the painter Emile Savitry, who played them the first jazz records to appear in France. A few years later he encountered violinist Stéphane Grappelli and urged him to try playing jazz on the classical violin. "It was Django's faith and Django's genius that blew away my fears," Grappelli recalled later. The two developed a musical bond and began a long-term collaboration in a group called the Quintet of the Hot Club of France. The name was clunky but the music was not: There was no drummer, and this gave the group an agile, reeling, free-spirited sound.

And the Hot Club did swing. Reinhardt plays with wild Gypsy restlessness and a classicist's respect for melody. His lines scamper and skitter far from conventional guitar practices; his strumming has the rousing triple-time fire of a musician who understood the needs of dancers. The recordings the group made early on, all documented on this budget-priced but lavish-sounding three-disc box, offer their sweetened interpretation of ragtime ("Tiger Rag" was a staple in live performance) as well as downcast melancholy blues and Reinhardt originals ("Nuages") drenched in wistfulness. The solos are usually delightful, as are the swooning, effusive exchanges between Reinhardt and Grappelli.

The group went on hiatus during World War II, and though it did re-form, it was never as compelling. Reinhardt was moving in different directions—an excellent document of his later, bebop-influenced electric-guitar sides is *Pêche à la mouche,* from 1947 and 1953. The earlier works, though, form the core of the Reinhardt legend—the jauntiness of the up-tempo romps, the wistful reflection of the ballads, the emotional expressivity of one Gypsy's guitar. If your needle is stuck on bebop and what came after, you're missing gems like these, which remain some of the most sublime, pleasurable jazz ever recorded.

GENRE: 🎷 Jazz. **RELEASED:** 2000, JSP. **KEY TRACKS:** "Tiger Rag," "Ain't Misbehavin'," "Nuages." **CATALOG CHOICE:** *Pêche à la mouche.* **NEXT STOP:** Claude Bolling: *Suite for Flute and Jazz Piano Trio.* **AFTER THAT:** Bireli Lagrene: *Roots to Django.*

Plaintive and Beautiful Whispers of a Revolution

Murmur

R.E.M.

Murmur's unkempt jangle opened up new possibilities for musicians and disaffected rock fans in the dark New Wave twilight of 1983. The debut album by the Athens, Georgia, four-piece R.E.M., it showed that the DIY aesthetic of punk didn't just have to mean fast and loud. Its schemes made room for shadowy melodies, abstruse (if not incomprehensible) lyrics, and chiming guitar arpeggios derived from the early records of the Byrds.

The band's plain, beautiful, and plaintive sounds, many of them from acoustic instruments, coalesced into something big. With this album R.E.M. blew tantalizing fresh air through the prefab world of rock, spearheading the movement that became known as "college rock" or "alternative rock." Curiously, much of *Murmur* doesn't exactly "rock" in the conventional sense. It's closer to strange, nocturnal folk—songs you might hear emanating from a campfire deep in the woods. Singer Michael Stipe's lyrics are both endlessly suggestive and inscrutable. Inspired by the metaphor-rich poetry of Patti Smith, Stipe writes in blinding torrents, concerning himself

R.E.M. formed in 1980 after Michael Stipe (far left) and guitarist Peter Buck (second from right) met in a record store.

with the meter of his phrases rather than their linear meaning. He once claimed that he was "blabbering" through the entire recording of the single "Radio Free Europe" (which was re-recorded for this album).

The other members of R.E.M.—guitarist Peter Buck, bassist Mike Mills, and drummer Bill Berry—have said that they were just learning how to play their instruments during the band's early days. They grew proficient by playing together. By *Murmur,* their sound is tightly knit—a refined and delicate weaving of needlepoint-precise guitar lines, each ringing with great and almost fierce clarity. Every song is a gem, and many of them offer glimpses of ideas R.E.M. would explore further on later albums. If you're familiar with any of the places R.E.M. visited during its hit-making years, on such albums as *Automatic for the People* and singles including "Losing My Religion" and the still dizzying "Orange Crush," check out where it started, on this wild, wistful, unassuming masterpiece that might be the most important rock record of the 1980s.

GENRE: 🅚 Rock. **RELEASED:** 1983, IRS. **KEY TRACKS:** "Radio Free Europe," "Talk About the Passion," "Pilgrimage." **F.Y.I.:** *Rolling* *Stone* magazine named *Murmur* the album of the year for 1983, over Michael Jackson's *Thriller* and the Police's *Synchronicity.* **CATALOG CHOICES:** *Fables of the Reconstruction; New Adventures in Hi-Fi.* **NEXT STOP:** Guadalcanal Diary: *Walking in the Shadow of the Big Man.* **AFTER THAT:** 10,000 Maniacs: *Our Time in Eden.*

Urgent Unkempt Grandeur

Let It Be

The Replacements

In the wise-beyond-his-years songs that twenty-four-year-old Paul Westerberg wrote for the third full-length Replacements album, there are raging hormones ("Gary's Got a Boner"), desperate Junior Casanova moves ("Sixteen Blue"), and frame-by-frame accounts of various rejections and embarrassments endured by awkward teenagers. A jaded romantic who once described himself as a "rebel without a clue," Westerberg dwells on those uncomfortable moments, chronicling the torments of growing up in agonizing, heart-ripped-open detail. His sharp, sardonic songs are a kind of American treasure—a knowing look back at the first-beer inebriated lunges and the all-consuming longings of restless kids desperate for companionship, aching to be anywhere that might be better than here.

The Replacements got together in 1979, in Minneapolis.

Westerberg's renderings of conflicted teenage feelings set the Replacements apart from every other scruffy rock band affiliated with the lo-fi postpunk explosion of the early 1980s. And by the time of this album, the Minneapolis band, originally called Dogbreath, seemed destined to break through into the rock mainstream. *Let It Be* should have done the trick—its songs range from abject dejection to blindingly upbeat giddiness to fist-in-the-air anthem stuff, and each balances catchy bubblegum hooks against gonzo rock delirium in a slightly different way. Sometimes Westerberg and his crew come right out and hit you over the head ("I Will Dare"), and sometimes they're surreptitious, as on "Unsatisfied," a sullen ode that gives voice to a vague generational restlessness felt by many in the Replacements' audience.

Let It Be was heavily salivated over by critics when it appeared. Since then, it has turned up regularly on lists of the Best Rock Albums Ever. But it never connected with a mass audience—some have suggested that the band's caterwauling, frequently inebriated and seriously erratic live performances didn't help win over doubters. That's a shame, because though it's always a hairpin turn from totally spinning out, this album, unlike much postpunk, has bracing and poignant growing-up stories to tell.

GENRE:  Rock. **RELEASED:** 1984, Twin/Tone. **KEY TRACKS:** "Sixteen Blue," "Androgynous," "Favorite Thing." **CATALOG CHOICES:** *Tim; Don't Tell a Soul; Pleased to Meet Me.* **NEXT STOP:** Meat Puppets: *Meat Puppets II.* **AFTER THAT:** Bob Mould: *Workbook.*

Countrypolitan Starts Here

Behind Closed Doors

Charlie Rich

Charlie Rich was the stealth soul singer of country music. The Arkansas native nicknamed the "Silver Fox" got his first break writing songs for Sun Records' Jerry Lee Lewis, and issued his first single, "Lonely Weekends," on a Sun subsidiary in 1959. Then he kicked around, mostly misunderstood, for more than a decade, recording rock, country, and rhythm and blues without consistent success. The tide turned when, in the early 1970s, he encountered veteran Nashville producer Billy Sherrill, who placed Rich's weathered and wounded voice in an almost-too-plush setting, with gentle rocking-chair rhythms and a busy string section. The result was a series of hits that virtually defined the crossover countrypolitan style; of them, *Behind Closed Doors* is the crown jewel.

Behind Closed Doors reached #1 on the *Billboard* Country chart.

The setting might be intentionally middle of the road, but that doesn't stop Rich from treating the songs, which mostly avoid Nashville's cheating hearts story line, like lost classics of bedroom soul. Rich projects an air of gruff cool. Like Ray Charles, whom he emulates, he escapes the velvet handcuff of posh tracks by singing with almost no affectation, emphasizing the weary realness of his voice. Also like Charles, Rich has no problem handling different styles: While the love songs (notably the title track and "The Most Beautiful Girl") make the soul influence clear, Rich is equally convincing interpreting sedate gospel hymns and an anything-but-sedate Neil Diamond–style production number ("Peace on You").

This album represents Rich's commercial peak—the title track and "The Most Beautiful Girl" both hit the upper reaches of the pop and country charts. It's perhaps more important as a template for the country crooner music of the '90s, though few imitators have matched Rich's gift for easygoing and sneakily compelling expression. Sam Phillips, the founder of Sun Records, put it this way: "I don't know anyone who has ever written or sung in a way that depicted more of the humanity of man, with greater melodic beauty, than Charlie Rich."

GENRE:  Country. **RELEASED:** 1973, Epic. **KEY TRACKS:** "A Sunday Kind of Woman," "Peace on You," "Behind Closed Doors." **CATALOG CHOICE:** *Pictures and Paintings.* **NEXT STOP:** Ted Hawkins: *The Next Hundred Years* (see p. 349). **AFTER THAT:** Arthur Alexander: *Lonely Just like Me.*

Tale-Spinning, Russian Style

Scheherazade

Nikolai Rimsky-Korsakov
Royal Concertgebouw Orchestra of Amsterdam (Kiril Kondrashin, cond.)

This symphonic tone poem centers on the legend of The Arabian Nights, in which a sultan, convinced of the faithlessness of women, has each of his wives killed the day after their wedding night. When he gets to Sultana Scheherazade, he encounters a woman skilled in the art of storytelling. Over a period of 1,001 nights, she enchants him with cliff-hanging fables and poems, delaying the inevitable. It takes 1,001 nights for the king to decide that she's faithful. The professorial Russian composer Nikolai Rimsky-Korsakov (1844–1908) initially furnished titles for each movement that referred to different tales, then removed them because he didn't want to link the music so closely to fixed text. This was wise: Each of *Scheherazade*'s long, winding melodies—among them are fanciful spinning motifs that suggest the moves of a dancer and episodes of shattering tragedy—provides its own narrative.

Rimsky-Korsakov conducted the premiere of *Scheherazade* on October 28, 1888, in St. Petersburg.

The key themes of each section are first stated by the violin, often alone. On this recording, the soloist is Herman Krebbers, who delivers the tales as though he's organizing a series of impulsively scrawled thoughts into a larger story line. Conductor Kiril Kondrashin hails from Russia, and has a deep sensitivity for the grit and vigor of the post-Tchaikovsky nationalism expressed by Rimsky-Korsakov and the other members of the so-called Mighty Five (Modest Mussorgsky, Mily Balakirev, Cesar Cui, and Alexander Borodin). Here, Kondrashin teases out the nationalistic flourishes (listen for the crisp, distinctly Russian theme-and-variations play of the strings around five minutes into the third movement).

Also here is Borodin's Second Symphony, in which the self-described "Sunday composer" (he made his living as a chemist) offers a idealized vision of Russia. It begins dimly, with a labored first movement, and ends with a dazzling, thoroughly transporting finale: That fourth movement, considered Borodin's best work, is notable for the way its pithy melodic bytes are developed, Beethoven style, into grand—and fiery—gestures.

GENRE: 🎵 Classical. **RELEASED:** 1980, Philips. **KEY TRACKS:** Rimsky-Korsakov: "The Sea and Sinbad's Ship," "The Story of the Kalender Prince." Borodin: fourth movement. **ANOTHER INTERPRETATION:** Kirov Orchestra (Valery Gergiev, cond.). **CATALOG CHOICE:** *Capriccio Espagnol,* London Symphony Orchestra (Charles Mackerras, cond.). **NEXT STOP:** Modest Mussorgsky: *Boris Godunov* (see p. 534). **AFTER THAT:** *Khachaturian Piano Concerto,* William Kapell, Boston Symphony Orchestra (Serge Koussevitzky, cond.).

The Pure Voice of a . . .

Perfect Angel

Minnie Riperton

S ome musicians defy the laws of nature. John Coltrane, the jazz saxophonist, played so rapidly during the "sheets of sound" phase of his career that it was impossible to pick out individual notes—the best you could do was to discern the general shapes. The classical pianist Arthur Rubinstein had such a distinct attack on the piano he made the wooden box sound like it was alive.

The R&B singer Minnie Riperton (1947–1979), who died after a battle with breast cancer, had a different kind of natural gift: the ability to sing clearly at the very top of an impossibly extended range. Unlike singers who creep up to the mountaintop for the final flourish of a song, Riperton went skyward at will, executing her ideas with the pinpoint precision of a flute virtuoso. Her manner was so nonchalant you forgot just how high above middle C she was. Nothing seemed beyond her range, whether she was singing rock (among her early recordings are several gems with a groundbreaking Chicago group called Rotary Connection) or jazz. Early in her career, when working as a receptionist at Chess Records, she contemplated a career in opera.

Determined to avoid using her range as a freak show attraction, Riperton played coy and casual in the early '70s, placing the emphasis on another innate skill: devastating timing. *Perfect Angel*, which was coproduced by Stevie Wonder, is her best shot, the most comfortable convergence of her cloud-dusting instrument and compelling songcraft. It's got Riperton's biggest single, the idyllic "Lovin' You"; a bouncing up-tempo workout ("Reasons"); and a Wonder-penned ode to self-discovery entitled "Take a Little Trip." Even before Riperton's death, the record was required listening for a generation of similarly equipped singers, and though many have copied her technique—Mariah Carey being the most famous—nobody has achieved the weeping-willow ease on display here.

***

GENRE: 🔵 R&B. **RELEASED:** 1974, Epic. **KEY TRACKS:** "Lovin' You," "Reasons," "The Edge of a Dream." **CATALOG CHOICES:** *Come to My Garden; Her Chess Years.* **NEXT STOP:** Mariah Carey: *Butterfly.* **AFTER THAT:** Mary J. Blige: *The Breakthrough.*

***

A Peak of Vocal Percussion

Lo último en la avenida

Ismael Rivera con Kako y Su Orquesta

O n this blistering date from 1971, Puerto Rican *sonero* Ismael Rivera sings like a drummer. That's a good thing. Though he tells his share of stories about good times in the neighborhood, Rivera spends just as much energy tossing out percussive vocal lines—on several of these songs, including the catcalling "El cumbanchero," he transforms his voice into an extra drum. His crisp, crackling attack recalls the hard slap of the bongo, and his perfectly placed accents propel the music in exactly the same way a great *conguero* (like Potato Valdes here) does. Parts of "La cumbita" find Rivera playfully imitating the rhythm players behind him, improvising as he goes along, thinking like a percussionist the whole time.

Rivera did play ancillary percussion on many of his recordings, and of all the great vocalists to emerge from Puerto Rico, he's the one with the strongest connection to rhythm. That is partly attributable to his background: Rivera grew up in Santurce, and among his neighbors was a percussionist and future bandleader, Rafael Cortijo. The two learned the island's traditional *bomba* and *plena* rhythms together, and later collaborated in one of the hottest Latin bands of the early

'60s, Cortijo y Su Combo. This release shows that Rivera's exacting sense of timing got better over the years: In front of *timbale* master Francisco Bastar's hardworking New York band, Rivera tears through these infectious tunes like the Charlie Parker of salsa—his ad-libs sound almost too inventive, and too relentless, to have been made up on the fly. But spontaneous they are—the handiwork of a singer who sends tricky polyrhythms flying through the music at odd angles, just like a drummer.

GENRE: 🌐 World/Puerto Rico.
RELEASED: 1971, Fania. **KEY TRACKS:** "El cumbanchero," "La cumbita," "El truquito." **CATALOG CHOICE:** Cortijo y Su Combo (featuring Ismael Rivera): *Baile con Cortijo y Su Combo.* **F.Y.I.:** The legendary Cuban singer Beny Moré named Rivera one of his all-time favorites. **NEXT STOP:** Pete "El Conde" Rodriguez: *El conde.* **AFTER THAT:** Roberto Roena y Su Apollo Sound: *4.*

A Peak of Jazz Activism

We Insist! Freedom Now Suite

Max Roach

Max Roach's *We Insist! Freedom Now Suite* is among a handful of jazz works to directly address slavery, racism, and the African American experience. On a purely musical level, it's arguably the most successful of them, because the drummer, a bebop-era veteran, does more than merely inventory the long list of injustices. With the help of a tremendous ensemble that includes three percussionists, he translates the frustration of the civil rights years into gales of vibrant sound—purposeful chants and grieving screams and inquisitive solos (from tenor legend Coleman Hawkins and others) that amplify the indignation of the title.

Roach (1924–2007) recognized that merely insisting on vague "change" was not enough—he had to make it "real" by confronting the protracted suffering of a people and the emotional scars that lingered over generations. He also recognized that the struggles were not unique to America: Several pieces look to Africa, enabling him to chart the diasporic connections between African, Afro-Cuban, and jazz rhythms. Still most of the pulse is derived from jazz. The critic Nat Hentoff, who was involved in the making of this record, said later that Roach regarded jazz as "an essential paradigm for constitutional democracy. In jazz each individual has a voice, but in order for it to work, the individuals must listen to each other."

Those involved in the five-part *Freedom Now* are clearly listening to each other; everyone calibrates his or her own contribution to align with the overall mission. The lyricist Oscar Brown Jr. reels off an account of a harsh slave driver, "Driva' Man," that is one chilling highlight, its message driven home by a needling, intensely focused improvisation from tenor saxophonist Coleman Hawkins. Then there's the work of Abbey Lincoln, the cool-headed singer then married to Roach: On the drums/vocals

Roach, center, participates at a sit-in at a white lunch counter.

duet called "Triptych: Prayer, Protest, Peace," Lincoln begins in a mood of deep introspection, then moves through a series of wordless moans, eddying cries, and shrieks that is unlike anything else in music—a riveting roar of feeling.

GENRE: 🎵 Jazz.
RELEASED: 1960, Candid.
KEY TRACKS: "Tears for Johannesburg," "Triptych," "Driva' Man." **CATALOG CHOICE:** *Clifford Brown and Max Roach* (see p. 119). **NEXT STOP:** Gil Scott-Heron: *Pieces of a Man* (see p. 684). **AFTER THAT:** Eugene McDaniels: *Headless Heroes of the Apocalypse* (see p. 487).

Jazz at the Brink of Unhinged

Featuring the Legendary Hasaan

The Max Roach Trio

Of all forms of music, jazz may be the most hospitable to mental instability. It takes a certain touch of rashness, if not madness, to pursue the as-yet-undiscovered. In real time. Without a map. The history books tell of extraordinarily gifted musicians (Thelonious Monk, Phineas Newborn) who struggled at various times with mental illness, but still managed to challenge their fellow musicians and push beyond the prevailing conventions of small-group jazz. Then there are those "differently wired" people who, despite great talent, weren't able to make a sustained contribution to music. Ibn Ali Hasaan, the Philadelphia pianist, belongs in that group.

Described by (usually tolerant) jazz musicians as eccentric and/or unstable, Hasaan made this one shockingly inventive record during a period of busy activity in the early

'60s, and then receded from view. At the time, Hasaan was an "it" child of East Coast jazz, an original voice whose performances at jam sessions (with Johnny Griffin and others) were recalled in reverent tones.

Hasaan's recorded debut was set up by one of his champions, drummer Max Roach. Roach headlined, but all the music was written by the pianist, and these tricky originals take the time-shifting intricacy of bebop to more extreme places, obscuring their logic beneath a layer of provocation. "Almost like Me" is a stomp written mostly in quarter notes that grows disturbingly zombielike as it progresses; the title of the opening tune,

"Three-Four vs. Six-Eight Four-Four Ways," offers a good indication of its metric convolutions, as well as its complexity. While it's possible to detect a dash of Monk in the clustered chords, Hasaan had his own way of playing—his inventions are absolute genius one minute and pure madness the next.

GENRE: 🎵 Jazz. **RELEASED:** 1965, Atlantic. **KEY TRACKS:** "Off My Back Jack," "Pay Not Play Not," "Hope So Elmo." **NEXT STOP:** Phineas Newborn Jr.: *A World of Piano!* (see p. 548). **AFTER THAT:** Thelonious Monk: *Solo Monk.*

Deep Space Swirls

Dreamtime Return

Steve Roach

Steve Roach's 1988 double-disc, inspired by visits to the Australian outback and the Aboriginal concept of "dreamtime," has been hyped as one of the pivotal works of ambient music. You may wonder why: It begins with the generic whooshing you'd expect from a NASA training film, and as it evolves acquires similar sounds typically used by film scorers to connote open planetary vistas. That's ambient music for you: To some, one minute its sweeping sounds evoke a great metaphysical vastness, to others that same material can seem a tired cliché.

Roach visited ancient Aboriginal sites in northern Australia during the development of this album.

Stick with *Dreamtime Return*, because after its garish opening segment, the music travels less expected pathways, with slow-moving textures luring listeners into evocations of tribal ritual. In Aboriginal mythology, "dreamtime" refers to a state of being in which the past, present, and future are experienced simultaneously. *Dreamtime*'s tales address the earth's origin, and the role of humans in it (the Aboriginal people believe every human event leaves a "record" in the land).

Inspired by these stories, Roach used a combination of synthesizers and ancient instruments, most notably the *dumbek* drum and the didgeridoo (that two-toned wind instrument native to Australia, played here by David Hudson), to create shape-shifting, constantly evolving atmospheres. *Dreamtime Return* is among a handful of pioneering works of what's sometimes called "Ethno-Ambient," though its rhythms are more aggressive than most music carrying that label. Moving from solemn, ceremonial beats to unmoored, tempoless explorations, Roach scatters tones and colors into brilliant arrays, and evolves them, ever so slowly, into a majestic long-distance journey. It may only be a simulation of dreamtime, but it's dazzlingly hypnotic all the same.

GENRE: 🌐 Electronica. **RELEASED:** 1988, Celestial Harmonies. (Reissued 2005, Projekt.) **KEY TRACKS:** "The Other Side," "The Ancient Day," "Looking for Safety." **CATALOG CHOICE:** *Trance Spirits.* **NEXT STOP:** David Byrne and Brian Eno: *My Life in the Bush of Ghosts* (see p. 136). **AFTER THAT:** Michael Brook: *Cobalt Blue.*

The Wild West, in Song

Gunfighter Ballads and Trail Songs

Marty Robbins

 estern mythmaking a high point on American television in 1959—that year there were some twenty dramas about the Wild West on the networks, including *Gunsmoke, Maverick,* and *Wanted: Dead or Alive.*

(Another of the best, *Bonanza,* would debut that fall.)

Even in those days, before television drove the big locomotive of popular culture, it was inevitable that singers would seize this trend, providing a soundtrack for the eternal chase between lawmen and outlaws. Marty Robbins's vivid concept album, *Gunfighter Ballads and Trail Songs,* hails from that moment. Recorded in April 1959 with a crew of singers and the excellent guitar tandem of Thomas Grady Martin and Jack H. Pruett, the album, with its epic tales of gunslinging lawlessness and deceit on the open prairie, struck a chord. The record became a hit, and one of its big singles, the memorable "El Paso," was the rare country song to reach the top of the pop charts. It brought Robbins one of the first Grammy awards for country music.

Gunfighter Ballads reached #6 on the *Billboard* Pop Albums chart.

"El Paso," which tells of a cowboy's obsessive love for a "Mexican maiden," benefits from Robbins's casual, smoldering vocal, and Martin's trembling south-of-the-border guitar ad-libs. It's one treasure among many here. Robbins idolized Gene Autry, and deployed a touch of the screen star's easygoing affect to make these clippity-clopping songs of saddle tramps and conniving outlaws as riveting as the Wild West itself. Or, at the least, the made-for-TV version.

GENRE: 🅞 Country. **RELEASED:** 1959, Columbia. **KEY TRACKS:** "El Paso," "Big Iron," "In the Valley," "Billy the Kid." **CATALOG CHOICE:** *Devil Woman.* **NEXT STOP:** Jim Reeves: *The Country Side of Jim Reeves.* **AFTER THAT:** Sonny James: *The Minute You're Gone.*

A Motown Cornerstone

The Ultimate Collection

Smokey Robinson and the Miracles

I n the course of an extended run fronting the Miracles and writing songs for other Motown acts, Smokey Robinson exhausted every permutation of the love song. He came up with definitive blunt dismissals ("Shop Around") and tender endearments ("My Girl"), songs that captured a jilted lover's brave face ("Tears of a Clown"), and songs that puzzled over love's ever-unfolding mysteries ("Ain't That Peculiar," a hit for Marvin Gaye). Robinson's often breezy tunes told truths about the nuances of romance and its conflicts, and threw light on notions that are often difficult to express in words. This gift prompted no less an authority than Bob Dylan to once proclaim Robinson as "America's greatest living poet."

The Miracles had over 50 hits on the American music charts.

You might not agree with Dylan after hearing one Smokey tune on oldies radio. Or maybe two. But listen to a bunch of them, back-to-back, and suddenly it's hard to muster enough superlatives to do this body of work justice. A powerhouse on several levels, Robinson is a writer capable of sketching the many permutations of love's pain, and a singer capable of putting you in close proximity to that feeling. He draws on these different skills in constantly surprising ways—sometimes singing forcefully (as on the shout "You Really Got a Hold on Me") but at other times, most notably on his eternally amazing ballad "Tracks of My Tears," suffusing his voice with a trembling, anguished sense of longing. The twenty-five tracks here include all the Top 10 hits Robinson sang with the Miracles (but not his versions of songs like "My Girl," which was a hit for the Temptations). One reason to select this over the many other available anthologies is to hear several B sides that should have been hits ("Choosey Beggar" and "Way Over There").

GENRE: 🌀 R&B. **RELEASED:** 1998, Motown. **KEY TRACKS:** "I Second That Emotion," "You've Really Got a Hold on Me," "Tracks of My Tears," "Tears of a Clown." **CATALOG CHOICES:** *Going to a Go-Go; Live!* **NEXT STOP:** The Supremes: *The Supremes Sing Holland-Dozier-Holland.* **AFTER THAT:** Marvin Gaye: *Anthology.*

So Light, So Clear . . .

The Voice of Lightness: Congo Classics, 1961–1977

Tabu Ley Rochereau

It's often said that truly great singers can sing anything—the phone book, a laundry list—and make it compelling. That isn't always hyperbole. Tucked inside this compilation of highlights from the long career of Congolese singing legend Tabu Ley Rochereau is a soap commercial. "Savon Omo," written by Rochereau and recorded in 1966 with the group African Fiesta, was used in an ad campaign for Omo laundry soap.

Heard here as a full four-minute tune, "Savon Omo" is not the most profound composition on this two-disc anthology, which contains some of the most persuasive ad-libbing in African pop. But it serves as an excellent demonstration of how an assured, impassioned singer can finesse (and redeem) ordinary material: First Rochereau gamely does his brand-building bit, repeating a fetching jingle-like phrase over and over. Then he initiates a call-and-response exchange with the background vocalists, and that's when things get interesting. Floating above the interlinked counterpoint of several agile electric guitars, he improvises in long torrents of wonderful (sometimes almost heroic) melody that venture far from the laundry. All ads should be this uplifting.

The aptly titled *The Voice of Lightness* traces Rochereau's evolution from roots in Congolese rumba (a huge craze in the '60s) to his development of *soukous*, the up-tempo rumba derivation that incorporates elements of American soul. In his conception, *soukous* is incessantly propulsive but also prayerful—there are moments when Rochereau's incantations resonate as devotional mantras, no matter if he's singing about deities or race relations, mortality or sex, the prowess of his various bands or (on the striking "Aon Aon") the allure of the wah-wah guitar.

The guitars are certainly worthy of attention; behind Rochereau, several different lead players crisscross and overlap in ways that are technically demanding, yet sound positively effortless. That's often true of Rochereau's music: From the early singles to the explosive two-part live showcase "Adeito," everything here has transfixing power, though of an unassuming, low-key sort. Rochereau's singing is a butterfly's symphony of wriggles and flutters, but don't be fooled: There's deep conviction behind it. That's really what sells the soap.

GENRE: 🌐 World/Congo. **RELEASED:** 2007, Sterns Music. (Recordings made 1961–1977.) **KEY TRACKS:** "Savon Omo," "Kasela," "Mama Ida," "Adeito (1 & 2)." **CATALOG CHOICE:** *Muzina*. **NEXT STOP:** Mbilia Bel: *Bel Canto: Best of the Genidia Years (1982–1987)*. **AFTER THAT:** Patience Dabany: *Patience Dabany*.

The Father of Country Music Sings (and Yodels)

The Essential Jimmie Rodgers

Jimmie Rodgers

Enjoyment of this, the first single-disc career survey of country music forefather Jimmie Rodgers, depends somewhat on your taste for tales of trouble and woe punctuated by yodeling. Known as the "Singing Brakeman" and the "Mississippi Blue Yodeler," the Mississippi-born Rodgers was a colorful figure who began working on the railroad at age fourteen. He performed in blackface as a young man, toured endlessly, and maintained an admirable work ethic: During his last recording session, he was so sick with tuberculosis he rested on a cot between takes. He died two days later.

His work as a brakeman had exposed him to all sorts of music—he absorbed blues and gospel and old-time folk songs, and allowed each to inform his own singing. The result was the sound we now know as "country"—firm and forthright declarations with hints of heartache (and the bittersweet blues) creeping in.

Rodgers deepened the emotions in his songs by yodeling. On his second session for RCA, in 1927, Rodgers did a blues-based song he wrote called "T for Texas" ("T for Texas, T for Tennessee, T for Thelma, that gal that made a wreck out of me") that was renamed "Blue Yodel No. 1" by RCA. On it, he punctuates each verse with a spry, gregarious yodel, an exotic torn-apart sound that Rodgers infects with twinges of the blues. The yodel became Rodgers's signature, and though he used the same techniques as the Swiss and others who relied on yodeling to communicate across mountain peaks, his tone is often mournful, sometimes emulating the sound of a train whistle in the distance.

Rodgers is revered for more than just that vocal flourish, which he once described as "curlicues." His original songs express a wry sense of humor and a deep connection to the lives of working people—among his famous tunes are "In the Jailhouse Now," "Pistol Packin' Papa," and

Fans nicknamed Rodgers the "Father of Country Music."

"Waiting for a Train." Even more critical to country music is his ear for nuance. Rodgers taught everyone who followed him—Hank Williams, Merle Haggard, Johnny Cash, Hank Snow, the whole crew—the gentle art of conveying feelings beyond words.

GENRE: 🌀 Country. **RELEASED:** 1997, RCA. (Original recordings made between 1927 and 1931.) **KEY TRACKS:** "Blue Yodel No. 1 (T For Texas)," "In the Jailhouse Now," "Memphis Yodel," "My Little Old Home Down in New Orleans," "Waiting for a Train." **CATALOG CHOICE:** *The Singing Brakeman.* **NEXT STOP:** Woody Guthrie: *Dust Bowl Ballads* (see p. 331). **AFTER THAT:** Ernest Tubb: *The Definitive Collection* (see p. 788).

The Hills Are Alive with . . .

The Sound of Music

Richard Rodgers and Oscar Hammerstein II
Original Motion Picture Soundtrack

There's no getting around *The Sound of Music*. It's part of the fabric of musical theater, championed as an artistic triumph in some quarters and regarded, no less affectionately, as kitsch in others. (Around the film's fortieth anniversary, there was an outbreak of interactive *Rocky Horror Picture Show*–style screenings, with audience members in nuns' habits singing along, and talking back to the screen.) Thanks to the song "Do-Re-Mi," lots of school kids effortlessly learn the notes of the major scale. The musical's first section offers a glimpse of prewar European upper-crust family life, while the second act provides a human perspective on the tumultuous events of 1930s Europe. It is corny and touching, bombastic and deliberate, stereotypical and idiosyncratic. This recording, from the blockbuster film, stayed in the Top 40 of *Billboard*'s Album charts for 161 weeks.

Whatever its shortcomings, the final collaboration between composer Richard Rodgers and lyricist Oscar Hammerstein II cannot be denied in one respect: Its songs are almost frighteningly memorable, a series of earworms that just won't take no for an answer. Writing melodies to celebrate the power of music is a tricky business at best, but with his opening title Rodgers goes there, boldly. His theme has a majestic and graceful sweep—it's exactly the series of notes you'd expect to burst forth from nature as some idealistic young heroine passes by. Really all of the show's major motifs can be appreciated not just as plot devices but hymns to the glory of music—from the step-wise ascension of "My Favorite Things" (sung primly here by Julie Andrews) to the comic caricatured yodeling of "The Lonely Goatherd," Rodgers and Hammerstein find ways to twist everyday sounds into swirls of wonder.

To appreciate just how strong *Sound of Music*'s

Julie Andrews, as Maria, dances on a hilltop in the 1965 film version of *The Sound of Music*.

individual songs are, seek out a few of the many reinterpretations that followed in the show's wake. Of particular note is John Coltrane's soprano saxophone journey through "My Favorite Things." Recorded while the film soundtrack was still selling like gangbusters, it finds Coltrane and his group reinventing the song, while exhibiting a deep reverence for the musical invention, and the gee-willickers innocence, of Rodgers's original theme.

GENRE: 😃 Musicals. **RELEASED:** 1965, RCA. **KEY TRACKS:** "The Sound of Music," "Sixteen Going on Seventeen," "Edelweiss," "My Favorite Things." **ANOTHER INTERPRETATION:** *Original Broadway Cast.* **NEXT STOP:** John Coltrane: *My Favorite Things.* **AFTER THAT:** Sarah Vaughan: *In the Land of Hi-Fi.*

The Voice of Portugal, Loud and Clear

The Art of Amália Rodrigues

Amália Rodrigues

This is a Pablo Neruda poem with wings. This is singing as a kind of journey into the soul, leading deeper than you might initially want to go. This is the coyness of Ella, the hurt of Billie Holiday, the brooding of João Gilberto.

Amália Rodrigues stops you in your tracks, flattens time, fills the air around you with a fine weepy mist and then, having rearranged your molecules, sends you on your sad way home.

You need not understand Portuguese to be transported by Rodrigues (1920–1999), the singer who defined and expanded the pensive and rueful style known as fado, which translates as "destiny." It's music that looks back on loves that might have been, with the singer

usually helped by guitar and Portuguese mandolin. Bypassing the brain entirely and speaking instead directly to the heart, the singer and actress created an incredible trove of sentimental, nostalgic songs. Over a career of several decades, she came to symbolize fado, and many Portuguese poets wrote lyrics tailored for her.

This anthology does a good job of collecting highlights from Rodrigues's peak years in the 1950s, and includes several pieces recorded in 1970 on her final masterpiece, *Com que voz.* The set contains fado classics as well as striking versions of Portuguese popular songs. The song that opens the set, "Nem as paredes confesso," offers a clue about how Rodrigues operates. The mood is one of murmuring reflection as Rodrigues sings about how she intends to keep the name of her lover a secret. "You may beg, you may cry, but I won't even tell the walls who is the man I love," she sings. As the song

Admirers dubbed Rodrigues *"Rainha do Fado"* (Queen of Fado).

nears its end, she adds a little aphorism that underscores her sense of the fleeting nature of pleasure: "Happiness," she sings solemnly, "is best enjoyed in secret."

GENRE: 🌐 World/Portugal. **RELEASED:** 1998, Blue Note. **KEY TRACKS:** "Nem as paredes confesso," "Vou dar de beber a dor," "Coimbra," "Maria Lisboa." **CATALOG CHOICE:** *Com que voz.*

NEXT STOP: Madredeus: *Ainda.* **AFTER THAT:** Misia: *Canto.*

The First Peak of a Cuban Maestro

Montuneando

Arsenio Rodríguez y Su Conjunto

It will probably take a Ray Charles–style biopic for the world to fully appreciate Arsenio Rodríguez, the blind composer and god of the Cuban six-string guitar known as the *tres.* Rodriguez was blinded at age seven, after he was kicked by a mule. He turned to music as a teenager, learning percussion, piano, and *tres.* By 1937, several of his original tunes, including the enduring "Bruca Manigua," had been recorded by vocalist Miguelito Valdés and Orquesta Casino de la Playa and were quickly becoming dance floor standards. Rodríguez developed his own small group in the early 1940s, and it quickly became a home for some of Cuba's finest, including the trumpet master Alfredo "Chocolate" Armenteros and Rodríguez's cousin, the vocalist Rene Scull. It departed from the traditional Cuban *son* ensembles by adding conga drum, piano, and additional trumpet players—a configuration that became known as the *conjunto.* Though the instrumentation was adopted by other Cuban groups, the Rodríguez ensemble stood apart. Listen to "Lo que dice usted" (or really anything here) to hear musicians who play with a restraint that recalls the great James Brown bands, yet can turn around and, in seconds, crank up the musical equivalent of a blazing bonfire.

By the time of these recordings, made between 1946 and 1950, Rodríguez was at the peak of his powers. His band swings with a more prounouced African kick than any other in Cuba. His *tres* playing is thrillingly agile, but he never grandstands; his slashing contributions to "Chicharronero" and others can be found deep in the (surprisingly clear for this era) mix. His songs, which became the core repertoire of countless Cuban small groups, have sturdy refrains that never wear out their welcome.

Rodríguez moved to New York in 1953, and though he made several strong records

(*Primitivo* catches his late period well), they pale next to *Montuneando* and the other albums he recorded at Havana's storied Egrem studios. Because of frosty U.S.-Cuban relations, these records can be hard to find in stores. That's a shame, because this suave-yet-potent dance music transcends politics, language, and geographical boundaries. It should be available to everyone.

GENRE: 🌐 World/Cuba. **RELEASED:** 1993, Tumbao. (Recordings made between 1946 and 1950.) **KEY TRACKS:** "Chicharronero," "El cerro tiene la llave," "Lo que dice usted." **CATALOG CHOICES:** *Primitivo; Arsenio dice.* **NEXT STOP:** Eddie Palmieri: *La perfecta* (see p. 573). **AFTER THAT:** Isaac Oviedo: *Routes of Rhythm,* Vol. 3.

A Time Capsule from a Famous Dance Floor

Live at the Palladium

Tito Rodriguez

From 1948 through its demise in the mid-'60s, the Palladium was *the* place to dance to Latin music in New York City. The hall, in a large second floor space at Broadway and 53rd Street, was home to the hottest bands in the country, and as a result drew skilled dancers of many races and classes. Some say the mambo craze took off here. It's the place where Tito Puente first made his mark, and where the lesser known but no less formidable Tito Rodriguez (1923–1973) held court regularly, entertaining crowds that often included movie stars and other celebrities. The singer and leader of the amazing band on this record, Rodriguez was born in Puerto Rico and moved to New York in 1940. By 1947 he was at the helm of his own band.

Fans call Rodriguez "El Inolvidable" (the Unforgettable).

According to the liner notes, this milestone of big-band Latin music was recorded at the club in 1959. But there's very little crowd noise, and only scattered applause. In fact *Live at the Palladium* sounds like a really sharp studio date; only the lively, high-octane solos and rippling percussion suggest a band caught up in the work of tantalizing the denizens of a packed dance floor.

"Live" or not, these ten selections showcase one of the most urbane dance bands of all time breezing through craftily arranged mambos, sultry cha-chas, and hard-grooving Afro-Cuban dance numbers. A young Eddie Palmieri is at the piano, and following his lead, the rhythm section digs in behind the horn players.

Latin music historians might argue that Rodriguez's early small-group sides or his later pop records are more essential—"Inolvidable," his biggest hit, shows what a devastating crooner he could be, while *Live at Birdland*, which features saxophonist Zoot Sims, exhibits an adventurous jazz side. Those records are nice, but as a time capsule of what went down on one of New York's most important dance floors, *Live at the Palladium* is unbeatable. Even if it didn't happen in front of a live audience.

GENRE: 🌐 World/Latin. **RELEASED:** 1960,

United Artists. **KEY TRACKS**: "Mama guela," "Liza," "Satin and Lace," "El monito y la girafa." **F.Y.I.**: In an interview in *Latin Beat* magazine, Eddie Palmieri once called this "one of the greatest albums that was ever recorded."

CATALOG CHOICES: *Live at Birdland; Mambo Mona; Three Loves Have I; Back Home in Puerto Rico.* **NEXT STOP:** Tito Puente/ Eddie Palmieri: *Masterpiece.* **AFTER THAT:** Charlie Palmieri: *Heavyweight.*

The Perfect Storm of Jangled-Nerve Guitars and Nervy Jagger

Exile on Main St

The Rolling Stones

At various times during the long run of the Rolling Stones, the band's rhythmic direction has been dictated primarily by singer Mick Jagger (*Some Girls*), or drummer Charlie Watts (*12 × 5, Voodoo Lounge*), or the songwriting tandem of Jagger and guitarist Keith Richards (*Let It Bleed*). One record, however, is primarily Richards's vision—the constantly surprising *Exile on Main St.* Throughout its four gloriously ragged LP sides, the Stones appear not as rock stars but as scrappers, tearing through mean old blues tunes and throwaway two-chord riffs in search of a less restrictive rock and roll language. The result: one of the most intense studio albums in rock history.

Exile is Richards's record almost by accident. The Stones left England several months before work began on the album, fleeing tax laws. Richards's French villa was available, and the group set up a mobile recording studio in the basement. Jagger wasn't around for the early sessions: His wife Bianca was about to give birth. Richards grumbled loudly about Jagger's absence, but it turned out to be a hidden blessing: It allowed the guitarist to work on his own terms, which at the time meant copious amounts of alcohol and illicit drugs. As the guitarist Mick Taylor recalled later, the setting

"... Within a few years the people who had written the reviews saying it was a piece of crap were extolling it as the best frigging album in the world."
—Keith Richards

was perfect for Richards. "All he had to do was fall out of his bed, roll downstairs and *voilà*, he was at work."

Faced with having to start the train by himself, Richards came up with the loose, spectacularly disheveled roar that infects the originals (notably "Happy," "Torn and Frayed," and the "living room version" of "Tumbling Dice") and the covers of storied blues ("Shake Your Hips," "Stop Breaking Down"). He sets up the mean groove that prevails throughout, a rhythm attack that's dark and dense and raw. The sense of new possibility no doubt helped inspire Jagger: It's possible to imagine the singer and lyricist turning up at the sessions, hearing the band ripping with merciless intensity, and realizing that the ante has been upped. His response: lyrics bristling with attitude (if not outright hostility), sung in a surly, visceral mood that equals and frequently exceeds that of the bloodthirsty music Richards and company are throwing down. Though *Exile* does contain a few "singles," it is much more a wall-to-wall album experience, a debauched marathon in which every track transfers a different jolt. If you haven't heard it straight through, you can't fully appreciate the extremes to which rock and roll can be pushed.

GENRE: 🎸 Rock. **RELEASED:** 1972,

Rolling Stones. **KEY TRACKS:** "Rocks Off," "Shake Your Hips," "Tumbling Dice," "Happy," "I Just Want to See His Face." **CATALOG CHOICE:** *Sticky Fingers.* **NEXT STOP:** Nirvana: *Nevermind* (see p. 553). **AFTER THAT:** Liz Phair: *Exile in Guyville* (see p. 596).

Get Satisfaction Here

Singles Collection: The London Years

The Rolling Stones

During a 2005 interview, Keith Richards was asked about the many recordings languishing in the Rolling Stones' overstuffed vault. He acknowledged there's a lot of material, and hinted that some was unfinished or otherwise deemed by vocalist Mick Jagger not worthy of release. "Sometimes we pile up more stuff than anybody can handle," he laughed, recalling that the hit "Start Me Up" was found six years after it was initially recorded. "It would take a comprehensive inventory, and we're not very comprehensive."

Until such a set comes to pass, and Richards suggests it'll be when he and his bandmates are dead, there are ways other than the original albums to appreciate the Stones' legacy, among them this chronologically arranged set of singles, complete with B sides. From early bursts like "Not Fade Away" and "Time Is on My Side," "Let's Spend the Night Together" and the immortal "(I Can't Get No) Satisfaction," this set charts the individual steps that led to a rock and roll dynasty. Though the band was, from its earliest days, intent on putting together coherent and well-paced albums, its singles stand as a separate legacy; they're some of the most rousing, melodically intricate

"I was always a singer. . . . I was one of those kids who just *liked* to sing."
—Mick Jagger

three-minute masterworks in rock history. And the B sides, many of them blistering blues played by students not content to be copycats, amount to an alternate history of the group—those looking for new reasons to be awed by the Stones are referred to the original "Off the Hook" or such covers as Willie Dixon's "I Just Want to Make Love to You" and "Little Red Rooster." The enduring chart-toppers have appeared on countless anthologies (with 1972's *Hot Rocks* still the best of them), but this head-spinning collection shows just how inventive the Stones were on a regular basis, before they took that "World's Greatest Rock and Roll Band" stuff too seriously.

GENRE: 🎸 Rock. **RELEASED:** 1989, Abkco. **KEY TRACKS:** "Satisfaction," "Little Red Rooster," "Let's Spend the Night Together." **CATALOG CHOICES:** *Out of Our Heads; Aftermath.* **NEXT STOP:** The Beatles: *Anthology.*

An Apex of Hard Bop

A Night at the Village Vanguard

Sonny Rollins

This isn't the Sonny Rollins record with the richest backstory—that distinction belongs to *The Bridge*, the record the saxophonist made after a period of self-imposed exile when he spent evenings practicing on Brooklyn's Williamsburg Bridge. This isn't the Rollins title with the famous battle—that's *Tenor Madness*, which features a spirited duel with John Coltrane. It's not the one with the first great jazz exploration of calypso, either: For that tune, Rollins's "St. Thomas," pick up *Saxophone Colossus*.

No, this record chronicles a few nights in the magical jazz year of 1957 when Rollins entertained patrons of the Village Vanguard with just his tenor, bass, and drums. At the time, the style known as hard bop was oriented mostly around harmony; virtually every band had either a piano player or a guitarist providing the basic framework of the songs. Dispensing with this configuration, Rollins gave himself a major challenge: As he played familiar tunes like "I've Got You Under My Skin" and "Softly, as in a Morning Sunrise," he had to establish at least an outline of the harmony to keep the group together. Most horn players avoid such an exposed setting, but its demands apparently did not bother Rollins. Throughout this thrillingly loose recording he creates fantastical figures that might not have occurred to him in a more conventional group setting. The openness proves ideal for Rollins's slippery improvisational style, and for drummer Elvin Jones, whose aggressive pulse, later heard in the Coltrane group, sparks marathon conversations, and short boxerlike jabs and taunts.

The Vanguard performances have been studied by generations of jazz musicians eager to learn the art of extended improvisation. Asked to look back on them decades later, Rollins downplayed their significance. "I always thought of myself as a work in progress. To me that was just another date."

GENRE: 🎵 Jazz. **RELEASED:** 1957, Blue Note. **KEY TRACKS:** "What Is This Thing Called Love," "I Can't Get Started," "Softly, as in a Morning Sunrise." **CATALOG CHOICE:** *Saxophone Colossus.* **NEXT STOP:** John Coltrane: *The Complete Live at the Village Vanguard.*

An Atypical Peak of California Pop

Heart like a Wheel

Linda Ronstadt

Ten love songs rendered with great care and Laurel Canyon laid-back-ness, Linda Ronstadt's plaintive *Heart like a Wheel* sounds like it belongs next to the records singer-songwriters like Neil Young and Jackson Browne were making in Southern California in the early '70s. It's got the soothing background vocals, and crop-dusting acoustic guitars that could have flown in from an Eagles session.

But in almost every way, it stands apart from that scene. Where the singer-songwriters proffered their own visions, former Stone Poneys singer Linda Ronstadt didn't write any songs—instead, she sought out little-known gems from emerging tunesmiths like Kate and Anna McGarrigle (see p. 489), who wrote the title track. And where the songwriters usually aimed for a unified mood, Ronstadt goes the other way, covering long-discarded soul hits ("The Dark End of the Street") and chipper Everly Brothers pop ("When Will I Be Loved") as well as more delicate meditations about love and the human spirit ("Heart like a Wheel").

The writerly notions are held together by Ronstadt's assured, easygoing lead vocals. In contrast to the oft-wistful (or apologetic) songwriters, she sings with a steely authority, using delicate pencil-sketch shades to underscore her lyrics. The album opens with

Heart like a Wheel spent 51 weeks on the *Billboard* Top 200 Album chart.

"You're No Good," the shout of betrayal that became her first number 1 single: Ronstadt belts it as though she wants to rattle the clock off the wall. Just when you get used to this firecracker persona—she's the roar Helen Reddy needed for "I Am Woman"—Ronstadt changes her tone dramatically, etching "Faithless Love" in a mood of dejection mixed with vulnerability. The temperament changes from song to song as Ronstadt shines light on the faint shadows, moments she treasures that others might have missed. She sings in a way that can make you think she wrote the music, and in a sense she did: Even though some of these songs kicked around for decades, they're completely reborn when she sings them.

GENRE: 🎸 Rock. **RELEASED:** 1974, Capitol. **KEY TRACKS:** "You're No Good," "When Will I Be Loved," "The Dark End of the Street," "Heart like a Wheel." **CATALOG CHOICE:** *Simple Dreams.* **NEXT STOP:** Jennifer Warnes: *Famous Blue Raincoat.* **AFTER THAT:** Nicolette Larson: *Nicolette.*

For New Horizons in Hip-Hop, Study . . .

Phrenology

The Roots

When the roulette wheel of life has, for unknown reasons, plopped you into the daily squabbles of deep South Philly instead of the placid leisure of the city's affluent Main Line, you can sit and moan, or you can be like water and flow around the obstacles. That's what the Roots did. They started out as a human jukebox able to fulfill any hip-hop requests, playing for change on the street. Making hip-hop supported not by turntables, but by a cohesive jazz-versed live band, the Roots developed a reputation as a powerhouse band. And through constant touring, it became the first-call hip-hop groove machine—an integral part of Jay-Z's excellent *Unplugged,* and an inspiration to both rappers and singers. At each step along a surprising evolutionary path, the Roots showed how hip-hop could benefit from genuine musicianship. Of the titles, *Things Fall Apart*, with its statement-of-devotion single "You Got Me," is the most accessible. *Phrenology*, however, comes closest to capturing the manic totality of the Roots.

Named for the arcane science of divining personality traits based on the shape of a person's head, *Phrenology* is a big old raspberry to every entrenched convention about hip-hop music. Its tracks are long, with elaborate interludes (one descends into a tempoless avant-garde phantasmagoria). Textures include abject noise and distorted rock guitars. Drummer Ahmir "?uestlove" Thompson, an astute scholar of black music whose vinyl collection exceeds 50,000 titles, discreetly updates rhythms fashionable generations before—check the blinged-out Bo Diddley beat that underpins

Drummer Ahmir "?uestlove" Thompson performs at a 2004 Roots concert.

the magnificent "Water," rapper Black Thought's tale of losing a comrade to drugs.

Some grooves have very little hip-hop in them—singer Jill Scott's "Complexity" is a seafaring samba, yet the Roots never seem pulled beyond their comfort zone. Even rock detours display a serious flow, with Black Thought—one of the elite hip-hop MCs to establish street credibility without going thug—thrashing through triple-time diatribes. These pulverizing tracks should be required listening for anyone intending to rap in public: Though filled with accounts of adversity, the rapper shows no strain. He just slides right along, like water, bound for someplace better.

GENRE: 🌐 Hip-Hop. **RELEASED:** 2002, MCA. **KEY TRACKS:** "Sacrifice," "Complexity," "Water," "The Seed 2.0." **CATALOG CHOICES:** *Things Fall Apart; The Roots Come Alive.* **NEXT STOP:** Jay-Z: *Unplugged.* **AFTER THAT:** Blackalicious: *Blazing Arrow.*

A Sumptuous Subterranean Trip

Avalon

Roxy Music

By the time Roxy Music got to *Avalon*, it was past its days as a brash upmarket glam band, past the escapades of the arty *Country Life*, and well beyond caring about conventionally configured hit singles. Instead, the British collective led by singer and pinup idol Bryan Ferry was completely obsessed with texture. This album recasts the pop song as a realm of lush, never-ending tactile pleasures.

There are standout compositions on *Avalon*. But the first thing that hits you are the dreamy environments—the pools of shimmering synthesizers, the formless enveloping fog of bass,

the sheen of high-gloss disco drums. Into these delicately etched scenes slinks Ferry, talking about love and longing in a voice of weary dejection. He shrugs through the title track and sings "More than This" like a crooner trapped in a time warp. Busted up though he might be, he can't help but play the suave romantic lead, ready for the next candlelit seduction scene.

Singing from a perch in the lonely shadows, he draws listeners out of the mundane and into a surreal funhouse, where high-life dandies go to contemplate the cosmos and nurse the romantic obsessions that are often their ruin.

On the cover: Lead singer Ferry's girlfriend, Lucy Helmore, wearing a medieval helmet and carrying a falcon.

Avalon's hypnotic, gorgeously languid sounds stand apart from almost everything else of its day—this is one of the most sumptuous listening experiences to come out of the 1980s. It's striking for its depth, the way its thick textures underscore the notion of love as an all-encompassing and sometimes

tragic pursuit. And for the way Ferry communicates, in scattered, stunningly apt images and anguished utterances that never rise above the setting marked "Simmering Torment."

GENRE: 🎸 Rock.
RELEASED: 1982, Warner Bros. **KEY TRACKS:** "Avalon," "More than This," "True to Life." **CATALOG CHOICES:** *For Your Pleasure; Country Life.* **NEXT STOP:** Brian Eno: *Another Green World* (see p. 258). **AFTER THAT:** Be Bop Deluxe: *Raiding the Divine Archive.*

Hello, It's Todd

Something/Anything?

Todd Rundgren

When a pop auteur sequesters himself in the studio intending to record every last squib himself, sometimes what comes out is a big ugly mess. And sometimes the result is a dizzying tour de force à la *Something/Anything?*, the most enduring statement from songwriter, multi-instrumentalist, producer, and conceptualist Todd Rundgren. Without him, pop of the 1970s would have been less melodic, and far less trippy. Rundgren's many influences take turns in the spotlight of this twenty-five-song tome—depending on the track, he's a Beatles disciple or a musician with a psychedelic jones, a student of AM radio or a singer who, having grown up in Philadelphia, totally gets blue-eyed soul. It's clear, from the start, that he's aiming high: The George Harrison–influenced opener "I Saw the Light" is a radiant single, and one of several pieces here ("Hello It's Me" is another) built around a lilting keyboard phrase. The remaining songs aren't a string of similar attempts at singles—there are grand stylistic lunges and wacky detours ("The Night the Carousel Burnt Down") and several roaring numbers that force Rundgren to bring in a band, and a blustery horn section.

Though Rundgren made lots of records after this one—both as a solo artist and the leader of the studiously progressive Utopia—he never distilled his influences so compellingly again. But he continued to make a contribution as a producer: Thank Rundgren for the party-time blast that is Grand Funk Railroad's *We're an American Band* and the ornate theatricality of Meat Loaf's *Bat out of Hell,* and for focusing the tremendous British art-pop pathfinders XTC on their best late album, *Skylarking* (see p. 878).

Maria." **CATALOG CHOICE:** *Hermit of Mink Hollow.* **NEXT STOP:** Steely Dan: *Can't Buy a Thrill.* **AFTER THAT:** Joe Jackson: *Big World.*

GENRE: 🎸 Rock. **RELEASED:** 1972, Bearsville. **KEY TRACKS:** "Hello It's Me," "I Saw the Light," "Wolfman Jack," "Black

Maria." **CATALOG CHOICE:** *Hermit of Mink Hollow.* **NEXT STOP:** Steely Dan: *Can't Buy a Thrill.* **AFTER THAT:** Joe Jackson: *Big World.*

A Fistful of Hip-Hop Firsts

Raising Hell

Run-DMC

Run-DMC was the first hip-hop act to embrace rock in a musically astute way (its breakthrough single was this album's collaboration with Aerosmith on the rock band's signature "Walk This Way"). The trio from Hollis, Queens, was the first hip-hop act to earn airtime on then-dismayingly-white MTV, the first to sell a million copies (this album eventually sold more than three million), and the first to establish many of hip-hop's narrative tropes—like rapping about sneakers ("My Adidas"), or boasting about vocabulary ("It's Tricky").

Run-DMC: from left, Jam Master Jay, Run, and DMC.

But with this, its third album, Run-DMC (rappers Joseph Simmons, aka Run, and Darryl McDaniels, aka DMC, and Jason Mizell, aka DJ Jam Master Jay, who was murdered at a recording studio in 2002) did something even more significant: The trio showed that hip-hop, then mostly a singles medium, could be album music. Its raps contain lyric references that function as recurring leitmotifs, animating several of the album's twelve tracks. These not only unify the work as a whole, they provide rappers Simmons and McDaniels (masters of the withering put-down) with a never-ending supply of material for riffing.

Raising Hell's fiery wordplay is matched (and sometimes overshadowed) by its genre-blind musical backdrops. These are the work of producer Rick Rubin, who'd started Def Jam with entrepreneur Russell Simmons (Joseph's brother) three years before work began on *Raising Hell.* A child of punk rock, Rubin offsets the Run-DMC raps with guitars that crunch even harder than Aerosmith's did—on "It's Tricky," Rubin transforms the guitar riff from the Knack's "My Sharona" into a massive goth attack. And he often runs DJ Jam Master Jay's turntables through rock sound effects too, with sometimes terrifying results.

Shrewdly, Rubin leaves the vocals untouched, so that it's possible to hear every last bit of the electrifying volleys between Simmons and McDaniels. These endure as some of the most intense point-counterpoint rapping in hip-hop history.

GENRE: 🎤 Hip-Hop. **RELEASED:** 1986, Def Jam. **KEY TRACKS:** "My Adidas," "Raising Hell," "Walk This Way," "It's Tricky." **CATALOG CHOICE:** *Run-DMC.* **NEXT STOP:** LL Cool J: *Mama Said Knock You Out.* **AFTER THAT:** The Beastie Boys: *Paul's Boutique* (see p. 57).

The Classic Cobra Recordings 1956–1958

Otis Rush

S ave this for a second stage of blues exploration. After you've heard renowned blues practitioners like B.B. King, Muddy Waters, and Howlin' Wolf, and have a sense of what the music sounded like in its heyday, the mighty left-handed guitarist and singer Otis Rush will astound you. Though little known outside of blues circles, Rush is hugely admired within that world, largely as a result of the singles he recorded for the Cobra label between 1956 and 1958. They're among the most satisfying pleasures in the music's deep history.

Rush was inspired to learn the guitar shortly after hearing Muddy Waters at a Chicago club. Not knowing much about the instrument, young Rush bought himself a guitar and played it left-handed, without changing the strings as some southpaw guitarists do. He began to develop a following in the clubs on the city's West Side; one night, the bassist, composer, and producer Willie Dixon, then working for the upstart Cobra label, heard Rush and convinced him to record. The first session, in the summer of 1956, yielded the steady-rolling Dixon tune "I Can't Quit You Baby," which reached the Top 10 on *Billboard*'s R&B charts.

This track and others establish Rush's signature—stinging, steady-handed guitar that frames a wild-eyed and almost unhinged vocal delivery. Rush sounds most at home doing slow blues—see "Groaning the Blues"—where his vibrating guitar sneaks into the spotlight one patient phrase at a time. But he's equally effective on the faster stuff, particularly hard-driving shuffles like "If You Were Mine." In fact, virtually everything here screams with the urgency that defined electric Chicago blues in the late '50s and early '60s. Though he recorded frequently after Cobra folded, Rush never got near this heat again.

GENRE: 😊 Blues. **RELEASED:** 2000, Fuel 2000. **KEY TRACKS:** "I Can't Quit You Baby," "Groaning the Blues," "If You Were Mine," "Double Trouble." **CATALOG CHOICE:** *Mourning in the Morning.* **NEXT STOP:** Magic Sam: *West Side Soul* (see p. 465).

see p. 465

The Circle Game

Tom Rush

T om Rush started his career as part of the old guard, a folk artist with a sonorous baritone and a healthy repertoire of traditional songs. Almost overnight, the Harvard grad (English lit, what else?) became something else—an early and effective champion of such songwriters as Joni Mitchell, Jackson Browne, and James Taylor. This album contains his captivating readings of songs from each of those writers, recorded just before their own recording careers took off. It's a key work, a foundation of the singer-songwriter explosion of the 1970s.

Like Tim Buckley (see p. 127) and others, Rush was a coffeehouse king awakened by the great experimentation happening in rock. *The Circle Game* is Rush's first attempt at a bigger canvas, and it pretty much has everything—an active string orchestra supports some tracks (Taylor's "Sunshine Sunshine"), while a kicky country band turns up on others (Charlie Rich's durable "So Long"). Rush doesn't do handstands to sell these tunes—he sounds like he just woke from a dream and is shaking off its effects. His low-key style

is particularly well suited to the music of Joni Mitchell. He gets deep into the feeling of internal restlessness that permeates "Urge for Going," and sings in a way that celebrates her precisely drawn images—those renegade clusters of stray words that resonate as exotic and familiar at the same time. Rush interprets Mitchell's songs with the care he gives his own (there are several of his originals here), and hearing his gentle readings, it's hard to believe that these songs, now part of the singer-songwriter "canon," were mostly unknown at the time.

GENRE: Ⓖ Folk. **RELEASED:** 1968, Elektra. **KEY TRACKS:** "Tin Angel," "Urge for Going," "No Regrets." **CATALOG CHOICE:** *Wrong End of the Rainbow.* **NEXT STOP:** Kris Kristofferson: *Kristofferson.* **AFTER THAT:** Jeff Buckley: *Grace* (see p. 126).

An Introduction to . . .

The World of Arthur Russell

Arthur Russell

Arthur Russell's world was really many worlds. The cellist, songwriter, and singer from Iowa was a part of the highbrow "new music" and multidisciplinary art scene at the New York performance art space known as the Kitchen. He provided backing for Allen Ginsberg's poetry readings. But Russell (1951–1992) was also the artist behind the first disco single on Sire Records—"Kiss Me Again," credited to Dinosaur L—and part of a rock collective called the Flying Hearts that sometimes included future Talking Heads singer David Byrne.

This single-disc collection, one of several to surface since Russell's death, from AIDS, in 1992, focuses on dance music. It does have a steady backbeat, but it's not exactly the same thing Justin Timberlake fans think of when they want to party. Russell favors cool open-

ended chords and oddly careening sound effects, many involving his multitracked cello. The vocal phrases are fairly straightforward—"Is It All Over My Face?," which has been cited as a key influence on the U.K. garage scene, is defined by repetitions of the title hook. But what surrounds them is often defiantly off-kilter and deliciously strange. It's art music for the dance floor.

Though much of this music was created in the early to mid-1980s, it aligns, sensibility-wise, with the cut-and-paste sample-wrangling that erupted a decade later. Russell's ideas about texture, and collision, presage some of the more radical fringes of electronica, just as his pop songs, collected on *Calling Out of Context*, anticipate the more recent work of Four Tet, Juana Molina (see p. 511), and others who create soundscapes on laptops rather than in recording studios. Russell never hit commercial paydirt, but his music points the way to a future where distinctions between highbrow and lowbrow become irrelevant.

GENRE: 🌐 Electronica. **RELEASED:** 2005, Soul Jazz. (Recordings made in the early '80s.) **KEY TRACKS:** "A Little Lost," "Wax the Van," "Go Bang," "Treehouse." **CATALOG CHOICE:** *Calling Out of Context.* **NEXT STOP:** Various Artists: *Journey into Paradise: The Larry Levan Story.* **AFTER THAT:** Ned Bartsch's Ronin: *Stoa.*

White-Hot Soul from the Motor City

"Devil with a Blue Dress On" and "Good Golly Miss Molly"

Mitch Ryder and the Detroit Wheels

The son of a big-band singer, William Levise started out in teen harmony groups, but not until the record producer Bob Crewe renamed him Mitch Ryder and his band the Detroit Wheels did his career get any traction.

The group's second recording for the Motor City's DynoVoice record label—a medley of Little Richard's "Jenny Jenny" and the Chuck Willis hit "C.C. Rider" entitled "Jenny Take a Ride"—became a hit, and established Ryder's "formula": medleys. Ryder's work in clubs taught him that a clever string of songs could keep people dancing. Though the individual tunes were held together by tenuous threads (sometimes just a drumbeat), they grew into mini-sensations, in part because of Ryder's gruff shout and his band's grind-it-out style.

"Devil with a Blue Dress On"/"Good Golly Miss Molly" is Ryder's shining moment. In three and a half minutes, Ryder and crew take two Little Richard classics on a joyride in a road-hogging drop-top V8. The rhythm section is all steady reliability—all Ryder has to do is ride around and shout at the appropriate times, and these undeniable songs take care of the rest.

Ryder, who is white, attracted the usual complaints about exploitation immediately after this became a hit—to some he was Pat Boone in shaggier duds. Ryder deserves better: He and his steady-rolling band showed that rock songs can be a renewable resource. Later generations got the message: Ryder lives in the brawny roar of early Bob Seger and fellow Detroiter Kid Rock, and his clever conjoining of "Devil with a Blue Dress On"/"Good Golly Miss Molly" figures into the epic medleys that are a fixture of concerts by Bruce Springsteen and the E Street Band. Much as Ryder did, Springsteen uses invigorated renderings of warhorses not to simply pay homage to the great rock past, but to make that spirit manifest in the here and now.

GENRE: 🎸 Rock. **RELEASED:** 1966, DynoVoice. **APPEARS ON:** *Devil with a Blue Dress On: Priceless Collection,* and many other hits compilations. (Look for one that also includes "Little Latin Lupe Lu.") **NEXT STOP:** Little Richard: *The Georgia Peach* (see p. 451). **AFTER THAT:** Bruce Springsteen and the E Street Band: *Live, 1975–1985.*

Kaija Saariaho ✦ Sade ✦ Dino Saluzzi ✦ Oumou Sangare ✦ Mongo Santamaria ✦ Santana ✦ Gustavo Santaolalla ✦ Moacir Santos ✦ Sasha ✦ Erik Satie ✦ Lalo Schifrin ✦ Arnold Schoenberg ✦ Franz Schubert ✦ Chico Science and Nação Zumbi ✦ Jill Scott ✦ Jimmy Scott ✦ Tony Scott ✦ Gil Scott-Heron ✦ Screaming Trees ✦ Márta Sebestyén and Muzsikás ✦ Pete Seeger ✦ Bob Seger and the Silver Bullet Band ✦ Andrés Segovia ✦ Sepultura ✦ Sex Pistols ✦ Shakira ✦ The Shangri-Las ✦ Ravi Shankar ✦ Sonny Sharrock ✦ Archie Shepp and Horace Parlan ✦ Michelle Shocked ✦ Wayne Shorter ✦ Wayne Shorter with Milton Nascimento ✦ Dmitri Shostakovich ✦ Jean Sibelius ✦ Sigur Rós ✦ Silly Wizard ✦ The Horace Silver Quintet ✦ Simon and Garfunkel ✦ Paul Simon ✦ Nina Simone ✦ Simply Red ✦ Frank Sinatra

S

✦ Frank Sinatra and Antonio Carlos Jobim ✦ The Sir Douglas Quintet ✦ Slayer ✦ Sleater-Kinney ✦ Percy Sledge ✦ Slum Village ✦ Sly and the Family Stone ✦ Bedřich Smetana ✦ Bessie Smith ✦ Elliott Smith ✦ Huey "Piano" Smith and His Clowns ✦ Jimmy Smith ✦ Lonnie Smith ✦ Patti Smith ✦ Willie "The Lion" Smith ✦ The Smiths ✦ Hank Snow ✦ Stephen Sondheim ✦ Sonic Youth ✦ The Soul Brothers ✦ Soundgarden ✦ Britney Spears ✦ Phil Spector ✦ Alexander "Skip" Spence ✦ Jimmie Spheeris ✦ Davy Spillane and Kevin Glackin ✦ Spiritualized ✦ Dusty Springfield ✦ Bruce Springsteen ✦ Carl Stalling ✦ The Stanley Brothers ✦ The Staple Singers ✦ Andy Statman ✦ Steeleye Span ✦ Steely Dan ✦ Stereolab ✦ Isaac Stern ✦ Cat Stevens ✦ Sufjan Stevens ✦ Rod Stewart ✦ Karlheinz Stockhausen ✦ The Stone Roses ✦ Johann Strauss II ✦ Richard Strauss ✦ Igor Stravinsky ✦ The Streets ✦ Jimmy Sturr and His Orchestra ✦ Jule Styne and Bob Merrill ✦ Sukay ✦ Donna Summer ✦ The Supremes ✦ The Swan Silvertones ✦ System of a Down

L'Amour de loin

Kaija Saariaho
Finnish National Opera (Esa-Pekka Salonen, cond.)

Here's the rare contemporary opera built around an extremely easy-to-follow story. It involves a medieval troubadour named Jaufre (played by Gerald Finley) and Clemence (Dawn Upshaw), the French-born countess of Tripoli. The two have heard of each other, and, like so many long-distance lovers in the age of Internet dating, they develop a deep longing, sight unseen. A third character, a woman known as the Pilgrim, shuttles messages back and forth. Most of the "action" involves this Pilgrim; each of the main characters unburdens to her in keening, contemplative stanzas. Aided by the Pilgrim, the two eventually get together in Act 5, though Jaufre arrives in Tripoli near death. This sends Clemence into a self-pitying swoon ("I am the widow of a man who did not know me!" she sings), and brings the realization that all love is distant and fleeting, dependent on a degree of imagination.

Saariaho, born in Finland, began composing in the late 1970s. Her early work used both acoustic and electronic instruments, and her pieces for chamber ensembles have drawn acclaim for their textural riches. Her music is light (and usually consonant) without being inconsequential. This DVD of the Peter Sellars production from Finland catches the piece's wide orchestral contrasts.

The two main characters are positioned on spiral staircases far apart, separated by water—the Pilgrim journeys to each in a Plexiglas boat. There's very little happening physically on stage, and that draws your attention to Saariaho's austere, slowly unfolding rhapsodies. At one point, the libretto describes how information is carried on the wind, by unseen angels. Get deep enough into Saariaho's contrasting lacy and brutish textures, and you can hear those whispering voices, carrying hints of ideas that the characters themselves can't quite articulate.

GENRE: 🎵 Opera. **RELEASED:** 2000, Deutsche Grammophon DVD. **KEY TRACKS:** Prelude to Act 4; Act 5. **CATALOG CHOICE:** *Portrait of Kaija Saariaho.* **NEXT STOP:** Osvaldo Golijov: *Ainadamar* (see p. 315).

Promise

Sade

Led by Nigerian-born beauty Sade Adu, the band known as Sade slithered onto the radio with the conga-spiced "Smooth Operator" in 1985. It was like a direct beam from Planet Eros: Here, in the age of synths, was an earthy essence as creamy as day spa body butter, with breathy vocals and melodies shimmering like satin sheets. Those desperate for something new to put next to Barry White in the romantico CD changer fell immediately for this aural aphrodisiac, cool and sophisticated and perfect for candlelight. Record execs had a term for it: "lifestyle music."

Promise held the #1 spot on both the U.S. and U.K. Album charts.

That first album, *Diamond Life*, was a bit erratic. By the follow-up, *Promise*, Sade and her gifted jazz-honed band of Brits fully refined the sound, by balancing vaguely exotic rhythmic undulations against catchy, wistfully sung hooks designed for the radio. Like "Smooth Operator," this album's lead single uses ersatz Latin rhythm, but "The Sweetest Taboo" is much more dramatic, a procession of catchy refrains propelled by hotel-lounge samba. The whole record percolates gently; often the only interruptions are Sade's sighs of rapture. And where earlier vocals are tentative, by the forlorn torch song "Is It a Crime," Sade sounds fully in control, communicating in a language of hurt bewilderment. The understatement she radiates serves the music well: *Promise* is an oasis of calm, one of few genuinely subtle records to emerge from the mostly shrill middle '80s.

GENRE: 🎵 R&B. **RELEASED:** 1985, Epic. **KEY TRACKS:** "Is It a Crime," "The Sweetest Taboo," "Jezebel." **CATALOG CHOICE:** *Love Deluxe*. **NEXT STOP:** Beth Orton: *Central Reservation* (see p. 568). **AFTER THAT:** Dido: *No Angel*.

New Age Space Tango from the Bill Evans of the **Bandoneón**

Cité de la musique

Dino Saluzzi

In his poem "Where Everything Is Music," the eleventh-century Sufi mystic Rumi describes music as a part of nature, a transitory resource that can always be replenished. "This singing art is sea foam, the graceful movements come from a pearl somewhere on the ocean floor."

Rumi might have been writing about a place like *Cité de la musique*, where the Argentine Dino Saluzzi imagines music that is fierce and definite and at the same time just a breeze. A master of the accordion-like *bandoneón*, Saluzzi began his career in the shadow of Astor Piazzolla—the legendary musician and composer who brought tango out of its slumber in the 1960s with incredibly intense and uncompromising music (see p. 599).

Saluzzi quickly differentiated himself from Piazzolla and others by concentrating on pure sound. He seeks luminous single notes, which he holds until they bead with sweat. His chord clusters are free of the wheeziness that plagues so much squeezebox music. His lines have folk-like echoes inside them, phrases that are at once comforting and eerie.

Though Saluzzi has recorded with various ensembles for several labels, many of his great works are found on ECM, the European jazz label known for its crystalline recordings. It's a nice fit, as Saluzzi's best work happens in airy, paper-thin atmospheres. On *Cité de la musique*, the *bandoneón* states a pensive theme and then trails away, leaving a lingering audio vapor trail. Sometimes Saluzzi sounds as if he's way out in the ozone, but since much of the music is rooted in tango, he's really just a block or two away. The explorations, aided by Saluzzi's son José (acoustic guitar) and Marc Johnson (bass), glimmer in unexpectedly poignant ways, haunting you well after the music has ended. Get inside these chamber-music conversations, with their quiet hints of heartbreak, and you may find yourself wishing it were possible to live in a city of music exactly like this.

GENRE: 🅑 Jazz. **RELEASED:** 1997, ECM. **KEY TRACKS:** "El rio y el abuelo," "Winter," "Cité de la musique." **CATALOG CHOICE:** *Rios.* **NEXT STOP:** Pat Metheny Group: *Letter from Home.* **AFTER THAT:** Gustavo Santaolalla: *Ronroco* (see p. 672).

A Musical Crusader Gives Some Sisterly Wisdom

Ko sira

Oumou Sangare

Malian singer Oumou Sangare specializes in songs about love, respect, and marriage. But the dynamo who possesses what is possibly the most agile voice in all of Africa doesn't have too many "happily ever after"

tales. Sangare is a crusader, a champion of women's rights. Her songs caution women to not believe the hype about marriage, and voice the frustrations of those who are sold by their families into forced marriages or polygamous relationships.

This is a radical stand for a woman in the male-dominated Islamic culture of Mali, and it has brought Sangare,

Sangare was a star by age 2.

birdlike flight paths, and after she's sung solo for a while, her background singers slide in for extended call-and-response exchanges. These showcase Sangare's flowing, endlessly surprising improvisations.

The musical inspiration behind *Ko sira* is undeniable—even those who don't agree with Sangare's message concede that her singing, and the economical

who is from the music-rich southern province of Wassoulou, much notoriety. Men have been known to protest outside her concerts, and she's been both hailed and scorned by politicians. None of this has deterred her. Sangare's second album, *Ko sira,* which means "Marriage Today," perfectly captures her warriorlike determination. As she exhorts her sisters to take control of their lives, Sangare sings with such clarity it is impossible to sense that anything radical or subversive (like, say, coping advice for a new bride) is going on. Her lines follow darting,

mix of traditional and modern instruments that surrounds it, is unique. She's the rare force who, having mastered the gentle art of persuasion, shifts gears and shouts with a conviction that rattles centuries-old assumptions. And that, all by itself, is a kind of miracle.

GENRE: 🌐 World/Mali. **RELEASED:** 1993, Nonesuch/World Circuit. **KEY TRACKS:** "Sigi kuruni," "Saa magni." **CATALOG CHOICE:** *Oumou.* **NEXT STOP:** Various Artists: *The Wassoulou Sound.*

No Decoration or Lavish Orchestration, Just . . .

Drums and Chants

Mongo Santamaria

The drum, Duke Ellington once said, is a woman. Which is to say, the drum is everything—inside it is the very essence of life. It is the clock and the time, and a mechanism for ordering the hours. In music of African origin, the drum carries the call to communion and serves as the heart of the ritual; it's the means of transcending the everyday and rising to higher levels of consciousness.

Of all the places where the drum commands reverence, Cuba stands apart. It's been a refinery for rhythms from Africa, and the place where complex iterations of pulse seem as natural as breathing. In Cuba, seemingly incompatible patterns gather into a symphonic percussive whole: The bells suggest one motion, the hand drums slap in a way that seems almost out of sync, and the *cascara*, that ever-present tapping of a stick hitting the side of a *timbale*, moves in a whole different orbit. Add them up and what emerges is a clustered complex groove that never feels complex.

The Cuban conga master Mongo Santamaria performed a great public service with *Drums and Chants*, a recording devoted to the fundamental pulses of Afro-Cuban music. Here, the interplay that's the bedrock of so much Latin music is the star. The entire record is devoted to interlocked conversations between drummers, and the parallel volleys between a solo vocalist and the chorus. The material is largely folkloric—there are *guaguanco* beats and sultry Colombian rumbas, and even several pieces built on the liturgical drumming of the Yoruba people (the deep, almost mystical *bata* drum that powers "Druma Kuyi")—but Santamaria replicates more than the patterns themselves. He gets the feeling, and the particular swing, behind each. It's as though he's pulling away a veil and laying bare some source code. This is essential for any investigation of the infinite permutations of rhythm.

GENRE: World/Cuba. **RELEASED:** 1978, Vaya. **KEY TRACKS:** "Margarito," "Ochun." **CATALOG CHOICE:** *Mongo Introduces La Lupe.* **NEXT STOP:** Tito Puente: *Top Percussion.* **AFTER THAT:** Batacumbele: *Con un poco de songo* (see p. 52).

The Linchpin of Latin Rock

Abraxis

Santana

With the introductory single "Evil Ways" and this explosive follow-up album, Carlos Santana and his namesake band made the crossroads of Latin dance music and rock into one of the most happening spots in the musical universe.

It was a zone of endless roiling percussion, magical extended guitar journeys, and rhythm that swayed like the hips of Mother Earth herself. If, as some in the press enthused, Santana was bringing revolution, it was with a sound as old as the hills. Tito Puente's "Oye como va," one of two chart-topping hits here, turns on a steady, effortlessly synchronized *son montuno* rhythm played exactly the way the Latin

Carlos Santana performing at the "Soul to Soul" concert in Ghana in 1971.

dance bands of the '50s did it. Except where Puente's brass usually saunters in to relieve the vocalist, Santana's version busts out the guitar like a streak of blue light, spinning a melody that fills the air with psychedelic flowers.

Likewise, the other FM favorite, "Black Magic Woman," fully integrates "rock" and "Latin" into one mighty pulse. Elsewhere on *Abraxis*, the group stretches in ways far more imaginative than the '90s jam bands ever did (for proof see the instrumental "Incident at

Neshabur," a suitelike showcase for the oscillating organ of Gregg Rolie).

Key to the enterprise is Santana, whose guitar has limitless powers of persuasion. Unlike those axmen who lean on the instrument's stun-gun attributes, Santana treats his guitar as a spirit vessel, fashioning long sustained tones into laser beams that cut right into the center of the music. Later, during the lean years of the '80s, the guitar and the percussion were the main reasons to listen to his bands. Here, though, Santana can practically coast, because everything's clicking.

GENRE: 🎸 Rock. **RELEASED:** 1970, Columbia. **KEY TRACKS:** "Oye como va," "Black Magic Woman/Gypsy Queen," "Incident at Neshabur," "Se a cabo." **CATALOG CHOICE:** *Caravanserai.* **NEXT STOP:** Malo: *Malo.* **AFTER THAT:** Chick Corea and Return to Forever: *Light as a Feather* (see p. 189).

Magnificent Instrumental Textures
from the Creator of the Brokeback Mountain Soundtrack

Ronroco

Gustavo Santaolalla

The folk instruments of the Andes, fixtures of subway stations and street corners all over the world, never sounded quite like this before. Growing up in Argentina, the composer and multi-instrumentalist Gustavo Santaolalla learned the special resonating characteristics of instruments like the *ronroco* (a ukulele-like four-stringed instrument originally made from an armadillo shell) and the *charango* (a five-stringed small guitar). He applied that knowledge to his shadowy original études, simple songs that celebrate the soulful tones each instrument produces. Though sometimes the *ronroco* is used on a distinctly plucked melody, it's often an element in a stringed-instrument latticework, part of fantastically billowing chord clusters.

Santaolalla's spare, reflective pieces exude the serenity of massage-table music, but they're hardly New Age meanderings—their sturdy and prideful melodies exhibit reverence for what sounds, at times, like folk songs from some long vanished culture.

The picturesque *Ronroco* was recorded at a heady moment for Santaolalla. He'd spent the previous few years producing some of the landmark works of rock en español, including critically acclaimed records by Café Tacuba (see p. 138). At the same time, his career as a film composer was taking off: Over the next few years his music would help define the thick moods of such films as *The Insider*, *The Motorcycle Diaries*, and *Brokeback Mountain*.

After *Ronroco*, Santaolalla went on to win 2 Academy Awards for Best Original Score.

If you've been transported by those soundtracks (and even if you haven't), seek this out: Its magnificent textures amount to a concentrated dose of Santaolalla's genius.

GENRE: 🌐 World/Argentina. **RELEASED:** 1998, Nonesuch. **KEY TRACKS:** "Jardin," "Del pago," "Atacana," "La vuelta." **CATALOG CHOICE:** *The Motorcycle Diaries*, Original Motion Picture Soundtrack.

NEXT STOP: Juana Molina: *Segundo* (see p. 511). **AFTER THAT:** Atahualpa Yupanqui: *Solo lo mejor de.*

A Big Band Sound like No Other

Coisas

Moacir Santos

This 1965 recording from Brazilian composer, arranger, and saxophonist Moacir Santos offers ten generically identified selections. "Coisas" means "things" in Portuguese, and each song is assigned just a number—

there's "Thing 1," "Thing 2," etc. It's a device, to be sure, but it has at least one positive effect: It encourages no preconceptions about what's coming.

That's exactly the way to approach this often beautiful coupling of Brazilian rhythm and jazz harmony. Santos's pieces begin with lighthearted melodies floating over rhythms derived from bossa nova. The themes seem slight at times, like caprices dashed off on a whim. Santos surrounds them with airy orchestrations that use the colors of the big band in new ways. His compositions reflect the influence of jazz legend Duke

"I think I was born with music." —Moacir Santos

Ellington: Born in poverty in rural Brazil of the 1920s, Santos ran away from a foster home at fourteen. He learned saxophone, and as a young man supported himself by playing in marching bands in Rio. He began writing music after hearing the Ellington band on record, and landed his first big job—writing music for Brazil's Radio Nacional—in the late 1950s.

Like Ellington, Santos wrote with the specific strengths and sonorities of his players in mind. For the ensemble passages, he seeks a kind of pastel lushness, and then asks the soloists to provide the heat. Many of these pieces feature ad-libs from Santos (he's remarkably dexterous on the big baritone saxophone), or the taciturn piano of Chaim Lavak. Recorded in three days, at a time when jazz in Brazil wasn't terribly adventurous, *Coisas* influenced such future giants as Sergio Mendes. It remains a shining example of cultural cross-pollination that enriches—and expands upon—its sources.

GENRE: 🌐 World/Brazil. **RELEASED:** 1965, Universal International. **KEY TRACKS:** "Thing 3," "Thing 5." **BUYER BEWARE:** The 2005 rerecording is less interesting. **CATALOG CHOICE:** *Saudade.* **NEXT STOP:** Abdullah Ibrahim: *African Space Program.* **AFTER THAT:** Chico O'Farrill: *Cuban Blues.*

From the Enchanted Dance Floor Mecca of Ibiza Comes . . .

Global Underground 013: Ibiza

Sasha

It takes more than a massive record collection to keep a dance floor in motion for hours on end. There's skill involved. And killer timing. And heart. All of that is in play on this craftily segued two-hour marathon of adrenaline-rush rhythm assembled by British DJ Sasha (real name: Alexander Coe). Recorded in 1999 to commemorate a particularly torrid stint at Space, a nightspot in the Spanish resort of Ibiza, it's ridiculously invigorating dance music that offers perspective on key details of the mixmaster's art.

The recording is not live. As with other titles in the Global Underground series, it replicates, exactly, the sequence of tunes patrons heard Sasha spin in Ibiza.

Credited with spearheading progressive house and trance music, Sasha has remixed tracks for Madonna, the Chemical Brothers, and others.

Working from the original song list, Sasha executes elaborate long-distance surges and sudden switchbacks with a smoothness that isn't always possible in performance. He begins the night like he knows people are just waking up; the first few tracks are low-key and almost ambient, simmering for minutes before anything as businesslike as a kick drum appears. The beats grow more insistent, and after an hour or so, Sasha is deep into his trancemaking tricks, juxtaposing woofer-pushing bass lines against dreamy textures against intricate percussion polyrhythms.

Each groove is plenty intricate. But Sasha, arguably the most musical DJ to emerge from the electronica boom of the 1990s, thinks big picture: Weaving BT's "Fibonacci Sequence" into FOB's "The Fly" into his own wriggling approximation of ecstasy, "Xpander," Sasha uses the transitions between each piece for fuel, and winds up hitting high-velocity peaks that pretty much smash to smithereens the notion that DJs aren't musicians. Very few conservatory-trained types could conceive of, much less execute, what Sasha achieves here.

GENRE: 〰 Electronica. **RELEASED:** 1999, Global Underground. **KEY TRACKS:** BT's "Fibonacci Sequence" into FOB's "The Fly," "Xpander," "Mercury & Solace," "Stage One,"

"Sacred." **CATALOG CHOICE**: Sasha and Digweed: *Northern Exposure.* **NEXT STOP**: | John Digweed: *Bedrock.* **AFTER THAT**: Various Artists: *Café Del Mar,* Vol. 5.

Quiet Reflection at the Piano

Gymnopédies, Gnossiennes

Erik Satie
Reinbert de Leeuw

The early piano works of Erik Satie (1866–1925) are the audio equivalent of slow-motion tai chi exercises. Melodies of arresting melancholy and overwhelming calm, they move as though suspended in molasses, with a deliberate grace. Very little ornamentation clutters up the foreground. Everything is measured: Each note is a halting step, the movement of a blind person navigating a strange house. The main ideas repeat at regular intervals, and for this reason, some consider Satie the father of New Age music. But when a master, such as the Amsterdam-born pianist Reinbert de Leeuw, digs into Satie, each new recurrence has its own temperament. The restatements come with distinct inflections—for Satie, a half-swallowed, barely glanced-at grace note can signify as much as a huge orchestral downbeat.

Satie referred to himself as a "phonometrician": someone who measures and writes down sounds.

Satie was a strange figure, an absinthe alcoholic who lived in a single-room Paris apartment, spent most of his time alone, and died of cirrhosis of the liver. He attended Paris Conservatoire but rarely showed up for classes. His primary source of income was work as a cabaret pianist. He was "discovered" by philosopher Jean Cocteau in 1915, well after he'd composed what became his most famous works (the ones heard here). This disc opens with the meditative "Gnossiennes," whose title was inspired by the Palace of Knossos in Crete. De Leeuw reduces the piece to its stark essence, following Satie's winding path as it stretches across barlines. On that suite and a similar one in waltz meter, "Gymnopédies," de Leeuw's rounded, contemplative phrasing puts listeners right inside Satie's mind-set, in a way that illuminates the composer's choices on almost a note-by-note basis. Satie starts a piece intending to make one point and one point only. Each chord is aimed at that ultimate goal—a singularity of focus that gives Satie's music the quality of an M. C. Escher maze: though these single-line themes seem nursery-rhyme simple at first, they exude a strange hypnotic resonance as they unfold—if you'll let them, they'll pull you away from everything you think you know about the world.

GENRE: 🎵 Classical. **RELEASED**: 2003, Universal. (Recorded in the 1970s.) **KEY TRACKS**: "Gymnopédies," "Gnossiennes," "Ogives." **OTHER INTERPRETATIONS**: Pascal Rogé: *3 Gymnopédies and Other Works;* Steve Hackett and John Hackett: *Sketches of Satie.* **NEXT STOP**: Leoš Janáček: *Piano Works* (see p. 391). **AFTER THAT**: Tangerine Dream: *Rubycon* (see p. 761).

Coolness in Every Scene

Bullitt

Lalo Schifrin
Original Motion Picture Soundtrack

Much film music of the late 1960s and early '70s carried a distinct echo of the music "the kids" were digging a few years before. It was easy to spot the opportunistic soundtracks, larded as they were with gimmicky, poorly executed attempts at rock and roll. At the same time, there were films that used rock and other pop elements successfully, integrating them in ear-stretching amalgamations that moved to the beat of contemporary life. Lalo Schifrin's *Bullitt* is one of the best.

Schifrin, who was born in Argentina, had provided music for several hit TV shows—that syncopated *Mission Impossible* theme is his—when he got the call for this 1968 Steve McQueen vehicle, which was shot on location in San Francisco. The music catches the wild wide-openness of the hilly city, and also helps underscore McQueen's famously calm demeanor: Everything smolders, nothing boils over. Schifrin is thinking chase scene right from the title theme, but it's the cue named "Shifting Gears" that establishes the pace, with dissonant strings cascading over a jarring groove. Hear this and you can almost see a battered coupe come flying over a hill, wheels well off the pavement.

Moods change suddenly in *Bullitt*, and so does the score: Even though the brass and string textures are plush, everything feels wound tight. Whether sketching a mod underworld, offering a moment of bossa nova calm (the muted-trombone tone poem "The Aftermath of Love"), or turning out a hard-swinging jazz boogaloo (check the kicky organ solo in "Hotel Daniels"), Schifrin doesn't merely appropriate trendy beats. He transforms them into vivid, eternally hip sounds.

GENRE: 🎷 Jazz. **RELEASED:** 1968, Warner Bros. **KEY TRACKS:** "*Bullitt* Main Title," "Shifting Gears," "The Aftermath of Love." **CATALOG CHOICES:** *Dirty Harry*, Original Motion Picture Soundtrack; *Black Widow*. **NEXT STOP:** Cliff Martinez: *Traffic*, Original Motion Picture Soundtrack.

Not the Scary Schoenberg

Gurrelieder

Arnold Schoenberg
Berlin Philharmonic (Sir Simon Rattle, cond.)

Those charged with luring paying customers to orchestra concerts tremble at the mention of Arnold Schoenberg (1874–1951). The modernist composer is responsible for some of the frostiest, most impenetrable works in the canon—he's the pioneer of "twelve tone" or serial music, a compositional method in which each tone of the chromatic scale functions in a predetermined series governing the harmonic and melodic "form" of the piece. They're a little like math problems in sound—they unfold at sharp angles and have been known to send patrons fleeing concert halls.

Schoenberg experienced his twelve-tone brainstorm, which he once predicted would "ensure the supremacy of German music for the next hundred years," in the early 1920s. *Gurrelieder* suggests that Schoenberg wasn't always so strident. In fact, before he became a dark prince, this imposing figure had quite the deft touch with smoldering romantic-era melodies: Sprinkled throughout this three-part composition, arguably his most important early work, are expansive and tuneful arias for five solo singers, accompanied by lush orchestrations reminiscent of Wagner.

When Schoenberg began the piece, in 1901, massive "event" compositions (like Gustav Mahler's Symphony No. 8, the "Symphony of a Thousand") were the rage. Schoenberg found a wild text—the poems of Danish writer Jens Peter Jacobsen, which tell of an illicit love affair between twelfth-century King Waldemar and a mistress, Tove, in the castle of Gurre—and concocted an unusual hybrid incorporating elements of song-cycle, oratorio, and opera. Schoenberg's vision required a massive ensemble: In addition to the five soloists, there's a three-part male chorus, an eight-part mixed chorus, and a huge orchestra.

Gurrelieder didn't actually premiere until 1913, and it offers a unique window into Schoenberg's evolution. The passages in the first two sections, like Tove's radiant "Sterne

"My works are 12-tone *compositions,* not *12-tone* compositions." —Arnold Schoenberg

jubeln" (sung here by soprano Karita Mattila), are bathed in placid tones and radiant consonance, with faint portents stirring in the low brass and strings. The appearance of the eerie Wood Dove in the middle of the piece shatters the tranquil "love" music of the first section and ushers in the shadowy, more macabre late scenes. Things get downright stormy in the third section: By the last few passages for solo voice and narrator, the orchestra has grown fitful, dissonant, and unpredictable, emitting splashes of notes that have scant connection to the vocals. Serialism is in the air.

That gradual shift in temperament is one of the many challenges involved in performing *Gurrelieder*. Another is sheer mass. On this version, recorded shortly after the terrorist attacks of September 11, 2001, British conductor Sir Simon Rattle focuses on the ruminating vocal melodies—in the liner notes, he says he thinks of the piece as the world's largest string quartet, and until the thundering chords of the finale, his version is striking for its intimacy. Rattle guides the Berlin Philharmonic as though determined to rehabilitate Schoenberg's image, to remind the world that before he was bit by the serialism bug, this composer made some downright gorgeous music.

GENRE: 🎵 Classical. **RELEASED:** 2002, EMI. **KEY TRACKS:** "Sterne jubeln," "Ein seltsamer Vogel ist so'n Aal," "Seht die Sonne!" **ANOTHER INTERPRETATION:** Deborah Voigt, Munich Philharmonic (James Levine, cond.). **CATALOG CHOICE:** *Transfigured Night,* Yo-Yo Ma and Walter Trampler, Juilliard String Quartet. **NEXT STOP:** Richard Wagner: *Gotterdämmerung* (see p. 840). **AFTER THAT:** Alban Berg: *Lulu Suite, Lyric Suite,* New York Philharmonic (Pierre Boulez, cond.).

Day Becomes Night, in a Heartbeat

Twelve Lieder, Moments musicaux

Franz Schubert
Elisabeth Schwarzkopf

S ome composers take an entire movement to tell a story. All Franz Schubert (1797–1828) needs is one well-deployed chord change. He slides from major to minor at an unexpected moment, and suddenly everything shifts:

Day becomes deep night, and what began as a pleasant tune develops a tempestuous undercurrent. The music of "Die junge nonne" lilts along in a bubble of serenity until the melody seems ready to end, fully resolved. But Schubert doesn't let go so easily; holding on to a series of tense suspended chords, he slows down the procession in a way that prolongs the conclusion.

Schubert wrote over 600 lieder during his career.

nist Edwin Fischer's anchoring accompaniment. Her singing illuminates Schubert's heady qualities. So, for that matter, does Fischer, both in the lieder and the fantastic "Moments musicaux" that close the disc. The piano piece, again an interconnected cycle, is notable for its shadows and understated sense of lyricism. Fischer treats it with spiritual reverence; at times, it sounds like he's playing a mass. His deep, carefully distilled phrasing celebrates the supremely organic singing quality of Schubert's lines, as though he's arguing that the composer is worthy of awe, not just admiration.

Schubert's primary medium was song; some consider him the father of the modern art song. These pieces, sung with authority by German soprano Elisabeth Schwarzkopf, show how he expanded the rigid form—usually ABA or ABAB—with gentle shifts of tonality and temperament. He arranged his songs into cycles, loosely linked "concept albums" centered on a theme; one set, "Winterreise," follows a man's progression into delirium as he walks out into the snow to die. It's heavy, chilling stuff. This set culls twelve of Schubert's stellar songs from different groupings, many of them written in the last eighteen months of his life.

Schwarzkopf understands that Schubert's schemes require open sky, and yet never flies at such elevation as to lose contact with pia-

GENRE: 🎵 Classical. **RELEASED:** 1953, EMI. **KEY TRACKS:** "Nachtviolin," "Die junge nonne," "Das lied im grünen," "Moments musicaux." **BUYER BEWARE:** There are many versions of Schubert lieder sung by Schwarzkopf; another on EMI, in the Great Recordings of the Century series, offers twenty-four lieder, but not "Moments musicaux." **NEXT STOP:** Edwin Fischer: *Brahms Piano Concerto No. 2,* Berlin Philharmonic (Wilhelm Furtwängler, cond.). **AFTER THAT:** Richard Strauss: *Der Rosenkavalier* (see p. 749).

Music During Wartime

Symphony No. 9

Franz Schubert

Berlin Philharmonic (Wilhelm Furtwängler, cond.)

If you're typically skeptical of the "Greatest Generation" hype about humanity during World War II, cue this up and believe. The scene: an early December evening in Berlin's Alte Philharmonie, 1942. War rages in Europe.

the players: the Berlin Philharmonic, led by Wilhelm Furtwängler (1886–1954), one of the conducting titans of the century. On the program: Schubert's Ninth Symphony, the summation of the romantic composer's formidable melodic gifts.

From the first downbeat, it's evident that everyone present—the musicians, the audience, the German engineers who captured the performance so accurately—is living in a state of crisis. Furtwängler brings the tumult of the world into his gestures; the intricate variations are delivered with outsized force, and every part, down to the last timpani roll, is executed with great purpose. War haunts the notes on the page, the breath of the players. Meanwhile, the music describes a place where cruelty on any scale seems unfathomable.

Schubert's primary theme is a long, meandering journey down a wooded lane. While Beethoven usually orients his symphonies around a terse repeated "hook" phrase, Schubert pursues an extended unbroken thought, a hefty paragraph filled with colorful ideas and inventive elaborations. Furtwängler catches the themes and their idyllic echoes in the development passages, but his eyes are trained on faraway vistas, the sloping mountains on the horizon. Check out the vivid second movement to hear how this expansive view yields a rousing effect. After a languid start, the conductor builds tension incrementally, with furtive dynamic swells. Eventually, after thirteen minutes, the orchestra becomes

impossible to stop, a river surging over its banks. The climax isn't all fury, however: Beneath the surface lurk tones of deep discontent, anguish, and choked-back rage.

Furtwängler was one of a small group of music luminaries who remained in Germany during the war and was known to have helped countless Jewish musicians escape. At his denazification trial, the conductor explained that he stayed because he thought the war would last only a few months, and saw himself as a caretaker of German music. He wasn't a Nazi sympathizer—many hear in his wartime recordings an intensity bordering on hostility, one man's coded protest of current events.

GENRE: 🎵 Classical. **RELEASED:** 2005, Opus Kura. (Recorded 1942.) **KEY TRACK:** Second movement. **COLLECTOR'S NOTE:** This recording, which also includes Brahms's *Variations on a Theme by Haydn,* is notable for a warmth and sonic detail that was far ahead of its time. Discovered when the Russians liberated Germany, it was among a number of wartime documents first made available on the Russian Melodiya label. **CATALOG CHOICE:** *Recordings 1942–1944,* Vol. 1 (includes Beethoven, Mozart, Schubert), Berlin Philharmonic (Wilhelm Furtwängler, cond.). **NEXT STOP:** Pyotr Tchaikovsky: *Symphony No. 6* (see p. 768). **AFTER THAT:** Ludwig van Beethoven: *The Nine Symphonies,* NBC Symphony Orchestra (Arturo Toscanini, cond.).

Beautiful Music, Haunted by Death

B-Flat Piano Sonata

Franz Schubert
Clifford Curzon

Franz Schubert (1797–1828) wrote this piece, his piano masterwork, in the last year of his life. He was dying of syphilis and mostly a recluse, but he spent his days churning out one great piece after another.

Scholars believe this and two other piano sonatas were completed in September 1828; all exhibit a fierce individuality not evident in his previous piano music. Around the same time, Schubert embarked on his unfinished final symphony, and it too is a leap, containing harmonic ideas that hint at directions taken by Mahler years later.

Something was clearly going on with Schubert, who despite some acclaim for his compositions was often broke and dependent on family and friends. His

In 1924, Curzon won the Royal Academy of Music's MacFarren Gold Medal.

late pieces share a stories-to-tell-before-I-sleep urgency, and a willingness to subvert long-entrenched compositional rules. They're also deeply moving: The B-Flat Sonata contains stunning elegiac melodies, themes that are beautiful in isolation and become more profound as they spread out and melt into each other. This is particularly true of the opening movement, which begins in murmuring quiet and dwells in a place of futility and resignation. The shadow of death hangs over each note, and Schubert sketches it perfectly, implying regret (or, at times, dread) without adding extra pathos. He shakes off the death-watch during the final movement, and just when things seem to brighten, the piece ends with a brief skirmish followed by a dramatic minor-key lunge into the abyss.

In chronology and temperament, Schubert is on the cusp between classicism and romanticism. He's attentive to form the way his classical predecessors were, yet he has the romantic's tendency toward rash expressions—his melodies are so loaded with ache you follow them just to see if he can sustain the mood. The often overlooked British pianist Clifford Curzon (1907–1982) accentuates Schubert's era-straddling duality. His tone is inviting and warm, but he maintains, through much of the piece, a teacher's inclination to emphasize structure over runaway feeling. There are plenty of lavish and dramatic versions of the B-Flat Sonata; Curzon's less-showy approach provides a clear view of what Schubert intended, and as a result, is a great way to encounter this magnificent music for the first time.

GENRE: 🎵 Classical. **RELEASED:** 1971, Decca. **KEY TRACK:** first movement. **ANOTHER INTERPRETATION:** Evgeny Kissin. **CATALOG CHOICE:** *Impromptus for Piano*, Murray Perahia. **NEXT STOP:** Johannes Brahms: *Fantasia Op. 116*, Eugen Jochum. **AFTER THAT:** Robert Schumann: *Piano Concerto*, Maurizio Pollini.

Da lama ao caos

Chico Science and Nação Zumbi

In the loose-limbed grooves of this first album by Brazil's Chico Science and Nação Zumbi, there are trace elements of James Brown (the tightly coiled rhythm guitar threaded throughout), Black Sabbath (the power chords), the Gap Band (the thumping stop-and-go bass lines), Korn (the hip-hop–style shouted vocals), Jimi Hendrix (the piercing lead guitar of "Rios, Pontes & Overdrives"), and suave African pop (the continent-hopping "Samba makossa").

None of these are rip-offs. Like previous generations of Brazilian musicians, vocalist and songwriter Science (1966–1997) and his band assimilate all sorts of music, and spit it back in a way that leaves only hints of their sources. Informed (and aided) by collage-style hip-hop beat-making, the band came along in the early '90s, at the time U.S. rockers were fusing metal and hip-hop with great commercial success. Science's crew takes the amalgamation to more sophisticated, polyrhythmic places. (They're Brazilian, after all.)

Science called his particular blending of funk, hip-hop, and rhythms native to the Recife region "Mangue Beat," a reference to the mud flats of the area. It proved almost instantly infectious: Not even a year after it began playing live, Science's band inspired several other outfits (see Cascabulho, p. 149) and began to attract the attention of such heavyweights as Gilberto Gil. Fed up with edgeless bossa nova lite, Brazilian youth rallied around *Caos,* and Science's rapid-fire rhythm-assassin vocals.

Science was killed in a car accident shortly after finishing the group's second album, *Afrociberdelia,* which was released in 1996. Although Nação Zumbi continued without him, Science's shoes were impossible to fill.

GENRE: 🌐 World/Brazil. **RELEASED:** 1994, Sony Brazil. (International release, 1995.) **KEY TRACKS:** "Rios, Pontes & Overdrives," "Samba makossa," "A cidade," "Maracatu de tiro certeiro." **CATALOG CHOICE:** *Afrociberdelia.* **NEXT STOP:** Carlinos Brown: *Omelette Man.* **AFTER THAT:** Cascabulho: *Hunger Gives You a Headache* (see p. 149).

Who Is Jill Scott? Words and Sounds, Vol. 1

Jill Scott

Give Beyoncé the form-fitting dress and Mariah the Blahnik heels; Jilly from Philly is the kind of girl who dashes out in sweats to put together a feast for her man after some early-morning loving. Scott's songs are the opposite of hot-action party-in-the-club gimmickry; one finds her describing an entire workday in anticipation of the evening of lust she's got planned. Another catches her sizing up a potential lover: "Your background, it ain't squeaky clean," she observes, adding, "Sometimes we all got to swim upstream."

Replacing the rampant Cristal-swilling fabulousness of commercial urban music with conversational observations about trust, romance, and devotion, Scott positions herself as a kind of anti-diva, the regular girl with an ear for poetry and a different notion about keeping it real. The songs on this astonishing debut ooze plenty of sex, but it's of the everyday variety—in Scott's world, sex is a beautiful and natural thing, not a weapon or a power center. These thoughts become radical when set to music that's far more imaginative than the automated thumps of Destiny's Child and countless others. There are ten kinds of smart music here, including a languid samba, a hard-swinging throwback to the soul-revue era, and several stupendously sung Philly-soul ballads.

Scott established the Blues Babe Foundation to help minority students pay for college.

A native of the tough streets of North Philadelphia, Scott was first heard sitting in with the pioneering hip-hop band the Roots (she coauthored the group's 1999 hit "You Got Me"). She went from being a spoken-word artist to frontwoman in an astoundingly short time—to understand why, cue up "A Long Walk" and marvel at her command of soaring lines and whiplashing rhythmic syncopations. Scott's second album, *Beautifully Human: Words and Sounds,* Vol. 2, continues in the same intensely musical vein, with Scott dispensing sharp commentary about senseless violence and the role of black men in the community.

GENRE: 🔘 R&B. **RELEASED:** 2000, Hidden Beach. **KEY TRACKS:** "Lyzel in E-Flat," "A Long Walk," "Slowly, Surely." **CATALOG CHOICES:** *Beautifully Human: Words and Sounds,* Vol. 2; *Experience: Jill Scott.* **NEXT STOP:** Erykah Badu: *Mama's Gun* (see p. 38). **AFTER THAT:** Bill Withers: *Still Bill* (see p. 871).

Ten Ballads in a Row Equals Pure Bliss

Falling in Love Is Wonderful

Jimmy Scott

Jimmy Scott was born with Kallmann's syndrome, a rare hereditary disease that inhibits hormonal development. This condition gave the five-foot-tall singer a perpetually boyish look, and prevented his voice from changing—his adult voice resembles that of a boy soprano's. "They called him 'Crying' Jimmy Scott because his voice just broke your heart," Ray Charles once said, as he recalled hearing Scott sing with the Lionel Hampton band in the 1950s.

Scott turned this handicap to his advantage. Through an on-again, off-again career spanning four decades, he perfected a sublime and unsettling contrast: He beams the optimism of youth, and at the same time his singing is informed by an adult knowledge of the bitterness and cruelty of romance. Ray Charles became Scott's champion, and when the R&B star started his Tangerine label in the early '60s, Scott was one of the first signings. Charles gave top-shelf arrangers Gerald Wilson and Marty Paich a simple mandate: He wanted Scott's voice cradled within a lush, string-heavy sound accented lightly by woodwinds.

Scott's small stature earned him the nickname Little Jimmy.

This turns out to be an ideal canvas. Singing songs associated with Frank Sinatra ("Someone to Watch Over Me," "How Deep Is the Ocean") and other crooners, Scott cultivates a mood of quietude that brings listeners into the emotional core of the songs. Everything here is syrup-slow—this is the rare instance where ten ballads in a row is pure bliss. Although there are moments when the tunes swell to a peak of emotion, Scott's everyday-casual phrases, the tossed-off half-forgotten ones, are just as memorable. He's one of those singers who can send shivers down your spine with the slightest of sighs.

The album, a career high, was responsible for one of Scott's "retirements" from the business. Shortly after it reached the marketplace, Herman Lubinsky, the owner of Scott's former label, Savoy, claimed the singer was still under contract and threatened to sue Tangerine. Charles withdrew the record before the press or the public could appreciate it. Exasperated, Scott stopped singing and took a job at a Cleveland hotel. He was lured back to music several times over the years, and in 1992 released an album called *All the Way* on Sire records, triggering a major comeback. Only after Lubinsky's death did *Falling in Love* return to circulation.

GENRE: 🎵 Vocals. **RELEASED:** 1962, Tangerine. (Reissued 2003, Rhino.) **KEY TRACKS:** "How Deep Is the Ocean," "They Say It's Wonderful," "If I Should Lose You." **CATALOG CHOICE:** *All the Way.* **NEXT STOP:** Billie Holiday: *Lady in Satin.* **AFTER THAT:** Bobby Purify: *Better to Have It.*

Find Your Center

Music for Zen Meditation and Other Joys

Tony Scott

This quietly engrossing album came about when the American jazz clarinetist Tony Scott visited Japan in the late 1950s. He was there to teach jazz and study traditional Japanese classical music, and after finishing a performance for radio, Scott encouraged the accompanying musicians to improvise with him using a common Japanese scale—the *chidori*—as a basis. The musician playing the *koto*, a harplike instrument, demurred, but the conductor, renowned composer Shinichi Yuize, embraced the challenge. Yuize hadn't done much improvising on the *koto*, but as he and Scott played they found a common harmonic framework. They were able to carry the spirit of the traditional music they'd just played into melodies that were created spontaneously.

Scott left Japan determined to record an album in the spirit of that impromptu meeting. In 1964, he returned to Japan and did: Throughout this set—which many consider to be the start of New Age music—Scott, Yuize, and Hozan Yamamoto, the master of the Japanese flute known as the *shakuhachi*, uncover music that's alive to the possibilities of the unfolding moment. The opening trio piece, "Is Not All One?," sets out a series of questioning long tones, and its contemplative drone sustains throughout everything that follows. The solo flights are few: Notice how Scott's clarinet cadenza on "San-Zen" is swept along by Yuize's one sweeping chordal flourish, with neither claiming the forefront. Similar dramatic exchanges crop up throughout, but sometimes the spirit connections are so placid and delicate they're imperceptible. They whisper a kind of Zen wisdom: Lower pulse rate, raise consciousness.

GENRES: 🌐 World/Japan 🎷 Jazz.
RELEASED: 1964, Verve. **KEY TRACKS:** "Is Not All One?," "San-Zen (Moment of Truth)," "A Quivering Leaf, Ask the Winds." **CATALOG CHOICE:** *South Pacific Jazz.* **NEXT STOP:** George Winston: *Autumn.* **AFTER THAT:** Keith Jarrett: *Spirits.*

We Interrupt This Program to Bring You . . .

Pieces of a Man

Gil Scott-Heron

When he wrote "The Revolution Will Not Be Televised," the scathing media critique that leads off this record, the poet and hip-hop progenitor Gil Scott-Heron envisioned a cataclysm so great it would disrupt even America's prime-time viewing habits. "*Green Acres, The Beverly Hillbillies,* and Hooterville Junction will no longer be so damned relevant, and women will not care if Dick finally gets down with Jane on *Search for Tomorrow,* because Black people will be in the street looking for a brighter day. . . . The Revolution will not be televised."

Electrifying when it first appeared on Scott-Heron's modest, voice-and-drums debut *Small Talk at 125th and Lenox,* "Revolution" got the full band treatment a year later on this follow-up album; it's this version that is most remembered now. Backed by a group of jazz luminaries—in addi-

In addition to his music, Scott-Heron published 4 books.

tion to pianist Brian Jackson, who accompanied the vocalist throughout this era, the band includes bassist Ron Carter, drummer Bernard Purdie, and flutist Hubert Laws—Scott-Heron rolls through verse after caustic verse. He riffs on race, politics, American escapism, and intolerance, leaving just enough room for the musicians to slip tasty responses into the margins. The result is a profound sound: Mind-expanding ideas set against simmering rhythms.

The son of a Jamaican soccer player, Scott-Heron was one of three young black students involved in the court-ordered integration of a public school in Jackson, Tennessee.

The experience eventually led him to the creative life. First he wrote poetry, then added hip rhythmic support—throughout this record and his other works from the same period (including the addiction rant "The Bottle"), Scott-Heron's lyrics question the status quo and mock the happy talk of politicians, encouraging listeners to think for themselves. That, of course, is a timeless notion: More than a generation later, when rap started to bubble up, old-timers hauled out this record to show kids how effective spoken-word delivery could really be. Plenty of hip-hop stars have acknowledged the debt—Chuck D of Public Enemy said in a 1994 interview that in his view, "everybody in rap has to know about Gil Scott-Heron, because in a sense, this rhythmic message music started with him."

GENRE: 🔵 R&B. **RELEASED**: 1971, Flying Dutchman. **KEY TRACKS**: "The Revolution Will Not Be Televised," "Home Is Where the Hatred Is," "Lady Day and John Coltrane." **CATALOG CHOICE**: *Winter in America*. **NEXT STOP**: Last Poets: *The Last Poets*. **AFTER THAT**: Public Enemy: *Fear of a Black Planet*.

A Heavy-Rock Meditation on Life and (Mostly) Death

Dust

Screaming Trees

The final song on this, the most underappreciated classic of the Seattle rock revolution, is called "Gospel Plow." It appropriates parts of a gospel standard favored by Pete Seeger and other folkies, and begins in the ageless cadence of an old-time spiritual. By the time the guitars kick in, vocalist Mark Lanegan has established himself as just another humble seeker who's a little bit scared of death. As the song unfolds, this character's spirit-quest takes him out in the big world, where keeping on the right side of cosmic accounts is a constant challenge, and the Grim Reaper is always trailing by a few steps. (The band members were familiar with this struggle: Before recording this swan song, they'd broken up several times because of substance abuse troubles.)

Dust is Screaming Trees' seventh and final album.

"Gospel Plow" hits all of the gruff-voiced Lanegan's sweet spots—it's got echoes of frontier Americana, a touch of bliss-seeking psychedelia, and lyrics sung off-handedly in a manner that's hopeful yet dour. It also turns on a trembling, undeniable refrain, buried though it may be under planks of industrial-strength guitar. Where Nirvana put the candy right out on the table, Lanegan and his cohorts dared listeners to dig. You have to get past the corrosive roar, past the foreboding lumberjack bluntness of Lanegan's vocals, past the ornate guitar countermelodies that crawl in the background. When you do, you'll discover that these are just plain great songs. Every last one of them.

GENRE: 🔴 Rock. **RELEASED**: 1996, Epic. **KEY TRACKS**: "Gospel Plow," "Dying Days." **CATALOG CHOICES**: *Sweet Oblivion*. Mark Lanegan solo: *Whiskey for the Holy Ghost*. **NEXT STOP**: Alice in Chains: *Dirt* (see p. 14).

The Careful Updating of Tradition

Márta Sebestyén and Muzsikás

Márta Sebestyén and Muzsikás

To understand why Márta Sebestyén is revered like a folk hero and adored like a rock star in Hungary, cue up "Három árva" from this, her first collaboration with the folk ensemble Muzsikás. Like much of her repertoire, it's music that's been handed down through generations, heard at family gatherings and the "dance houses" that are a key locus of social life in Hungary.

Though she sings the age-old themes the way they might have been heard decades ago, Sebestyén doesn't play the tune totally straight. One nontraditional anchor, a strummed acoustic guitar, gives the music unexpected coffeehouse openness. As the piece unfolds, the tone of her voice changes; what began as a weary lament grows more urgent, outgoing. Similar flickers of modernity pop up all over this amazing set, as the musicians respond to Sebestyén's sometimes eerie (and extremely mood-specific) singing with strident chord clusters and animated fiddle outbursts.

Sebestyén has done laudable work preserving the rural dances and folk songs of Hungary and Transylvania—several projects, most notably *The Bartók Album*, contain the folk songs that were appropriated by Béla Bartók, Zoltán Kodály, and others, interpreted the way the composers likely first encountered them. On those albums as on this one, Sebestyén savors the timeless themes. It's as though she finds the wisdom of the ages inside them, and no matter how much is going on around her, Sebestyén makes sure that those illuminations shine through.

GENRE: 🌐 World/Hungary. **RELEASED:** 1987, Hannibal. **KEY TRACKS:** "Három árva," "Hajnali nóta." **CATALOG CHOICES:** *The Bartók Album; Blues for Transylvania.* **NEXT STOP:** Abdelli: *Among Brothers.* **AFTER THAT:** Irén Marik: *From Bach to Bartók.*

A High Expression of American Idealism

We Shall Overcome: The Complete Carnegie Hall Concert

Pete Seeger

Near the end of the first half of this recording, which documents Pete Seeger's June 8, 1963, appearance at Carnegie Hall, the guitarist and folk singer makes oblique reference to the "events" in Birmingham, Alabama. He explains that he visited the area, one front in the civil rights movement, a few weeks before. As he shares a brief set of the songs he heard there, more than a few in the crowd sing along.

Particularly on "Keep Your Eyes on the Prize," it sounds as though this audience knows the words, even the appended verses that speak directly of the struggle for civil rights. Once he's got the crowd locked in a powerful unison, Seeger strays away from the melody, adding a slightly errant, deliberately scruffy harmony vocal. With that, the storied hall becomes a church and Seeger its choirmaster—the dedicated soul whose idealism inspires congregants and makes profound social change seem possible.

That's classic Pete Seeger: There's no outrage in his delivery, yet he somehow stirs outrage in his listeners. A founding father of modern folk, Seeger intends nothing more than to raise consciousness, and just by singing his tales of hardship and hymns of struggle, he does exactly that. This uniformly strong two-disc set contains the complete concert and includes most of his well-known songs. It serves as an excellent introduction to the vast Seeger trove of protest music, folk songs from across the globe, and children's songs. It's essential listening for anyone who wants to understand American idealism.

Seeger's songs are appeals to basic right-

"Any darn fool can make something complex; it takes a genius to make something simple."
—Pete Seeger

mindedness, governed by a universal golden-rule view of justice. Though they're now indelibly linked to the tumult of the 1960s, they resonate beyond that era, because they speak so eloquently about compassion, understanding, and dignity. When Seeger begins another sing-along, "We Shall Overcome," he urges his listeners to "go and help those people down in Birmingham and Mississippi . . . and maybe we'll see this song come true." And then he sings in that unshakable way of his. Pretty soon his believing becomes contagious, spreading possibility. And look where that eventually led: A reprehensible chapter in American history came to an end.

GENRE: 🎵 Folk. **RELEASED:** 1964, Columbia. **KEY TRACKS:** "We Shall Overcome," "Mrs. McGrath," "A Hard Rain's A-Gonna Fall," "Keep Your Eyes on the Prize," "I Ain't Scared of Your Jail." **CATALOG CHOICE:** *If I Had a Hammer: Songs of Hope and Struggle.* **NEXT STOP:** Bruce Springsteen: *The Seeger Sessions.* **AFTER THAT:** John Jacob Niles: *My Precarious Life in the Public Domain.*

The Rock and Roll Road, Immortalized

"Turn the Page"

Bob Seger and the Silver Bullet Band

Bob Seger, the Detroit rocker whose bellowing ballad "Like a Rock" was used in pickup truck ad campaigns, wrote "Turn the Page" back when he was leading a band that openly emulated the hard-driving style of Mitch Ryder's Detroit Wheels. Seger hadn't yet authored the hits that would put him on the plush upper-tier touring circuit later in the '70s. But he'd been playing rock long enough to know the loneliness of life on the endless highway, and with "Turn the Page," he captured the vague sense of dislocation, and the overpowering need for normalcy, that settles in after a few weeks of hard touring.

In the verses, Seger talks in the first person about his experiences—telling how he's taunted for his long hair and haunted by the girl he met at the last stop. But in the choruses he takes himself out of the frame to watch from a distance, shifting into the second person to follow his rocker persona on stage, giving his all and at the same time going through the motions, questioning and possibly mocking his ambitions. Toggling back and forth between confessionals and scene-sketches, Seger creates an enduring, passionately wrought portrait that reduces most rock "road songs" to dust.

"Turn the Page" originally appeared on *Back in '72*, an album that mixed Seger originals with strong interpretations of several rock clas-

The first record Seger ever bought was *Come Go with Me* by the Del Vikings.

sics (among them the Allmans' "Midnight Rider"). Never issued on CD, that album has been in legal limbo for more than a decade. The version of "Turn the Page" in common circulation is a 1975 performance at Detroit's Cobo Arena, one of Seger's first headlining gigs. It's electrifying. There's Seger singing with the raspy, full-throated commitment of his "Night Moves" and "Like a Rock" prime about the lonely touring life of stardom that was just around the corner for him. You can almost smell the diesel fumes.

GENRE: 🎸 Rock. **RELEASED:** 1973, Reprise. **APPEARS ON:** *"Live" Bullet; Greatest Hits, Vol. 2.* **ANOTHER INTERPRETATION:** Metallica: *Garage, Inc.* **NEXT STOP:** Gregg Allman: *Laid Back.* **AFTER THAT:** Kid Rock: *Cocky.*

Six Strings and Truth

The Art of Segovia

Andrés Segovia

Ah, the classical guitar: It's always at least pleasant. The performer may not be world-class, the piece may be only marginally interesting, and yet the sound of the instrument (alone or with orchestra) is so soothing, so peaceful, it can atone for gaps in technique or conception.

The legendary Andrés Segovia (1893–1987) never depended on that free pass. By the time he was performing concerts, in his early twenties, the self-taught Segovia had developed a singular tone and distinctive attack resembling that of flamenco guitarists. He also had an impressive ability to make the instrument "sing" even when he was playing demanding technical passages. But his repertoire was limited—there wasn't

much music written expressly for the classical guitar. Segovia crusaded to change that: As his fame grew, he transcribed works by Bach and Chopin (including the latter's Preludes, one of which, No. 7, is here), and cajoled and commissioned composers to write "serious" music for him. Among those who took up the challenge was Mexican composer Manuel Ponce (whose colorful "Theme, Variations, and Finale" Segovia recorded in 1954) and Spanish composer Federico Moreno Torroba (whose "Romance de los pinos," recorded in 1960, is breathtaking).

This two-disc overview includes some of Segovia's most lyrical recordings, many made in the early '50s when he was at his peak. It offsets modern pieces written for guitar with vivid transcriptions: To fully appreciate Segovia's ability to recast music intended for other instruments, check the excerpt from Edvard Grieg's "Lyric Pieces," or Alexander Scriabin's Prelude No. 4 in E-Flat Minor.

Those enchanted by classical guitar need not stop at Segovia, who was the main brand name for much of the twentieth century. The Australian John Williams, a Segovia student

Segovia received honorary PhDs from 10 universities.

who features a more fastidious technique, continued his mentor's repertory crusade by championing the neglected but amazing guitar-oriented work of Paraguayan composer Agustín Barrios.

GENRE: 🎻 Classical.
RELEASED: 2002, Deutsche Grammophon. **KEY TRACKS:** Edvard Grieg: "Lyric Pieces." Alexander Scriabin: Five Preludes. Joaquín Rodrigo: "Fantasio para un gentilhombre." **CATALOG CHOICE:** *1927–1939 Recordings,* Vol. 1. **NEXT STOP:** John Williams: *From the Jungles of Paraguay: John Williams Plays Barrios.* **AFTER THAT:** Various Artists: *Essential Guitar: 33 Guitar Masterpieces.*

Brazilian Metal, More Than a Novelty

Roots

Sepultura

Before this album it's safe to say that much of the rock world viewed Brazilian heavy-metal band Sepultura as a novelty—competent imitators who could be dismissed the same way the cognoscenti write off French hip-hop MCs and Japanese crooners. But after *Roots,* the fearsome four-piece from Belo Horizonte became unassailable: Nobody in metal anywhere cranked with such primal intensity.

Released just as the "alternative metal" of Korn and others hit big in the U.S., *Roots* is a masterwork of pressure-cooked aggression that marks a turning point for Sepultura (which is the Portuguese word for "grave"). On its previous five albums, the band sang mostly in English, and proffered riffs that bore the unmistakable influence of Metallica.

This time, vocalist Max Cavalera and his cohorts embrace their heritage—singing in Portuguese, while integrating African and Brazilian percussion (the instruments used on "Dusted" include the West African *djembe* drum and a "rusted propane tank" played by Max's brother Igor). The repetitive polyrhythms, which incorporate ancient ritual elements and field recordings of the Xavante Indians, help Sepultura bust the plodding stutter-stomp of metal into a million spectacular pieces.

GENRE: 🎸 Rock. **RELEASED:** 1996, Roadrunner. **KEY TRACKS:** "Roots Bloody Roots," "Straighthate," "Breed Apart." **CATALOG CHOICE:** *Chaos A.D.* **NEXT STOP:** Slipknot: *Slipknot.* **AFTER THAT:** System of a Down: *Toxicity* (see p. 758).

Punk Version 1

Never Mind the Bollocks Here's the Sex Pistols

Sex Pistols

For better and worse, this thirty-nine-minute blast of loud and proud scruffiness has become punk's ground zero. That's not to say it's the best punk record, or even necessarily the first. But it was the first one to tantalize, to terrorize, and eventually galvanize a large part of the rock-speaking world. And it remains an essential document for understanding the music's cyclical upheavals: When the Sex Pistols exploded, rock was mostly Foreigner. Safe stuff, with few aspirations toward rattling the status quo.

The Sex Pistols charged into the ring with an unruly sound, and an us-against-them ideology that disaffected kids everywhere understood immediately. These four musicians, barely competent on their instruments, took up the cause of England's unemployed and downtrodden, the legions of young people trampled by bad economics. As John Lydon (aka Johnny Rotten) said years later: "If we had an aim, it was to force our own working-class opinions into the mainstream, which was unheard of in pop music at the time."

Force them they did, with help from a rampaging guitar-as-blunt-instrument attack and manager Malcom McLaren's formidable hype machine. Early gigs were newsworthy for rowdy behavior (the band was known to spit on and taunt its audiences) that led to, in several instances, near-riots. McLaren seized upon the notoriety, using television appearances and outrageous altercations with media to fan the flames,

The Sex Pistols: from left, Paul Cook, Sid Vicious, Johnny Rotten, and Steve Jones.

and by the time this album arrived, a sense of full-on revolt was in the air.

Never Mind the Bollocks doesn't really need any hype. Its snarled refrains and bellicose chants—"No future for you!" Rotten sneers throughout "God Save the Queen"—signal that this is a profoundly different rock and roll enterprise. The songwriting's minimal. There's, like, zero finesse in the playing. And yet when the band lunges into "Pretty Vacant" or "Anarchy in the U.K.," it unleashes an undeniable force, leading to explosions of awesome magnitude that proved key to the then-developing ethos of punk. Fans loved the Sex Pistols because the band's music mirrored and magnified the decay they saw all around them. People who loathed the band considered its music (and its tactics) fresh evidence of society's decline. Both sides, at least, agreed on the existence of a downward spiral.

GENRE: 🎸 Rock. **RELEASED:** 1977, Warner Bros. **KEY TRACKS:** "Holidays in the Sun," "No Feelings," "Pretty Vacant," "Anarchy in the U.K.," "God Save the Queen." **CATALOG CHOICE:** Public Image Ltd (Lydon's next band): *Second Edition.* **NEXT STOP:** Ramones: *Ramones* (see p. 631). **AFTER THAT:** The Damned: *Damned Damned Damned.*

A Peak of Latin Pop

¿Dónde están los ladrones?

Shakira

Texas-born Latin pop star Selena cracked the door in the 1980s. The Cuban American singer Gloria Estefan knocked it open a little wider, through a series of singles ("Conga") that made Afro-Cuban rhythm an accessible exotic for middle America. And then Shakira, from Colombia, came along in 1998 with this album of seductive pan-American pop and rock. Latin crossover has never been the same.

On one level, Shakira's story is about pure ambition. After her 1996 album *Pies descalzos* brought her to stardom throughout Latin America, she set her sights on conquering North America. She hired Emilio Estefan (Gloria's husband and business Svengali), who put together a team of musicians and producers skilled at repurposing Latin rhythm for global consumption. This was a savvy move, as in the eyes of U.S. labels, the Estefans were proven hit-makers and could do no wrong. Shakira got the red-carpet welcome. Her flamethrowing voice and adventuresome songs did the rest.

Though *¿Dónde están los ladrones?* has Spanish lyrics, the music pulls from a rich smorgasbord of world rhythms—there are updates of her homeland's stately *cumbia*, explorations of percussive funk, and moments that glance at urban New York–style salsa. Shakira's mother is Colombian and her father is from Lebanon, and on one track,

the stellar "Ojos asi," she cannily blends elements from those disparate worlds into an unexpectedly entrancing groove. Where many in Latin pop strive for simple and repetitive words, Shakira writes as though in a romantic poet's reverie; her elegant, deeply felt images put the lyrics of many she was compared to—Estefan, Alanis Morissette—to shame.

The album's title, *Where Are the Thieves?*, refers to a setback Shakira suffered in the early stages of the project: Her luggage, including a briefcase that contained lyrics she'd been writing, was stolen at the Bogotá airport. Demoralized, she was forced to start essentially from scratch.

Dónde están, which sold over eight million copies worldwide, was the end of an era for Shakira: After this, she tarted herself up a bit, and began singing in English. On one bit of begging-for-a-hit salaciousness, she proudly proclaims that her "hips don't lie." Those hips, and the rest of her, offer more profound truths here.

GENRE: 🌐 World/Colombia.
RELEASED: 1998, Columbia.
KEY TRACKS: "Ojos asi," "Ciega, sordomuda," "Si te vas," "No creo."
CATALOG CHOICE: *Laundry Service.*
NEXT STOP: Selena: *Amor prohibido.* **AFTER THAT:** Bloque: *Bloque* (see p. 100).

Shakira released 8 of this album's 11 tracks as singles.

The Quintessential Teen Melodrama

"Leader of the Pack"

The Shangri-Las

Underpinned by the revving of the recording engineer's Harley-Davidson, this 1964 smash is the best example of a crowded subgenre: The tragic tale of young love. The song is the sorrowful reflection of a teenager who falls for the leader of a biker gang. Her parents don't approve. She defends him. Finally they demand that she cut him loose. She breaks the news, and as he drives away, she begs him to "go slow." He evidently doesn't listen, because behind an instrumental passage is the sound of squealing brakes and shattering glass.

The narrative has all the subtlety of a made-for-TV movie, but as rendered by the Shangri-Las—two sets of sisters from Queens, New York, who began singing together just a year before this song rocketed up the charts— "Leader of the Pack" is also somehow touching. The lead vocal, by Mary Weiss, conveys just enough desperation to seem "real," a sense

The girl group called themselves the Shangri-Las after a restaurant in Queens.

that's reinforced by the keening girl-group harmonies.

Other "tragedy" songs came before this one, but the chart-topping success of "Leader" sparked a melodrama stampede on the pop charts. The Shangri-Las made particularly effective ones: Subsequent hits included woeful tales about abandonment ("I Can Never Go Home Anymore") and heartbreak ("He Cried") that follow the "Leader" formula to the letter.

GENRE: ✪ Pop. **RELEASED:** 1964, Red Bird. **APPEARS ON:** *The Ultimate Shangri-Las.* **CATALOG CHOICE:** Mary Weiss: *Dangerous Game.* **NEXT STOP:** Various Artists: *Girl Group Sounds Lost and Found.*

First Thought, Best Thought?

Three Ragas

Ravi Shankar

We tend to see figures like Ravi Shankar—the sitar master from India who is often called the first "world music" superstar—as on a life journey with music, constantly sharpening skills in pursuit of unattainable mastery. That may be a romantic notion. What if Shankar hit the grand slam on his first attempt at reaching a Western audience, way back in 1956? What if all the experience he acquired subsequently turned out to be not really necessary? What if, in his refinement of the intricate systems that underpin the Indian raga, he lost something more elusive than technical command—a sensibility that allowed him to get beyond notes and the intricate counting sequences in order to communicate in beams of pure energy?

This, Shankar's first long-playing recording, invites such questions. For while his later output is plenty awe-inspiring, there are sparks of almost paranormal divine inspiration pulsing through this music. You can hear that intensity in the thrashing chords of the twenty-eight-minute opener "Raga Jog," and in the morning devotional "Raga Ahir Bhairav," which Shankar explores in double-time and later triple-time bursts. The improvisations are humble yet audacious; they uphold the pattern and, at the same time, seek release from it. They're notable for incredibly precise feats of sitar pitch-bending, extravagant slurred swoops that extend half an

Shankar was a student of the Indian *sarod* player Baba Allauddin Khan.

octave or more, and are played with such microtonal control they might fry the synapses of anyone who ever tried to make a guitar "talk."

Although Shankar went on to make many breathtaking albums—including the well-known *At the Monterey International Pop Festival* and the George Harrison–produced *Chants of India*, which offers imaginative musical settings of Sanskrit chants from ancient Hindu scriptures—*Three Ragas* remains something special. In the liner notes to the remastered edition, Shankar acknowledges as much: "When I hear this I feel the spirit of freshness and the vigor of youth in it."

GENRE: 🌐 World/India. **RELEASED:** 1956, World Pacific. (Reissued 2000, Angel.) **KEY TRACKS:** "Raga Jog," "Raga Ahir Bhairav." **CATALOG CHOICES:** *At the Monterey International Pop Festival; Chants of India.* **NEXT STOP:** Nikhil Banerjee: *Afternoon Ragas, Rotterdam 1970.*

A Jazz Road Not Taken

Ask the Ages

Sonny Sharrock

Sonny Sharrock started out translating the shrieks of free-jazz horn players into the language of the electric guitar. Then, for a while, he cranked up corrosive power chords and shuddering waves of feedback, fashioning a dialect from turmoil. Then he tore out for points unknown. Sharrock's music is among the most genre-blind in all of guitardom, and *Ask the Ages*, which he recorded three years before his sudden and premature death in 1994, is his magnum opus. It's one of the most mind-expanding records of the 1990s.

At various times on these originals, Sharrock and his band (master drummer Elvin Jones, bassist Charnett Moffett, and saxophonist Pharoah Sanders) sound like they're working in a New York jazz club, and their mission is to dismantle the conventions and niceties that prevail there. "As We Used to Sing" is built on modal chords similar to those used by John Coltrane when he recorded for Impulse and still had Jones behind him. In Sharrock's hands, these same chords rattle with something akin to brute force. The melody, however, is simple and sweet, reminiscent of early Neil Young. Inside that contrast is a clue to Sharrock's intentions: He's making jazz-informed music for rock ears.

All of *Ask the Ages* fits that paradigm. The opener, "Promises Kept," begins with a straight-up declarative theme, but within two minutes Sharrock and Sanders have drifted far out into a fitfully atonal interstellar orbit. Other tunes (like "Who Does She Hope to Be?") position simple lines against calm, almost sedate backdrops. Once he's set the scene, Sharrock works to expand the original moods. His solos are dotted with bloodthirsty lunges into metal or jazz skronk, but they're never just a look-at-me freak show or aggression for its own sake. With Sharrock, even the most quirky guitar tactics have a musical purpose. Referencing Jimi Hendrix one minute and Jim Hall the next, Sharrock sounds like he's on an ideological crusade, and in a sense he is: *Ask the Ages* amounts to a fitful, brilliant, brave assault on guitar orthodoxy.

GENRE: 🎷 Jazz. **RELEASED:** 1991, Axiom. **KEY TRACKS:** "Promises Kept," "As We Used to Sing," "Many Mansions." **CATALOG CHOICES:** *Guitar; Green Line* (with Steve Marcus). **NEXT STOP:** Derek Bailey: *Ballads.*

A Shock from Shepp

Goin' Home

Archie Shepp and Horace Parlan

In the 1970s, musicians who'd surged to the forefront of the jazz avant-garde a decade earlier faced unexpected career challenges. The New York saxophonist Archie Shepp, for example, was big stuff when the visceral, fire-breathing "freedom sound" was developing. But by the mid-'70s, that flame was cinders, a marginalized subset of jazz expression. Some artists switched gears to play tamer jazz. Some lunged more aggressively toward the stratosphere. For a brief time anyway, Shepp found gospel.

Goin' Home, Shepp's duet with pianist Horace Parlan, was recorded in 1977 but not released until 1985; it's the polar opposite of the bellicose braying that was the saxophonist's signature in the '60s. On such enduring melodies as "Go Down Moses" and "Swing Low Sweet Chariot," Shepp and Parlan (the Pittsburgh native who worked with Charles Mingus for a time) play with plainspoken simplicity. The overall tone is one of reverence.

Much of this record is tempoless, a mood that gives the themes an extra shot of majesty. As Shepp sings "Sometimes I Feel like a Motherless Child" in the pip-squeak upper register of his soprano saxophone, Parlan listens closely without adding too much, eventually contributing apt and unobtrusive chords. Several pieces find Shepp echoing his wilder Impulse years (see "Amazing Grace," which Parlan sets up as an ambling stride exercise). But even then, the saxophonist hints at rebellion in supremely melodic fashion. And both improvisers, working together, do whatever is necessary to bring the spirit to the forefront.

GENRES: 🎷 Jazz ✝ Gospel. **RELEASED:** 1985, SteepleChase. **KEY TRACKS:** "Swing

Low Sweet Chariot," "Sometimes I Feel like a Motherless Child," "Amazing Grace." **CATALOG CHOICES:** Shepp: *Three for a Quarter, One for a Dime.* Parlan: *Us Three.* **NEXT STOP:** Steve Lacy and Mal Waldron: *Hot House* (see p. 438).

Nothing's Shocking with . . .

Short Sharp Shocked

Michelle Shocked

During her performances, the irreverent folksinger-songwriter Michelle Shocked makes it a point to urge her audiences to get involved in music. Play or sing every day, she tells people, because "music is too important to be left to the professionals."

Shocked is living proof of that idea. She grew up in Gilmer, Texas, but after a rocky childhood tour of army bases, she left her mother and sought out her estranged father, who introduced her to country music and blues. Shocked bounced around a lot, living in San Francisco and Amsterdam; she was "discovered" while working as a volunteer at a folk festival in Kerrville, Texas. A producer heard her, and recorded what became *The Texas Campfire Tapes* on a portable cassette machine in a field, with crickets chirping in the background. That led to bigger things: This, her second effort, was recorded in Hollywood and produced by veteran Pete Anderson (Dwight Yoakam's musical director). It's got Shocked playing guitar and singing with the steadying support of a full band. Her voice, which exudes an errant, almost punkish energy, is more front-and-center than it was on *The Texas Campfire Tapes.*

Happily, the upmarket surroundings don't overshadow Shocked's songs, which share truths and shine light on injustices in a deft, almost subliminal way. Singing as though

Michelle Shocked, seen here in 2003, standing atop her tour bus in New York City.

she's got no time for niceties, Shocked kicks out raucous blues double entendres (the shuffling "If Love Was a Train"), paints a bleak portrait of where she grew up ("Memories of East Texas"), and summons a leftist's indignation to interpret Jean Ritchie's haunted Rust Belt lament "The L&N Don't Stop Here Anymore." Yet when she wants to, Shocked can reel off a conventional narrative—the lovely "Anchorage" is a series of letters to an old friend that ruminate on the diverging paths of their lives. True to her code, Shocked doesn't deliver these sparkling tunes like a professional folkie determined to enlighten (or scold) listeners; she lets her feisty character shine through. As a result, *Short Sharp Shocked* feels like an evening spent around a fire with friends, with one great storyteller holding forth.

GENRES: 🎸 Rock 🎤 Folk. **RELEASED:** 1988, Mercury. **KEY TRACKS:** "Hello Hopeville," "Graffiti Limbo," "Anchorage," "If Love Was a Train." **CATALOG CHOICE:** *The Texas Campfire Tapes.* **NEXT STOP:** Ani DiFranco: *Dilate.* **AFTER THAT:** Vic Chesnutt: *Is the Actor Happy?* (see p. 162).

Jazz Composition at Its Most Wrenching

Juju

Wayne Shorter

Vincent van Gogh once defined an artist's work this way: "Always seeking without absolutely finding. . . . I am seeking. I am striving. I am in with all my heart." Jazz musicians generally fit that profile; the saxophonist and composer Wayne Shorter epitomizes it. Among his special gifts is the ability to write music that comes from a place of deep immersion. His pealing, jagged melodies establish an avenue of inquiry, and then his improvisations draw listeners deeper—into tangles of emotion, mystic unknowables waiting beneath the surface.

The recordings Shorter made for Blue Note Records, beginning with *Night Dreamer* and *Juju*, from 1964, are the epic journals of a seeker. To create them, Shorter—who was, at the time, a part of Miles Davis's famed '60s quintet—rejected conventional ideas about composing for a hard-bop jazz group. His forms are more elaborate than what had come before. His rhythms combine broken swing and languid African pulses in a loose, perpetually jagged update of Afro-Cuban rhythm.

Of all the zillions of records with a tenor saxophone at the center, including those made by Shorter's friend John Coltrane (to whom he was frequently compared), this one is among the most wrenching, a song cycle of plaintive cries and beseeching declarations. Like so much great music, it thrives on the balance of opposing forces—in these tunes, which have been studied endlessly by musicians, brainy upheavals are tangled up with pure singing from the heart. Shorter's pursuit is not always tidy, as big ideas are sometimes left hanging, unresolved, along the way. But it is always rousing. And its energy is contagious: Listen to how the rhythm section follows Shorter, getting fully behind his quest. Everyone senses that Shorter is striving toward something metaphysical—and possibly unattainable. Like him, they're immersed in the search itself, not the finding.

GENRE: 🎵 Jazz. **RELEASED:** 1964, Blue Note. **KEY TRACKS:** "Juju," "House of Jade," "Mahjong." **CATALOG CHOICES:** *Speak No Evil; The All-Seeing Eye.* **NEXT STOP:** Joe Henderson: *Power to the People* (see p. 355). **AFTER THAT:** McCoy Tyner: *The Real McCoy* (see p. 792).

The Best-Ever Conjoining of Brazilian Music and Jazz

Native Dancer

Wayne Shorter featuring Milton Nascimento

Native Dancer hails from the middle 1970s, that heady time when jazz musicians rushed to embrace non-Western rhythms and ideas. Most of the end products were dismal—the jazzers didn't bother to learn the musical languages they were appropriating. Listening now, some give off the nasty smell of fast-buck exploitation.

Wayne Shorter, then a member of the fusion supergroup Weather Report (see p. 849), avoided this trap. For his wondrous investigation of Brazilian music, the saxophonist and composer sought one of its most distinctive voices, singer-songwriter Milton Nascimento. Together, the two built an ensemble drawn from both worlds—several of the Brazilian musicians had worked on Nascimento's breakthrough *Clube da Esquina* (see p. 540), and the jazzers included pianist Herbie Hancock—and then set out to explore Nascimento's airy rhapsodies (as well as several Shorter originals) in a loose, free-floating atmosphere.

The defining idea is understatement: This is some of the most delicate, sensitive ensemble playing ever filed under jazz fusion. Even when the rhythm is a percolating Afro-Brazilian funk, the musicians provide the minimal backing necessary to establish the pulse, and then get out of the way. This throws the spotlight onto the flowing, constantly morphing conversation between Shorter and Nascimento, two distinct voices in search of the same ecstasy. Nascimento frequently sings in a childlike falsetto, and on several pieces, notably "Ponta de Areia," his stately theme inspires impish, darting counterlines from Shorter. The discourse is lively and liquid, and kissed with deferential sweetness—it's as though Shorter and Nascimento sense that these languid and often pensive tunes are precious, and so is the simpatico language they've developed to interpret them.

GENRE: 🄿 Jazz. RELEASED: 1974, Columbia. **KEY TRACKS:** "Ponta de Areia," "Beauty and the Beast," "Ana Maria." **CATALOG CHOICES:** Shorter: *Alegria.* Nascimento: *Milton.* **NEXT STOP:** George Duke: *A Brazilian Love Affair.* **AFTER THAT:** Joni Mitchell: *Shadows and Light.*

Working Within the System

Symphony No. 5

Dmitri Shostakovich
Royal Concertgebouw Orchestra (Bernard Haitink, cond.)

A leitmotif of Dmitri Shostakovich's career is the way he dealt with tough critics in high places. After his racy opera *Lady Macbeth of Mtsensk* premiered in 1936, the official Soviet newspaper *Pravda*—in a review some believe was written by Stalin himself—dismissed the work as "muddle instead of music." Shortly after, the ruling Politburo, which considered the arts to be a propaganda tool that needed close regulation, was moved to issue decrees about what was acceptable in music. One dictated that "All aspects of music should be subordinate to melody and such melody should be clear and singable."

Shostakovich (1906–1975) shelved the piece he'd been preparing, the wild Symphony No. 4, and set out to salvage his career with the more conventional Symphony No. 5, which he wrote in three months in 1937 and later intimated was an atonement of sorts. It's a dramatic course correction. From the opening thematic nugget, the early passages are exceedingly tuneful, with a lyricism Shostakovich hadn't displayed previously. Then, particularly in the final movement, come harrumphing jackbooted marches and other bombastic flourishes, the kinds of showy episodes a composer might churn out with a party boss looking over his shoulder. One parlor game involves trying to guess Shostakovich's intentions in this piece: Some hear, in the brawnier passages, a sarcastic comment on the absolutism of Soviet life, while others hear a composer simply trying to survive within the system, to keep on keeping on.

"[Shostakovich] succeeded in forging a musical language of colossal emotional power."
—David Fanning

The third movement, Largo, is where Shostakovich most audibly stops worrying about official pressure; in the carefully wrought version led by Dutch conductor and violinist Bernard Haitink, the drama stretches over fifteen minutes. The string episodes carry a hint of challenge; they don't question authority outright, they merely seethe against it internally. Amsterdam's terrific Royal Concertgebouw Orchestra picks up on that buried tension, and magnifies it just enough. As often happens with this piece, the orchestra sounds somber in one passage and sardonic the next, extremes that are so vivid, they overshadow conjecture about the composer's intent.

This disc also features Shostakovich's Ninth Symphony, a light work (usually lasting just twenty-six minutes) that bears the influence of Mozart as well as the romantic-era composers. Shostakovich once described it as a "joyful little piece," predicting that "musicians will like to play it, and critics will delight in blasting it."

GENRE: 🎼 Classical. **RELEASED:** 1993, Decca. **KEY TRACK:** third movement (Largo). **ANOTHER INTERPRETATION:** New York Philharmonic (Leonard Bernstein, cond.). **CATALOG CHOICE:** Symphony No. 8, Chicago Symphony Orchestra (Georg Solti, cond.). **NEXT STOP:** Sergey Prokofiev: *Romeo and Juliet* (see p. 617).

A Russian Super Summit

Violin Concerto No. 1
Cello Concerto No. 1

Dmitri Shostakovich

Violin: *David Oistrakh, New York Philharmonic (Dimitri Mitropoulos, cond.)*
Cello: *Mstislav Rostropovich, Philadelphia Orchestra (Eugene Ormandy, cond.)*

Having already reined in the wilder elements of his music in response to government scrutiny (see previous page), Russian composer Dmitri Shostakovich spent the years after World War II tangled in a complicated dance with authority. The music he wrote during this period operates on several levels: Its surfaces offer enough "people's" content to please the party (victory marches and other nods to Russian bravery), while underneath he slips in more subversive, often bitterly ironic notions.

It's tempting to hear Shostakovich's works as facile patriotic outbursts embedded with cryptic hints; they're more than that. The gifted composer held onto his soul, and shared it in the beautiful, almost confessional cadenzas and solo passages of these two soliloquies for orchestra. The Violin Concerto, written in 1948 but not premiered until 1955, follows the format of Shostakovich's Fifth and Tenth symphonies; it begins with a slow movement, with languid extended lines that seem born of idle reflection. That's followed by a raucous second movement influenced by folk dance (think drunken comrades after a party meeting), a lyrical third, and a victory march finale. At each turn, soloist David Oistrakh, a Russian, stretches the themes out, savoring their myriad dimensions; note the clarity he brings to the tricky rhythmic extrapolations of the final movement.

The cello concerto is played by another Russian superpower, Mstislav Rostropovich with the Philadelphia Orchestra under Eugene Ormandy, which for a while was the welcoming committee for Russian composers in the U.S. Here the second movement, marked "moderato," is spellbinding. It's a study in the extended development of brief melodic "cells" that plays out in half steps and haunted-house shivers from the cello in its upper register.

Ormandy doesn't catch the jumpy nervousness of some Shostakovich lines—that fire is more audible throughout Mitropoulos's reading of the Violin Concerto. But Ormandy and the Philadelphians provide Rostropovich with something equally precious: sumptuous shimmers that cradle and cushion the cello. The sheer sound is one reason this performance towers over others: Few groups bring Shostakovich's enveloping textures to life so vividly.

GENRE: 🎻 Classical. **RELEASED:** 1956, 1960, Columbia. (Reissued 1998, Sony Classical.) **KEY TRACKS:** Violin Concerto: first movement. Cello Concerto: second movement. **CATALOG CHOICE:** *String Quartets Nos. 2, 3, 7, 8 & 12,* Borodin Quartet. **NEXT STOP:** Ludwig van Beethoven: *Triple Concerto,* David Oistrakh, Mstislav Rostropovich, Sviatoslav Richter, Cleveland Symphony Orchestra (George Szell, cond.). **AFTER THAT:** Aram Khachaturian: *Piano Concerto,* William Kapell, Boston Symphony Orchestra (Serge Koussevitzky, cond.).

Music for the Adventure Film Inside Your Head

Symphony No. 5, Symphony No. 7

Jean Sibelius
Boston Symphony Orchestra (Sir Colin Davis, cond.)

Portions of the first movement of Symphony No. 5—particularly the nervous-making strings that ratchet up the tension around three minutes in—may remind listeners of those action films where a damsel in distress is hanging from the precipice of a tall building, awaiting rescue. Finnish composer Jean Sibelius (1865–1957) gives the string players the task of manufacturing portent; for long stretches the music suggests mounting danger, until suddenly the lifeline snaps and we're on a collision course with calamity. The third movement contains more hurtling-toward-the-inevitable exposition, as well as a sweeping melody fitting for the final reel of an epic film.

A painstaking composer known for his nationalistic "Finlandia" and the pomp-filled march cadences of Symphony No. 2, Sibelius never wrote the same thing twice; each of his major works has its own system and logic, with highly individual devices (unresolved cloudy tones in the strings, intricate birdlike pecks from the winds) serving as unifying elements. No. 5 premiered in 1915, and then Sibelius spent four years revising it. He finished the dense, single-movement No. 7 in 1924.

The structure of No. 7 is plenty radical, but that's not why the piece is Sibelius's greatest. Its themes connect facets of symphony and tone poem, with hyper-descriptive images in the winds supported by broad punctuating chords from the brass and low strings. At times, his sustained tones and ostinatos echo those of Beethoven's Pastoral Symphony and Berlioz's acid-tripping *Symphonie fantastique* (see p. 82). But throughout this piece, Sibelius sounds like he's chasing a single thought, following it along a rocky trajectory. He rarely circles back to restate anything "familiar," or to provide a traditional symphonic toehold (though the fifth segment feels a bit like a scherzo). And after spending most of the twenty-two-minute

"If I cannot write a better symphony than my Seventh, then it shall be my last."   —Sibelius

work in pursuit, Sibelius ends it not with any flag-waving, but a single marathon chord that resolves abruptly. Some consider it the most distinctive finale in the entire symphonic repertoire.

This is the first of three recordings of Sibelius's works helmed by British conductor Sir Colin Davis. The performances are lively, and extremely attentive. Though he obviously knows how the story ends, Davis engineers each plot twist to maximize the surprise. He spreads that on-edge energy through the ensemble and then to everyone within earshot.

GENRE: 🎻 Classical. **RELEASED:** 1975, Philips. (Reissued 2001.) **KEY TRACKS:** Symphony No. 5: first movement. Symphony No. 7: first and third movements. **CATALOG CHOICE:** *Lemminkäinen Suite,* Iceland Symphony Orchestra (Petri Sakari, cond.). **NEXT STOP:** Hector Berlioz: *Symphonie fantastique* (see p. 82). **AFTER THAT:** Aram Khachaturian: *Spartacus,* Royal Philharmonic Orchestra (Yuri Temirkanov, cond.).

Icelandic Rockers Glimpse the Future

Ágætis byrjun

Sigur Rós

The title of this album, the second effort from Icelandic grandeur merchants Sigur Rós, translates roughly as "Good Start." But it's more than that—it's a dispatch from some vast and exotic realm, a fantastical frozen Narnia where keening voices echo in the upper atmosphere.

Ágætis byrjun was named Iceland's "Album of the Century" when it was released there in 1999. After the band made several tours of Europe, the album won worldwide

release in 2001; by the following year, Sigur Rós was performing at festivals and adjusting to life as a Next Big Thing. Rock fans starved for something majestic found themselves hooked: It didn't matter that most of the lyrics were sung in either Icelandic, or a made-up language its members called "Hopelandic." The words were far less important than the way Jón Þor Birgisson sang them, in an angelic true-believer falsetto.

To someone weaned on U2, say, the Sigur Rós maelstrom can be a mindblower, a wondrous dream state that's planted in Pink Floydy space rock but has a touch of spiritual fervor (and even, at times, optimism) peeking through. The pieces, mostly somber processionals, are augmented with slowly oscillating synthesizers and inventive writing for strings. Yet the slow churn rarely leads to the expected fireworks-erupting peaks of anthem rock (for that, see Sigur Rós's more accessible

Lead singer Jónsi Birgisson often plays his guitar with a cello bow.

2005 release, *Takk*). Instead, Sigur Rós—which, after this album, built a recording studio in a drained indoor swimming pool—seeks refuge on some barren icy tundra far away from rock and roll, and manages, through sheer dedication and a taste for extremely lavish sonics, to lure others to it.

GENRE: 🎸 Rock.
RELEASED: 2001, MCA. (Icelandic release: 1999.) **KEY TRACKS:** "Svefn-g-englar," "Ný batteri." **CATALOG CHOICE:** *Takk*. **NEXT STOP:** Pink Floyd: *Ummagumma*. **AFTER THAT:** Spiritualized: *Ladies and Gentlemen We Are Floating in Space* (see p. 732).

Spellbinding Scottish Fables, Jigs, and Reels

Wild and Beautiful

Silly Wizard

The "young rover" is a familiar figure in Irish and Scottish ballads. He leaves his home to sail off for grand adventures, expecting that his lady will await his return. "If I Was a Blackbird," the opening track on the aptly titled *Wild and Beautiful*, turns the tables: The rover returns just in time to wave good-bye to his lover, who's embarking on a journey of her own. The young man is initially stung by this, and then overtaken by melancholy; by the time Andy Stewart, Silly Wizard's lead voice, finishes the tale, the rover is rueful. He's learned the meaning of loss.

That twist is characteristic of Silly Wizard, which formed in Edinburgh in 1971 and disbanded in the late 1980s. A band of traditional musicians,

This is Silly Wizard's fourth album.

they were expert at twisting folk standbys and familiar songs into new, and often revealing, configurations. On "Blackbird," for example, the instrumental backdrop is typically calm and measured, while the harmony vocals on the refrain stretch out wildly, becoming increasingly haunting as the tale progresses. Stewart adapted the song from several different versions handed down by members of his family, and wrote two verses of his own. These additions show the group's finesse: They make the rover's plight clear without laying on too much pathos. (The Wizards save *that* for the tragic ode "The Fisherman's Song.")

One of the most dynamic traditional ensembles in Scottish music, Silly Wizard was esteemed not just for Stewart's heavy-heart vocals, but also for instrumental pieces that showcase the deft accordion of Phil Cunningham and the fiddle playing of his brother, Johnny. Among this album's treasures is a song called "The Pearl," a chamber-music rhapsody written by Phil Cunningham to mark his parents' thirtieth wedding anniversary. It is pure, undiluted sweetness.

GENRE: 🌐 World/Celtic. **RELEASED:** 1981, Shanachie. **KEY TRACKS:** "If I Was a Blackbird," "The Pearl," "The Fisherman's Songs." **CATALOG CHOICES:** *Caledonia's Hardy Sons; Glint of Silver.* **NEXT STOP:** The House Band: *Stonetown.* **AFTER THAT:** Hank Dogs: *Bareback.*

Rikki Don't Lose Your Father's Number

Song for My Father

The Horace Silver Quintet

Walter Becker and Donald Fagan of Steely Dan knew what they were doing when they seized the groove of Horace Silver's 1964 "Song for My Father" as the backdrop for "Rikki Don't Lose That Number."

The first single from *Pretzel Logic* (1974) isn't expressly "about" jazz. Instead, it seeks to portray the shady characters clustered in music clubs, unglamorous souls involved in elaborate between-set machinations to cop the next buzz. With its kicky broken bossa nova beat, Silver's tune serves Steely Dan as a kind of cultural marker, a last holdout on corner-bar jukeboxes during that changing of the guard moment in the 1960s when soul was ascending and jazz becoming esoterica.

The cover features a photograph of Silver's father, John.

"Song for My Father" endures because Silver, one of the most underappreciated composers in jazz, never let his music lapse into the theoretical. Just about everything on this hard-bop classic has an inviting pulse and an ethos of low-key island cool. The pianist's father was black, of Portuguese descent, from Cape Verde; his mother had both Irish and African ancestors. Much of Silver's writing is steeped in the looseness of African music. "Que pasa?" is a vaguely Afro-Cuban jaunt, while "The Natives Are Restless Tonight" alternates between a brisk samba and equally breakneck swing. It's one of many Silver tunes that travel intricate pathways yet never sound cerebral.

Song contains music from three separate record dates, with differing personnel—it's one of the few Blue Note albums of the period that took more than a day to make. Silver outlines his tunes in a clean and spare manner, with a minimum of bluster; his rendering of Ornette Coleman's ballad "Lonely Woman" is a minor masterpiece in the key of disconsolate. Silver's grounded playing style connects potentially faddish rhythms to the pulse of the urban world, not just the jazz world—which is one reason people who have only a casual jazz jones, acquired from exposure to stuff like Steely Dan, seek this out.

GENRE:  Jazz. **RELEASED:** 1964, Blue Note. **KEY TRACKS:** "Song for My Father," "The Natives Are Restless Tonight," "Que pasa?," "Lonely Woman." **CATALOG CHOICES:** *Horace-Scope; In Pursuit of the Twenty-seventh Man.* **NEXT STOP:** Bobby Timmons: *This Here Is Bobby Timmons.* **AFTER THAT:** Joe Henderson: *Inner Urge.*

Not the Clichéd Version of the '60s

Bridge Over Troubled Water

Simon and Garfunkel

This album, the last that Simon and Garfunkel recorded, serves as an effective counterbalance to the clichés that have grown up around American culture of the 1960s. The era is forever associated with a rampant flower-powered euphoria; Simon, the songwriter, specializes in pieces that sit idly and contemplate life in America from the window seat of a bus (or a subway bench, with a Peruvian folk band playing "El condor pasa" on the opposite platform).

The era is often portrayed as a time of unity, a moment of almost utopian togetherness, but Simon writes as an outsider, and some of his best songs take the perspective of an alienated, isolated young man. ("The Boxer" follows one such soul as he hustles in Manhattan.) The '60s stand for heedless free love; in Simon's songs, emotional entanglement brings heavy consequences and duties. The title song expresses devotion and empathy in terms more likely to resonate with an adult than some headstrong hippie: "When you're weary, feeling small," goes one verse, "I'll take your part." Simon is a deceptive lyricist—he starts out describing the scenery, and pretty soon he's drawn listeners deep into the thoughts of his complicated, often conflicted characters.

Simon (front) and Garfunkel's (back) *Bridge Over Troubled Water* won 6 Grammy awards.

Every tune on *Bridge* conveys a slightly different perspective, and inhabits a different mood: There are moments of withering cynicism ("Keep the Customer Satisfied") and euphoric expressions of teenage romance ("Cecilia"), personal reflections ("The Only Living Boy in New York") and pieces that swell with the aspirations of millions ("The Boxer"). Each song is a marvel of introspection, and also concision—Simon communicates deep tangles of emotion in coded bursts. And each provides listeners with something even more elusive—a quiet respite from the exuberant noise of pop culture in the Age of Aquarius.

GENRE:  Rock. **RELEASED:** 1970, Columbia. **KEY TRACKS:** "Bridge Over Troubled Water," "The Boxer," "El condor pasa," "Cecilia." **CATALOG CHOICES:** *Bookends; The Graduate.* **NEXT STOP:** Elliott Smith: *XO* (see p. 716). **AFTER THAT:** Laura Nyro: *Eli and the Thirteenth Confession* (see p. 558).

Paul's Excellent Global Adventures

Graceland

Paul Simon

Paul Simon once said the inspiration for *Graceland* came from a cassette of South African "township jive" he'd listened to over and over. Enamored, the singer and songwriter eventually invited South African musicians to join him for an experiment. Simon captured basic rhythm tracks in Africa (with a band anchored by the impossibly nimble bassist Bakithi Khumalo), and then spent months singing along with those sketches, developing songs. Once he had an outline, he enlisted the heavenly chorus of Ladysmith Black Mambazo, which until this project had primarily sung a capella. He then added accordion from Louisiana zydeco master Rockin' Dopsie, and the East Los Angeles band Los Lobos, and his own (often talk-sung) vocals.

PAUL·SIMON
GRACELAND

Graceland was added to the United States National Recording Registry in 2006.

From this ingredient list came a simmering, savory stew, music that was profoundly connected to the earth—but not tethered to any one region. Simon picked up bits of African pop but didn't cop every attribute of the indigenous styles—he was going for pastiche, a mingling of "roots" musics, and his assimilation was so thorough it's impossible to pinpoint where the African influence ends, say, and the gospel one begins. This wasn't the first time Simon explored rhythms from exotic locales—his 1980 film and soundtrack *One Trick Pony* contains a perky Caribbean fantasia entitled "Late in the Evening," which was a minor hit. *Graceland* represents the singer-songwriter's most concerted attempt at integrating diverse styles. It came out around the same time as similarly outward-looking integrationist experiments from Peter Gabriel and others, and is credited with helping to popularize African music in the U.S. and Europe.

The success encouraged Simon to keep going. He followed the drums of Africa across the slave routes, to Brazil, and on the entrancing *The Rhythm of the Saints* again sought collaboration with indigenous specialists, pairing them with several of *Graceland*'s African musicians. These exchanges inspired an even broader range of songs—there is a dejected metropolitan love ode ("She Moves On") next to a poetic revery in waltz time ("Further to Fly") next to a mystical journey built around Brazilian vocalist Milton Nascimento ("Spirit Voices") that is among the most evocative pieces in Simon's songbook. The monumental *Graceland* is generally considered Simon's masterpiece, but the hybrid spirit he sought there is more fully realized on *The Rhythm of the Saints*, where it sounds like the rivers of Africa and Brazil are running parallel, proud and unstoppable.

GENRE: ✪ Pop. **RELEASED:** 1986, Warner Bros. **KEY TRACKS:** "Diamonds on the Soles of Her Shoes," "Graceland." **CATALOG CHOICE:** *The Rhythm of the Saints.* **NEXT STOP:** Various Artists: *The Indestructible Beat of Soweto* (see p. 814). **AFTER THAT:** Peter Gabriel: *So.*

More than Four Women

Anthology

Nina Simone

In the song-drama "Four Women," one of several Nina Simone originals on this career overview released shortly after she died in 2003, at age seventy, the classically trained pianist and singer assumes the identities of four black female archetypes—the wise, long-suffering laborer, the whore, the militant, and the confused child of mixed-race parents. Each is distinct, stepping out of a different period novel. Through changes in inflection and dialect, Simone forces her listeners to confront those characters, feel their humanity, sense their struggles. By the time the song ends, you know about more than just four isolated women; you know about womanhood and pride, dignity and the tangled politics of identity and race.

It's always that way with Simone: Whether she's singing some overworked show tune or one of her own cautionary essays about struggle ("To Be Young, Gifted, and Black," a bona fide standard, is included here), there is deep perspective in her phrasing, some connection to life beyond the velvet banquette. She rarely throws herself completely into extremes like "happy" or "sad"—hers is complex music in the key of bittersweet, complete with the messier aspects that jazz divas sometimes gloss over. Her love songs, like the wrenching "I Loves You Porgy,"

have the weary, worn-down countenance of the soldier returning from violent battle; her protest songs ("Mississippi Goddam" is the most famous) are delivered with a romantic's blue-sky idealism.

Simone's most memorable material carries the core truths of blues and gospel, yet she's always stretching beyond those roots—she incorporates the fevered repetitions of '60s soul and the open hurt of Billie Holiday (there's a harrowing, almost disgusted treatment of "Strange Fruit" here). As she evolved, she became a high priestess of nuance who, by slipping traces of anger and elation and lust and frustration into the margins, provided meanings and implications that weren't there before.

GENRES: 🎧 Jazz 🎤 Vocals. **RELEASED:** 2003, RCA. **KEY TRACKS:** "Mississippi Goddam," "To Be Young, Gifted, and Black." **CATALOG CHOICE:** *Four Women*. **NEXT STOP:** Jill Scott: *Who Is Jill Scott?*, Vol. 1 (see p. 681).

Blue-Eyed Soul from a British Redhead

Picture Book

Simply Red

Face it: The track record of white people doing black music isn't all that stellar. Start with Pat Boone's unswinging covers of Little Richard, which outsold the originals and remain an outrage of exploitation, and work your way up the time line. What you find is one feeble approximation after another. Even the mega-selling acts of blue-eyed soul don't exactly thrive under long-term scrutiny. Hall & Oates? Great singing, three for-the-ages songs, and after that you can figure out why the luncheonette was abandoned. George Michael? Please.

On the short list of white vocalists who instinctively understand the fine art of singing soul—Boz Scaggs, Van Morrison, David Bowie circa *Young Americans*—belongs Mick Hucknall, the leader of Simply Red. With this surprising debut album, Hucknall and a band of Stax-worshipping rhythm players turn out natty (if occasionally overly synthesized) songs that embrace the basic song styles and strategies of soul—but are never cheap knockoffs. "Money's Too Tight (to Mention)," for example, is built on a disco shoop, but it

Mick Hucknall (pictured) is the driving force and only permanent member of Simply Red.

uses the plush trappings of Philadelphia soul—shivering strings and O'Jays-style male-harmony choruses—to shout down the unfeeling Reagan-era response to poverty.

Blue-eyed soul ultimately works on the strength of the songs, and there lies the real story of *Picture Book*. From the opening plea "Come to My Aid" to the rousing "Jericho" to the gentle "Holding Back the Years" to the grumbling funk of "(Open Up the) Red Box," these ten pieces celebrate and then revitalize the basic teachings of old soul in ways even the glammed-out New Wave kids of the '80s could appreciate.

GENRE: 🎸 Rock. **RELEASED:** 1985, Elektra. **KEY TRACKS:** "Holding Back the Years," "Come to My Aid," "Jericho," "Heaven." **NEXT STOP:** Boz Scaggs: *Silk Degrees*. **AFTER THAT:** James Hunter: *People Gonna Talk*.

Swing Is Here

Songs for Swingin' Lovers

Frank Sinatra

We put Frank Sinatra on to snap a party to life. Or to sulk after the party's over. Or to grapple with whatever we don't understand about human nature. Because embedded in his music is something

more consequential than those cream-of-the-crop top-shelf notes—there are ideas about how to carry oneself, navigate the social graces, engage the world. Sinatra sings as though the shape of his next phrase might actually have impact on his destiny. And, by extension, our own.

Of course, that's how singers rolled back in the days when they ruled Las Vegas. Even then, Sinatra's attention to detail was singular.

Honoring Sinatra with a Grammy Legend Award in 1994, U2 lead singer Bono described the singer's gift this way: "Comin' through with the big stick, the aside, the quiet compliment, good cop/bad cop all in the same breath."

Songs for Swingin' Lovers is one of the best showcases for that dizzying sequence of uppercuts and jabs, in which unbridled cocksure exuberance is followed by moments of anguished soul-searching. It's among the early collaborations between Sinatra and arranger Nelson Riddle, and it shows how even when the rhythms are designed to not rattle the china, Sinatra somehow rattles the soul. On chart after ambling chart, each one decorated with a slightly different set of studio-orchestra colors, the Chairman of the Board demonstrates all the little ways exacting placement and phrasing can light up the room. His lines fall fitfully against the pattering rhythms. Or they glide along, gently increasing altitude, helped aloft by trembling strings. Or, on the reading of "Love Is Here to Stay" that is one of several definitive performances here, his phrases are steeped in a besotted, lovestruck haze.

No other American singer entertained this way, in sly bursts that formed their own iconographic musical language. Even within the canon of Sinatra "swing" records there are huge differences: *Swingin' Session and More*, perhaps Sinatra at his most barn-burning, is a blur of up-tempo jazz offset by one hall-of-fame ballad ("I Concentrate on You"), while *A Swingin' Affair* seeks a bluesier swagger. Bono called him a "singer who makes other men poets," and it takes about thirty seconds, on any track on any Sinatra record with the word "swing" in the title, to hear why.

Sinatra, seen sporting his signature debonair style, was a member of the famous Rat Pack.

GENRE: 🎤 Vocals. **RELEASED:** 1956, Capitol. **KEY TRACKS:** "Love Is Here to Stay," "I've Got You Under My Skin," "We'll Be Together Again," "Old Devil Moon." **CATALOG CHOICES:** *Come Dance With Me; Swingin' Session and More.* **NEXT STOP:** Tony Bennett: *Basie Swings, Bennett Sings.* **AFTER THAT:** Dinah Washington: *Dinah Jams.*

Love Trouble, Made Beautiful

Sings for Only the Lonely

Frank Sinatra

The time, as the classic taproom ode "One for My Baby" tells us, is quarter to three. In the thick haze of this album, though, it feels later. And lonelier. These are the wee small hours when Frank Sinatra, world's greatest saloon singer, is in his element, presiding over a kind of barstool catharsis that spreads the hurt around. He tells about the great love that has crumbled (or is crumbling). His voice trembles, and every tick is part of the portrait of a brave former romantic in defeat. He plays this type with great empathy, as a wounded Everyman—one of so many characters who lurk in the lounge nursing their disappointment, bending the ear of the barkeep, seeking consolation in the woozy hues of jazz and cocktails.

The sad songs come one after another on this album, Sinatra's definitive ballad collection. They include grand rushes of futile hope

("What's New?"), self-pitying realizations ("Guess I'll Hang My Tears Out to Dry"), and moments of delicious, carefully wrought bittersweetness ("Spring Is Here"). Each selection touches on a different aftershock of romance: Following one chorus of "Willow Weep for Me" that catches Sinatra at what sounds like a rock-bottom low point, arranger Nelson Riddle begins the last stanza with a woeful descending string line that plunges the mood deeper into despair. The moment is so heavy you may find yourself actually relieved when the song ends.

This album consists of fourteen downers in a row. Even skilled singers have trouble sus-

taining that type of spell. Sinatra, though, flour-ishes. One or two slow weepers is not enough for him. He needs every one of these songs to even begin to address the wonder of romance and the endlessness of its disappointments.

GENRE: 🎵 Vocals. **RELEASED:** 1958, Capitol. **KEY TRACKS:** "Angel Eyes," "What's New?," "Willow Weep for Me," "One for My Baby," "Spring Is Here." **CATALOG CHOICES:** *In the Wee Small Hours; Sinatra & Strings; September of My Years.* **NEXT STOP:** Jimmy Scott: *Falling in Love Is Wonderful* (see p. 682). **AFTER THAT:** Chet Baker: *Let's Get Lost* (see p. 40).

Ol' Blue Eyes Meets the Picasso of Bossa Nova

Francis Albert Sinatra & Antonio Carlos Jobim

Frank Sinatra and Antonio Carlos Jobim

Frank Sinatra founded Reprise Records in 1960 because he wanted to call his own shots. During the label's first few years, a period when he was also recording for Capitol to finish his contract there, he surrounded himself with great talents, and cultivated an atmosphere of anything-goes artistic collaboration. In addition to the hard-swinging records with the Count Basie Orchestra (*Sinatra/Basie* and *Sinatra at the Sands* being the most famous), Sinatra spear-headed a thoughtful meeting with Duke Ellington (*Francis A. & Edward K.*), and had a hit duet with his daughter Nancy, "Something Stupid."

Jobim was a pioneer of the Brazilian bossa nova style.

Francis Albert Sinatra & Antonio Carlos Jobim is easily the most astounding of these gatherings, and one of the absolute high points

of the 1960s. Sinatra might have come late to bossa nova—the Stan Getz/João Gilberto (see p. 308) phenomenon happened in 1963, and this wasn't issued until '67—but he threw himself into it. Sinatra sneaks inside Jobim's fragile, lament-ing lines, and makes himself right at home. As happens with so many of his vocal per-formances, Sinatra teases out the unstated emotions drifting behind the words and between the sea-grass backgrounds of arranger Claus Ogermann. Sinatra underplays so brilliantly he makes it seem as though the Brazilian composer, who's on guitar and sometimes vocals here, *is* the star of the show.

And in one sense Jobim is the star—his regal music challenges singers like no other music does. You can tell the singer was completely absorbed in the composer's ethos by the way he interprets several pieces not written by Jobim, including "I Concentrate on You." These utilize sullen, hotel-lounge bossa beats, and Sinatra reframes their melodies to conform to his collaborator's singular languidness. By the time he's finished, he's morphed them into Jobim tunes—no small feat.

GENRE:  Vocals. **RELEASED:** 1967, Reprise. **KEY TRACKS:** "Corcovado," "How Insensitive," "I Concentrate on You." **CATALOG CHOICE:** *Sinatra/Basie.* **NEXT STOP:** Sarah Vaughan: *Brazilian Romance.* **AFTER THAT:** Cannonball Adderley: *Cannonball's Bossa Nova.*

An Underappreciated American Voice

Mendocino

The Sir Douglas Quintet

In sound-bite terms, Doug Sahm's legacy boils down to one wild garage-rock freak-out that became an unlikely hit ("She's About a Mover") and a few plaintive pop songs ("Mendocino" being the most well known) that later influenced such hit-makers as Jimmy Buffett. But as a founding member of the Texas Tornados, Sahm helped bring *norteño* (a rural style of music from the north of Mexico, often featuring accordion) to the U.S., and he ws a singer of such disarming earnestness that other singers have a hard time convincingly covering his songs. (Listen to the plaintive "Texas Me" here, and see if you can imagine another singer doing it.)

Mendocino is the Sir Douglas Quintet's third album.

Singer and songwriter Sahm (1941–1999) was a Texas renaissance man, and one of the most musically significant cult artists of the rock era. This 1969 album, written when Sahm was living in Northern California and missing his home state, contains some of his most touching songs, and features the strongest lineup of the Sir Douglas Quintet. This band had to be good: Sahm had the singular ability to absorb disparate styles of music into the same song, and make them sound like they belong together. The raucous "She's About a Mover," which the group originally cut in 1966 and rerecorded here, is a typical amalgam: It's a rampaging boogaloo expressed through the keening innocence of '50s pop. Other tunes, including the oddly exuberant "Sunday Sunny Mill Valley Groove Day" that was left off the original LP, surround peppy rock or Tex-Mex beats with spacey psychedelic atmospheres—to amazing effect.

This album is the best way to first encounter Sahm, who counted Bob Dylan and Willie Nelson among his friends and fans. It shows Sahm at the moment when his ideas about music were rapidly coalescing, and his zanier lyrics were backed up by a band that could seemingly make the most ordinary tune sound like the kind of party you never want to leave.

GENRE:  Rock. **RELEASED:** 1969, Smash/Mercury. **KEY TRACKS:** "Mendocino," "Texas Me," "She's About a Mover." **CATALOG CHOICE:** The Texas Tornados: *The Texas Tornados*. **NEXT STOP:** Boz Scaggs: *Boz Scaggs*. **AFTER THAT:** Bela Fleck and the Flecktones: *Bela Fleck and the Flecktones*.

Grisly, Gruesome, Great

Reign in Blood

Slayer

I t took heavy metal musicians years to build a teensy-weensy bit of credibility, to get beyond the ghoulish and cartoonish. It takes Slayer twenty-eight minutes to torch all that well-intentioned imaging work.

The blistering-fast *Reign in Blood* is full metal anarchy, an assault that blurs elements of speed metal and punk, thrash metal and devil-worshipping hard rock into tremendous menace. It is easily the most intense record of the mid-'80s and one of the more significant heavy rock statements of all time.

Nothing is sacred with Slayer. The album opens with a "tribute" of sorts to Nazi commander Josef Mengele, the so-called "Angel of Death." Columbia Records, Slayer's label, found the words to this song so reprehensible its executives refused to distribute the album. (Geffen Records immediately picked it up and made it into a hit.)

Things don't exactly get cheery after that opening. Produced by Rick Rubin, *Reign in Blood* is a series of hard-hitting, if often tongue-in-cheek, psychodramas, each terrifying in its own special way. Lead singer and bassist Tom Araya dispenses delighted proclamations of derangement ("Criminally Insane"), mocks the horror-film heroine who says her prayers ("Jesus Saves"), and ponders the end of life ("Postmortem") in a way that

The members of Slayer together in 1986, the year *Reign in Blood* was released.

loads as much mental torment as any whiplash-fast song can hold.

The words are hardly the primary Slayer selling point. The band, which formed in Huntington Beach, California, in 1982, builds its songs around the switchblade accuracy of guitarists Kerry King and Jeff Hanneman. Rather than just stomp in the typical metal fashion (à la Megadeth), these two specialized in ultra-fast chromatic lines, crisscrossing riffs, and other devices that demand serious technical skill. That's the Slayer psych-out: Even when they're cranking superfast metal thunder, the band moves with a stalker's grace.

GENRE:  Rock. **RELEASED:** 1986, American/Geffen. **KEY TRACKS:** "Raining Blood," "Criminally Insane," "Postmortem." **COLLECTOR'S NOTE:** The expanded edition offers a bonus track ("Aggressive Perfector") and an amazing remix of "Criminally Insane." **CATALOG CHOICE:** *Seasons in the Abyss*. **NEXT STOP:** Pantera: *Vulgar Display of Power* (see p. 575). **AFTER THAT:** Corrosion of Conformity: *Blind*.

Misfit Rock, All-Girl Division

Call the Doctor

Sleater-Kinney

"Little Mouth," one of twelve songs on this panicky gem of latter-day punk, begins with a curt, dismissive "Damn you." Then Corin Tucker, the primary singer of the Olympia, Washington, three-piece Sleater-Kinney, repeats herself—except this time, her voice is an octave higher and she's practically shrieking. What follows is ninety seconds of pulverizing harangue, sung as one long extended blur and accompanied by guitars that slide around to hit several pitches at once. You don't have to process the words ("dam-aged-goods!") to sense the fury, and that's one reason the female trio Sleater-Kinney burns so brightly: They specialize in a caterwauling, totally abrasive roar that won't leave you alone.

Sleater-Kinney in 1996: Carrie Brownstein, Lora Macfarlane, and Corin Tucker.

Gnashing and noisy, full of tirades about being a misunderstood girlfriend and an objectified woman, *Call the Doctor* captures Sleater-Kinney at the first of several career peaks. Its strident vocals push right to the edge of reasonableness: Tucker and Carrie Brownstein both sing and play guitar, sometimes teaming up for powerful unison vocals, but often going their separate ways to explore more frazzled emotions. As one dispenses the main taunt, the other drifts in the faraway ether, adding barbed and often shouted commentary or encouragement. The band consists of just two guitars and drums; without an anchoring bass presence, everything feels tense, and almost impossibly keyed-up. On "Stay Where You Are" and "Little Mouth," the result is music that's at once ragged and triumphant, hooky and histrionic.

Sleater-Kinney, which got its name from a service road off of Interstate 5 in Lacey, Washington, wasn't the only '90s band to embrace those contrasts. But it took them further than most, and, like all the great provocateurs of punk had done before them, gleefully exploited the extremes; when Tucker declares "I Wanna Be Your Joey Ramone," she mixes a fan's worshipful devotion and a jaded rocker's oh-please into the same thought. This album established Sleater-Kinney, and after it, the group tore into slightly different realms, ending up in the thick tangles of *The Woods*, one of the most musically astute reckonings of Led Zeppelin–era classic rock ever undertaken by a punk band. That album turns out to be the group's last: In late 2006, Sleater-Kinney announced that it was going on indefinite hiatus. For those who love visceral, short-fuse rock and roll, this is a huge loss.

GENRE: 🎵 Rock. **RELEASED:** 1996, Chainsaw. **KEY TRACKS:** "Call the Doctor," "Little Mouth," "Stay Where You Are," "Good Things," "I Wanna Be Your Joey Ramone." **CATALOG CHOICES:** *The Woods; All Hands on the Bad One.* **NEXT STOP:** Liz Phair: *Exile in Guyville* (see p. 596). **AFTER THAT:** L7: *Bricks Are Heavy.*

The Mysteries of Love, Lesson One

"When a Man Loves a Woman"

Percy Sledge

When you get right down to it, every truly important bit of life wisdom can be found on a well-stocked jukebox. Wanna know what love is? Dial up "When a Man Loves a Woman," the first single from Alabama-born soul singer Percy Sledge. It's an excellent lesson in what it means to be devoted to somebody. Hear it just once and you know Sledge, a former hospital orderly, is speaking from experience—about spending his last dime and putting up with all manner of mistreatment just to hold on to what he's got.

Sledge has said that he carried around the refrain for years before the song was written, and it's easy to see why: It's a melody

Sledge wrote this song after his girlfriend left him. It hit #1 on *Billboard*'s Hot 100.

made for pleading, a graceful rainbow arc that holds all the romance (and concomitant distress) a singer can muster. The famed Atlantic Records producer Jerry Wexler once described it as "a holy love hymn," and certainly Sledge's edge-of-tears performance has lots to do with that: He's not singing to entertain. He's testifying.

"When a Man Loves a Woman" was among the first Southern soul singles to reach the top of the pop charts; it utterly typifies the region's magical gritty aura. Though Sledge wrote most of the tune, because he wasn't savvy about the music business, he gave away song credit to two backing musicians who'd helped him refine the piece. Following its success, Sledge recorded a string of albums and successful singles for Atlantic; these are spirited affairs, invested with the unshakable sincerity that defines this gem. If the subsequent works are less prominent in the Great Big Jukebox of Knowledge, that's probably because "When a Man Loves a Woman" says so much.

GENRE: 🏵 R&B. **RELEASED:** 1966, Atlantic. **APPEARS ON:** *When a Man Loves a Woman; It Tears Me Up: The Best of Percy Sledge.* **NEXT STOP:** Otis Redding: *Otis Blue* (see p. 636).

The Playbook for a Ton of '90s Hip-hop

Fantastic, Vol. 1

Slum Village

For the most part, the lure of this touchstone of '90s hip-hop isn't the wordplay. In fact, the crude sexual boasts and outsized proclamations of rhyme-assassin prowess from the members of this Detroit crew often feel like first drafts, as though the rappers are just messing around, intending to put "final" vocals on later.

What's going on behind the words is another story. *Fantastic* is the world's first peek into the overstuffed bag of tricks developed by the producer known as Jay Dee or J Dilla (born Jimmy Yancey, he died in 2006 after a long illness). A genius of collage and collision, Jay Dee was the rare hip-hop beatmaker whose every groove is instantly identifiable, blessed with a signature rhythmic "feel." *Fantastic*, Vol. 1 was made in four days in Jay Dee's basement, with the rappers doing their thing to a simple drum track. The producer told the rappers to "imagine" a more elaborate production behind them, which he added after the fact (most hip-hop is made the other way around, with the music first). Sure enough, Jay Dee augmented the raps with burbling James Brownish bass lines, rubbery electric pianos, and all sorts of sampled sorcery.

First as singles and then as an album, these tracks became an underground phenom-

"We break rules, we do things other people wouldn't do."
—Slum Village cofounder Baatin

enon in Detroit clubs—their up-tempo agitations influenced Eminem and the D12 crew—and soon the Slum Village sound spread throughout the East Coast, particularly among those looking for something besides confrontational gangsta sounds. Ahmir "?uestlove" Thompson, the drummer of the Roots, recalls that the earthy musical textures of *Fantastic* spread like wildfire through the hip-hop ranks, influenc-

ing what he and others were doing: "Hands down this album birthed the neo-soul movement," he argues, adding that everyone from the Roots to D'Angelo to Erykah Badu copped bits of Jay Dee's hypersyncopated approach. "It was a new way to present raw funk in a contemporary sense."

GENRE: 🎤 Hip-Hop. **RELEASED:** 1996, Donut Boy. **KEY TRACKS:** "Keep It On (This Beat)," "Players," "Look of Love (Remix)." **CATALOG CHOICE:** *Fantastic*, Vol. 2. **NEXT STOP:** The Roots: *Things Fall Apart*. **AFTER THAT:** Erykah Badu: *Mama's Gun* (see p. 38).

Taking Things Higher, Whether You Go or Not

Stand!

Sly and the Family Stone

tand! is the crystallizing moment for Sly and the Family Stone. On the three records before it, former Bay Area radio DJ Sly Stone and his band aimed for, and often reached, a kinky confluence of rock and funk and vaudeville

camp that was downright addictive—and totally unlike anything else happening at the time. This album seized that musical scheme for different ends—to spread the psychedelic idealism (some would say utopianism) that was bubbling through the counterculture.

Recognizing he couldn't simply talk in the abstract about inclusion, Stone developed music that breathed that way, with tightly wound grooves, and tag-team vocal exchanges between men and women, black people and white people, music snobs and street punks.

The band urged listeners to believe in themselves ("Stand!") and wasn't the least corny about it. It envisioned a world where being compassionate, being "Everyday People," was more important than skin color or bank balance. Its sharp commentaries on race spoke out against intolerance no matter where it came from—the caustic hiss "Don't call me Nigger, Whitey" is followed immediately by its inverse, "Don't call me Whitey, Nigger."

Sly and the Family Stone in 1968.

Released in May 1969, *Stand!* didn't explode until August, in the wake of the band's galvanizing performance at the Woodstock festival. (In its review, *Rolling Stone* compared the festival to a battle of the bands won by Sly and company, who took revelers to "their own majestically freaked-out stratosphere.")

Seven of these nine slices of delirious perfection turned up on the radio (the other two are extended jams). All of it has the feeling of limitless possibility on the horizon, and the belief that brotherhood is worth fighting for. George Clinton, whose groups Parliament and Funkadelic are unthinkable without Sly, put it this way in a 2006 interview in *The Washington Post*: "Sly was like all the Beatles and all of Motown in one. He was the baddest thing around."

GENRE: 🎵 R&B. **RELEASED:** 1969, Epic. **KEY TRACKS:** All of them. **CATALOG CHOICES:** *Fresh; Anthology.* **NEXT STOP:** Shuggie Otis: *Inspiration Information* (see p. 568). **AFTER THAT:** N.E.R.D.: *In Search of . . . .*

A River, Immortalized in Music

Má vlast

Bedřich Smetana
Czech Philharmonic (Rafael Kubelík, cond.)

Lots of pieces attempt to describe the majesty of water, but most are somewhat generic—their undulations could describe any vast ocean or raging river. Not so with the detailed sketch "Vltava," the best-known section of this six-part poem for orchestra. Czech composer Bedřich Smetana's intention was to celebrate specific traits of the Moldau River, a fixture of daily life in Prague. Starting from trickling headwaters well north of the city, he uses different musical devices to evoke the path of the river: Early on the music is distinguished by furtive little splashes of melody, the "talk" of small creeks and brooks. As the river gathers force, the melodies lengthen, becoming more stately. By the time the segment ends, you feel the reverence Smetana (1824–1884) felt watching the wide river flow through his city.

The other sections offer glimpses of life in Prague—*Má vlast* is often mentioned as an example of the "nationalistic" music fashionable during Smetana's time, in which composers strove to immortalize the unique character traits of their homelands. The river scenes do this in consistently stirring ways, even if, ironically, the primary "Vltava" theme was borrowed from the Swedish folk song "Ack Värmeland, du sköna." Meanwhile elsewhere in the piece, Smetana seems to be torn between writing love letters to his city and cranking out military-style marches. This version features the Czech Philharmonic, whose membership know the river well. Recorded at the Prague Spring festival in 1990 shortly after the Velvet Revolution, it was guided by conductor Rafael Kubelík. Without doing too much flag-waving, Kubelík goes for big swells of feeling rather than distantly picturesque shades, allowing the performance to bubble over with the pride of a hometown experiencing profound renewal.

GENRE: 🎵 Classical. **RELEASED:** 1990, Supraphon. **KEY TRACK:** "Vltava / The Moldau." **F.Y.I.** During the years he spent writing and scoring *Má vlast*, Smetana completely lost his hearing. **ANOTHER INTERPRETATION:** Czech Philharmonic (Václav Talich, cond.). **NEXT STOP:** Modest Mussorgsky/Maurice Ravel: *Pictures at an Exhibition* (see p. 634).

The Amazing Travels of an Empress

The Essential Bessie Smith

Bessie Smith

There's no such thing as too much Bessie Smith. However, should you require an abbreviated tour of the earth-rattling vocal power and zillion-watt personality of the "Empress"—the first true superstar of the blues—begin with four selections from this two-disc career overview. Start with "Graveyard Dream Blues," one of the many death-haunted tunes in her repertoire; it shows how, without abandoning her feminine grace, Smith caught the woeful grittiness of male blues singers who outnumbered her on the tent-show circuit of the 1920s. (Smith, who, as legend has it, was tutored by the great Ma Rainey, learned to sing in those revues; they often lacked amplification, and as a result she was forced to develop the commanding vocal presence that became her calling card.)

Then cue up "Need a Little Sugar in My Bowl," recorded in 1931 with pianist Clarence Williams, to hear Smith's salacious side, the way she managed explicit talk about sex entirely through coy and playful double entendre. After that, seek out "On Revival Day" to hear her blend the blues, entertainment, and spirituality into a fervent sound that influenced generations of performers from Sister Rosetta Tharpe (see p. 771) to Aretha Franklin (see p. 288). Finally, check out one of the many songs that takes Smith away from blues form, like the version of "Alexander's Ragtime Band" featuring pianist Fletcher Henderson (see p. 354) or one of her last recordings, "Do Your Duty," an attempt to change her style to appeal to fans of swing. Both prove that as persuasive as she was singing blues, Smith had great jazz timing and an ear for sweet

In 2002, Smith's "Down-Hearted Blues" was chosen for the Library of Congress's National Recording Registry.

melody. She could make the most challenging stuff seem effortless.

Considering that Smith recorded more than 160 songs during her career, such a small sampling can hardly do her legacy justice. Still, these tracks should get you hooked on this extraordinary performer, whose spirit illuminates much subsequent blues singing. Smith was also a resilient woman: By age nine, she'd lost both her mother and father and soon after began performing for spare change outside nightclubs in Chattanooga, Tennessee. Smith zoomed from bit player in tent shows to a full-blown star who traveled by private train car, and fell just as quickly. She died from injuries suffered in a car accident in 1937, shortly after being invited to perform at Carnegie Hall as part of John Hammond's Spirituals to Swing concert (see p. 811), leaving future generations to wonder what might have happened if the Empress had gotten a second act.

GENRE: 🔵 Blues. RELEASED: 1997, Columbia. KEY TRACKS: "Jail-House Blues," "St. Louis Blues," "On Revival Day." FURTHER INQUIRY: Chris Albertson's *Bessie* is the definitive Smith biography. NEXT STOP: Lucille Bogan: *Shave 'Em Dry: The Best of Lucille Bogan*. AFTER THAT: Alberta Hunter: *Amtrak Blues*.

Artful Miniatures of Classic Pop

XO

Elliott Smith

Elliott Smith was a welcome rarity in the melodically challenged 1990s. He was a singer-songwriter who related to the raw emotions vented by grunge singers, but was also conversant in the highly textured expressions of the Beatles and other pop tunesmiths.

The Oregon native, who got his start in the influential postpunk band Heatmiser, was a troubled soul—he was found dead in his L.A. apartment in 2003, the victim of knife wounds to the chest that may or may not have been self-inflicted. He battled addiction for years, even during a rare period of intense visibility—in 1997, when his song "Miss Misery," featured in the film *Good Will Hunting*, was nominated for an Oscar, he performed it on the awards show in a listless haze that kept his many curious new fans at arm's length.

For a long time, though, Smith was able to manage, and use, the despair he was feeling. His lyrics tell of having "static in my head, the reflected sound of everything," and yet his music is uncluttered, even crystalline, notable for its poised and cautiously buoyant melodies. He specialized in disquieting songs of self-recrimination, artful miniatures that examine feelings of dislocation through the serene prism of classic pop. The subject was often inner turmoil, yet no sirens scream inside his songs: At the postgrunge moment when most rock auteurs were expected to purge and vent, Smith held his disappointments close, and let them seep through in breathy, carefully considered whispers. You could be fully immersed in the bittersweetness before the words even had a chance to sink in.

The songs of *XO* have a touch of Kurt Cobain's disaffected-youth attitude-mongering, but it is conveyed in song structures that descend directly from the Beatles. Every last one is a gem—the two parlor-music waltzes, the ambling "Independence Day," the hurtling

"Bled White," and the acoustic-guitar-and-voice fugue "Tomorrow Tomorrow." Too hip for the radio and too smart for indie rock, they remain a rare pinnacle of craft in an era when primitivism ruled. Rarely have accounts of being blown apart sounded so well put together.

GENRE: 🎸 Rock. **RELEASED:** 1998, Dreamworks. **KEY TRACKS:** "Tomorrow Tomorrow," "Bled White." **CATALOG CHOICE:** *From a Basement on the Hill.* **NEXT STOP:** Iron and Wine: *Our Endless Numbered Days.*

Party Time at the Piano

This Is . . .

Huey "Piano" Smith and His Clowns

If you believe the history books, Huey "Piano" Smith is a forgotten footnote. He was never king of the boogie-woogie-influenced R&B explosion that happened in New Orleans during the 1950s—such luminaries as Professor Longhair and Eddie Bo held that distinction. Smith was never the most famous of the city's fast-rising rock piano giants, either; Fats Domino overshadowed him in almost every way.

But cue up virtually any of the singles Smith and his band the Clowns recorded for Ace Records in the late '50s, and prepare for a jolt. Here is some of the most deliriously giddy party-time music ever captured on tape. These up-tempo dance-floor jumps and cat-calling blues are highly concentrated magic elixirs—press Play and watch the cares of the day melt away. Smith's original songs seem simple: "Rockin' Pneumonia and the Boogie Woogie Flu" (one of several "disease" songs in his canon), "Sea Cruise" (later a hit for Frankie Ford), and "Little Liza Jane" amount to a series of riffs and shouts, sung with suave nonchalance by frequent guest vocalist Bobby Marchan. Still, the draw is Smith's scooting, relentlessly rollicking rhythm section, which shuttles along in grand New Orleans style, moving with the unstoppable force of a freight train and the curve-hugging grace of a sports car.

GENRE: 🎤 R&B. **RELEASED:** 1998, Music Club. **KEY TRACK:** "Don't You Just Know It." **NEXT STOP:** Professor Longhair: *New Orleans Piano* (see p. 616). **AFTER THAT:** Dave Bartholomew: *Spirit of New Orleans.*

What, Exactly, Went On Back There?

Back at the Chicken Shack

Jimmy Smith

Jimmy Smith, the man who established the sound and the vocabulary of the Hammond B3 organ in jazz, recorded a massive amount of music under his own name. Some of his best-known works are simple blues-based blowing sessions—see *The Sermon*, which begins with a twenty-minute throwdown. And a bunch of his records are whiplash-inducing displays of technique, like *Groovin' at Small's Paradise*, a highly caffeinated two-disc blur of watch-me-dazzle dexterity.

Sometimes when Smith lets his fingers (and his toes, via the foot pedals that push out the bass lines) do all the walking, his sheer speed overwhelms the delicate back-and-forth of jazz communication. That's why *Back at the Chicken Shack* is such a treasure: For whatever reason, Smith resists the showboating impulse here, focusing on coy, furtive moves instead. These are low-pressure jaunts through blues and standards ("On the

Smith was honored with the NEA Jazz Masters Award in 2005.

Sunny Side of the Street"), conversations that breeze along and eventually culminate in exciting shout choruses. Smith dazzles, as expected, when he solos, but is equally impressive as an accompanist: His spiked chords and sassy rejoinders snap the grooves into high definition, and practically force tenorman Stanley Turrentine and guitarist Kenny Burrell to keep things simple.

GENRE: 🎵 Jazz. **RELEASED:** 1960, Blue Note. **KEY TRACKS:** "Back at the Chicken Shack," "Minor Chant," "On the Sunny Side of the Street." **CATALOG CHOICES:** *The Sermon; Groovin' at Small's Paradise.* **NEXT STOP:** Kenny Burrell: *Blue Bash.*

Mr. Smith, Working in the Long Shadow of Mr. Brown

Live at the Club Mozambique

Lonnie Smith

For a long time in the late '60s and '70s, players from all corners of popular music found themselves under the spell of James Brown. With his severe, instantly identifiable groove, the Godfather of Soul established a rhythm aesthetic that spread quickly—pop guitarists copped the articulate rhythm parts, jazz drummers emulated the precision-machined patterns. Even a fleet-fingered technician like Lonnie Smith, the organ player, caught the bug: When he really gets going on "Love Bowl" from this sizzling live date, Smith abandons jazz entirely in order to attack a single chord over and over again. That's how Brown played the organ (see

The Jazz Journalists Association named Smith "Organ Keyboardist of the Year" in 2003, 2004, and 2005.

Soul Pride: The Instrumentals, p. 121), and Smith's accompanists, already tuned to the JB funk frequency, pick up the reference. They put a little extra grease into the backbeats, encouraging Smith to carry his jabbing repetitions further into the twilight zone.

Smith's group includes frequent accomplices George Benson on guitar and Ronnie Cuber on baritone saxophone, the core band that drives

Benson's 1966 major-label debut *It's Uptown.* Here, playing Smith's original blues and boogaloo tunes, the musicians focus on the simple percolating JB-style vamps, and slip the cerebral jazz stuff into the solos—check out the blazing-fast "Seven Steps to Heaven" and "Scream," which features a roaring turn by Cuber and one of the most earthy, gut-level statements Benson ever recorded.

Brown's counterintuitive approach to rhythm—that mix of exactitude and nonchalance—is something special. It is one reason this record, which was made on an average night in 1970 at Detroit's famed Club Mozambique, eclipses just about everything filed under soul-jazz, including important works by saxophonist Lou Donaldson and guitarist Grant Green. Lots of jazz musicians respected James Brown; few were able to extend his ideas the way Smith and his group do here.

GENRE: 🎷 Jazz. **RELEASED:** 1995, Blue Note. (Recorded in 1970.) **KEY TRACKS:** "Scream," "Love Bowl," "Seven Steps to Heaven." **CATALOG CHOICE:** *Boogaloo to Beck.* **NEXT STOP:** Lou Donaldson: *Everything I Play Is Funky.* **AFTER THAT:** George Benson: *It's Uptown.*

The Journey of a Great Rock Poet Begins

Horses

Patti Smith

Patti Smith once described her artistic enterprise as "three-chord rock merged with the power of the word." She didn't mean just any old words. From the very first line of this endlessly praised debut—"Jesus died for somebody's sins, but not mine"—Smith uses incendiary poetry as her guitar substitute, her rage-maker. She howls. She brays. She hurls language in sprays of outrage, mocking piety one minute and making solemn prayerful incantations the next. A romantic with deep appreciation for life's beauty, Smith is also a rebel in the great rock tradition, and an artist as bent on cultural confrontation as the Beat poets were. This confluence of perspectives—worlds not so peacefully coexisting—is at the heart of her debut album, *Horses.*

Patti Smith Horses

"*[Horses]* tore my limbs off and put them back on in a whole different order."   —Michael Stipe

Horses is an unusual beast, a series of manifestos and vignettes with wild torrents of words flung against the music at odd angles. Tilting headfirst at complacency, Smith spins several images at once, while riding three chords as far away from party-time escapism as anyone's ever gone. She's so good at reanimating rock that when she seizes an old warhorse—the Wilson Pickett hit "Land of a Thousand Dances"— as part of her triptych "Land," it comes out all disfigured, with an almost nuclear glow.

Smith grew up in rural New Jersey and, after dropping out of college and working factory jobs, fled to Manhattan in 1967. She became romantically linked with the photographer Robert Mapplethorpe, who encouraged her to perform and later bankrolled her early recording sessions. In 1975, Smith headlined a two-month residency at CBGB; she was discovered there by Clive Davis and signed to Arista Records.

This album, produced by the Velvet Underground's John Cale, was released in December 1975, and immediately hailed by critics as a major work. It established Smith as a galvanizing force, if not the most important woman in rock. The rare punk neoclassicist, she acknowledged the titans of classic rock (notably Bob Dylan and Van Morrison) while distancing herself from rock cliché. Her subsequent works, notably the big-beat-bold *Easter* and the poignant grief cycle *Gone Again*, bolster that initial impression—even if, ironically, her legacy now extends to the fiercely independent riot grrls who were direct descendents and the even poppier Avril Lavignes of the world, who came later.

GENRE: 🎸 Rock. **RELEASED:** 1975, Arista. **KEY TRACKS:** "Gloria," "Land," "Elegie," "Free Money." **CATALOG CHOICES:** *Easter; Gone Again.* **NEXT STOP:** PJ Harvey: *Rid of Me.* **AFTER THAT:** Ani DiFranco: *Out of Range.*

Hear How . . .

The Lion Roars! His Greatest 1934–1944

Willie "The Lion" Smith

During the Depression years, one of the ways people in New York made ends meet was to hold informal house concerts featuring well-known musicians, usually piano players. These "rent parties" were sometimes uproarious events. One star of the circuit, the pianist Willie "The Lion" Smith, recalled that "about a hundred people would crowd into a seven-room flat until the walls bulged and the main door was often split wide open."

Through these informal, off-the-books affairs, Smith (1897–1973) and others developed sizable reputations for rocking out—while refining the intricate conventions of "stride piano," which fused elements of ragtime, the blues, and boogie-woogie. This is music of superhuman dexterity: On many of the performances in this anthology, Smith can be heard operating as a one-man rhythm section, pumping out a repetitive bass line

"The Lion" playing at a "rent party" at the Park Lane Hotel on February 17, 1939.

while also dishing sharp, hard-swinging chords. It's music of synapse-frying intricacy, but rarely is that the first impression: A gregarious entertainer and raconteur, Smith always sounds like he's just having fun.

This anthology gathers recordings Smith made during his peak years. The Newark, New Jersey, native began playing professionally after returning from combat duty in World War I (where, he told people later, he earned that "Lion" nickname for his bravery), and quickly found himself in demand. The early tracks are drawn from sessions he did as a sideman, backing the clarinetist Mezz Mezzrow and others. Later highlights include pieces from Smith's group called His Cubs—among them his original "Echoes of Spring" (1935), which has a sweet, almost disarming lyricism. Then come piano solos like the aptly named "Finger Buster" (1939), which find Smith contrasting beautiful rhapsodic melodies with high-energy ragtime-derived impromptus that utilize the piano's full range. These might sound quaint today, but they startled plenty of musicians at the time, influencing such essential voices as Duke Ellington (who wrote "Portrait of the Lion" for him) and Thelonious Monk.

GENRE: 🎷 Jazz. **RELEASED:** 1998, Living Era. **KEY TRACKS:** "Harlem Joys," "Echoes of Spring," "The Swampland Is Calling Me," "Strange Fruit." **CATALOG CHOICE:** *The Lion and the Lamb*. **NEXT STOP:** Albert Ammons and Meade "Lux" Lewis: *The First Day* (see p. 20). **AFTER THAT:** Various Artists: *Stride Piano Summit*.

A Literary Dude Finds a Way to Rock

The Queen Is Dead

The Smiths

The Smiths typify one of the classic oppositional dynamics that define many rock bands: The singer, a self-described "well-read" chap named Morrissey, appears as the wounded poet in his garret, musing loftily about the perilous machinations of love. The band, meanwhile, is much scruffier—led by rhythmically astute guitarist Johnny Marr, it specializes in breezy, chiming, quintessentially buoyant music.

Lots of acts have milked that contrast. But few have taken it to the delightful extremes that define the Smiths' third album, *The Queen Is Dead*.

Here are silly word puns blown up to the preposterous ("Frankly, Mr. Shankly," "Some Girls Are Bigger than Others"), and songs that present the great poets as trading-card superheroes ("Cemetry Gates," which finds Morrissey giving his friend John Keats and William Butler Yeats and keeping Oscar Wilde for himself). Here are distraught accounts about the end of an affair (the weepy "I Know It's Over") and rampaging Stones-

"I decided [to call us the Smiths] because it was the most ordinary name, and I think it's time that the ordinary folk of the world showed their faces." —Morrissey

style rockers about saying the wrong thing ("Bigmouth Strikes Again," with its curiously empathetic line, "Now I know how Joan of Arc felt as the flames rose to her Roman nose and her Walkman started to melt").

The Queen Is Dead often turns up on those Best Albums of All Time lists, and though the band has publicly disagreed with that appraisal, it is the album that best captures the droll humor and musical extravagances that made the Smiths so riveting. Perhaps stung by the mostly negative reaction to his scolding previous work *Meat Is Murder*, Morrissey slings sensual images while sharing the darkness in his heart (talking about the cemetery, he tells his friend, "Let's go where we're wanted"). Meanwhile, Marr and the rhythm section blaze trails toward an idealized zone of rock (and sometimes pop) sunshine. Their runaway exuberance magnifies and sometimes mocks Morrissey's gloomy desperation. One vivid illustration comes on "There Is a Light That Never Goes Out": The singer makes a morbid declaration—"If a ten-ton truck kills the both of us, to die by your side, well, the pleasure and the privilege is mine"—and the band just cruises right along, barely noticing that Morrissey traffic snarl on the side of the road.

GENRE: 🎸 Rock. **RELEASED:** 1986, Sire. **KEY TRACKS:** "There Is a Light That Never Goes Out," "Cemetry Gates," "The Boy with the Thorn in His Side," "Bigmouth Strikes Again." **CATALOG CHOICES:** *Strangeways Here We Come.* Morrissey solo: *You Are the Quarry.* **NEXT STOP:** Magnetic Fields: *69 Love Songs* (see p. 465). **AFTER THAT:** The Pet Shop Boys: *Very.*

Canada's Great Country Kingpin, the "Singing Ranger"

The Essential

Hank Snow

Easily the most significant country music star to hail from Nova Scotia, Hank Snow (1914–1999) had a disciplined voice, and diction that was clear and decidedly cornpone-free. From his 1950 breakthrough,

a Jimmie Rodgers–style rail-rider's song called "I'm Movin' On," Snow showed that it wasn't necessary to sound like a mountain man to sing country. One of his signature hits, "I've Been Everywhere" (1962), is a precursor of sorts to hip-hop: Over a brisk clippety-clop, Snow dispenses a deftly rhymed list of places he's been and troubles he's seen.

That song is known to most through Johnny Cash's cover, which has been used in several television ads. Snow sings it with such precision, it becomes a display of narrative skill and pure verbal dexterity. The dude's itinerary is impressive, but even more impressive is the way he links the dots on the map.

After the runaway success of "I'm Movin' On," which stayed at the top of the charts for twenty-one weeks, Snow was invited to perform on the *Grand Ole Opry*, and became a regular.

When Snow was 14, he ordered his first guitar from Eaton's catalog for $5.95.

(He was directly responsible for Elvis Presley's Opry bow in 1954, and briefly comanaged the Memphis singer.) Between 1949 and 1980, Snow placed eighty-five singles on the country charts. This collection gathers highlights from Snow's singles career (his albums are notoriously less-than-satisfying affairs). It includes the lighthearted courting song "Would You Mind," a spellbinding confession called "I Don't Hurt Anymore," and a crackerbox of clichés, "Unwanted Sign upon Your Heart," that Snow transforms into an unexpected thing of beauty.

GENRE: 🎵 Country. **RELEASED:** 1997, RCA. **KEY TRACKS:** "I'm Movin' On," "I've Been Everywhere," "Would You Mind," "I Don't Hurt Anymore." **CATALOG CHOICE:** *Blues for My Blue Eyes.* **NEXT STOP:** Jimmie Rodgers: *The Essential Jimmie Rodgers* (see p. 652).

Night Time Is the Right Time

A Little Night Music

Stephen Sondheim
Original Broadway Cast

Early in *A Little Night Music*, his tale of foolish romance in the Swedish countryside, Stephen Sondheim establishes three major characters with three distinct songs. "Now" introduces Fredrik Egerman, a lawyer whose girl bride is still a virgin after eleven months of marriage. "Later" shares the thoughts of Henrik, Fredrik's son, who's in divinity school but in love with his stepmother. "Soon" begins with the bride, Anne, responding to Fredrik's advances. Before long, the three themes intersect in a burst of carefully coordinated counterpoint. As the thoughts of these smart, perhaps too smart, people vie for prominence, their impulses converge in a hormonally charged and tastefully buttoned-down cacophony.

A Little Night Music won the New York Drama Critics' Circle Award and the Tony Award for Best Musical.

And that's just the opening gambit. Though it's got knotty moments, much of this musical, which draws its title from Mozart and some inspiration from Ingmar Bergman's *Smiles of a Summer Night* (1957), is lighter and more immediately accessible than most Sondheim—without sacrificing the composer's arch wit or his knack for enchanting spiral-staircase melodies. Much of the music is written in 3/4 time, and yet never dissolves into a waltzapalooza. On some tunes, Sondheim offers traces of tempo in the distance; others have no organizing pulse at all. He tosses out lots of different rhythms and devices, and somehow avoids the mannered air of so much theater music.

A Little Night Music is home to some of Sondheim's wittiest lyrics. Fredrik, wondering when the "right" moment might be, observes: "Now, as the sweet imbecilities tumble so lavishly onto her lap, there are two possibilities: A, I could ravish her, or B, I could nap." It also contains his one big hit. "Send In the Clowns," sung here by Glynis Johns, is that rare perfectly formed jewel—a showstopping solo that pulls listeners through hurt, disappointment, malaise, anger, and obsession with disarming ease. Johns sings the stately theme with a matron's stoicism; she uses the weathered imperfection of her voice to underscore the message, knowing that those imperfections (the singing she can't quite manage) make the music devastating. "Send In the Clowns" freezes time for just a little while, long enough for Sondheim to catch some truth about the corrosive nature of regret, but not so long that his characters tire of the waltz.

GENRE: 😊 Musicals. **RELEASED:** 1973, Columbia. **KEY TRACKS:** "Now," "Later," "Soon," "The Glamorous Life," "A Weekend in the Country," "Send In the Clowns." **CATALOG CHOICE:** *Company,* Original Broadway Cast. **NEXT STOP:** Jule Styne: *Gypsy,* Original Broadway Cast. **AFTER THAT:** Jerry Herman: *Mame,* Original Broadway Cast.

The Slasher Musical

Sweeney Todd Live at the New York Philharmonic

Stephen Sondheim
George Hearn, Patti LuPone, New York Choral Artists,
New York Philharmonic (Andrew Litton, cond.)

Though it's written for the Broadway stage and intended to be interpreted by singing actors conversant in Tin Pan Alley, *Sweeney Todd* can also be considered an opera. Its significant dramatic moments unfold in music, and its ensemble passages contain back-and-forth volleys reminiscent of Mozart.

Stephen Sondheim wrote the music after seeing Christopher Bond's 1973 play, which is based on assorted folktales that have scared British children since the 1820s. As on his other theater projects, Sondheim developed an entire musical "language" for the show; for this, the music is tightly wound, in the manner of a Hitchcock thriller, with occasional respites for languid contemplation in the shadows. When the narrative hints at the gratuitous violence of low-budget slasher films, the music supplies a shivering string effect or sudden death-rattle symphonic chords.

Sondheim's textures have no equal in musical theater. When he intends for us to feel compassion, he finds a sly, and utterly perfect, way to bathe the theater in that mood. Similarly, his characters do not stride out and proclaim their motivations, as often happens in current musicals; instead, we learn about their desires and drives as they bounce off other people or their surroundings. Both Sweeney and the sailor, Anthony Hope, reveal their inner lives—Sweeney's dark and complicated,

Sweeney Todd tells the story of the Demon Barber of Fleet Street.

Anthony's sunny and uncomplicated—with their respective views of London. And in "The Worst Pies in London," Mrs. Lovett condemns her pie-selling rival Mrs. Mooney in ways that make it clear this is who she'd rather be, at least from a mercantile standpoint.

This performance is an illustration of what can happen when opera companies adapt Broadway material. These re-creations, which began in earnest with Leonard Bernstein in the mid-'80s, often featured operatic voices in lead roles—and were generally dismissed by show people as inferior. This one is carefully cast, with opera singers in the supporting roles and two Broadway veterans, George Hearn and Patti LuPone, in the leads. LuPone brings perfect theatrical diction to her role, jolting each line alive without shattering the subtlety necessary for Sondheim. And Hearn, who'd done the original road production and was then considered past his prime, lunges into the Epiphany scene, when he embarks on his reign of terror, with a youthful intensity; where that early piece tends to exhaust singers for the remainder of the work, he grows stronger and more melodically confident. Both singers get nice support from the New

York Philharmonic, which pumps Sondheim's themes to a mighty and majestic hugeness. Most Broadway scores would seem slight under such treatment. This one blossoms.

GENRE: 🎭 Musicals. **RELEASED:** 2000, NYP. **KEY TRACKS:** "Epiphany," "The Worst Pies in London." **CATALOG CHOICE:** *Passion,* Original Broadway Cast. **NEXT STOP:** Various Artists: *Send In the Clowns: The Ballads of Stephen Sondheim.* **AFTER THAT:** Adam Guettel: *The Light in the Piazza.*

New Rock Ecstasy

Daydream Nation

Sonic Youth

❝ It takes a teenage riot to get me out of bed right now." With these words, from the opening track of this highly influential double album, Thurston Moore articulates the basic stance that has served Sonic Youth for decades: In tones both ironic and openly derisive, the New York art-punk band positions itself at a lofty remove, away from the squall of everyday rock culture. Four contrarians fed up with the posing and the hype that ruled rock in the 1980s, they're suspicious of scenesters and fads. Yet they're still fans. They hold out hope for new rock ecstasy. Amazingly, this album actually

Sonic Youth formed in 1981 in New York City.

helped inspire some: After grunge erupted in the early '90s, many of its key practitioners, including Nirvana's Kurt Cobain, identified Sonic Youth as a primary inspiration.

Sonic Youth had been recording for six years when it made this radical racket. The band began in the early '80s, blasting the rock status quo with tools borrowed from guitarist and noise-manipulating composer Glenn Branca. Gradually Moore, bassist Kim Gordon (his wife), guitarist Lee Ranaldo, and drummer Steve Shelley came to appreciate the benefits of song form, and by this album had arrived at a potent meta-rock, in which bludgeoning guitars and swarming-insect drones support disciplined shouted refrains.

This is a different kind of teenage riot: After delivering its snarly vocal harangues, Sonic Youth dives into unruly long-form guitar explorations that are the real meat of the album. These are headstrong and improvisational; Among the most breathtaking are "Rain King," which describes an eerie utopia, and "Silver Rocket," an extended foray into corrosive noise. For all the off-kilter chaos, Sonic Youth exhibits an attraction/revulsion complex with classic rock. Its songs glance at such established figures as Jimi Hendrix, Joni Mitchell, and Neil Young, suggesting that these insurrectionists do, on some level, have respect for their elders.

GENRE: 🎸 Rock. **RELEASED:** 1988, Enigma. (Reissued 2007, Geffen.) **KEY TRACKS:** "Teen Age Riot," "Rain King," "'Cross the Breeze," "Eric's Trip," "Silver Rocket." **CATALOG CHOICES:** *Dirty; Goo; Washing Machine.* **NEXT STOP:** Smashing Pumpkins: *Mellon Collie and the Infinite Sadness.* **AFTER THAT:** Nirvana: *In Utero.*

Township Jive Without Borders

The Rough Guide to the Soul Brothers

The Soul Brothers

Every eight bars of "Isiphiwo"—one of twenty stellar grooves on this career overview of South African legends the Soul Brothers—brings a slight change of scenery. The tune begins with Moses Ngwenya's Hammond B3 organ, and a big flourish that resembles a Baptist call to worship. That phrase forms the basic outline of a groove, and when the rhythm section enters, it kicks out a high-stepping version of South Africa's signature beat, "township jive." Then the two voices start singing; as they repeat a single phrase several times, their twinned declaration has the fire of Southern soulman Otis Redding in stereo. That verse is followed by a horn section riff that sends things back to the township again. On and on it goes, spongy groove spinning into deep verse, the lightness of dance music supported by the sound of strong, purposeful souls gathered in worship.

Not all of the Soul Brothers' material has that range, but it all speaks to the internationalization of pop music—and how even the most potent indigenous style can be expanded and enhanced by contact with the outside world.

First known as the Groovy Boys, the Soul Brothers caught fire when Ngwenya and singer David Masondo joined forces in 1976, after discovering a shared love for reggae and American R&B. Determined to push indigenous South African music in new directions, they blended enthusiastic pop refrains with rolling, propulsive rhythms. The sound caught on quickly, and for a while in the 1980s, the Soul Brothers were among the few "rock star"–type acts in South Africa, putting out at least one album per year. This overview, which contains hits from just about every phase of the band's storied career, offers huge helpings of that indestructible beat. It's a great way to encounter one of the underappreciated trailblazers of African pop.

GENRE: 🌐 World/South Africa.
RELEASED: 2001, Rough/World Music Network. **KEY TRACKS:** "Mama ka s'bongile," "Isiphiwo." **CATALOG CHOICE:** *Jive Explosion.* **NEXT STOP:** Mahlathini and the Mahotella Queens: *Paris/Soweto* (see p. 467).

Superintense, Superunlikely, Superfantastic

Superunknown

Soundgarden

Green River was the first Seattle grunge band—its EP *Come on Down*, considered by some to be the hallowed blueprint of the sound, appeared in 1985. Nirvana was, of course, the all-time grunge sales champ. But by a long mile, the most musically adept band to emerge from the scene was Soundgarden.

Give *Superunknown* thirty seconds and you will understand why. The opener, "Let Me Drown," plunges listeners right into the eye of a storm—or a gamer's alternative-reality dungeon—where everything gets swirled around and rearranged. The hiccuping rhythm feels like a panic in progress, the kind that gets your adrenaline rushing as options narrow. Atop that foundation come cascading waves of guitar that are the band's killer app: Through the magic of multitracking, Kim Thayil sets demanding étude-book exercises against kaleidoscopic textures, yet plays everything with the brutal heavy hand of a metal god.

With that drama unfolding behind him, singer Chris Cornell doesn't have to do much. But on the urgent "Let Me Drown" and throughout this record, he uses his voice as another instrumental texture—check out the superintense "Mailman," where the payoff line "I know I'm headed for the bottom, but I'm riding you all the way" is delivered in a tone of deliberate, almost sadistic menace. Cornell sounds like he's settling scores, railing at forces far more mighty

"Superunknown relates to birth in a way."
—Chris Cornell

than he, an impression enhanced through studio effects: At the song's peak, his voice reverberates like it's bouncing around a vast canyon.

Similar thrills await on each of the fifteen tracks of this masterwork, as the band discovers endlessly interesting ways to pump Cornell's torments to a grand epic level. Sometimes these involve a guitar-symphony attack that resembles *Physical Graffiti*–era Led Zeppelin. And sometimes the backing is more elemental, closer to grunge. And though a few tunes do explore the pet grunge theme of alienation, many more offer dark, bracing musings on life and death. These are transmissions from a superfantastical subterranean world that's far from the fashionable and the trendy. And this record is the only way to go there.

GENRE: 🎵 Rock. **RELEASED:** 1994, A&M. **KEY TRACKS:** "Let Me Drown," "Fell on Black Days," "Superunknown," "Limo Wreck." **CATALOG CHOICE:** *Badmotorfinger.* **NEXT STOP:** Metallica: *Master of Puppets* (see p. 499). **AFTER THAT:** Temple of the Dog: *Temple of the Dog.*

The Only Britney That Matters

"Toxic"

Britney Spears

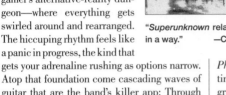

Britney Spears's oeuvre is filled with songs about taboo attraction—pop confections that freeze the moment when lust becomes a dangerous obsession, or, more often, when she realizes that whoops, she's led another poor man down the road to ruin.

Most of these transgression tales are audio soft porn, with melodies as threadbare as the outfits la diva Spears wore in the big-budget videos. Not "Toxic." Though the message is totally typical—she knows better, but she's addicted to that dangerous kiss—the means of conveying it are unique, a blur of Bollywood strings and last-roundup cowboy guitars and chittering electronic beats. Over these shifting elements, Spears sings the hypnotic refrain in a twisting swirl that screams, "Somebody help," because these feelings inside are careening out of control. For once, she's actually believable.

The most successful of the pinups who followed the Madonna handbook to pop stardom in the '90s, Spears hadn't had a Top 40 hit in three years when she began recording her fourth album, *In the Zone*, which appeared in late 2003. Like her previous albums, this one relied on a cluster of producers, and for "Toxic," which became the album's second single, she turned to the then-unknown Swedish team of Bloodshy and Avant. The duo organized the song into

Spears has sold over 83 million records worldwide.

episodes—the brief "verse" section features Spears in a breathless falsetto, followed by a moment of odd electronic buzzing, followed by the psychedelic patchwork of that sticky chorus. Though the sounds in some sections are pretty far-fetched—one wonders whether Spears even knows that the strings here are a winking reference to the soundtracks of countless Indian movies—when combined like this, they lead to something far more electric than the average naughty-girl pop song.

GENRE: ⭐ Pop. **RELEASED:** 2003, Jive.
APPEARS ON: *In the Zone; Greatest Hits.*
NEXT STOP: The Raspberries: "Go All the Way."
AFTER THAT: Christina Aguilera: *Stripped.*

The Wall of Sound

Back to Mono

Phil Spector

More is always more in the musical schemes of Phil Spector. Whenever you hear a '60s-era production with echoey voices, five or six guitar parts, nearly as many keyboards, and perfectly aligned maracas and other percussion shaking and rattling underneath, it's safe to assume that the enigmatic Spector created it, or inspired it. The Bronx-born, L.A.-based multi-instrumentalist revolutionized record production with his elaborate multitracking, which became immortally known as the "Wall of Sound." Spector himself was more loquacious, saying he specialized in "little symphonies for the kids," calling his sound a "Wagnerian approach to rock and roll."

Spector's first hit, with his own group the Teddy Bears, came in 1958, when he was still in high school; he appropriated the thought inscribed on his father's gravestone ("To Know Him Was to Love Him") as the chorus of a song, and had a Top 10 hit. After a short try at college (UCLA), Spector dedicated himself to the music business. His break came in 1960, when some L.A. producers he'd been apprenticing with sent him to New York to work with the songwriting team of Jerry Leiber and Mike Stoller. Spector hit it off with the pair right away, co-writing "Spanish Harlem" with Leiber, which became a hit for Ben E. King, and playing the guitar break in the middle of the Drifters' "On Broadway." Spector formed his first record company in 1961 (Philles Records), to showcase the talents of a girl group known as the Crystals.

Over the next three years, Spector was responsible for twenty successive smash hits, from the Crystals' "Da Doo Ron Ron" to the Ronettes' "Be My Baby" to Darlene Love's "Chapel of Love" to the Righteous Brothers' "You've Lost That Lovin' Feelin'." These and many more towering productions are collected in the chronologically arranged mega-anthology *Back to Mono*, which offers splendid transfers of the original hits. That dizzyingly dense sound you hear on CD is exactly what Spector heard in the control room, and (mostly) what made it onto those jukebox 45s.

The producer, whose sound directly influenced Brian Wilson during the Beach Boys' *Pet Sounds* days, didn't stay on top forever. After one track he considered his best work—"River

The 4-disc *Back to Mono* contains recordings made from 1958 to 1969.

Deep, Mountain High," which he recorded with Tina Turner singing—didn't connect in the U.S., Spector became a producer for hire, working on John Lennon's *Imagine* (see p. 446), George Harrison's *All Things Must Pass* (see p. 345), and Leonard Cohen's *Death of a Ladies' Man*. Eventually, Spector became a recluse, and he was later charged with murder in a 2003 shooting at his mock castle near L.A.

Back to Mono is not only wall-to-wall with wall-of-sound hits, it also includes all of *A Christmas Gift for You*, arguably the most exuberant holiday set in rock history.

GENRE: 🎸 Rock. **RELEASED:** 1991, Abkco. **KEY TRACKS:** All of them. **NEXT STOP:** Various Artists: *The Brill Building Sound.* **AFTER THAT:** Burt Bacharach: *The Look of Love.*

A Singer-Songwriter Path Not Taken

Oar

Alexander "Skip" Spence

Just before this was recorded in 1968, Alexander "Skip" Spence spent six months in the psychiatric prison ward at New York's Bellevue Hospital. He'd threatened a bandmate with an ax during the making of the second

Moby Grape record, and was not only kicked out of the band but deemed a threat to himself and others. Upon his release, Spence bought a motorcycle and drove to Nashville, carrying several pads full of song lyrics. There, according to legend, he set up shop in a studio, and recorded these oddly riveting and achingly beautiful songs in four days, playing all the instruments and producing the music himself. The result stands as his peak musical achieve-

ment. It's also his artistic epitaph: Though he was briefly involved in Moby Grape reunions and assorted projects, he never recorded his own music professionally again.

Because of the circumstances of its creation, *Oar* is sometimes lumped in with other records made by rock's certifiably unhinged denizens—Pink Floyd's Syd Barrett, the raconteur Daniel Johnston. That shortchanges Spence. From the opening refrain of "Little

Hands," which has a touch of John Lennon acidity, it's clear that this is an auteur with a firm grasp on structure, and an ear for doleful melodies that are far more sophisticated than most "savant-art."

Spence covers significant stylistic range—*Oar* contains folk songs fractured into absurd hallucinations, a couple of straightforward rockers, and a country waltz that shows off his

Spence died from lung cancer in 1999, when he was 52.

grave baritone. These are feats of great loner reflection, with ethereal vocals that hang heavily in the air and tangles of overlapping guitar carrying on their own conversation. At first, you can't help but appreciate the craft, then

the sheer openhearted loveliness of the melodies. Later it becomes clear that Spence is hardly even at the controls. He's working so fast he has to trust the details to the goodwill of the universe, and he gets lucky: These dashed-off songs are full of happy accidents and assorted amazingness.

GENRE: 🎸 Rock.
RELEASED: 1969, Columbia.
KEY TRACKS: "Little Hands," "Diana," "War Is Peace," "Books of Moses." **CATALOG CHOICE:** Moby Grape: *Moby Grape.* **NEXT STOP:** Syd Barrett: *The Madcap Laughs.*
AFTER THAT: Nick Drake: *Pink Moon.*

A Lost Classic from a California Singer-Songwriter

Isle of View

Jimmie Spheeris

The L.A.-born Jimmie Spheeris followed the road not taken by other California singer-songwriters of the early '70s. Where most tunesmiths (the Byrds, Neil Young, et al.) sought the declarative directness of country,

Spheeris had his head in faraway clouds. Everything he sang oozed an almost beatific hippie idealism. His ethereal notions carried over into his lyrics, which told tales of winged gods coming through the smog to deliver messages of hope. (Hey, it was the '70s.)

Spheeris was discovered by Clive Davis, and this debut was issued in 1971—in the wake of Young's *After the Gold Rush* (see p. 885) and just before Jackson Browne's first album. Despite a pleasantly spacey voice (think Duncan Sheik on downers),

Spheeris's parents owned and operated a traveling carnival called the Majick Empire.

and more than a few disarmingly poetic turns of phrase, Spheeris managed to attract only a cult following. That's a shame, because the contemplative *Isle of View* has much to recommend it—stirring little songs about nature and assorted phantasmagoria like "I Am the Mercury," the slow-motion plea "Come Back," and the gorgeous and unconventional string writing from Beck's dad David Campbell (legend has it that Beck, age eleven months, was a regular at these sessions). None of Spheeris's three subsequent titles for Columbia Records—the last two made with musicians who, like Spheeris, had joined the Church of Scientology—registered much of an impact either. Spheeris dropped out of sight in the late '70s, and had just completed work on a comeback when he was killed by a drunk driver in 1984. He left what might best be described as a small legacy—it took a letter-writing campaign in 1997 to bring his music to compact disc—but that doesn't diminish the placid chamber pop pleasure that is *Isle of View*.

GENRE: 🎸 Rock. **RELEASED:** 1971, Columbia. **KEY TRACKS:** "Come Back," "I Am the Mercury," "For Roach." **CATALOG CHOICE:** *The Dragon Is Dancing*. **NEXT STOP:** Duncan Sheik: *Phantom Moon*. **AFTER THAT:** Laura Veirs: *Year of Meteors*.

Through the Magic Pipes Comes . . .

Forgotten Days

Davy Spillane and Kevin Glackin

Behold the uilleann pipes. They look like some Victorian-era plumbing apparatus, an absurd bassoonlike contraption through which, it seems, nothing elegant could possibly ever emerge. But close your eyes, because the sound they make is not what you'd expect. It's an enveloping, otherworldly tone, hollow and haunting, like a transmission beamed straight from some celestial Middle Earth cavern. A tone so pure it cuts through modern artifice.

Davy Spillane became entranced with the pipes early. He began playing them at age twelve, and his concert career started when he was sixteen.

Spillane makes all of his own instruments.

Within a few years he was playing in rock bands (one esteemed ensemble, Moving Hearts, was described as a "Celtic Little Feat"), writing breathtaking rock-influenced ballads, and finding unconventional applications for the instrument.

Forgotten Days is the flip side to those extroverted explorations, and one of the most conventional recordings Spillane has done. A series of cleverly arranged traditional songs featuring just the uilleann pipes and the fiddle of Kevin Glackin, it's an ideal setting for appreciating Spillane's paranormal dexterity, and his knack for manipulating the tone of the pipes to give each piece a distinctive emotional shading. Spillane and Glackin gallop in brisk unisons, and like longtime dancing partners, easily switch between lead and accompaniment roles. Their music sometimes races past, and even at the fast tempos the duo takes obvious delight not just in the phrases, but the sonorities they discover. Those tones, magical blends of hearts moving in graceful sync, make this essential. Especially for people who associate Celtic music with Lucky Charms commercials.

GENRE: 🌐 World/Celtic. **RELEASED:** 2001, Barrowstone. **KEY TRACKS:** "The Pigeon on the Gate/Within a Mile of Dublin," "The Golden Eagle/The Rights of Man." **CATALOG CHOICE:** Moving Hearts: *Moving Hearts*. **NEXT STOP:** Horslips: *The Tain*. **AFTER THAT:** Lúnasa: *The Merry Sisters of Fate*.

The Path to Illumination, with Many Twists and Turns

Ladies and Gentlemen We Are Floating in Space

Spiritualized

This album's cover is designed to resemble the label commonly affixed to prescription drugs in the U.K. The back warns "For aural administration only. . . . Use only as directed by a physician." Just about every song recommends drugs, legal or otherwise, as helpful in easing the pain of a devastating romantic setback. Or to obliterate nasty memories.

But this is no ordinary drug record. Its twelve elaborately sculpted tracks, many using symphonic orchestration and/or a gospel choir, form a kind of journal—an inquiry into how far one should go to relieve (or temporarily forget about) distress. Principal songwriter Jason Pierce, whose love affair with interstellar possibility began when he was part of the minimalist British rock band Spacemen 3, starts out by seeking to inspire warm fellow feeling, via an old-fashioned idealistic rock anthem called "Come Together." (No relation to the Beatles' tune.) Then he tries introspection ("All of My Thoughts"). He longs for companionship. He spends some time in pursuit of more abstract notions (the swirling instrumental "No God Only Religion"). By the last song, "Cop Shoot Cop," he's poking around some shady alleys, seeking transcendence in the blues.

Though mind-altering substances may be at work, this music isn't gratuitously spacey. Cosmic, yes, but in the old-school sense: Here is a grand sound ideally suited to the perpetually unfinished wrestling match with the imponderables of life. Gospel is referenced overtly several times, and *Ladies and Gentlemen* shares gospel's quest to know and understand greater powers. But as he writes his hymns for lost souls, Pierce isn't seeking comfortable numbness—more like illumination. The drugs are one means. This fervent music is another, even more powerful, one. And there are no nasty side effects.

GENRE: 🎸 Rock. **RELEASED:** 1997, Arista. **KEY TRACKS:** "No God Only Religion," "Electricity," "Cop Shoot Cop." **CATALOG CHOICE:** *Laser Guided Melodies.* **NEXT STOP:** Pink Floyd: *Wish You Were Here.*

Soul of a Different Stripe, via London

Dusty in Memphis

Dusty Springfield

Shortly after she arrived in Memphis to record this album, British singer Dusty Springfield found herself overwhelmed. Producers Jerry Wexler, Arif Mardin, and Tom Dowd had brought her to the famed American Studios, where they intended to record, and casually pointed out where Wilson Pickett stood to do his vocals. She was awestruck. "You know, you kind of freeze at that point," Springfield recalled later. "Being English, it's very hard to explain how we love and worship these people."

As a result of her jitters, Springfield found it impossible to work in Memphis. So she recorded the lead vocals of *Dusty in Memphis* in New York. For the first and only time in her career, she sang with just the basic rhythm tracks to guide her—the string parts and other sweetening hadn't been recorded yet. She seized the Memphis band's steady, nothing-fancy backing, and paid more attention to rhythm than she had before. This helped her get something almost paramusical onto the tape, a smoldering fire that distinguished the ballads (the wise Carole King–Gerry Goffin "No Easy Way Down") and the assertive, whiplashing grooves ("Son of a Preacher Man") and every song in between.

Dusty in Memphis isn't a soul album in

"I think she is the greatest white singer that there ever has been."
—Elton John

the strict sense. It's an album of great pop songs done soulfully. And make no mistake: The eleven selections on the original (the Deluxe Edition contains a bunch of less satisfying bonus tracks) are all great songs, among them a poignant Randy Newman ode about a spat overheard through thin walls ("I Don't Want to Hear It Anymore"). Despite the top-shelf material and Springfield's spacious, sometimes mysterious vocal performances, the album wasn't a hit when it came out—it peaked at number 99 on the *Billboard* Albums chart, and sold fewer than 100,000 copies its first year. Only much later, when the dust of 1969 cleared, did this delicate marvel find its audience.

GENRE: 🎵 Vocals. **RELEASED:** 1969, Atlantic. **KEY TRACKS:** "No Easy Way Down," "Son of a Preacher Man," "I Don't Want to Hear It Anymore." **CATALOG CHOICE:** *A Brand New Me.* **NEXT STOP:** Norah Jones: *Feels like Home.*

"The Door's Open but the Ride, It Ain't Free"

Born to Run

Bruce Springsteen

Born to Run is the basic rock and roll impulse—we gotta get out of this place—blown up larger than life and written in the block letters of flashing neon signs. In this American classic of the open road, New Jersey singer and guitarist Bruce Springsteen follows small-time toughs, would-be Casanovas, and unsuspecting pretty girls on desperate, and often ill-fated, quests for a payoff, a kiss, a chance at glory on Highway 9. The opening image—"The screen door slams, Mary's dress waves"—suggests the unremarkable start of a shore-town

date, but nobody in these high-revving songs is passive. Mary and everyone else are chasing down some type of destiny. Springsteen brings you into their anxiety, through breathless stanzas that not only express but share the aspirations of his characters. For these people, staying put means rotting; escape is the last chance power try, the final grab at redemption.

Few rock albums breathe with the romance of life's possibilities the way *Born to Run* does. Springsteen has said that as he was writing "Thunder Road," "Jungleland," "Backstreets," and the other operatic marvels here, he recognized he'd need to create a sonic vocabulary massive enough to carry the narratives. With help from his redoubtable Asbury Park crew, one of the most assured bands ever to play rock and roll, he got that, exactly. *Born to Run* encompasses the wild-eyed innocence of early rock and the muscular torque of the great bar bands. The beats charge forward with Cadillac swagger and Porsche finesse; the guitars are engines revving. Everything surrounding the meat-and-potatoes—the yowling sad-dude saxophone of Clarence Clemens, those pinpoint chimes from the glockenspiel, dancing upper-octave piano arpeggios spilling from some ballet studio—becomes an elegant, perfect counterpoint.

Each of these songs is a suite defined by distinct episodes—a songwriting approach

Born to Run's iconic cover photo was shot by Eric Meola.

Springsteen largely abandoned after this, in favor of tighter and less sprawling pieces. There are sudden pensive pauses, tempo changes, and massive crescendos that underscore the overwhelming drama in the lyrics. The music on this album is riddled with ups and downs—the fireworks-blazing exuberance of that "pulling out of here to win" line in "Born to Run" is eclipsed, moments later, by the despairing 4 A.M. wail that echoes through "Jungleland." Those mood swings help Springsteen realize another of his goals for *Born to Run*: In a documentary about the making of the album, he recalls that he wanted it to feel as though "it could all be taking place on an endless summer night."

GENRE: 🎸 Rock. **RELEASED:** 1975, Columbia. **KEY TRACKS:** "Thunder Road," "Born to Run," "She's the One," "Night," "Backstreets," "Jungleland." **CATALOG CHOICES:** *Darkness on the Edge of Town; The River; Nebraska.* **NEXT STOP:** The Who: *Who's Next* (see p. 859). **AFTER THAT:** U2: *War.*

A Cartoon Universe in Sound

The Carl Stalling Project

Carl Stalling
Warner Brothers Studio Orchestra

Some pop culture pundits argue that it's possible to glean a fair understanding of the world just by watching old cartoons. If that's even a teensy bit true, part of the edification comes through sound:

The music accompanying short animated films—particularly those made by Warner Brothers during the 1936–1958 tenure of composer Carl Stalling—greatly enhances the story, capturing not just the madcap action but the essential quirks of the characters, their underlying motivations.

Bugs Bunny and the others in those classic cartoons don't talk much, and Stalling took advantage of that, using pirouetting bits of mood music as a kind of shorthand. One scene would culminate with a thundering orchestral peak, and then might come a serenely trilling solo piccolo to signify the calm after the storm. Stalling's scores are outsized schemes of tension and release, cut to fit the ever-changing requirements of the cat-and-mouse chase.

Stalling worked for Warner Brothers from 1936 to 1958.

Listening without the visuals may initially seem pointless—these "tunes" don't unfold in routine or expected ways, that's for sure. But Stalling was a resourceful appropriator, lacing his scores with bits of ethnic music, weird orchestral effects (one is called "Anxiety Montage"), or references to the classics (for several generations now, kids have associated his twist on the "Valkyrie" leitmotif, from Richard Wagner's *Die Walküre* (see p. 839), with Elmer Fudd's immortal "Kill the Wabbit"). Worth it for the sliding-down-banisters pennywhistles and the clanging metal-on-metal smashups and muted-trumpet scowls, these delightful scores might send you flying off the cliff, but they'll have you smiling all the way down.

GENRE: 🎷 Jazz. **RELEASED:** 1990, Warner Bros. **KEY TRACKS:** "Anxiety Montage," "Dinner Music for a Pack of Hungry Cannibals," "Putty Tat Trouble." **NEXT STOP:** Raymond Scott: *Reckless Nights and Turkish Twilights.* **AFTER THAT:** Ennio Morricone: *The Good, the Bad, and the Ugly.*

What the Angel Band Might Sound Like

The Complete Columbia Recordings

The Stanley Brothers

It's difficult to find a bad Stanley Brothers record. The Virginia brothers Carter (who died in 1966) and Ralph (still kicking and busier than ever thanks to the film *O Brother, Where Art Thou?*) had a songbook that wasn't terribly huge. Over an extended career, they recorded multiple versions of many originals, including the mythic "Man of Constant Sorrow." As a result, even the low-budget anthologies sold in truck stops are fine introductions. This single-disc set, which contains recordings from 1949 to 1952, offers great performances (and sparkling CD transfers) of the group's core repertoire.

The Stanley Brothers, who called themselves the Clinch Mountain Boys when they first got together in 1947, were unjustly less famous than bluegrass pioneers Bill Monroe or Flatt and Scruggs, but their influence on country music is inescapable. The basics of the Stanley sound didn't change much from the duo's first recordings (on the regional Rich-R-Tone label) to these masterful performances from the late '40s: This is humble, affect-free singing, often in wide and brotherly harmony, that offers stories of tragic deaths (often of children) and expressions of undying faith.

The recordings the Stanleys made during a three-year stint at Columbia rank among the duo's most creative. Most of the twenty-two tracks are originals, and several of them ("Drunkard's Hell," "Pretty Polly," "Man of Constant Sorrow") represent a fresh, uncluttered approach to Monroe's bluegrass. These tunes carry the wisdom of mountain-dwellers and wanderers, and they're delivered in calm, level-headed, pretension-free tones. More fervor creeps into the selections that are outright expressions of faith: When these two describe how the "Angels Are Singing (in

The Stanley Brothers performed on the *Farm and Fun Time* radio show for over 10 years.

Heaven Tonight)," even the most cynical urban sophisticates might find themselves shaken or, at the very least, stirred.

GENRE: 🌎 Country.
RELEASED: 1996, Columbia.
KEY TRACKS: "Angels Are Singing (in Heaven Tonight)," "Man of Constant Sorrow," "Gathering Flowers for the Master's Bouquet." **CATALOG CHOICES:** *Earliest Recordings: The Complete Rich-R-Tone 78s; Man of Constant Sorrow.* **NEXT STOP:** Patty Loveless: *Mountain Soul.*

They'll Take You There

The Best of the Staple Singers

The Staple Singers

Here's an illustration of inspiration in action. Among those who heard the early speeches of the Reverend Martin Luther King was a guitar player by the name of Roebuck "Pops" Staples, who'd been kicking blues-tinged gospel around Chicago for a few years. The words about equality and respect and opportunity inspired him to make changes in his music. "When Dr. King started preaching," Staples's daughter Yvonne recalled after her father's death in 2000, "Pops said, 'I think we can sing it.' That's what he felt. . . . He lived the life. He believed that the world could be made a better place for all of us."

For a run of several years, the Staple Singers became the musical embodiment of that idealism. The family band sang about respect and decency, and cast the struggle for equality in human, empathetic terms.

"Pops" and his singing daughters, Mavis, Cleotha, and Yvonne.

They became a conscience of the pop charts: Their earthy call-and-response songs, huge hits like "I'll Take You There" and lesser-known gems like "Be What You Are," soldiered toward the higher ground in a way that brought people of all races and circumstances along. Theirs was an affirming, positive approach to spirituality. The Staple Singers could rouse an audience the way the great gospel quartets did, but they never lectured anybody about skipping church.

With the help of producer Al Bell and the musicians of Memphis, Tennessee, and Muscle Shoals, Alabama, the group found unexplored territory between pop-gospel and gritty rhythm and blues. The first burst came in 1968, with a song called "Heavy Makes You Happy"; from there, the group churned out original message songs and imaginative covers, including stunning versions of Otis Redding's "(Sittin' on) the Dock of the Bay" and the Band's "The Weight," that depended on the brawny, determined voice of daughter Mavis Staples. Supporting this vocal blend is an unobtrusive band led by the outfit's true secret weapon—the guitarist and patriarch, Pops Staples. Listen closely to discover a wizard of the deep background, serving up fills and crying lead-lines that are devastatingly concise. The words of the Staple Singers are plenty righteous by themselves, but it's his delicate, tasteful asides that speed this music heavenward.

GENRES: 🕇 Gospel 🍺 R&B. **RELEASED:** 1986, Stax. **KEY TRACKS:** "Respect Yourself," "The Weight," "I'll Take You There." **CATALOG CHOICE:** Mavis Staples with Lucky Peterson: *Spirituals and Gospel*. **NEXT STOP:** The Rance Allen Group: *The Best of the Rance Allen Group*. **AFTER THAT:** Andrae Crouch: *His Best*.

Dance with the Mystics

Between Heaven and Earth: Music of the Jewish Mystics

Andy Statman

Full of swollen storm-cloud chords and somber instrumental echoes of ancient incantations, *Between Heaven and Earth* is Jewish music for people who are feeling burned out on the zippy gaiety of klezmer.

On these nine gently engrossing and sometimes New Agey excursions, clarinetist Andy Statman and an attentive jazz-schooled backing group tackle a series of prayer melodies used by Hasidic mystics to induce heightened awareness. These are simple themes, many brushed with a mournful undercurrent, and Statman takes advantage of their openness: He frequently goes off on squiggly rubato tangents that uncover beauty in a kind of exploratory slow motion. Central to the vibe of discovery is pianist Kenny Werner, who frames Statman's pitch-bending elegies with perfectly placed chordal clusters. He and the others operate in an atmosphere of communal seeking; rather than providing the expected firm rhythm, the musicians appear more interested in *davening*, or praying. Statman and his accomplices have deep backgrounds in jazz, and on several of these selections, the improvisations flow in the direction of the avant-garde at its transcendence-seeking zenith.

Two guests seize and amplify that spirit: Mandolinist David Grisman links Statman's mystic airs to the everyday sounds of the Appalachian hills, while banjo master Bela Fleck lures Statman into an agitated dance, "Purim," that contrasts with the reverential, sometimes even awed tone that pervades everything else here.

GENRE: 🌐 World. **RELEASED:** 1997, Shanachie. **KEY TRACKS:** "You Were Revealed," "Adir," "Yonah." **CATALOG CHOICE:** *Nashville Mornings, New York Nights*. **NEXT STOP:** Don Byron: *Tuskegee Experiments*. **AFTER THAT:** Alvin Batiste: *Marsalis Music Honors Alvin Batiste*.

Another Answer to the Vexing Question: "How Much to Rock?"

Parcel of Rogues

Steeleye Span

Every British folk act of the '60s and '70s eventually came to the crossroads where "folk" and "rock" converge. When Fairport Convention arrived there in 1969 (see *Liege and Lief*, p. 268), the group led by guitarist Richard Thompson brokered an innovative truce between styles that many traditionalists believed (Bob Dylan notwithstanding) should remain separate. Even some members of Fairport had reservations—the bassist Ashley Hutchings left the band to join the nascent Steeleye Span, because its music at the time was defiantly "folk." That only lasted a few years, and after several more

Parcel of Rogues is Steeleye Span's fifth album.

personnel changes, Steeleye Span wound up at the same crossroads. It added electric guitars and a drummer, and made this magical album.

Like *Liege*, the lively *Parcel of Rogues* is an imaginative integration, not a radical upheaval. There are almost tribal rhythms that carry the otherworldly voice of Maddy Prior, whose airy soprano harks back centuries. Prior is strangely affecting even when singing such esoteric pieces as "Alison Gross," the gorgeously harmonized

tale of an ugly witch. There are traditional songs so thoroughly rejiggered as to be unrecognizable: "Cam Ye o'er Frae France" uses rockish textures to conjure suffocating doom. Also here are several perky instrumentals that rely on both traditional dancing-fiddle passages and wah-wah guitar. Imagine a wandering troubadour whose stock-in-trade is sad songs stumbling into a hippie pagan ritual in the idyllic British countryside—that's the spirit behind *Parcel of Rogues*. The old-timer wants to jam, and the kids aren't so far gone that they've forgotten the old songs. A good time is had by all.

GENRE: 🎵 Folk. **RELEASED:** 1973, Chrysalis. (Reissued 1989, Shanachie.) **KEY TRACKS:** "Alison Gross," "Cam Ye o'er Frae France." **CATALOG CHOICE:** *Below the Salt.* **NEXT STOP:** Pentangle: *Cruel Sister.*

An Apex of Studio Perfection

Aja

Steely Dan

Walter Becker and Donald Fagan of Steely Dan had a reputation for fanatical persnicketiness. Working on the later Steely Dan records, they were known to spend expensive days in the studio chasing an ideal thwack on the snare drum, endlessly tweaking (and debating) barely perceptible shadings of sound. The hired guns, crucial to Steely Dan starting with the 1975 *Katy Lied,* were sometimes baffled by the process. (Fagan once recalled that people would leave their sessions saying things like "But we didn't play any music today.") Still, the ends did justify the means: On the level of pure sonic wizardry, Steely Dan records shine like crazy diamonds. Their razor focus and futuristic gleam catch a sonic ideal nobody else imagined.

The darkly acidic *The Royal Scam* (1976) marks the beginning of the Dan's obsessive phase, and the lean *Aja* represents its apex. The seven (!) tracks exist in a kind of hyper-real state, where each snare drum hit is a dagger to the heart. Songs that start with shooping, instantly accessible backbeats wind up deep in graduate metaphysics, where abstraction rules and the "angular banjos" mentioned in the title track serve as pathways to illumination. Embedded within these tunes are chord sequences more demanding than you'll find in most jazz, some built on a tonality Becker and Fagan called "mu major." These provide a platform for broiling extended solos, from

Becker on impossibly liquid electric guitar, from the furtive Wayne Shorter on saxophone, and from drummer Steve Gadd, whose melodic excursion through the title track is one of the great drum solos of all time.

Aja marks the rare occasion when a pair of wisecracking music obsessives managed an elaborate, unapologetically sophisticated end run around the lowest-common-denominator mentality of pop radio. Yes, there's a killer sense of the hook at work here. But Becker and Fagan are not going to spoon-feed anybody. Your ears have to adjust to *their* palette. This happened, en masse, upon *Aja*'s release: Several of the songs became radio hits, and the album went on to sell millions. One explanation for the album's success might be the tones Becker and Fagan spent all that time obsessing over. Most music from 1977 sounds like it was made in 1977. *Aja* is timeless.

GENRE: 🎸 Rock. **RELEASED:** 1977, MCA. **KEY TRACKS:** "Deacon Blues," "Aja," "Black Cow." **CATALOG CHOICES:** *Pretzel Logic; The Royal Scam; Gaucho.* **NEXT STOP:** Donald Fagan: *The Nightfly.* **AFTER THAT:** The Blue Nile: *Hats.*

Life in a Blender

Emperor Tomato Ketchup

Stereolab

When the Jetsons go for a family drive, this is what might be playing in their hovercraft. As the beloved animated TV series of the '60s did, Stereolab's fourth album *Emperor Tomato Ketchup* offers a stylized

(and idealized) vision of the future—it's a friendly new frontier, with technological solutions waiting around every corner and possibilities expanding in all directions. The music bubbles along, sleekness epitomized, gliding boldly toward some space-age bachelor pad. Where everything old—even those buoyantly

optimistic singing groups of the 1960s, like the Association—can be rejiggered into something wondrous and new again.

Few rock acts have repurposed the random detritus of pop culture quite as spectacularly as Stereolab did on this, its most fully realized statement. The collective led by multi-instrumentalist Tim Gane manipulates small recurring loops similar to those used by hip-hop beatmakers and electronica DJs into richly textured collages. These include spry skating-rink organ and arena-rock guitar machinations (see "The Noise of Carpet").

Lead voice Laetitia Sadier and expert harmony singer Mary Hansen pick up on the junior-jumble spirit of the instrumentals, spiking the songs with abstract ideas from theoretical philosophers and leftist thinkers. Sometimes they sing the surreal and cerebral lyrics in close harmony. But more often, their winsome voices move in parallel orbits and carefully synchronized exchanges of call-and-response.

Emperor aligns with similarly spirited works of life-in-a-blender juxtaposition from

Emperor Tomato Ketchup is also the name of a 1971 Japanese film.

Beck (see p. 64), the Beastie Boys (see p. 57), and others of its day. It's a triumph of assimilation, in which disconnected ideas become part of a cohesive, if slightly surreal, scheme. Some critics called the result "post rock," but really no shorthand designation does justice to these alluring sounds, which come zooming in from some distant utopia, offer glimpses of life there, and then speed silently away.

GENRE: 🎸 Rock. **RELEASED:** 1996, Elektra. **KEY TRACKS:** "The Noise of Carpet," "Metronomic Underground," "Anonymous Collective." **CATALOG CHOICE:** *Transient Random Noise Bursts with Announcements.*
NEXT STOP: Os Mutantes: *Mutantes* (see p. 536). **AFTER THAT:** Beck: *Midnite Vultures.*

Fire from the Violin

Lalo: Symphonie Espagnole
Bruch: Violin Concerto No. 1

Isaac Stern
Philadelphia Orchestra (Eugene Ormandy, cond.)

Yes, a few notes don't arrive exactly on schedule. There's fuzz around some of them, and a few outright flubs too. But if you're looking for a soloist to pull you inside a piece and show you what really matters about it, seek out the fiery violinist Isaac Stern.

Stern (1920–2001) was born in the Ukraine, but his family moved to San Francisco when he was an infant. He began music studies at age eight, and by fifteen had made his debut—with the San Francisco Symphony. Blessed with a robust tone, he became one of the most prolific recording artists in classical music, and he is among the all-time best at going with the gut. Many classical stars chase unassailable technical perfection; on this recording and others, Stern appears willing to sacrifice persnickety details in order to discover—and tease out—the heart music beyond the notation. He is unruly, and volatile—at times during the up-tempo sections of Edouard Lalo's five-movement *Symphonie Espagnole*, it sounds as though he's using his instrument to chop wood. Then, when things get too reckless, he'll deliver a line so invested with intention it encapsulates the feeling of the entire piece.

With dazzling declarative themes that vault into the nosebleed register, *Symphonie Espagnole* is perfect for Stern. Composed in 1874, it is among the most famous pieces by Edouard Lalo, who was born in France of Spanish parents. Despite his heritage, Lalo doesn't load the piece up with the "Spanish" scales that were in fashion at the time—only the last two movements contain overt regional references. The fourth is a choice Stern showpiece: Moving with a sleepwalker's serenity, the violinist modulates his customary scene-stealing ways, focusing on slight shifts in tone color and vibrato to underscore the emotional crosscurrents of the piece.

The Max Bruch concerto, which premiered in 1866, is in some ways an even better platform for Stern's heated style. After an initial bit of exploratory wandering that has the character of a cadenza, the music settles into a calm processional gait for the primary theme. Stern begins it as if weeping, and he labors over the fragile line as the orchestra spreads out a heart-tugging chord sequence beneath him. Here and in the equally strong closing movement, Stern makes the most of Bruch's songlike melodies. With broad and sometimes excited gestures, he points right at the specific aspects of the line that tear him up, nudging them into the spotlight. Where some soloists worry about balancing precise execution with emotional communication, Stern charges ahead, making such concerns seem academic. He might gloss over some notes and lunge fitfully at others, but in the context of such lively and illuminating performances, those glitches are tiny, trifling things.

GENRE: 🎻 Classical. **RELEASED:** 1967, Columbia. (Reissued 2007, Sony Classical.) **KEY TRACKS:** Lalo: fourth movement. Bruch: first movement. **F.Y.I:** Cellist Yo-Yo Ma once named this among his favorite recordings, calling it "Isaac Stern at his best. There's nothing more to say." **CATALOG CHOICE:** Mendelssohn, Tchaikovsky: *Violin Concertos,* Philadelphia Orchestra (Eugene Ormandy, cond.). **NEXT STOP:** Nathan Milstein: *Beethoven and Brahms Violin Concertos,* Pittsburgh Symphony (William Steinberg, cond.).

Ohhh, Baby, Baby, It's a Wild World

Tea for the Tillerman

Cat Stevens

Pop music is home to seekers, earnest Hermann Hesse–reading types who are (as one song title here declares) "on the road to find out" and more than willing to send back dispatches. Born in England to Greek parents, Cat Stevens (Steven Demetre Georgiou) wasn't the first such soul. But he was among the most successful. For several years starting in 1970, he made spiritual inquiry—and introspection—seem a vital and necessary part of a young person's life.

Starting with a sonic palette somewhere between the late Beatles and the then-rising California singer-songwriters, Stevens created homily-rich songs that portrayed internal questing as a richly rewarding, and possibly sexy, pursuit. He wrote koans about religion, sometimes exhibiting a profound skepticism. He sang about technology, loss of innocence (most poignantly on "Where Do the Children Play?"), and the eternal struggles between brash youth and experience.

Tea for the Tillerman catches Stevens at his most brazen as a thinker and his most daring as a pop auteur; the record he issued six months after this one, *Teaser and the Firecat*, has the more simplistic singles "Morning Has Broken" and "Peace Train." This album is wound tighter, and takes more rhythmic chances; at times its questioning feels somewhat more severe. These are pluses: The sudden shifts of tempo jolt listeners from complacency, and the (few) varied musical approaches give Stevens's notions about romance (the search for a "Hard Headed Woman," the sketch of "Sad Lisa") an almost mystical aura.

Stevens adopted the Muslim name Yusuf Islam in 1977.

Amazingly, Stevens's contribution to pop endures despite his well-publicized conversion to Islam in 1977, and his harsh condemnation of Western idol worship that followed. It's fine if he doesn't want to be a star anymore. But his choice doesn't change the resonance of these serene, entrancing hymnlike works, created at a time when Stevens was wandering "the road to find out."

GENRE: 🎸 Rock. **RELEASED:** 1970, A&M. **KEY TRACKS:** "Where Do the Children Play?," "Wild World," "But I Might Die Tonight," "Longer Boats," "Father and Son." **CATALOG CHOICE:** *Teaser and the Firecat.* **NEXT STOP:** Donovan: *Sunshine Superman.* **AFTER THAT:** Jim Croce: *You Don't Mess Around with Jim.*

Two Down, Forty-eight to Go

Illinoise

Sufjan Stevens

At first people thought Sufjan Stevens was joking. After garnering big acclaim for his second solo effort *Greetings from Michigan: The Great Lakes State* (2003), the singer, songwriter, and nu-folk mystic from Michigan told interviewers he intended to create a series of albums of original songs, one for each state in the union. A grand and quixotic plan a social studies teacher could love, this project seemed likely to exhaust Stevens's considerable compositional resources—even as it earned him a place in the novelty-music hall of fame.

Then came the even more inventive *Illinoise,* and suddenly Stevens's modest proposal didn't seem like such a joke. These smart and occasionally subversive songs cel-

ebrate the salient characteristics of Illinois: The album opens with a wide-eyed expression of awe about the possible existence of aliens, "Concerning the UFO Sighting Near Highland, Illinois." From there, Stevens involves such notable figures as the poet Carl Sandburg (who visits Stevens in a dream), the notorious gangster Al Capone, and the serial killer John Wayne Gacy, using the characters as springboards for all sorts of writerly pondering. The local color functions in the manner of a TV-news crawl at the bottom of the screen—it's a sidelight, not the main show. Stevens's observations on human nature are so trenchant, they transcend state lines.

Stevens sprinkles impressive helpings of ear candy through these diverse tunes—scruffy alt-rock hooks, broad-shouldered arena anthems, and sneaky, sophisticated melodies that occupy a little-explored zone between folk reflection and the jazz stratosphere. A gifted multi-instrumentalist, he thinks in terms of texture and color, and on this record spends more time creating lush settings than worrying about vocal perfection. He knows he's not the kind of singer who's going to wow anybody, and his deliberately low-affect approach—a disarmingly candid all's-swell-in-the-meditation-room demeanor—suits the songs of *Illinoise* perfectly.

GENRE: 🎸 Rock. **RELEASED:** 2005, Asthmatic Kitty. **KEY TRACKS:** "Concerning the UFO Sighting Near Highland, Illinois," "The Black Hawk War," "John Wayne Gacy, Jr.," "The Tallest Man, the Broadest Shoulders." **CATALOG CHOICE:** *Greetings from Michigan: The Great Lakes State.* **NEXT STOP:** Devendra Banhart: *Smokey Rolls Down Thunder Canyon.* **AFTER THAT:** Jim O'Rourke: *Eureka.*

Every Song Paints a Different Picture and . . .

Every Picture Tells a Story

Rod Stewart

Yes, he's foisted plenty of stinky music on the world—the disco-era lowlight "Do Ya Think I'm Sexy" or the four (!) tortured volumes of standards that make up much of his output in the '90s and beyond.

But in 1971, Rod Stewart could do no wrong. He was an exotic kind of belter, with a bourbon-blessed voice that sounded totally torn up at the beginning of the night, and got better from there. His band the Faces had honed a swaggering, almost bawdy brand of blues-rock that was drawing well on both sides of the Atlantic, and would reach its recorded peak with *A Nod Is as Good as a Wink . . . to a Blind Horse* later in the year.

Overshadowing the solid Faces stuff is Stewart's third solo album—a jaw-dropper that is unlike anything rowdy Rod the Mod had done before. Though backed by the Faces, he isn't leaving everything on the stage as he did with the band—these performances are closer to confessional soul, wistful and uncharacteristically reflective. The material ranges from an early-rock classic ("That's All Right," which Stewart interpolates with "Amazing Grace") to a totally reinvented Temptations hit ("I'm Losing You") to a Dylan song ("Tomorrow Is a Long Time") to the great seduction tale "Maggie May," which was the B side of the first single and became a radio hit after DJs, unprompted, started playing it.

That first single, Tim Hardin's "Reason to Believe," ranks among rock's all-time great covers. It closes the album, a pensive wee-hours

Rod Stewart performing at New York's Madison Square Garden in 1971.

nightcap. Though he's strutted around elsewhere, here Stewart plays the sad rogue, puzzling over clues left by a lover who's suddenly vacated the premises. Sounding alternately resigned and defiant, Stewart broods and bawls through Hardin's melody like he really wants to understand what went wrong. His sincerity is audible, and touching; it makes the song, and really the entire album. Stewart had plenty of hits after this, but he never sounded as genuine again.

GENRE: 🎸 Rock. **RELEASED:** 1971, Mercury. **KEY TRACKS:** All of them. **CATALOG CHOICE:** Faces: *A Nod Is as Good as a Wink.* **NEXT STOP:** Jeff Beck: *Truth.* **AFTER THAT:** The Black Crowes: *Shake Your Money Maker.*

Icy Voices Hooked on Phonics

Stimmung

Karlheinz Stockhausen
Theater of Voices (Paul Hillier, cond.)

Like many of his peers in the avant-garde, German composer Karlheinz Stockhausen (1928–2007) conceived of his pieces as full-blown conceptual events, in which context and structural ingenuity are often as important as the notes. One of his string quartets requires each of the four musicians to be stationed in a different helicopter. Among his later pieces are long, deliberately obscure operas that are extended meditations on each day of the week.

The beguiling choral work *Stimmung*, written during the winter of 1968 in a snowbound house on Long Island Sound, isn't quite so outlandish. The concept here is about syllables and their overtones, and what happens to a single indivisible kernel of sound—the repetition of a vowel, say—as it is repeated. Inspired by the technique known as "overtone singing," Stockhausen studied which elements of speech produced particularly striking sounds, and wrote short passages in which a primary tone, usually produced at whisper-like low volume, triggers fantastical

Stockhausen said that the snow on the frozen Long Island Sound was "the only landscape I really saw during the composition of the piece."

clusters and far-flung extensions of the root chord. In some ways, the piece, which is usually performed with the singers in a circle, explores motific development in ways similar to those of Beethoven's Diabelli Variations—except where Beethoven poured forth an endless stream of melodic elaborations, Stockhausen uses chanting and long tones and mouth and throat effects (captured by positioning the microphone extremely close to the singers) to create stunning and majestic sweeps of sound. The textures become the variations.

"Stimmung" means "tuning," and one of the piece's challenges has to do with pitch: Each singer is tasked with sustaining his or her tone as the harmonic scheme changes ever so slightly (or radically) around it. The Copenhagen-based Theater of Voices, led by vocal-ensemble magician Paul Hillier, magnifies the contrasts and collisions, savoring the magnetic pull of adjoining half steps. They render Stockhausen's rippling waves with remarkable clarity, drawing listeners into each isolated fragment of its icy soundscape. Their singing makes the piece accessible, but beware: This can be creepy on headphones.

GENRE: 🎼 Classical. **RELEASED:** 2007, Harmonia Mundi. **KEY TRACKS:** "Model 1," "Model 4," "Model 27." **CATALOG CHOICE:** *Gruppen,* WDR Sinfonieorchester Köln (Peter Eötvös, cond.). **NEXT STOP:** Luciano Berio: *Sinfonia for Eight Voices and Orchestra* (see p. 81). **AFTER THAT:** Nico Muhly: *Speaks Volumes.*

The Glorious Beginnings of Madchester

The Stone Roses

The Stone Roses

When the Stone Roses started in the late 1980s, the notion of mingling elements of rock with rave culture was outlandish. Not anymore: In the aftermath of the singles from this massively successful album,

bands (first in the band's hometown of Manchester, then London, and later the U.S.) began pursuing the idea in earnest—among the successful were Happy Mondays, Inspiral Carpets, and later Kula Shakur. Some became massive. Some disappeared quickly. None ever quite equaled the crazed confluence of wiggly grooves, pinging guitars, and blissed-out vocals that distinguish this album.

"It's timeless. It still sounds fresh." —Ian Brown

What's incredible about *The Stone Roses* is how unelectronic it is: Though the band was deeply influenced by acid house and other dance styles, it didn't simply sample existing material. Instead, it sought to re-create the hypnotic beat in a rock context. Drummer Reni (Alan John Wren) translated the relentless pulses of house into vital, breathing, human grooves—one example of his genius is the gently rolling "Waterfall," a perpetual-motion machine in 4/4 time.

The songs, written by guitarist John Squire and vocalist Ian Brown, build on that rhythmic churn. They contain unabashedly positive refrains and sweet psychedelic melodies like "I Wanna Be Adored," carefully speared guitar melodies and lovely, elaborate vocal harmonies (see "She Bangs the Drums" and "Elephant Stone") that hark back to the radiant pop of the mid-1960s. Each a different exploration, the songs flow together beautifully: This is one of the few albums of its time that remains thrilling until the last song.

GENRE: 🎸 Rock. **RELEASED:** 1989, Silvertone/RCA. **KEY TRACKS:** "Waterfall," "She Bangs the Drums," "I Wanna Be Adored," "I Am the Resurrection." **BUYER BEWARE:** The original CD version of this suffers from odd sonic inconsistencies. Seek out later remastered versions, or the 1995 *The Complete Stone Roses.* **NEXT STOP:** Happy Mondays: *Bummed.* **AFTER THAT:** Kula Shakur: *K.*

A Double Shot of Viennese Finery

Die Fledermaus/ New Year's Concert

Johann Strauss II

Vienna Philharmonic (Clemens Krauss, cond.)

Here are two distinct slivers of history: an excellent representation of the Johann Strauss operetta *Die Fledermaus* and the first recording of the Vienna Philharmonic's now annual "New Year's" concert, which is devoted to the waltzes and polkas of the city's heritage, many written by the Strauss family.

Performed here without between-songs spoken dialogue, *Die Fledermaus* is a polarizing work—some dismiss it as provincial fluff, others hold it up as some of the best music of the nineteenth century. Even its detractors have to acknowledge this much: There's genius in these melodies, broadly lyrical lines that carry character portraits while glancing at subtle undercurrents of human emotion. Strauss (1825–1899) was a master of the local delicacy, the Viennese waltz, and uses it to tell a saucy tale about rich people acting out sexually at a masquerade ball. The plot resembles that of Mozart's *The Marriage of Figaro*, and like that work contains episodes of brash cavorting as well as more introspective moments. "Ach, meine Herr'n und Damen" is a simple motif that approximates the cadences of hearty (and contagious) laughter. A bit later, in the "Csardas: Klage der Heimat," Hilde Gueden (as Rosalinde) sings in lavish descending spirals "around" the melody, in a way that suggests an inescapable regret.

The conductor, Clemens Krauss, was working with the Vienna Philharmonic during World War II; among his ideas was a free concert

Johann Strauss was hailed as "the Waltz King" during his lifetime.

celebrating Austrian music, an affirmation of culture while the population, still suffering hardship, rebuilt the city's hallowed performance spaces. The concert became a tradition on New Year's Day, and is now broadcast live throughout Europe. Disc two of the surprisingly crisp transfer contains what's known as "New Year's" concert No. 1, from September 1951. It opens with Strauss's magnificent "Tales from the Vienna Woods," which features the Viennese zither. In this excellent rendering, it's possible to hear not only the orchestra's customary precision, but its uniquely "Viennese" phrasing: As the music swells to mark some key culminating point in the waltz, the group, en masse, pauses ever so slightly. Turns out this "lilt" is polarizing too: Some conductors believe it can be taught, while others contend it never feels right unless it's in your bones. Which it clearly is here.

GENRES: 🏴 Opera 🎼 Classical.
RELEASED: 1992, Decca. **KEY TRACKS:**
Die Fledermaus: "Ach, ich darf nicht hin zu dir!,"
"Also, noch verschärft die Strafe?" *New Year's
Concert:* "Tales from the Vienna Woods," "The
Dragonfly," "Egyptian March." **ANOTHER
INTERPRETATION:** *Die Fledermaus,*

Berlin Philharmonic (Herbert von Karajan, cond.). **CATALOG CHOICE:** *19 Waltzes,* Wiener Johann-Strauss Kammerorchester (Willi Boskovsky, cond.). **NEXT STOP:** W. A. Mozart: *The Marriage of Figaro* (see p. 528). **AFTER THAT:** Richard Strauss: *Capriccio,* Elisabeth Schwarzkopf, Philharmonia Orchestra (Wolfgang Sawallisch, cond.).

Music of Godlike Power

Also sprach Zarathustra

Richard Strauss
Berlin Philharmonic (Karl Böhm, cond.)

In his classic of existential philosophy *Thus Spoke Zarathustra,* Friedrich Nietzsche wrote, "Whenever your spirit wants to speak in images, pay heed; for that is when your virtue has its origin and beginning." Composer Richard Strauss did pay heed. His 1896 orchestral tone poem is subtitled "Freely After Nietzsche." Through a series of vividly imagined and sometimes gimmicky scenes, Strauss seeks to evoke the spirit of Nietzsche's "Superman," and the world of new possibility he is charged with shaping. The piece begins with one of the most famous openings in all of music—a gathering-storm mass of chords that surge and crest and then crack apart, an episode Strauss intended to symbolize the dawn of man. From there, *Zarathustra* visits increasingly abstract realms, each utilizing new combinations of instruments. Strauss's scoring is masterly: He uses towering chords (some from a full theater organ) and dense images to draw listeners into the trembling moment when the shell is cracking apart, and new worlds are being born. With this version, the Berlin Philharmonic captures both the heavy celestial thunder and the microscopic tensions of Strauss's orchestrations.

Strauss's opening sequence served as the anchor for Stanley Kubrick's *2001: A Space*

"I now comfort myself with the knowledge that I am on the road I want to take."
—Richard Strauss
(on composing tone poems)

Odyssey; it's an utterly perfect union of sound and image. Since then, the music has served as the backdrop for countless less-artistic advertisements and campy TV send-ups. Some critics say that Kubrick was the best thing to happen to an overblown, and often pretentious, piece that is historically significant primarily as a warm-up for Strauss's opera career. But what a warm-up: Those cresting brass long tones call from several galaxies over, beckoning all within earshot to really think for a minute about space, and man's role within it.

GENRE: 🎷 Classical. **RELEASED:** 1958, Deutsche Grammophon. **KEY TRACKS:** Opening, "Science" section. **ANOTHER INTERPRETATION:** *2001: A Space Odyssey,* Philadelphia Orchestra (Eugene Ormandy, cond.). **CATALOG CHOICE:** *Salome,* Teresa Stratus, Vienna Philharmonic (Karl Bohm, cond.). **NEXT STOP:** Gustav Holst: *The Planets* (see p. 364). **AFTER THAT:** Modest Mussorgsky: *A Night on Bald Mountain,* New York Philharmonic (Leonard Bernstein, cond.).

A Deep Dark Difficult "Black Diamond" of an Opera

Elektra

Richard Strauss

Birgit Nilsson, Vienna Philharmonic (Sir Georg Solti, cond.)

Not all music is supposed to be digested in one sitting. Sometimes music has to seep into the nervous system over a period of prolonged exposure. There may be some work involved in understanding it. This is, of course, a tough sell in our instant-gratification age: We know what we like and that's what we buy. In an earlier, pre-iTunes period, choices were more limited, and people would actually sit down and listen to music that repulsed or challenged or terrified them. They didn't expect their own aesthetic to be affirmed every time they pressed Play. These brave souls may not have ended up cherishing every piece they were listening to, but by repeatedly confronting aspects of the musical universe that they found difficult, they broadened their horizons.

For many people who don't listen to opera regularly, Strauss's *Elektra*, one of the much-hallowed "great operas," may be rough sledding. Historians insist there is important music waiting inside this piece, which premiered in 1909 and was the first of many collaborations between Strauss and playwright Hugo von Hofmannsthal. Ears weaned on pop, trained to expect the hook that arrives within the first thirty seconds of a tune, may think otherwise. Strauss did write hooks, but his are not easily repeated advertising slogans. Instead, they're extended paragraphs, thoughts crashing on top of thoughts. It can take several encounters before the themes clarify. As the piece goes on, what began as a trickle of ideas, gathers force: Parts of the "Recognition Scene" in which Elektra first sees the brother she thought was dead are not for those seeking a meditative haven.

Elektra is a tale of revenge based on the writings of Sophocles, and so has overtones of Greek tragedy. It opens with a scene of musical and physical brutality among the maids of a palace, and gets darker from there—when we first meet Elektra, she's being kept with the dogs. Strauss evidently wants to jolt his listeners; that opening, and much of what follows, pushes standard tonality to its limits, with odd chords splayed over several octaves. His techniques, which he largely abandoned in subsequent works like *Der Rosenkavalier* (see next page), are arresting for their sheer drama, the way they conjure storm clouds in the background.

This version, with the Vienna Philharmonic, is among the greatest. Led by conductor Sir Georg Solti, whose edge-of-your-seat urgings are palpable, it features Birgit Nilsson in the title role. A sensitive soprano able to summon tremendous power on demand, Nilsson sings in shuddering outbursts that lure you into the *Elektra* terror, and radiate a severe beauty that can pull you back to the piece again and again.

GENRE: 😊 Opera. **RELEASED:** 1967, EMI. **KEY TRACKS:** Act 1: "Allein! Weh, ganz, allein"; Act 2: "Nun denn, allein," "Orest!" **ANOTHER INTERPRETATION:** Astrid Varnay, Kölner Rundfunkorchester. **CATALOG CHOICE:** *Capriccio,* Elisabeth Schwarzkopf, Nicolai Gedda, Philharmonia Orchestra (Wolfgang Sawallisch, cond.). **NEXT STOP:** Richard Wagner: *The Ring Trilogy,* Birgit Nilsson, Vienna Philharmonic (Georg Solti, cond.). **AFTER THAT:** Hector Berlioz: *Requiem,* Boston Symphony Orchestra (Charles Munch, cond.).

Trysts and Turns of Viennese Aristocracy

Der Rosenkavalier

Richard Strauss

*Elisabeth Schwarzkopf, Otto Edelmann, Christa Ludwig,
Philharmonia Orchestra (Herbert von Karajan, cond.)*

Much of the dialogue in Richard Strauss's final opera *Capriccio* centers on a parlor debate about what's most important in opera—words or music? Strauss wrestled with this question throughout his life, answering at times with grand instrumental flourishes (see *Elektra*, the work preceding *Der Rosenkavalier*, previous page) and at other times with chatty duets and trios (for example, see the sister/sister discussion in the first act of *Arabella*).

A chronicle of the trysts and turns of the Viennese aristocracy, *Der Rosenkavalier* doesn't put Strauss definitively on the side of words or music. Instead it offers spine-tingling displays of both. The text, by German playwright Hugo von Hofmannsthal, has nicely developed characters contending with lust, duplicity, and, occasionally, big, literary ideas. Strauss surrounds them with sumptuously upholstered themes, many strong enough to grab the spotlight as instrumental motifs. (Parts of this have been "adapted" for the symphony orchestra; the key material translates well as a suite of symphonic "songs.")

Strauss was at a crossroads when he began *Der Rosenkavalier*. On his two previous large works, he'd pushed the envelope, with harmonies that dance on the line dividing tonality and atonality. This time he elected to step back a bit; it's a work of consolidation that aspires to the compactness of his tone poems and the knotty, slow-to-resolve tension of his chamber works. The music is mostly consonant, and there are moments of breathtaking melody—including the closing tableau of Act 1, in which the aristocratic Marschallin, sung lavishly by Elisabeth Schwarzkopf, confronts the conflicted reality of her affair with a much younger boy toy.

Marschallin goes missing in the second act, but reappears in the third as a deus ex machina, untangling the relationships and cases of mistaken identity (it's a comic opera, so there's lots of cross-dressing and subterfuge). In the course of this, she participates in a sublime trio with her former beau Octavian (sung by Christa Ludwig) and another aristocratic girl, Sophie (Teresa Stich-Randall), that is among the great culminating moments in opera. As conducted by the great Herbert von Karajan, the section that begins with "Mein Gott" sounds like it was written for these three singers. They establish a precise yet intimate mood, and sustain it throughout their exchanges, while at the same time handling Strauss's technically daunting aerial melodies. Beware: After experiencing this performance of the famous trio, the big flag-waving finales of other operas may seem like empty bluster.

GENRE: 🎵 Opera. **RELEASED:** 1957, EMI. **KEY TRACKS:** Act 1: "Die Zeit"; Act 2: "Herr Baron von Lerchenau!"; Act 3: "Mein Gott." **ANOTHER INTERPRETATION:** Felicity Lott, Anne Sofie von Otter, Vienna State Opera (Carlos Kleiber, cond.; DVD). **CATALOG CHOICE:** *Arabella,* Dietrich Fischer-Dieskau, Lisa Della Casa, Bavarian State Opera Orchestra (Joseph Keilberth, cond.). **NEXT STOP:** Leonard Bernstein: *Candide,* Christa Ludwig, Nicolai Gedda, London Symphony Orchestra (Leonard Bernstein, cond.).

If You Care About Melody, You Need This

Four Last Songs

Richard Strauss

Jessye Norman, Leipzig Gewandhaus Orchestra (Kurt Masur, cond.)

With these meditations on the end of life, Richard Strauss deftly pulls off what composers had been trying (mostly in vain) to do for the previous hundred years: Write endless melodies. Not running-at-the-mouth gibberish, but substantial lines that have shape and lyricism but don't conform to conventional "song" lengths. These pieces, sung rhapsodically by Jessye Norman, seem to go on and on, always resolving yet never resolved, questing without ever circling back. Remarkably, they don't wander. As Norman finishes one of the beautiful phrases, the orchestra comes along and takes the handoff, surging just enough to earn the right to follow such a luminous presence.

The third song, "Beim Schlafengehen," is of particular note in this regard. An elegy that moves at a floating crawl, it is an engrossing processional, in which one brilliant phrase adds resonance to the preceding ones. Though the music moves slowly, Norman sings the extended lines as though spreading joy and pain evenly across the sound spectrum, taking care not to miss any spots. Her sustained notes catch all the voluptuousness of Strauss's ideas without smothering or distorting their shapes.

These songs are Strauss's last major work, finished only months before his death, at age eighty-five, in 1949. Filled with verses about coming to terms with death, they're a classic swan song. Indeed, "In Abendrot" begins with a focused burst of string tone, an enveloping sound that suggests a long look down the tunnel of blue light into the next world.

This disc also contains one of the very few concert pieces by Richard Wagner. The individual songs of *Wesendonck Lieder* are among the shortest stand-alone works in an output marked by its epic scale. Norman sings them as though trying to compensate for their compactness, by magnifying each emotional ripple.

GENRE: 🎻 Classical. **RELEASED:** 1982, Philips. **KEY TRACKS:** All of them. **NEXT STOP:** Wagner: *Tristan und Isolde* (see p. 838).

Sun-Kissed Morning Dew on an Idyllic Hillside

The Rite of Spring

Igor Stravinsky

Cleveland Symphony Orchestra (Pierre Boulez, cond.)

Like many students of music, Trey Anastasio, the guitarist and leader of the rock band Phish, had his mind blown by Igor Stravinsky (1882–1971). In the liner notes to a compilation of the Russian composer's work,

Anastasio describes his eureka moment: "When I first listened to Stravinsky's music, it was like a lightbulb went off—'Oh, you can do anything you want!'"

This is a common reaction to Stravinsky, the great modernist whose landmark ballets—most famously *The Rite of Spring* but also the two preceding works, *Petroushka* and *Firebird*—cleared away long-unquestioned and seriously atrophied rules governing composition. They're "changing of the guard" pieces that celebrate the dense new world of the industrial age, replacing parlor staidness with vivid, proudly asymmetrical episodes.

Stravinsky's lines might not resolve in customary ways; there is, nonetheless, extreme rigor in his work. His music rearranges the formats and structures known to arts patrons of his day—this is perhaps one reason the 1913 Paris premiere of *The Rite of Spring* erupted in a riot within the first five minutes. Likewise, harmonies in Stravinsky are not exclusively "consonant" or "dissonant"—they're both at once, with layers of unusual chords creating a bed of nails for themes that describe a tranquil spring morning or, later, a ritual sacrifice. Stravinsky finds power in these contrasts. Check out the character-establishing early scenes of *Petroushka*, which follows the exploits of a lonely puppet. The grandly animated lines are offset by dark, unsettling counter-themes that

Time magazine named Stravinsky one of the 100 most influential people of the twentieth century.

foreshadow sinister doings.

The Rite of Spring was written as a ballet, but is more often experienced as concert music. It opens with a lone bassoon, playing a Ukrainian folk song. From there, Stravinsky offers fleeting tastes from an overloaded buffet of melodic delights: whimsical fantasies in the high winds, passages featuring the low strings that call for a serrated saw instead of a bow.

This performance is conducted by Pierre Boulez, the French composer and conductor who is regarded as one of the most astute interpreters of modern music. Boulez brings out the folk elements of the *Rite* but is careful not to exaggerate them; under his direction, the Cleveland Orchestra renders the episodic flights with flashes of fire rather than a steady flame, and this suits the piece better. Go into the *Rite* as deeply as Boulez does here, and pretty soon you'll be awed not just by the limitless possibilities, but by the metadiscipline Stravinsky brings to the music's details.

GENRE: 🎸 Classical. **RELEASED:** 1973, Columbia. **KEY TRACKS:** *The Rite of Spring*: "The Spring Divinations," "Dance of the Earth." *Petroushka*: Act 1. **CATALOG CHOICES:** *Symphony of Psalms; The Rake's Progress.* **NEXT STOP:** Béla Bartók: *Music for Strings, Percussion, and Celesta* (see p. 47).

The True Confessions of a London Slacker

Original Pirate Material

The Streets

This droll, self-aware debut follows the rather ordinary exploits of a British slacker who spends his nights drinking, carousing, playing video games, and pursuing all sorts of self-indulgences. Its songs are anti-anthems, odes celebrating those who aren't on the fast track aspiring to a better life. Their author, a young white MC and producer named Mike Skinner, comes across as the antithesis of the amped-up Beastie Boys, who shouted about how you've got to fight for your right to party. He's so perpetually wasted, he's lost the will to fight for anything.

Skinner's tales unfold over an unusual British beatbox style called "garage" (which

Original Pirate Material **peaked at #10 on the U.K. Albums chart.**

later evolved into "grime")—terse rhythms that move at faster-than-hip-hop tempos, with very little adornment. The multitalented Skinner made most of the album himself, at home, in between work shifts at fast-food joints; his irreverent narratives (and occasional confessions) are delivered in a working-class accent, and are shot through with a sense of minimum-wage futility. Several tracks, including "Geezers Need Excitement," find Skinner developing whole theories of life out of conversations overheard on the bus; other songs, like "Same Old Thing," relegate the

rapping to the sidelines, throwing the emphasis on the dance floor syncopations.

As a rapper, Skinner's nothing special—the draw is less his herculean delivery than the story he's telling, and the inventive sampled sounds he uses to tell it. Skinner admits as much on a statement of purpose called "Sharp Darts": "One day I hope to earn some hard royalties from a bit of sample robbery, hook burglary, noise thievery, or wholesale piracy." He's hardly a pirate. Skinner does here what all the hip-hop greats do: He transforms common slacker desires into strikingly universal screeds.

GENRE: 🎤 Hip-Hop. **RELEASED:** 2002, Vice. **KEY TRACKS:** "Turn the Page," "Sharp Darts," "Same Old Thing," "Geezers Need Excitement." **CATALOG CHOICE:** *A Grand Don't Come for Free*. **NEXT STOP:** Dizzee Rascal: *Boy in da Corner* (see p. 227). **AFTER THAT:** Lady Sovereign: *Vertically Challenged*.

The Sound of Beer

Polkapalooza

Jimmy Sturr and His Orchestra

J immy Sturr provides whatever it is polka people need—hot tunes, boisterous beats, a little humor—when they gather in hotel ballrooms and church basements to do their thing. There's camp involved, sure. And chutzpah.

Sturr, who formed his first band when he was eleven and has been recording since the '60s, is an example of an artist working a cliché until it's cool—whenever hipsters get around to embracing polka, he'll be there, cranking out the spinning dances some consider "the sound of beer."

On this, his 101st album, clarinetist and arranger Sturr and his polished band play the traditional two-stepping stuff with great aplomb—it is, after all, their meat and potatoes. (For proof, see the version of "Pennsylvania Polka," sung by Johnny Karas. It's timeless.) But as the kooky title of this disc demonstrates,

Sturr recognizes the value of showbiz; he lets accordionist Gene Bartkiewicz or fiddler Frankie Urbanovitch steal the spotlight with jaw-dropping displays of virtuosity that are the polka equivalent of the ten-minute arena-rock drum solo. And Sturr reaches beyond the oompah a few times, most boldly when he invites the great Mexican accordionist Flaco Jiménez to guest on the sizzling instrumental "Bayou Pon Pon." This is anything but trying-to-get-paid polka.

Sturr's recordings have won 17 out of the 23 Grammy Awards given for Best Polka Album.

This is totally assured dance music, made by curious musicians intent on spreading joy as far and wide as possible.

GENRE: 🌐 Country.
RELEASED: 1999, Rounder.
KEY TRACKS: "Pennsylvania Polka," "Bayou Pon Pon," "Polka Fever," "Lovers Waltz."
CATALOG CHOICE: *Dance with Me.* **NEXT STOP:** Frankie Yankovic: *I Wish I Was Eighteen Again.* **AFTER THAT:** Brave Combo: *Polkas for a Gloomy World.*

Barbra in Pre-Diva Days

Funny Girl

Jule Styne and Bob Merrill
Original Broadway Cast Recording

In her hit-making heyday, Barbra Streisand was among the most over-esteemed singers in pop music history, a diva in every unsavory connotation of the term. This Broadway classic of her early career proves she didn't start out that way. As Fanny Brice, unlikely comic star of the Ziegfeld Follies, Streisand offers careful, character-sensitive readings of great songs. She interprets the music with humor and humanity, and though her voice doesn't have the fullness it would develop later, it is supremely believable. That can't be said of many of her recordings of the 1970s and '80s—where she's a sturdy voice whose bombastic and emotionally manipulative gestures place ego-fulfillment above considerations of melody.

With *Funny Girl*, Streisand appears

Styne composed over 1,500 songs during his career.

as a key cog in an overall entertainment machine—not the whole machine. She gets the lion's share of composer Jule Styne's songs—twelve, including several duets and ensemble numbers—and yet never seems to be hogging the spotlight. She actually *earns* the spotlight. And apparently it didn't come easily: The show had a famously troubled pre-Broadway history, as it took Streisand a year, and help from several acting coaches, to arrive at the characterization that would eventually bring her a Best Actress Oscar for the film version.

754 STYNE • SUKAY

Funny Girl is one of the great showbiz musicals. It's an ugly-duckling story about Brice, whose breakthrough moment with the Follies, told through the song "His Love Makes Me Beautiful," comes when she's asked to play a bride. She arrives onstage in a full wedding costume—but with a pillow underneath, ostensibly pregnant. The visual gag makes her a star, and Styne, one of the great melodists among theater composers, provides her with suitably strong material the rest of the way. The gems include "Don't Rain on My Parade" and "The Music That Makes Me Dance," which Streisand interprets with wonderful grace and a light touch. The score requires Streisand to be brash and funny and sympathetic, sometimes within the same verse. She more than manages this hat trick, singing with great timing and indomitable spirit, as though she recognizes it's up to her to make listeners realize how special these melodies are.

GENRE: 😊 Musicals. **RELEASED:** 1964, Capitol. **KEY TRACKS:** "Sadie Sadie," "Rat Tat Tat," "The Music That Makes Me Dance," "Don't Rain on My Parade." **ANOTHER INTERPRETATION:** Original Motion Picture Soundtrack (also starring Streisand). **BUYER BEWARE:** *Funny Lady*, the sequel, is to be avoided. **CATALOG CHOICE:** *Gypsy*, Original Broadway Cast. **NEXT STOP:** Frank Loesser: *Guys and Dolls*, 1992 Broadway Revival.

Not Your Average Subway Buskers

Cumbre

Sukay

If your knowledge of Andean mountain music begins and ends with those trios that play "El cóndor pasa" on subway platforms, prepare for a jolt. Sukay brings the traditional music of Bolivia, Chile, and Peru to life in super-extreme high-definition. The variously sized pan flutes pop as though propelled by hot, volcanic breath from the center of the earth. The stringed instruments, notably the small ten-string *charango*, are strummed in urgent fleet-fingered code. The feeling is of irrepressible energy—even when the melodies are heavy-hearted (which is often), the music flutters with glorious, birdlike buoyancy.

Sukay was formed in 1974 by an American singer, Quentin Howard, and a Swiss multi-instrumentalist, Edmund Badoux. After travels through South America, the group settled in San Francisco; regular international tours sparked wide interest in indigenous Andean music, and established the group among the elite in a suddenly growing genre. (One indication of Sukay's meteoric rise: *Charango* master Eddy Navia left his group, the esteemed Bolivian band Salve Andina, to join Sukay in 1978, and the Argentine classical guitarist Enrique Coria followed several years later.)

Cumbre is an excellent showcase for Sukay's hallmark—exacting ensemble play. Navia, Coria, and the pan flutist Alcides Mejia follow traditional performance practices handed down for generations: Moving as a unit, they honor the contours of tunes every Andean group is expected to play (the trembling rhapsody "Desde lejos," a winsome arrangement of "El cóndor pasa") without going to great extremes to sexy things up. A bit more risk-taking happens on the Navia originals, pieces distinguished by open-vista melodies (the title track) and fetchingly sincere refrains ("Tinkuna") that can sometimes resemble rustic village songs. Everything, though, is driven by Sukay's spry ensemble cohesion, which charges these stirring originals and minor-key folk songs with undeniable electricity.

GENRE: 🌐 World/Andes. **RELEASED:** 1990, Sukay Records. **KEY TRACKS:** "Tierra de vicuñas," "Tinkuna," "El cóndor pasa," "Desde lejos." **CATALOG CHOICE:** *Music of the Andes.* **NEXT STOP:** Inti-Illimani: *Antologia Vol. 1, 1973–1978.* **AFTER THAT:** Rumillajta: *Wiracocha.*

A Dance Floor Milestone

"I Feel Love"

Donna Summer

Donna Summer first experienced fame in 1975 via the brazen moaning and sexy breathing that made her debut single, "Love to Love You Baby," a worldwide smash. She parlayed that novelty hit into an influential career: Over the next four years, she and producers Georgio Moroder and Pete Bellotte created a string of songs that defined and then transcended disco. "I Feel Love," from the erratic *I Remember Yesterday* (1977), was among the team's first and most significant experiments—a wickedly bouncy synthesized utopia that foreshadowed house, techno, and other forms of electronic dance music of the '80s and '90s. Forward-looking producer Brian Eno pronounced the song "the future of music" when he heard it.

Summer had hit songs in the *Billboard* Top 40 every year from 1977 to 1984.

At the very least, it's the sound of restless producers having a little what-the-hell-let's-try-this fun. Unlike most of Summer's hits, "I Feel Love" is minimal—a few lines of lyric, an ingratiating beat, simple keyboards. Its genius is in repetition: The popcorn-popping keyboard parts and busy bass lines move in cool, steady loops that cycle around at regular intervals. This backdrop is so beguiling Summer doesn't need to do much, and she doesn't—her cooing vocal hook seems to just float on top of the arrangement.

This track showed that Summer, then a rising star, had some artistic range. After it, on such torrid albums as *Bad Girls,* she and her production team began to explore styles that stretched well beyond the dance floor. Several tunes built on rock and funk backbeats became chart-topping singles, but none have aged as well as this iconoclastic wonderment of a song. Despite its disco-era origins, "I Feel Love" crackles with rhythmic vitality. Still.

GENRE: 🎤 R&B. **RELEASED:** 1977, Casablanca. **APPEARS ON:** *I Remember Yesterday; The Donna Summer Anthology.* **CATALOG CHOICES:** *Bad Girls; The Donna Summer Anthology.* **NEXT STOP:** Gloria Gaynor: *Never Can Say Goodbye.* **AFTER THAT:** Chic: *C'est Chic* (see p. 163).

Supreme Radio Nectar

"You Keep Me Hangin' On"

The Supremes

If someone forced you to pick one song that epitomizes Motown's hit-making machine at its peak, an obvious choice might be "Stop in the Name of Love," the 1965 number 1 hit by the Supremes that's become a karaoke standby. Or maybe the bouncy "Baby Love," which reached the top the year before, or the philosophical "You Can't Hurry Love." Written and produced by the team of Holland-Dozier-Holland, these are all essential texts, consummate marriages of craft and inspiration that remain without peer in pop music.

Go a bit farther into the discography, and you soon encounter another of the twelve (!) chart-topping singles the Supremes generated between 1964 and 1969: "You Keep Me Hangin' On." It's the highest of the high, the most action-packed three minutes of radio nectar ever recorded by Diana Ross and her crew, a song that never gets old even though it's been covered endlessly. An ode to a dead-end

The successful singing group originally formed under the name the Primettes in 1959.

relationship, this was the first single from the 1966 album *The Supremes Sing Holland-Dozier-Holland.* Later it became a hit for Vanilla Fudge in 1968, and again in the '80s when sung by Kim Wilde. (It's also been interpreted by Wilson Pickett, Rod Stewart, and Madness.)

"You Keep Me Hangin' On" started as an experiment. After generating a string of chart-topping hits that followed a bouncy,

upbeat formula, Lamont Dozier and brothers Brian and Eddie Holland felt comfortable challenging the singers a bit—with a more aggressive rock-style beat, and a meatier subject. The single-note guitar phrase that's the song's foundation was inspired, Dozier said later, by the Morse code sound of a radio news flash. Around it, the Motown rhythm section builds a groove that exists in some magical netherworld between "rock" and "soul," unifying those styles in a way few had done before.

The result is the last great Holland-Dozier-Holland effort for the Supremes. The songwriting and production team parted ways with Motown the following year, leaving behind this dizzying and highly habit-forming single, the rare oldies-radio staple that sounds like it was made yesterday.

GENRES: 🎙 R&B ✴ Pop. **RELEASED:** 1966, Motown. **APPEARS ON:** *The Supremes Sing Holland-Dozier-Holland.* **CATALOG CHOICE:** *The Ultimate Collection.* **NEXT STOP:** The Four Tops: *Anthology* (see p. 287). **AFTER THAT:** The Pointer Sisters: *Best of the Pointer Sisters.*

A Cornerstone of Gospel Singing

The Swan Silvertones/ Saviour Pass Me Not

The Swan Silvertones

O n these twenty-three hymns and revival tent standbys, the Swan Silvertones sing like they know the job description calls for more than singing. They expect to reassure the faithful, rescue the wayward,

galvanize the undecided, and along the way generate a little something for the collection plate. If, in the course of doing that, they wind up creating group singing that has the spontaneity of jazz and the raw feeling of soul, well, consider that a bonus from the Great Beyond.

As Claude Jeter, the lead singer, begins telling about "How I Got Over" or envisions "Peace in the Valley," his cohorts gather around him in clusters of deep-toned brother-

The a cappella group changed their name from the Four Harmony Kings when they began a radio show sponsored by the Swan Bakery Company.

attributable to the voices— Jeter and usually Solomon Womack handling leads, with two tenors, a baritone, and a bass who changed several times over the years—and part was the work of arranger Paul Owens, who added wide Four Freshman–style harmonies. By the time the Swans recorded these two classic albums, the group expanded to include a guitarist, the great Linwood Hargrove, as well as a rhythm section anchored by jazz bass-ist Bob Cranshaw that main-

hood, dispensing uh-huhs and amens that spur the discussion forward. On "Mary Don't You Weep," for example, Jeter moves from the familiar verses into deep elaborations, using slight blues-singer inflections for emphasis. Every now and then he tosses out a few extemporaneous lines, at one point singing, "I'll be a bridge over deep water if you just trust my name." Years later, that aside inspired Paul Simon's "Bridge Over Troubled Water."

Jeter formed the Swan Silvertones in Coalwood, West Virginia, in 1938. Recordings started in the mid-1940s, first on the King label, and within a few years the gospel circuit was abuzz about the Swans, which one gospel radio DJ, Joe Bostic Jr., once described as "smooth as polished glass." That's largely

tained an easygoing swing.

Be prepared to hunt for this title. Vee Jay went bankrupt in 1965, and since then the catalog has been in and out of print. It was pressed most recently by the reissue label Collectables and subsequently allowed to again go out of print. Rest assured: This music is worth the search.

GENRE: ♊ Gospel. **RELEASED:** *Swan*: 1959, *Saviour*: 1962, both on Vee Jay. (Reissued 2001, Collectables.) **KEY TRACKS:** "Mary Don't You Weep," "Peace in the Valley," "Saviour Pass Me Not," "Amazing Grace." **CATALOG CHOICE:** *Love Lifted Me*. **NEXT STOP:** The Caravans: *The Best of the Caravans* (see p. 143). **AFTER THAT:** The Blind Boys of Mississippi: *The Original Five Blind Boys*.

Metal, Chopped and Chiseled

Toxicity

System of a Down

The average Slayer-worshiping suburban American headbanger wasn't prepared for System of a Down when its over-torqued debut appeared in the summer of 1998. By the time the band returned with this even more blistering follow-up in September 2001, things were different: Within weeks metalheads were hailing System as the future of the genre. Then Korn and Tool fans jumped on board. Pretty soon *Toxicity* spread everywhere.

System of a Down relies on the same loud and sludgy power chords favored by hundreds of metal bands—except the L.A.-based foursome plays them twice or three times as fast, with serrated-saw lead guitar jutting from the mix. Where the lords of metal tend to keep the same groove going for a while, SOAD chops up its tunes into little episodes, some of which reflect the influence of Frank Zappa in his more absurdist moments. And where most singers in metal stick to a prescribed set of topics—raw anger, alienation, and the almighty next buzz—Armenian lead singer Serj Tankian agitates, surprisingly eloquently, about the U.S. government's abuses of power, and the inner thoughts of suicide bombers. (He's also the rare frontman inclined to find the humor in his over-the-top tirades; sometimes it's possible to hear him chuckling or injecting sly self-deprecating asides.)

Toxicity captures the band's range, and

Toxicity has sold over 6.5 million copies worldwide.

its rage. It's prog-rock muscle-flexing offset by goth darkness, a touch of thrash offset by a balancing hint of early '90s alternative rock. Its outbreaks of full-metal menace are followed by brisk and galvanizing funk rhythms, and those are followed by moments when the dust settles and something even more audacious, like a brave little lullaby melody, appears.

The assault is a dense one, but it never feels like gratuitous metal rebellion in the key of noise: As Tankian and his crew blaze through "Prison Song," "Chop Suey!," and the mostly inscrutable "Jet Pilot," it's possible to hear them discarding all the tiresome posturing that's attached to heavy metal, the snide intolerance, the insularity, and the xenophobia. With the slate clean, they tear out in search of the next frontier. Only to discover about ten frontiers. Maybe more.

GENRE: 🎵 Rock. **RELEASED:** 2001, American. **KEY TRACKS:** "Chop Suey!," "Prison Song," "Jet Pilot." **CATALOG CHOICE:** *System of a Down*. **NEXT STOP:** Tool: *Aenima*. **AFTER THAT:** The Mars Volta: *The Bedlam in Goliath* (see p. 476).

Taj Mahal ✦ Talking Heads ✦ Tangerine Dream ✦ Taraf de Haïdouks ✦ Howard Tate ✦ Art Tatum ✦ Cecil Taylor ✦ James Taylor ✦ Pyotr Ilyich Tchaikovsky ✦ Television ✦ The Temptations ✦ 10cc ✦ Sister Rosetta Tharpe ✦ Mikis Theodorakis ✦ 13th Floor Elevators ✦ Leon Thomas ✦ Richard and Linda Thompson ✦ Big Mama Thornton ✦ Cal Tjader ✦ The Tokens ✦ Toots and the Maytals ✦ Mel Tormé ✦ Peter Tosh ✦ Ali Farka Touré ✦ Touré Kunda ✦ Allen Toussaint ✦ Ralph Towner ✦ Traffic ✦ T. Rex ✦ A Tribe Called Quest ✦ Lennie Tristano ✦ Ernest Tubb ✦ 2Pac ✦ Özel Türkbas ✦ Big Joe Turner ✦ Ike and Tina Turner ✦ McCoy Tyner

T

All Natural, and Refreshingly Doctrine-Free

The Natch'l Blues

Taj Mahal

Taj Mahal (born Henry Saint Clair Fredericks) was the perfect bluesman for the trippy mixing bowl of the late 1960s. The New York–born singer and guitarist knew rural blues—he studied some ethnomusicology at the University of Massachusetts while majoring in animal husbandry—but he wasn't a slave to the Delta style, or urban Chicago blues either. And he wasn't a purist. After he moved to Santa Monica in 1965, his first band was a rock combo with guitarist Ry Cooder and future Spirit drummer Ed Cassidy. After he became a solo artist, Fredericks took a stage name—Taj Mahal—that came to him in a dream. He began recording a fanciful blend of ragtime and blues—his mission was to go deeper than the British blues-rock "revival." Through an impressive career, he's applied the spirit of the blues to music from Africa and the Caribbean—the most stunning of these cultural exchanges is *Kulanjan*, which features Mali's Toumani Diabaté (see p. 221), the virtuoso of the intricate African stringed instrument known as the *kora*.

On this, his second album, Mahal's approach to the blues is already extremely inclusive. He begins with a steamrolling Delta shuffle chopped out on steel-bodied guitar, and then veers into "Corinna," which has an ambling West Coast backbeat not unlike those proffered by the Grateful Dead. There are also several Otis Redding–style R&B shouters, bits of hard, wiry funk ("Cuckoo"), and a few pieces with pianist Al Kooper that approach the tale-spinning of the Band ("She Caught the Katy").

Throughout, Mahal presents himself as an affable storyteller sharing wry perspectives on human nature. On the original stomp "Done Changed My Way of Living," Mahal borrows an old punch line to complain about those tiresome L.A. gold diggers who have "a handful of gimme, a mouth full of much obliged." The line turns up in blues from the 1950s, but when Mahal sings it, with a unique blend of bitterness and bemusement, it sounds like a brand-new thought.

GENRE: 🔵 Blues. **RELEASED:** 1968, Columbia. **KEY TRACKS:** "Corinna," "Cuckoo," "She Caught the Katy." **CATALOG CHOICE:** *Kulanjan.* **NEXT STOP:** Blind Willie McTell: *The Definitive* (see p. 492). **AFTER THAT:** Ted Hawkins: *Songs from Venice Beach.*

Not the Same as It Ever Was

Remain in Light

Talking Heads

The Talking Heads started out as purveyors of jerky, self-conscious minimalist rock unlike anything happening in New York punk in the 1970s. After a string of acclaimed albums, the band ended up trapped in an absurdist sideshow of its own making—with David Byrne, aka the guy in the big suit, spewing non sequiturs over tepid funk rhythms.

The Talking Heads added 7 musicians for the tour supporting this album.

In between, beginning with "I Zimbra" (from 1979's *Fear of Music*) and continuing through this album and the next, the Talking Heads reigned as one of the most invigorating, intense, dauntingly original rock bands in the world. *Remain in Light* marks the moment when everything—from the big "vision" to the little details—falls into place. The key puzzle piece is rhythm: Before starting work on this monster, the foursome and producer Brian Eno set out to globalize typical foursquare rock grooves. They took what the band already did well—those sharp guitar spikes and pummeling up-and-down backbeats—and punched them up with elements of loose-limbed West African dance pop, up-tempo soul-revue send-ups, and syncopations that cut across the music at unexpected angles.

Talk about an awakening. From the mystical opening notes of "Born Under Punches," it's clear that virtually everything about the Talking Heads' enterprise is different. Less spastic. More streamlined. Reborn as a groove machine with libido-enhancing powers, the rhythm section (drummer Chris Frantz and bassist Tina Weymouth) kicks out a cryptic code that's reinforced by the intricate overlapping rhythm guitar circuits of Jerry Harrison and guest Adrian Belew. The pulse becomes so strong, it sweeps even the congenitally uptight Byrne into the dance. Through oblique, seemingly disconnected exclamations ("This is not my beautiful house!" "Facts are useless in an emergency!"), Byrne presents himself as the bewildered Everyman who no longer trusts his thinking, but isn't quite comfortable enough to surrender to the flow of the irrational rhythm. That mind-body conflict is typical of the juxtapositional genius of *Remain in Light*. These unexpectedly glorious tunes balance brains against instinct, pop hookcraft against ancient ritual, art concept against the primal urge to dance.

GENRE: 🎸 Rock. **RELEASED:** 1980, Sire.
KEY TRACKS: "Crosseyed and Painless,"
"The Great Curve," "Once in a Lifetime."
CATALOG CHOICES: *The Name of This Band Is the Talking Heads; Speaking in Tongues.*
NEXT STOP: Beck: *Odelay.* **AFTER THAT:**
Sonic Youth: *Daydream Nation* (see p. 725).

A Portal to the Inner Cosmos

Rubycon

Tangerine Dream

You know those fancy spas, the ones that advertise how they'll bring you to your mellow place and, for a premium fee, lead you through calming meditations and salt scrubs and such? They don't want you to know about records like this. For a whole lot less money, Tangerine Dream will chill you out, loosen the grip of the grid, and help you transition to a quieter, more reflective state of mind.

The music Tangerine Dream made during the mid-1970s, its most creative period, has been described as "space ambience" and "stoner nirvana." It's all that and an EPCOT ride too, a tour through vast desolate lunar landscapes (or a hyperreal simulation). This two-part piece continues the basic ideas the German trio, formed by Edgar Froese in 1967, explored so skillfully on its previous album *Phaedra*, the oft-maligned ambient milestone that put the group in the Top 20 of the British Album charts for the first time. There are lush cascades of echo-chamber sound and slow-moving swirls of otherworldly strings created on the tape-based instrument known as the mellotron.

But *Rubycon* adds more rhythmic synthesizer blips, recurring patterns that pulsate beneath the surface. And its "Part Two" is much darker than anything on *Phaedra*: Propelled by solemn electronically generated male voices, it begins in the murky oceanic depths. As the voices trail off, the music seems to brighten, slowly ascending until, in the final moments, glimmers of daylight poke through. This voyaging vision of sound, ever-unfolding and not quite ever arriving, has been imitated endlessly since 1975. But somehow its admirers haven't quite captured the openness and faraway grandeur of Tangerine Dream.

GENRES: 〰 Electronica 🎸 Rock.
RELEASED: 1975, Virgin. **KEY TRACKS:** "Rubycon," "Rubycon (Part II)." **CATALOG CHOICES:** *Phaedra; Stratosfear.* **NEXT STOP:** Klaus Schulze: *Moondawn.* **AFTER THAT:** David Torn: *Cloud About Mercury.*

What It Sounds Like When Gypsies Frolic

Taraf de Haïdouks

Taraf de Haïdouks

When it really gets moving, the Romanian Gypsy band Taraf de Haïdouks makes music that borders on the frantic. Playing fiddles and accordions and bells, the group gives off a strange combination of madcap energy and coolheaded precision. The musicians slalom and swerve from theme to theme, pumping up adrenaline as they go. They could be kids embroiled in a paintball strategy game, or detectives trailing a suspect through a bustling urban market.

Some of the Taraf songs actually do immortalize the capers of common Gypsy thieves. The Haïdouks are known as Robin Hood–like characters; the band's name translates as "band of brigands." These musicians from the village of Clejani,

The band is known as "Taraful Haiducilor" in Romania.

which is south of Bucharest, range in age from twenty to eighty. They belong to a lineage of Gypsy musicians known as *lăutari*, who have handed down the traditional songs and dances heard at weddings, funerals, and harvest celebrations for generations. This, the group's first international release, presents that music in all its ranging glory—evidently, the Gypsies don't like to stay in one musical zone for too long.

Among the treasures are the animated "Hora ca la ursari," which translates to "The

Bear-Leader's Circle Dance," and the "Hora din caval" (Shepherd's Circle Dance), which both sound as if they'd be favorites at rowdier family reunions. Other pieces favor the tempo of slow, mourning ballads that have the heavy woe of Eastern European history woven in. Still, this is living music, not "heritage museum" stuff. As David Harrington of the Kronos Quartet noted, Taraf de Haïdouks "take their listeners to the essence of music; that place where the bow meets the string and a world of action follows."

GENRE: 🌐 World/Romania. **RELEASED:** 1999, Nonesuch. **KEY TRACKS:** "Dragoste de la Clejani," "Hora ca la ursari," "Turceasca." **CATALOG CHOICE:** *The Continuing Adventures of . . .* **NEXT STOP:** Manu Chao: *Clandestino* (see p. 154). **AFTER THAT:** Kevin Johansen: *Sur o no sur.*

A Phantom Classic of Soul

Get It While You Can

Howard Tate

Between 1966 and 1968, the singer Howard Tate and songwriter-producer Jerry Ragovoy developed a sound that stands slightly apart from everything else happening in R&B at the time. They featured horns just like Otis Redding and others in Memphis did, but deployed them with more restraint. They borrowed from the blues, but in tiny doses. Recording mostly in New York, they emphasized the preacher-like determination of Tate's voice, creating a suave, upmarket soul. These efforts were embraced by musicians—B.B. King, Janis Joplin, and Jimi Hendrix all covered material from this set—and mostly ignored by the public. *Get It While You Can* generated three songs that reached the Top 20 on the R&B charts and then disappeared quickly. Adding insult to injury, it's been reissued haphazardly, making it another of the phantom classics of soul singing.

The indifference took its toll on Tate. After cutting singles for several labels, he dropped out of sight in the early '70s,

Tate was born August 14, 1939, in Macon, Georgia.

fell victim to drug and alcohol abuse, and spent time homeless on the streets of Camden, New Jersey. Following a religious awakening, he slowly put his life back together, and was working as a minister when, in 2000, a radio DJ sought an answer to the question, Whatever happened to Howard Tate? Ragovoy didn't know; he'd told friends he thought Tate was dead. Eventually the singer reemerged, renewed his collaboration with Ragovoy, and recorded a sturdy comeback (*Rediscovered*, 2003). When he performed in England, Tate was greeted with a hero's welcome.

Get It While You Can inspires that kind of reverence. Its songs are short, most under three minutes, and driven by Tate's at once casual and urgent entreaties. Everything he sings is intensely rhythmic, but in a low-key way; where the big shots of soul leaned on their rhythm sections to provide spark, Tate creates it all by himself, at times pushing the musicians with snappy drill-sergeant declarations. These are Tate's only showy moments: Never terribly fancy or super-athletic, he rarely lets loose with an Otis Redding–style shout. Instead, Tate brings exactly what the songs need, and nothing more. He puts heart behind every line, trusting that his plainspoken delivery can, in the right setting, be just as persuasive. This is the right setting.

GENRE: 🌐 R&B. **RELEASED:** 1966, Verve. **KEY TRACKS:** "Ain't Nobody Home," "Glad I Knew Better," "Stop," "Get It While You Can," "Look at Granny Run Run." **CATALOG CHOICE:** *Rediscovered*. **NEXT STOP:** James Carr: *You Got My Mind Messed Up* (see p. 143). **AFTER THAT:** Solomon Burke: *Rock 'n Soul*.

Jazz Piano at Blazing Speed

Piano Starts Here

Art Tatum

From the very start, Art Tatum (1909–1956) was diabolical. The Ohio-born pianist begins one of his first recordings, a radio broadcast of "Tiger Rag" from 1933, with a series of calm chords that suggests he's about to play a ballad. It's a supreme fake-out: What follows is a high-speed chase through the possibilities of solo improvisation, led by a musician with a rampaging imagination. He darts between ragtime fantasias and blistering exhibitions of technical mastery, sometimes "answering" a taunt played by his right hand at the top of the keyboard with a booming bass rejoinder near the bottom. This dizzying excursion has no equal in jazz: At times, it sounds like Tatum, who was legally blind, is carrying on a conversation between three or four distinctly different musicians, among them one who's fixated on Fats Waller, another who's anticipating bebop.

The man didn't just have big hands, he had big ears—and an exhaustive repertoire of popular songs at his fingertips. Just about everything Tatum plays crackles with a lively wit and a determination to surprise, if not delight. And all of it has a distinct touch: that fleet and springy attack that none of his imitators fully caught.

To fathom Tatum, start with *Piano Starts Here*, which offers the famed "Tiger Rag" and equally legendary studio performances from his heyday. To hear what the mighty pianist sounded like when he was playing for fun, track down the jaw-dropping *God Is in the House*, culled from private after-hours performances in 1940 and 1941 recorded by Jerry Newman, then a Columbia University student. These show Tatum tempering his dazzle reflex, and offering thoughtful elaborations on familiar melodies ("Sweet Lorraine," "Georgia on My Mind"), and dancing blithely through solos that are impossibly complex. This is Tatum in his element, in a nightclub, where fans (including composer George Gershwin) could sit close to watch his fingers. Pianist Eddie Heywood once said, "The more I hear him, the more convinced I am that I'd better quit playing and drive a truck." Tatum did that to people.

GENRE: 🎹 Jazz. **RELEASED:** 1995, Columbia. **KEY TRACKS:** "Tiger Rag," "Yesterdays," "Willow Weep for Me." **CATALOG CHOICES:** *God Is in the House; The Tatum Group Masterpieces*, Vol. 3. **NEXT STOP:** Oscar Peterson: *At the Concertgebouw.* **AFTER THAT:** Gonzalo Rubalcaba: *The Blessing*.

Making the Piano Talk, in a Different Language

Silent Tongues

Cecil Taylor

At times when Cecil Taylor is really punishing the piano, you get the sense he might have been happier as a saxophone player. He likes the chords and the sheer mass of sound the piano offers, but wants more individual expression. He mashes distinct sonorities into dancing blurs of color, changes ordinary melodies into rattling spasms of percussion.

For both his phenomenal technique and his unorthodox approach, Taylor is revered as a free-jazz pathfinder—and derided as a provocateur bent on terrorizing those who expect every eighty-eight-key contraption to yield cocktail-hour pleasantries. Taylor's music is, to be sure, challenging stuff. And it's also undeniably personal. It can take years to fully digest the ideas he is pondering, but only a few notes to know that it's him playing. He's one of those rare musicians able to instantly overcome the anonymity of the piano.

"I try to imitate on the piano the leaps in space a dancer makes."
—Cecil Taylor

This solo performance, from the 1974 Montreux Jazz Festival, is an excellent way to first encounter Taylor. It's got his trademark tumult (see the two-part "Crossing"), moments of unexpected melodicism ("After All"), and, of course, outbreaks that come from such an instinctual place, and are so totally unhinged, you suspect even a great mind like Taylor would have trouble re-creating them.

GENRE: 🎵 Jazz. **RELEASED:** 1974, Freedom/Black Lion. **KEY TRACKS:** "After All," "Crossing." **CATALOG CHOICE:** *Conquistador.* **NEXT STOP:** Anthony Braxton: *The Montreux/Berlin Concerts.* **AFTER THAT:** Marilyn Crispell: *Spirit Music.*

Sonic Comfort Food

Sweet Baby James

James Taylor

If you're a guy, you need this on the shelf as a symbol of your sensitivity. *Sweet Baby James* sends prospective girlfriends the tacit signal that you can kick back and be mellow. If you're a girl, you need this because for several generations now, your sisters have turned to James Taylor, in winter, spring, summer, or fall, whenever they needed a friend. This is Taylor's breakthrough, and one of the first singer-songwriter records to make a virtue of sensitive-guy introspection. After it, Taylor, whose music incorporates bits of country and gospel, became a big star and, later, a chardonnay accompaniment for warm summer nights.

As his career progressed, Taylor buffed the edges of his confessional approach until it became glossy L.A. soft-rock. This album's desultory and downcast odes, among them the title track and "Country Road," argue that the edges were crucial to his art. The best songs here start at a shattered emotional pitch; they follow sad and somewhat lost characters as they try to pick up the pieces. "Fire and Rain," which was allegedly inspired by a suicide in a mental institution where Taylor had been a patient, is among several songs that express

Sweet Baby James has sold over 3 million copies in the U.S.

a basic human desire to help. Such compassion can come off as corny; yet Taylor, with his rumpled aw-shucks delivery, conveys tender and genuine concern. It's this plainspoken Everyguy tone that brings people back to *Sweet Baby James*: Lots of singer-songwriters tell of dire circumstances and the hope that's nearly lost. Few manage to make the troubles fade as Taylor does, in a voice so reassuring and warm it can give a lifelong pessimist faith in the future.

GENRE: 🎸 Rock. **RELEASED:** 1970, Warner Bros. **KEY TRACKS:** "Country Road," "Fire and Rain," "Sweet Baby James," "Anywhere like Heaven." **CATALOG CHOICE:** *James Taylor.* **NEXT STOP:** Neil Young: *Harvest.* **AFTER THAT:** Steve Forbert: *Jackrabbit Slim.*

Two Great Concertos from the Russian Tunesmith

Violin Concerto
Piano Concerto No. 1

Pyotr Ilyich Tchaikovsky

Nathan Milstein, Vienna Philharmonic (Claudio Abbado, cond.);
Martha Argerich, Royal Philharmonic Orchestra (Charles Dutoit, cond.)

Tchaikovsky's Piano Concerto No. 1 elicits extreme responses. It's a hugely popular work that's programmed often and reliably draws crowds. Yet it's sometimes dismissed as lightweight; even those who admit enjoying it might describe it as a guilty pleasure. The disparate reactions can be traced back to the same thing: the tunes. These gorgeous rhapsodies rise up out of thin air, move into the spotlight like they own the place, and sweep listeners into a rare state of melody bliss.

Somehow this doesn't satisfy classical music's scholars and fussbudgets. They complain that the theme that rises up during the first movement, a grand Big Tune that might be expected to undergo extensive variation, completely disappears. This simply isn't done—composers are expected to value their lines, not use them as glorified billboards and then discard them. Yet that's what happens. The wily pianist Martha Argerich, whose rendering positively sparkles, points out the splendor of the tune while leaving behind no comment on the composer's puzzling choices. Not her job.

But listen to the second movement, and its plaintiveness suggests another possibility: Maybe Tchaikovsky (1840–1893) was such a melody machine, he could afford to let some go by without milking them for every last drop of drama. He's certainly tapped into a seemingly inexhaustible source of ideas here: This song without words moves from one lovely expansive thought to another, held together with clever inversions and ingenious reharmonizations. As Argerich mood-lights each theme, the orchestra, conducted by her husband, Charles Dutoit, offers a transparent, never intrusive support that lets the Tchaikovsky melodies meander.

The Violin Concerto is more straightforward structurally. And more demanding from a technical standpoint. Leopold Auer, the violinist for whom it was written, initially said it was unplayable, adding that the violin was constantly being yanked in opposite directions. Auer eventually made peace with Tchaikovsky's intentions, and wrote a set of bowings for the piece.

Like the piano work, it's ceaselessly lyrical, full of instrumental "songs" cleverly placed within the architecture of the concerto. But it is also incredibly demanding: Five minutes into the first movement, Tchaikovsky serves up melodies thick and fast, not caring at all about where the violinist's fingers might be in relation to where he's sending them next. That passage challenges some violinists, who labor to adhere to the tempo. Nathan Milstein has no such trouble. He fits the melodies together effortlessly, and uses a technique called "portamento"—the gliding between pitches that went out of fashion after World War II—to add emotional resonance to the lines. Cool under pressure and flexible, he does whatever is necessary to honor Tchaikovsky's rash and dizzying themes.

GENRE: 🎵 Classical. **RELEASED:** 1998, Deutsche Grammophon. **KEY TRACKS:** Piano Concerto: second movement. Violin Concerto: first movement. **CATALOG CHOICE:** *The Nutcracker* (see below). **NEXT STOP:** Ludwig van Beethoven: *The Five Piano Concertos,* Alfred Brendel. **AFTER THAT:** *Brahms Violin Concerto,* David Oistrakh, Cleveland Symphony Orchestra (George Szell, cond.).

Visions of Sugarplums

The Nutcracker

Pyotr Ilyich Tchaikovsky
Kirov Orchestra (Valery Gergiev, cond.)

Yes, there are reasons to simply *listen* to the *Nutcracker.* Some would argue that it's actually preferable to experience Tchaikovsky's fanciful ballet without the seasonal trappings, without having to follow the toy soldiers and the sugarplum fairies as they tumble through their annual rituals. That's because the suggestions and intimations of motion start with the orchestra. Strip away the visual cues, and what you encounter is inventive, wide-extremes scoring and boisterous melodies that bounce from one section to another—in some ways this is a concerto for orchestra. Besides, any composer who can create a charming dance out of the pushing and shoving of wooden figures has some kind of mojo working.

Tchaikovsky's final ballet, the *Nutcracker* was composed between 1891 and 1892, and was most often heard as an abridged orchestral suite until the 1960s, when ballet companies worldwide embraced it. Throughout the first act, he creates a tranquil children's playroom scene. There's no dark storminess, not even so much as a bass fiddle. He begins with racing, stair-climbing lines for the violins, and within minutes, listeners are swept into a child's fidgety Christmas Eve anticipation. The energetic, sometimes sharply rhythmic themes help illustrate the onstage pantomimes of Act 1—Clara's imaginary journey with the Nutcracker and the battle with malevolent mice. Act 2 pretty much dispenses with plot altogether; it's a series of exuberant dances, each with its own idiosyncratic orchestration. To conjure the mythic Sugarplum Fairy, Tchaikovsky uses little more than tartly plucked strings and celesta.

"[Music] is a faithful friend, protector, and comforter, and for its sake alone, life in this world is worth living." —Tchaikovsky

Animation is the name of the game with the *Nutcracker*, and the Kirov Orchestra's version, guided by Russian conductor Valery Gergiev, at times feels electrically charged. Gergiev brings out the quirks of the score but doesn't linger over them—everything moves at a breezy clip. How breezy? Most recordings of the piece are spread over two compact discs; this version fits, if just barely, on one.

GENRE: 🎼 Classical. **RELEASED:** 1998, Philips. **KEY TRACKS:** "Scene and Waltz of the Snowflakes," "Grandfather Dance," "Pas de deux: Variation 2 (Dance of the Sugarplum Fairy)." **CATALOG CHOICE:** *Swan Lake,* Philadelphia Orchestra (Wolfgang Sawallisch, cond.). **NEXT STOP:** Aram Khachaturian: *Spartacus,* Vienna Philharmonic (Ernest Ansermet, cond.). **AFTER THAT:** Igor Stravinsky: *Firebird Suite,* Atlanta Symphony Orchestra and Chorus (Robert Shaw, cond.).

The Illest from Ilyich

Symphony No. 6 "Pathétique"

Pyotr Ilyich Tchaikovsky
Leningrad Philharmonic (Evgeny Mravinsky, cond.)

There's a fine line between deep personal pathos and self-absorbed bathos, and with this, his last symphony, Pyotr Ilyich Tchaikovsky rides it like a daredevil. He gets tangled up in tones of overwhelming sorrow, and then leaps into the swollen, outsized drama that was a trademark of his ballets. Where Beethoven's dark moments hold an undercurrent of hope and faith in humanity, Tchaikovsky lets the despair just be despair, with no redeeming third-act heroics waiting in the wings.

The rare symphonic work that doesn't end on a note of triumph, this was written quickly, in a matter of weeks during the spring of 1893. But it feels like the product of marathon brooding. Its subtitle, suggested by Tchaikovsky's brother Modest, translates from Russian not as "pathetic" but as "deeply affecting the emotions," and that's an excellent description of its lure. Both the opening movement—a structurally innovative fever-dream of episodic bursts and impulsive mood changes—and the lurching, decidedly unheroic odd-meter 5/4 "waltz" are saturated with feeling, governed by the composer's pursuit of intense melodic rapture.

Composed in the wake of his failed marriage, Symphony No. 6 is regarded as Tchaikovsky's masterwork. He conducted its premiere in October of 1893, and died nine days later, a victim of cholera.

Of the many versions of this piece available, this one recorded in 1956 by the Leningrad, with Russian conductor Evgeny Mravinsky, is particularly radiant. It's supple in ways Russian orchestras of the cold-war era often were not, and fully charged with the romance Tchaikovsky embedded in the score. The package includes Tchaikovsky's fourth and fifth symphonies as well.

GENRE: 🎵 Classical. **RELEASED:** 1961, Deutsche Grammophon. **KEY TRACK:** first movement. **CATALOG CHOICE:** *1812 Overture, Capriccio Italien,* Chicago Symphony Orchestra (Daniel Barenboim, cond.). **NEXT STOP:** Sergey Rachmaninoff: *Works for Piano and Orchestra,* Raphael Orozco, Royal Philharmonic Orchestra (Edo de Waart, cond.).

An Unpunk Punk-Era Manifesto

Marquee Moon

Television

For a moment there in the mid-'70s, it looked like guitar rock had pretty much run its course. The major works of the British blues-influenced bands (Led Zeppelin, Deep Purple) were in the past, and the American iterations, like Aerosmith, were blatant copycats. The most influential band in the U.S. was nearly unknown, those dystopian explorers the Velvet Underground. The most promising rising stars, like the Ramones, were savage primitivists with limited skills. Then came *Marquee Moon.*

Television's debut amounts to a radical rethinking of rock guitar. The singer and primary songwriter Tom Verlaine and his technically adept lead player, Richard Lloyd, did not bludgeon listeners. They needled them instead, with fantastic barbed-wire melodies and sprocketed counterlines. The New York band's sound was

Robert Mapplethorpe took this portrait of the band.

built on the precise alignment of several contrasting motifs: Verlaine would establish a rhythmic phrase, against which Lloyd would splatter defiant, often deliriously dissonant, melodies. "There weren't many bands where the two guitars play rhythm and melody back and forth, like a jigsaw puzzle," Lloyd said in an interview marking *Marquee Moon*'s 2003 reissue. "It was what we were obsessed with when we recorded." This twin-guitar attack inspired bands across the rock spectrum—scruffy alt-rockers (the Pixies), noise specialists (Sonic Youth), and big arena acts like U2. (The Edge, U2's guitarist, simulates the intricate Television sound all by himself, with effects pedals.)

With their extended instrumental sections, impenetrable moods (see "Torn Curtain"), and often-lofty lyrics ("I fell right into the arms of Venus de Milo," goes one), the songs of *Marquee Moon* advanced ideas far more ambitious than those of the New York punk brigade. Television knew its rock history (traces of Chuck Berry and the early Rolling Stones creep into songs like "Friction") and, more important, knew what it needed to avoid—the cursory punk snarl. That knotted-up and spectacular sound drew massive love from critics, and has since been cited as a cornerstone of modern rock—*Marquee Moon* is number 128 on *Rolling Stone* magazine's list of the 500 Greatest Albums of All Time. Yet Television hasn't connected with a large audience, suffering commercially for an innocent crime: This band was way too hip for the room.

GENRE: 🎸 Rock. **RELEASED:** 1977, Elektra. **KEY TRACKS:** "Friction," "Venus," "Torn Curtain." **CATALOG CHOICE:** *Live at the Old Waldorf, 6/29/78.* **NEXT STOP:** Sonic Youth: *Daydream Nation* (see p. 725). **AFTER THAT:** The Soft Boys: *Underwater Moonlight.*

"And You Know It"

"Ain't Too Proud to Beg"

The Temptations

Sitting in the Memphis office of his longtime producer Willie Mitchell one day, Al Green talked about the key requirement of soul—how a singer has to make every last plea seem not simply plausible, but urgent in that all-consuming live-or-die way. It's a quality Green (see p. 323), one of the best baby-take-me-back singers of all time, has brought to a long list of great songs. And, to be sure, his peers—Otis Redding, Ray Charles—have etched equally personal entries in the book of love. But to Green, one of the all-time great examples was sung by David Ruffin of the Temptations: "Ain't Too Proud to Beg."

"It doesn't take but two lines and you feel that this man is torn up," Green said, talking about the 1966 recording, which is essentially a Ruffin solo feature. "He says, 'I got a looooove so deep, in the pit of my heart,' and from then on, there is just no ques-

From left: Melvin Franklin, Paul Williams, Eddie Kendricks, David Ruffin, Otis Williams.

tion about it. He's all the way in this thing. He's not ashamed to come and plead to you, baby. He's going to do whatever it takes. . . . By the time he gets to the line we all know—'Ain't too proud to beg and you know it'—well damn right you know it. That's meat, man. That kind of singing turns people around. They go, 'He means that, don't he?' That's soul singing right there."

GENRE: 🎤 R&B. **RELEASED:** 1966, Motown. **APPEARS ON:** *Gettin' Ready.* **CATALOG CHOICE:** David Ruffin: *David, the Unreleased Album.* **NEXT STOP:** Al Green: *Let's Stay Together.* **AFTER THAT:** Eddie Kendricks: *Eddie Kendricks.*

The Moodiest Hit Single Ever

"I'm Not in Love"

10cc

"If all music has expressive value," Aaron Copland writes in his classic book *What to Listen for in Music*, "then the composer must become conscious of the expressive value of his theme." That basic theorem has special resonance for the art of the three-minute pop song, in which a single emotional "value" is often hammered repeatedly. The brooding "I'm Not in Love," an unlikely smash hit in 1975, is an example of this, though its theme is communicated not merely through words or melodies, but its enveloping atmosphere. The "theme" amounts to a short recurring declaration ("I'm not in love . . ."), and every sound around it is downcast, disconsolate, and enervated, reinforcing the denial. The heavily processed backing voices seem listless, as if they can't get up off the couch. The synthesizers swirl into pretty puddles of sound, and when the tempo falls abruptly away in the middle, what's left is an oddly captivating musical mist.

Rarely do creators of pop songs dare to venture so deeply down one tunnel, in pursuit of a sound to match a theme. That's perhaps why this song, the most evocative from the coloristic and often experimental British art-pop band, endures: You hear the first notes and you know that for the next few minutes, you'll be caught within an inescapable malaise that's the total antithesis of a typical silly love song.

GENRE: 🎸 Rock. **RELEASED:** 1975, Mercury. **APPEARS ON:** *The Original Soundtrack.* **CATALOG CHOICE:** *Deceptive Bends.* **NEXT STOP:** Sparks: *Kimono My House.* **AFTER THAT:** Talk Talk: *Spirit of Eden.*

The Rosetta Stone

Complete Recorded Works in Chronological Order, 1938–1947

Sister Rosetta Tharpe

Sister Rosetta Tharpe was among the wildest figures in American music of the 1940s. That's saying something considering that the decade saw the birth of bebop and the heyday of jump blues. By trade and by faith, the native of Cotton Plant, Arkansas, was a gospel singer. She also played mean guitar—in an authoritative, rhythmic way that remains instantly identifiable. From the start of her professional career in 1938, Tharpe didn't limit herself to churches and revival tents: Incurring the wrath of the pious, she took her music into nightclubs, where she informed revelers that the Lord's train would not carry any drinkers to the promised land. She rocked hard decades before there was rock and roll, jammed with jazz and blues musicians, and performed with Cab Calloway at the Cotton Club. These associations—and her swinging, genre-blurring recordings—made her the first gospel trailblazer, a "crossover" artist who approached spiritual music with a spritz of showbiz.

When Tharpe began performing at age 4, she was known as "Little Rosetta Nubin, the singing and guitar-playing miracle."

Tharpe had a fixed repertoire; she recorded the same pieces (like "This Train" and "Down by the Riverside") over and over again, with different backing. This three-disc set begins with solo recordings and late '30s works with Lucky Millinder's orchestra that set forth the basic Tharpe style—a shouting, declamatory vocal offset by incessantly swinging rhythm guitar. After more solo sides (including a trembling "Nobody Knows, Nobody Cares"), Tharpe hit her stride in 1944 when she began a decade-long collaboration with the Sammy Price Trio. The combination of Tharpe's crisp rhythm

guitar and pianist Price's heavy, boogie-woogie left hand was downright radical in the pre-rock era, and remains incendiary to this day. Tharpe roars through blues songs with devotional lyrics, and old-time spirituals ("Strange Things Happening Every Day"), as though every tune is a new chance to nudge wayward souls toward the straight and narrow. Part of her jubilation, though, is musical: She's finally found musicians who can keep up with her hard-charging style, and she's going to ride that locomotive as far as it will take her.

GENRE: ✝ Gospel. **RELEASED:** 2001, Document. (Also available as *The Original Soul Sister* on Proper.) **KEY TRACKS:** "Didn't It Rain," "Strange Things Happening Every Day," "This Train," "Rock On," "Down by the Riverside." **CATALOG CHOICE:** *Gospel Train.* **NEXT STOP:** Willie Mae Ford Smith: *Mother Smith and Her Children.* **AFTER THAT:** Marion Williams: *My Soul Looks Back.*

"Zorba" and Then Some

The Best of Mikis Theodorakis

Mikis Theodorakis

Those who know the wistful music of the 1964 film *Zorba the Greek* have a sense of the persuasive power of Mikis Theodorakis. Like Béla Bartók and a handful of others, Theodorakis writes melodies that spring from and celebrate the soul of his country—for a time his music was a kind of surrogate ambassador, a "symbol" of modern Hellenic culture. Yet the ethnicity isn't exclusionary: Anyone with a pulse can love these hymns to an elusive deity and songs that make a lover's wistfulness sound noble.

Theodorakis is a unique figure in music. Though known mostly for "Zorba" and similar popular songs, he's also a prolific composer of contemporary classical music—he's written ballets, symphonies, cantatas, film scores, and operas. He began composing as a teenager and at seventeen gave his first performance—

with a choir he'd assembled himself. Later he studied at conservatories in Athens and Paris (one teacher was Olivier Messiaen; see p. 497), and then, upon returning to Greece, began investigating his country's musical traditions. This yielded treasure right away: A main theme of *Zorba* is derived from the "Syrtaki dance," a traditional dance that originated on the island of Crete.

This collection offers a sampling of Theodorakis's output, with emphasis on his songs and smaller pieces. The excerpts from *Zorba*, particularly the "Love Dance," ooze a lazy, breathtaking lyricism, while other instrumental pieces, including "Strike of the Pick," capture the lively swirling music heard at Greek weddings. Several pieces were written after the outspoken composer, a leftist who's

since become part of the Greek legislature, was put in a prison camp by the fascist Greek government; among these is the oddly calm "They Were Imprisoned."

Though the *Best of* doesn't represent the full sweep of Theodorakis's contribution, it's a great starting point—a way to hear how a man, deeply moved by the beauty and character of his country, repays the debt in song.

GENRE: 🌐 World/Greece. **RELEASED:** 1999, Delta. **KEY TRACKS:** "The Sad Lady," "Love Dance," "They Were Imprisoned." **CATALOG CHOICES:** *Litany; El-Las/Canta Theodorakis* (with María del Mar Bonet). **NEXT STOP:** Savina Yannatou and Primavera en Salonica: *Sumiglia*. **AFTER THAT:** Melina Kana: *Portrait*.

Psychedelic Rock, with Emphasis on the Psyche

Easter Everywhere

13th Floor Elevators

The 1960s opened so many doors. Suddenly seekers like Tommy Hall, whose instrument was the electric jug, found themselves playing in rock bands like the 13th Floor Elevators. And singers like Roky Erickson, who later struggled with mental illness (he spent years in an institution where he was subjected to electroshock and other radical therapies), became oracles of the acid age. In this time of rapidly expanding consciousness (and unusual tolerance for cultural quackery), bands that walked their own twisted road could become voices of a generation even before they fully developed a "voice."

The 13th Floor Elevators were among the trippier of those outfits. Formed in a garage in Austin, Texas, the band had a minor hit called "You're Gonna Miss Me" in 1966, which was included on the debut *The Psychedelic Sounds of the 13th Floor Elevators. Easter Everywhere,* the considerably more disciplined

follow-up, cranks up the band's strengths while occasionally pushing toward more extreme psychedelic weirdness. Erickson can be heard yelping and occasionally babbling about assorted inner crises. When he drops the veil and chooses to flat-out rock, as on "She Lives (in a Time of Her Own)," he's unexpectedly effective, a frontman who knows how to harness his demons.

Erickson, who's cultivated an adoring following for his subsequent solo works, seems to turn on the crazy at will: Tucked between the audacious cuts and the hallucinogenic explorations are more tender contemplations that feature his remarkably focused vocals—the original "I Had to Tell You," a cover of Bob

Dylan's "It's All Over Now, Baby Blue." These showcase the inventive work of guitarist Stacy Sutherland, whose fills and meandering asides are one reason this music endures still. Listen carefully and you'll hear that the consequential action is often going on behind him, as the musicians scramble to follow him into those trippier realms.

GENRE: 🎸 Rock. **RELEASED:** 1967, International Artists. **KEY TRACKS:** "She Lives (in a Time of Her Own)," "Slip Inside This House." **CATALOG CHOICES:** Roky Erickson: *Never Say Goodbye.* **NEXT STOP:** Daniel Johnston: *Fun.* **AFTER THAT:** ? and the Mysterians: *96 Tears.*

Summoning a Rarely Heard Side of Free Jazz

Spirits Known and Unknown

Leon Thomas

Leon Thomas was a journeyman singer with a scattered résumé (Mary Lou Williams, Rahsaan Roland Kirk) when he joined saxophonist Pharoah Sanders's group in 1968. Suddenly, with Sanders's guidance, the topics of his daily conversations became an integral part of his art. Thomas (1937–1999) had things to say about the war in Vietnam and the state of race relations—at times he could sound like the dashiki-wearing radical wandering the student union expounding on society's evils. Thomas relied on musicians versed in free jazz to underscore his message—and proved that music long associated with confrontational shrieking could open minds and soothe souls.

Thomas was born in East St. Louis, Illinois.

This album, the singer and poet's debut, opens with the song Thomas made famous on Sanders's *Karma* (1969), "The Creator Has a Master Plan." This version is slightly calmer but just as cosmic; Thomas sings like he wants to liberate his listeners from the prison of their conventional expectations, and he deploys all kinds of tricks to do so. Among his favorites is a slow, undulating, yodel-like incantation that resembles sounds made by Native American singers. He uses this device instead of "scat-singing" in his ad-libs, to call forth spirits known and unknown.

Spirits catches the range of Thomas's art: It positions his protest song "Damn Nam (Ain't Goin' to Vietnam)" alongside the Horace Silver classic "Song for My Father," and features a fired-up Sanders on three cuts, including a roiling version of the saxophonist's "Malcolm's Gone." Many free jazzers talked and chanted on their records during this period, but rarely did they sound as immersed in the moment as Thomas does here.

GENRES: 🎷 Jazz 🎤 Vocals. **RELEASED:** 1969, Flying Dutchman/Bluebird. **KEY TRACKS:** "The Creator Has a Master Plan," "Echoes," "Malcolm's Gone," "A Night in Tunisia." **COLLECTOR'S NOTE:** The 2002 reissue includes eight jazz standards that were recorded with a big band in 1958 but never released. They're snapshots of a tamer Thomas. **CATALOG CHOICE:** *Live in Berlin.* **NEXT STOP:** Gil Scott-Heron: *Reflections.*

One of the All-Time Great Breakup Records

Shoot Out the Lights

Richard and Linda Thompson

There's nothing accidental about the order of songs on this strong-minded album, which takes just thirty-eight minutes to tell its story. It begins with a plea, "Don't Renege on Our Love," that voices a long-shot hope that a romance can be salvaged. From there, the duo of Richard and Linda Thompson—a married couple who'd been working together in various bands that followed Fairport Convention in the late '60s—trace the gradual (and jarring) final stages of love. They catch the cautiousness of daily communication in "Walking on a Wire," and anger in "Just the Motion." As things grow increasingly sour, Richard Thompson's grim outlook takes over; both the macabre "Did She Jump" and the closing "Wall of Death" describe a level of torment and desperation more common in novels than pop songs.

When they started work on this, Richard and Linda were a relatively stable couple, followers of an ecstatic Sufi brand of Islam who'd issued a series of trenchant folk-rock albums (*I Want to See the Bright Lights Tonight* is the best). They recorded and then scrapped a first set of tunes (several tracks are included on Richard's anthology *Watching the Dark*), and during the second round of sessions, which yielded this brilliantly sung record, the couple began having problems. After they finished recording, the Thompsons held off on releasing *Shoot Out* because Linda was pregnant; by the time it appeared,

in 1982, they were strictly a professional couple. They began one U.S. tour during which Richard brought his mistress on the road with them, making it west across the country before calling it quits. Richard completed the tour heading back east playing solo.

Produced by Joe Boyd, the American responsible for the recordings of Nick Drake and others, *Shoot Out the Lights* catches a tension and exposed-nerve edginess that was rare in the British folk-rock of the day. Its instrumental tone—harsh, hurtling spears of electric guitar punctuating blunt expressions of hurt—is remarkable whether you take its lyrics as an autobiographical account of a real dissolution or just a songwriterly device.

GENRES: 🎤 Folk 🎸 Rock. **RELEASED:** 1982, Hannibal. (Rykodisc's 1991 reissue contains a bonus track, "Living in Luxury.") **KEY TRACKS:** "Walking on a Wire," "Shoot Out the Lights," "Did She Jump," "Wall of Death." **CATALOG CHOICES:** Richard Thompson: *Hand of Kindness.* Linda Thompson: *Fashionably Late.* **NEXT STOP:** Suzanne Vega: *Solitude Standing* (see p. 827). **AFTER THAT:** Scott Walker: *Scott 4.*

Richard and Linda Thompson married in October 1972.

Watch Out for Big Mama

Hound Dog: The Peacock Recordings

Big Mama Thornton

Even if she hadn't recorded a stack of never-equaled jump-blues singles, Big Mama Thornton would have a place in the history books— as the singer whose 1952 version of "Hound Dog" inspired young Elvis Presley to cut the tune.

Cue up Thornton's version and prepare to be amazed. The tempo's slower. The rhythm section, borrowed from the Johnny Otis orchestra, is relaxed—we're way farther South than Elvis was. The hard-living Thornton (1926–1984), who was born in Alabama and was discovered singing in Houston, takes it upon herself to supply all of the fire. She's done with the little puppy dog who's hanging around her door, and she uses her blast furnace of a voice to tell him so. From her first utterance, she completely owns the tune: Placing each shout just so, she turns ordinary lyrics into ridiculing taunts. Hearing her "encourage" guitarist Pete Lewis during the solo break—issuing commands like a displeased dog owner—is an experience not to be missed.

Thornton's "Hound Dog" was #1 on the *Billboard* R&B charts for 7 weeks.

Thornton claimed she'd written "Hound Dog," but lost a lawsuit with the songwriting team of Jerry Leiber and Mike Stoller over authorship rights. She recorded several of the duo's other tunes during this period, however, including the equally dismissive "I Smell a Rat." Another great Leiber/Stoller performance is "Hard Times," the slinking slow lament which boasts thrilling stop-time ad-libs that amount to a complete textbook on singing the blues.

GENRE: 🟤 Blues. **RELEASED:** 1992, Peacock/MCA. **KEY TRACKS:** "Hound Dog," "They Call Me Big Mama," "You Don't Move Me No More," "I Smell a Rat." **CATALOG CHOICE:** *The Vanguard Years.* **NEXT STOP:** Memphis Minnie: *Hoodoo Lady* (see p. 495). **AFTER THAT:** Koko Taylor: *Koko Taylor.*

Plenty of Good Vibes Here

Primo

Cal Tjader

Pick up any Cal Tjader record from the late '50s through the early '70s, and you can usually count on this much: Whether the style is Latin jazz or boogaloo or straight salsa (Tjader recorded them all convincingly), the music will swing. The side-men will bring plenty of heat. The California-based Tjader (1925–1982) will dazzle on the vibraphone for a few brief moments, but mostly his solos will be models of percussive mellowness—not for nothing did some wags refer to Tjader's music as "mambo without the migraine."

Tjader taught himself to play the vibraphone, drums, bongos, and congas.

So it goes on Tjader's best-known effort, the 1964 booga-loo *Soul Sauce*, which is often credited with commercializing the soul-jazz explosion. Pleasant and reasonably groovy, *Soul Sauce* is a great way to start exploring Tjader—especially if you're in the market for a suave bachelor-pad ethos of retro hipness.

To hear the vibraphonist simmering in slighty hotter surroundings, seek out the more obscure *Primo*. Recorded in 1970, this set is a profound departure—it's a daring, guns-blazing cranked-to-eleven New York salsa all-star jam. Its explorations are far more con-tentious, and imbued with a strutting sense of purpose, than most of the pleasant-sounding discs in the vibraphonist's large discography.

Credit for this goes largely to pianist Charlie Palmieri, the spark plug on countless Latin classics, who (along with Tito Puente) wrote the *Primo* arrangements. Palmieri is a ferocious accompanist, and watch out when it's his turn to solo: He plays electric piano on most of the ten tracks, alter-nating between deftly threaded bebop and heavy, hammer-ing attacks. Both Palmieri and Tjader hit full stride on "Gringo City," the title of which might have been an affectionate dig at the vibraphon-ist—who was esteemed by many in the Latin music community as the hippest Anglo on the scene. That's heavy praise, and it doesn't take long with this record (or, for that matter, *Soul Sauce*) to hear him earn it.

GENRE: 🎵 Jazz. **RELEASED:** 1970, Fantasy. **KEY TRACKS:** "Mama Aguela," "Gringo City," "Tanga," "Azucar Mama." **CATALOG CHOICES:** *Soul Sauce; The Monterey Concert.* **NEXT STOP:** Mongo Santamaria: *La bamba.* **AFTER THAT:** Charlie Palmieri: *Either You Have It or You Don't.*

A Song You Never Forget

"The Lion Sleeps Tonight"

The Tokens

Written and recorded by a South African entertainer named Solomon Linda in 1939, "The Lion Sleeps Tonight" is the prototypical simple song that quickly becomes an "ear worm"—first its *wem-oh-weh* baritone chant lodges in your cortex, followed by that soaring falsetto theme. You can find yourself singing the song even if you haven't heard it in years.

It's been having that effect since Linda's

original, entitled "Mbube" (The Lion) in Zulu, first caught on in his homeland, where it trig-gered a new approach to a cappella singing that came to be called "mbube." The sweet refrain eventually spread around the world: Pete Seeger recorded a folk version in the early '50s, and then a Brooklyn doo-wop group called the Tokens took lyrics credited to the pop producer George Weiss and recorded this well-known rendition, which became a hit in 1961. It's quite an extraordinary intermingling—a tune bursting with pop innocence that's at the same time distinctly exotic.

The Tokens formed at Abraham Lincoln High School in Brooklyn in 1955.

Over 130 versions of the song have been recorded since, including several associated with the Disney hit *The Lion King*. Incredibly, Linda's family did not benefit from this inescapable work—he died in 1962 with twenty-two dollars to his name. After a 2000 article in *Rolling Stone* documented how Linda had been systematically cheated by businessmen, several U.S. record executives got involved to rectify the situation. An out-of-court settlement was reached in February 2006 that forces the U.S. publisher of the song to pay the family royalties dating from 1987, a term that includes the film and Broadway runs of *The Lion King*.

GENRE: ✪ Pop.
RELEASED: 1961, RCA Victor.
APPEARS ON: *The Tokens*. **ANOTHER INTERPRETATION:** Ladysmith Black Mambazo on *Spike and Co.: Do It a Cappella*. **NEXT STOP:** Mbongeni Ngema: *Sarafina!*, Original Broadway Cast Recording.

A Definitive Slice of Early Reggae

Funky Kingston/In the Dark

Toots and the Maytals

If Bob Marley is reggae's spiritual guide, Frederick "Toots" Hibbert is the singer who embodies the music's resolute soul. The leader of the hard-grooving band called the Maytals, Hibbert sings in a voice of sweet agitation, with a commitment that has earned him comparisons to Memphis legend Otis Redding. But from the early days of his career, Hibbert—whose 1968 single "Do the Reggay" may possibly have given Jamaican music its trade name (disputes exist)—managed to be both rousing in a party-time-soul-revue way and sweet in a loverman way. Without ever sounding like he was straining to turn on the charm.

When it was first released in the U.S. in

Toots & the Maytals have a record 31 #1 songs in Jamaica.

1975, *Funky Kingston* was a ten-track singles compilation designed to capitalize on the surge of international curiosity about reggae. It drew from two Toots and the Maytals Jamaican titles, *Funky Kingston* and the follow-up *In the Dark*, and included "Pressure Drop," the frantic classic Hibbert wrote for the film *The Harder They Come*. This 2003 set offers everything from the original masters, but thankfully omits the horn section and other sweetening that was added later for export.

"Pressure Drop" alone is worth the price of admission: It gathers bits of ska and early reggae into a groove that's way too hyped for ganja. The remaining songs showcase Hibbert's mastery of call-and-response. The disc offers one trance-inducing original after another—from the deep and rubbery pulse of "Funky Kingston" to the gently rocking "Redemption Song," a prayer called "Time Tough," and a prison song, "54-46 Was My Number." There are also several noteworthy covers, including an over-the-top "Louie Louie," and a treatment of John Denver's "Take Me Home Country Roads" that winds up being anything but a novelty—as Hibbert's relentless grind-it-out voice transforms a limp little throwaway into something that sounds scarifyingly like a lost soul classic.

GENRE: 🌐 World/Jamaica. **RELEASED:** 2003, Island. (*Funky Kingston* originally issued 1973; *In the Dark* issued 1973.) **KEY TRACKS:** "Time Tough," "54-46 Was My Number," "Pressure Drop," "Take Me Home Country Roads." **CATALOG CHOICE:** *Live* (1980). **NEXT STOP:** Hugh Mundell: *Africa Must Be Free by 1983* (see p. 532). **AFTER THAT:** Yabby You: *Jesus Dread*.

Velvet Fog in the Footlights

Swings Shubert Alley

Mel Tormé

In the '50s, every saloon singer and jazz crooner had at least a few show tunes in his or her back pocket. The sashaying melodies and brainy structures of Cole Porter, the Gershwins, and the other Broadway bigs were acid tests for aspiring song-stylists—if you couldn't make a classic like Comden and Green's "Just in Time" enchanting, you probably shouldn't be charging admission.

Mel Tormé understood this. By 1960, he'd issued several well-regarded records that established him as a jazz-leaning craftsman with good showbiz instincts. Still, his approach was a bit tame; he'd earned that "Velvet Fog" nickname not just for the enveloping quality of his voice, but because he'd stripped all harshness and abrasion from his game.

This collection, his fifth collaboration with the masterly arranger Marty Paich, is Tormé's most convincing attempt at letting his

Tormé wrote more than 250 songs during his career, including "The Christmas Song."

inner swinger loose. Where many singers treat big-band backing as ornamentation, Tormé gets right next to the horns, positioning his voice somewhere between the trumpets and trombones, where he can send the music sideways by dipping out of key for a split second. Tormé's sometimes blithe, sometimes campy enthusiasm spreads to the soloists, and on "Whatever Lola Wants" both alto saxophonist Art Pepper and the late, criminally underappreciated trombone virtuoso Frank Rosolino take spirited turns that spice up the endeavor. Even here, though, Tormé never sounds like he's showing off. His art is in his little curlicue twists and (very) brief scatted ad-libs, animated gestures that slyly enhance the swing while making clear he's not lost in any kind of fog.

GENRE: 🎤 Vocals. RELEASED: 1960, Verve. KEY TRACKS: "On the Street Where You Live," "A Sleepin' Bee," "Whatever Lola Wants." CATALOG CHOICE: *Mel Tormé and the Marty Paich Dek-Tette.* NEXT STOP: Tony Bennett: *The Essential Tony Bennett.* AFTER THAT: Frank Sinatra: *Songs for Swingin' Lovers* (see p. 706).

The Best Tosh Ever

Live at the One Love Peace Concert

Peter Tosh

Billed as a gathering of the greatest names in reggae, Kingston's 1978 One Love Peace Concert was also intended to promote peace among warring Jamaican political factions. At one point Bob Marley, the show's headliner, brought then Prime Minister Michael Manley and his rival, Edward Seaga, on stage for a handshake—hoping that a show of solidarity might quell the violence then raging in Jamaica's slums.

If Marley was determined to make peace, his former bandmate Peter Tosh arrived that day with a different agenda: to advocate for the legalization of marijuana and shout down hypocrisy of all types. Performing with the politicians sitting in the second row, Tosh summons a passion that might startle those who know his laconic and laid-back 1976 debut, *Legalize It.* Amped up and agitated, he roars through diatribes about cultural imperialism ("400 Years") and issues boastful street threats (the ska-tinged "Stepping Razor") with a severe, this-is-business tone that presages gangsta rap. Tosh sings as though reggae is a conduit for higher consciousness, a way for people of differing ideologies to discuss abstract ideas like "justice" and "equal rights."

Tosh was nicknamed "Stepping Razor" for his biting temper.

By the time the set is over, after a medley of "Legalize It" and the best-known song Tosh composed for the Wailers, "Get Up, Stand Up," Tosh has dispensed several passionate harangues, including one that lasts seven minutes. The concert's pinnacle comes on the solemn "Burial," as Tosh's band, led by bassist Robbie Shakespeare and amazing drummer Sly Dunbar, punctuates his message with slyly subversive background music.

Tosh's discography contains several other rousing live documents with considerably better fidelity, but *The One Love Peace Concert* marks an intense high point in Tosh's long career.

GENRE: 🌐 World/Jamaica. RELEASED: 2000, JAD. KEY TRACKS: "Legalize It/Get Up, Stand Up," "Burial/Speech." CATALOG CHOICE: *Legalize It.* AFTER THAT: Bunny Wailer: *Blackheart Man.* NEXT STOP: Steel Pulse: *Earth Crisis.*

Hypnotic African Blues

The River

Ali Farka Touré

O ften called "the African John Lee Hooker," Malian singer and guitarist Ali Farka Touré (1939–2006) shared at least one key trait with the late Mississippi Delta blues legend: the ability to make mesmerizing music out of seemingly insignificant repetitive phrases.

These phrases are at the center of *The River*, Touré's consummate melding of blues and African music. Touré begins each piece with a prancing motif that sets the tempo, and the members of his ensemble—including drummers who keep time clicking sticks—fall into an entrancing procession. They repeat the same phrase endlessly, adding slight variations; the static backdrop gives Touré room to improvise both vocally and on his treble-heavy electric guitar. His wailing flatted-third melodies sometimes align with blues tradition; the rhythms behind him are fairly laid-back. In much the way Hooker did, Touré builds his testimony one fractured line at a time, until a song like "Heygana," a tribute to a mountain, takes on the massiveness of its subject.

Touré was born in the village of Kanau on the banks of the Niger River.

Touré is not exclusively a bluesman here. He rarely follows the twelve-bar form of the Western blues and his guitar playing embodies quintessentially African rhythmic perseverance. But his music evokes the languid pace of life in the Mississippi Delta. It draws from the blues' emotional reservoir and talks about the same universal troubles. This is gracefully visionary music by a Malian nobleman who cultivated a profound two-way connection between Mother Africa and the American South.

GENRE: 🌐 World/Mali. **RELEASED:** 1990, Mango. **KEY TRACKS:** "Heygana," "Toungere," "Kenouna." **CATALOG CHOICE:** *In the Heart of the Moon* (with Toumani Diabaté). **NEXT STOP:** Toumani Diabaté: *New Ancient Strings* (see p. 221). **AFTER THAT:** John Lee Hooker: *Alone*.

Brotherly Singing from Africa

Paris-Ziguinchor Live

Touré Kunda

T he Touré brothers of Casamance in southern Senegal deserve a spot alongside the Everly Brothers and the Gibbs of Bee Gees fame on the short list of the world's great singing siblings. Aligning for powerful unisons or splitting off to improvise melodies of shamanic intensity, the three—Ismalia, Sixu Tidiane, and Ousmane (a fourth, Amadou, died after collapsing during a 1983 performance)—crafted a sound drawn equally from ancient griot chants and modern African pop.

This 1984 concert begins with hand drums and voice: For more than two minutes, the three brothers shout out to various African regions, shifting the rhythmic emphasis from 4/4 to 6/8 every eight measures. A compressed version of tribal ritual, the exchanges prime the crowd for what follows—an hour of trance-inducing prayers and chants, kept aloft by kicky Africanized reggae (a rhythm the band described with the phonetic term *djambaadong*), polyrhythmic funk, and featherweight samba. All of it is passionately sung, the sound of three contrasting voices seeking one euphoria.

Paris-Ziguinchor Live arrived at an interesting moment—mid-1984, two years before Paul Simon's *Graceland* (see p. 704) transformed African music into a cosmopolitan accessory for the urban hip, and just as established figures like Youssou N'Dour were developing international followings. The Touré brothers had spent years kicking around Paris. Unlike many of their peers seeking international success, the Touré brothers weren't interested in tradition. They surrounded themselves with diverse musicians—the band here includes a German keyboardist, a French guitarist, and percussionists from several African nations. This "mini U.N." approach yielded an unexpectedly rich, heady music, an instrumental attack every bit as intense as the Touré brothers' beseeching, nearly wailing, vocals.

GENRE: 🌐 World/Senegal. **RELEASED:** 1984, Celluloid (France). **KEY TRACKS:** "Sayla," "Sidi yella." **NEXT STOP:** Youssou N'Dour: *Immigrés* (see p. 542). **AFTER THAT:** Baaba Maal: *Djam leelii* (see p. 462).

Big Hits from the Phil Spector of New Orleans

Finger Poppin' and Stompin' Feet

Allen Toussaint

Easily the most influential "unknown" in New Orleans music, Allen Toussaint is one of those Zelig figures who only *seems* invisible—his fingerprints are everywhere. The pianist, singer, and songwriter got his start filling in on Fats Domino sessions, and from there was hired by the Minit label to help develop talent; his hits for the label are collected on the spunky, rollicking *Finger Poppin'*. Then he helped develop the soul-funk that erupted in New Orleans in the late 1960s—his productions put the Meters on the map—and went on to create significant hits in the 1970s, including the LaBelle classic "Lady Marmalade." Through it all, Toussaint has preferred the low light of the studio to neon-sign popularity. As a result, he remains criminally underappreciated.

To begin to understand his influence, start with the mashed-potato backbeats and seemingly slight nonsense riffs of *Finger Poppin'*, among them Jessie Hill's inspired strut "Ooh Poo Pah Doo," Toussaint's first hit for the Minit label. These showcase his production style, which might be described as lean and mean: Building arrangements around a horn section and his own clipped piano accompaniments,

Toussaint gives his singers lots of room to stretch. That puts the emphasis on zany personalities like Ernie K-Doe, whose classic complaint "Mother-In-Law" is here. (Toussaint has said it's his favorite production, and it was the first New Orleans R&B record to hit number 1 on the pop charts.) Among the lesser-known gems are two by the deep-voiced Benny Spellman, "Fortune Teller" (which was later covered by the Rolling Stones) and "Lipstick Traces (on a Cigarette)."

Toussaint began a solo career in the early '70s. Highlights from that period, gathered on *The Allen Toussaint Collection,* show a completely different side of his talent. Recognizing that his voice wasn't suited to up-tempo shouts, he wrote sly, creeping-in-the-back-door odes with unas-

Toussaint's songs have been covered by everyone from Devo to Warren Zevon.

suming, slyly gorgeous melodies like "What Do You Want the Girl to Do?," a hit for Boz Scaggs. Taken together, these titles show two sides of the Toussaint talent: The boisterous *Finger Poppin'* singles get the party started, and then the earthy, more reflective tunes on *The Toussaint Collection* provide the perfect late-night respite, for when those stompin' feet get tired.

GENRE: 🎙 R&B.
RELEASED: 2002, EMI. (Original recordings made in 1960–1962.) **KEY TRACKS:** "Mother-in-Law," "Ooh Poo Pah Doo." **CATALOG CHOICES:** *The Allen Toussaint Collection; Southern Nights.* **NEXT STOP:** The Meters: *The Original Funkmasters.* **AFTER THAT:** The Neville Brothers: *Yellow Moon.*

Chamber Jazz, on the Astral Plane

Solstice

Ralph Towner

Modern recording technology presents improvising artists with a profound dilemma: To overdub or not to overdub? And when one does overdub, what effect does this have on music that's ostensibly created "in the moment"? Does the enhanced palette expand possibilities or constitute a form of sonic deception?

Ralph Towner's *Solstice* stands as one of the most inventive, musically astute responses to this conundrum. The guitarist and three other musicians—Jan Garbarek on saxophone and flute, Eberhard Weber on bass and cello, Jon Christensen on drums—play the themes mostly live, all together in the same room. Then, on the agile "Nimbus" and others, the same players add additional parts. Garbarek creates a fantasia for multiple flutes; Weber weaves his cello between the existing bass line and Towner's hyperarticulate acoustic guitar. Rather than inflate things to orchestral mass, Towner, who adds piano on several tracks, wisely retains the conversational quality of a live performance. The result is a contemplative chamber jazz, with animated melodies and solos that extend the fragile elegance of the themes.

A founding member of the '70s world-music group Oregon, Towner is among the elite conceptual jazz thinkers. His restrained use of multitracking to add textural detail sets *Solstice* apart from much jazz of the 1970s. The emphasis is on sound: Manfred Eicher, ECM's founder, who produced the album (and many of the label's other landmarks), seeks an absolute purity of tone, a great-outdoors openness that lets every attack ring organically. This makes it possible to savor discrete elements deep inside the music—like the dancing ticks from Christensen's cymbals, or the scorpion sting of Garbarek's soprano saxophone, or Towner's twelve-string guitar,

which sometimes swells into a hundred-string behemoth, enveloping everything inside its warm sonority. These sounds are so quietly alluring, and so fully realized, they render questions like "Is it live or is it multi-tracked?" academic.

GENRE: 🅐 Jazz. **RELEASED:** 1975, ECM. **KEY TRACKS:** "Nimbus," "Winter Solstice," "Oceanus." **F.Y.I.:** Pat Metheny, who got his start recording for ECM, counts this among his favorite recordings. **CATALOG CHOICE:** *Old Friends, New Friends.* **NEXT STOP:** Keith Jarrett: *Belonging.* **AFTER THAT:** Bill Frisell: *Lookout for Hope.*

The High Spark of Jazz-Rock

John Barleycorn Must Die

Traffic

After a turbulent year in the spotlight as part of the supergroup Blind Faith (see p. 98), Steve Winwood began 1970 disillusioned with the music business and facing an all-too-common reality: He and Traffic, the band that broke up when Blind Faith came knocking, owed United Artists two more records. The keyboardist and singer, then twenty-two, went into the studio right away, composing songs for what he expected would be his first solo album (working title: *Mad Shadows*). A few songs in, wanting more musical energy than he could generate himself, Winwood asked two of his old cronies from Traffic, drummer and sometime singer-lyricist Jim Capaldi and woodwind player Chris Wood, to stop by. Before long, Traffic was reborn.

Keyboardist and singer Steve Winwood led several incarnations of Traffic.

John Barleycorn Must Die collects the music the three made during a feverish round of sessions; there are long expanses of jamming

punctuated by brief sections featuring Winwood's searing vocals, a template Traffic would use on later works. *Barleycorn* retains the crusading spirit of the band's first two albums while moving into even more improbable realms—among them old English balladry (the title cut), jazz-rock fusion (the instrumental "Glad," a most original appropriation of New Orleans–style piano), existential rock ("Empty Pages"), and an introspective shade of soul ("Stranger to Himself").

The band's range is impressive, as is its unconventional instrumentation—at times Winwood supplies bass on the organ, and is accompanied by just drums and saxophone. Still, the salient characteristic of *John Barleycorn,* and what separates it from everything else of its day, is its earthy, unpressured feel. The tunes, most written by Winwood and Capaldi, sound like they sprouted during superfriendly jam sessions. Though they're built on strong fundamentals—old-fashioned verse-chorus discipline—they're ruled by a marvelous wildness, a sense that the ad-libbed explorations are as important as the hooks. Later, Traffic and others got snarled in brain-cramping attempts at prog-rock wonkery. Here, though, the band sounds utterly grounded. As the grooves percolate effortlessly along, it becomes clear that unity, not any technical skill, is what makes the music levitate.

GENRE: 🎸 Rock. **RELEASED:** 1970, Island. **KEY TRACKS:** "Glad," "Freedom Rider," "Empty Pages," "Stranger to Himself." **CATALOG CHOICE:** *The Low Spark of High Heeled Boys.* **NEXT STOP:** Jefferson Airplane: *Surrealistic Pillow.* **AFTER THAT:** Caravan: *Cunning Stunts.*

A Banging Classic

Electric Warrior

T. Rex

The major hit from the British proto-glam band T. Rex, "Bang a Gong (Get It On)" is a rock classic with an afterlife that nearly overshadows its original impact. It has helped sell cars (Mitsubishi) and spaghetti sauce (Ragú), and its hormone-driven exhortations have wormed into countless movies, including *Moulin Rouge* and *Billy Elliot.* The song has been used so much it's become a kind of shorthand, filmic code for the wayward, slightly troubled "dirty sweet" girl.

Oddly, no matter how much commerce or symbolism is attached to "Bang a Gong," this cool-strutting three-minute miracle from 1971 retains a hint of outsider menace. This comes primarily from the slightly spacey head-in-the-clouds orientation of Marc Bolan, the corkscrew-curled vocalist and driving force. Bolan approaches rock as both a musical and a mythmaking challenge—at times it seems he's tuned to some otherworldly frequency nobody else is picking

Lead singer Marc Bolan left school at 15 and became a model before starting a band.

up. *Electric Warrior* taps into that transmission, while reflecting the greatness and the rampant excess that distinguished rock circa 1971. Some of its best tunes, the trippy "Cosmic Dancer" and "Jeepster," resonate as ridiculously pretentious and insanely beautiful in the same instant.

When this album was released, Bolan was already a big star in the U.K. He was then seen as something of a preposterous figure in the U.S., but not anymore.

He looms as a kind of linchpin now, one of the few to transfer the lofty disconnected ideas floating around early '70s rock—blues and boogie, ethnic rhythms, ornate orchestral textures—into something visionary. How visionary? This album taught David Bowie and Mott the Hoople the meaning of glam, helped hard rock bands get in touch with their inner druid, and presaged the feral abandon of punk. The spirit of T. Rex lives still in the garagey hooks of the Strokes and the disinterested cool of the White Stripes, and really whenever the sudden urge to get it on strikes.

GENRE: 🎸 Rock. **RELEASED:** 1971, Reprise. **KEY TRACKS:** "Bang a Gong (Get It On)," "Jeepster." **CATALOG CHOICE:** *The Ultimate Collection.* **NEXT STOP:** Mott the Hoople: *All The Young Dudes.* **AFTER THAT:** New York Dolls: *New York Dolls.*

"No time for hibernation, only elation"

The Low End Theory

A Tribe Called Quest

Even before gangsta rap became a huge commercial force in 1994, hip-hop was trapped in an unfortunate lowest-common-denominator feedback loop. MCs who specialized in violent and/or misogynist messages were sold to suburban teenagers as next-generation sages, creating demand for hip-hop that valued party-time nihilism over enlightened expression. Their success encouraged subsequent waves of opportunistic copycats, until so-called "consciousness rap" became a tiny subgenre, off in the margins.

There was very little for smart MCs to gain by speaking out against this status quo in 1991. A Tribe Called Quest did anyway, boldly, loudly, and with great humor. On the aptly titled *The Low End Theory*, MCs Q-Tip and Phife Dawg and DJ Ali Shaheed Muhammad created a caustic commentary that endures as one of the most important hip-hop albums of all time.

The MCs, who grew up in Queens, directly attacked what they saw as hip-hop's blind spots—one recurring subject is the dim-wittedness of the music business, from the overhyped fake-rhyming stars to the sleazy promoters who take advantage of them. Another is the genre's treatment of women:

In 2006, *Time* magazine called *The Low End Theory* one of the 100 best albums of all time.

On "Butter," a cad finds himself confounded by a strong woman named Flo—and suddenly realizes how he's treated previous girlfriends. Set to a nicely distended Weather Report sample, that track is one of several with messages that run counter to the strong-man posturing of so much hip-hop. Another equally severe lesson is titled "The Infamous Date Rape."

Underpinning these screeds is resourceful music that looks far beyond kick/snare boom-bap. Quest looks for beats in unusual places, drawing on old jazz and blues records and stray instrumental sounds (like the vibraphone on "Vibes and Stuff," or jazz legend Ron Carter's bass line on "Verses from the Abstract") to create terse sonic schemes. These sound terrifically loose, yet are carefully developed, and they're at least part of the reason *The Low End Theory* remains thrilling: Where rap hit-makers load everything and the kitchen sink into their gaudy tales of excess, Quest stays close to the ground and away from gimmicks, so that nothing mucks up the message.

GENRE: 🎤 Hip-Hop. **RELEASED:** 1991, Jive. **KEY TRACKS:** "Excursions," "Buggin'

Out," "The Infamous Date Rape." **CATALOG CHOICE:** *Midnight Marauders.* **NEXT STOP:** Common: *Like Water for Chocolate.* **AFTER THAT:** Mos Def and Talib Kweli: *Mos Def and Talib Kweli Are Black Star* (see p. 525).

The Musings of a Jazz Thinker

Tristano/The New Tristano

Lennie Tristano

Everybody who followed jazz in the 1950s had an opinion about Lennie Tristano (1919–1978). He was hailed by some (including Beat writer Jack Kerouac, who mentioned this album several times) as a major conceptualist, a musician who gathered ideas from bebop and West Coast cool jazz into a cerebral sound. Others dismissed his compositions as cluttered schemes designed to show off runaway technique, and dismissed his playing as too detached—he could sound like a math professor solving elaborate equations. The common rap was that there was no heat, no "soul," in his playing.

1955's *Tristano* is hailed for its experiments with overdubbing and altered tape speed.

It took a long time for the blind Chicago native to win widespread acceptance in jazz. Listening to this title, which combines two of his most significant releases, the chill becomes understandable. Tristano's elongated, almost babbling melody lines seem calculated; the solos that follow are equally thoughtful, yet visit harmonic zones not in common jazz usage. In the space of a single passage, he can sound like a visionary who's way ahead of the times and an iconoclast who's lost in his own reality.

With the perspective of time, those contrasts are exactly what make Tristano a treasure. *Tristano/The New Tristano,* which combines a 1955 release with one from 1962,

includes live dates with his best quartet, the one featuring saxophonist Lee Konitz, as well as daunting and sophisticated unaccompanied jazz piano (several tunes find Tristano overdubbing multiple lines, a move that was itself controversial). The group had been together for some time; its previous albums, *Intuition* and *Crosscurrents,* are notable for their wily, journeying themes. Everyone involved knew exactly what Tristano wanted: a smooth and steady swing with no fireworks, and solos that sprouted ideas like weeds. Konitz (and many others) had to work to attain that stream of consciousness. Whenever Tristano sat down to play, it was just always there, instantly.

GENRE: 🎵 Jazz. **RELEASED:** 1955, 1962, Atlantic. (Reissued 1994.) **KEY TRACKS:** "Requiem," "You Go to My Head," "All the Things You Are," "Deliberation." **CATALOG CHOICES:** *Intuition; Crosscurrents* (not available as of press time). **NEXT STOP:** The Jimmy Giuffre Three: *1961* (see p. 313). **AFTER THAT:** Miles Davis: *Birth of the Cool.*

The Best Way to Encounter the Texas Troubadour

The Definitive Collection

Ernest Tubb

The next time some airbrushed contemporary country star like Toby Keith attempts another half-baked revival of old-time honky-tonk music, haul out the hard stuff: the plain and oddly perfect recordings of Ernest Tubb (1914–1984).

Tubb's singles stand among the greatest examples of honky-tonk, that rowdy slice-of-life style that was born in the South and nurtured in Texas roadhouses in the 1930s. These are simple tunes studded with corny couplets about being in love, missing a lover, getting lost in drink. And they're defined by lonesome and deliciously succinct guitar melodies; Tubb was one

Tubb was inducted into the Country Music Hall of Fame in 1965.

of the first country artists to have a hit single backed by electric guitar (his 1940 breakthrough "Walking the Floor Over You"). Most of his subsequent works feature sparkling breaks from either Jimmy Short, steel guitarist Jerry Byrd, or Tommy "Butterball" Paige.

Central to the enterprise is Tubb's straightforward delivery. His voice is roughened and unremarkable, and he approaches these songs in an offhand way that's surprisingly endearing. He makes simplicity a virtue, singing about the tragedy of war ("Soldier's Last Letter") and the joy of a reunion ("It's Been So Long, Darling," one of several singles celebrating the end of World War II) with the same straightforward demeanor. With Tubb, there are no put-on airs, no frills, just the core of the song.

A sharecropper's son from Crisp, Texas, Tubb began his career openly emulating the blue yodels of Jimmie Rodgers (see p. 652),

and got his break in 1936 when Rodgers's widow, Carrie, championed him. His nascent career was nearly derailed in 1939—he damaged his voice by singing too soon after a tonsillectomy. This proved a blessing: He couldn't yodel anymore, and his voice acquired the sandpapery, almost weary tone that defines his mature work. That sound, restored to full glory on this nicely remastered collection of Tubb's career peaks, enchanted country fans, led to a series of duets with Loretta Lynn (the best of them, "Mr. & Mrs. Used to Be," is here), and made him a fixture at the Grand Ole Opry for four decades. Despite all that, Tubb's star is in recession—he's one of those legends who has been overlooked by recent generations. That'll change. This is 100-proof music, too strong to be ignored for long.

GENRE: ◔ Country. **RELEASED:** 2006, MCA/Universal. (Original recordings 1941–1967, Decca.) **KEY TRACKS:** "Walking the Floor Over You," "Soldier's Last Letter," "Tomorrow Never Comes," "I Love You Because," "Mr. & Mrs. Used to Be," "Waltz Across Texas." **CATALOG CHOICE:** *Live 1965.* **NEXT STOP:** Conway Twitty and Loretta Lynn: *The Definitive Collection.* **AFTER THAT:** Lefty Frizzell: *Look What Thoughts Can Do* (see p. 290).

"Live my life as a thug until the day I die . . ."

All Eyez on Me

2Pac

Ever since Tupac Shakur's violent death, there have been persistent rumors that the New York–born rapper is, in fact, alive somewhere, and still on the run from the various evil forces that conspired against him during a 1996 drive-by shooting in Las Vegas. This notion would explain Shakur's rather incredible posthumous output—more records bearing his name have been released since his death than during his lifetime. Where the "martyr in exile" theory falls apart is in the music itself: None of the posthumous output gets within the same ZIP code as the creativity displayed here, on this double-disc of illuminated

2Pac began recording *All Eyez on Me* just a few hours after his release from prison.

and belligerent dynamite that's schooled every would-be thug who ever rocked a microphone.

When Shakur, or 2Pac, recorded this, he was already deep into gangsta mythology and the real-life exploits that fueled it. His previous album, *Me Against the World*, came out while he was in prison, serving time on a sexual assault conviction. *All Eyez on Me* is his fourth record, and as he implies with the title, he'd been affected by several years of living in the spotlight. He sounds somewhat paranoid, quick to draw conclusions about people and their motives; on "Only God Can Judge Me," he muses, "Perhaps I was blind to the facts, stabbed in the back, I couldn't trust my own homies, just a bunch a dirty rats." Throughout, he talks of loyalty as though it's a rare and precious thing. His descriptions of violence are dramatic and mean-spirited and funny, sometimes all at once.

Among Shakur's enduring contributions to hip-hop is his effective use of R&B-style hooks, repetitive and often sung catchphrases. These offset the brutality of the *All Eyez* raps and provide the songs with basic structure. "Can't C Me," one of several tightly wound Dr. Dre productions, features the sepulchral vocals of George Clinton doing a P-Funk thing; "All About U" contains a refrain sung by Nate Dogg over a beat that flirts with disco.

This was Shakur's first effort for L.A.-based Death Row Records. Between the time of its release, in February 1996, and his murder in September, Shakur visited the studio regularly, and the music he recorded, much of it released posthumously under the nom de rap Makaveli, hews to generic thug narratives at the expense of the more cosmic observations of his earlier work. Sure, the shoot-'em-ups and street confrontations are skillful, but they're missing the introspective dimension that lifts this album above so much of the posturing gangsta jive that came after it.

GENRE: 🅣 Hip-Hop. **RELEASED:** 1996, Death Row. **KEY TRACKS:** "California Love," "All Eyez on Me," "Skandalous," "Ambitionz as a Ridah." **CATALOG CHOICE:** *Me Against the World*. **NEXT STOP:** Snoop Dogg: *Doggystyle*. **AFTER THAT:** 50 Cent: *Get Rich or Die Tryin'*.

Oh, Those Steamy Turkish Nights

How to Make Your Husband a Sultan

Özel Türkbas

Disregard the cheesy cover and the how-to title (and the step-by-step photographs in the CD booklet). This is actually a fine document of Turkish nightclub music from the 1960s. It was put together by Özel Türkbas,

the belly dancer who, with this record, began a campaign to take "the art of domestic seduction" international. Her ploy worked: The record sold 150,000 copies in the U.S. and over a million in Turkey, and was the first of several Türkbas hits.

Put this on, and the first image isn't of some scantily dressed cosmopolitan housewife of the era sashaying around snapping finger cymbals. It's more like a public celebration or a scene from a bustling dance hall, where the band is cranking out brisk, precise music that has everybody moving. Built around the wizardry of clarinetist Mustafa Kandıralı, this ensemble slithers and undulates, creating swirling waves of hypnotic rhythm.

Türkbas in full regalia.

Several pieces leave room for improvised variations, and that's where things heat up. Kandıralı and violinist Cevdet Çağla keep the dance rhythm going while unspooling extended technically demanding embellishments. Like the swing-era musicians who had more to offer than "In the Mood," they manage to slip in subversive, jaw-dropping runs without shirking their main responsibility, accompanying dancers.

GENRE: 🌐 World/Turkey. **RELEASED:** 1969, Traditional Crossroads. **KEY TRACKS:** "Taksimler," "Tokat," "Tin Tin." **NEXT STOP:** Ivo Papasov and His Orchestra: *Balkanology* (see p. 576).

The Baddest Bartender Ever

Big, Bad, and Blue

Big Joe Turner

Big Joe Turner sang in a way that made musicians who'd played thousands and thousands of twelve-bar blues choruses sit up, take notice, and then turn up the heat. The Kansas City shouter had a famously powerful voice—

according to legend, he could rock a nightclub without any amplification. He delivered his hard-swinging mix of boogie, R&B, and jump

blues with a nonchalance that belied its roof-rattling. Some singers worked; Turner partied. Amazingly, the extra-large Turner had that ability from the very start of his career, which is documented on the early selections of this torrid three-disc anthology. Recalling his first performing opportunity, Turner remembered being sixteen or seventeen and penciling on a mustache to enter Kansas City's Backbiter's Club. A few years later, he could be heard singing at the Sunset Club with pianist Pete Johnson. Except he wasn't up on stage: Mary Lou Williams, the great jazz pianist from Kansas City, remembers that Turner would sing from behind the bar while serving customers. "I don't think I'll ever forget the thrill of listening to Big Joe shouting . . . while mixing drinks."

Big, Bad, and Blue documents the key points in the evolution of a prolific artist. The early sides, several featuring pianist Johnson, positively sizzle. Turner took Johnson's rhythm-centered approach to boogie, then added swinging horns, more jittery rhythms, and a tomcatting irreverence. The combination made him a star, a "boss of the blues" with a voice as big and boisterous as any America has produced.

GENRE: 🔘 R&B. **RELEASED:** 1994, Rhino/ Atlantic. **KEY TRACKS:** "Piney Brown Blues," "Flip, Flop & Fly," "Boogie Woogie Country Girl." **CATALOG CHOICE:** *I've Been to Kansas City* (featuring collaborations with Art Tatum). **NEXT STOP:** Louis Jordan: *The Best of Louis Jordan* (see p. 412). **AFTER THAT:** Wynonie Harris: *Bloodshot Eyes.*

The Hits from a Soul Revue like None Other

Proud Mary

Ike and Tina Turner

Tina Turner claimed a lot of pop culture face time in the 1980s. Helped along by a series of passionately sung ballroom-pop bonbons— "Private Dancer," "What's Love Got to Do with It"—the singer mounted a full-scale comeback, enchanting younger generations who maybe knew "Proud Mary" from oldies stations. For a while Turner was everywhere—with high-energy tours and a celebrated memoir telling all about the lean years with her abusive husband, guitarist Ike Turner (1931–2007).

Any record executive worth his payola budget should have seen this second coming as an opportunity to sell stuff from the "early days," when Turner was the most ferocious shouter on two legs. Alas, to get the full story, the Tina-obsessed have been forced to buy several hits packages from competing

Ike and Tina won a Grammy for "Proud Mary" in 1972.

labels, of varying sonic quality. This one is the best of the spotty field; it offers the charting hits but lacks the larger-than-life Phil Spector production of "River Deep, Mountain High," a single George Harrison once described as "a perfect record from start to finish." (That track is included on the Spector box *Back to Mono*; see p. 728.)

Still, the thrilling singles of *Proud Mary* serve as an introduction to the screaming cyclone of sound that was the Ike and Tina Revue. The title hit, which deserves its own shrine in the annals of pop, was one of several covers this duo transformed into platforms for Tina's famously gritty voice. (Others here include the Beatles' "Come Together," Sly and the Family Stone's "I Want to Take You Higher," and the Rolling Stones' "Honky Tonk Woman.") These and other less familiar tracks depend on Ike's terse, groove-conscious guitar—personal failings aside, this man was a master of the minimal Memphis backbeat with a knack for pushing his rhythm sections into a higher gear. Of course they're just trying to keep up with Tina, who revs at a level few humans ever reach.

GENRE: 🔘 R&B. **RELEASED:** 1991, EMI. **KEY TRACKS:** "Proud Mary," "Come Together," "Nutbush City Limits," "Honky Tonk Woman." **CATALOG CHOICE:** *Live in '71*, a CD/DVD combo recorded in Europe. Though it lacks modern production, this hot concert offers most of the hits. **NEXT STOP:** Ruth Brown: *Miss Rhythm* (see p. 123). **AFTER THAT:** Betty Wright: *Betty Wright Live.*

An Apex of Hard Bop

The Real McCoy

McCoy Tyner

J ohn Coltrane once described his longtime pianist McCoy Tyner this way: "He can take anything, no matter how weird, and make it sound beautiful." When Tyner recorded this hallmark of hard bop, he'd spent six years

in the Coltrane group perfecting the alchemic art of changing "weird" to "beautiful." He managed this primarily through the chords he played behind 'Trane: Where most jazz accompanists supported soloists with tight little clusters, Tyner used bold wide intervals—usually fourths, stacked into a massive two-handed power-chord attack—that gave the music the feeling of vast openness. A keen

Tyner began playing the piano when he was 13 years old.

listener, Tyner would follow the saxophonist's moves, punctuating phrases with jolting crashes of thunder. His chords are invitations, or outright challenges—"come explore *these* vistas."

Tyner was so integral to Coltrane's "sound" that it is downright startling to hear the pianist clearing out horizons for a different soloist—here, tenorman Joe Henderson, who scoots around in twisty circles, filling the spaces Tyner leaves. The five original compositions offer

Tyner's vision of hard bop, and it's surprisingly inclusive: The opener "Passion Dance" is built on a recurring phrase that suggests tribal ritual, while "Blues on the Corner" is a carefree Sunday stroll, and the stunning "Search for Peace" offers a moment of inward-looking tranquility. As with many of this era's best jazz compositions, the tunes are a starting point. It doesn't take long for Tyner and his crew to veer off the grid, and seek possibilities out in the upper atmosphere. That's where the real *Real McCoy* can be found.

GENRE: 🎷 Jazz. **RELEASED:** 1967, Blue Note. **KEY TRACKS:** "Passion Dance," "Contemplation." **CATALOG CHOICE:** *Enlightenment.* **NEXT STOP:** Bobby Hutcherson: *Components* (see p. 375). **AFTER THAT:** Joe Henderson: *Inner Urge.*

Francisco Ulloa ✦ Ultramagnetic MCs ✦ Uncle Tupelo ✦ United Sacred Harp Musical Association ✦ Usher ✦ U2 ✦ Ritchie Valens ✦ Dave Van Ronk ✦ Los Van Van ✦ Townes Van Zandt ✦ Edgar **U, V** Varèse ✦ Various Artists ✦ Sarah Vaughan ✦ Stevie Ray Vaughan and Double Trouble ✦ Suzanne Vega ✦ Caetano Veloso and Gilberto Gil ✦ Caetano Veloso ✦ The Velvet Underground ✦ Giuseppe Verdi ✦ Heitor Villa-Lobos ✦ Antonio Vivaldi ✦ Kevin Volans

Ultramerengue

Francisco Ulloa

Before the rise of the big Dominican dance bands in the 1960s, merengue was mostly made by groups of three or four musicians. These *tipico* bands centered on the tambora drum, which pumps out the pulse, and either the accordion or the four-stringed *cuatro* guitar—instruments that provide the harmony as well as the repetitive riffs, called *jaleos,* that keep dancers swirling. (In contemporary bands, the *jaleos* are usually handled by long-winded saxophonists.)

Zipping along at ultrafast tempos, *merengue tipico* returned to prominence in the late 1980s through the efforts of musicians such as accordionist Francisco Ulloa. In his hands, the music can feel like a tornado uprooting everything in its path—it's exciting and just a bit out of control. Formerly employed in agriculture (where one of his specialties was caring for palm trees) the native of Puerto Plata is a master of the squeezebox, and one of the few figures in Dominican music conversant in both traditional rural styles and the more modern dance floor derivations.

Ultramerengue showcases not just this broad range—its fourteen tracks include a snappy rewrite of an old Colombian folk song, several boleros, and a *pambiche,* which is slower and more sensual than "hot" merengue—but also Ulloa's preternatural composure. As the rhythm of this supercharged dance music careens wildly, he pumps out leapfrogging, impossibly tricky phrases that defy the laws of accordion physics.

GENRE: 🌐 World/Dominican Republic. **RELEASED:** 1992, Green Linnett. **KEY TRACKS:** "Juanita Morel," "La carta," "La negra Tomasa," "Ay Mami," "Dominga, que linda eres," "La Tinajita." **CATALOG CHOICE:** *Merengue.* **NEXT STOP:** Cieguito de Nagua: *Aprovechate.* **AFTER THAT:** Silvério Pessoa: *Batidas urbanas.*

Critical Beatdown

Ultramagnetic MCs

Before they started rapping, the four principals of the Ultramagnetic MCs (Ced-Gee, Kool Keith, Moe Luv, and T. R. Love) were part of two prominent New York break-dancing crews—the New York City Breakers and People's Choice. When the chance came to rap in 1984, they took what they knew about creating a party on the street and applied it in the recording studio, first on dizzying singles lampooning the perceived excesses of rappers ("Ego Trippin'") and then on *Critical*

Beatdown, which stands as one of the most ferocious debuts in the history of hip-hop.

Critical Beatdown is a full-on audio assault. It has songs with grabby catch-phrases worthy of a big-budget pop record; dense, relentlessly funky sample collages; and rapid-fire outbursts designed to, as rapper Kool Keith quips at one point, "make your dome piece spin like a windmill."

Ultramagnetic MCs formed in 1984.

That's not just boasting; the Ultramags' multisyllabic proclamations of prowess are supported by all kinds of musical trickery, from intentionally indistinct atmospheres ("Feelin' It") to stomping piano riffs (the proud "Mentally Mad"). The crew's ideas about sound swept through hip-hop quickly—Public Enemy mentioned *Critical Beatdown* as one inspiration for *It Takes a Nation of Millions to Hold Us Back* (see p. 618), and other hip-hop heads credit the album with establishing the very notion of "alternative rap," which focuses on enlightened discussions of community and responsibility.

The *Beatdown* grooves have turned up on lots of electronic pop since. (The British rave-rock pioneers Prodigy borrowed bits of the title track for their massive single "Smack My Bitch Up"; Prodigy producer Liam Howlett once called the album "the raw demo essence of hip-hop.") Amazingly, only one of the four MCs remains a creative force in music today—the hyper-kinetic Kool Keith, who has recorded as Dr. Dooom and the funky intergalactic gynecologist Dr. Octagon.

GENRE: 🎤 Hip-Hop. **RELEASED:** 1988, Next Plateau. **KEY TRACKS:** "Ease Back," "Ego Trippin'," "Give the Drummer Some," "Funky," "Bait." **CATALOG CHOICE:** Dr. Octagon: *Dr. Octagonecologyst.* **NEXT STOP:** Public Enemy: *Fear of a Black Planet.* **AFTER THAT:** DJ Shadow: *Endtroducing* (see p. 229).

The Swan Song of a Trailblazing Band

Anodyne

Uncle Tupelo

Uncle Tupelo crawled out of the factory town of Belleville, Illinois, in 1990, making loud Clash-like guitar noises while playing strange homemade hillbilly songs. The band, led by songwriters Jay Farrar (who went on to form Son Volt) and Jeff Tweedy (who molded Wilco, see p. 860), wasn't the first band to create "alternative country" or "Americana" music, or to blend electric guitars with banjos and mandolins. But it was the first since Gram Parsons to effectively expand the style's mythology, with a mix of gingham and leather, Woody Guthrie's wisdom and the Minutemen's rage.

This is the last of four Uncle Tupelo albums. All are populated with conniving drifters, miners courting danger, and other hard-luck cases one might encounter on the lonesome highway. The musical textures start out in a thick haze of feedback, and gradually, with each album, acquire clarity and nuance. By the time of its third effort, live-in-the-studio *March 16–20, 1992*, the band's emphasis had shifted completely—to delicately embroidered acoustic atmospheres supporting weighty, sometimes abjectly spooky murder-ballad narratives.

With *Anodyne* Uncle Tupelo circles back to rock, in an amazing way. The overall vibe is front-porch music made by a group of friends. But the band allows undercurrents of anger and dislocation to bubble to the surface of its songs. Everything is charged with possibility and volatility. Even when the arrangements are pleasant and straightforward, songs like the indignant "We've Been Had" feel like unsettled punk-rock powder kegs.

The tunes are often credited to Farrar and Tweedy as a tandem, but that is purely for publishing purposes: The two are in different

orbits. Farrar's apocalyptic, transcendence-seeking odes pull listeners into a desolate, often grim landscape, while Tweedy's chipper two-beat curiosities and open-hearted love songs offer a comfortable resting place, if not a touch of hope. This deft balance of opposing forces (country against rock, bitter against sweet, contentment against disillusionment) makes *Anodyne* riveting from start to finish.

GENRE: 🅡 Rock. **RELEASED:** 1993, Sire/Reprise. **KEY TRACKS:** "The Long Cut," "Give Back the Key to My Heart," "Chickamauga," "Anodyne," "We've Been Had." **CATALOG CHOICE:** *March 16–20, 1992.* **NEXT STOP:** Sixteen Horsepower: *Folklore.* **AFTER THAT:** The Jayhawks: *Tomorrow the Green Grass.*

No Harp, Just Voices

Southern Journey, Vol. 9: Harp of a Thousand Strings

United Sacred Harp Musical Association Singing Convention

Participants in Sacred Harp singing, the American tradition of worship song that's sometimes called "Shape Note" singing, are divided into four groups according to vocal range. Sopranos, altos, tenors, and baritones

each occupy a side of a square; they face each other when they sing, with the leader, often just a member of the choir, in the middle. No accommodation is made for an audience. Congregants sing for each other, for hours and hours. (Some involved in the music, which has enjoyed an explosion of popularity in recent years, suggest that the fervent intensity might be compromised by too many onlookers.) When musicologist Alan Lomax recorded this on September 12, 1959, at a convention in Alabama, the group went through over a hundred songs in a day, stopping only for the traditional meal they call "dinner on the grounds."

The mass of voices doesn't necessarily

generate intricate harmony. There's some here (see the psalm tune "David's Lamentation"), but more often, the group sings in open fourths and fifths, a hollowed-out sound that aligns Sacred Harp with early liturgical music from Europe. The songs, notated by shapes (different notes of the scale are represented by geometric figures such as squares and triangles), come in several types: In addition to the psalm-based pieces, there are folk tunes out of the English or Irish vocal tradition ("Wondrous Love"), lively revivalist tunes ("Homeward Bound"), and what are called fuguing tunes, rhythmically intricate pieces (like "Greenwich" and "Sherburne") in which the various parts start out singing independent lines. These culminate in rousing unison finales.

Music is the centerpiece of the annual Sacred Harp conventions, of course, but there's also fellowship. Lomax's surprisingly crisp field recording captures the sound of a community, finding strength in the sounds they only get to hear when they're all together, making them.

GENRES: 🌐 Folk ✝ Gospel. **RELEASED:** 1996, Rounder/Alan Lomax Collection. **KEY TRACKS:** "Homeward Bound," "Weeping Mary," "David's Lamentation," "Wondrous Love." **NEXT STOP:** Various Artists: *Religion Is a Fortune*. **AFTER THAT:** The Hilliard Ensemble: *Pérotin*.

Little Things Take This over the Top

Confessions

Usher

"Caught Up," one of the five (!) singles to chart from this megahit by Atlanta singer Usher Raymond, starts out sounding like every other competent but ultimately empty R&B single of recent vintage.

There's an uptight little vocal melody that requires Ush to apply his golden pipes to exactly four notes. Underneath that is a club-ready whomping beat that sounds like it was inspired by a drum corps rehearsal.

Nothing much, in other words, is particularly new. And yet the wily Usher keeps things interesting—just by the writhing, utterly "caught up" way he sings about this girl. He's a dramatist of the dropping-bread-crumbs school, sprinkling isolated thoughts that pull you into the refrain. And that refrain, when it arrives, is not shy: For months this was the most concentrated dose of ear candy available on the radio. It's where Usher makes like Michael Jackson circa "Billie Jean," playing the misunderstood victim. As he tells how the girl's got him wrung

out, he goes through every Jacko contortion, and sometimes even multitracks several vocals together, in a Marvin Gaye–like cascade. All it takes is a few spins through the title phrase to get addicted. Usher's wriggling leads, which are slightly different each time, do the rest.

Like many contemporary R&B projects, *Confessions* patches together tracks by different big-name producers. "Caught Up" is one of several pieces by the duo of Andre Harris and Vidal Davis, who'd worked similar magic for Jackson and Jill Scott. Their tunes sit alongside sumptuous ballads ("Burn," produced by Jermaine Dupri) and one thrilling club jam ("Yeah!," produced by Lil' Jon, with a cameo by Ludacris). Usually such record-making-by-committee results in a wandering, diffuse product—several hot tracks followed by filler. But Usher, smoothness personified,

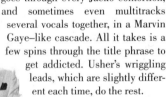

With *Confessions*, Usher became the first solo artist in pop music history to have 3 singles in *Billboard*'s Hot 100 Top 10 at the same time.

gets everything to mesh, making this one of the most creative examples of post-millennial urban pop.

GENRE: 🎙 R&B. **RELEASED:** 2004, Arista.

KEY TRACKS: "Caught Up," "Confessions Part 2," "Yeah!," "Throwback." **CATALOG CHOICE:** *My Way.* **NEXT STOP:** Luther Vandross: *Ultimate Collection.* **AFTER THAT:** Beyoncé: *Dangerously in Love.*

"Tear Down the Walls That Hold Me Inside"

The Joshua Tree

U2

U2 started out in 1976 as a zealot's idea of a great rock band. Furious about bloodshed in Ireland and racism everywhere, the Irish four-piece charged full-speed-ahead toward the power grid, fueled by self-righteousness and a razor-sharp rhythm guitar spearing holes in the upper atmosphere. They were true believers, and their stirring sound made not just the cause du jour, but belief itself, infectious: Being in a crowd when U2 was rattling off "Sunday Bloody Sunday" or "New Year's Day," you felt like you stood for something.

U2 (clockwise from top left): Adam Clayton, the Edge, Bono, and Larry Mullen Jr.

And then, fame happened. After spending years cultivating that scrappy underdog image, suddenly Bono and his pals were rock stars. This had uncomfortable implications—who wants to crusade alongside a self-righteous billionaire? As Bono acknowledged later in interviews, the band sensed that its tone had to change. And it did: *The Joshua Tree* is U2's vision quest, a tear through the vast open spaces of mythic America in search of illumination, if not personal truth. There's doubt in these songs with youthful idealism replaced by a slightly wary sense of the world.

Shifting the focus from outrage at external forces to frustration at internal vexations, U2 redirected its crusade: This is an album about turning inward, confronting that existential void, and living to tell about it. The refrains remind that fame and fortune isn't everything ("I Still Haven't Found What I'm Looking For"), and how the search for understanding can be overwhelming (the album opens with "Where the Streets Have No Name," and after a two-minute instrumental surge that is one of the great crescendos in rock, the first words are "I want to run, I want to hide, I want to tear down the walls that hold me inside").

That's one giant-sized statement of intention and it serves as a kind of mission statement: Every phrase uttered by Bono the bell-ringer embodies a touch of that restlessness. Every pummeling, military-march backbeat—and this album, which was produced by sound-sculpting experts Daniel Lanois and Brian Eno, is full of them—is aimed at breaking the chains, bursting out of the old patterns, finding new clarity. Some great rock affirms life as it is. This sweeping, majestic album is concerned with possibilities and ideals not yet glimpsed. It doesn't tear down the walls for you, but it does provide the impetus, and maybe even some of the tools, for doing the demolition yourself.

GENRE:  Rock. **RELEASED:** 1987, Island. **KEY TRACKS:** "Where the Streets Have No Name," "I Still Haven't Found What I'm Looking For," "With or Without You," "Running to Stand Still." **CATALOG CHOICES:** *The Unforgettable Fire; How to Dismantle an Atomic Bomb.* **NEXT STOP:** Peter Gabriel: *So.* **AFTER THAT:** Midnight Oil: *Diesel and Dust.*

Es Para Bailar

"La Bamba"

Ritchie Valens

Ritchie Valens has at least two significant rock-trivia claims to fame: The Los Angeles native is regularly identified as the "first Hispanic rock star." And because he was on the same ill-fated plane that killed the Big Bopper and Buddy Holly in 1959, he's one of rock's original road tragedies, forever part of "the day the music died."

Valens was seventeen at the time of the crash. He was just beginning to attract national attention as a hit-maker—he'd performed his first single "Come On, Let's Go," four months before on *American Bandstand*—and had only completed one full album of material. Valens's second single was "Donna," a ballad he wrote for his real-life girlfriend; "La Bamba" was on the flip side.

Valens's professional career lasted only 8 months.

Where "Donna" resembles countless mild-mannered '50s love songs, "La Bamba" is a shot of unrestrained wildcat exuberance unlike anything else. Building on the simple shooping beat of maracas, Valens creates a guitar melody for the ages, merging Chuck Berry–style riffs with the nimble lines of Mexican mariachi music—in fact, "La Bamba" is an adaptation of a traditional Mexican wedding song. Valens sings in phonetic Spanish (he'd been raised speaking only English), delivering the ridiculously catchy lines with such energy, no translation is necessary. This is one of the first instances of a rock song toppling language and cultural barriers.

Passionately covered by Los Lobos (see p. 453) for the 1987 Valens biopic of the same name, "La Bamba" is one of those watershed moments that tends to overshadow everything else. That's not fair to Valens, whose spry guitar inventions (see "Come On, Let's Go," "Bonie Maronie," and others on any decent compilation) exhibit a boundless energy that suggests had he missed that plane, Valens might really have gone on to shake up the music world.

GENRE:  Rock. **RELEASED:** 1958, Del-Fi. **APPEARS ON:** *Rockin' All Night: The Best of Ritchie Valens.* **ANOTHER INTERPRETATION:** Los Lobos: *La Bamba, Original Motion Picture Soundtrack.* **NEXT STOP:** Chan Romero: *Hippy Hippy Shake.* **AFTER THAT:** Los Lobos: *How Will the Wolf Survive?*

The Mayor of MacDougal Street, in His Prime

Inside Dave Van Ronk

Dave Van Ronk

These songs—blues laments, haunting spirituals such as "Motherless Child," and enduring ballads like "Poor Lazarus"—were frequently part of Dave Van Ronk's performances in Greenwich Village in the early

1960s. And as a result, they seeped into the consciousness of several generations of aspiring folk musicians and pop singer-songwriters. On the scene at the exact moment the folk revival gained traction, Van Ronk (1936–2002) was heard regularly at places like the Gaslight and Gerde's Folk City. His shows became magnets for such fresh-off-the-bus musicians as Bob Dylan.

A critic once called Van Ronk a "walking museum of the blues."

disc, *Folksinger* and *Inside Dave Van Ronk*, were both recorded in April 1962. The first features just his voice and guitar, the second adds dulcimer, autoharp, and twelve-string guitar. They stand not just as a high point of his art, but among the most important artifacts of the folk revival: Where some of his peers were writing brainy and somewhat detached odes, Van Ronk was digging deep into the songbook

Van Ronk was one of the few white performers who credibly sang the blues. A big man, his severe, husky voice was well suited to the style, as was his elemental, never flashy guitar accompaniment. While others wrote originals based on traditional forms, Van Ronk stuck to the source material, reinterpreting allegorical songs like "Samson and Delilah" in rousing, often surprising ways.

The two stellar albums repackaged on this

of the American experience, and creating music that resonates in still-wrenching ways.

GENRE: 🎧 Folk. **RELEASED:** 1962, Fantasy. (Reissued 1969.) **KEY TRACKS:** "Samson and Delilah," "Cocaine Blues," "Long John," "He Was a Friend of Mine," "Poor Lazarus," "Motherless Child," "Stackerlee." **CATALOG CHOICE:** *Black Mountain Blues.* **NEXT STOP:** Bob Dylan: *The Freewheelin' Bob Dylan.*

The Zippiest Van Van Ever

¡Ay Dios, ampárame!

Los Van Van

Salsa scholars are prone to calling veteran dance band Los Van Van, which was founded by bassist Juan Formell in 1969, "the Cuban Beatles." It's not an entirely reckless comparison: Like the Beatles, this ensemble has both refined and transcended established forms, as well as broadened the orchestral possibilities for everyone working in the genre. Its sly arrangements show how an ornate tangle of violins, trombones, synthesizers, and three lead singers can operate as one mighty machine.

Watch Los Van Van perform in a packed club, and you might get an additional impression: This band is also the Cuban Rolling Stones—raucous and wild, well skilled at pushing dancers toward the kind of bliss that's possible even with clothes on. This isn't always easy to hear on their studio recordings, of which many, alas, are dim and compressed affairs that inadequately capture the band's polyrhythmic attack.

This problem is rectified by the crisp *¡Ay Dios, ampárame!*, perhaps the best representation of Los Van Van on disc. It was recorded shortly after the rhythm-centered dance offshoot

Los Van Van was among the first Cuban groups to incorporate synthesizers and drum machines into its music.

known as *timba* swept Havana in the early '90s; as it has done with previous dance crazes, Los Van Van takes *timba* to new heights in terms of complex arrangement—anyone who says synths don't belong in salsa is referred to "Soy todo" here. The powerhouse band's energy doesn't overwhelm the singers, particularly gritty-voiced Mayito, whose taunting ad-libs include riffs on Santeria deities and the challenges of keeping a romance alive in modern Havana. Essential for any comprehensive library of dance music.

GENRE: 🌐 World/Cuba. **RELEASED:** 1996, Caribe. **KEY TRACKS:** "Deja la ira," "Soy todo," "De igual a igual." **CATALOG CHOICE:** *Lo ultimo en vivo.* **NEXT STOP:** NG La Banda: *En la calle.* **AFTER THAT:** The Fania All Stars: *Commitment.*

The Poet at His Peak

Live at the Old Quarter

Townes Van Zandt

A mong those who love the late Texas singer and songwriter Townes Van Zandt, debates rage about which album is his best, and whether or not he was more persuasive when he was sober, drunk, or getting there.

But there's general agreement on this: The best way to hear him was in a small club, where, accompanying himself on acoustic guitar, he'd share devastating tales of romantic devotion and its flip side, isolation.

The scion of an aristocratic Texas oil family, Van Zandt (1944–1997) came by his poetry with difficulty. He was diagnosed with manic depression as a young man, and treated with insulin shock therapy. This damaged his long-

term memory, and created problems when he consumed alcohol, which was frequently. He began recording in 1968, and despite several attempts at working within the mainstream music business—he even moved to Nashville briefly in the late '70s—he eventually became a semi-recluse, touring when he needed money and recording only occasionally. Meanwhile his stature grew as his songbook was raided by Willie Nelson and others.

This 1973 performance, taped at a small club in a rundown part of Houston, provides a vivid picture of his gifts. Van Zandt plays originals from his first several albums, mixing wry storyteller blues ("Fraternity Blues," "Talking Thunderbird Blues") with affect-free love songs ("If I Needed You") and poignant troubadour odes ("For the Sake of the Song," one of his all-time best). These compact, taciturn songs are plenty smart, and not at all pretentious—Van Zandt hides bitterness like a Texas poker champ, and delivers his lines, even the torn-up-inside confessions, in an offhand, almost deadpan

Van Zandt cited Lightnin' Hopkins and Bob Dylan as influences.

way that makes them absolutely riveting.

GENRE: 🌑 Country.
RELEASED: 1973, Tomato. (Reissued 2008, Fat Possum.)
KEY TRACKS: "Pancho & Lefty," "To Live Is to Fly," "For the Sake of the Song," "Waiting 'Round to Die." **CATALOG CHOICE:** High, Low, and In Between. **F.Y.I.:** Steve Earle called Van Zandt "the best songwriter in the whole world, and I'll stand on Bob Dylan's coffee table in my cowboy boots and say that." **NEXT STOP:** Gram Parsons: GP/Grievous Angel (see p. 581). **AFTER THAT:** Jimmie Dale Gilmore: After Awhile.

The Odd Sonic Schemes of an Off-Putting Visionary

The Complete Works

Edgar Varèse

Royal Concertgebouw Orchestra (Riccardo Chailly, cond.)

In March 1997, Flaming Lips frontman Wayne Coyne assembled more than forty cars on one level of a parking garage in Austin, Texas. He gave each driver a cassette tape with music he'd prepared on it, and told the participants

to roll down the windows or open the doors and crank up the volume. At his exact cue, the drivers hit Play, unleashing an odd sonic chase scene—with short melodic motifs rolling from one end of the garage to the other.

This audio "sculpture," which was performed for an audience estimated at over a thousand, had historical precedent—most obviously "Poème electronique," Edgar Varèse's

The writer Henry Miller once called Varèse "the stratospheric Colossus of Sound."

riveting installation for the Brussels World's Fair in 1958. Varèse (1883–1965) intended his piece to be played on three synchronized tape recorders, with the signals fed to multiple amplifiers and speakers. One of the most important early examples of tape-based composition, it begins with the tolling of far-off bells, and progresses through devices typical of the French composer's more traditional music—there are slide whistles and sirens, rhythmic tapping, and odd far-off squiggles that approximate gull calls. Each sound is a discrete "event" that functions somewhat like an image in a poem; the relationships between the episodes are unclear, and the listener is left to ponder the unusual juxtapositions.

The "Poème," Varèse's last completed work, arrived at a time when most electronic music had the resonance of a monotone doorbell. Though many criticized its abstractions, it has grown in stature. One reason is that Varèse didn't adhere to any single preexisting "system," like serialism, that defined much composition in the early twentieth century. Instead, his great works rely on a variety of techniques. They're governed by sharp-stick orchestral provocations one minute, highly ordered, almost Stravinsky-like motifs another, and pure gimmickry (the police sirens that terrorize "Amériques," rendered with great zest by Riccardo Chailly and the Royal Concertgebouw Orchestra here) the next. Such a mishmash of techniques anticipates the scattershot evolution of music in the second half of the twentieth century, and makes Varèse a patron saint of sonic scheming. His concepts still thrive in audio "installations" in art galleries and, every now and then, some crowded parking garage.

GENRE: 🎼 Classical. **RELEASED:** 1998, London. **KEY TRACKS:** "Poème electronique," "Amériques," "Ecuatorial." **NEXT STOP:** Frank Zappa: *The Yellow Shark.* **AFTER THAT:** The Flaming Lips: *Zaireeka.*

The Mother Lode of American Music

Anthology of American Folk Music

Various Artists, edited by Harry Smith

Superlatives fly whenever people talk about the *Anthology of American Folk Music,* a massive compendium of American musical history assembled by an eccentric scholar named Harry Smith and issued in 1952, at the height of Joseph McCarthy's anti-Communist witch hunt. Many musicians, Joan Baez among them, have described the set as a catalyst—these are the records that turned the light on for them, and helped them understand the majesty and inescapable humanity of American roots music. John Fahey, the folk artist and scholar, gauges the *Anthology*'s impact this way in the liner notes to the 1997 CD edition: "I'd match the *Anthology* up against any other single compendium of important information ever assembled."

That's not an overstatement. Here, on six CDs enhanced with multimedia content, are the building blocks of American music, the essential DNA of the blues, jazz, gospel, country, and then some. The information is strung together in a way that tells stories and builds mythologies—indeed, part of its genius is in Smith's organization, which divides the discoveries into sections devoted to "Ballads," "Social Music," and "Songs." The offerings include wild-eyed screamers (Charley Patton), fleet-fingered mountain banjo pickers (Clarence Ashley), medicine-show veterans (Jim Jackson), well-known song rescuers (the Carter Family), and woefully unknown Cajun characters (Joseph Falcon). Just about every selection has been influential in some way since the *Anthology*'s release. Not only did Smith reintroduce artists who'd been forgotten for years, he encouraged investigation into long-dormant styles and provided the troubadours of '50s folk with an abundance of source material.

Decades after the *Anthology* had made its mark, Smith was quoted as saying, "I'm glad to say that my dreams came true: I saw America changed through music." If that's even a bit accurate, it's because Smith set out to document not just music, but the way music functioned in American society. He showed how one generation can benefit from the sounds that captivated past generations. In seeking the ongoing musical conversations that traveled between old and young, black people and white people, rich and poor, city dwellers

and those isolated by miles, he paints a picture of an America connected by sound—and stories—long before it was connected by high-speed Internet and superhighways.

GENRE: 🔟 Folk. **RELEASED:** 1952, Folkways. (Reissued 1997.) **KEY TRACKS:** Furry Lewis: "Kassie Jones Pts. 1 and 2." Mississippi John Hurt: "Frankie." Joseph Falcon: "Acadian One-Step." Rev. Moses Mason: "John the Baptist." **NEXT STOP:** John Fahey: *The Transfiguration of Blind Joe Death* (see p. 268). **AFTER THAT:** Bob Dylan: *Highway 61 Revisited* (see p. 243).

The Origins of New York Hip-Hop

The Best of Sugar Hill Records

Various Artists

Several things were key to the early development of hip-hop. One was location: The style started at block parties in the South Bronx and (later) Queens, in forbidding neighborhoods notable for their abandoned tenement buildings and neglected playgrounds. Following the example of Jamaican artists, the early pioneers of rap set up on street corners, with just turntables and primitive amplification. They drew curious listeners by spinning thumping disco records and encouraging young poets to rhyme over them.

Equally fortuitous was the presence of Sylvia Robinson, the founder of Sugar Hill Records. At the exact moment hip-hop started to bubble, Robinson, a music business veteran who'd run disco labels in the '70s, got involved with several of its most promising personalities. She not only perceived the commercial potential of hip-

Melle Mel (above) was the main songwriter for Grandmaster Flash and the Furious Five.

hop, she knew what it would take, business-wise, to make it more than a momentary fad—it was her idea to unite three of the nascent scene's individual rappers as a unit called the Sugar Hill Gang.

There are fifteen tracks on this anthology of early Sugar Hill. Some sound dated now, some are surprisingly entertaining, and at least two remain absolutely essential to the canon. First there's the 1979 "Rapper's Delight," the pioneering yarn featuring Robinson's handpicked team of rap talents. The first rap smash hit, it was built around the beat of Chic's disco gem "Good Times" rerecorded by studio musicians, and featured boasts and taunts in common circulation at the time. Seeing the notoriety Sugar Hill got for the track, which has sold over eight million copies, the DJ Grandmaster Flash—the developer of the techniques of "cutting" and "scratching" vinyl records in rhythmic ways that became the backbone of hip-hop rhythm—signed with Sugar Hill in 1980. After several head-spinning singles, Flash and his rappers dropped "The Message" in 1982.

This was Sugar Hill's second genre-rocking explosion. To this point most rap hits were little more than idle boasts; here Melle Mel bluntly describes street life, talking about "Broken glass everywhere, people pissin' on the stairs, you know they just don't care." Many rappers who rose to prominence later, including Chuck D of Public Enemy and Queen Latifah, have said that it was "The Message" that first inspired them, and it's easy to hear why. Latifah once called it a "crystal ball perspective of life in the ghetto," but it's more than that. It's also a monster on the dance floor.

GENRE: 🎤 Hip-Hop. **RELEASED:** 1994, Sugar Hill/Rhino. **KEY TRACKS:** Sugar Hill Gang: "Rapper's Delight." Grandmaster Flash and the Furious Five: "The Message," "White Lines (Don't Do It)." **CATALOG CHOICE:** Grandmaster Flash: *Salsoul Jam 2000.* **NEXT STOP:** Run-DMC: *Raising Hell* (see p. 663). **AFTER THAT:** Kurtis Blow: *Kurtis Blow.*

The Coolest Reclamation Project in Music History

Buena Vista Social Club

Various Artists

When guitarist Ry Cooder and producer Nick Gold went around Havana looking for singers and instrumentalists who'd made their mark in the pre-Castro heyday of *son,* they didn't expect to find one legend (the vocalist Ibrahim Ferrer) working as a messenger for a shoeshine operation, or another (pianist Rubén González) playing for gymnastics classes. They also didn't expect that the simple act of bringing these veterans into a recording studio, a place many hadn't visited in thirty years, would lead to such warm and affirmative music—much less an international sensation.

Buena Vista Social Club was recorded in just 6 days.

Cooder recalled later that his first emotion was dismay: "It seemed obvious to me that these people, who were like legends to some of us, had been completely disregarded at home." Still, Cooder discovered, the musicians and singers had grown wary. "They had been through the carpetbagger thing before, where people would come and make a record with them and never pay. When we started I felt we needed to earn their trust . . . so we got them to tell stories."

Those stories led the group back to some old favorites of Cuban music from the 1950s—the swaying *son* rhythms of "Chan Chan" and the famed bolero "Dos gardenias." Cooder recorded everything live in a well-preserved state-run studio, and took care to re-create the classic sounds, at times just slipping in ethereal guitar commentary.

The result is easy-sipping genius of the highest order.

The initial *Buena Vista*, and a Wim Wenders film documenting the project, created demand for worldwide tours and more recordings in that Old Havana spirit. Cooder obliged with several subsequent records; the best of them is *The Buena Vista Social Club Presents Ibrahim Ferrer*, which was the first time in the captivatingly gruff singer's forty-odd-year career that he ever had his name on the front of an album. Recorded two years after the round-robin initial session, this one is even more lustrous. The band's tighter, and Ferrer responds to it with vivid, heart-heavy singing—he's plenty fiery yet completely in control of that wiggly-worm hipsway that remains a Cuban secret.

GENRE: 🌐 World/Cuba. **RELEASED:** 1997, Nonesuch/World Circuit. **KEY TRACKS:** "Chan Chan," "Dos gardenias." **CATALOG CHOICE:** *The Buena Vista Social Club Presents Ibrahim Ferrer.* **NEXT STOP:** Trio Matamoros: *Todos sus exitos.* **AFTER THAT:** Septeto Habanera: *Seventy-five Years Later.*

From a Small Label, a Mighty Roar

Cameo-Parkway, 1957–1967

Various Artists

The history of American popular music is more than performers and movements—it's also about the regional recording labels that documented and nurtured each nascent scene and dance craze. These often small operations, run by musicians or songwriters or engineers, were more nimble than the large established national outfits, and more attuned to the fast-changing tastes of young America. Among the best known of these are Sun Records, which captured the musical explosion going on in Memphis in the 1950s, and Motown, which did the same in Detroit in the 1960s. But there were other less-glamorous outfits that were nearly as influential, including Philadelphia's Cameo-Parkway, the twin imprints that gave the world Chubby Checker, Bobby Rydell, and a long list of incandescent and often overlooked singles.

Founded with borrowed funds by a music teacher named Bernie Lowe, Cameo (and later Parkway) was run out of the basement of Lowe's home. It started in 1956 and the very next year had, with its sixth 45-RPM single, a smash hit: "Butterfly," written by Lowe and his lyricist partner Kal Mann, and recorded by a South Philly rockabilly guitarist named Charlie Gracie. More hits followed, and many of them were first heard on a then-local TV show called *Bandstand*, a "dance" show featuring Philly teens. The program went national in 1957, but because it was taped in Philadelphia, Cameo-Parkway was often asked to supply talent on short notice. *Bandstand*'s host, Dick Clark, returned the favor by alerting Lowe to fast-spreading dance trends; it was his tip that convinced Lowe to rerecord "The Twist," a Hank Ballard song. The first single for a former butcher-shop employee Chubby Checker (né Ernest Evans), "The Twist" became an international sensation.

This four-disc set, a comprehensive reissue of the label's vast holdings, plays like a dream shuffle from a torrid decade of pop music. It contains big singles, from Checker's "Pony Time" to Dee Dee Sharp's "Mashed Potato Time" to the Orlons' "South Street" to the Mysterians' famed slice of psychedelic rock "96 Tears." It also offers early glimpses of artists who went on to success later—among them Patti LaBelle, the persuasive Philly-soul singer Bunny Sigler, and Detroit rocker Bob Seger. Taken together, these provide one clue why Cameo-Parkway didn't ever grab the kind of recognition Motown enjoyed: It didn't have one "sound," but many, scattered across all corners of the pop universe.

GENRE: 🎸 Rock. **RELEASED:** 2005, Abkco. **KEY TRACKS:** Chubby Checker: "The Twist." The Dovells: "Bristol Stomp." The Orlons: "The Wah Watusi." Bobby Rydell: "Wild One." Charlie Gracie: "Butterfly." **NEXT STOP:** Various Artists: *The Philly Sound.* **AFTER THAT:** Various Artists: *Eccentric Soul,* Vol. 1: *The Capsoul Label.*

The Concert That Started Rock Activism

The Concert for Bangladesh

Various Artists

Pull this out whenever your faith in the power of music begins to wane. Go directly to Billy Preston's spine-chilling "That's the Way God Planned It," which is performed with a star-studded house band. Turn it up. Listen as the organist and singer takes a packed Madison Square Garden through several minutes of uplift—first a purposeful sing-along hymn, then a rollicking double-time jubilee. It's pure bolts of energy, live on stage.

This set is worth the retail price just for that track. And for the opening raga, which features Ravi Shankar (see p. 692) and Ali Akbar Khan (see p. 421) in a beautiful twenty-minute discourse. And for five well-chosen songs by Bob Dylan, who'd only performed on stage once in the previous five years. His set includes "A Hard Rain's A-Gonna Fall" and "Just like a Woman," which features background vocals by Leon Russell and the concert's organizer, George Harrison, along with Ringo Starr on tambourine.

It's worth having just to hear Russell link the Stones' "Jumpin' Jack Flash" to the Coasters' doo-wop classic "Youngblood." And it's also essential for Harrison's turn, which features songs from *All Things Must Pass* as

Sales of this album raised $15 million for Bangladesh relief.

well as several Beatles compositions. Among these is "While My Guitar Gently Weeps." Eric Clapton is on stage, and he and Harrison engage in one of the more thrilling two-man guitar explorations in rock. As they finish each other's thoughts, the two extend and amplify the song's intent: You haven't heard the full gamut of gentle (and not so) guitar weeping until you've heard this.

Organized by George Harrison to help Bengalis made homeless by the 1970 Bhola cyclone, the August 1971 concert stands as the first large-scale example of rock activism. Its successes were more than monetary: Harrison and his cohorts focused the attention of the West on problems in a remote, far less affluent part of the world, and showed generations of celebrities how to use their media profile to raise cash and consciousness. Many significant fund-raising events have happened since; few have been as musically consequential as *The Concert for Bangladesh.*

GENRE: 🎸 Rock. **RELEASED:** 1971, Apple. **KEY TRACKS:** Billy Preston: "That's the Way God Planned It." George Harrison: "My Sweet Lord," "While My Guitar Gently Weeps," "Awaiting on You All." Bob Dylan: "A Hard Rain's A-Gonna Fall," "Just like a Woman." **COLLECTOR'S NOTE:** The concert is now available on DVD, and it includes performances that did not make the original album. **NEXT STOP:** Various Artists: *Farm Aid.* **AFTER THAT:** Billy Preston: *Ultimate Collection.*

Lots of Big Names Making (Surprise!) Big Music

Concert of the Century

Various Artists

Hype being what it is, there's reason to mistrust anything that calls itself the "Concert of the Century." Much like "one-night-only summit meetings" in jazz, galas of concert performers are usually staid occasions designed to generate piles of cash, with considerations of art secondary to those of scheduling and star power. This affair, organized by the violinist Isaac Stern to benefit Carnegie Hall, is different. It showcases the pianist Vladimir Horowitz playing chamber music with Stern and cellist Mstislav Rostropovich, and accompanying the German art-song titan Dietrich Fischer-Dieskau.

Concert of the Century celebrates Carnegie Hall's 85th anniversary.

Horowitz didn't usually appear as an accompanist; this version of Robert Schumann's *Dichterliebe*, one of the greatest German song cycles, is his only recording with a vocalist. It's spectacular. Like many singers, Fischer-Dieskau had a set approach to a piece, particularly one like the *Dichterliebe*, which follows a poet's progress through spiraling waves of heartbreak. Horowitz pays attention to the text, yet manages to nudge the vocalist away from easy and obvious renditions. The piece is a series of song fragments somewhat akin to the rock-era "concept album," with bits of song held together by a governing narrative theme. Horowitz plays as though he's interested in magnifying the ambiguities of Schumann's lines, and often his left hand floats between pulses rather than committing to a particular tempo. This atmosphere of fluidity and conditional give-and-take lures Fischer-Dieskau into one of the most electrifying, tension-filled performances of his forty-year career.

Horowitz shines on the Tchaikovsky Piano Trio as well, despite the fact that his initial entrance has all the subtlety of a 3 A.M. wake-up call. Once he calibrates his attack for the setting, Horowitz snaps off wondrously alert chords that serve as a kind of backbone, conveying organizing authority without big dictatorial gestures. Other highlights include Leonard Bernstein conducting Beethoven's "Leonore" overture and Bach's D Minor Concerto for Two Violins with Stern and Yehudi Menuhin.

GENRE: 🎼 Classical. **RELEASED:** 1976, Columbia. (Reissued 1991, Sony.) **KEY TRACKS:** Schumann: *Dichterliebe.* Tchaikovsky: Piano Trio. **NEXT STOP:** Robert Schumann: *Kreisleriana,* Vladimir Horowitz.

The '70s, in One Handy Package

Dazed and Confused

Various Artists

Original Motion Picture Soundtrack

Had director Richard Linklater managed to sneak Bachman-Turner Overdrive's "Takin' Care of Business" (and maybe the Led Zeppelin song that gave his 1993 film about '70s stoner kids its title) onto this fourteen-cut nostalgia trip, he would have encapsulated the experience of teendom in the Me Decade.

As it is, the *Dazed and Confused* soundtrack gets scarifyingly close. It's a proud parade of guilty pleasures, songs that burrowed into the consciousness of any kid with a Kiss Army patch on his jean jacket. Appropriately, there's a range—Nazareth's proto-power-ballad "Love Hurts" sits next to ZZ Top's archetypical Texas shuffle "Tush," and Sweet's laughably stilted "Fox on the Run" is offset by classic rebellion anthems (such as Alice Cooper's "School's Out") and heavy-lidded stomps (Foghat's "Slow Ride").

Scores of compilations are devoted to the hits of this era, but this one beats them all, largely because of its utterly perfect sequence.

Reportedly, one-sixth (!) of the film's budget was spent on soundtrack rights.

Starting with the kerranging chords of Rick Derringer's "Rock and Roll Hootchie Koo," the most intense one-hit wonder of all time and a must for any rock collection, it pulls listeners through a series of thumping anthems and arena sing-alongs, each more emblematic of the era than the one before. It might have been an average hour on rock radio in the hazy '70s, but today it sounds like pure genius.

GENRE: 🅡 Rock. **RELEASED:** 1993, Warner Bros. **KEY TRACKS:** ZZ Top: "Tush." Rick Derringer: "Rock and Roll Hootchie Koo." Foghat: "Slow Ride." **NEXT STOP:** Deep Purple: *Machine Head* (see p. 216). **AFTER THAT:** Bachman-Turner Overdrive: *II*.

Doo wop, doo wop, doo wop, doo wop

The Doo Wop Box

Various Artists

Only a handful of boxed sets are recommended in this book—in part because the often pricey multi-CD collections are designed for obsessives and completists, not average fans. There are, however, some areas where an extensive anthology is the best starting point. Doo-wop, the free-spirited singing style that began on street corners and in rec halls in the late 1940s, is one of them. It's certainly possible to build a library of great vocal-harmony-group singles one at a time. But it would take forever, and even then you'd probably miss some of the terrific lesser-known groups that light up *The Doo Wop Box*.

Significant research went into this anthology. Each disc covers a distinct historical period—doo-wop's origins (1948–1955), its role in early rock (1955–1957), its golden age (1957–1959), and subsequent revivals (1959–1987). Each represents the most prominent acts of the era: Disc two, which is devoted to early rock, begins with the spry "Speedoo" by the Cadillacs, followed by the massive hit "Why Do Fools Fall in Love" by Frankie Lymon and the Teenagers, with the Flamingos and the Clovers following in short order. But interspersed between the familiar blasts of exuberance are two mid-tempo ballads by Lee Andrews and the Hearts, one of the many lesser-known groups to

Frankie Lymon and the Teenagers were inducted into the Vocal Group Hall of Fame in 2000.

come out of the doo-wop hotbed of Philadelphia. Andrews sings "Tear Drops" as though he can't shake a love-related malaise; his voice has a dreamy, faraway gaze that makes the song haunting.

There are plenty of similarly underloved acts waiting to be discovered here—and just like the big stars, they specialize in creamy caramel harmonies, jittery beats, and boundless optimism. By organizing this chronologically, and alternating between the expected megahits and lesser-known tunes that are just as compelling, curators Bob Hyde and Walter DeVenne counter the perception of doo-wop as a passing fad, showing how the form evolved from slapdash street corner crooning to endlessly beguiling vocal choreography.

GENRE: ✪ Pop. **RELEASED:** 1994, Rhino. **KEY TRACKS:** Lee Andrews and the Hearts: "Tear Drops." The Teenagers featuring Frankie Lymon: "Why Do Fools Fall in Love." The Clovers: "Devil or Angel." **NEXT STOP:** Various Artists: *The Doo Wop Box*, Vol. 2.

The Ring-a-Ding of . . .

The Fabulous Swing Collection

Various Artists

When it was great, swing was a wonderful evening of dancing. The rest of the time, it was just swanky background music played by men in tuxedos. The swing era gave us titans like Benny Goodman, Count Basie, and Duke Ellington (see p. 317, 50, and 252 respectively), and scads of other brassy big bands whose legends were built one ballroom at a time. Most of these had a hit or two—swing was about individual songs—that turned on an opulent idea of rhythm, an infectious and easygoing glide that kept the dance floor in motion.

As good as many of these bands were, and as often as they recorded, their legacies amount to scattered individual singles. So the best way to really get the sound—and, more important, the feel—of these sultans is via one of the countless compilations devoted to the era. Believe the title of this one: RCA, which recorded many of the great bands of the 1930s and '40s, gathered these nineteen tracks from its vast holdings, and sure enough, they're all fabulous. In addition to the recordings that have become ubiquitous shorthand for swing—Glenn Miller's "In the Mood," Tommy Dorsey's "Opus One"—there are blithe and beautiful melodies (Dorsey's "Marie"),

demanding arrangements (Charlie Barnet's blazing "Cherokee"), flashes of individual greatness (clarinetist Artie Shaw's "Non Stop Flight"), and barnstorming band theme songs (Glen Grey's "Casa Loma Stomp"). Not recommended for those determined to sit still and listen.

GENRE: 🎷 Jazz. **RELEASED:** 1998, RCA. **KEY TRACKS:** All of them. **NEXT STOP:** Various Artists: *The Fabulous Big Band Collection.* **AFTER THAT:** Duke Ellington and His Orchestra: *Never No Lament* (see p. 252).

A Social and Musical Landmark

From Spirituals to Swing

Various Artists

A talent scout with an uncanny sense of what was coming next, John Hammond probably had more influence on the music of the twentieth century than any other nonmusician—he was responsible for discovering and recording Count Basie, Bob Dylan, Bruce Springsteen, Aretha Franklin, and Stevie Ray Vaughan, among many others. Despite such a list, the modest, liberal-leaning Hammond considered one night in 1938 to be among his most important accomplishments: the all-star From Spirituals to Swing concert, an extravaganza that was the first "integrated" program at Carnegie Hall.

From Spirituals to Swing chronicles two concerts at Carnegie Hall in 1938 and 1939.

The original intent was to pay tribute to Bessie Smith, who'd died some fourteen months before. Hammond assembled an evening, sponsored by the Communist journal *New Masses,* that would showcase all forms of "American Negro Music" (as the program read): raw rural blues and ripping boogie-woogie and then-blooming swing. The talent lineup

included the Basie band, the blindingly fast pianist Albert Ammons (heard in several settings, including torrid three-piano conversations with Meade "Lux" Lewis and Pete Johnson), bluesmen Big Bill Broonzy and Sonny Terry, and the pioneering gospel quartet known as Mitchell's Christian Singers.

The evening's written program reminded concertgoers that most of the performers "are making their first appearance before a predominantly white audience." The notes encouraged listeners to respond informally to the music, closing with a plea: "May we ask that you forget you are in Carnegie Hall?" The august venue doesn't seem to impact the musicians much—Basie's crew churns out the "hot" jazz that was then the rage, while Broonzy startles the crowd on "It Was Just a Dream." The *From Spirituals to Swing* box set collects related studio recordings (including, most curiously, spoken artist introductions Hammond appended in the 1950s prior to the concert's initial release) and performances from a sequel in 1939. Not all are sparkling gems—the sound is inevitably fuzzy, some selections are merely okay—but they catch the first moment black American music was presented as art, not just some exotic entertainment.

GENRES: 🎵 Jazz 🔵 Blues. **RELEASED:** 1959, Vanguard. (Reissued 1999.) **KEY TRACKS:** Sister Rosetta Tharpe and Albert Ammons: "Rock Me." Count Basie and His Orchestra: "One O'Clock Jump." Benny Goodman Sextet: "I Got Rhythm." **FURTHER INQUIRY:** *John Hammond on Record: An Autobiography* finds the talent scout recalling his encounters with some of the greatest musicians of the twentieth century.

"This Train's Got the Disappearing Railroad Blues"

Great American Train Songs

Various Artists

Railroad travel has probably inspired more indisputably great songs than any other mode of transport. Sure, cars are lust objects and planes are great when you need to get far away fast. But a train—lonesome whistle blowing, mighty engines thrumming down the tracks—that's a king-sized myth in motion.

The songs on this collection immortalize individual trains and their operators—the fearsome "Wabash Cannonball" (sung here by Willie Nelson), the superfast "Orange Blossom Special" (Bill Monroe), the "Rock Island Line" (Johnny Cash). But these legends, even

This classic collection pays tribute to the great American railroad.

the towering ones, often transcend particulars. These songs are slices of life from frontier America, an era when optimism ran high and railroads built by hammers and anvils and sweat connected people with their dreams. For a long stretch of the twentieth century, the rails represented possibility, opportunity, escape; as a result, they inspired songs about loneliness ("Waitin' for a Train"), the aftershocks of desire ("Heartbreak Express"), and, really, every

human emotion. At the same time, the rhythms of train travel have inspired countless musical approximations: To feel the graceful shuttling motion of a steam train, check out "Rock Island Line," which is built on a steady, unshakable backbeat. Listen to a bunch of train songs back-to-back, and you may feel like you're hearing the grand parade of American history, from westward expansion through the industrial revolution, chugging by.

Until, that is, you get to Steve Goodman's majestic "City of New Orleans." That song, considered by some to be the ultimate train song, laments the inelegant demise of railroad culture—the "disappearing railroad blues." Written in the early '70s and made into a hit by Arlo Guthrie in 1972, "City of New Orleans" is a pattering, easygoing sketch of life on the rails: As the Illinois Central train from Chicago to New Orleans ambles along, Goodman tells of the rogues in the club car playing penny-a-point poker, and the mothers with their babes rocked to sleep by the motion. He sings in a way that lets you know a grand and romantic part of America is vanishing, and it's worth caring about. If you don't sense it in the first verse, it'll hit you in the second, where Goodman describes how the sons of Pullman porters and the sons of engineers perceive the trains their fathers ride every day. "Magic carpets made of steel," he calls them.

GENRES: 🌑 Country 🎵 Folk.
RELEASED: 2003, Green Hill. **KEY**
TRACKS: Dolly Parton: "Heartbreak Express."
Elvis Presley: "Mystery Train." Willie Nelson:
"Wabash Cannonball." Bill Monroe: "Orange
Blossom Special." Steve Goodman: "City of New
Orleans." **F.Y.I.:** The refrain of "City of New
Orleans" gave the ABC-TV morning show *Good
Morning America* its name. **NEXT STOP:**
Arlo Guthrie: *Hobo's Lullaby.* **AFTER THAT:**
The Grateful Dead: *American Beauty* (see p. 322).

The Prayer Leaders Sing

The Great Cantors

Various Artists

Behold a man singing with such force it sounds like his rib cage is rattling. And another who's so wrapped up in an ancient melody, he seems almost lost. And another whose prayer for sustenance and well-being comes across like crying and singing and begging all at once.

These men are Jewish cantors, spirit guides who sing the forever questing prayers that frame Hebrew services. Their music is mostly made by a lone solo voice, sometimes supported by a choir; when a cantor performs in concert, the accompaniment may expand to include piano or organ. Their material is drawn from prayer

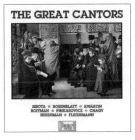

This features 8 cantors sharing peak performances.

texts—the songs here seek blessings for the month ahead ("Yehi rotzon milfonecho" is sung by Gershon Sirota, who died in the Warsaw Ghetto in 1943), mark important festivals (Salomo Pinkasovicz's "Ochiloh loeil"), and are heard at the start of Morning Prayers (Hermann Fleishmann's "Toras haschem t'mimo").

This anthology offers stellar performances from eight of the legendary cantors of the twen-

tieth century. Each has his own way of interpreting and embellishing text: Joseph Rosenblatt, who was born in Ukraine and emigrated to the U.S. in 1912, dashes off marvelously intricate spiraling lines that have the immediacy of jazz improvisation; Fleishmann, a lyric baritone, sings with a sober, earthbound deliberation. The strategies may be different, but the end result in each case is the same: Through these voices comes trembling and thundering affirmation of life.

Asked by *The New York Times* to share some of his favorite recordings, jazz pioneer Ornette Coleman (see p. 181) chose Rosenblatt's devotional incantations heard here: "He's making the sound of what he's experiencing as a human being, turning it into the quality of his voice."

GENRE: 🌐 World/Hebrew. **RELEASED:** 1990, Pearl. **KEY TRACKS:** Joseph Rosenblatt: "Av horachamim," "Tikanto Shabbos." David Roitman: "V'haarev no."

Berele Chagy: "In shenkel arein." Hermann Fleishmann: "Toras haschem t'mimo." **NEXT STOP:** Laura Wetzler: *Kabbalah: Songs of the Jewish Mystics*. **AFTER THAT:** Nusrat Fateh Ali Khan: *Mustt Mustt*.

From the Townships a New Kind of Jive

The Indestructible Beat of Soweto

Various Artists

Spend some time with these songs, which were recorded in Soweto between 1980 and 1984, and you may develop renewed appreciation for the indomitable human spirit. The musicians and singers represented on this compilation were creating this lighthearted, incredibly buoyant music during the South African apartheid. Though they make veiled acknowledgment of the political situation, these musicians are not overtly in the protest business—they're entertainers singing about courtship and gossip, and they're interested in creating a rhythmic escape. They do this with impressive style, a sound that is both ebullient and marked by fierce determination.

In 1987 *The Indestructible Beat of Soweto* won the *Village Voice*'s Pazz and Jop Poll for Best Record.

This anthology gathers music heard on Soweto radio in the early 1980s, the moment when the upbeat dance style known as *mbaqanga* swept through the townships of South Africa. The *mbaqanga* beat was not exactly brand-new (it contains elements of township jive and *marabi*, popular forms of the 1960s, as well as jazz and R&B), and some of the singers, including Mahlathini (see p. 467) and the inspired Amaswazi Emvelo, were established names. But the springy grooves carry the force of radical newness. They're like a blast of Black Sabbath after a steady diet of the Carpenters.

It only takes a few moments in the company of these suave syncopations to understand why Paul Simon and other rock artists were so enchanted by this music. (Ladysmith Black Mambazo, the choir that collaborated with Simon on *Graceland*, performs the transfixing "Nansi imali" here; this and other tunes could have provided Simon inspiration for his project.) More individual is Amaswazi Emvelo, whose "Thul'ulalele" is like a church service in miniature. These radiant, gloriously synchronized voices aren't ignoring what they face out in the world every day. They're just shifting the focus higher. Liberating themselves from the well-documented hatred and intolerance, they choose to celebrate light, joy, possibility—qualities that help make this music truly indestructible.

GENRE: 🌐 World/South Africa. **RELEASED:** 1986, Shanachie. **KEY TRACKS:** Ladysmith Black Mambazo: "Nansi imali." Umahlathini Nabo: "Qhde manikiniki." **NEXT STOP:** Mzwakhe Mbuli: *Resistance Is Defence*. **AFTER THAT:** Soweto Gospel Choir: *Voices from Heaven*.

The Exploits of an Unstoppable Reggae Production Machine

The Mighty Two

Various Artists

O ne miracle of reggae is the way it overcomes sameness: Almost every roots-reggae song has the same syncopated rhythm guitar part, the same beat structure (and tempo), and bass lines that travel the same familiar paths. And yet, the best reggae artists mold those building blocks into highly individual music.

Production is a key differentiating element, and for an astounding run beginning in 1975, the team known as the Mighty Two—producer and label entrepreneur Joe Gibbs and engineer Errol Thompson—had some serious mojo working. Immediately after combining forces, the two veterans put together a formidable house band known as the Professionals, which included such future stars as bassist Robbie Shakespeare, drummer Sly Dunbar, and guitarist Earl "Chinna" Smith. Then they began cranking out singles and terrifically imaginative full albums for Dennis Brown, Culture, the Mighty Diamonds, Peter Tosh, and others. Many Mighty Two productions were only known to Jamaicans, but a few, notably Culture's 1977 *Two Sevens Clash*, became global successes.

This compilation serves as an excellent introduction to the Gibbs-Thompson partnership. It has several hall-of-fame singles—Brown's "Money in My Pocket," the Mighty Diamonds' irrepressibly tuneful "Ghetto Living"—as well as expansive dub journeys and rarities. The works by lesser-known artists, including the talented Dennis Walks, show that the Mighty Two brought the same keen instincts—an inventive and uncluttered sonic sorcery—to the studio every day, no matter who was singing.

GENRE: 🌐 World/Jamaica. **RELEASED:** 1990, Heartbeat. **KEY TRACKS:** Joe Gibbs and the Professionals: "Rockers Dub." Prince Far-I: "Heavy Manners." Dennis Brown: "Money in My Pocket." The Mighty Diamonds: "Ghetto Living." **NEXT STOP:** Culture: *Two Sevens Clash.* **AFTER THAT:** The Mighty Diamonds: *Deeper Roots.*

Surprisingly Melodic Percussion

Music from the Morning of the World

Various Artists

T his recording of tuned percussion, an early classic of world music, was the work of a curious amateur. In 1966, David Lewiston quit his job as a financial journalist in New York and went to Bali to see what he could hear. He carried a portable tape recorder, one of the very first stereo models. Relying entirely on locals he met, he found his way to accomplished traditional musicians. He'd record these inventive gamelan (gong) orchestras, then take notes on the pieces—though not an ethnomusicologist, Lewiston jotted down the meanings and significances of each piece, documenting the rituals behind the music. His notes are an education in themselves.

MUSIC FROM THE MORNING OF THE WORLD
The Balinese Gamelan
&
Ketjak: The Ramayana Monkey Chant

Recorded in Bali by David Lewiston

This album was the first release in what would eventually become the influential Explorer series.

In a *New York Times* profile, Lewiston explained that he was driven entirely by what he called "the pleasure principle." He sought traditional music that intrigued him, and made sure that the musicians involved were comfortable. "If it's enjoyable, it'll be reflected in the music making. These aren't session musicians. These guys are farmers, and when they get together for music, it's basically to have a good time."

Music from the Morning of the World captures that—in surprisingly accurate (for 1966) audio. The clang and ring of the gamelan is powerful as an individual sound, but when a group of percussionists gather, the massed result can be overwhelming—rhythms that chatter and overlap in hypnotic ways, with little two- and three-note pitched phrases dancing on top. Lewiston definitely caught musicians in a comfort zone: In the excerpt of the "Barong Dance," the group slows and stops and switches meter as though guided by a paranormal force, each attack perfectly coordinated. Similar unity informs the music on the disc that's most familiar to tourists, the "Ketjak (Monkey) Dance": This is percussion as theater, and choreography, and a path to illumination. All at once.

GENRE: 🌐 World/Indonesia. **RELEASED:** 1967, Nonesuch Explorer. **KEY TRACKS:** "Gamelan Gong: Barong Dance," "Ketjak Dance." **COLLECTOR'S NOTE:** The entire Explorer series was reissued in 2003; among its other treasures are *Bali: Gamelan of the Love God.* **NEXT STOP:** Konono No. 1: *Congotronics* (see p. 431). **AFTER THAT:** Henry Kaiser and David Lindley: *A World Out of Time* (see p. 416).

A Secret History of '60s Rock

Nuggets: Original Artyfacts from the First Psychedelic Era

Various Artists

E xplorers by nature, musicians are often the first to recognize the works discarded by previous generations. Many times their discoveries are private epiphanies, shared with a small circle of friends and fellow obsessives. Not so with *Nuggets*: In 1972, the record executive Jac Holzman and guitarist and music journalist Lenny Kaye (later an integral part of the Patti Smith Group) assembled what they considered the best American garage rock of the middle and late 1960s. Their initial double album (and the much-expanded four-CD box issued in 1998) spotlighted chart-topping singles from one-hit wonders, minor regional bands that barely made the radio, and lots of devilishly inspired music in between.

The very first track, "I Had Too Much to Dream (Last Night)," by the Electric Prunes, is a good example of the curatorial bent: A Top 20 hit in 1966, it's a snarly Stones-influenced rocker, with a hook that should have made it a classic. Its loose pulsating energy sets the tone for what follows: over a hundred three-minute blasts of attitude and musical acumen. Heard one after another, these disciplined and sometimes deliriously unruly tunes are footnotes to the Official History, the stuff that scholars focused on the Great Bands (the Beatles, Cream, the Rolling Stones, etc.) often miss. The *Nuggets* compilers aren't saying that the Swingin' Medallions

The album's liner notes contain one of the first uses of the term "punk rock."

are as important as Cream, just that the South Carolina band made a few songs like "Double Shot (of My Baby's Love)" that deserve a bit of bandwidth in the big time capsule.

GENRE: 🎸 Rock.
RELEASED: 1998, Rhino. (Original issue 1972, Elektra.)
KEY TRACKS: Sagittarius: "My World Fell Down." Captain Beefheart and His Magic Band: "Diddy Wah Diddy." The Electric Prunes: "I Had Too Much to Dream (Last Night)." The Sir Douglas Quintet: "She's About a Mover." The Knickerbockers: "Lies." **BUYER BEWARE:** There are some Nuggets knockoffs on the market, and even Rhino's subsequent U.K.-oriented *Nuggets II* isn't as consistently strong. **NEXT STOP:** The Sir Douglas Quintet: *Mendocino* (see p. 709). **AFTER THAT:** The Dukes of Stratosphear: *Psonic Psunspot.*

The Soundtrack That Brought Bluegrass Back

O Brother, Where Art Thou?

Various Artists
Original Motion Picture Soundtrack

When it first appeared in 2000, Joel and Ethan Coen's retelling of the *Odyssey* as a Depression-era morality story didn't have much impact. As a film, it was a little bit odd, though haunting in spots. But people left theaters humming the prominently featured songs, rerecordings of hymns, and old-time laments that helped the Coens evoke the ethics and beliefs of a simpler time. That triggered a phenomenon. Within a year the soundtrack had sold over five million copies, renewed interest in classic bluegrass and traditional American music, and spawned an extensive concert tour and a slew of subsequent releases. For a while, any performer with a speck

of bluegrass in the back catalog was opportunistically riding the *O Brother* bandwagon.

There are only a few vintage recordings among the nineteen songs here (one, "Po' Lazarus," credited to J. Carter and Prisoners, was recorded in 1955 by folklorist Alan Lomax); the rest were produced by T-Bone Burnett in a spare style reminiscent of the single-microphone, wax-cylinder recordings of the 1930s. Nothing mucks up these homespun tunes, which provide a gravitas the film occasionally lacks. With its tales of infants dying and calamitous journeys, bluegrass turns out to be eerily dramatic, and such performers as Alison Krauss, the Soggy Bottom Boys, and the Cox Family function in the manner of a Greek chorus, offering empathy and gossipy wisdom. Among the many perfect moments uniting music and visuals, there's the climactic scene at a Ku Klux Klan rally: Here, the

The film's stars (from left): John Turturro, George Clooney, and Tim Blake Nelson.

sepulchral voice of bluegrass pioneer Ralph Stanley is heard singing "O Death." All by himself. It's an amazing song made more chilling, if that were possible, in this context.

GENRE: ☼ Country.
RELEASED: 2000, Lost Highway. **KEY TRACKS:** Ralph Stanley: "O Death." Soggy Bottom Boys: "Man of Constant Sorrow." J. Carter and Prisoners: "Po' Lazarus." **NEXT STOP:** Ralph Stanley: *Saturday Night/Sunday Morning.*

The Ageless Music of China

Phases of the Moon: Traditional Chinese Music

Various Artists

S everal times on this captivating overview, what sounds like a woman's fragile contralto appears, offering an animated, twisting-in-the-wind melody. But it isn't a singer. It's the *erhu,* a two-stringed violinlike instrument that,

when played by a master such as Wang Guotong, acquires eerie voice-like characteristics, evoking quiet sobbing or playful laughter. Coming from silk strings, such vivid expressions can be unsettling at first, but as the melodies of "The Moon Mirrored in the Pool" unfold, they become familiar, even soothing.

Phases . . . mixes traditional and contemporary compositions.

The *erhu* is one of the instruments that is central to China's traditional music. This collection, performed by the China Recording Company in 1980 and released on CBS Records in the West in 1991, offers glimpses of others. Among them: the zith-

erlike *qin,* a plucked instrument notable for its sharp articulation; bamboo Chinese vertical and transverse flutes, and the four-stringed *pipa,* which has between nineteen and twenty-six frets and a warm resonance similar to the mandolin. Each gets a turn in the spotlight—one joy of this collection is hearing how these diverse and exotic instruments resonate when they're at the forefront of an ensemble.

In China, traditional melodies are often linked to specific images. The musicians are expected to bring landscape-painting titles, like "Spring on the Pamir Plateau," to life.

To do this, they pluck strings just so, sustain breathy long tones, and essay swooping lyrical lines that suggest a bird in flight. These effects require deep concentration and phenomenal control—it takes methodical, highly disciplined execution to make music feel this effortless. It's a rigorous type of virtuosity, yet the players never exhibit any strain. In profoundly tranquil tones, they conjure flowing water and beautiful moonlit lakes, not merely describing nature but aligning every aspect of the music with it.

GENRE: 🌐 World/China. **RELEASED:** 1991, CBS. **KEY TRACKS:** "The Moon Mirrored in the Pool," "Days of Emancipation," "Spring on the Pamir Plateau." **BUYER BEWARE:** Much of what is marketed as "traditional" Chinese music in the West is shoddy synthesizer-heavy reworkings of folk songs. Look for some indication of traditional instruments. **NEXT STOP:** The Guo Brothers and Shung Tian: *Yuan.* **AFTER THAT:** Lei Qiang: *Chinese Traditional Erhu Music,* Vol. 1.

If Greeks Sang the Blues . . .

Rembetica: Historic Urban Folk Songs from Greece

Various Artists

Any music born in hashish dens and dependent on the impassioned singing of societal outcasts has something to tell the world. The style Greeks know as *rembetica* blossomed after the end of the Turco-Greek war in 1922,

when thousands of Greeks who'd been living in Turkey (and throughout Asia Minor) were repatriated. These returnees flocked to seaport towns like Piraeus and were seen as undesirables—in part because they brought elements of Turkish culture, including music and hashish.

The songs of *rembetica* are concerned with hopeless love and desperate attempts to stay alive, contempt for authority and dread over the hardships awaiting in jail. The singers, liberated by the hashish, seek ecstasy through flowing, sometimes wandering musical entreaties; they're accompanied by the distinctive sound of the stringed *bouzouki* and other ancient instruments. Because of its emotional forthrightness, *rembetica* has been compared to the blues,

Historic Urban Folk Songs from Greece

Rembetica loosely translates to "the blues of the Aegean."

but a more precise allegory is Appalachian folk balladry: Like the great balladeers, the singers of *rembetica* seek transcendence through verse after verse that offers florid elaboration on the basic tale.

This disc offers tracks from some of the genre's greats, both historical figures and more modern performers who've revived the core style. No hashish is required to appreciate these fervent yet gentle love odes, laments, and quests for illumination.

GENRE: 🌐 World/Greece. **RELEASED:** 1992, Rounder. **KEY TRACKS:** Andonis Dalgas: "Sousta politiki." Yiannis Tsanakas: "Rast gazel." Rita Abatzi: "O psilos." **NEXT STOP:** Savina Yannatou: *Sumiglia.*

Ah Ah Ah Ah Still Stayin' Alive

Saturday Night Fever

Various Artists
Original Motion Picture Soundtrack

Disco warped the world. It transformed ordinarily rhythm-impaired white people into wriggling masses of flesh, and gave them humiliating dances to do in public (see "The Hustle"). It tantalized club owners, who discovered that suddenly it was possible to fill the room just by hiring a DJ. This put lots of bands out of work, and in many cities permanently changed the live-music climate. Disco weakened the demand for albums by pop craftsmen and singer-songwriters; some executives blame it for the sharp downturn in the entire record business in 1979.

This document, an essential piece of any cultural history of the 1970s, captures the moment when disco was a marginally interesting musical enterprise. It was a very brief moment. Six months before this, the only defensible disco was Donna Summer (see p. 755). Two years after this monster hit, which eventually sold twenty-five million copies, the individual songs had been ubiquitous on the radio for so long, backlash was inevitable.

Heard now, removed from the frenzy, *Saturday*

John Travolta became an international star after playing Tony Manero in this blockbuster.

Night Fever remains striking for the deft shimmer of Arif Mardin's production, and the sharp, hook-atop-hook songwriting of the Bee Gees. The three Australian Gibb brothers, who'd been exploring disco and funk rhythms on two albums before this one, wrote a set of themes (for themselves and others including Tavares) sturdy enough to endure beyond the moment of hotness—including one shining pop ballad, "How Deep Is Your Love." Much was made of the trio's Chipmunkian brotherly harmonies, but few focused on *what* they were singing—radiant refrains that essentially say, "Even if you never go out in platform shoes and polyester, somehow, some way, you should be dancing."

GENRE: ✪ Pop.
RELEASED: 1977, RSO.
KEY TRACKS: Bee Gees: "Jive Talkin'," "Night Fever," "How Deep Is Your Love." **F.Y.I.:** The working title of the film was "Tribal Rites on a Saturday Night." **CATALOG CHOICE:** The Bee Gees: *Odessa.* **NEXT STOP:** Dr. Buzzard's Original Savannah Band: *Dr. Buzzard's Original Savannah Band.* **AFTER THAT:** Various Artists: *A Tom Moulton Mix* (see p. 823).

The Best of an Underappreciated Scene

Ska Bonanza: The Studio One Ska Years

Various Artists

S ka is a mongrel. Though often described as the Jamaican response to American rock and roll, it also contains traces of New Orleans swing, as well as elements of R&B *mento* music, the Jamaican folk dance style. When gently stirred together, and framed by the steady lilt of an electric guitar hitting the offbeats, the result is a buoyant, instantly uplifting groove.

Ska coalesced in the mid-'60s around musicians assembled by the producer Clement Dodd, first at Federal Records and then at his famed Studio One. These players, among them reggae guitarist Ernest Ranglin, saxophonist Tommy McCook, and keyboardists Jackie Mittoo and Aubrey Adams, understood that the music had to be at once loose, like island music, and tight, like Southern R&B, to succeed. As this compilation demonstrates, the collective caught that elusive balance right away, both on kicky instrumentals (the set opener "Nimble Foot Ska") and when backing one of the scene's emerging vocalists (like Alton Ellis, whose "My Heaven" is a straight-up doo-wop ballad).

This two-disc survey captures a wide range of early ska, augmenting the radio singles with more experimental material. Among its treasures are several tunes featuring the "house band," the Skatalites, early ska attempts by Bob Marley and the Wailers, and agitated jive outbreaks by Don Drummond. Like many ska entertainers, Drummond recognized that he needed great musicians to put the sound across, and he sought to keep them happy by showcasing their talents. As a result, many of his singles have instrumental breaks featuring such enchanting soloists as Roland Alphonso, whose talkative saxophone was a key part of "the sound of young Jamaica."

GENRE: 🌐 World/Jamaica. **RELEASED:** 2006, Heartbeat/Rounder. **KEY TRACKS:** The Skatalites: "Black Sunday." Alton Ellis: "My Heaven." Don Drummond: "Man in the Street." **NEXT STOP:** Desmond Dekker and the Aces: *Action!* **AFTER THAT:** Jackie Mittoo: *Wishbone.*

Transfixing Sounds from the Rain Forests of South America and the Caribbean

The Spirit Cries

Various Artists

F or those who live under its canopy (and, for that matter, pretty much everyone who breathes), the rain forest is a life-giver—the source of shelter, basic sustenance, and crucial medicinal plants. It's also the meeting point between the earthly and spirit worlds. Appeals to higher powers are common in the music of the South American and Caribbean rain forest, as are quests for higher states of consciousness. On these transfixing field recordings, made between 1947 and 1987, the people of once-isolated cultures in Panama, Peru, Belize, and elsewhere share the music that helps speak to and summon the spirit forces that are so central to their lives.

This music—a mix of grieving songs, social dances, prayers, and healing rituals that have been handed down for generations—is wild and unkempt, shot through with unrestrained feeling. The performers aren't entertainers; they sing to accomplish things. On the first of several "Abaimahani" songs of mourning from the Garifuna people of Belize, Alphonsa Casmino can be heard trembling as she sings the melody, which came to her in a dream. Her voice weary and frail, she honors her deceased sister through a series of upturned, ascending lines—each one a fresh question for the heavens.

Other highlights include the somber incantations of a Choco Indian shaman from Colombia, who drives feverish spirits away by singing while shaking a palm frond ("Healing Song"); the synched-up exchanges between lead voice and chorus that define the songs of the Peruvian Ashaninka people, and the rhythmic solo singing, marked by wide intervallic leaps, of the Shipibo from Peru.

All the cultures represented on this set, which was curated by Grateful Dead drummer Mickey Hart from collections in the Library of Congress's Endangered Music Project, have at least one thing in common: Their ways of life have been under siege, threatened by deforestation, climate change, and the destruction of ancestral homelands deep within the forests. That makes this collection something of a window onto a vanishing world: If the rain forests are destroyed, it's only a matter of time before these stark and devastating songs disappear, too—each an irretrievable loss.

GENRE: 🌐 World/Latin America.
RELEASED: 1993, Rykodisc. **KEY TRACKS:** "Shipibo Song," "Ashaninka Songs," "Healing Song," "Grating Song," "Abaimahani." **NEXT STOP:** Various Artists: *Mbuti Pygmies of the Ituri Rainforest.* **AFTER THAT:** Various Artists: *Music of Indonesia 7: Music from the Forests of Riau and Mentawai.*

A Glittering Example of Show Business

Stormy Weather

Various Artists

Original Motion Picture Soundtrack

T he plot's pretty lean, but the lineup of musical talent involved in this big-budget 1943 picture more than compensates. By the time Cab Calloway, as his hi-dee-ho hipster self, kicks off the variety show that becomes the film's opulent finale, we've already heard Fats Waller romp through "Ain't Misbehavin'," Lena Horne sing "Stormy Weather," and a duet between Horne and Bill "Bojangles" Robinson on "I Can't Give You Anything but Love."

A song-and-dance extravaganza featuring an all–African American cast, *Stormy Weather* hails from a time when the music really carried a musical. True, not every song is as memorable as Horne's signature "Stormy Weather," the Harold Arlen–Ted Koehler classic that appears near the end of the film. Horne treats the tune as a moody lament; she observes that since her man left, it "keeps raining all the time," her phrases registering as a series of inconsolable aches. Horne's performance here ranks easily among the most memorable interpretations of an American standard. But everything moves with showbiz zip, and there are times when some of the lesser-known singers—like Mae Johnson, who does "I Lost My Sugar in Salt Lake City"—strut right in and surprise everybody. Heck, Horne

Lena Horne and Bill "Bojangles" Robinson brighten the scene of *Stormy Weather*.

surprises too, hamming like a blithe showgirl on the jungle-tinged novelty "Diga Diga Doo." And watch out when the Calloway band gets

involved. The second half of the soundtrack offers several band showcases—"Jumpin' Jive," a sizable Calloway hit, is rendered as if the band were doing it for the first time, and there's a treatment of "Body and Soul" that shows that the rhythm didn't always have to be red-hot for this band to be great.

GENRES: 🎭 Musicals 🎤 Vocals. **RELEASED:** 1943, Twentieth Century–Fox. **KEY TRACKS:** "Stormy Weather," "Ain't Misbehavin'," "Jumpin' Jive." **NEXT STOP:** Lena Horne: *At the Sands.* **AFTER THAT:** Cab Calloway: *Are You Hep to the Jive?*

The Origins of the Dance Remix

A Tom Moulton Mix

Various Artists

The brainstorm hit Tom Moulton, a music-biz promotion exec turned male model, at a nightclub on Fire Island, New York, in the early '70s. Wouldn't it be great if somebody extended disco songs for dancers?

At that time, DJs played the three-minute single version of a song; when one hit finished, they'd just start another one. This created lots of "churn" on the dance floor, as patrons fled songs they didn't like. "I just thought it was a shame that the records weren't longer, so people could really start getting off," Moulton recalls in the liner notes of this two-disc set, which chronicles what happened after that brainstorm. Moulton, the father of the

"I get such pleasure and joy out of taking something and trying to bring it to another level."
—Tom Moulton

dance remix, created a new way to experience music.

As disco crested in the mid-'70s, Moulton convinced several labels to give him access to the master tapes of singles. He took the songs apart, emphasizing percussion breaks and recurring guitar and keyboard riffs over the "hooks" from the radio versions. (Gloria Gaynor's response after hearing Moulton's mix of an early single: "I don't sing much.") His next innovation had to do with delivery: He and engineer José Rodriguez put the remixes on twelve-inch vinyl singles, which allowed for longer tracks and better fidelity, particularly in the bass frequencies.

Those developments helped accelerate the growth of disco—and much subsequent urban music, including hip-hop. Moulton's mixes are fascinating musical expansions that show how an initial inspiration can be reassembled into countless alternate ones. The collection includes several dazzlingly reborn hits (Eddie Kendricks's 1973 hit "Keep On Truckin'") and at least as many underappreciated gems—including BT Express's "Peace Pipe" and Orlando Riva Sound's super-funky 1977 "Moonboots." This isn't a definitive history of disco—it's more a time-trip back to Studio 54 during the frenzied years, when you didn't have a prayer of getting on the floor. These mixes are a big reason why.

GENRE: 🎵 R&B. **RELEASED:** 2006, Soul Jazz. **KEY TRACKS:** Eddie Kendricks: "Keep On Truckin'." MFSB: "Love Is the Message." BT Express: "Peace Pipe." Orlando Riva Sound: "Moonboots." **NEXT STOP:** Various Artists: *Journey into Paradise: The Larry Levan Story.* **AFTER THAT:** Various Artists: *Salsoul Presents: Disco Trance and Cosmic Flavas.*

What's Playing in the Chill Room

Trainspotting

Various Artists
Original Motion Picture Soundtrack

Trainspotting is one in a long string of film soundtracks from the 1990s to feature staggering assemblages of big-name talent. It's better than just about all of them. It begins with one of the great pulverizing rock anthems of 1977, Iggy Pop's "Lust For Life," and from there features indelible truth-telling tracks from Lou Reed ("Perfect Day," from 1972) and New Order (the upbeat "Temptation," from 1982), and a gorgeous Brian Eno study in melancholy, "Deep Blue Day." These are interspersed with pieces written expressly for the film—an upbeat bit of pop dance hall from Pulp ("Mile End"), a slice of quintessential Brit pop (Blur's "Sing"), the spacey, dub-style, ten-minute title instrumental from Primal Scream.

The film, based on Irvine Welsh's bestselling novel about club kids with drug dependen-

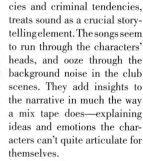

Trainspotting gathers important rock recordings from the 1970s, '80s, and '90s.

cies and criminal tendencies, treats sound as a crucial storytelling element. The songs seem to run through the characters' heads, and ooze through the background noise in the club scenes. They add insights to the narrative in much the way a mix tape does—explaining ideas and emotions the characters can't quite articulate for themselves.

And like a great mix tape, *Trainspotting* is riveting because it exists within carefully defined sonic parameters. Though it draws on many styles and eras, it has an aura, a signature print. Each of these pieces in some way underscores an element of the story, catching the vague sense of gloom and desperation that unites these sad characters. The mood becomes the star, connecting often balkanized worlds, establishing a through-line that is actually stronger on the soundtrack than it is in the film. Though it appeared during a curious pop-culture moment when rock bands and suddenly hot electronica stars were sniffing around to see what each might steal from the other, it's no scattershot kitchen-sink mashup: Very few compilations of music capture—and sustain—a mood as thrillingly and completely as *Trainspotting* does.

GENRES: ⓚ Rock ⓦ Electronica. **RELEASED:** 1996, EMI. **KEY TRACKS:** Iggy Pop: "Lust for Life." Brian Eno: "Deep Blue Day." New Order: "Temptation." Primal Scream: "Trainspotting." Blur: "Sing." **F.Y.I.:** In 2007, *Vanity Fair* ranked *Trainspotting* the seventh best film soundtrack in history. **NEXT STOP:** Dirty Vegas: *Dirty Vegas.* **AFTER THAT:** Various Artists: *Hacienda Classics.*

Opening Spirit Pathways

World of Gnawa

Various Artists

The Gnawa brotherhoods of Morocco chase ecstasy—and express devotion—through drums and chants. In nighttime rituals notable for both their games and their solemnity, these Islamic seekers trade repeated call-and-response phrases: A lead voice issues a strident, sometimes taunting idea, and the others around the circle answer back. Accompanying (and often dictating the pace of) this communication is a nimble, mesmerizing rhythm from the *tabi*, a double-sided drum played with olive-wood sticks, and large metal castanets called *qareqeb*. The three-stringed *guinbri*, which is either plucked or slapped, provides sketchy harmony.

Gnawa music gets its driving rhythm from West Africa (the polyrhythms traveled with slaves to Morocco) and its devotional orientation from Islam. This makes a powerful combination, especially when delivered by impassioned voices like those captured on the compilation *World of Gnawa*, which was recorded in Morocco and features many of the form's ace practitioners. A pronounced mystical "spirit" drives every selection, from the opening call to ritual ("Aada 1," a twelve-minute appeal to the prophet Muhammad intended to "purify" the intentions of the assembled musicians) to songs dedicated to wandering Sufi mystics and others hoping to be whisked into a trance state. The musicians invariably reach that state—just by locking into the propulsive, endlessly varied rhythms. Even pieces that last twenty minutes seem to fly by.

There have been a number of Western attempts at harnessing the Gnawa spirit—jazz pianist Randy Weston has recorded several albums with Moroccan musicians. These often focus on the more surface "entertainment" aspects of Gnawa ritual. The well-annotated *World of Gnawa*, which includes English translations of the lyrics, goes much deeper.

GENRE: 🌐 World/Morocco. **RELEASED:** 2001, Rounder. **KEY TRACKS:** "Aada 1," "Neqsha," "Hammadi." **NEXT STOP:** Randy Weston: *The Splendid Master Gnawa Musicians of Morocco.* **AFTER THAT:** Grateful Dead: *Fillmore West 1969.*

A Magical Night with the Husky-Voiced Queen

Live in Japan

Sarah Vaughan

Jazz vocal music peaked on September 24, 1973. On that night, Sarah Vaughan gave a concert at the Sun Plaza Hall in Tokyo. She and her trio went through many of the tunes she'd been singing for decades— "There Will Never Be Another You," "On a Clear Day," "Bye Bye Blackbird"—in other words, the jazz singer's songbook.

Virtually every one of the twenty-seven songs on this set offers an unsurpassed thrill. Though Vaughan's studio records (including her magical 1954 *Sarah Vaughan with Clifford Brown* and the equally joyous *Swingin' Easy* from the same year) are considered definitive post-bebop singing, *Live in Japan* improves on these landmarks. It finds Vaughan linking the flirtatious, breezing-along style of her early years to more cerebral pursuits, including bold top-to-bottom reconceptions of familiar melodies. She drapes extended phrases across the rhythm in almost haphazard fashion, rendering normal notions of tempo irrelevant. She rewrites some themes to make them much hipper—"Like Someone in Love" has a touch of Coltrane in it, while "My Funny Valentine" aims for the pastel colors associated with pianist Bill Evans. There's a rare moment when Vaughan, the most musically astute of vocalists, steps behind the piano to accompany herself on an ethereal "The Nearness of You," gently (and at times almost invisibly) framing her smoldering vocals.

Another highlight is Antonio Carlos Jobim's "Wave," which Vaughan starts as a majestic and super-slow ballad. When the bossa nova pulse kicks in on the second chorus, it brings with it breathtaking vistas. Like all great music, this "Wave" offers nothing less than a new way of seeing the world. That one track is enough to take your breath away. And then along comes another perfect little miracle, and then another, until the show's over. That's when it hits you: This all happened on one night.

GENRES: 🅘 Jazz 🅥 Vocals. **RELEASED:** 1974, Mainstream/Columbia. **KEY TRACKS:** "Wave," "Like Someone in Love," "My Funny Valentine." **CATALOG CHOICES:** *Swingin' Easy; In the Land of Hi-Fi; Brazilian Romance.* **NEXT STOP:** Shirley Horn: *You Won't Forget Me.* **AFTER THAT:** Carmen McRae: *Carmen Sings Monk* (see p. 491).

A Texas-Size Shot of Blues Guitar

The Sky Is Crying

Stevie Ray Vaughan and Double Trouble

Posthumous collections of material from the deep vaults are usually grab bag affairs—a few shining moments surrounded by tracks that were left on the cutting room floor for a reason. The opposite is true of *The Sky Is Crying,* the first such collection released after Texas guitar hotshot Stevie Ray Vaughan died in a helicopter crash in 1990. These ten uniformly strong studio performances, recorded between 1984 and 1989, map the appetites and proclivities of the mighty maestro of the pitch-bend.

One of the last discoveries of legendary ear John Hammond (Bob Dylan, Bruce Springsteen, and Billie Holiday were among his earlier finds), Vaughan had the chops to astound people. But he used them wisely. These outtakes display flashes of technical wizardry yet are more notable for their restraint, moments when Vaughan clears away thickets of blues guitar cliché with wrenching single-note laser beams of emotion.

And as on the solid but often erratic studio records he put together while alive, Vaughan makes those discoveries across an impressive range of styles: *Sky* includes one of his signature Hendrix covers, "Little Wing," ǡ trip through Lonnie Mack's "Wha down-tempo treatment of jazz gui̇ Burrell's "Chitlins con Carne" that is notable for its gentle octaves and questioning, impossibly liquid phrases. There's also an extremely rare acoustic moment, "Life by the Drop," that reinforces a less-obvious aspect of Vaughan's art: He'd attack his instrument with an almost terrifying savagery, then turn around and melt your heart with some improbable guitar outbursts that sounded, for all the world, like the sky really was crying.

GENRE: 🔵 Blues. **RELEASED:** 1991, Epic. **KEY TRACKS:** "Little Wing," "Chitlins con Carne," "Life by the Drop." **CATALOG CHOICE:** *Texas Flood.* **NEXT STOP:** Joe Louis Walker: *Blue Soul.* **AFTER THAT:** Roy Buchanan: *Sweet Dreams: The Anthology.*

Folk-Pop Exploded

Solitude Standing

Suzanne Vega

"My name is Luka, I live on the second floor." Thus begins New York pop-folk songwriter Suzanne Vega's disquieting story of a city kid's attempt to deal with a volatile (and seemingly violent) home situation. Vega focuses not on the details of the kid's plight but on his awkwardness. She sketches his brave front—and the way it barely hides his fear, his sense of being overwhelmed.

The song, one of several radio hits on *Solitude Standing,* sparked nationwide discussion about the domestic abuse of children. One reason it touched a nerve is its undeniable catchiness. Vega goes for exuberant refrains cush-

Solitude Standing went multiplatinum in the U.S.

ioned by cooing background vocals—if there ever was an effective counterbalance to a bleak and disturbing scene, this runaway musical optimism is it.

"Luka" is but one highlight of the entrancing *Solitude Standing,* the follow-up to Vega's critically lauded 1985 debut. Where her first collection centered on meditative acoustic guitar and lots of breathless words, this one, made with the help of downtown New York musicians, presents Vega using colors and shades and shadowy orchestrations. The album ranges from pure pop to almost ambient meditations, and every track resonates differently. The title tune alternates between a steady rock pulse and ethereal free-falling passages that seem borne from a daydream. "Calypso" is a gorgeously liquid homage to undersea explorers, while "Ironbound/Fancy Poultry" floats effortlessly between 3/4 and 4/4 time to sketch a Newark street scene.

Solitude Standing yielded another improbable hit—the cinema-verité "Tom's Diner," which Vega sings a cappella. This song, which was remixed by the British producers DNA first without her permission then with her blessing, became a massive club hit the following year. It has now been redone over thirty different ways, by Destiny's Child, Lil' Kim, and others. When audio engineer Karlheinz Brandenburg was developing the MP3 audio format for computers, he used the original "Tom's Diner" as a test, explaining that if he could get the program to translate Vega's warm voice, it could translate anything.

GENRES: Pop 🅕 Folk. **RELEASED:** 1987, A&M. **KEY TRACKS:** "Solitude Standing," "Ironbound/Fancy Poultry," "Calypso." **CATALOG CHOICE:** *Suzanne Vega.* **NEXT STOP:** Laura Veirs: *Year of Meteors.* **AFTER THAT:** Maria Muldaur: *Maria Muldaur* (see p. 531).

The Grace of Brazil, the Fire of Rock

Tropicália 2

Caetano Veloso and Gilberto Gil

When veteran music stars try to return to their glory days, what usually comes out is a messy, pathetic echo—see *Bat Out of Hell II*. Happily *Tropicália 2*, the reprise of the pathfinding collaboration between Brazilian songwriters Caetano Veloso and Gilberto Gil, is a marked exception to this rule. It was recorded in 1993, twenty-five years after *tropicália*, the radical cultural movement they spearheaded, opened up young Brazil to the ideas of rock and roll, Andy Warhol, and surrealism.

Influenced by the great flowering of late '60s rock in Britain and America, Veloso and Gil integrated its sensibility into a psychedelic whirl that first and foremost affirmed Brazil. It was a celebration of cultural identity

Rolling Stone called *Tropicália 2* a "historic collaboration between Brazil's two 50-something songwriting giants at the peak of their powers."

and at the same time a sneaky subversion of it.

Of course, by 1993, much of pop music trafficked in this type of crafty global mixing, with regional distinctions invoked as quaint curiosities or novelty items. The mission of *Tropicália 2* might be summed up as one of reverse revolution, or recontextualization: As they lay pretty themes over beachcombing Afro-Brazilian grooves, Veloso and Gil seek the shards of heritage worth preserving. They invoke goddesses of the Candomblé faith ("Dada"), use samba phrases to quietly decry the persistence of racism in the world ("Haiti"), and explore parallels between Brazilian art film and music ("Cinema novo").

Throughout, there's the sense that these two thinkers—Veloso the unrepentant musical adventurer and Gil, who became Brazil's minister of culture in 2003 (another instance of a former radical joining the establishment)—are taking stock, reflecting on *tropicália's* impact. They've grown from hell-raisers into perceptive and often elegant poets; now when they sing of Brazil, they do so with reverence and a touch of contrition, celebrating things they may have sneered at in their heady youth. This gives *Tropicália 2* an incredibly rich perspective. As Veloso and Gil expand the basic sound, they reconnect with—and extend—the rebel impulse that got *tropicália* going in the first place.

GENRE: 🌐 World/Brazil. **RELEASED:** 1994, Nonesuch. **KEY TRACKS:** "Haiti," "As coisas," "Cinema novo," "Baião atemporal." **CATALOG CHOICES:** Veloso: *Caetano Veloso*. Gil (with Jorge Ben): *Gil e Jorge.* **NEXT STOP:** Dorival Caymmi: *Caymmi e seu violão* (see p. 153). **AFTER THAT:** Raul Seixas: *Gita.*

Rare Beauty from a Former Enfant Terrible

Livro

Caetano Veloso

Imagine an intersection on the outskirts of Rio, a busy place where the cosmopolitan and the rustic converge. From one direction comes a drum troupe, happily pounding out a rhythm that lures hip-hop kids into a dance.

From the opposite direction, the breeze carries traces of an orchestra—twittering pastel flutes and strings and muted trumpets. As often happens on the street, the sounds don't smash against each other in direct collision. Instead they flow into a single sensory impression, an ever-shifting river of sound.

Caetano Veloso's incandescent *Livro* might have been conceived in such a spot. Its songs express the yearnings common to so much Brazilian music—lust and sadness and the longing for whatever is far away—in a language that bubbles with and thrives on deep contrasts. This music is rooted in a rumbling funk foundation, but it's got moody Gil Evans–ish orchestrations on top. It's somewhat samba, but also a touch arty, with moments where the beat falls away and some drifting tempoless rhapsody (about the magic awaiting inside books, among other things) takes over.

Veloso began this project in search of rhythms that could transcend generational differences. He'd been listening to American neo-soul singer D'Angelo (see p. 204), known for his canny updates of Marvin Gaye, and was convinced that a similar Brazilian confluence of old and new could yield interesting sounds. Veloso studied the street rhythms played in the favelas, the urban slums ringing Brazil's cities, and collaborated with several troupes. He ended up with more than just generic samba beats jacked up with a hip-hop kick: *Livro's* agitated yet ever-sensual polyrhythms are an acoustic version of a DJ's collage creation, with Veloso's tender vocals thrown in, almost as an afterthought.

Those vocals are the most riveting Veloso has committed to tape since the early 1980s. Singing with featherweight lightness, Veloso nuzzles and caresses the serpentine melodies. All the songs rely on Veloso's natural understatement, but of special note is his love letter to New York City, "Manhata." Sung in a voice filled with quiet awe, it's the rare city song that celebrates all the external romance of the place while revealing something of its often-hidden heart as well.

GENRE: 🌐 World/Brazil. **RELEASED:** 1997, Nonesuch. **KEY TRACKS:** "Manhata,"

"Os passistas," "Voce e minha." **F.Y.I.:** Beck, whose *Mutations* was partly inspired by Veloso, describes the Brazilian legend's music this way: "The different little sounds and ideas that run through his records are like a bunch of little jewels. Any one of them could change your life." **CATALOG CHOICE:** *Estrangeiro*. **NEXT STOP:** Gilberto Gil: *Quanta*. **AFTER THAT:** D'Angelo: *Brown Sugar* (see p. 204).

One of the Most Influential Rock Albums of All Time

The Velvet Underground and Nico

The Velvet Underground

Recorded mostly over two days in 1966, *The Velvet Underground and Nico* was "produced" by the artist and conceptualist Andy Warhol during the period of his multimedia Exploding Plastic Inevitable road show.

Warhol, whose iconic banana image is on the cover, insisted that the German model-actress Nico sing on the album, and according to guitarist Lou Reed, made sure the group was able to do what it wanted to do artistically. Nonetheless, years later, multi-instrumentalist John Cale credited Tom Wilson with handling most of the production, saying that Warhol "didn't do anything."

At any rate, the musicians didn't need much help: They'd already developed their own language, with knotted guitars and assorted foreboding dissonances occupying center stage. Cale, guitarist and songwriter Lou Reed, drummer Maureen Tucker, and guitarist Sterling Morrison developed a thrilling and totally unique approach to rock and roll. The concept took elements of Beat-poet stream of consciousness and added gritty realism and aggrandized notions of escape—Don DeLillo in 4/4 time. The songs follow nihilists, antisocial artistes, and other rogues as they endure the hassles of scoring drugs and struggle with all manner of sexual deviance. (Reed took the band name from a book on sadomasochism.)

The three comparatively mellow songs featuring Nico—"I'll Be Your Mirror," "All Tomorrow's Parties," and "Femme Fatale"—set her glassy-eyed detachment against heated rhythm section surges, fractured shards of junkyard guitar, and drones from Cale's viola. The remainder of the album features Reed singing his own songs, among them several that bring a literary fatalism to the junkie life ("I'm Waiting for the Man," "Heroin") and others that chase a new kind of rock abandon ("Run Run Run").

Everything has the electricity of the new running through it. Hearing *The Velvet Underground and Nico* now, it's impossible to miss those Velvet fingerprints on so much of the music that came after—glam, noise, punk, and grunge, not to mention the fervent poetry of Patti Smith and the odd shadows of R.E.M. *Rolling Stone* calls this "the most prophetic rock album ever made," and that might actually be an understatement.

GENRE: 🎸 Rock. **RELEASED:** 1967, Verve. **KEY TRACKS:** "All Tomorrow's

Parties," "I'll Be Your Mirror," "I'm Waiting for the Man," "Heroin," "Run Run Run." **CATALOG CHOICES:** *White Light/White Heat; Peel Slowly and See* (five-CD set). **NEXT STOP:** R.E.M.: *Fables of the Reconstruction.* **AFTER THAT:** Dream Syndicate: *The Days of Wine and Roses.*

An Exotic Love Triangle

Aida

Giuseppe Verdi
*Leontyne Price, Jon Vickers,
Chorus and Orchestra of the Rome Opera (Sir Georg Solti, cond.)*

*A*ida might be set in North Africa, but it's grand Italian opera with all the trimmings. It's got the languid, deliberating arias that are among Giuseppe Verdi's signature contributions to the form. It's got moments of

big flag-waving pageantry that operagoers of his day expected. Naturally there's a tangled love triangle, with subplots of jealousy and deception that unspool gradually.

And the melodies Verdi (1813–1901) gave his title character—sung here by Leontyne Price, in the recording that established her as the preeminent Aida of the twentieth century—are incredibly

On the cover: Leontyne Price as Aida.

demanding. They require the soprano, playing a captured Ethiopian princess, to deliver outbursts of tremendous force. And then, seconds later, the score shifts, requiring the singer to produce quiet and deliciously tender high-register long tones, which are sustained almost beyond the limits of human breath. Price handles those challenges with unsurpassed poise, and astounding vocal warmth. (Listen to her third-act aria "Qui Radamas verra!," which exists in a suspended state of floating, ethereal brilliance.)

Despite Verdi's attempts to "regionalize" the music with snake-charmer curlicues and modes intended to reflect the exotic locale, the most striking musical themes of *Aida* are solidly European. There's a healthy

dose of block-chord heroism, most overtly in the famous "Triumphal March" scene that features the Egyptian army parading war treasures and Ethiopian prisoners (including Aida's father) while chanting "Glory to Egypt!" Just as often, though, the deeply moving music occurs in more intimate moments, like the duet between the Egyptian princess Amneris (played by Rita Gorr) and the man she expects will become her husband, the military general Radames (sung with intense authority by Jon Vickers). And just about every time she sings, whether solo or with others, the African American Price brings her character's deep conflicts to the fore. She obviously relates to the plight of an Ethiopian princess forced into servitude, but is equally compelling contemplating what it means to fall in love with a man who helped conquer her nation. The conflict informs her every phrase.

Price's sense of purpose radiates throughout the production, and creates, with help from the measured tempi and conservative shadings of conductor Sir Georg Solti, an *Aida* for the ages. In some *Aida* readings, the showy over-the-top scenes trample the luminous quieter music. Not here. We get all the glory—and all the doubt—Verdi intended.

GENRE: ⊗ Opera. **RELEASED:** 1962, Decca. **KEY TRACKS:** Act 1: "Celeste Aida," "Gloria al Eggito"; Act 2: "Vieni, o guerriero vindice"; Act 3: "Qui Radamas verral," "O terra, addio." **ANOTHER INTERPRETATION:**

Price recorded *Aida* again in 1970, for RCA, and has identified that as her preferred version. **CATALOG CHOICE:** *La traviata,* Maria Callas, Giuseppe di Stefano, Orchestra and Chorus of La Scala (Carlo Maria Giulini, cond.). **NEXT STOP:** Georges Bizet: *Carmen* (see p. 89). **AFTER THAT:** Giacomo Puccini: *Madama Butterfly,* Mirella Freni, Luciano Pavarotti, Vienna Philharmonic (Herbert von Karajan, cond.).

A Somber Shot of Verdi

Requiem

Giuseppe Verdi
Leontyne Price, Jussi Björling,
Vienna Philharmonic and Chorus (Fritz Reiner, cond.)

This is Verdi for people who consider opera a hokey way to tell a story: It's got the big ballooning vocal declarations forever associated with Italian opera—Verdi wrote this just after *Aida,* arguably his career peak—but little of the turgid storyline, as the text is drawn from the Catholic requiem mass. It has moments of deep, inward-looking orchestral murmuring, but few of opera's contrived "climax" scenes.

And the subject is death, that opera standby. The Requiem was occasioned by two deaths that affected Verdi—the demise of Gioachino Rossini in 1868 and the 1873 passing of Tuscan novelist Alessandro Manzoni. Verdi wasn't a devout Catholic, but he hints at the unyielding fire-and-brimstone absolutism of the Roman Catholic church without dishing the usual stern warnings from an angry God. Where other composers (including Fauré) used the requiem's mystical incantations to bow to an almighty power, Verdi took a more distanced view. He wrote as though confronting the human fear of death. The vocal lines, sung here by the authoritative soprano Leontyne Price and the storied tenor Jossi Björling, are epic pleas for mercy.

This charged performance was also historic: It was the only time Price and Björling, two

operatic greats of different generations, crossed paths. Price was in her early thirties, and months away from making her debut at the Metropolitan Opera. Björling, the enormously popular Swedish tenor who sings with an unexpectedly youthful demeanor, would be dead within a year. Under direction from Hungarian conductor Fritz Reiner, the soloists transform Verdi's bursts of illumination into riveting music. Even if you don't follow the text, you can't escape the restless, heavy-hearted questioning Verdi brought to this extended mourning ritual.

GENRE: ⊗ Classical. **RELEASED:** 1960, Decca. **KEY TRACKS:** "Offertorio," "Sanctus," "Recordare," "Lacrimosa." **ANOTHER INTERPRETATION:** Angela Gheorghiu, Roberto Alagna, Berlin Philharmonic and Swedish Radio Chorus (Claudio Abbado, cond.). **CATALOG CHOICE:** *Macbeth,* Alfredo Giacomotti, Orchestra and Chorus of La Scala (Claudio Abbado, cond.). **NEXT STOP:** Gabriel Fauré: *Requiem* (see p. 272).

A For-the-Ages Pairing of Composer and Conductor

Falstaff

Giuseppe Verdi

*Frank Guarrera, Teresa Stich-Randall, Giuseppe Valdengo,
NBC Symphony Orchestra (Arturo Toscanini, cond.)*

As a young cellist, Arturo Toscanini (1867–1957) participated in the 1887 premiere of Giuseppe Verdi's *Otello*. Upon hearing *Falstaff*, which was first performed in 1893, Toscanini sent Verdi a famous three-word note: "Grazie, grazie, grazie." The two became acquainted, and as Toscanini's reputation as a charismatic conductor grew, they inevitably discussed music. This association gives Toscanini's Verdi recordings a special straight-from-the-source resonance—we're hearing a keen interpreter who has firsthand knowledge of the composer's intent.

The lively, intensely animated *Falstaff* is Verdi's final opera; like its predecessor *Otello*, it recasts Shakespeare for operatic voices. But unlike *Otello*, its libretto conflates elements of two works, *The Merry Wives of Windsor* and *Henry IV*, into one story—a comedy about a fat drunken knight, Falstaff, who concocts a scheme to get money out of two of Windsor's more attractive widows. The narrative isn't riveting, but the music easily transcends that shortcoming—this is Verdi communicating in melodic bursts and brief musical poems that convey the essence of a character or a situation with stunning concision. Where *Otello* is riddled with devices the composer used before, *Falstaff* has a pronounced boldness, and a level of invention (audible in the contrapuntal exchanges between voices and orchestra) that extends well beyond his previous works.

In the *New Grove Dictionary of Music and Musicians* entry on Toscanini, this recording

Verdi composed over 30 operas during his career.

is singled out as a monument to the conductor's "vitality and interpretive insight." Listen first to the elements that are directly under Toscanini's control—the brisk pace, the clean textures, the sudden power-surge crescendos that rise from the orchestra's back row. There's no dithering on his stage, and no excessive ornamentation; even this lighthearted opera is serious business. Then listen to the way Toscanini supports the singers, using precise orchestral colors to throw contrast onto Verdi's soaring vocal lines. The maestro with the photographic memory doesn't steamroll through the score; he frames it in absolute terms, so that a casual listener might discern something of its structure.

That authority is one reason Toscanini cuts such a towering figure in twentieth-century music. He was known to be fearsome in rehearsal, a stickler for detail. Still, musicians loved him. Spend time with this and you'll hear why. He was forever pushing his orchestra toward ecstatic peaks of music-making that aren't always accessible to mortals.

GENRE: 🎵 Opera. **RELEASED:** 1950, RCA. (Reissued 2000.) **KEY TRACKS:** Act 1: "Falstaff m'ha canzonetta"; Act 2: "È sogno? o realtà?"; Act 3: "Epilogue." **CATALOG**

CHOICE: *Rigoletto,* Joan Sutherland, Luciano Pavarotti, London Symphony Orchestra (Richard Bonynge, cond.). **NEXT STOP:** Johannes Brahms: *The Four Symphonies,* NBC Symphony Orchestra (Arturo Toscanini, cond.). **AFTER THAT:** Jean Sibelius: Symphonies Nos. 1 and 2, NBC Symphony Orchestra (Leopold Stokowski, cond.).

The Best from Brazil's Fiercly Nationalistic Composer

Bachianas brasileiras

Heitor Villa-Lobos

*Victoria de los Ángeles, Orchestre National de la Radiodiffusion Française
(Heitor Villa-Lobos, cond.)*

G ive it up for the composer who is not ashamed of his homeland. The inventive and often misunderstood Heitor Villa-Lobos (1887–1959) took an almost argumentative stand, in interviews, to answer criticism that he was merely a repurposer of folk songs. "Yes, I'm Brazilian—very Brazilian," he was once quoted as saying. "In my music, I let the rivers and seas of this great Brazil sing. I don't put a gag on the tropical exuberance of our forests and our skies, which I intuitively transpose to everything I write."

The breathtaking beauty of Brazil does define Villa-Lobos—it's there in his active streams of melody and graceful, poignant intervallic leaps. Like Bartók, Villa-Lobos did his share of musicological digging; he spent time in the Amazon rain forests with his guitar, learning the folk songs of various remote tribes. Some of what he brought back has the feeling of a pastiche, slides taken on vacation. But not these works, which have become his signature. The *Bachianas*—essays for orchestra, voice, and various solo instruments that Villa-Lobos wrote over many years—attempt to pour the endlessly warm, flowing character of Brazil into a sturdy Bach-style structure.

There's nothing quite like the *Bachianas* in the orchestral repertoire. Though Villa-Lobos starts with folk melodies, he immediately carries them into the dark forest of his imagination, where they sprout oversized counterlines and unlikely melodic rejoinders.

These wandering "subthemes" are often as lyrical as the original source material. Through them Villa-Lobos teases out ideas and emotions lurking in the background, transforming plain folk themes into the music equivalent of three-dimensional chess.

It can take several encounters with the *Bachianas* before all of the rich layers and seemingly slight (but actually huge) inventions clarify. Certain recordings—like those featuring legendary Spanish soprano Victoria de los Ángeles on this collection—can speed that process. This is a restrained reading, with tropical exuberance muted just a bit. That allows the composer's subtle undercurrents, which intertwine pleasure and misery in that quintessentially Brazilian way, to shine through.

GENRE: 🎵 Classical. **RELEASED:** 1958, EMI. **KEY TRACKS:** Bachianas Nos. 2, 5, 9. **ANOTHER INTERPRETATION:** *Alma Brasileira: Music of Villa-Lobos,* Renée Fleming, New World Symphony (Michael Tilson Thomas, cond.). **CATALOG CHOICE:** Guitar Concerto, Julian Bream, London Symphony Orchestra (André Previn, cond.). **NEXT STOP:** Cello Trio: *Tango Brasileiro.* **AFTER THAT:** Wayne Shorter: *Alegria.*

To Everything, There Is a Season

The Four Seasons

Antonio Vivaldi
Janine Jansen

A few notes into the sprite-like "La primavera," the opening theme of this violin concerto, and you might find yourself anticipating a public television pledge drive, or a BBC Special Report, or some *Saturday Night Live* parody of uppercrust snobbery. It's been used that way so often, it's come to represent everything starchy and pretentious. That's not fair to Antonio Vivaldi (1678–1741), the Italian composer whose repertoire includes animated concertos and beautiful choral works. An ordained priest who spent much of his professional life at a school for orphaned girls in Venice, Vivaldi has of course had no

Jansen began to study the violin at age 6.

control over the modern-day appropriation (and misappropriation) of his most famous piece. Consider it a price of fame.

Those who know only the haughty sound-bite may be surprised to discover there's really cool, picturesque music inside *The Four Seasons*. Unlike Bach and other Germanic baroque composers, Vivaldi came up with scintillating melodies, and sent them out into the world with just enough fanfare to perk up listeners' ears. He didn't often engage in discursive "elaborations" on the themes, choosing instead to move quickly on to the next one. The most vivid moments in this piece, generally considered his best, seize upon specific aspects of each season: When the winds pick up in the winter section, they register as lashing, stabbing sounds, like ice hitting a roof. The summer section, "L'estate," opens in a thick slow mood, a listlessness brought on by heat. Later in the season, a joyous, scampering game of chase

breaks out; in one particular highlight of this recording, the Dutch violinist Janine Jansen interprets the passage with a wildcatting, almost hyperalert, animation.

Jansen's rendering of Vivaldi, with a small chamber group that includes several members of her family, has little of the condescending "let me show you baroque" affectation of some modern concert soloists. Though gifted as an instrumentalist, Jansen's most valuable asset may be curiosity: Using exacting articulation, Jansen plays as though imagining what these pieces might have sounded like echoing through the parlors and ballrooms of Venice. Sometimes she disregards the composer's tempo markings, adding slight rallentandos and telling pauses. With those "loosening up" effects, Jansen brings Vivaldi's melodies out of that metric uniformity that can make baroque a code-crunching exercise, and into a more open, flowing atmosphere where their musical riches can blossom.

GENRE: 🎷 Classical. **RELEASED:** 2005, Decca. **KEY TRACKS:** "L'estate," "L'inverno." **CATALOG CHOICE:** *Dixit Dominus RV 807*, Körnerscher Sing-Verein Dresden (Peter Koop, cond.). **NEXT STOP:** George Frideric Handel: *Water Music* (see p. 342). **AFTER THAT:** Lorraine Hunt Lieberson: *Handel Arias*.

The Evolution of a Composer

Hunting: Gathering

Kevin Volans
The Duke Quartet

When South Africa–born Kevin Volans began writing *White Man Sleeps* in the early 1980s, he had one overriding ambition. "I didn't want to Westernize African music," Volans told *BBC Music Magazine* of his intention for the piece that first brought him fame. "I wanted to Africanize Western music."

Tall order. But Volans, who'd then just finished an eight-year stint studying with and serving as a teaching assistant for Karlheinz Stockhausen (see p. 744) in Cologne, managed to do exactly that. A series of short, mysterious dances built on African rhythms, *White Man Sleeps* was originally intended for an eclectic conglomeration of "early" instruments including harpsichord and viola da gamba. The Kronos Quartet (see p. 196) asked Volans to recast it for string quartet, and recorded it on *Pieces of Africa*, which became one of the top-selling string quartet records of all time. Since then, that piece and a follow-up, *Hunting: Gathering*, have been recorded by other string groups; this version, by the London-based Duke Quartet, is loose and improvisational, rendering Volans's scores as a series of flickering beats and psychedelic flashpoints.

Fashioning small, carefully chopped rhythmic cells into recurring patterns, Volans transports the percussive nature of African music into a concert context—getting the intensity while carefully avoiding exploitation. At times on both *White Man* and *Hunting*, he has the strings approximate the sound of ritual drums way off in the distance; as they travel, the patterns acquire tones and chords and the occasional rhapsodic solo. The Duke treats each crest as a magical event, linking the trance elements of African groove with the equally mesmeric repetitions of minimalism.

Volans became a citizen of Ireland in the 1990s, and since then has gradually filtered the African influences from his work. String Quartet No. 6, which closes the Duke set, was written in 2000 for two string quartets (or one willing to play along with a prerecorded track). It replaces the syncopated hijinks of his earlier work with chords struck in pairs, as echoes or precisely juxtaposed mirror-image counterpoints. The piece is as captivating as his agitated early compositions—just slower, more contemplative. Volans has said he was seeking to eliminate thematic matter entirely; he wanted the piece to feel like a blank slate. The Duke Quartet conjures that sense, making emptiness signify in surprising ways for twenty-six totally engrossing minutes.

GENRE: 𝄞 Classical. **RELEASED:** 2002, Black Box. **KEY TRACKS:** String Quartet No. 1: "Fifth Dance." String Quartet No. 2: "II." String Quartet No. 6. **ANOTHER INTERPRETATION:** Both Nos. 1 and 2 were recorded by the Kronos Quartet on its excellent *Pieces of Africa*. **CATALOG CHOICE:** *Cicada, Duets*, Mathilda Hornsveld, Jill Richards, Matteo Fargion. **NEXT STOP:** William Chapman Nyaho: *Piano Music by Composers of African Descent*. **AFTER THAT:** Nico Muhly: *Mother Tongue*.

Richard Wagner ✦ Rufus Wainwright ✦ Tom Waits ✦ Fats Waller ✦ William Walton ✦ War ✦ The Clara Ward Singers ✦ Dionne Warwick ✦ Dinah Washington ✦ Muddy Waters ✦ Weather Report ✦ Andrew Lloyd Webber and Tim Rice ✦ Kurt Weill and Bertolt Brecht ✦ Gillian Welch ✦ Kanye West ✦ Speedy West and Jimmy Bryant ✦ Randy Weston ✦ Kenny Wheeler ✦ Barry White ✦ The White Stripes ✦ Chris Whitley ✦ The Who ✦ Wilco ✦ The **W** Wild Tchoupitoulas ✦ Hank Williams ✦ Joe Williams with the Count Basie Orchestra ✦ Lucinda Williams ✦ Marion Williams ✦ Mary Lou Williams ✦ The Tony Williams Lifetime ✦ Sonny Boy Williamson II ✦ Bob Wills and His Texas Playboys ✦ Cassandra Wilson ✦ Jackie Wilson ✦ Bill Withers ✦ Stevie Wonder ✦ Wu-Tang Clan ✦ Robert Wyatt ✦ Tammy Wynette

Love und Death, Wagner Style

Tristan und Isolde

Richard Wagner

Vienna State Opera (Christian Thielemann, cond.)

The famed "love duet" in the second act of Richard Wagner's *Tristan und Isolde* is not just another memorable opera moment. As with many things Wagner (1813–1883), it's larger than life, a meeting of big voices that spirals into something of a marathon. When the first act ends, Tristan has ingested what he believes is a death potion, served up by the spiteful Isolde in a moment of vengeance. Unbeknownst to either, Isolde's maid has swapped the cocktail for a love potion, and in Act 2 the pair marvel at and celebrate the circumstances that have drawn them together.

This inspires a seventeen-minute extravaganza on the notion of death in love. Isolde, sung here by the persuasive Deborah Voigt, is in a tizzy; from the first notes, she belts with a double-forte fervor. Tristan (here played by Thomas Moser) is equally forceful. As the scene progresses, their exchanges become more torrid, propelled not by conventional recurring "motifs" (rarely does Wagner repeat) but tense chromatic passages that push to sharp, almost shouted climaxes.

Wagner once explained it was his need to "vent his feelings musically" that led him to compose *Tristan und Isolde*, which debuted in 1865. Oh, he vents—that's a given. But that's not all he does. Despite a few overheated love scenes (like the duet from Act 2) and orchestrations that are downright severe at times, this is a work of surprising sensuality—each bit of simmering musical tension becomes an integral part of the narrative. Many scholars fix the start-

"I have devised in my mind a *Tristan und Isolde,* the simplest, yet most full-blooded musical conception imaginable."
—Richard Wagner

ing point for modern atonality here, in Wagner's constantly shifting key centers; at the time of the premiere, some heard these devices as vented feelings run too far amok. One critic who reviewed the premiere, Edward Hanslick, complained, "The Prelude to *Tristan und Isolde* reminds me of the old Italian painting of a martyr whose intestines are slowly unwound from his body on a reel."

The spry Vienna State Opera Orchestra is well suited to the whipsaw nature of Wagner; the ensemble follows conductor Christian Thielemann's intelligent delineation of the opera's peaks and valleys. Though Voigt has spent her career singing Verdi (a stroll in the park when compared with the more conceptual Wagner), she brings great lucidity to Isolde, drawing equally on vocal accuracy and dramatic commitment to make her scenes, and by extension the entire work, sparkle.

GENRE: 😊 Opera. **RELEASED:** 2004, Deutsche Grammophon. **KEY TRACK:** Act 2. **ANOTHER INTERPRETATION:** Kirsten Flagstad, Philharmonia Orchestra (Wilhelm Furtwängler, cond.). **CATALOG CHOICE:** *Die Walküre* (see next page). **NEXT STOP:** Carl Orff: *Carmina Burana,* Orchestra of the Deutsche Oper Berlin (Eugen Jochum, cond.).

Warning: Do Not Grab This Ring Casually

Die Walküre

Richard Wagner
Bayreuth Festival Orchestra (Joseph Keilberth, cond.)

There's nothing even remotely casual about Richard Wagner's four-part Ring cycle. It is the ultimate operatic epic, a thundering, weighty experience with the scope to enchant not just opera lovers but video gamers and fanatics immersed in Dungeons and Dragons–style role-play. Written over twenty-six years, it takes sixteen hours to perform from start to finish; a festival in Bayreuth, Germany, where this version was recorded live, undertakes the job every few years, drawing obsessed fans from around the world. Its tale—about a gold ring stolen from Rhine maidens by an evil dwarf named Alberich—spins through allegories about power, greed, and original sin. The "hero," a human warrior who does the bidding of the gods to help return the ring, doesn't even appear until Part Three.

This recording is of *Die Walküre*, which is Part Two, the most popular of the episodes and the one that best stands alone. It begins with a storm-tossed character named Siegmund (played here by Ramón Vinay), who picks up a strange vibe from the woman, Sieglinde (played by Gré Brouwenstijn), who has given him shelter. Turns out she is, in fact, his sister. They are Walsungs, creatures who are half god and half human, and in the first of several incestuous plot-twists, they fall in love. They have a son, Siegfried the warrior, who needs two more operas to get the gold back where it belongs.

Time is no object to the grandiose Wagner: The three acts of *Die Walküre*, which debuted in 1870, stretch over four compact discs. Each act contains at least one for-the-ages scene. The opening act's extended love duet, "Winterstürme," finds Siegmund and Sieglinde rhapsodizing through melodically understated declarations that will surprise anyone who associates Wagner with bombast. The great composer, who drew inspiration from German and Nordic sagas and mythologies, saves the big guns for Act 2, where it's possible to hear what happens when the headstrong characters enter a collision course. Then there's the final act, which may remind modern listeners of an intergalactic battle scene from *Star Wars*.

This 1955 recording is considered one of two definitive modern readings—Sir Georg Solti's 1965 version is the other. This one takes a more "old school" approach to Wagner's text: By '65, opera singers were emphasizing tone production over the actual telling of the story. This recording, like many earlier interpretations of Wagner, finds the singers focusing on the meaning of the words first. The difference, one of intent, is significant: Here, everyone is immersed in the story. Swept away by Wagner's foreboding allegories, they're worried less about perfect notes than relaying the larger-than-life truths and consequences of the text. Which are many.

GENRE: 🎵 Opera. **RELEASED:** 2006, Testament. (Recorded 1955.) **KEY TRACKS:** "Winterstürme," "Wotan's Farewell," "Ride of the Valkyries." **ANOTHER INTERPRETATION:** Vienna Philharmonic (Georg Solti, cond.). **CATALOG CHOICE:** *Gotterdämmerung* (see next page). **NEXT STOP:** Richard Strauss: *Der Rosenkavalier* (see p. 749).

Gods Wreaking Havoc from on High

Götterdämmerung

Richard Wagner

Birgit Nilsson, Wolfgang Windgassen, Dietrich Fischer-Dieskau, Vienna Philharmonic (Sir Georg Solti, cond.)

Thⁱˢ is some of the most thrilling music ever made on Planet Earth. Its massive peals of sound flatten the notion that classic opera can't equal—or surpass—the sheer raw power of guitar-driven contemporary music. Its harsh chords amount to the basic DNA of heavy metal—the good, dramatic kind. Its bellowing vocal lines demand extraordinary energy (and discipline); some opera stars simply can't hack Wagner. There are extra-large distraught outbursts from the singers and equally extreme flashes from the brass. And it's got one of the longest arias in recorded opera history—the finale, Brünnhilde's "Immolation" scene.

Götterdämmerung, which premiered in 1874, brings Richard Wagner's sixteen-hour Ring cycle to a tumultuous close. It is the most challenging section, in part because Wagner has lots of loose ends to tie up. His devilishly complex intertwined plots require a slew of villains. These are introduced during the eventful Act 1, and their machinations lead to the death of Siegfried in Act 3, which has Christ-like significance—he died for the world's sinful greed. Brünnhilde burns everything down, and it's as though she hit some biblical reset button: The slate is wiped clean, the world begins anew.

There are many *Götterdämmerung* recordings; none can top the precision of this 1964 studio effort led by Sir Georg Solti. It's got a dream-team cast—Birgit Nilsson (Brünnhilde), Wolfgang Windgassen (Siegfried), Dietrich Fischer-Dieskau (Gunther)—that would have been too expensive for a live production. Solti approached the task as though shooting a movie (in some cases, a full day's work yielded only twenty recorded minutes of usable music),

and pushed the Vienna Philharmonic to a more brusque, edgy sound than it usually achieved. In fact, some critics, suspecting mixing-board trickery, describe the sound of the ensemble as "surreal." To hear Solti at his best, check out the stormy horn entrance in the third act, which explodes into the spotlight like a racehorse leaping from the gate. It's grand, but somehow not bombastic.

Wagner was, of course, temperamentally disposed to the oversized—many of the *Götterdämmerung* highlights are thundering, larger-than-life passages. There are times when the singers seem to inflate their voices to properly execute the themes—listen to Fischer-Dieskau putting his most majestic voice forward throughout, or Nilsson's enraged aria in the third act, an excellent showcase for her gleaming high notes. Though Wagner wrote memorable choruses in other operas, the one in the third act is the only one in the whole entire Ring cycle. It's tremendous—a two-hanky requiem for the gods in twilight, complete with deep existential questions from the mortals, who look warily to the heavens and wonder: What now?

GENRE: 🎙 Opera. **RELEASED:** 1964, Decca. (Reissued 1997.) **KEY TRACKS:** "Wintersturme," "Hoiho, Hagen!," "Heil dir, Gunther," "War das sein Horn?" **ANOTHER INTERPRETATION:** Astrid Varnay, Bayreuther Festspiele Orchester. **CATALOG**

CHOICE: *Die Meistersinger,* Herbert Lippert, Chicago Symphony Orchestra (Georg Solti, cond.). **NEXT STOP:** Birgit Nilsson: *Sings Richard Wagner and Richard Strauss.* **AFTER THAT:** John Adams: *Nixon in China,* Orchestra of St. Luke's (Edo de Waart, cond.).

You Want This One

Want One

Rufus Wainwright

By the time he made his third album, the enormously gifted pianist, singer, and songwriter Rufus Wainwright had lived through his share of tumult. He was born into a family of musicians—his mother is Kate McGarrigle, of the Quebec McGarrigles (see p. 489), and his father is folksinger and humorist Loudon Wainwright III, who immortalized his infant son's early proclivities with the song "Rufus Is a Tit Man." The couple divorced when Rufus was young, and looking back, he recalls being devastated by it. If anything, the family business complicated things. After his critically fawned-over debut in 1998, Wainwright had public feuds with his dad, celebrated his homosexuality, struggled openly with addiction to crystal meth, and did flamboyant things like re-creating the entire program of Judy Garland's legendary 1961 performance at Carnegie Hall (see page 300).

Want One was followed by a sequel, *Want Two,* in 2004.

A moody tunesmith with an ear for opera and a taste for the killer knock-you-off-your-feet hook, Wainwright reached a creative peak with his third album, *Want One,* which stands among the most florid, downright ambitious song cycles in pop history.

How ambitious? Track one begins as a solemn processional, a little melody hummed by monks as they file into morning prayers. Three minutes later, it's ballooned into a *Clockwork Orange* carnival, with a pealing orchestra storming center stage. The "theme" it plays is an interpolation of Maurice Ravel's *Bolero,* and Wainwright sails above it, singing about the happy headlines he'd like to see on the front page of *The New York Times.* From there, *Want One* is by turns glorious and garish. Its songs ponder romantic obsession in every flavor imaginable: There are vulnerable little jazz waltzes ("Vicious World") and lazy, lilting music-theater dance routines ("Harvester of Hearts"), anthems that try, in vain, to pin down vague longing ("I Don't Know What It Is"), futile declarations ("My phone's on vibrate for you"), and amped-up guitar rockers ("Movies of Myself," a caustic comment on reality TV and the self-mythologizing impulse). At one point Wainwright describes his writing as "a bucket of rhymes I threw up somewhere," but don't believe him: His slouchy, just-woke-up singing is the only casual thing about this stunner.

GENRE: 🎵 Rock. **RELEASED:** 2003, Dreamworks. **KEY TRACKS:** "Harvester of Hearts," "Oh What a World," "Movies of Myself," "Go or Go Ahead," "Vibrate." **CATALOG CHOICES:** *Poses; Want Two.* **NEXT STOP:** Elliott Smith: *XO* (see p. 716). **AFTER THAT:** Duncan Sheik: *Brighter/Later.*

Street Cabaret of the Downtrodden and Forgotten

Rain Dogs

Tom Waits

Tom Waits is the American poet of lost causes. The people in his songs are forever coming up just short, mocked by fate and taunted by all sorts of unseen cosmic troubles. His unsavory sailors, stubble-bearded drifters, and grumbling Bowery bums are usually involved in roguish activity—*Rain Dogs,* his despairing *Leaves of Grass,* opens with the barked declaration "We sail tonight for Singapore." Waits follows along as the ragtag crew blunders into momentous doomed events. The cast of characters changes from song to song, but all of them seem to get caught up in similarly sordid and desperate schemes, and Waits tells their

"If I want a sound, I usually feel better if I've chased it and killed it. . . ."   —Tom Waits

stories with the fond bemusement of a distant relative. He watches as they get one last shot, when they put all the chips on the table. And being the sympathetic sort, he stands dutifully by when things don't work out, serenading them as they turn tail and head for home.

Waits has been staging this sort of street cabaret for decades, since the rambling poetics of his debut, *Closing Time* (1973), and the more campy maneuvers of *Swordfishtrombones* (1983). *Rain Dogs* is the most elaborate, and the most musically varied, of his works. It's also the basic template for much of what he's done since.

A sprawling suite that hides considerable musical ambitions behind spectacularly disheveled sounds, *Rain Dogs* serves up greasy lowlife America, scrambled. It features the gravel-voiced singer and songwriter fronting a restless postmodern parade band of clip-clopping mallet instruments and wayward guitars; at times this group inspires him to croon like a plastered Louis Armstrong wannabe. Among the nineteen uniformly stunning tracks are a brisk rum boogie ("Jockey Full of Bourbon"), a concise pop anthem ("Hang Down Your Head"), a fantastical update of jive swing ("Walking Spanish"), a dusty country song that sounds like a zillion-year-old standard ("Blind Love"), an absurd tarantella ("Tango till They're Sore"), and a wobbly swagger ("Big Black Mariah") that turns typical blues imagery sideways.

By the time this incredible journey ends, *everything* is sideways. The down and out becomes opulent, kissed with a romance of the nocturnal that makes the tidy, orderly daytime world seem hollow. It's almost a magic trick, this transformation, because it has less to do with the assimilation of musical styles than Waits's ability to pull enduring truths from the clutter. Drink long enough at his table, and you too might begin to see these sad-sack characters as heroes.

GENRE: 🎸 Rock. **RELEASED:** 1985, Island. **KEY TRACKS:** "Clap Hands," "Jockey Full of Bourbon," "Big Black Mariah," "Downtown Train," "Blind Love." **CATALOG CHOICES:** *Closing Time; Foreign Affairs; Nighthawks at the Diner.* **NEXT STOP:** Randy Newman: *Good Old Boys.* **AFTER THAT:** John Cale: *Vintage Violence.*

The Best from an Early Jazz Showman

If You Got to Ask, You Ain't Got It

Fats Waller

Thomas "Fats" Waller, the pianist, composer, and bandleader, represents a pinnacle of jazz as bug-eyed rampantly exuberant show music. Not art music. His band offered snappy arrangements and great soloists, yet for all its slickness, it mostly prized having fun—a kind of campy, shuffling fun that shoots through the music at a hundred miles per hour. Joking and cavorting, Waller and his bands—usually billed as "Fats Waller and His Rhythm"—specialized in a blithe, and instantly infectious, swing.

Along with Louis Armstrong, the New York–born Waller (1904–1943) was a key architect of early jazz. A prodigy on the piano, Waller was also schooled in the organ

In 2004, Waller's "Ain't Misbehavin'" was listed in the National Recording Registry.

works of J. S. Bach, and received additional education from Harlem stride master James P. Johnson (see p. 401). Blessed with a light, effervescent touch, Waller linked elements of stride, boogie-woogie, and ragtime into jaw-dropping displays: Seek out the impressive "Honey Hush," recorded in 1939, to hear an early foreshadowing of jump blues and rock and roll, a simple tune propelled by a rollicking, bawdy beat. Waller's spry rhythm is just one part of his contribution: He's among the most prolific composers of his era, responsible for such immortal party-time themes as "The Joint Is Jumpin'." Several songs he wrote early in his career—including "Ain't Misbehavin'" and "Honeysuckle Rose"—became instant

standards, crucial to the repertoire of virtually everyone who played jazz in the 1930s.

Though Waller's recording career was brief, he managed to leave his mark across an impressive range of music. This set divides his output into three categories: There's a disc devoted to delirious originals he sang with a winking, insouciant air; another focusing on hardworking jazz instrumentals that showcase his pianistic flair and ability to swing intensely while his drummers play lightly with brushes; and a third that features his interpretations of popular songs by George Gershwin and others. Together they offer a complete picture of Waller as creative force and show-business wizard, a performer who could play circles around his competition and, with every step, spread his own brand of sheer delight.

GENRE: 🅘 Jazz. **RELEASED:** 2006, RCA. **KEY TRACKS:** "Honeysuckle Rose," "I'm Crazy About My Baby," "You Ain't the Only Oyster in the Stew," "Ain't Misbehavin'." **CATALOG CHOICE:** *Handful of Keys.* **NEXT STOP:** Jelly Roll Morton: *Birth of the Hot* (see p. 524). **AFTER THAT:** Eubie Blake: *That's Ragtime!*

The Best from an Early Bloomer

Symphony No. 1 and Belshazzar's Feast

William Walton
City of Birmingham Orchestra (Sir Simon Rattle, cond.)

Put this on to contemplate what it means to reach an artistic peak early in life. British composer William Walton (1902–1983) was in his early thirties when he finished his first symphony. It begins at a rushing gallop with many instruments hammering away at a single note, then splits off into brief episodes that transfer the headstrong rush of youth into sound. Later in his career, Walton showed a deep understanding of melody, but most of his work is concerned with rhythmic churning—tempos that shift and collide like tectonic plates. Walton invests each with a pronounced sense of drama, making excellent use of gnarled harmonies. Those accustomed to Mozart-style orderly chordal resolutions will find in Walton an approach to tension and release that is ear-stretching—but not off-putting.

Four years earlier, Walton had premiered *Belshazzar's Feast*, a cantata that is a more extroverted statement. On this recording, conductor Sir Simon Rattle creates grand gestures using unorthodox bowing techniques and other devices. His handling of the pieces is animated: He recognizes that Walton works best when the musicians match the vigor of the material.

By 1939, these two pieces and several others, including the coronation march *Crown Imperial*, had vaulted Walton to stardom. He was hailed as the most important British composer of the day, but he mistrusted the praise. That year, in an interview, he noted: "I've gone through the first halcyon periods and am just about ripe for my critical damnation." The words proved prophetic: Though he composed into the 1950s, Walton's later works were met with derision, and he never contributed anything as riveting as these two landmark pieces again.

GENRE: 🎵 Classical. **RELEASED:** 2000, EMI. **KEY TRACKS:** Symphony No. 1: first movement. *Belshazzar's Feast*: "Thus Spake Isaiah." **CATALOG CHOICE:** *Violin Concerto*, Joshua Bell, Baltimore Symphony (David Zinman, cond.).

Asking the Musical Question . . .

Why Can't We Be Friends?

War

To the musicians of War, the question "Why Can't We Be Friends?" was never abstract. The L.A. group chronicled the challenges and day-to-day desperation of inner-city life—its poignant 1972 album

The World Is a Ghetto echoed ideas Marvin Gaye put forth the year before in *What's Going On?* (see p. 304). War didn't just inventory problems, however: The band was interested in solutions. Many of the songs on this album talk about brotherhood and human connection, advocating compassion as an essential step toward neighborhood peace.

That spirit is reflected in the music. War drew elements from all corners of the Los Angeles metroplex, and made them sound like they belonged together. In the addictive songs of *Why Can't We Be Friends?*, chunky reggae beats connect with the Delta-derived harmonica lines of its star soloist Lee Oskar. *Timbale*-sparked salsa worms its way into a flamboyant funk party. There's pan-cultural spice, but not in a corny "we're all okay in the global village" way—the

In the music video for "Low Rider," the album cover "sings" a part of the song.

chants are tinged with an activist's sense of indignation. Also here is the at once rustic and futuristic "Low Rider," a suave jam for the ages built on grumbling, almost indecipherable bass vocals.

The singles (the title track and the endlessly sampled "Low Rider") offer a basic outline of the War strategy, and the album tracks, like the four-part suite "Leroy's Latin Lament," go deeper, demonstrating how a boisterous meeting of (often contentious) tribes can yield music of undeniable strength.

GENRE: 🎵 R&B. **RELEASED:** 1975, United Artists. (Reissued 1992.) **KEY TRACKS:** "Low Rider," "Leroy's Latin Lament," "Why Can't We Be Friends?" **CATALOG CHOICES:** *All Day Music; The World Is a Ghetto.* **NEXT STOP:** Mandrill: *Composite Truth.* **AFTER THAT:** Malo: *Malo.*

From the Amen Corner to the Street Corner

Take My Hand, Precious Lord

The Clara Ward Singers

It couldn't have been easy out there on the gospel highway in the America of the 1940s and '50s. The quartets and quintets of singers, most of them African American, heard the call and went on the road intending to spread the joy they'd found. Inevitably, this took them to the South and other places where black strangers, even those singing songs of joy and faith and forgiveness, were not exactly welcome. What they encountered along the way—routine bigotry, meanness, mistrust—would test anyone's faith. Singer Marion Williams, who was a key member of the Clara Ward Singers during the 1950s, recalls travel as a daily trial. "We couldn't use the bathrooms on the highway. If they did have

one for us, there was a sign on the door that said 'Colored.'"

Somehow these challenges did not adversely affect the Ward Singers, five powerful women whose unflappable enthusiasm and intricate harmonizing can still raise goose bumps. One of the early gospel acts to perform in nonchurch venues (and the very first to work a Las Vegas lounge), the Ward Singers appeared onstage wearing glittering dresses and lavish jewels, and within minutes their exceedingly determined vocalizing would melt any resistance in the room. They had help, of course: a songbook filled with just about every revival-meeting standard, as well as current gospel hits, imaginatively arranged by leader Ward to take advantage of the theatrical whoops of her soloists.

This disc showcases many of the Ward Singers' signature songs. It's divided between studio recordings made in the late '50s and a sizzling live performance (featuring the dynamic lap-steel guitarist Sammy Fein) at New York's Town Hall from 1958. The program offers a comprehensive picture of one of gospel's most sparkling ensembles. The Wards were solid on the fundamentals of traditional gospel, and at the same time not content to preach to the converted. Like the great Sister Rosetta Tharpe (see p. 771) and others, they take the word from the amen corner, pump it up to overdrive, and send it out into the world beyond church. Where it might actually do some good.

GENRE: ✛ Gospel. **RELEASED:** 1996, MCA. (Original recordings issued 1958, 1960.) **KEY TRACKS:** "Take My Hand, Precious Lord," "You'll Never Walk Alone," "I Found the Keys to the Kingdom." **CATALOG CHOICE:** *Meetin' Tonight.* **NEXT STOP:** The Caravans: *The Best of the Caravans* (see p. 143). **AFTER THAT:** The Fairfield Four: *Standing in the Safety Zone.*

A Chance Encounter That Led to Consummate Pop Craft

The Dionne Warwick Collection

Dionne Warwick

Dionne Warrick and Burt Bacharach were just two striving professionals, scuffling to get paid, when they met in a recording studio in 1961. She was part of the Gospelaires (a familial singing group that had backed Ben E. King on the monster hit "Stand by Me"), who'd been hired that day to sing backing vocals for the Drifters. He, a pianist who'd done road time with Vic Damone and Marlene Dietrich, was the author of a song the Drifters were cutting called "Mexican Divorce." Bacharach invited Warrick to sing on some pop songs he and lyricist Hal David had just written. The next year, the team's first single, "Don't Make Me Over"—one of the first songs with a feminist message to reach the Top 40 in the rock era—carried a typographical error: Warrick was identified as Warwick.

Over her career, Warwick placed 56 hits on the *Billboard* Hot 100 chart.

The name stuck, and so did the collaboration: Over the next eight years, through the turbulent period associated with the overlapping frenzies of Elvis Presley, the Beatles, and the Summer of Love, Warwick, Bacharach, and David established an alternate pop reality, a sparkly pristine universe where poise and sophistication reigned.

That these opulent tunes, which include "Walk On By," "Do You Know the Way to San José," and the eternally slinky bossa "The Look of Love," are the result of a chance encounter is enough to make you wonder about the caprice of fate. Warwick's crystalline voice showed up at the exact moment Bacharach and David's compositional style—with its demanding intervallic leaps and torrents of words, and chord changes that hint at (but never wallow in) melancholy—began to mature. She doesn't simply sing what the two wrote; her agile, affectation-free delivery elevates the fragile melodies, making them seem at once regal and windswept. Her style is so conversational, it's easy to miss how elegantly she's shaping the music. The next time somebody complains about pop as a reckless realm of shouters and louts, insist on silence and cue up any of the twenty-four tracks here—immaculate productions that have a quiet, unassuming way of saying it all.

GENRES: ⭐ Pop 🎵 Vocals. **RELEASED:** 2004, WEA International. **KEY TRACKS:** "I'll Never Fall in Love Again," "The Look of Love." **CATALOG CHOICE:** *Promises, Promises / I'll Never Fall in Love Again.* **NEXT STOP:** Whitney Houston: *Whitney Houston* (see p. 370). **AFTER THAT:** Amy Winehouse: *Back to Black.*

She Earns the Exclamation Point!

Dinah!

Dinah Washington

inah Washington's discography has two clearly delineated sides: This and other casual jazz records she made with small combos in the 1950s, and the more elaborate titles that followed her 1959 crossover move

(and biggest hit) *What a Difference a Day Makes.*

Washington didn't change her singing style much when she went uptown—the plush orchestra dates still rely on her wise delivery and knack for communicating lingering bitterness. In his autobiography, arranger Quincy Jones recalls her singing this way: She could "take the melody in her hand, hold it like an egg, crack it open, fry it, let it sizzle, reconstruct it, put the egg back in the box and back in the refrigerator and you would've still understood every single syllable."

The lavish studio sides are pleasant, but to encounter Washington at her peak, seek out the early stuff. *Dinah!*, recorded in 1955, is an excellent place to begin exploring this emotional cyclone of a singer, who was mar-

Fans call Dinah Washington "Queen of the Blues."

ried seven times and struggled openly with her weight (she died, at age thirty-nine, after ingesting a mix of diet pills and alcohol). Though the lure throughout is Washington's crisp delivery, she gets plenty of help: Hal Mooney's hip horn charts are cut from the Sinatra swing book, and on the slower numbers, the strings are refreshingly unobtrusive.

Listen as the alert backing trio (pianist Wynton Kelly, drummer Jimmy Cobb, bassist Keeter Betts) lures the singer into extravagant slow-motion wails, or, just as frequently, provides a firm anchor for her raw, perpetually wounded ballad persona, and you'll hear how great instrumentalists can inspire a singer. The trio practically forces Washington to dig deep and give her all. And she does. Among this set's definitive performances are a fetchingly bluesy "All of Me," and a simultaneously poised and fiery treatment of "Smoke Gets in Your Eyes."

GENRES: 🅙 Jazz 🅥 Vocals. RELEASED: 1956, EmArcy. (Reissued 1991, Verve.) KEY

TRACKS: "All of Me," "Smoke Gets in Your Eyes," "A Cottage for Sale." CATALOG CHOICE: *What a Difference a Day Makes.* NEXT STOP: Marlena Shaw: *Marlena.* AFTER THAT: Betty Carter: *The Audience with Betty Carter.*

One Jaw-Dropping Night in a Blues Legend's Life

At Newport 1960

Muddy Waters

A master of sweetly crying guitar leads and flip jazz-like vocal phrases, Waters was rarely less than inspired when tape was rolling. His discography contains a tall stack of definitive records—early singles for Chess (collected on various hits packages) that depend on his already leathery voice, mid-career titles (*Folk Singer,* 1964) that present him in an "unplugged" acoustic context, and the late rock-tinged collaborations with Johnny Winter (*Hard Again,* 1977) that have a stinging energy you might not expect from an elder statesman.

Still, in the great wandering of an epic blues life, one night stands out: Waters's 1960 performance at the Newport Jazz Festival. The Chicago-based singer and guitarist got the gig after highly acclaimed tours in Europe in 1958 and 1959 had raised his profile, and this performance, which anchored a blues evening, helped expand Waters's reputation beyond the Chicago clubs he called home. Released the following year, the live album took that even further; it's routinely cited as an inspiration by then up-and-coming British blues guitarists such as Eric Clapton, Jimmy Page, and Jeff Beck (many of whom eventually performed with Waters).

The set list is essentially Muddy Waters's

"Muddy was a master of just the right notes."
—Bluesman John Hammond Jr.

greatest hits. It's lacerating Chicago blues and clever reworkings of songs the man born McKinley Morganfield had been playing since he was discovered by musicologist Alan Lomax in the Mississippi Delta in the 1940s. There's the immortal Willie Dixon tune "(I'm Your) Hoochie Coochie Man" and the pleading "Baby Please Don't Go" (this is perhaps Waters's most riveting vocal rendition of the song) and a ripping "I've Got My Mojo Working." The focus is less on individual heroics than galvanizing group interplay, and the band, which includes rollicking pianist Otis Spann and harmonica virtuoso James Cotton, hits hot stride on the opener, "I Got My Brand on You" and then, miraculously, sustains it. Check out the way Cotton contributes to the locomotion of "Tiger in Your Tank." He positions his harmonica right alongside the guitar, thinking of himself as another rhythm instrument. And away they go, romping. Hear that, and it's easy to understand why those future guitar legends were so inspired. It rocks.

from the original and four bonus studio tracks recorded a month after the Newport appearance. **CATALOG CHOICES:** *The Real Folk Blues/More Real Folk Blues; Electric Mud; Hard Again.* **NEXT STOP:** B.B. King: *Live at the Regal* (see p. 426). **AFTER THAT:** Buddy Guy: *Damn Right, I've Got the Blues* (see p. 332).

GENRE: 🙂 Blues. **RELEASED:** 1960, Chess/MCA. **KEY TRACKS:** "Baby Please Don't Go," "I Got My Brand on You," "(I'm Your) Hoochie Coochie Man," "Soon Forgotten." **BUYER BEWARE:** Several versions of this have been released; the best is the one from 2001, which offers serious audio upgrades

---

Forecast Calls for . . .

Heavy Weather

Weather Report

Weather Report started in 1970 as an experiment by refugees from the interstellar space explorations of Miles Davis circa *In a Silent Way*. At that time, jazz-rock fusion was open-ended, anarchy-seeking stuff, often built on displays of wild intensity. Within a few years, as keyboardist Joe Zawinul and saxophonist Wayne Shorter developed distinct compositional signatures, Weather Report made it something else—lurking, shadowy, multidimensional music propelled by agile Afro-Latin grooves.

By the time of *Heavy Weather*, the band's seventh studio album, the transformation was nearly total: The long solos that dominated Davis's records were gone, replaced by busy themes and stray ad-libs scribbled in the margins. Melodies more overtly occupied center stage—in parts of "Teen Town" and the plaintive "A Remark You Made," the theme is delivered by Jaco Pastorius, the pioneer who showed the world how the fretless bass could sing.

The music of *Heavy Weather* is thoroughly scripted, yet feels totally free—cue up "Birdland," the album's "single," to experience one of the only homages to jazz history

In 1977, *Down Beat* magazine chose *Heavy Weather* as Album of the Year.

that doesn't look backward. Over a gum-snapping backbeat, Zawinul conjures the full textural richness of a big band using synthesizers. Pastorius, wound as tightly as a drum, rumbles in and out of the spotlight, inserting his bass as another lead voice, effortlessly linking the infectious swing to his own favorite groove music, Stax-Volt R&B. Shorter darts from foreground to background like he's in the middle of a Spy vs. Spy chase. And by the time the group slams into the shout chorus, you feel like you've been riding a hipster bullet train that started back in the Count Basie 1930s, and won't stop till it hits Tomorrowland.

GENRE: 🎷 Jazz. **RELEASED:** 1977, Columbia. **KEY TRACKS:** "Palladium," "Teen Town," "A Remark You Made," "Birdland." **CATALOG CHOICES:** *Black Market; Mr. Gone; 8:30.* **NEXT STOP:** Jaco Pastorius: *Word of Mouth.* **AFTER THAT:** Passport: *Iguacu.*

Heaven on Their Minds

Jesus Christ Superstar

Andrew Lloyd Webber and Tim Rice
Original Cast Recording

Okay, so the source material—the story of Jesus—was pretty good. And the idea of adding a rock backbeat and turning it into a parable on the messianic worship of celebrity, that was inspired. But what separates this project from virtually everything else Andrew Lloyd Webber, the British treacle merchant, and lyricist Tim Rice developed together is the tunes—alternately spangley and cathedral-worthy, full of conflict and overrun with the bustle that followed this miracle worker and his large entourage everywhere.

The songs trace the last few weeks in the life of Jesus Christ, using rock backbeats, slang, and other modern allusions to change, slightly, the biblical context. Though it's not the first rock musical—that distinction might go to the far less hooky *Hair*, or even *Bye Bye Birdie*—*Jesus Christ Superstar* is the first to arrive with its own distinct sound, a set of signature character cues and motifs that connect into what's technically an operetta, since there's no spoken dialogue in the whole thing. When the story gets tense, the band provides gnarled, hectic accompaniment; the moment of Judas's betrayal is set against a staccato electric guitar figure that dramatizes a traitor's roiling inner conflict. Judas, played here by rocker Murray Head, shines throughout; an even bigger rock star, Deep Purple's Ian Gillan, plays Jesus. When our protagonists are stealing a quiet moment—see Yvonne Elliman's restive confession "I Don't Know

Andrew Lloyd Webber (left) and Tim Rice (right) won the Tony Award for Best Original Score for *Jesus Christ Superstar*.

How to Love Him"—the music catches a placid, idyllic mood, but much of *Superstar*, even the crowd scene "Hosanna," ripples with an undercurrent of turmoil. Unlike later Rice–Lloyd Webber collaborations, virtually every one of these songs gets under your skin without being overbearingly emotional.

Jesus Christ Superstar incited outrage from religious leaders when it arrived on Broadway in 1971. It became a massive hit and, in another delicious pop culture irony, within a few years was credited for sparking renewed interest in religion among young people. What's more, this soundtrack is frequently mentioned by subsequent generations of rockers as a formative listening experience. Sure, it's heavy and symbolic, but it's also riveting, the unlikely Sunday school lesson that's also a guilty pleasure.

GENRE: 😊 Musicals. **RELEASED:** 1970, MCA. **KEY TRACKS:** "What's the Buzz/ Strange Thing Mystifying," "I Don't Know How to Love Him," "Damned for All Time/Blood Money." **ANOTHER INTERPRETATION:** Original Motion Picture Soundtrack. **CATALOG CHOICE:** *Evita*, Original Broadway Cast. **NEXT STOP:** Anything but *Godspell*.

Pride, Envy, Anger, Sloth, Greed, Gluttony, Lust

The Seven Deadly Sins

Kurt Weill and Bertolt Brecht

Lotte Lenya, Wilhelm Bruckner-Ruggeberg

A tale of two sisters seeking fortune in America, Kurt Weill's last collaboration with lyricist Bertolt Brecht is one of the great allegorical stories of the twentieth century. When the story opens, the two women (one's a singer, the other a dancer; both are named Anna) set out ostensibly to help their poor family build a house in Louisiana, and during stops at various U.S. cities they collide with the deadly sins. The irony is, every time they resist one of the über sins, they commit a greater injustice to humanity. The sins serve as a satirical device: Anna 2 does wrong only when she does not commit the sin, and each time she learns the mercantile lesson that anything that brings financial success is morally okay. The full title of the work: "The Seven Deadly Sins of the Petty Bourgeoisie."

When he was 18, Weill moved to Berlin to study with Engelbert Humperdinck.

Weill and his wife/muse Lotte Lenya left Germany in 1933, after his name appeared on a Hitler hit list. They fled to Paris where, that year, Weill and Brecht concocted this piece, which is Weill's most symphonic theater work. In the past, the collaboration had been driven by Brecht's texts; here, in what was the duo's final joint effort, Weill took wild musical chances. The sinning plays out through broad, fetchingly melodic tunes—sturdy themes that hold up independently of any story line.

Lenya handles the dual roles of Anna 1, the practical-minded primary singer, and Anna 2, the emotional, artistic dancer. Their contrasting personalities help Brecht tell a tale in which conventional notions of moral-ity are turned upside down. Lenya's thin voice and super-fast vibrato didn't fall pleasantly on American ears at first. Her career faltered until after Weill died in 1950. Her voice deepened, her characterizations sharpened, and in the 1960s she became a reliable character actress (a landlord in the Broadway *Cabaret*, an evil Russian spy in *From Russia with Love*). These recordings were made with an ad hoc orchestra in Germany in the mid-1950s, and they show that despite her frail instrument, Lenya brought an imposing authority to her character. She conveys the moral gray areas of the text without any irony or exaggerated self-consciousness. By holding back her own judgment about the sisters and their sins, she brings listeners closer to each situation, where they can draw their own conclusions.

GENRE: 😀 Musicals. **RELEASED:** 1997, MHK. (Recorded 1955.) **KEY TRACKS:** "Anger (Molto Agitato)," "Lust (Moderato)." **COLLECTOR'S NOTE:** This is bundled with *Berlin Theatre Songs*, which contains songs from several Brecht/Weill productions. **CATALOG CHOICE:** *Threepenny Opera*, 1954 New York Cast. **NEXT STOP:** The Dresden Dolls: *Yes, Virginia . . . .*

Timeless Truth-Telling

Time (The Revelator)

Gillian Welch

Gillian Welch begins this journey with a song about identity, how it is shaped and transformed, and how only time can reveal who's genuine and who's "queen of the fakes and imitators." It's helpful to keep those cautionary words in mind as the rest of *Time* unfolds. They serve as a preamble, of sorts, for Welch's delicate inquiry—sketches and portraits of people caught in the middle of various deceptions, haunted by memories they can't shake and otherwise messed with by Papa Time. The weary-voiced singer and songwriter's two previous albums brought postmodern lyrical ideas to old-timey Appalachian balladry. With this work, she goes beyond being an imitator. She pours the forthright tone associated with the legendary Carter Family into songs shot through with modern ambivalence, poetic accounts of cell phone–tethered life. These range from meditations on faulty memory ("My First Lover," whom she describes as "tall and breezy with his long hair down, but he gets a little hazy when I think of him now") to a fable about rock and roll heroism ("Elvis Presleys Blues") to an expression of near biblical wanderlust ("I Dream a Highway," which lasts over fourteen minutes and invokes Lazarus, Gram Parsons, and Emmylou Harris).

Welch was born in Manhattan. She calls her style "American Primitive," though critics consider her a catalyst of the alternative-country "Americana" style. Her songs are

"Tradition informs everything I do, but it's not what I do."
—Gillian Welch

rustic and at the same time gimlet-eyed, wise about the world. Both Welch and her musical partner David Rawlings sing and play guitar; she strums placidly while he scatters terse jabs and gingham-print chords all over the place. Their voices intertwine beautifully, with Rawlings sometimes supplying high, hollowed-out harmonies that provide an extra shot of lonesomeness.

After being hailed and scorned for the scholarly appropriations of her first two records, Welch made other changes this time around—she told one interviewer that she conceived this as a set of rock songs, to be played on acoustic instruments. Even when the mood is front-porch plaintive, Welch's songs speak to a moment being lived right now, not some quaint olden-days curio. Changing lanes between pensive balladry and wrenching blues, Welch and Rawlings create hazy out-of-time dream sequences that belong to no one genre. But speak the truths of many.

GENRE: 🌐 Country. **RELEASED:** 2001, Almo Sounds. **KEY TRACKS:** "Dear Someone," "Ruination Day, Part 2," "Revelator," "I Dream a Highway." **CATALOG CHOICE:** *Hell Among the Yearlings.* **NEXT STOP:** Iris DeMent: *Infamous Angel.* **AFTER THAT:** Victoria Williams: *Loose.*

The Product of a Heavy Awakening

College Dropout

Kanye West

I n 2002, the hip-hop producer Kanye West—then known for severe, sizzling beats that anchored super-successful hits for Jay-Z and others—survived a serious car accident. Its aftermath brought a reality check, in which West

realized he wanted to do more than just make beats and turn knobs in the studio. Though he'd broken his jaw (it was wired shut), West began writing raps while still in the hospital, including one from this album that became a hit, "Through the Wire," which graphically describes the accident and his subsequent awakening.

The physical recovery took a while. But by West's own account, the attitude change was instantaneous. *College Dropout* is the confession of a wickedly talented, high-rolling beatmaker whose priorities have been reordered. It's a savagely erudite screed on racism and the socioeconomic conditions of African Americans, a meditation on fate, an audacious lampoon of infomercials, and an outright booty call.

It's also the extremely rare hip-hop record to talk directly about faith. In one verse of "Jesus Walks," West says he knows that kind of talk limits his commercial prospects—that radio won't "spin" an overly religious song.

He doesn't care: He goes right back to the pulpit on the very next track, saying, "Whenever I open my heart, my soul or my mouth, a touch of God rings out."

West's message is carried by the same terse, nothing-but-the-essentials production style that put him in demand initially. On "Through the Wire," West speeds up Chaka Khan's vocals (from her hit "Through the Fire") until they're a chipmunk-like blur, but not so much that the original's eargrabbing melody is lost. Other tracks tap the Bacharach/David songbook or draw from collages of defiantly odd sound scraps; several anticipate the more elaborate orchestrations that West (with help from Fiona Apple's producer Jon Brion) would pursue on the otherwise less daring 2005 follow-up, *Late Registration*.

GENRE: 🎵 Hip-Hop.
RELEASED: 2004, Roc-A-Fella.
KEY TRACKS: "Through the Wire," "Slow Jamz," "I'll Fly Away," "Jesus Walks."
CATALOG CHOICE: *Late Registration.*
NEXT STOP: Jay-Z: *The Blueprint.* **AFTER THAT:** N.E.R.D.: *In Search Of . . . .*

West's *College Dropout* was voted Best Album of the Year by *Rolling Stone, Spin,* and the *Village Voice* Pazz & Jop critics' poll.

Beware: Flaming Guitars

Stratosphere Boogie

Speedy West and Jimmy Bryant

Purveyors of quickstepping boogies and clippety-clopping two-steps, guitarists Speedy West and Jimmy Bryant were a well-matched tandem. West played pedal steel, and specialized in swooping melodies. Bryant, the first guitarist to endorse the Fender Telecaster, played six-string with an accountant's precision. The chugging and choogling traveling music they made was ahead of its time. And, apparently, slightly too space-age for mainstream tastes.

West and Bryant first met at a Los Angeles club in 1948. After several years of studio work—backing Tennessee Ernie Ford and Kay Starr—they began recording as a duo in 1952, and

Between 1950 and 1955, West (left) played on over 6,000 recordings with 177 different artists.

over the next four years met with sporadic success. Radio stations didn't play the duo. The Nashville establishment certainly didn't know what to make of the wild West-Bryant instrumentals, which sent the pedal-steel-plus-standard-guitar attack of Bob Wills and His Texas Playboys (see p. 868) to Jetsonian outer limits.

The recordings collected on *Stratosphere Boogie* are freewheeling and astonishing, explosions of guitar derring-do without equal. Here is bebop with a twang ("The Night Rider"), fiddle tunes brushed with a touch of Hawaiian soul ("Old Joe Clark"), and weepers that show West sliding and swooping over the fretboard ("Sleepwalker's Lament"). The music feels alive and off-the-cuff, because that's how West and Bryant made it. In the liner notes, West recalls that they'd each bring two songs to a session. Neither heard the other's material until it was time to record. "We did that on purpose so we had a spontaneous sound."

GENRE: ◯ Country. **RELEASED:** 1952–1956, Capitol. (Reissued 1995, Razor & Tie.) **KEY TRACKS:** "Stratosphere Boogie," "Old Joe Clark," "Speedin' West," "The Night Rider." **NEXT STOP:** Les Paul: *Crazy Rhythm*.

A Jazz Landmark Inspired by Mother Africa

The Spirits of Our Ancestors

Randy Weston

There was lots of talk about ancestors and forefathers floating around the jazz world in the early 1990s. Wynton Marsalis, media darling, was everywhere, preaching a respect-the-tradition approach that won many followers among young jazz musicians. Some veterans responded as well—Keith Jarrett's *Standards* trio showed how old tunes, the Marsalis-approved "classic" repertoire of jazz, could be reworked into newly vital platforms.

Randy Weston, the often-overlooked pianist and composer who was born in Brooklyn in 1926, entered this discussion from a different direction: Forget about honoring the well-documented exploits of Louis Armstrong and the other jazz greats, he suggested, and concentrate on Mother Africa, the headwater from which so much music has flowed. This two-CD suite, recorded over three days in 1991, stands as one of the most imaginative explorations of "world jazz" ever recorded, a series of picturesque "scenes" conjuring village life from the perspective of urbane jazzers.

A series of originals inspired by folk tunes, *Spirits* begins with Weston's solo piano fantasy, "African Village Bedford-Stuyvesant 1," which

In 1955, Weston was voted New Star Pianist in *Down Beat* magazine's International Critics' Poll.

links stride-style rhythms to angular modern chordal splashes. That's a clue about what's to come: music that, in celebrating Africa, gleefully scrambles the jazz time line. A medium-sized ensemble arrives for "The Healers," playing a rustic melody that arranger Melba Liston, a frequent Weston collaborator, scored to make several horns sound like a parade band. The soloists all rise to the challenges of these ambling pieces: Eager to expand upon Weston's earthy, contrivance-free motifs, they move as though guided by wise ancestral spirits.

GENRE: 🎵 Jazz. **RELEASED:** 1992, Antilles. **KEY TRACKS:** "African Village Bedford-Stuyvesant 1," "African Cookbook," "The Call," "African Sunrise," "A Prayer for Us All." **CATALOG CHOICES:** *Tanjah; The Splendid Master Gnawa Musicians of Morocco.* **NEXT STOP:** Abdullah Ibrahim: *Soweto.* **AFTER THAT:** Dudu Pukwana: *In the Townships.*

Pure Lyricism from the Trumpet

Gnu High

Kenny Wheeler

From Louis Armstrong through Dizzy Gillespie and the hard bop master Woody Shaw, the trumpet has usually attracted extroverts and dazzlers. Kenny Wheeler, the enormously talented trumpeter and composer, began to change that in the 1970s—his playing emphasizes softer textures and less grandstanding approaches. On the astounding *Gnu High*, he plays the flügelhorn, a close relative of the trumpet that has a slightly more rounded tone, and favors scampering, musing phrases over reveille bursts that scream, "Look at me!" With this record and several that follow it, Wheeler suggests that brass can sing, and sing sweetly.

Few jazz musicians treat it that way. And even fewer write tunes that demand such tonal nuance. Wheeler specializes in languid, questioning themes that practically force him to think in expansive terms when soloing. The title suite, which lasts nearly thirteen minutes, moves through long rubato passages into broken samba-like grooves and, eventually, a more assertive choppy swing. When Wheeler makes his entrance, he doesn't barge in; rather, he glides, taking care not to step too heavily on any one beat. Follow closely as he develops his solos, however: Wheeler frequently ventures into the trumpet's extreme upper register, where brute force is often needed, and somehow hangs onto his innate sense of lyricism. Believe the title: His high notes are a new kind of high.

Gnu High is also notable as the rare date from this period where Keith Jarrett appears in a supporting role. The pianist totally "gets" Wheeler's tunes—at times on "Smatter," which features a solo-piano interlude, Jarrett generates flowing melodies with such facility, you might think he wrote the tune. That's also a function of tone: Because Wheeler's sound is so warm and inviting, everyone around him plays that way too.

GENRE: 🎵 Jazz. **RELEASED:** 1975, ECM. **KEY TRACKS:** "Smatter," "Gnu Suite." **CATALOG CHOICE:** *Double, Double You.* **NEXT STOP:** Keith Jarrett: *My Song* (see p. 394). **AFTER THAT:** Woody Shaw: *Rosewood.*

The Maestro of Satin Sheets and Candlelight

Can't Get Enough

Barry White

Though based on the West Coast and often associated with disco, the songwriter, producer, and deep-voiced love god Barry White (1944–2003) made his biggest artistic contribution during the heyday of smooth,

orchestral Philly soul. In 1973 and 1974, White and/or his Love Unlimited Orchestra were inescapable on the radio and, alongside the O'Jays and Isaac Hayes, helped trigger one of pop music's gaudiest outbreaks of polished symphonics. In that two-year period alone, White's recordings generated more than sixteen million dollars in sales.

White's 1974 release *Can't Get Enough* is the most consistent in his discography, and an all-time classic of baby-making bedroom soul. It begins, as many White projects do, with an opulent instrumental. "Mellow Mood Part 1" serves as a showcase for the band of ace session musicians White kept on retainer, which included rhythm guitarist Melvin "Wah-Wah" Watson and Crusaders'

Can't Get Enough is White's third album.

bassist Wilton Felder. Then comes "You're the First, the Last, My Everything," a driving disco anthem that became the blueprint for big hits by Donna Summer and others. It might just be the one track that best epitomizes the songwriting and production innovations of disco.

From there White dishes a few trademark spoken-word bended-knee declarations (including the one from the album's other massive hit, "Can't Get Enough of Your Love, Babe") interspersed with shining string fantasias. White was frequently derided as a one-trick artist, and it's true that as a singer, he did rely on a limited repertoire of quiet groans and deeply worshipful postcoital crooning. But what he couldn't do with his voice he did with his orchestra: Like nothing before or since, these inventive arrangements cook forever on low flame, creating an ideal setting for an evening of bliss.

GENRE: 🎵 R&B. **RELEASED**: 1974,

Twentieth Century. **KEY TRACKS**: "You're the First, the Last, My Everything," "Can't Get Enough of Your Love, Babe," "Oh Love, Well We Finally Made It." **CATALOG CHOICE**: *Stone Gon'.* **NEXT STOP**: George Benson: *Breezin'.* **AFTER THAT**: Al Green: *The Belle Album.*

A "Track One" for the Ages, and Then Some

Elephant

The White Stripes

In *High Fidelity,* Nick Hornby's 1996 novel (and the subsequent feature film) about record worship, the clerks in the local shop spend their days organizing everyday life into lists. There are debates over the all-time best party songs, the best side one, track one, and so on. No fine point escapes these aesthetes, who relate every possible human experience to three-minute songs.

Elephant, the fourth album from the Detroit duo known as the White Stripes, would likely have been a favorite in that store, not least because it opens with one savage blast of rock and roll, a quintessential track one that telegraphs the big rock noise to follow. "Seven Nation Army" transforms a lover's declaration of devotion ("A seven-nation army couldn't hold me back") into a crusade framed by a guitar riff that incorporates great hooks from British blues-rock of the late '60s and brash American arena fare of the '70s.

The White Stripes—guitarist, singer, and songwriter Jack White, drummer and singer Meg White—first attracted attention in 2001 with a fuzzed up, irreverent take on the blues and an ear for quirky pop songs (the best known is the disarmingly sweet "Fell in Love with a Girl"). *Elephant* finds the duo in its comfort

"If you study the picture carefully, Meg and I are elephant ears in a head-on elephant."
—Jack White

zone—its pop leanings are evident on "Hypnotise," while the swaggering "Ball and Biscuit" reaches new heights of blues derangement. At the same time, it expands the Stripes' raw sound, with lilting piano and country-style guitar strumming, and, on the bizarro breakup song "There's No Home for You Here," lugubrious, defiantly out-of-time shards of metal guitar.

Incredibly, there's no letup in this cannily sequenced fourteen-song romp. Follow the White Stripes through simple hooks, prog-rock darkness, and campy vaudeville routines, and it becomes clear that this band didn't just come up with a killer track one. It made one of the most consistently riveting rock records of all time.

GENRE: 🎸 Rock. **RELEASED**: 2003, V2. **KEY TRACKS**: "Seven Nation Army," "There's No Home for You Here," "Black Math," "Ball and Biscuit." **CATALOG CHOICE**: *White Blood Cells.* **NEXT STOP**: Smashing Pumpkins: *Mellon Collie and the Infinite Sadness.* **AFTER THAT**: The Hives: *Tyrannosaurus Hives.*

A Distorted Roots-Rock Roar

Living with the Law

Chris Whitley

This album appeared in 1991, as the back-to-the-roots "Americana" movement was gaining steam. It towers above just about everything else filed under that description. While most of the genre's young practitioners treated Hank Williams or Muddy Waters songs as sacred texts, Chris Whitley (1960–2005) assimilated and then torched those influences. He said he had no interest in preserving the blues—or, for that matter, keeping anything pure. He sought, instead, to connect worlds. Building on thick tangles of guitar and plaintive cries, he opened up the trove of American roots music to postpunk kids who'd yet to discover the meaning of Robert Johnson.

In 2001, *The New York Times* called Whitley "restless . . . evoking Chet Baker and Sonic Youth as much as Robert Johnson."

Living with the Law, Whitley's debut, unfolds in a sultry too-hot-to-care haze. The guitarist sings in dejected bursts and he often sounds less like a Delta bluesman than a weary farmhand trapped in the high-intensity headlights of a world he doesn't understand. Around his vocals are shimmering atmospheres from the steel-bodied guitar and carefully speared lead guitar lines, which Whitley plays with such force they rattle.

What holds this raggedy mess together are the songs, disciplined vignettes that could be chapters in an extended drifter narrative. Whitley writes in a way that shows his understanding of blues tropes, and when he climbs into his weary falsetto to tell about the trouble he has staying on the straight and narrow, you believe him. There's panic in his voice, and it doesn't belong exclusively to the blues—or to him. It's universal.

GENRES: 🎸 Rock 🎵 Blues. **RELEASED:** 1991, Columbia. **KEY TRACKS:** "Big Sky Country," "I Forget You Every Day," "Dust Radio." **CATALOG CHOICE:** *Soft Dangerous Shores.* **NEXT STOP:** Daniel Lanois: *Acadie.* **AFTER THAT:** Son Volt: *Trace.*

"There's a Lot I Could Do with a Freak"

Tommy

The Who

In the September 1968 double issue of *Rolling Stone*, the Who's Pete Townshend talked at length about his vision for his band's next project. It was to be the tale of a boy struck deaf, dumb, and blind after witnessing a murder at a young age.

The narrative would follow Tommy's trials, his recovery and transformation into a pop-culture sensation—if not a messianic figure. The music, Townshend said, would have to "explain what happens, that the boy elevates and finds something which is incredible."

That's pretty much how *Tommy* turned out, give or take a few nonsensical ditties. The first "rock opera" and still the best, Townshend's song cycle has an unusually complex (and often disturbing) plot, but never leans too heavily on it. Each key "scene"—from early ones involving relatives and schoolyard bullies taking advantage of Tommy to triumphant later ones chronicling his unlikely breakthrough as a "Pinball Wizard"—is explored through fetchingly memorable songs. As in opera, kernels of melody crop up at strategic points to knit the story together. For example, the vocal declaration "We're Not Gonna Take It" comes near the end of the work, but its theme has been in the air from the start—it's integral to the overture (where it's played by solo French horn) and appears in the background of several subsequent scenes.

Tommy was later produced on the stage and turned into a film.

The songs of *Tommy* catch Townshend at his most trenchant—check out the way he uses the zealous, pealing tones of a church choir to ponder blind devotion and idol-worship ("See Me, Feel Me/Listening to You"). Throughout, the guitarist attends to the fine points of craft and storytelling, yet never gets so Operaman that he forgets his strong suit: charged-up refrains of fire-breathing defiance ("We're Not Gonna Take It," "I'm Free"). These are more than songs—they're affirmations of rock as a path to understanding and maybe even redemption. Hear just one of them, and you may find yourself swept right into the world of that miraculous deaf, dumb, and blind kid, who somehow puts people in touch with what it means to be alive.

GENRE: 🎸 Rock. **RELEASED:** 1969, MCA. **KEY TRACKS:** "We're Not Gonna Take It," "I'm Free," "Underture," "Pinball Wizard," "See Me, Feel Me/Listening to You." **CATALOG CHOICES:** *Quadrophenia; The Who Sell Out.* **NEXT STOP:** The Soundtrack of Our Lives: *Behind the Music.* **AFTER THAT:** Oasis: *(What's the Story) Morning Glory?*

Rock Rebellion Writ Large

Who's Next

The Who

Take all the gazillions of well-intentioned rock anthems written since this came out in 1971. Load them into boom boxes and press Play at the same time. The mass of sound won't get anywhere near the earth-rattling righteousness of Roger Daltrey singing "Won't Get Fooled Again" with guitarist Pete Townshend, bassist John Entwistle, and drummer Keith Moon clanging mightily behind him.

One of the great rock albums, *Who's Next* almost didn't happen. Attempting to follow up the band's massive 1969 hit *Tommy*, Townshend wrote a sprawling suite of somewhat futuristic songs he called *Lifehouse,* which he intended as another opera. It fell apart. Townshend suffered a nervous breakdown. When he returned, he revisited a few of the *Lifehouse* pieces, writing new songs from them. *Who's Next* is what emerged. It's the moment when Townshend arrived at a balance of brute power and oppositional provocation that was unlike anything in rock before. It was loud and at the same time learned. Its feistiness made it an inspiration for much that followed: Without this, there would be no U2. No Clash. No Pearl Jam.

Every track on *Who's Next* is its own universe. Starting with the synthesizer-studded "Baba O'Riley," a lament about the "teenage wasteland" that is arguably the greatest album-opener in rock history, the Who charges through a series of amazingly disciplined and totally visceral songs. One, "Love Ain't for Keeping,"

wrestles with the meaning of commitment. Another, "Behind Blue Eyes," complains about being forever misunderstood. Townshend's focused writing keeps the rhythm section perpetually on the verge of volcanic eruption, while Daltrey, CEO of Indignation Incorporated, stands like a sentry on the precipice, warning the members of his tribe about the perils ahead. No matter how many times you've heard these songs on the radio, it's impossible to listen casually: By the time the final blitzkrieg, "Won't Get Fooled Again," hits, you're part of the army, ready to battle duplicity wherever it festers.

GENRE: 🎸 Rock. **RELEASED:** 1971, MCA. **KEY TRACKS:** "Baba O'Riley," "Behind Blue Eyes," "Bargain," "Won't Get Fooled Again." **CATALOG CHOICES:** *The Who Sell Out; Live at Leeds* (original version). **NEXT STOP:** U2: *War.* **AFTER THAT:** Pearl Jam: *Vs.*

Art Beats the Business

Yankee Hotel Foxtrot

Wilco

The story of this album is just too good not to tell. Even if you've heard it a zillion times, and know every parry and thrust of the struggle between Earnest Rock Band and Evil Megacorp, there's something heartwarming about how it ends up. It's the extremely rare victory for art over the craven greed that so often rules the music business.

Veteran band (Wilco) turns in a rousing, challenging new album. Evil Record Company (Reprise) is not so roused, and suggests changes, among them the inclusion of a "single" the band has somehow overlooked. Band says, "See ya." Legal wrangling ensues. Eventually the band breaks free, and sends the challenging music to other labels. Several are interested, and when said album (*Yankee Hotel Foxtrot*) appears on Nonesuch, which, ironically, is owned by the same big conglomerate

that owns Reprise, it's met with nearly universal critical raves. Though it's been available as a free download for months, it becomes a commercial success, making the evil label look colossally stupid.

Even without all the drama, *Yankee Hotel Foxtrot* is notable—it's the album where principal songwriter Jeff Tweedy's art sprouts new dimensions. A tunesmith who, as part of Uncle Tupelo (see p. 795), developed distinctive approaches to front-porch country-folk and snarling rock, Tweedy pushes past what worked for him on previous projects. He discovers not one new voice, but several. His declarative love songs ("I'm the Man Who Loves You") cut straight to the chase in an almost uncomfortably vulnerable way; then, on songs like "Kamera," his images float around in a cloudy upper atmosphere, supported by blips and radio static (the album's title is derived from shortwave lingo) and planks of droning guitar dissonance.

On the cover: a picture of Marina City in Wilco's hometown of Chicago.

Tweedy's inspired by these startling sounds, so much so that he rhapsodizes on several songs about music as a great elixir—it's a "Radio Cure" for loneliness, or the speediest way to "turn your orbit around." Individually or en masse, the songs on *Yankee Hotel Foxtrot*

and the even more adventurous follow-up, *A Ghost Is Born*, do exactly that.

GENRE: 🎸 Rock. **RELEASED:** 2002, Nonesuch. **KEY TRACKS:** "I Am Trying to Break Your Heart," "Radio Cure," "Jesus, Etc.," "War on War." **FURTHER INQUIRY:** Filmmaker Sam Jones chronicled this record's backstory in the documentary *I Am Trying to Break Your Heart.* **CATALOG CHOICES:** *Summerteeth; A Ghost Is Born.* **NEXT STOP:** Joe Henry: *Short Man's Room.* **AFTER THAT:** The Arcade Fire: *Funeral.*

The Secret Heartbeat of the Crescent City

The Wild Tchoupitoulas

The Wild Tchoupitoulas

Inside the beautifully harmonized battle cries of the Mardi Gras Indians dwells the secret heartbeat of New Orleans. At once jovial and diffident, these songs provide a window into the mystical aspects of the place. They're simple and infectious chants, echoes from a world kept hidden backstage most of the year, part of the exotic beads-and-feathers culture that blooms, magically, each February in the parades and celebrations of Fat Tuesday.

Those chants have resounded with extra urgency in the years since Hurricane Katrina devastated the city. But this is no quaint cultural-heritage document. Here, the call-and-response exchanges of voodoo priests and the taunts of the tribes are transformed into

The band takes its name from Tchoupitoulas Street in New Orleans.

radical and righteous-sounding dance music. The rhythms are all suitable for spirited strutting—there's a slow, undulating prance through "Meet de Boys on the Battlefront," and a version of "Iko Iko" (the group's revision of the Dixie Cups' 1965 hit) built on a terse chank-a-chank grind. In typical New Orleans fashion, no overt effort is audible in this funk—it's casual music made for striding down boulevards, drink raised overhead, backfield in motion, without a care.

Even in the Crescent City, that high-stepping revelry doesn't just happen. The Wild Tchoupitoulas had been part of the parade scene for years when the leader, Big Chief Jolly (George Landry), asked his cousins, members of the Neville family, to bolster the tribe's music, as an experiment. The sound was a success, and pretty soon Landry's tribe was in the studio. With guidance from ace producer Allen Toussaint (see p. 782), Landry and his crew tear through their energetic, crowd-revving chants one after another, creating a joyous album-length medley. While the vocals are incredible, the rhythm-section interplay between the Nevilles and members of the Meters makes this, the Wild Tchoupitoulas' only album, essential.

(According to one legend, this was the session at which the Neville Brothers became a band.) Everything percolates effortlessly along, with jabbering organ, thumping bass, and greasy drumbeats coalescing into something that's highly combustible and impossible to resist. Those who love the Neville Brothers will find the roots of that band's galvanizing, superkinetic, grin-producing groove here.

GENRES: 😊 Blues 🎸 Rock. **RELEASED:** 1976, Mango. **KEY TRACKS:** "Hey Pocky A Way," "Brother John," "Meet de Boys on the Battlefront." **CATALOG CHOICE:** The Neville Brothers: *Fiyo on the Bayou.* **NEXT STOP:** The Dirty Dozen Brass Band: *Voodoo.* **AFTER THAT:** The Soul Rebels: *Rebelution.*

The Best of the Hillbilly Shakespeare

Forty Greatest Hits

Hank Williams

The professional recording career of Hank Williams, the country singer-songwriter who did more to immortalize the lonesome road than any other, lasted all of six years. In that time, Williams (1923–1953) wrote a series of songs that still epitomize the plainspoken essence of country music—weepers like "Your Cheatin' Heart" and "I'm So Lonesome I Could Cry," blithe up-tempo tunes like "You're Gonna Change (or I'm Gonna Leave)," and the roaring shuffle "Move It on Over." Williams released jukebox classics with incredible regularity—in 1949 he hit the Top 10 with seven different singles—but it wasn't until after his death, and the rise of the long-playing phonograph record, that most fans could appreciate the magnitude of his output. Turns

"I reckon I've written a thousand songs and had over 300 published." —Hank Williams

out he generated enough material to fill a ten-CD box set.

Unfortunately, the people charged with preserving Williams's work were somewhat reckless. Shortly after he died (in the backseat of his new Cadillac while being driven to a New Year's Day show in Canton, Ohio), there came a wave of "altered" recordings—strings were added to some tunes, and others had the original mono mixes reprocessed into horrendous fake stereo. Later, there were posthumous duets with family members. This collection focuses on the original singles and choice B sides, wisely avoiding those extra-large judgment lapses.

These forty songs present Williams as the key link between the rural wildness of early country and the suave, sophisticated honky-tonk of the modern era. And they spotlight his primary areas of concentration—upbeat and lighthearted tunes ("Hey Good Lookin'"), deeply wounded balladry ("Cold, Cold Heart," which, incredibly, was issued as a B side), and zesty gospel ("I Saw the Light"). All of it is essential, a reliable map to the restless America, where lonely hearts ride even lonelier roads.

GENRE: 🌐 Country. **RELEASED:** 1978, Mercury. (Reissued 2000.) **KEY TRACKS:** "Moanin' the Blues," "Jambalaya (on the Bayou)," "Cold, Cold Heart," "Lovesick Blues," "I'm So Lonesome I Could Cry." **CATALOG CHOICES:** *Hank Williams as Luke the Drifter*. **NEXT STOP:** The Louvin Brothers: *Satan Is Real* (see p. 455). **AFTER THAT:** Hank Williams Jr.: *Whiskey Bent and Hell Bound*.

All Right, OK, This Wins

Count Basie Swings, Joe Williams Sings

Joe Williams with the Count Basie Orchestra

When Joe Williams took over for Jimmy Rushing as the singer in a retooled 1954 edition of the Count Basie band, some longtime fans were worried. After all, nobody in all of jazz or blues had the steamrolling power of Rushing. The lanky Williams (1918–1999), who told one interviewer he spent his twenties playing baseball and goofing around, couldn't touch his predecessor on that score. But he did have something else—a buoyant and refined style, a way of phrasing that nicely complemented the barreling brawn of the Basie band. Where Rushing would reach out and grab listeners, Williams used a suave cosmopolitan cool to lure them in. Still, as Williams recalled years later, this didn't help him win fans among Basie loyalists immediately. "It took them years before they finally decided, 'So it isn't Jimmy Rushing.'"

This is Williams's first recording with Basie. It's also his career peak, and a near-

Swings/Sings was recorded in July 1955 in New York.

perfect exhibition of the band-singer art. It starts with a crackling, high-energy update of Williams's first signature song with Basie, "Every Day I Have the Blues." Arranged by the great Ernie Wilkins, the chart goes against most big-band-with-vocal conventions: The band starts with several choruses of simple blues, building anticipation for more than a minute and a half before Williams enters. The brass is so hot there's no need for vocal fireworks, but Williams drops some anyway—spine-chilling ad-libs that test the agility of his rich, buttery baritone. By his last chorus, when he really lets loose, you can tell Williams is awed by this hard-swinging band, and doing what he can to keep up.

Actually, that admiration is audible throughout *Sings/Swings*. Williams approaches "Teach Me Tonight" the way a Basie soloist would—as a test of gentlemanly restraint, catching the tune's ribald possibilities without ever veering into salaciousness. He bounces through "All Right, OK, You Win" in a glib and playful mood, and when he slows down a bit, to render the bluesy "Please Send Me Someone to Love," Williams makes like he's nearly given up on the romance business. Basie's crew follows him (or maybe pushes him) right to the brink of despair, empathizing with that pain while wringing every last musical possibility from it.

GENRES: Jazz Vocals. **RELEASED:** 1955, Clef. **KEY TRACKS:** "Every Day I Have the Blues," "Teach Me Tonight," "All Right, OK, You Win." **CATALOG CHOICE:** *Presenting Joe Williams with the Thad Jones/Mel Lewis Jazz Orchestra*. **NEXT STOP:** Jimmy Rushing: *Jimmy Rushing Sings the Blues*. **AFTER THAT:** Jimmy Witherspoon: *The Spoon Concerts*.

A Good Downer from a Poet of the Gravel Roads

Sweet Old World

Lucinda Williams

Texas-based singer and songwriter Lucinda Williams spent eight years writing her self-titled third album—a relationship chronicle that yielded hits for Mary Chapin Carpenter ("Passionate Kisses") and others, and contained one of the all-time great expressions of love's bitterness, "Changed the Locks." Having gone so deeply into that realm, it was probably inevitable that Williams would seek something different for the follow-up, *Sweet Old World*, which arrived four years later.

And what a difference: These eleven originals (and a version of Nick Drake's "Which Will") amount to an extended meditation on death, from someone who has obviously grieved a few times. When Williams sings, "See what you lost when you left this world" on the title track, her subsequent list of the little things worth celebrating is delivered in cracked and aching tones, like she's trying to remind herself, not the departed, about what pleasure means. Williams's voice is well suited to this emotional place: She can sound wracked

In 2002, *Time* called Williams "America's best songwriter."

and vulnerable even when she's belting out an up-tempo blues.

Telling stories about unexpected suicides, breakups, and lesser tragedies, Williams manages to convey loss without wallowing in despair. There's anger bubbling inside these songs, and resentment, and also that fragile minute-to-minute hope shared by survivors. The themes are mostly dour, sure, but because Williams's eye is so sharp and her voice so believable, *Sweet Old World* is the good kind of downer.

GENRE: Country. **RELEASED:** 1992, Chameleon. **KEY TRACKS:** "Six Blocks Away," "Pineola," "Sweet Old World." **CATALOG CHOICE:** *Lucinda Williams*. **NEXT STOP:** Rosanne Cash: *Interiors*. **AFTER THAT:** Amy Rigby: *Diary of a Mod Housewife*.

Strong, as in Superhuman

Strong Again

Marion Williams

Marion Williams begins this, her best solo album, by making a list of troubles that might be helped by prayer. Cancer. Gambling. Alcoholism. Whatever the habit or affliction, the indomitable Williams is committed to trying to get things moving in the right direction. To that end, she closes every verse with this simple declaration: "I got your name on the prayer list."

Sung by anyone else, such a ploy would seem routine gospel showbiz. But Williams shares her "Prayer List" in a way that's believable, even reassuring. She mentions the scourges diabetes and AIDS with a shiver. (In the case of diabetes, she had some personal experience: Williams's mother lost both legs to the disease.) Still, when Williams comes to the part about praying, there's peace in the valley. She sounds like she knows that if she prays, something is gonna happen.

That quality of unshakable faith is present in Williams's best recordings—which include notable works as part of Clara Ward Singers (see p. 845). This one, which finds her in front of a small ensemble, is notable for the song selection: In addition to tearing up gospel standbys like "O Happy Day" and "Working on a Building," Williams does a breathtaking tempoless version of "Sometimes I Feel like a Motherless Child," followed by an impassioned reworking of Billie Holiday's "God Bless the Child."

In truth, it really doesn't matter whether Williams sings a prayer list or a grocery list. Seconds after she drops one of those blistering ad-libs, the music roars to life, and suddenly long-shot miracles don't seem so unlikely anymore.

GENRE: ✝ Gospel. **RELEASED:** 1991, SpiritFeel/Shanachie. **KEY TRACKS:** "O Happy Day," "Prayer List," "If You See My Savior," "Working on a Building." **F.Y.I.:** Little Richard once acknowledged that his signature "Whoooo" was inspired by Marion Williams. **CATALOG CHOICE:** *If We Ever Needed the Lord Before.* **NEXT STOP:** Bessie Griffin: *Recorded Live at "The Bear" in Chicago* (see p. 328). **AFTER THAT:** Dorothy Love Coates: *A City Built Four Square.*

The Stars Align for These Astrological Portraits

Zodiac Suite

Mary Lou Williams

On a Sunday in 1945, jazz pianist Mary Lou Williams (1910–1981) told the listeners of her WNEW radio program that for each of the next twelve weeks she'd be premiering a new piece of music based on a different sign of the zodiac. Her basic idea, she wrote in the liner notes of what became her first extended work, was to write music that reflected the temperaments and traits of each sign, as represented by artists such as Art Tatum (Libra) and Lena Horne (Cancer), many of them her friends. "I have always thought of astrology as understanding one of the influences that molds man's destiny, and I have given the signs the musical interpretation which I feel they warranted."

Williams received Guggenheim Fellowships in 1972 and 1977.

She'd already written the first three before that broadcast. And then, writer's block descended. "I couldn't write any more, my inspiration had left me," she told a jazz historian. So she did what any alert jazz musician would: She made things up on the fly, composing while she was playing. Remarkably, the music never wanders: Ranging from old-fashioned stride to beautifully contemplative rubato fantasias, Williams explores themes that might have been in her composition notebook for years. "Aries," for one, is sublime, as is the drifting, vaguely disquieted introduction of "Cancer."

Williams did formalize the *Suite,* eventually drawing on her arranging experience with Andy Kirk's Clouds of Joy to create an orchestral score for a concert at New York's Town Hall in December 1945. But the versions heard here, which are mostly solo with bass accompaniment on some tunes, are more interesting—they're spare and wondrous examples of "spontaneous composition" that encompass the whole renegade history of jazz but never sound like a history lesson.

GENRE: 🎷 Jazz. **RELEASED:** 1945, Asch. (Reissued 1977, Folkways.) **KEY TRACKS:** "Libra," "Cancer," "Aries." **CATALOG CHOICE:** *Zoning.* **NEXT STOP:** Duke Ellington: *The Far East Suite* (see p. 253). **AFTER THAT:** Andy Kirk and His Clouds of Joy: *Jukebox Hits of 1936–1949.*

The Most Exciting Jazz-Rock Fusion

Emergency!

The Tony Williams Lifetime

❝Emergency!" begins with a press roll on the snare drum, an age-old device used by jazz drummers to rally the troops. Within seconds, though, the spark-plug percussionist Tony Williams (1945–1997) has wiped out all vestiges of tradition, and we're into some thrashing, whiplashing backbeat that's closer to Jimi Hendrix than anything swing. The electric guitar of John McLaughlin, who first played with Williams in the bands of Miles Davis, slices the air. Lurking in the background is organist Larry Young, whose chords have a clipped, Morse code urgency. For nine thrilling minutes, these three musicians travel through various tempos—some brisk uptempo jazz, some stomping rock, some outright space jamming—and follow an equal number of moody tangents. When, near the end, there's an audible exclamation, a "whoo!," it's clear that this is not another jazz attempt to "cash in" on rock, it's serious business.

In the liner notes of a Lifetime anthology, Williams says that after leaving Davis's group, he began listening to Hendrix, Cream, and the MC5: "My drumming had become more aggressive and that was the direction that I wanted to follow." This trio quickly became the most vital realization of that sound.

McLaughlin and Young prove excellent companions. Though other power trios followed this one, few ever achieved the sense of commitment, the shared taste for fast-rising and sustained insurrections. Just about every track finds him trampling stylistic barriers,

and deploying different types of provocations—Williams's improvisational reflexes are so toned it seems that every moment brings some new rhythmic challenge. Very few titles filed under jazz fusion exceed *Emergency!* in thrills per minute.

GENRE: 🅙 Jazz. **RELEASED:** 1969, Polydor. **KEY TRACKS:** "Emergency!," "Vashkar," "Spectrum." **CATALOG CHOICES:** *Lifetime; Tokyo Live.* **NEXT STOP:** Mahavishnu Orchestra: *Birds of Fire.* **AFTER THAT:** Billy Cobham: *Spectrum.*

This Blues Brings Eyesight to the Blind

One Way Out

Sonny Boy Williamson II

The odd case of Sonny Boy Williamson illustrates how identity can be fluid in the blues. The youngest of twenty-one children from Glendora, Mississippi, singer and harmonica player Aleck "Rice" Miller got his big

break hosting *King Biscuit Time*, the first national blues radio show, in 1941. The show's sponsor (Interstate Grocery Company) believed it could sell more if Miller presented himself as Chicago harmonica star John Lee (whose stage name was "Sonny Boy" Williamson). The two didn't resemble each other in looks or playing style, but somehow the identity-theft ruse worked, enhancing Miller's employability on the blues circuit. Only after Lee was murdered did Miller, whose likeness appeared on boxes of Sonny Boy corn meal, proclaim himself the "real" Sonny Boy.

Williamson was known to hold his harmonica between his top lip and his nose and play with no hands.

The itinerant bluesman turned up looking for work at Chess Records in August 1955; bassist Willie Dixon, who was there, remembers that

Williamson carried his harps in a case, told great stories about the Delta, and had his playing "just about together." A contract was signed on the spot, and the harmonica man's first session—with Muddy Waters's band—happened within days.

One Way Out collects Williamson's early Chess singles, and rarities that were left off his (erratic) early albums. All showcase his positively massive roar on the blues harp, and his comparatively casual singing style. Williamson was a wry blues parodist—check his spot-on imitation "Like Wolf," which allegedly incurred Howlin' Wolf's wrath—and a supremely confident bandleader who linked his hot rural style with the subtle big-city Chicago rhythm.

When he gets things rolling, on the imploring "Work with Me" and other tracks here, he sets off his vocal declarations with lusty, hard-blowing two-bar harmonica rejoinders, harrowing solos in miniature. Williamson contributed a boatload of enduring blues images—"Born Blind" tells of a woman so in touch with her sexuality, she brings "eyesight to the blind," while "One Way Out," famously interpreted by the Allman Brothers, is the prototypical panic attack of a cheating lover. But it's the primal sound Williamson uses to communicate them that makes him one of a kind.

GENRE: 🔵 Blues. RELEASED: 1975, Chess/MCA. KEY TRACKS: "Born Blind," "Work with Me," "One Way Out." CATALOG CHOICE: *Help Me.* NEXT STOP: Muddy Waters: *Hard Again.* AFTER THAT: The Allman Brothers Band: *At Fillmore East* (see p. 16).

The Sizzle of Western Swing

The Tiffany Transcriptions, Vols. 2 and 3

Bob Wills and His Texas Playboys

Bob Wills, the great popularizer of Western swing, was first and foremost an entertainer. No matter what type of music his band was playing—and the musicians he surrounded himself with were fluent in blues and jazz and popular song—the lanky Texan worked to make it exciting. When the rhythm was heating up, he goaded his players with a loud "whoooot" shout or something similar, and often interjected words of encouragement while a solo was under way. On Vol. 3's sprightly version of Duke Ellington's "Take the A Train," recorded for radio broadcast in the '40s, he cuts into an energetic chorus by the electric mandolin player Tiny Moore to get the band to crank things up a notch. "Let's straighten out, boys, get Tiny a little loose." Right away the drums snap out a tighter beat, and Moore, one of the Texas Playboys' great soloists, responds with a series of aggressive, rhythmically intense phrases. The band would likely have reached that zone anyway, but as Wills well knew, just making the suggestion drew listeners in, made them participants.

These two volumes contain the essential spirit of Western swing—Vol. 2 gathers live-in-the-studio versions of Wills's most famous songs (including "Take Me Back to Tulsa" and "Steel Guitar Rag"), while Vol. 3 shows the band working through jazz and blues standards, a key part of its live repertoire. Wills didn't see the styles as isolated: He was one of the first figures in American music to achieve widespread fame by blending traits from different genres. His band brought a jazz sense of open-ended improvisation to traditional country songs, and an infectious, almost boogie-woogie dance-floor jump to songs usually heard as laments. Longtime Playboys guitarist Eldon Shamblin recalled that the diversity was a key part of Wills's plan: "Bob didn't restrict the people that worked for him to any type (of music), you got a good variety of things to do." That approach separates Wills, still, from all the Western swing slingers that came later: No small group of its time covered as much stylistic territory.

GENRE: ⚫ Country. RELEASED: 1994, Rhino. KEY TRACKS: Vol. 2: "Steel Guitar Rag," "Ida Red." Vol. 3: "I'm a Ding Dong

Daddy," "It's Your Red Wagon," "Take the A Train." **CATALOG CHOICE:** *The Essential Bob Wills and His Texas Playboys.* **F.Y.I.:** A series of live performances recorded for radio broadcast in the 1940s, the Tiffany Transcriptions number ten volumes. **NEXT STOP:** Spade Cooley: *Spadella.* **AFTER THAT:** The Hot Club of Cow Town: *Swingin' Stampede.*

The Light from One Smoldering Candle

Blue Light 'til Dawn

Cassandra Wilson

Cassandra Wilson started out as a jazz singer, doing gigs with several innovative bands (including Brooklyn's experimental M-Base collective) and at the same time recording typical jazz-singer let-me-entertain-you stuff—"Night and Day" and "Blue Skies" and shooby dooby dooby. Eventually the Mississippi-born New York–based vocalist, who reigned among the elite jazz singers of the 1980s, became restless, and began to look beyond torch songs for inspiration.

So she looked outside of jazz for inspiration. In interviews, she's recalled how she began seeking new challenges for her voice, a mighty instrument blessed with husky overtones and an alluringly smoky woodish hue. She began to integrate gospel and blues and pop songs into her performances, eventually assimilating them into music that blurs genre distinctions entirely. *Blue Light 'til Dawn* is the first album to capture that shift. It features wondrously spare, molasses-slow versions of Robert Johnson ("Come On in My Kitchen," "Hellhound on My Trail"), Philly soul (Thom Bell and Linda Creed's "Children of the Night," a hit for the Stylistics), pop (Van Morrison's "Tupelo Honey"), and torch song ("You Don't Know What Love Is").

Working with a small group of inventive New York jazzers, emphasizing hand drums

Down Beat magazine named Wilson Female Jazz Vocalist of the Year for three straight years beginning in 1994.

and percussion over trap set, Wilson cultivates the opposite of dazzle—hers is an inviting, shadow-filled sound that calls from a lonesome bayou. Atmosphere dictates everything that happens on these tracks, and helps knit together pieces from disparate ends of popular music. It also guides Wilson's vocals: Her sullen "Hellhound" wanders far from typical blues woe, yet winds up an apt, weary summation of it all the same.

Blue Light became an adult contemporary hit, and set Wilson on the course she's pursued since. Subsequent albums find her personalizing ever more unusual tunes (the Monkees' "Last Train to Clarksville"). The records are all engrossing and shaped by extremely sensitive musicianship, but *Blue Light* has something more—the renegade energy of one who, having taken a flying leap, is just discovering a new mode of expression.

GENRES: 🎵 Jazz ⬤ Vocals. **RELEASED:** 1993, Blue Note. **KEY TRACKS:** "Tupelo Honey," "Hellhound on My Trail." **CATALOG CHOICES:** *New Moon Daughter; Blue Skies.* **NEXT STOP:** India.Arie: *Acoustic Soul.*

The Collected Greatness of the Black Elvis

The Very Best of Jackie Wilson

Jackie Wilson

Though his discography is erratic, Jackie Wilson looms as one of the underappreciated titans of popular music, a dynamo who taught generations of performers—from Patti LaBelle to Michael Jackson— how to bring it live. Combining his hurt, ever-impassioned loverman singing with rapid spins and splits and dancing feats of considerable skill, Wilson earned his title "Mr. Excitement" every night. Dionne Warwick, whose first national touring gig was opening for Wilson, recalls learning the fine art of galvanizing a crowd from him: "He always gave his audiences pure excitement." Even Elvis Presley was enamored: Between takes during the 1956 recording of *The Million Dollar Quartet*, the King can be heard raving about Jackie Wilson's live performance of "Don't Be Cruel."

A former boxer who grew up in Detroit, Wilson (1934–1984) could pump an ordinary song into a showstopping event. With him, the draw was rarely the song itself—it was what happened to it. He'd swoon as though in the grip of a paranormal force, or wind up pleading on his knees. He would combine extravagant blues dips, melismatic U-turns, and controlled trills (see the blithe, blazing-hot "Reet Petite") into a finely wrought emotional appeal.

Wilson was one of the most persuasive singers popular music has produced. Alas, this is not always reflected in his recording career, which was plagued by mismanagement. Early on, he enlivened jump blues and swing tunes with Billy Ward and the Dominoes, but as a solo artist he also got sidetracked doing schmaltzy pop. The tragedy of this becomes clear when you hear a song written by Berry Gordy Jr. before he started Motown: The doo-wop-tinged "Lonely Teardrops," one of Wilson's six Top 10 pop hits, demonstrates his gift for forthright confessional singing, while later singles (like "Baby Workout") exhibit a more assertive rhythmic swagger. Wilson proved that the combination of those traits could be incendiary—he's an important bridge between up-tempo '50s R&B and the more thoughtful, personal style of soul that Ray Charles made famous. Known for a stretch in the '60s as "the Black Elvis," Wilson earned the comparison with his sharp sense of timing and incandescent passion. To hear a singer leaving it all on the studio floor, cue up the 1967 gem "(Your Love Keeps Lifting Me) Higher and Higher" or really anything here. It doesn't get much better than this.

GENRE: 🎤 R&B. **RELEASED:** 1993, Brunswick/Ace. **KEY TRACKS:** "Lonely Teardrops," "Baby Workout," "I'll Be Satisfied," "I Get the Sweetest Feeling," "(Your Love Keeps Lifting Me) Higher and Higher." **NEXT STOP:** Clyde McPhatter: *Clyde McPhatter.* **AFTER THAT:** Ben E. King: *Don't Play That Song.*

During his long career, Jackie Wilson recorded over 50 hit singles.

He Said "Lean on Me" and Everybody Did

Still Bill

Bill Withers

From the moment he appeared in 1971, Bill Withers ran counter to the prevailing wisdom of the record industry. As an African American singer, he understood soul. But he specialized in thoughtful, gentle music—his songs had the earthbound wisdom of country or folk in them, and a grown-up's perspective on life's challenges.

This wasn't an easy sell. And Withers, who'd waited more than a decade for his chance to record, did not change to suit the industry. Born and raised in Slab Fork, West Virginia, the youngest in a family of six kids, Withers worked as a milkman and on an auto assembly line during his twenties, singing and writing songs in his spare time. He eventually moved to Los Angeles, where he found work installing bathrooms on Boeing aircraft. He saved money to make tapes of his songs, and at first encountered total rejection, as he recalled in an interview in *Blues and Soul* magazine: "I had tapes all over the place but nothing happened."

Clarence Avant, the president of Sussex Records, heard Withers in 1970 and reacted differently. He paired the singer and guitarist with the Memphis rhythm section led by keyboardist and producer Booker T. Jones (plus guitarist Stephen Stills, who offset Withers's acoustic strumming with piercing leads), and encour-

In the summer of 1972, Bill Wither's "Lean on Me" was #1 on the *Billboard* pop and R&B charts.

aged him to do his own material. The result, *Just as I Am*, yielded a strong single ("Ain't No Sunshine") and a wise song that should have become a standard, "Grandma's Hands."

Withers followed that with *Still Bill*, one of the most eloquent records ever filed under "Rhythm and Blues." These are shades-of-gray stories, full of a mature understanding of human nature: "Use Me" describes a lover's total, damaging devotion; "Lean on Me" uses hymnlike chords as the backdrop for an open-hearted offering of support; "Who Is He (and What Is He to You)?" shows what happens when obsession devolves into paranoid suspicion. Even when reflecting on weighty matters, Withers cultivates a mood of unflappable calm, making everything sound like a lazy summer evening on the front porch.

GENRE: 🎙 R&B. **RELEASED:** 1972, Sussex/Columbia. **KEY TRACKS:** "Lonely Town, Lonely Street," "Use Me," "Lean on Me," "Take It All In and Check It All Out." **CATALOG CHOICE:** *Just as I Am.* **NEXT STOP:** Jill Scott: *Beautifully Human: Words and Sounds*, Vol. 2. **AFTER THAT:** Amos Lee: *Last Days at the Lodge.*

The Vision of Wonder

Innervisions

Stevie Wonder

Stevie Wonder's transition from child star to self-reliant artist began with (what else?) a contract dispute. In 1971, when he turned twenty-one, the blind multi-instrumentalist negotiated for, and eventually received, complete control over his music—the sounds, the words, the mixes, everything. Motown wasn't happy at first, but what followed was an explosion of creativity that reverberated powerfully throughout the music world and beyond. Between *Where I'm Coming From* (his first self-produced work, issued in 1971) and *Songs in the Key of Life* (1976), Wonder created four milestone albums, one right after another. These mind-blowing works represent a confluence of craft and heaven-sent inspiration not attained since. They've all got buoyant, stretchy-elastic rhythms, and refrains so resolutely positive they defy gravity, and lyrics of substance. Wonder's incredible string of classics expand the definition of "message music" to include hard-grooving, instantly addictive radio songs.

The New York Times called Wonder a "force of nature."

Following the example of labelmate Marvin Gaye (whose 1971 album *What's Going On*, see p. 304, was one of Motown's early forays into social commentary), Wonder began addressing the problems of urban America on his magical 1972 release, *Talking Book*. With *Innervisions*, he cranks things up a notch. He writes idealized prayers and strident calls to awareness about drug abuse ("Too High," perhaps the funkiest antidrug song of all time). He tackles poverty and racism (the striving "Higher Ground," as well as the seven-minute narrative about the struggles of a Southern family, "Living for the City") and then sermonizes more generally on the evils of arrogance ("He's Misstra Know-It-All").

Wriggling through graceful vocal melodies and ad-libs as daring as those from any jazz musician, Wonder speaks truth to power. But he doesn't harangue: Everything comes wrapped in Wonder's resolutely bright, indomitable spirit—particularly on the sun-splashed "Golden Lady" and "Don't You Worry 'bout a Thing," a blithe fantasy in *son montuno* rhythm that comes near the end of the record. One of his indisputable flashes of radio genius, "Don't You Worry," turns on the Spanish phrase *Todo está bien chévere* (Everything's gonna be alright). Listening to Wonder sing, it's almost impossible not to share that feeling.

GENRE: 🎧 R&B. **RELEASED:** 1973, Tamla/Motown. **KEY TRACKS:** "Golden Lady," "Higher Ground," "Don't You Worry 'bout a Thing," "Too High." **CATALOG CHOICES:** *Talking Book; Fulfillingness' First Finale.* **NEXT STOP:** Curtis Mayfield: *Superfly.* **AFTER THAT:** Donny Hathaway: *Everything Is Everything* (see p. 348).

An All-Day Player That Never Gets Old

Songs in the Key of Life

Stevie Wonder

C onsider what it takes for a blind recording artist to capture ideas in the studio. There are the usual problems of positioning oneself correctly at an instrument, and the challenges of keeping a constant distance to the

microphone—quality takes can be ruined by a simple turn of the head. Then there is the not-small problem of lyrics. On this, his magnum opus, Stevie Wonder sang most of the lead vocals just after hearing the lines spoken into his headphones.

Think about that the next time you hear any of these twenty-one incandescent songs, which include one of the all-time funkiest looks back at childhood ("I Wish") and a prayer for the ages ("Love's in Need of Love Today") and a bursting-with-life samba ("Another Star"). Wonder sings all of them in an unbroken spirit stream, even though every few seconds he's being prompted with the next line in his ear. Miraculously, he's not thrown by this. He wriggles and tumbles through the lines as though he's riding river rapids. Nothing about these vocals—*nothing*—feels premeditated.

Songs in the Key of Life was #1 on the *Billboard* Top 200 Album chart for 14 weeks.

When he began work on *Songs,* Wonder had issued five albums, all classics, in the preceding thirty-nine months. He made a public decision to slow down for this collection; the musicians involved recall that in addition to spending time refining each track, Wonder kept writing (and in some cases recording) right up until the mixing sessions. The final product, which took two years to complete, contains seventeen thoughtful and undeniable songs originally issued on two vinyl records (plus a four-song "something's extra"). There is no filler.

GENRE: 🎤 R&B. **RELEASED:** 1976, Tamla/Motown. **KEY TRACKS:** All of them. **CATALOG CHOICE:** *Hotter than July.* **NEXT STOP:** Shuggie Otis: *Inspiration Information* (see p. 568).

The First Salvo from a Crew That Changed the Hip-Hop Game

Enter the Wu-Tang (36 Chambers)

Wu-Tang Clan

T he poet Samuel Taylor Coleridge once defined prose as "words in their best order," and poetry as "the best words in their best order." Following that thought, hip-hop might be described as "the best words in their best order over the best beat."

The debut of the Wu-Tang Clan, a nine-member collective from Staten Island, ranks among the most creative examples of this, an exhibition of word-slinging that moves with snapping, karate-chopping efficiency—and, no accident, was largely inspired by the elaborate rituals and mythology of martial arts films.

First assembled by the DJ and MC known as RZA (Robert Diggs) at a time when the locus of hip-hop creativity had shifted to the West Coast, the Wu developed tracks with a brutally lean backbeat crunch. Incorporating samples from martial arts films as well as jazz and old R&B records, RZA created dark, lurking-in-the-shadows vibes, and then let his super-imaginative supporting cast build on the menace. Though this is a debut record made by largely unknown talents, each MC hits the microphone with a distinct sound and approach—Ol' Dirty Bastard raps in a nasal singsong, Raekwon delivers his thoughts in a rat-a-tatting stutter, Method Man deploys a stoner mumble, Ghostface Killah affects a tone of almost overwhelmed grimness. That's one remarkable thing about *Enter*: There are

The 1978 martial arts film *The 36th Chamber of Shaolin* inspired the album's title.

enough rappers involved to field a baseball team, and most tracks are done in a fresh, freewheeling round-robin style involving several of them, yet somehow the individual voices are highly differentiated. By the time this engrossing set of battle rhymes ends, you *know* these characters.

And after this album hit, the world got to know them much better. As *Enter the Wu-Tang* was embraced by the hip-hop nation, the collective became a dynasty of sorts, with various MCs embarking on solo careers. Some released albums that are hip-hop classics in their own right. Still, to fully appreciate the collective it's necessary to start here, at the beginning, when its members were concerned with choosing words carefully, putting them in the best order, and delivering them with thrilling rhythmic exactitude.

GENRE: 🎤 Hip-Hop. **RELEASED:** 1993, Loud. **KEY TRACKS:** "Method Man," "Clan in da Front," "Protect Ya Neck," "C.R.E.A.M." **CATALOG CHOICES:** *The W.* Method Man: *Tical.* Ol' Dirty Bastard: *Best of.* **NEXT STOP:** Mobb Deep: *Infamous.* **AFTER THAT:** A Tribe Called Quest: *Midnight Marauders.*

A Record of Fate and Its Consequences

Rock Bottom

Robert Wyatt

As a member of the pioneering band Soft Machine, Robert Wyatt helped establish the renegade tone and sense of adventure that became central to progressive rock of the early 1970s, particularly the music of Pink Floyd.

The inventive drummer and singer left Soft Machine in late 1971, forming the short-lived, mostly instrumental Matching Mole. In the spring of '73, Wyatt began working on the material for this album. On June 1, the night before his new ensemble was to rehearse for the first time, he fell from a fourth-floor window and suffered severe spinal cord injuries. "I spent three months lying flat on my back, gazing at the ceiling of a surreal public dormitory amongst twenty others whose lives had also radically changed in a split second," Wyatt writes in the liner notes.

On the album Wyatt dedicated lyrics to his wife, the poet Alfreda Benge.

Wyatt learned to live in a wheelchair, and months later returned to the music he'd planned to record. Despite the circumstances of its creation, *Rock Bottom* isn't morose—like many of Wyatt's subsequent solo records, it offers quaint country garden landscapes and spacey, open-ended environments that support cryptic lyrics. Nursery rhymes and fables figure prominently here, as do expressions of awe and admiration for Alfreda Benge, who later became his wife. (Among them is this enduring endearment: "Your lunacy fits neatly with my own.") Wyatt, who plays keyboard and sings since he's unable to play drums, creates deeply engrossing ambient tapestries to surround his (sometimes impish) wordplay. This album relies on the knotty musical strategies associated with art rock, but uses them in more intimate, approachable ways, with carefully sculpted peaks and valleys. Check the intro-

duction to "Little Red Riding Hood Hit the Road," which lasts three engrossing minutes: Winding through several different keys and rhythmic motifs, the piece careens between splattering trumpet solos and watercolor keyboard textures in a slow, measured ramp-up. By the time Wyatt's fragile falsetto appears, he's prepared his listeners for literally anything. In terms of sweep, invention, and gradually mounting tension, this is one of the greatest stage-setting introductions in all of rock.

Rock Bottom sets the tone for Wyatt's solo career—its stylistic leaps and chord sequences turn up on many subsequent recordings. It is, however, more oriented toward fantasy than most of his later work; his discography includes embittered song cycles like *Cuckooland* (2003), a dismayed, scathing attack on the policies of large Western democracies.

GENRE: 🎸 Rock. **RELEASED:** 1974, Virgin. **KEY TRACKS:** "Little Red Riding Hood Hit the Road," "A Last Straw," "Alifib." **CATALOG CHOICES:** *Cuckooland; Old Rottenhat.* Soft Machine: *Third.* **NEXT STOP:** Caravan: *Cunning Stunts.* **AFTER THAT:** National Health: *Of Queues and Cures.*

An Introduction to the "First Lady of Country Music"

Anniversary: Twenty Years of Hits

Tammy Wynette

Many singers associated with Nashville's Golden Age in the 1960s are remembered for one towering song. In the case of Tammy Wynette (1942–1998), it's "Stand By Your Man," the jukebox classic of sisterly advice. Cowritten by Wynette and her producer Billy Sherrill, it was one of five number 1 hits for Wynette in 1968 and 1969, and subsequently became her theme. A mid-tempo song with swollen string fanfares and a killer refrain, it consistently ranks among the all-time best in polls of country fans—in 2003, it topped Country Music Television's list of the 100 Greatest Songs in Country Music. It's also been derided by feminists; in an interview with *60 Minutes* during her husband's first presidential campaign, Hillary Clinton said she "wasn't some little woman standing by my man like Tammy Wynette." Wynette, who'd long argued that the song was not about female subservience but mutual support, demanded—and received—an apology from Clinton.

By the time she recorded "Stand," Wynette was well-schooled in the ways of the world, and the deceitfulness of men. Born in Mississippi, she was raised by her grandmother; as a teenager, she moved to Birmingham, Alabama, to be with her mother. Wynette married at seventeen, and quickly had three children. She and her first husband divorced before her third child was born, leaving her a single mom. She started singing as a second job, and after a bit of local success, moved to Nashville in 1966. That year she

Wynette's duets with onetime husband George Jones earned the pair the nickname "the President and First Lady" of country music.

signed to Epic Records and began working with Sherrill.

Wynette's life experience comes through in her songs. She can project steely resolve when necessary, and she can also pour on the motherly empathy, particularly on songs that are sensitive to a child's view, like the sad "D-I-V-O-R-C-E." After Wynette and George Jones began dating in 1968, her recording activity expanded to include a series of duets with him. These remain some of the most enduring tandem love songs in all of popular music; and several, including the stoic "We're Gonna Hold On," are here. In addition, this anthology contains some of Wynette's most wrenching album sides, and a sampling of the pathos-filled tearjerkers that became her standard fare in the later '70s. They're shining examples of solid country-politan craft, and Wynette's unaffected ache of a voice transforms them into art.

GENRE: ⚫ Country. **RELEASED:** 1987, Epic. **KEY TRACKS:** "Apartment No. 9," "D-I-V-O-R-C-E," "Stand By Your Man." **CATALOG CHOICE:** George Jones and Tammy Wynette: *Sixteen Biggest Hits*. **NEXT STOP:** Loretta Lynn: *Don't Come Home A-Drinkin' (with Lovin' on Your Mind)*. **AFTER THAT:** Tanya Tucker: *What's Your Mama's Name*.

X ✦ XTC ✦ Goro Yamaguchi ✦ The Yardbirds ✦ Yes ✦ Faron Young ✦ Larry Young ✦ Lester Young ✦ Neil Young ✦ Frank Zappa ✦ Tom Zé ✦ Warren Zevon ✦ The Zombies ✦ ZZ Top

X, Y, Z

The Most Delirious X-Plosion of West Coast Punk

Wild Gift

X

Wild Gift time-machines fifty years of rebel music into one mighty squall. Recorded quickly in 1981 as the follow-up to X's incendiary (and unexpectedly successful) debut *Los Angeles*, its songs have the twitchy blues-guitar arpeggios of Chuck Berry and the death-ray stare of underfed New York punks. At the same time, the tunes carry hints of '50s girl-group innocence and traces of the woozy raunch of the Doors. (The album was produced by Doors keyboardist Ray Manzarek.) Sometimes the music sounds like primal anarchy. Sometimes it veers closer to rec-hall rockabilly.

With this full-tilt tumult, X linked the insurgent sensibility of punk to a more varied musical attack, and in the process avoided the posturing that reduced many acts to safety-pin-wearing cartoons. In all of punk, for example, there's never been an admission quite like "We're Desperate," or an end-of-the-love-affair ode like the wry, knowing "When Our Love Passed Out on the Couch." In real life, the love was still new: *Wild Gift* was recorded shortly after bassist and singer John Doe and singer Exene Cervenka were married. Many of the songs, notably the addictively catchy "White Girl" and the leering "The Once Over Twice," find the pair struggling to honor the commitment, mull-ing the risks of infidelity. As Cervenka recalls in the liner notes: "Some of the songs carried feelings both of us were having but couldn't act on because we were married."

Wild Gift didn't exactly tear up the charts. But from here, X continued to grow in unusual ways, pushing its punk-rockabilly further while developing a reputation for fiery live performances. The Doe/Cervenka marriage ended in the late '80s, and X dissolved soon after; Doe's first solo album (*Meet John Doe*) is a criminally neglected blast of rousing righteousness. Still, *Wild Gift* remains the gem, the moment when four believers living somewhere off of Santa Monica Boulevard took rusty parts from the rock and roll scrap heap, and slapped together a new American maelstrom.

GENRE: 🎸 Rock. **RELEASED:** 1981, Slash. **KEY TRACKS:** "When Our Love Passed Out on the Couch," "We're Desperate." **CATALOG CHOICE:** *Los Angeles.* **NEXT STOP:** The Blasters: *The Blasters.*

In the Shadow of the Beatles, and Still a Universe Away

Skylarking

XTC

It's impossible to overstate the influence of the Beatles on musicians who grew up in the 1960s and '70s. The quartet's sunny, visionary records eventually impacted just about everyone involved in music, from singers to symphonists.

The Beatles changed long-entrenched notions of vocal harmony, overhauled verse-chorus song form, and fully exploited the creative possibilities of multitrack recording. Worshippers have been contending with (if not puzzling over) these innovations ever since.

In the crowded pantheon of post-Beatles pop, XTC looms as one of the few bands to not simply learn from the Fab Four, but to take the inspiration into significant new realms. The

Singer and guitarist Andy Partridge called *Skylarking* "a summer's day baked into one cake."

British outfit built around singer-songwriter Andy Partridge and bassist-songwriter Colin Moulding started out in 1977 as a New Wave guitar band. Its first few records are notable for their determined edginess—jabbing, jolting guitar lines support easy-to-remember hooks. That sound worked for a while, through the aptly named *Drums and Wires* (1979). And then, somewhat suddenly, XTC went arty. Partridge and Moulding began augmenting the guitars with keyboard parts, and elaborate string-orchestra padding, and "Strawberry Fields"–ish vocal processing. By the time the band made this gem, which was produced by Todd Rundgren, another Beatles obsessive, its sound resembled *Abbey Road*. Except the lyrics come with a cynical New Wave smirk.

Skylarking is XTC confronting the Beatles

influence, after years of running from it. The overall organization recalls James Joyce's *Ulysses*—it follows some too-sensitive souls through the activities of a single day. The curtain opens with the sound of crickets chirping in the morning ("Summer's Cauldron"), and then rolls through moments of reflection and idyllic late-afternoon frolics ("Grass"), eventually ending with a child's bedtime prayers (the plaintive "Dear God," which was added to the sequence after it became a hit in the U.S.). *Skylarking* is the result of equal parts rash inspiration and painstaking craft. It's possible to hear the Beatles influence, but on much of this metaphysically minded work of chamber pop brilliance, the melodies are all XTC. And sheer ecstasy.

GENRE: 🅡 Rock. **RELEASED:** 1986, Geffen. **KEY TRACKS:** "Grass," "That's Really Super, Supergirl," "Ballet for a Rainy Day," "Season Cycle," "Dear God." **COLLECTOR'S NOTE:** The remastered 2002 version contains "Mermaid Smile," a sparkling song that was excised from the original version to make room for "Dear God." **CATALOG CHOICES:** *Drums and Wires; English Settlement; Nonsuch.* **NEXT STOP:** Todd Rundgren: *Something/Anything?* (see p. 662).

The Calming Breath

Shakuhachi Music: A Bell Ringing in the Empty Sky

Goro Yamaguchi

Used for centuries in China and then Japan, the *shakuhachi* flute is considered by some to be a path to enlightenment. To the Zen students of the Fuke sect, it is also a vital part of training—*suizen*, or blowing meditation, is aimed at not just the creation of beautiful tones but the development of deep breath control. A master flutist can make the air dance, or "create a life in one long breath."

On the two extended pieces that make up this solo disc, the gifted Goro Yamaguchi (1933–1999) pretty much exhausts what the five-hole bamboo *shakuhachi*, which is played vertically like a recorder, can do. His performances have moments of

NASA included an excerpt from this album on the Voyager Golden Record, which was sent into space.

astounding technique, but more often a deep sense of clarity and composure—qualities that make this music ideal for meditation. Early in the first piece, "Depicting the Cranes in Their Nest," Yamaguchi executes carefully controlled swoops and pitch-bends that evoke a young bird's anxious first flights, and the accompanying parental trepidation. In the second piece, sweeping long tones depend upon Yamaguchi's poised and steady airstream—at times it's possible to almost feel the air shooting across the tone holes, and sense how, just using breath, he's gently shading the music. (Both pieces also contain

more pronounced inflections, moments where quick finger work signals abrupt changes of emotional temperature.)

Though the long, elaborate lines can seem extemporaneous, *shakuhachi* music does have a structure, with distinct melodic passages that unfold in sequence. The title selection was written by a Zen priest named Kyochiku after a dream about enlightenment; it is laced with religious meanings, and is considered one of the most technically demanding tunes in the repertoire. According to the liner notes, which offer a concise history of *shakuhachi* music, it is also the most frequently performed. Go deeply into the mood of calming beauty and contented introspection Yamaguchi sustains for fifteen (!) minutes, and you may appreciate why.

GENRE: 🌐 World/Japan. **RELEASED:** 2007, Nonesuch Explorer. (Original release 1969.) **KEY TRACKS:** "Depicting the Cranes in Their Nest," "A Bell Ringing in the Empty Sky." **NEXT STOP:** Reiko Kimura and Tadashi Tajima: *Music for Koto.*

One Hatchling from the British Invasion Guitar Incubator

Over Under Sideways Down (U.S.)/ Roger the Engineer (U.K.)

The Yardbirds

A t different times during its brief existence (1962–1968), the Yardbirds had Eric Clapton, Jeff Beck, and/or Jimmy Page on lead guitar. As dynasties go, that's possibly the best ever in rock, on par with the New York

Yankees home run club from Babe Ruth through Mickey Mantle and Roger Maris. This album, the band's first to be conceived as an

album and not merely a collection of singles, documents the Beck era and includes several early tracks with Page. It's essential listening for anyone who cares about rock guitar.

Each axman's tenure brought a corresponding shift in sound. The Yardbirds started out playing a jittery blues rock, with Clapton, then a staunch blues purist, providing Delta-obsessed leads. When the band started to move away from blues with the soaring single "For Your Love," Clapton left in disgust, joining John Mayall's Bluesbreakers. Beck came aboard ready to try different styles and loosened up the band. His stinging, crystal-clear sound drives the determinedly weird "Hot House of Omagarashid," a wordless chant (drawn, allegedly, from Gregorian chant) splayed over a twisted Bo Diddley beat, and "He's Always There," a straight pop hook embellished with psychedelic guitar musings.

Beck and Page played together for a brief time, on the foreboding "Happenings Ten Years Time Ago"; "Psycho Daisies" features Page on bass. These tracks solidified the Yardbirds' reputation for sonic mayhem; it's a treasure trove of piercing leads, thick distortion, and other guitar sound-shaping tricks.

The Page era of the Yardbirds is most

The Yardbirds in 1965.

notable for a record that's not available—the March 1968 Anderson Theater concert in New York that was very briefly issued by Epic as *Live Yardbirds! Featuring Jimmy Page*. It was recorded shortly before the Yardbirds dissolved around Page, and he was forced to assemble the lineup that became Led Zeppelin. The live set offers moments of savage guitar intensity ("Dazed and Confused") and an extended guitar exploration, "White Summer," that directly foreshadows Led Zeppelin in its conjoining of blues and traditional folk song (in this case, "She Moves Through the Fair"). Later, Page recast the tune on the first Led Zeppelin record, as "Black Mountain Side." And the rest, as they say, is history.

GENRE: 🎸 Rock. **RELEASED:** 1966, Epic. (Reissued 2004, Repertoire.) **KEY TRACKS:** "Over Under Sideways Down," "The Nazz Are Blue," "Hot House of Omagarashid," "Jeff's Boogie," "Psycho Daisies," "Stroll On." **CATALOG CHOICE:** *Live Yardbirds! Featuring Jimmy Page.* **NEXT STOP:** The Who: *The Who Sings My Generation.* **AFTER THAT:** Jeff Beck: *Wired.*

The Beginnings of Radio-Friendly Prog Rock

The Yes Album

Yes

This is the rare progressive rock album that doesn't scream, "We Are Musicians, Take Us Seriously," in the first thirty seconds. Though its lyrics talk cosmic gibberish about glimpsing heaven and the goodness of human souls and the role of Starship Troopers in the galaxy, the music underneath is a model of discipline. The Yes rhythm section, anchored by drummer Bill Bruford, hops between different time signatures as casually as most people cross the street. No matter what the keening, skyscraping vocalist Jon Anderson sings, the band pounds out music that's heavy and celestial, rhythmically agile and exultant.

Rock historians point to *Fragile*, the album that followed this one, as the definitive Yes. Although it contains the breakthrough single "Roundabout" (the biggest prog-rock hit of all time) it splinters into tracks showing off the prodigious talents of each individual musician. *The Yes Album* is, by contrast, all about the group—here are five confident musicians journeying through extended suites ("Starship Trooper"), executing dramatic shifts of tempo with enviable precision. The seeds of "Roundabout" are here—check out the chord sequence that defines "A Venture" and the Zen philosophy of "Perpetual Change."

The Yes Album is Yes's third album.

More significant, there are several songs that show Anderson striving to make his music accessible, while retaining its road-map complexities: Though it wasn't nearly the hit "Roundabout" was, "Your Move/All Good People" is a feast of hooks, instantly singable and still somehow deep.

GENRE: 🎸 Rock.
RELEASED: 1971, Atlantic.
KEY TRACKS: "Your Move/All Good People," "Starship Trooper," "Yours Is No Disgrace," "Perpetual Change." **CATALOG CHOICES:** *Fragile; Close to the Edge.* **NEXT STOP:** Emerson, Lake, and Palmer: *Brain Salad Surgery* (see p. 256). **AFTER THAT:** Pink Floyd: *Piper at the Gates of Dawn.*

The Hillbilly Heartthrob, Immortalized

The Complete Capitol Hits of Faron Young

Faron Young

The great American credo "Live Fast, Love Hard, Die Young" was the first song Faron Young recorded after his Army hitch was up in 1954. Young (1932–1996) didn't write the song (Nashville DJ Joe Allison did), but he imbued it with all the wildcat energy of one just sprung from a long-standing obligation. It is the essence of early rock rebellion, before such rebellion became a codified (and commodified) part of rock and roll.

When "Live Fast" was released, Young had a built-in audience for his work: Because he'd experienced a bit of success (with the single "Goin' Steady") before entering the service, the military featured him in a weekly radio show heard on two thousand stations. The singer and guitarist, born in Shreveport,

Louisiana, said later that the publicity did him a "world of good." After his release, he capitalized on the exposure with a string of energetic honky-tonk hits, collected here, that made him a star; by late 1955, when rock and roll exploded, Young was possibly the biggest attraction in country music, and one of the form's few talents who knew, instinctively, how to appeal to younger listeners.

Young did this by bringing a bit of honky-tonk rhythm and teen-idol pop sheen to his art—for a while, he was known as the "Hillbilly

Heartthrob." Though he wrote (or cowrote) some singles, he was also esteemed as a sharp eye for talent, recording early songs by Willie Nelson ("Hello Walls," a number 1 hit), Don Gibson, and others. Sonically, most of Young's singles of the '50s are best described as "nothing fancy"—just nice warm vocals atop neatly appointed small-band accompaniment, following the general path of his idol, Hank Williams. But they're charming and energetic,

Young was discovered while singing at his local Optimist Club.

and graced with a hint of the abandon that became a key ingredient of all the fast-living rock and roll that followed.

GENRE: 🌐 Country.
RELEASED: 2004, Collector's Choice. **KEY TRACKS:** "Live Fast, Love Hard, Die Young," "If You Ain't Lovin' (You Ain't Livin')," "That's the Way I Feel," "I Hear You Talkin'." **NEXT STOP:** Merle Haggard: *Mama Tried* (see p. 334). **AFTER THAT:** Wynn Stewart: *After the Storm.*

Post-Bop Jazz Organ Starts (and Pretty Much Ends) Here

Unity

Larry Young

In the original liner notes accompanying this thrilling 1965 jazz date, organist Larry Young (1940–1978) enthuses about the pulse maintained by Elvin Jones, who was, at the time, just ending a five-year association with pathfinding saxophonist John Coltrane. The way Jones plays "lets you do whatever you feel on top of the rhythm," Young explains. For an organ player working in the shadow of such greats as Jimmy Smith, that freedom unlocked the door to another world: On this album Young becomes the first wizard of the Hammond B3 to step out of the barn-burning bebop-and-blues game to explore

Unity is Larry Young's fifth album.

more freely, in the manner of the horn players and pianists of the day.

Mostly what Young seeks is jazz in the mold of Coltrane's "My Favorite Things," with open plateaus stoked by Jones's lashing rhythms. Young surrounds himself with musicians

who are similarly inclined—the trumpeter Woody Shaw, who was twenty at the time, brings a youthful irreverence, while tenor saxophonist Joe Henderson specializes in odd, unconventionally shaped ideas.

Working through three Shaw originals (the opener, "Zoltan," borrows a riff from Hungarian composer Zoltán Kodály), and several less complex themes (including the standard "Softly, As in a Morning Sunrise"), Young and group pursue the crashing peaks of Coltrane, but more temperately, like woodcarvers intent on precision. An alert accompanist, Young peppers the soloists with zinging chord clusters that push things forward. Young's solos are equally memorable—feats of dancing scale-like lines interrupted by bold, crosscutting lunges. His turn on "Softly" is a model of highly individual hard-bop soloing, with dashes of dissonant harmony around the edges.

Young continued this exploration, both under his own name and with others—the guitarist Grant Green, and, in the early '70s, as part of drummer Tony Williams's fusion-leaning Lifetime (see p. 866). Young might not have been the all-time speed demon of the jazz organ, but he pushed the instrument in ways nobody else even dreamed about.

GENRE:  Jazz. **RELEASED:** 1966, Blue Note. **KEY TRACKS:** "Softly, As in a Morning Sunrise," "Zoltan," "Monk's Dream." **CATALOG CHOICE:** *Into Something*. **NEXT STOP:** Lonnie Liston Smith: *Astral Traveling*. **AFTER THAT:** Jimmy Smith: *Root Down*.

A Peak from Prez

The "Kansas City" Sessions

Lester Young

The porkpie hat. The horn cocked at a crazy angle, big eyes bugging. The tremor of vibrato that suggests maybe he's got the shakes. The brainy phrases that seem to float in a different airspace from the rest of the music.

Lester Young (1909–1959), jazz original, was the kind of figure who'd let the myths precede him onto the bandstand. And then when it came time to solo, he'd create more.

Young was key to the development of bebop kingpin Charlie Parker (the young player studied Young's early recordings with Count Basie). An icon of cool way before "cool jazz" hit in the 1950s, Young hung with Billie Holiday (see p. 362) on some of her classics too. In between, on his own records, he established a jazz of poise and utter incandescence. This record catches a small but significant sliver of that.

Recorded by a small group of Basie musicians (called the Kansas City Six) in moments stolen away from the big band in 1938 and 1944, these sessions benefit from a freewheeling attitude, a kind of furloughed-soldier

Billie Holiday nicknamed Young "Prez," short for president.

irreverence, that is rare for the times. This light feeling sparks exceptional solos—grooving on that Basie heartbeat, Young makes outbursts of intricate saxophone slide easily along. His playing is fluid and yet also riddled with unexpected switchbacks, and when he digs into a standard, like "Them There Eyes," his scissoring phrases have an air of modernity.

The conventional assessment of Lester Young is that his best work happened before World War II—he encountered recurring racial hostility during his military service, struggles that some biographers believe led him into alcoholism. The 1944 recordings here, made shortly after his discharge, are as exuberant as those from before the war, yet Young's solos are tinged with new restraint, a willingness to hang back. Later in the '40s and early '50s, the man Billie Holiday called "Prez" for his regal bearing was one of the few swing-era musicians to transition to more modern styles. He became less interested in dazzling people than conjuring thick mood pieces; the beautifully recorded *With the Oscar Peterson Trio* from 1952 showcases Young as a deep thinker whose every line feels fully composed, in the manner of a lyric.

GENRE:  Jazz. **RELEASED:** 1997, Commodore. **KEY TRACKS:** "Them There Eyes," "Pagin' the Devil," "I Got Rhythm." **CATALOG CHOICES:** *With the Oscar Peterson Trio; The Complete Alladin Sessions.* **NEXT STOP:** The Count Basie Orchestra: *Best of 1937–1939.* **AFTER THAT:** Gene Ammons and Sonny Stitt: *Boss Tenors.*

The Many Moods of Neil

After the Gold Rush

Neil Young

Not long after this, his third solo record, Canadian-born, California-based rock troubadour Neil Young began thinking about his albums as explorations of distinct moods. He'd gather a bunch of country-rock meditations under one roof (*Harvest*, from 1972, is the first and best of his peaceful easy titles), or pursue aggressive guitar rock (*Rust Never Sleeps*) with his bloodthirsty band Crazy Horse. This drilling-deep approach helped Young create a discography of thematically unified albums, many of them classics.

Young was inducted into the Rock and Roll Hall of Fame twice—for his solo work and as a member of Buffalo Springfield.

The sprawling *After the Gold Rush* presents Young at his most diverse, with brooding folk songs followed by rabid rock howls. Each selection is modest, more quick sketch than finished portrait: There are quaint little questioning songs ("Tell Me Why") that are the aural equivalent of needlepoint samplers. There are haunting thoughts on the rape of the earth (the title track, with its prescient line "Look at Mother Nature on the run in the nineteen seventies"), and songs that express lovers' idealism ("Only Love Can Break Your Heart"). And there is also "Southern Man," arguably Young's all-time most harrowing performance. Expressing outrage over the lingering racism of the American South, Young tells of phantom screams and "bullwhips cracking" with a wobbly fury in his voice, his indignation echoed by haywire spears of furious and beautiful electric guitar.

Because of its variety, *After the Gold Rush* is an excellent starting point for sustained exploration of Young. Those enthralled by "Southern Man" might investigate *Tonight's the Night, Sleeps with Angels,* and the rousing *Live Rust.* Those who resonate with "Tell Me Why" might next make room for *Harvest,* or its surprisingly strong sequel *Harvest Moon.* Truth is, after you lock into the Neil Young wavelength, the style and the setting don't much matter. The draw is his enigmatic and revelatory songs, which have a way of finding clarity regardless of what's around them.

GENRE: 🅡 Rock. **RELEASED:** 1970, Reprise. **KEY TRACKS:** "Tell Me Why," "After the Gold Rush," "Southern Man." **CATALOG CHOICES:** *Harvest; Tonight's the Night; Ragged Glory; Sleeps with Angels; Harvest Moon; Rust Never Sleeps/Live Rust.* **NEXT STOP:** Crosby, Stills, Nash, and Young: *Déjà Vu* (see p. 195). **AFTER THAT:** Creedence Clearwater Revival: *Cosmo's Factory.*

A Primer on One Devious Daredevil

The Best Band You Never Heard in Your Life

Frank Zappa

Frank Zappa (1940–1993) was an American original, a wry satirist disguised as a crude jokester, a bandleader whose daredevil deviousness regularly pushed the musicians around him to the threshold of genius.

Oh yeah, and he shredded the electric guitar like nobody else. For most of his life, though, he was dismissed as a crank. It took a flurry of outrageously diverse releases just before and after his death to change that impression.

A restless explorer, Zappa is hard to pin down. His artistic contribution ranges from conceptual rock (*Uncle Meat*) to ribald satire (*Sheik Yerbouti*) to cerebral jazz fusion (*Hot Rats*) to ambitious theater works (*Thing Fish*) to challenging contemporary classical compositions (*The Yellow Shark*) that require a steel-trap mind to execute correctly.

Frank Zappa recorded over 75 albums during his career.

Although you probably need ten Zappa albums to fully "get" his genius, this live set, culled from the 1988 tour that was Zappa's last big rock sojourn, offers a thrilling representation of this mayhem-maker's incredible range. As it opens, Zappa tells the crowd that he's met Johnny Cash that day, and in preparation for a guest appearance, Zappa

and the band work up Cash's "Ring of Fire" as a slow, skanky reggae. Cash doesn't show (his wife got sick), but Zappa and band play it anyway, expanding its original meaning to include jokes about hemorrhoids. That sets the tone for a nothing-sacred set that includes an irreverent romp through Ravel's *Boléro*, a campy send-up of Led Zeppelin's "Stairway to Heaven," and a demonic "Sunshine of Your Love" that inspires Zappa's unhinged near-delirious guitar genius. There are also chipper versions of Zappa originals "Zoot Allures," "The Torture Never Stops," and "Lonesome Cowboy Burt," one of several songs with new lyrics commenting on the then-recent fall of televangelist Jimmy Swaggart.

Every track contains at least one moment of jaw-dropping instrumental dazzle—a stickler for precision, Zappa led one of the most accomplished, well-rehearsed bands in rock history. Though completists will argue that studio versions of some songs are better, *The Best Band* serves as a spirited primer on one of the twentieth century's most provocative musical thinkers. If you don't like this, you'll probably never get Zappa.

GENRE: 🎸 Rock. **RELEASED:** 1993, Rykodisc. **KEY TRACKS:** "Ring of Fire," "Zombie Wolf," "Cosmic Debris," "Purple Haze." **CATALOG CHOICES:** *We're Only in It for the Money; Hot Rats; Zoot Allures; The Yellow Shark.* **NEXT STOP:** Captain Beefheart and His Magic Band: *Safe as Milk.* **AFTER THAT:** The Mars Volta: *The Bedlam in Goliath* (see p. 476).

The Ravings of a Visionary Song Insurgent

Fabrication Defect

Tom Zé

Tom Zé has spent a career of some forty years being forever too hip for the room. Which, in the context of Brazilian popular music, is no small accomplishment. Zé got his first exposure via *tropicália,* the movement spearheaded by Gilberto Gil and Caetano Veloso that happily doused tradition with a spritz of irreverent experimentation. That's where Zé lived, and for a long stretch of the 1970s he made defiantly unconventional song cycles with strong political messages. These were embraced by his fellow artists but failed to attract many paying customers. Later in the decade, at a time when samba had fallen out of favor, Zé's *Estudando o samba* repositioned the national dance as a kind of rarefied art music. It was this record that first drew David Byrne, the former Talking Heads frontman and founder of Luaka Bop records, into the Zé orbit, and helped give the iconoclastic Zé, who once described his work as "spoken and sung journalism," an international profile.

Fabrication Defect tells the story of people who are turned into androids by economic exploitation.

Fabrication Defect, which was released in 1998, finds Zé again out of step with the culture of his homeland. Or, at least, appearing out of step. It's a joyous, cluttered caravan of ideas: Potent African hand-drumming sits alongside generic drum machine bossa beats. The half-crazed rantings of a street-corner prophet alternate with the somber chants of what sounds like an obscure mystical sect. And everything is built around looped clanging sounds. Zé's fourteen enumerated "Defects" (among them, curiosity and political ambition) align him, sensibility-wise, with the patchwork electronic pop happening in the U.S. and England at the time. Indeed, this record segues magically with contemporaneous recordings by Beck and Stereolab, among others. It's proof that no matter how zany or misunderstood or ahead of the curve a musician may be at home, there are always some like-minded souls out there, somewhere.

GENRE: 🌐 World/Brazil. **RELEASED:** 1998, Luaka Bop. **KEY TRACKS:** "Defect 1: Gene," "Defect 4: Emeré." **CATALOG CHOICE:** *Estudando o samba.* **NEXT STOP:** Os Mutantes: *Mutantes* (see p. 536).

Jackson Browne Called Him the "First and Foremost Proponent of Song Noir"

Excitable Boy

Warren Zevon

Warren Zevon's third album is filled with sad sacks, schemers, and strange characters who could have wandered from the pages of 1950s-era pulp novels. Among his creations are a crazed mercenary killer named Roland; pampered and self-obsessed elites wreaking havoc with the lethal combination of "Lawyers, Guns, and Money"; and the denizens of a bizarre stalker underworld ("Werewolves of London"). Then there's the weirdo of the title track, who murders his date for the Junior Prom. The townsfolk shake their heads as they gossip: He always was an excitable boy.

These songs are delivery systems for the wit and wisdom of a black humorist (a trenchant observer of humanity who more than once was compared to Mark Twain), and so often operate on several levels at once. They're freakshow-on-the-sidewalk portraits, and at the same time caustic commentaries on a nihilistic society obsessed with escaping reality whenever possible. Like Randy Newman and a handful of others, Zevon (1947–2003) weaves acute observations into his narratives; the lyrics might be acidic, but they're also unapologetically smart, laced with references to history and thinly disguised outrage over current events. As he follows the exploits of "Roland the Headless Thompson Gunner," for example, Zevon slips in questions about the misadventures and miscalculations of U.S. foreign policy. And no matter what message is carried by the words, Zevon's unkempt,

Zevon's *Excitable Boy* reached #8 on the *Billboard* pop album charts.

defiantly casual delivery offers another level of comment, the audio equivalent of a raised eyebrow.

Zevon had that sardonic edge from the start—his debut is even more astringent. But after this, Zevon, the son of a professional gambler, descended into a years-long vodka binge that hindered his output. Though subsequent works contain smatterings of genius, *Excitable Boy* is Zevon's most fully realized album, and the one that established him as a refreshingly dour voice in an L.A. singer-songwriter scene defined by puppy-dog sweetness. It's also his most varied collection, with straightforward three-chord rock anthems ("Lawyers, Guns, and Money"), anxious attempts at funk ("Nighttime in the Switching Yard"), and one forthright piano ballad ("Accidentally like a Martyr"). A sincere, beautifully wrought song, it's the one to play for people who think Zevon spent his whole career howling like a werewolf.

GENRE: 🎸 Rock. **RELEASED:** 1978, Asylum. **KEY TRACKS:** "Lawyers, Guns, and Money," "Excitable Boy," "Accidentally like a Martyr." **CATALOG CHOICE:** *Warren Zevon.* **NEXT STOP:** Randy Newman: *Good Old Boys.* **AFTER THAT:** Jackson Browne: *Late for the Sky* (see p. 124).

Thoughtful Psychedelia

Odessey and Oracle

The Zombies

"Time of the Season," the only hit from this wondrous and revelatory album, was recorded after the members of the Zombies agreed to break up. "We were all very testy at that time," guitarist Chris White recalled in the notes to the anthology *Zombie Heaven*. "We knew we were going to break up, so it was, 'Let's get this thing finished, let's get out of here.'"

All recall the studio environment as being tense, with the song's composer, keyboardist Rod Argent, imperiously instructing singer Colin Blunstone how to deliver the melody. Eventually they finished "Time of the Season," and walked away expecting little from it. The song was released as a single in 1969, nearly a year after the band said farewell, and it became a massive hit in the U.S. The success led some curious seekers to the album, where they encountered one of the most florid and ambitious song cycles of the rock era. From a distance, *Odessey and Oracle* can sound like an unretouched photo from the age of flower power. But it's deeper than that, and more challenging. While some tracks move in a drifty Donovan-ish head-in-the-clouds way, others position psychedelic colors—coming from such instruments as the aptly named mellotron keyboard—within crisp, rock-rhythm contexts. The best of these are "Hung Up on a Dream" and "Changes," artifacts from a long-ago season when trippy experiments weren't all that far from what lit up the airwaves.

GENRE: 🎸 Rock. **RELEASED:** 1968, Columbia. (Reissued 2004, with bonus tracks, Fuel 2000.) **KEY TRACKS:** "Time of the Season," "Hung Up on a Dream," "Friends of Mine," "Changes." **CATALOG CHOICE:** *Zombie Heaven*. **NEXT STOP:** Pink Floyd: *Meddle*. **AFTER THAT:** Donovan: *Sunshine Superman*.

Hell-Raisers Play the Blooze

Tres Hombres

ZZ Top

The first thing you notice about the opening of "La Grange," the ZZ Top breakthrough, is the controlled force with which Billy Gibbons's fingers hit the strings. He's playing a rhythm guitar line that's rattled around jukejoints of blues lore, one John Lee Hooker popularized (and likely pioneered) with "Boogie Chillun." Gibbons plays it like he's tapping out a secret code. There are only a few notes, and he places them exactingly, so the phrase just skips along. When the bass and drums check in after a few verses, they kick things into a loud whomp, but at the center of it all is that same original line, trucking hard, cutting through any and all radio static.

That one phrase propels everything—the song, this surprisingly strong album, really the entire career of ZZ Top, the shit-kicking Texas trio that amped up shuffling "blooze" into music that flattened stoner kids in suburban arenas.

Tres Hombres, ZZ Top's third effort, hit the charts in August 1973, at a moment when blues-rock was peaking: That same month saw the release of the debut from Lynyrd Skynyrd, a flashy band featuring three lead guitarists, and the Allman Brothers Band's highest-charting album, *Brothers and Sisters*. ZZ was a different animal—in part because of its nothing-fancy instrumentation (guitar, bass, drums), and also its sharp balance of thunder and finesse:

Dusty Hill and Billy Gibbons at a 1973 concert in Statesboro, Georgia.

Throughout *Tres Hombres*, the band's loud-proud heaviness is offset by the ornery Gibbons, who carves his solos with a scalpel.

Alas, the Top took a sordid turn in the early '80s, with a series of leering and overly synthesized hit records (*Afterburner*) that were saddled with cartoonishly absurd videos. Those artifacts from a grim time are rusting on blocks in the pop-culture junkyard, while *Tres Hombres* is still on the road—a sleek, streamlined machine for the ages.

GENRE: 🎸 Rock. **RELEASED:** 1973, Warner Bros. **KEY TRACKS:** "Jesus Just Left Chicago," "La Grange," "Precious and Grace." **CATALOG CHOICE:** *Fandango!* **NEXT STOP:** Lynyrd Skynyrd: *One More from the Road.* **AFTER THAT:** Robin Trower: *Bridge of Sighs.*

108 More Recordings to Know About

To arrive at the final 1,000 Recordings to Hear Before You Die, I considered many other works—in some cases I found it necessary to explore an artist's entire discography. Following are some of the particularly strong selections I encountered—titles that I very much wanted to include.

Richard Adler and Jerry Ross: *The Pajama Game*, Original Broadway Cast (Musicals)

John Anderson: *Wild and Blue* (Country)

Louis Andriessen: *De Staat*, Arnold Schoenberg Choir (Reinbert de Leeuw, cond.) (Classical)

Joan Armatrading: *Joan Armatrading* (Rock)

Dorothy Ashby: *In a Minor Groove* (Jazz)

Susana Baca: *Susana Baca* (World/Peru)

Devendra Banhart: *Smokey Rolls Down Thunder Canyon* (Rock)

Syd Barrett: *The Madcap Laughs* (Rock)

Beck: *Odelay* (Rock)

Blood Sweat and Tears: *Blood Sweat and Tears* (Rock)

Boards of Canada: *The Campfire Headphase* (Electronica)

Pierre Boulez: *Répons*, Ensemble InterContemporain (Pierre Boulez, cond.) (Classical)

Chico Buarque: *Construção* (World/Brazil)

Vashti Bunyan: *Just Another Diamond Day* (Folk)

Terry Callier: *Occasional Rain* Jazz, (Folk)

Betty Carter: *The Audience with Betty Carter* (Jazz, Vocals)

Nat King Cole: *Love Is the Thing* (Vocals)

John Coltrane: *Giant Steps* (Jazz)

Country Gentlemen: *Yesterday and Today Vol. 1* (Country)

Miles Davis: *Live-Evil* (Jazz)

Nick Drake: *Pink Moon* (Folk)

Champion Jack Dupree: *Blues from the Gutter* (R&B, Blues)

Bob Dylan: *Live 1964—Concert at Philharmonic Hall* (Rock)

Eggs Over Easy: *Good 'n' Cheap* (Rock)

Joe Ely: *Honky Tonk Masquerade* (Country)

English Beat: *Special Beat Service* (Rock)

EPMD: *Business as Usual* (Hip-Hop)

The Flatlanders: *More a Legend Than a Band* (Folk, Country)

Bob Gibson and Bob Camp: *At the Gate of Horn* (Folk)

João Gilberto: *Live in Montreux* (World/Brazil)

Michael Harrison: *Revelation* (Classical)

Joe Henderson: *Inner Urge* (Jazz)

Joe Henry: *Trampoline* (Rock)

Mike Heron: *Smiling Men with Bad Reputations* (Rock)

Richard "Groove" Holmes: *On Basie's Bandstand* (Jazz)

Janis Ian: *Between the Lines* (Folk, Rock)

Indigo Girls: *Indigo Girls* (Folk, Rock)

INXS: *Kick* (Rock)

Jackson do Pandeiro: *Como Tem Zéna Paraíba—O Melhor De* (World/Brazil)

Jethro Tull: *Aqualung* (Rock)

Beau Jocque and the Zydeco Hi-Rollers: *Pick Up On This!* (R&B)

Billy Joel: *Turnstiles* (Rock)

Kepa Junkera: *Bilbao 00:00h* (World/Spain)

Aram Khachaturian: *Piano Concerto*, William Kapell, Boston Symphony Orchestra (Serge Koussevitzky, cond.) (Classical)

Kinky: *Kinky* (Electronica)

Andy Kirk and His Clouds of Joy: *Jukebox Hits 1936–1949* (Jazz)

Kool and The Gang: *Live at the Sex Machine* (R&B)

Kris Kristofferson: *Kristofferson* (Country)

Jonathan Larson: *Rent*, Original Broadway Cast (Musicals)

Furry Lewis: *In His Prime (1927–1928)* (Blues)

Nick Lowe: *Pure Pop for Now People* (Rock)

Witold Lutosławski: *Piano Concerto*, Krystian Zimerman, BBC Symphony Orchestra (Witold Lutosławski, cond.) (Classical)

Samba Mapangala and Orchestre Virunga: *Virunga Volcano* (World/Congo)

Branford Marsalis: *Renaissance* (Jazz)

Wynton Marsalis: *J Mood* (Jazz)

Prince Nico Mbarga: *Aki Special* (World/Nigeria)

Felix Mendelssohn: *Songs Without Words*, Andras Schiff (Classical)

Pat Metheny and Ornette Coleman: *Song X* (Jazz)

M.I.A.: *Arular* (Electronica)

Mbongeni Ngema: *Sarafina!*, Original Broadway Cast (Musicals)

Van Morrison: *It's Too Late to Stop Now* (Rock)

Ohio Players: *Fire* (R&B)

Osibisa: *Hot Flashback Vol. 1* (World/Ghana)

Harry Partch: *Revelation in the Courthouse Park* (Classical)

Jaco Pastorius: *Word of Mouth* (Jazz)

Tom Petty and the Heartbreakers: *Damn the Torpedos* (Rock)

Pink Floyd: *Wish You Were Here* (Rock)

Plug: *Drum 'n' Bass for Papa* (Electronica)

Baden Powell and Vinicius de Moraes: *Os Afro Sambas* (World/Brazil)

Professor Longhair: *Crawfish Fiesta* (R&B)

Maurice Ravel: *Daphnis et Chloë; La Valse*, Berlin Philharmonic (Pierre Boulez, cond.) (Classical)

R.E.M.: *Fables of the Reconstruction* (Rock)

Terry Riley: *In C* (Classical)

Rockpile: *Seconds of Pleasure* (Rock)

Roberto Roena y Su Apollo Sound: *4* (World/Latin)

Rolling Stones: *Beggers Banquet* (Rock)

Sonny Rollins: *The Bridge* (Jazz)

Rush: *Grace Under Pressure* (Rock)

Boz Scaggs: *Silk Degrees* (Rock)

Shirley Scott: *Queen of the Organ* (Jazz)

Thione Seck and Raam Daan: *XV Anniversary Live!* (World/Senegal)

Artie Shaw: *The Centennial Collection* (Jazz)

Wayne Shorter: *Speak No Evil* (Jazz)

Dmitri Shostakovich: *Lady Macbeth of Mtsensk*, Nicolai Gedda, London Philharmonic Orchestra (Mstislav Rostropovich, cond.) (Opera)

Judee Sill: *Heart Food* (Rock)

Sly and the Family Stone: *Fresh* (R&B)

Specials: *Specials* (Rock)

Bruce Springsteen: *Nebraska* (Rock)

Bruce Springsteen: *Darkness on the Edge of Town* (Rock)

Steely Dan: *Pretzel Logic* (Rock)

Sting: *Nothing Like the Sun* (Rock)

The Stylistics: *Round Two* (R&B)

Supertramp: *Crime of the Century* (Rock)

Joan Sutherland, Marilyn Horne, and Luciano Pavarotti: *Great Duets and Trios* (Opera)

Tabala Wolof: *Sufi Drumming of Senegal* (World/Senegal)

10,000 Maniacs: *Our Time in Eden* (Rock)

Tinariwen: *Amassokoul* (World/Tuareg)

Urge Overkill: *Saturation* (Rock)

Van Halen: *1984* (Rock)

Various Artists: *The Complete Stax-Volt Singles 1959–1968* (R&B)

Various Artists: *Guitar Paradise of East Africa* (World/Africa)

Various Artists: *Spirits of Life: Haitian Vodou* (World/Haiti)

The Verve: *Urban Hymns* (Rock)

Meredith Willson: *The Music Man*, Original Motion Picture Soundtrack (Musicals)

Jimmy Witherspoon: *The 'Spoon Concerts* (Jazz, Blues)

Yabby You: *Jesus Dread (1972–1977)* (World/Jamaica)

Neil Young: *Tonight's the Night* (Rock)

Los Zafiros: *Bossa Cubana* (World/Cuba)

Sources

The following is intended to help curious listeners track down the music in this book. There are many shops and online sites devoted to every musical sub-speciality; below are some retailers that I found useful in the course of researching the book. Also, readers can visit 1000recordings.com, which has links to buy most of the book's recommended albums.

GENERAL

amazon.com
itunes.com
bn.com
borders.com
tower.com
emusic.com

CLASSICAL AND OPERA

Arkiv Music
arkivmusic.com

DANCE, ELECTRONICA

Breakbeat Science
breakbeatscience.com

611 Records
611records.com

HIP-HOP

UndergroundHipHop
undergroundhiphop.com

Fat Beats
fatbeats.com
406 6th Avenue, 2nd Floor
New York, NY 10011
(212) 673-3883

JAZZ

Jazz Record Mart
jazzmart.com
27 East Illinois Street
Chicago, IL 60611
(800) 684-3480 or
(312) 222-1474

Downtown Music Gallery
downtownmusicgallery.com
342 Bowery
New York, NY 10012
(800) 622-1387

Other Music
(also rock, electronica, world, avant-garde)
othermusic.com
15 East 4th Street
New York, NY 10003
(212) 477-8150

RARITIES

Dusty Groove
dustygroove.com
1120 North Ashland Avenue
Chicago, IL 60622
(888) 387-8947

GEMM
gemm.com

WORLD MUSIC

General

National Geographic World Music
worldmusic.national
  geographic.com

World Music Institute
worldmusicinstitute.org
(212) 545-7536

Brazil

Modern Sound
modernsound.com.br

Reggae

Jammyland
jammyland.com
(212) 614-0185

Latin

Descarga
descarga.com
(800) 377-2647

African

Stern's Music
sternsmusic.com

Arabic

Rashid's Music Sales
rashid.com
(800) 843-9401

Musical Genres Indexes

COUNTRY

ELECTRONICA

FOLK

GOSPEL

HIP-HOP

JAZZ

MUSICALS

OPERA

POP

R&B

ROCK

VOCALS

☐ The Four Freshman, *The Four Freshman and Five Trombones*, 286

☐ Serge Gainsbourg, *Histoire de Melody Nelson*, 296–97

☐ Judy Garland, *Judy at Carnegie Hall*, 300–301

☐ Billie Holiday, *The Ultimate Collection*, 362–63

☐ Shirley Horn, *Close Enough for Love*, 367–68

☐ Eddie Jefferson, *The Jazz Singer*, 394–95

☐ Norah Jones, *Come Away with Me*, 409

☐ Lambert, Hendricks, and Ross, *The Hottest New Group in Jazz*, 438–39

☐ Peggy Lee, *Black Coffee*, 444

☐ Julie London, *At Home/Around Midnight*, 454

☐ Johnny Mathis, *Open Fire, Two Guitars*, 482

☐ Carmen McRae, *Carmen Sings Monk*, 491

☐ Les Paul with Mary Ford, *The Best of the Capitol Masters: Ninetieth Birthday Edition*, 586

☐ Edith Piaf, *The Voice of the Sparrow*, 598–99

☐ Louis Prima, *The Wildest!*, 612

☐ Jimmy Scott, *Falling in Love Is Wonderful*, 682–83

☐ Nina Simone, *Anthology*, 705

☐ Frank Sinatra, *Songs for Swingin' Lovers*, 706–7

☐ Frank Sinatra, *Sings for Only the Lonely*, 707–8

☐ Frank Sinatra and Antonio Carlos Jobim, *Francis Albert Sinatra & Antonio Carlos Jobim*, 708–9

☐ Dusty Springfield, *Dusty in Memphis*, 732–33

☐ Leon Thomas, *Spirits Known and Unknown*, 774

☐ Mel Tormé, *Swings Shubert Alley*, 779–80

☐ Various Artists, *Stormy Weather*, 822–23

☐ Sarah Vaughan, *Live in Japan*, 826

☐ Dionne Warwick, *The Dionne Warwick Collection*, 846–47

☐ Dinah Washington, *Dinah!*, 847–48

☐ Joe Williams with the Count Basie Orchestra, *Count Basie Swings, Joe Williams Sings*, 863–64

☐ Cassandra Wilson, *Blue Light 'til Dawn*, 869

WORLD

☐ Manu Chao, *Clandestino*, 154–55

☐ Codona, *Codona 3*, 178–79

☐ Joi, *We Are Three*, 406–7

☐ Andy Statman, *Between Heaven and Earth: Music of the Jewish Mystics*, 737

Algeria

☐ Khaled, *N'ssi, N'ssi*, 421

Andes

☐ Sukay, *Cumbre*, 754–55

Angola

☐ Waldemar Bastos, *Pretaluz*, 51–52

Argentina

☐ Carlos Gardel, *The Best of Carlos Gardel*, 299–300

☐ Juana Molina, *Segundo*, 511

☐ Astor Piazzolla, *Tango: Zero Hour*, 599–600

☐ Gustavo Santaolalla, *Ronroco*, 672–73

Armenia

☐ Djivan Gasparyan, *I Will Not Be Sad in This World*, 302

Brazil

☐ Jorge Ben, *Africa/Brazil*, 76–77

☐ Lô Borges, *Lô Borges*, 106

☐ Cartola, *Cartola*, 147

☐ Cascabulho, *Hunger Gives You a Headache*, 149–50

☐ Dorival Caymmi, *Caymmi e seu violão*, 153

☐ Djavan, *Luz*, 228–29

☐ Bebel Gilberto, *Tanto tempo*, 310–11

☐ João Gilberto, *João Gilberto*, 311–12

☐ Ilê Aiyê, *Canto negro*, 379–80

☐ Antonio Carlos Jobim, *The Composer of "Desafinado" Plays*, 397–98

☐ Antonio Carlos Jobim and Elis Regina, *Elis & Tom*, 398–99

☐ Os Mutantes, *Mutantes*, 536

☐ Milton Nascimento with Lô Borges, *Clube da esquina*, 540–41

☐ Hermeto Pascoal, *Slaves Mass*, 583–84

☐ Baden Powell, *O universe musical de Baden Powell*, 607

☐ Elis Regina, *Como & porque*, 639–40

☐ Moacir Santos, *Coisas*, 673–74

☐ Chico Science and Nação Zumbi, *Da lama ao caos*, 681

☐ Caetano Veloso and Gilberto Gil, *Tropicália 2*, 828–29

☐ Caetano Veloso, *Livro*, 829–30

☐ Tom Zé, *Fabrication Defect*, 887

Bulgaria

☐ The Bulgarian Women's National Radio and Television Chorus, *Le mystère des voix bulgares*, 130–31

☐ Ivo Papasov and His Orchestra, *Balkanology*, 576

Cameroon

☐ Manu Dibango, "Soul Makossa," 222–23

Cape Verde

☐ Cesaria Evora, *Cesaria*, 266

Celtic

☐ The Bothy Band, *Old Hag You Have Killed Me*, 107–8

☐ The Boys of the Lough, *Live at Passim*, 110

☐ The Chieftains, *The Chieftains 4*, 165

☐ The Clancy Brothers and the Dubliners, *Irish Drinking Songs*, 169–70

☐ Clannad, *Macalla*, 170–71

☐ De Danann with Mary Black, *Song for Ireland*, 215–16

- Various Artists, *The Mighty Two*, 815
- Various Artists, *Ska Bonanza: The Studio One Ska Years*, 821

Japan

- Kodo, *Live at Acropolis, Athens, Greece*, 430–31
- Tony Scott, *Music for Zen Meditation and Other Joys*, 683–84
- Goro Yamaguchi, *Shakuhachi Music: A Bell Ringing in the Empty Sky*, 879–80

Klezmer

- Itzhak Perlman, *Live in the Fiddler's House*, 593

Latin

- Ray Barretto, *Barretto Power*, 45–46
- Rubén Blades and Willie Colón, *Siembra*, 93–94
- Celia Cruz and Johnny Pacheco, *Celia y Johnny*, 197–98
- Larry Harlow, *Salsa*, 343
- Eddie Palmieri, *La perfecta*, 573–74
- Eddie Palmieri, *Eddie Palmieri*, 574–75
- Tito Puente and His Orchestra, *Dance Mania!*, 621–22
- Tito Rodriguez, *Live at the Palladium*, 656–57

Latin America

- Various Artists, *The Spirit Cries*, 821–22

Madagascar

- Henry Kaiser and David Lindley with Musicians from Madagascar, *A World Out of Time*, 416

Mali

- Toumani Diabaté and Ballake Sissoko, *New Ancient Strings*, 221
- Salif Keita, *Moffou*, 420
- Oumou Sangare, *Ko sira*, 670
- Ali Farka Touré, *The River*, 781

Mauritania

- Dimi Mint Abba and Khalifa Ould Eide, *Moorish Music from Mauritania*, 2–3

Mexico

- Café Tacuba, *Cuatro caminos*, 138
- Nati Cano's Mariachi los Camperos, *¡Viva el mariachi!*, 141
- Flaco Jiménez, *Squeeze Box King*, 397

Middle East

- Ofra Haza, *Fifty Gates of Wisdom: Yemenite Songs*, 352–53

Morocco

- Various Artists, *World of Gnawa*, 825

Nigeria

- King Sunny Ade, *The Best of the Classic Years*, 11
- I. K. Dairo and His Blue Spots, *Definitive Dairo*, 202
- Fela Kuti and the Afrika 70, *Confusion/Gentleman*, 436

Pakistan

- Nusrat Fateh Ali Khan and Party, *In Concert in Paris*, 422–23

Puerto Rico

- Cortijo y su Máquina del Tiempo, *La Máquina del Tiempo*, 190
- Cheo Feliciano, *Cheo*, 274
- El Gran Combo de Puerto Rico, *30 Aniversario*, 322
- Héctor Lavoe, *De ti depende*, 439–40
- Ismael Rivera con Kako y Su Orquesta, *Lo último en la avenida*, 646–47

Portugal

- Madredeus, *O espírito da paz*, 464
- Amália Rodrigues, *The Art of Amália Rodrigues*, 654–55

Romania

- Taraf de Haïdouks, *Taraf de Haïdouks*, 762–63

Russia

- Huun-Huur-Tu, *The Orphan's Lament*, 376

Senegal

- Baaba Maal (with Mansour Seck), *Djam leelii*, 462
- Youssou N'Dour, *Immigrés*, 542–43
- Orchestra Baobab, *Pirates Choice*, 565–66
- Touré Kunda, *Paris-Ziguinchor Live*, 781–82

South Africa

- Mahlathini and the Mahotella Queens, *Paris/Soweto*, 467–68
- The Soul Brothers, *The Rough Guide to the Soul Brothers*, 726
- Various Artists, *The Indestructible Beat of Soweto*, 814

Spain

- Camarón de la Isla, *La leyenda del tiempo*, 139–40

Tanzania

- Remmy Ongala and Orchestre Super Matimila, *Songs for the Poor Man*, 564

Trinidad

- Mighty Sparrow and Lord Kitchener, *Sixteen Carnival Hits*, 503–4

Turkey

- Özel Türkbas, *How to Make Your Husband a Sultan*, 790

Venezuela

- Los Amigos Invisibles, *Arepa 3000: A Venezuelan Journey into Space*, 19

Zimbabwe

- Thomas Mapfumo and the Blacks Unlimited, *Chimurenga Singles, 1976–1980*, 473

Occasions Indexes

S ometimes you're looking for music to help set a mood. The following indexes list recordings that can do just that. Not every track on every album will reflect the theme, but one or more will. Happy listening!

COCKTAIL HOUR

Almost as important as the swizzle sticks, delightful tunes for when it's time to kick back with a cool libation.

❑ Johnny Adams, *The Real Me: Johnny Adams Sings Doc Pomus*, 8

❑ The Cannonball Adderley Quintet, *At the Lighthouse*, 10

❑ Arthur Alexander, *The Ultimate Arthur Alexander*, 13–14

❑ Mose Allison, *Allison Wonderland*, 15–16

❑ Herb Alpert and the Tijuana Brass, *Whipped Cream and Other Delights*, 18–19

❑ Fred Astaire, *Steppin' Out: Astaire Sings*, 28–29

❑ Chet Atkins and Les Paul, *Chester and Lester*, 29–30

❑ Harry Belafonte, *Live at Carnegie Hall*, 72–73

❑ Tony Bennett and Bill Evans, *The Tony Bennett–Bill Evans Album*, 78–79

❑ Art Blakey and the Jazz Messengers, *Moanin'*, 95

❑ Bobby "Blue" Bland, *Two Steps from the Blues*, 95–96

❑ Clifford Brown–Max Roach Quintet, *Clifford Brown and Max Roach*, 119

❑ Lord Buckley, *His Royal Hipness*, 127

❑ Sonny Clark, *Cool Struttin'*, 172

❑ Nat King Cole and His Trio, *The Complete After Midnight Sessions*, 180–81

❑ John Coltrane and Johnny Hartman, *John Coltrane and Johnny Hartman*, 183–84

❑ Bing Crosby, *A Centennial Anthology of Decca Recordings*, 194–95

❑ Bobby Darin, *That's All*, 206–7

❑ Sammy Davis Jr., *I Gotta Right to Swing*, 212–13

❑ Paul Desmond with Jim Hall, *Take Ten*, 220

❑ Ella Fitzgerald, *Ella Fitzgerald Sings the Cole Porter Songbook*, 279

❑ Ella Fitzgerald and Louis Armstrong, *Ella and Louis*, 280

❑ The Four Freshmen, *The Four Freshmen and Five Trombones*, 286

❑ Serge Gainsbourg, *Histoire de Melody Nelson*, 296–97

❑ Erroll Garner, *Concert by the Sea*, 301–2

❑ Stan Getz and João Gilberto, *Getz/Gilberto*, 308–9

❑ Dexter Gordon, *Go!*, 318

❑ Billie Holiday, *The Ultimate Collection*, 362–63

❑ Shirley Horn, *Close Enough for Love*, 367–68

❑ Ahmad Jamal, *But Not for Me: Live at the Pershing*, 387–88

❑ Etta James, *Tell Mama*, 389

❑ Little Willie John, *The Very Best of Little Willie John*, 400

❑ George Jones, *The Grand Tour*, 408–9

❑ Ernesto Lecuona, *The Ultimate Collection: Lecuona Plays Lecuona*, 441–42

❑ Peggy Lee, *Black Coffee*, 444

❑ Les McCann and Eddie Harris, *Swiss Movement*, 486–87

❑ Hank Mobley, *Soul Station*, 508–9

❑ The Modern Jazz Quartet, *European Concert*, 509–10

❑ Wes Montgomery, *Smokin' at the Half Note*, 516–17

❑ Oliver Nelson, *The Blues and the Abstract Truth*, 543

❑ Phineas Newborn Jr., *A World of Piano!*, 548–49

❑ Charlie Parker, *Charlie Parker with Strings*, 578–79

❑ Les Paul with Mary Ford, *The Best of the Capitol Masters: Ninetieth Birthday Edition*, 586

❑ The Oscar Peterson Trio, *Night Train*, 595–96

❑ Charlie Rich, *Behind Closed Doors*, 644

❑ Nina Simone, *Anthology*, 705

❑ Frank Sinatra, *Songs for Swingin' Lovers*, 706–7

❑ Dusty Springfield, *Dusty in Memphis*, 732–33

❑ Cal Tjader, *Primo*, 776–77

❑ Sarah Vaughan, *Live in Japan*, 826

❑ Dinah Washington, *Dinah!*, 847–48

❑ Muddy Waters, *At Newport 1960*, 848–49

❑ Joe Williams with the Count Basie Orchestra, *Count Basie Swings, Joe Williams Sings*, 863–64

❑ Cassandra Wilson, *Blue Light 'til Dawn*, 869

❑ Lester Young, *The "Kansas City" Sessions*, 884–85

GET THE PARTY STARTED

From ever-popular standbys (Motown hits) to up-tempo electronica, the secret weapons used by DJs to get people of all ages moving and grooving.

❑ Mitch Ryder and the Detroit Wheels, "Devil with a Blue Dress On" and "Good Golly Miss Molly," 666

❑ Huey "Piano" Smith and His Clowns, *This Is . . .*, 717

❑ Britney Spears, "Toxic," 727–28

❑ The Streets, *Original Pirate Material*, 751–52

❑ Donna Summer, "I Feel Love," 755

❑ The Supremes, "You Keep Me Hangin' On," 756

❑ Talking Heads, *Remain in Light*, 760–61

❑ Big Mama Thornton, *Hound Dog: The Peacock Recordings*, 776

❑ Toots and the Maytals, *Funky Kingston/In the Dark*, 778–79

❑ Allen Toussaint, *Finger Poppin' and Stompin' Feet*, 782–83

❑ Big Joe Turner, *Big, Bad, and Blue*, 790–91

❑ Ultramagnetic MCs, *Critical Beatdown*, 794–95

❑ Ike and Tina Turner, *Proud Mary*, 791–92

❑ Usher, *Confessions*, 797–98

❑ Various Artists, *The Best of Sugar Hill Records*, 804–5

❑ Various Artists, *Dazed and Confused*, 809

❑ Various Artists, *The Fabulous Swing Collection*, 810–811

❑ Various Artists, *Saturday Night Fever*, 820

❑ Various Artists, *A Tom Moulton Mix*, 823–24

❑ Fats Waller, *If You Got to Ask, You Ain't Got It*, 843

❑ War, *Why Can't We Be Friends?*, 844–45

❑ The White Stripes, *Elephant*, 857

❑ The Wild Tchoupitoulas, *The Wild Tchoupitoulas*, 861–62

❑ Jackie Wilson, *The Very Best of Jackie Wilson*, 870

❑ Stevie Wonder, *Innervisions*, 872

MUSIC TO INSPIRE REFLECTION

Calm, centering sounds for contemplating the cosmos.

❑ Dimi Mint Abba and Khalifa Ould Eide, *Moorish Music from Mauritania*, 2–3

❑ John Adams, *Harmonium*, 6

❑ Mahmoud Ahmed, *Éthiopiques, Vol. 7: Erè Mèla Mèla*, 12

❑ Aphex Twin: *Selected Ambient Works 85–92*, 22–23

❑ J. S. Bach, *The Well-Tempered Clavier, Book 1*, 35

❑ J. S. Bach, *Mass in B Minor*, 36

❑ The Band, *The Band*, 44

❑ Samuel Barber, *Adagio for Strings*, 44–45

❑ Béla Bartók, *Six String Quartets*, 46–47

❑ Waldemar Bastos, *Pretaluz*, 51–52

❑ Ludwig van Beethoven, *Missa Solemnis*, 67–68

❑ Benedictine Monks of the Abbey of St. Maurice and St. Maur, Clervaux, *Salve Regina: Gregorian Chant*, 77–78

❑ Vishwa Mohan Bhatt and Ry Cooder, *A Meeting by the River*, 86

❑ Paul Bley, *Fragments*, 96–97

❑ The Blind Boys of Alabama, *Spirit of the Century*, 97–98

❑ Bonnie "Prince" Billy, *I See a Darkness*, 102–3

❑ Boukman Eksperyans, *Kalfou Danjere*, 108–9

❑ Bright Eyes, *I'm Wide Awake, It's Morning*, 115–16

❑ Jackson Browne, *Late for the Sky*, 124–25

❑ The Bulgarian Women's National Radio and Television Chorus, *Le mystère des voix bulgares*, 130–31

❑ Neko Case, *Fox Confessor Brings the Flood*, 150–51

❑ Johnny Cash, *American Recordings*, 152

❑ Tracy Chapman, *Tracy Chapman*, 155–56

❑ Hariprasad Chaurasia, *Raga Darbari Kanada*, 159

❑ Sonny Chillingworth, *Endlessly*, 165–66

❑ Frédéric Chopin, *Nocturnes*, 168

❑ Van Cliburn, *Rachmaninoff: Piano Concerto No. 3; Prokofiev: Piano Concerto No. 3*, 173–74

❑ Jimmy Cliff, *The Harder They Come*, 174–75

❑ Leonard Cohen, *Songs of Leonard Cohen*, 179–80

❑ John Coltrane, *A Love Supreme*, 183

❑ Karen Dalton, *It's So Hard to Tell Who's Going to Love You the Best*, 203–4

❑ Miles Davis, *Kind of Blue*, 208

❑ Miles Davis Quintet, *In a Silent Way*, 210–11

❑ De Danann with Mary Black, *Song for Ireland*, 215–16

❑ Toumani Diabaté and Ballake Sissoko, *New Ancient Strings*, 221

❑ Nick Drake, *Five Leaves Left*, 235–36

❑ Bob Dylan, *Blood on the Tracks*, 245–46

❑ Brian Eno, *Ambient 1: Music for Airports*, 259–60

❑ Alejandro Escovedo, *Gravity*, 261

❑ Bill Evans Trio, *Sunday at the Village Vanguard/Waltz for Debby*, 263–64

❑ Fairport Convention, *Liege and Lief*, 268–69

❑ Roberta Flack, "The First Time Ever I Saw Your Face," 280–81

❑ Jan Garbarek and Ralph Towner, *Dis*, 299

❑ Djivan Gasparyan, *I Will Not Be Sad in This World*, 302

❑ João Gilberto, *João Gilberto*, 311–12

❑ Henryk Górecki, *Symphony No. 3, Op. 26: Symphony of Sorrowful Songs*, 319

ROMANCE ENHANCERS

This music and candlelight . . . pretty much all you need.

CARDIO WORKOUT

Rhythm music from all over the world to elevate your heart rate.

PLAY THIS FOR THE KIDS

Selections to spark a lifelong love of music. Ideal for jaded Guitar Hero stars who think they've heard everything.

❑ ABBA, *Gold*, 2

❑ The Abyssinian Baptist Choir, *Shakin' the Rafters*, 4–5

❑ The Almanac Singers, *Complete General Recordings*, 17–18

❑ Albert Ammons and Meade "Lux" Lewis, *The First Day*, 20

❑ Louis Armstrong, *The Complete Hot Fives and Hot Sevens*, 26–27

❑ Erykah Badu, *Mama's Gun*, 38

❑ The Balfa Brothers, *The Balfa Brothers Play Traditional Cajun Music*, 41–42

❑ Béla Bartók, *Concerto for Orchestra; Music for Strings, Percussion, and Celesta*, 48–49

❑ The Beach Boys, "Good Vibrations," 54

❑ The Beatles, *A Hard Day's Night*, 58

❑ The Beatles, *Rubber Soul*, 58–59

❑ Harry Belafonte, *At Carnegie Hall*, 72–73

❑ Leonard Bernstein and Stephen Sondheim, *West Side Story*, 84–85

❑ Blind Blake, *Ragtime Guitar's Foremost Fingerpicker*, 94

❑ Jerry Bock and Sheldon Harnick, *Fiddler on the Roof*, 100–101

❑ James Booker, *New Orleans Piano Wizard Live!*, 104–5

❑ Boston, *Boston*, 107

❑ The Caravans, *The Best of the Caravans*, 143

❑ The Original Carter Family, *The Carter Family: 1927–1934*, 145–46

❑ Pablo Casals, *J. S. Bach, Suites for Cello*, Vols. 1 and 2, 149

❑ Chicago, *The Chicago Transit Authority*, 164

❑ The Chieftains, *The Chieftains 4*, 165

❑ Frédéric Chopin, *Ballades and Scherzos*, 166–67

❑ The Coasters, "Yakety Yak," 176–77

❑ Joe Cocker, *Mad Dogs and Englishmen*, 178

❑ Sam Cooke and the Soul Stirrers, *Sam Cooke with the Soul Stirrers*, 186

❑ Dick Dale and His Del-Tones, *King of the Surf Guitar*, 202–3

❑ Miles Davis Quintet, *Highlights from the Plugged Nickel*, 209–10

❑ The Dixie Chicks, *Wide Open Spaces*, 226

❑ Michael Doucet and BeauSoleil, *Bayou Deluxe*, 233–34

❑ Bob Dylan, *Highway 61 Revisited*, 243–44

❑ The Eagles, *Hotel California*, 248

❑ Ramblin' Jack Elliott, *The Essential Ramblin' Jack Elliott*, 255–56

❑ Tal Farlow, *The Swinging Guitar of Tal Farlow*, 270–71

❑ Fleetwood Mac, *Fleetwood Mac*, 284–85

❑ Judy Garland, *Judy at Carnegie Hall*, 300–301

❑ George Gershwin, *Porgy and Bess*, 307–8

❑ Benny Goodman and His Orchestra, *The Complete 1938 Carnegie Hall Concert*, 317

❑ The Grateful Dead, *American Beauty*, 322–23

❑ Woody Guthrie, *Dust Bowl Ballads*, 331–32

❑ The Jimi Hendrix Experience, *Are You Experienced*, 355–56

❑ Jerry Herman, *Hello, Dolly!*, 357–58

❑ Vladimir Horowitz, *Horowitz at the Met*, 368–69

❑ The Incredible String Band, *The Hangman's Beautiful Daughter*, 380–81

❑ Burl Ives, *The Wayfaring Stranger*, 382

❑ Joe Jackson, *Night and Day*, 384

❑ Elton John, *Goodbye Yellow Brick Road*, 399

❑ Lonnie Johnson, *The Original Guitar Wizard*, 403

❑ Robert Johnson, *The Complete Recordings*, 404

❑ Henry Kaiser and David Lindley with Musicians from Madagascar, *A World Out of Time*, 416

❑ The Kinks, *The Kinks Are the Village Green Preservation Society*, 427–28

❑ Leadbelly, *Where Did You Sleep Last Night?*, 440–41

❑ Led Zeppelin, *How the West Was Won*, 443–44

❑ Jerry Lee Lewis, *Live at the Star Club, Hamburg*, 448

❑ Lyle Lovett, *Joshua Judges Ruth*, 458–59

❑ Henry Mancini, *Breakfast at Tiffany's*, 472

❑ Bob Marley and the Wailers, *Natty Dread*, 474–75

❑ John Mayall with Eric Clapton, *Blues Breakers*, 484–85

❑ Curtis Mayfield, *There's No Place like America Today*, 485–86

❑ The Mighty Diamonds, *Right Time*, 502–3

❑ Joni Mitchell, *Court and Spark*, 507–8

❑ Bill Monroe, *The Music of Bill Monroe*, 513–14

❑ Milton Nascimento with Lô Borges, *Clube da esquina*, 540–41

❑ Ricky Nelson, *Greatest Hits*, 544

❑ Harry Nilsson, *Nilsson Schmilsson*, 551

❑ Laura Nyro, *Eli and the Thirteenth Confession*, 558

❑ Odetta, *Odetta Sings Ballads and Blues*, 561–62

❑ King Oliver and His Creole Jazz Band, *Off the Record: The Complete 1923 Jazz Band Recordings*, 563

❑ Ivo Papasov and His Orchestra, *Balkanology*, 576

❑ Charlie Parker, *A Studio Chronicle, 1940–1948*, 577–78

❑ Dolly Parton, *Coat of Many Colors*, 583

☐ Les Paul with Mary Ford, *The Best of the Capitol Masters: Ninetieth Birthday Edition*, 586

☐ Peter, Paul and Mary, *Peter, Paul and Mary*, 594–95

☐ Bud Powell, *The Amazing Bud Powell*, Vol. 1, 607–8

☐ Sergey Rachmaninoff, *His Complete Recordings*, 626–27

☐ Richard Rodgers and Oscar Hammerstein II, *The Sound of Music*, 653–54

☐ Jimmie Rodgers, *The Essential Jimmie Rodgers*, 652–53

☐ Sonny Rollins, *A Night at the Village Vanguard*, 659

☐ Pete Seeger, *We Shall Overcome: The Complete Carnegie Hall Concert*, 686–87

☐ Paul Simon, *Graceland*, 704

☐ Willie "The Lion" Smith, *The Lion Roars! His Greatest 1934–1944*, 720–21

☐ The Stanley Brothers, *The Complete Columbia Recordings*, 735–36

☐ Steely Dan, *Aja*, 738–39

☐ Art Tatum, *Piano Starts Here*, 764

☐ Pyotr Ilyich Tchaikovsky, *The Nutcracker*, 767–68

☐ Sister Rosetta Tharpe, *Complete Recorded Works in Chronological Order, 1938–1947*, 771–72

☐ The Tokens, "The Lion Sleeps Tonight," 777–78

☐ United Sacred Harp Musical Association Singing Convention, *Southern Journey, Vol 9: Harp of a Thousand Strings*, 796–97

☐ Ritchie Valens, "La bamba," 799

☐ Various Artists, edited by Harry Smith, *Anthology of American Folk Music*, 803–4

☐ Various Artists, *The Doo Wop Box*, 809–10

☐ Various Artists, *O Brother, Where Art Thou?*, 817–18

☐ Speedy West and Jimmy Bryant, *Stratosphere Boogie*, 854

☐ Stevie Wonder, *Songs in the Key of Life*, 873

ROADTRIP SOUNDTRACK AM

There may be traffic, but with this music playing, it'll be green lights on the straightaway—inside the car, anyway. Upbeat selections for daytime driving; moodier ones for night.

☐ Fiona Apple, *When the Pawn . . .*, 23–24

☐ The Beatles, *Revolver*, 59–60

☐ Buffalo Springfield, *Retrospective*, 129–30

☐ Johnny Cash, *At Folsom Prison*, 151–52

☐ Chicago, *The Chicago Transit Authority*, 164

☐ Patsy Cline, *The Patsy Cline Collection*, 175–76

☐ Lester Flatt, Earl Scruggs, and the Foggy Mountain Boys, *Foggy Mountain Jamboree*, 282–83

☐ Emmylou Harris, *Pieces of the Sky*, 344–45

☐ Jascha Heifetz, *Brahms, Tchaikovsky Violin Concertos*, 353

☐ Waylon Jennings, *Honky Tonk Heroes*, 395–96

☐ Booker Little, *Out Front*, 450–51

☐ Magic Sam, *West Side Soul*, 465

☐ The Dave Matthews Band, *The Gorge*, 482–83

☐ John Mayall with Eric Clapton, *Blues Breakers*, 484–85

☐ Blind Willie McTell, *The Definitive Blind Willie McTell*, 492

☐ Charles Mingus, *Mingus Ah Um*, 504

☐ Wes Montgomery, *Smokin' at the Half Note*, 516–17

☐ Bill Monroe, *The Music of Bill Monroe*, 513–14

☐ Milton Nascimento with Lô Borges, *Clube da esquina*, 540–41

☐ Nitty Gritty Dirt Band, *Will the Circle Be Unbroken*, 554

☐ Marty Robbins, *Gunfighter Ballads and Trail Songs*, 650

☐ Santana, *Abraxis*, 671–72

☐ Sleater-Kinney, *Call the Doctor*, 711

☐ Hank Snow, *The Essential*, 722

☐ The Staple Singers, *The Best of the Staple Singers*, 736–37

☐ T. Rex, *Electric Warrior*, 785–86

☐ Muddy Waters, *At Newport 1960*, 848–49

☐ Hank Williams, *Forty Greatest Hits*, 862–63

ROADTRIP SOUNDTRACK PM

☐ The Allman Brothers Band, *At Fillmore East*, 16–17

☐ The Band, *The Band*, 44

☐ James Booker, *New Orleans Piano Wizard Live!*, 104–5

☐ Solomon Burke, *Don't Give Up on Me*, 131–32

☐ Burning Spear, *Marcus Garvey*, 132

☐ Vic Chesnutt, *Is the Actor Happy?*, 162–63

☐ Codona, *Codona 3*, 178–79

☐ Ry Cooder, *Paradise and Lunch*, 185

☐ Bob Dylan, *Love and Theft*, 246

☐ Fleetwood Mac, *Then Play On*, 283–84

☐ Rory Gallagher, *Irish Tour 1974*, 297–98

☐ Merle Haggard, *Mama Tried*, 334–35

☐ John Lee Hooker, *John Lee Hooker Plays and Sings the Blues*, 365–66

☐ Lightnin' Hopkins, *Lightnin' Hopkins*, 367

☐ Bobby Hutcherson, *Components*, 375–76

☐ Robert Johnson, *The Complete Recordings*, 404

☐ Janis Joplin, *Pearl*, 410–11

☐ Led Zeppelin, *Led Zeppelin II*, 442–43

☐ Baaba Maal (with Mansour Seck), *Djam leelii*, 462

LAZY SUNDAY MORNING

Tranquil music for when you don't have anywhere to rush off to.

HEADPHONE JOURNEY

Incredible tones and textures for spacing out, as well as recordings that reward particularly close listening.

SUPERMAN'S EARBUDS

Music that glimpses the heroic; ideal for getting pumped up to deliver a presentation, save a damsel from a burning building, etc.

❏ Alice in Chains, *Dirt*, 14–15

❏ The Arcade Fire, *Neon Bible*, 24–25

❏ Bad Brains, *I Against I*, 37

❏ The Beach Boys, *Pet Sounds*, 55

❏ Ludwig van Beethoven, *String Quartets, Opp. 131, 135*, 66–67

❏ Ludwig van Beethoven, *Symphonies Nos. 1–9*, 70–71

❏ Ludwig van Beethoven, *Violin Concerto*, 496–97

❏ Black Flag, *Damaged*, 91–92

❏ Boston, *Boston*, 107

❏ Café Tacuba, *Cuatro caminos*, 138

❏ Johnny Cash, *At Folsom Prison*, 151–52

❏ The Clash, *London Calling*, 172–73

❏ Elvis Costello and the Attractions, *Armed Forces*, 190–91

❏ Bob Dylan, *Blonde on Blonde*, 244–45

❏ Fishbone, *Truth and Soul*, 278

❏ Aretha Franklin, *Amazing Grace*, 289–90

❏ Fugazi, *Repeater*, 291–92

❏ Gang of Four, *Entertainment!*, 298

❏ Marvin Gaye, *What's Going On*, 304

❏ Green Day, *American Idiot*, 325–26

❏ George Frideric Handel, *Messiah*, 341

❏ The Jimi Hendrix Experience, *Are You Experienced*, 355–56

❏ Hüsker Dü, *Zen Arcade*, 374–75

❏ Iggy and the Stooges, *Raw Power*, 378–79

❏ Mahalia Jackson, *The Apollo Sessions: 1946–1951*, 384–85

❏ Jane's Addiction, *Ritual de lo Habitual*, 392

❏ Kodo, *Live at Acropolis, Athens, Greece*, 430–31

❏ The Mahavishnu Orchestra with John McLaughlin, *The Inner Mounting Flame*, 466–67

❏ Gustav Mahler, *Symphony No. 9*, 470–71

❏ Thomas Mapfumo and the Blacks Unlimited, *Chimurenga Singles, 1976–1980*, 473

❏ Bob Marley and the Wailers, *Exodus*, 475–76

❏ MC5, *Kick Out the Jams*, 488

❏ Yehudi Menuhin, *Beethoven Violin Concerto, Mendelssohn Violin Concerto*, 496–97

❏ Metallica, *Master of Puppets*, 499

❏ Ministry, *The Mind Is a Terrible Thing to Taste*, 505

❏ Mother Love Bone, *Apple*, 526–27

❏ My Morning Jacket, *It Still Moves*, 537–38

❏ Nirvana, *Nevermind*, 553

❏ Pantera, *Vulgar Display of Power*, 575–76

❏ Pearl Jam, *Ten*, 588–89

❏ The Police, *Synchronicity*, 603–4

❏ Public Enemy, *It Takes a Nation of Millions to Hold Us Back*, 618–19

❏ Radiohead, *OK Computer*, 627–28

❏ Max Roach, *We Insist! Freedom Now Suite*, 647–48

❏ The Rolling Stones, *Exile on Main St*, 657–58

❏ Franz Schubert, *Symphony No. 9*, 679

❏ Sepultura, *Roots*, 689

❏ Sleater-Kinney, *Call the Doctor*, 711

❏ Sly and the Family Stone, *Stand!*, 713–14

❏ Sonic Youth, *Daydream Nation*, 725

❏ Soundgarden, *Superunknown*, 726–27

❏ Bruce Springsteen, *Born to Run*, 733–34

❏ Karlheinz Stockhausen, *Stimmung*, 744–45

❏ Richard Strauss, *Also sprach Zarathustra*, 747

❏ System of a Down, *Toxicity*, 758

❏ A Tribe Called Quest, *The Low End Theory*, 786–87

❏ U2, *The Joshua Tree*, 798–99

❏ Richard Wagner, *Götterdämmerung*, 840–41

❏ Kanye West, *College Dropout*, 853

❏ The Who, *Tommy*, 858–59

❏ The Who, *Who's Next*, 859–60

❏ Stevie Wonder, *Innervisions*, 872

❏ X, *Wild Gift*, 878

❏ Frank Zappa, *The Best Band You Never Heard in Your Life*, 886–87

Classical and Opera Composers Index

Classical and Opera Performers Index

P

Page, Christopher, 320

Panerai, Rolando, 620

Patzak, Julius: *Mahler: Das Lied von der Erde*, 470

Pavarotti, Luciano:

Amore: Romantic Italian Love Songs, 148

Donizetti: L'elisir d'amore, 214

Puccini: La bohème, **619–20**

Puccini: Madama Butterfly, 832

Puccini: Turandot, **620–21**

Verdi: Rigoletto, 340, 834

Pears, Peter:

Britten: Death in Venice, 117

Britten: Peter Grimes, 117

Perahia, Murray:

Great Pianists Series, 328

Schubert: Impromptus for Piano, 680

Perlman, Itzhak:

Beethoven: Piano Trios, Vol. 2, 66

Beethoven: Violin Concerto, 497

Live in the Fiddler's House, **593**

Mozart: Violin Sonatas, 34

Philadelphia Orchestra:

David Bowie Narrates Peter and the Wolf, 617

Lalo: Symphonie espagnole; Bruch: Violin Concerto No. 1, **740–41**

Mendelssohn, Tchaikovsky: Violin Concertos, 741

Rachmaninoff: His Complete Recordings, 627

Shostakovich: Cello Concerto No. 1, **698–99**

Tchaikovsky: Swan Lake, 768

2001: A Space Odyssey, 747

Philharmonia Orchestra and Chorus:

Beethoven: Missa solemnis, **67–68**

Beethoven: Violin Concerto, **496–97**

Brahms: A German Requiem, 36

Handel: Messiah, 341

Mahler: Das Lied von der Erde, **469–70**

Mozart: Don Giovanni, 529

Ravel: Piano Concerto in G; Rachmaninoff: Piano Concerto No. 4, **501–2**

Rossini: The Barber of Seville, 529

Strauss: Capriccio, 747, 748

Strauss: Der Rosenkavalier, **749**

Wagner: Tristan und Isolde, 838

Pires, Maria João: *Chopin: Nocturnes*, **168**

Pittsburgh Symphony: *Beethoven and Brahms Violin Concertos*, 741

Podger, Rachel: *Bach: Violin Concertos*, 35

Polish Festival Orchestra: *Chopin: Piano Concertos Nos. 1 and 2*, **167–68**

Pollini, Maurizio:

Chopin: Études, 450

Schumann: Piano Concerto, 680

Polyansky, Valery: *Rachmaninoff: The Bells, Symphonic Dances*, 626

Prades Festival Orchestra: *Schumann: Cello Concerto*, 66

Prague National Theater Orchestra and Chorus: *Martinů: Julietta*, **479**

Previn, André:

Britten: Four Sea Interludes from Peter Grimes, 117

Villa-Lobos: Guitar Concerto, 834

Price, Leontyne:

Verdi: Aida, **831–32**

Verdi: Requiem, **832**

Q

Quilico, Gino, 154

R

Rachmaninoff, Sergey: *His Complete Recordings*, **626–27**

Radio France Philharmonic Orchestra and Chorus: *Bizet: Carmen*, **89–90**

Chabrier: Le roi malgré lui, **153–54**

Raphael Ensemble: *Brahms: String Sextets, Nos. 1 & 2*, 113

Rattle, Sir Simon:

Adams: Harmonielehre, 6

Bruckner: Symphony No. 4, 471

Gershwin: Porgy and Bess, **307–8**

Maw: Odyssey Symphony, 484

Schoenberg: Gurrelieder, **676–77**

Walton: Symphony No. 1 and Belshazzar's Feast, **844**

RCA Symphony Orchestra:

Horowitz Plays Rachmaninoff: Concerto No. 3, Sonata No. 2, 627

Puccini: La bohème, 620

Reiner, Fritz:

Bartók: Concerto for Orchestra; Music for Strings, Percussion, and Celesta, **47–48**

Brahms, Tchaikovsky Violin Concertos, **353**

Horowitz Plays Rachmaninoff: Concerto No. 3, Sonata No. 2, 627

Mussorgsky: A Night on Bald Mountain, 83

Respighi: Pines of Rome, 67, 83

Verdi: Requiem, **832**

Reinhard Goebel: *Bach: Brandenburg Concertos*, 33

Reuss, Daniel: *Stravinsky: Les Noces*, 373

Richards, Jill: *Volans: Cicada Duets*, 836

Richter, Sviatoslav:

Bach: The Well-Tempered Clavier Book 1, 369

Beethoven: Triple Concerto, 699

Brahms: Piano Concerto No. 2, **113–14**

Liszt: The Two Piano Concertos, The Piano Sonata, **449–50**

Schumann: Piano Concerto, 627

Riegel, Kenneth: *Liszt: Faust Symphony*, 450

Rogé, Pascal:

Gershwin: Concerto in F with Ravel: Concerto in G, 307

Satie: 3 Gymnopédies and Other Works, 675

General Index

G

Credits

FRONT COVER AND SPINE: Johann Sebastian Bach (1685–1750)
   Bust by Carl Ludwig Seffner (1861–1932), 1895
   COLLECTION: Bachhaus Eisenach/Neue Bachgesellschaft e. V.
   PHOTO OF BUST: André Nestler, Eisenach, Germany

BACK COVER: Eric Mencher

A–Z: p. 2 AP Images, p. 4 Tom Copi/Michael Ochs Archives, p. 5 Michael Ochs Archives/Getty Images, p. 6 Carlo Allegri/Getty Images, p. 8 Michael Ochs Archives/Getty Images, p. 9 Samir Hussein/Getty Images, p. 10 Michael Ochs Archives/Getty Images, p. 11 Courtesy of Shanachie Entertainment, p. 14 Michael Ochs Archives/Getty Images, p. 15 (top) Annamaria DiSanto/WireImage, p. 15 (bottom) Michael Ochs Archives/Getty Images, p. 16 Michael Ochs Archives/Getty Images, p. 17 Gjon Mili/Time & Life Pictures/Getty Images, p. 19 AP Images, p. 21 Hulton Archive/Getty Images, p. 24 Ethan Miller/Getty Images, p. 26 AFP/Getty Images, p. 27 AP Images, p. 28 AP Images, p. 34 Hulton Archive/Getty Images, p. 37 Jim Steinfeldt/Michael Ochs Archives/Getty Images, p. 38 AP Images, p. 41 (top) AP Images, p. 42 Michael Ochs Archives/Getty Images, p. 43 Lisa Haun/Michael Ochs Archives/Getty Images, p. 44 Michael Ochs Archives/Getty Images, p. 45 Hulton Archive/Getty Images, p. 49 Roger Viollet/Getty Images, p. 50 AP Images, p. 51 AP Images, p. 53 Fin Costello/Redferns/Retna, p. 57 Paul Natkin/WireImage, p. 63 Redferns Picture Library, p. 64 Roger Viollet/Getty Images, p. 66 Time & Life Pictures/Getty Images, p. 69 Hulton Archive/Getty Images, p. 72 AP Images, p. 73 AP Images, p. 75 Arthur Siegel/Time & Life Pictures/Getty Images, p. 77 Eric Cabanis/AFP/Getty Images, p. 81 Erich Auerbach/Hulton Archive/Getty Images, p. 82 Pierre Petit/Hulton Archive/Getty Images, p. 84 Hank Walker/Time & Life Pictures/Getty Images, p. 85 AP Images, p. 89 Stephanie Chernikowski/Michael Ochs Archives/Getty Images, p. 90 Hulton Archive/Getty Images, p. 92 (bottom) Michael Ochs Archives/Getty Images, p. 94 Michael Ochs Archives/Getty Images, p. 95 AP Images, p. 96 Michael Ochs Archives/Getty Images, p. 98 Michael Ochs Archives/Getty Images, p. 101 AP Images, p. 104 Courtesy of SONY BMG Music Entertainment, p. 109 AP Images, p. 111 Don Emmert/AFP/Getty Images, p. 112 Hulton Archive/Getty Images, p. 114 Erich Auerbach/Hulton Archive/Getty Images, p. 115 Michael Ochs Archives/Getty Images, p. 116 AP Images, p. 117 (top) Frank Mullen/WireImage, p. 118 (top) Frank Driggs Collection/Hulton Archive/Getty Images, p. 118 (bottom) Michael Ochs Archives/Getty Images, p. 122 Michael Ochs Archives/Getty Images, p. 124 Michael Ochs Archives/Getty Images, p. 125 Hulton Archive/Getty Images, p. 126 Courtesy of SONY BMG Music Entertainment, p. 128 Michael Ochs Archives/Getty Images, p. 129 Robin Platzer/Time & Life Pictures/Getty Images, p. 130 Michael Ochs Archives/Getty Images, p. 135 Victor Blackman/Hulton Archive/Getty Images, p. 138 Kevin Mazur/WireImage, p. 139 Jan Galperin, p. 140 Redferns Picture Library, p. 142 Hulton Archive/Getty Images, p. 144 Michael Ochs Archives/Getty Images, p. 148 AP Images, p. 151 AP Images, p. 155 (bottom) AP Images, p. 156 Tom Copi/Michael Ochs Archives/Getty Images, p. 161 Tom Copi/Michael Ochs Archives/Getty Images, p. 163 Charlyn Zlotnik/Michael Ochs Archives/Getty Images, p. 166 Time & Life Pictures/Getty Images, p. 168 Marion Kalter/akg-images, p. 170 Courtesy of SONY BMG Music Entertainment, p. 172 Redferns Picture Library, p. 173 Courtesy of SONY BMG Music Entertainment, p. 174 AP Images, p. 175 Michael Ochs Archives/Getty Images, p. 176 Michael Ochs Archives/Getty Images, p. 177 Michael Ochs Archives/Getty Images, p. 180 (top) Roz Kelly/Michael Ochs Archives/Getty Images, p. 180 (bottom) Michael Ochs Archives/Getty Images, p. 181 Michael Ochs Archives/Getty Images, p. 186 AP Images, p. 187 AP Images, p. 188 AP Images, p. 191 Michael Ochs Archives/Getty Images, p. 193 Evening